Who Is This Book For?

Visual Studio 2010 Express is available for download **completely free of charge** from Microsoft's web site. You won't need to invest in any other software in order to follow all of the exercises in this book. All you will need is a computer with Microsoft Windows XP, Windows Vista or Windows 7 (recommended).

If you are an absolute beginner and want to master the art of creating interactive data-driven web sites with ASP.NET and C# you've found the right book.

The book will teach you to create and maintain ASP.NET websites, using Visual Studio, the industry-standard development tool. The express version of Visual Studio is used in this book. This can be downloaded **completely free of charge** from Microsoft's web site.

The book begins by showing you how to install Visual Studio 2010 Express and explore some of its most important features. You'll then learn the basic web technologies of HTML, CSS and JavaScript.

With this solid grounding in web technologies, it is then possible for you to understand how C# and ASP.NET 4.0 combine to create dynamic, interactive, data-driven web applications.

Because data-driven web applications require a database, the book will also teach you how to use Microsoft's new LINQ technology to easily integrate a database.

The emphasis throughout this book is on solid, professional coding practices and techniques. Instead of simple code snippets the book takes you through the process of developing a high-quality, sophisticated web application. By the end of the course you will have a working and complete application that can be used as the basis for your own real-world commercial projects.

This book is for users who:

- Want to take the first step towards a career in web development.

- Are absolute beginners with little or no previous exposure to ASP.NET, C# and other web technologies.

- Are already comfortable with using Windows and a web browser.

- Want to understand the core web technologies of HTML, CSS and JavaScript.

- Want to become proficient with Visual Studio, the industry-standard development tool.

- Want to learn C#, the world's most widely-used professional programming language.

- Want to learn to use ASP.NET 4.0 to create data-driven, dynamic web applications.

Simon Smart

Learn ASP.NET 4.0, C# and Visual Studio 2010 Essential Skills with The Smart Method

Published by:

The Smart Method Ltd
Burleigh Manor
Peel Road
Douglas, IOM,
Great Britain
IM1 5EP

Tel: +44 (0)845 458 3282 Fax: +44 (0)845 458 3281

E-mail: sales@LearnASP4.com
Web: www.LearnASP4.com (this book's dedicated web site)

Printed and bound in the EEC

FIRST EDITION

International Standard Book Number (ISBN10): 0-9554599-6-6
International Standard Book Number (ISBN13): 978-0-9554599-6-2

1 2 4 6 8 10 9 7 5 3

About the Author

Simon Smart has spent the last 10 years working in almost every aspect of software development, from accounting systems to manufacturing machinery programming. Over the course of his career he has seen software move away from desktop machines and towards web-based applications like the ones covered in this book.

Starting with the earliest versions of ASP he experienced its growth into ASP.NET 4, spending many long hours finding out what works and what doesn't.

Simon always found books and documentation about ASP.NET to be of limited use, even to the experienced. In 2011 he set out to write his own book, hoping to pass on the knowledge gained in his years working as a programmer.

In his spare time, Simon can be usually be found in the outdoors, roaming the forests and hills looking for new places to explore. His dad finds this amusing, particularly when it's raining.

Author's Acknowledgements

Kind words can be short and easy to speak, but their echoes are truly endless.

Mother Teresa, Catholic Nun (1910-1997)

Special thanks are due to my father Mike Smart, the founder of The Smart Method, who encouraged me to put my years of experience in .NET programming to use in writing this book.

I would also like to thank my girlfriend Emillie Long, whose advice and encouragement helped immensely.

Special thanks are also due to Jack Smart, Jen Stowell and Gord Hill who provided much useful feedback, improving the book greatly.

Finally, I would like to thank the readers of this book. It is my fondest hope that this book will give many people the first step they need to embark upon a career of web application development.

Contents

Session Five: C# Variables   149

Session Six: C# Classes, Namespaces and Methods   181

Session Eleven: Using data controls   301

Session Twelve: Build a complete ASP.NET site   323

Index   351

Introduction

Welcome to *Learn ASP.NET 4.0, C# and Visual Studio 2010 Essential Skills with The Smart Method*. This book has been designed to enable students to master essential ASP.NET skills by self-study. The book is equally useful as courseware in the classroom.

Smart Method publications are continually evolving as we discover better ways of explaining or teaching the concepts presented.

Feedback

At The Smart Method we love feedback – be it positive or negative. If you have any suggestions for improvements to future versions of this book, or if you find content or typographical errors, the author would always love to hear from you via e-mail to:

feedback@LearnASP4.com

Future editions will always incorporate your feedback so that there are never any known errors at time of publication.

If you have any difficulty understanding or completing a lesson, or if you feel that anything could have been more clearly explained, we'd also love to hear from you. We've made hundreds of detail improvements to our books based upon reader's feedback and continue to chase the impossible goal of 100% perfection!

Downloading the sample files

In order to use this book it is sometimes necessary to download sample files from the Internet. The sample files are available from:

http://www.LearnASP4.com

Type the above URL into your web browser and you'll see the link to the sample files at the top of the home page.

Problem resolution

If you encounter any problem downloading or using the sample files please send an e-mail to:

feedback@LearnASP4.com

We'll do everything possible to quickly resolve the problem.

Typographical Conventions Used In This Book

This guide consistently uses typographical conventions to differentiate parts of the text.

When you see this	Here's what it means
Right-click on *My Project* in the Solution Explorer and then click *Build* from the shortcut menu.	Italics are used to refer to text that appears in a menu, a dialog, or elsewhere within the Visual Studio application. At times, italics may also be used for emphasis or distinction.
Click File→New Project....	Click on the *File* menu and choose *New Project...* from the drop-down menu.

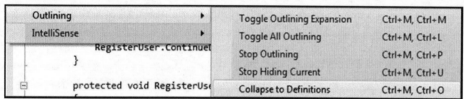

Click Edit→Outlining→ Collapse To Definitions.	Click on the *Edit* menu and look for the *Outlining* sub-menu. Click the *Outlining* menu and then click on *Collapse to Definitions*.

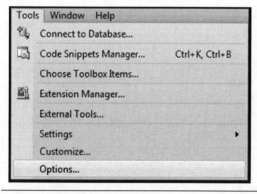

Click Tools→Options...→Formatting→ Server tag→Assembly definition.	This is a more involved example. 1. Click the *Tools* menu, and then click the *Options...* button. A new dialog pops up. 2. Click on the *Formatting* group in the *Options* dialog. 3. Drop down the *Server Tag* list and click *Assembly definition*.
Type **int X;** on the next line.	Whenever you are asked to actually type something on the keyboard it is shown in bold faced text.
Press **<Ctrl>** + **<Z>**.	You should hold down the **Ctrl** key and then press the **Z** key.

Toolbox

When a lesson tells you to click a button, an image of the relevant button will often be shown either in the page margin or within the text itself.

note

If you switch to *Design* view and click on the properties of an object in the *Properties* window, you'll notice a short description of the property…

If you want to read through the book as quickly as possible, notes which usually expand a little on the lesson text, may be ignored.

important

Do not click the Delete button at this point as to do so would erase the entire table.

Whenever something can easily go wrong, or when the subject text is particularly important, you will see the *important* sidebar.

You should always read important sidebars.

tip

Moving between tabs using the keyboard

You can also use <Ctrl>+<Tab> on the keyboard to cycle through all of the tabs you have open.

Tips add to the lesson text by showing you shortcuts or time-saving techniques relevant to the lesson.

The bold text at the top of the tip box enables you to establish whether the tip is appropriate to your needs without reading all of the text.

In this example you may not be interested in keyboard shortcuts so you do not need to read further.

anecdote

I worked on an ASP.NET project for a gaming company a couple of years ago…

Sometimes I add an anecdote gathered over the years from my work or from other areas of my experience.

If you simply want to learn ASP.NET as quickly as possible, ignore anecdotes.

trivia

The Mosaic browser

Before 1993, the Internet was very different to the way it is today…

Sometimes I indulge myself by adding a little piece of trivia in the context of the skill being taught.

Just like my anecdotes you can ignore these if you want to. They won't help you to learn ASP.NET any better!

If you are not completing the course incrementally use the sample file: **Lesson 5-1** to begin this lesson.

When there is a sample file (or files) to accompany a session, the file name will be shown in a folder icon.

You can download the lesson or file from: *www.Learnasp4.com.* Detailed instructions are given in: *Lesson 1-3: Set up the development environment.*

Putting the Smart Method to Work

Visual Studio version and service pack

This edition was written using *Visual Web Developer 2010 Express Service Pack 1* running under the *Microsoft Windows 7 Service Pack 1* operating system. You'll discover how to confirm that your computer is running these versions during *Lesson 1-2: Check your Visual Studio and Windows version*.

If you are using an earlier operating system (for example Windows XP or Windows Vista) this book will be equally relevant, but you may notice small differences in the appearance of some of the screen grabs in the book. This will only occur when describing an operating system (rather than a Visual Studio) feature.

This book is written purely for Visual Studio 2010 Express and, due to changes in this version, some features may not be available in earlier or later versions (such as 2005 and 2008).

Sessions and lessons

The book is arranged into Sessions and Lessons. In a *Smart Method* course a Session would generally last for between forty-five and ninety minutes. Each Session would represent a continuous period of interactive instruction followed by a coffee break of ten or fifteen minutes.

When this book is used for self-instruction I recommend that you do the same. You'll learn better if you lock yourself away, switch off your telephone and complete the whole session without interruption. The memory process is associative, and each lesson within each session is very closely coupled (contextually) with the others. By learning the whole session in one sitting, you'll store all of that information in the same part of your memory and should find it easier to recall later.

The experience of being able to remember all of the words of a song as soon as somebody has got you "started" with the first line is an example of the memory's associative system of data storage.

It is highly recommend that you do take a break between sessions and spend it relaxing rather than catching up on your e-mails. This gives your brain a little idle time to do some data sorting and storage.

Read the book from beginning to end

Many books consist of disassociated self-contained chapters, often all written by different authors. This approach works well for pure reference books (such as encyclopedias). The problem with this approach is that there's no concept of building knowledge upon assumed prior knowledge, so the text is either confusing or unduly verbose as instructions for the same skill are repeated in many parts of the book.

This book is more effective as a learning tool because it takes a holistic approach. You will learn ASP.NET 4.0 in the same way you would be taught during one of our *Smart Method* courses.

In our classroom courses it's often the case that a delegate turns up late. One golden rule is that we can't begin until everybody is present, as each hands-on lesson builds upon skills taught in the previous lesson.

I strongly recommend that you read the book from beginning to end in the order in which it is written. Because of the unique presentational style, you'll hardly waste any time reading about things that you already know and even the most advanced ASP.NET developer will find some nugget of extremely useful information in every session.

How this book avoids wasting your time

> Nobody has things just as he would like them. The thing to do is to make a success with what material I have.
>
> *Dr. Frank Crane (1861–1928), American clergyman and journalist*

The only material available to me in teaching you ASP.NET is the written word and sample files. I'd rather have you sitting next to me in a classroom, but Frank Crane would have told me to stop complaining and use the tools I have in the most effective way.

Over the years I have read many hundreds of computer text books. Most of my time was wasted. The main problem with most books is having to wade through thousands of words just to learn one important technique. Not reading everything could mean missing that one essential insight.

This book utilizes some of the tried and tested techniques developed after teaching vast numbers of people during many years of delivering *Smart Method* classroom courses.

As you'll see in this section, many presentational methods are used to help you to avoid reading about things you already know, or things that are of little interest.

Why our classroom courses work so well

In our classroom courses we don't waste time teaching skills that the delegates already know. If it is clear that the delegate already understands a skill no time is wasted explaining it, but if the delegate has difficulty, more information is given until success is demonstrated.

Another key to learning effectively is to teach only the best way to accomplish a task. For example, you can comment code by typing two forward slashes or you can click the shortcut buttons on the toolbar. Because typing forward slashes is the easiest, fastest and most intuitive method, only this is practised in the classroom. In the book we do mention the alternatives, but only in a sidebar.

How this book mimics our classroom technique

Here's a lesson step:

---

tip

Comment shortcuts using the toolbar

You can quickly comment and uncomment code using the comment buttons on the toolbar:

1 Add a basic comment.

1. Add a new line before:

   return RoundNumber(FirstNumber + SecondNumber);

2. Add a comment with the code:

   //Add FirstNumber and SecondNumber

   You'll see that the comment is shown in green.

If you already know how to add a comment, read only the line: *Add a basic comment* and just do it. Don't waste your time reading anything else.

Read the smaller print only when the information is new to you.

If you're in a hurry to learn only the essentials, as fast as possible, don't bother with the sidebars unless they are labeled **important**.

Read the sidebars only when you want not to miss anything and have the time and interest.

Avoiding repetition

> 2   Open the code-behind file of *default.aspx*.
>
> You learned how to do this in: *Lesson 1-7: Manage a project with the Solution Explorer.*

In this book (and in our classroom courses) we do not wish to waste your time with reiteration.

In a classroom course, a delegate will sometimes forget something that has already been covered that day. The instructor must then try to get the student to remember and drop little hints reminding them about how they completed the task earlier.

This isn't possible in a book, so I've made extensive use of cross references in the text pointing you back to the lesson in which the relevant skill was learned. The cross references also help when you use this book as a reference work but have forgotten the more basic skills needed to complete each step.

Use of American English

American English (rather than British English) spelling has been used throughout. This is because the help system and screen elements all use American English spelling, making the use of British English confusing.

Examples of differences are the British English spelling: *Colour* and *Dialogue* as opposed to the American English spelling: *Color* and *Dialog*.

Because this book is available worldwide, much care has been taken to avoid any country-specific terminology. For example, in most of the English speaking world, apart from North America, the symbol # is referred to as the **hash sign**, so the term *hash* is used throughout this book.

First page of a session

1/ The first page begins with a quotation, often from an era before the age of the computer, that is particularly pertinent to the session material. As well as being fun, this helps us to remember that all of the real-world problems we solve with technology have been around for a long time.

3/ The session objectives *formally* state the precise skills that you will learn in the session.

At the end of the session you should re-visit the objectives and not progress to the next session until you can honestly agree that you have achieved them.

In a *Smart Method* course we never progress to the next session until all delegates are completely confident that they have achieved the previous session's objectives.

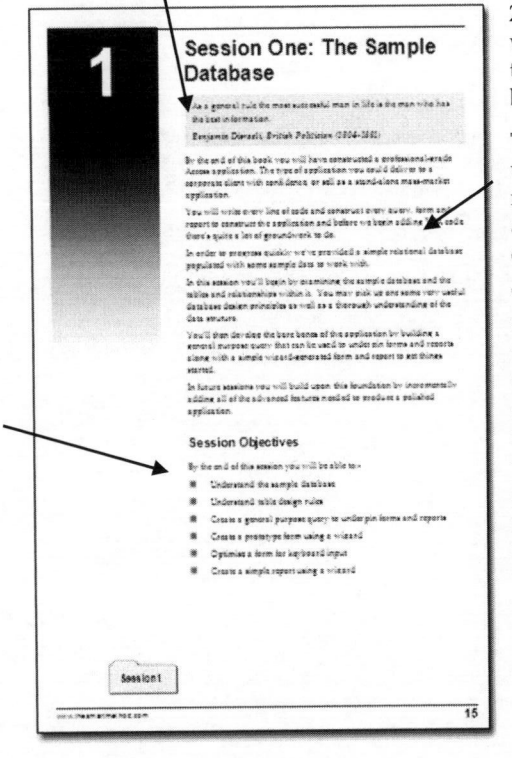

2/ In the next few paragraphs we *informally* summarise why the session is important and the benefits that can be gained.

This is important because without motivation adults do not learn. For adults, learning is a means to an end and not an end in itself.

The aim of the introduction is to motivate your retention of the skills that will be taught in the following session by allowing you to preview the relevance of the material that will be presented. This may subconsciously put your brain into "must remember this" mode—assuming, of course, that the introduction convinces you that the skills will be useful to you!

Every lesson is presented on two facing pages

> Pray this day, on one side of one sheet of paper, explain how the Royal Navy is prepared to meet the coming conflict.
>
> *Winston Churchill, Letter to the Admiralty, Sep 1, 1939*

Winston Churchill was well aware of the power of brevity. The discipline of condensing thoughts into one side of a single sheet of A4 paper resulted in the efficient transfer of information.

A tenet of our teaching system is that every lesson is presented on *two* facing sheets of A4. We've had to double Churchill's rule as they didn't have to contend with screen grabs in 1939!

If we can't teach an essential concept in two pages of A4 we know that the subject matter needs to be broken into two smaller lessons.

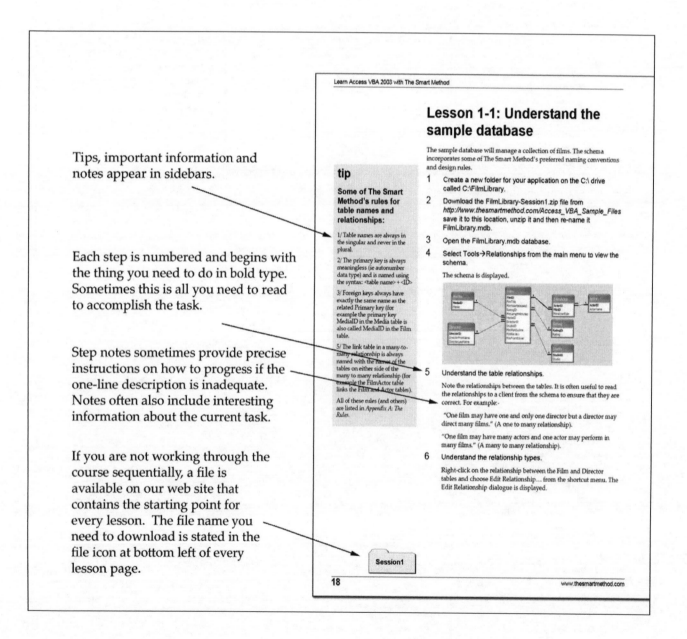

Tips, important information and notes appear in sidebars.

Each step is numbered and begins with the thing you need to do in bold type. Sometimes this is all you need to read to accomplish the task.

Step notes sometimes provide precise instructions on how to progress if the one-line description is inadequate. Notes often also include interesting information about the current task.

If you are not working through the course sequentially, a file is available on our web site that contains the starting point for every lesson. The file name you need to download is stated in the file icon at bottom left of every lesson page.

Learning by participation

Tell me, and I will forget. Show me, and I may remember. Involve me, and I will understand.

Confucius (551-479 BC)

Confucius would probably have agreed that the best way to teach IT skills is hands-on (actively) and not hands-off (passively). This is another of the principal tenets of the *Smart Method* teaching system. Research has backed up the assertion that you will learn more material, learn more quickly, and understand more of what you learn, if you learn using active, rather than passive methods.

For this reason pure theory pages are kept to an absolute minimum with most theory woven into the hands-on sessions either within the text or in sidebars. This echoes the teaching method in Smart Method courses, where snippets of pertinent theory are woven into the lessons themselves so that interest and attention is maintained by hands-on involvement, but all necessary theory is still covered.

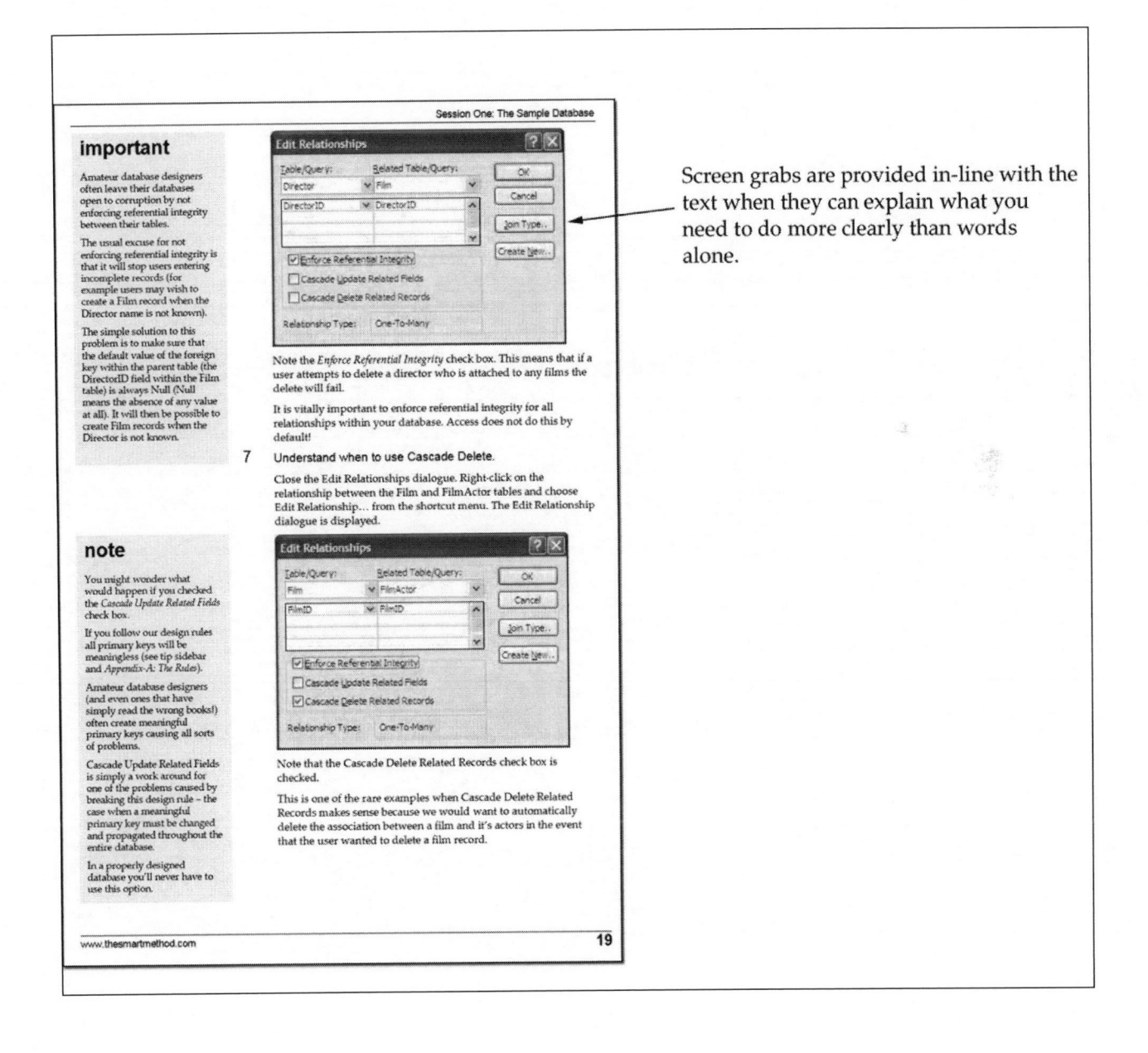

Session One: Getting Started with Visual Studio

> Man is a tool-using animal. Without tools he is nothing, with tools he is all.
>
> *Thomas Carlyle, Scottish Writer (1795-1881)*

All of the tools you need to work with ASP.NET are now available as a **free** download from Microsoft under the name Visual Studio Express. Visual Studio Express lacks some of the advanced features of the professional Visual Studio versions, but its interface is nearly identical.

Instructions for downloading and installing Visual Studio are included at the start of this session.

Visual Studio is a complex application with hundreds of features. In this session, you're going to create a very simple project and explore some of the basic functionality of Visual Studio.

Session Objectives

By the end of this session you will be able to:

- Install Visual Studio
- Check your Visual Studio and Windows version
- Set up the development environment and download the sample files
- Set up Windows for development
- Create an ASP.NET Web Application project
- Create an ASP.NET Web Site project
- Manage a project with the Solution Explorer
- Run a project in debug mode
- View .aspx pages in Source and Design views
- Use automatic formatting
- Expand and collapse code regions
- Change properties in Design view
- Change properties in Source view
- Add controls to a page with the Toolbox
- Use the QuickTasks menu
- Get help

Lesson 1-1: Install Visual Studio

If you are using Windows XP or Windows Vista, the procedure is almost the same as described here for Windows 7. You should be able to figure out the differences!

1   Download Visual Studio Express.

1. Open Internet Explorer and navigate to:
    http://www.microsoft.com/express/Web/

2. Click the *Install* button (if you don't see this see sidebar).

A warning dialog will probably appear.

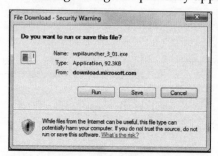

If the warning dialog doesn't appear, you should be taken straight to the screen shown in step 4.

3. Click *Run*.

    Another warning dialog will appear.

4. Click *Yes* (or perhaps *Run*).

5. Several progress bars and dialogs will pop up as the Web Platform Installer is installed.

    Eventually, you will see this screen (or a similar one):

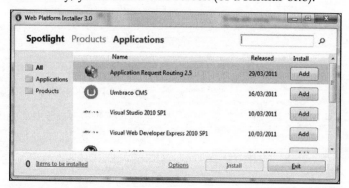

6. Click *Visual Web Developer Express 2010 SP1* (by the time you read this book it may be SP2, or an even later number).

7. Click *Add*.

Visual Web Developer Express 2010 SP1	10/03/2011	Add

note

It won't install on my computer!

There are many different ways that you can re-configure windows to prohibit installation of applications or to simply not allow anything to be downloaded from the web.

If you have firewall or anti-virus software, it is quite possible that this has been configured to block downloads.

If your computer is part of a corporate network, it is likely that your IT department has blocked users from installing new programs.

We can't offer technical support for Microsoft installation issues – you'll have to ask Microsoft for help if you really think that their site is down or faulty!

note

My Internet connection is too slow to download

Visual Studio is quite a large download, so it's recommended you have a reasonably fast Internet connection available.

Even with a fast connection, it can take several hours to install all of the Visual Studio tools. At times nothing may seem to be happening for long periods of time, but don't switch off your computer…be patient!

8. Click *Install*.

A list of terms and conditions will be displayed.

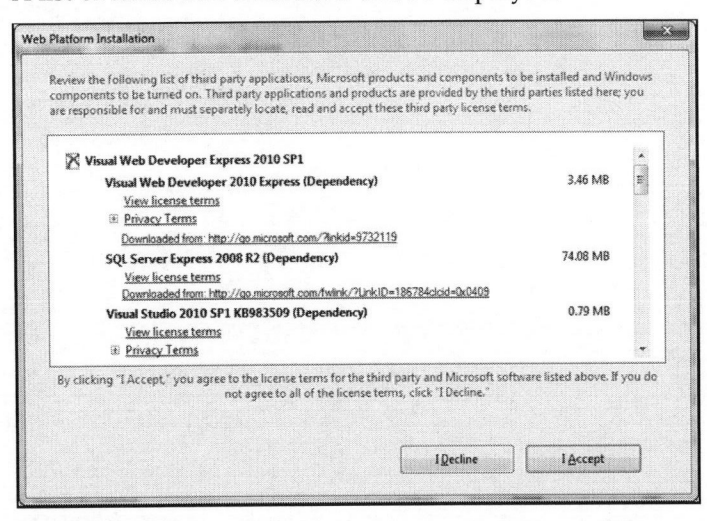

9. Click *I Accept*.

10. Another dialog may be displayed, asking you to configure SQL Server (you won't see it if SQL Server is already installed).

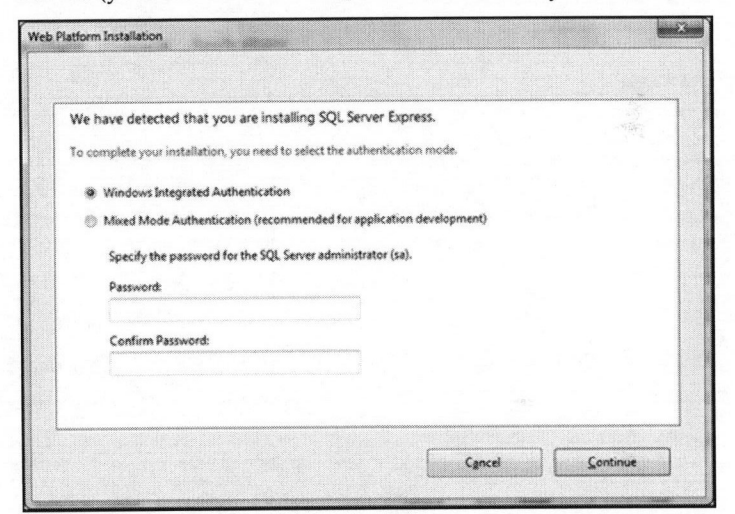

11. Click *Windows Integrated Authentication*.

12. Click *Continue*.

Visual Studio will now be downloaded and installed. This can take several hours on some systems.

During the installation, you may be prompted to restart your computer.

2   Start Visual Studio

After installing Visual Studio you should see "Microsoft Visual Web Developer 2010 Express" in your Start Menu.

Click on the program as shown below to start Visual Studio.

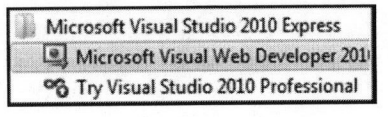

Lesson 1-2: Check your Visual Studio and Windows version

Microsoft sometimes refers to Visual Studio 2010 Express as *Visual Web Developer 2010 Express*. This book refers to it as "Visual Studio".

Visual Studio 2010 Express is a freeware version of the Visual Studio IDE (Integrated Development Environment) optimized for web application development.

Microsoft provides this version free of charge for students and hobbyists so that they can learn to use Visual Studio without having to purchase the product.

1 Open Visual Studio (if it isn't open already).

2 Check your Visual Studio version.

Click Help→About Microsoft Visual Web Developer 2010 Express.

Microsoft Visual Studio 2010	Microsoft .NET Framework
Version 10.0.40219.1 SP1Rel	Version 4.0.30319 SP1Rel
© 2010 Microsoft Corporation.	© 2010 Microsoft Corporation.
All rights reserved.	All rights reserved.

The two version numbers shown above are the important ones. This book was written using Microsoft Visual Studio Version *10.0.40219.1 SP1Rel* and Microsoft .NET Framework Version *4.0.30319 SP1Rel*.

If you have an earlier version, please follow the steps in *Lesson 1-1: Install Visual Studio* to upgrade to the latest version. Some users have reported that they had to uninstall and re-install Visual Studio in order to upgrade.

If you have a later version it's not a problem, but some of the things described in this book might behave slightly differently.

3 Check your operating system version.

Click the *System Info* button on the dialog you opened in the previous step.

You should see your operating system name and version in the top-right corner of the dialog that appears.

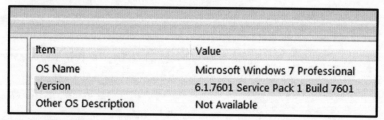

Item	Value
OS Name	Microsoft Windows 7 Professional
Version	6.1.7601 Service Pack 1 Build 7601
Other OS Description	Not Available

Microsoft Windows 7 Version 6.1.7601 Service Pack 1 is the version of Windows that is used for the screenshots in this book.

You can still use this book if you have Windows XP, Windows Vista or a different version of Windows 7, but some of the items described in this book may behave slightly differently.

4   Close the *System Information* dialog.

5   Click *OK* to close the *About Microsoft Visual Web Developer 2010 Express* dialog.

6   Close Visual Studio.

Lesson 1-3: Set up the development environment and download the sample files

1 Open Visual Studio (if it isn't open already).

2 Enable Expert Settings.

To access the full range of Visual Studio's features, you must enable Expert Settings.

To do this, click Tools→Settings→Expert Settings.

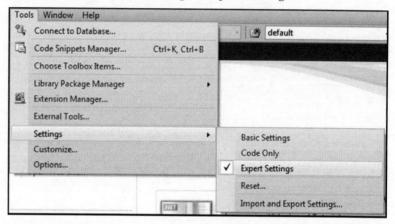

In the *Basic Settings* and *Code Only* modes you can access only a limited sub-set of Visual Studio's features. Only *Expert Settings* allows you to use every feature of Visual Studio.

3 Reset the window layout.

1. Click Window→Reset Window Layout.

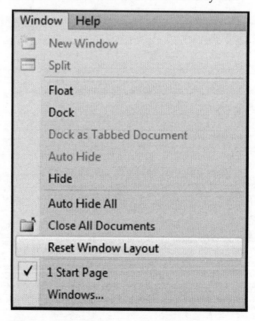

2. When prompted to confirm click *Yes*.

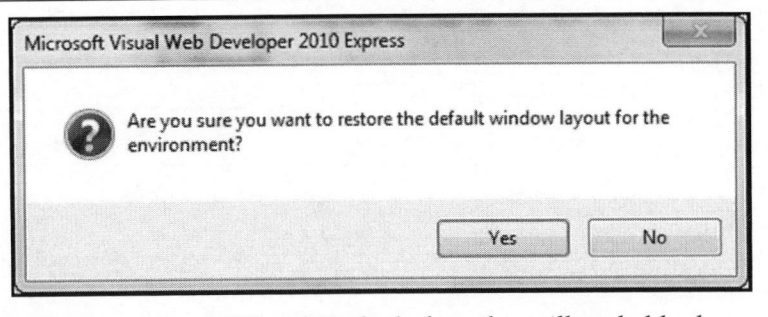

If you have never used Visual Studio before, this will probably do nothing. If you have used it before, however, it will reset the window layout so that it matches the screenshots you will see in this book.

If you ever accidentally change the layout of Visual Studio's windows by closing a toolbar or dragging a window out of its position, you can always reset the layout back to the default by using this option.

4   Download the sample files.

1. Go to www.LearnASP4.com using your web browser.

2. Click the *Files* button on the top toolbar.

3. Download the sample files.

I recommend that you extract the sample files to a folder named: *C:\Practice\ASP.NET*. This will maintain consistency with the screen grabs and instructions in the book.

Lesson 1-4: Set up Windows for development

Microsoft go out of their way to make Windows easy to use for non IT professionals. They worry that untrained users may delete vital system files, so they hide them by default. Microsoft also feel that the concept of file extensions may confuse normal users.

While this is great for ordinary office workers, as a professional developer you don't want Windows to hide anything from you.

1 Open Windows Explorer.

Right-click Windows start button and select *Open Windows Explorer* from the shortcut menu.

2 Browse to the C:\Practice\ASP.NET\Images folder.

note

If you are using Windows XP

If you are using Windows XP, you won't have an *Organize* menu available.

To access the *Folder Options* dialog in Windows XP, simply click: Tools→Folder Options.

3 Stop Windows from hiding file extensions.

1. Click Organize→Folder and search options.

   The *Folder Options* dialog appears.

2. Click the *View* tab at the top of the dialog.

3. Un-tick the *Hide extensions for known file types* box if it is ticked.

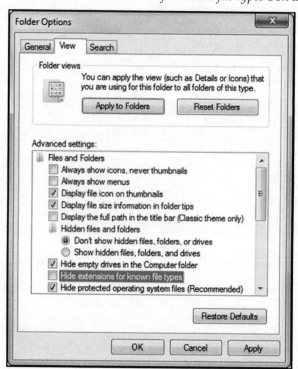

note

File extensions

Every useful file in Windows has an *extension*, which is placed at the end of the file name after a dot (for example *.jpg, .png, .txt*).

File extensions tell Windows what type of file the file is. If you were to rename *balloon.jpg* to *balloon.txt*, Windows would no longer treat the file as an image and would try to treat it as a text file instead.

File extensions are very important when working with web sites. While browsing the internet, you have probably noticed web addresses ending in *.htm, .html* and *.aspx*.

You'll be working with these file types in the course of this book.

4.   Click *OK*.

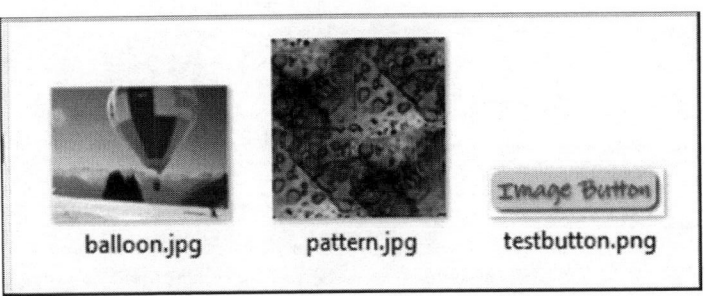

You will notice that the name of the balloon image now ends in *.jpg*.

The *.jpg* was actually there all the time, but Windows was hiding it to simplify its interface.

The *.jpg* part of the file is known as its *extension* (see sidebar).

4   Stop Windows from hiding files.

Some files are *hidden* by default. Unless you change the default settings, Windows will not display these files at all.

For a normal user hidden files wouldn't present a problem, but as a developer it's essential to be able to see all of the files that exist.

1.   Reopen the *Folder Options* dialog by clicking Organize→Folder and search options.

2.   Click the *View* tab.

3.   Click *Show hidden files, folders, and drives.*

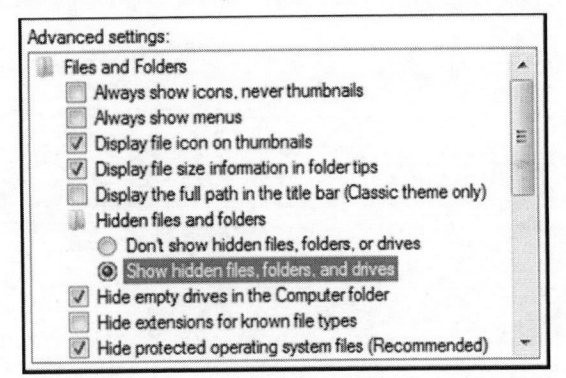

4.   Click *OK*.

Windows will now display all files, even if they are hidden.

Lesson 1-5: Create an ASP.NET Web Application project

An ASP.NET Web Application project is the starting point in creating an ASP.NET web site. Projects contain all of the web pages, images and other files that are needed to create a web site.

In this lesson, you'll create an ASP.NET Web Application project.

1   Open Visual Studio.

2   Create a new Web Application project.

1.   Click File→New Project....

2.   Click *Visual C#* in the left-hand pane.

This book will teach you about the C# programming language, not the Visual Basic programming language (see sidebar).

3.   Click *ASP.NET Web Application* in the central pane.

4.   Enter **My Project** into the *Name* box.

Notice that the *Solution name* box automatically copies what you enter.

5.   Click the *Browse...* button and browse to C:/Practice/ASP.NET (or the folder where you placed your sample files). Then click the *Select Folder* button.

6.   Make sure the *Create directory for solution* box is ticked.

7.   Click *OK*.

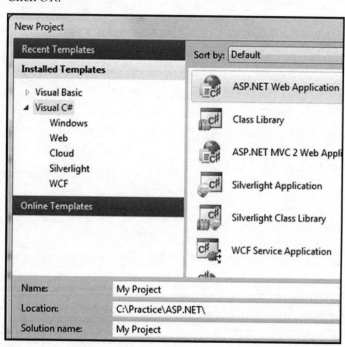

You have just created your first ASP.NET Web Application project. Visual Studio will automatically open it (this may take a little time).

note

What are the other project types?

When creating a new project, you'll notice there are lots of other project types besides the one you chose in this lesson.

In this book, you'll only be using the *ASP.NET Web Application* and *ASP.NET Empty Web Application* project types, but many of the others will be covered in the next book in this series: *Learn ASP.NET 4.0, C# and Visual Studio 2010 Expert Skills with The Smart Method.*

note

ASP.NET MVC web applications

MVC stands for: *Model, View, Controller.* It's a programming methodology where all code is separated into those three groups.

MVC web application projects exist for programmers who want to design their web applications using the MVC methodology.

ASP.NET isn't really designed for the MVC methodology, so MVC projects tend to be harder to work with than standard web applications, especially if you're new to programming.

For this reason, you won't use MVC projects in this book.

note

Why am I learning C# and not Visual Basic?

Visual Studio offers you the choice of working in Visual C# or Visual Basic.

In this book, you will learn the basics of C#, rather than Visual Basic. This is because C# is a more sought-after skill.

Several surveys have shown that there are more jobs advertised for C# developers than Visual Basic, so your skills will be more marketable by choosing C#.

Regardless of this, C# and Visual Basic are very similar indeed. If you learn C#, you should find that Visual Basic is very easy to pick up.

note

My Project.suo

The *.suo* file is hidden by default, so you will only see it if you have configured Windows to display hidden files.

The *.suo* file is used to store settings for your project, and will be automatically updated through Visual Studio.

You will never have to open it directly.

3 Open the new project.

1. Close Visual Studio.

2. Navigate to your sample files folder using Windows.

3. Open the new *My Project* folder that has appeared.

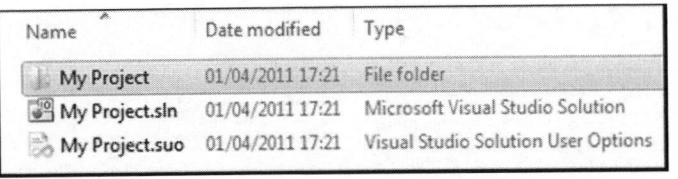

You will see another *My Project* folder and a file called *My Project.sln*.

My Project.sln is the *solution* file. The solution file tells Visual Studio which files are in your project. If you double-click on it, your project will be opened in Visual Studio.

4. Open the *My Project* folder by double-clicking on it.

Name	Date modified	Type
Account	01/04/2011 17:20	File folder
App_Data	01/04/2011 17:20	File folder
bin	01/04/2011 17:20	File folder
obj	01/04/2011 17:20	File folder
Properties	01/04/2011 17:20	File folder
Scripts	01/04/2011 17:20	File folder
Styles	01/04/2011 17:20	File folder
About.aspx	01/04/2011 17:20	ASP.NET Server Page
About.aspx.cs	01/04/2011 17:20	Visual C# Source file
About.aspx.designer.cs	01/04/2011 17:20	Visual C# Source file
Default.aspx	01/04/2011 17:20	ASP.NET Server Page
Default.aspx.cs	01/04/2011 17:20	Visual C# Source file
Default.aspx.designer.cs	01/04/2011 17:20	Visual C# Source file
Global.asax	01/04/2011 17:20	ASP.NET Server Application
Global.asax.cs	01/04/2011 17:20	Visual C# Source file
My Project.csproj	01/04/2011 17:21	Visual C# Project file
My Project.csproj.user	01/04/2011 17:21	Visual Studio Project User Options file
Site.Master	01/04/2011 17:20	ASP.NET Master Page
Site.Master.cs	01/04/2011 17:20	Visual C# Source file
Site.Master.designer.cs	01/04/2011 17:20	Visual C# Source file
Web.config	01/04/2011 17:20	XML Configuration File
Web.Debug.config	01/04/2011 17:20	XML Configuration File
Web.Release.config	01/04/2011 17:20	XML Configuration File

This folder has lots of items in it! These are the files that contain all of the code and content for your site.

You'll notice a file named *My Project.csproj*. This is the *project* file.

Projects are very similar to solutions. You can open your project by double-clicking *My Project.csproj*, just as you can open it by double-clicking *My Project.sln*. The major difference is that a solution can contain several projects.

In the course of this book you'll only work with one project at a time, so it doesn't matter which file you use to open your projects.

5. Open the project by double-clicking the solution or project file.

Lesson 1-6: Create an ASP.NET Web Site project

As well as Web Application projects, you can also create Web Site projects. A Web Site is very similar to a Web Application, but it is not compiled.

Compiling offers many advantages, making the Web Application the preferred application type (see sidebar), but for completeness you'll also learn how to create a Web Site project in this lesson.

1 Open Visual Studio (if it isn't open already).

2 Create a new Web Site project.

1. Click File→New Web Site....

2. Click *Visual C#*.

3. Click *ASP.NET Web Site*.

4. Click the *Browse...* button and browse to the folder where you placed your sample files, then click the *Open* button.

5. Append the text **\My Web Site** to the box showing the path to your Sample Files folder.

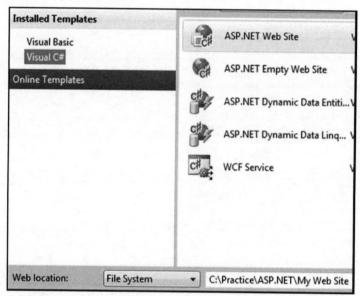

6. Click *OK*.

7. Click *Yes* to create the folder if prompted.

A new web site is automatically created and opened.

3 Open the Web Site.

1. Close Visual Studio.

2. Navigate to your sample files folder using Windows.

3. Open the new *My Web Site* folder that has appeared.

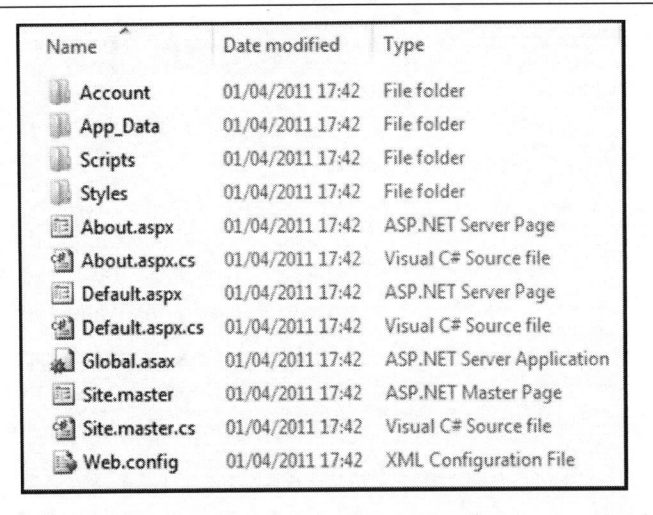

This is quite different to your Web Application project!

When you created your Web Application, a *.csproj* file and a *.sln* file were created to tell Visual Studio which files are included in the project. Web Sites don't use these files; instead they assume that all of the files in the same folder are part of the Web Site. This means that you can't open a Web Site in the same way as you can open a Web Application.

You'll only be using Web Applications from this point on, but it's useful to know how to open a Web Site.

4. Open Visual Studio.

5. Click File→Open Web Site...

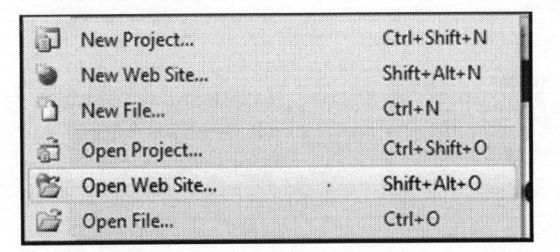

6. Browse to the *My Web Site* folder and click *Open*.

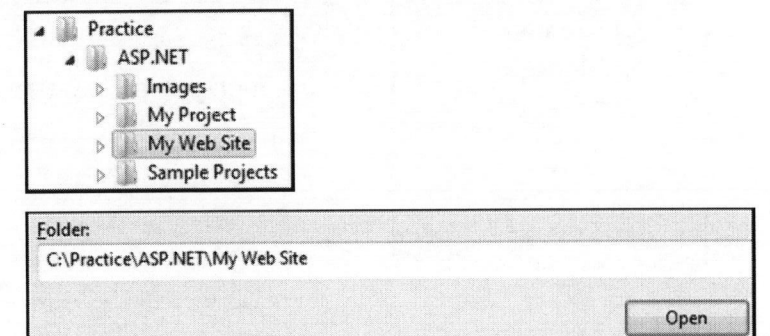

The web site is opened.

Lesson 1-7: Manage a project with the Solution Explorer

The *Solution Explorer* window can be found at the top-right of the Visual Studio screen. It displays all of the web pages and other objects that are in your current solution and allows you to edit them. It also enables you to add files to your project and remove them.

When you created *My Project* in *Lesson 1-5: Create an ASP.NET Web Application project*, a lot of different files were automatically added to it. In this lesson you'll learn how to open some of those files, add new files and remove files.

1   Open *My Project* from your sample files folder.

    1.   Click File→Open Project.

    2.   Click the *My Project.sln* file in the *My Project* subfolder of your Sample Files folder.

    3.   Click *Open*.

Alternatively, you can navigate to your Sample Files folder and double-click on *My Project.sln* as you did in: *Lesson 1-5: Create an ASP.NET Web Application project.*

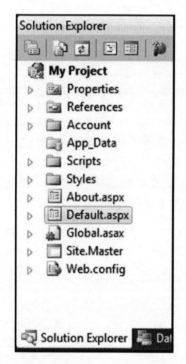

2   Double-click *Default.aspx* in the *Solution Explorer*.

This will open the HTML code of *Default.aspx* in the main window. You can open any file in your project by double-clicking it in this way.

Don't worry if you don't understand any of the code displayed yet. By the time you've finished this course you'll completely understand what it all means.

An aspx file acts as a web page and can be understood by a web browser. You may have noticed some web addresses ending with .aspx while browsing the Internet.

Default.aspx is normally the 'home page' of a web site.

3   Open the 'code-behind' file of *Default.aspx*.

    1.   Expand *Default.aspx* by clicking the small arrow to the left of it in the *Solution Explorer*.

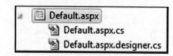

    2.   Double-click *Default.aspx.cs*

This will open the C# 'code-behind' file of *Default.aspx* in the main window.

You won't understand any of the C# code you see in this file yet, but by the end of this book it will all make sense to you.

Every .aspx file has a code-behind file. The code-behind files are actually separate files, but they are grouped together by the solution explorer for clarity.

If you are not completing the course incrementally use the sample file: **Lesson 1-6** to begin this lesson.

Sample files with the starting point for each lesson are also provided for all of the other lessons in this session.

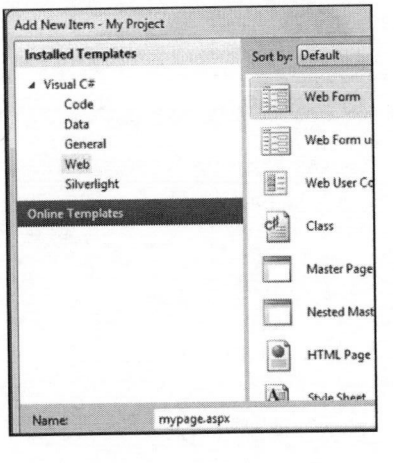

You can also open the code-behind file by right-clicking on *Default.aspx* and then clicking *View Code* from the shortcut menu.

4   Add a new page to the project.

1. Right-click on *My Project* in the *Solution Explorer* and then click Add→New Item… from the shortcut menu.

2. Click *Web* in the left pane of the dialog and then click *Web Form* from the top of the center panel.

3. Enter **mypage.aspx** in the *Name* box and then click *Add*.

You have now added a new page to your project. Visual Studio helpfully opens its HTML code for you. You will also see that *mypage.aspx* has appeared in the Solution Explorer.

5   Add a new folder to the project.

Adding a folder is very similar to adding a folder in Windows.

1. Right-click on *My Project* in the Solution Explorer and then click Add→New Folder from the shortcut menu.

    The new folder is created and its default name (*NewFolder1*) is highlighted, ready for you to type a meaningful name.

2. Type **Images** as the name of your new folder and press **<Enter>**.

6   Add an image to the *Images* folder.

1. Right-click on the *Images* folder and then click Add→Existing Item… from the shortcut menu.

2. Navigate to your sample files folder and choose the file *balloon.jpg* in the *Images* folder, then click *Add*.

    This will take a copy of *balloon.jpg* and place it in your project's *Images* folder. You can use this method to add any file to your project.

7   Remove the *About.aspx* page.

1. Right-click on the *About.aspx* page and then click *Delete* from the shortcut menu.

2. Click *OK*.

If you check your Recycle Bin, you'll find that the *About.aspx* page has been moved there.

8   Exclude *balloon.jpg* from the project.

1. Right-click on the *balloon.jpg* file you added in step 6.

2. Click *Exclude From Project* from the shortcut menu.

You'll see that *balloon.jpg* disappears from your project, but if you check the *Images* folder using Windows you'll see that the file is actually still there.

By excluding *balloon.jpg*, you have stopped it from being included in the web site when it is published, but you haven't actually deleted the file from the project.

This is useful when you want to remove something from a project but aren't sure if you might need it again later.

Lesson 1-8: Run a project in debug mode

Now that you've created a project it would be useful to see it in action. Visual Studio has a virtual web server that lets you test your site without needing to upload it to the Internet.

In this lesson you'll learn how to start the virtual web server to see the pages that were automatically created as part of your web application.

1   Open *My Project* from your sample files folder (if it isn't already open).

2   Start Debugging.

   1.   Double-click *Default.aspx* to open it.

   2.   Click Debug→Start Debugging.

You can also use the shortcut button on the toolbar, which looks like a 'play' button.

After a short delay, the *Default.aspx* page will be displayed in your web browser.

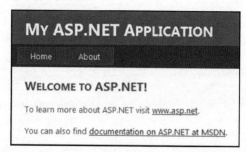

The path in the address bar of your browser will look something like: *http://localhost:51332/Default.aspx*

Localhost is the web address of your own computer. When you started debugging, Visual Studio started a virtual web server on your computer at this address so that you can test your project.

Note that if you click the *About* button you will see an error. This is because you deleted the *About.aspx* file in: *Lesson 1-7: Manage a project with the Solution Explorer.*

3   Close your browser.

Close your browser now. This will bring you back to Visual Studio and stop debugging.

4   Change the start page to *mypage.aspx.*

   1.   Right-click on *mypage.aspx* in the *Solution Explorer* and then click *Set As Start Page* from the shortcut menu.

   2.   Start debugging.

If you can't do this, see the sidebar: *Manually stopping debugging.*

You'll find that this time the path that is opened is: *http://localhost:51332/mypage.aspx.* You didn't put anything on mypage.aspx, so the page will be blank.

trivia

Web browser market share

In 2004, it was estimated that over 90% of web users were using Microsoft's Internet Explorer browser but by December 2010 Internet Explorer's share of the browser market was below 50%.

So what changed? In 2004, the Firefox browser was released, boasting many new features that Internet Explorer lacked such as tabbed browsing. By December 2010, Firefox was being used by approximately 30% of Internet users.

The browser with the next largest market share as of December 2010 was Google Chrome. This was released in 2008 and quickly gained around 10% of the market.

The other major browsers at the time of writing are Apple's Safari, Opera and a growing number of people using mobile devices to browse the Internet (such as Android Smart phones, iPhones and iPads).

As a professional web developer, you'll probably want to test your web applications in Internet Explorer, Firefox and Chrome along with any other browsers that you think your users may have.

Because you have set *mypage.aspx* as the start page, it will always appear when you start debugging.

5 **Change the browser used for debugging.**

1. Close your web browser.

2. Right-click on *Default.aspx* in the *Solution Explorer* and then click *Browse With...* from the shortcut menu.

   A dialog will appear showing all of your installed browsers.

3. Click *Internet Explorer* and then click *Set as Default*.

   This will make Internet Explorer the default browser for debugging this project (if it wasn't already).

4. Click *Browse* to view the page with Internet Explorer.

   If this doesn't work, make sure that any instances of Internet Explorer are closed and try again.

5. Close Internet Explorer to return to Visual Studio.

Most web developers need to test that their sites work in several browsers (see sidebar).

6 **Cause a build error.**

When you start debugging, your project is 'built'. This is another word for compiled (for more on this see sidebar in: *Lesson 1-6: Create an ASP.NET Web Site project*).

When your project is built, all of its code is checked for errors. If there are any major errors, the virtual web server won't be able to start and Visual Studio will try to tell you why.

1. Double-click *Default.aspx.cs* or right-click on *Default.aspx* and click *View Code* from the shortcut menu.

2. Type some nonsense in the space shown.

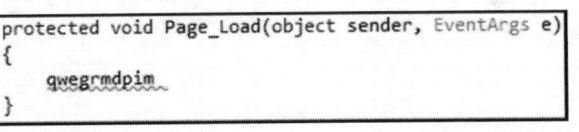

```
protected void Page_Load(object sender, EventArgs e)
{
    qwegrmdpim
}
```

   You'll notice that the text you typed is underlined in red. Visual Studio has already noticed that there's something wrong with this code.

3. Try to start debugging.

   A dialog will appear, warning you that there are build errors and asking if you'd like to use the last successful build instead.

4. Click *No*.

5. Delete the nonsense and start debugging again.

   mypage.aspx displays properly this time (though, of course, it is empty).

7 **Close your web browser.**

8 **Close Visual Studio.**

note

The languages browsers understand

Web browsers need to understand three languages in order to display a website to you.

HTML code is found in individual web pages. It contains the content of the page and has some control over its layout. You'll learn a lot more about HTML in: *Session Two: Understanding Web Sites*.

CSS (Cascading Style Sheets) are used to control the layout and style of an entire web site. The correct use of CSS keeps the appearance of every page in the website consistent. Some amateur web sites do not use Cascading Style Sheets but they are found in all professional sites. You'll learn more about CSS later in: *Lesson 2-8: Work with CSS*.

JavaScript code is used to perform special actions in the visitor's web browser such as pop-up windows. You'll learn more about JavaScript in: *Lesson 2-11: Work with JavaScript*.

ASP.NET allows you to add C# code to a web site that allows the site to react to the visitor's input, connect to databases and do other useful and amazing things.

A browser can't understand C# code. The web server generates HTML code "on the fly" from the C# code you write.

For example, when you use a search engine and click the "Search" button, the C# code at the web server queries a database containing millions of web page details. It then generates an HTML page containing the search results and sends them back to your web browser. This book is about ASP.NET and focuses upon C# code, but it also covers the basics of the other three languages.

Lesson 1-9: View .aspx pages in Source and Design views

ASPX files can be viewed in two different ways. *Design* view allows you to work with the web page visually and *Source* view allows you to work with the web page's HTML code. This lesson will show you how to work with both views.

1   Open *My Project* from your sample files folder.

2   Open the HTML code of *mypage.aspx*.

To open the HTML code of *mypage.aspx*, simply double-click on it in the *Solution Explorer*. HTML stands for HyperText Markup Language (see sidebar).

3   Add some text.

In the code window you will see a gap between two lines saying *<div>* and *</div>*.

1.   Type **Welcome to My Project!** into the space between *<div>* and *</div>*.

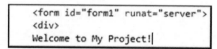

2.   Start debugging.

If you are unable to start debugging, you have probably left the web page open from the last debug session. If this is the case, click the *Stop Debugging* button ▣ on the *Debug* toolbar. The green *Start Debugging* button ▶ will then light up.

When debugging starts, you will see the text appear on the web page.

3.   Close the web browser.

4   Switch to *Design* view.

Click the *Design* button at the bottom of the code window.

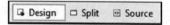

The web page and its layout are displayed visually.

5   Switch to *Split* view.

Click the *Split* button at the bottom of the code window.

The *Split* view simply displays both *Design* and *Source* views simultaneously.

6   Change text in *Design* view.

You can change text in *Design* view in the same way as you would in *Source* view.

1. Click the *Design* button.

2. Click in the white space after *Welcome to My Project!*

3. Type: **Hello world!**

7   Switch back to *Source* view.

Click the *Source* button next to the *Design* button you clicked in the previous step.

Notice how Visual Studio has automatically added HTML code to correctly code the text you simply typed in Design view.

```
<form id="form1" runat="server">
<div>
    Welcome to My Project!
    Hello World!</div>
</form>
```

8   Save changes to the file.

You may have noticed that when you made changes to *mypage.aspx*, an asterisk (*) appeared next to its name on its tab.

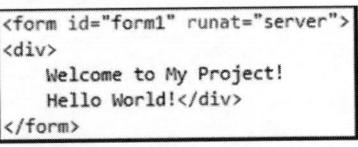

The asterisk indicates that changes have been made to the file. If you were to try to close the tab, you would be warned that you had unsaved changes.

Click File→Save mypage.aspx.

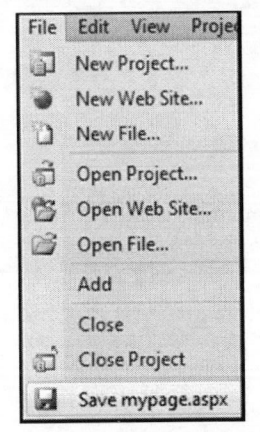

The asterisk disappears.

You can also press <**Ctrl**>+<**S**> to save the tab you currently have open.

9   Close Visual Studio.

Lesson 1-10: Use automatic formatting

As you saw in *Lesson 1-9: View .aspx pages in Source and Design views*, *Design* view makes it very easy to make changes to your web pages. However, when you make changes in *Design* view the code that is created is often messy and hard to understand in *Source* view.

Fortunately, Visual Studio comes with a great automatic formatting feature that will tidy up the code for you!

1   Open *My Project* from your sample files folder.

2   Open the HTML code of *mypage.aspx*.

3   Make the HTML code messy.

At the moment the HTML code isn't perfect, but it's still quite easy to read. However, HTML code can often get very messy and hard to understand.

1.   Add some extra spaces before your *Welcome to My Project!* text.

```
<body>
    <form id="form1" runat="server">
    <div>
                            Welcome to My Project!
        Hello world!</div>
    </form>
</body>
```

2.   Remove the line break between *<form>* and *<div>*.

```
<body>
    <form id="form1" runat="server">    <div>
                            Welcome to My Project!
        Hello world!</div>
    </form>
</body>
```

3.   Remove the line breaks between the last instances of *</div>*, *</form>*, *</body>* and *</html>*.

```
<body>
    <form id="form1" runat="server">    <div>
                        Welcome to My Project!
        Hello world!</div>    </form></body></html>
```

Your code is now quite badly messed up! You could correct the formatting manually, but there is a much easier way.

4   View *mypage.aspx* in your browser.

It's interesting to note that your web browser doesn't care how badly formatted the HTML code is, it still displays the page in exactly the same way as it did before.

5   Close your browser and return to Visual Studio.

6   Automatically fix the page formatting.

tip

Changing automatic format settings

Generally speaking, it's a good idea to stay with Microsoft's default settings for formatting code. If you personalize it you may find that, when working in a team environment, other developers find your code confusing.

However, if you're an experienced web developer working alone, you might have a preferred way of formatting your code that is different to Microsoft's default settings.

If so, you can change the formatting behaviour of Visual Studio by clicking Tools→Options→Text Editor.

You can also take a short cut to the appropriate settings by right-clicking in an HTML code window and then clicking *Formatting and Validation...* from the shortcut menu.

The screenshots in this book all use Microsoft's default formatting.

note

Use automatic formatting frequently as you work through this book

This book won't tell you to use automatic formatting again after this point, but feel free to use it if the code you add in later lessons doesn't match what is shown in the screenshots.

The screenshots in this book will always show the code correctly formatted.

1. Open *mypage.aspx* in *Source* view (if it isn't open already).

2. Click Edit→Format Document.

You'll see that the code is rearranged and the formatting looks sensible again!

```
<body>
    <form id="form1" runat="server">
    <div>
        Welcome to My Project!
    </div>
    </form>
</body>
```

This option works in all of the document types you have opened so far. It is extremely useful when code looks messy and hard to read as it will automatically tidy everything up!

7   Open the code-behind file of *Register.aspx* in the *Account* folder.

You learned how to do this in: *Lesson 1-7: Manage a project with the Solution Explorer.*

The code on this page still won't make any sense to you yet, but you'll understand all of it by the end of this course.

8   Mess up the formatting of the C# code.

Automatic formatting works with C# too.

Add different numbers of spaces before the lines of code to make them hard to read.

```
        protected void RegisterUser_CreatedUser(c
        {
FormsAuthentication.SetAuthCookie(RegisterUser.U

                string continueUrl = RegisterUs
    if (String.IsNullOrEmpty(continueUrl))
                                            {
                continueUrl = "~/";
        }

                Response.Redirect(continueU

}

        }
```

It's now confusing enough to scare even the most experienced programmers!

9   Fix the C# code automatically.

Click Edit→Format Document.

The code is automatically formatted correctly, making it a lot more readable.

```
protected void RegisterUser_CreatedUser(ob
{
    FormsAuthentication.SetAuthCookie(Regi

    string continueUrl = RegisterUser.Cont
    if (String.IsNullOrEmpty(continueUrl))
    {
        continueUrl = "~/";
    }
    Response.Redirect(continueUrl);
}
```

Lesson 1-11: Expand and collapse code regions

In Visual Studio, you often need to work with large amounts of HTML and C# code. To help you to deal with such large amounts of code, Visual Studio provides the ability to expand and collapse the code into regions. This allows you to get an overview of the code and expand only the parts you are interested in.

In this lesson you'll expand and collapse code in both a C# and an HTML file.

1   Open *My Project* from your sample files folder.

2   Expand and collapse C# code regions.

tip

Collapse to Definitions

Although you can expand and collapse code using the + and – icons as you do in this lesson, there are a few advanced ways to expand and collapse your code.

If you click:

Edit→Outlining→ Collapse to Definitions

…your code will be collapsed so the biggest areas of code are hidden.

This is often the most useful way to view your code as you can then selectively expand only the code you want to see.

    1.   Open the code-behind file of *Register.aspx*, which is in the *Account* folder.

      (You learned how to do this in: *Lesson 1-7: Manage a project with the Solution Explorer*).

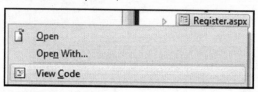

      The content of the C# code-behind file is displayed.

```
namespace My_Project.Account
{
    public partial class Register : System.Web.UI.Page
    {
        protected void Page_Load(object sender, EventArgs e)
```

      Code-behind files contain C# code which is used to turn a static read-only HTML web page into a dynamic ASP.NET page. Dynamic pages can execute code when users perform actions such as clicking on web page buttons.

    2.   Click the minus icon (⊟) next to the line:
      namespace My_Project.Account

```
namespace My_Project.Account...
```

      You'll see that the code below it seems to disappear! Don't worry though, this is a feature of Visual Studio that allows you to collapse blocks of code in order to simplify the view when a page contains a large amount of code.

    3.   Expand the code again by clicking the plus sign icon (⊞).

```
namespace My_Project.Account
{
    public partial class Register : System.Web.UI.Page
    {
        protected void Page_Load(object sender, EventArgs e)
```

      You can use any of the plus and minus icons on the page to expand and collapse different areas of code.

3 Open the HTML code of *Register.aspx*.

Simply double-click on *Register.aspx* in the *Solution Explorer*.

4 Expand and collapse HTML code regions.

1. Wait for the ⊟ buttons to appear.

Visual Studio takes some time to process an HTML file before the buttons will appear to expand and collapse its code.

Sometimes the buttons don't appear at all (even after waiting some time). If this happens close the file and reopen it.

```
<asp:Content ID="BodyContent" runat="server" Conte
    <asp:CreateUserWizard ID="RegisterUser" runat=
        <LayoutTemplate>
            <asp:PlaceHolder ID="wizardStepPlaceho
            <asp:PlaceHolder ID="navigationPlaceho
        </LayoutTemplate>
        <WizardSteps>
            <asp:CreateUserWizardStep ID="Register
                <ContentTemplate>
                    <h2>
```

2. Click the first ⊟ button, next to *<asp: Content*.

```
<%@ Page Title="Register" Language="C#" MasterPageFi
    CodeBehind="Register.aspx.cs" Inherits="My_Proje

<asp:Content ID="HeaderContent" runat="server" Conte
</asp:Content>
<asp:Content ID="BodyContent" ...>...</asp:Content>
```

Again, all of the page's code seems to disappear! But as before, it has just been collapsed out of sight.

3. Expand the code again by clicking the ⊞ button.

The code reappears.

```
<asp:Content ID="BodyContent" runat="server" Conte
    <asp:CreateUserWizard ID="RegisterUser" runat=
        <LayoutTemplate>
            <asp:PlaceHolder ID="wizardStepPlaceho
            <asp:PlaceHolder ID="navigationPlaceho
        </LayoutTemplate>
        <WizardSteps>
            <asp:CreateUserWizardStep ID="Register
                <ContentTemplate>
                    <h2>
```

5 Close Visual Studio.

Lesson 1-12: Change properties in Design view

You might have noticed the *Properties* window under the *Solution Explorer*. In this lesson you'll use it to change the properties of some things on web pages while in *Design* view.

1 Open the *ShiningStone* project from your sample files folder.

It can be found in the *Sample Projects* sub-folder.

2 Open the HTML code of *buy.aspx* and switch to *Design* view.

Switch to *Design* view by clicking the *Design* button at the bottom of the code window.

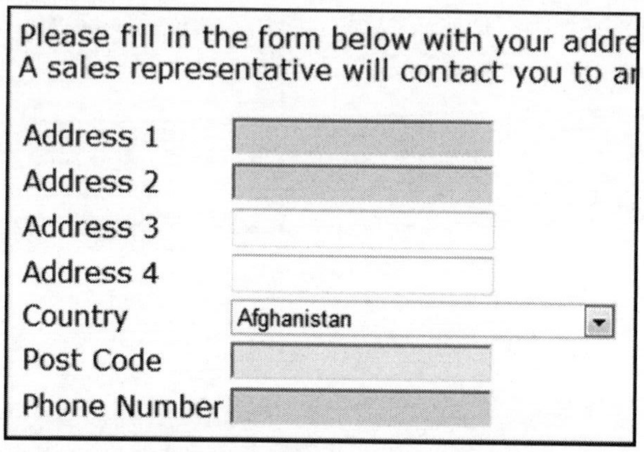
Please fill in the form below with your addr
A sales representative will contact you to a
Address 1
Address 2
Address 3
Address 4
Country
Afghanistan
Post Code
Phone Number

3 Open the *buy.aspx* page in your browser.

Click the *Start Debugging* shortcut button.

<u>OR</u>

Right-click on *buy.aspx* in the Solution Explorer and then click *View in Browser* from the shortcut menu.

It may take some time for the web page to appear. This is normal when debugging.

Try entering text into the text boxes and selecting a country using the drop down menu.

4 Change the color of a text box.

1. Close your web browser to stop debugging.
2. Click the blue text box next to *Post Code*.

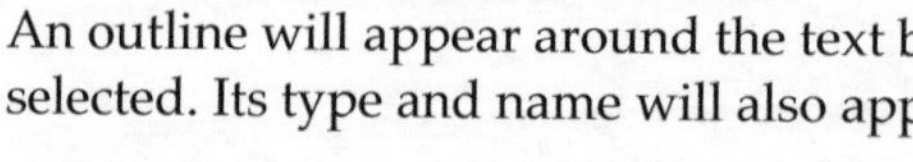
asp:TextBox#TextBoxPostCode
Post Code

An outline will appear around the text box to indicate that it is selected. Its type and name will also appear above it.

If you look at the *Properties* window, you'll see that the bar at the top has also changed to indicate the name of the control you have selected.

Properties
TextBoxPostCode System.Web.UI.WebControls.TextBox

note

Web colors

On web pages, colors are usually defined using hex (short for hexadecimal) codes.

Hexadecimal is a counting system used by computers which has the numbers 0 to 9 as well as the letters A-F. This means that 1B in hexadecimal would actually be 12 in the decimal counting system we're used to.

Hex color codes are actually 3 hexadecimal numbers put together to define a color.

The first number indicates how much red is in the color, the second how much blue and the third how much green.

This means that black would be #000000 because it has absolutely no red, blue or green.

White would be #FFFFFF, the maximum amount of every color.

The brightest possible red would be #FF0000, with 255 parts red and 0 parts blue and green.

This color coding system allows for 16,777,216 possible colors.

note

Other Properties

If you switch to *Design* view and click on the properties of an object in the *Properties* window, you'll notice a short description of the property appears at the bottom of the window.

There are so many possible properties that they won't all be covered in this book, but by using the descriptions you can quickly learn the purpose of each property.

3. Look for the *BackColor* property in the *Properties* window.

   This property controls the background color of the text box (see *Web colors* sidebar for more information).

4. Click in the box that currently says *#CCFFFF*.

   A box with three dots appears on the right-hand side of the box.

5. Click on that box and a dialog will appear prompting you to choose a color.

6. Click any color you like and then click *OK*.

7. Click on a different text box and you will see that the color of the *Post Code* text box has changed to the selected color.

5 Change the ID property of a control.

1. Click the *Submit Order* button.

   You should see the name *ButtonSubmitOrder* shown at the top of the *Properties* window.

2. Scroll down to the *ID* property (it's at the end of the list if you are viewing properties in categorized view – see sidebar) and change it to: **ButtonSend**

   You will notice that the name of the button has changed above the *Submit Order* button and at the top of the *Properties* window.

   The *ID* property is the property that ASP.NET uses to tell controls apart. You will cover this in more depth in: *Lesson 4-1: Name controls correctly.*

3. Change the *ID* of the button back to: **ButtonSubmitOrder**

6 Select *TextBoxAddress1* from the drop-down menu at the top of the *Properties* window.

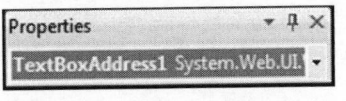

You will see that the *Address 1* text box is highlighted in the *Design* view the same as it would be if you had clicked on it.

This method of selecting objects is useful when you have a very crowded page or when there are hidden elements on the page.

7 Close Visual Studio.

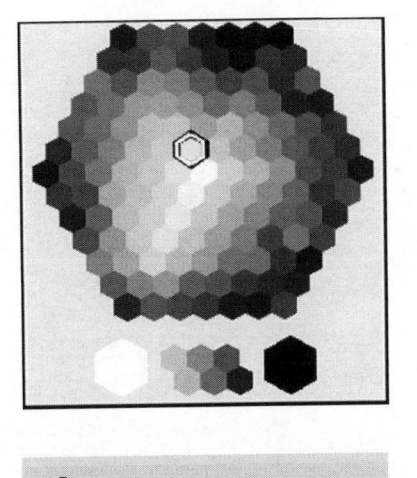

tip

Viewing properties in alphabetical order

By default, Visual Studio shows properties in categories that can be collapsed and expanded by using the small arrows to the left of each group.

You can change the properties window to show properties in alphabetical order by clicking the *alphabetical* icon at the top of the window:

The A-Z view is useful when you know a property name but cannot remember its category.

You can switch it back to grouping by categories by clicking:

The screenshots in this book use the default *Categorized* view.

Lesson 1-13: Change properties in Source view

In the last lesson you changed properties using *Design* view, but it's also possible to do the same thing in *Source* view. This is useful when your page contains hidden elements or is too complicated for *Design* view to display properly. Some developers prefer to work in *Source* view most of the time.

In this lesson, you'll use *Source* view to change the properties of controls on your page.

1 Open *ShiningStone* from your sample files folder.

   It can be found in the *Sample Projects* sub-folder.

2 Open *buy.aspx* in *Source* view.

   After opening *buy.aspx* you can switch to *Source* view by clicking the *Source* button at the bottom of the window.

3 Change control properties in *Source* view using the *Properties* window.

   1. Click on the line that begins:

      `<asp:TextBox ID="TextBoxAddress1"`

      The line should be highlighted in gray. You will see that *TextBoxAddress1* is automatically selected in the *Properties* window.

      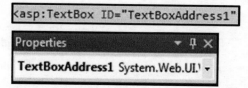

   2. In the *Properties* window, Type **Enter Address** into the *Text* property and press **<Enter>**.

      After a brief delay *Enter Address* appears on *TextBoxAddress1's* line in the *Code Window*.

      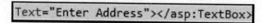

   3. View *buy.aspx* in your browser.

      You'll see that changing the *Text* property has placed the text *Enter Address* inside the *Address 1* text box. The *Text* property is useful when you want to display default text in a text box control.

      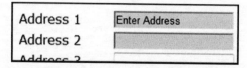

   4. Close your browser and return to Visual Studio.

5. Delete the text you entered from the *Text* property and press **<Enter>**.

You will see that the text has been removed from the code.

```
BackColor="#FFCCCC"></asp:TextBox>
```

6. View *buy.aspx* in your browser again.

You'll see that the text has been removed from the text box.

7. Close your browser and return to Visual Studio.

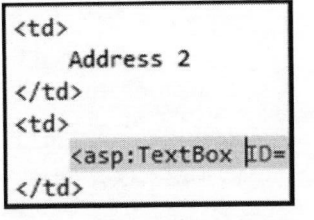

Whenever you change properties using the *Properties* window, the page's code (visible in *Source* view) is being updated. This also works the other way around: if you change properties in *Source* view, they will change in the *Properties* window.

4   Manually change properties in *Source* view.

Although you can use the *Properties* window to change properties while in *Source* view, *Source* view is really intended to be used to edit code manually.

1. Click in the space just after *<asp:TextBox* underneath *Address 2*.

```
<td>
    Address 2
</td>
<td>
    <asp:TextBox ID=
</td>
```

2. Type **Text="Enter Address"**, followed by a space.

```
<td>
    Address 2
</td>
<td>
    <asp:TextBox Text="Enter Address" ID="
</td>
```

You have just manually set the *Text* property of *TextBoxAddress2*.

3. View *buy.aspx* in your browser.

You'll see that the text has been placed in the second text box, just as you'd expect.

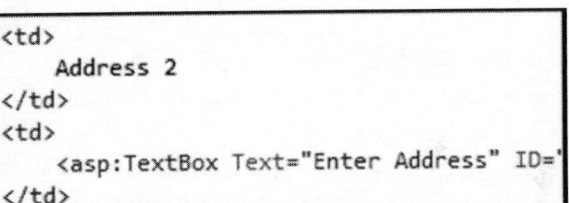

4. Remove the *Text* property by deleting the code you added.

```
<td>
    Address 2
</td>
<td>
    <asp:TextBox ID="TextBoxAddress2"
</td>
```

Source view can be useful, as it displays all of a page's code. There are some things that *Design* view is incapable of displaying, but *Source* view will always contain everything.

5   Close Visual Studio.

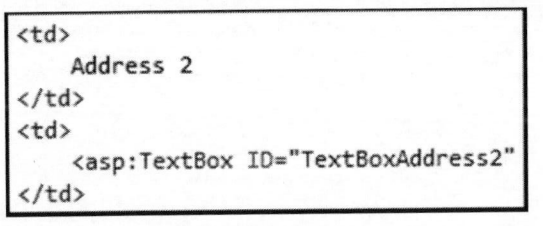

Lesson 1-14: Add controls to a page with the Toolbox

You now know how to navigate through a project and make basic changes to the controls on your pages. Using the *Toolbox*, you can add controls to your pages by simply dragging and dropping them.

1   Open *My Project* from your sample files folder.

2   Open the HTML code of *mypage.aspx* and switch to *Design* view.

     You learned how to do this in: *Lesson 1-9: View .aspx pages in Source and Design views.*

3   Expand the Toolbox.

     1.   Click the *Toolbox* icon on the top left of the screen.

        The *Toolbox* will appear.

     2.   Click the *Auto Hide* icon (⊟) to the right of the top bar of the *Toolbox* to pin it to the window.

        This will stop it from overlapping your page and stop it from disappearing automatically (see sidebar).

4   Expand the *Standard* category in the *Toolbox* (if it isn't already expanded)

     This is done the same way as in the *Solution Explorer* and *Properties Window.*

     Click the ▷ icon next to the *Standard* category (unless it is already expanded).

     The *Standard* category contains the most commonly-used controls.

5   Add a button control to the page.

     Click and drag a *Button* control from the *Toolbox* onto your page, underneath the text you added earlier.

     You will see that a button has been created called *Button1.*

6   Switch to *Source* view.

7   Add a *TextBox* control in *Source* view.

     1.   In the same way as you did with the *Button*, drag a *TextBox* control from the *Toolbox* onto the *Code Window.*

        Try to drop the *TextBox* just before the line that contains the button you added earlier (the line that begins *<asp:Button*).

```
<asp:TextBox ID="TextBox1" runat="server"></asp:TextBox>
<asp:Button ID="Button1" runat="server" Text="Button" />
```

        Some code is added to the page for your new *TextBox* control.

---

tip

Auto Hide

You may have noticed that the *Solution Explorer, Properties Window* and *Toolbox* all have the same 'pin' icon in the top-right corner of their windows:

⊟

This button switches on and off *Auto Hide*. When *Auto Hide* is switched on, the window will automatically minimize away from the screen when it is not in use. By auto-hiding your windows, you can get a large unobstructed view of the main window.

Feel free to experiment with *Auto Hide*. Remember that you can always reset your window layout to default by clicking Window→ Reset Window Layout.

---

2. Switch back to *Design* view.

You will see that the new text box control has been inserted before the button.

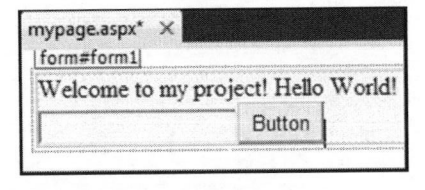

8 Add an *HTML* control.

1. Switch to *Design* view if you're not in that view already.

2. Collapse the *Standard* category in the *Toolbox*.

3. Expand the *HTML* category in the *Toolbox*.

4. Drag an *Input (Reset)* control onto your page after your button.

Your page should now look like this:

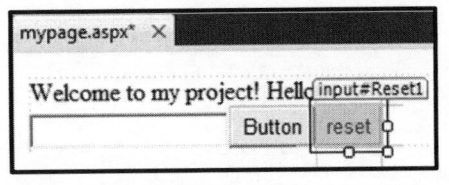

9 Add a *Calendar* control.

You will find the *Calendar* control in the *Standard* category of the *Toolbox*.

In the same way you added the last two controls, add a *Calendar* control to the page. Try to place it before your text box.

Your page should now look like this:

10 Save your changes and close Visual Studio.

Lesson 1-15: Use the QuickTasks menu

You've now learned how to add controls and change their properties, but some controls come with extra features that can only be accessed using the *QuickTasks* menu.

You'll use the *QuickTasks* menu in this lesson.

1   Open *My Project* from your sample files folder (if it isn't already open).

2   Open *mypage.aspx* and switch to *Design* view.

3   Click the Calendar control you added in the last lesson.

4   Open the *QuickTasks* menu for the calendar.

When a *QuickTasks* menu is available for a control, a small arrow icon will appear on the top right-hand side of the control when you select it in *Design* view.

Click the arrow icon ▣ to open the *QuickTasks* menu.

5   Auto Format the calendar using *QuickTasks*.

1.   Click *Auto Format...* in the Calendar control's *QuickTasks* menu.

A dialog will appear from which you can select a format for your calendar.

2.   Click the *Simple* calendar format and click *OK*.

Your calendar should now look like this:

<	January 2011					>
Mo	**Tu**	**We**	**Th**	**Fr**	**Sa**	**Su**
27	28	29	30	31	1	2
3	4	5	6	7	8	9
10	11	12	13	14	15	16
17	18	19	20	21	22	23
24	25	26	27	28	29	30
31	1	2	3	4	5	6

Of course, your own calendar will show the current month and date.

6   View the code that was added by the QuickTask.

Switch to *Source* view. You will see that a lot of code was added to your page when you applied the Auto Format.

If you were very patient, you could set all of those properties yourself using the skills you've learned so far, but Auto Format makes your life a lot easier.

Most *QuickTasks* help to speed up tasks that would usually require you to set a lot of properties manually.

note

Other controls that use QuickTasks

Only a few of the *Standard* ASP.NET controls use *QuickTasks*, mostly the ones that display lists of items.

The more complex controls, especially the ones under the *Data* category have many different *QuickTasks* options.

For now it is only important that you know how to access the *QuickTasks* menu.

Any important *QuickTasks* will be covered in detail as the relevant control is introduced later in the book.

7   Add a *DropDownList* control between the *TextBox* and *Button* controls.

Using the skills you learned in *Lesson 1-14: Add controls to a page with the Toolbox*, add a *DropDownList* control to the page. You'll find it in the *Standard* category of the *ToolBox*.

Try to place it between your *TextBox* and *Button* controls.

8   Use *QuickTasks* to add items to your *DropDownList*.

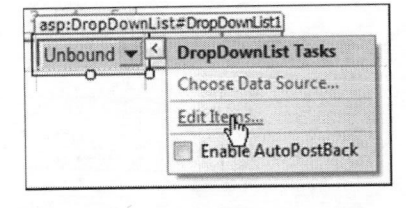

1. Open the *QuickTasks* menu for your new *DropDownList* and click *Edit Items....*

    A dialog will appear.

2. Click the *Add* button to add a new item to your *DropDownList*.

3. Fill in the *Text* property (in the right-hand panel of the dialog) with **Yes** and press **<Enter>**.

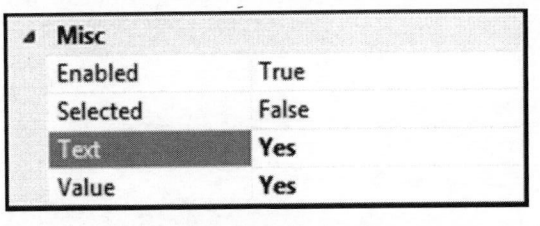

    You will see that the *Value* property is automatically set to match the *Text* property.

    You will explore the *DropDownList* control in detail in: *Lesson 4-7: Use drop down lists*.

4. Add another item by clicking *Add*. This time set its *Text* property to: **No**

5. Click *OK*.

6. Start debugging.

    You will see that your *DropDownList* now has the choices *Yes* and *No* available.

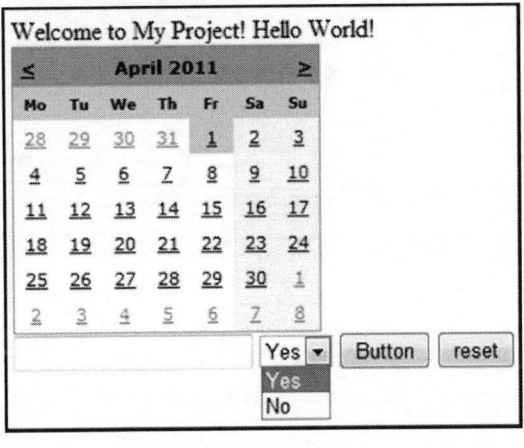

    If you look at the page in *Source* view, you'll see that the following lines of code were added by the QuickTask:

    <asp:ListItem>Yes</asp:ListItem>
    <asp:ListItem>No</asp:ListItem>

9   Save your changes and close Visual Studio.

---

note

In the case of the *DropDownList* control, you could also have accessed the *Items* dialog through its *Items* property in the *Properties* window. However, *QuickTasks* options sometimes allow you to do things that are not possible simply by using *Design* view and the *Properties* window.

In some cases, a QuickTask will allow you to use a simple dialog to quickly create complex code that would otherwise take an enormous amount of effort to type in manually.

Lesson 1-16: Get help

Although this book will teach you all of the skills you need to work with ASP.NET, it won't cover every single control and possible line of code.

Microsoft provides a huge library of help and reference files for ASP.NET called MSDN. This provides comprehensive documentation for every part of the .NET framework (see sidebar).

1   Open Visual Studio.

2   Click Help→View Help.

A dialog may appear asking if you want to allow Visual Studio to display help files from the Internet.

If the dialog appears, click *Yes*.

A web browser window will open displaying Microsoft's homepage for Visual Studio 2010.

3   Search MSDN for the DropDownList control.

Enter **dropdownlist** into the search box in the top-left corner and click the magnifying glass icon to search.

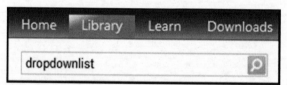

4   Click on the first search result that appears.

DropDownList Class (System.Web.UI.WebControls)
Represents a control that allows the user to select a single it
msdn.microsoft.com/en-us/library/system.web.ui.webcontrol

Everything you could ever want to know about the DropDownList control is displayed.

A lot of the help file won't make much sense to you at the moment. You'll probably recognize the list of properties and their descriptions and will be able to understand some of the example code.

5   Check the .NET version of the help file.

At the time of writing there have been 5 versions of the .NET framework and Microsoft has help files for each one.

To make sure you're looking at the correct help file, check the text at the top of the screen just underneath the title. It should say *.NET Framework 4*. If it doesn't, simply click on the *Other Versions* drop-down and select *.NET Framework 4*.

6   Ask for help in the MSDN forums.

As well as the reference documentation available from MSDN, Microsoft has an online forum available where you can discuss Visual Studio and ASP.NET.

To access the forums, close the web browser and click: Help→MSDN Forums (from the Visual Studio menu). The web page will then appear in a tab inside Visual Studio.

If you click the *Ask a Question* button, you will be prompted to register an MSDN Profile and will then be able to ask your question.

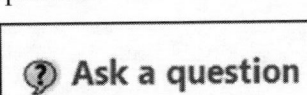

7   Search the Internet for help.

Besides Microsoft's documentation and forums, the Internet is full of other development communities and tutorials.

Sometimes the best way to find the answer to a specific problem is to use your favorite search engine.

If you search for **ASP.NET dropdownlist** using a search engine, you will probably see the MSDN page you looked at earlier appear at the top of the results, along with many other results from different places around the web.

8   Close Visual Studio.

Session 1: Exercise

1   Create a new *ASP.NET Web Application* project in your sample files folder called: **Exercise1**

2   Add a new *Web Form* item to the project called: **mypage.aspx**

3   Add a *Calendar* control to the *mypage.aspx* page.

4   Use *QuickTasks* to *Auto Format* the Calendar control to the *Colorful 1* scheme.

5   Change the *ID* property of the Calendar control to: **CalendarColorful**

6   Add a new folder to the project called: **Images**

7   Add the *pattern.jpg* file from the *Images* folder in your sample files folder to your new *Images* folder.

8   Add a HTML *Image* control to the page using the *HTML* category of the *ToolBox*.

9   Set the *Src* property of the new *Image* control to: **Images/pattern.jpg**

10   Delete the *About.aspx* page.

11   Set *mypage.aspx* to be the project's start page.

12   Start the project in debug mode.

13   Save your work.

If you need help slide the page to the left

Session 1: Exercise Answers

These are the four questions that students find the most difficult to answer:

Q 7	Q 6	Q 5	Q 3
1. Right-click on the *Images* folder in the *Solution Explorer*. 2. Click: Add→ Existing Item... from the shortcut menu. 3. Browse to the *C:\Practice\ASP.NET\Images* folder. 4. Click on *pattern.jpg* and then click *Add*. This was covered in: *Lesson 1-7: Manage a project with the Solution Explorer.*	1. Right-click on *Exercise1* in the *Solution Explorer*. 2. Click Add→ New Folder from the shortcut menu. 3. Type the name: **Images** This was covered in: *Lesson 1-7: Manage a project with the Solution Explorer.*	1. Click on the calendar in *Design* view. 2. Scroll down in the *Properties* window until you see the *ID* property. 3. Click in the box that currently says *Calendar1* and change the text to: **CalendarColorful** This was covered in: *Lesson 1-12: Change properties in Design view.*	1. Double-click on *mypage.aspx* in the *Solution Explorer*. 2. Click on the *Design* button at the bottom of the main panel. 3. Drag a *Calendar* control from the *ToolBox* to the page. This was covered in: *Lesson 1-14: Add controls to a page with the Toolbox.*

If you have difficulty with the other questions, here are the lessons that cover the relevant skills:

1   Refer to: Lesson 1-5: Create an ASP.NET Web Application project.

2   Refer to: Lesson 1-7: Manage a project with the Solution Explorer.

4   Refer to: Lesson 1-15: Use the QuickTasks menu.

8   Refer to: Lesson 1-14: Add controls to a page with the Toolbox.

9   Refer to: Lesson 1-12: Change properties in Design view.

10   Refer to: Lesson 1-7: Manage a project with the Solution Explorer.

11   Refer to: Lesson 1-8: Run a project.

12   Refer to: Lesson 1-8: Run a project.

13   Refer to: Lesson 1-9: View .aspx pages in Source and Design views.

Session Two: Understanding Web Sites

2

> All truths are easy to understand once they are discovered; the point is to discover them.
>
> *Galileo Galilei, Italian scientist (1564 - 1642)*

Microsoft has long realized that there are two (almost) completely different resources needed to create excellent web applications: web designers and web developers. They even provide two tools, one for each discipline (Visual Studio for web developers and Expression Web for web designers).

Web developers are mainly concerned with the functionality of a web application, which they enable using ASP.NET and C# technologies.

Web designers are mainly concerned with the appearance of web pages, which they enable using three completely different technologies: HTML, CSS and JavaScript.

In this session it is assumed that you have no existing web design skills. It is included because you'll need to understand basic web design to put your C# and ASP.NET skills into context.

Many readers of this book will already be very comfortable with web design technologies. Even if you are in this category you should still complete this session as it also includes some important background information about ASP.NET and C#.

Session Objectives

By the end of this session you will be able to:

- Understand HTML bold, italic and heading tags
- Understand HTML paragraph and break tags
- Understand the aspx page structure
- Use the title, meta, link and script tags
- Create an HTML table
- Navigate HTML with the tag navigator
- Display images and links on a page
- Work with CSS
- Use the CSS Properties window
- Use the div and span tags
- Work with JavaScript
- Work with HTML forms

Lesson 2-1: Understand HTML bold, italic and heading tags

You've already touched on HTML a few times in this book, enough to understand that it is a vital part of every web site.

This lesson covers some of the basics of writing HTML code.

1   Open *HTMLTest* from your sample files folder.

You will find this in the *Sample Projects* subfolder.

2   Open *default.aspx* in *Source* view.

3   Add some text.

1. Type the following into the gap between *<div>* and *</div>*:

    This is paragraph 1

    ```
    <body>
        <form id="form1" runat="server">
        <div>
            This is paragraph 1
        </div>
        </form>
    </body>
    ```

2. Switch to *Design* view and you'll see that the text appears on the page.

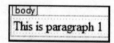

4   Make the text bold.

The *<b>* tag makes text bold.

1. Switch to *Source* view.

2. Change the paragraph to look like this:

    This is <b>paragraph 1</b>

    ```
    <div>
        This is <b>paragraph 1</b>
    </div>
    ```

    When you type the first <b> tag you'll see IntelliSense at work (see sidebar).

    Everything between <b> and </b> will be made bold.

3. Switch back to *Design* view.

    You'll see that the text *paragraph 1* is now displayed in bold.

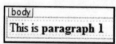

5   Make text italic.

The *<i>* tag works in the same way as the *<b>* tag to make text italic.

1. Switch back to *Source* view again.

2. Change the paragraph to look like this:

<i>This is <b>paragraph 1</b></i>

```
<div>
    <i>This is <b>paragraph 1</b></i>
</div>
```

Everything between *<i>* and *</i>* will be made *italic*. Note that this includes the contents of the *<b>* tag.

When tags are put inside other tags like this, it is called 'nesting'.

3. Switch back to *Design* view.

This time you'll see that the whole paragraph is italic, with the words *paragraph 1* in bold and italic.

```
body
This is paragraph 1
```

Notice the order of the closing tags. It's important that you close the tags in the same order in which you opened them.

6 **Make text into a heading.**

1. Return to *Source* view.

2. Add a new line before the existing text.

3. Add the following code:

<h1>This is the page heading</h1>

```
<div>
    <h1>This is the page heading</h1>
    <i>This is <b>paragraph 1</b></i>
</div>
```

4. Switch to *Design* view.

You'll see that the contents of the *h1* tag are very big and bold!

5. Return to *Source* view.

6. Change your *<h1>* and *</h1>* tags into **<h2>** and **</h2>**tags.

```
<div>
    <h2>This is the page heading</h2>
    <i>This is <b>paragraph 1</b></i>
</div>
```

7. Switch to *Design* view.

You'll see that *h2* is slightly smaller than *h1* (see sidebar for more).

```
body
This is the page heading

This is paragraph 1
```

Lesson 2-2: Understand HTML paragraph and break tags

In this lesson, you'll use the HTML paragraph and break tags to break up text on your page.

1   Open *HTMLTest* from your sample files folder.

You will find it in the *Sample Projects* subfolder.

2   Open *default.aspx* in *Source* view.

3   Add paragraph tags to the HTML code.

One of the most basic tags in HTML is the paragraph tag. Paragraph tags do just what they say: they break up text into paragraphs.

1. Add a new line after the text: *paragraph 1*.

2. Type the following on the new line:

    This is paragraph 2

    ```
    <div>
        <h2>This is the page heading</h1>
        <i>This is <b>paragraph 1</b></i>
        This is paragraph 2
    </div>
    ```

3. Switch to *Design* view and you'll see that both of the pieces of text have been put on the same line, even though they're on different lines in your HTML code. This is because web browsers ignore white space.

    ```
    This is paragraph 1 This is paragraph 2
    ```

4. Switch back to *Source* view and add *<p>* tags to contain both the text: *This is paragraph 1* and *This is paragraph 2*:

    <p><i>This is <b>paragraph 1</b></i></p>
    <p>This is paragraph 2</p>

    ```
    <div>
        <h2>This is the page heading</h1>
        <p><i>This is <b>paragraph 1</b></i></p>
        <p>This is paragraph 2</p>
    </div>
    ```

5. Switch back to *Design* view.

    You'll see that the text has now been separated into two paragraphs.

    ```
    This is paragraph 1

    This is paragraph 2
    ```

4   Break up a paragraph with break tags.

Although paragraph tags are useful for breaking text into paragraphs, sometimes you will want to put line breaks inside paragraphs without starting a new paragraph. For this you will use the break tag: *
*

1. Switch to *Source* view.

2. Add the following text on a new line after the two paragraphs:

   <p>Mary had a little lamb
   Its fleece was white as snow
   And everywhere that Mary went
   The lamb was sure to go</p>

   ```
   <div>
       <h2>This is the page heading</h1>
       <p><i>This is <b>paragraph 1</b></i></p>
       <p>This is paragraph 2</p>

       <p>Mary had a little lamb
       Its fleece was white as snow
       And everywhere that Mary went
       The lamb was sure to go</p>
   </div>
   ```

3. Switch to *Design* view.

   You'll see that although you've put the text in a paragraph of its own, everything is still on one line inside that paragraph.

   > *This is **paragraph 1***
   >
   > This is paragraph 2
   >
   > Mary had a little lamb Its fleece was white as snow And eve

   You might be thinking that you could fix this by putting every line inside a pair of *<p>* tags, but doing that would cause gaps to appear between the lines by default (see sidebar).

   The answer is the break tag. The break tag just inserts a single line break wherever it is placed.

4. Switch to *Source* view and change the text to the following:

   **<p>Mary had a little lamb
**
   **Its fleece was white as snow
**
   **And everywhere that Mary went
**
   The lamb was sure to go</p>

   ```
   <p>Mary had a little lamb<br />
   Its fleece was white as snow<br />
   And everywhere that Mary went<br />
   The lamb was sure to go</p>
   ```

   Note that the break tag is a self-closing tag (see sidebar).

5. Start Debugging.

   Your page should now look like this:

   > http://localhost:49882/default.aspx
   >
   > ## This is the page heading
   >
   > *This is **paragraph 1***
   >
   > This is paragraph 2
   >
   > Mary had a little lamb
   > Its fleece was white as snow
   > And everywhere that Mary went
   > The lamb was sure to go

note

<% %> Tags

In ASP.NET it is actually possible to put C# code directly onto an HTML web page by putting it between <% and %> tags.

ASP.NET's precursor was simply known as ASP and had no code-behind files, so all of the C# code was put on the aspx page inside <% %> tags.

Since ASP.NET introduced code-behind files, it is very rare to see this done today.

trivia

HTML and the W3C

You've probably noticed the links to *w3.org* in the *DOCTYPE* and *html* tags. This is the web site of the World Wide Web Consortium or W3C.

The W3C are responsible for defining international standards for the Internet.

Before the W3C began to define recognized standards, web browsers often disagreed hugely on the correct way to interpret HTML.

Since the introduction of the W3C's standards there are a lot fewer incompatibilities between browsers.

Newer versions of HTML may appear at any time as the W3C refines and improves the HTML and CSS languages. You can see that, in this case, the web page complies with the *XHTML 1.0 Transitional* standard. This is a very mature standard (finalized in 2002) that is well supported by all modern browsers.

Unfortunately, some browsers still don't fully comply with the W3C's standards, so it is still necessary to test your sites thoroughly in every type of browser you think your users may have.

Lesson 2-3: Understand the aspx page structure

Although Visual Studio automatically creates the basic elements of an HTML page for you, it's important to understand the purpose of each element.

In this lesson you'll manually create the different parts of a structured HTML web page.

1 Open *HTML Test* from your sample files folder.

2 Open *emptypage.aspx* in *Source* view.

This page contains only the bare bones of an *.aspx* web page.

3 Understand the *Page* tag.

The first tag is enclosed in <% tags (see sidebar). This line is never sent to web browsers and is used instead to inform ASP.NET which programming language and code-behind file to use for this page.

```
<%@ Page Language="C#" AutoEventWireup="true" CodeBehi
```

You should never have to change this line in the course of this book.

4 Understand the *DOCTYPE* tag.

The *DOCTYPE* tag is the first thing that a web browser reads. It tells the web browser which web standard was used to create the page so that it can interpret the HTML code correctly.

```
<!DOCTYPE html PUBLIC "-//W3C//DTD XHTML 1.0 Transiti
```

This line is needed because there are several different versions of HTML defined by the Web Consortium or W3C (see sidebar).

Again, you should never have to change this line.

5 Add a *<head>* tag.

The next tags you'll see are opening and closing *<html>* tags. These tell the browser that the code inside the tags is HTML.

Between the *<html>* and *</html>* tags, add the following:

<head>

</head>

```
<html xmlns="http://www.w3.org/1999/xhtml">
    <head>

    </head>
</html>
```

The *head* tag doesn't contain any of the page's content, but instead is used to contain other information about the page. You'll learn more about the *head* tag in: *Lesson 2-4: Use the title, meta, link and script tags*.

6 Add a *<body>* tag.

Everything that you actually see in a web browser is contained between two *body* tags. In the last lesson, all of the text you added was nested inside the *body* tags.

After the *</head>* line, add the following:

<body>

</body>

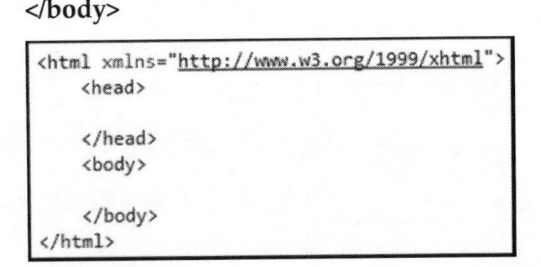

7   Add a form.

If you look back at *default.aspx*, you'll notice that the only thing missing from this page is the *form* tag. You'll learn more about forms in: *Lesson 2-12: Work with HTML Forms.*

For ASP.NET controls to work correctly, they need to be nested inside *form* tags. The code between the form tags runs on the server (see sidebar).

Since ASP.NET controls will be displayed on the web page, the *form* tag needs to be inside the *body* tags.

Add the following text inside the *body* tag:

<form id="form1" runat="server">

</form>

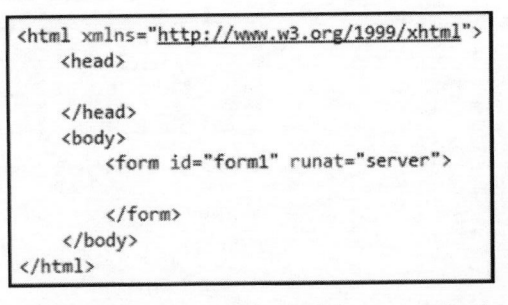

You've now created the full framework of an ASP.NET web page, capable of using ASP.NET controls and C# code.

Of course, this is normally created automatically when you add a new page to the project.

8   Save your changes and close Visual Studio.

note

runat="server"

When an HTML tag is marked with *runat="server"* it becomes available to ASP.NET instead of being a normal 'static' tag.

This means that you can modify its contents using C# code, which you will start doing in: *Lesson 3-1: Change properties with C#.*

For this reason, any ASP.NET controls have to be inside a form with *runat="server"* to work correctly.

Although you could place 'static' HTML content outside the *form* tag, it is best to keep all of your page's content between the *<form>* and *</form>* tags.

ASP.NET will only allow you to have one form with *runat="server"* per page.

You'll learn more about forms in: *Lesson 2-12: Work with HTML Forms.*

Lesson 2-4: Use the title, meta, link and script tags

You created a pair of *<head>* tags in: *Lesson 2-3: Understand the aspx page structure*. These define a head section which contains other tags to define information about the page that is not displayed in the web browser.

In this lesson you'll learn about three of the tags that can be added to the head section: the *title, meta, link* and *script* tags.

1   Open *HTMLTest* from your sample files folder.

2   Open *headtest.aspx* in *Source* view.

This is another empty, bare-bones aspx page.

3   Set the page's title.

1.   Click between the *<title>* and *</title>* tags and type:
Head Tags

2.   View the page in your browser.

You'll see that the page title has been picked up and is displayed in the page's tab.

3.   Close the web browser.

4   Add a favicon using the *link* tag.

1.   Add the following tag after the *title* tag:

<link rel="shortcut icon" href="/favicon.ico" />

```
<head runat="server">
    <title>Head Tags</title>
    <link rel="Shortcut Icon" href="/favicon.ico">
</head>
```

2.   View the page in your browser.

You should see a 'smiley face' icon appear next to your page's title. This is called a *favicon*. See the sidebar if your favicon doesn't appear.

4.   Close the web browser.

5   Add a page description using the *meta* tag.

Meta tags are used to provide information about your page to web browsers. They are also often read by search engines to gather information about your page to display in search results.

Add the following tag to your *<head>* tag:

<meta name="description" content="A test page" />

```
<head runat="server">
    <title>Head Tags</title>
    <link rel="Shortcut Icon" href="/favicon.ico">
    <meta name="description" content="A test page" />
</head>
```

note

Meta tags and search engines

In the 1990's, meta tags were often the only thing indexed by search engines. Because of this they were extremely important to a page's search engine ranking.

In recent years, however, search engines have moved away from meta tags and towards more complex analysis of pages to determine search engine ranking.

Meta tags still shouldn't be ignored, but they no longer have the importance they once had.

There are many other Meta tags that are used for different purposes. Several of these are used to provide enhanced information to search engines.

The contents of meta tags aren't directly visible to people visiting your site.

6 Link a CSS stylesheet using the *link* tag.

You've seen CSS mentioned briefly a few times. CSS is used to consistently apply an appearance and layout to web pages across a site.

The *link* tag can be used to add a reference to a CSS stylesheet in order to allow it to apply a standard style this page.

1. Add the following to your *<head>* tag:

   <link rel="stylesheet" href="/styles/allred.css" />

   ```
   <head runat="server">
       <title>Head Tags</title>
       <link rel="Shortcut Icon" href="/favicon.ico">
       <meta name="description" content="A test page" />
       <link rel="stylesheet" href="/styles/allred.css" />
   </head>
   ```

2. View the page in your browser.

   You'll see that linking the stylesheet has made the background of your page turn red! *Allred.css* is a very basic stylesheet. You'll learn to create more interesting stylesheets in: *Lesson 2-8: Work with CSS.*

3. Close the web browser.

7 Link a JavaScript file using the *script* tag.

In *Lesson 1-9: View .aspx pages in Source and Design views,* you might have read the sidebar saying that there are three main languages understood by web browsers. The first two are HTML and CSS. The only language you haven't seen in action is JavaScript.

1. Add the following text to your *<head>* tag:

   <script type="text/javascript" src="/scripts/alert.js"></script>

   ```
   <head runat="server">
       <title>Head Tags</title>
       <link rel="Shortcut Icon" href="/favicon.ico">
       <meta name="description" content="A test page" />
       <link rel="stylesheet" href="/styles/allred.css" />
       <script type="text/javascript" src="/scripts/alert.js"></script>
   </head>
   ```

   Note that *script* tags cannot be self-closing. You must have an opening *<script>* and a closing *</script>* tag for them to work.

2. View the page in your browser.

   This time a popup window will appear when your page loads.

Making messages appear in popups is only one of the most basic things JavaScript can do. You'll learn a little more about JavaScript in: *Lesson 2-11: Work with JavaScript.*

Lesson 2-5: Create an HTML table

Another important feature of HTML is the ability to create tables. If you've ever worked with Microsoft Excel, you should be familiar with tables of data laid out in a series of rows and columns.

In this lesson, you'll see how an HTML table can be created automatically and manually by hand-writing code.

1   Open *HTMLTest* from your sample files folder.

2   Open *tabletest.aspx* in *Design* view.

3   Automatically create a table using the design tools.

    1.   Click Table→Insert Table.

    The *Insert Table* dialog appears.

    2.   Click *OK*, without changing any settings.

    A table will appear, outlined in dotted lines.

    3.   Click in each of the table's four cells and fill them in as shown:

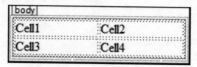

4   Add a row to the table using HTML.

    1.   Switch to *Source* view.

    You will see that the table is made up of 3 different HTML tags: *<table>*, *<tr>* and *<td>*.

    The *<tr>* and *<td>* tags define table rows and table cells. They must be contained in a *table* tag to be recognized as part of a table.

    You'll notice that the text you added is all contained in the *<td>* tags.

    2.   Add some blank space before the *</table>* tag.

    3.   Add the following code in the space:

    <tr>
    <td>Cell5</td>
    <td>Cell6</td>
    </tr>

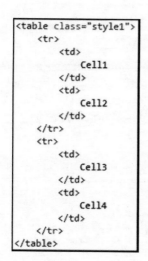

```
<table class="style1">
    <tr>
        <td>
            Cell1
        </td>
        <td>
            Cell2
        </td>
    </tr>
    <tr>
        <td>
            Cell3
        </td>
        <td>
            Cell4
        </td>
    </tr>
</table>
```

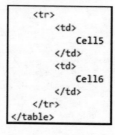

```
    <tr>
        <td>
            Cell5
        </td>
        <td>
            Cell6
        </td>
    </tr>
</table>
```

Remember that you can use automatic formatting to automatically indent the table code as shown. You learned how to do this in: *Lesson 1-10: Use automatic formatting*.

4. Switch back to *Design* view.

5. You'll see that a new row has been added containing the cells *Cell5* and *Cell6*.

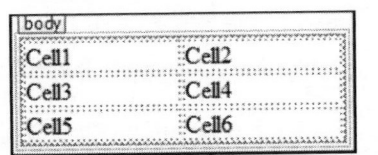

5 Merge cells in *Design* view.

1. Click and drag from *Cell1* to *Cell2* so that both cells are highlighted.

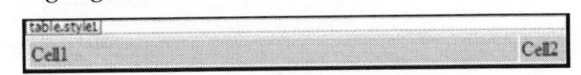

2. Click Table→Modify→Merge Cells.

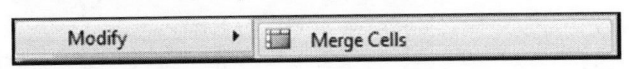

You'll see that the top two cells have now been merged into one big cell.

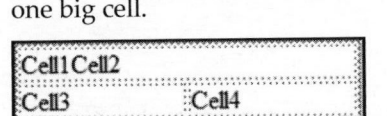

3. Replace the text in the top cell with: **TitleCell**

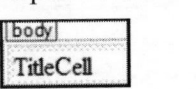

4. Switch back to *Source* view.

You'll see that the cell has been merged by changing it into a single *td* tag with a *colspan* property of 2, because it spans two columns.

```
<td colspan="2">
    TitleCell
</td>
```

6 Make *TitleCell* into a heading cell.

There is a special kind of cell for headings called *th*.

1. Change the *<td>* tag for *TitleCell* into a *<th>* tag.

```
<th colspan="2">
    TitleCell
</th>
```

2. Switch to *Design* view.

You'll see that the text has been automatically made bold and centered.

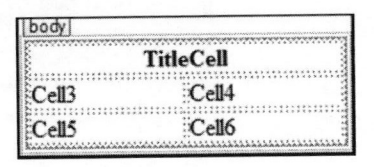

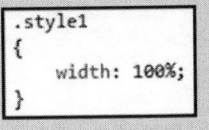

Lesson 2-6: Navigate HTML with the tag navigator

As you have learned already in this session, HTML is made up of a series of tags that are nested inside each other.

In large HTML files, it can become increasingly difficult to relate what you see in *Design* view to the code in *Source* view. Fortunately, Visual Studio provides you with the tag navigator, which shows at a glance which tag you have selected and which tags it is nested inside.

1   Open *HTML Test* from your sample files folder.

2   Open *tabletest.aspx* in *Design* view.

3   Navigate nested tags using the tag navigator.

    1.   Click in one of your table's cells.

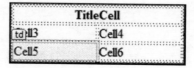

    The tag navigator should appear at the bottom of the screen.

    If the tag navigator doesn't appear, close any browser windows you have open and try closing and reopening *tabletest.aspx*.

    The navigator shows you which tag you currently have selected and the hierarchy of the tags it is nested inside.

    You can see that the *td* tag you have selected is nested inside a *tr* tag, which is inside a *table* tag, which is inside a *div* tag, which is inside a *form* tag, which is inside the *body* tag, which is inside the *html* tag.

    2.   Select the entire table row using the tag navigator.

    You can select any of the tags in the navigator by clicking on them. Click on the *<tr>* button to select the whole table row.

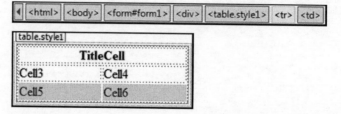

    Now the entire row is selected. If this doesn't work for you try clicking the <td> button again followed by the <tr> button.

    Notice as well that the *<tr>* tag is selected in the *Properties* window (if your properties window has disappeared you need to reset your window layout to default as described in: *Lesson 1-3: Set up the development environment*).

3. Select the entire table using the tag navigator.

Click the *<table.style1>* tag in the tag navigator to select the entire table.

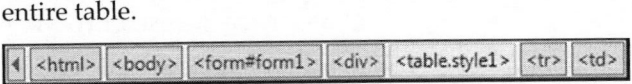

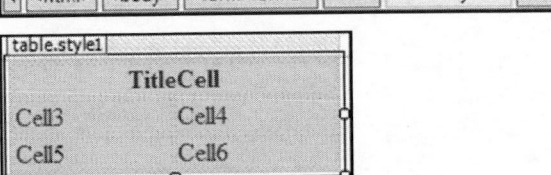

Again, you'll see that the *table* tag is selected in the *Properties* window, ready for you to change its properties.

4 **Select only a tag's content using the tag navigator.**

1. Click on *Cell5*.

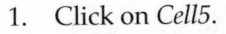

2. Hover your mouse cursor over the *<tr>* button in the tag navigator.

You'll notice that a black down arrow appears to the right of the button. This indicates that there is a drop-down menu.

3. Click the down arrow next to *<tr>* and then click *Select Tag Content* from the drop-down menu.

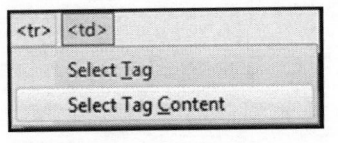

Now only the text inside the *<tr>* tag is selected!

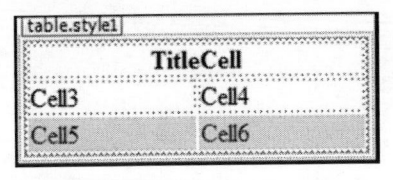

4. Press **<Delete>**.

The contents of the cells are deleted, but the cells themselves are left intact.

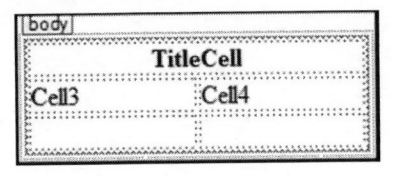

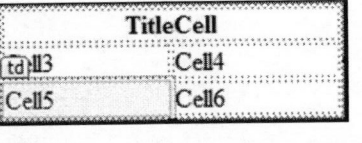

note

Deleting

A lot of Visual Studio's interface is standardized across the application. Deleting is a good example.

Pressing the **<Delete>** key will delete whatever you currently have selected, whether it is a control in *Design* view or a file in the *Solution Explorer*.

The same is true if you right-click and then click *Delete* from the shortcut menu.

Lesson 2-7: Display images and links on a page

With the skills you've learned so far in this session, you're close to being able to create useful HTML pages.

This lesson will show you how to add hyperlinks and images to a page.

1 Open *HTML Test* from your sample files folder.

2 Open *linktest.aspx* in *Design* view.

3 Create a link in *Design* view.

   1. Type the following text onto the page:

   The Smart Method

   2. Select the text either by clicking and dragging or by using the tag navigator to select the *div* tag content (you learned how to do this in: *Lesson 2-6: Navigate HTML with the tag navigator*).

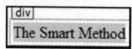

   3. Click Format→Convert to Hyperlink....

   A dialog appears.

   4. Type **http://www.learnasp4.com** into the dialog and click *OK*.

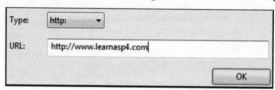

   5. View *linktest.aspx* in your browser and try clicking on the link.

   The LearnASP4.com web site home page appears.

   6. Close the browser and return to *Design* view.

4 Change the link's properties using *Design* view.

   1. Click on your link in *Design* view.

   The *Properties* window should display <A> as its selected object. The <a> tag is used to define an HTML hyperlink.

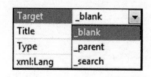

   2. Change the *Target* property of the link to **_blank** using the *Properties* window.

   You'll notice that the *Target* property has a drop-down menu. It is quicker to choose *_blank* from the drop-down list than to type it in manually

   3. View the page in your browser and click on the link.

   This time you'll see that the link opens in a new window.

   4. Close the web browser.

5 Add a link in *Source* view.

   1. Switch to *Source* view.

2. After the pair of <a></a> tags that define the hyperlink to *The Smart Method* add the following hyperlink code:

**<a href="http://www.learnmicrosoftexcel.com">
Learn Excel</a>**

```
<div>
    <a href="http://www.learnasp4.com" target="_blank">The Smart Method</a>
    <a href="http://www.learnmicrosoftexcel.com">Learn Excel</a>
</div>
```

3. Switch back to *Design* view.

You will see that the HTML tag you added has created a link.

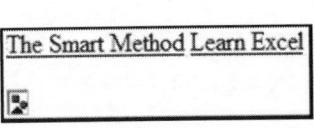

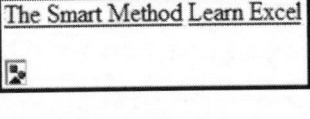

6 Add an image in *Design* view.

As you did in *Lesson 1-14: Add controls to a page with the Toolbox*, drag an *Image* control from the *HTML* category of the *Toolbox* onto the page, below the links.

7 Set the image path in *Design* view.

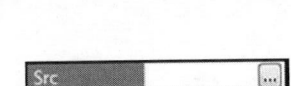

1. Select the I*mage* element and find the *Src* property in the *Properties* window.

If the *Src* property is not visible, it is because you have either added a standard image control instead of an HTML image control or because you have placed the image control inside the hyperlink <*a*> tags.

2. Click the *browse* icon next to the *Src* property (⬚) and select *balloon.jpg* from the *images* folder.

3. Click *OK*.

The image now appears on the page. Note that the *Src* property has been set to *images/balloon.jpg*. This is the *path* to the image (see sidebar).

8 Change the image path in *Source* view.

1. Switch to *Source* view.

2. Change the *src* property of the *img* tag to: **images/pattern.jpg**

```
<img alt="" src="images/pattern.jpg" />
```

3. Switch back to *Design* view.

You will see that the image has changed.

You should now have a good idea of how to change properties using both the *Design* and *Source* views.

9 Save your changes and close Visual Studio.

---

note

Paths

If you're a seasoned Windows and Internet user, you probably understand that paths are used to tell computers which folder a file is in.

In this lesson, the images you need to display are in the *images* folder, so the path begins with *images*.

If an image called image.jpg was in a sub-folder of *images* called *photos*, the path would be:

images/photos/image.jpg

HTML paths are always relative to the current location of the page. If your page was in a folder called *pages*, you'd need to use the following path to get to the *images* folder:

../images/image.jpg

../ in a path means to go up one level (ie to the folder that this folder is in).

If paths are getting confusing, using the browse feature, as you do in this lesson, will always return the correct path.

Lesson 2-8: Work with CSS

CSS is the language used to define the styles of elements on modern web pages. CSS has over a hundred different properties you can use to define styles and there are many different CSS techniques used to create the pages you see on the Internet.

Covering every CSS property and technique would be the subject matter for an entire book in itself, but you will briefly cover some of the most important ones in this lesson.

1   Open *HTMLTest* from your sample files folder.

2   Open *csstest.aspx* in *Source* view.

3   Link the *csstest.css* stylesheet from the *styles* folder.

Add the following tag to the page's head section (anywhere in the area between the *<head>* and *</head>* tags):

```
<link rel="Stylesheet" href="/styles/csstest.css" />
```

4   Create a CSS class.

CSS classes are ways of grouping style properties together in CSS and giving them a name. Elements on your page can then be referenced to the name of the class in order to use its styles.

1.   Double-click on *csstest.css* in the *Styles* folder to open it for editing. Note that the file is currently empty.

2.   Add the following text to the CSS file:

```
.BigText
{
    font-size: xx-large;
}
```

```
csstest.css  ×
    .BigText
    {
        font-size: xx-large;
    }
```

You just created a CSS class called *BigText* that makes the text of any HTML tag that references it extra, extra large.

5   Assign the BigText class to an HTML tag.

Now that you've created a class, you need to assign it to an element on the page for it to affect anything.

1.   Open *csstest.aspx* in *Source* view.

2.   Change the line that says *<div id="Div1">* to the following:

```
<div id="Div1" class="BigText">
```

```
<div id="Div1" class="BigText">
    <p>Paragraph 1</p>
    <p>Paragraph 2</p>
    <p>Paragraph 3</p>
</div>
```

Note that CSS class names are case sensitive so *bigtext* wouldn't work.

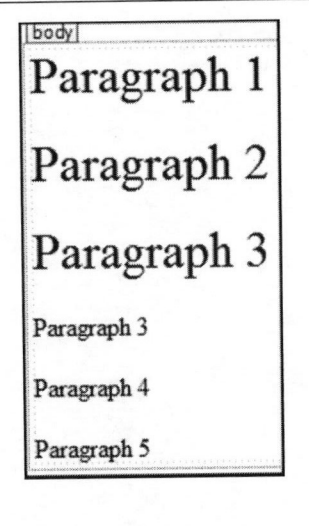

3. Switch to *Design* view.

   You'll see that the text of all of the elements nested inside *Div1* has been made extra, extra large.

6 **Create a CSS identifier.**

Identifiers are similar to classes, but instead of using the *class* property they automatically attach themselves to any element with the same *ID* property. It is easier to understand identifiers by seeing them in action:

1. Open *csstest.css*.

2. Add the following text:

   #Div2
   {
      color: White;
      background-color: Blue;
   }

```
.BigText
{
    font-size: xx-large;
}

#Div2
{
    color: White;
    background-color: Blue;
}
```

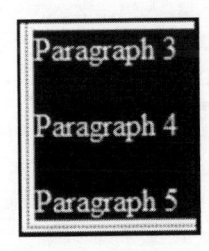

3. Switch back to *csstest.aspx* in *Design* view.

   As you can see, the identifier has set the text color to white and the background color to blue for all elements within the div tags that have the ID *Div2*.

7 **Use inline CSS.**

Although it's best practice to keep all of your styles in separate CSS files, you can also place CSS code directly into the *style* property of an HTML tag.

1. Switch back to the *Source* view of *csstest.aspx*.

2. Change the code of *<p>Paragraph 1</p>* to the following:

   <p style="font-size: xx-small">Paragraph 1</p>

```
<div id="Div1" class="BigText">
    <p style="font-size: xx-small">Paragraph 1</p>
    <p>Paragraph 2</p>
    <p>Paragraph 3</p>
</div>
```

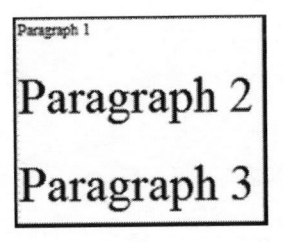

3. Switch back to *Design* view.

   You'll see that *Paragraph 1* now has smaller text than the other paragraphs.

   Inline CSS always overrides any style set by the *class* property.

ASP.NET often automatically generates inline CSS when converting ASP.NET controls into HTML code.

Lesson 2-9: Use the CSS Properties window

note

Other common CSS properties

In this session you learn how to modify text and background colors.

Other common CSS properties are:

font-family
Used to select the fonts used by text.

display
Used to change how the element is displayed. Most often used to hide elements by setting to *none*.

position
Used to change how the element is positioned on the page.

top and *left*
Used to set an element's position, depending on how the *position* property is set.

text-align
Used to align text and nested elements to the left, right, center, etc.

vertical-align
Used to set how text and nested elements are aligned vertically.

padding
Adds space to the inside of the element.

margin
Adds space to the outside of the element.

To make it easier to work with CSS, Visual Studio provides the *CSS Properties* window.

By using it in *Design* view, you can very easily create and modify CSS styles.

1   Open *HTMLTest* from your sample files folder.

2   Open *csstest.aspx* in *Design* view.

3   Display the *CSS Properties* window.

Click View→CSS Properties.

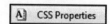

4   Modify the *BigText* style using the CSS Properties window.

1.   Select *Div1* using the drop-down menu in the *Properties* window (the normal *Properties* window, not the *CSS Properties* window).

You'll see that the *.BigText* style you created in *Lesson 2-8: Work with CSS* is shown in the *Applied Rules* box at the top of the *CSS Properties* window. It also shows that *BigText* comes from the file *csstest.css*.

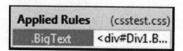

Towards the top of the *CSS Properties* list, you can see the *font-size* property, which is part of the *.BigText* CSS class.

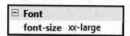

Beneath *font-size*, you'll see a complete list of the CSS properties that are available. You can use the *CSS Properties* window to set them just like you set properties in the *Properties* window.

2.   Using the drop-down menu in *CSS Properties*, change the *font-size* from **xx-large** to **xx-small**.

You'll see the change happen immediately in the *Design* panel.

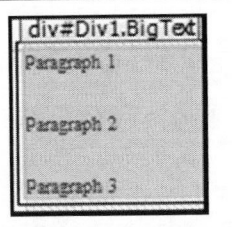

note

CSS 3

At the time of writing CSS has had 3 versions, but Visual Studio's list of CSS properties is only complete up to CSS version 2.

CSS version 2 is almost universally supported by modern web browsers, while support for CSS 3 is very inconsistent.

You can still use CSS 3 properties in Visual Studio, but you will have to type them into your CSS files manually and Visual Studio may mark them with warnings as it does not recognize them as valid CSS.

CSS 3 properties will probably be added to Visual Studio when web browser support for them improves.

3. Open *csstest.css* from the *styles* folder.

   You'll see that the *.BigText* class has been automatically changed.

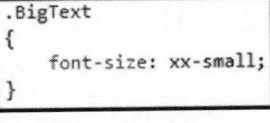

```
.BigText
{
    font-size: xx-small;
}
```

5   **Add a new style using the CSS Properties window.**

1. Open csstest.aspx in Design view.

2. Select *Div1* using the drop-down menu in the *Properties* window (if it isn't selected already).

3. **Either**

   Clear the *Class* property in the *Properties* window.

   Or

   Right-click on *.BigText* in the *Applied Rules* section of the *CSS Properties* window and then click *Remove Class* from the shortcut menu.

   This removes the reference to *.BigText* from *Div1*. You'll see the text return to its normal size except for the first line.

4. Right-click in the *Applied Rules* box in the *CSS Properties* window and then click *New Style...* from the shortcut menu.

   The *New Style* dialog will appear.

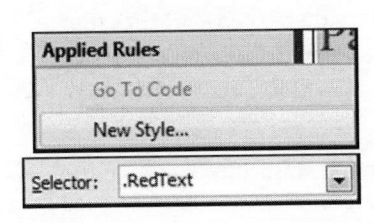

5. Enter **.RedText** into the *Selector* box (be careful not to enter two dots by mistake as the dialog doesn't select the existing dot).

   This is the name of your new CSS class, which will work in exactly the same way as the *BigText* class you created in: *Lesson 2-8: Work with CSS*.

6. Choose *Existing style sheet* from the *Define in* drop-down.

   This tells the dialog that you want to create your style in an existing *.css* file instead of creating another one or creating an inline style.

7. Choose *styles/csstest.css* from the *URL* drop-down.

8. Choose *Red* from the *color* drop-down.

9. Click *OK*.

   You'll see that the text in *Div1* is now displayed in red.

10. Open *csstest.css*.

    You'll see that a new *.RedText* class has been automatically created through the dialog.

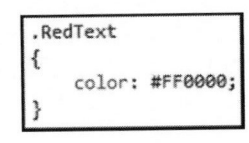

```
.RedText
{
    color: #FF0000;
}
```

Lesson 2-10: Use the div and span tags

In *Lesson 2-8: Work with CSS* you applied a CSS style to *div* tags, but you might be wondering exactly what a *div* is.

Div and *span* tags (which will be covered in this lesson) are used as containers for your page's content in order to apply a CSS style to multiple elements. In this lesson, you'll work with the *div* tag and its partner the *span* tag.

1   Open *HTMLTest* from your sample files folder.

2   Open *divspantest.aspx* in *Source* view.

3   Add two *div* tags containing some text.

1.   Add the following HTML in the space between the *form* tags:

<div id="Div1">Div1</div>
<div id="Div2">Div2</div>

```
<form id="form1" runat="server">
    <div id="Div1">Div1</div>
    <div id="Div2">Div2</div>
</form>
```

2.   Switch to *Design* view.

You'll see that the two *div* tags are displayed, but that they are on separate lines, despite the fact you didn't use any *p* or *br* tags. This is because the *div* tag automatically starts a new line after its closing tag.

You'll also notice that both of the *div* tags have picked up a background color. This is because there is a CSS stylesheet linked to this page (*divspantest.css*) that defines styling properties for any tag with the ID property *Div1* or *Div2*. Later in this lesson you will edit the linked stylesheet.

4   Add two *span* tags with text.

1.   Switch to *Source* view and add the following HTML after the two *div* tags:

<span>Span1</span>
<span>Span2</span>

```
<form id="form1" runat="server">
    <div id="Div1">Div1</div>
    <div id="Div2">Div2</div>
    <span>Span1</span>
    <span>Span2</span>
</form>
```

2.   Switch to *Design* view.

You'll see that the pieces of text held in the *span* tags are shown side by side. Unlike *div*, the *span* tag doesn't add any line breaks automatically.

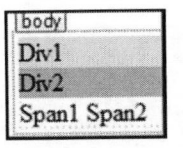

5 Use CSS to set the size of the *Div2* element.

1. Open *divspantest.css* from the *Styles* folder.

You'll see the identifier classes that have already been created for *Div1* and *Div2*.

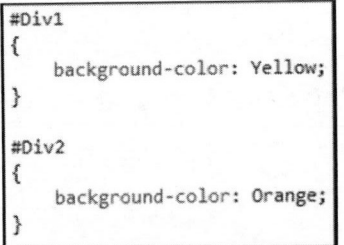

2. Add the following to the #*Div2* identifier:

width: 300px;
height: 300px;

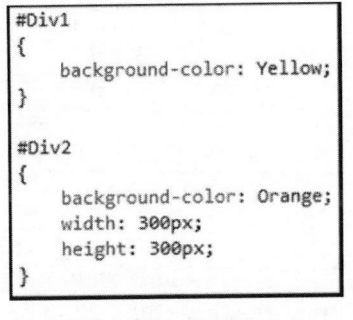

Switch back to *divspantest.aspx* and you'll see that the *Div2* box has increased in size thanks to your CSS.

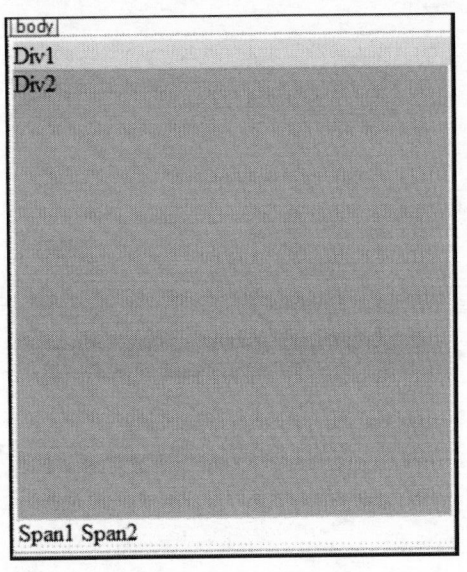

Most modern web sites use a combination of *div* and *span* tags with CSS to create their layouts and style their content.

Some ASP.NET controls automatically create *div* and *span* tags. You'll see this in action in: *Lesson 3-1: Change properties with C#.*

trivia

JavaScript and browser compatibility

Thanks to the efforts of the W3C, HTML and CSS are now run in very similar ways across all of the major browsers. JavaScript, however, still has very bad cross-browser compatibility.

Writing JavaScript that would work in every browser used to require a lot of programming to account for the peculiarities of different browsers.

Fortunately, JQuery does all of that for you.

JQuery is a JavaScript library with a lot of useful functions. Most importantly, all of its functions are cross-browser compatible.

If you look in the *scripts* folder of this lesson's project, you'll see the JQuery files.

ASP.NET doesn't automatically generate JQuery code, although it does include the JQuery files with every new Web Application project.

Because ASP.NET doesn't use JQuery you won't cover it in this book, but it is a wonderful resource if you work with JavaScript in the future.

Lesson 2-11: Work with JavaScript

As well as HTML and CSS the remaining language recognized by a web browser is JavaScript. JavaScript is code that can be used to add interactive features to web pages without having to obtain information from the server. For this reason it is called client-side code (in IT terminology a browser is referred to as a "client").

Although you won't need to write any JavaScript in order to create basic ASP.NET sites, it's important that you can recognize it when you see it as ASP.NET will automatically add JavaScript to a lot of pages.

1   Open *HTMLTest* from your sample files folder.

2   Open *scripttest.aspx* in *Source* view.

You'll see that a link to *scripttest.js* has already been added to this page.

```
<script type="text/javascript" src="/scripts/scripttest.js"></script>
```

3   Add inline JavaScript.

In the same way as CSS, you can add JavaScript directly to the page instead of having it in a separate file. But just like with CSS, it is best practice to keep your JavaScript code in separate files.

1.   Add the following code to the *head* tag, under the existing *script* tag pair:

```
<script type="text/javascript">
    alert("Hello!");
</script>
```

```
<head runat="server">
    <title></title>
    <link rel="Stylesheet" href="/s
    <script type="text/javascript"
    <script type="text/javascript">
        alert("Hello!");
    </script>
</head>
```

2.   View *scripttest.aspx* in your browser (*Design* view isn't capable of executing JavaScript).

You should see your message pop up on the screen. This is one of the most basic JavaScript functions.

3.   Close your browser and remove the JavaScript code you just added.

4   Assign a JavaScript function to a page element's onclick event.

1.   Return to *scripttest.aspx* in *Source* view.

2.   Change the code of *<div id="Button">* to:

<div id="Button" onclick="ClickMessage()">

```
<div id="Button" onclick="ClickMessage()">
    Click Me!
</div>
```

note

ASP.NET and JavaScript

Many of ASP.NET's special functions are accomplished using JavaScript, but you might never know this as it's all generated automatically behind the scenes.

Although there's a lot more to know about JavaScript, the basic understanding provided by this lesson will enable you to complete and understand all of the lessons in this book.

note

Client-Side and Server-Side

JavaScript is *Client-Side* code. This means it runs on the computer of the person visiting your web site, not on the web server that is hosting your web site.

Because JavaScript is client-side, you can never rely on it running: the visitor might have disabled JavaScript in their browser settings.

The C# code you'll be learning later on is *Server-Side* and can't be directly interfered with by visitors to your site.

3. Open the page in your browser.

Click Me!

4. Click the *Click Me!* Button.

Clicked!

You'll see a message pop up as before. If you look in *scripttest.js* in the *Scripts* folder, you'll see the JavaScript *function* that caused this to happen.

By adding the function's name to the div's *onclick* property, you've made it run when the div is clicked.

5 **Change colors with JavaScript.**

1. Close your browser and open the *scripttest.js* file.

   You'll find it in the *scripts* folder of the project.

2. Replace the line *alert("Clicked!");* with:

   **document.getElementById("Button")
   .setAttribute("style", "background-color: red;");**

   ```
   function ClickMessage() {
       document.getElementById("Button")
       .setAttribute("style", "background-color: red;");
   }
   ```

   This might seem like a complicated piece of code, but if you break it down into its components it's not so difficult.

   document.getElementById("Button")
   This tells JavaScript to search the page for an element with an ID of *Button*. The blue *div* on the page is called *Button*, so it will find that.

   setAttribute("style", "background-color: red;");
   This tells JavaScript to set the *style* property of the tag to *background-color: red;*. You used the *style* property in *Lesson 2-8: Work with CSS*.

   You've already set the *ClickMessage()* function to run when the *div* is clicked. When the user clicks on the *div*, the JavaScript will change the div's HTML code to the following:

   <div id="Button" style="background-color: red;" onclick="ClickMessage()">Click Me!</div>

3. View *scripttest.aspx* in your browser.

4. Click on the *Click Me!* div.

   The color of the div changes when it is clicked.

   Click Me!

6 Save your changes and close Visual Studio.

Lesson 2-12: Work with HTML Forms

HTML forms are the only mechanism available in HTML that is able to send information to the web server. All of the buttons and text boxes you've added in previous lessons have been *form controls*.

HTML forms are relatively simple, but they are the backbone of ASP.NET.

1 Open *HTMLTest* from your sample files folder.

2 Open *formstest.htm* in *Design* view.

   An *.htm* file is a pure HTML file that doesn't contain any of ASP.NET's special features. Browsers will recognize HTML files with both the *.htm* and *.html* file extensions but *.htm* is the file extension favored by Visual Studio.

   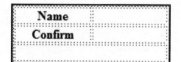

   You should recognize the design as an HTML table with some text in the cells. This is going to be your form.

3 Add an HTML Text input control.

   1. Add an *Input (Text)* control from the *HTML* category of the *Toolbox* to the cell to the right of *Name*.

   The *Input (Text)* control is the HTML equivalent of the ASP.NET *TextBox* control, which you'll learn about in: *Lesson 4-4: Use text boxes*.

   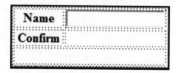

   2. Set the *Name* property of the new control to: **Name**

   The *Name* property is used to identify the data that will be sent by the form (see sidebar).

4 Add an HTML Checkbox input control.

   1. In the same way as you did in the last step, add an *Input (Checkbox)* control in the cell next to *Confirm*.

   The *Input (Checkbox)* control is the HTML equivalent of the ASP.NET *CheckBox* control, which you'll learn about in: *Lesson 4-5: Use check boxes*.

   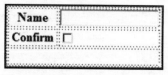

   2. Set the *Name* property of the new checkbox to: **Confirm**

5 Add an HTML Submit input control.

---

note

The Name property

You have to set the *Name* property in this lesson because you're using a pure HTML form.

When you start using ASP.NET's controls later on you won't need to worry about the *Name* property anymore because ASP.NET will handle it automatically.

note

Unix and Windows Web servers

Pure HTML code such as you see in this lesson can be run on any web server. That's not true of ASP.NET code, however.

ASP.NET web sites must be hosted on a server running the Windows operating system and Microsoft's IIS web server software.

Many web hosting services on the Internet use the open-source Linux operating system and Apache web server software instead. There's a big cost saving associated with this approach as the web hosting service doesn't have to purchase any software (Linux and Apache are both freeware).

While Apache doesn't support ASP.NET it does support a similar (also open-source) set of technologies based upon the PHP programming language.

PHP is an open source alternative to ASP.NET which is favored by hobbyists.

Many web bulletin boards can be found with passionate arguments about whether PHP or ASP.NET is "best". There's no real answer to this question but many agree that PHP is more suitable for smaller projects while ASP.NET makes it easier to work with large and complex projects.

Add an *Input (Submit)* control from the *HTML* category of the *Toolbox* to the bottom cell of the table.

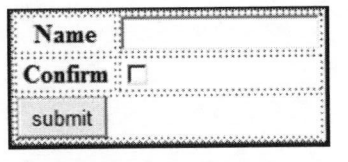

The *Input (Submit)* HTML control is used to send the contents of the form to the server. It's the equivalent of the ASP.NET *Button* control, which you'll learn more about in: *Lesson 4-2: Use button controls*.

6 Set the *action* of the form.

1. Switch to *Source* view.

2. You'll see that there are no *asp* elements on this page at all. This is a pure HTML page that could be served by any web server to any web browser (see sidebar).

3. Set the *action* property of the *form* tag to: **formsubmit.aspx**

    You can do this by adding the property to the tag using the code **action="formsubmit.aspx"** or by clicking on the *form* tag and using the *Properties* window to set the *Action* property.

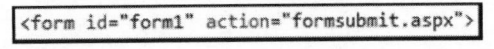

The *action* property tells the form where to send the data that the user has entered when the submit button is clicked.

formsubmit.aspx is an ASP.NET page that will process the data and display it.

When using aspx pages, you'll never need to manually set the *action* property. You'll learn more about how ASP.NET sends and receives data in: *Lesson 3-11: Send data between pages*.

7 Submit the form.

1. View *formstest.htm* in your browser.

2. Fill in the form and click *submit*.

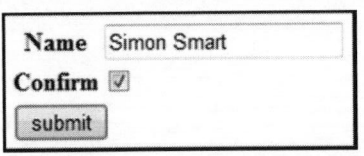

You are redirected to *formsubmit.aspx*, which receives the data you entered and displays it.

> Your name is: *Simon Smart*
> You ticked *confirm*.

Almost everything ASP.NET does revolves around this system of HTML forms sending data to the web server. Visual Studio generates most of the HTML code that makes this work automatically, but with the knowledge you've gained from this lesson you should be able to understand what it is doing behind the scenes.

Session 2: Exercise

1   Open *exercise.aspx* within the *HTMLTest* sample project in *Source* view.

2   Set the page title in the head section to: **Session 2 Exercise**

3   Add a link to the CSS file called *layout.css*. It can be found in the *styles* folder.

4   Add a pair of *div* tags to the page (between the form tags).

5   Type the text **Site Name** between the *div* tags.

6   Set the *class* property of the *div* tags to the CSS class: **header**

7   Switch to *Design* view and add an HTML table to bottom of the page.

8   Remaining in *Design* view, merge the bottom two cells of the HTML table.

9   In the first cell of the HTML table, type the text: **Site**

10   Switch to *Source* view and make the *Site* text bold using HTML.

11   Switch to *Design* view and type the text: **Learn ASP 4 web site** into the top-right table cell.

12   Make the text you have just typed a hyperlink to: *http://www.learnasp4.com.*

13   Add an HTML image element to the bottom row of the table and reference it to the *pattern.jpg* image in the i*mages* folder.

14   Using the *CSS Properties* window, set the *color* CSS property of the *Site Name* text to: **White**

15   Add a link to the JavaScript file *exercise.js*. It can be found in the *scripts* folder.

16   Add JavaScript code to *exercise.js* to display a pop-up message.

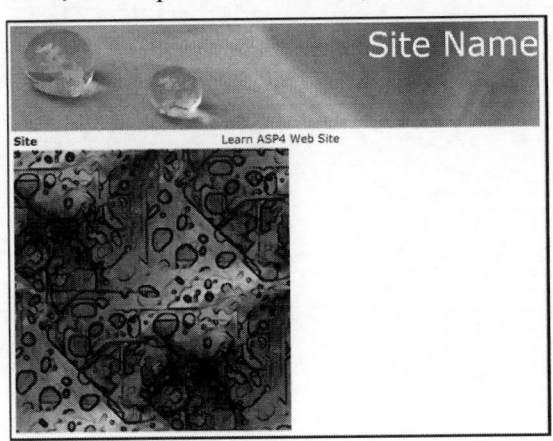

HTMLTest - start   **HTMLTest - end**

If you need help slide the page to the left

Session 2: Exercise Answers

These are the four questions that students find the most difficult to answer:

Q 14	Q 8	Q 7	Q 6
1. Switch to *Design* view.	1. Switch to *Design* view.	1. Switch to *Design* view.	1. Switch to *Source* view.
2. Click on the *header* div so it is highlighted.	2. Click and drag from the bottom-left cell of the table to the bottom right, so they are both highlighted.	2. Click below the *header* div.	2. Modify the *div* tag to:
<DIV> should appear as the selected item in the *Properties* window.		3. Click Table→ Insert Table.	**<div class="header"> Site Name </div>**
3. Click View→ CSS Properties.	3. Click Table→Modify→ Merge Cells.	4. Click OK on the dialog that appears.	This was covered in: *Lesson 2-10: Use the div and span tags.*
4. Open the drop-down list next to *color* in the *CSS Properties* window and click the white box.	This was covered in: *Lesson 2-5: Create an HTML table.*	This was covered in: *Lesson 2-5: Create an HTML table.*	
This was covered in: *Lesson 2-9: Use the CSS Properties window.*			

If you have difficulty with the other questions, here are the lessons that cover the relevant skills:

1   Refer to: Lesson 1-7: Manage a project with the Solution Explorer.

2   Refer to: Lesson 2-4: Use the title, meta, link and script tags.

3   Refer to: Lesson 2-4: Use the title, meta, link and script tags.

4   Refer to: Lesson 2-10: Use the div and span tags.

5   Refer to: Lesson 2-10: Use the div and span tags.

9   Refer to: Lesson 2-5: Create an HTML table.

10   Refer to: Lesson 2-1: Understand HTML bold, italic and heading tags.

11   Refer to: Lesson 2-5: Create an HTML table.

12   Refer to: Lesson 2-7: Display images and links on a page.

13   Refer to: Lesson 2-7: Display images and links on a page.

15   Refer to: Lesson 2-4: Use the title, meta, link and script tags.

16   Refer to: Lesson 2-11: Work with JavaScript.

Session Three: ASP.NET Web Pages

> You cannot open a book without learning something.
>
> *Confucius, Chinese philosopher (551BC – 479BC)*

At this point you have a good grounding in how HTML, CSS and JavaScript are all interpreted by a web browser in order to display a web page.

In this session you'll see how ASP.NET integrates with HTML, CSS and JavaScript to create exciting interactive web sites.

You'll also write your first C# code in this session.

Session Objectives

By the end of this session you will be able to:

- Change properties with C#
- Add event handlers to Controls
- Use Breakpoints
- Use Watches and Locals
- Understand the Exception object
- Understand the Page object
- Understand Request and Response
- Understand PostBack
- Work with ViewState
- Move between pages using C#
- Send data between pages
- Use Session
- Edit the Web.config file

note

default.aspx .designer.cs

You've probably noticed that when you expand an .aspx file, there's a file called *[filename].aspx.designer.cs* as well as *[filename].aspx.cs*.

This file is used by the *Design* view of the Visual Studio interface. All of the code inside it is automatically generated and you will never have to edit it.

important

C# and semicolons (;)

You'll notice that the line of code you add in this example ends in a semi-colon.

Semi-colons are required by C# to indicate the end of a line of code. You might have noticed in *Lesson 2-11: Work with JavaScript* that JavaScript uses the same convention.

You'll notice, however, that the code that defines the method doesn't have a semi-colon at the end of it.

Lines that 'contain' other code using { and } don't need semi-colons because the { and } define the area they affect.

Because C# doesn't consider a line of code to be finished until it sees a semi-colon, you can split a long line of code onto multiple lines without causing any problems.

If you are not completing the course incrementally use the sample file: **Lesson 3-1** to begin this lesson.

Sample files with the starting point for each lesson are also provided for all of the other lessons in this session.

Lesson 3-1: Change properties with C#

You've already worked with HTML controls and briefly viewed ASP.NET's code-behind files.

In this lesson, you'll use some very basic C# code to change the properties of controls on a web page.

1   Open *CSharpTest* from your sample files folder.

2   Open *default.aspx* in *Design* view.

3   Add a *Label* control from the *Standard* category of the *Toolbox*.

4   Set the *ID* of the new *label* control to: **LabelOutput**

5   Open the code-behind file of *default.aspx*

You learned how to do this in: *Lesson 1-7: Manage a project with the Solution Explorer.*

6   Add some code to set the *Text* property of the label.

You can see the C# code that goes with *default.aspx* on this page. At the moment, the important part is:

protected void Page_Load(object sender, EventArgs e)
{
}

```
protected void Page_Load(object sender, EventArgs e)
{

}
```

This is a *method*. Methods are the way C# code is organized into pieces that can be run individually.

The *Page_Load* method is an *event handler*. An event handler is a special type of method that runs in response to something happening. In this case the event that triggers the event handler is the page loading. You'll learn more about event handlers in: *Lesson 3-2: Add event handlers to Controls.*

The { and } symbols show where the method begins and ends. Everything between the { and } is part of the method. As you can see, at the moment the method is empty.

1.   Add the following line of C# code in the gap between the { and }.

LabelOutput.Text = "Hello world!";

```
protected void Page_Load(object sender, EventArgs e)
{
    LabelOutput.Text = "Hello world!";
}
```

```
http://localhost:51998/default.aspx

Hello world!
```

2. View the page in your browser.

You'll see that the *Text* property of the label was changed when the page loaded.

7 Examine what ASP.NET has done.

1. View *default.aspx* in your browser, if it isn't visible already.

2. View the source of the page.

   To do this in *Internet Explorer*, right-click on the page and then click *View Source* from the shortcut menu.

   You should see a line of code that says:

   <span id="LabelOutput">Hello world!</span>

```
<div>

    <span id="LabelOutput">Hello world!</span>

</div>
```

3. Close your browser and return to *default.aspx* in *Source* view.

   Compare the label code here. It should say:

   *<asp:Label ID="LabelOutput" runat="server"
   Text="Label"></asp:Label>*

```
<asp:Label ID="LabelOutput" runat="server" Text="Label"></asp:Label>
```

When a user requests your page, the web server converts the *asp:* controls into HTML that their web browser can understand.

The real power of ASP.NET is in the use of event handlers and C# code to change the properties of elements on the page in response to user interaction, making pages interactive.

8 Add some code to make the label's text bold.

1. Switch back to *default.aspx.cs* (the code-behind file).

2. Add the following line of code on the next line of the *Page_Load* event handler:

   LabelOutput.Font.Bold = true;

```
protected void Page_Load(object sender, EventArgs e)
{
    LabelOutput.Text = "Hello world!";
    LabelOutput.Font.Bold = true;
}
```

This piece of code is a little different to the last one (see sidebar).

3. View the page in your browser.

   You'll see that the text has been made bold by the C# code that you added.

```
http://localhost:50085/default.aspx

Hello world!
```

Lesson 3-2: Add event handlers to Controls

An *event handler* is a piece of code that is triggered by something happening. In the last lesson you worked with the *Page_Load* event, which runs whenever a page loads.

In this lesson you'll add some more events to the page.

1 Open *CSharpTest* from your sample files folder.

2 Open *default.aspx* in *Design* view.

3 Add a *Button* control from the *Standard* category of the *Toolbox*.

Place it after the *Label* you added in: *Lesson 3-1: Change properties with C#.*

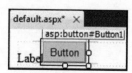

note

Changing events in Source view

Although you can use the *Properties* window to change properties in *Source* view you are unable to add events in this view.

If you select an ASP.NET control in *Source* view, you'll see that the *events* icon disappears from the *Properties* window.

4 Set the *ID* property of the new button to: **ButtonChangeText**

5 Add a *Click* event handler to the button.

1. Make sure you are in *Design* view.

2. Select the *Button* so *ButtonChangeText* appears in the *Properties* window.

3. Click the *events* button 🗲 in the *Properties* window.

   It can be found just below the drop-down menu.

   You will see a list of the possible events for the *Button* control.

4. Double-click in the empty box next to *Click*.

   You will be automatically taken to the code-behind file of *default.aspx* and will see that some code has been automatically added:

```
protected void ButtonChangeText_Click(object sender, EventArgs e)
{

}
```

   This is the *event handler* for the button's *click* event. When the button is clicked, any code between the { and } will be run.

5. Add the following line of code to the new event handler:

   LabelOutput.Text = "Text changed!";

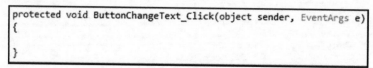

note

The order of events

In this lesson you have two events both trying to set the *Text* property of a label control, but the *click* event 'wins'. This is because the events are always processed in a certain order.

When the button is clicked, the page reloads and the *Page_Load* event sets the label's text to *Hello World!* At a later point in time the *Click* event occurs and sets the label control's text property to *Text Changed!*

On a real web site you'd probably try to avoid this and make sure that only one piece of code affects the label at a time.

6. View the page in your browser and click the button.

You'll see that the text in the label is changed. This is because the *click* event comes after the *Page_Load* event (see sidebar).

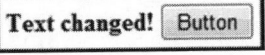

7. Close your web browser.

6 Add a *Calendar* control to the page from the *Standard* category of the *Toolbox*.

7 Change the *ID* property of the *Calendar* control to: **CalendarSelect**

If your *Properties* window is still displaying *Events* you will have to switch back to *Properties* by clicking the *Properties* icon.

8 Add an event handler to the *Selection Changed* event of the *Calendar* control.

1. In the same way as you did for the button, select the calendar in *Design* view and then click the *events* button in the *Properties* window.

Action
DayRender
SelectionChanged
VisibleMonthChanged

As you can see, *Calendar* has a different set of events to *Button*. You'll learn more about the events of different controls in: *Session Four: ASP.NET Controls.*

2. Double-click in the empty box next to *SelectionChanged* in the *Properties* window.

The *SelectionChanged* event happens when the user selects a date from the calendar.

3. Add the following code to the event handler that is automatically generated:

LabelOutput.Text = CalendarSelect.SelectedDate.ToString();

```
protected void CalendarSelect_SelectionChanged(object sender,
{
    LabelOutput.Text = CalendarSelect.SelectedDate.ToString();
}
```

This code will set the *Text* property of your label to the date that was selected in the calendar.

You will learn about *ToString* in: *Lesson 5-9: Convert variables using cast and ToString.*

4. View the page in your browser.

5. Click on a date in the calendar.

You will see that the event handler code runs and the label is filled in with the date that was selected.

9 Close your web browser and Visual Studio.

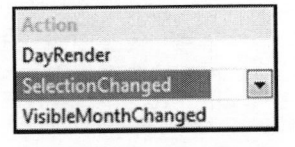

Lesson 3-3: Use Breakpoints

So far, you've been able to tell that your code is working properly by running it and seeing the results. When things don't work the way you expect them to, it is helpful to be able to get a closer look at what is going wrong.

Breakpoints let you pause your code and examine the current state of the application.

1 Open *CSharpTest* from your sample files folder.

2 Open *default.aspx.cs* (The code-behind file of *default.aspx*).

3 Add a breakpoint to the *CalendarSelect_SelectionChanged* event handler.

   1. Click on the line of code that sets *LabelOutput*'s *Text* property in the *CalendarSelect_SelectionChanged* event handler.

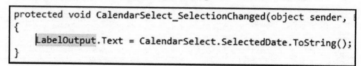

```
protected void CalendarSelect_SelectionChanged(object sender,
{
    LabelOutput.Text = CalendarSelect.SelectedDate.ToString();
}
```

   2. Right-click on the line and then click Breakpoint→Insert Breakpoint from the shortcut menu.

      The line will be highlighted in red, and a red circle will appear in the bar to the left. This indicates that a breakpoint is present.

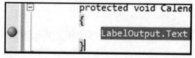

4 Inspect properties while code is running.

   1. Run *default.aspx* in Debug mode (see sidebar).

   2. Click on a date in the calendar.

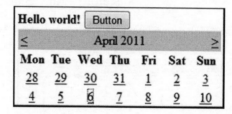

      You should be automatically brought back to Visual Studio with the line you added a breakpoint to highlighted in yellow.

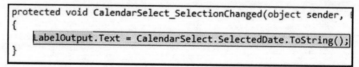

```
protected void CalendarSelect_SelectionChanged(object sender,
{
    LabelOutput.Text = CalendarSelect.SelectedDate.ToString();
}
```

      Your web application is now paused at the point where you placed the breakpoint.

   3. Examine the current *Text* of *LabelOutput*.

You can quickly see the current values of properties by hovering your mouse cursor over them. Hover your cursor over the *.Text* part of *LabelOutput.Text*.

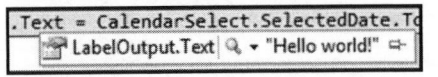

You can see that the current value of *LabelOutput.Text* is: *Hello world!*

4. View the rest of the properties of the *LabelOutput* control.

    By hovering your mouse cursor over *LabelOutput* itself and expanding the categories by clicking the + symbol, you can see the rest of *LabelOutput*'s properties.

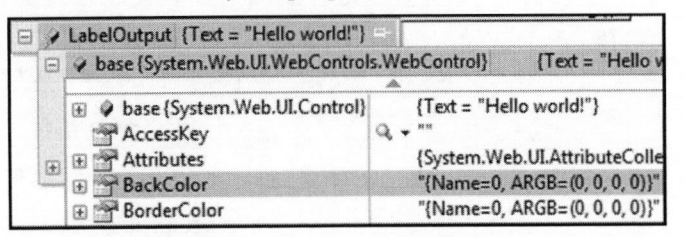

5   Step through code using the *Debug* tools.

Although it's useful to see the properties at your breakpoint, it's even more useful to be able to step through your code line by line and see what is affected.

1. Click Debug→Step Over.

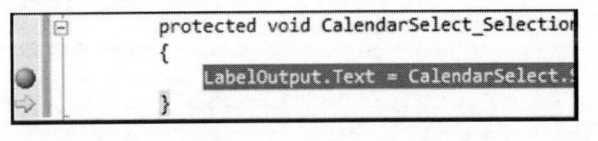

You will see that the next line is highlighted in yellow and has a small yellow arrow in the bar to the left. You have now stepped through the last line and onto this one.

Because you stepped through the last line, it will have updated the label's text.

2. Check the *Text* property of *LabelOutput*.

    As you did before, move your mouse cursor over *.Text* in the *LabelOuput.Text* code.

    You'll see that the text has been updated.

    LabelOutput.Text ⚲ ▾ "31/12/2010 00:00:00"

3. Click Debug→Continue.

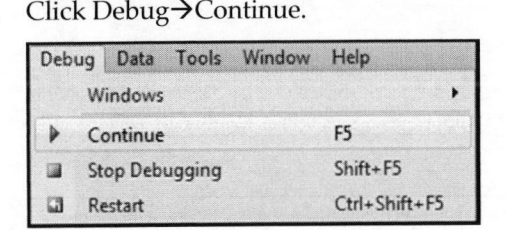

You will be sent back to your web browser and the site will continue running as normal.

You can also continue running by clicking the 'play' button on the toolbar (see sidebar).

97

---

note

The Debug Toolbar

As well as using the *Debug* menu, you can use the icons on the Debug toolbar.

▶ ‖ ▢ ⬙

These allow you to continue, pause, stop and restart debugging.

These correspond to *Step Into*, *Step Over* and *Step Out*.

The difference between these isn't obvious at the moment, but will make more sense in: *Session Six: C# Classes, Namespaces and Methods.*

For now you only need to use *Step Over*.

Lesson 3-4: Use Watches and Locals

In *Lesson 3-3: Use Breakpoints,* you learned how to pause your application at certain points in order to inspect the current state of controls and values. However, by using that technique you can inspect only the values of objects that your code directly refers to.

Using the *Watch* and *Locals* windows, you can inspect any values that are available, regardless of whether or not your code makes reference to them.

1 Open *CSharpTest* from your sample files folder.

2 Open *default.aspx.cs* (The code-behind file of *default.aspx*).

3 Start debugging.

4 Click on a date in the calendar.

> The breakpoint you added in *Lesson 3-3: Use Breakpoints* should pause the code inside the *CalendarSelect_SelectionChanged* event handler.

5 View properties using the *Locals* window.

1. Click the *Locals* button at the bottom-left of the screen.

The *Locals* window will appear (if it wasn't visible already).

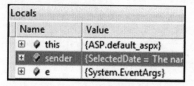

Locals contains all of the properties that are currently available to your code in a tree structure. It's not always the easiest way to find what you're looking for, but it always contains everything.

2. Expand *this* by clicking the plus-sign icon next to it.

The *this* object is the object that contains your code. In this case, *this* is your aspx page.

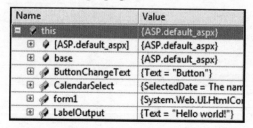

3. Expand *LabelOutput* in the *Locals* window.

You will see the properties of the *LabelOutput* control displayed.

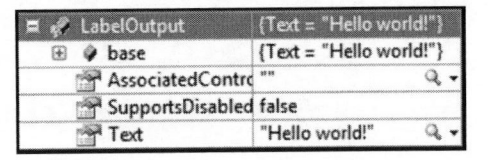

Note that these are only properties that have a value. You could view a complete list of the control's properties by expanding *base*.

4. Return to the web browser by clicking Debug→Continue.

6   View properties using the *Watch* window.

The *Watch* window works very similarly to the *Locals* window, but you can choose the values you want to appear in it. It's usually a much more convenient way of inspecting values in your application.

1. Click on a date on the calendar again.

    Your code should pause at the breakpoint once more.

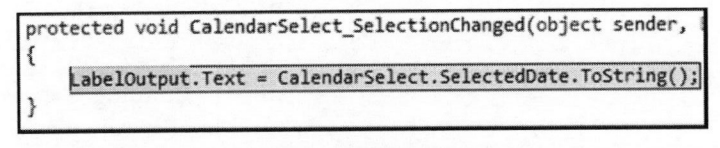

2. Display the *Watch* window by clicking the *Watch* button at the bottom-left of the screen.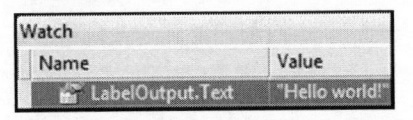

3. Select *LabelOutput.Text* by clicking and dragging your mouse cursor over it.

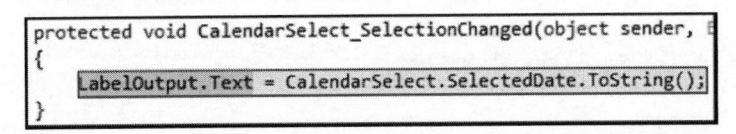

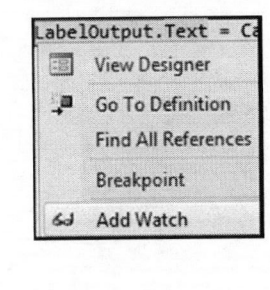

4. Right-click on the highlighted text and then click *Add Watch* from the shortcut menu.

    LabelOutput.Text and its current value appear in the *Watch* window.

Watch	
Name	Value
LabelOutput.Text	"Hello world!"

5. Use *Step Over* to step to the next line.

    You'll see that the value is updated in the *Watch* window. The *Watch* window is very useful for keeping an eye on the current values of important properties.

Watch	
Name	Value
LabelOutput.Text	"31/03/2011 00:00:00"

    You'll be using the *Watch* window more in the coming lessons.

7   Stop debugging and close Visual Studio.

Lesson 3-5: Understand the Exception object

So far all of your code may have run without any problems, but unfortunately that won't always be so. When things do go wrong, Visual Studio will do its best to tell you what the problem is.

You've already seen a build error in *Lesson 1-8: Run a project*, but those only appear when Visual Studio is able to detect a problem before the code runs.

Exceptions appear when something goes wrong while the code is running. By looking at the exception, you will hopefully be able to work out what the problem is.

1   Open *CSharpTest* from your sample files folder.

2   Open *debugme.aspx.cs* (The code-behind file of *debugme.aspx*).

> There is some code in here that you won't recognize, but the important thing is that it's going to cause an error by trying to divide by zero.
>
> You will understand everything that this code is doing after: *Lesson 5-10: Perform basic mathematical operations.*

3   Cause an exception.

1.   Start debugging to view *debugme.aspx* in Debug mode.

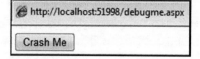

2.   Click the *Crash Me* button.

> You should be brought back to Visual Studio. If not, switch back to it manually without closing the browser window.

You will see the line that caused the exception highlighted in yellow and a box showing the details of the exception.

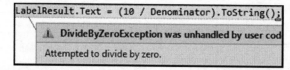

This exception is very obvious. The error message at the top tells you that it was caused by attempting to divide by zero.

Unfortunately not all error messages are as easy to understand.

4   Use troubleshooting tips.

You'll notice that the *Exception* window shows a list of *Troubleshooting tips*. You can click on them to read articles relevant to the problem, which might help you to fix it.

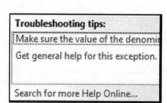

You can also click *Search for more Help Online...* to be redirected to a search page which will allow you to search Microsoft's articles for anything relevant.

5   View the details of the exception.

An exception isn't just an error message; it has properties, just like the controls on your page.

Actions:
View Detail...
Enable editing
Copy exception detail to the clipboard

note

null

You can see two *null* values for properties in the screenshots of the *Exception* object and you might have noticed them in a few other properties you saw earlier.

null is a value that literally means 'nothing'. A property with a value of *null* is considered not to have a value.

It's important to note that there's a difference between 0 and *null*, since 0 is a number and *null* is the absence of a number.

You'll learn more about *null* in: *Lesson 5-12: Understand null.*

1. Click the *View Detail...* link in the *Exception* box.

2. Expand *System.DivideByZeroException* by clicking the arrow.

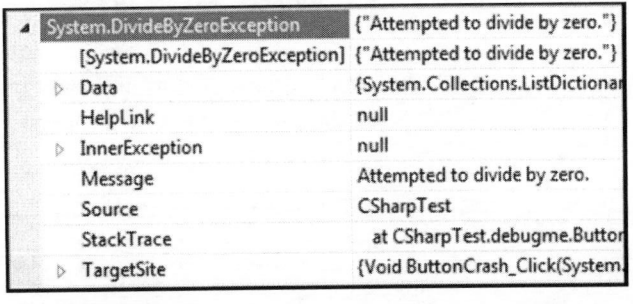

The most important properties of the exception are *InnerException, Message, Source* and *StackTrace*.

InnerException will contain another exception if this one had a deeper cause. Essentially, the Inner Exception is the exception that caused this one. Since this exception didn't have a deeper cause, the Inner Exception is *null* (see sidebar).

Message is the error message you've already seen displayed on the main exception box.

Source is the *namespace* that caused the error. You'll learn about namespaces in: *Lesson 6-4: Work with namespaces.*

StackTrace shows the operation that caused the error. If you read it you'll see that the first line tells you that it originated in *debugme.ButtonCrash_Click.*

6   Fix the problem.

This error happened because the number the code divided by was zero. You can fix this by changing the number.

1. Click *OK* and stop debugging.

    Either close your web browser or click Debug→Stop Debugging.

2. Change the line *int Denominator = 0;* to:

    int Denominator = 2;

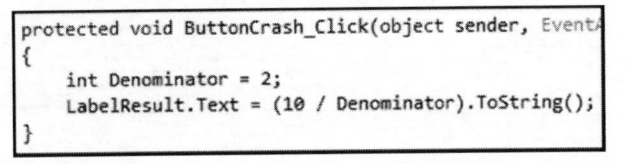

3. View the page in Debug mode and click the button.

You will see that there is no longer an error. Instead the result of 10 divided by 2 is displayed.

Lesson 3-6: Understand the Page object

Every *.aspx* page has an object behind it called the *Page* object which contains a lot of useful properties about the status of the page.

In this lesson you'll inspect the *Page* object and view some of the more important parts of it.

1   Open *CSharpTest* from your sample files folder.

2   Open *default.aspx.cs* (the code-behind file of *default.aspx*).

3   Add a breakpoint to the *ButtonChangeText_Click* event.

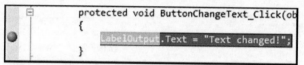

Right click on the line that begins *LabelOutput.Text* and click Breakpoint→Insert Breakpoint or click in the gray bar to the left of the line.

4   Run *default.aspx* in Debug mode and click the button.

Your code should pause at the breakpoint.

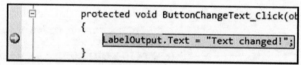

5   Display the Watch window.

Click the *Watch* tab, at the bottom left hand side of the screen, to display the *Watch* window if it's not visible already.

6   Clear all current watches.

Right-click in the *Watch* window and then click *Clear All* from the shortcut menu.

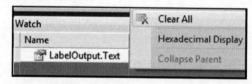

This will clear any existing watches from the window.

7   Manually add a watch for *Page*.

1.   Click in the empty box under *Name* in the *Watch* window.

2.   Type **Page** into the box and press <**Enter**>.

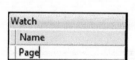

A watch will be added for the *Page* object.

8   Expand *Page* in the *Watch* window.

Expand the *Page* object to view its properties by clicking the + sign next to it in the *Watch* window.

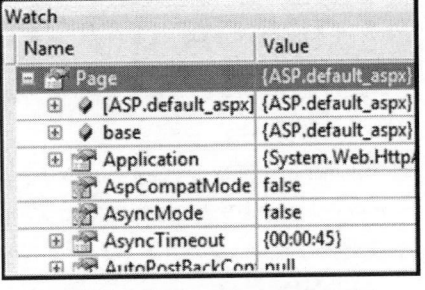

9   Add a watch for *Page.Controls*.

As you can see, the *Page* object has an overwhelming number of properties, most of which won't make much sense to you at the moment.

The *Page* object can be thought of as a container for absolutely everything on an ASP.NET page.

1. In the same way as you did for *Page*, add a watch for:
    Page.Controls

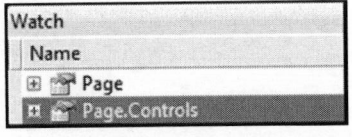

2. Expand *Page.Controls*.

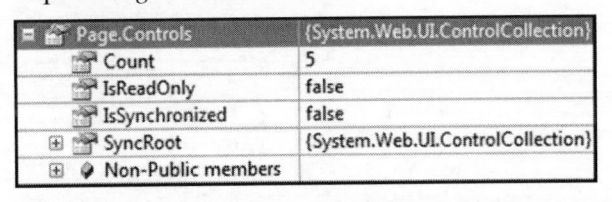

You will see that the *Count* property is 5. This is because *Page.Controls* is a collection containing 5 controls. You'll learn all about collections in: *Lesson 8-2: Create a collection*.

10   View properties of *LabelOutput* through the *Page* object.

Add the following watch to the *Watch* window:

Page.FindControl("LabelOutput")

⊞ 🖳 Page	{ASP.default_aspx}
⊞ 🖳 Page.Controls	{System.Web.UI.ControlCollection}
⊞ ◈ Page.FindControl("LabelOutput")	{Text = "Hello world!"}

You will see that the *LabelOutput* control is found within the *Page* object and its *Text* property is displayed. The controls in the *Page* object are more specifically contained in the *Page.Controls* collection (see sidebar). *FindControl* makes it easy to locate a specific control.

As you've seen already, you don't need to use *Page.FindControl* under normal circumstances. You've only done this to illustrate that everything you add to a page becomes part of the *Page* object.

You'll examine some other important parts of the *Page* object in the rest of this session.

11   Stop debugging and close Visual Studio.

Lesson 3-7: Understand Request and Response

On 'plain' HTML web pages, a web browser sends a request to a web server and the web server responds by sending back the page's HTML code.

ASP.NET works in-between receiving the request from the browser and sending the response back to them, and you can see this in action by inspecting the *Page.Request* and *Page.Response* objects.

1   Open *CSharpTest* from your sample files folder.

2   Open *requestresponse.aspx.cs* (The code-behind file of *requestresponse.aspx*).

3   Add a breakpoint to the *Page_Load* event handler.

You might be wondering how to add a breakpoint to an event handler that doesn't have any code in it; if you try to set a breakpoint on a blank line, it won't let you.

Instead, set the breakpoint on the line with the } sign on it.

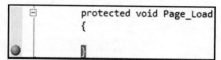

4   Run *requestresponse.aspx* in Debug mode.

Your code should be paused almost immediately, as the breakpoint is reached as soon as the page loads.

5   Clear any existing watches and add a watch for *Page.Request*.

This was covered in: *Lesson 3-6: Understand the Page object.*

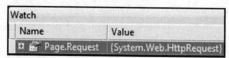

6   Inspect *Page.Request*.

The *Page.Request* object contains all of the information that was sent by the visitor to the page.

1.   Expand *Page.Request* and find *UserAgent* in the properties list.

The *UserAgent* property tells you which browser the visitor is using.

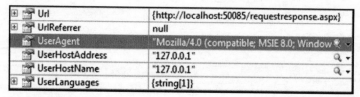

In a slightly cryptic way the text informs me that I am using Microsoft Internet Explorer 8 (MSIE 8.0). This will be different if you are using a different browser.

2. Look at the other properties of *Page.Request*.

   UserHostAddress shows the IP address of the visitor (127.0.0.1 or ::1 means it is your own machine).

   Url shows the web address the visitor entered to get to this page.

7   Manipulate *Page.Response*.

1. Stop debugging and remove the breakpoint.

2. Run *requestresponse.aspx* in Debug mode.

   You will see that it is filled with 'Lorem Ipsum' dummy text.

   > **http://localhost:50085/requestresponse.aspx**
   >
   > Lorem ipsum dolor sit amet, consectetur adipiscir
   > urna. Donec mattis nulla justo, ac aliquam risus. (
   > ut feugiat et, consequat sit amet mi. Maecenas int
   > vel interdum venenatis, felis eros viverra risus, vita
   > aliquet id blandit diam congue. Phasellus tincidunt

3. Stop debugging and return to the code-behind file of *requestresponse.aspx*.

4. Add the following code to the *Page_Load* event handler:

   Page.Response.Write("Hello world!");
   Page.Response.End();

   ```
   protected void Page_Load(object sender, EventArgs e)
   {
       Page.Response.Write("Hello world!");
       Page.Response.End();
   }
   ```

5. Run *requestresponse.aspx* in Debug mode.

   You'll see that the big block of text that was on the page has disappeared and been replaced by *Hello World!*.

   > **http://localhost:50085/requestresponse.aspx**
   >
   > Hello world!

   This happened because you ended the page's response to the visitor early. If you hadn't ended the response, the web server would have gone on to add the page's content to the response.

   By using *Page.Response.Write*, as you did in this example, you can add content directly to the web server's response without it being on the .aspx page at all. This is useful for testing and debugging purposes, but it is better practice to use a control on the page to display content.

   ASP.NET allows you to 'listen' to the user's *Request* and modify the web server's *Response* appropriately. In practice you will rarely need to access the *Page.Request* and *Page.Response* objects directly.

8   Close Visual Studio.

note

About PostBack

You learned earlier that JavaScript is client-side code, while the C# code in code-behind files is server-side code. Server-side code can only run when the browser posts back to the server.

One advantage of this is that server-side code can't be seen by visitors to your site. C# server-side code can also do some things that JavaScript can't, such as accessing a database.

The down-side of PostBack is that the user has to send a request back to the server every time they want the page to update and the whole page needs to be re-loaded. If you have large pages, this can make them significantly slower.

JavaScript can change pages without posting back to the server, which makes it much faster. However, it is less secure than server-side code and has some limitations.

Using web services, it is possible for JavaScript and C# to work together and only update certain parts of the page. This is known as AJAX.

AJAX isn't covered by this book, but you'll learn all about it in the next book in this series: *Learn ASP.NET 4.0, C# and Visual Studio 2010 Expert Skills with The Smart Method.*

Lesson 3-8: Understand PostBack

In *Lesson 2-12: Work with HTML Forms*, you created an HTML form that sent (or *posted*) data to another page. ASP.NET normally uses a form to *post* data back to the same page; this is called *PostBack*.

By using *PostBack*, the user sends data to your web site without moving between pages. ASP.NET's controls expect this, and you can use it to your advantage.

1   Open *CSharpTest* from your sample files folder.

2   Open the code-behind file of *postbacktest.aspx*.

3   See PostBack in action.

   1.   View *postbacktest.aspx* in your browser.

   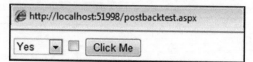

   2.   Click the button that says *Click Me*.

   You should notice a brief 'flicker' as the page reloads. This is because the page's form was submitted and the data 'posted back'.

   3.   Choose an item from the drop-down list.

   You'll notice that this time there was no flicker. By default, changing the value of a drop-down doesn't cause the form to be submitted.

   4.   Click the check-box.

   You'll notice this doesn't cause a post-back either.

   5.   Close your web browser and return to Visual Studio.

4   Use C# code to check if the page has posted back.

   1.   Add the following code to the *Page_Load* event handler:

   LabelIsPostBack.Text = Page.IsPostBack.ToString();

   ```
   protected void Page_Load(object sender, EventArgs e)
   {
       LabelIsPostBack.Text = Page.IsPostBack.ToString();
   }
   ```

   Page.IsPostBack is a value that tells you whether the page has been posted back. *ToString* converts the value into text.

   2.   View *postbacktest.aspx* in your browser.

You will see that the label at the top of the page says *False*. This means that the page currently hasn't been posted back. The user has just loaded the page and hasn't clicked on any controls yet.

3. Click the button.

You'll see that the label changes to say *true*. This means the user has submitted the form and posted back some data.

This is useful because it allows you to make some of your code only run when the user has posted back. You'll see how this can be done in: *Lesson 7-1: Use the if statement.*

4. Close your web browser.

note

How ASP.NET posts back without a button

In the HTML form you created in *Lesson 2-12: Work with HTML Forms*, the only way to submit the form was to click a button.

In this lesson you've seen that ASP.NET can submit its form when other things happen. It does this by automatically generating JavaScript to submit the form.

If you open the page in your browser and view the source (right-click and *View Source* in Internet Explorer), you'll see that ASP.NET has added lines with *javascript:__doPostBack*. This JavaScript causes the form to be submitted.

Because JavaScript is client-side code, you should always be aware that someone browsing your site might have disabled JavaScript, in which case the post-back will not work.

5 **Make a non-PostBack control post back.**

Earlier you saw that the *DropDownList* and *CheckBox* controls don't automatically post back when you click on them. If your page needs to be updated when the user changes one of these controls, you might want them to post back. Fortunately, it can be done.

1. Open *postbacktest.aspx* in *Design* view.

2. Select the *DropDownListPostBack* control.

3. Set the control's *AutoPostBack* property to: **True**

You learned how to do this in: *Lesson 1-12: Change properties in Design view.*

4. View the page in your browser.

5. Try changing the value of the drop-down list.

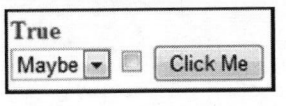

You'll see that this time the page posts back and the label at the top confirms this.

The *AutoPostBack* property is available on most controls that don't automatically post back.

6 **Close Visual Studio.**

Lesson 3-9: Work with ViewState

Have you ever used an online form and become really annoyed when all of the contents of the controls disappeared after a post-back? This is the problem that *ViewState* elegantly solves.

In this lesson you'll see *ViewState* in action and discover how you can also use *ViewState* to store values of your own

1   Open *CSharpTest* from your sample files folder.

2   Open *viewstatetest.aspx* in *Design* view.

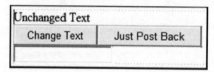

You'll see that there is a label control, two button controls and a text box control.

3   See ViewState in action.

1. View *viewstatetest.aspx* in your browser.

2. Click the *Change Text* button.

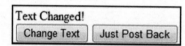

You'll see that the label at the top of the screen changes to say: *Text Changed!*

3. Click the *Just Post Back* button.

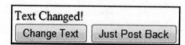

You'll see that the label continues to say *Text Changed!* even after the page is posted back; the *state* of the label has been maintained thanks to *ViewState*.

4. See the hidden *ViewState* data.

As you've done before, view the source of the page by right-clicking (in Internet Explorer) and then clicking *View Source* from the shortcut menu.

5. Look for the *aspNetHidden* div near the top of the page.

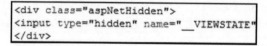

The middle line contains all of the *ViewState* data. It looks like nonsense because it's encrypted, but it is easy to decrypt using tools available on the Internet so don't rely on it to be secure.

4   Disable ViewState and see the difference.

1. Close your browser and return to the *Design* view of *viewstatetest.aspx*.

2. Change the *EnableViewState* property of the *LabelText* control to: **False**

3. View *viewstatetest.aspx* in your browser.

4. Click the *Change Text* button.

You'll see the text change as before.

5. Click the *Just Post Back* button.

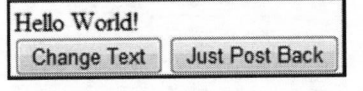

This time the state of the label hasn't been maintained by *ViewState*, so the label's text reverts to its original value.

5   Store a value in *ViewState*.

As well as letting ASP.NET automatically store the values of your controls in *ViewState*, you can also use *ViewState* to store values of your own.

1. Open the code-behind file of *viewstatetest.aspx*.

2. Put the following code in the *Page_Load* event handler:

ViewState["MyText"] = "Hello World!";

```
protected void Page_Load(object sender, EventArgs e)
{
    ViewState["MyText"] = "Hello World!";
}
```

This code will store the text *Hello World!* in *ViewState*, next to a *key* of *MyText*. The key is used to retrieve the text from *ViewState*.

3. Replace the code in the *ButtonChangeText_Click* event handler with:

LabelText.Text = ViewState["MyText"].ToString();

```
protected void ButtonChangeText_Click(object sender, EventArgs e)
{
    LabelText.Text = ViewState["MyText"].ToString();
}
```

This sets the *Text* property of the *LabelText* control to the value you stored under *MyText* in *ViewState*.

4. View the page in your browser.

5. Try clicking the *Change Text* button.

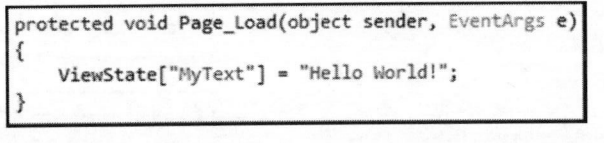

You'll see that the text *Hello World!* is retrieved from *ViewState* and displayed in the *Label*.

Storing values in ViewState is useful when you have a value that you need to keep after a post-back but don't want to put it in a visible control on the page.

anecdote

ViewState troubles

I was once called upon to urgently solve a problem while another developer was away on holiday. His web application had suddenly stopped working and nobody knew why.

The page in question had a large table that was populated with data from a database and *ViewState* had been left on.

Because *ViewState* makes the browser send back the state of the control, the browsers were sending back a huge amount of data every time the page posted back. This made the page run very slowly, but didn't actually stop it from working.

Over time, as the database grew, more and more data was being sent back until, on that day, it exceeded the request limit of 4 megabytes and ASP.NET stopped it from working.

After simply disabling *ViewState* on the table, everything worked perfectly again.

Lesson 3-10: Move between pages using C#

You should now have a pretty good idea of how ASP.NET works on a single page. You know how to change the properties of elements on the page and capture the data that the user has entered.

Although you learned how to create HTML hyperlinks in *Lesson 2-7: Display images and links on a page*, there are also ways to move between pages using C#.

1   Open *CSharpTest* from your sample files folder.

2   Open the code-behind file of *movepage1.aspx*.

3   Move to *movepage2.aspx* with *Page.Response.Redirect*.

You learned about the *Page.Response* object in *Lesson 3-7: Understand Request and Response*. By using its *Redirect* method, you can send the browser to a different page.

1.   Add the following code to the *ButtonMove_Click* event handler:

Page.Response.Redirect("movepage2.aspx");

```
protected void ButtonMove_Click(object sender, EventArgs e)
{
    Page.Response.Redirect("movepage2.aspx");
}
```

2.   View *movepage1.aspx* in your browser.

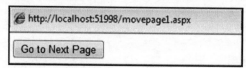

3.   Click the button.

You'll see that you are redirected to *movepage2.aspx*.

Welcome to page 2!

Note that the address bar shows that you are on *movepage2.aspx* now.

4   Move to the next page with a hyperlink.

1.   Close your browser and open *movepage1.aspx* in *Source* view.

2.   Add an HTML link after the button using the code:

<a href="movepage2.aspx">Next Page</a>

```
<div>
    <asp:Button ID="ButtonMove" runat="ser
        onclick="ButtonMove_Click" />
    <a href="movepage2.aspx">Next Page</a
</div>
```

3.   View *movepage1.aspx* in your browser.

4.   Click the *Next Page* link.

You'll see that this has exactly the same result as *Response.Redirect*.

5   Move to the next page with *Page.Server.Transfer*.

You haven't looked at the *Server* object yet. The *Server* object contains methods to tell the web server to carry out certain operations. For now you're interested in the *Transfer* method.

1.   Close your browser and return to the code-behind file of *movepage1.aspx*.

2.   Replace your *Page.Response.Redirect* line of code with:

Page.Server.Transfer("movepage2.aspx");

```
protected void ButtonMove_Click(object sender, EventArgs e)
{
    Page.Server.Transfer("movepage2.aspx");
}
```

3.   View *movepage1.aspx* in your browser.

4.   Click the button.

You'll see that once again you are redirected to *movepage2.aspx*, but look at the address bar:

The browser still thinks you're on *movepage1.aspx*! This is one of the major differences with *Server.Transfer*.

Server.Transfer switches to the new page internally, but doesn't tell the browser. From the perspective of the person viewing your site, they haven't changed pages at all.

Using *Server.Transfer* also keeps a reference to the previous page, as you'll see in: *Lesson 3-11: Send data between pages*.

6   Close your browser and Visual Studio.

Lesson 3-11: Send data between pages

You now know how to retrieve data from a page, access the properties of controls and transfer between pages, but quite often you'll want the site to remember something the user has entered on a previous page after they move to a new page.

In this lesson you'll learn a few of the ways to send data from one page to another.

1   Open *CSharpTest* from your sample files folder.

2   Open *passdata1.aspx* in *Design* view.

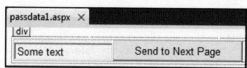

You'll see that there is a text box and a button on the page. You're going to write code that will send the contents of the text box to another page, which will display it.

3   Send data using *PreviousPage*.

If you use *Server.Transfer* to move between pages, you can actually access the *Page* object of the previous page.

1. Open the code-behind file of *passdata1.aspx*.

2. Add the following code to the *ButtonSend_Click* event handler:

    Page.Server.Transfer("passdata2.aspx");

    ```
    protected void ButtonSend_Click(object sender, EventArgs e)
    {
        Page.Server.Transfer("passdata2.aspx");
    }
    ```

    As mentioned in *Lesson 3-10: Move between pages using C#*, *Server.Transfer* will keep a link open to the previous page.

3. View *passdata1.aspx* in your browser.

4. Change the text in the text-box if you wish and then click the *Send to Next Page* button.

    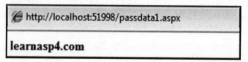

    You'll see that *passdata2.aspx* has picked up the data and displayed it, but because you used *Server.Transfer*, you still appear to be on *passdata1.aspx*.

5. View the code-behind file of *passdata2.aspx*.

    You will see the following code:

    LabelReceivedData.Text =
    ((TextBox)Page.PreviousPage.FindControl("TextBoxText")).Text;

note

Advantages and disadvantages of *QueryString*

Sending values with *QueryString* is one of the best ways to send values between pages when you don't mind exposing them to the user.

The major disadvantage of *QueryString* is that the values can be very easily tampered with by the user. If you have, for example, a *documentid* value in the query string, the user could very easily change it in order to bypass security and access any document in the system.

You could create a secure system with *QueryString*, but you would have to incorporate a way to check that the user has access to the resource they have requested.

This is the code that retrieves *TextBoxText* from the previous page and sets the *Label* on this page to its *Text* property. It probably looks a little confusing at the moment. You won't be able to fully understand this code until you've completed: *Lesson 5-9: Convert variables using cast and ToString.*

Page.PreviousPage is a link to the *Page* object you came from.

FindControl("TextBoxText") looks for the *TextBoxText* control on the previous page.

4 Send data using *QueryString.*

The QueryString method is the most widely used method of sending data between pages.

While browsing the Internet, you might have noticed that sometimes web addresses look something like:

www.[site].com/[page].aspx?page=10&product=13

The values after the question mark are *QueryString* values, and you can use them to send data between pages.

1. Open the code-behind file of *passdata1.aspx.*

2. Replace the *Page.Server.Transfer* line of code with:

**Page.Response.Redirect
("passdata3.aspx?text=" + TextBoxText.Text);**

```
protected void ButtonSend_Click(object sender, EventArgs e)
{
    Page.Response.Redirect("passdata3.aspx?text=" + TextBoxText.Text);
}
```

3. View *passdata1.aspx* in your browser.

4. Change the text in the text-box if you wish and then click the *Send to Next Page* button.

http://localhost:51998/passdata3.aspx?text=learn...

learnmicrosoftexcel.com

You'll see that *passdata3.aspx* has retrieved the text you entered and displayed it.

If you look at the address bar, you can see how the text was sent to *passdata3.aspx.*

http://localhost:51211/passdata3.aspx?text=learnmicrosoftexcel.com

5. Close your browser and view the code-behind file of *passdata3.aspx.*

You'll see that the text was retrieved using *Page.Request.QueryString.*

```
if (Page.Request.QueryString["text"] != null)
{
    LabelReceivedData.Text = Page.Request.QueryString["text"];
}
```

You'll fully understand this code later in the course, after completing: *Lesson 7-1: Use the if statement.*

Lesson 3-12: Use Session

In *Lesson 3-11: Send data between pages,* you saw how you can use *Server.Transfer* and *Response.Redirect* to send values between pages.

Session is another way of transferring values between pages, but session values don't just travel between pages, they remain in place for as long as a user's session lasts.

When a user first sends a *Request* to the web server, they are assigned a *Session* which keeps track of them until it has been 20 minutes (by default) since their last *Request.* The session is then said to have "timed out".

1   Open *CSharpTest* from your sample files folder.

2   Store a value using *Session.*

   1.   Open the code-behind file of *passdata1.aspx.*

```
protected void ButtonSend_Click(object sender, EventArgs e)
{
    Page.Response.Redirect("passdata3.aspx?text=" + TextBoxText.Text);
}
```

   2.   Replace the line beginning with *Page.Response.Redirect* line with the following code:

   Session["Text"] = TextBoxText.Text;

```
protected void ButtonSend_Click(object sender, EventArgs e)
{
    Session["Text"] = TextBoxText.Text;
}
```

This code stores the contents of *TextBoxText.Text* (ie the text the user types into the text box) in *Session* under the key of *Text.*

Session keys work in exactly the same way as the *ViewState* key you used in: *Lesson 3-9: Work with ViewState.*

3   Retrieve a value from *Session.*

   1.   Open the code-behind file of *passdata4.aspx.*

```
public partial class passdata4 : System.Web.UI.Page
{
    protected void Page_Load(object sender, EventArgs e)
    {

    }
}
```

   2.   Add the following code to the *Page_Load* event handler:

   LabelReceivedData.Text = Session["Text"].ToString();

```
protected void Page_Load(object sender, EventArgs e)
{
    LabelReceivedData.Text = Session["Text"].ToString();
}
```

This code will retrieve the value stored under the *Text* key from *Session* and display it in a *Label* control on the page.

4   Transfer the value.

1. Open the code-behind file of *passdata1.aspx*.

```
protected void ButtonSend_Click(object sender, EventArgs e)
{
    Session["Text"] = TextBoxText.Text;
}
```

2. Add the following line of code to the *ButtonSend_Click* event handler:

Page.Response.Redirect("passdata4.aspx");

```
protected void ButtonSend_Click(object sender, EventArgs e)
{
    Session["Text"] = TextBoxText.Text;
    Page.Response.Redirect("passdata4.aspx");
}
```

As you learned in *Lesson 3-10: Move between pages using C#*, this will send the user to the *passdata4.aspx* page after placing the contents of the *TextBox* in *Session["Text"]*.

passdata4.aspx will then retrieve the value from *Session* and display it.

3. View *passdata1.aspx* in your browser.

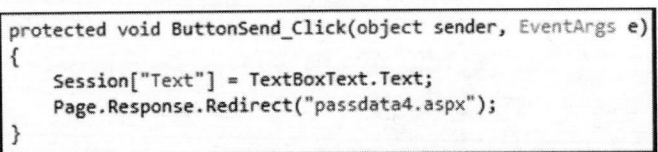

4. Change the text in the text-box if you wish and then click the *Send to Next Page* button.

You will see that the data has been sent to *passdata4.aspx* which has retrieved it from *Session* and displayed it.

5   Close Visual Studio.

Lesson 3-13: Edit the Web.config file

note

XML

XML isn't actually a specific programming language; it's really a standard for storing information. The HTML code you wrote earlier was a form of XML.

XML always works as a series of nested tags enclosed in < and > symbols, which open and close in the same way HTML tags do.

The *Web.config* file recognizes different tags to HTML, but basically works the same way.

Because XML can be used to store any kind of value in a hierarchy it's an extremely versatile way to store data.

You might have been wondering what the *Web.config* file does, as you've seen it in every project you've worked on so far.

Web.config is an XML file (see sidebar) which contains settings to tell the web server how to handle your web site. By changing the settings in *Web.config* you can modify many important settings.

Changing settings in Visual Studio often automatically makes changes to your *Web.config* file.

1   Open *CSharpTest* from your sample files folder.

2   Open *Web.config.*

You will see that there is actually very little code inside the *Web.config* file. This is because you are using ASP.NET 4. ASP.NET 4 automatically manages a lot of things that had to be in *Web.config* in previous versions.

```xml
<?xml version="1.0"?>

<!--
    For more information on how to configure your ASP.NET ap
    http://go.microsoft.com/fwlink/?LinkId=169433
    -->

<configuration>
    <system.web>
        <compilation debug="true" targetFramework="4.0" />

    </system.web>
</configuration>
```

3   Use *Web.config* to switch *customErrors* on.

customErrors is a setting that determines whether ASP.NET displays the details of error messages to visitors to the site.

On a live site, the details of errors should be hidden from visitors as they contain glimpses into the site's code which may be a security risk.

1.   Add the following line of code to *Web.config* inside the *system.web* tag:

<customErrors mode="On"></customErrors>

```xml
<configuration>
    <system.web>
        <compilation debug="true" targetFramework="4.0" />
        <customErrors mode="On"></customErrors>
    </system.web>
</configuration>
```

2.   View *crashme.aspx* in your browser.

Either do this by right-clicking on it and clicking *View in Browser* from the shortcut menu or by opening it and clicking Debug→Start Without Debugging.

You need to view the page without debugging, as otherwise Visual Studio will stop execution before the error is shown.

You will see that a *Runtime Error* dialog is displayed, but it offers no further details of the error itself. In fact, it shows instructions of how to modify your *Web.config* file to show the error details.

```
Runtime Error

Description: An application error occurred on the server. The curren

Details: To enable the details of this specific error message to be view
<customErrors> tag should then have its "mode" attribute set to "Remote(
```

4   Switch *customErrors* off.

1. Close your browser and return to *Web.config*.

2. Change the *customErrors* line to:

   \<customErrors mode="Off">\</customErrors>

3. View *crashme.aspx* in your browser.

   This time you will see the full details of the error message, as you have switched off *customErrors*.

```
Attempted to divide by zero.

Description: An unhandled exception occurred during the execution of the

Exception Details: System.DivideByZeroException: Attempted to divide by
```

   You will also see a snippet of code that shows which line caused the error. This is the reason *customErrors* shouldn't be switched off on a live web server, as it might show code that could help someone break into your system.

```
Line 13:            {
Line 14:                int Zero = 0;
Line 15:                int Crash = 1 / Zero;
Line 16:            }
Line 17:        }
```

   There is a third setting for *customErrors* called *RemoteOnly* (see sidebar).

5   Extend the length of sessions.

In *Lesson 3-11: Send data between pages,* you learned that a user's session on an ASP.NET site lasts for 20 minutes after their last request, but that is only the default. Using *Web.config,* you can make sessions last longer.

1. Close your browser and open *Web.config*.

2. Add the following line inside the *system.web* tag:

   \<sessionState timeout="60">\</sessionState>

```
<system.web>
    <compilation debug="true" targetFramework="4.0" />
    <customErrors mode="Off"></customErrors>
    <sessionState timeout="60"></sessionState>
</system.web>
```

   This will make sessions last for 60 minutes instead of 20.

   There are many, many other settings that can be changed in *Web.config,* but for now it is just important that you understand what *Web.config* does and how you can edit its settings.

6   Close Visual Studio.

Session 3: Exercise

1   Open the *CSharpTest* sample project and open *exercise.aspx*.

2   Disable *ViewState* on the *TextBoxText* control by setting its *EnableViewState* property to: **False**

3   Add a *Click* event handler to the *ButtonChangeText* control.

4   Add code to the new *Click* event handler to set the *Text* property of the *TextBoxText* control to: **The Smart Method**

5   Add a *Click* event handler to the *ButtonSendData* control.

6   Add code to the *ButtonSendData* control's *Click* event to move to *passdata2.aspx* using *Server.Transfer*.

7   Set a breakpoint in the *Click* event of *ButtonSendData*.

8   Run *exercise.aspx* in Debug mode and type some text into the text box.

9   Click *Send Data* and then use the *Watch* window to get the value of *TextBoxText.Text*.

10   Stop debugging and add code to the *ButtonSendData* control's *Click* event handler to store the *Text* of the *TextBoxText* control in *Session* under the key of *Text*.

11   Change the *ButtonSendData* control's *Click* event handler to redirect the user to *passdata4.aspx* using *Response.Redirect* instead of *Server.Transfer*.

CSharpTest - start

CSharpTest - end

If you need help slide the page to the left

Session 3: Exercise Answers

These are the four questions that students find the most difficult to answer:

Q 9	Q 7	Q 6	Q 3
1. Run *exercise.aspx* in Debug mode by clicking: Debug→Start Debugging. 2. Click on the *Send Data* button. Your code will be paused. 3. Return to the code-behind file of *exercise.aspx* if you aren't automatically sent there. 4. Click on the *Watch* button at the bottom of the screen. 5. Click in an empty box in the *Watch* window and type: **TextBoxText.Text** 6. Press <**Enter**>. This was covered in: *Lesson 3-3: Use Breakpoints.*	1. Open the code-behind file of *exercise.aspx*. 2. Right-click on the *Page.Server.Transfer* line in the *ButtonSendData_Click* event handler. 3. Click: Breakpoint→ Insert Breakpoint from the shortcut menu. This was covered in: *Lesson 3-3: Use Breakpoints.*	1. Open the code-behind file of *exercise.aspx*. 2. Add the following code to the *ButtonSendData_Click* event handler: **Page.Server. Transfer("passdata2.aspx");** This was covered in: *Lesson 3-10: Move between pages.*	1. Open *exercise.aspx* in *Design* view. 2. Select the *ButtonChangeText* control by clicking on it. 3. Click on the *Events* button in the *Properties* window. ⚡ 4. Double-click in the empty box next to *Click*. This was covered in: *Lesson 3-2: Add event handlers to Controls.*

If you have difficulty with the other questions, here are the lessons that cover the relevant skills:

1   Refer to: Lesson 1-7: **Manage a project with the Solution Explorer.**

2   Refer to: Lesson 3-9: **Work with ViewState.**

4   Refer to: Lesson 3-1: **Change properties with C#.**

5   Refer to: Lesson 3-2: **Add event handlers to Controls.**

8   Refer to: Lesson 1-8: **Run a project in debug mode.**

10   Refer to: Lesson 3-11: **Send data between pages.**

11   Refer to: Lesson 3-10: **Move between pages.**

Session Four: ASP.NET Controls

4

> A designer knows he has achieved perfection not when there is nothing left to add, but when there is nothing left to take away.
>
> *Antoine de Saint-Exupéry, French writer and aviator (1900 – 1944)*

In this session you'll work with the different controls ASP.NET has to offer in greater depth and gain an understanding of what they can do.

You'll also learn some of the best practices for naming controls and structuring your pages.

Session Objectives

By the end of this session you will be able to:

- Name controls correctly
- Use button controls
- Use label and literal controls
- Use text boxes
- Use check boxes
- Use radio buttons
- Use drop down lists
- Use the RequiredFieldValidator control
- Use other validation controls
- Use common properties

Lesson 4-1: Name controls correctly

Almost every time you've added a control in this book, you've changed its ID property instead of leaving it at the default value. Using consistent names for your controls is one of the most important things to do when working with C# or ASP.NET.

Whenever you create a control, you should always set its ID property to something meaningful before doing anything else with it.

In this lesson, you'll create a number of controls and set their ID properties according to the naming convention used by this book.

1   Open *My Project* from your sample files folder.

2   Add a new Web Form called: **namingtest.aspx**

You learned how to do this in: *Lesson 1-7: Manage a project with the Solution Explorer.*

3   Switch to *Design* view.

4   Add an ASP.NET *Label* control to the page.

You learned how to do this in *Lesson 1-14: Add controls to a page with the Toolbox.*

5   Add three ASP.NET *Button* controls to the page.

Your page should now look like this:

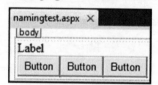

6   Set the *Text* properties of the buttons.

1.   Set the *Text* property of the first button to: **Monday**

2.   Set the *Text* property of the second button to: **Tuesday**

3.   Set the *Text* property of the third button to: **Wednesday**

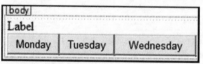

7   Name the buttons correctly.

At the moment you have buttons that say *Monday, Tuesday* and *Wednesday* on them, but their ID properties still say *Button1, Button2* and *Button3.*

Although you could work with them this way, it would be very confusing when you looked at the code as you'd have no idea which button was which without checking the page.

1.   Set the *ID* property of *Button1* to: **ButtonMonday**

2.   Set the *ID* property of *Button2* to: **ButtonTuesday**

3.   Set the *ID* property of *Button3* to: **ButtonWednesday**

If you are not completing the course incrementally use the sample file: **Lesson 4-1** to begin this lesson.

Sample files with the starting point for each lesson are also provided for all of the other lessons in this session.

8 Name the label correctly.

This book always uses the convention [Control Type][Name], which is always in Mixed Case.

Using this convention, it's always easy to understand which type of control the code is working with and what it does.

Set the *ID* property of the *Label1* control to: **LabelDay**

9 See IntelliSense at work.

1. Add a *Click* event handler to the *ButtonMonday* control.

    You learned how to do this in: *Lesson 3-2: Add event handlers to Controls.*

2. Type **Button** into the code window (inside the new event handler).

    You'll notice that the *IntelliSense* menu appears.

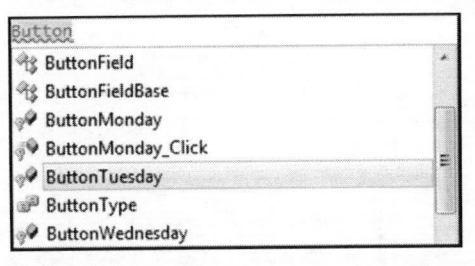

    Because you named all of your buttons properly, you can see all of them listed together in the *IntelliSense* menu at a glance.

3. Delete the *Button* text you just added.

4. Type **Label** into the *Code* window.

    You'll see the *IntelliSense* menu appear again.

5. Choose *LabelDay* by double-clicking on it.

    Alternatively, scroll down to it using the arrow keys and press **<Enter>**.

    You'll learn more about *IntelliSense* in: *Lesson 5-1: Use IntelliSense.*

6. Add **.Text = "Monday";** to the end of the line.

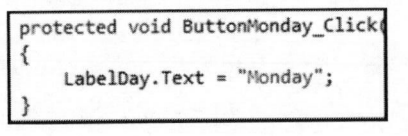

    With this code, you can see at a glance that the *ButtonMonday* control will set the *LabelDay* label's text to *Monday* when clicked.

    If you hadn't named your controls, here is how it would have looked:

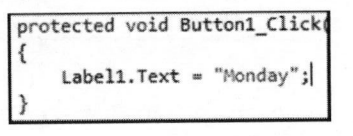

    As you can see, by naming your controls you have made your code a lot easier to understand and work with.

Lesson 4-2: Use button controls

note

Button events

If you look at the available events for each of the button controls, you'll see that there are a few other events in addition to *Click*.

Using any event other than *Click* for a button is extremely rare.

You've already worked with the *Button* control quite a bit at this point, but there are a few different types of button control that act in a similar way.

You'll learn about the different types of button controls in this lesson.

1   Open *My Project* from your sample files folder.

2   Add a new Web Form called: **controlstest.aspx**

3   Open *controlstest.aspx* in *Design* view.

4   Add a *Button* control to the page.

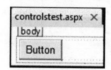

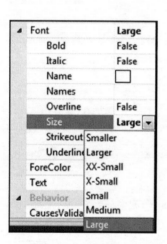

5   Set the properties of the *Button* control.

1.   Set the *ID* property of the button to: **ButtonTest**

2.   Set the *Text* property of the button to: **Standard Button**

3.   Set the *BackColor* property of the button to: **Black**

   You learned how to set the *BackColor* property in *Lesson 1-12: Change properties in Design view.*

4.   Set the *ForeColor* property of the button to: **White**

5.   Set the *Font Size* property of the button to: **Large**

   To do this, you will need to expand the *Font* property in the *Properties* window. You can then select the size from a drop-down menu.

   Your button should now look like this:

   As you can see, you have quite a lot of control over the appearance and style of your buttons.

tip

The *LinkButton* and HTML

It is possible to put any valid HTML code into a *LinkButton*'s *Text* property. This code will appear inside a pair of HTML <a> </a> tags when sent to the browser.

This allows advanced developers to make any part of an HTML page into a button.

6   Add a *LinkButton* to the page, below the *Button*.

The *LinkButton* control behaves in exactly the same way as a button, but the server will convert it into an HTML <a> tag rather than an HTML *Input (Submit)* control.

This control appears to be a hyperlink but acts like a button. Unlike a hyperlink, it posts back using JavaScript code.

7   Set the properties of the *LinkButton*.

1. Set the *ID* of the link button to: **LinkButtonTest**

2. Set the *Text* of the link button to: **Link Button**

3. Set the *ForeColor* of the link button to: **Red**

4. Set the *Font Bold* property of the link button to: **True**

8　Add an *ImageButton* to the page, below the *LinkButton*.

It will actually appear just after the *LinkButton.* This is because of the way the page is structured at the moment, and isn't something to worry about.

The *ImageButton* control, as you might expect, is a button that uses an image. Note that unlike the *LinkButton* control, the *ImageButton* doesn't need to use any JavaScript to submit the form.

9　Add *testbutton.png* to the *Images* folder.

You will find *testbutton.png* in the *C:\Practice\ASP.NET\Images* folder.

You learned how to add files to a project in: *Lesson 1-7: Manage a project with the Solution Explorer.*

10　Set the properties of the *ImageButton*.

1. Set the *ID* of the image button to: **ImageButtonTest**

2. Set the *ImageURL* of the image button to:
   ~/Images/testbutton.png

   You can either type this in or use the browse button next to the property to find the image (see sidebar for explanation of the tilde)

3. Set the *AlternateText* of the image button to **Test Image Button** (see sidebar).

The *Button, LinkButton* and *ImageButton* controls provide a choice of three different appearances for your buttons.

11　Remove the controls from the page.

You're going to be using *controlstest.aspx* to test controls through the rest of this session, so you need to remove the buttons before continuing.

To do this, select them in *Design* view and either press <**Delete**> or right-click and then click *Delete* from the shortcut menu.

Lesson 4-3: Use label and literal controls

You've already worked with the *Label* control several times. Using a label control is probably the easiest way to make a piece of text on a page accessible to your C# code.

In this lesson you'll learn a little bit more about the capabilities of label controls and about the similar *Literal* control.

1 Open *My Project* from your sample files folder.

2 Open *controlstest.aspx* in *Design* view.

3 Add a *Label* control to the page.

4 Set the properties of the *Label* control.

   1. Set the *ID* property to: **LabelTest**

   2. Change the *Text* property to: **Test Label**

   3. Set the *Font Bold* property to: **True**

      Most controls that contain text have the same text formatting properties as *Label* controls.

5 Add a *Literal* control to the page, next to the *Label* control.

The *Literal* control looks a little strange. This is because it doesn't have any *Text*, so a placeholder is shown instead (see sidebar).

6 Set the properties of the *Literal* control.

   1. Set the *ID* property of the Literal control to: **LiteralTest**

   2. Set the *Text* property of the Literal control to: **Test Literal**

You'll notice there are a lot fewer properties for a *Literal* control than there are for a *Label* control. You'll see why in a moment.

7 See the difference between *Label* and *Literal* controls.

   1. View *controlstest.aspx* in your browser.

   2. View the source of the page.

      As you've done before, right-click in Internet Explorer and then click *View Source* from the shortcut menu.

```
<span id="LabelTest" style="font-weight:bold;">Test Label</span>
Test Literal
```

You can see that the *Label* has been converted into a *span* tag by the server. The server has converted the *Font Bold* property to inline CSS.

The *Literal* sends exactly what you put into its *Text* property to the browser. This is the reason it has so few properties. The server will never change it in any way. This is useful when you want to use C# to place HTML code directly onto the page.

The *Label* control is the best choice when you simply want to display text in the user's browser.

8 **Use the *Load* event.**

1. Close your browser and return to *controlstest.aspx* in *Design* view.

2. Select *LabelTest* and add a *Load* event handler to it.

   Do this in the same way as you added the *Click* event handler to your buttons earlier: Select the control, click the *Events* button (in the *Properties* window) and double-click in the empty box next to *Load*.

3. Add the following code to the *Load* event handler of *LabelTest*:

   LabelTest.Text = "Label Load Event Fired!";

   ```
   protected void LabelTest_Load(object sender, Ev
   {
       LabelTest.Text = "Label Load Event Fired!";
   }
   ```

4. View *controlstest.aspx* in your browser.

   You will see that the *Text* property of the label was updated when the page loaded.

   http://localhost:51760/controlstest.aspx

   Label Load Event Fired! Test Literal

The *Load* events (for each control on the page) happen immediately after the *Page_Load* event. You'd see the same effect if you put the code into the *Page_Load* event handler instead.

In general, it's better to use the *Page_Load* event handler rather than the *Load* event handlers of each individual control. This keeps all of the code that runs when the page loads in the same place.

The person viewing your site can't interact directly with *Label* or *Literal* controls, so there are no other important events.

9 **Remove the controls.**

Remove both the *Label* and *Literal* controls.

10 **Remove the *LabelTest_Load* event handler.**

1. Try running the project in *Debug* mode.

   You'll find it is unable to run. This is because you left the event handler code for the *Label* control behind after you deleted it, and it no longer makes sense to ASP.NET.

2. Remove the *LabelTest_Load* event handler.

   Simply open the code-behind file and delete the event handler.

3. Try running the project again.

   This time it will be able to start.

11 **Close Visual Studio.**

note

The other events of label and literal controls

As well as the *Load* event, you'll notice the *Init, PreRender* and *Unload* events. These correspond to *Page_Init, Page_PreRender* and *Page_Unload* in the same way as *Load* corresponds to *Page_Load*.

You'll also see *DataBinding* and *Disposed*.

Disposed happens when the control is removed from the web server's memory, which will happen after the control has been converted to HTML and sent to the user's web browser.

DataBinding is a special event that only happens if the control is attached to a data source, such as an SQL database. You'll learn more about binding data to controls in: *Lesson 11-8: Bind data to a control using C#.*

It isn't just the *Label* and *Literal* controls that have these events; they're available on every ASP.NET control. In practice, however, it is very rare to have to use them. You won't need to use any of these events throughout the rest of this book.

Lesson 4-4: Use text boxes

You've already worked with the *TextBox* control a few times. It's one of the most common controls in ASP.NET. The TextBox control provides the easiest way to allow users of your site to input text.

1 Open *My Project* from your sample files folder.

2 Open *controlstest.aspx* in *Design* view.

3 Add a *TextBox* control to the page.

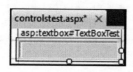

4 Set the ID of the *TextBox* control to: **TextBoxTest**

You now have a text box with the default properties.

5 Make *TextBoxTest* bigger.

1. Set the *Width* of the *TextBoxTest* control to: **300px**

2. Set the *Height* of the *TextBoxTest* control to: **75px**

3. View the page in your browser.

4. Type some text into the text box.

You'll see that although the text box has lots of room, the text all stays on the top line.

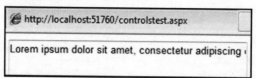

5. Close the browser.

6 Make *TextBoxTest* work with multiple lines.

1. Set the *TextMode* property of *TextBoxTest* to: **MultiLine**

2. View the page in your browser.

3. Try typing in some text.

This time the text is spread across multiple lines.

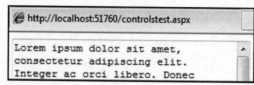

4. Close the browser.

7 Set the width in columns.

As well as setting the width of a text box in pixels, you can also set it using columns. A column is a single letter.

1. Clear the *Width* property of *TextBoxTest*.

Simply remove the text from the property.

2. Set the *Columns* property of *TextBoxTest* to: **50**

It's up to you how you prefer to specify the width of a text box.

8 Use the *TextChanged* event.

1. Add a *TextChanged* event handler to *TextBoxTest*.

    You learned how to do this in: *Lesson 3-2: Add event handlers to Controls*.

2. Put the following code in the event handler:

    Response.Write(TextBoxTest.Text);

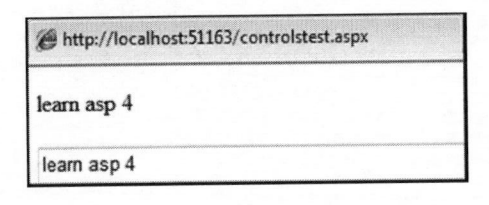

3. View the page in your browser.

4. Type in some text.

    Nothing actually happens as the *TextChanged* event isn't fired. This is because the page hasn't been posted back, so the server doesn't know that the text has been changed.

5. Close your browser and return to *controlstest.aspx*.

6. Add a *Button* control to the page, and set its ID property to: **ButtonSubmit**

7. View the page in your browser.

8. Type some text into the text box and click the button.

    This time the page posts back. The server sees that the text has been changed, so the *TextChanged* event fires and your C# code adds the text to the top of the *Response*.

9. Click the button again without changing the text.

    The text hasn't changed since last time, so *TextChanged* doesn't fire when the page posts back this time.

10. Close the browser.

9   **Set the maximum length of the text box.**

1. Set the *MaxLength* property of the *TextBoxTest* control to: **10**

2. View the page in your browser.

3. Type some text into the text box.

    Unfortunately, the *MaxLength* property has no effect. The user can still enter as much text as they like.

4. Close the browser and set the *TextMode* property of the *TextBoxTest* control back to: **SingleLine**

5. View the page in your browser.

6. Type some text into the text box.

    This time the text is limited correctly. Unfortunately, *MaxLength* does not work with *MultiLine* text boxes.

10 **Close the browser and remove the controls and code.**

As you did in the previous lessons, remove the controls from the page.

Don't forget to remove the *TextBoxTest_TextChanged* event handler from the code-behind file.

> **note**
>
> **AutoPostBack**
>
> When a *TextBox* control has its *AutoPostBack* property set to *True*, it will submit the form as soon as the user clicks away from the text after editing it.
>
> This property is rarely used for *TextBox* controls.

Lesson 4-5: Use check boxes

In this lesson you'll learn more about the *CheckBox* control, which you've only seen very briefly at this point.

A check box is simply a box that the user can check or un-check. You have probably seen them while browsing the Internet.

1   Open *My Project* from your sample files folder.

2   Open *controlstest.aspx* in *Design* view.

3   Add a *CheckBox* control to the page.

4   Set the ID property of the *CheckBox* control to: **CheckBoxTest**

You'll see that much like the *Literal* control, the *CheckBox* displays a placeholder containing its *ID* unless you set its *Text* property.

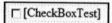

5   Make the *CheckBoxTest* control checked by default.

Set the *Checked* property of the *CheckBoxTest* control to: **True**

You'll see that the control is now checked by default.

6   Set the *Text* property of the *CheckBox* control to: **Confirm**

You'll see that the text appears to the right of the CheckBox.

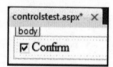

7   Set the *TextAlign* property of the *CheckBox* control to: **Left**

This will make the text appear to the left of the *CheckBox* instead of to the right.

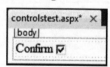

8   Add a *CheckedChanged* event handler.

1.   In the same way as you've done before, add a *CheckedChanged* event handler to the *CheckBoxTest* control.

You learned how to do this in: *Lesson 3-2: Add event handlers to Controls.*

The *CheckedChanged* event happens when the user ticks or unticks the *CheckBox*.

2.   Add the following code to the *CheckedChanged* event handler:

Response.Write(CheckBoxTest.Checked.ToString());

```
protected void CheckBoxTest_CheckedChanged(object se
{
    Response.Write(CheckBoxTest.Checked.ToString());
}
```

This will write the *Checked* property of the checkbox to the page.

3. View *controlstest.aspx* in your browser.

4. Un-check *CheckBoxTest*.

Nothing happens despite the *CheckedChanged* event being in place.

This is because the form hasn't been posted back.

9 **Make the *CheckBoxTest* control post back when it is clicked.**

1. Close the browser and return to *controlstest.aspx* in *Design* view.

2. Set the *AutoPostBack* property of the *CheckBoxTest* control to: **True**

3. View *controlstest.aspx* in your browser.

4. Un-check *CheckBoxTest*.

This time you'll see the page post back when you click the check box and the event handler code will write the current status of the *CheckBox* onto the screen. *True* means the box is checked, *False* means the box is un-checked.

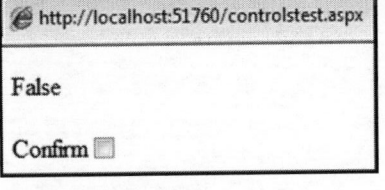

5. Check the *CheckBox* again.

You'll see the page post back again and the event handler displays *True*, since the box is now checked.

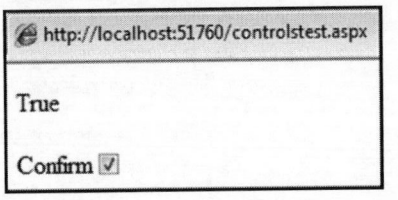

Instead of setting the *AutoPostBack* property, you could also have added a button to the page as you did in: *Lesson 4-4: Use text boxes.*

10 **Close the browser and remove the controls and code.**

Remove the controls from the page.

Don't forget to remove the *CheckBoxTest_CheckedChanged* event handler from the code-behind file.

11 **Close Visual Studio.**

Lesson 4-6: Use radio buttons

You haven't used the *RadioButton* control yet in this book, but it's likely that you've seen radio buttons while browsing the Internet.

Radio buttons are very similar to check boxes, but only allow the user to choose one option at a time. You'll learn more about the *RadioButton* control in this lesson.

1   Open *My Project* from your sample files folder.

2   Open *controlstest.aspx* in *Design* view.

3   Add a *RadioButton* control to the page.

You'll see that a placeholder containing the *ID* is shown in exactly the same way as with the *CheckBox* control.

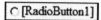

4   Set properties of the new *RadioButton* control.

    1.   Set the *ID* property to: **RadioButtonChoice1**

    2.   Set the *Text* property to: **Choice 1**

5   Add another *RadioButton* control to the page.

Try to add it below the first one.

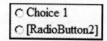

6   Set the properties of the new *RadioButton* control.

    1.   Set the *ID* property to: **RadioButtonChoice2**

    2.   Set the *Text* property to: **Choice 2**

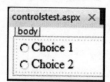

7   See the *RadioButton* control in action.

    1.   View *controlstest.aspx* in your browser.

    2.   Click on each of the radio buttons.

You'll see that they both become selected with no way to de-select them. This isn't the way you want things to work.

This is because you haven't told the two radio buttons that they belong to the same group yet.

8   Assign the two radio buttons to a group.

    1.   Close the browser and return to *controlstest.aspx* in *Design* view.

    2.   Set the *GroupName* property of both of the radio buttons to: **Choices.** (Be careful not to add any trailing spaces).

3. View *controlstest.aspx* in your browser.

4. Click on each of the radio buttons.

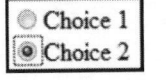

This time you're only able to select one choice at a time, which is how radio buttons are supposed to work.

Note that if you had used a *RadioButtonList* control instead (see sidebar), the *GroupName* properties would be automatically assigned.

5. Close your browser.

9 **Make *RadioButtonChoice1* selected by default.**

Set the *Checked* property of the *RadioButtonChoice1* control to: **True**

You'll see that the first choice is now selected by default.

10 **Use the *CheckedChanged* event.**

1. Add a *CheckedChanged* event handler to the *RadioButtonChoice1* control.

This event handler will fire when the first radio button is checked or unchecked.

2. Add the following code to the new event handler:

Response.Write(RadioButtonChoice1.Checked.ToString());

```
protected void RadioButtonChoice1_CheckedChanged(object se
{
    Response.Write(RadioButtonChoice1.Checked.ToString());
}
```

This code will write *True* or *False* onto the screen depending on whether *RadioButtonChoice1* is selected or not.

3. View *controlstest.aspx* in your browser.

4. Try clicking on each of the *RadioButton* controls.

As with the *CheckBox* control, the *RadioButton* control doesn't automatically post back by default, so nothing happens.

5. Close the browser and set the *AutoPostBack* properties of *RadioButtonChoice1* and *RadioButtonChoice2* to: **True**

6. View *controlstest.aspx* in your browser again.

7. Try clicking on each of the *RadioButton* controls.

You'll see that the event handler works when you click on *Choice 1*, but nothing happens when you click on *Choice 2*. This is because although *Choice 2* is posting back it doesn't have an event handler.

This could easily be fixed by giving the *RadioButtonChoice2* control a *CheckedChanged* event handler as well.

8. Close the browser.

11 **Remove the controls and event handler code.**

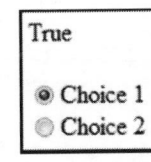

Lesson 4-7: Use drop down lists

note

Other list-based controls

In previous lessons, the *CheckBoxList* and *RadioButtonList* controls were mentioned, both of which work in a similar way to *DropDownList* controls.

BulletedList and *ListBox* controls are also based on lists and are also very similar.

Everything you learn about the *DropDownList* control in this lesson can be applied to the other list-based controls as well.

You learned a little about the *DropDownList* control in: *Lesson 1-15: Use the QuickTasks menu*.

The *DropDownList* control is a little different to the controls you've worked with so far in this session. List-based controls contain multiple items each with their own set of properties. They also have properties and events that affect every item in the list.

1   Open *My Project* from your sample files folder.

2   Open *controlstest.aspx* in *Design* view.

3   Add a *DropDownList* control to the page.

4   Set the *ID* of the new *DropDownList* to: **DropDownListTest**

5   Add items to the *DropDownList*.

You might remember doing this in: *Lesson 1-15: Use the QuickTasks menu*.

1.   Click *Edit Items…* from the *QuickTasks* menu of *DropDownListTest*.

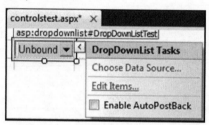

2.   Add a new item to the list.

3.   Set the new item's *Text* property to: **Product 1**

4.   Set the new item's *Value* property to: **1**

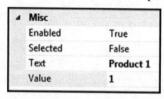

5.   In the same way, create a **Product 2** item with a *Value* of: **2**

6.   Create a **Product 3** item with a *Value* of: **3**

7.   Click *OK*.

You might be wondering what the *Value* property is for. Items in *DropDownLists* are allowed to have both a *Text* value (that is shown to the user) and another *Value* that is hidden from the user but is visible to your C# code.

The *Value* is especially useful when your *DropDownList* control is linked to items in a database (see sidebar).

6   Use the *SelectedIndexChanged* event.

note

List-based controls and databases

List-based controls can be made to retrieve their lists from a database instead of typing them in manually.

You'll learn how to do this in: *Lesson 11-2: Attach a data source to a control*.

As well as the *Text* and *Value* properties, each item in a *DropDownList* control is automatically assigned a unique *Index* number (see sidebar).

1. Add a *SelectedIndexChanged* event handler to the *DropDownListTest* control.

2. Add the following code to the event handler:

   Response.Write(DropDownListTest.SelectedValue);

   This code will write the *Value* of the item that the user has selected onto the top of the web page.

3. Add a new line inside the event handler (after the previous line) with this code:

   Response.Write("<br />");

   This code will simply add an HTML break tag after the *Value*. This HTML tag adds a line break.

4. Add a new line inside the event handler (after the previous line) with this code:

   Response.Write(DropDownListTest.SelectedItem.Text);

   This code will write the contents of the *Text* property of the selected item.

5. Add another line to place a <br /> tag after the previous line:

   Response.Write("<br />");

6. Add one more line to the event handler:

   Response.Write(DropDownListTest.SelectedIndex);

   This will write the *Index* property of the selected item (see sidebar).

```
protected void DropDownListTest_SelectedIndexChanged(ob
{
    Response.Write(DropDownListTest.SelectedValue);
    Response.Write("<br />");
    Response.Write(DropDownListTest.SelectedItem.Text);
    Response.Write("<br />");
    Response.Write(DropDownListTest.SelectedIndex);
}
```

7. View *controlstest.aspx* in your browser.

8. Change the value in the *DropDownList*.

   You'll see that, once again, nothing happens because the page hasn't been posted back.

9. Close the browser, return to *Design* view and then set the *AutoPostBack* property of *DropDownListTest* to: **True**

10. View *controlstest.aspx* in your browser again.

11. Change the value in the *DropDownList*.

    This time the event handler runs and each of the relevant properties are displayed.

7 Remove the controls and event handler code.

Lesson 4-8: Use the RequiredFieldValidator control

You now know how to work with the controls needed to create almost any online form. One thing you'll often want to do with online forms is to validate the user's input to make sure they are entering everything correctly.

Although you could validate input using a combination of C# and JavaScript, ASP.NET provides a series of controls that will automatically generate the validation code for you. The *RequiredFieldValidator* is one of these.

1   Open *ShiningStone* from your sample files folder.

2   Open *buy.aspx* in *Design* view.

This is the form a visitor to the site would use to buy a product. It isn't finished yet, and one thing it needs is validation.

3   Add a *RequiredFieldValidator* control to the page.

Drag a *RequiredFieldValidator* control from the *Validation* category of the *Toolbox* so that it is just after the textbox following *Address 1*.

Address 1		RequiredFieldValidator

A *RequiredFieldValidator* simply makes sure that the user has entered something into the control it validates. In this case you're going to make it validate that text has been entered into the *TextBoxAddress1* control.

4   Set the properties of the new *RequiredFieldValidator* control.

1. Set the *ID* property to: **RequiredFieldValidatorAddress1**

2. Set the *Text* property to: *****

    This is the message that will appear if the control fails to validate, ie if the user doesn't fill in the field.

3. Set the *ControlToValidate* property to: **TextBoxAddress1**

    The *ControlToValidate* property tells the validator which control it is going to check.

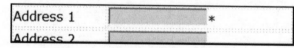

5   See *RequiredFieldValidator* in action.

1. View *buy.aspx* in your browser.

2. Click *Submit Order* without entering anything into any of the text boxes.

    You will see that the page doesn't post back and your * text appears where you placed your *RequiredFieldValidator*.

3. Type something into the *Address 1* text box.

---

note

Validation groups

You already know that an ASP.NET page is implemented using one (and only one) form that typically includes all page content.

This can cause a problem.

Imagine you had a log-in section at the top of your web page containing two fields: *User Name* and *Password*.

When the user tried to log in, (in this example), validation would fail because *Address 1* was blank.

Validation groups solve this problem.

All validation controls have a *ValidationGroup* property which is blank by default. This means that, by default, all controls belong to the same Validation Group.

If you wished to associate some form controls with a submit button (in this example the *User Name* and *Password*) you would set the *ValidationGroup* property of these controls to the same value. When the user clicked the submit button control, validation rules would then be applied only to the *User Name* and *Password*.

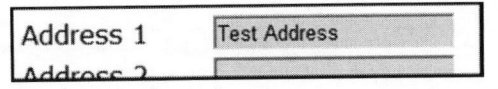

4. Click *Submit Order*.

   This time the page posts back without problems.

5. Close the web browser.

6 Validate using C#.

Although the messages you've seen displayed so far are very fast and helpful, the web server implements them using JavaScript. A malicious user could bypass your validation by simply disabling JavaScript.

Fortunately, you can use C# to very easily check that the user hasn't somehow bypassed your validation rules.

1. Open the code-behind file of *buy.aspx*.

2. Add the following code to the *ButtonSubmitOrder_Click* event handler:

   if (Page.IsValid) Response.Write("OK!");

   ```
   protected void ButtonSubmitOrder_Click(object
   {
       if (Page.IsValid) Response.Write("OK!");
   }
   ```

   This will re-check the user input against all validators on the page and only write *OK!* if all validation rules succeed. This is a very useful security enhancement.

   This code uses an *if* statement. You'll learn all about them in: *Lesson 7-1: Use the if statement*.

3. View the page in your browser.

4. Enter some text into the *Address1* text box.

   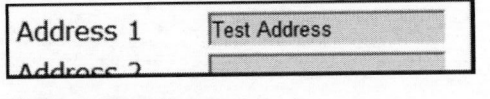

5. Click *Submit Order*.

   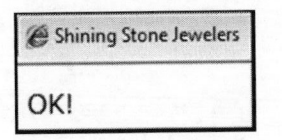

   You'll see that the page submits and the C# test succeeds. If you'd disabled JavaScript to try to bypass the validation, the C# test wouldn't succeed and you wouldn't see *OK!*.

7 Close Visual Studio.

Lesson 4-9: Use other validation controls

The *RequiredFieldValidator* control is very useful, but Visual Studio comes with other validation controls to help you make sure your users have entered the right values into your forms.

The *RangeValidator* control allows you to check that the user has entered the correct type of value and allows you to restrict the value to a range.

The *ValiationSummary* control lets you easily display a list of validation error messages to let the user know what they have entered incorrectly.

1   Open *ShiningStone* from your sample files folder.

2   Open *buy.aspx* in *Design* view.

3   Add a *RangeValidator* control next to *Phone Number*.

     The *RangeValidator* control is intended to restrict a value to a specific type and range.

     Add a *RangeValidator* control to the right of the *Phone Number* text box control.

4   Set the properties of the new *RangeValidator* control.

     1.   Set the *ID* property to: **RangeValidatorPhoneNumber**

     2.   Set the *Text* property to: *****

     3.   Set the *ControlToValidate* property to: **TextBoxPhoneNumber**

     4.   Set the *Type* property to: **Integer**

        The *Type* property makes sure that the contents of the validated control are of a certain type. Setting it to *Integer* will make sure that the user enters a whole number into the *TextBoxPhoneNumber* control.

     5.   Set the *MinimumValue* property to: **0**

     6.   Set the *MaximumValue* property to: **999999**

     The *MinimumValue* and *MaximumValue* properties control which numbers the *RangeValidator* will accept as valid. In this case, if the number is below 0 or above 999999, it will be considered invalid. This will restrict users to phone numbers with six digits or less.

5   See the *RangeValidator* control in action.

     1.   View *buy.aspx* in your browser.

     2.   Enter some text into the *Address 1* text box.

Address 1	Test Address
Address 2	

     3.   Enter **999999** into the *Phone Number* text box.

Phone Number	999999

note

Advanced validation controls

Along with the *RequiredFieldValidator* and *RangeValidator* controls you'll see the *CompareValidator*, *CustomValidator* and *RegularExpressionValidator* controls.

The *CompareValidator* control is used when you want to validate by comparing one control with another.

The *CustomValidator* control allows you to enter your own JavaScript code to be used for validation.

The *RegularExpressionValidator* control allows you to validate using a Regular Expression. Regular Expressions aren't covered in this book, but you can learn more about them in the Expert Skills book in this series.

---

4. Click: *Submit Order*.

> **Shining Stone Jewelers**
>
> OK!

The form submits because *999999* is within the range of the *RangeValidator*.

5. Enter **9999999** into the *Phone Number* text box.

> Phone Number | 9999999

6. Click *Submit Order*.

> Phone Number | 9999999 | *

This time the validator error message appears because *9999999* is higher than the *MaximumValue*.

In a real project you would probably use a *RegularExpressionValidator* control to make sure the user enters a valid phone number (see sidebar).

7. Close the web browser.

6 Add a *ValidationSummary* control.

As well as displaying error messages next to the controls themselves, you can use a *ValidationSummary* control to show a list of validation problems.

1. Add a *ValidationSummary* control below the *Submit Order* button.

2. Set the *ID* of the new *ValidationSummary* to: **ValidationSummaryBuy**

The *ValidationSummary* control will automatically pick up the *ErrorMessage* properties from any other validation controls on the page.

7 Set error messages for your validation controls.

1. Set the *ErrorMessage* property of the *RequiredFieldValidatorAddress1* control to: **Address 1 Required**

2. Set the *ErrorMessage* property of the *RangeValidatorPhoneNumber* control to: **Invalid Phone Number**

8 Try out the *ValidationSummary*.

1. View *buy.aspx* in your browser.

2. Enter **abc** in the *Phone Number* text box.

3. Click the *Submit Order* button.

The validation summary is displayed, showing the *ErrorMessage* properties, along with the asterisks from the *Text* properties.

> • Address 1 Required
> • Invalid Phone Number

> Submit Order
>
> • Error message 1.
> • Error message 2.

Lesson 4-10: Use common properties

You've become familiar with the properties of the most common controls in this session, but you've probably noticed that there are a few properties that are common to all controls.

In this lesson you'll look at some of the common properties and learn what they do.

1   Open *My Project* from your sample files folder.

2   Open *controlstest.aspx* in *Design* view.

3   Add some controls to the page.

1. Add a *Label* control and name it: **LabelTest**

2. Add a *Button* control and name it: **ButtonTest**

3. Add a *Calendar* control and name it: **CalendarTest**

Label	Button					
<		February 2011				>
Mon	**Tue**	**Wed**	**Thu**	**Fri**	**Sat**	**Sun**
31	1	2	3	4	5	6
7	8	9	10	11	12	13
14	15	16	17	18	19	20
21	22	23	24	25	26	27
28	1	2	3	4	5	6
7	8	9	10	11	12	13

4   Change the *Font* properties.

1. Set the *Font Underline* property of the *LabelTest* control to: **True**

2. Set the *Font Underline* property of the *ButtonTest* control to: **True**

3. Set the *Font Underline* property of the *CalendarTest* control to: **True**

You'll see that the property has the same effect on each control. The *Font* properties are available on all controls that contain text.

5   Use the *Visible* property.

All ASP.NET controls have a *Visible* property. If *Visible* is set to *False*, the HTML from the control is never sent to the user's browser.

1. Set the *Visible* property of the *CalendarTest* control to: **False**

2. View *controlstest.aspx* in your browser.

You'll see that the *CalendarTest* control doesn't appear. If you view the source of the page in Internet Explorer, you'll see that it isn't just hidden, it is completely omitted from the page.

```
<div>

    <span id="LabelTest" style="text-decor
    <input type="submit" name="ButtonTest"

</div>
```

3. Close the browser.

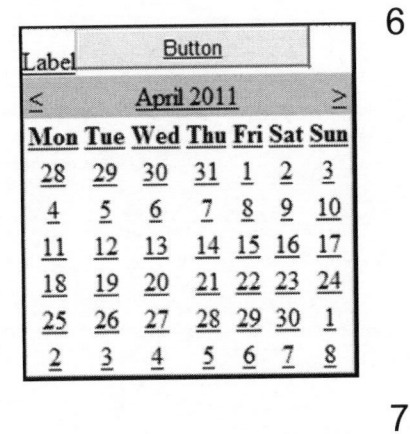

6 **Use the *Height* and *Width* properties.**

Almost every control has *Height* and *Width* properties that can be used to determine their size.

1. Set the *Width* property of the *ButtonTest* control to: **150px**

2. Set the *Width* property of the *CalendarTest* control to: **10px**

   As you can see, the *Calendar* control only shrinks slightly. This is because it can't shrink smaller than the content inside it.

   If you were to reduce the *Font Size* property of the *CalendarTest* control it would shrink to a smaller size.

7 **Use the *CSSClass* property.**

When you set a control's styles using its properties, the web server automatically creates CSS code to display them on the page.

It's more efficient and organized to keep your CSS in a different file and assign CSS classes to your controls. You can do that on almost every control using the *CSSClass* property.

1. Add a link to the *Site.css* file in the *Styles* folder.

   Switch to *Source* view and add the following line to the *<head>* tag:

   <link href="Styles/Site.css" rel="stylesheet" type="text/css" />

2. Switch back to *Design* view.

   You'll see that the CSS file has taken effect and the page's colors have changed.

3. Set the *CSSClass* property of the *LabelTest* control to: **failureNotification**

4. Set the *CSSClass* property of the *ButtonTest* control to: **failureNotification**

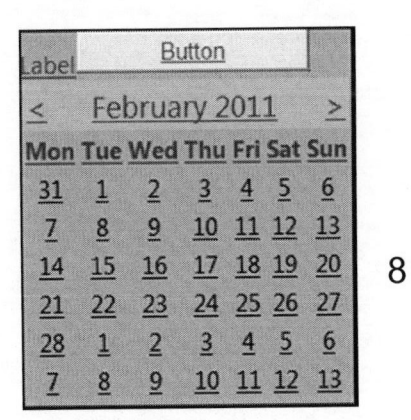

5. Set the *CSSClass* property of the *CalendarTest* control to: **failureNotification**

You'll see that the font becomes red and slightly larger due to applying the CSS class. You'll also notice that it is still underlined. This is because any properties you set on the controls themselves will override the CSS class.

8 **Remove the controls and code.**

Remember to remove the reference to the CSS file.

Session 4: Exercise

1   Open the *ShiningStone* sample project and open *buy.aspx* in *Design* view.

2   Set the maximum length of each of the address text box controls to 50.

3   Make each of the address text boxes 50 columns wide.

4   Add a *CheckBox* control in the space before the *Submit Order* button.

5   Set the *Text* property of the *CheckBox* control to: **I accept the terms and conditions**

6   Set the *CheckBox* ID property to: **CheckBoxAcceptTerms**

7   Add a *RequiredFieldValidator* control next to the *Address 2* text box and set it up appropriately.

8   Add a *RequiredFieldValidator* next to the *Post Code* text box and set it up appropriately.

9   Make the background color of the *Post Code* text box match the background color of the *Address 1* text box.

10   Make the font of the *Submit Order* button bold.

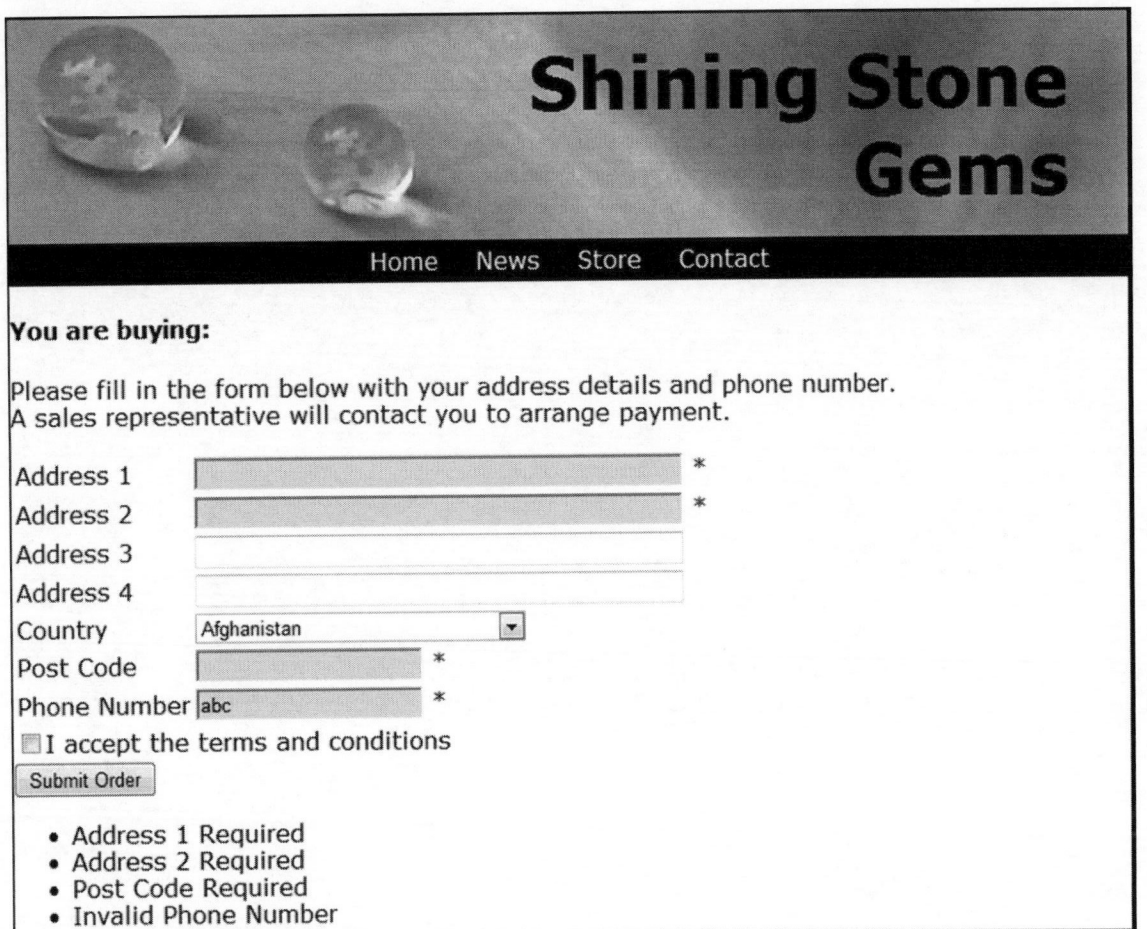

Session 4: Exercise Answers

These are the four questions that students find the most difficult to answer:

Q 9	Q 7	Q 6	Q 2
1. Open *buy*.aspx in *Design* view.	1. Open *buy*.aspx in *Design* view.	1. Open *buy*.aspx in *Design* view.	1. Open *buy*.aspx in *Design* view.
2. Click one of the pink text boxes.	2. Drag a *RequiredFieldValidator* from the *Validation* category of the *Toolbox* to the space after *TextBoxAddress2*.	2. Select *CheckBox1* and set its *ID* property to:	2. Select each of the address text box controls by clicking on them.
3. Look at the *BackColor* property.	3. Select the *RequiredFieldValidator*.	**CheckBoxAcceptTerms**	3. Set the *MaxLength* property of each text box control to: **50**
You will see it is *#FFCCCC*.	4. Set the *ID* property to:	This was covered in: *Lesson 4-1: Name controls correctly.*	This was covered in: *Lesson 4-4: Use text boxes.*
4. Click the *Post Code* text box.	**RequiredFieldValidatorAddress2**		
5. Set the *BackColor* property to: **#FFCCCC**	5. Set the *Text* property to: *****		
This was covered in: *Lesson 1-12: Change properties in Design view.*	6. Set the *ErrorMessage* property to: **Address 2 Required**		
	7. Set the *ControlToValidate* property to: **TextBoxAddress2**		
	This was covered in: *Lesson 4-8: Use the RequiredFieldValidator control.*		

If you have difficulty with the other questions, here are the lessons that cover the relevant skills:

1   Refer to: Lesson 1-7: Manage a project with the **Solution Explorer.**

3   Refer to: Lesson 4-4: Use text boxes.

4   Refer to: Lesson 4-5: Use check boxes.

5   Refer to: Lesson 4-5: Use check boxes.

8   Refer to: Lesson 4-8: Use the RequiredFieldValidator control.

10   Refer to: Lesson 4-10: Use common properties.

Session Five: C# Variables

> Numbers constitute the only universal language.
>
> *Nathanael West, American author and screenwriter (1903 – 1940)*

So far you've mostly worked with Visual Studio's visual features and haven't written a lot of C# code.

From this point on you'll start to learn a lot more about C# and how it fits in with the pages you design, starting with variables.

A variable is a container for a value. The value could be a number, a piece of text, a date or any one of the large number of variable types C# understands.

In this session you'll learn about the different types of variable C# can understand and how they can interact with each other.

Session Objectives

By the end of this session you will be able to:

- Use IntelliSense
- Create a variable
- Use string variables properties and methods
- Use integer variables
- Use floating point variables
- Use Boolean variables
- Use DateTime variables
- Convert variables using Convert and Parse
- Convert variables using cast and ToString
- Perform mathematical operations
- Use the Math library for advanced mathematics
- Understand null
- Use object and var variables

Lesson 5-1: Use IntelliSense

You've already seen IntelliSense quite a few times in the previous sessions but have mostly ignored it. The IntelliSense menu is the menu that appears as you're typing code, providing suggestions for what you might mean.

IntelliSense is one of Visual Studio's most useful features, and you'll learn more about how to use it in this lesson.

1   Open *ShiningStone* from your sample files folder.

2   Open the code-behind file of *buy.aspx*.

3   See the IntelliSense Menu.

1. Add a new line to end of the *ButtonSubmitOrder_Click* event handler.

2. Type **textbox** on the new line.

   The IntelliSense menu will appear, showing all available objects that contain the text *textbox*.

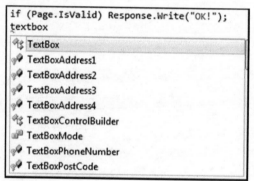

4   Select *TextBoxAddress1* from the IntelliSense menu.

1. Highlight *TextBoxAddress1*.

   You can do this either by clicking on it or scrolling down to it with the arrow keys.

   A box appears on the right giving you some information about the selected item.

   > TextBox buy.TextBoxAddress1
   > TextBoxAddress1 control.

   It's not particularly useful in this case, but it can help you when you're not sure exactly what you're looking for.

2. Choose *TextBoxAddress1*.

   You can decide *TextBoxAddress1* is what you were looking for by either double-clicking on it or pressing <**Enter**>.

   IntelliSense will automatically fill in the name.

5   See the properties of the *TextBoxAddress1* control using IntelliSense.

Press: <.>

This will make IntelliSense list the properties of the *TextBoxAddress1* control.

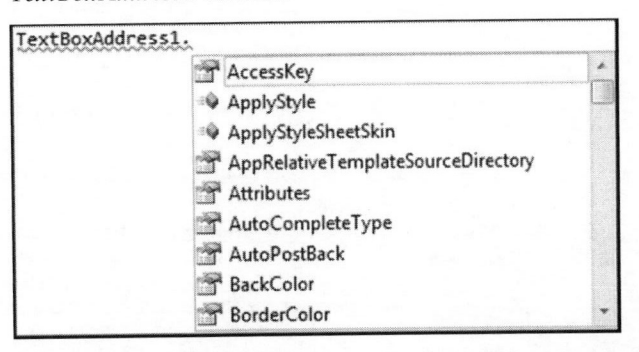

You can scroll up and down the large list of properties by either using the scrollbar with the mouse or using the arrow keys.

You can see all of the text box's properties in this list, plus a few items with different icons, such as *ApplyStyle*, as seen in the screenshot. *ApplyStyle* is a method (see sidebar).

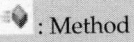
6 Select the *Text* property using IntelliSense.

1. Scroll down to the *Text* property either using the arrow keys or the scrollbar.

2. Refine the search by typing: **te**

   While IntelliSense is displayed, you can keep typing to narrow down your search to items that contain what you typed.

   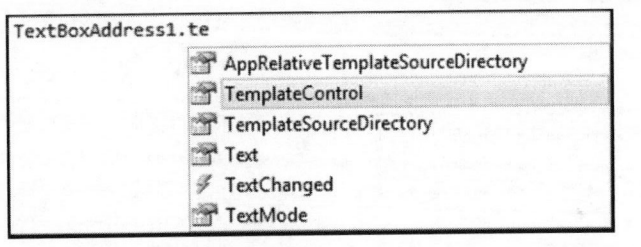

3. Make sure *Text* is selected.

   If you used the mouse to scroll down to *Text*, you will need to click on it.

   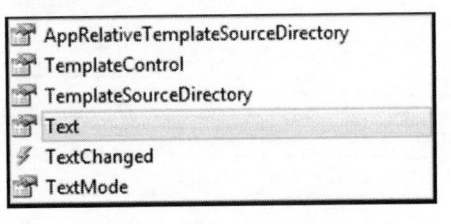

4. Press <**Enter**> or double-click on *Text*.

   Once again, you'll see that the text is automatically filled in.

   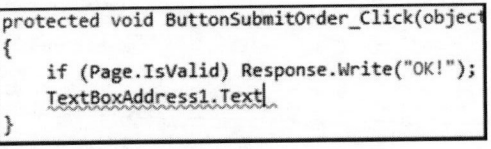

7 Remove the line of code you added.

8 Close Visual Studio.

Lesson 5-2: Create a variable

note

Visual Studio warnings

In *Lesson 1-8: Run a project in debug mode,* you saw that code with errors is underlined in red. In this lesson, you see some code underlined in green.

Green underlining indicates a warning rather than an error. If you hover your mouse cursor over the marked line, you will see the warning Visual Studio is giving you.

In this case, Visual Studio is just warning you that the *TestString* variable isn't being used for anything. As soon as you add some code to make use of the variable, the green underline will disappear.

Warnings won't stop you from running a project. They are there only for information purposes.

1 Open *ShiningStone* from your sample files folder.

2 Open the code-behind file of *buy.aspx.*

3 Add a string variable to the *Page_Load* event handler.

Add the following code to the *Page_Load* event handler:

string TestString = "Hello World!";

```
protected void Page_Load(object sender, EventArgs e)
{
    string TestString = "Hello World!";
}
```

A variable can be thought of as a container for data. You have created a new *string* variable called *TestString* which contains the text *Hello World!* You'll notice that *TestString* is underlined in green. This is a warning message (see sidebar).

A *string* variable always contains text. You'll learn more about strings in: *Lesson 5-3: Use string variable properties and methods.*

4 Set the *Text* property of the *TextBoxAddress1* control to the value of *TestString.*

1. Add a new line to the *Page_Load* event handler.

2. Type: **TextBoxAddress1.Text**

3. Look to the side of the IntelliSense menu.

```
string TextBox.Text
Gets or sets the text co
```

The first word (string) tells you that the Text property of a TextBox control can be manipulated in the same way as a string variable. You could have guessed that by the fact that it can contain a piece of text.

4. Complete the line of code so it appears as follows:

TextBoxAddress1.Text = TestString;

```
protected void Page_Load(object sender,
{
    string TestString = "Hello World!";
    TextBoxAddress1.Text = TestString;
}
```

You may notice that as you began to type *TestString* it appeared in the IntelliSense menu.

5. View *buy.aspx* in your browser.

```
Address 1        Hello World!
```

You'll see that the *Address 1* text box displays *Hello World!* This is because your code copied the text stored in the variable to the *Text* property of the control.

6. Close your web browser.

5 Change the value of the *TestString* variable.

The reason variables are called variables is that their values can vary. *TestString* doesn't have to stay at the value you defined when you created it. In fact it is very easy to change its value.

1. Add a new line after the one where you created *TestString*.

2. Put the following code on your new line:

TestString = "Please enter address";

This will change the value of the *TestString* variable from *Hello World!* to *Please enter address*. This technique works with any kind of variable.

```
protected void Page_Load(object sender,
{
    string TestString = "Hello World!";
    TestString = "Please enter address";
    TextBoxAddress1.Text = TestString;
}
```

3. View *buy.aspx* in your browser.

You'll see that because the value of the *TestString* variable was changed, the new value is used in the text box.

4. Close the web browser.

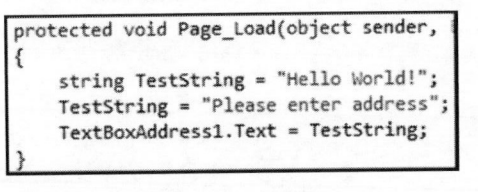

6 Remove all code from the *Page_Load* event handler.

7 Create a variable using the text from a control.

As well as setting a control's properties from a variable, you can set a variable from a control's properties.

1. Add the following line of code to the end of the *ButtonSubmitOrder_Click* event handler:

string Address1 = TextBoxAddress1.Text;

This creates a new string variable called *Address1*. It also sets the value of the variable to a copy of the contents of the *Text* property of the *TextBoxAddress1* control.

2. Add the following line of code after the last one you added:

Response.Write(Address1);

This will write contents of the string variable you created to the page.

```
protected void ButtonSubmitOrder_Click(objec
{
    if (Page.IsValid) Response.Write("OK!");
    string Address1 = TextBoxAddress1.Text;
    Response.Write(Address1);
}
```

3. View *buy.aspx* in your browser.

4. Fill in the highlighted text boxes (the text boxes have been highlighted to indicate that they are required fields).

You may rememeber that in: *Lesson 4-9: Use other validation controls* you set a rule that the *Phone Number* had to be a number between 0 and 999999 so make sure that your phone number is within this range.

5. Press *Submit Order*.

The text you entered is written to the screen after the validation message you added earlier.

note

String means exactly the same as *string*

If you look carefully in the IntelliSense menu when typing *string*, you'll notice that there's also an entry called *String* (where the first letter is capitalized).

In code, *String* means exactly the same thing as *string*.

So which is the better writing style?

All of Microsoft's examples use the lower-case version and, for that reason, I've used the same in the code examples in this book.

There's also a very good argument to suggest that the upper-case version represents better coding practice because *String* is the 'real' name of the string type in the .NET library.

There are similar alternative names for some other variable types, as you will see later in this session.

```
OK!
Address 1
```

Lesson 5-3: Use string variable properties and methods

1   Open *ShiningStone* from your sample files folder.

2   Open the code-behind file of *buy.aspx*.

3   Attach two strings together.

As well as setting the value of a string, as you did in *Lesson 5-2: Create a variable*, you can join two strings together using a + sign. Joining two strings together is also called *concatenating*.

1.   Add a new line after: *string Address1 = TextBoxAddress1.Text;*

2.   Put the following code on the new line:

   Address1 = "<br />" + Address1;

```
if (Page.IsValid) Response.Write("OK!");
string Address1 = TextBoxAddress1.Text;
Address1 = "<br />" + Address1;
Response.Write(Address1);
```

This code will add an HTML break tag (*
*) to the beginning of the *Address1* string variable.

You learned about the HTML break tag in: *Lesson 2-2: Understand HTML paragraph and break tags.*

3.   View *buy.aspx* in your browser.

4.   Fill in the required fields appropriately and click *Submit Order*.

   You'll see that the *Address1* string is now displayed on its own line because of the HTML *
* tag you added to it.

5.   Close your web browser.

4   Find out the length of a string.

C#'s string variables offer a number of useful properties and methods. One of the most useful properties is *Length*.

1.   Add a new line at the end of the *ButtonSubmitOrder_Click* event handler.

2.   Put the following code on the new line:

   Response.Write("(" + Address1.Length + ")");

```
protected void ButtonSubmitOrder_Click(object ser
{
    if (Page.IsValid) Response.Write("OK!");
    string Address1 = TextBoxAddress1.Text;
    Address1 = "<br />" + Address1;
    Response.Write(Address1);
    Response.Write("(" + Address1.Length + ")");
}
```

You're actually joining 3 strings together here: an *opening bracket*, the *Length* property of the string and a *closing bracket*. This will show the length (number of characters) of the string in brackets.

3. View *buy.aspx* in your browser.

4. Fill in the required fields as before and click *Submit Order*.

This time you'll see the length of the text you entered plus 5 (the number of characters in the <br /> tag) in brackets after the text.

5. Close the browser.

```
OK!
test address 1 (21)
```

5 Use the *ToUpper* method of the string variable to make a string all UPPER CASE.

Sometimes you might want to convert a string to upper case. Fortunately, C# makes this very easy.

1. Replace:

Response.Write(Address1);

With:

Response.Write(Address1.ToUpper());

2. Open *buy.aspx* in your browser and test it in the same way as you have previously.

You'll see that the Address 1 text is displayed in UPPER CASE.

You can use *ToLower()* in the same way to make a string all lower case. *ToUpper* and *ToLower* are methods (see sidebar).

3. Close the web browser.

6 Use the *Replace* method to remove all of the spaces from a string.

You can use the *Replace* method to replace letters inside a string.

1. Add a new line after: *Address1 = "<br />" + Address1;*

2. Add the following code on the new line:

Address1 = Address1.Replace(" ","");

This code will remove all of the spaces from the *Address1* string. By changing the contents of the two sets of double quotation marks, you can replace any part of the string with any other string.

```
if (Page.IsValid) Response.Write("OK!");
string Address1 = TextBoxAddress1.Text;
Address1 = "<br />" + Address1;
Address1 = Address1.Replace(" ","");
Response.Write(Address1.ToUpper());
Response.Write("(" + Address1.Length + ")");
```

3. Open *buy.aspx* in your browser and test it again.

Make sure you enter some text with spaces into the *Address 1* text box. You'll see that the spaces are removed from the string when it is displayed on the page after submitting.

4. Close the web browser.

7 Remove all of the code from the *ButtonSubmitOrder_Click* event handler.

Lesson 5-4: Use integer variables

An integer variable contains a whole number (a number with no decimal places).

Strings and integers make up the majority of variables in most ASP.NET applications.

1   Open *ShiningStone* from your sample files folder.

2   Open the code-behind file of *buy.aspx*.

3   Create an integer variable.

    1.   Add the following code to the *Page_Load* event handler:

```
int TestInt = 10;
Response.Write(TestInt);
```

```
protected void Page_Load(obj
{
    int TestInt = 10;
    Response.Write(TestInt);
}
```

    This code creates a new *int* variable called *TestInt* with a value of 10 and writes it to the page.

    2.   View *buy.aspx* in your browser.

    You will see the number displayed when the page loads.

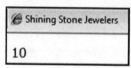

    3.   Close the web browser.

4   Add a value to the *TestInt* variable.

Because C# understands that the *int* variable is a number rather than a piece of text, you can perform mathematical operations with it such as adding, subtracting, multiplying and dividing.

    1.   Add the following line of code before the *Response.Write(TestInt);* line:

```
TestInt = TestInt + 5;
```

    This code will add 5 to the value of the *TestInt* variable.

```
protected void Page_Load(obj
{
    int TestInt = 10;
    TestInt = TestInt + 5;
    Response.Write(TestInt);
}
```

    2.   View *buy.aspx* in your browser.

    You will see that *15* is displayed on the page (the sum of 10 + 5).

---

note

short, *int* and *long*

Along with *int*, there are two other integer variable types: *short* and *long*.

Much like *string* and *String*, the *int* variable has another name in the .NET framework which means exactly the same thing: *Int32*.

An *Int32* is a 32-bit integer. This means that an int32 (or int) can hold a number from minus 2,147,483,647 to 2,147,483,647 and takes up 32 bits of memory.

short and *long* correspond to the "real" variables of *Int16* and *Int64*. An *Int16* variable can hold a number from minus 32,767 to 32,767 and an *Int64* can hold a number from minus 9,223,372,036,854,775,807 to 9,223,372,036,854,775,807!

If you found your integers were using too much memory, you would probably convert them to *short* if you knew that they would never exceed 32,767.

long is useful on the rare occasions where you need to work with numbers greater than 2,147,483,647.

General practice is to use *int* for all integer variables and only to change them to *short* or *long* if it becomes necessary.

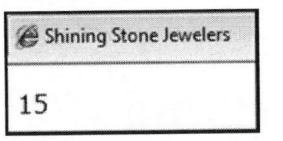

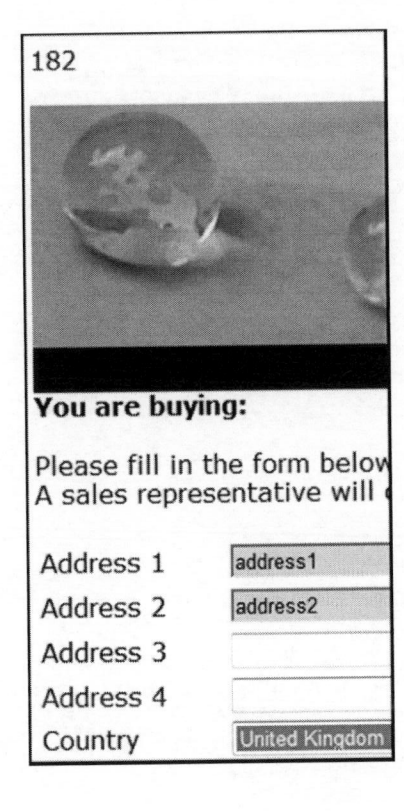

3. Close the web browser.

5 **Retrieve the SelectedIndex property from a drop-down list control to indicate the user's choice.**

Some properties of controls are integers, such as the *SelectedIndex* property of a *DropDownList* control.

1. Add the following line of code before the *Response.Write(TestInt);* line:

    TestInt = DropDownListCountry.SelectedIndex;

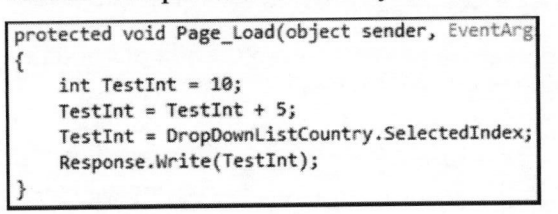

```
protected void Page_Load(object sender, EventArg
{
    int TestInt = 10;
    TestInt = TestInt + 5;
    TestInt = DropDownListCountry.SelectedIndex;
    Response.Write(TestInt);
}
```

2. View *buy.aspx* in your browser.

3. Complete the form.

    Make sure to choose a country from the drop-down list.

4. Click *Submit Order*.

    You'll see that the *index* value for the country you selected is displayed.

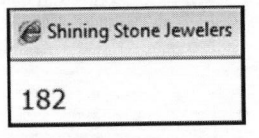

5. Change the country in the drop-down list.

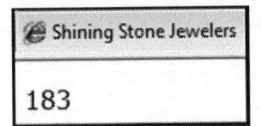

6. Click *Submit Order* again.

    You'll see that the index number changes.

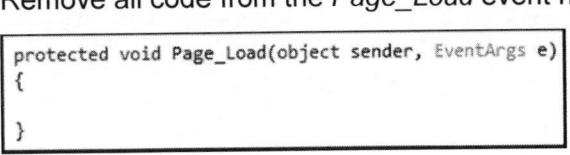

In a real-world web application you'd usually use the *SelectedValue* property instead of the *SelectedIndex* property to identify a user's drop-down choice. To keep things simple, we didn't use the *SelectedValue* property because it is a string rather than an integer.

6 **Remove all code from the *Page_Load* event handler.**

```
protected void Page_Load(object sender, EventArgs e)
{

}
```

Lesson 5-5: Use floating point variables

Integers are great for working with whole numbers, but there will often be times when you will want to work with numbers that have decimal places, such as when working with currency values.

In C#, numbers with decimal places are stored as *floating point* numbers. The mathematics behind them is beyond the scope of this book, but you'll learn how to create and work with them in this lesson.

1   Open *ShiningStone* from your sample files folder.

2   Open the code-behind file of *buy.aspx*.

3   Add a float variable.

   1.   Add the following code to the *Page_Load* event handler:

      float TestFloat = 3.14159f;
      Response.Write(TestFloat);

      This code creates a new *float* variable called *TestFloat* with a value of 3.14159 and writes it to the page.

      You need to end a *float* value with an *f* in order for it to be recognised as a *float* value.

      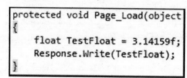

      ```
      protected void Page_Load(object
      {
          float TestFloat = 3.14159f;
          Response.Write(TestFloat);
      }
      ```

   2.   View *buy.aspx* in your browser.

      You will see that the number is displayed on the screen when the page loads.

      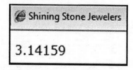

   3.   Close your web browser.

4   Understand the accuracy problem.

   Floating point values are only accurate within certain parameters (see sidebar).

   1.   Calculate **3.14159 * 3.14159** using a calculator or Microsoft Excel.

      You should find that the correct result is: *9.8695877281*

      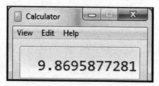

   2.   Change the second line of code you added in the previous step to the following:

Response.Write(TestFloat * 3.14159);

```
protected void Page_Load(object sender,
{
    float TestFloat = 3.14159f;
    Response.Write(TestFloat * 3.14159);
}
```

3. View *buy.aspx* in your browser.

   You will see that the result that is returned is:
   9.86958810009003. That's because a float is only accurate up to
   7 digits!

4. Close your browser.

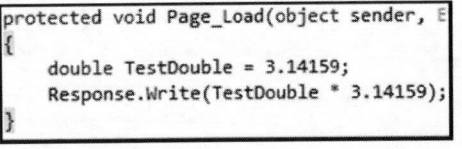

5 Fix the accuracy problem.

   The *double* type is accurate up to at least 15 digits, so it should be
   capable of calculating the result correctly.

   1. Change your code to:

      double TestDouble = 3.14159;
      Response.Write(TestDouble * 3.14159);

```
protected void Page_Load(object sender, E
{
    double TestDouble = 3.14159;
    Response.Write(TestDouble * 3.14159);
}
```

      Remember how you had to put an f after the float value? You
      don't need to put any symbol after *double* values.

   2. View *buy.aspx* in your browser.

      This time you will see the correct result of *9.8695877281*.

   3. Close your browser.

6 Change the code to use a *decimal* variable instead of a
   double variable.

   1. Change the code to:

      decimal TestDecimal = 3.14159m;
      Response.Write(TestDecimal * 3.14159m);

```
protected void Page_Load(object sender, Eve
{
    decimal TestDecimal = 3.14159m;
    Response.Write(TestDecimal * 3.14159m);
}
```

      You'll notice that you add an *m* to the end of the decimal
      number in much the same way as you added an *f* for the *float*.

   2. View *buy.aspx* in your browser.

      Again, the result will be correct: *9.8695877281*

7 Remove the code you added to the *Page_Load* event
   handler.

Lesson 5-6: Use Boolean variables

You've already seen a lot of Boolean values when working with control properties. Wherever you saw a property that could be set to either *true* or *false*, you were looking at a Boolean value.

Booleans are always either *true* or *false* and are perfect for anything that can be expressed as a yes or no answer. In this lesson you'll work with a Boolean variable.

1   Open *ShiningStone* from your sample files folder.

2   Open the code-behind file of *buy.aspx*.

3   Add a *bool* variable.

> ## note
>
> ### Empty *bool* variables
>
> If you don't tell C# what value a *bool* has when you create it, C# will give it the default value of *false*.
>
> Normally Booleans can never be *null*: they can only be *true* or *false*.
>
> There is a special technique that can be used to create a nullable Boolean. You'll learn how to do this in: *Lesson 5-12: Understand null*.

1.   Add the following code to the *Page_Load* event handler:

bool TestBool = true;
Response.Write(TestBool);

This code creates a new *bool* variable called *TestBool* and sets it to *true*.

```
protected void Page_Load(obje
{
    bool TestBool = true;
    Response.Write(TestBool);
}
```

2.   View *buy.aspx* in your browser.

You will see that *True* is displayed.

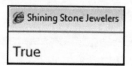

3.   Close the browser.

4   Change the value of the Boolean.

You can easily change the value of a Bool variable in the same way as you would change the value of any other variable.

1.   Add the following line of code after the *bool TestBool = true;* line:

TestBool = false;

Notice that there are no inverted commas around *true* and *false*. They are not strings, but built-in values that C# understands.

```
protected void Page_Load(obje
{
    bool TestBool = true;
    TestBool = false;
    Response.Write(TestBool);
}
```

2.   View *buy.aspx* in your browser.

You'll see that the value has been changed and *False* is displayed.

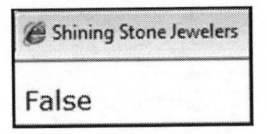

3. Close your web browser.

5 Set the bool variable to the opposite of its current value.

Booleans support logical operators, which you'll learn more about in: *Lesson 7-3: Use basic logical operators*. By using the exclamation mark (or NOT operator), you can change the bool variable to the opposite of its current value.

This is useful when there is something you want to toggle on or off.

1. Change the *TestBool = false;* line to:

    TestBool = !TestBool;

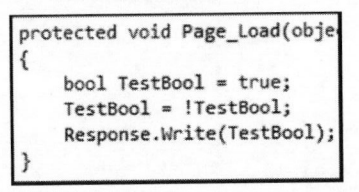

```
protected void Page_Load(obje
{
    bool TestBool = true;
    TestBool = !TestBool;
    Response.Write(TestBool);
}
```

2. View *buy.aspx* in your browser.

    You'll see *False* displayed again: the opposite of *True*.

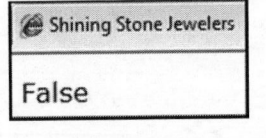

3. Close your web browser.

4. Change the *bool Testbool = true;* line to:

    bool TestBool = false;

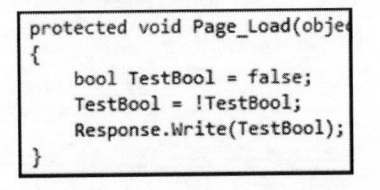

```
protected void Page_Load(obje
{
    bool TestBool = false;
    TestBool = !TestBool;
    Response.Write(TestBool);
}
```

5. View *buy.aspx* in your browser.

    This time *True* is displayed: the second line of code has changed *TestBool* to its opposite. *True* is the opposite of *False*.

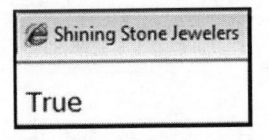

6. Close the web browser.

6 Remove all code from the *Page_Load* event handler.

note

Empty *DateTime* variables

If you create a *DateTime* variable without a value, its value will be *null*. You'll learn about *null* in: *Lesson 5-12: Understand null.*

Unlike the other variable types you've worked with so far, there isn't a simple way to manually assign a value to a *DateTime* variable.

You will almost always create a date based on the value of a *Calendar* control or using *DateTime.Now*.

If you wanted to create a new *DateTime* variable containing an arbitrary date and time you'd do so by specifying arguments when creating a new instance of the *DateTime* class.

You'll learn how to do this in: *Lesson 6-2: Create an instance of a class.*

note

Regional calendars

Different calendars are used by different countries. The *DateTime* object supports all of these, but it will default to the calendar that is used by the computer that the web application is running on.

It's important to bear in mind that the web server you eventually place your site on may be using a different calendar to the computer you are developing the application on.

ASP.NET calls the regional rules for formatting dates, numbers, etc the *culture.*

You can use the *globalization* tag in the *Web.config* file to make sure your site always runs using your chosen culture rather than using the culture of the server it is running on.

Lesson 5-7: Use DateTime variables

The *DateTime* variable is possibly the most specialized variable in C#. It is, as you would expect, used to store dates and times.

Date and time are often the most difficult things to work with in programming, since date and time systems are very complex. Fortunately, the *DateTime* variable does a lot of the work for you.

1   Open *ShiningStone* from your sample files folder.

2   Open the code-behind file of *buy.aspx.*

3   Add a *DateTime* variable.

1.   Add the following code to the *Page_Load* event handler:

DateTime TestDateTime = DateTime.Now;
Response.Write(TestDateTime);

```
protected void Page_Load(object sender, Ev
{
    DateTime TestDateTime = DateTime.Now;
    Response.Write(TestDateTime);
}
```

The *Now* property of *DateTime* always contains the current date and time.

When the page loads, this code will create a new *DateTime* variable containing the current date and time and output it to the page.

2.   View *buy.aspx* in your browser.

```
20/04/2011 11:48:48
```

The date above represents 20th April 2011 in UK format. If your date and time are formatted differently from the example above see the *Regional calendars* sidebar for an explanation.

3.   Close your browser.

4   Use the *AddDays* method to add three days to the *DateTime* variable.

The *DateTime* variable has several methods that allow you to easily manipulate the date and time stored inside it.

1.   Add the following line of code after the *DateTime TestDateTime = DateTime.Now;* line:

TestDateTime = TestDateTime.AddDays(3);

```
protected void Page_Load(object sender, EventArgs e)
{
    DateTime TestDateTime = DateTime.Now;
    TestDateTime = TestDateTime.AddDays(3);
    Response.Write(TestDateTime);
}
```

This code adds 3 days to value of the *TestDateTime* variable. This means that the result that is output to the page should be 3 days later than today.

2. View *buy.aspx* in your browser.

3. Close your browser.

> 23/04/2011 11:48:07

You can use the other *Add* methods of *DateTime* to add hours, months, years, etc. to a *DateTime* variable's value.

5 **Use the *Month* property to display the month from the value of the *DateTime* variable.**

Sometimes you'll just want to get a single component from a date, such as the month or year. The *DateTime* variable has properties that allow you to easily extract each component.

1. Change the *Response.Write(TestDateTime);* line to:

   Response.Write(TestDateTime.Month);

   ```
   DateTime TestDateTime = DateTime.Now;
   TestDateTime = TestDateTime.AddDays(3);
   Response.Write(TestDateTime.Month);
   ```

   You might notice in the IntelliSense menu that the *Month* property is an *int* value.

2. View *buy.aspx* in your browser.

   You'll see that just the month is displayed as an integer.

3. Close your browser.

All of the components of the date have their own property. For example, you could get the year of the date using the *TestDateTime.Year* property.

6 **Use the *ToShortDateString* method to display the date in a shorter format.**

The *DateTime* variable offers a few methods that will format the date in different ways.

1. Change the *Response.Write(TestDateTime.Month);* line to:

   Response.Write(TestDateTime.ToShortDateString());

   ```
   DateTime TestDateTime = DateTime.Now;
   TestDateTime = TestDateTime.AddDays(3);
   Response.Write(TestDateTime.ToShortDateString());
   ```

   This will display a shorter date string. Notice that there are other similar methods such as *ToShortTimeString* and *ToLongDateString*.

2. View *buy.aspx* in your browser.

   > 23/04/2011

You can customize the date string in a more sophisticated way using the *ToString* method. You'll learn how to do this in: *Lesson 5-9: Convert variables using cast and ToString.*

7 **Remove all code from the *Page_Load* event handler.**

Lesson 5-8: Convert variables using Convert and Parse

You now know how to create and work with the most common variable types in C#, but it's often necessary to convert variables from one type to another.

In this lesson you'll learn some of the ways you can convert variables.

1   Open *ShiningStone* from your sample files folder.

2   Open the code-behind file of *buy.aspx*.

3   Create a *string* variable.

Add the following to the *ButtonSubmitOrder_Click* event handler:

string PhoneNumberText = TextBoxPhoneNumber.Text;

```
protected void ButtonSubmitOrder_Click(object sender,
{
    string PhoneNumberText = TextBoxPhoneNumber.Text;
}
```

As you've seen before, this will create a *string* variable called *PhoneNumberText* that contains the text entered into the *TextBoxPhoneNumber* control.

4   Convert the contents of the *string* variable to *int* data using *Convert*.

In *Lesson 4-9: Use other validation controls,* you added a *RangeValidator* control with a *Type* property of *Integer*. This means that the user can only enter integer values into the *TextBoxPhoneNumber* control.

Because you know the *TextBoxPhoneNumber* control's *Text* property will contain an integer, it will always be possible to convert the *string* variable from its *Text* property into an *int* variable.

Add the following code on the next line:

int PhoneNumber = Convert.ToInt32(PhoneNumberText);

```
protected void ButtonSubmitOrder_Click(object sender, EventArgs e)
{
    string PhoneNumberText = TextBoxPhoneNumber.Text;
    int PhoneNumber = Convert.ToInt32(PhoneNumberText);
}
```

This converts the contents of the *PhoneNumberText* string variable into integer data which is stored in a new variable called *PhoneNumber*.

You could then perform mathematical operations on the *int* variable; something you couldn't do with a *string* variable.

You'll notice that there are lots of *Convert.To* options in the IntelliSense menu, including all of the types you've worked with in this session.

5   Convert the contents of the *int* variable to *float* data using *Convert.*

Add the following code on the next line:

float PhoneNumberFloat = Convert.ToSingle(PhoneNumber);

```
protected void ButtonSubmitOrder_Click(object sender, EventArgs e)
{
    string PhoneNumberText = TextBoxPhoneNumber.Text;
    int PhoneNumber = Convert.ToInt32(PhoneNumberText);
    float PhoneNumberFloat = Convert.ToSingle(PhoneNumber);
}
```

Note that the method for converting to *float* is *ToSingle* rather than *ToFloat.* This is because the 'real' name of the *float* type is *Single* (see: *Lesson 5-5: Use floating point variables - sidebar*).

You could use the new *float* variable to carry out mathematical operations with decimal places, something you couldn't do with *string* or *int* variables.

6   Convert the contents of the *string* variable to *int* data using the alternative *Parse* method.

Replace the *int PhoneNumber…* line with:

int PhoneNumber = int.Parse(PhoneNumberText);

```
protected void ButtonSubmitOrder_Click(object sender, EventArgs e)
{
    string PhoneNumberText = TextBoxPhoneNumber.Text;
    int PhoneNumber = int.Parse(PhoneNumberText);
    float PhoneNumberFloat = Convert.ToSingle(PhoneNumber);
}
```

The *Parse* method is an alternative to the *Convert* method, although it only converts from *string* to other types. There is a parse method available for all of the types you have worked with in this session.

7   Convert the contents of the *string* variable to *float* data using *Parse.*

Replace the *float PhoneNumberFloat…* line with:

float PhoneNumberFloat = float.Parse(PhoneNumberText);

```
protected void ButtonSubmitOrder_Click(object sender, Even
{
    string PhoneNumberText = TextBoxPhoneNumber.Text;
    int PhoneNumber = int.Parse(PhoneNumberText);
    float PhoneNumberFloat = float.Parse(PhoneNumberText);
}
```

Here you're using the *Parse* method to convert the *PhoneNumberText* string data into *float* data.

8   Close Visual Studio.

note

The TryParse method

If the *Parse* or *Convert* methods are not able to convert a variable, an exception is generated. Exceptions were covered in: *Lesson 3-5: Understand the Exception object.*

The *TryParse* method doesn't cause an exception if conversion is impossible.

TryParse is covered in the Expert Skills book in this series.

Lesson 5-9: Convert variables using cast and ToString

In this lesson, you'll use the *ToString* conversion method to convert any variable into a *string* and use the *cast* method to force C# to recognize a variable as a certain type.

1 Open *ShiningStone* from your sample files folder.

2 Open the code-behind file of *buy.aspx*.

3 Convert the contents of an *int* variable into *string* data using the*ToString* method.

You've seen the *ToString* method used a few times already in this book. Almost every type of variable has a *ToString* method that allows you to change its data into string data.

Add the following line to the end of the *ButtonSubmitOrder_Click* event handler:

string PhoneNumberText2 = PhoneNumber.ToString();

```
protected void ButtonSubmitOrder_Click(object sender, Event
{
    string PhoneNumberText = TextBoxPhoneNumber.Text;
    int PhoneNumber = int.Parse(PhoneNumberText);
    float PhoneNumberFloat = float.Parse(PhoneNumberText);
    string PhoneNumberText2 = PhoneNumber.ToString();
}
```

This converts the integer data in the *PhoneNumber* variable to string data and stores it in the new *PhoneNumberText2* string variable.

4 Format a date using *ToString*.

The *ToString* method behaves differently for different variable types. For some variable types, you can change how the resulting string is formatted by providing a *format string* as an argument.

Arguments are the values you enter in the brackets when you call a method. You'll learn more about arguments in: *Lesson 6-6: Create methods with arguments*.

1. Add the following code to the *Page_Load* event handler:

DateTime TodaysDate = DateTime.Now;
string FormattedDate = TodaysDate
.ToString("dd MMM yyyy");
Response.Write(FormattedDate);

```
protected void Page_Load(object sender, EventArgs e)
{
    DateTime TodaysDate = DateTime.Now;
    string FormattedDate = TodaysDate.ToString("dd MMM yyyy");
    Response.Write(FormattedDate);
}
```

This code creates a *DateTime* variable called *TodaysDate* containing today's date. The date is then converted into a string using the *ToString* method with an argument of *dd MMM yyyy* (this is a *format String* - see sidebar).

note

Format strings

In this lesson, you can see a basic format string to show a common representation of a date.

There are many different symbols you can use in date format strings, but these are some of the most common:

d : Day
M : Month
y : Year
h : Hour
m : Minute
s : Second

You can learn more about date format strings from Microsoft's help files.

The *format string* tells the *ToString* method to display a 2-digit day, a 3-letter month and a 4-digit year.

2. View *buy.aspx* in your browser.

   You'll see that the date is formatted correctly.

3. Close your browser.

Shining Stone Jewelers

07 Apr 2011

5 Use *cast* to eliminate ambiguity.

The last way of converting variables is called *casting*. Casting is usually used when the type of the variable is ambiguous. For example, when faced with a value such as 123.45 C# cannot determine whether the number represents a float, double or decimal value.

1. Remove all code from the *Page_Load* event handler.

2. Add the following code to the *Page_Load* event handler:

   decimal DecimalNumber = 100.75;

   ```
   protected void Page_Load(object sender, EventArgs e)
   {
       decimal DecimalNumber = 100.75;
   }
   ```

   The number *100.75* will be underlined in red, and if you move your cursor over it you'll see that it is not being recognized as a decimal value. In *Lesson 5-5: Use floating point variables*, you discovered one solution for this problem when you postfixed the number with the letter *m*.

   Using a *cast*, however, you can make sure that the value is recognized as a decimal even without the *m*.

3. Change the code to the following:

   decimal DecimalNumber = (decimal)100.75;

   ```
   protected void Page_Load(object sender, EventArgs e)
   {
       decimal DecimalNumber = (decimal)100.75;
   }
   ```

   Putting the type in brackets before the number *casts* it to that type. Note that you could have done the same thing with the *Convert.ToDecimal* method.

4. Add the following code on the next line:

   float FloatNumber = (float)DecimalNumber;

   ```
   protected void Page_Load(object sender, EventArgs e)
   {
       decimal DecimalNumber = (decimal)100.75;
       float FloatNumber = (float)DecimalNumber;
   }
   ```

   Here you have used *cast* to convert the *decimal* value into a *float* value.

   There aren't *Convert* and *Parse* methods for all variable types, but *cast* works for every type.

6 Remove all code from both event handlers.

Lesson 5-10: Perform basic mathematical operations

You did some basic mathematics when working with integers and floating point numbers, but in this lesson you'll learn about all of the basic mathematical operations available to you.

1   Open *My Project* from your sample files folder.

2   Add a new web form to the project called: **calculator.aspx**

You learned how to do this in: *Lesson 1-7: Manage a project with the Solution Explorer.*

3   Add two new *TextBox* controls to the page.

Call the text boxes **TextBoxFirstNumber** and **TextBoxSecondNumber**.

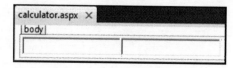

4   Add a *Label* control to the page.

1. Add a *Label* control to the page, below the two text boxes.

2. Name the *Label* control: **LabelResult**

3. Clear the *Text* property of the *LabelResult* control.

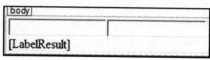

5   Add a button that will add the contents of the two text boxes.

1. Add a *Button* control to the page.

2. Set the *ID* property of the *Button* control to: **ButtonCalculate**

3. Set the *Text* property of the *ButtonCalculate* control to: **Calculate**

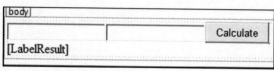

4. Add a *Click* event handler to the *ButtonCalculate* control.

Add the following code to the *ButtonCalculate_Click* event handler:

```
double FirstNumber =
Convert.ToDouble(TextBoxFirstNumber.Text);
double SecondNumber =
Convert.ToDouble(TextBoxSecondNumber.Text);
double Result = FirstNumber + SecondNumber;
LabelResult.Text = Result.ToString();
```

```
protected void ButtonCalculate_Click(object sender, EventArgs e)
{
    double FirstNumber = Convert.ToDouble(TextBoxFirstNumber.Text);
    double SecondNumber = Convert.ToDouble(TextBoxSecondNumber.Text);
    double Result = FirstNumber + SecondNumber;
    LabelResult.Text = Result.ToString();
}
```

This code hopefully makes sense to you by now.

The text from each text box is placed into a *double* variable, then the two doubles are added together and placed into another *double* variable called *Result*. Finally, *Result* is converted into a string and displayed in the *LabelResult* control.

5. View *calculator.aspx* in your browser.

6. Enter some numbers into the text boxes and press the button.

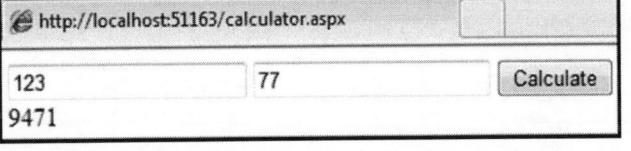

The result of adding the two numbers together appears in the *Label* control.

7. Close your browser.

6 Change the calculation to multiply the two numbers.

This should be very straightforward to you by now.

1. Change the line:

double Result = FirstNumber + SecondNumber;

to:

double Result = FirstNumber * SecondNumber;

```
protected void ButtonCalculate_Click(object sender, EventArgs e)
{
    double FirstNumber = Convert.ToDouble(TextBoxFirstNumber.Text);
    double SecondNumber = Convert.ToDouble(TextBoxSecondNumber.Text);
    double Result = FirstNumber * SecondNumber;
    LabelResult.Text = Result.ToString();
}
```

2. View *calculator.aspx* in your browser.

3. Enter some numbers into the text boxes and press the button.

> http://localhost:51163/calculator.aspx
>
> | 123 | 77 | Calculate |
> 9471

You'll see that this time the numbers are multiplied.

In the same way, you can subtract using the minus operator - and divide using the forward slash operator: /.

7 Close Visual Studio.

---

note

Brackets (or Parentheses)

You can use brackets to eliminate ambiguity in mathematical operations, for example:

*int X = (1 + 2) * 2;*

...would make X equal 6.

*int X = 1 + (2 * 2);*

...would make X equal 5.

note

Modulo

Modulo is rarely seen outside of programming.

You can perform a modulo operation using the % symbol in the same way as you'd use the other mathematical operators (such as + and -).

Modulo divides two numbers and returns the remainder after dividing. For example 112 % 100 would return 12.

note

Shortcuts

There are a few shortcuts to perform the most basic mathematical operations.

Assume you have created an *int* variable called *Number*.

Number++;
Adds 1 to *Number*.

Number--;
Subtracts 1 from *Number*.

Number += 123;
Adds 123 to *Number*.

Number -= 123;
Subtracts 123 from *Number*.

Number *= 123;
Multiplies *Number* by 123.

Number /= 123;
Divides *Number* by 123.

Lesson 5-11: Use the Math library for advanced mathematics

As well as basic addition, subtraction, multiplication and division, C# offers a host of advanced mathematical functions inside the *Math* library.

In this lesson, you'll discover some of the most useful methods in the *Math* library.

1 Open *My Project* from your sample files folder.

2 Open the code-behind file of *calculator.aspx*.

3 Use the *Math* functions to raise one number to the power of the other.

1. Change the line:

    *double Result = FirstNumber * SecondNumber;*

    to:

    double Result = Math.Pow(FirstNumber, SecondNumber);

    ```
    double FirstNumber = Convert.ToDouble(TextBoxFirstNumber.Text);
    double SecondNumber = Convert.ToDouble(TextBoxSecondNumber.Text);
    double Result = Math.Pow(FirstNumber, SecondNumber);
    LabelResult.Text = Result.ToString();
    ```

    This is the first method you've used that needs more than one argument. The first argument is the number to be raised (*FirstNumber*) and the second is the number to raise to (*SecondNumber*). You'll learn about this in greater depth in: *Lesson 6-6: Create methods with arguments.*

    After you type *Math.*, you'll see a list of all of the functions you can use with *Math.*

2. View *calculator.aspx* in your browser.

3. Enter some numbers into the text boxes and press the button.

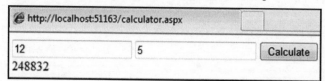

In this example the first number is raised to the power of the second (12^5).

You could also have done this more easily using the ^ operator. You used the *Pow* method as an introduction to the *Math* library.

4 Use the *Round* method of the the *Math* library to round a result to 2 decimal places.

1. Close your browser and return to the code-behind file of *calculator.aspx.*

2. Replace the *double Result...* line with:

double Result =
Math.Round(FirstNumber + SecondNumber, 2);

```
double FirstNumber = Convert.ToDouble(TextBoxFirstNumber.Text);
double SecondNumber = Convert.ToDouble(TextBoxSecondNumber.Text);
double Result = Math.Round(FirstNumber + SecondNumber, 2);
LabelResult.Text = Result.ToString();
```

This code adds *FirstNumber* and *SecondNumber* together, but the *Math.Round* method will round the result to 2 decimal places.

The *Round* method has two arguments: the number to round and the required number of decimal places. By changing the second argument (which is currently 2), you can change the number of decimal places returned.

You'll learn more about arguments in: *Lesson 6-6: Create methods with arguments.*

3. View *calculator.aspx* in your browser.

4. Enter some numbers with decimal places and click the button.

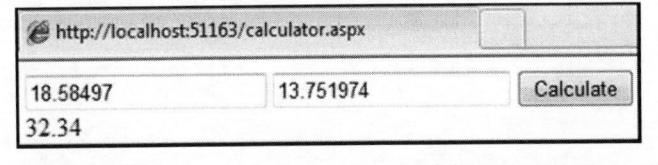

The numbers are added together and the result is rounded to 2 decimal places.

5   Use the *Math* functions to get the larger of two numbers.

1. Close your browser and return to the code-behind file of *calculator.aspx.*

2. Replace the *double Result…* line with:

double Result = Math.Max(FirstNumber, SecondNumber);

```
double FirstNumber = Convert.ToDouble(TextBoxFirstNumber.Text);
double SecondNumber = Convert.ToDouble(TextBoxSecondNumber.Text);
double Result = Math.Max(FirstNumber, SecondNumber);
LabelResult.Text = Result.ToString();
```

This code will return the larger of the two numbers entered into the text boxes.

3. View *calculator.aspx* in your browser.

4. Enter some numbers and click the button.

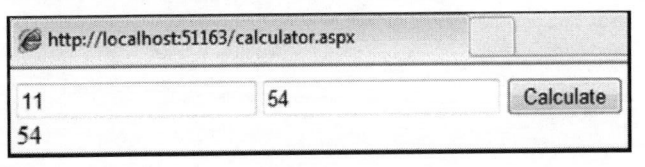

The largest number is displayed.

You can also use *Math.Min* to get the smaller of two numbers.

Lesson 5-12: Understand null

null is C#'s concept of 'nothing'. If you create a variable without giving it a value, it will often have a value of *null*.

1 Open *My Project* from your sample files folder.

2 Open the code-behind file of *calculator.aspx*.

3 Add a null string.

1. Add the following code to the *Page_Load* event handler:

   string NullString;
   string EmptyString = "";

2. Set a breakpoint at the end of the *Page_Load* event handler.

   You learned how to do this in: *Lesson 3-3: Use Breakpoints*.

   ```
   protected void Page_Load(obje
   {
       string NullString;
       string EmptyString = "";
   }
   ```

3. Right-click *calculator.aspx* in the *Solution Explorer* and select *Set As Start Page* from the shortcut menu.

4. Run *calculator.aspx* in *Debug* mode.

   You learned how to do this in: *Lesson 1-8: Run a project in debug mode*.

   ```
   protected void Page_Load(obj
   {
       string NullString;
       string EmptyString = "";
   }
   ```

   When the page loads, it will be pause at the breakpoint and you will be returned to the code editor.

5. Check the values of the *NullString* and *EmptyString* variables.

   Hover your mouse cursor over the names *NullString* and *EmptyString* in the code editor to see their values.

   You will see that *NullString* has a value of *null*, while *EmptyString* has an empty *string* instead of *null*.

The distinction between *null* and an empty string is an important one. You can perform all string methods on an empty string, but many methods would cause an exception if you tried to use them with a *null* string.

If you tried to set the *Text* property of a label control to *null*, for example, it would cause an exception.

4 Add a null int.

1. Stop debugging by clicking the stop button.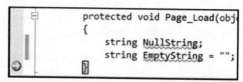

2. Add the following line of code to the end of the *Page_Load* event handler:

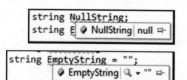

int NullInt;

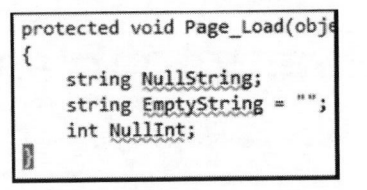

3. Run the page in Debug mode.

4. When the code pauses, check the value of *NullInt*.

You'll see that rather than being null, the value is 0. This is because int isn't nullable by default. A normal int can never have a null value (and most of the time that's exactly what you want).

If you were to try to set *NullInt* to null using *NullInt = null;* you would see an error.

5. Stop debugging by clicking the stop button.

5   Make the *int* nullable.

There are times when you want an *int*, or other non-nullable variable to contain a null value, especially when working with databases as you'll discover in: *Lesson 12-6: Create a Search page.*

Fortunately, it's very easy to make a variable nullable.

1. Change the *int NullInt;* line to the following:

int? NullInt;

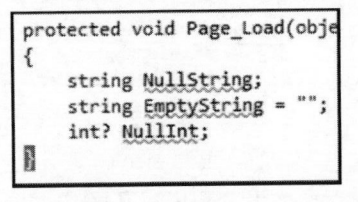

Putting the question mark after *int* makes it nullable! You can do this with other non-nullable types, for example *double?* and *DateTime?* would create nullable versions of those types.

You can't create a *string?* because *string* is already nullable.

2. Run the page in *Debug* mode.

3. Check the value of *NullInt*.

This time you'll see that *NullInt* has a *null* value.

4. Stop debugging by clicking the stop button.

6   Remove the code you added to the *Page_Load* event handler.

7   Remove the breakpoint.

Lesson 5-13: Use object and var variables

An object is a self-contained piece of code that has its own set of properties, methods and events.

The .NET library that C# uses is actually a library of objects. Just about everything in C# is an object. Controls, web pages and even variables are all objects. In this lesson you'll learn about the *object* and *var* variable types.

1   Open *My Project* from your sample files folder.

2   Open the code-behind file of *calculator.aspx*.

3   Modify your code to use the *object* variable type.

You used the *double* variable type for your calculations on this page, which is the correct approach, but since a *double* variable is an object you can also use an *object* variable.

An object variable can store any type of data. You typically use them when you need to store data but do not know its type in advance.

Change the first line of code in *ButtonCalculate_Click* to the following:

**object FirstNumber =
Convert.ToDouble(TextBoxFirstNumber.Text);**

```
protected void ButtonCalculate_Click(object sender, EventArgs e)
{
    object FirstNumber = Convert.ToDouble(TextBoxFirstNumber.Text);
    double SecondNumber = Convert.ToDouble(TextBoxSecondNumber.Text);
    double Result = Math.Max(FirstNumber, SecondNumber);
    LabelResult.Text = Result.ToString();
}
```

You'll notice that the line that performs the calculation is indicating an error using a red underline. This is because the *Math.Max* method expects numeric arguments and doesn't know what to do with an *object* variable.

> **note**
>
> **GetType**
>
> You can use the *GetType* method of an *object* variable to return its current type.

4   Cast the *object* variable's value to a *double*.

You can still make this code work by casting the *object* variable to a *double* variable type for the purposes of this calculation.

Change the *double Result…* line to:

**double Result = Math.Max((double)FirstNumber,
SecondNumber);**

```
object FirstNumber = Convert.ToDouble(TextBoxFirstNumber.Text);
double SecondNumber = Convert.ToDouble(TextBoxSecondNumber.Text);
double Result = Math.Max((double)FirstNumber, SecondNumber);
LabelResult.Text = Result.ToString();
```

The error disappears. You could also have solved the problem by converting the value of the *object* to a *double* with the *Convert.ToDouble* method.

5   Put today's date into the *object*.

Because an *object* doesn't have a fixed type, it is capable of storing any type of data.

1. Add the following line of code after the *object FirstNumber…* line:

FirstNumber = DateTime.Now;

```
object FirstNumber = Convert.ToDouble(TextBoxFirstNumber.Text);
FirstNumber = DateTime.Now;
```

This changes the value of the *FirstNumber* variable to today's date.

You can now see why C# needs to be explicity told the type of data that is stored in an *object*. It could literally be anything!

2. Remove the line that sets the *FirstNumber* variable to today's date.

Obviously trying to convert a *DateTime* to a *double* would cause an exception if you tried to run this code.

6   Use a *var* variable type.

Just like the object variable type, the *var* variable type can be used to store data of any type. But there's an important twist.

The *var* data type establishes its type when it is created. From that point forward the type cannot be changed and the variable can be used in exactly the same way as the type it has assumed.

1. Change the first line of code in *ButtonCalculate_Click* to the following:

var FirstNumber = Convert.ToDouble(TextBoxFirstNumber.Text);

2. Remove the cast from the *double Result…* line:

double Result = Math.Max(FirstNumber, SecondNumber);

```
var FirstNumber = Convert.ToDouble(TextBoxFirstNumber.Text);
double SecondNumber = Convert.ToDouble(TextBoxSecondNumber.Text);
double Result = Math.Max(FirstNumber, SecondNumber);
LabelResult.Text = Result.ToString();
```

3. View *calculator.aspx* in your browser and test the form.

The calculation works without any problems. Even without casting the *var* to a *double*, C# knows that the *FirstNumber* variable's type is *double*. This is simply because you put a *double* value into the variable when you created it, causing it to assume the double variable type.

4. Close your web browser.

7   Change the code back to use *double*.

Although the calculation will still work perfectly using *object* and *var* variables, it is best to use exactly the types you want whenever possible. Change the first line from a *var* back to a *double*:

Session 5: Exercise

1   Open the *My Project* sample project and open *calculator.aspx* in design view.

2   Add a new *Button* control to the page called: **ButtonCalculate2**

3   Add a *Click* event handler to the *ButtonCalculate2* control.

4   Create a *string* variable called **PIString** in the *ButtonCalculate2_Click* event handler with a value of: **"3.14159265"**

5   Create a *double* variable called **PIDouble** in the same event handler and set its value to the value of the *PIString* variable by using the *Convert* method.

6   Create an *int* variable in the same event handler called **CircleRadius** with a value of: **19**

7   Create a *double* variable in the same event handler called **CircleCircumference** with a value of: **PIDouble * CircleRadius**

8   Use the *Pow* function from the *Math* library to raise the *CircleCircumference* variable to the power of 2.

9   Convert the *CircleCircumference* variable to a *string* using the *ToString* method. Call the *string*: **OutputCircumference**

10   Create a *DateTime* variable called **TodaysDate** containing today's date.

My Project - start

My Project - end

If you need help slide the page to the left

Session 5: Exercise Answers

These are the four questions that students find the most difficult to answer:

Q 9	Q 8	Q 5	Q 4
Use the following line of code: **string OutputCircumference = CircleCircumference .ToString();** This was covered in: *Lesson 5-8: Convert variables using Convert and Parse.*	Use the following line of code: **CircleCircumference = Math.Pow (CircleCircumference, 2);** This was covered in: *Lesson 5-11: Use the Math library for advanced mathematics.*	Use the following line of code: **double PIDouble = Convert.ToDouble(PIString);** This was covered in: *Lesson 5-8: Convert variables using Convert and Parse.*	Use the following line of code: **string PIString = "3.14159265";** This was covered in: *Lesson 5-3: Use string variable properties and methods.*

If you have difficulty with the other questions, here are the lessons that cover the relevant skills:

1   Refer to: Lesson 1-7: Manage a project with the Solution Explorer.

2   Refer to: Lesson 1-14: Add controls to a page with the Toolbox.

3   Refer to: Lesson 3-2: Add event handlers to Controls.

6   Refer to: Lesson 5-4: Use integer variables.

7   Refer to: Lesson 5-10: Perform basic mathematical operations.

10   Refer to: Lesson 5-7: Use DateTime variables.

6

Session Six: C# Classes, Namespaces and Methods

> Though this be madness, yet there is method in it.
>
> *William Shakespeare, English poet and playwright (1564 – 1616)*

Classes can be thought of as containers that C# code is separated into.

All C# code must be contained within a class. For example, the code-behind files that are automatically created with your pages are classes.

.NET programming may seem complicated with its hierarchical system of classes and extensive library of functions, but it's really not all that difficult.

In this session you'll learn the essentials of how to use C# classes, and even to create some classes of your own.

Session Objectives

By the end of this session you will be able to:

- Create a class
- Create an instance of a class
- Use the .NET library
- Work with namespaces
- Create and use methods
- Create methods with arguments
- Create methods that return a value
- Create a private method
- Createa a static method
- Create and dispose of instances
- Create class constructors

Lesson 6-1: Create a class

C# code is organized into classes, which can have properties, methods and events.

Classes can be thought of as templates from which any number of instances of the class (also called objects) may be created.

In previous lessons you created many variables. You were actually creating many instances of the relevant variable's class.

For example, the *DateTime* class defines all of the properties, methods and events of a *DateTime* variable.

In this lesson you'll create a brand new class of your own.

note

Everything in an ASP.NET application is a class

You might remember that C#'s code-behind files end in *.cs*, the same file extension as *MyClass.cs*. That's because they are classes too!

An ASP.NET application consists of many classes co-operating with each other to produce the web site you see in your browser.

note

Protection levels

In this lesson you created both your property and your method using the prefix *public*.

public means that the property or method is available within any instance created from the class. For example the *Text* property of a *Label* control is a public property of the *Label* class.

If you'd created a property with the prefix *private*, it would only be available to code inside the class. In other words it would be hidden in any instance created from the class.

public and *private* are called *protection levels*.

You'll learn more about protection levels in: *Lesson 6-8: Create a private method*.

1   Open *My Project* from your sample files folder.

2   Create a new class.

   1. Right-click *My Project* in the *Solution* Explorer and then click Add→New Item... from the shortcut menu.

   2. Click *Web* under the *Installed Templates* list on the left-hand side.

   3. Click *Class* from the central list of item types.

   4. Name the class: **MyClass.cs**

   5. Click *Add*.

   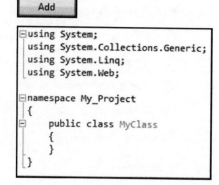

```
using System;
using System.Collections.Generic;
using System.Linq;
using System.Web;

namespace My_Project
{
    public class MyClass
    {
    }
}
```

   Your new class will appear in the *Solution Explorer* and its code will be automatically displayed.

3   Add a property to your class.

   Add the following line of code to your class:

   public int IntProperty;

```
public class MyClass
{
    public int IntProperty;
}
```

If you are not completing the course incrementally use the sample file: **Lesson 6-1** to begin this lesson.

Sample files with the starting point for each lesson are also provided for all of the other lessons in this session.

This will create a new property called *IntProperty* in your class, using the *int* data type.

You will be able to access this new property using: *MyClass.IntProperty*

4   Add a method to your class.

1.   Add the following code to your class:

public void AddToProperty()
{
}

```
public class MyClass
{
    public int IntProperty;
    public void AddToProperty()
    {
    }
}
```

This will create a new method called *AddToProperty*.

You will be able to call the new method using: *MyClass.AddToProperty()*

2.   Add the following code inside the *AddToProperty* method:

IntProperty = IntProperty + 1;

```
public void AddToProperty()
{
    IntProperty = IntProperty + 1;
}
```

This method will add 1 to the value of the *IntProperty* property when it is called.

You can see how you can use classes to create your own objects when none of the built in classes provide the functionality you need.

5   Close Visual Studio.

Lesson 6-2: Create an instance of a class

Before you can use your class you must create an instance of it. You can do this in almost exactly the same way as you would with a variable.

In this lesson, you'll create and use an instance of the class you created in: *Lesson 6-1: Create a class.*

1   Open *My Project* from your sample files folder.

2   Open the code-behind file of *calculator.aspx.*

3   Create an instance of your class.

Add the following code to the *Page_Load* event handler:

MyClass MyClassInstance = new MyClass();

```
protected void Page_Load(object sender, EventArgs e)
{
    MyClass MyClassInstance = new MyClass();
}
```

This creates a new instance of *MyClass* called *MyClassInstance.*

As you can see, creating instances of classes is very similar to creating variables.

4   Use the instance.

You can use an instance of your class in exactly the same way as you'd use a variable.

1. Add the following line of code to the end of the *Page_Load* event handler:

MyClassInstance.IntProperty = 10;

```
protected void Page_Load(object sender, EventArgs e)
{
    MyClass MyClassInstance = new MyClass();
    MyClassInstance.IntProperty = 10;
}
```

This will set the *IntProperty* property of the *MyClassInstance* object to *10.*

2. Add the following line of code on the next line:

MyClassInstance.AddToProperty();

```
protected void Page_Load(object sender, EventArgs e)
{
    MyClass MyClassInstance = new MyClass();
    MyClassInstance.IntProperty = 10;
    MyClassInstance.AddToProperty();
}
```

In *Lesson 6-1: Create a class*, you created the *AddToProperty* method which adds 1 to the *IntProperty* property.

3. Add the following line of code on the next line:

Response.Write(MyClassInstance.IntProperty);

```
protected void Page_Load(object sender, EventArgs e)
{
    MyClass MyClassInstance = new MyClass();
    MyClassInstance.IntProperty = 10;
    MyClassInstance.AddToProperty();
    Response.Write(MyClassInstance.IntProperty);
}
```

This will output the value of the *IntProperty* property of the *MyClassInstance* object onto the page so that you can check whether the method worked.

Since you set the *IntProperty* property to *10* and then called the *AddToProperty* method once, you are expecting a result of *11*.

4. View *calculator.aspx* in your browser.

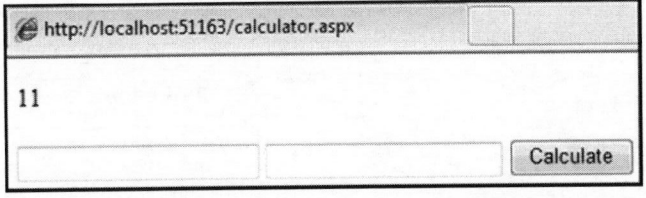

The number *11* appears at the top of the screen as expected.

5. Close your browser.

5 Remove the code you added to the *Page_Load* event handler.

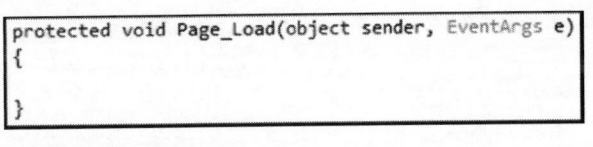

6 Close Visual Studio.

Lesson 6-3: Use the .NET library

You have already used several components of the .NET framework, but you have only seen a tiny fraction of what is available.

In this lesson you'll use the *using* keyword in your class to enable quick access to an even larger selection of objects from the .NET framework.

1   Open *My Project* from your sample files folder.

2   Open *MyClass.cs*.

3   Examine the *using* lines.

At the top of the class, you'll see the *using* lines that were added automatically:

```
using System;
using System.Collections.Generic;
using System.Linq;
using System.Web;
```

These lines are all references to different parts (or *namespaces*) of the .NET framework (see sidebar).

You'll learn more about namespaces in: *Lesson 6-4: Work with namespaces*.

4   Add a new method to the *MyClass* class called *TestMethod*.

As you did with the *AddToProperty* method, add the following code to add another method to the class:

public void TestMethod()
{
}

```
public void AddToProperty()
{
    IntProperty = IntProperty + 1;
}
public void TestMethod()
{
}
```

5   Create a *StringBuilder* object from the .NET library.

The *StringBuilder* object is a more advanced version of the *string* variable that is designed to work better with very large strings. It's in the *System.Text* namespace, so it isn't easily available by default.

Add the following code to the *TestMethod* method:

System.Text.StringBuilder TestStringBuilder =
new System.Text.StringBuilder();

```
public void TestMethod()
{
    System.Text.StringBuilder TestStringBuilder =
        new System.Text.StringBuilder();
}
```

This creates a new instance of the *StringBuilder* class called *TestStringBuilder*.

Notice that you have to type *System.Text.* in order to access the *System.Text* namespace.

6 Add a reference to *System.Text*.

Although it's easy enough to type *System.Text* when you need something from the *System.Text* namespace, this may make your code harder to read and more cumbersome to edit.

Fortunately a short-cut to any namespace may be created by adding a new *using* line.

1. Add the following line of code to the *using* lines at the top of the page:

   using System.Text;

   ```
   using System.Linq;
   using System.Web;
   using System.Text;
   ```

   This will create a short-cut so that objects in the *System.Text* namespace can be accessed directly.

2. Change the *System.Text.StringBuilder...* line to:

   StringBuilder TestStringBuilder = new StringBuilder();

   ```
   public void TestMethod()
   {
       StringBuilder TestStringBuilder = new StringBuilder();
   }
   ```

   This is a lot easier to read.

   Note that if the *using* line had not been added, this code would have caused a build error.

7 Close Visual Studio.

© 2011 The Smart Method Ltd

187

---

note

Namespace confusion

Using a reference to a namespace makes your code a little less readable.

System.Text.StringBuilder

... makes it clear that the *StringBuilder* class is defined in the *System.Text* namespace.

StringBuilder

... does not make it clear which namespace *StringBuilder* originated from.

Fortunately, you can easily see which namespace an object originates from by hovering your mouse cursor over it.

If you try this with *StringBuilder* you'll see which namespace it originated from and a short description of what the class does.

```
StringBuilder TestStringBu
class System.Text.StringBuilder
Represents a mutable string of ch
```

Lesson 6-4: Work with namespaces

You worked with some of the namespaces of the .NET framework in *Lesson 6-3: Use the .NET library*, but your project has namespaces of its own too.

For most projects you won't need to change the namespaces that are automatically generated, but it's useful to understand what they do and how to modify them if you need to.

1   Open *My Project* from your sample files folder.

2   Open *MyClass.cs*.

3   Change the namespace of the *MyClass* class.

    1.   Look for the following line of code:

```
namespace My_Project
```

    This line tells C# that everything inside its curly brackets { } is part of the *My_Project* namespace.

    Whenever you create a project, a default namespace is created with the same name as the project. Because this project is called *My Project*, everything is placed in the automatically-generated *My_Project* namespace by default.

    2.   Change the *namespace* line to:

    namespace CustomClasses

```
namespace CustomClasses
{
    public class MyClass
```

    3.   Open the code-behind file of *calculator.aspx*.

    4.   Try adding the following code to the *Page_Load* event handler:

    MyClass MyClassInstance = new MyClass();

```
protected void Page_Load(object sender, Event
{
    MyClass MyClassInstance = new MyClass();
}
```

    You'll immediately see errors appear, and will notice that *MyClass* is not displayed in the IntelliSense menu.

    This same line of code worked fine in *Lesson 6-2: Create an instance of a class*. That was because *calculator.aspx.cs* shared the same namespace as the *MyClass* class (*My_Project*).

    5.   Change the *MyClass…* line of code to:

    CustomClasses.MyClass MyClassInstance = new CustomClasses.MyClass();

```
protected void Page_Load(object sender, EventArgs e)
{
    CustomClasses.MyClass MyClassInstance =
        new CustomClasses.MyClass();
}
```

    Now that you've told your code to look in the *CustomClasses* namespace, it can find *MyClass* without any problems.

By using namespaces, you can separate your classes into their own groups. This keeps the number of items in the IntelliSense menu manageable.

4 **Add a reference to the *CustomClasses* namespace.**

Just as you did with the *System.Text* namespace in *Lesson 6-3: Use the .NET library*, you can also add references to your own namespaces.

1. Add the following line to the *using* lines at the top of *calculator.aspx*'s code-behind file:

    using CustomClasses;

    ```
    using System.Web.UI;
    using System.Web.UI.WebControls;
    using CustomClasses;
    ```

2. Change the *CustomClasses.MyClass...* line back to:

    MyClass MyClassInstance = new MyClass();

    ```
    protected void Page_Load(object sender, Even
    {
        MyClass MyClassInstance = new MyClass();
    }
    ```

As you can see, by adding a reference, you can directly access everything in the *CustomClasses* namespace.

5 **Add a sub-namespace.**

The namespaces of the .NET framework don't just have a single level, but are arranged in a hierarchy. It's very easy to create the same kind of hierarchy yourself.

1. Return to *MyClass.cs*.

2. Change the *namespace* line to:

    namespace CustomClasses.TestClasses

    ```
    namespace CustomClasses.TestClasses
    ```

    This tells C# that the *MyClass* class is in the *TestClasses* namespace, which is inside the *CustomClasses* namespace.

3. Return to the code-behind file of *calculator.aspx*.

    ```
    MyClass MyClassInstance = new MyClass();
    ```

    You'll see that the reference to *MyClass* is showing an error again. That's because *MyClass* isn't in the *CustomClasses* namespace any more, so it can't be found.

4. Add the following reference:

    using CustomClasses.TestClasses;

    ```
    using System.Web.UI.WebControls;
    using CustomClasses;
    using CustomClasses.TestClasses;
    ```

    This has fixed the error by making the *TestClasses* sub-namespace available to the page.

    You could also have accessed the *MyClass* class by typing *CustomClasses.TestClasses.MyClass*.

Lesson 6-5: Create and use methods

You have already created a method in: *Lesson 6-1: Create a class*. In this lesson you'll create a new class with some more useful methods.

1   Open *My Project* from your sample files folder.

2   Create a new class named: **CalculatorFunctions.cs**

       You learned how to do this in: *Lesson 6-1: Create a class*.

       This class will be used to perform useful mathematical functions.

3   Add properties to the class.

      1.   Add a public *double* property called: **FirstNumber**

      2.   Add another public *double* property called: **SecondNumber**

      3.   Add a third public *double* property called: **Result**

       Your class should look like this:

```
public class CalculatorFunctions
{
    public double FirstNumber;
    public double SecondNumber;
    public double Result;
}
```

4   Create a method to add *FirstNumber* and *SecondNumber* together.

      1.   Add a new method using the following code:

       public void Add()
       {
       }

       This creates a new method called *Add*. The word *void* means that the method doesn't return a value, but you'll learn more about that in: *Lesson 6-7: Create methods that return a value*.

      2.   Add the following code to the *Add* method:

       Result = FirstNumber + SecondNumber;

```
public void Add()
{
    Result = FirstNumber + SecondNumber;
}
```

       This will add together the values of the *FirstNumber* and *SecondNumber* properties and place the result in the *Result* property.

5   Create methods for other common mathematical functions.

      1.   Add a **Subtract** method that works in exactly the same way as the *Add* method.

       The code should be:

```
public void Subtract()
{
    Result = FirstNumber - SecondNumber;
}
```

public void Subtract()
{
    Result = FirstNumber - SecondNumber;
}

2. Add a **Multiply** method in the same way.

3. Add a **Divide** method in the same way.

6 Call your methods.

1. Open the code-behind file of *calculator.aspx*.

2. Remove all code from the *ButtonCalculate_Click* event handler.

3. Add the following code to the *ButtonCalculate_Click* event handler:

CalculatorFunctions Functions = new CalculatorFunctions();

```
protected void ButtonCalculate_Click(object sender, EventArgs e)
{
    CalculatorFunctions Functions = new CalculatorFunctions();
}
```

This creates a new instance of the *CalculatorFunctions* class called *Functions*.

4. Add the following code on the next line:

Functions.FirstNumber = Convert.ToDouble(TextBoxFirstNumber.Text); Functions.SecondNumber = Convert.ToDouble(TextBoxSecondNumber.Text);

```
CalculatorFunctions Functions = new CalculatorFunctions();
Functions.FirstNumber = Convert.ToDouble(TextBoxFirstNumber.Text);
Functions.SecondNumber = Convert.ToDouble(TextBoxSecondNumber.Text);
```

This sets the *FirstNumber* and *SecondNumber* properties of the *Functions* object to the values entered in the textboxes.

5. Add the following code on the next line of the event handler:

Functions.Add();

This calls the *Add* method defined in the *CalculatorFunctions* class. It will add together the *FirstNumber* and *SecondNumber* properties and put the result into the *Result* property.

6. Add the following code on the next line:

LabelResult.Text = Functions.Result.ToString();

This displays the value of the *Result* property in *LabelResult*.

```
CalculatorFunctions Functions = new CalculatorFunctions();
Functions.FirstNumber = Convert.ToDouble(TextBoxFirstNumber.Text);
Functions.SecondNumber = Convert.ToDouble(TextBoxSecondNumber.Text);
Functions.Add();
LabelResult.Text = Functions.Result.ToString();
```

All of the mathematics on the *calculator.aspx* page is now done by your *CalculatorFunctions* class. If you like, try it out by viewing *calculator.aspx* in your browser.

Lesson 6-6: Create methods with arguments

Although the *CalculatorFunctions* class works, it could be a lot easier to use. Rather than setting two properties in order to perform calculations, you could make the numbers into arguments of each of the methods.

By using arguments, you can make methods accept values when they are called. You'll change your mathematical methods to use arguments in this lesson.

1   Open *My Project* from your sample files folder.

2   Open *CalculatorFunctions.cs*.

3   Remove the *FirstNumber* and *SecondNumber* properties.

Since you will be providing these numbers through arguments, you don't need the properties any more.

```
public class CalculatorFunctions
{
    public double Result;
    public void Add()
    {
        Result = FirstNumber + SecondNumber;
    }
}
```

Some errors will appear when you remove the properties.

4   Change all methods to require arguments.

1.   Change the line that starts the *Add* method to:

public void Add(double FirstNumber, double SecondNumber)

```
public void Add(double FirstNumber, double SecondNumber)
{
    Result = FirstNumber + SecondNumber;
}
```

This makes the *Add* method ask for two *double* variables called *FirstNumber* and *SecondNumber* when you call it.

Since the arguments have the same names as the properties you removed in the previous step, you don't need to make any further changes to the code.

2.   Add arguments to the *Subtract*, *Multiply* and *Divide* functions in the same way so there are no more errors.

5   Call the *Add* method from the *calculator.aspx* page.

Since you've changed the *Add* method to require arguments instead of using properties, you'll need to change how you call it.

```
Functions.FirstNumber =
Functions.SecondNumber
Functions.Add();
```

1.   Open the code-behind file of *calculator.aspx*.

Some of your code will be marked in red because it is no longer valid.

2.   Remove all code from the *ButtonCalculate_Click* event handler.

3. Add the following code to the *ButtonCalculate_Click* event handler:

**double FirstNumber = Convert.ToDouble(TextBoxFirstNumber.Text);
double SecondNumber = Convert.ToDouble(TextBoxSecondNumber.Text);**

```
protected void ButtonCalculate_Click(object sender, EventArgs e)
{
    double FirstNumber = Convert.ToDouble(TextBoxFirstNumber.Text
    double SecondNumber = Convert.ToDouble(TextBoxSecondNumber.Te
}
```

This will create *FirstNumber* and *SecondNumber* variables containing the numbers that were entered by the user.

4. Add the following code on the next line of the event handler:

CalculatorFunctions Functions = new CalculatorFunctions();

```
double FirstNumber = Convert.ToDouble(TextBoxFirstNumber.Text);
double SecondNumber = Convert.ToDouble(TextBoxSecondNumber.Text);
CalculatorFunctions Functions = new CalculatorFunctions();
```

This creates an instance of the *CalculatorFunctions* class called *Functions*.

5. Add the following code on the next line of the event handler:

Functions.Add(FirstNumber, SecondNumber);

```
double FirstNumber = Convert.ToDouble(TextBoxFirstNumber.Text);
double SecondNumber = Convert.ToDouble(TextBoxSecondNumber.Text);
CalculatorFunctions Functions = new CalculatorFunctions();
Functions.Add(FirstNumber, SecondNumber);
```

This calls the *Add* method with the *FirstNumber* and *SecondNumber* variables as arguments.

6. Add the following code on the next line of the event handler:

LabelResult.Text = Functions.Result.ToString();

```
double FirstNumber = Convert.ToDouble(TextBoxFirstNumber.Text);
double SecondNumber = Convert.ToDouble(TextBoxSecondNumber.Text);
CalculatorFunctions Functions = new CalculatorFunctions();
Functions.Add(FirstNumber, SecondNumber);
LabelResult.Text = Functions.Result.ToString();
```

The majority of the methods in the .NET library require arguments. Some of them can even accept multiple sets of arguments. This is called *overloading* (see sidebar).

6 Test the new functionality.

1. View *calculator.aspx* in your browser.

2. Fill in the two boxes with numbers and click the *Calculate* button.

```
3.5                        0.5              Calculate
4
```

You'll see that the calculation works correctly.

7 Close your browser and close Visual Studio.

Lesson 6-7: Create methods that return a value

note

What are functions?

In C#, the code for creating methods that return values is almost exactly the same as the code for methods that don't return a value.

Visual Basic, however, has a clear distinction between the two. Methods that return a value are called *functions* in Visual Basic.

In C#, methods are usually referred to as methods regardless of whether they return a value or not.

This information is provided because you might hear some developers use the word function when they refer to a method that returns a value.

Your *CalculatorFunctions* class is more useful now, but it would be even easier to use if it didn't store the results of calculations in the *Result* property.

In this lesson you'll convert your mathematical methods so that they return results by themselves.

1 Open *My Project* from your sample files folder.

2 Open *CalculatorFunctions.cs*.

3 Remove the *Result* property.

Since the methods are going to return values by themselves, you won't need the *Result* property to store results any more.

Errors will appear when you do this, but you'll fix the errors in the course of this lesson.

4 Change your methods to return values.

1. Change the line that starts the *Add* method to:

public double Add(double FirstNumber, double SecondNumber)

```
public double Add(double FirstNumber, double SecondNumber)
{
    Result = FirstNumber + SecondNumber;
}
```

You've changed the method from *public void* to **public double**. This tells C# that the method will return a *double* value.

void is used for methods that don't return any values.

2. Change the line inside the *Add* method to:

return FirstNumber + SecondNumber;

```
public double Add(double FirstNumber, double SecondNumber)
{
    return FirstNumber + SecondNumber;
}
```

return tells the method to return its value. Note that the *return* line will always end the method, so any code placed after this line will never run.

3. Make the *Subtract, Multiply* and *Divide* methods return a *double* value in the same way as you did with the *Add* method.

Simply change *void* to **double** in each method and replace *Result* = with: **return**

5 Call the *Add* method on the *calculator.aspx* page.

You will need to change how you call the *Add* method to account for the fact that it now returns a value.

1. Open the code-behind file of *calculator.aspx*.

You'll see that some of your code is marked in red because it is no longer valid.

```
Functions.Add(FirstNumber, SecondNumber);
LabelResult.Text = Functions.Result.ToString();
```

2. Change the *Functions.Add...* line to:

double Result = Functions.Add(FirstNumber, SecondNumber);

```
protected void ButtonCalculate_Click(object sender, EventArgs e)
{
    double FirstNumber = Convert.ToDouble(TextBoxFirstNumber.Text);
    double SecondNumber = Convert.ToDouble(TextBoxSecondNumber.Text);
    CalculatorFunctions Functions = new CalculatorFunctions();
    double Result = Functions.Add(FirstNumber, SecondNumber);
    LabelResult.Text = Functions.Result.ToString();
}
```

This will store the value returned by the *Add* method in a new *double* variable called *Result*.

3. Change the line that sets the *LabelResult.Text* property to:

LabelResult.Text = Result.ToString();

```
protected void ButtonCalculate_Click(object sender, EventArgs e)
{
    double FirstNumber = Convert.ToDouble(TextBoxFirstNumber.Text);
    double SecondNumber = Convert.ToDouble(TextBoxSecondNumber.Text);
    CalculatorFunctions Functions = new CalculatorFunctions();
    double Result = Functions.Add(FirstNumber, SecondNumber);
    LabelResult.Text = Result.ToString();
}
```

This uses the *Result* variable you created on the previous line instead of the property of the *Functions* class you used in: *Lesson 6-6: Create methods with arguments.*

6 Test your code.

1. View *calculator.aspx* in your browser.

2. Fill in the two boxes with numbers and click the *Calculate* button.

| 3141 | 59 | Calculate |
| 3200 | | |

You'll see that the calculation works correctly using your class method.

3. Close your browser.

Using arguments and return values is best practice when creating methods.

7 Close Visual Studio.

note

Why return values?

You might be wondering why returning a value from your methods is better than setting a property as you did in earlier lessons.

In this case it's undoubtedly better because it eliminates potential errors.

Previously there was no way of knowing which calculation had produced the result found in the *Result* variable.

There's nothing stopping you from taking whichever approach you think is best for whatever you're trying to achieve.

Lesson 6-8: Create a private method

So far all of the methods and properties you've created have been *public*, meaning they can be accessed freely when an instance of the class is created (or *instantiated*).

public is a protection level. You can use different protection levels to change the accessibility of methods and properties. You'll learn how to use the *private* protection level in this lesson.

1   Open *My Project* from your sample files folder.

2   Open *CalculatorFunctions.cs*.

3   Add a private method.

Add the following method to the *CalculatorFunctions* class:

private double RoundNumber(double Number)
{
    return Math.Round(Number, 2);
}

```
public class CalculatorFunctions
{
    private double RoundNumber(double Number)
    {
        return Math.Round(Number, 2);
    }
}
```

This method accepts a *double* value as an argument and returns it as a *double* value rounded to 2 decimal places.

What makes it different to the methods you've added so far is that it is *private*. This means it can only be accessed within the class itself.

4   Try to access the *RoundNumber* method from *calculator.aspx*.

   1.   Open the code-behind file of *calculator.aspx*.

   2.   Add a new line at the end of the *ButtonCalculate_Click* event handler.

   3.   Type the following on the new line:

   Functions.

Functions.
Add
Divide
Equals
GetHashCode
GetType
Multiply
Subtract
ToString

The IntelliSense menu should appear. This lists all of the methods in the *Functions* object, which is an instance of the *CalculatorFunctions* class.

4. Look for the *RoundNumber* method in the IntelliSense menu.

You won't see it, as it's not accessible. If you tried to use *Functions.RoundNumber* here, you would get an error message.

5. Remove the *Functions.* text you added.

```
protected void ButtonCalculate_Click(object sender, EventArgs e)
{
    double FirstNumber = Convert.ToDouble(TextBoxFirstNumber.Text);
    double SecondNumber = Convert.ToDouble(TextBoxSecondNumber.Text);
    CalculatorFunctions Functions = new CalculatorFunctions();
    double Result = Functions.Add(FirstNumber, SecondNumber);
    LabelResult.Text = Result.ToString();
}
```

5   **Use the *RoundNumber* method inside *CalculatorFunctions.cs*.**

1. Return to *CalculatorFunctions.cs*.

2. Change the *return* line in the *Add* method to:

return RoundNumber(FirstNumber + SecondNumber);

```
public double Add(double FirstNumber, double SecondNumber)
{
    return RoundNumber(FirstNumber + SecondNumber);
}
```

You won't see any error messages this time. The *RoundNumber* function is available because your code is inside the *CalculatorFunctions* class.

Anything that is created with the *private* protection level can only be accessed inside its own class.

3. Open *calculator.aspx* in your browser and test the calculation to confirm that it is rounding correctly.

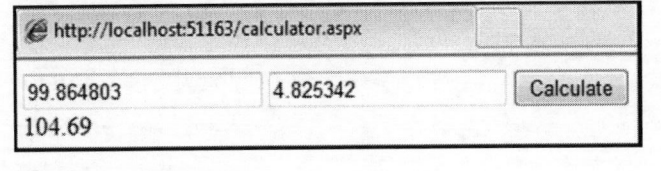

http://localhost:51163/calculator.aspx

| 99.864803 | 4.825342 | Calculate |
104.69

4. Close your browser.

6   **Close Visual Studio.**

important

Static properties are bad programming practice

Static methods can be very useful but static properties are a very bad idea.

When you create a static property it is available to your entire application. This means that every class in the application is able to change its value. For this reason you can never be sure what value the static property has, rendering it worthless.

The use of static properties can introduce many errors that are almost impossible to debug.

My advice is to never use them in your code.

Lesson 6-9: Create a static method

In order to use all of the properties and methods you've created in the *CalculatorFunctions* class so far, you have had to first create an instance of the class.

Some properties, such as the *DateTime.Now* property you saw in *Lesson 5-7: Use DateTime variables,* can be accessed without creating an instance of the class.

These are called *static* properties and methods. You'll create some in this lesson.

1   Open *My Project* from your sample files folder.

2   Open *CalculatorFunctions.cs.*

3   Make the *Add* method static.

A static method can be called without creating an instance of its class. The methods in the *Math* class you saw in *Lesson 5-11: Use the Math library for advanced mathematics* were all static methods.

Change the line that begins the *Add* function to:

public static double Add(double FirstNumber, double SecondNumber)

```
public static double Add(double FirstNumber, double SecondNumber)
{
    return RoundNumber(FirstNumber + SecondNumber);
}
```

All you need to do to make a method static is to add the word *static* after its protection level. You can do exactly the same thing to make classes and properties static.

Note that you should avoid using static properties wherever possible (see sidebar).

4   Make the *RoundNumber* method static.

You will see an error inside your *Add* method. If you move your mouse cursor over the error, you'll see a message complaining that the *RoundNumber* method is not static.

Static methods are isolated from non-static methods, since non-static methods can only be used via an instance of the class. The only way to allow the *Add* method to call the *RoundNumber* method is to make the *RoundNumber* method static as well.

In the same way as you did with the *Add* method, make the *RoundNumber* method static:

private static double RoundNumber(double Number)

```
private static double RoundNumber(double Number)
{
    return Math.Round(Number, 2);
}
```

The errors disappear.

```
public static double Add(double FirstNumber, double SecondNumber)
{
    return RoundNumber(FirstNumber + SecondNumber);
}
```

5 **Call the static method from the *calculator.aspx* page.**

Because the *Add* method is now static, you no longer need to create an instance of the class to call it.

1. Open the code-behind of *calculator.aspx*.

2. Remove the line:

   CalculatorFunctions Functions = new CalculatorFunctions();

```
protected void ButtonCalculate_Click(object sender, EventArgs e)
{
    double FirstNumber = Convert.ToDouble(TextBoxFirstNumber.Text);
    double SecondNumber = Convert.ToDouble(TextBoxSecondNumber.Text);
    double Result = Functions.Add(FirstNumber, SecondNumber);
    LabelResult.Text = Result.ToString();
}
```

Since you're using a static method, you don't need an instance of the class any more.

The line that calls the *Add* method is now marked as an error. This is because the *Functions* instance of the *CalculatorFunctions* class no longer exists.

3. Change the line beginning with *double Result* to:

   double Result = CalculatorFunctions.Add(FirstNumber, SecondNumber);

```
protected void ButtonCalculate_Click(object sender, EventArgs e)
{
    double FirstNumber = Convert.ToDouble(TextBoxFirstNumber.Text);
    double SecondNumber = Convert.ToDouble(TextBoxSecondNumber.Text);
    double Result = CalculatorFunctions.Add(FirstNumber, SecondNumber);
    LabelResult.Text = Result.ToString();
}
```

4. Open *calculator.aspx* in your browser.

5. Test the calculation.

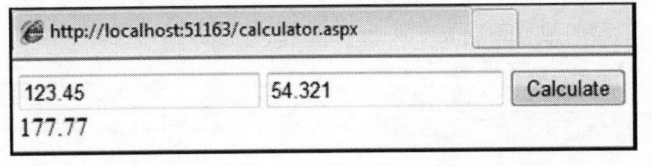

You'll see that it still works without any problems, but you've reduced the amount of code needed to call the method by making it static.

Static methods are ideal when the method stands alone and has no properties. The calculations in the *CalculatorFunctions* class are a perfect example of this.

6 **Close Visual Studio.**

Lesson 6-10: Create and dispose of instances

You've already created an instance of your own class and have seen how static methods work.

In this lesson you'll learn about best practice when working with classes.

1 Open *ShiningStone* from your sample files folder.

2 Open the code-behind file of *buy.aspx*.

3 Create a new instance of a data class.

The *ShiningStone* project has a LINQ data class that allows it to communicate with its database. You'll learn how to use the LINQ data class in *Lesson 10-3: Retrieve a single row of data using LINQ*. For now it's a good class to practice creating and disposing of instances.

1. Add the following code to the *ButtonSubmitOrder_Click* event handler:

   ShiningStoneDataContext Data = new ShiningStoneDataContext();

   ```
   protected void ButtonSubmitOrder_Click(object sender, EventArgs e)
   {
       ShiningStoneDataContext Data = new ShiningStoneDataContext();
   }
   ```

   This creates a new instance of the *ShiningStoneDataContext* class called *Data*.

2. Add the following code on the next line:

   Data.SubmitChanges();

   This method won't actually do anything at this stage. It's just an example of a method that you might call from the *Data* instance.

   ```
   protected void ButtonSubmitOrder_Click(object sender, EventArgs e)
   {
       ShiningStoneDataContext Data = new ShiningStoneDataContext();
       Data.SubmitChanges();
   }
   ```

4 Dispose of the *Data* instance.

Many classes have a method called *Dispose*. The *Dispose* method is used to clear the class from memory.

Some classes don't have *Dispose* methods. This is usually because they don't have any properties that stay in memory.

A LINQ data class like the *ShiningStoneDataContext* class can load a lot of data into memory when it is used, so it is good practice to dispose of it as soon as you no longer need it.

Add the following line of code on the next line:

Data.Dispose();

note

Garbage collection

C# has a garbage collector that automatically disposes of objects that are no longer in scope.

In this case, for example, the C# garbage collector would dispose of the *Data* instance after *ButtonSubmitOrder_Click* was finished, since it wouldn't be usable any more.

Despite this, it's always best to dispose of instances when you can, since the garbage collector doesn't always clean up memory immediately.

```
protected void ButtonSubmitOrder_Click(object sender, EventArgs e)
{
    ShiningStoneDataContext Data = new ShiningStoneDataContext();
    Data.SubmitChanges();
    Data.Dispose();
}
```

This will remove the *Data* instance from memory. If you were to try to work with the *Data* instance after this line, you would cause an exception.

5   Use the *using* statement to automatically dispose of an instance.

As well as disposing of instances using the *Dispose* method, you can use a *using* statement to automatically dispose of an instance.

Note that working with *using* statements inside your code is different to the *using* statements at the top of the page.

1.   Remove the code you added to the *ButtonSubmitOrder_Click* event handler.

2.   Add the following code to the *ButtonSubmitOrder_Click* event handler:

using (ShiningStoneDataContext Data =
new ShiningStoneDataContext())
{
    Data.SubmitChanges();
}

```
protected void ButtonSubmitOrder_Click(object sender, EventArgs e)
{
    using (ShiningStoneDataContext Data = new ShiningStoneDataContext())
    {
        Data.SubmitChanges();
    }
}
```

This does exactly the same thing as calling the *Dispose* method, but is much easier to understand and work with.

The *using* statement creates the *Data* instance and then automatically disposes of it after the last curly bracket *}*.

6   Close Visual Studio.

Lesson 6-11: Create class constructors

A constructor is a method that runs whenever an instance of a class is created. In this lesson you'll learn how to use constructors and add them to your own classes.

1   Open *My Project* from your sample files folder.

2   Open *MyClass.cs*.

3   Add a constructor to the class.

    1.   Add the following method to the class:

        public MyClass()
        {
        }

        This is a simple constructor. Any code you put inside it will run when an instance of the class is created.

        In order to be recognized as a constructor, the method must have the same name as the class it belongs to.

        Notice how the syntax differs from a normal method. There is no *void* (or other return value type) specified before the method name. This syntax is peculiar to constructors.

```
public MyClass()
{
    IntProperty = 15;
}
```

    2.   Add the following code to the constructor:

        IntProperty = 15;

        This will set the *IntProperty* property to *15* whenever a new instance of the class is created.

4   See the constructor in action on the *calculator.aspx* page.

    1.   Open the code-behind file of *calculator.aspx*.

        In *Lesson 6-4: Work with namespaces,* you created an instance of the *MyClass* class in the *Page_Load* event handler.

    2.   Put a breakpoint at the end of the *Page_Load* event handler.

        You learned how to do this in: *Lesson 3-3: Use Breakpoints.*

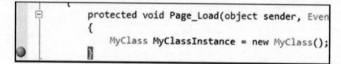

    3.   Run *calculator.aspx* in debug mode.

    4.   When the code is paused, check the value of the *MyClassInstance.IntProperty* property.

        You'll see that the constructor has set the value of the property to 15.

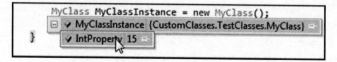

5. Stop debugging but leave the breakpoint in place.

5 **Add arguments to your constructor.**

Just like any other method, constructors can have arguments.

1. Return to *MyClass.cs*.

2. Change the code of the constructor to:

public MyClass(int StartingNumber)
{
    IntProperty = StartingNumber;
}

```
public MyClass(int StartingNumber)
{
    IntProperty = StartingNumber;
}
```

This adds an argument to the constructor called *StartingNumber* and sets the *IntProperty* property to the number provided in the argument.

This should look very familiar to you. It's exactly the same as adding arguments to any other method. This was covered in: *Lesson 6-6: Create methods with arguments*.

6 **Instantiate the *MyClass* class with arguments.**

1. Return to the code-behind file of *calculator.aspx*.

```
MyClass MyClassInstance = new MyClass();
```

You'll see that the line creating the instance of the *MyClass* class is now marked as an error.

This is because it's trying to create an instance of the *MyClass* class without providing the required argument.

2. Change the code in the *Page_Load* event handler to:

MyClass MyClassInstance = new MyClass(17);

```
MyClass MyClassInstance = new MyClass(17);
```

This provides the number 17 as the constructor argument.

This means that when the constructor runs, it will set the value of *IntProperty* to 17.

You could provide any *int* value for this argument.

3. Run *calculator.aspx* in debug mode.

The breakpoint should still be in place, so execution should be paused at the end of *Page_Load* event handler.

4. Check the value of the *MyClassInstance.IntProperty* property.

You'll see that the constructor has set the value of the property to 17.

```
MyClassInstance {CustomClasses.TestClasses.MyClass}
    IntProperty  17
```

5. Stop debugging and remove the breakpoint.

Session 6: Exercise

1   Open the *My Project* sample project and add a new class called: **Circle.cs**

2   Add a public *double* property to the *Circle* class called: **CircleCircumference**

3   Add a public method to the *Circle* class called: **CalculateDiameter**

4   Make the *CalculateDiameter* method return a *double* value.

        (Don't worry about the indicated error, this will be overcome in question 6).

5   Make the *CalculateDiameter* method ask for a *double* argument called: **Radius**

6   Add code to the *CalculateDiameter* method to multiply the *Radius* argument by 2 and return the result.

7   Add a constructor to the *Circle* class.

8   Make the constructor require a *double* value as an argument called: **Circumference**

9   Make the constructor set the *CircleCircumference* property to the value of the *Circumference* argument.

10   Make the *CalculateDiameter* method static.

11   Add a new Web Form to the project called: **circlecalculator.aspx**

12   Open the code-behind file of *circlecalculator.aspx*.

13   Add code to the *Page_Load* event handler to create an instance of the *Circle* class named **MyCircle** using a *Circumference* argument of: **50**

14   Add code on the next line to create a new *double* variable called: **MyCircleDiameter**

15   Add code on the next line to call the static *CalculateDiameter* method of the *Circle* class with a *Radius* argument of **7.95**, storing the resulting value in the *MyCircleDiameter* variable.

        (Remember that *CalculateDiameter* is a static method and is called in a different way to normal methods).

16   Add code to output the value of *MyCircleDiameter* using *Response.Write*.

17   View *circlecalculator.aspx* in your browser.

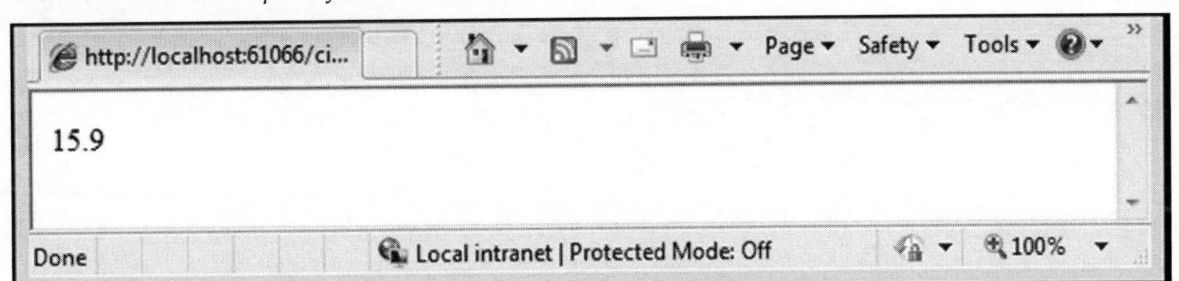

My Project - start

My Project - end

If you need help slide the page to the left

Session 6: Exercise Answers

These are the four questions that students find the most difficult to answer:

Q 10	Q 7	Q 6	Q 3
Change the line that starts the *CalculateDiameter* method to: **public static double CalculateDiameter (double Radius)** This was covered in: *Lesson 6-9: Create a static method.*	Use the following code: **public Circle()** **{** **}** This was covered in: *Lesson 6-11: Create class constructors.*	Use the following line of code: **return Radius * 2;** This was covered in: *Lesson 6-7: Create methods that return a value.*	Use the following code to add the public method: **public void CalculateDiameter()** **{** **}** This was covered in: *Lesson 6-5: Create and use methods.*

If you have difficulty with the other questions, here are the lessons that cover the relevant skills:

1   Refer to: Lesson 6-1: Create a class.

2   Refer to: Lesson 6-1: Create a class.

4   Refer to: Lesson 6-7: Create methods that return a value.

5   Refer to: Lesson 6-6: Create methods with arguments.

8   Refer to: Lesson 6-11: Create class constructors.

9   Refer to: Lesson 6-11: Create class constructors.

11   Refer to: Lesson 1-7: Manage a project with the Solution Explorer.

12   Refer to: Lesson 1-7: Manage a project with the Solution Explorer.

13   Refer to: Lesson 6-11: Create class constructors.

14   Refer to: Lesson 5-5: Use floating point variables.

15   Refer to: Lesson 6-9: Create a static method.

16   Refer to: Lesson 3-7: Understand Request and Response.

17   Refer to: Lesson 1-8: Run a project in debug mode.

Session Seven: C# Logical constructs and error handling

> Logic and mathematics are nothing but specialised linguistic structures.
>
> *Jean Piaget, Swiss psychologist and philosopher (1896 – 1980)*

Now that you know how C# code is structured and organized, it's time to add some programming logic to enable your code to respond intelligently to different conditions.

In this session you'll learn the basics of programming logic and a little more about best coding practice.

Session Objectives

By the end of this session you will be able to:

- Use the if statement
- Use else and else if
- Use basic logical operators
- Use advanced logic
- Use get and set
- Use try and catch to handle errors
- Use comments
- Use summaries

note

Single line *if* statements

As well as using curly brackets {}, you can put an *if* statement on a single line. For example:

if (Page.IsValid)
Response.Write("Validation OK");

Of course, this is useful only if you have just one line of code you intend your *if* statement to run.

Some programmers prefer to use the curly brackets even when they want to run only a single line of code, as this is more consistent and makes the code easier to understand.

important

The = assignment operator and the == equality operator

Some programming languages use the equals sign (=) for both assignment and equality.

C# uses the double equals sign (==) for equality and the single equals sign (=) for assignment.

Examples

AcceptedTerms = true

Assigns the value of *true* to the *AcceptedTerms* Boolean variable.

AcceptedTerms == true

Checks whether the value of the *AcceptedTerms* variable is equal to *true*. Returns *true* if it does, and *false* if it doesn't.

If you are not completing the course incrementally use the sample file: **Lesson 7-1** to begin this lesson.

Sample files with the starting point for each lesson are also provided for all of the other lessons in this session.

Lesson 7-1: Use the if statement

1 Open *ShiningStone* from your sample files folder.

2 Open the code-behind file of *buy.aspx*.

3 Create an *if* statement.

1. Remove all existing code from the *ButtonSubmitOrder_Click* event handler.

2. Add the following code to the event handler:

   bool AcceptedTerms = CheckBoxAcceptTerms.Checked;

   ```
   protected void ButtonSubmitOrder_Click(object sender, EventArgs e)
   {
       bool AcceptedTerms = CheckBoxAcceptTerms.Checked;
   }
   ```

   This code should make sense to you by now. It creates a Boolean variable called *AcceptedTerms* which will be *true* if the *CheckBoxAcceptTerms* control is checked and *false* if it is not.

   You created the *CheckBoxAcceptTerms* control in the session 4 exercise.

3. Add the following code on the next line:

   if (AcceptedTerms == true)
   {
   }

   This is the first time you've seen the == equality operator. See sidebar for more on this.

   This is a very simple *if* statement. As you can see, the code is very similar to the code you used to create methods. Everything inside the curly brackets { } will only run if the *AcceptedTerms* variable has a value of *true*.

   In other words, the code inside the curly brackets { } will only run if the user has checked the *CheckBoxAcceptTerms* control.

4. Add the following code inside the *if* statement (between { }):

   Response.Write("Terms OK");

   ```
   protected void ButtonSubmitOrder_Click(object sender, EventArgs e)
   {
       bool AcceptedTerms = CheckBoxAcceptTerms.Checked;
       if (AcceptedTerms == true)
       {
           Response.Write("Terms OK");
       }
   }
   ```

5. View *buy.aspx* in your browser.

6. Complete the form (without checking *I accept the terms and conditions*) and then click the *Submit Order* button.

   The page will post back, but nothing interesting will happen.

> Shining Stone Jewelers
>
> Terms OK

7. Check the *I accept the terms and conditions* box.

8. Click *Submit Order* again.

   This time the logical test in the *if* statement returns true and *Terms OK* appears on the page.

4 Create a nested *if* statement.

As you can see, it's quite simple to test for a single condition. You can make your program's logic more complex by putting *if* statements inside other *if* statements.

Just like putting HTML tags inside each other, this is known as *nesting*.

1. Close your browser and return to the code-behind file of *buy.aspx*.

2. Add the following code inside the *if* statement you created before:

   if (Page.IsValid)
   {
      Response.Write("Validation OK");
   }

```
protected void ButtonSubmitOrder_Click(object sender, EventArgs e)
{
    bool AcceptedTerms = CheckBoxAcceptTerms.Checked;
    if (AcceptedTerms == true)
    {
        Response.Write("Terms OK");
        if (Page.IsValid)
        {
            Response.Write("Validation OK");
        }
    }
}
```

As you may remember from *Lesson 4-8: Use the RequiredFieldValidator control*, *Page.IsValid* is the server-side confirmation that your form's validation controls are happy with the form's content.

The *if* statement will now check if the *AcceptedTerms* variable is *true* and will only check the *Page.IsValid* property if so.

You might want to do this if you intend to reject the user's order if they do not accept the terms and conditions (making any further validation checks pointless).

3. View *buy.aspx* in your browser.

4. Complete the form without checking the *CheckBoxAcceptTerms* control and click the *Submit Order* button.

   Nothing happens. The *CheckBoxAcceptTerms* control wasn't checked so neither of the *if* statements succeed.

5. Check the *CheckBoxAcceptTerms* control and submit the form again.

   This time both *if* statements succeed and the results are shown on the page.

> Shining Stone Jewelers
>
> Terms OKValidation OK

6. Close your web browser.

Lesson 7-2: Use else and else if

The *if* statements you've used so far are great for testing a single condition, but sometimes you need to test for multiple conditions with different outcomes for each condition.

This could be done by creating separate *if* statements for every condition, but it's easier and tidier to use *else* and *else if* to do this.

In this lesson you'll use *else* and *else if* to extend the logic of your *if* statements.

1   Open *ShiningStone* from your sample files folder.

2   Open the code-behind file of *buy.aspx*.

3   Add an *else* statement.

Add the following code at the end of the *ButtonSubmitOrder_Click* event handler:

**else
{
    Response.Write
    ("You must accept the terms and conditions to continue");
}**

```
if (AcceptedTerms == true)
{
    Response.Write("Terms OK");
    if (Page.IsValid)
    {
        Response.Write("Validation OK");
    }
}
else
{
    Response.Write("You must accept the terms and conditions to continue");
}
```

This follows on from the *if* statement that checks if the *CheckBoxAcceptTerms* control is checked. As you might have guessed, it will run if the *CheckBoxAcceptTerms* control is not checked.

else mean 'otherwise', ie if the *CheckBoxAcceptTerms* control is checked, write *Terms OK*, otherwise write *You must accept the terms and conditions to continue*.

4   Add an *else if* statement.

As well as using *else* to run some code if an *if* statement's logic fails, you can use *else if* to create chains of logical procedures.

1.   Add the following code to the end of the *ButtonSubmitOrder_Click* event handler:

**string SelectedCountry =
DropDownListCountry.SelectedItem.Text;**

```
        Response.Write("You must accept the terms and conditions to
}
string SelectedCountry = DropDownListCountry.SelectedItem.Text;
```

This will put the name of the country chosen from the drop-down list into a *string* variable called *SelectedCountry*.

2. Add the following code on the next line:

    if (SelectedCountry == "Canada")
    {
       Response.Write("We cannot currently deliver to Canada");
    }

    As you know from *Lesson 7-1: Use the if statement*, this checks if the selected country is *Canada* and outputs the shown text if it is.

3. Add the following code on the next line:

    else if (SelectedCountry == "United Kingdom")
    {
       Response.Write("Eligible for free delivery");
    }

    Because you used *else if,* this *if* statement will follow on from the first one. It will only run if the value of the *SelectedCountry* variable is not *Canada*, but is *United Kingdom*.

4. Add the following code on the next line:

    else
    {
       Response.Write("Standard delivery charges apply");
    }

```
string SelectedCountry = DropDownListCountry.SelectedItem.Text;
if (SelectedCountry == "Canada")
{
    Response.Write("We cannot currently deliver to Canada");
}
else if (SelectedCountry == "United Kingdom")
{
    Response.Write("Eligible for free delivery");
}
else
{
    Response.Write("Standard delivery charges apply");
}
```

This ends the chain of logic. It will only run if the value of the SelectedCountry variable is not *Canada* or *United Kingdom*.

5. View *buy.aspx* in your browser.

    Try completing the form and setting the *Country* drop-down list to *Canada, United Kingdom* and any other country to see the difference.

Shining Stone Jewelers

Terms OKValidation OKWe cannot currently deliver to Canada

Because *Response.Write* is being used, the text is all output together at the top of the page. In the final version of this page, you'd use a *Label* control to show the results instead.

Lesson 7-3: Use basic logical operators

You should be able to create a great deal of programming logic with the techniques you've already learned in this session, but you can use *logical operators* to make your *if* statements even more powerful.

1 Open *ShiningStone* from your sample files folder.

2 Open the code-behind file of *buy.aspx*.

3 Use && to check two conditions in a single *if* statement.

&& is the *AND* logical operator.

By using *&&*, you can check many different conditions in a single *if* statement.

1. Change the *if (AcceptedTerms…* line to:

    if (AcceptedTerms == true && Page.IsValid)

    This makes the single *if* statement check both conditions. The code inside the *if* statement will only run if both the *AcceptedTerms* variable and the *Page.IsValid* property are *true*.

2. Remove the following code:

    if (Page.IsValid)
    {
    **   Response.Write("Validation OK");**
    }

    Since your first *if* statement now handles the *Page.IsValid* property as well, you don't need this any more.

```
if (AcceptedTerms == true && Page.IsValid)
{
    Response.Write("Terms OK");
}
else
{
    Response.Write("You must accept the ter
}
```

4 Use || to check if either condition is true.

| | is the *OR* logical operator.

By using | |, you can check if any of several conditions are true. *&&* is different because it will only run if every condition is true.

1. Return to the code-behind of *buy.aspx*.

2. Change the *else if (SelectedCountry…* line to:

    else if (SelectedCountry == "United Kingdom"
    | | SelectedCountry == "Ireland")

```
else if (SelectedCountry == "United Kingdom"
    || SelectedCountry == "Ireland")
{
    Response.Write("Eligible for free delivery");
}
```

By using the || operator, you've made the *if* statement execute its code if the value of the *SelectedCountry* variable is either *United Kingdom* or *Ireland*.

3. View *buy.aspx* in your browser.

4. Complete the form and try selecting either *United Kingdom* or *Ireland* from the drop-down menu.

> Terms OKValidation OKEligible for free delivery

You'll see that both options cause the *if* statement to run and print *Eligible for free delivery* at the top of the page.

5. Close your browser.

5 Use *!* to check if a condition is not true.

! is the *NOT* operator. You have actually used it once already in: *Lesson 5-6: Use Boolean variables*.

So far all of your *if* statements have been used to check if a condition was *true*. You can use *!* to check if a condition is false. Of course, you could also use == *false* to accomplish the same result, but the *!* operator requires less code.

1. Return to the code-behind file of *buy.aspx*.

2. Change the *if (AcceptedTerms...* line to:

if (!AcceptedTerms == true || !Page.IsValid)
{
    Response.Write
    ("You must accept the terms and conditions to continue");
}

```
if (!AcceptedTerms == true || !Page.IsValid)
{
    Response.Write("You must accept the term
}
```

As you can see, by using the *!* operator, you've made the *if* statement do the opposite of what it did previously.

You'll notice that you also use the || (OR) operator instead of the && (AND) operator.

This is because you want the code to run if either the value of the *AcceptedTerms* variable is *false* (NOT true) or the value of the *Page.IsValid* property is *false* (NOT true).

3. Remove the redundant code:

else
{
  Response
  .Write("You must accept the terms and conditions to continue");
}

```
bool AcceptedTerms = CheckBoxAcceptTerms.Checked;
if (!AcceptedTerms == true || !Page.IsValid)
{
    Response.Write("You must accept the terms and conditions to
}
string SelectedCountry = DropDownListCountry.SelectedItem.Text;
if (SelectedCountry == "Canada")
```

---

note

Other ways to use !

The *!* operator is more versatile than the others, and can be used in a number of ways.

For example, if you had a *bool* variable called *MyBool*, all of the following would check if the value of *MyBool* is *false*:

if (MyBool != true)

if (!MyBool == true)

if (!MyBool)

In *Lesson 7-4: Use advanced logic* you'll learn about bracketing logical operators, which can be used to make logical operations even more versatile.

Lesson 7-4: Use advanced logic

You now know how to check for multiple conditions using logical operators. Even more can be done by using brackets to control precedence in the same way as you would with mathematical operations.

1   Open *ShiningStone* from your sample files folder.

2   Open the code-behind file of *buy.aspx*.

3   Remove all of the code from the *ButtonSubmitOrder_Click* event handler.

You're going to start from the beginning again and try to make the logic as streamlined as possible.

4   Create a complex *if* statement.

1. Add the following code to the *ButtonSubmitOrder_Click* event handler:

   string SelectedCountry = DropDownListCountry.SelectedItem.Text;

   ```
   protected void ButtonSubmitOrder_Click(object sender, EventArgs e)
   {
       string SelectedCountry = DropDownListCountry.SelectedItem.Text;
   }
   ```

   You need this code to extract the name of the selected country from the dropdown list control.

2. Add the following code to the next line:

   if (Page.IsValid
   && CheckBoxAcceptTerms.Checked
   && SelectedCountry == "United Kingdom"
   || SelectedCountry == "Ireland")
   {
       Response.Write("Logic succeeded!");
   }

   ```
   if (Page.IsValid
       && CheckBoxAcceptTerms.Checked
       && SelectedCountry == "United Kingdom"
       || SelectedCountry == "Ireland")
   {
       Response.Write("Logic succeeded!");
   }
   ```

   Here's the logic you're trying to define:

   The page must be valid AND The terms and conditions checkbox must be checked.

   AND also…

   The selected country must be either the United Kingdom OR Ireland.

   Unfortunately the code above does not model this correctly.

note

Multi-line *if* statements

As you can see in the screenshot to the right, you can put C# code across multiple lines to make it easier to read.

Whether you do this or not is up to you. Personally I prefer to keep my *if* statements on a single line and only break them up if they are very long.

3. View *buy.aspx* in your browser.

4. Complete the form, selecting *Ireland* from the *Country* drop-down and leaving the *terms and conditions* checkbox unchecked.

   Although the *terms and conditions* checkbox was left unchecked, the *if* statement still executed its code. This is because there were no brackets to clarify precedence.

   Here's what C# saw:

   The terms and conditions check box isn't checked

   AND

   The SelectedCountry is not United Kingdom

   …. So that's a fail on two counts… except you then indicated:

   OR Selected Country == Ireland

   … which is *true* so C# thought you wanted to run the code.

   To solve the problem you need to add brackets to tell C# what you really meant. In other words you need to define precedence rules. This is indicated by the use of brackets like this:

   (The page must be valid AND The terms and conditions checkbox must be checked)

   AND

   (The selected country must be either the United Kingdom OR Ireland.)

5 Close your browser and add brackets to clarify precedence.

1. Change the *if* statement to the following:

   **if ((Page.IsValid && CheckBoxAcceptTerms.Checked)
   && (SelectedCountry == "United Kingdom"
   || SelectedCountry == "Ireland"))**

```
if (
    (Page.IsValid && CheckBoxAcceptTerms.Checked)
    &&
    (SelectedCountry == "United Kingdom" || SelectedCountry == "Ireland")
)
{
    Response.Write("Logic succeeded!");
}
```

5. View *buy.aspx* in your browser.

6. Complete the form, selecting *Ireland* from the *Country* drop-down and leaving the *terms and conditions* check box unchecked.

   This time nothing happens, since the *terms and conditions* checkbox isn't checked.

7. Check the *terms and conditions* check box and resubmit the form.

   This time all of the logic you specified succeeds and the code runs.

Lesson 7-5: Use get and set

There are two special methods you can add to a property: *get* and *set*. It's fairly rare to want to do this, but it's important that you understand the technique.

1   Open *ShiningStone* from your sample files folder.

2   Open the code-behind file of *buy.aspx*.

3   Create a *bool* property.

In lesson *Lesson 6-1: Create a class (sidebar),* you discovered that your code-behind file is actually a class.

You can add properties to your code-behind files, just as you would add a property to any other class.

Add the following code (outside any event handlers):

private bool AcceptedTerms;

```
public partial class buy : System.Web.UI.Page
{
    protected void Page_Load(object sender, EventArgs e)
    {

    }

    private bool AcceptedTerms;
}
```

This creates a normal *bool* property that can be accessed only within the code-behind file, since it is private.

There's very rarely any reason to make properties in a code-behind file public.

4   Add a *get* method to the property.

By adding a *get* method, you can change what is returned when any code requests the value of the property.

1.   Change the property code to the following:

private bool AcceptedTerms
{
  get
  {
    return true;
  }
}

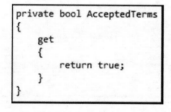

Note that there is no longer a semi-colon after *AcceptedTerms*.

This very simple *get* method will always return *true* whenever anything asks for the value of the *AcceptedTerms* property.

The *AcceptedTerms* property is now also read-only. If you tried to change the value of *AcceptedTerms* you would see an error.

2.   Change the *return true;* line to:

return CheckBoxAcceptTerms.Checked;

note

Uses for *get* and *set*

get and *set* can be used to add logic to any property when its value is set or retrieved.

Everything you can achieve with *get* and *set* can be done using other techniques that you've already learned. For this reason most developers rarely make use of *get* and *set*.

get and *set* are particularly useful, however, when you want to store a value in ViewState.

You learned about setting ViewState values in: *Lesson 3-9: Work with ViewState*.

By setting a ViewState value in the *set* method and retrieving it using a *get* method, you can make ViewState values easier to work with.

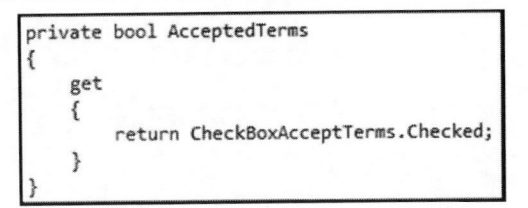

Now the *AcceptedTerms* property will always have the same value as the *Checked* property of the *CheckBoxAcceptTerms* control.

5   Add a *set* method to the variable.

At the moment the *AcceptedTerms* property will retrieve the value of *CheckBoxAcceptTerms.Checked*, but the property is read-only so you can't set its value.

1.   Add the following code after the end of the *get* method:

set
{
    CheckBoxAcceptTerms.Checked = value;
}

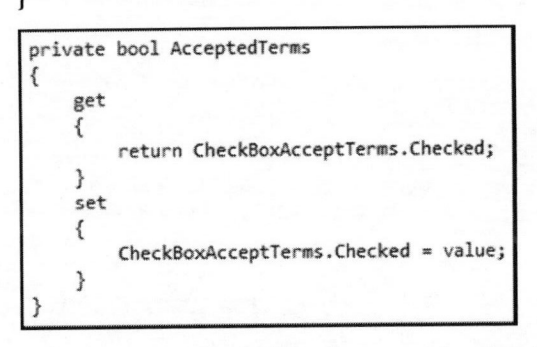

value acts as a placeholder for any value that is assigned to the property.

This code will set the *CheckBoxAcceptTerms.Checked* property to the value that is provided if you change the value of the *AcceptedTerms* property.

2.   Add the following code to the *Page_Load* event handler:

AcceptedTerms = true;

```
protected void Page_Load(object sender, EventArgs e)
{
    AcceptedTerms = true;
}
```

Since assigning a value uses the *set* method, the *CheckBoxAcceptTerms* control will be checked when the page loads.

3.   View *buy.aspx* in your browser.

☑ I accept the terms and conditions
Submit Order

You'll see that the checkbox is is checked. The *set* method successfully passed the assigned value to the control's *Checked* property.

4.   Close your browser.

Lesson 7-6: Use try and catch to handle errors

Unfortunately, no matter how hard you try to limit the possibility of errors they will still happen, usually because the user did something you didn't expect.

Fortunately, you can use the *try* and *catch* statements to handle errors without the page crashing and displaying an ugly error page.

1 Open *My Project* from your sample files folder.

2 Open the code-behind file of *Default.aspx*.

3 Add code that will cause an exception.

If you think back to *Lesson 3-5: Understand the Exception object*, you'll remember that one of the easiest ways to cause an exception (error) is to try to divide by zero.

Add the following code to the *Page_Load* event handler:

int Zero = 0;
int Error = 1 / Zero;

```
protected void Page_Load(object sender, EventArgs e)
{
    int Zero = 0;
    int Error = 1 / Zero;
}
```

4 View *Default.aspx* in your browser.

If your code pauses, minimize your browser and then press the continue button. ▶

You will see an error page.

Server Error in '/' Application.

Attempted to divide by zero.

5 Handle the error using *try* and *catch*.

1. Close your browser.

2. Change the code in the *Page_Load* event handler to the following:

```
try
{
    int Zero = 0;
    int Error = 1 / Zero;
}
catch
{
}
```

```
try
{
    int Zero = 0;
    int Error = 1 / Zero;
}
catch
{
}
```

This C# code will try to run the code between the first set of curly brackets { } (the *try* statement) and will only run the code between the second set (the *catch* statement) if an exception occurs.

Since there is no code in the *catch* statement, nothing will happen if there is an error. This is known as *swallowing* the error, and is considered to be bad practice.

3. View *Default.aspx* in your browser.

MY ASP.NET APPLICATION

This time the page displays normally. The error still happened, but your *try* and *catch* code handled it.

4. Close your browser.

6 Retrieve details of the error in the *catch* statement.

If you want to tell the user what went wrong or record any errors in a log, you can retrieve the *Exception* object in your *catch* statement.

You examined the *Exception* object in: *Lesson 3-5: Understand the Exception object*.

1. Change the *catch* line to the following:

catch (Exception Ex)

This is very similar to adding an argument to a method, as you did in: *Lesson 6-6: Create methods with arguments*. It creates a variable called *Ex* which contains the *Exception* object generated by the error.

2. Add the following code to the *catch* statement (between the curly brackets { }):

Response.Write(Ex.Message);

```
catch (Exception Ex)
{
    Response.Write(Ex.Message);
}
```

This will output the *Message* property of the *Exception* object to the top of the browser window.

3. View *Default.aspx* in your browser.

This time the error message appears at the top of the page.

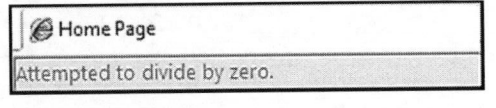
Home Page

Attempted to divide by zero.

4. Close your browser.

Lesson 7-7: Use comments

You can tell when code has been written by a true professional because it is easy to understand and maintain. Using a consistent naming convention and following best practice is part of this, but adding comments to your code can help immensely.

The best programmers always add comments to their code wherever it might be confusing. In this lesson you'll discover several different ways of adding comments.

1   Open *My Project* from your sample files folder.

2   Open *CalculatorFunctions.cs*.

3   Add a basic comment.

    1.   Add a new line before:

       return RoundNumber(FirstNumber + SecondNumber);

    2.   Add a comment to the new line with the code:

       //Add FirstNumber and SecondNumber

```
public static double Add(double FirstNumber, double SecondNumber)
{
    //Add FirstNumber and SecondNumber
    return RoundNumber(FirstNumber + SecondNumber);
}
```

You'll see that the comment is shown in green.

By adding the two forward-slashes, you defined the piece of text as a comment. Comments don't affect the code in any way; their only purpose is to explain the code to someone reading it.

4   Use /* */ to comment a large area.

    1.   On the line before the *Divide* method, type:

       /*

    This begins a commented area.

    2.   On the line after the end of the *Divide* method, type:

       */

    This ends the commented area.

```
/*
public double Divide(double FirstNumber, double SecondNumber)
{
    return FirstNumber / SecondNumber;
}
*/
```

Because it's commented, the *Divide* method can no longer be called. It won't be recognized as a method any more, since it's now considered to be a comment.

This technique is used widely and is known as "commenting out" a method. It is more useful than deleting the method because if you later find that you need it again you only need to remove the comment markers.

tip

Comment shortcuts

You can quickly comment and uncomment code using the comment buttons on the toolbar:

Clicking these buttons will comment or uncomment whatever code is currently selected. You can use them to comment and uncomment large amounts of code very quickly.

These buttons work on HTML and JavaScript code as well as C#.

You can use /* */ comments to create large, multi-line comments.

3. Remove the comment marks from the *Divide* method so it is recognized as a method again.

```
public double Divide(double FirstNumber, double SecondNumber)
{
    return FirstNumber / SecondNumber;
}
```

5 Add a comment at the end of a line.

It's often tidier to add your comments at the end of the line they explain rather than before it. This is known as an "in-line comment".

1. Remove the line:

   //Add FirstNumber and SecondNumber

2. Change the line:

   return RoundNumber(FirstNumber + SecondNumber);

   to:

   return RoundNumber(FirstNumber + SecondNumber);
   //Add FirstNumber and SecondNumber

```
public static double Add(double FirstNumber, double SecondNumber)
{
    return RoundNumber(FirstNumber + SecondNumber); //Add FirstNumber and SecondNumber
}
```

This is usually the best way to comment short lines of code.

6 Add a comment in mid-line using /* */.

Using /* */, you can even add comments in the middle of a line of code. This can make it confusing to look at, so think carefully before doing so.

1. Change the line:

   public double Divide(double FirstNumber, double SecondNumber)

   to:

   public double Divide(double FirstNumber,
   double SecondNumber /* Denominator */)

```
public double Divide(double FirstNumber, double SecondNumber /* Denominator */)
{
    return FirstNumber / SecondNumber;
}
```

2. Remove the *Denominator* comment. You're going to replace it with something more useful in the next lesson.

```
public double Divide(double FirstNumber, double SecondNumber)
{
    return FirstNumber / SecondNumber;
}
```

7 Close Visual Studio.

Lesson 7-8: Use summaries

In *Lesson 5-1: Use IntelliSense*, you saw that descriptions of methods and arguments appear in the IntelliSense menu.

You can add these descriptions to your own classes by using XML summaries. You'll create some of these in this lesson.

1   Open *My Project* from your sample files folder.

2   Open *CalculatorFunctions.cs*.

3   Examine a summary from the .NET library.

    1.   Add a new line to one of the event handlers.

    2.   On the new line, type: **Math.Round**

       This will cause the IntelliSense menu to appear.

> decimal Math.Round(decimal d, int decimals, MidpointRounding mode) (+ 7 overload(s))
> Rounds a decimal value to a specified number of fractional digits. A parameter specifies how to round the value if it is midway between two other numbers.

       You will see that the description of the *Math.Round* method is: *Rounds a decimal value to a specified number of fractional digits…*

    3.   Type an opening bracket: **(**

       This should cause the IntelliSense menu to change to show the description of the method's arguments. If it doesn't, delete what you've typed and retype:

       Math.Round(

> ▲ 1 of 8 ▼ decimal Math.Round(**decimal d**)
> Rounds a decimal value to the nearest integral value.
> *d: A decimal number to be rounded.*

       You'll see that the method has a *decimal* argument called *d*, which has the description: *A decimal number to be rounded*.

       You can use the black arrows or arrow keys on your keyboard to see the different groups of arguments that the method is able to process.

    4.   Delete the *Math.Round* line of code.

4   Add an XML summary.

    1.   Add a new line before the *RoundNumber* method.

    2.   Type three forward slashes: ///

```
///
private static double RoundNumber(double Number)
```

       As soon as you type the last forward slash, the framework for an XML summary will automatically be created.

```
/// <summary>
///
/// </summary>
/// <param name="Number"></param>
/// <returns></returns>
private static double RoundNumber(double Number)
```

note

When to use summaries

Summaries aren't always necessary. Event handlers on your pages don't often need summaries since it is usually already clear what they do.

It is good practice to add summaries to every new class you create.

Use your best judgment when working on classes that were automatically created by Visual Studio (such as code-behind files).

note

The *<returns>* tag

You didn't populate the *<returns>* tag in this lesson, but you probably guessed that it is used to describe the value the method returns.

The *returns* description isn't visible in the IntelliSense menu so it would only be visible to someone looking at the class itself.

The *returns* tag is also read by Visual Studio's automatic documentation tool (see below)

note

Automatic documentation

Summaries aren't just useful for making your code easier to read. Visual Studio can use them to automatically create documentation for your code.

You can learn about automatic documentation in the Expert Skills book in this series.

5   Add the method description.

1. Type the following on the blank line between the *<summary>* tags:

    Rounds a number to two decimal places.

    ```
    /// <summary>
    /// Rounds a number to two decimal places.
    /// </summary>
    ```

2. Add a new line to the *Add* method.

3. On the new line, type: **RoundNumber**

    The IntelliSense menu appears, and you can see that your method now has a description just like the ones from the .NET library.

    ```
    double CalculatorFunctions.RoundNumber(double Number)
    Rounds a number to two decimal places.
    ```

4. Remove the *RoundNumber* code from the *Add* method.

6   Add a description for the *Number* argument.

1. Add the following inside the *<param>* tags in the summary:

    Number to be rounded.

    ```
    /// <summary>
    /// Rounds a number to two decimal places.
    /// </summary>
    /// <param name="Number">Number to be rounded.</param>
    /// <returns></returns>
    ```

2. Add a new line to the *Add* method.

3. On the new line, type: **RoundNumber(**

    The bracket is needed to open the description of the arguments.

    You'll see that the *Number* argument is now described at the bottom of the summary.

    ```
    double CalculatorFunctions.RoundNumber(double Number)
    Rounds a number to two decimal places.
    Number: Number to be rounded.
    ```

4. Remove the *RoundNumber* code you added to the *Add* method.

    ```
    public static double Add(double FirstNumber, double SecondNumber)
    {
        return RoundNumber(FirstNumber + SecondNumber); //Add FirstNu
    }
    ```

By using summaries, you can make your code even easier for other developers to use and maintain. They are extremely useful when working in a team environment.

7   Close Visual Studio.

Session 7: Exercise

1   Open the *Spark* sample project and open *viewtransactions.aspx* in *Design* view.

2   Add a *SelectedIndexChanged* event handler to the *DropDownListSelectedPeriod* control.

3   Add an *if* statement to the event handler that checks if the value of the *DropDownListSelectPeriod* control's *SelectedValue* property is equal to: **"2010"**

4   If the value of the property is **"2010"**, make your *if* statement change the *Panel2010.Visible* property to **true** and the *Panel2011.Visible* property to **false.**

5   Use *else if* to check if the value of the property is **"2011"**. If it is, set the *Panel2011.Visible* property to **true** and the *Panel2010.Visible* property to **false.**

6   Open viewtransactions.aspx in your browser and test your code.

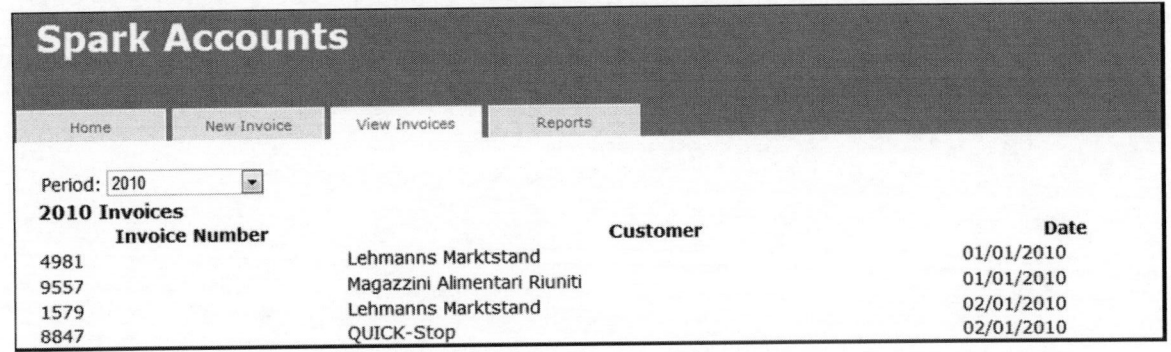

7   Close your browser and open the code-behind file of *newtransaction.aspx*.

8   Add an *if* statement to the start of the *ButtonSubmit_Click* event handler to check if the value of the *DropDownListCustomer* control's *SelectedValue* property is **"6"**, **"9"** or **"11"**. If so, set the *Text* property of the *LabelError* control to:
That customer is currently out of use

9   Add an *else* statement to the *ButtonSubmit_Click* event handler which will run if the value of the property is not **"6"**, **"9"** or **"11"**.

10   Add *try* and *catch* statements to the *ButtonSubmit_Click* event handler and place any error messages in the *Text* property of the *LabelError* control.

11   Add a comment to the *CalculateVAT* method to explain what it does. (VAT or Value Added Tax is a sales tax levied in Europe).

12   Add a summary to the *CalculateVAT* method and populate it with useful descriptions.

Spark - start

Spark - end

If you need help slide the page to the left

Session 7: Exercise Answers

These are the four questions that students find the most difficult to answer:

Q 10	Q 9	Q 8	Q 4
Add the code: **try** **{** ...at the very beginning of the event handler. At the very end of the event handler, add: **}** **catch (Exception Ex)** **{** 　**LabelError.Text =** 　**Ex.Message;** **}** This was covered in: *Lesson 7-6: Use try and catch to handle errors.*	After the end of your last *if* statement, add the code: **else** **{** **}** This was covered in: *Lesson 7-2: Use else and else if.*	Use the following lines of code: **string CustomerID = DropDownListCustomer .SelectedValue;** **if (CustomerID == "6"** **|| CustomerID == "9"** **|| CustomerID == "11")** **{** 　**LabelError.Text =** 　**"That customer is** 　**currently out of use.";** **}** This was covered in: *Lesson 7-3: Use basic logical operators.*	Use the following lines of code: **if** **(DropDownListSelectPeriod .SelectedValue == "2010")** **{** 　**Panel2010.Visible = true;** 　**Panel2011.Visible = false;** **}** This was covered in: *Lesson 7-1: Use the if statement.*

If you have difficulty with the other questions, here are the lessons that cover the relevant skills:

1　　Refer to: Lesson 1-7: Manage a project with the Solution Explorer.

2　　Refer to: Lesson 3-2: Add event handlers to Controls.

3　　Refer to: Lesson 7-1: Use the if statement.

5　　Refer to: Lesson 7-2: Use else and else if.

6　　Refer to: Lesson 1-8: Run a project in debug mode.

7　　Refer to: Lesson 1-7: Manage a project with the Solution Explorer.

11　　Refer to: Lesson 7-7: Use comments.

12　　Refer to: Lesson 7-8: Use summaries.

Session Eight: C# Collections and Loops

> My mind seems to have become a kind of machine for grinding general laws out of large collections of facts.
>
> *Charles Darwin, English naturalist (1809 – 1882)*

Believe it or not, you now know almost all of the basic principles of writing C# code!

After this session, you'll be spending the rest of the book applying what you've learned to access databases and create useful dynamic web sites.

In this session, the last on C# code, you'll learn how to deal with collections of objects and iterate through them.

Session Objectives

By the end of this session you will be able to:

- Create an array
- Create a collection
- Iterate through a collection using a foreach loop
- Iterate through a collection using a for loop
- Use break and return

Lesson 8-1: Create an array

Arrays are the simplest type of collection in C#, but they are also the most limited. Using an array, you can store multiple values in a single variable.

1   Open *Spark* from your sample files folder.

2   Open *Utilities.cs*.

This is a static class. As you may remember from *Lesson 6-9: Create a static method,* this means that it can be used without creating an instance of the class.

3   Add a public method to the class.

Use the following code:

public static string GetBlockedCustomers()
{
}

```
public static class Utilities
{
    public static string GetBlockedCustomers()
    {
    }
```

When complete, this method will return a list of blocked customer ID numbers as an array.

4   Create a string array in the new method.

Create an array using the following code:

string[] Customers = new string[3];

```
public static string GetBlockedCustomers()
{
    string[] Customers = new string[3];
}
```

string[] defines a new array of *string* variables. You can place square brackets *[]* after any type of variable to create an array of that type.

The *[3]* means that the new array will be able to contain three strings.

5   Populate the array.

It's easy to set the values in an array:

1. Add the following code to set the value of the first element in the array: **Customers[0] = "6";**

2. Add the following code to set the second value in the array: **Customers[1] = "9";**

3. Set the third value using similar code: **Customers[2] = "11";**

```
public static string GetBlockedCustomers()
{
    string[] Customers = new string[3];
    Customers[0] = "6";
    Customers[1] = "9";
    Customers[2] = "11";
}
```

tip

Dynamic arrays

Although you can't change the size of an array without recreating it, a new array will automatically size itself if you specify the contents when you create it.

Using this syntax uses less code, so it can be ideal for short arrays such as the one you create in this lesson.

You could create this lesson's array in a single line of code, as follows:

string[] Customers =
new string[]{"6","9","11"};

If you are not completing the course incrementally use the sample file: **Lesson 8-1** to begin this lesson.

Sample files with the starting point for each lesson are also provided for all of the other lessons in this session.

Your array will now contain the values *6, 9* and *11*.

You might think that you should be assigning a value to *Customers[3]*, but as you can see, the first element's index number is *[0]*.

When you created a *string[3]* array, you created a string array with 3 elements: [0], [1] and [2]. That's because all collections in C# are zero based. This was discussed in: *Lesson 4-7: Use drop down lists (zero-based indexing sidebar).*

<table>
<tr><td>

note

Multidimensional arrays

The array you create in this lesson has a single dimension, but it's possible to create multidimensional arrays with elements such as *string[1,7]*. These are useful for situations where you have a grid of data.

Multidimensional arrays are covered in depth in the Expert Skills book in this series.

</td></tr>
</table>

6   Make the method return the array.

   1.   Change the line that starts the method to:

   public static string[] GetBlockedCustomers()

   The *string[]* return value is needed to tell the method that it will return an array rather than a single string.

   2.   Add the following line at the end of the method:

   return Customers;

```
public static string[] GetBlockedCustomers()
{
    string[] Customers = new string[3];
    Customers[0] = "6";
    Customers[1] = "9";
    Customers[2] = "11";
    return Customers;
}
```

This will return the *Customers* array when the method is called.

7   Test the array on the *newstransaction.aspx* page.

   1.   Open the code-behind file of *newtransaction.aspx*.

   2.   Find the line that checks *CustomerID* numbers.

```
if (CustomerID == "6" || CustomerID == "9" || CustomerID == "11")
{
    LabelError.Text = "That customer is currently out of use.";
}
```

You created this line in the session 7 exercise so it may not be identical to the above example.

   3.   Change the code to:

   if(Utilities.GetBlockedCustomers().
   Contains(DropDownListCustomer.SelectedValue))

```
if (Utilities.GetBlockedCustomers().Contains(DropDownListCustomer.SelectedValue))
{
    LabelError.Text = "That customer is currently out of use";
}
```

By using the *Contains* method of the array, you have simplified the *if* statement considerably. If you had 50 customers you wanted to block this would almost be a necessity, although you would normally use a database to store a list that long.

By using an array, you have centralized your list of blocked customers and made it much easier to work with.

Lesson 8-2: Create a collection

Collections are a more advanced way of storing multiple values inside a single object. Unlike arrays, which have a fixed size once they are created, you can add and remove items from collections. For most purposes collections are more convenient to work with than arrays.

In this lesson you'll create a *List* collection and add some items to it.

1   Open *Spark* from your sample files folder.

2   Open *Utilities.cs*.

3   Remove the contents of the *GetBlockedCustomers* method.

4   Create a *List* collection.

Add the following code to the *GetBlockedCustomers* method:

List<string> BlockedCustomers = new List<string>();

```
public static string GetBlockedCustomers()
{
    List<string> BlockedCustomers = new List<string>();
}
```

This creates a new *List* collection that can contain only *string* variables.

You can put any data type between the < > marks to create a list of that type. *List<int>* would create a list of *int* variables, for example.

If you wanted a *List* to contain more than one type of variable, you would have to use a *List<object>*, but you would then have to convert the objects back to their original types when you retrieved them.

tip

Quick lists

Just like with arrays, you can populate a *List* with a single line of code.

You could have created the *List* used in this lesson by simply typing:

List<string> BlockedCustomers = new List<string>()
{ "6", "9", "11" };

Of course, the huge advantage of lists is their ability to add and remove items.

5   Add items to the *List*.

1.   Add the following code to add a value to the *List*.

BlockedCustomers.Add("6");

```
public static string GetBlockedCustomers()
{
    List<string> BlockedCustomers = new List<string>();
    BlockedCustomers.Add("6");
}
```

As you can see, it's very easy to add a value to a list.

2.   Add the following code to add the other two values to the list:

BlockedCustomers.Add("9");
BlockedCustomers.Add("11");

```
public static string GetBlockedCustomers()
{
    List<string> BlockedCustomers = new List<string>();
    BlockedCustomers.Add("6");
    BlockedCustomers.Add("9");
    BlockedCustomers.Add("11");
}
```

You now have a list containing the three strings that you previously stored in an array in: *Lesson 8-1: Create an array.*

note

Other types of collection

If you look at the *using* lines at the top of the class, you'll see *System.Collections.Generic*. This is where the *List* class is defined, and it contains other types of collection too.

Try typing the following into any event handler:

System.Collections.Generic.

...and you'll see a list of collection types in the IntelliSense menu.

- KeyValuePair<>
- LinkedList<>
- LinkedListNode<>
- List<>
- Queue<>
- SortedDictionary<>
- SortedList<>
- SortedSet<>
- Stack<>

Two of the most useful are:

Dictionary
Works the same way as a *List*, but allows you to give each value a *Key*, which you can use to retrieve the value. This is very similar to the way *ViewState* and *Session* work, as you may recall from: *Lesson 3-11: Send data between pages.*

SortedList
Very similar to a *List*, but has methods to easily sort the contents.

For most purposes the *List* collection is the best choice.

6   Remove an item from the *List*.

You can remove an item from a list using the *Remove* method. Add the following code to the end of the method:

BlockedCustomers.Remove("11");

```
BlockedCustomers.Add("11");
BlockedCustomers.Remove("11");
```

7   Retrieve a single item from a *List*.

Lists have zero-based index numbers just like arrays. You can retrieve the second item from the list and put its value into a *string* variable with the code:

string SecondCustomer = BlockedCustomers[1];

```
BlockedCustomers.Remove("11");
string SecondCustomer = BlockedCustomers[1];
```

8   Make the method return the *List*.

You learned how to return values from methods in: *Lesson 6-7: Create methods that return a value.*

1.   Change the line that defines the method to:

public static List<string> GetBlockedCustomers()

Unsurprisingly, you need to set the return value of the *GetBlockedCustomers* method to *List<string>* in order to return the *List* collection.

2.   Add the following line at the end of the method:

return BlockedCustomers;

```
public static List<string> GetBlockedCustomers()
{
    List<string> BlockedCustomers = new List<string>();
    BlockedCustomers.Add("6");
    BlockedCustomers.Add("9");
    BlockedCustomers.Add("11");
    BlockedCustomers.Remove("11");
    string SecondCustomer = BlockedCustomers[1];
    return BlockedCustomers;
}
```

This will return the *List* collection when the method is called.

9   Use the *List*.

1.   Open the code-behind file of *newtransaction.aspx*.

2.   Find the line:

**if (Utilities.GetBlockedCustomers()
.Contains(DropDownListCustomer.SelectedValue))**

```
if (Utilities.GetBlockedCustomers().Contains(DropDownListCustomer.SelectedValue))
{
    LabelError.Text = "That customer is currently out of use";
}
```

You'll notice there are no errors appearing. The *List* collection has a *Contains* method just like an array so there's no need to change the code here at all!

Lesson 8-3: Iterate through a collection using foreach

One of the most common things you'll need to do with collections is to iterate through each item in the collection. Iterating through a collection is a little like flicking through the pages in a book.

If you knew the number of items in a collection, you could directly address them using *Collection[0], Collection[1]*, etc. but most of the time you won't know in advance how many items your collection has.

In this lesson you will use a *foreach* loop to iterate through each item in a collection.

1   Open *My Project* from your sample files folder.

2   Open *CalculatorFunctions.cs*.

3   Add a method to total all of the numbers in a list of *int* variables.

> You should be quite familiar with creating methods by now. Use the following code:
>
> **public static int TotalNumbers(List<int> ListToTotal)**
> **{**
> **}**
>
> ```
> public static int TotalNumbers(List<int> ListToTotal)
> {
>
> }
> ```
>
> This method accepts a *List<int>* collection as an argument and returns an *int* value. When this method is complete it will add up the values of each element in the *ListToTotal* collection and then return the total.
>
> This method is *static*, so you won't need to create an instance of the *CalculatorFunctions* class to call the method.

4   Create an *int* variable called: **Total**

> To return the total as an *int* value, you'll need to create an *int* variable to return. Create one in the *TotalNumbers* method using the following code:
>
> **int Total = 0;**
>
> ```
> public static int TotalNumbers(List<int> ListToTotal)
> {
>     int Total = 0;
> }
> ```
>
> The *Total* variable is assigned a value of *0*. You'll add the value of each element in the *ListToTotal* collection to the *Total* variable as you iterate through them.

5   Iterate through each item in *ListToTotal* using *foreach*.

> Add the following code to the *TotalNumbers* method:

foreach (int NumberToTotal in ListToTotal) { }

```
int Total = 0;
foreach (int NumberToTotal in ListToTotal)
{

}
```

The *NumberToTotal* variable is called the *Iteration Variable*. The code will loop through all of the items in the *ListToTotal* collection. For each iteration, the value of the current item will appear in the *NumberToTotal* iteration variable.

6 **Add code to sum the total in the *Total* variable.**

Add the following code inside the curly brackets following the *foreach* statement:

Total = Total + NumberToTotal;

As the *foreach* statement iterates through each item in the *ListToTotal* collection, their values will be added to the *Total* variable.

7 **Add code to return the total value.**

At the end of the method, you'll need to return the *Total* variable using: **return Total;**

```
int Total = 0;
foreach (int NumberToTotal in ListToTotal)
{
    Total = Total + NumberToTotal;
}
return Total;
```

8 **Try out the method on the *calculator.aspx* page.**

1. Open the code-behind file of *calculator.aspx*.

2. Remove all code from the *ButtonCalculate2_Click* event handler.

3. Add code to the method to create a *List* of *int* variables, containing some values:

   List<int> ListToTotal = new List<int>() { 12, 17, 135 };

   This *List* collection contains the integer values 12, 17 and 135. Therefore its total should come to 164.

4. Add code to call the method from the *CalculatorFunctions* class and output the result:

   int Total = CalculatorFunctions.TotalNumbers(ListToTotal);
   Response.Write(Total);

```
protected void ButtonCalculate2_Click(object sender, EventArgs e)
{
    List<int> ListToTotal = new List<int>() { 12, 17, 135 };
    int Total = CalculatorFunctions.TotalNumbers(ListToTotal);
    Response.Write(Total);
}
```

5. View *calculator.aspx* in your browser and click the second button (named *Button*).

   The number *164* is displayed, showing that your method totaled the numbers correctly!

http://localhost:51163/calculator.aspx

164

Lesson 8-4: Iterate through a collection using a for loop

foreach is a really easy way to iterate through each item in a collection, but it has a major limitation. You can't modify the value in the iteration variable.

Another way to loop through all of the items in a collection is using a *for* loop. *for* loops don't have to be used with collections, they can be used for any piece of code that you want to run several times.

1   Open *My Project* from your sample files folder.

2   Open *CalculatorFunctions.cs*.

3   Create a new method called: **AddToNumbers**

Your new method is going to take a *List* collection containing *int* variables and add an *int* value to each item in the collection.

Use the following code:

public static void AddToNumbers(int AmountToAdd, List<int> Numbers)
{
}

```
public static void AddToNumbers(int AmountToAdd, List<int> Numbers)
{

}
```

4   Create a *for* loop to iterate through the *List* collection.

1. Store the number of items in the *List* collection in a variable using:

    int NumberOfNumbers = Numbers.Count;

    This isn't strictly necessary, but it will make the next step easier to understand.

2. Add the following code:

    for (int Counter = 0; Counter < NumberOfNumbers; Counter++)
    { }

```
public static void AddToNumbers(int AmountToAdd, List<int> Numbers)
{
    int NumberOfNumbers = Numbers.Count;
    for (int Counter = 0; Counter < NumberOfNumbers; Counter++)
    {

    }
}
```

This is the *for* loop. If you look at each part of it in turn it is easier to understand:

int Counter = 0
This creates a new *int* variable called *Counter* with a value of zero that will identify the current iteration in the loop.

Counter < NumberOfNumbers

This logical test determines when the loop will end. In this case, the loop will run as long as the value of *Counter* is less than the value of *NumberOfNumbers*.

Counter++

This code runs at the end of each iteration. In this case, it adds one to the value of the *Counter* variable (You learned about ++ in: *Lesson 5-10: Perform basic mathematical operations*).

Any code placed between the curly brackets will run as many times as there are items in the *Numbers* collection.

5 Add code to add a value to each item in the collection.

Add the following code inside the *for* loop:

Numbers[Counter] = Numbers[Counter] + AmountToAdd;

```
public static void AddToNumbers(int AmountToAdd, List<int> Numbers)
{
    int NumberOfNumbers = Numbers.Count;
    for (int Counter = 0; Counter < NumberOfNumbers; Counter++)
    {
        Numbers[Counter] = Numbers[Counter] + AmountToAdd;
    }
}
```

By using the *Counter* variable, you can access each item in the *Numbers* collection by its index, just as you did with arrays in: *Lesson 8-1: Create an array*.

Here, you're adding the value of the *AmountToAdd* variable onto the value of each item in the *Numbers* collection as you iterate through the collection.

6 Try out the method on the *calculator.aspx* page.

1. Open the code-behind of *calculator.aspx*.

2. Add a new line after the *List<int> ListToTotal…* line.

3. Call the *AddToNumbers* method on the new line, using the following code:

CalculatorFunctions.AddToNumbers(10, ListToTotal);

```
protected void ButtonCalculate2_Click(object sender, EventArgs e)
{
    List<int> ListToTotal = new List<int>() { 12, 17, 135 };
    CalculatorFunctions.AddToNumbers(10, ListToTotal);
    int Total = CalculatorFunctions.TotalNumbers(ListToTotal);
    Response.Write(Total);
}
```

This code calls your method, which will add 10 to each of the numbers in the *ListToTotal* collection. If it works correctly, you can expect the total to be *194* (12 + 10 + 17 +10 + 135 + 10).

4. View *calculator.aspx* in your browser and click the second button (named *Button*).

The number *194* is displayed, indicating that your method worked correctly!

note

Passing arguments by reference and by value

All of the simple variable types (such as *int, string, bool* and *double*) are, by default, sent to methods *by value* when used as arguments.

Some variable types (such as *List* collections) are sent to methods *by reference* when used as arguments.

The reason that the *AddToNumbers* method was able to permanently change the values in the *ListToTotal* collection was because the collection was sent *by reference*.

You'll learn more about sending variables *by reference* and *by value* in the Expert Skills book in this series.

For the moment, all you need to know is that methods can only permanently change the values of arguments when they are passed by reference.

http://localhost:51163/calculator.aspx

194

Lesson 8-5: Use break and return

You've already used *return* to return a value from a method, but *return* and the similar *break* can also be used to escape from loops (but this is poor programming practice – see sidebar).

In this lesson you'll use *break* and *return* to escape from a loop.

1   Open *My Project* from your sample files folder.

2   Open *CalculatorFunctions.cs*.

3   Make the *AddToNumbers* method stop iterating when it encounters a value of 17 using *break*.

Using *break*, you can exit out of a loop without exiting the method.

1. Add the following code immediately after the first curly bracket of the *for* loop:

   if (Numbers[Counter] == 17)
   {
      break;
   }

```
public static void AddToNumbers(int AmountToAdd, List<int> Numbers)
{
    int NumberOfNumbers = Numbers.Count;
    for (int Counter = 0; Counter < NumberOfNumbers; Counter++)
    {
        if (Numbers[Counter] == 17)
        {
            break;
        }
        Numbers[Counter] = Numbers[Counter] + AmountToAdd;
    }
}
```

   This is a simple *if* statement that checks if the current item in the *Numbers* collection has a value of *17*. When this value is encountered it exits the *for* loop using *break*.

2. View *calculator.aspx* in your browser and click the *Button* button.

   ```
   http://localhost:51163/calculator.aspx

   174
   ```

   This time you'll see a total of *174* rather than the *194* you were expecting. This is because your loop stops when it encounters a value of *17*, so instead of:

   $(12 + 10) + (17 + 10) + (135 + 10) = 194$

   ...you're seeing:

   $(12 + 10) + 17 + 135 = 174$

3. Close your browser.

important

Using *break* and *return*

It is best practice to avoid using *break* and *return* in loops wherever possible.

Instead of using *break* in this example, it would have been better to use a simple *if* statement.

The reason that this is best practice is because methods are expected to run from beginning to end through a logical process. Exiting in the middle of that process makes your code harder to understand.

It's still important to recognize *break* and *return*, since not all programmers will stick to that standard.

4 Make the *AddToNumbers* method perform an operation after exiting the loop.

1. Add the following code to the end of the *AddToNumbers* method, outside the *for* loop's curly brackets:

Numbers[0] = Numbers[0] + 999;

```
public static void AddToNumbers(int AmountToAdd, List<int> Numbers)
{
    int NumberOfNumbers = Numbers.Count;
    for (int Counter = 0; Counter < NumberOfNumbers; Counter++)
    {
        if (Numbers[Counter] == 17)
        {
            break;
        }
        Numbers[Counter] = Numbers[Counter] + AmountToAdd;
    }
    Numbers[0] = Numbers[0] + 999;
}
```

2. View *calculator.aspx* in your browser and click *Button* again.

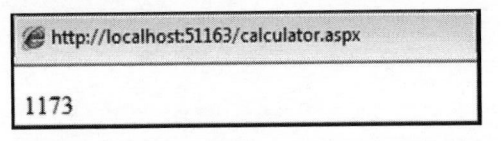

http://localhost:51163/calculator.aspx

1173

This time you'll see that the total comes to *1173*. Your calculation is now:

(12 + 10) + 17+ 135 + 999 = 1173

Although your *break* exited from the *for* loop, it didn't exit the method. This meant that the code following the closing curly bracket of the loop was executed.

3. Close your browser.

5 Change *break* to *return*.

As you might have guessed, *return* will exit the entire method rather than just exiting the loop.

1. Change your *break* to: **return**

```
public static void AddToNumbers(int AmountToAdd, List<int> Numbers)
{
    int NumberOfNumbers = Numbers.Count;
    for (int Counter = 0; Counter < NumberOfNumbers; Counter++)
    {
        if (Numbers[Counter] == 17)
        {
            return;
        }
        Numbers[Counter] = Numbers[Counter] + AmountToAdd;
    }
    Numbers[0] = Numbers[0] + 999;
}
```

2. View *calculator.aspx* in your browser and click *Button*.

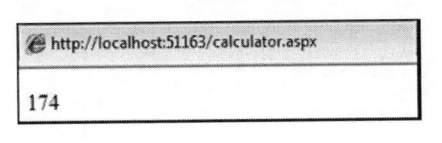

http://localhost:51163/calculator.aspx

174

You'll see that the total is now *174*, as it was earlier in this lesson. The method terminated when *return* was encountered in your code. The line that added *999* was never reached.

break and *return* can be used in the same way in a *foreach* or *while* loop.

Session 8: Exercise

1   Open the *My Project* sample project and create a new class called: **MyData.cs**

2   Add a new public method called **GetNumbers**, which returns an array of *int* variables.

    (You'll see an error at this stage as you have not yet created code that returns a value).

3   Create an array of *int* variables called **Numbers** in the *GetNumbers* method containing the numbers: **1, 1, 3, 5, 8** and make the method return the array.

    (The previously flagged error should disappear as soon as you specify the return value).

4   Add a new public method called **GetNames**, which returns a *List* of *string* variables.

    (You'll see an error at this stage as you have not yet created code that returns a value).

5   Create a *List* of *string* variables called **Names** in the *GetNames* method containing the names: **"Mike"**, **"Simon"**, **"Emily"** and make the method return it.

    (The previously flagged error should disappear as soon as you specify the return value).

6   Add a new public method called **ProcessNames**, which doesn't return a value.

7   Create a *List* of *string* variables called **NamesToProcess** in the *ProcessNames* method and populate it with the *List* collection returned by the *GetNames()* method.

8   Use a *for* loop to loop through the list of names and make each one upper case using the *ToUpper* method of the *string* variable type.

9   Add a new public method called **AppendNames** which returns a *string* value.

    (You'll see an error at this stage as you have not yet created code that returns a value).

10   In the new method, add a *foreach* loop which loops through the names returned by the *GetNames* method and appends them all to a single *string* variable. Make the method return the *string*.

11   Add a new page called **test.aspx** and use the *Page_Load* event handler to call the *AppendNames* method of the *MyData* class and output the return value to the top of the web page.

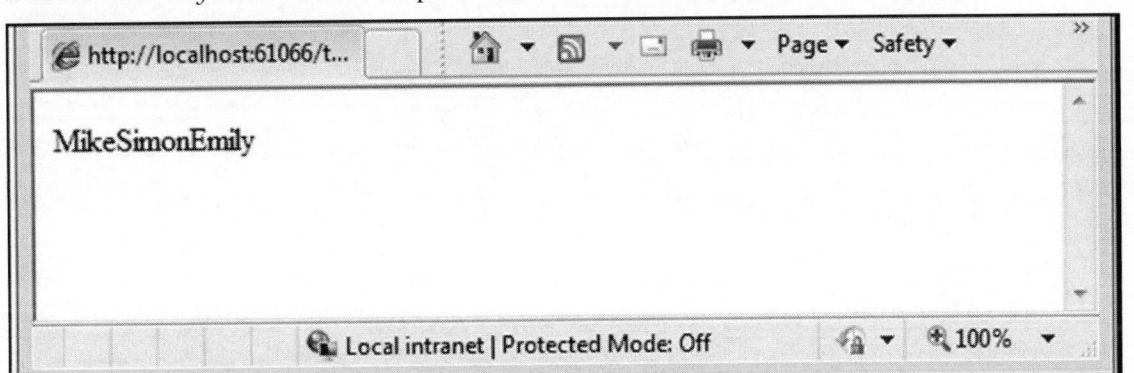

Session 8: Exercise Answers

These are the four questions that students find the most difficult to answer:

Q 10	Q 8	Q 5	Q 3
| Use the following code:<br><br>```
public string
AppendNames()
{
   string
   AppendedNames = "";
   foreach (string Name
   in GetNames())
   {
      AppendedNames =
      AppendedNames +
      Name;
   }
   return
   AppendedNames;
}
```<br><br>This was covered in: *Lesson 8-3: Iterate through a collection using foreach.* | Use the following code:<br><br>```
public void
ProcessNames()
{
   List<string> Names =
   GetNames();
   for (int Counter = 0;
   Counter <
   Names.Count;
   Counter++)
   {
      Names[Counter] =
      Names[Counter]
      .ToUpper();
   }
}
```<br><br>This was covered in: *Lesson 8-4: Iterate through a collection using a for loop.* | Use the following code:<br><br>```
public List<string>
GetNames()
{
   List<string> Names =
   new List<string>();
   Names.Add("Mike");
   Names.Add("Simon");
   Names.Add("Emily");
   return Names;
}
```<br><br>It is also possible to do this using less code.<br><br>This was covered in: *Lesson 8-2: Create a collection.* | Use the following code:<br><br>```
public int[]
GetNumbers()
{
   int[] Numbers =
   new int[5];
   Numbers[0] = 1;
   Numbers[1] = 1;
   Numbers[2] = 3;
   Numbers[3] = 5;
   Numbers[4] = 8;
   return Numbers;
}
```<br><br>It is also possible to do this using less code.<br><br>Both this and the alternative technique were covered in: *Lesson 8-1: Create an array.* |

If you have difficulty with the other questions, here are the lessons that cover the relevant skills:

1   Refer to: Lesson 6-1: Create a class.

2   Refer to: Lesson 6-7: Create methods that return a value, Lesson 8-1: Create an array.

4   Refer to: Lesson 6-7: Create methods that return a value, Lesson 8-2: Create a collection.

6   Refer to: Lesson 6-5: Create and use methods.

7   Refer to: Lesson 8-2: Create a collection.

9   Refer to: Lesson 6-7: Create methods that return a value.

11   Refer to: Lesson 1-7: Manage a project with the Solution Explorer, Lesson 6-2: Create an instance of a class, Lesson 3-7: Understand Request and Response.

Session Nine: Authentication

> Even paranoids have real enemies.
>
> *Delmore Schwartz, American poet and writer (1913 – 1966)*

One of the most common requirements for a dynamic web application is the ability for your users to create accounts and log in to a member's area. This process is called *authentication*.

In the early days of the web creating a login system was a very complicated process, but ASP.NET makes it surprisingly easy to create a secure login system without writing any C# code.

In this session you'll learn everything you need to set up a web site with user accounts and a member's area.

Session Objectives

By the end of this session you will be able to:

- Use .NET's built-in security features
- Manage a site with ASP.NET Configuration
- Change authentication types
- Use the Login control
- Customize the Login control
- Use the CreateUserWizard control
- Use other login controls
- Add folder-level security
- Set up roles
- Use C# to limit access
- Use the security wizard

Lesson 9-1: Use .NET's built-in security features

Back in *Lesson 1-5: Create an ASP.NET Web Application project*, you created a standard project. The default project already contains a login system of its own! If you don't need anything more advanced, you can simply customize the pages that are created for you.

In this lesson, you'll look at the pages that are created automatically and see how they can be used.

1   Open Visual Studio.

2   Create a new *ASP.NET Web Application* project called **My Membership** in your sample files folder.

   You first learned how to do this in: *Lesson 1-5: Create an ASP.NET Web Application project*.

3   Create a new account.

   1.   View *register.aspx* in your browser.

        You will find it in the *Account* folder.

   2.   Complete the form using the password **learnasp**. Make a careful note of your chosen *User Name* as you will need it later.

   3.   Click *Create User*.

        You have now created a user account and will be automatically logged in.

        Welcome **ssmart**! [Log Out]

4   Log out of the site.

   To log out, simply click the *Log Out* button in the top-right corner of the page.

   Welcome **ssmart**! [Log Out]

   Alternatively, close the window and reopen it from *Visual Studio*.

5 Log in to the site with your new username and password.

1. Close your browser window if it is open.

2. View *Login.aspx* in your browser.

   Login.aspx can be found in the *Account* folder.

3. Enter your username and password.

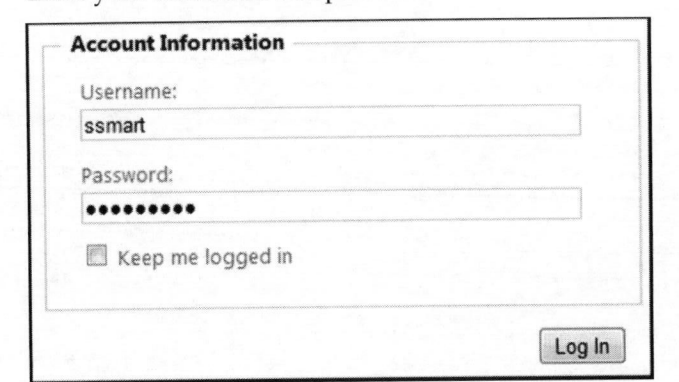

   Enter the username and password for the account you created earlier in this lesson.

4. Click *Log In*.

   You will once again be logged into the site.

   As you can see, it's very easy to create a site with login capabilities by simply customizing the automatically-generated pages.

   You'll learn more about customizing the default ASP.NET application in: *Lesson 12-1: Use a master page*.

   In the rest of this session you'll learn more about how the ASP.NET authentication system works and learn to create similar pages yourself.

6 Close your web browser and close Visual Studio.

Lesson 9-2: Manage a site with ASP.NET Configuration

In the previous lesson you saw how easily you can set up a site to allow registration and membership, but you might be wondering how you can manage your members and change security settings.

You can do this very easily using the *ASP.NET Configuration* utility.

1 **Open *MyMembership* from your sample files folder.**

2 **Open the *ASP.NET Configuration* utility.**

tip

You can also access the *ASP.NET Configuration* utility by clicking the shortcut button at the top of the *Solution Explorer:*

1. Open *Default.aspx* in *Source* view.

   You need to have a page open in order for the *Project* menu to be available.

2. Click Project→ASP.NET Configuration.

   The *ASP.NET Configuration* utility will start in a new browser window.

3 **View existing users.**

note

The Provider tab

As you'll see later in this session, ASP.NET has many controls that can be dropped onto the page to automatically interface with the membership database.

The provider is a class that provides all of the services these controls need to function.

If you had very specialized membership requirements you could write your own provider class, but this isn't usually necessary.

The provider tab allows you to specify an alternate custom provider in these rare cases.

1. Click *Security*, either at the top of the page or in the table.

   The security tab will open.

2. Click *Manage Users*.

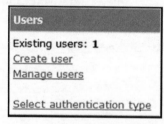

As you can see, you could create a user here using the *Create user* option, but you could just as easily use the *Register.aspx* page on your site.

You will see a list of existing users. At the moment there is only one user, which you created in: *Lesson 9-1: Use .NET's built-in security features*. As you can see, you can easily edit and delete the user from here.

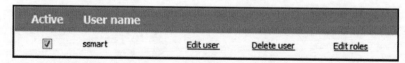

Active	User name			
☑	ssmart	Edit user	Delete user	Edit roles

You will learn about roles in: *Lesson 9-9: Set up roles*.

If you are not completing the course incrementally use the sample file: **Lesson 9-2** to begin this lesson.

Sample files with the starting point for each lesson are also provided for all of the other lessons in this session.

4 **Define email settings.**

note

Taking your application offline

You might have noticed the *Take offline* option on ASP.NET Configuration utility's *Application* tab.

If you click this option, your site will be taken offline. When the site is offline, none of the pages or files in the site will be accessible.

note

Configuring your provider

The *ASP.NET Configuration* utility is unfortunately limited in some areas. There are a number of important settings you can only change by editing the *Web.config* file.

If you open *Web.config* and look for the *AspNetSqlMembershipProvider* element, you will see that it has settings such as *minRequiredPasswordLength*, which determines how long a user's password must be.

The only way to change these settings is to change them manually in *Web.config*.

To enable your application to send email, you need to configure its email settings. You can do that easily using the *ASP.NET Configuration* utility.

1. Click the *Application* tab at the top of the screen.

    The settings on this page come from your *Web.config* file. You learned about *Web.config* settings in: *Lesson 3-13: Edit the Web.config file*.

    Most of the options on this page are quite self-explanatory. *Application Settings* are your own custom application properties. You won't use them in this book but they are covered in the Expert Skills book in this series.

2. Click *Configure SMTP e-mail settings*.

3. Complete the form with valid e-mail settings.

    Valid email settings aren't essential for any of the lessons in this book, so you can skip this step if you don't have access to a mail server.

    If you'd like to set up email anyway, you can use google's free email service by signing up for a *GMail* account at *http://www.gmail.com*.

    If you are using *GMail*, the following settings were correct in May 2011 (but as with all things on the web they may change):

Server Name:	**smtp.gmail.com**
Server Port:	**587**
From:	**[Your gmail address]**
Authentication:	**Basic**
Sender's user name:	**[Your gmail address]**
Sender's password:	**[Your gmail password]**

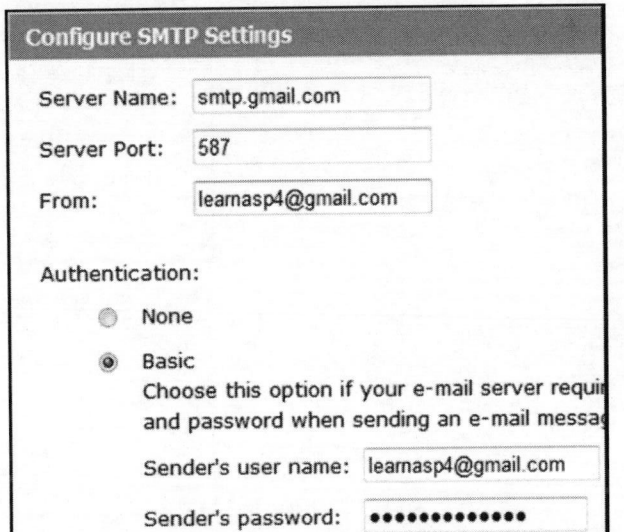

4. Click *Save*.

    Email settings are important if you want to use security features that send emails to the user, such as when the user forgets their password.

5   Close your browser and close Visual Studio.

Lesson 9-3: Change authentication types

In *Lesson 9-1: Use .NET's built-in security features,* you created a web site where users can log in with a username and password. This is called *Forms* authentication.

Forms authentication is perfect for web sites on the Internet, but it can be cumbersome if you're making a site that is only going to be used on an internal network (known as an *intranet* site).

You can use *Windows* authentication to allow your site to automatically recognize the user by their Windows username and password when used on an internal network (saving them the bother of logging in).

1   Open *MyMembership* from your sample files folder.

2   Open the *ASP.NET Configuration* utility.

3   Switch the authentication type to *Windows*.

    1.   Click *Security,* either at the top of the page or in the table.

    The security tab will open.

    2.   Click *Select Authentication Type.*

    A page will appear, prompting you to choose between *From the Internet* and *From a local network.*

    3.   Click *From a local network.*

> **How will users access your site?**
>
> ○ **From the internet**
>
> Select this option if users will access your using a web form. The site will use forms a you store in a database.
>
> ● **From a local network**
>
> Select this option if users will access your built-in Microsoft Windows authentication t password will be able to access your site.

    This is the *Windows* authentication setting.

    4.   Click *Done.*

    The button is in the bottom-right corner.

Because you are now using Windows authentication, you will no longer be able to manage users using the *ASP.NET Configuration* utility. You can't use both *Windows* and *Forms* authentication at the same time.

Note that you will no longer be able to log in using the user name and password created earlier.

---

note

Windows authentication on the Internet

Although *Forms* authentication is the preferred form of authentication on the Internet, it's still possible to use *Windows* authentication on Internet sites.

If you use *Windows* authentication on an Internet site (as opposed to intranet), visitors will be prompted to log in when they first attempt to access any page on the site.

A visitor to a site using *Windows* authentication will have to provide a valid Windows username and password for the network the site is hosted on.

Using Windows authentication on the Internet is generally not a good idea.

> **Users**
>
> The current authentication type is **Windows**. User management from within this tool is therefore disabled.
> Select authentication type

5. Close the *ASP.NET Configuration* utility.

4 **Test Windows authentication.**

1. View *Default.aspx* in your browser.

> Welcome **ssmart**! [Log Out]

In the top-right corner you will see your windows username. The new authentication method has automatically authenticated you without requiring you to log in!

See the sidebar if this doesn't happen automatically.

2. Close your browser.

5 **Switch back to *Forms* authentication.**

1. Open the *ASP.NET Configuration* utility.

2. Click the *Security* tab.

3. Click *Select Authentication Type.*

4. Click *From the Internet.*

> How will users access your site?
>
> ● **From the internet**
>   Select this option if users will access your using a web form. The site will use forms a you store in a database.
>
> ○ **From a local network**
>   Select this option if users will access your built-in Microsoft Windows authentication t password will be able to access your site.

5. Click *Done.*

You'll see that the options to create and manage your *Forms* users are available again and that the existing user has re-appeared.

> **Users**
>
> Existing users: **1**
> Create user
> Manage users
>
> Select authentication type

6. Close the *ASP.NET Configuration* utility.

6 **Close Visual Studio.**

Lesson 9-4: Use the Login control

So far, you've used only automatically-generated pages to log in and register accounts. By using the controls from the *Login* category of the *Toolbox* you can easily add these features to pages of your own.

1 Open *MyMembership* from your sample files folder.

2 Add a new web form page named: **mylogin.aspx**

You first did this in: *Lesson 1-7: Manage a project with the Solution Explorer.*

3 Open *mylogin.aspx* in *Design* view.

4 Add a *Login* control to the page.

1. Drag the *Login* control from the *Toolbox* onto the page.

   You will find it under the *Login* category of the *Toolbox*.

   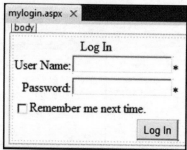

2. Set the *ID* of the new *Login* control to: **LoginMyPage**

5 Make the *Login* control redirect when the user logs in successfully.

The *Login* control would already allow a user to log in without any problems, but since there are no links on this page, it would be better if it redirected the user to another web page after they log in. Fortunately, it's easy to do so using the *LoggedIn* event.

1. Add a *LoggedIn* event handler to the *LoginMyPage* control.

   You first added event handlers to controls in: *Lesson 3-2: Add event handlers to Controls.*

2. Add the following code to the event handler:

   Response.Redirect("Default.aspx");

---

note

Logging in with C#

As well as using the *Login* control, you can use the *System.Web.Security* namespace of the .NET library to log in using C#.

Assuming your username and password were in text boxes called *TextBoxUsername* and *TextBoxPassword*, you could use the following code:

System.Web.Security.Membership .ValidateUser (TextBoxUsername.Text, TextBoxPassword.Text);

This method returns *true* and logs the user in if the username and password are correct and returns *false* if not.

```
protected void LoginMyPage_LoggedIn(object sender, EventArgs e)
{
    Response.Redirect("Default.aspx");
}
```

note

Returning to a page using a ReturnUrl query string value

Often you'll want to make a Log In page available from many pages on your web site.

When this is the case you'll often want your user to return to the previous page after logging in.

You can do this by calling your login page with a *ReturnUrl* query string value. For example:

<a href= "mylogin.aspx?ReturnUrl= about.aspx"> Log In</a>

The above HTML code would create a hyperlink with the text *Log In*. After logging in the user would be returned to the *about.aspx* web page.

Youcan use this technique with any page that contains a *Login* control.

You learned about query strings in: *Lesson 3-11: Send data between pages.*

6   Test the *Login* control.

1.   View *mylogin.aspx* in your browser.

2.   Enter the login details of the user you created earlier, but deliberately get the password wrong.

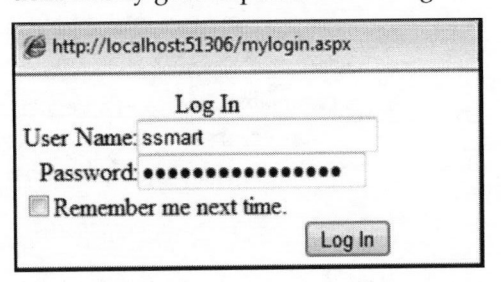

3.   Click *Log In*.

> Your login attempt was not successful. Please try again.
> [Log In]

You'll see an error message. You entered the wrong password and weren't able to log in, so the *LoggedIn* event didn't fire.

You could customize the error message by changing the *FailureText* property of the *Login* control.

4.   Enter the correct login details and then click *Log In* again.

This time you are logged in and sent to the *Default.aspx* page by the code you added. If you look in the top-right corner of the page, you'll see confirmation that you are logged in.

> Welcome **ssmart!** [Log Out]

5.   Close your browser.

7   Close Visual Studio.

Lesson 9-5: Customize the Login control

The *Login* control can be customized using properties in the same way as every other control, but in order to customize it further you can convert it into a template.

Converting a control to a template splits the control into several individual elements, allowing you to customize the layout and style of the control even further.

The *Login* control is an excellent example of this, but there are several other controls you can convert to templates using the same techniques that you'll use in this lesson.

1   Open *MyMembership* from your sample files folder.

2   Open *mylogin.aspx* in *Source* view.

```
<asp:Login ID="LoginMyPage" runat="server" onloggedin="LoginMyPage_LoggedIn">
</asp:Login>
```

You will see that the *Login* control is defined by a single pair of tags. This is fine if you're happy to customize it using its properties, but it won't allow you to change the layout of the control.

3   Convert the *Login* control to templates.

1. Switch to *Design* view.

2. Choose *Convert to Template* from the *QuickTasks* menu of the *LoginMyPage* control. You learned about the *QuickTasks* menu in: *Lesson 1-15: Use the QuickTasks menu.*

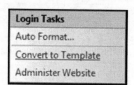

3. Switch back to *Source* view.

```
<asp:Login ID="LoginMyPage" runat="server" OnLoggedIn="LoginMyPage_LoggedIn">
    <LayoutTemplate>
        <table cellpadding="1" cellspacing="0" style="border-collapse: collap
            <tr>
                <td>
                    <table cellpadding="0">
                        <tr>
                            <td align="center" colspan="2">
                                Log In
                            </td>
                        </tr>
                        <tr>
                            <td align="right">
                                <asp:Label ID="UserNameLabel" runat="server"
                            </td>
```

You'll see that the *Login* control has been converted into an HTML table which you can customize.

Note that controls will only be recognized as part of the *Login* control if they are inside the *LayoutTemplate* tags, and their *ID* properties must not be changed from the automatically generated values.

4   Customize the *Login* control.

1.   Select the *User Name:* label in *Design* view.

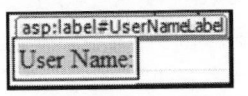

2.   Set the *Text* property of the *Label* control to: **UID:**

You wouldn't have been able to change this text before you converted the *Login* control to a template.

3.   Change the *Text* property of the *Password:* label to: **PWD:**

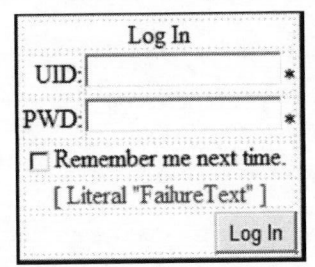

5   Replace the *Log In* button with a *LinkButton* control.

1.   Select the *Log In* button control and view its properties.

The *CommandName* property contains the *Login* keyword. This tells the *Login* control to log the user in when the button is clicked.

2.   Delete the *Log In* button.

3.   Add a *LinkButton* control to the previous location of the *Log In* button.

> ☐ Remember me next time.
> [Literal "FailureText"]
>   LinkButton

If you're having trouble getting the *LinkButton* control to appear in the right place, click in the table cell first and then add the *LinkButton* control.

4.   Set the *ID* property of the new *LinkButton* control to: **LinkButtonLogin**

5.   Set the *Text* property of the *LinkButton* control to: **Log In**

6.   Set the *CommandName* property to the keyword: **Login**

6   Try out your customized *Login* control.

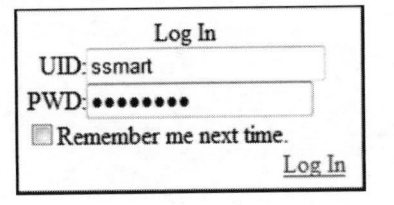

1.   View *mylogin.aspx* in your browser.

2.   Fill in the correct details and click *Log In*.

3.   You will be logged in correctly.

> Welcome **ssmart!** [Log Out]

7   Close your browser and close Visual Studio.

Lesson 9-6: Use the CreateUserWizard control

The *CreateUserWizard* control is used on the automatically-generated *Register.aspx* page you saw in: *Lesson 9-1: Use .NET's built-in security features.*

In this lesson, you'll add a *CreateUserWizard* control to a page of your own and use it to create a new user.

1 Open *MyMembership* from your sample files folder.

2 Add a new page called: **myregister.aspx**

3 Add a *CreateUserWizard* control to the page.

   1. Open *myregister.aspx* in *Design* view.

   2. Add a *CreateUserWizard* control from the *Login* category of the *Toolbox*.

      This creates a standard form for registering a new account.

4 Customize the *CreateUserWizard* control.

   1. Set the *ID* of the *CreateUserWizard* control to: **CreateUserWizardMyPage**

   2. Use *Auto Format* from the *QuickTasks* menu to apply the *Professional* format to the control. You learned about the *QuickTasks* menu in: *Lesson 1-15: Use the QuickTasks menu.*

5 Create a user using your new page.

   1. View *myregister.aspx* in your browser.

   2. Complete the form using the password: **learnasp**

note

Settings in *Web.config*

Some settings that influence your membership provider can only be changed in *Web.config*.

In this lesson, security questions and answers aren't requested because of the *Web.config* setting:

requiresQuestionAndAnswer= "false"

This part of the login process is called the *Create User* step.

You'll see that the *Security Question* and *Security Answer* fields don't appear on the page. This is because of the settings in *Web.config* (see sidebar).

3. Click *Create User*.

> **Complete**
> Your account has been successfully created.
> Continue

This part of the login process is called the *Complete* step.

The new user is created.

4. Close your web browser.

6 Convert the *CreateUserWizard* control into a template.

Just like the *Login* control, you can customize either, or both, steps of the *CreateUserWizard* control by converting them into templates.

You first encountered the concept of customizing controls with templates in: *Lesson 9-5: Customize the Login control*.

1. Open *myregister.aspx* in *Design* view.

2. Choose *Customize Complete Step* from the *QuickTasks* menu of the *CreateUserWizard* control.

> Customize Create User Step
> Customize Complete Step
> Administer Website

The *Complete* step is converted into a template and made editable.

3. Change the *Your account has been successfully created* text to:

Thank you for registering an account!
Click Continue to proceed!

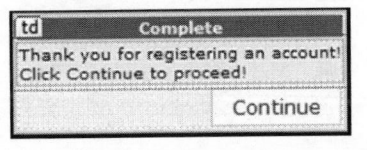

By using the customization options in the *QuickTasks* menu, you can fully customize each step of the *CreateUserWizard* control.

If your registration process has many special requirements it may be easier to create your own registration form and then use the *System.Web.Security.Membership.CreateUser* method to create users (see sidebar).

note

Creating users with C#

Just as you can log in using C#, you can create users by using the *System.Web.Security* namespace.

To create a new user, call the *System.Web.Security.Membership .CreateUser* method.

This method has several sets of arguments that you can use for different registration requirements.

Note that if you try to send the method a password that doesn't meet the requirements you've defined in *Web.config*, you will cause an error.

7 Close Visual Studio.

Lesson 9-7: Use other login controls

In this lesson you will learn how to use the other controls in the *Login* category of the *Toolbox*.

1   Open *MyMembership* from your sample files folder.

2   Add a new page to the project called: **mylogin2.aspx**

3   Open *mylogin2.aspx* in *Design* view.

4   Add a *Login* control to the page.

    1.   Drag a *Login* control onto the page from the *Login* category of the *ToolBox*.

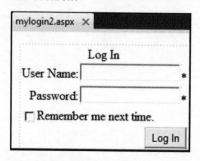

    2.   Set the *ID* of the *Login* control to: **LoginMyPage**

    3.   Use *Auto Format* from the *QuickTasks* menu to set the new *Login* control to the *Professional* format.

       You first used *Auto Format* in: *Lesson 1-15: Use the QuickTasks menu.*

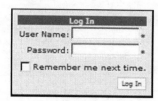

5   Add a *LoginName* control to the page.

The *LoginName* control displays the username of the logged-in user. You've seen it in the top-right corner of the automatically-generated pages.

It will be blank unless the user is logged in.

    1.   Drag a *LoginName* control onto the page from the *Login* category of the *Toolbox*.

       Put the new control below the *LoginMyPage* control.

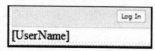

    2.   Set the *ID* of the new control to: **LoginNameMyPage**

    3.   View *mylogin2.aspx* in your browser.

    4.   Log in using the username and password you created earlier.

If you are not completing this course incrementally, the login details in the sample file will be:

Username: **ssmart**
Password: **learnasp**

You will see that the *LoginName* control now displays your username.

5.   Close your browser.

6   Add a *LoginStatus* control to the page.

The *LoginStatus* control shows either a *Login* or *Logout* hyperlink, depending on whether or not a user is logged in. Clicking *Login* will send the user to the login page, clicking *Logout* will log them out, and all without writing any code at all!

1.   Drag a *LoginStatus* control onto your page from the *Login* category of the *Toolbox*.

Place it just after your *LoginName* control.

[UserName]Login

2.   Set the *ID* of the new control to: **LoginStatusMyPage**

3.   View *mylogin2.aspx* in your browser.

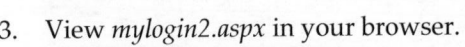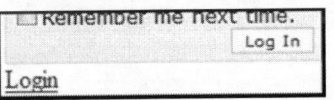

You will see that the *LoginStatus* control is currently displaying a *Login* link, since you are not currently logged in.

4.   Log in using the same username and password you used earlier in this lesson.

You will see that the *LoginStatus* control now shows a *Logout* link.

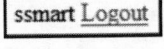

5.   Click the *Logout* link.

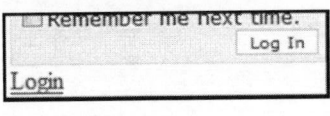

You are logged out.

6.   Click the *Login* link.

You will be redirected to *Login.aspx*. This is because it has been selected as the *loginUrl* in *Web.config* (see sidebar).

7   Close your web browser and Visual Studio.

---

note

loginUrl

If you look in *Web.config*, you will see the tag:

<forms loginUrl="~/Account/Login.aspx" timeout="2880" />

The *loginUrl* property here defines the *Account/Login.aspx* page as the default login page.

The *LoginStatus* control will automatically send users to this address if they click its *Login* link.

The user is also sent to the default login page if they attempt to access a page that they do not have access to.

Lesson 9-8: Add folder-level security

You will sometimes want to have pages that are accessible only to certain users. For example you might have an administration page which you want only system administrators to be able to access.

Fortunately, ASP.NET gives you a very easy way to set up page security, although it is limited to securing the contents of a folder rather than an individual page.

1 Open *MyMembership* from your sample files folder.

2 Create an admin page.

1. Add a new folder to the project called: **Admin**

   You learned to add new folders in: *Lesson 1-7: Manage a project with the Solution Explorer.*

2. Add a new page to the *Admin* folder called: **default.aspx**

   Because it is named *default.aspx*, if a user navigates to *www.yoursite.com/Admin* the page will automatically be displayed.

3 Create a new access rule.

1. Open the *ASP.NET Configuration* utility.

2. You learned how to do this in: *Lesson 9-2: Manage a site with ASP.NET Configuration.*

3. Click the *Security* tab.

4. Click *Create access rules*.

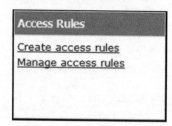

5. Click the *Admin* folder on the left.

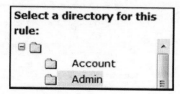

6. Click *Anonymous Users*.

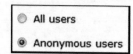

Anonymous users are users who have not logged in.

7. Click *Deny* on the right.

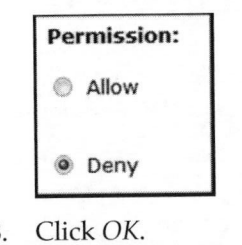

8. Click *OK*.

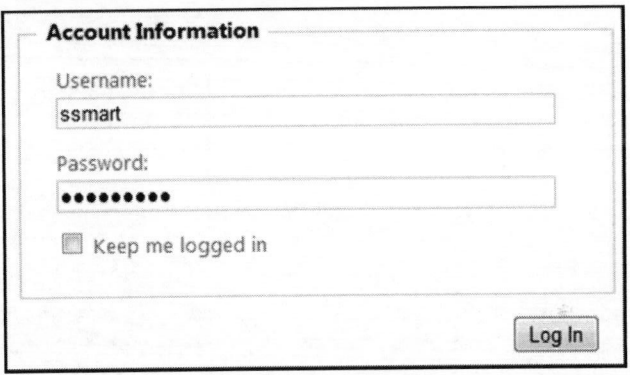

9. Close the *ASP.NET Configuration* utility.

This rule will make sure that only users who have logged in will be able to access pages in the *Admin* folder.

4 **Try out your access rule.**

1. View *Default.aspx* (from the *Admin* folder) in your browser.

   Since you are not logged in by default, you will be denied access and will be automatically redirected to the login page.

2. Log in with your username (the one you created in: *Lesson 9-1: Use .NET's built-in security features*).

After logging in, you will be automatically redirected to *default.aspx* in the *admin* folder.

   Since it is a blank page you won't actually see anything on the page, but before you logged in you were unable to access it at all.

3. Close your browser.

5 **Close Visual Studio.**

Lesson 9-9: Set up roles

If you have a lot of users, it's useful to be able to group them together into roles. All members sharing the same role can then be given the same access rights.

By using roles, you can make your access rules much simpler and make your site's security easier to manage.

1   Open *MyMembership* from your sample files folder.

2   Create a role called: **Normal User**

    1.   Open the *ASP.NET Configuration* utility.

    2.   Click the *Security* tab.

    3.   Click *Enable Roles*.

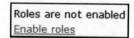

Roles are not enabled
Enable roles

       By default, roles are disabled. You have to enable them in order to use them.

    4.   Click *Create or Manage roles*.

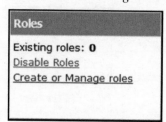

Roles

Existing roles: **0**
Disable Roles
Create or Manage roles

    5.   Enter **Normal User** into the text box.

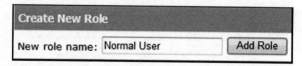

Create New Role

New role name: Normal User   [Add Role]

    6.   Click *Add Role*.

       You have now created a role.

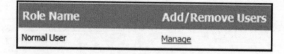

Role Name	Add/Remove Users
Normal User	Manage

3   Assign a user to the role.

    1.   Click the *Manage* button next to the *Normal User* role.

    2.   Use the search functions to find the first user you created.

       Either enter the username into the text box and click *Find User* or click on the letter of the alphabet that your username begins with.

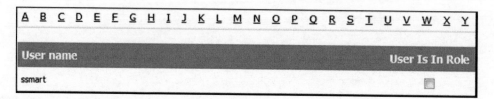

A B C D E F G H I J K L M N O P Q R S T U V W X Y
User name   **User Is In Role**
ssmart   ☐

3. Tick the *User Is In Role* box.

    Your user account is now part of the *Normal User* group.

4. Click *Back*.

    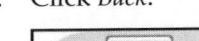

4   Add an access rule for the role.

1. Click the *Security* tab at the top of the page to return to the main *Security* page.

2. Click *Manage access rules*.

    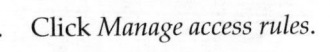

3. Click the *Admin* folder on the left.

    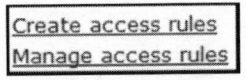

4. Click *Add New Access Rule*.

    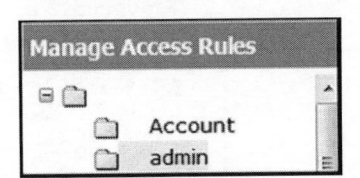

    The rule automatically applies to the *Normal User* role by default as this is the only role that currently exists.

    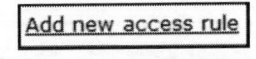

5. Click *Deny*.

    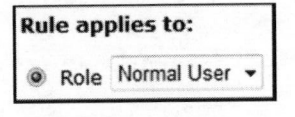

6. Click *OK*.

    Your permissions now deny both members of the *Normal User* role and people who have not logged in from accessing the *Admin* folder.

    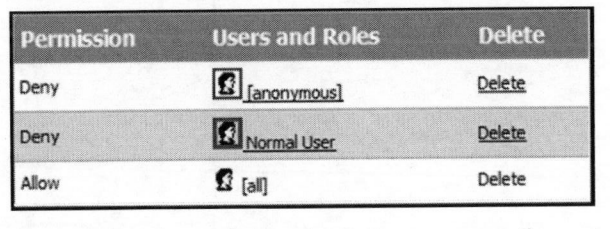

    By combining roles and access rules, you can easily control which users can access which folders.

5   Close your browser and close Visual Studio.

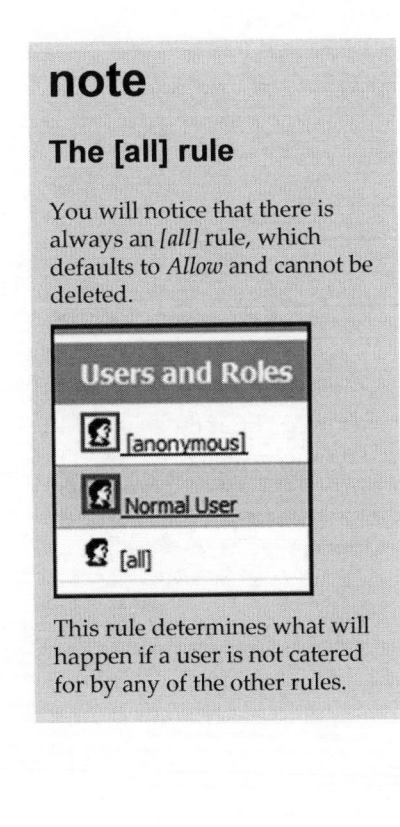

note

The [all] rule

You will notice that there is always an *[all]* rule, which defaults to *Allow* and cannot be deleted.

This rule determines what will happen if a user is not catered for by any of the other rules.

Lesson 9-10: Use C# to limit access

As well as using the options in the *ASP.NET Configuration* utility, you can use certain C# methods and properties to check whether a user is logged in and redirect them accordingly.

1 Open *MyMembership* from your sample files folder.

1 Open the code-behind file of *About.aspx*.

2 Make the page only available to logged-in users with C#.

    1. Add the following code to the *Page_Load* event handler:

```
if (!Page.User.Identity.IsAuthenticated)
{
    Response.Redirect("~/Account/Login.aspx");
}
```

```
protected void Page_Load(object sender, EventArgs e)
{
    if (!Page.User.Identity.IsAuthenticated)
    {
        Response.Redirect("~/Account/Login.aspx");
    }
}
```

note

Page.User.Identity .Name

In this lesson you use the *Page.User.Identity .IsAuthenticated* property to check whether the user is logged in.

The *Page.User.Identity.Name* property will contain the username of the logged-in user if the user is logged in.

The *Page.User.Identity.IsAuthenticated* property returns *true* if the user is logged in and *false* if they are not.

You leaned about using the tilde (~) within paths in*: Lesson 4-2: Use button controls (sidebar).* You learned about the NOT operator (!) in: *Lesson 7-3: Use basic logical operators.*

    2. View *Default.aspx* in your browser.

    3. Click the *About* link.

You will be redirected to *Login.aspx* by the code you added because you are not logged in.

    4. Log in.

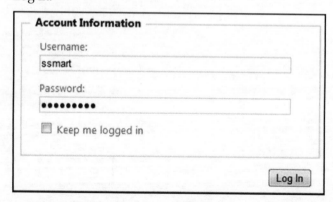

If you are not working through this course sequentially, the sample file for this lesson uses Username: **ssmart**, Password: **learnasp**.

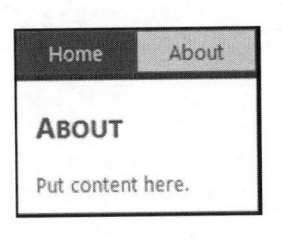

You will be sent back to *Default.aspx*.

5. Click the *About* link.

   This time you are able to access the page because you are logged in.

3   **Make the page only available to the *Normal User* role.**

   1. Close your browser and return to the code-behind file of *About.aspx*.

   2. Change the *if* statement in the *Page_Load* event handler to:

      if (!Page.User.IsInRole("Normal User"))

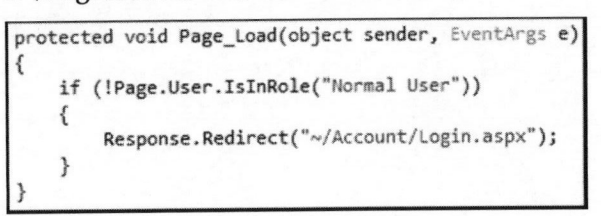

```
protected void Page_Load(object sender, EventArgs e)
{
    if (!Page.User.IsInRole("Normal User"))
    {
        Response.Redirect("~/Account/Login.aspx");
    }
}
```

   This code will redirect the user if they are not assigned to the *Normal User* role.

   3. View *Default.aspx* in your browser.

   4. Click the *About* link.

   Because you're not logged in, you are redirected to the login page. This happens because *IsInRole* returns *false* for users that are not logged in, as well as for logged in users that are not members of the *Normal User* group.

   5. Log in again as the user you assigned to the *Normal User* role in: *Lesson 9-10: Use C# to limit access*. In the sample file for this lesson this is user: **ssmart**, password **learnasp**.

   6. Click the *About* link.

      This time you are able to access the page because you are logged in as a user that has the *Normal User* role.

   7. Log out.

   8. Log in as your second user (the one you created in: *Lesson 9-6: Use the CreateUserWizard control*). In the sample file for this lesson this is user: **ssmart2**, password **learnasp**.

      This user doesn't have the *Normal User* role.

   9. Try to access the *About* page.

      You are redirected to the login page. This user doesn't have the *Normal User* role so the user doesn't pass the *IsInRole* check.

   10. Close your web browser.

   Note that in a real-world application this implementation could confuse your users. See sidebar for details of how you could make this application more friendly.

Lesson 9-11: Use the security wizard

note

Adding security to existing sites

In order for ASP.NET security to work, an *ASPNETDB.MDF* file is required. This is the database file that will contain all user information.

If the file is not present, it will be automatically added when you run the *ASP.NET Configuration* utility.

As well as using the individual security configuration pages in the *ASP.NET Configuration* utility, you can use the security wizard to set up your site's security on a step-by-step basis.

1   Open *MyMembership* from your sample files folder.

2   Open the *ASP.NET Configuration* utility.

3   Click the *Security* tab.

4   Start the security wizard.

   1.   Click
Use the security Setup Wizard to configure security step by step.

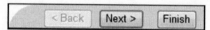

     The first page of the security wizard will appear. This page gives a brief explanation of what the security wizard does.

   2.   Click *Next* at the bottom-right of the screen.

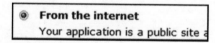

5   Select the authentication method.

The next page is almost identical to the one you used to set the authentication method in: *Lesson 9-3: Change authentication types.*

   1.   Click *From the Internet* (if it isn't selected already).

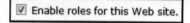

   2.   Click *Next.*

6   See provider information.

The page you're on now is only useful if you're using a custom provider. Providers were explained in: *Lesson 9-2: Manage a site with ASP.NET Configuration (sidebar).*

Click *Next.*

7   Enable or disable roles.

The next step allows you to enable or disable roles.

   ☑ Enable roles for this Web site.

Leave roles enabled and click *Next.*

8   Add a role called: **Manager**

This page allows you to add roles, just as you did in: *Lesson 9-9: Set up roles.*

   1.   Enter *Manager* into the *New Role Name* text box.

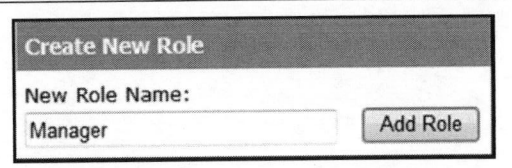

2. Click *Add Role*.

The *Manager* role appears on the *Existing Roles* list, along with the *Normal User* role created earlier.

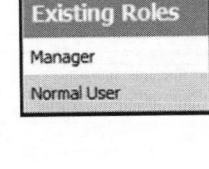

3. Click *Next*.

9 View the *Create User* page.

This page allows you to create new users. It uses the *CreateUserWizard* control you learned about in: *Lesson 9-6: Use the CreateUserWizard control*.

Click *Next*.

10 Add an access rule.

The next page allows you to add access rules, just as you did in *Lesson 9-8: Add folder-level security*.

1. Expand the folder on the left by clicking the + sign.

A list of all of the folders in your site appears.

2. Click the *Admin* folder on the left.

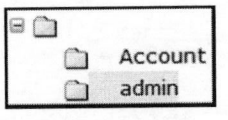

You will see the rules you created earlier.

3. Select the *Manager* role from the dropdown menu.

4. Click *Allow*.

5. Click *Add This Rule*.

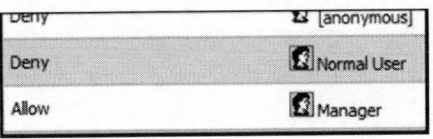

You will see a new rule appear, allowing users with the *Manager* role to access all files in the *Admin* folder.

11 Complete the wizard.

Click the *Finish* button to close the wizard. Note that you could have clicked *Finish* at any time if you wanted to end the wizard early.

It's up to you whether you prefer to use the wizard to set up ASP.NET security settings or use the individual pages. They both do exactly the same thing.

Session 9: Exercise

1 Create a new *ASP.NET Web Application* in your sample files folder, named: **Session9**

2 Start the project in *Debug* mode, view its pages and then close your web browser.

(This is necessary because the project must be built before the *ASP.NET Configuration* utility will work properly. Starting debugging causes the project to be built).

3 Open the *ASP.NET Configuration* utility for your new project.

4 Enable roles for the application.

5 Add a new role called: **Moderator**

6 Add a new folder to the project called: **Moderate**

7 Add a new *aspx* page to the *Moderate* folder called: **default.aspx**

8 Add a *Calendar* control to your new page.

9 Use the *ASP.NET Configuration* utility to add access rules to allow only users with the *Moderator* role to access the *Moderate* folder.

10 Create a new user account and assign it to the *Moderator* role.

11 Attempt to view the new *default.aspx* page in the *Moderate* folder in your browser.

12 Log in when prompted using the user you created in step 10.

If all of the above questions were completed correctly you will now see the new *default.aspx* file in the *Moderate* folder.

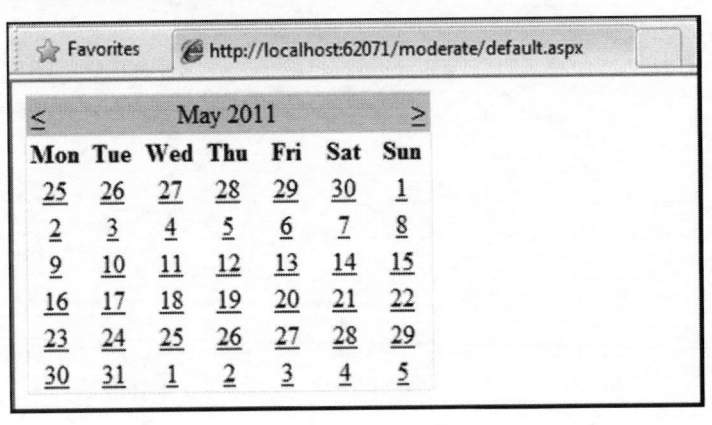

Session9 - end

If you need help slide the page to the left

Session 9: Exercise Answers

These are the four questions that students find the most difficult to answer:

Q 10	Q 9	Q 5	Q 3
1. Open the *ASP.NET Configuration* utility (if it isn't open already). 2. Click the *Security* tab. 3. Click *Create user*. 4. Complete the form. 5. Check the *Moderator* box. 6. Click *Create User*. This was covered in: *Lesson 9-1: Use .NET's built-in security features.*	1. Open the *ASP.NET Configuration* utility. 2. Click the *Security* tab. 3. Click *Manage Access Rules*. 4. Click the *Moderate* folder on the left. 5. Click *Add new access rule*. 6. Click *Allow*. 7. Click *OK*. 8. Click *Add new access rule*. 9. Click *Anonymous Users*. 10. Click Deny. 11. Click *OK*. This was covered in: *Lesson 9-8: Add folder-level security.*	1. Open the *ASP.NET Configuration* utility. 2. Click the *Security* tab. 3. Click *Create or Manage roles*. 4. Type **Moderator** into the *New role name* text box. 5. Click *Add Role*. This was covered in: *Lesson 9-9: Set up roles.*	Click Project→ ASP.NET Configuration. Alternatively, click the icon in the *Solution Explorer*: This was covered in: *Lesson 9-2: Manage a site with ASP.NET Configuration.*

If you have difficulty with the other questions, here are the lessons that cover the relevant skills:

1   **Refer to: Lesson 1-5: Create an ASP.NET Web Application project.**

2   **Refer to: Lesson 1-8: Run a project in debug mode.**

4   **Refer to: Lesson 9-9: Set up roles.**

6   **Refer to: Lesson 1-7: Manage a project with the Solution Explorer.**

7   **Refer to: Lesson 1-7: Manage a project with the Solution Explorer.**

8   **Refer to: Lesson 1-14: Add controls to a page with the Toolbox.**

11   **Refer to: Lesson 9-1: Use .NET's built-in security features.**

12   **Refer to: Lesson 9-1: Use .NET's built-in security features.**

Session Ten: Accessing Data

> As a general rule, the most successful man in life is the man who has the best information.
>
> *Benjamin Disraeli, British Prime Minister (1804 – 1881)*

Almost every ASP.NET web site has a database of some kind. For example, online shops have databases filled with products, customer details and orders.

Being able to interact with a database is almost always required when writing interactive web sites.

In this session you'll learn how to use Microsoft's new LINQ technology to allow your website to interact with a database by creating web pages that are able to read, write and edit data.

Session Objectives

By the end of this session you will be able to:

- Work with SQL databases in Visual Studio
- Add LINQ data classes to a project
- Retrieve a single row of data using LINQ
- Retrieve multiple rows of data using LINQ
- Sort results and called Stored Procedures using LINQ
- Check whether a record exists using LINQ
- Update database records using LINQ
- Insert database records using LINQ
- Delete database records using LINQ
- Use LINQ with collections

note

Database types

Visual Studio is capable of working with any type of SQL-compliant database.

Visual Studio works best with Microsoft's SQL Server database product, but it is entirely possible to use other database types such as Access, Oracle and MySQL.

The free Express version of SQL Server was automatically installed on your machine when you installed Visual Studio.

note

The *App_Data* folder

The *App_Data* folder is a special folder which ASP.NET assumes will contain any databases used by a web site.

If you right-click on the first item displayed in the *Solution Explorer* and then click Add→*Add ASP.NET Folder*, you will see that there are a number of other 'special' ASP.NET folders which are expected to contain certain things.

For now, the *App_Data* folder is the only one that is important.

Lesson 10-1: Work with SQL databases in Visual Studio

SQL (Structured Query Language) is a query language that allows computer applications to add, edit and delete data from a database.

Whenever your application interacts with a database it does so by constructing an SQL query.

You don't need to learn SQL to access data in your projects because ASP.NET provides classes which generate SQL for you.

1   Open *My Project* from your sample files folder.

2   Add a new SQL database to the project called: **MyDatabase.mdf**

   1.   Right-click on *My Project* in the *Solution Explorer* and click Add→New Item… from the shortcut menu.

   2.   Click *Data* in the panel on the left.

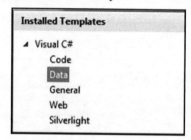

   3.   Click *SQL Server Database* in the center panel.

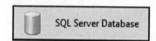

   4.   Type **MyDatabase.mdf** into the *Name* text box.

   5.   Click *Add*.

   You will be prompted to place the new database in the *App_Data* folder of the site, rather than the main folder.

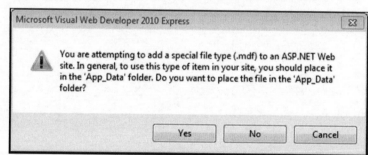

   6.   Click *Yes*.

   You have now added a new database to your project. Of course, it is completely empty.

   In a typical work environment database design is done by a specialized team member called a DBA (database administrator).

If you are not completing the course incrementally use the sample file: **Lesson 10-1** to begin this lesson.

Sample files with the starting point for each lesson are also provided for all of the other lessons in this session.

Most ASP.NET programmers do not have database design skills, but have the skills needed to access data from a database designed by a DBA. If you are interested in database design there are many books on this subject.

You don't need any database design skills to complete this book as sample databases are provided to work with.

3 Open *Spark* from your sample files folder.

The *Spark* project already has its own database, named *Spark.mdf.*

4 View the *Spark.mdf* database.

1. Expand the *App_Data* folder in the *Solution Explorer.*

2. Double-click *Spark.mdf.*

After a short delay, you will be transferred to the *Database Explorer* window.

The *Database Explorer* appears in the same area as the *Solution Explorer.* You can switch back to the *Solution Explorer* by clicking on the *Solution Explorer* tab at the bottom of the window.

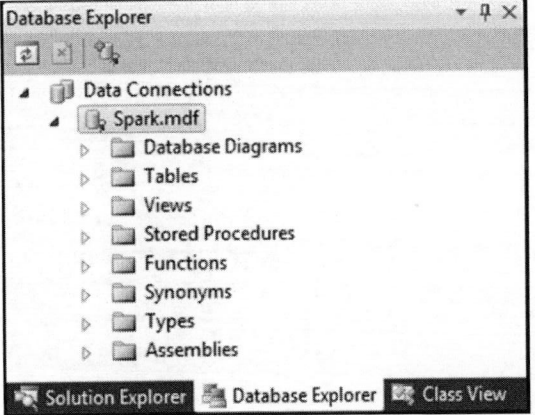

5. Expand the *Tables* folder in the *Database Explorer.*

You will see that the *Spark* database contains the *Customer* and *Invoice* tables.

Tables are the containers that databases store their data in. Database tables are similar to spreadsheets as they contain tables of information divided into rows and columns.

5 View the contents of the *Customer* table.

Right click the *Customer* table and click *Show Table Data* from the shortcut menu. After a few seconds, the contents of the table will appear in the central panel of Visual Studio.

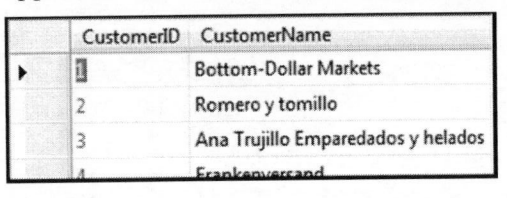

You are able to edit the data in the table by changing the values in the cells.

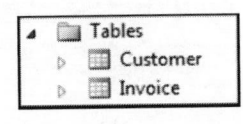

Lesson 10-2: Add LINQ data classes to a project

LINQ, which stands for Language Integrated Query, is a relatively new addition to .NET which makes working with databases much easier.

Before LINQ, programmers would usually create their own set of classes to generate the SQL needed to interact with a database. This took a lot of time and effort.

ASP.NET's LINQ classes automatically create the SQL needed to interact with your data, making it unnecessary to learn SQL. LINQ also streamlines the development process by removing the need to create your own data access classes.

1   Open *Spark* from your sample files folder.

2   Add LINQ data classes to the project.

     1.   Right-click on *Spark* in the *Solution Explorer* and click Add→New Item… from the shortcut menu.

     2.   Click *Data* in the left panel.

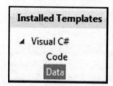

     3.   Click *LINQ to SQL Classes* in the center panel.

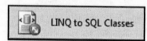

     4.   Type **Spark.dbml** into the *Name* text box.

     5.   Click *Add*.

The *dbml* file will be added and will automatically be opened, displaying what it calls the *Object Relational Designer*.

> The Object Relational Designer allows you to visualize data classes in your code.
>
> Create data classes by dragging items from **Database Explorer** or **Toolbox** onto this design surface.

Although your LINQ data class file has been created, you need to tell it to add classes for the objects in your database using this designer.

3   Add a table to your LINQ classes.

     1.   Open the *Database Explorer* by clicking its tab underneath the *Solution Explorer*.

     2.   Expand the *Spark.mdf* database.

     3.   Expand the *Tables* folder.

     4.   Click and drag the *Customer* table from the *Tables* folder onto the *Object Relational Designer* in the central panel.

     The table will appear in the LINQ designer panel.

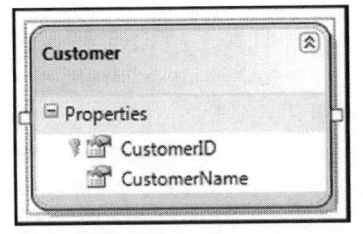

Your LINQ file now contains a class for the *Customer* table, which allows you to easily search and update the table using the C# code you'll learn later in this session.

4   Add the *Invoice* table to your LINQ classes.

In the same way as you did with the *Customer* table, drag the *Invoice* table onto the LINQ designer.

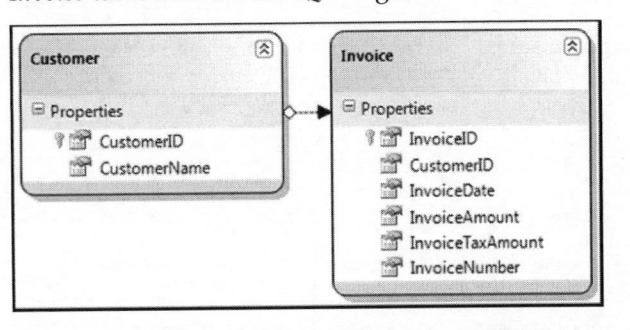

The *Invoice* table is now available to your LINQ classes.

You'll notice the arrow between the two tables. This indicates the presence of a *relationship* between the tables.

The line and arrow tell you that each customer may have many invoices.

LINQ classes allow you to very easily find all of the invoices for any customer and to find the customer for any invoice. You'll see this in action in: *Lesson 10-4: Retrieve multiple rows of data using LINQ*.

5   Add a stored procedure to your LINQ classes.

Stored procedures are similar to methods, but are stored inside the database. Stored procedures contain SQL code that can manipulate data in ways that would be difficult using C#. In a team environment, stored procedures are usually written by the DBA.

The stored procedure in this example finds the highest invoice number in the *Invoice* table.

1.   Expand the *Stored Procedures* folder in the *Database Explorer*.

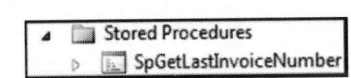

2.   Drag the *SpGetLastInvoiceNumber* procedure onto the LINQ designer.

The stored procedure will appear in the right panel of the *Linq Designer*.

SpGetLastInvoiceNumber ()

Now that the stored procedure is part of the LINQ data class, you can call it just like any other C# method. You'll do this in: *Lesson 10-5: Sort results and call stored procedures using LINQ*.

Lesson 10-3: Retrieve a single row of data using LINQ

In this lesson, you'll see how easily you can extract the data you want from a database using LINQ.

1   Open *Spark* from your sample files folder.

2   Open the code-behind file of *reports.aspx*.

3   Create an instance of your LINQ data class.

Create an instance of your data class with the *using* statement. This causes the class to automatically dispose of itself (see sidebar).

Add the following code to the *Page_Load* event handler:

using (SparkDataContext Data = new SparkDataContext())
{
}

```
protected void Page_Load(object sender, EventArgs e)
{
    using (SparkDataContext Data = new SparkDataContext())
    {
    }
}
```

The LINQ data class always appends *DataContext* to the name you give it. You provided the name *Spark.dbml*, so the class is called *SparkDataContext*. You've just created an instance of the class called *Data*.

4   Use the data class to retrieve a customer record from the database.

When you added the *Customer* table to the LINQ classes in the last lesson, a *Customer* class was automatically created. The *Customer* class is used to represent rows of data in the *Customer* table.

1. Add the following code inside the *using* statement:

    Customer MyCustomer = Data.Customers.First();

    ```
    using (SparkDataContext Data = new SparkDataContext())
    {
        Customer MyCustomer = Data.Customers.First();
    }
    ```

    This gets the first row from the *Customers* table and puts it in an object called *MyCustomer*, which is an instance of the *Customer* class.

2. On the next line (inside the *using* statement), type:

    MyCustomer.

    You will see the IntelliSense menu for *MyCustomer*. As you can see, it has *CustomerID* and *CustomerName* as properties.

    The *CustomerID* property is an *int* and the *CustomerName* property is a *string*. You already know how to work with these types.

note

LINQ Query and Lambda syntax

There are two ways to use LINQ. You can use the lambda expressions you see in this lesson or a 'query' syntax which looks more like SQL code.

Unless you're familiar with SQL the lambda syntax is easier to understand, so all examples in this book use that approach.

Here's what this lesson's code would look like using the 'query' approach:

Customer MyCustomer = (from Customer in Data.Customers where Customer.CustomerID == 5 select Customer).Single();

note

Getting data without using LINQ

Before LINQ, databases were usually accessed using the *System.Data.SqlClient* namespace of the .NET library.

System.Data.SqlClient is still available, but it requires a lot more code to use. This method also requires you to either use stored procedures or SQL code.

LINQ has made this approach obsolete but you may still see it used in older projects.

You'll also notice the *Invoices* property. Using *Invoices*, you can get a collection of invoices that belong to the customer stored in the *MyCustomer* object.

3. Delete the *MyCustomer.* text you just added.

5 Output the customer name.

1. Type the following code on the next line:

LabelReport.Text = MyCustomer.CustomerName;

```
using (SparkDataContext Data = new SparkDataContext())
{
    Customer MyCustomer = Data.Customers.First();
    LabelReport.Text = MyCustomer.CustomerName;
}
```

The *CustomerName* property is a string, so you can display it in the label.

2. View *reports.aspx* in your browser.

> Bottom-Dollar Markets

Bottom Dollar Markets will appear on the page: the first customer in the *Customers* table.

3. Close your browser.

6 Get a specific customer.

1. Change the *Customer MyCustomer…* line to:

Customer MyCustomer = Data.Customers
 .Single(Customer => Customer.CustomerID == 5);

```
using (SparkDataContext Data = new SparkDataContext())
{
    Customer MyCustomer = Data.Customers
            .Single(Customer => Customer.CustomerID == 5);
    LabelReport.Text = MyCustomer.CustomerName;
}
```

This code will search the *Customer* table for a customer record with a *CustomerID* of 5 and return the record as an instance of the *Customer* class.

This code inside the *Single* method looks a little strange. It's what's called a *Lambda Expression*. All you need to understand about a lambda expression is that the part before the => is an alias to be used to identify the database table.

In this example you used *Customer* as an alias to avoid confusion. It is possible to use any combination of letters as an alias.

2. View *reports.aspx* in your browser.

> Lehmanns Marktstand

This time *Lehmanns Marktstand* appears on the page.

If you compared this with the table data using the *Database Explorer*, you'd see that *Lehmanns Marktstand* has a *CustomerID* of 5.

Lesson 10-4: Retrieve multiple rows of data using LINQ

In the previous lesson, you retrieved a single row of data from a database and stored it in an object. LINQ can also retrieve multiple rows and put them into a collection of objects.

1   Open *Spark* from your sample files folder.

2   Open the code-behind file of *reports.aspx*.

3   Remove the code inside the *using* statement.

You're going to create a new LINQ query, so get rid of the old one.

```
protected void Page_Load(object sender, EventArgs e)
{
    using (SparkDataContext Data = new SparkDataContext())
    {

    }
}
```

4   Use the data class to retrieve multiple rows.

In *Lesson 10-3: Retrieve a single row of data using LINQ,* you retrieved a single customer from the *Customer* table in the database. This time you're going to retrieve several records from the *Invoice* table.

Add the following code inside the *using* statement:

var Invoices = Data.Invoices
       .Where(Invoice => Invoice.InvoiceAmount > 990);

```
using (SparkDataContext Data = new SparkDataContext())
{
    var Invoices = Data.Invoices
        .Where(Invoice => Invoice.InvoiceAmount > 990);
}
```

This code retrieves a collection of *Invoice* objects from the *Invoice* table of the database with *InvoiceAmount* values greater than 990.

See the sidebar for more information about why you're using the *var* type instead of a *List* collection for this.

5   Output the list of invoices on the page.

Because *Invoices* is a collection, you'll need to use *foreach* to iterate through the collection in order to display its contents on the screen.

You learned about *foreach* in: *Lesson 8-3: Iterate through a collection using foreach.*

1. Add a *string* variable on the next line to contain the HTML that will be output:

    string Output = "";

2. Add a *foreach* loop to iterate through the *Invoices* collection:

    foreach (Invoice InvoiceToOutput in Invoices)
    {
    }

note

LINQ collections and var

As you may recall from *Lesson 5-13: Use object and var variables,* using the *var* variable type is usually bad practice.

When working with LINQ, the *var* variable type is actually the preferred type since, in some cases, you will not know in advance the type of object that LINQ will return.

You learned about the *var* type in: *Lesson 5-13: Use object and var variables.*

It is also possible to convert the LINQ output to a *List* by using the *ToList* method.

For example:

*List<Invoice> Invoices =
Data.Invoices.Where
(Invoice =>
Invoice.InvoiceAmount > 990)
.ToList();*

LINQ criteria

In both of the examples you've worked with so far, your LINQ queries have used only a single criteria (in this example: InvoiceAmount > 990)

You can use any of the logical operators to build your criteria expression.

(For more on logical operators see: *Lesson 7-3: Use basic logical operators*).

For example, to get all invoices that have either an *InvoiceAmount* greater than 900 or a *CustomerID* of 5 you could use the LINQ code:

*Data.Invoices.Where
(Invoice =>
Invoice.InvoiceAmount > 900
|| Invoice.CustomerID == 5);*

3. Make the *foreach* loop add the *InvoiceNumber* property from each *Invoice* object to the *Output* string variable:

Output += InvoiceToOutput.InvoiceNumber;
Output += "<br />";

4. Place the value of *Output* on the page (outside the *foreach* loop):

LabelReport.Text = Output;

```
var Invoices = Data.Invoices
    .Where(Invoice => Invoice.InvoiceAmount > 990);
string Output = "";
foreach (Invoice InvoiceToOutput in Invoices)
{
    Output += InvoiceToOutput.InvoiceNumber;
    Output += "<br />";
}
LabelReport.Text = Output;
```

6 View *reports.aspx* in your browser.

You'll see the invoice numbers of the invoices with values above 990 displayed.

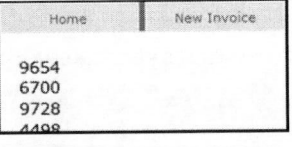

7 Use LINQ to 'drill-down' through relationships.

In *Lesson 10-2: Add LINQ data classes to a project*, you saw that the *Customer* and *Invoice* tables were linked by a line with an arrow, indicating a relationship between the two tables.

Because there is a relationship, you can very easily 'drill-down' from your *Invoice* objects to the *Customer* objects they belong to.

1. Close your browser if it is open.

2. Add the following code at the beginning of your *foreach* statement:

Output += InvoiceToOutput.Customer.CustomerName;
Output += " - ";

```
foreach (Invoice InvoiceToOutput in Invoices)
{
    Output += InvoiceToOutput.Customer.CustomerName;
    Output += " - ";
    Output += InvoiceToOutput.InvoiceNumber;
    Output += "<br />";
}
```

As you can see, you can access the properties of the *Customer* associated with the *Invoice* by simply using its *Customer* property. This works with any table that has a relationship.

A correctly designed database will always have relationships defined.

3. View *reports.aspx* in your browser.

Because of the code you added, the *CustomerName* now appears next to the *InvoiceNumber* in the browser window.

4. Close your browser.

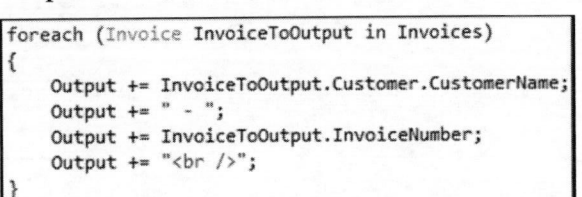

Lesson 10-5: Sort results and call stored procedures using LINQ

You now know the basics of querying a database using LINQ, but LINQ offers many more methods to accomplish some more advanced queries.

1 Open *Spark* from your sample files folder.

2 Open the code-behind file of *reports.aspx*.

note

Other LINQ functions

You can do even more advanced queries in LINQ using methods such as *Sum*, *Average* and *Count*.

These are explored in more depth in the Expert Skills book in this series.

3 Sort the LINQ results.

At the moment, the results of your query are being returned in no particular order.

Fortunately, you can use the *OrderBy* method to sort your results.

1. Remove the semicolon from the end of the *var Invoices…* code line and append the following code:

   .OrderBy(Invoice => Invoice.InvoiceNumber);

   ```
   var Invoices = Data.Invoices
       .Where(Invoice => Invoice.InvoiceAmount > 990)
       .OrderBy(Invoice=>Invoice.InvoiceNumber);
   ```

2. View *reports.aspx* in your web browser.

   As you might have guessed, your results are now sorted by *InvoiceNumber*, from lowest to highest.

   ```
   Lehmanns Marktstand - 1266
   Lehmanns Marktstand - 1579
   B's Beverages - 3122
   ```

3. Close your browser.

4. Change *.OrderBy* to: **.OrderByDescending**

   ```
   var Invoices = Data.Invoices
       .Where(Invoice => Invoice.InvoiceAmount > 990)
       .OrderByDescending(Invoice=>Invoice.InvoiceNumber);
   ```

5. View *reports.aspx* in your web browser.

   Now your results are sorted from highest *InvoiceNumber* to lowest.

   ```
   Hanari Carnes - 9728
   B's Beverages - 9726
   Island Trading - 9654
   ```

6. Close your browser.

4 Get only the top 5 results from the database.

By using the *Take* method, you can return only the number of results you want.

1. Remove the semicolon from the end of the *var Invoices…* code line and append the following code:

   .Take(5);

```
var Invoices = Data.Invoices
    .Where(Invoice => Invoice.InvoiceAmount > 990)
    .OrderByDescending(Invoice => Invoice.InvoiceNumber)
    .Take(5);
```

2. View *reports.aspx* in your browser.

```
Hanari Carnes - 9728
B's Beverages - 9726
Island Trading - 9654
Ana Trujillo Emparedados y helados - 8869
Hanari Carnes - 7615
```

Only the top 5 invoice numbers are displayed.

3. Close your browser.

By using the *OrderBy* and *Take* methods together, you can retrieve the top or bottom values from any database table.

5   Call a stored procedure using LINQ.

In *Lesson 10-2: Add LINQ data classes to a project*, you added a stored procedure to your LINQ data classes.

Stored procedures can do pretty much anything with a database, and LINQ makes it very easy to call them.

1. Remove all of the code inside your *using* statement.

2. Add the following code inside the *using* statement:

int LastInvoice = Data.SpGetLastInvoiceNumber();

```
using (SparkDataContext Data = new SparkDataContext())
{
    int LastInvoice = Data.SpGetLastInvoiceNumber();
}
```

This calls the *SpGetLastInvoiceNumber* stored procedure and puts its return value into an *int* variable called *LastInvoice*.

Stored procedures can be called anything, but I always prefix them with *Sp* to make them easier to find in the IntelliSense list.

3. Add the following code inside the *using* statement:

LabelReport.Text = LastInvoice.ToString();

```
using (SparkDataContext Data = new SparkDataContext())
{
    int LastInvoice = Data.SpGetLastInvoiceNumber();
    LabelReport.Text = LastInvoice.ToString();
}
```

This will output the last invoice number onto the page.

4. View *reports.aspx* in your browser.

```
9987
```

You should see the number *9987* appear: the highest invoice number in the *Invoices* table.

6   Close your browser and close Visual Studio.

---

note

Stored procedure methods

In this example, the stored procedure doesn't need any arguments and simply returns an *int* value, but stored procedures can have arguments and return values, just like any other method.

You can use the IntelliSense description of stored procedure methods to check what arguments the method requires and the type of value it returns.

---

note

LINQ or Stored Procedures?

Stored procedures can do everything LINQ can do and will usually be faster and more efficient.

Using stored procedures for everything seems ideal, but having hundreds of stored procedures in a database often becomes unmanageable and difficult to maintain.

I recommend using LINQ for simple, everyday queries and stored procedures for anything more complicated, or if you see performance issues.

Lesson 10-6: Check whether a record exists using LINQ

There will be times when you'll need to run a LINQ query without being sure whether it will find any records in the database. When returning multiple records using the *Where* method this will simply return an empty collection, but when using the *Single* method it will cause an exception.

In this lesson you'll write LINQ code to check if a single record exists and only return a result if so.

1 Open *Spark* from your sample files folder.

2 Open the code-behind file of *reports.aspx*.

3 Write code to return a single record.

In *Lesson 10-3: Retrieve a single row of data using LINQ,* you used the *Single* method to return a single row of data. If the row of data hadn't existed it would have caused an exception.

1. Remove all code from the *using* statement.

2. Add the following code inside the *using* statement:

**Customer CheckCustomer = Data.Customers
.Single(Customer => Customer.CustomerID == 99);**

```
using (SparkDataContext Data = new SparkDataContext())
{
    Customer CheckCustomer = Data.Customers
        .Single(Customer => Customer.CustomerID == 99);
}
```

3. Add the following code on the next line:

LabelReport.Text = CheckCustomer.CustomerName;

```
using (SparkDataContext Data = new SparkDataContext())
{
    Customer CheckCustomer = Data.Customers
        .Single(Customer => Customer.CustomerID == 99);
    LabelReport.Text = CheckCustomer.CustomerName;
}
```

4. View *reports.aspx* in your browser.

Server Error in '/' Application.

Sequence contains no elements

You will see an error message. This is because there is no record in the database for customer ID 99 so the *Single* method generates an exception.

You could use *try* and *catch* to work around this, but it's better to avoid that approach because you can make your code work without causing an exception.

You learned about *try* and *catch* in: *Lesson 7-6: Use try and catch to handle errors.*

5. Close your browser.

4 **Add code to check whether the record exists.**

1. Change the *Single* method to: **SingleOrDefault**

   The *SingleOrDefault* method works in exactly the same way as *Single,* but it will return *null* if the record doesn't exist instead of causing an exception.

   ```
   Customer CheckCustomer = Data.Customers
       .SingleOrDefault(Customer => Customer.CustomerID == 99);
   LabelReport.Text = CheckCustomer.CustomerName;
   ```

note

FirstOrDefault

The *FirstOrDefault* method works in a similar way to the *SingleOrDefault* method.

2. View *reports.aspx* in your browser.

   > # Server Error in '/' Application.
   >
   > *Object reference not set to an instance of an object.*

   You will see another error. This time it's because the *CheckCustomer* object is *null,* so the code can't set *LabelReport.Text* to the value of its *CustomerName* property.

   You can fix this with a simple *if* statement.

3. Close your browser.

4. Change the *LabelReport.Text…* line to:

   if (CheckCustomer == null)
   {
       LabelReport.Text = "Customer does not exist!";
   }
   else
   {
       LabelReport.Text = CheckCustomer.CustomerName;
   }

   ```
   using (SparkDataContext Data = new SparkDataContext())
   {
       Customer CheckCustomer = Data.Customers
           .SingleOrDefault(C => C.CustomerID == 99);
       if (CheckCustomer == null)
       {
           LabelReport.Text = "Customer does not exist!";
       }
       else
       {
           LabelReport.Text = CheckCustomer.CustomerName;
       }
   }
   ```

   This will check if the returned *Customer* object is *null.* If the return value is *null,* the text *Customer does not exist!* is displayed instead of the return value.

5. View *reports.aspx* in your browser.

   > Customer does not exist!

   You'll see that your code does not cause an exception and instead shows that customer ID 99 does not exist.

6. Close your browser.

Lesson 10-7: Update database records using LINQ

You're not limited to simply retrieving and displaying data from your database, you can very easily update it too.

In this lesson you'll update some rows in your database using LINQ.

1   Open *Spark* from your sample files folder.

2   Open the code-behind file of *reports.aspx*.

3   Retrieve an invoice from the database.

1.   Remove all code from the *using* statement.

2.   Add code to retrieve a single invoice record from the database:

**Invoice MyInvoice = Data.Invoices.Single
(Invoice => Invoice.InvoiceID == 1882);**

3.   Add code to output the invoice to the page:

**LabelReport.Text = MyInvoice.InvoiceNumber;
LabelReport.Text += "<br />";
LabelReport.Text += MyInvoice.InvoiceAmount.ToString();**

```
using (SparkDataContext Data = new SparkDataContext())
{
    Invoice MyInvoice = Data.Invoices.Single
        (Invoice => Invoice.InvoiceID == 1882);
    LabelReport.Text = MyInvoice.InvoiceNumber;
    LabelReport.Text += "<br />";
    LabelReport.Text += MyInvoice.InvoiceAmount.ToString();
}
```

4.   View *reports.aspx* in your browser.

```
2431
526.1200
```

The *InvoiceNumber* and *InvoiceAmount* of the invoice are displayed.

4   Add a button to update the invoice.

1.   Close your browser and open *reports.aspx* in *Design* view.

2.   Add a *Button* control to the page.

Place the button control after the *LabelReport* control.

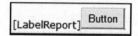

3.   Call the button: **ButtonUpdateInvoice**

4.   Set the *Text* property of the button to: **Update Invoice**

5.   Add a *Click* event handler to the button.

5   Update the invoice record.

1.   Copy and paste the code from your *Page_Load* event handler into your *ButtonUpdateInvoice_Click* event handler.

note

The SubmitChanges method

The *SubmitChanges* method will commit any changes you have made to your database.

If you have a large collection of data you want to update, you still only need to call the *SubmitChanges* method once.

LINQ will keep track of any changes made prior to committing them to the database.

```
2431
526.1200  Update Invoice
```

note

Keeping the page up to date

In this lesson you update the invoice that is displayed on the page, but the page doesn't immediately display the changes you made.

Ideally, you would store the code that retrieves and displays the invoice details in a separate method that is called by both the *Page_Load* and *ButtonUpdateInvoice_Click* event handlers.

Of course this approach wouldn't be very efficient as the method would be called twice when the button was clicked.

You'll discover a more efficient solution in: *Lesson 12-8: Create a Checkout page.*

```
2431
123.0000  Update Invoice
```

2. Remove the three lines of code that set the value of *LabelReport.Text* from your *ButtonUpdateInvoice_Click* event handler.

```
protected void ButtonUpdateInvoice_Click(object sender, EventArgs e)
{
    using (SparkDataContext Data = new SparkDataContext())
    {
        Invoice MyInvoice = Data.Invoices.Single
            (Invoice => Invoice.InvoiceID == 1882);
    }
}
```

3. Add code to change the *InvoiceAmount* property of the invoice.

MyInvoice.InvoiceAmount = 123;

```
Invoice MyInvoice = Data.Invoices.Single
    (Invoice => Invoice.InvoiceID == 1882);
MyInvoice.InvoiceAmount = 123;
```

4. View *reports.aspx* in your browser and click *Update Invoice*.

Nothing happens. LINQ doesn't update the database unless you specifically tell it to.

5. Close your browser.

6. Add the following code to the *using* statement in the *ButtonUpdateInvoice_Click* event handler:

Data.SubmitChanges();

```
Invoice MyInvoice = Data.Invoices.Single
    (Invoice => Invoice.InvoiceID == 1882);
MyInvoice.InvoiceAmount = 123;
Data.SubmitChanges();
```

This tells LINQ to update the database with any changes you make.

7. View *reports.aspx* in your browser and click *Update Invoice* again.

The value did update, but this isn't apparent as the updated value isn't displayed on the screen. That is because the code in the *Page_Load* event is executed before the code in the *Click* event (see: *Lesson 3-2: Add event handlers to Controls*).

Your *Page_Load* event handler will have to run again to retrieve the updated value.

(See sidebar for a discussion of a solution to this problem).

8. Refresh the page.

Using your browser's refresh button, refresh the page.

Now you will see the updated value (*123*).

As you can see, simply changing the properties of your LINQ objects and then calling the *SubmitChanges* method allows you to update any of the values stored in your database.

You can also do this with collections of data by using a *foreach* loop and calling the *SubmitChanges* method once it has finished (see sidebar).

Lesson 10-8: Insert database records using LINQ

As well as retrieving and updating database records, you can use LINQ to add new records using a similar technique.

In this lesson you'll use LINQ to make the *New Invoice* page functional.

1   Open *Spark* from your sample files folder.

2   View *newtransaction.aspx* in design view.

New Invoice

Customer	Unbound ▾
Invoice Number	*
Amount	**
Tax Amount (20%)	**

[LabelError]

Submit

Your invoice was successfully added.

This web page is not yet functional. Eventually you'll be able to choose a customer from the drop-down list and add a new customer invoice.

3   Open the code-behind file of *newtransaction.aspx*.

4   Create a new instance of your *DataContext* class.

Add a new *using* statement inside the *else* statement to create a new instance of the *SparkDataContext* class:

using (SparkDataContext Data = new SparkDataContext())
{
}

```
else
{
    using (SparkDataContext Data = new SparkDataContext())
    {
    }
}
```

note

Naming of controls

If you look at the page in *Design* view, you'll notice that the names of the controls on the page closely match the names of the properties in the database.

This is best practice. If a control is used to display or set a value in a database, its name should match the name of the database field it displays or sets.

5   Create a new instance of the *Invoice* class.

In previous lessons, you've retrieved an *Invoice* object from the database by using the *SparkDataContext* class. In this lesson you want to add a new invoice, so you need to create a new instance of the *Invoice* class.

Add the following code inside the *using* statement:

Invoice NewInvoice = new Invoice();

```
else
{
    using (SparkDataContext Data = new SparkDataContext())
    {
        Invoice NewInvoice = new Invoice();
```

As you should recall from *Lesson 6-10: Create and dispose of instances*, this code creates a new instance of the *Invoice* class called *NewInvoice*.

6   Set the new invoice's properties.

1. Add the following code after the line that creates the *NewInvoice* object:

NewInvoice.CustomerID = 5;

```
Invoice NewInvoice = new Invoice();
NewInvoice.CustomerID = 5;
```

The *Customer* dropdown isn't functional yet, so you're setting the *CustomerID* manually for now to test the page.

In *Lesson 11-2: Attach a data source to a control,* you'll make the *Customer* dropdown automatically retrieve every customer in the database.

2. Add code to set the other properties according to the controls on the page:

NewInvoice.InvoiceNumber = TextBoxInvoiceNumber.Text;
NewInvoice.InvoiceAmount =
Convert.ToDecimal(TextBoxAmount.Text);
NewInvoice.InvoiceTaxAmount =
Convert.ToDecimal(TextBoxTaxAmount.Text);

3. Add code to set the date and time:

NewInvoice.InvoiceDate = DateTime.Now;

```
NewInvoice.CustomerID = 5;
NewInvoice.InvoiceNumber = TextBoxInvoiceNumber.Text;
NewInvoice.InvoiceAmount =
    Convert.ToDecimal(TextBoxAmount.Text);
NewInvoice.InvoiceTaxAmount =
    Convert.ToDecimal(TextBoxTaxAmount.Text);
NewInvoice.InvoiceDate = DateTime.Now;
```

7 **Tell LINQ to send the data to the database.**

Just creating an *Invoice* object and calling the *SubmitChanges* method isn't enough. You need to specifically tell LINQ to insert the record.

1. Tell LINQ which record needs to be inserted into the *Invoice* table:

Data.Invoices.InsertOnSubmit(NewInvoice);

2. Call the *SubmitChanges* method to insert the record.

Data.SubmitChanges();

```
NewInvoice.InvoiceTaxAmount =
    Convert.ToDecimal(TextBoxTaxAmount.Text);
NewInvoice.InvoiceDate = DateTime.Now;
Data.Invoices.InsertOnSubmit(NewInvoice);
Data.SubmitChanges();
```

8 **Add code to tell the user that the invoice was added successfully.**

Add the following code after the *SubmitChanges* line:

PanelAddInvoice.Visible = false;
PanelConfirmAdded.Visible = true;

This will hide the panel containing the new invoice details and show a panel with the confirmation text.

9 **Test *newtransaction.aspx.***

1. Open *newtransaction.aspx* in your browser and complete the form.

2. Click *Submit.*

The confirmation text appears on the page.

---

note

InvoiceID

When setting the properties of the *Invoice* object, you might have noticed that there's an *InvoiceID* property that you don't set.

InvoiceID is the table's unique *primary key,* which is automatically maintained by the database.

In most well-designed databases, the primary key is automatically maintained.

tip

Inserting a collection

As well as inserting a single *Invoice* object using the *InsertOnSubmit* method, you can insert a collection of *Invoice* objects (such as a *List<Invoice>*) by using the *InsertAllOnSubmit* method.

```
Data.SubmitChanges();
PanelAddInvoice.Visible = false;
PanelConfirmAdded.Visible = true;
```

```
Your invoice was successfully added.
```

---

note

Deleting records

It is best practice never to delete records from databases.

In the old days of computing disk space was at a premium so old records were physically deleted.

These days disk storage space is very cheap so it is useful to keep deleted records in case the user needs to recall them later.

Ideally, instead of deleting a record, you should update it with a property to indicate that the record should be treated as if it did not exist.

note

Database permissions

If you are working with a remote database server, you will need to be given a username and password that has permission to access it.

The database administrator can allow or disallow a user to view, update, insert or delete records.

If you don't have permission to carry out an action on the database, an exception will be generated.

Lesson 10-9: Delete database records using LINQ

You can now retrieve, update and insert database records using LINQ. The only common database operation you haven't covered is deleting.

1 Open *Spark* from your sample files folder.

2 Open the code-behind file of *reports.aspx*.

3 Remove the *ButtonUpdateInvoice* control and its code.

1. Remove the *ButtonUpdateInvoice_Click* event handler.

2. Open *reports.aspx* in *Design* view.

3. Delete the *ButtonUpdateInvoice* control.

4 Add a new button control.

1. Add a new *Button* control where the *ButtonUpdateInvoice* control used to be.

2. Name the new button: **ButtonDeleteInvoice**

3. Set the *Text* property of the button to: **Delete Invoice**

4. Add a new *Click* event handler to the *ButtonDeleteInvoice* control.

```
[LabelReport]     Delete Invoice
```

5 Create a new instance of your LINQ *DataContext* class in the new event handler.

using (SparkDataContext Data = new SparkDataContext())
{
}

```
protected void ButtonDeleteInvoice_Click(object sender, Ev
{
    using (SparkDataContext Data = new SparkDataContext())
    {

    }
}
```

6 Retrieve an *Invoice* object for the invoice currently displayed on the page.

Before you can delete an invoice, you need to retrieve an *Invoice* object that matches the invoice you want to delete.

Copy the code that retrieves the invoice currently displayed from the *Page_Load* event handler and paste it into your *ButtonDeleteInvoice_Click* event handler (inside the *using* statement):

Invoice MyInvoice = Data.Invoices
.Single(Invoice => Invoice.InvoiceID == 1882);

```
using (SparkDataContext Data = new SparkDataContext())
{
    Invoice MyInvoice = Data.Invoices
        .Single(Invoice => Invoice.InvoiceID == 1882);
}
```

You now have an *Invoice* object which you're going to delete from the database.

note

Deleting a collection

In the same way you can insert a collection of database rows using the *InsertAllOnSubmit* method, you can delete a collection of database rows using the *DeleteAllOnSubmit* method.

7   Tell LINQ to delete the invoice.

Deleting a record is very similar to inserting one:

1.   Tell LINQ which record needs to be deleted from the *Invoice* table:

     Data.Invoices.DeleteOnSubmit(MyInvoice);

2.   Call the *SubmitChanges* method to delete the record:

     Data.SubmitChanges();

```
using (SparkDataContext Data = new SparkDataContext())
{
    Invoice MyInvoice = Data.Invoices
        .Single(Invoice => Invoice.InvoiceID == 1882);
    Data.Invoices.DeleteOnSubmit(MyInvoice);
    Data.SubmitChanges();
}
```

8   Test your code.

1.   View *reports.aspx* in your browser.

     You will see that the page still retrieves the details of the invoice with the InvoiceID of *1882*.

```
2431
526.1200   Delete Invoice
```

2.   Click the *Delete Invoice* button.

3.   Refresh the page.

     You will see an exception! Your code successfully deleted the record from the database but this has introduced an error.

```
Server Error in '/' Application.

Sequence contains no elements
```

     The error ocurrs because your *Page_Load* event handler is trying to use the *Single* method to get invoice ID 1882 which no longer exists.

9   Fix the error.

1.   Close your browser and return to the code-behind file of *reports.aspx*.

2.   In the *Page_Load* event handler, change *1882* to: **1883**

```
Invoice MyInvoice = Data.Invoices
    .Single(I => I.InvoiceID == 1883);
```

3.   View *reports.aspx* in your browser.

```
5129
304.4700   Delete Invoice
```

     There is no longer an error: your code was able to find invoice ID *1883*.

     You could also have fixed the error by changing the *Page_Load* event handler to use the *SingleOrDefault* method instead of the *Single* method and then handling the possibility of a *null* value. You did this in: *Lesson 10-6: Check whether a record exists using LINQ.*

Lesson 10-10: Use LINQ with collections

The LINQ code you've learned in this session doesn't just work with databases; you can use it on any collection!

1   Open *Spark* from your sample files folder.

2   Open the code-behind file of *reports.aspx*.

3   Remove all code from the *Page_Load* event handler.

4   Remove the *ButtonDeleteInvoice_Click* event handler.

5   Remove the *ButtonDeleteInvoice* control from the page.

6   Retrieve the customer collection from the *Utilities* class.

In the *Page_Load* event handler, call the *Utilities.GetBlockedCustomers* method to get back the collection of *string* variables you created in *Lesson 8-2: Create a collection* and put it in a variable named: **BlockedCustomers**

List<string> BlockedCustomers = Utilities.GetBlockedCustomers();

```
protected void Page_Load(object sender, EventArgs e)
{
    List<string> BlockedCustomers = Utilities.GetBlockedCustomers();
}
```

7   Retrieve a single item using the *Single* method.

In exactly the same way as you did in *Lesson 10-3: Retrieve a single row of data using LINQ,* you can use LINQ to retrieve a single item from a collection. Of course, this time it will be a *string* value instead of a *Customer* object.

Add the following code to the *Page_Load* event handler:

string SingleCustomer = BlockedCustomers
.Single(CustomerID => CustomerID == "6");

```
List<string> BlockedCustomers = Utilities.GetBlockedCustomers();
string SingleCustomer = BlockedCustomers
    .Single(CustomerID => CustomerID == "6");
```

Because the items in the *BlockedCustomers* collection don't have any properties, you can use the alias (*CustomerID*) on its own to represent the values in the collection.

8   Test your code.

1. To display the value of the *SingleCustomer* string variable in the label on the page add the following code:

LabelReport.Text = SingleCustomer;

```
List<string> BlockedCustomers = Utilities.GetBlockedCustomers();
string SingleCustomer = BlockedCustomers
    .Single(CustomerID => CustomerID == "6");
LabelReport.Text = SingleCustomer;
```

2. View *reports.aspx* in your browser.

6

You will see the number 6 appear on the page. It was found in the collection and output by your code.

3. Close your browser.

9 Retrieve multiple items from the BlockedCustomers collection using LINQ's *Where* method.

You do this in exactly the same way as you did in: *Lesson 10-4: Retrieve multiple rows of data using LINQ.*

1. Remove code, so that you are left with just the line beginning: *List<string> BlockedCustomers…*

```
protected void Page_Load(object sender, EventArgs e)
{
    List<string> BlockedCustomers = Utilities.GetBlockedCustomers();
}
```

2. Use the *Where* LINQ method to return a sub-set of items from the list collection.

var SubList = BlockedCustomers
.Where(CustomerID => CustomerID == "6"
|| CustomerID == "9" || CustomerID == "99");

```
List<string> BlockedCustomers = Utilities.GetBlockedCustomers()
var SubList = BlockedCustomers
    .Where(CustomerID =>
            CustomerID == "6"
        || CustomerID == "9"
        || CustomerID == "99");
```

This will search the *BlockedCustomers* collection for items with the values *6, 9* or *99* and put the results into a new collection called *SubList*.

10 Output the list to the page.

Use a *foreach* loop to display the resulting values in the *LabelReport* control.

foreach (string CustomerID in SubList)
{
    LabelReport.Text += CustomerID;
    LabelReport.Text += "<br />";
}

```
foreach (string CustomerID in SubList)
{
    LabelReport.Text += CustomerID;
    LabelReport.Text += "<br />";
}
```

11 Test your code.

View *reports.aspx* in your browser.

6
9

You will see that the numbers *6* and *9* appear, but *99* does not. That is because it wasn't found in the collection.

LINQ can make working with collections very easy, but you should be careful not to let it impact performance (see sidebar).

note

LINQ and performance

When you use LINQ on a database, it creates SQL code which is used by the database to retrieve your information.

Databases don't have to look through every record in the database to find the one you need. They use indexes to speed up searching.

When you use LINQ with collections, it actually does the equivalent of a *foreach* loop, looking through every value in the collection in order to find the ones you want. With large collections, this can be a slow process that is demanding on the computer running it.

Be aware of this when using LINQ with collections.

Session 10: Exercise

1   Open the *Session10* project from your sample files folder.

2   Add *LINQ to SQL Classes* to the project. Call the file: **Session10.dbml**

3   Add the *Customer* table from the *Spark* database to the *LINQ to SQL Classes*.

4   Add the *SpGetLastInvoiceNumber* stored procedure from the *Spark* database to the *LINQ to SQL Classes*.

5   Open the code-behind file of *Default.aspx*.

6   Add code to the *Page_Load* event handler to retrieve a *Customer* object with the *CustomerID* of 7 and display the object's *CustomerName* property in the *TextBoxEditCustomerName* control.

7   Add *Click* event handlers to the *ButtonAddCustomer* and *ButtonSaveCustomer* controls.

8   Add code to the *ButtonSaveCustomer_Click* event handler to retrieve the customer with the *CustomerID* of 7 and set its *CustomerName* property to the value entered in the *TextBoxEditCustomer* control.

9   Add code to the *ButtonSaveCustomer_Click* event handler to commit the changes to the *CustomerName* property to the database by calling the *SubmitChanges* method.

10   Add code to the *ButtonAddCustomer_Click* event handler to add a new record to the *Customer* table in the database.

      Set the new record's *CustomerName* property to the value of the *TextBoxNewCustomerName.Text* property.

      (Remember to use the *InsertOnSubmit* method before the *SubmitChanges* method).

11   Add *try* and *catch* code to all three event handlers and put the *Message* property of any exceptions into the *LabelError.Text* property.

12   View and test the *default.aspx* page in your browser.

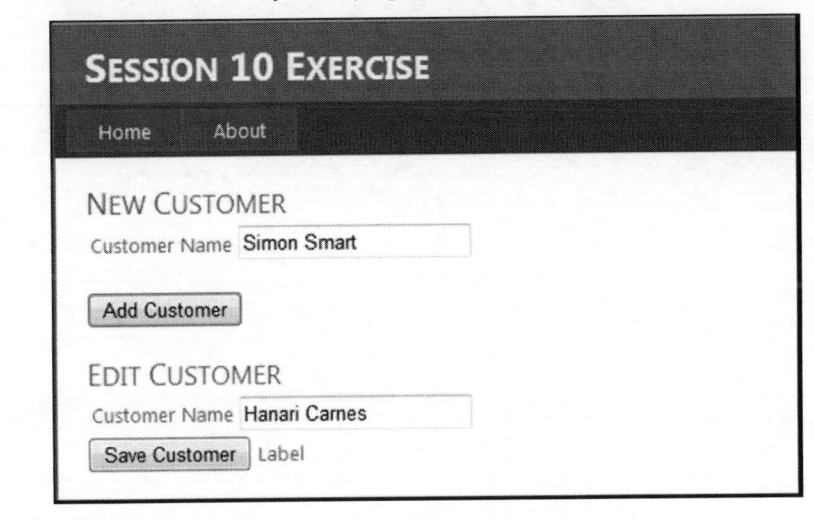

Session10 - start   Session10 - end

If you need help slide the page to the left

Session 10: Exercise Answers

These are the four questions that students find the most difficult to answer:

Q 11	Q 10	Q 8	Q 6
1. Enclose your code in the following: **try** **{** *[Code]* **}** 2. Add the following: **catch** **(Exception Ex)** **{** **LabelError** **.Text = Ex** **.Message;** **}** This was covered in: *Lesson 7-6: Use try and catch to handle errors.*	Use the following code: **using (Session10DataContext Data = new Session10DataContext())** **{** **Customer NewCustomer = new Customer();** **NewCustomer** **.CustomerName = TextBoxNewCustomer Name.Text;** **Data.Customers** **.InsertOnSubmit (NewCustomer);** **Data.SubmitChanges();** **}** This was covered in: *Lesson 10-8: Insert database records using LINQ.*	Use the following code: **using (Session10DataContext Data = new Session10DataContext())** **{** **Customer MyCustomer = Data.Customers** **.Single (Customer => Customer .CustomerID == 7);** **MyCustomer** **.CustomerName = TextBoxEditCustomer Name.Text;** **}** This was covered in: *Lesson 10-7: Update database records using LINQ.*	Use the following code: **using (Session10DataContext Data = new Session10DataContext())** **{** **Customer MyCustomer = Data .Customers.Single (Customer => Customer .CustomerID == 7);** **TextBoxEditCustomer Name.Text = MyCustomer .CustomerName;** **}** This was covered in: *Lesson 10-3: Retrieve a single row of data using LINQ.*

If you have difficulty with the other questions, here are the lessons that cover the relevant skills:

1   Refer to: Lesson 1-7: Manage a project with the Solution Explorer.

2   Refer to: Lesson 10-2: Add LINQ data classes to a project.

3   Refer to: Lesson 10-2: Add LINQ data classes to a project.

4   Refer to: Lesson 10-2: Add LINQ data classes to a project.

5   Refer to: Lesson 1-7: Manage a project with the Solution Explorer.

7   Refer to: Lesson 3-2: Add event handlers to Controls.

9   Refer to: Lesson 10-7: Update database records using LINQ.

12   Refer to: Lesson 1-8: Run a project in debug mode.

Session Eleven: Using data controls

> Errors using inadequate data are much less than those using no data at all.
>
> *Charles Babbage, English mathematician (1792 – 1871)*

Using the code you learned in the last session along with your knowledge of ASP.NET controls and HTML, you can already create a web application that reads and writes data to a database.

However, ASP.NET comes with several controls that can do a lot of the work for you, making creating data-centric web pages even easier.

In this session, you'll work with some of these controls and see how you can easily interact with databases without needing to write any code at all!

Session Objectives

By the end of this session you will be able to:

- Use the LinqDataSource control
- Attach a data source to a control
- Use the GridView control
- Add sorting and paging to a GridView
- Add editing features to a GridView
- Use the DetailsView control
- Use the SqlDataSource control
- Bind data to a control using C#

Lesson 11-1: Use the LinqDataSource control

The easiest way to bind data to a control on a page is to use a data source control. There are a few of these in the *Data* category of the *Toolbox*, but in this lesson you're going to use the *LinqDataSource* control.

The *LinqDataSource* control retrieves data using *LINQ to SQL Classes*.

1   Open *Spark* from your sample files folder.

2   Open *newtransaction.aspx* in *Design* view.

3   Add a *LinqDataSource* control to the page.

Drag a *LinqDataSource* control from the *Data* category of the *Toolbox* onto the page. Place it just before the *Customer* drop down.

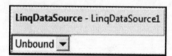

note

Placing data sources

In this lesson you place the *LinqDataSource* control near the *DropDownList* control it is going to populate, but the placement of a data source control doesn't matter.

Data sources aren't visible to people visiting the page, so you can put them wherever seems most logical.

4   Configure the *LinqDataSource* control.

1. Set the *ID* property of the *LinqDataSource* control to: **LinqDataSourceCustomer**

2. Click *Configure Data Source...* from the *QuickTasks* menu of the *LinqDataSource* control.

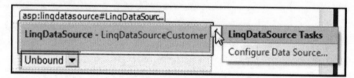

This opens the configuration dialog for the control.

3. Make sure *Spark.SparkDataContext* is selected.

In the first step of configuration, you select which LINQ data context (ie dbml file) to use.

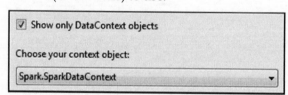

Since you only have one it should already be selected. If it isn't, select it.

4. Click *Next*.

5. Select the table to retrieve data from.

This data source is going to retrieve a list of customers for the *DropDownListCustomer* control to use, so select the *Customers* table from the *Table* dropdown.

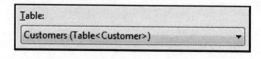

If you are not completing the course incrementally use the sample file: **Lesson 11-1** to begin this lesson.

Sample files with the starting point for each lesson are also provided for all of the other lessons in this session.

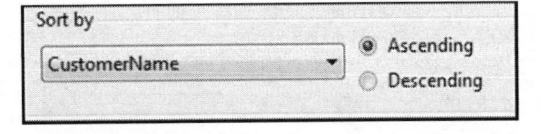

6. Click *OrderBy....*

This opens a dialog to configure sorting. Sorting works exactly the same way as using the *OrderBy* and *OrderByDescending* methods in LINQ (see: *Lesson 10-5: Sort results and call stored procedures using LINQ*).

7. Select *CustomerName* and *Ascending.*

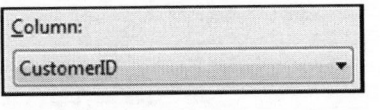

8. Click *OK.*

9. Click *Where....*

This opens a dialog to configure query criteria, which work the same way as the *Single* and *Where* methods in LINQ (see: *Lesson 10-3: Retrieve a single row of data using LINQ*).

10. Select *CustomerID* from the *Column* drop-down.

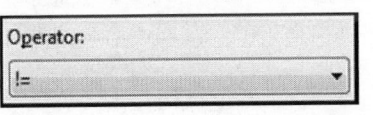

This tells the *LinqDataSource* control that *CustomerID* is the database column you want to use for your criteria.

11. Select *!=* from the *Operator* drop-down.

This is the 'does not equal' operator. You learned about it in: *Lesson 7-3: Use basic logical operators.*

12. Select *None* from the *Source* drop-down.

The *Source* drop-down allows you to tell your data source to retrieve a value from several different sources (see sidebar).

In this case, you want a value that doesn't change. *None* allows you to type in the value you want to use.

13. Enter **5** into the Parameter Properties *Value* text box.

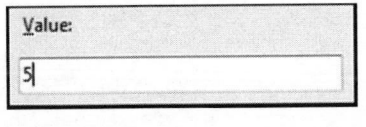

14. Click *Add.*

Your new parameter has been added. This data source will now retrieve everything from the *Customer* table except for *CustomerID* 5.

15. Click *OK.*

16. Click *Finish.*

note

Other *Source* options

In this lesson, you use the *None* source to specify your own value for a parameter, but you can choose between several sources.

Control
Retrieve a value from a control on the page.

Cookie
Retrieve a value from a cookie.

Form
Retrieve a value from:
Page.Request.Form

Profile
Retrieve a value from a user profile.

QueryString
Retrieve a value from:
Page.Request.QueryString

Session
Retrieve a value from a *Session* variable.

Route
Retrieve a value from a URL.

Lesson 11-2: Attach a data source to a control

In this lesson, you'll attach the *LinqDataSource* control you created in *Lesson 11-1: Use the LinqDataSource control* to the *DropDownListCustomer* control.

1   Open *Spark* from your sample files folder.

2   Open *newtransaction.aspx* in *Design* view.

3   Set the data source of the *DropDownListCustomer* control to *LinqDataSourceCustome*r.

    1. Click *Choose Data Source...* from the *QuickTasks* menu of *DropDownListCustomer*.

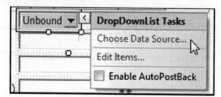

    2. Select the *LinqDataSourceCustomer* control from the first drop-down list.

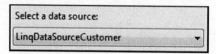

      This is the *LinqDataSource* control you created in: *Lesson 11-1: Use the LinqDataSource control*.

    3. Select *CustomerName* from the second drop-down list.

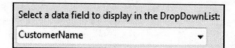

      This tells the *DropDownList* control to display *CustomerName*. This is the value that will be shown on the page and will be stored in the *DropDownListCustomer.SelectedItem.Text* property.

    4. Select *CustomerID* from the third drop-down list.

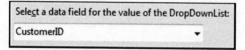

      This determines the hidden value that will accompany each item in the drop-down list control. The value will be stored in the *DropDownListCustomer.SelectedValue* property.

    5. Click *OK*.

      Your data source is now linked to your control. When the page is viewed, the list of customers will be automatically displayed in the *DropDownList* control.

4   View *newtransaction.aspx* in your browser.

You will see that the drop-down list has been populated.

Ana Trujillo Emparedados y helados ▼
Ana Trujillo Emparedados y helados
Bottom-Dollar Markets
B's Beverages
Cactus Comidas para llevar
Frankenversand
Hanari Carnes
Island Trading
La maison d'Asie
Magazzini Alimentari Riuniti
Morgenstern Gesundkost
QUICK-Stop
Romero y tomillo

note

Other controls to attach data sources to

You can attach a data source to the *BulletedList, CheckBoxList, ListBox* and *RadioButtonList* controls in exactly the same way as you attach one to a *DropDownList* control.

There are also more advanced data controls in the *Data* category such as the *GridView* control, which you'll use in: *Lesson 11-3: Use the GridView control.*

5   Inspect the properties of the *DropDownListCustomer* control.

The *QuickTasks* menu makes things easier in this case, but it doesn't do anything you can't do by manually setting the properties of the *DropDownList* control.

1.   Close your browser.

2.   Examine the *DataSourceID* property of the *DropDownList* control.

DataSourceID	LinqDataSourceCustomer

This determines which data source control the *DropDownList* control uses. As you can see, it's currently *LinqDataSourceCustomer*.

You could change the data source by changing this property.

3.   Examine the *DataTextField* property.

DataTextField	CustomerName

This is the field that is displayed in the *DropDownList* control. It is currently *CustomerName*.

4.   Examine the *DataValueField* property.

DataValueField	CustomerID

This is the field that is stored in the hidden value of each item in the drop-down list. It is currently *CustomerID*.

Whether you prefer to use the *QuickTasks* dialog or set the properties manually is up to you.

6   Add an item to the *DropDownList* control control manually.

1.   Use the *Edit Items…* QuickTasks dialog to add a new item to the *DropDownListCustomer* control with the *Text*:
      -- Select Customer --

      You first did this in: *Lesson 1-15: Use the QuickTasks menu.*

2.   View *newtransaction.aspx* in your browser.

      You'll see that your item isn't displayed. That's because it was overwritten by the items from the database. Fortunately this is easy to fix.

3.   Close your browser and set the *AppendDataBoundItems* property of the *DropDownListCustomer* control to: **True**

      This means that items from the database will be added to the *DropDownList* control instead of overwriting any existing items.

4.   View *newtransaction.aspx* in your browser.

      This time your manually-added item stays where it is.

-- Select Customer --
-- Select Customer --
Ana Trujillo Emparedados y helados
Bottom-Dollar Markets
B's Beverages
Cactus Comidas para llevar
Frankenversand
Hanari Carnes
Island Trading
La maison d'Asie
Magazzini Alimentari Riuniti
Morgenstern Gesundkost
QUICK-Stop
Romero y tomillo

Lesson 11-3: Use the GridView control

The *GridView* control is an extremely flexible control that allows you to retrieve and display data in an automatically-generated table.

In this lesson you'll create a basic *GridView* control that displays invoices in order of date.

1 Open *Spark* from your sample files folder.

2 Open the code-behind file of *reports.aspx.*

3 Remove the existing code from the *Page_Load* event handler.

4 Add a *LinqDataSource* control to the page.

   1. Open *reports.aspx* in *Design* view.

   2. Add a new *LinqDataSource* control after the *LabelReport* control.

   3. Name the new control: **LinqDataSourceInvoice**

   4. Configure the data source to retrieve records from the *Invoice* table, sorted by *InvoiceDate* in ascending order.

     You learned to do this in: *Lesson 11-1: Use the LinqDataSource control.*

5 Add a *GridView* control to the page.

   1. Add a *GridView* control from the *Data* category of the *Toolbox.*

     Place it after the *LinqDataSourceInvoice* control.

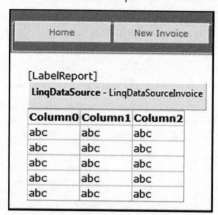

   2. Set the *ID* property of the *GridView* control to: **GridViewInvoice**

   3. Set the *EnableViewState* property of the *GridView* control to **False** (see sidebar).

6 Set the data source of the *GridView* control.

Choose *LinqDataSourceInvoice* from the *Choose Data Source* drop-down in the *QuickTasks* menu for the *GridView* control.

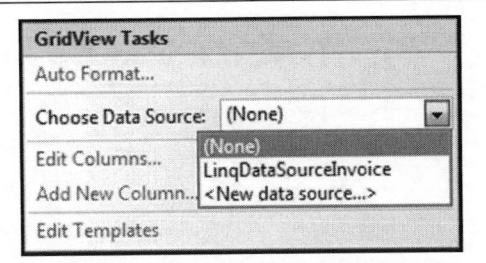

You will see that the columns from the database table are automatically added to the *GridView* control!

InvoiceID	CustomerID	InvoiceDate	InvoiceAmount	InvoiceTaxAmount	InvoiceNumber
0	0	13/04/2011 00:00:00	0	0	abc

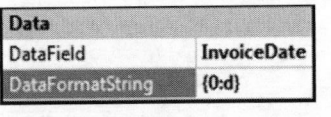

7 Edit the *GridView* control's columns.

1. Click *Edit Columns…* from the *QuickTasks* menu of the *GridView* control.

   The *Fields* dialog will appear.

2. Click *InvoiceID* in the *Selected Fields* list.

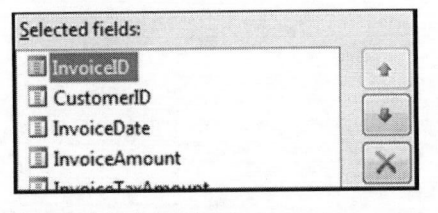

3. Click the *Delete* button to remove it.

4. Delete the *CustomerID* field in the same way.

5. Click the *InvoiceDate* field.

   The field's properties are displayed in the *BoundField properties* panel.

6. Scroll down to the *DataFormatString* property and set it to: **{0:d}**

Data	
DataField	InvoiceDate
DataFormatString	{0:d}

   This is a data format string. It's different to the format strings that you can use in the *ToString* method (see sidebar).

7. Set the *DataFormatString* of the *InvoiceAmount* and *InvoiceTaxAmount* fields to: **{0:c}**

8. Click *OK*.

   You'll see that the date and value fields are now easier to read.

8 Format the *GridView* control.

The *GridView* control looks nicer now, but it's not as attractive as it could be. You can use *Auto Format* to change that very easily.

1. Click *Auto Format…* from the *QuickTasks* menu of the *GridView* control.

2. Choose the *Classic* format and then click *OK*.

Lesson 11-4: Add sorting and paging to a GridView

GridView controls are often used to display data for reporting purposes. For example, the *GridView* control you created in *Lesson 11-3: Use the GridView control* shows a list of invoices.

Being able to sort data and break a long list into a number of shorter pages makes a report much easier for a user to work with. In this lesson, you'll add sorting and paging to your *GridView* control.

1   Open *Spark* from your sample files folder.

2   Open *reports.aspx* in *Design* view.

3   Enable sorting and paging features.

    1. Set the *AllowPaging* property of the *GridViewInvoice* control to: **True**

    Page number links appear at the bottom of the *GridView* control. You can further customize paging using the other properties in the *Paging* category.

    2. Set the *AllowSorting* property of the *GridViewInvoice* control to: **True**

    This allows the user to change the sort order of the *GridView* control by clicking on the column names at the top of the table.

You can also enable sorting and paging by using the *Enable Paging* and *Enable Sorting* check boxes in the *QuickTasks* menu.

4   Try out sorting and paging.

    1. View *reports.aspx* in your browser.

    2. Click the *InvoiceNumber* heading on the *GridView* control.

InvoiceDate	InvoiceAmount	InvoiceTaxAmount	InvoiceNumber
6/30/2010	$264.03	$52.81	1000
7/29/2010	$199.27	$39.85	1002
1/20/2011	$904.50	$180.90	1002
1/21/2010	$52.88	$10.58	1007
1/18/2011	$871.90	$174.38	1008
10/21/2010	$287.35	$57.47	1012
3/6/2010	$587.79	$117.56	1013
8/4/2010	$38.16	$7.63	1013
3/16/2010	($82.46)	($16.49)	1018
5/23/2010	$80.62	$16.12	1023
1 2 3 4 5 6 7 8 9 10 …			

The data will be sorted by *InvoiceNumber*, from lowest to highest. The actual currency prefix you will see ($ in the above example) may be different on your computer. That's because it reflects the locale of your computer.

note

Limitations of sorting and paging

ASP.NET's automatic sorting and paging functions are great for simple sorting and paging, but have some limitations.

Sorting can only support one sort at a time. For example you can't sort by both *InvoiceDate* and *InvoiceAmount*.

Sorting and paging can also be problematic when binding data to a *GridView* using C#, as you will see in: *Lesson 11-8: Bind data to a control using* C#.

3. Click the *InvoiceNumber* heading again.

InvoiceDate	InvoiceAmount	InvoiceTaxAmount	InvoiceNumber
8/6/2010	$117.51	$23.50	9987
7/4/2010	$421.15	$84.23	9974
9/18/2010	$856.01	$171.20	9974
10/18/2010	$158.21	$31.64	9970
4/27/2010	$116.45	$23.29	9966
9/22/2010	$453.62	$90.72	9962
2/14/2011	$128.65	$25.73	9958
4/25/2010	$303.52	$60.70	9954
5/20/2010	$371.63	$74.33	9951
2/9/2011	$892.76	$178.55	9947

12345678910…

Now the data is sorted by *InvoiceNumber* from highest to lowest.

4. Click the number *5* from the page numbers at the bottom of the *GridView* control.

InvoiceDate	InvoiceAmount	InvoiceTaxAmount	InvoiceNumber
3/24/2010	($885.83)	($177.17)	9818
9/26/2010	$468.44	$93.69	9817
8/19/2010	$99.37	$19.87	9816
12/31/2010	$443.65	$88.73	9815
2/26/2010	$141.92	$28.38	9813
6/17/2010	$224.61	$44.92	9812
5/6/2010	$310.53	$62.11	9811
9/24/2010	$364.66	$72.93	9803
12/19/2010	$400.97	$80.19	9798
7/9/2010	$877.94	$175.59	9797

12345678910…

You will be taken to the fifth page of data.

5. Click the three dots … after page number 10.

InvoiceDate	InvoiceAmount	InvoiceTaxAmount	InvoiceNumber
8/18/2010	$937.21	$187.44	9521
2/10/2010	$759.87	$151.97	9516
12/6/2010	$460.22	$92.04	9515
5/2/2010	$572.05	$114.41	9511
1/9/2010	$665.41	$133.08	9508
3/14/2010	$245.74	$49.15	9497
8/27/2010	$927.57	$185.51	9488
2/19/2011	$824.93	$164.99	9485
8/9/2010	$515.70	$103.14	9484
7/13/2010	$477.99	$95.60	9477

…11 12 13 14 15 16 17 18 19 20 …

You are taken to page number 11 and shown the next 10 page numbers.

As you can see, adding sorting and paging features to your *GridView* control is very easy indeed!

Lesson 11-5: Add editing features to a GridView

GridView controls can do more than just display information. By using some of their more advanced features, you can set them up to edit and even delete records automatically!

1 Open *Spark* from your sample files folder.

2 Open *reports.aspx* in *Design* view.

3 Add editing buttons to the *GridView* control.

1. Click *Edit Columns…* from the *QuickTasks* menu of the *GridViewInvoice* control.

2. Expand *CommandField* in the *Available fields* list.

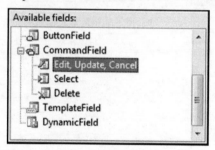

3. Click *Edit, Update, Cancel*.

4. Click *Add*.

5. Use the 'up' arrow to move your *Edit, Update, Cancel* field to the top of the list.

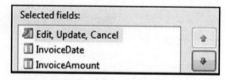

This will make your *Edit, Update* and *Cancel* buttons appear in the first column of the table.

6. Click *OK*.

Notice the *Edit* links on the left of the control. The *Edit, Update* and *Cancel* links aren't very nice to look at by default. See the sidebar for information on customizing them.

4 Try out the editing features.

1. View *reports.aspx* in your browser.

2. Click one of the *Edit* links next to a record.

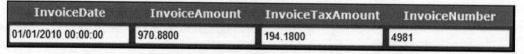

InvoiceDate	InvoiceAmount	InvoiceTaxAmount	InvoiceNumber
01/01/2010 00:00:00	970.8800	194.1800	4981

The fields will change into text boxes, allowing you to edit their values.

3. Change the *InvoiceNumber* value to: **TSM-185**

note

Customizing the *GridView* control further

From this book, you've learned to use ASP.NET's automatic features to easily create a *GridView* that can access and edit data.

By using more advanced fields such as the *ButtonField* and *TemplateField*, you can customize the behavior of your *GridView* controls even further.

You'll learn more about this in: *Lesson 12-4: Create a Products page*.

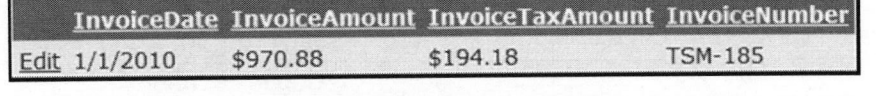

4. Click the *Update* link.

> Server Error in '/' Application.
>
> *LinqDataSource 'LinqDataSourceInvoice' does not support*

An exception will appear. This is because the *LinqDataSource* control doesn't allow you to update records by default.

5. Close the browser window and return to Visual Studio.

6. Set the *EnableUpdate* property of the *LinqDataSourceInvoice* control to: **True**

   (You can also enable updating using the *QuickTasks* menu).

7. View *reports.aspx* in your browser and try changing an invoice number to **TSM-185** again.

InvoiceDate	InvoiceAmount	InvoiceTaxAmount	InvoiceNumber
Edit 1/1/2010	$970.88	$194.18	TSM-185

This time the record updates successfully.

8. Close the browser window and return to Visual Studio.

5 Add delete buttons to the *GridView* control.

1. Return to the *Edit Columns* dialog of the *GridViewInvoice* control by using the *QuickTasks* menu.

2. Add a *Delete* field from the *CommandField* category.

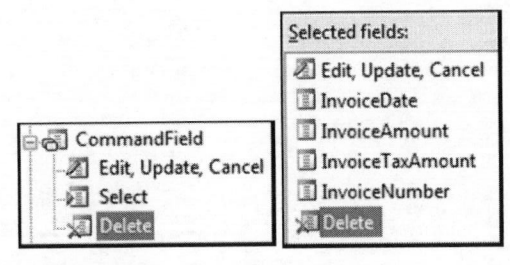

note

The *Select* CommandField

Along with *Edit*, *Update*, *Cancel* and *Delete*, you'll notice *Select*.

The *Select* field allows the user to select a row in the *GridView*, which will be highlighted and will be accessible by your C# code as: *GridView.SelectedRow*

The only reason to use a *Select* field is if you intend to use C# code to take an action depending upon the selected row.

When a *Select* field is clicked, the *SelectedIndexChanged* event of the *GridView* runs.

3. Click *OK*.

4. Set the *EnableDelete* property of the *LinqDataSourceInvoice* control to: **True**

   Just like you needed to set the *EnableUpdate* property to *True* in order to update records, you must set the *EnableDelete* property to *True* in order to delete records.

   As long as you don't set these properties to *True*, you can be assured that your *LinqDataSource* controls will never update or delete any records.

5. View *reports.aspx* in your browser.

6. Try deleting a record by clicking one of the *Delete* buttons.

The record is deleted from the database.

Lesson 11-6: Use the DetailsView control

There are several other data controls, including *DataList, DetailsView, FormView, ListView* and *Repeater*. Of these, only the *DetailsView* control has the convenient *Edit Fields* dialog that the *GridView* control has. The other controls use templates, which you may recall from: *Lesson 9-5: Customize the Login control.*

In this lesson, you'll work with the *DetailsView* control.

1   Open *Spark* from your sample files folder.

2   Open *reports.aspx* in *Design* view.

3   Add a *DetailsView* control to the page.

   1. Drag a *DetailsView* control from the *Data* category of the *Toolbox* onto the page.

   2. Set the *ID* property of the new *DetailsView* control to: **DetailsViewInvoice**

   3. Use the *Choose Data Source* drop-down in the *QuickTasks* menu of the *DetailsView* control to set its data source to *LinqDataSourceInvoice*.

      You did this in: *Lesson 11-2: Attach a data source to a control.*

      The fields from the *Invoice* table should appear in the *DetailsView* control. If they don't, click *Refresh Schema* from the *QuickTasks* menu and click *No* if prompted (see sidebar).

InvoiceID	0
CustomerID	0
InvoiceDate	24/03/2011 00:00:00
InvoiceAmount	0
InvoiceTaxAmount	0
InvoiceNumber	abc

      As you can see, a *DetailsView* control is similar to a *GridView* control, but it only displays one record at a time and displays the data in rows instead of in columns.

4   Enable paging on the *DetailsView* control.

   Enable paging on the *DetailsView* control in exactly the same way as you did with the *GridView* control in: *Lesson 11-4: Add sorting and paging to a GridView.*

   This adds page numbers that allow you to move between records in the *DetailsView* control.

5   Add editing features to the *DetailsView* control.

   1. Tick the *Enable Editing* box in the *QuickTasks* menu of the *DetailsView* control.

      This does exactly the same thing as adding an *Edit, Update, Cancel* field manually (as you did in: *Lesson 11-5: Add editing features to a GridView*).

important

Refresh fields and keys

If you have to click the *Refresh Schema* option to bring back the columns for a control, a dialog may appear asking: *Would you like to regenerate the GridView column fields and data keys using the selected data source schema?*

If you click *Yes*, the columns in your *GridView* control will be regenerated and all of the customization you have made will be lost.

You should almost always click *No* if you see this dialog.

note

The *DataList, FormView, ListView* and *Repeater* controls

The *DataList, FormView, ListView* and *Repeater* controls all use templates rather than convenient dialog boxes.

This means you have to customize them by working in *Source* view rather than simply changing properties and using *QuickTasks* dialogs.

DataList
Similar to *DetailsView*, but displays multiple records at once and can only be customized using templates.

FormView
Almost identical to *DetailsView*, but uses templates instead of the *Edit Columns* dialog.

ListView
Extremely flexible control with a dialog to customize it in various ways, but cannot be customized fully without editing the code manually in *Source* view.

Repeater
The control *ListView* is based on. No dialogs of any kind: you have to configure the control manually in *Source* view.

You will learn more about working with templates and the *ListView* control in the Expert Skills book in this series.

2. View *reports.aspx* in your browser.

3. Click the *Edit* button in the *DetailsView* control.

4. Modify the values and click *Update*.

InvoiceID	2183
CustomerID	5
InvoiceDate	01/01/2010 00:00:00
InvoiceAmount	444
InvoiceTaxAmount	111
InvoiceNumber	TSM-1
Update Cancel	

Your updated record will be shown in the *GridView* control above, as well as in the *DetailsView* control.

5. Close the browser window and return to Visual Studio.

6   Make the *DetailsView* control insert a record.

One thing a *DetailsView* control can do that a *GridView* control can't is to automatically add new records to a database.

1. Use the *Edit Fields* dialog of the *DetailsView* control to add a *New, Insert, Cancel* field from the *CommandField* category.

> InvoiceNumber
> Edit, Update, Cancel
> New, Insert, Cancel

2. Set the *EnableInsert* property of the *LinqDataSourceInvoice* control to: **True**

Just like *EnableUpdate* and *EnableDelete*, you need to set *EnableInsert* to *True* to allow records to be inserted through your *LinqDataSource* control.

3. View *reports.aspx* in your browser.

4. Click *New* on the *DetailsView* control.

5. Complete the *DetailsView* control's form to add an invoice for CustomerID 5 as shown.

CustomerID	5
InvoiceDate	01 Jan 1980
InvoiceAmount	9986
InvoiceTaxAmount	153
InvoiceNumber	TSM-2
Insert Cancel	

6. Click *Insert*.

7. You will see your new invoice appear in the *GridView* control as well as the *DetailsView* control.

	InvoiceDate	InvoiceAmount	InvoiceTaxAmount	InvoiceNumber	
Edit	1/1/1980	$9,986.00	$153.00	TSM-2	Delete

8. Close the browser window and return to Visual Studio.

7   Delete the *DetailsViewInvoice* control.

Lesson 11-7: Use the *SqlDataSource* control

For any new projects I would recommend that you always use the *LinqDataSource* control and not the *SqlDataSource* control.

LINQ is Microsoft's newer (and better) technology.

The reason I'm showing you how to use the *SqlDataSource* control is that you may work on older projects that were created before the LINQ technology became available.

The *SqlDataSource* control is very similar to the *LinqDataSource* control, but instead of accessing data via your LINQ classes, it interacts directly with the database.

1   Open *Spark* from your sample files folder.

2   Open *reports.aspx* in *Design* view.

3   Add a *SqlDataSource* control to the page.

    1.   Add a *SqlDataSource* control just after the *LinqDataSource* control.

    2.   Set the *ID* property of the *SqlDataSource* control to: **SqlDataSourceInvoice**

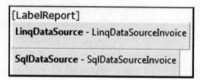

4   Configure the *SqlDataSource* control.

    1.   Click *Configure Data Source* from the *QuickTasks* menu of the *SqlDataSourceInvoice* control.

       A dialog will appear.

    2.   Select *SparkConnectionString* from the drop-down menu.

       The connection string tells the *SqlDataSource* how to connect to your database. Visual Studion automatically added *SparkConnectionString* to *Web.config* when the database was added to the project.

    3.   Click *Next*.

       A configuration dialog will appear that is similar to the configuration dialog for a *LinqDataSource* control.

    4.   Select *Invoice* from the *Name* drop-down.

Name:
Invoice

You will notice some code in the *SELECT Statement* box. This is the automatically-generated SQL code that will be sent to the database.

> SELECT statement:
>
> SELECT * FROM [Invoice]

5. Click *ORDER BY...*

   A sorting dialog will appear that is almost identical to the one for the *LinqDataSource* control.

6. Set the *SqlDataSource* control to sort by *InvoiceDate*.

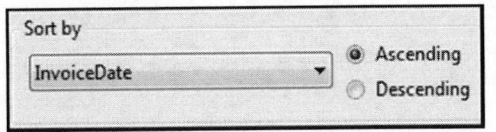

7. Click *OK*.

   You will notice that some more SQL code has been added to sort the results.

> SELECT statement:
>
> SELECT * FROM [Invoice] ORDER BY [InvoiceDate]

   This *SqlDataSource* control now does exactly the same thing as the *LinqDataSourceInvoice* control on the page.

8. Click *Next*.

9. Click *Finish*.

5   Use the new data source.

1. Use the *QuickTasks* menu of the *GridView* control to set its data source to: **SqlDataSourceInvoice**. Click *No* when asked if you wish to refresh the data. If you were to click *Yes* you'd lose all of the formatting you applied earlier in this session.

2. View *reports.aspx* in your browser.

   You will see that the data is returned without any problems.

3. Click *Edit* and try to update one of the records.

   You will see an exception.

> # Server Error in '/' Application.
>
> *Updating is not supported by data source*

SqlDataSource controls can't update records unless you add SQL code to the control's *UpdateQuery* property.

6   Switch back to the *LinqDataSource* control.

1. Close your browser.

2. Use the *QuickTasks* menu of the *GridView* control to change its data source back to: **LinqDataSourceInvoice**. Remember to click *No* when prompted.

3. Delete the *SqlDataSourceInvoice* control.

Lesson 11-8: Bind data to a control using C#

Although it's very easy to use the *LinqDataSource* control to connect a control to a database, you can also use the LINQ code you learned in *Lesson 10-3: Retrieve a single row of data using LINQ* to do the same thing.

Using C# instead of data source controls is helpful when you need more flexibility on your pages. For example, you can use *if* statements to return different sets of data depending on different conditions. You'll see how useful this can be in: *Lesson 12-6: Create a Search page*.

1 Open *Spark* from your sample files folder.

2 Open *reports.aspx* in *Design* view.

3 Delete the *LinqDataSourceInvoice* control.

You're going to connect the database to the *GridView* control manually, so you don't need the *LinqDataSource* control anymore.

4 Remove the data source property from the *GridView* control.

Remove the text from the *DataSourceID* property of the *GridViewInvoice* control so that it is blank.

```
DataSourceID
```

Click *No* when prompted to refresh the *GridView* control's fields.

tip

Binding to other controls

You can bind data to any control that has a *DataSource* property by using the techniques learned in this lesson.

The data you bind to your controls doesn't have to be created by LINQ; you can use any collection as a data source.

5 Add code to retrieve the data.

1. Open the code-behind file of *reports.aspx*.

2. Add the following code to the *Page_Load* event handler:

   using (SparkDataContext Data = new SparkDataContext())
   {
      var Invoices = Data.Invoices
      .OrderBy(Invoice=>Invoice.InvoiceDate);
   }

```
protected void Page_Load(object sender, EventArgs e)
{
    using (SparkDataContext Data = new SparkDataContext())
    {
        var Invoices = Data.Invoices
        .OrderBy(Invoice => Invoice.InvoiceDate);
    }
}
```

This code retrieves the contents of the *Invoices* table sorted by *InvoiceDate* and places it into a collection called *Invoices*.

6 Bind the data to the *GridView* control.

1. Add the following code to the *using* statement:

   GridViewInvoice.DataSource = Invoices;

```
var Invoices = Data.Invoices
.OrderBy(Invoice => Invoice.InvoiceDate);
GridViewInvoice.DataSource = Invoices;
```

This provides the *GridView* control with the data returned by *LINQ*. Since the *Invoice* objects all have names that correspond to the items in the table, the columns that were automatically generated by the *LinqDataSource* control earlier will continue to work without any problems.

If you were to use data from a different table, you would have to set up your *GridView* control's columns to match the new table.

2. Add the following code on the next line:

GridViewInvoice.DataBind();

```
var Invoices = Data.Invoices
.OrderBy(Invoice => Invoice.InvoiceDate);
GridViewInvoice.DataSource = Invoices;
GridViewInvoice.DataBind();
```

Without this line, the data will not appear in the control. Whenever you change a control's data source property, you must call the *DataBind* method before the new data will be displayed.

7 **See the code in action.**

1. View *reports.aspx* in your browser.

InvoiceDate	InvoiceAmount	InvoiceTaxAmount	InvoiceNumber
01/01/1980	9986.0000	153.0000	TSM-2
01/01/2010	444.0000	111.0000	TSM-1
01/01/2010	91.3500	18.2700	9557

2. Click *Edit, Delete* or one of the page numbers.

You will see an exception. Without the *LinqDataSource* control to handle these events they will not work (see sidebar).

3. Close your browser.

8 Add a *PageIndexChanging* event to the *GridView* control.

You can create your own event handler to enable the *GridView* control to use paging.

1. Add a *PageIndexChanging* event handler to the *GridViewInvoice* control.

2. Add the following code to the new event handler:

GridViewInvoice.PageIndex = e.NewPageIndex;
GridViewInvoice.DataBind();

```
protected void GridViewInvoice_PageIndexChanging(ob
{
    GridViewInvoice.PageIndex = e.NewPageIndex;
    GridViewInvoice.DataBind();
}
```

This will enable the paging features to work.

Note that an object called *e* is often passed into an event handler as an argument. In this case the *NewPageIndex* property of the *e* object must be provided to the *GridView* control in order for it to move to the next page.

---

note

Adding *Edit* and *Delete* functionality to your *GridView* control

The easiest way to allow editing and deleting of records in a *GridView* is to use a *LinqDataSource* control.

If you bind data to your control manually, you can still use the *GridView* control's automatic functions by adding *RowEditing* and *RowDeleting* event handlers.

You will learn more about this topic in the Expert Skills book in this series.

```
Server Error in '/' Application.

The GridView 'GridViewInvoice' fired event
```

note

Efficient querying

Since the LINQ code in this lesson is in the *Page_Load* event handler, the database will be queried every time the page posts back.

On this page, that isn't a problem, but it's inefficient to re-query the database if the data hasn't changed.

You can make your queries more efficient by using an *if* statement along with the *Page.IsPostBack* property.

You'll make use of this technique in: *Lesson 12-8: Create a Checkout page.*

Session 11: Exercise

1   Open the *Spark* project from your sample files folder.

2   Open *customer.aspx* in *Design* view.

3   Add a *LinqDataSource* control to retrieve records from the *Customer* table, sorted by *CustomerName*. Name your new control *LinqDataSourceCustomer*.

4   Add a *GridView* control and attach it to the *LinqDataSource* control.

5   Enable sorting and paging for the *GridView* control.

6   Add *Command fields* to the *GridView* control to edit and delete records.

7   Use *AutoFormat* to make the *GridView* control more presentable.

8   Add a *DropDownList* control to the page. Name your new control: **DropDownListCustomer**

9   Add C# code to the *Page_Load* event handler of *customer.aspx* to retrieve the contents of the *Customer* table and place it in the *DropDownList* control.

10   Set the *DropDownList* control's *DataTextField* property to **CustomerName** and the *DataValueField* property to **CustomerID**.

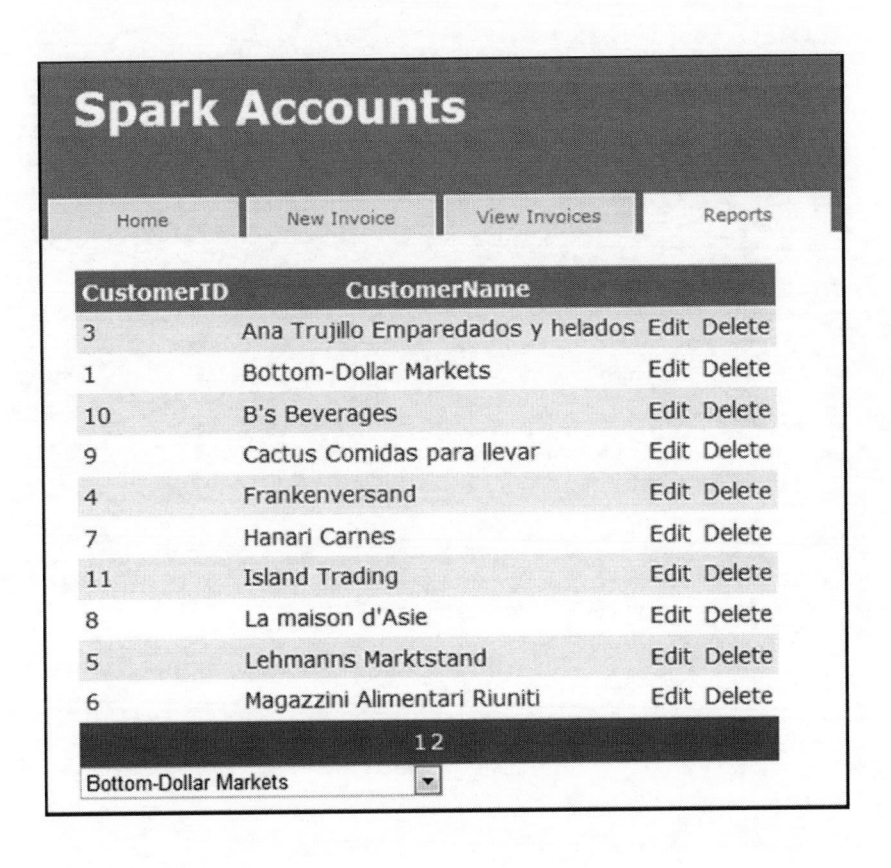

Session 11: Exercise Answers

These are the three questions that students find the most difficult to answer:

Q 9	Q 6	Q 3

Use the following code:
 	
using (SparkDataContext Data = new SparkDataContext())
{
   DropDownListCustomer
   .DataSource = Data.Customers;
   DropDownListCustomer
   .DataBind();
}
 	
This was covered in:
Lesson 11-8: Bind data to a control using C#.
	1. Click *Edit Columns...* in the QuickTasks menu of the *GridView* control.
	
	2. Expand the *CommandField* category in the *Available Fields* list.
	
	3. Click *Edit, Update, Cancel* from the *CommandField* category.
	
	4. Click *Add*.
	
	5. Click *Delete* from the *CommandField* category.
	
	6. Click *Add*.
	
	7. Click *OK*.
	
	This was covered in:
	Lesson 11-5: Add editing features to a GridView.
		1. Add a *LinqDataSource* control to the page.
		
		2. Set the *ID* property of the new control to: **LinqDataSourceCustomer**
		
		3. Click *Configure Data Source...* from the QuickTasks menu of the control.
		
		4. Ensure that *Spark.SparkDataContext* is selected and click *Next*.
		
		5. Ensure that *Customers(Table<Customer>)* is selected in the *Table* drop-down.
		
		6. Click *OrderBy...*
		
		7. Ensure *CustomerName* is selected in the *Sort by* drop-down.
		
		8. Click *OK*.
		
		9. Click *Finish*.
		
		This was covered in:
		Lesson 11-1: Use the LinqDataSource control.

If you have difficulty with the other questions, here are the lessons that cover the relevant skills:

1   Refer to: Lesson 1-7: Manage a project with the Solution Explorer.

2   Refer to: Lesson 1-7: Manage a project with the Solution Explorer.

4   Refer to: Lesson 11-3: Use the GridView control.

5   Refer to: Lesson 11-4: Add sorting and paging to a GridView.

7   Refer to: Lesson 1-15: Use the QuickTasks menu.

8   Refer to: Lesson 1-14: Add controls to a page with the Toolbox.

12

Session Twelve: Build a complete ASP.NET site

> We have finished the job. What shall we do with the tools?
>
> *Haile Selassie, Ethiopian statesman (1892 – 1975)*

You've now mastered all of the essential skills needed to work with ASP.NET, C# and Visual Studio.

You've worked with all of the major ASP.NET controls, you've learned how to create all of the most important programming structures in C# and you've used the most important features of Visual Studio.

With the skills you've learned, you have a solid foundation upon which to further develop you C# code and Visual Studio skills.

In this session, you'll put your skills to use by finishing the *SmartMethodStore* project, a simple e-commerce site with products, a shopping cart and many advanced features.

Session Objectives

By the end of this session you will be able to:

- Use a master page
- Handle errors with Global.asax
- Log errors to a database
- Create a Products page
- Create a Shopping Cart
- Create a Search page
- Add functionality to a Search page
- Create a Checkout page
- Create a Payment page
- Implement security
- Publish a site

Lesson 12-1: Use a master page

A master page is a way of storing your site layout in a single file, which you can then assign to many pages. The automatically-generated site created when you create a new *ASP.NET Web Application* includes a master page.

note

Whether to use master pages

Master pages provide a convenient way to create multiple pages based on a single template. By using a master page, you can avoid having to manually update each page when a minor change is made to your site layout.

The disadvantage of master pages if that you lose the ability to completely customize each page.

Whether you prefer to use master pages or not is up to you.

A good compromise between using master pages and having complete code on every page is *Web User Controls*. You can learn about them in the Expert Skills book.

1   Open *SmartMethodStore* from your sample files folder.

2   Open *Site.Master* in *Design* view.

As you can see, a master page looks exactly the same as any other .aspx page.

3   Examine the *Content PlaceHolder* control.

The *ContentPlaceHolder* is a special control that's only available on master pages. It's used to define areas that can be edited on pages that use the master page.

The *ContentPlaceHolder* appears in the *Standard* category of the *Toolbox*.

1. Select the *MainContent* control.

    The easiest way to do this is to select *MainContent* from the drop-down list at the top of the *Properties* window.

    This is a *ContentPlaceHolder*. It doesn't have any interesting properties, but it will create an editable region for all pages that use this master page.

2. Open *Default.aspx* in *Design* view.

    As you can see, *Default.aspx* uses the *Site.Master* master page.

3. Select the *BodyContent* control.

    This is the *ContentPlaceHolder* control you saw on the master page. You can edit only the contents of the *ContentPlaceHolders* on this page. Everything else is provided by the master page.

4. Switch to *Source* view.

If you are not completing the course incrementally use the sample file: **Lesson 12-1** to begin this lesson.

Sample files with the starting point for each lesson are also provided for all of the other lessons in this session.

```
<%@ Page Title="Home Page" Language="C#" MasterPageFile="~/Site.master" AutoEventW:

<asp:Content ID="HeaderContent" runat="server" ContentPlaceHolderID="HeadContent">
</asp:Content>
<asp:Content ID="BodyContent" runat="server" ContentPlaceHolderID="MainContent">
    <h2>
        Welcome to The Smart Method <i>Store</i>!
```

As you can see, the only controls on this page are the *HeaderContent* and *BodyContent* controls. These controls are the local copies of the *HeadContent* and *MainContent* placeholders defined on the master page.

At the top of the page, you can see the master page referenced in the *MasterPageFile* property.

4   Add a new page which uses a master page.

1. Open the *New Item...* dialog from the *Solution Explorer*.

2. Choose *Web form using Master Page* from the *Web* category.

3. Name the new page: **products.aspx**

4. Click *Add*.

   You will be prompted to select which master page to use.

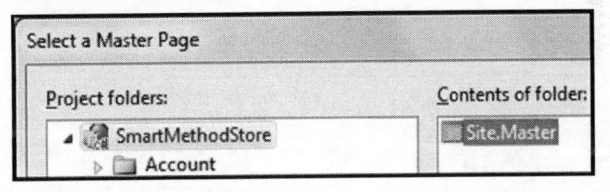

   Your site currently has only one master page: *Site.Master*. If you had more master pages, you could select a different one by using this dialog.

5. Click *OK*.

6. Switch to *Source* view, if you aren't already in that view.

   You will see that *Content* controls linked to the *ContentPlaceHolder* controls in the master page have been created automatically.

```
<asp:Content ID="Content1" ContentPlaceHolderID="HeadContent"
</asp:Content>
<asp:Content ID="Content2" ContentPlaceHolderID="MainContent"
</asp:Content>
```

7. Enter the following HTML code inside the *MainContent* placeholder:

   <h2>Products</h2>

```
<asp:Content ID="Content2" ContentPlac(
    <h2>Products</h2>
</asp:Content>
```

8. View *products.aspx* in your browser.

   You will see that ASP.NET has used the master page to create an attractive web page that displays the content you have added to the placeholder.

Lesson 12-2: Handle errors with Global.asax

The *Global.asax* file is automatically created when you create a new *ASP.NET Web Application* project.

Global.asax contains event handlers that are related to your application and user sessions. *Global.asax* also contains an event handler that runs whenever an error happens anywhere in your application.

By using *Global.asax*, you can intercept every error that happens on your site. There are other event handlers in *Global.asax* that can also be useful (see sidebar).

1　Open *SmartMethodStore* from your sample files folder.

2　Open *Global.asax*.

```
public class Global : System.Web.HttpApplication
{
    void Application_Start(object sender, EventArgs e)...
```

You will see the automatically-created event handlers:

Application_Start
Runs when your site is started by the web server.

Application_End
Runs when your site is stopped by the web server.

Application_Error
Runs whenever there is a server error on your site.

Session_Start
Runs when a user arrives at your site and starts a new session (see: *Lesson 3-12: Use Session*).

Session_End
Runs when a user's session ends.

3　Add an error page to your application.

The default error screen that appears in ASP.NET is not very nice to see. Creating a page to display in case of errors is good practice.

1. Add a new *Web Form using Master Page* named: **error.aspx**

2. Add the following HTML code to the *MainContent* area of *error.aspx*:

   <h2>Something went wrong</h2>
   <p>We're sorry, but something went wrong with your request. If you continue to have problems, please contact support.</p>

4　Add redirection code to the *Global.asax* file.

note

Using the other *Global.asax* event handlers

It's rare to need to modify the other event handlers in *Global.asax*.

The most likely use of the *Session_Start* and *Session_End* events would be to log details of users when they arrive at your site.

You can add other event handlers to *Global.asax*. There are many other application events that *Global.asax* can handle.

A useful example is the *Application_AuthenticateRequest* event, which runs before any page is served to a user. Some programmers use this to implement their own custom log-in systems (when they have special requirements that go beyond ASP.NET's built-in security features).

1. Open *Global.asax*.

2. Add the following code to the *Application_Error* event handler:

   Response.Redirect("~/error.aspx");

   ```
   void Application_Error(object sender, EventArgs e)
   {
       // Code that runs when an unhandled error occurs
       Response.Redirect("~/error.aspx");
   }
   ```

   Note that you can also set the default error page in the *ASP.NET Configuration* utility. You may have noticed the option when you worked through: *Lesson 9-2: Manage a site with ASP.NET Configuration*.

   Setting the error page in the *ASP.NET Configuration* utility is very easy and convenient, but *Global.asax* allows you to do more than just redirect the user, as you'll see in: *Lesson 12-3: Log errors to a database*.

5 **Test your redirection code.**

1. Open *Default.aspx* in your browser.

2. Replace *Default.aspx* in the browser's web address bar with **qqqqqq.aspx** (a page that does not exist).

   > http://localhost:50542/qqqqqq.aspx

   You are automatically redirected to your site's error page instead of being shown a standard error.

   SOMETHING WENT WRONG

   We're sorry, but something went wrong with your request.

6 **Close Visual Studio.**

Lesson 12-3: Log errors to a database

By adding some LINQ database code to your *Global.asax* file, you can log any errors that happen on your site to a database.

Keeping a log of errors that happen on your site is good practice, as it helps you to track down and fix any problems that occur, even if they are not reported by your users.

If you had several web applications (on a corporate intranet, for example), you could even use this technique to centralize your error logging into a single database, allowing you to see all application problems in one place.

1   Open *SmartMethodStore* from your sample files folder.

2   Open *Global.asax*.

3   Add code to log all errors to a database.

   Although the error handling code you added in *Lesson 12-2: Handle errors with Global.asax* is useful, you could have done the same thing using the *ASP.NET Configuration* utility (you learned to use this in: *Lesson 9-2: Manage a site with ASP.NET Configuration*).

   Manually adding code to *Global.asax* allows you to customize error handling to a far greater extent.

   1.   Add *LINQ to SQL Classes,* naming the LINQ file: **Store.dbml**

       You learned how to do this in *Lesson 10-2: Add LINQ data classes to a project.*

   2.   Add all database tables from the *Store* database to your new LINQ classes.

       You learned how to do this in *Lesson 10-2: Add LINQ data classes to a project.*

   3.   Open *Global.asax*.

   4.   Add the following code to the beginning of your *Application_Error* event handler:

       ```
       using (StoreDataContext Data = new StoreDataContext())
       {
           Exception ExceptionToLog = Server.GetLastError();
           Error NewError = new Error();
           NewError.ErrorMessage = ExceptionToLog.Message;
           NewError.ErrorStackTrace = ExceptionToLog.StackTrace;
           NewError.ErrorURL = Request.Url.ToString();
           NewError.ErrorDate = DateTime.Now;
           Data.Errors.InsertOnSubmit(NewError);
           Data.SubmitChanges();
       }
       ```

       This code uses the *Server.GetLastError* method to retrieve an *Exception* object (called *ExceptionToLog*) containing details of the last error that occurred on the web server. You learned about the *Exception* object in: *Lesson 3-5: Understand the Exception object*.

The code then needs to log the information in the *ExceptionToLog* object by adding a new row to the *Error* table in the *Store* database. It does this by creating a new *Error* object (representing a row in the *Error* table) called *NewError*.

The error details are then transferred from the *ExceptionToLog* object to the *NewError* object and inserted into the database.

This process is covered in more depth in: *Lesson 10-8: Insert database records using LINQ*.

```
void Application_Error(object sender, EventArgs e)
{
    // Code that runs when an unhandled error occurs
    using (StoreDataContext Data = new StoreDataContext())
    {
        Exception ExceptionToLog = Server.GetLastError();
        Error NewError = new Error();
        NewError.ErrorMessage = ExceptionToLog.Message;
        NewError.ErrorStackTrace = ExceptionToLog.StackTrace;
        NewError.ErrorURL = Request.Url.ToString();
        NewError.ErrorDate = DateTime.Now;
        Data.Errors.InsertOnSubmit(NewError);
        Data.SubmitChanges();
    }
    Response.Redirect("~/error.aspx");
}
```

4   Test your error logging.

1. View the site in your browser.

2. Attempt to navigate to a URL that doesn't exist.

    http://localhost:50542/sdfdsf.aspx

    You should be redirected to the error page, just as you were in: *Lesson 12-2: Handle errors with Global.asax*.

    SOMETHING WENT WRONG

    We're sorry, but something went wrong with your request.

    This time, however, the error was also written to the *Error* table of the *Store* database.

3. Close your web browser.

4. View the contents of the *Error* table using the *Database Explorer*.

    You learned how to do this in: *Lesson 10-1: Work with SQL databases in Visual Studio*.

    You will see that the details of the error have been recorded in the table.

ErrorID	ErrorURL	ErrorMessage
1	http://localhost:50542/sdfdsf.aspx	File does not exist.
NULL	NULL	NULL

5   Close Visual Studio.

note

The *GridView ImageField*

You learned about *GridView* fields in: *Lesson 11-3: Use the GridView control*.

In this lesson you use an *ImageField* to display an image in a *GridView* control.

The only thing that makes an *ImageField* different to a normal *GridView* field is that it can automatically generate the HTML code needed to display an image.

In this example, paths to images are stored in the *ProductImageUrl* field in the *Product* table.

Lesson 12-4: Create a Products page

1   Open *SmartMethodStore* from your sample files folder.

2   Open *products.aspx* in *Design* view.

3   Add a *LinqDataSource* control to the page called: **LinqDataSourceProduct**

4   Configure the *LinqDataSource* control to retrieve all records from the *Product* table and sort them by *ProductName* in ascending order.

You learned how to do this in: *Lesson 11-1: Use the LinqDataSource control*.

5   Add a *GridView* control to the page called: **GridViewProduct**

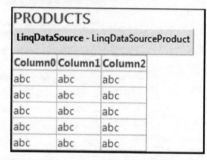

6   Link the *GridViewProduct* control to *LinqDataSourceProduct*.

You learned to do this in: *Lesson 11-3: Use the GridView control*.

7   Configure your *GridView* control.

1. Set the *ShowHeader* property of the *GridView* control to: **False**

2. Open the *Edit Columns…* dialog of the *GridViewProduct* control using the *QuickTasks* menu.

3. Remove the *ProductID* and *ProductImageUrl* fields from the *Selected fields* pane.

4. Add an *ImageField* to the *Selected fields* pane from the *Available fields* pane and set the *DataImageUrlField* property of the new *ImageField* to: **ProductImageUrl** (see sidebar).

5. Use the arrows to move the *ImageField* to the top of the *Selected fields* pane.

6. Set the *DataFormatString* of the *ProductPrice* column to: **{0:c}**

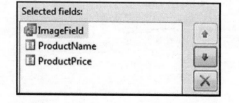

7. Click *OK*.

8. Use *Auto Format...* from the *GridView* control's *QuickTasks* menu to set the format to *Classic*.

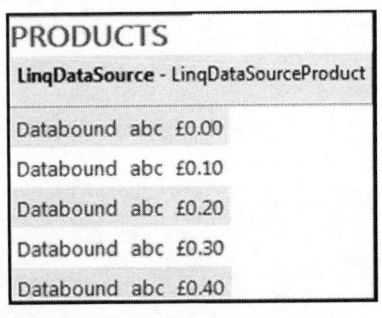

8 Create buttons to add products to the shopping cart.

The *ButtonField* causes a post-back when it is clicked, and fires the *RowCommand* event handler.

1. Open the *Edit Columns...* dialog of the *GridViewProduct* control.

2. Add a *ButtonField* to the *Selected fields* pane from the *Available fields* pane.

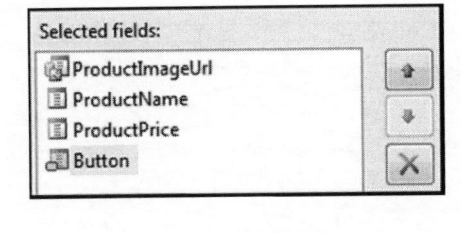

3. Set the *Text* property of the new *ButtonField* to: **Add to cart**

4. Set the *CommandName* property of the *ButtonField* to: **AddToCart**

   The *CommandName* property is used to determine which button field has been clicked.

5. Click *OK*.

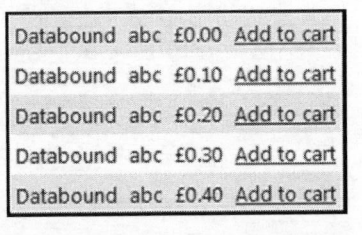

In *Lesson 12-5: Create a Shopping Cart* you'll add code that will add the selected product from the *GridView* control to the shopping cart when the *ButtonField* is clicked.

9 Test *products.aspx* in your browser.

Lesson 12-5: Create a Shopping Cart

1   Open *SmartMethodStore* from your sample files folder.

2   Open *products.aspx* in *Design* view.

3   Add code to add the selected product to the shopping cart.

    1.   Add a *RowCommand* event handler to the *GridView* control.

       You learned to do this in: *Lesson 3-2: Add event handlers to Controls.*

       The *RowCommand* event runs when the user clicks a *ButtonField.*

    2.   Add the following code to the *GridViewProduct_RowCommand* event handler:

       if (e.CommandName == "AddToCart")
       {
       }

```
protected void GridViewProduct_RowCommand(
{
    if (e.CommandName == "AddToCart")
    {
    }
}
```

       This isn't strictly necessary, since you only have one *ButtonField.*

       If you had more than one, you could tell which *ButtonField* had been clicked by checking the *e.CommandName* property against the *CommandName* properties you gave to each *ButtonField.*

    3.   Add the following code inside the *if* statement:

       int RowClicked = Convert.ToInt32(e.CommandArgument);

```
if (e.CommandName == "AddToCart")
{
    int RowClicked = Convert.ToInt32(e.CommandArgument);
}
```

       The *CommandArgument* property contains the index number of the row that was clicked. This will be used in the next step to retrieve the *ProductID.*

       You learned about the *e* object in: *Lesson 11-8: Bind data to a control using C#*

    4.   Add the following code:

       **int ProductID = Convert.ToInt32
       (GridViewProduct.DataKeys[RowClicked].Value);**

```
int RowClicked = Convert.ToInt32(e.CommandArgument);
int ProductID = Convert.ToInt32
    (GridViewProduct.DataKeys[RowClicked].Value);
```

       The *Value* property of the *GridViewProduct.DataKeys* collection contains the *ProductID* of the row clicked.

    5.   Add the following code:

       List<int> ProductsInCart = (List<int>)Session["Cart"];

```
int RowClicked = Convert.ToInt32(e.CommandArgument);
int ProductID = Convert.ToInt32
    (GridViewProduct.DataKeys[RowClicked].Value);
List<int> ProductsInCart = (List<int>)Session["Cart"];
```

As you learned in: *Lesson 3-12: Use Session*, the *Session* object can contain a collection of objects of different types. These objects can be retrieved using a key (in this case you've decided to use *Cart* as the key).

It is common practice to implement a shopping cart by storing the cart items in a *Session* collection (but see sidebar for alternative techniques).

If the user hasn't added any items to their cart yet, the *Cart* collection will not exist and a *null* value will be returned.

Note that values stored in the *Session* object have a type of *object* (this was covered in *Lesson 5-13: Use object and var variables*). For this reason you need to cast the object into the correct type (in this case *List<int>*). You learned about casting in: *Lesson 5-9: Convert variables using cast and ToString*.

6. Add the following code:

   if (ProductsInCart == null)
   {
       ProductsInCart = new List<int>();
   }

   As discussed in the previous step, *ProductsInCart* will be null if the user hasn't added any products yet. In this case the above code creates a new *List* collection.

   You learned about creating *List* collections in: *Lesson 8-2: Create a collection*.

7. Add the following code:

   ProductsInCart.Add(ProductID);

   When the code has established that the *List* collection exists it adds the *ProductID* to the collection.

8. Add the following code:

   Session["Cart"] = ProductsInCart;

   ```
   if (e.CommandName == "AddToCart")
   {
       int RowClicked = Convert.ToInt32(e.CommandArgument);
       int ProductID = Convert.ToInt32
           (GridViewProduct.DataKeys[RowClicked].Value);
       List<int> ProductsInCart = (List<int>)Session["Cart"];
       if (ProductsInCart == null)
       {
           ProductsInCart = new List<int>();
       }
       ProductsInCart.Add(ProductID);
       Session["Cart"] = ProductsInCart;
   }
   ```

   Finally, the updated *List* collection (shopping cart) is stored in the *Session* object.

   You'll retrieve it again on the checkout page you create in: *Lesson 12-8: Create a Checkout page*.

Lesson 12-6: Create a Search page

Although the site doesn't currently have very many products, there may come a time when there are too many for users to easily scroll through.

In this lesson you'll add a search page to enable users to easily find products.

In this example the search functionality is only provided on a single page. You could use the same techniques to put search capabilities on your *Products* page, or even on the master page to make it available throughout the site.

In this lesson you'll create the user interface for the search page. In: *Lesson 12-7: Add functionality to a Search page* you'll add code to make the page work.

1   Open *SmartMethodStore* from your sample files folder.

2   Open *search.aspx* in *Design* view.

3   Add an HTML table to the bottom of the page.

   1. Click Table→Insert Table.

      The *Insert Table* dialog appears.

   2. Uncheck *Specify Width*.

   3. Click *OK*.

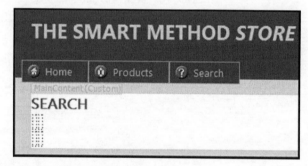

4   Populate the table with text and controls.

   1. Type **Product Name:** into the first cell.

   2. Add a *TextBox* control to the second cell on the top row named:
      TextBoxProductName

   3. Type **Price Below:** into the first cell on the next row.

   4. Add a *TextBox* control to the last empty cell called:
      TextBoxPriceBelow

   5. Add a third row to the table.

      You can do this by right-clicking on last row of the table and then clicking Insert→Row Below from the shortcut menu.

note

Formatting problems

You might find that the text you type into the table is very large and in all caps. If so, it's because you placed yout table inside the *H2* tags that the page title is in.

To correct this, you will have to go into *Source* view and move the *</h2>* tag so it is just after the *Search* text.

6. Add a *Button* control to the first cell of the new row named: **ButtonSearch**

7. Set the *Text* property of the *ButtonSearch* control to: **Search**

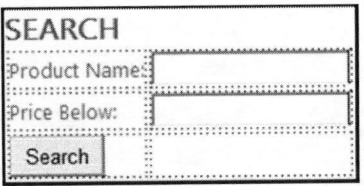

5 Copy the *GridView control* from the *products.aspx* page to the *search.aspx* page.

You'll need a *GridView* control to display the search results. Fortunately, you have already created one on the *Products* page that does everything you need.

1. Open *products.aspx* in *Design* view.

2. Copy the *GridViewProduct* control.

3. Return to *search.aspx* in *Design* view.

4. Paste the *GridView* onto the page.

   After pasting the *GridView* control, you might need to go into *Source* view to move it so that it is outside the table.

```
</table>
<asp:GridView ID="GridViewProduct" runat="server"
```

5. Clear the *DataSourceID* property of the *GridView* (click *No* when prompted).

6. Open the code-behind file of *products.aspx* and copy the entire *GridViewProduct_RowCommand* event handler.

7. Open the code-behind file of *search.aspx* and paste in the event handler just after the end of the *Page_Load* event handler.

```
public partial class search : System.Web.UI.Page
{
    protected void Page_Load(object sender, EventArgs e)
    {

    }
    protected void GridViewProduct_RowCommand(object sender, GridVie
    {
        if (e.CommandName == "AddToCart")
        {
            int RowClicked = Convert.ToInt32(e.CommandArgument);
            int ProductID = Convert.ToInt32
                (GridViewProduct.DataKeys[RowClicked].Value);
            List<int> ProductsInCart = (List<int>)Session["Cart"];
            if (ProductsInCart == null)
            {
                ProductsInCart = new List<int>();
            }
            ProductsInCart.Add(ProductID);
            Session["Cart"] = ProductsInCart;
        }
    }
```

Lesson 12-7: Add functionality to a Search page

1   Open *SmartMethodStore* from your sample files folder.

2   Open *search.aspx* in *Design* view.

3   Add code to search the database.

1. Add a *Click* event handler to the *ButtonSearch* control.

2. Add a *using* statement to the *ButtonSearch_Click* event handler:

    using (StoreDataContext Data = new StoreDataContext()) { }

    ```
    protected void ButtonSearch_Click(object sender, EventArgs e)
    {
        using (StoreDataContext Data = new StoreDataContext())
        {
        }
    }
    ```

3. Add the following code inside the *using* statement:

    string ProductName = TextBoxProductName.Text;

    ```
    using (StoreDataContext Data = new StoreDataContext())
    {
        string ProductName = TextBoxProductName.Text;
    }
    ```

    This puts the text entered into the *TextBoxProductName* control into a *string* variable called *ProductName*

4. Add the following code inside the *using* statement:

    ```
    string ProductName = TextBoxProductName.Text;
    decimal? PriceBelow = null;
    ```

    decimal? PriceBelow = null;

    The question mark after decimal denotes a nullable *decimal* variable. You learned about nullable variables in: *Lesson 5-12: Understand null.*

    The code also initializes the variable with a value of *null.*

5. Add the following code inside the *using* statement:

    ```
    decimal? PriceBelow = null;
    if (TextBoxPriceBelow.Text.Length > 0)
    {
        PriceBelow =
        Convert.ToDecimal(TextBoxPriceBelow.Text);
    }
    ```

    if (TextBoxPriceBelow.Text.Length > 0)
    {
    ** PriceBelow =**
    ** Convert.ToDecimal(TextBoxPriceBelow.Text);**
    }

    This code converts the contents of the *TextBoxPriceBelow* control to *decimal* only if the text box is not empty.

    This means that the *PriceBelow* variable will remain null if the user has not entered any text into the textbox.

    Note that this will cause an exception if the user enters non numeric data into the textbox. You could fix this by using *try* and *catch* or by using a validation control to ensure that the value is a valid decimal.

6. Add the following LINQ code to the *ButtonSearch_Click* event handler (inside the *using* statement):

var SearchResults = Data.Products.Where
    (Product =>
    (Product.ProductName.Contains(ProductName)
    || ProductName.Length == 0)
    &&
    (Product.ProductPrice <= PriceBelow
    || PriceBelow == null));

```
var SearchResults = Data.Products.Where
    (Product =>
    (Product.ProductName.Contains(ProductName) || ProductName.Length == 0)
    &&
    (Product.ProductPrice <= PriceBelow || PriceBelow == null));
```

You learned about logical operators in: *Lesson 7-3: Use basic logical operators* and in *Lesson 7-4: Use advanced logic.*

You learned how to retrieve records using LINQ in*: Lesson 10-4: Retrieve multiple rows of data using LINQ.*

Product.ProductName.Contains(ProductName)

This expression returns products with a *ProductName* that contains the text entered into the search box.

|| ProductName.Length == 0

By using the OR operator a blank search box will return all records (this is normally how search boxes are implemented).

(Product.ProductPrice <= PriceBelow
|| PriceBelow == null))

This code works in a similar way. If a *PriceBelow* has been entered by the user only products with prices below or equal to the entered price are returned.

7. Add the following code on the next line inside the *using* statement:

GridViewProduct.DataSource = SearchResults;
GridViewProduct.DataBind();

```
    (Product.ProductPrice <= PriceBelow || PriceBelow == null));
GridViewProduct.DataSource = SearchResults;
GridViewProduct.DataBind();
```

This code displays the search results in the *GridView* control.

Your search page is now fully functional!

4   Test your search page.

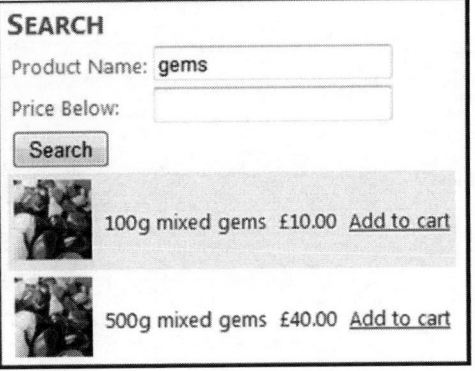

Lesson 12-8: Create a Checkout page

Earlier, you wrote code to allow users to add products to their shopping cart. Now you need a page where your users can view their shopping cart, remove items from it and go on to pay for the products they want to buy.

1   Open *SmartMethodStore* from your sample files folder.

2   Open *checkout.aspx* in *Design* view.

3   Add a *GridView* control to display the shopping cart.

    1.   Copy and paste the *GridViewProduct* control from *search.aspx* to the bottom of *checkout.aspx*.

SHOPPING CART			
Databound	Databound	Databound	Add to cart
Databound	Databound	Databound	Add to cart
Databound	Databound	Databound	Add to cart
Databound	Databound	Databound	Add to cart
Databound	Databound	Databound	Add to cart

    2.   Open the *Edit Columns…* dialog from the *QuickTasks* menu of the *GridView* control.

    3.   Change the *Text* property of the *Add To Cart* field to: **Remove from cart**

    4.   Change the *CommandName* property to: **RemoveFromCart**

    5.   Click OK.

4   Add code to remove items from the shopping cart.

    1.   Add a *RowCommand* event handler to the *GridViewProduct* control.

    2.   Add the following code to the event handler:

```
if (e.CommandName == "RemoveFromCart")
{
    int RowClicked = Convert.ToInt32(e.CommandArgument);
    int ProductID = Convert.ToInt32
    (GridViewProduct.DataKeys[RowClicked].Value);
    List<int> ProductsInCart = (List<int>)Session["Cart"];
    ProductsInCart.Remove(ProductID);
    Session["Cart"] = ProductsInCart;
}
```

This is very similar to the code you added *in Lesson 12-5: Create a Shopping Cart,* but it removes items from the shopping cart instead of adding them.

5   Add a method to retrieve the products from the database.

    1.   Add a new private method just after the *Page_Load* event handler:

note

Extending the page

This page works fine, but it doesn't have some of the features you might have seen on other sites, such as product quantities and a total cost.

To do this, you could create a new class with properties for both ProductID and quantity.

The Expert Skills book in this series will also teach you more skills to help you implement this and other features.

```
private void GetProductsFromCart()
{
}
```

2. Add code to the method:

```
if (Session["Cart"] != null)
{
    using (StoreDataContext Data = new StoreDataContext())
    {
        List<int> Cart = (List<int>)Session["Cart"];
        var Products = Data.Products.
        Where(Product => Cart.Contains(Product.ProductID))
        GridViewProduct.DataSource = Products;
        GridViewProduct.DataBind();
    }
}
```

This code retrieves records from the database that match the product ID numbers stored in the shopping cart collection and displays them in the *GridViewProduct* control.

6   Add code to call the *GetProductsFromCart* method.

Before your page will retrieve any data, it will need to need to call your method.

1. Add the following code to the *Page_Load* event handler:

```
if (!Page.IsPostBack)
{
    GetProductsFromCart();
}
```

This will call your method and retrieve the shopping basket when the user first loads the page.

2. Add the following to the end of the *GridViewProduct_RowCommand* event handler:

GetProductsFromCart();

This calls your method to refresh the *GridView* control after an item has been removed from the shopping cart.

```
if (e.CommandName == "RemoveFromCart")
{
    int RowClicked = Convert.ToInt32(e
    int ProductID = Convert.ToInt32(Gr

    List<int> ProductsInCart = (List<i
    ProductsInCart.Remove(ProductID);
    Session["Cart"] = ProductsInCart;
    GetProductsFromCart();
}
```

7   Add a *Button* control to continue to payment.

1. Open *checkout.aspx* in *Design* view.

2. Add a *Button* control to the page named:
    ButtonContinueToPayment

3. Set the *Text* property of the button to: **Continue to Payment**

4. Add a *Click* event handler to the button.

5. Add code to the new event handler to redirect the user to *pay.aspx*:

    Response.Redirect("~/pay/pay.aspx");

8   Test the checkout page.

You'll need to begin at the products page and then add some items to the shopping cart.

```
SHOPPING CART
Databound  Databound  Databound  Re
Databound  Databound  Databound  Re
Databound  Databound  Databound  Re
Databound  Databound  Databound  Re
Databound  Databound  Databound  Re
       Continue to Payment
```

note

Internet payment providers

The vast majority of web sites use third party payment providers to process credit card payments.

The most popular payment provider is PayPal, which you've probably heard of. PayPal accepts all major credit cards and is relatively easy to integrate into your site using the skills you've learned in this book.

As an alternative to storing your own transactions, many payment providers offer a complete online storefront, meaning that all you have to do is send your users to the correct link to buy your products.

Lesson 12-9: Create a Payment page

The purpose of this page is to record and store delivery addresses and orders, before sending the user to whichever payment provider you use to handle their payment details (see sidebar).

1 Open *SmartMethodStore* from your sample files folder.

2 Open *pay.aspx* (from the *pay* folder) in *Design* view.

You'll see that the controls to enter the address have already been created to save time. You could easily create this form yourself.

3 Add code to write an *Order* record to the database.

Before sending the user to your payment provider, you need to record their order details.

1. Add a *Click* event handler to the *ButtonContinueToPayment* control.

2. Add the following code to the *ButtonContinueToPayment_Click* event handler:

   using (StoreDataContext Data = new StoreDataContext())
   {
   }

   ```
   protected void ButtonContinueToPayment_Click(object sender,
   {
       using (StoreDataContext Data = new StoreDataContext())
       {
       }
   }
   ```

   As usual, you need to create an instance of the LINQ class to connect to the database.

3. Add code to the *using* statement to create and populate a new *Order* object.

   Order NewOrder = new Order();
   NewOrder.OrderAddress1 = TextBoxOrderAddress1.Text;
   NewOrder.OrderAddress2 = TextBoxOrderAddress2.Text;
   NewOrder.OrderTown = TextBoxOrderTown.Text;
   NewOrder.OrderRegion = TextBoxOrderRegion.Text;
   NewOrder.CountryID =
   Convert.ToInt32(DropDownListCountry.SelectedValue);
   NewOrder.OrderPostCode = TextBoxOrderPostCode.Text;

   This creates an *Order* object and populates its address details.

4. Add other details to the *Order*:

   NewOrder.OrderPaid = false;
   NewOrder.OrderSent = false;
   NewOrder.UserName = Page.User.Identity.Name;

   This sets the *OrderPaid* and *OrderSent* flags to *false*, so the order is marked as unpaid and unsent. It also sets the *UserName* to the username of the currently logged-in user.

In the next lesson you'll add security to make sure that a user must be logged in to place an order.

```
using (StoreDataContext Data = r
{
    Order NewOrder = new Order(
    NewOrder.OrderAddress1 = Te:
    NewOrder.OrderAddress2 = Te:
    NewOrder.OrderTown = TextBo:
    NewOrder.OrderRegion = Text
    NewOrder.CountryID = Conver
    NewOrder.OrderPostCode = Te:
    NewOrder.OrderPaid = false;
    NewOrder.OrderSent = false;
    NewOrder.UserName = User.Id
    Data.Orders.InsertOnSubmit(
    Data.SubmitChanges();
}
```

4 Commit the record to the database.

Add the following code:

Data.Orders.InsertOnSubmit(NewOrder);
Data.SubmitChanges();

This sends the record to the database.

5 Record the list of products for the order.

As well as storing the address details in your database, you'll want to store the list of products the user ordered.

To store the list of products, you will add the contents of the shopping card to the *OrderProduct* table in the database. You can do this by using a *foreach* loop.

1. Add the following code inside the *using* statement:

    List<int> Products = (List<int>)Session["Cart"];

    This retrieves the shopping cart from the *Session* object.

```
using (StoreDataContext Data = new
{
    Order NewOrder = new Order();
    NewOrder.OrderAddress1 = TextE
    NewOrder.OrderAddress2 = TextE
    NewOrder.OrderTown = TextBoxOr
    NewOrder.OrderRegion = TextBox
    NewOrder.CountryID = Convert.T
    NewOrder.OrderPostCode = TextE
    NewOrder.OrderPaid = false;
    NewOrder.OrderSent = false;
    NewOrder.UserName = User.Ident
    Data.Orders.InsertOnSubmit(New
    Data.SubmitChanges();

    List<int> Products = (List<int
    foreach (int ProductID in Proc
    {
        OrderProduct NewOrderProdu
        NewOrderProduct.OrderID =
        NewOrderProduct.ProductID
        Data.OrderProducts.InsertC
    }
    Data.SubmitChanges();
}
```

2. Add the following code:

    foreach (int ProductID in Products)
    {
    　　OrderProduct NewOrderProduct = new OrderProduct();
    　　NewOrderProduct.OrderID = NewOrder.OrderID;
    　　NewOrderProduct.ProductID = ProductID;
    　　Data.OrderProducts.InsertOnSubmit(NewOrderProduct);
    }
    Data.SubmitChanges();

    This code cycles through the list of products in the shopping cart and adds them to the *OrderProduct* table. They're linked to the *Order* table by the *OrderID*.

    Note that you only need to call the *SubmitChanges* method once. This was covered in: *Lesson 10-8: Insert database records using LINQ.*

6 Send the user to your payment system.

There are many different payment systems available on the Internet, all of which operate differently.

For now, just mark the end of the event handler with the following commented line:

//Send user to payment system here

7 Close Visual Studio.

Lesson 12-10: Implement security

Using the skills you learned in *Session Nine: Authentication,* it's time to add security to the site.

1   Open *SmartMethodStore* from your sample files folder.

2   Open the *ASP.NET Configuration* utility.

> You learned how to do this in: *Lesson 9-2: Manage a site with ASP.NET Configuration.*

3   Enable roles.

> You learned how to do this in: *Lesson 9-9: Set up roles.*

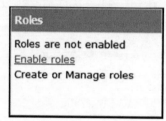

4   Add a role called: **Admin**

> You learned how to do this in: *Lesson 9-9: Set up roles.*

5   Create an *administrator* user.

> Create a user named **administrator** and assign it to the *Admin* role using **learnasp** as the password.

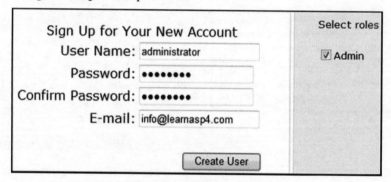

6   Create an access rule to only allow users with the *Admin* role to access the *admin* folder.

> You learned how to do this in: *Lesson 9-8: Add folder-level security.*

1. Open the *Security* tab of the *ASP.NET Configuration* utility.

2. Click *Create access rules.*

3. Click the *admin* folder.

4. Create a rule to allow *Admin* users access to the *admin* folder.

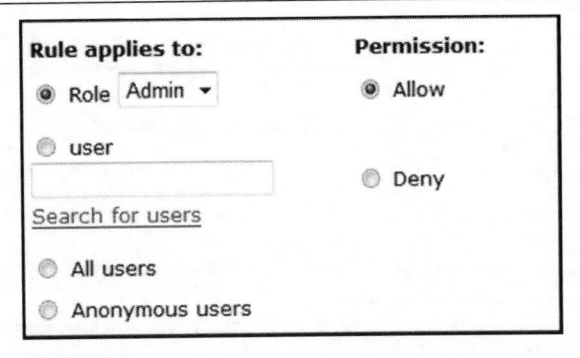

5. Click OK.

6. Return to the *Create access rules* form.

7. Create a rule to deny all other users access to the *admin* folder.

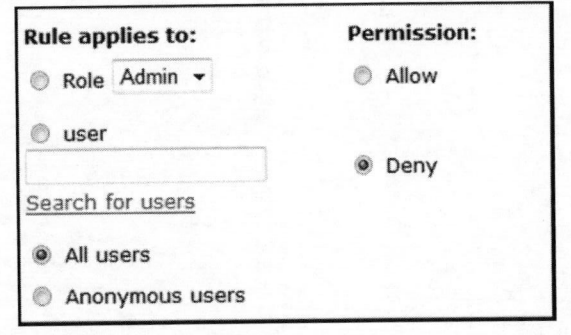

8. Click OK.

Now only users with the *Admin* role will be allowed to access the pages in the *admin* folder.

7   Create an access rule to only allow logged-in users to access the *pay* folder.

You need to make sure the user is logged-in when they access the *pay.aspx* page so that you can link orders to user accounts. You can do this by creating an access rule.

1. Open the *Create access rules* form again.

2. Click the *pay* folder.

3. Add a rule to deny anonymous users.

Rule applies to:	Permission:
⦿ Role Admin ▾	⦿ Allow
⦿ user	
	⦿ Deny
Search for users	
⦿ All users	
⦿ Anonymous users	

4. Click OK.

Now only users who are logged in will have access to the *pay* folder.

8   Close Visual Studio.

Lesson 12-11: Publish a site

Your site is now finished, although you could add a lot of tweaks and imp rovements using the skills you've learned in this book.

The final step is to publish the site so that it can be used by a web server.

1   Open *SmartMethodStore* from your sample files folder.

2   Open the *Publish* dialog.

Right-click on *SmartMethodStore* in the *Solution Explorer* and click *Publish...* from the shortcut menu.

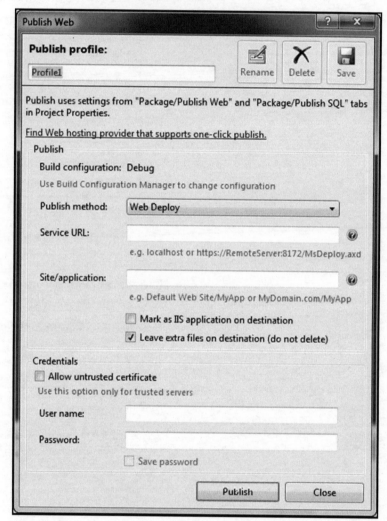

The *Publish* dialog appears. Using this dialog, you can publish your site using a variety of methods.

3   Publish the site to a folder on your computer.

Although you can publish the site directly to a server using the *Publish* dialog's other methods (see sidebar), it's usually easier to publish it to a folder on your computer and then move it to the server yourself.

By publishing the site to a folder on your computer, you can also keep copies of each published version of the site.

---

note

Publish profiles

You can create multiple sets of publishing settings using publish profiles. You can manage your publish profiles using the top part of the *Publish* dialog.

To create a second publish profile, click <*New...*> from the *Publish profile* drop-down menu.

---

note

Other publish methods

As well as publishing the site to a place on your computer, as you do in this example, you can use the following other methods:

Web Deploy
A method that publishes your web site directly to the web server. *Web Deploy* is a service that isn't supported by every web host; your host should supply the required settings.

FTP
The most common way of connecting to remote web servers is using FTP (file transfer protocol). By using the FTP option, you can copy your site directly to the web server. FTP details should be provided by your web host.

FPSE
FPSE stands for FrontPage Server Extensions. It is another way of publishing directly to a web server that is supported by some hosts. As with the other options, settings should be provided by your host.

In general, the simplest way to publish your web site is either to publish to your own computer and then copy the files using FTP, or to use the FTP option to directly publish your site to the server.

This is a good idea, as you can quickly revert back to an earlier version if a problem is discovered with a newer version.

1. Choose *File System* from the *Publish method* drop-down.

    The window shrinks considerably.

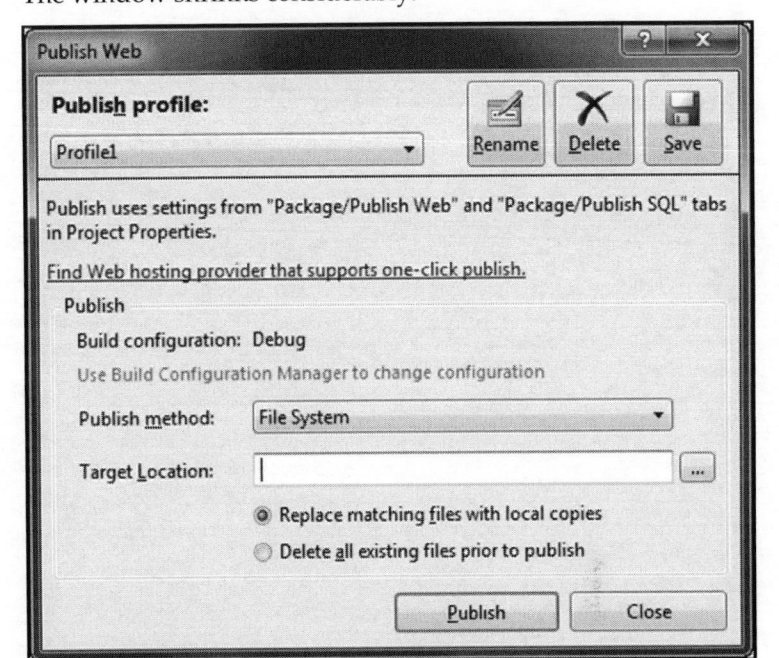

2. Click the ⸛ icon next to *Target Location*.

3. Navigate to your sample files folder and click *Open*.

4. Add a back-slash and the date to the end of the path.

    You don't want the site to be published directly into your sample files folder, this will place it in a subfolder with the date you entered.

5. Click *Publish*.

    The site will now be published to the location you specified.

4   **View the published files.**

    Navigate to the folder you published the site to and view the files.

    You'll notice that there are no longer any *.cs* files with your *.aspx* files. This is because they have been compiled into the *bin* folder.

    The site is now ready to be published to any Microsoft IIS web server. The files simply need to be copied to the server.

5   **Close Visual Studio.**

Session 12: Exercise

1 Open the *SmartMethodStore* project from your sample files folder.

2 Open *products.aspx* from the *admin* folder.

3 Add a *LinqDataSource* control to the page which retrieves all entries from the *Product* table.

4 Add a *GridView* control and link it to the *LinqDataSource*.

5 Add the ability to update and delete products to the new *GridView* control.

6 Add a *DetailsView* control linked to the same *LinqDataSource* control.

7 Add the ability to insert a new product to the *DetailsView* control.

8 Open *orders.aspx* from the *admin* folder.

9 Add *LinqDataSource* and *GridView* controls to display all records from the *Order* table where *OrderSent* is *false* and *OrderPaid* is *true*.

10 Add a *ButtonField* to the *GridView* control and set its *Text* property to: **Send Order**

11 Add a *RowCommand* event handler to your *GridView* control that will set the selected order's *OrderSent* property to *true* when the *Send Order ButtonField* is clicked.

THE SMART METHOD *STORE*

Home	Products	Search

ProductID	ProductName	ProductPrice	ProductImageUrl		
1	Large amethyst crystal geode	150.0000	images/geode-tn.jpg	Edit	Delete
2	Small amethyst crystal geode	20.0000	images/geode-tn.jpg	Edit	Delete
3	Snowflake obsidian keyring	5.0000	images/keyring-tn.jpg	Edit	Delete
4	Large amethyst stone	5.0000	images/amethyst-tn.jpg	Edit	Delete
5	100g mixed gems	10.0000	images/mixedgems-tn.jpg	Edit	Delete
6	500g mixed gems	40.0000	images/mixedgems-tn.jpg	Edit	Delete

ProductID	1
ProductName	Large amethyst crystal geode
ProductPrice	150.0000
ProductImageUrl	images/geode-tn.jpg
New	

SmartMethodStore - start

SmartMethodStore - end

If you need help slide the page to the left

Session 12: Exercise Answers

These are the four questions that students find the most difficult to answer:

Q 11	Q 9	Q 7	Q 5

1. Add a *RowCommand* event handler to your *GridView* control.
 	
2. Add the following code:
 	
int RowClicked = Convert.ToInt32 (e.CommandArgument);
 	
int OrderID = Convert.ToInt32 (GridViewOrder.DataKeys[RowClicked].Value);
 	
using (StoreDataContext Data = new StoreDataContext())
{
   Order OrderToSend = Data.Orders
   .Single(Order =>
   Order.OrderID == OrderID);
   OrderToSend
   .OrderSent = true;
   Data.SubmitChanges();
}
GridViewOrder.DataBind();
 	
This was covered in: *Lesson 12-4: Create a Products page.*
	1. Add a new *LinqDataSource* to the page.
	
	2. Click *Configure Data Source* from the *QuickTasks* menu of the *LinqDataSource.*
	
	3. Click *Next.*
	
	4. Choose *Orders* from the *Table* drop-down.
	
	5. Click *Where…*
	
	6. Choose *OrderSent* from the *Column* drop-down.
	
	7. Choose == from the *Operator* drop-down.
	
	8. Choose *None* from the *Source* drop-down.
	
	9. Type **False** into the *Value* box.
	
	10. Click *Add* and repeat the process for the *OrderPaid* property with a value of: **True**
	
	12. Add a *GridView* control and link it to the *LinqDataSource.*
	
	This was covered in: *Lesson 11-1: Use the LinqDataSource control.*
		1. Open the *Edit Columns* dialog from the *QuickTasks* menu of the *DetailsView* control.
		
		2. Add a *New, Insert, Cancel* field from the *CommandField* category.
		
		3. Click OK.
		
		4. Set the *EnableInsert* property of your *LinqDataSource* to: **True**
		
		This was covered in: *Lesson 11-6: Use the DetailsView control.*
			1. Open the *Edit Columns* dialog from the *QuickTasks* menu of the *GridView* control.
			
			2. Add an *Edit, Update, Cancel* field from the *CommandField* category.
			
			3. Add a *Delete* field from the *CommandField* category.
			
			4. Set the *EnableUpdate* and *EnableDelete* properties of your *LinqDataSource* to: **True**
			
			This was covered in: *Lesson 11-5: Add editing features to a GridView.*

If you have difficulty with the other questions, here are the lessons that cover the relevant skills:

1   Refer to: Lesson 1-7: Manage a project with the Solution Explorer.

2   Refer to: Lesson 1-7: Manage a project with the Solution Explorer.

3/4   Refer to: Lesson 11-3: Use the GridView control.

6   Refer to: Lesson 11-6: Use the DetailsView control.

8   Refer to: Lesson 1-7: Manage a project with the Solution Explorer.

10   Refer to: Lesson 12-4: Create a Products page.

Index

B

D

G

N

O

P

Also Available From The Smart Method®

Become an ASP.NET Expert with our Expert Skills book.

DEVELOPING PARALEGAL SKILLS

ETHICS WATCH

PARALEGAL TODAY: THE LEGAL TEAM AT WORK

ROGER LEROY MILLER • MARY MEINZINGER

EIGHTH EDITION

Options.

We understand that affordable options are important. Visit us at cengage.com to take advantage of our new textbook rental program, which can be bundled with our MindTap products!

Over 300 products in every area of the law: MindTap, textbooks, online courses, reference books, companion websites, and more—Cengage helps you succeed in the classroom and on the job.

Support.

We offer unparalleled course support and customer service: robust instructor and student supplements to ensure the best learning experience, custom publishing to meet your unique needs, and sales representatives always ready to provide you with dependable service.

Feedback.

As always, we want to hear from you! Your feedback is our best resource for improving the quality of our products. Contact your sales representative or write us at the address below if you have any comments about our materials or if you have a product proposal.

Accounting and Financials for the Law Office • Administrative Law • Alternative Dispute Resolution • Bankruptcy Business Organizations/Corporations • Careers and Employment • Civil Litigation and Procedure • CP Exam Preparation • Computer Applications in the Law Office • Constitutional Law • Contract Law • Criminal Law and Procedure • Document Preparation • Elder Law • Employment Law • Environmental Law • Ethics • Evidence Law • Family Law • Health Care Law • Immigration Law • Intellectual Property • Internships • Interviewing and Investigation • Introduction to Law • Introduction to Paralegalism • Juvenile Law • Law Office Management • Law Office Procedures • Legal Research, Writing, and Analysis • Legal Terminology • Legal Transcription • Media and Entertainment Law • Medical Malpractice Law • Product Liability • Real Estate Law • Reference Materials • Social Security • Torts and Personal Injury Law • Wills, Trusts, and Estate Administration • Workers' Compensation Law

---

5 Maxwell Drive
Clifton Park, New York 12065-2919

For additional information, find us online at: **cengage.com**

PARALEGAL TODAY: THE LEGAL TEAM AT WORK

ROGER LEROY MILLER • MARY MEINZINGER

CENGAGE

Australia • Brazil • Canada • Mexico • Singapore • United Kingdom • United States

Paralegal Today: The Legal Team at Work
8th Edition
Roger LeRoy Miller and Mary Meinzinger

SVP, Higher Education & Skills Product: Erin Joyner

VP, Higher Education & Skills Product:
Michael Schenk

Product Director: Matthew Seeley

Associate Product Manager: Abbie M. Schultheis

Product Assistant: Nick Perez

Learning Designer: Mara C. Vuillaume

Senior Content Manager: Betty L. Dickson

Senior Digital Delivery Lead: Beth Ross

Director, Marketing: Neena Bali

Executive Marketing Manager: Mark Linton

IP Analyst: Ashley Maynard

IP Project Manager: Nick Barrows

Production Service: SPi Global, Inc.

Designer: Erin Griffin

Cover Image Source: iStock 518501343
iStockPhoto.com/wdstock; iStock
863497494 iStockPhoto.com/PeopleImages;
iStock 1125703789 iStockPhoto.com/damircudic;
Shutterstock 649123297 I.Friedrich/
ShutterStock.com

Text Designer: Joe Devine

Interior Image Source:
1316614421 fizkes/ShutterStock.com
1477336865 fizkes/ShutterStock.com

For product information and technology assistance, contact us at
Cengage Customer & Sales Support, 1-800-354-9706 or
support.cengage.com.

For permission to use material from this text or product,
submit all requests online at **www.cengage.com/permissions.**

Library of Congress Control Number: 2020949410

Book Only ISBN: 978-0-3574-5405-3
Package ISBN: 978-0-3574-5406-0

Cengage
200 Pier 4 Boulevard
Boston, MA 02210
USA

Cengage is a leading provider of customized learning solutions with employees residing in nearly 40 different countries and sales in more than 125 countries around the world. Find your local representative at **www.cengage.com.**

To learn more about Cengage platforms and services, register or access your online learning solution, or purchase materials for your course, visit **www.cengage.com.**

Printed in the United States of America
Print Number: 01   Print Year: 2021

To Jo,
Your publishing success is well deserved. May you
continue to create best sellers for years to come.

R.L.M.

To Jer,
Rest in peace.
Your loving daughter.

MMU

Brief Contents

Appendices

Contents

CHAPTER 3   The Inner Workings of the Law Office | 54

CHAPTER 4   Ethics and Professional Responsibility | 85

CHAPTER 5   Sources of American Law | 119

PART 2　Legal Procedures and Paralegal Skills　174

Developing Paralegal Skills: Creating a User-Friendly Document   244

Office Tech and Cybersecurity: Online "Plain English" Guidelines   249

Developing Paralegal Skills: Effective Editing   250

Featured Contributor: Tips for Making Legal Writing Easier   252

Ethics Watch: Letters and the Unauthorized Practice of Law   260

Developing Paralegal Skills: Reviewing Attorney-Generated Documents   261

CHAPTER 9   Legal Writing: Form and Substance | 241

Featured Contributor: Pretrial Preparation   270

Developing Paralegal Skills: File Workup   276

Developing Paralegal Skills: A Checklist for Drafting a Complaint in a Federal Civil Case   282

CHAPTER 10   Civil Litigation: Before the Trial | 269

Ethics Watch: Keeping Client Information Confidential 292

Developing Paralegal Skills: Deposition Summaries 300

Developing Paralegal Skills: Electronic Discovery 305

Office Tech and Cybersecurity: The Costs of Electronic Discovery 306

CHAPTER 11 Conducting Interviews and Investigations | 315

Developing Paralegal Skills: Thinking through a Fraud Investigation 317

Featured Contributor: Ten Strategies for Effective Interviews and Investigations 326

Office Tech and Cybersecurity: Communicating through Graphics 330

Ethics Watch: Interviewing Clients and the Unauthorized Practice of Law 331

Developing Paralegal Skills: Checking the Accident Scene 336

Developing Paralegal Skills: Accessing Government Information 342

CHAPTER 12 Trial Procedures | 350

PART 3   Key Elements of the Law   420

CHAPTER 14   Tort Law, Product Liability, and Consumer Law | 421

CHAPTER 15   Contracts and Intellectual Property Law | 453

CHAPTER 16   Real Property and Insurance Law | 485

CHAPTER 17   Family Law and Estates | 509

CHAPTER 18   Business Organizations and Employment Law | 538

CHAPTER 19   Bankruptcy and Environmental Law | 572

Appendices

Preface

The paralegal profession continues to grow. The Bureau of Labor Statistics estimates that the number of practicing paralegals will expand on average by four thousand a year. At the same time, there is constant evolution in how legal services are provided. More and more services are delivered online, though clients still generally prefer the assurance that comes from personal contact. The human dimension is not going away.

In keeping with these developments, *Paralegal Today*, Eighth Edition, covers the traditional topics needed in paralegal education, while emphasizing the many online tools now available. We use real-world examples in the text plus substantive features to add interest to the subject matter. Those who have used the text before know how extensive the supplements package is.

All key areas of paralegal studies are covered in *Paralegal Today*, Eighth Edition: careers, ethics and professional responsibility, pretrial preparation, trial procedures, criminal law, legal interviewing and investigation, legal research and analysis, online legal research, and legal writing. The book also provides in-depth coverage of substantive law, including bankruptcy, contracts, intellectual property, torts, product liability, real property, estates, business organizations, and family law.

A Practical, Focused Approach

This book has been streamlined in response to user comments. Some instructors believed the book had too many features, which tended to distract from the core messages. For the Eighth Edition, the design has been simplified to keep the focus on the main messages in each chapter. The substantive content has not been reduced. In editing the new edition, we solicited input from law professors, practitioners, and a law librarian to be sure the content is current and well rounded.

In addition to the substantive content covered in each chapter, *Paralegal Today*, Eighth Edition, presents practical advice and "hands-on" activities for paralegals-to-be. Exercises at the end of each chapter provide opportunities for students to review their knowledge and to apply the concepts and skills discussed in the chapter. A special introduction to the student, *Skill Prep*, which precedes Chapter 1, contains practical advice and tips on how to master the legal concepts and procedures presented in the text. The lessons there also apply later, on the job.

Paralegal Today, Eighth Edition, illustrates paralegal working environments and on-the-job situations. Each chapter includes challenges to a paralegal's ethical obligations. These realistic situations give students a better understanding of how seemingly abstract ethical rules affect the legal tasks performed by attorneys and paralegals.

An Emphasis on Technology

We have made sure that *Paralegal Today*, Eighth Edition, is the most up-to-date text available. We include features and materials in this edition that show how developments in technology are affecting the law, the legal workplace, and paralegal tasks.

In particular, we have added an all-new feature titled *Office Tech and Cybersecurity* in each chapter. These materials will help students learn how to take advantage of technology to enhance their work quality and productivity as paralegals.

The Organization of This Textbook

As paralegal instructors know, materials should be presented in such a way that students can build their skills and knowledge base block by block. This is a difficult task because, no matter where you begin, you will need to refer to some information that has not yet been presented to students. For example, if you try to explain on the first or second day of class what paralegals do, you will necessarily have to mention terms that may be unfamiliar to students, such as *deposition* and *procedural law*. In this text, the authors have attempted to organize the topics discussed in such a way that students are not mystified by terms and concepts not yet covered.

Content Sequence

We have attempted to accommodate the needs of paralegal instructors as much as possible by organizing the text into three basic parts.

- Part 1 (Chapters 1–6) focuses primarily on the paralegal profession—its origins and development, the wide array of paralegal careers, the requirements and procedures that students can expect to encounter in the legal workplace, and the threshold ethical responsibilities of the profession. Part 1 also discusses the structure of the American legal system—the sources of law and the courts.

- Part 2 (Chapters 7–13) looks in detail at legal procedures and paralegal skills. The student learns about the basic procedural requirements in civil and criminal litigation, as well as the skills involved in conducting interviews and investigations, legal research and analysis, and legal writing.

- Part 3 (Chapters 14–19) focuses on substantive law. The areas of law treated in this part of the text include torts, product liability, consumer law, contracts, intellectual property, insurance, real property, estates, family law, business organizations, employment, bankruptcy, and environmental law. Additionally, the chapters covering substantive law include many numbered, highlighted examples to provide real-world illustrations of the legal concepts being discussed.

A Flexible Arrangement

We believe that this organization of the materials allows the greatest flexibility for instructors. Although to a certain extent each chapter in the text builds on information contained in previous chapters, the chapters and parts can also be used independently. In other words, instructors who wish to change the sequence of topics to fit their course design preferences, or who do not want to use all the chapters, will find it easy to do so.

Key Features in Every Chapter

As mentioned earlier, the Eighth Edition features a new *Office Tech and Cybersecurity* feature in every chapter. In addition, we include the other learning features to instruct and pique interest.

Office Tech and Cybersecurity (New to This Edition)

A new feature called *Office Tech and Cybersecurity* appears in each chapter of the Eighth Edition. This feature focuses on how working in an online world affects various aspects of paralegal work. It also shows how paralegals can use technology to their benefit for greater productivity while warning of the potential dangers of being "connected." Some of the new *Office Tech and Cybersecurity* features include the following:

- Deploying Cybersecurity in a Law Firm (Chapter 2)
- E-Communications and Confidentiality (Chapter 4)
- Cybersecurity and Government Contracting (Chapter 15)
- Cybersecurity and Digital Assets (Chapter 17)

Developing Paralegal Skills

The *Developing Paralegal Skills* feature presents hypothetical examples of paralegals at work to help your students develop crucial paralegal skills. Numbering at least two per chapter, the feature includes checklists and practical tips. Some examples are the following:

- Interviewing a Client (Chapter 1)
- Creating a Trust Account (Chapter 3)
- File Workup (Chapter 10)
- Thinking through a Fraud Investigation (Chapter 11)
- Preparing for Property-Settlement Negotiations (Chapter 17)

Ethics Watch

The *Ethics Watch* feature typically takes a student into a hypothetical situation that clearly presents an ethical problem. All are tied to specific ethical principles of NALA, The Paralegal Association, the National Federal of Paralegal Associations (NFPA), or the American Bar Association (ABA). When possible, students are told what they should and should not do in the particular situations discussed. In some instances, consultation with a supervising attorney is necessary. Some examples include the following:

- Paralegal Expertise and Legal Advice (Chapter 1)
- Social Events and Confidentiality (Chapter 4)
- Using Secondary Sources (Chapter 7)
- Wills and Paralegal Supervision (Chapter 17)

Featured Contributor Articles

Each chapter of *Paralegal Today*, Eighth Edition, contains a *Featured Contributor* article written by an educator or an expert in the field. These unique articles offer practical tips and real-world insights on some aspect of paralegal work relating to the topic covered in the chapter. Here are examples of new *Featured Contributor* articles for this edition:

- Tips for Effective Communication (Chapter 3)
- Securing Client Information in the Digital Age (Chapter 4)
- Pretrial Preparation (Chapter 10)
- Ten Strategies for Effective Interviews and Investigations (Chapter 11)

OFFICE TECH AND CYBERSECURITY

ONLINE RESOURCES FOR PARALEGALS

Many career resources are available online. To keep your skills up to date and to stay on top of developments in the law, you should regularly check such resources.

Paralegal Associations

Many paralegals belong to NALA or to NFPA, discussed earlier. Both organizations offer excellent gateways for paralegal resources. NALA's website (**nala.org**) displays information on many professional certification and continuing education programs. It also provides links to state and local affiliated organizations. The NFPA website (**paralegals.org**) offers a continuing education calendar, a gateway to legal research sites, and a variety of career advice.

American Bar Association

The ABA is not just for lawyers. The Standing Committee on Paralegals (**americanbar.org/groups/paralegals/**) provides career information, continuing education, directories, a gateway to blogs by paralegals, and information on hundreds of paralegal education programs.

Bryan Garner's Legal Writing Site

America's most celebrated legal writing guru, law professor Bryan Garner, is best known for his books, which include *The Redbook: A Manual on Legal Style and Legal Writing in Plain English*. He is the editor of the famous *Black's Law Dictionary*. Garner's website, **lawprose.org**, offers a bibliography of articles on legal writing, a schedule of legal writing seminars, and other relevant links.

The Paralegal Gateway

Paralegal Gateway on Facebook focuses on job advice, examples of successful résumés and interviews, and networking tools such as LinkedIn. It also offers links to continuing education resources.

Legal News

Law firms produce a wide range of online newsletters and sites on specific areas of law. In addition, the LawProf blog network (**lawprofessorblogs.com**) provides many subject-specific blogs (known as *blawgs*) by law professors that offer commentary on new cases, statutes, and news from trustworthy sources. Using online resources will keep you up to date on relevant developments in law.

DEVELOPING PARALEGAL SKILLS

INTERVIEWING A CLIENT

Brenda Lundquist is a paralegal in a small firm. Her responsibilities include interviewing divorce clients. Using a standard set of forms, Brenda meets with a prospective client and obtains information about the reasons for the divorce, finances and assets, and desired custody arrangements. This information is needed to assist the supervising attorney in determining whether to take the case. The information also helps Brenda to prepare documents to be filed with the court should the attorney represent the client. Brenda enjoys the work because she likes helping people, and often people who are getting divorced need both emotional and legal support.

Checklist for Client Interviews

- Plan the interview in advance.
- Print out forms and checklists to use during the interview.
- Introduce yourself as a paralegal.
- Explain the purpose of the interview to the client.
- Communicate your questions precisely.
- Listen carefully and be supportive, as necessary.
- Summarize the client's major concerns.
- Give the client a "timeline" for what will happen in the legal proceedings.

ETHICS WATCH

PARALEGAL EXPERTISE AND LEGAL ADVICE

Paralegals often have deep knowledge in specific areas of law. If you specialize in environmental law, for example, you will become familiar with environmental claims. When working with a client on a matter involving an environmental agency, you might be tempted to advise the client on which type of action would be most favorable to him or her. Never do so. Only attorneys may give legal advice, and paralegals who give legal advice risk penalties for the unauthorized practice of law. Whatever legal advice is given to the client must come directly from the attorney.

If you speak to a client, the advice must reflect exactly (or nearly exactly) what the attorney said with no modification and must be communicated to the client as directed by the attorney. After consulting with your supervising attorney, for example, you can say to the client that the attorney "advises that you do all that you can to settle the claim as soon as possible."

The rule prohibiting the unauthorized practice of law is stated in Section 1.8 of the NFPA *Model Code of Ethics and Professional Responsibility*: "A paralegal shall comply with the applicable legal authority governing the unauthorized practice of law in the jurisdiction in which the paralegal practices." It is also required by the NALA *Code of Ethics and Professional Responsibility*, Canon 4: "A paralegal must use discretion and professional judgment commensurate with knowledge and experience but must not render independent legal judgment in place of an attorney."

Reprinted by permission of the National Federation of Paralegal Associations, Inc. (NFPA®), paralegals.org. Copyright 1975, Adopted 1975, Revised 1979, 1986, 1995, 2007. Reprinted with permission of NALA, The Paralegal Association. Inquiries should be directed to NALA, 1516 S. Boston, #200, Tulsa, OK 74119, nala.org.

FEATURED CONTRIBUTOR

TIPS TO JUMPSTART YOUR PARALEGAL CAREER

Antoinette France-Harris, J.D.

BIOGRAPHICAL NOTE
Antoinette France-Harris has been a licensed attorney since 1998. She began her legal career with a New York firm where she specialized in corporate and estate planning matters. After establishing herself as a successful transactional attorney, she decided to relocate to Georgia in 2002. Initially, she worked in-house for Fortune 1000 companies, and then, she became a solo practitioner. Her firm's areas of specialization included real estate, corporate, estate planning, and family law transactions.

In 2010, Professor Harris began teaching Paralegal Studies full time at Atlanta Technical College. In addition, she acted as department chair for two years before becoming assistant professor in Legal Studies at Clayton State University in August 2014. She is now an associate professor at Clayton State. Professor Harris has received a B.S. from Harvard University, an M.S.W. from Columbia University, and a J.D. from the University of Pennsylvania.

This is a great time to become a paralegal! Opportunities exist in various legal specialties, including bankruptcy, family, and environmental law. So, how does one get started? This article is designed to provide some useful strategies to launch a career in paralegalism. The list is by no means exhaustive, but it will give the reader a starting point on this exciting journey.

... continuously enhance your education...

degree. Others who already have a bachelor's in a different field might consider a post-baccalaureate certificate in paralegalism instead. Even paralegals who received on-the-job training report that obtaining a degree has opened doors to promotions and salary increases and makes it easier to transition from one employer to the next.

Tip 1: Formal Education

Generally, people become paralegals either through on-the-job training or formal education. Many paralegal jobs require an associate's degree. For broader appeal, job seekers might pursue a bachelor's

Tip 2: Never Stop Learning—Continuing Legal Education

In this perpetually changing and increasingly technological legal industry, it is important to continuously enhance your education and skills to keep pace. An easy way to do so is by attending

Other Special Pedagogical Features

As before, we have included a number of special pedagogical features, discussed below.

Chapter Outlines

On every chapter-opening page, a *Chapter Outline* lists the first-level headings within the chapter. These outlines allow you and your students to tell at a glance what topics are covered in the chapters.

Chapter Objectives

In every chapter, just following the *Chapter Outline*, we list primary *chapter objectives*. Your students will know immediately what is expected of them as they read each chapter.

Vocabulary and Margin Definitions

Legal terminology is often a major challenge for beginning paralegal students. We use an important pedagogical device—margin definitions—to help your students understand legal terms. Whenever an important term is introduced, it is highlighted in the text and defined in the margin of the page.

At the end of each chapter, all these terms are listed in alphabetical order in *Key Terms and Concepts*, along with the page number on which each appears. Your students can examine this list to make sure that they understand all of the important terms introduced in the chapter. All the terms are also listed and defined in the *Glossary* at the end of the text. Spanish equivalents to many important legal terms in English are provided in a separate glossary in Appendix G.

corporate law
Law that governs the formation, financing, merger and acquisition, and termination of corporations, as well as the rights and duties of those who own and run the corporation.

contract
An agreement (based on a promise or an exchange of promises) that can be enforced in court.

CHAPTER SUMMARY

TODAY'S PROFESSIONAL PARALEGAL

What Is a Paralegal?

The definition of *paralegal* varies within the legal community, but most definitions distinguish between the work of a paralegal and a legal assistant. Paralegals perform many of the tasks traditionally handled by attorneys. A paralegal is qualified by education, training, or work experience to be employed by a law office, corporation, governmental agency, or other entity. A paralegal performs delegated substantive legal work, for which a lawyer is responsible.

What Do Paralegals Do?

1. *Typical tasks*—Paralegals may perform the following duties: interviewing and maintaining contact with clients and witnesses, locating and interviewing wit-

2. *Duties often vary*—Paralegals perform different functions depending on where they work and on their abilities and experience. Duties vary according to the size of the

Chapter Summaries

We have included a chapter summary at the conclusion of each chapter in the Eighth Edition. Each summary conveys important concepts from the chapter. This visually appealing format facilitates the students' review of the chapter contents.

Exhibits and Forms

To help illustrate important forms, letters, memoranda, and so forth relating to paralegal work, many exhibits are filled in with hypothetical data. Exhibits of this type in *Paralegal Today*, Eighth Edition, include those listed below:

- A Sample Client Bill (Chapter 3)
- A Sample Settlement Agreement (Chapter 6)
- A Sample Demand Letter (Chapter 9)
- Memorandum in Support of a Motion to Suppress (Chapter 13)

Chapter-Ending Materials for Review and Study

Every chapter contains chapter-ending pedagogical materials designed to provide a wide variety of assignments for your students. The chapter-ending pedagogy begins with the chapter summaries, followed by the *Key Terms and Concepts*, which we have already mentioned. These elements are followed by the materials described below.

Questions for Review

Every chapter includes a number of straightforward questions for review. These questions are designed to test students' knowledge of the basic concepts discussed in the chapter.

Ethics Questions

Because of the importance of ethical issues in paralegal training, we have also included one or more ethical questions at the end of each chapter. Each question presents a hypothetical situation, followed by one or two questions about what the paralegal should do to resolve the dilemma.

Practice Questions and Assignments

The hands-on approach to learning paralegal skills is emphasized in the practice questions and assignments that appear at the end of each chapter. A particular situation is presented, and the student is asked to actually carry out an assignment.

Group Projects

Each chapter provides an assignment designed to promote teamwork, usually for groups of four students, with specific instructions for each student's tasks.

Appendices

To make this text a reference source for your students, we have included the appendices listed below.

A   NALA's *Code of Ethics and Professional Responsibility*
B   NALA's *Model Standards and Guidelines for the Utilization of Paralegals*
C   NALS *Code of Ethics and Professional Responsibility*
D   NALA's Certification Program
E   NALS Certification
F   The Constitution of the United States
G   Spanish Equivalents for Important Legal Terms in English

For Users of the Seventh Edition

Those of you who have used the Seventh Edition of *Paralegal Today* will want to know some of the major changes that have been made for the Eighth Edition. Generally, major elements in the Seventh Edition—including the text, exhibits, features, and end-of-chapter pedagogy—have been revised or updated as necessary to reflect new laws, procedures, and technological developments. We also constantly revise for added clarity and accuracy.

In the interest of streamlining, we dropped the *In the Office* feature. A new feature titled *Office Tech and Cybersecurity* replaces the previous *Technology and Today's Paralegal* feature. The new feature retains some of the previous material but reflects the growing concern about online security and the increasing use of technical tools in practice. We constantly work to improve the text and thank users of previous editions, as well as other paralegal educators, for advice.

Revisions to Selected Chapters

Every chapter has been revised for accuracy and timeliness of content. Next, we summarize some specific changes to the text.

- **Chapter 1: Today's Professional Paralegal.** Updated coverage of professional paralegal organizations' certifications, including materials on the new definition of *paralegal*, which was adopted by the American Bar Association (and others) in 2020. (Note that Appendix D also details the 2018 modifications to NALA's Certified Paralegal examination.)

- **Chapter 3: The Inner Workings of the Law Office.** A new subsection discussing the issues that have been raised by the Me Too movement and its implications in the workplace, as well as an updated Exhibit on *Timeslip*. A new *Office Tech and Cybersecurity* outlines "Proper and Effective E-Mail Communications," and a new *Featured Contributor* article examines "Ten Tips for Effective Communications" in the paralegal landscape.

- **Chapter 5: Sources of American Law.** New materials include three new *Chapter Objectives* on the American legal system, two margin definitions (per curiam *opinion* and *Islamic law system*), a new section on the new United States–Mexico–Canada Agreement (USMCA), and another on the Islamic law system (*sharia*). A new *Office Tech and Cybersecurity* feature discusses "Cyber Issues and Sources of Law."

- **Chapter 7: Legal Research and Analysis.** Three updated Exhibits reflect 2019 and 2020 citations, as well as new materials on slip opinions and unofficial reporters, the uses of case syllabuses, and using judicial opinions for research.

- **Chapter 8: Online Legal Research.** Three new *Chapter Objectives* on legal resources online, a new subsection on SSRN.com, and another on advanced technology services. Five of the chapter's Exhibits are updated to show current screens for major legal research services and websites.

- **Chapter 10: Civil Litigation: Before the Trial.** Four new *Chapter Objectives* and two new margin definitions (*judicial economy* and *sovereign immunity*), as well as a new *Featured Contributor* article titled "Pretrail Preparation."

- **Chapter 11: Conducting Interviews and Investigations.** Additional coverage of proper processes and techniques for interviews and investigations, including a new section on initial interviews, discussions on details to consider before interviews and investigations, and how to handle client interviews. A new margin definition (*crimes of moral turpitude*) and a new *Featured Contributor* article titled "Ten Strategies for Effective Interviews and Investigations."

- **Chapter 12: Trial Procedures.** Expanded coverage of protecting confidential information and of electronic evidence in a courtroom.

- **Chapter 17: Family Law and Estates.** Four new *Chapter Objectives* on family law, a new numbered example on child-custody, and new materials discussing modern DNA testing's effects on paternity and adoption lawsuits. New details on surrogacy, frozen embryos and divorce, and a new section on "asset protection trusts." A new *Office Tech and Cybersecurity* feature titled "Cybersecurity and Digital Assets" for estate-planning purposes. Two new *Ethics Questions* in the end-of-chapter pedagogy.

- **Chapter 18: Business Organizations and Employment Law.** New numbered examples illustrating piercing the corporate veil, professional corporations, and types of stock. A new subsection on retaliatory discharge and another on religious discrimination. New materials touch on gender identity and sexual orientation under "Employment Discrimination." A new *Office Tech and Cybersecurity* feature titled "Corporate Data Security."

Supplements Available for the Eighth Edition

Instructor Resources

Additional instructor resources for this product are available online. Instructor assets include an Instructor's Manual, Educator's Guide, PowerPoint® slides, and a test bank powered by Cognero®. Sign up or sign in at www.cengage.com to search for and access this product and its online resources.

MindTap

CENGAGE
MINDTAP

MindTap for *Miller/Paralegal Today, The Legal Team at Work* is a highly personalized fully online learning platform of authoritative content, assignments, and services offering you a tailored presentation of course curriculum created by your instructor. MindTap for *Miller/Paralegal Today, The Legal Team at Work* guides you through the course curriculum via an innovative learning path where you complete reading assignments, annotate your readings, complete homework, and engage with quizzes and assessments. MindTap includes a variety of web apps known as "MindApps"—allowing functionality like having the text read aloud to you, as well as MindApps that allow you to synchronize your notes with your personal Evernote account. MindApps are tightly woven into the MindTap platform and enhance your learning experience.

How MindTap helps students succeed?

- Use the Progress App to see where you stand at all times—individually and compared with the highest performers in your class.

- ReadSpeaker reads the course material to you.
- MyNotes provides the ability to highlight text and take notes that link back to the MindTap material for easy reference when you are studying for an exam or working on a project.
- A glossary that is only a click away.
- Flashcards are pre-created to help you memorize the key terms.

Not using MindTap in your course?

- It's an online destination housing ALL your course material and assignments, neatly organized to match your syllabus.
- It is loaded with study tools that help you learn the material more easily.
- To learn more, go to www.cengage.com/mindtap or ask your instructor to try it out.

Please note that the Internet resources provided in this book are of a time-sensitive nature, and URL addresses often change or may be deleted.

Acknowledgments for Previous Editions

Numerous careful and conscientious individuals have helped us in this undertaking from the beginning. We continue to be indebted to those whose contributions helped to make previous editions of *Paralegal Today* a valuable teaching/learning text. We particularly thank the following paralegal educators for their insightful criticisms and comments:

Laura Barnard
Lakeland Community College, OH

Lia Barone
Norwalk Community College, CT

Carol Brady
Milwaukee Area Technical College, WI

Rhonda Brashears
Certified Paralegal, TX

Debra Brown
Coastline Community College, CA

Chelsea Campbell
Lehman College, NY

Linda S. Cioffredi
Woodbury College, VT

Lora C. Clark
Pitt Community College, NC

Jeptha Clemens
Northwest Mississippi Community College, MS

Arlene A. Cleveland
Pellissippi State Technical Community College, TN

Lynne D. Dahlborg
Suffolk University, MA

Kevin R. Derr
Pennsylvania College of Technology, PA

Bob Diotalevi
Florida Gulf Coast University, FL

Donna Hamblin Donathan
Marshall University Community College, OH

Dora Dye
City College of San Francisco, CA

Wendy B. Edson
Hilbert College, NY

Jameka Ellison
Everest University, FL

Leslie Sturdivant Ennis
Samford University, AL

Pamela Faller
College of the Sequoias, CA

OrsolyaFuri
Bridgewater State College, MA

Gary Glascom
Cedar Crest College, PA

ReginaGraziani
University of Hartford, CT

Dolores Grissom
Samford University, AL

Paul D. Guymon
William Rainey Harper College, IL

Sharon Halford
Community College of Aurora, CO

Vera Haus
McIntosh College, NH

Linda Wilke Heil
Central Community College, NE

Jean A. Hellman
Loyola University, IL

Melinda Hess
College of Saint Mary, NE

Louise Hoover
Rockford Business College, IL

Marlene L. Hoover
El Camino College, CA

Susan J. Howery
Yavapai College, AZ

Jill Jasperson
Utah Valley State College, UT

Melissa M. Jones
Samford University, AL

Deborah Winfrey Keene
Lansing Community College, MI

Jennifer Allen Labosky
Davidson County Community College, NC

Dora J. Lew
California State University, East Bay, CA

TerriLindfors
Globe University/ Minnesota School of Business, MN

Mary Hatfield Lowe
Westark Community College, AR

Gerald A. Loy
Broome Community College, NY

Brian McCully
Fresno City College, CA

Paula Montlary
Florida Career College, FL

Linda Mort
Kellogg Community College, MI

Constance Ford Mungle
Oklahoma City University, OK

H. Margaret Nickerson
William Woods College, MO

Martha G. Nielson
University of California, San Diego, CA

Elizabeth L. Nobis
Lansing Community College, MI

Joy D. O'Donnell
Pima Community College, AZ

Anthony Piazza
David N. Myers College, OH

Francis D. Polk
Ocean County College, NJ

Ruth-Ellen Post
Rivier University, NH

Elizabeth Raulerson
Indian River Community College, FL

Kathleen Mercer Reed
University of Toledo, OH

Lynn Retzak
Lakeshore Technical Institute, WI

Evelyn L. Riyhani
University of California, Irvine, CA

Melanie A. P. Rowand
California State University, East Bay, CA

Vitonio F. San Juan
University of La Verne, CA

Susan F. Schulz
Southern Career Institute, FL

Sean Scott
St. Petersburg College, FL

Joanne Spillman
Westwood College Online, CO

Roger Stone
Hilbert College, NY

John G. Thomas III
Northampton County Community College, PA

Derek Thomson
Bryant & Stratton College, NY

Loretta Thornhill
Hagerstown Community College, MD

Julia Tryk
Cuyahoga Community College, OH

Stonewall Van Wie III
Del Mar College, TX

Lorrie Watson
Orangeburg Calhoun Technical College, SC

Anita Whitby
Park University, MO

Acknowledgments for the Eighth Edition

During the preparation of the Eighth Edition of *Paralegal Today*, several professionals offered us penetrating criticisms, comments, and suggestions for improving the text. While we haven't been able to comply with every request, the reviewers listed below will see that many of their suggestions have been taken to heart.

- **Lynn Crossett**, Texas State University, TX
- **Dora J. L. Dye**, City College of San Francisco, CA
- **Emma Wright Fletcher**, University of Cincinnati, OH
- **Wendie Witzke**, Western Technical College, WI

We also are grateful to the following authors of the *Featured Contributor* articles in *Paralegal Today*, Eighth Edition, for enhancing the quality of our book with their tips and illuminating insights into paralegal practice:

- **John Bell**, Greenville Technical College, SC
- **Deborah Bouchoux**, Georgetown University, DC
- **Kristine Condon**, Kankakee Community College, IL
- **Matt Cornick**, Clayton State University, GA
- **John DeLeo**, Central Penn College, PA
- **Ceaser Espinoza**, El Centro College, TX
- **Antoinette France-Harris**, Clayton State University, GA
- **Regina Graziani**, University of Hartford, CT
- **P. Darrel Harrison**, San Diego Miramar College, CA
- **Daniel Hinkel**, Corporate counsel, GA
- **Robyn Ice**, Tulane University, LA
- **Steven Kempisty**, Bryant & Stratton College, NY
- **Judith Mathers Maloney**, Molloy College, NY
- **Tom McClure**, Illinois State University, IL
- **Bill McSorley**, Midlands Tech, SC
- **William Putman**, Paralegal educator/author, NM
- **Kenneth O'Neil Salyer**, Education consultant, KY
- **Angela Schneeman**, Paralegal and author, MN
- **Janis Walter**, University of Cincinnati, OH

In preparing this text, we were also the beneficiaries of the expertise brought to the project by the editorial and production staff of Cengage Learning. Our Product Manager, Abbie Schulthesis, put together a supplements package that is without parallel in the teaching and learning of paralegal skills. Mara Vuillaume, our Learning Designer, was also incredibly helpful in putting together the teaching/learning package. We also wish to thank Betty Dickson, Senior Content Project Manager, for her assistance throughout the production process.

A number of other individuals contributed significantly to the quality of *Paralegal Today*, Eighth Edition. We wish to thank Roger Meiners for his assistance in creating what we believe is the best introductory paralegal text on the market today. We also thank Suzanne Jasin for her special efforts on the project. Finally, we are indebted to the staff at SPi Global, Inc., our compositor, whose ability to generate the pages for this text quickly and accurately made it possible for us to meet our ambitious printing schedule.

We know that we are not perfect. If you or your students have suggestions on how we can improve this book, write to us. That way, we can make *Paralegal Today* an even better book in the future. We promise to answer every communication that we receive.

Roger LeRoy Miller
Mary Meinzinger

A Paralegal Skills Module

fizkes/Shutterstock.com

WHAT'S INSIDE

After reading this skills module, you will be better prepared to . . .

- *Make good choices*
  (College Prep, p. xxxiii)

- *Manage your time*
  (Time Prep, p. xxxiv)

- *Be engaged in your studies*
  (Study Prep, p. xxxvi)

- *Study for quizzes and exams*
  (Test Prep, p. xxxix)

- *Read your textbook efficiently*
  (Read Prep, p. xl)

- *Write quality papers*
  (Write Prep, p. xlii)

- *Make a presentation*
  (Presentation Prep, p. xlvi)

Welcome

With this course and this textbook, you've begun what we hope will be a stimulating and thought-provoking journey into the study of law. In this course, you will learn about the paralegal profession, the basic structure of the legal system, and substantive law, such as torts and criminal law. You'll also learn about procedural issues, such as civil litigation and criminal procedure. This book will help you develop paralegal skills, including legal research and writing, interviewing, and investigation. Building your base of knowledge will get you well on your way to a great future as a paralegal.

We have developed this skills module to help you get the most out of this course and textbook. Whether you are a recent high school graduate moving on to college or a working professional continuing your education, what you want most when you study is **RESULTS**. You want to become familiar with the issues and ideas presented in this textbook so that you can talk about them during class and remember them as you prepare for exams and assignments. Natural talent alone will not ensure your success as a paralegal; you also must develop effective study skills and good work habits. This study skills module is designed to help you do just that. With tips on lifestyle decisions, time management, how to be more engaged when you study, how to get the most out of your textbook, how to prepare for quizzes and exams, how to write papers, and how to prepare and deliver a presentation, this guide will help you develop the skills you need to be the best learner you can be.

College Prep

It takes several things to succeed in a college class—especially concentration and commitment to your studies. To do this, you need energy. When you are full of energy, time seems to pass quickly, and it is easier to get things done. As you know, when you don't have energy, time feels as if it is dragging, and even your favorite activities can feel like a burden. To have the energy you need to be a great college learner, it is important to make good lifestyle choices.

Here are some suggestions to help you succeed as a student and prepare for your future career.

- Too often, we become so busy with other aspects of our lives that we neglect our health. It is crucial that you eat a balanced diet, exercise regularly, and get enough sleep. If you don't take care of your physical well-being, other areas of your life will suffer. Research shows that people who are physically active learn better in school.

- Most people who succeed have a plan: they know what they want to accomplish and when. Do you have a life plan for after college? If not, you can start by making a list of your lifetime goals, even though they may change later on. You can also create a career plan that includes a list of skills you will need to succeed. Then, in addition to your classes, choose outside activities that will help you develop the skills that can lead to a good job.

- Whenever we do something new, whether in college or in other areas of life, we usually aren't very good at it. We can always benefit from feedback from those who are accomplished in that area, such as instructors or people working in a given field. Therefore, welcome feedback that is offered to you, and if it isn't given, ask for it.

- Do you want to become a better writer? Your college probably has a writing center with resources to help you with your writing assignments. If not, you should be able to find a tutor who will help you figure out what you are trying to communicate and how to put it effectively on paper. Clear writing is a critical skill for paralegals.

- Do you want to become a better public speaker? Consider using your campus's audiovisual resources to sharpen this essential skill. Record yourself giving a presentation, and then critique your performance. Invite a few friends to give their reaction, too. Join a school organization such as a debate or drama club to gain confidence in front of a live audience. Being comfortable talking to strangers is a much-needed skill for most paralegals.

- Learn to be a good listener. Hearing is not the same thing as listening, and many people are not good listeners. People often hear what they want to hear. We all filter information through our own experiences and interests. When talking with friends, instructors, or family members, focus carefully on what they say, as you may learn something unexpected. To be a good paralegal, you will need to listen well to attorneys' instructions and to clients, too.

- Be very careful about what you post on the Internet. A good rule of thumb is, "Don't post anything that you wouldn't want the world to know." Many employers search the Internet for information concerning potential employees, and one embarrassing photo, comment, or tweet can have long-term negative consequences. Law firms are particularly careful about hiring people with good character.

- Practice good record-keeping skills. Filing systems are an easy way to keep track of your money. First,

iStock.com/Wavebreakmedia

{ Most people who succeed have a plan. }

label file folders for different categories related to your personal finances, such as paycheck stubs, bank statements, and receipts from purchases. If you find you need another category, just set up a new folder. Paralegals must have excellent file systems. Do it in your own life now, and it will come naturally on the job.

- Be thankful for the people who care about you. Your family and good friends are a precious resource. When you have problems, don't try to solve them by yourself. Don't focus on disappointments. Talk to the people in your life who want you to succeed and be happy, and listen to their advice.

- No doubt you have seen people jump to conclusions that were not correct. Critical thinking is a crucial skill for paralegals, and, as with any other skill, you will get better at it with practice. Whether you are considering a friend's argument, a test question, a major purchase, or a personal problem, carefully weigh the evidence, balance strengths and weaknesses, and make a reasoned decision.

- Rather than worrying about approval from others, seek approval from the person who matters the most—yourself. Your conscience will tell you when you are doing the right thing. Don't let worries about what others think run—or ruin—your life.

> **If you don't take care of your physical well-being, other areas of your life will inevitably suffer.**

Time Prep

Doing well in college-level courses involves a lot of work. You have to go to class, read the textbook, pay attention to lectures, take notes, complete homework assignments, write papers, and take exams. On top of that, there are other things in your life that call for your time and attention. You have to take care of your home, run daily errands, take care of family, spend time with friends, work a full- or part-time job, and find time to unwind. With all that you're involved in, knowing how to manage your time is critical if you want to succeed as a learner.

The key to managing your time is knowing how much time you have and using it well. At the beginning of every term, you should evaluate how you use your time. How much time do you spend working? Caring for your home and family? Watching TV or movies? Studying? Keep a record of what you do hour by hour for a full week. Once you see where all your time goes, you can decide which activities you might change in order to manage your time more effectively. If you think you are busy in college, wait until you are a practicing paralegal! Then, time management will be even more critical.

Here are some other helpful tips on how to make the most of your time.

- Plan your study schedule in advance. At the beginning of each week, allocate time for each subject that you need to study. If it helps, put your schedule on a calendar computer program or on your smartphone for efficient daily planning. Learning to schedule tasks you need to complete and recording upcoming deadlines will serve you well when you are a paralegal.

- Don't be late for classes, meetings, or other appointments. If you find that you have trouble being on time, adjust your planning to arrive ten minutes early to all engagements. That way, even if you are "late," you will still be on time. It is critical to learn to be prompt for clients and court matters.

- To reduce the time spent looking for information on the Internet, start with a clear idea of your research task. Use a trusted search engine, and focus only on the subject at hand. Do not allow yourself to be sidetracked by other activities such as checking e-mail or social networking.

- Set aside a little time each day to assess whether you are on track to meet the requirements in all your classes, whether that involves studying for a test, writing a paper, or completing a group project. Don't let deadlines "sneak up" on you. A calendar program or app can help you keep track of target dates and can even give you friendly reminders.

- Nothing wastes more time—or is more aggravating—than having to redo schoolwork that was somehow lost on your computer. Back up all of your important files periodically. You can copy them onto an external hard drive or a USB flash drive.

- Concentrate on doing one thing at a time. Multitasking is a trap we often fall into that leads to doing several things quickly but poorly. When you are studying, don't carry on a text conversation with a friend or have one eye on the Internet.

- Set goals for yourself, not only with schoolwork but also with responsibilities in other areas of your life. If you tell yourself, "I will have this task done by Monday at noon and that other task finished before dinner on Wednesday," you will find it much easier to balance the many demands on your time.

- Regularly checking e-mail and text messages not only interrupts the task at hand, but is also an easy excuse for not working. Set aside specific times of the day to check and answer e-mail, and, when necessary, make sure that your cell phone is off or out of reach. A reply text can wait until you complete your work.

- Sometimes, a task is so large that it seems impossible, making it more tempting to put off. When given a large assignment, break it into a series of small assignments. Then, make a list of the assignments, and as you finish each one, give yourself the satisfaction of crossing it off your list.

- Many of us have a particular time of day when we are most alert, whether early morning, afternoon, or night. Plan to do schoolwork during your most efficient time, and set aside other times of the day for activities that do not require serious concentration.

- Slow down! Some people think they are getting more work done by rushing, but that often leads to poor decisions, mistakes, and errors of judgment, all of which waste time. Work well, not quickly, and you will save time.

- In marketing, *to bundle* means to combine several products. In time management, it means combining two activities to free up some time. For example, if you need to exercise and want to socialize, bundle the two activities by doing activities with your friends. Take along some schoolwork when you head to the laundromat—you can get a lot done while you're waiting for the spin cycle to end. Or, you can record class lectures (ask the professor for permission) so that you can review class material while you're running errands.

- Develop a habit of setting time limits for tasks, both in and out of school. You will find that with a time limit in mind, you will waste less time and work more efficiently, a prized skill among paralegals.

- A Chinese adage goes, "The longest journey starts with a single step." If you are having trouble getting started on a project or assignment, identify the first task that needs to be done. Then do it! This helps avoid time-wasting procrastination.

iStock.com/pixelfit

Study Prep

What does it take to be a successful student? Success does not depend on how naturally smart you are. Successful students and paralegals aren't born, they're made. What this means is that even if you don't consider yourself naturally "book smart," you can do well in this course by developing study skills that will help you understand, remember, and apply key concepts in school and on the job.

There are five things you can do to develop good study habits:

- Be engaged.
- Ask questions.
- Take notes.
- Make an outline.
- Mark your text.

Be Engaged

If you've ever heard elevator music, you know what easy listening is like—it stays in the background. You don't pay attention to it, and you probably forget it after a few minutes. That is *not* what you should be doing in class. You have to be engaged. Being *engaged* means listening to discover (and remember) something. As you listen with attention, you will hear what your instructor believes is important. One way to make sure that you are listening attentively is to take notes. Doing so will help you focus on the professor's words and will help you identify the most important parts of the lecture.

Ask Questions

If you are really engaged in a course, you will ask a question or two whenever you do not understand something. You can also ask a question to get your instructor to share her or his opinion on a subject. However you do it, true engagement requires you to be a participant in your class. The more you participate, the more you will learn (and the more your instructor will know who you are!).

Take Notes

Note taking has a value in and of itself, just as outlining does. The physical act of writing makes you a more efficient learner, since you must think about what you are writing. In addition, your notes provide a guide to what your instructor thinks is important. That means you will have a better idea of what to study before the next exam if you have a set of notes that you took during class. Paralegals usually take notes while listening to work instructions, doing research, or talking to clients or witnesses. It is a skill that increases the quality and accuracy of results.

Make an Outline

As you read through each chapter of this textbook, you might make an outline—a simple method for organizing information. You can create an outline as part of your reading or at the end of your reading. Or you can make an outline when you reread a section before moving on to the next one. The act of physically writing an outline will help you retain the material, thereby giving you a better chance of earning a higher grade. Even if you make an outline that is no more than the headings in this text, you will be studying more efficiently than you would be otherwise.

To make an effective outline, you have to be selective. Outlines that contain all the information in the text are not very useful. Your objectives in outlining are, first, to identify the main concepts and, then, to add details that support those main concepts.

Your outline should consist of several levels written in a standard format. The most important concepts are assigned Roman numerals; the second most important, capital letters; the third most important, numbers; and the fourth most important, lowercase letters. Here is a quick example from part of Chapter 12:

I.   **Trial Procedures**
   A. Preparing for trial
   B. Contacting and preparing witnesses
      1. Contacting witnesses and issuing subpoenas
      2. Preparing witnesses for trial
         a. Tell witnesses what to expect
         b. Role playing
         c. Numerous details
   C. Exhibits and displays
   D. The trial notebook

Legal "Shorthand"

Members of the legal profession usually use abbreviations and symbols as part of a shorthand system to allow for greater efficiency when taking notes. Rather than writing out common legal terms, here are some of the shorthand abbreviations and symbols often used:

Δ or D	defendant
π or P	plaintiff
≈	similar to
≠	not equal to, not the same as
[	therefore
a/k/a	also known as
atty	attorney
b/c or b/cz	because
b/p	burden of proof
cert	*certiorari*
dely	delivery
dep	deposition
disc	discovery
JML	judgment as a matter of law
JNOV	judgment *non obstante veredicto* (notwithstanding the verdict)
JOP	judgment on the pleadings
juris or jx	jurisdiction
K	contract
mtg	mortgage
n/a	not applicable
neg	negligence
PL	paralegal
Q	as a consequence, consequently
§ or sec	section
s/b	should be
S/F	Statute of Frauds
S/L	statute of limitations

You can expand on this list by creating and using other symbols or abbreviations. Once you develop a workable shorthand system, routinely use it in the classroom and then carry it over to your job. Most organizations you will work for will also use symbols and abbreviations, which you can add to your shorthand system.

Mark Your Text

Because you own your textbook for this course, you can greatly improve your learning by marking your text. By doing so, you will identify the most important concepts of each chapter, reinforce your knowledge as you mark, and at the same time make a handy study guide for reviewing material at a later time.

Different Ways of Marking

The most common form of marking is to underline important points. The second most common method is to use a felt-tipped highlighter, or marker, in yellow or some other transparent color. Marking also includes circling, numbering, using arrows, jotting brief notes, or any other method that allows you to remember things when you go back to skim the pages in your textbook prior to an exam.

Why Marking Is Important

Marking is important for the same reason that outlining is—it helps you to organize the information in the text. It allows you to become an active participant in the mastery of the material. Researchers have shown that the physical act of marking, just like the physical acts of note taking and outlining, helps you better retain the material. The clearer the material is organized in your mind, the more you'll remember. Studies indicate that active readers (those who engage with the text by outlining or marking) typically do better on exams. One reason this may be true is that outlining and/or marking require sharper concentration, and greater concentration facilitates greater recall.

Two Points to Remember When Marking

Read one section at a time before you do any extensive marking. You can't mark a section until you know what is important, and you can't know what is important until you read the whole section. Don't mark too extensively. Just as an outline cannot contain everything that is in a text (or, with respect to note taking, in a lecture), marking the whole book isn't useful. If you do mark the whole book, when you go back to review the material, your markings will not help you remember what was important.

The key to marking is *selective* activity. Mark each page in a way that allows you to see the most important points at a glance. You can follow up your marking by adding information to your subject outline.

With these skills in hand, you will be well on your way to becoming a great student. Here are a few more hints that will help you develop effective study skills.

- Put a check mark next to material that you do not understand. After you have completed an entire chapter, take a break. Then, work on better comprehension of the checkmarked material.

- As a rule, do schoolwork as soon as possible after class. The longer you wait, the more likely you will be distracted by television, video games, phone calls from friends, or social networking.

- Many students are tempted to take class notes on a laptop computer. This is a bad idea for two reasons. First, it is hard to copy diagrams or take other "artistic" notes on a computer. Second, it is easy to get distracted by checking e-mail or surfing the Web. (Notice, too, how many people look over the shoulders of other students who are surfing the Web rather than paying attention.)

- We study best when we are free from distractions such as the Internet, phones, and our friends. That's why your school library is often the best place to work. Set aside several hours a week of "library time" to study where you can concentrate in peace and quiet. When you are working as a paralegal, being able to devote quiet attention to material is a key skill.

- Reward yourself for studying! From time to time, allow yourself a short break so you can surf the Internet, go for a jog, take a nap, or do something else that you enjoy. These interludes will refresh your mind and enable you to study longer and more efficiently.

- A neat study space is important. Staying neat forces you to stay organized. When your desk is covered with piles of papers, notes, and textbooks, things are being lost even though you may not realize it. The only work items that should be on your desk are those that you are working on that day.

- Often, studying involves pure memorization. To help with this task, create flash (or note) cards. On one side of the card, write the question or term. On the other side, write the answer or definition. Then, use the cards to test yourself on the material.

- Mnemonic (ne-*mon*-ik) devices are tricks that increase our ability to memorize. A well-known mnemonic device is the phrase ROY G BIV, which helps people remember the colors of the rainbow—red, orange, yellow, green, blue, indigo, violet. You can create your own mnemonics for whatever you need to memorize. The more fun you have coming up with mnemonics for yourself, the more useful they will be.

- Take notes twice. First, take notes in class. Then, when you get back home, rewrite your notes. The rewrite will act as a study session by forcing you to think about the material. Invariably, it will lead to questions that are crucial to the study process.

- By turning headings or subheadings in all of your textbooks into questions—and then answering them—you will increase your understanding of the material.

- Multitasking while studying is generally a bad idea. You may think that you can review your notes and watch television at the same time, but your ability to study will almost certainly suffer. It's OK to give yourself Internet or TV breaks from schoolwork, but do not combine the two.

Test Prep

You have worked hard reading your textbook, paying close attention in class, and taking good notes. Now it's test time, when that hard work pays off. To do well on an exam, of course, it is important that you learn the concepts in each chapter as thoroughly as possible; however, there are additional strategies for taking exams. You should know which reading materials and lectures will be covered. You should also know in advance what type of exam you are going to take—essay or objective or both. (Objective exams usually include true/false, fill-in-the-blank, matching, and multiple-choice questions.) Finally, you should know how much time will be allowed for the exam. By taking these steps, you will reduce any anxiety you feel as you begin the exam, and you'll be better prepared to work through the entire exam.

Follow Directions

Students are often in a hurry to start an exam, so they don't bother to read the instructions. The instructions can be critical, however. In a multiple-choice exam, for example, if there is no indication that there is a penalty for guessing, then you should never leave a question unanswered. Even if only a few minutes are left at the end of an exam, you should guess on the questions about which you are uncertain.

Additionally, you need to know the weight given to each section of an exam. In a typical multiple-choice exam, all questions have equal weight. In other types of exams, particularly those with essay questions, different parts of the exam carry different weights. You should use these weights to apportion your time accordingly. If the essay portion of an exam accounts for 20 percent of the total points on the exam, you should not spend 60 percent of your time on the essay.

Finally, you need to make sure you are marking the answers correctly. Some exams require a No. 2 pencil to fill in the dots on a machine-graded answer sheet. Other exams require underlining or circling. In short, you have to read and follow the instructions carefully.

Objective Exams

An objective exam consists of multiple-choice, true-false, fill-in-the-blank, or matching questions that have only one correct answer. Students usually commit one of two errors when they read objective-exam questions: (1) they read things into the questions that do not exist, or (2) they skip over words or phrases. Most test questions include key words such as:

- all
- never
- always
- only

If you miss any of these key words, you may answer the question wrong even if you know the information. Consider the following example:

> True or False? All cases in which one person kills another person are considered murder.

In this instance, you may be tempted to answer "True," but the correct answer is "False," because the charge of murder is only brought in cases in which one person *intentionally* killed another. In cases in which a person unintentionally killed another, the charge is manslaughter.

Whenever the answer to an objective question is not obvious, start with the process of elimination. Throw out the answers that are clearly incorrect. Typically, the easiest way to eliminate incorrect answers is to look for those that are meaningless, illogical, or inconsistent. Often, test authors put in choices that make perfect sense and are indeed true, but they are not the answer to the question under study.

If you follow the above tips, you will be well on your way to becoming an efficient, results-oriented student. Here are a few more suggestions that will help you get there.

- Instructors usually lecture on subjects they think are important, so those same subjects are also likely to be on the exam. This is another reason to take extensive notes in class.

- Review your lecture notes immediately after each class, when the material is still fresh in your mind. Then, review each subject once a week, giving

> Grades aren't a matter of life and death, and worrying about them can have a negative effect on your performance.

yourself an hour to go back over what you have learned. Reviews make tests easier because you will feel comfortable with the material.

- At times, you will find yourself studying for several exams at once. When this happens, make a list of each study topic and the amount of time needed to prepare for that topic. Then, create a study schedule to reduce stress and give yourself the best chance for success.

- When preparing for an exam, you might want to get a small group together (two or three other students) for a study session. Discussing a topic out loud can improve your understanding of that topic and will help you remember the key points that often come up on exams.

- Some professors make old exams available, either by posting them online or putting them on file in the library. Old tests can give you an idea of the kinds of questions the professor likes to ask. You can also use them to take practice exams.

- Cramming just before the exam is a dangerous proposition. Cramming tires the brain unnecessarily and adds to stress, which can severely hamper your testing performance. If you've studied wisely, have confidence that you will recall the information when you need it.

- Be prepared. Make a list of everything you will need for the exam, such as pens or pencils, a watch, and a calculator. Arrive at the exam early to avoid having to rush, which will only add to your stress. Good preparation helps you focus on the task at hand.

- Be sure to eat before taking a test. Having some food in your stomach will give you the energy you need to concentrate. Don't go overboard, however. Too much food or heavy foods will make you sleepy during the exam.

> **Cramming just before the exam is a dangerous proposition.**

- When you first receive your exam, look it over quickly to make sure that you have all the pages. If you are uncertain, ask your professor or exam proctor. This initial scan may uncover other problems as well, such as illegible print or unclear instructions.

- If the test requires you to read a passage and then answer questions about that passage, read the questions first. This way, you will know what to look for as you read.

- With essay questions, look for key words such as "compare," "contrast," and "explain." These will guide your answer. If you have time, make a quick outline. Most importantly, get to the point without wasting your time (or your professor's) with statements such as "There are many possible reasons for . . . ."

- When you finish a test early, your first instinct may be to hand it in and get out of the classroom as quickly as possible. It is always a good idea, however, to review your answers. You may find a mistake or an area where some extra writing will improve your grade.

- Grades aren't a matter of life and death, and worrying too much about a single exam can have a negative effect on your performance. Keep exams in perspective. If you do poorly on one test, it's not the end of the world. Rather, it should motivate you to do better on the next one.

Read Prep

This textbook is the foundation for your introduction to paralegal studies. It contains key concepts and terms that are important to understanding law and the practice of law. This knowledge will be important not only for you to succeed in this course but for your future paralegal career. For this reason, it is essential that you develop good reading skills so that you can get the most out of this textbook and other class materials.

All students know how to read, but reading for a college-level course goes beyond being able to recognize words on a page. Students must read to learn. Read a chapter with the goal of understanding its key points and how it relates to other chapters. In other words, you have to be able to explain what you read. To do this, you need good reading habits and skills, which are necessary for success as a paralegal.

Reading for Learning Requires Focus

Reading (and learning from) a textbook is not like reading a newspaper, magazine, or novel. The point of reading for learning isn't to get through the material as fast as you can or to skip parts to get to the stuff you think is most interesting. A textbook is a source of deep information about a subject. The goal of reading a textbook is to learn as much of that information as you can. This kind of reading requires concentration. When you read to learn, you have to make an effort to focus on the book and tune out other distractions so that you can comprehend and remember the information you have read.

> **How to read this book:**
> 1. Preview.
> 2. Read in detail.
> 3. Review.

Reading for Learning Takes Time

When reading your textbook, you need to go slow. The most important part of reading for learning is not how many pages you get through or how fast you get through them. Instead, the goal is to learn the key concepts that are presented in each chapter. To do that, you need to read slowly, carefully, and with great attention. It will be the same on the job—careful reading is essential in legal work.

Reading for Learning Takes Repetition

Even the most well-read scholar will tell you that it's difficult to learn from a textbook just by reading through it once. To read for learning, you have to read assigned material a number of times. This doesn't mean, though, that you just sit and read the same section three or four times. Instead, you should follow a preview-read-review process. The sections that follow provide a good guide.

The First Time

The first time you read a section of the book, you should preview it. During the preview, pay attention to how the chapter is formatted. Look over the title of the chapter, the section headings, and highlighted or bold words. This will give you a good preview of the important ideas in the chapter. You should also pay close attention to any graphs, illustrations, or figures that are used in the chapter, since these provide a visual illustration of important concepts. You should also give special attention to the first and last sentence of each paragraph. First sentences usually introduce the main point of the paragraph, while last sentences usually sum up what was presented in the paragraph.

The goal of previewing is to identify the main idea of the section. Of course, you may not be able to come up with a detailed answer yet, but that's not the point of previewing. Instead, the point is to develop some general ideas about what the section is about so that when you do read it in full, you know what to look for.

The Second Time

After the preview, you'll want to read through the passage in detail. During this phase, it is important to read with a few questions in mind: What is the main point of this paragraph? What does the author want me to learn from this? How does this relate to what I read before? Keeping these questions in mind will help you be an attentive reader who is actively focusing on the main ideas of the passage.

After you have completed a detailed read of the chapter, take a break so that you can rest your mind (and your eyes). When you resume studying, you should write up a summary or paraphrase of what you just read. You don't need to produce a detailed, lengthy summary of the whole chapter. Instead, try to come up with a brief paraphrase that covers the most important ideas of the chapter. This paraphrase will help you remember the main points of the chapter, allow you to check the accuracy of your reading, and provide a good guide for later review.

The Third Time (and Beyond)

After you've finished a detailed reading of the chapter, you should take the time to review the chapter (at least once, but maybe even two, three, or more times). During this step, you should review each paragraph and the notes you made, asking this question: "What was this paragraph about?" At this point, you'll want to answer the question in some detail, drawing on what you learned during your first two readings.

Reading with others is also a great way to review the chapter. After completing the reading individually, group members should meet and take turns sharing what they learned from their reading. Explaining the material to others will reinforce and clarify what you already know. It also provides an opportunity to learn from others. Gaining another perspective on a passage will increase your knowledge, since different people will key in on different things during a reading.

Whether you're reading your textbook for the first time or reviewing it for the final exam, here are a couple of tips that will help you be an attentive and attuned reader.

1. Set Aside Time and Space

To read effectively, you need to be focused and attentive, and that won't happen if your phone is buzzing with text messages every two minutes, if the TV is on in the background, or if you're surrounded by friends or family. Similarly, you won't be able to focus on your book if you're trying to read in a room that is too hot or too cold, or sitting in an uncomfortable chair. So when you read, find a quiet, comfortable place that is free from distractions where you can focus on one thing—learning from the book.

2. Take Frequent Breaks

Reading your textbook shouldn't be a test of endurance. Rest your eyes and your mind by taking a short break every twenty to thirty minutes. The concentration you need to read attentively requires lots of energy, and you won't have enough energy if you don't take frequent breaks. Studies indicate that hard concentration can rarely go beyond thirty minutes, as our minds need small rest breaks.

3. Keep Reading

Effective reading is like playing sports or a musical instrument—practice makes perfect. The more time that you spend reading, the better you will be at learning from your textbook. Your vocabulary will grow, and you'll have an easier time learning and remembering information in all your courses.

Write Prep

A key part of succeeding as a student is learning how to write well. Whether writing papers, presentations, essays, or even e-mails to your instructor, you have to be able to put your thoughts into words and do so with force, clarity, and precision. In this section, we outline a three-phase process that you can use to write virtually anything.

1. Getting ready to write
2. Writing a first draft
3. Revising your draft

Phase 1: Getting Ready to Write

First, make a list. Divide the ultimate goal—a finished paper—into smaller steps that you can tackle right away. Estimate how long it will take to complete each step. Start with the date your paper is due and work backwards to the present. For example, if the due date is December 1 and you have about three months to write the paper, give yourself a cushion and schedule November 20 as your target completion date. Plan what you want to get done by November 1, and then list what you want to get done by October 1.

How to Pick a Topic

To generate ideas for a topic, any of the following approaches work well:

- **BRAINSTORM WITH A GROUP.** There is no need to create in isolation. You can harness the energy and the natural creative power of a group to help you.

- **SPEAK IT.** To get ideas flowing, start talking. Admit your confusion or lack of clear ideas. Then just speak. By putting your thoughts into words, you'll start thinking more clearly.

- **USE FREE WRITING.** Free writing, a technique championed by writing teacher Peter Elbow, is also very effective when trying to come up with a topic. There's only one rule in free writing: Write without stopping. Set a time limit—say, ten minutes—and keep your fingers dancing across the keyboard the whole time. Ignore the urge to stop and rewrite. There is no need to worry about spelling, punctuation, or grammar during this process.

Refine Your Idea

After you've come up with some initial ideas, it's time to refine them:

- **SELECT A TOPIC AND WORKING TITLE.** Using your instructor's guidelines for the paper or speech, write down a list of topics that interest you. Write down all of the ideas you think of in two minutes. Then choose one topic. The most common pitfall is selecting a topic that is too broad. "Trial Procedure" is not a useful topic for your paper. Instead, consider something narrow that can be accomplished with some detail, such as "Motions for Judgment Notwithstanding the Verdict."

- **WRITE A THESIS STATEMENT.** Clarify what you want to say by summarizing it in one concise sentence.

This sentence, called a *thesis statement*, refines your working title. A thesis is the main point of the paper; it is a declaration of some sort. You might write a thesis statement such as "Motions for judgment notwithstanding the verdict (JNOV) have a low success rate but are an essential tool in obtaining a favorable outcome for a client."

Set Goals

Effective writing flows from a purpose. Think about how you'd like your reader or listener to respond after considering your ideas.

- If you want to persuade someone to your point of view, make your writing clear and logical. Support your assertions with evidence.

- If your purpose is to move the reader into action, explain exactly what steps to take and offer solid benefits for doing so.

To clarify your purpose, state it in one sentence—for example, "The purpose of this paper is to discuss and analyze how motions for JNOV are constructed and presented at trial."

Begin Research

In the initial stage, the objective of your research is not to uncover specific facts about your topic. That comes later. First, you want to gain an overview of the subject. You must first learn enough about such motions and how they are used to be able to explain them to others.

Make an Outline

An outline is a kind of map. When you follow a map, you avoid getting lost. Likewise, an outline keeps you from wandering off topic. To create your outline, follow these steps:

1. Review your thesis statement, and identify the three to five main points you need to address in your paper to support your thesis that such motions are worth filing.

2. Next, look closely at those three to five major points or categories, and think about what minor points or subcategories you want to cover in your paper. Your major points are your big ideas; your minor points are the details you need to fill in under each of those ideas.

3. Ask for feedback. Have your instructor or a classmate review your outline and offer suggestions for improvement. Did you choose the right categories and subcategories? Do you need more detail anywhere? Does the flow from idea to idea make sense?

Do In-Depth Research

Three-by-five-inch index cards are an old-fashioned but invaluable tool for in-depth research. Simply write down one idea or piece of information per card. This makes it easy to organize—and reorganize—your ideas and information. Organizing research cards as you create them saves time. Use rubber bands to keep *source cards* (cards that include the bibliographical information for a source) separate from *information cards* (cards that include nuggets of information from a source) and to maintain general categories.

When creating your cards, be sure to:

- Copy all of the information correctly.

- Always include the source and page number on information cards.

- Be neat and organized. Write legibly, using the same format for all of your cards.

In addition to source cards and information cards, generate *idea cards*. If you have a thought while you are researching, write it down on a card. Label these cards clearly as containing your own ideas.

Phase 2: Writing a First Draft

To create your draft, gather your index cards, and confirm that they are arranged to follow your outline. Then write about the ideas in your notes. It's that simple. Look at your cards and start writing. Write in paragraphs, with one idea per paragraph. As you complete this task, keep the following suggestions in mind:

- **REMEMBER THAT THE FIRST DRAFT IS NOT FOR KEEPS.** You can worry about quality later; your goal at this point is simply to generate lots of words and lots of ideas.

- **WRITE FREELY.** Many writers prefer to get their first draft down quickly and would advise you to keep writing, much as in free writing. Of course, you may pause to glance at your cards and outline. The idea is to avoid stopping to edit your work.

- **BE YOURSELF.** Let go of the urge to sound "official" or "scholarly," and avoid using unnecessary big words or phrases. Instead, write in a natural voice. Address your thoughts not to the teacher but to an intelligent student or someone you care about. Visualize this person, and choose the three or four most important things you'd say to her about the topic.

- **MAKE WRITING A HABIT.** Don't wait for inspiration to strike. Make a habit of writing at a certain time each day.

- **GET PHYSICAL.** While working on the first draft, take breaks. Go for a walk. Speak or sing your ideas out loud. From time to time, practice relaxation techniques and breathe deeply.

- **HIDE THE DRAFT IN YOUR DRAWER FOR A WHILE.** Schedule time for rewrites before you begin, and schedule at least one day between revisions so that you can let the material sit. The brain needs that much time to disengage itself from the project.

Phase 3: Revising Your Draft

During this phase, keep in mind the saying, "Write in haste; revise at leisure." When you are working on your first draft, the goal is to produce ideas and write them down. During the revision phase, however, you need to slow down and take a close look at your work. One guideline is to allow 50 percent of writing time for planning, researching, and writing the first draft. Then use the remaining 50 percent for revising.

There are a number of especially good ways to revise your paper:

1. Read it out loud.

The combination of voice and ears forces us to pay attention to the details. Is the thesis statement clear and supported by enough evidence? Does the introduction tell your reader what's coming? Do you end with a strong conclusion that expands on what's in your introduction rather than just restating it?

2. Have a friend look over your paper.

This is never a substitute for your own review, but a friend can often see mistakes you miss. Remember, when other people criticize or review your work, they are not attacking you. They're just commenting on your paper. With a little practice, you will learn to welcome feedback because it is one of the fastest ways to approach the revision process.

3. Cut.

Look for excess baggage. Avoid at all costs and at all times the really, really terrible mistake of using way too many unnecessary words, a mistake that some student writers often make when they sit down to write papers for the various courses in which they participate at the fine institutions of higher learning that they are fortunate enough to attend. (Example: The previous sentence could be edited to "Avoid unnecessary words.") Also, look for places where two (or more) sentences could be rewritten as one. Resist

the temptation to think that by cutting text you are losing something. You are actually gaining a clearer, more polished product. For maximum efficiency, make the larger cuts first—sections, chapters, pages. Then go for the smaller cuts—paragraphs, sentences, phrases, words.

4. Paste.

In deleting both larger and smaller passages in your first draft, you've probably removed some of the original transitions and connecting ideas. The next task is to rearrange what's left of your paper or speech so that it flows logically. Look for consistency within paragraphs and for transitions from paragraph to paragraph and section to section.

5. Fix.

Now it's time to look at individual words and phrases. Define any terms that the reader might not know, putting them in plain English whenever you can. In general, focus on nouns and verbs. Using too many adjectives and adverbs weakens your message and adds unnecessary bulk to your writing. Write about the details, and be specific. Also, check your writing to ensure that you are:

- Using the active voice. Write *"The research team began the project"* rather than (passively) *"A project was initiated."*

- Writing concisely. Instead of *"After making a timely arrival and perspicaciously observing the unfolding events, I emerged totally and gloriously victorious,"* be concise with *"I came, I saw, I conquered."*

- Communicating clearly. Instead of *"The speaker made effective use of the television medium, asking in no uncertain terms that we change our belief systems,"* you can write specifically, *"The reformed criminal stared straight into the television camera and shouted, 'Take a good look at what you're doing! Will it get you what you really want?'"*

6. Prepare.

In a sense, any paper is a sales effort. If you hand in a paper that is wearing wrinkled jeans, its hair tangled and unwashed and its shoes untied, your instructor is less likely to buy it. To avoid this situation, format your paper following accepted standards for margin widths, endnotes, title pages, and other details. Ask your instructor for specific instructions on how to cite the sources used in writing your paper. You can find useful guidelines in the *MLA Handbook for Writers of Research Papers*, a book from the Modern Language Association. If you cut and paste material from a Web page directly into your paper, be sure to place that material in quotation marks and cite the source. Before referencing an e-mail message, verify the sender's identity. Remember that anyone sending e-mail can pretend to be someone else. Use quality paper for the final version of your paper. For an even more professional appearance, bind your paper with a plastic or paper cover.

7. Proofread.

As you ease down the home stretch, read your revised paper one more time. This time, go for the big picture and look for the following using this proofreading checklist:

- A clear thesis statement.

- Sentences that introduce your topic, guide the reader through the major sections of your paper, and summarize your conclusions.

- Details—such as quotations, examples, and statistics—that support your conclusions.

- Lean sentences that have been purged of needless words.

- Plenty of action verbs and concrete, specific nouns.

- Finally, look over your paper with an eye for spelling and grammar mistakes. Use contractions sparingly if at all. Use your word processor's spell-check, by all means, but do not rely on it completely as it will not catch everything.

When you are through proofreading, take a minute to savor the result. You've just witnessed something of a miracle—the mind organizing diverse ideas into a creative work of art! That's the *aha!* in writing.

Academic Integrity: Avoiding Plagiarism

Using another person's words, images, or other original creations without giving proper credit is called *plagiarism*. Plagiarism amounts to taking someone else's work and presenting it as your own—the equivalent of cheating on a test. The consequences of plagiarism can range from a failing grade to expulsion from school. Plagiarism can be unintentional, as some students don't understand the research process. Sometimes they leave writing until the last minute and don't take the time to organize their sources of information. Also, some people are raised in cultures where identity is based on group membership rather than individual achievement. These students may find it hard to understand how creative work can be owned by an individual.

To avoid plagiarism, ask an instructor where you can find your school's written policy on this issue. Don't assume that you can resubmit a paper you wrote for another class for a current class; many schools will regard this as plagiarism even though you wrote the paper. The basic guidelines for preventing plagiarism are to cite a source for each phrase, sequence of ideas, or visual image created by another person. While ideas cannot be copyrighted, the specific way that an idea is *expressed* can be. You also need to list a source for any idea that is closely identified with a particular person. The goal is to clearly distinguish your own work from the work of others. There are several ways to ensure that you do this consistently.

- **IDENTIFY DIRECT QUOTES.** If you use a direct quote from another writer or speaker, put that person's words in quotation marks. If you do research online, you might find yourself copying sentences or paragraphs from a Web page and pasting them directly into your notes. This is the same as taking direct quotes from your source. To avoid plagiarism, identify such passages in an obvious way.

- **PARAPHRASE CAREFULLY.** Paraphrasing means restating the original passage in your own words, usually making it shorter and simpler. Students who copy a passage word for word and then just rearrange or delete a few phrases are running a serious risk of plagiarism. Remember to cite a source for paraphrases, just as you do for direct quotes. When you use the same sequence of ideas as one of your sources—even if you have not paraphrased or directly quoted—cite that source.

- **NOTE DETAILS ABOUT EACH SOURCE.** For books, details about each source include the author, title, publisher, publication date, location of publisher, and page number. For articles from print sources, record the article title and the name of the magazine or journal as well. If you found the article in an academic or technical journal, also record the volume and number of the publication. A librarian can help identify these details. If your source is a Web page, record as many identifying details as you can find—author, title, sponsoring organization, URL, publication date, and revision date. In addition, list the date that you accessed the page. Be careful when using Web resources, as not all websites are considered legitimate sources. Wikipedia, for instance, may not be regarded as a legitimate source for certain information; the National Institute of Justice's website, however, is acceptable.

- **CITE YOUR SOURCES AS ENDNOTES OR FOOTNOTES TO YOUR PAPER.** Ask your instructor for examples of the citation format to use. You do not need to credit wording that is wholly your own, nor do you need to credit general ideas, such as the suggestion that people use a to-do list to plan their time. But if you borrow someone else's words or images to explain an idea, do give credit.

Presentation Prep

In addition to reading and writing, your success as a student will depend on how well you can communicate what you have learned. Most often, you'll do so in the form of presentations. Many people are intimidated by the idea of public speaking, but it really is just like any other skill—the more often you do it, the better you will get. Developing a presentation is similar to writing a paper. Begin by writing out your topic, purpose, and thesis statement. Then carefully analyze your audience by using the strategies listed below.

If your topic is new to listeners . . .

- Explain why your topic matters to them.
- Relate the topic to something that they already know and care about.
- Define any terms that they might not know.

If listeners already know about your topic . . .

- Acknowledge this fact at the beginning of your speech.
- Find a narrow aspect of the topic that may be new to listeners.
- Offer a new perspective on the topic, or connect it to an unfamiliar topic.

If listeners disagree with your thesis . . .

- Tactfully admit your differences of opinion.
- Reinforce points on which you and your audience agree.
- Build credibility by explaining your qualifications to speak on your topic.
- Quote experts who agree with your thesis—people whom your audience is likely to admire.
- Explain to your audience that their current viewpoint has costs for them and that a slight adjustment in their thinking will bring significant benefits.

If listeners might be uninterested in your topic . . .

- Explain how listening to your speech can help them gain something that matters deeply to them.
- Explain ways to apply your ideas in daily life.

Remember that audiences generally have one question in mind: *"So what?"* They want to know that your presentation relates to their needs and desires. To convince people that you have something worthwhile to say, think of your main topic or point. Then see if you can complete this sentence: "I'm telling you this because . . . ."

Organize Your Presentation

Consider the length of your presentation. Plan on delivering about one hundred words per minute. Aim for a lean presentation—enough words to make your point but not so many as to make your audience restless. Leave your listeners wanting more. When you speak, be brief, and then be seated. Presentations are usually organized in three main parts: the introduction, the main body, and the conclusion.

1. The introduction.
Rambling presentations with no clear point or organization put audiences to sleep. Solve this problem by making sure your introduction conveys the point of your presentation. The following introduction, for example, reveals the thesis and indicates exactly what's coming. It conveys that the speech will have three distinct parts, each in logical order:

> Prison overcrowding is a serious problem in many states. I intend to describe prison conditions around the country, the challenges these conditions create, and how various states are addressing the issue.

Some members of an audience will begin to drift during any speech, but most people pay attention for at least the first few seconds.

Highlight your main points in the beginning sentences of your speech. People might tell you to open your introduction with a joke, but humor is tricky. You run the risk of falling flat or offending somebody. Save jokes until you have plenty of experience and know your audiences well. Also avoid long, flowery introductions in which you tell people how much you like them and how thrilled you are to address them. If you lay it on too thick, your audience won't believe you. Get down to business, which is what the audience wants. Draft your introduction, and then come back to it after you have written the rest of your presentation. In the process of creating the main body and conclusion, your thoughts about the purpose and main points of your speech might change.

2. The main body.
The main body of your speech accounts for 70 to 90 percent of your presentation. In the main body, you develop your ideas in much the same way that you develop a written paper. Transitions are especially important in presentations. Give your audience a signal when you change points. Do so by using meaningful pauses, verbal emphasis, and transitional phrases: "On the other hand, until the public

realizes what is happening to children in these countries . . ." or "The second reason police officers use *Miranda* cards is . . . ." In long presentations, recap from time to time. Also, make it a point to preview what's to come. Hold your audience's attention by using facts, descriptions, expert opinions, and statistics.

3. The conclusion.

At the end of the presentation, summarize your points, and draw your conclusion. You started with a bang; now finish with drama. The first and last parts of a presentation are the most important. Make it clear to your audience when you have reached the end. Avoid endings such as "This is the end of my presentation. Are there any questions?" A simple standby is "So, in conclusion, I want to reiterate three points: First . . . ." When you are finished, stop speaking. Although this sounds quite obvious, a good presentation is often ruined by a speaker who doesn't know when, or how, to wrap things up.

Support Your Presentation with Notes and Visuals

To create speaking notes, you can type out your presentation in full and transfer key words or main points onto a few three-by-five-inch index cards. Number the cards so that if you drop them, you can quickly put them in order again. As you finish the information on each card, move it to the back of the pile. Write information clearly and in letters large enough to be seen from a distance. The disadvantage of the index card system is that it involves card shuffling, so some speakers prefer to use outlined notes.

You can also create supporting visuals. Presentations often include visuals such as PowerPoint slides or handwritten flip charts. These visuals can reinforce your main points and help your audience understand how your presentation is organized. They also serve to trigger your memory about what you should say to flesh out the bullet points in your visuals. Use visuals to *complement* rather than *replace* speech. If you use too many visuals or if they are too complex, your audience might focus on them and forget about you.

- Use fewer visuals rather than more. For a fifteen-minute presentation, a total of five to ten slides is usually enough.

- Limit the amount of text on each visual. Stick to key words presented in short sentences or phrases and in bulleted or numbered lists.

- Use a consistent set of plain fonts. Make them large enough for all audience members to see.

- Stick with a simple, coherent color scheme. Use light-colored text on a dark background or dark text on a light background.

Overcome Fear of Public Speaking

Surveys indicate that the fear of public speaking is the number one fear for many people. For those who harbor this fear, being overlooked by an audience in favor of visuals may be exactly what they hope for! Ideally, though, while many of us may not be able to eliminate fear of public speaking entirely, we can take steps to reduce and manage it. The following tips will help you conquer any fear you might feel at the thought of public speaking.

- **PREPARE THOROUGHLY.** Research your topic thoroughly. Knowing your topic inside and out can create a baseline of confidence. To make a strong start, memorize the first four sentences that you plan to deliver, and practice them many times. Delivering them flawlessly when you're in front of an audience can build your confidence for the rest of your speech.

- **ACCEPT YOUR PHYSICAL SENSATIONS.** You have probably experienced the physical sensations that are commonly associated with stage fright: dry mouth, a pounding heart, sweaty hands, muscle jitters, shortness of breath, and a shaky voice. One immediate way to deal with such sensations is simply to notice them. Tell yourself, "Yes, my hands are clammy. Yes, my stomach is upset. Also, my face feels numb." Trying to deny or ignore such facts can increase your fear. In contrast, when you fully accept sensations, they start to lose power. While speakers often feel nervous, they do not look that nervous. Members of the audience are there to listen and are sympathetic.

- **FOCUS ON CONTENT, NOT DELIVERY.** If you view presentations simply as an extension of a one-to-one conversation, you will realize that the goal is not to perform but to communicate your ideas to an audience just as you would explain them to a friend. This can reduce your fear of speaking. Instead of thinking about yourself, focus on your message. Your audience is more interested in what you have to say than in how you say it. Forget about giving a "speech." Just give people valuable ideas and information that they can use.

Practice Your Presentation

The key to successful public speaking is practice. While it's good to use practice sessions to memorize the contents of your speech, these sessions are also important times to work on how you use your voice and body as you speak. To make your practice time efficient and beneficial, follow the tips below, and run through your speech two or three (or more) times until you're ready to deliver a professional, polished presentation.

- **PRACTICE IN THE ROOM IN WHICH YOU WILL DELIVER YOUR PRESENTATION.** Ideally, you will be able to practice your presentation where it will be given. If that is not possible, at least visit the site ahead of time so you are comfortable with your surroundings. Also make sure that the materials you need for your presentation, including any audiovisual equipment, will be available when you need them and that you know how to use them.

- **USE YOUR "SPEAKER'S VOICE."** When you practice, do so in a loud voice. Your voice sounds different when you talk loudly, and this fact can be unnerving. Get used to it early on. People do not like to strain to hear what you have to say.

- **MAKE A RECORDING.** Many schools have video recording equipment available for student use. Use it while you practice, and then view the finished recording to evaluate your presentation. Did your speech cover your main points in a clear, logical fashion? Did you speak at an appropriate rate, neither too fast nor too slow? Pay special attention to your body language—your posture, your eye contact, and how you used your hands.

- **LISTEN FOR REPEATED WORDS AND PHRASES.** Examples of unwanted filler words include *you know*, *kind of*, and *really*, plus *uh*, *umm*, and *ah*. To get rid of them, try to notice them every time they pop up in your daily speech.

- **KEEP PRACTICING.** Avoid speaking word for word, as if you were reading a script. When you know your material well, you can deliver it in a natural way. Practice your presentation until you could deliver it in your sleep, then run through it a few more times. You do not want to hide behind a computer monitor or stare at your script while you read it. You know the material, so you only need visual triggers on PowerPoint slides or note cards.

Deliver Your Presentation

When the time comes to deliver your presentation, your practice will help you to feel confident and self-assured. It's important to dress appropriately for the occasion, because the clothing you choose to wear delivers a message that's as loud as your words. Consider how your audience will be dressed, and then choose a wardrobe based on the impression you want to make. It shows respect for the audience to be dressed professionally.

Before you begin, get the audience's attention. If people are still filing into the room or adjusting their seats, they're not ready to listen. Wait for the audience to settle into their seats before you begin.

For a great presentation, keep these tips and reminders from your practice sessions in mind:

- **PROJECT YOUR VOICE.** When you speak, do it loudly enough to be heard. Avoid leaning over your notes or a computer monitor.

- **MAINTAIN EYE CONTACT.** When you look at people, they become less frightening. Remember, too, that it is easier for the audience to listen to someone when that person is looking at them. Find a few friendly faces around the room, and imagine that you are talking to each of these people individually.

- **NOTICE YOUR NONVERBAL COMMUNICATION AND YOUR BODY LANGUAGE.** Be aware of what your body is telling your audience. Contrived or staged gestures will look dishonest. Hands in pockets, twisting your hair, chewing gum, or shifting your weight from one foot to the other will detract from your speech and make you appear less polished.

- **WATCH THE TIME.** You can increase the impact of your words by keeping track of the time during your presentation. It's better to end early than to run late.

- **PAUSE WHEN APPROPRIATE.** Beginners sometimes feel they have to fill every moment with the sound of their voice. Release that expectation. Give your listeners a chance to make notes and absorb what you say.

- **HAVE FUN.** Chances are that if you lighten up and enjoy your presentation, so will your listeners.

Reflect on Your Presentation

Review and reflect on your performance. Did you finish on time? Did you cover all of the points you intended to cover? Was the audience attentive? Did you handle any nervousness effectively? Welcome evaluation from others. Most of us find it difficult to hear criticism about our speaking. Be aware of resisting such criticism, and then let go of your resistance. Listening to feedback will increase your skill.

iStockPhoto.com/PeopleImages

PART 1

The Paralegal Profession

CHAPTER

1

Today's Professional Paralegal

CHAPTER OBJECTIVES

After completing this chapter, you will be able to:

- Compare the varying definitions of *paralegal*.
- Describe the major tasks paralegals perform.
- List the professional associations for paralegals.
- Explain the scope of and options for paralegal education and training.
- Define *certification*, and describe the paralegal certifications currently available.
- Describe the key skills and attributes of the professional paralegal.
- Discuss the future of the paralegal profession.

Introduction

The career of a paralegal can be exciting, challenging, and rewarding. Over time, law firms have been giving greater responsibilities to paralegals. Opportunities for paralegals to work outside of law firms (such as in corporations or government agencies) are also expanding. As the profession has grown, the average paralegal salary has increased. In 2020, several sources reported the average or median pay for a paralegal to be between $51,000 and $55,000 a year. Experienced paralegals can earn substantially more.

How do you know if you want to become part of this dynamic profession? The first step is to become familiar with what a paralegal is, the kinds of work paralegals do, and what education and skills are needed. These topics are covered in this chapter. In Chapter 2, you will learn about where paralegals work and how to get a job as a paralegal. As you read through this book, remember that this is only an introduction to the profession and the starting point of your education. You should supplement what you learn in the classroom by networking with paralegals in professional environments. In today's competitive job market, whom you know can be as important as what you know in getting the job you desire.

What Is a Paralegal?

In the past, the terms *paralegal* and *legal assistant* have been used synonymously in the legal community. As noted below, however, some legal organizations prefer to make distinctions between these terms in their respective definitions.

Definition of Paralegal

In 2020, the **American Bar Association (ABA)** removed the term *legal assistant* from its definition of *paralegal*. The ABA wanted to recognize a distinction between the work done by paralegals and that of legal assistants. The new ABA definition reads as follows:

> A **paralegal** is a person qualified by education, training, or work experience who is employed or retained by a lawyer, law office, corporation, governmental agency or other entity and who performs specifically delegated substantive legal work, for which a lawyer is responsible.[1]

The Paralegal Association (NALA), which is the largest national organization of paralegals, starts its definition of *paralegal* with the term *legal assistant,* making the two terms synonymous.

The **National Federation of Paralegal Associations (NFPA)** is another large paralegal association. Members of the NFPA were concerned that some attorneys refer to their secretaries as legal assistants and so wanted to distinguish the role of paralegals as professionals. The NFPA gives the following definition for *paralegal*:

> A Paralegal is a person, qualified through education, training or work experience to perform substantive legal work that requires knowledge of legal concepts and is customarily, but not exclusively, performed by a lawyer. This person may be retained or employed by a lawyer, law office, governmental agency or other entity or may be authorized by administrative, statutory or court authority to perform this work. Substantive shall mean work requiring recognition, evaluation, organization, analysis, and communication of relevant facts and legal concepts.[2]

American Bar Association (ABA)
A voluntary national association of attorneys. The ABA's mission is: To serve equally our members, our profession and the public by defending liberty and delivering justice as the national representative of the legal profession.

paralegal
A person qualified by education, training, or work experience who is employed or retained by a lawyer, law office, corporation, governmental agency or other entity and who performs specifically delegated substantive legal work, for which a lawyer is responsible.

The Paralegal Association (NALA)
The largest national paralegal association in the United States; formed in 1975. NALA is actively involved in paralegal professional development.

National Federation of Paralegal Associations (NFPA)
A large paralegal association in the United States; formed in 1974. NFPA is actively involved in paralegal professional development.

American Association for Paralegal Education (AAfPE)
A national organization of paralegal educators; the AAfPE was established in 1981 to promote high standards for paralegal education.

Yet another major organization, the **American Association for Paralegal Education (AAfPE)**, provides the following definition:

Paralegals perform substantive and procedural legal work as authorized by law, which work, in the absence of the paralegal, would be performed by an attorney. Paralegals have knowledge of the law gained through education, or education and work experience, which qualifies them to perform legal work. Paralegals adhere to recognized ethical standards and rules of professional responsibility.[3]

Expanding Roles

Paralegals today perform many functions that traditionally were performed by attorneys. That is why the U.S. Department of Labor predicts growth in the paralegal profession will continue "much faster than the average for all occupations." Paralegals perform substantive legal work for which they are trained through education, experience, or (usually) both.

What Do Paralegals Do?

Paralegals assist attorneys in many ways. The following is a sample of some tasks that paralegals typically perform in a law office. Keep in mind that today's paralegals work in many nontraditional settings, including corporations, government agencies, courts, insurance companies, and real estate firms—indeed, in almost any entity that uses legal services. Throughout this book, you will read about the specific tasks that paralegals perform in different settings.

A Sampling of Paralegal Tasks

Typically, paralegals perform the following duties:

- *Conduct client interviews and maintain contact with clients*—provided that the client is aware of the status and function of the paralegal, who does not give legal advice.

- *Locate and interview witnesses*—gather relevant facts and information about a lawsuit, for example.

- *Conduct legal investigations*—obtain, organize, and evaluate information from sources such as police reports, medical records, photographs, court documents, experts' reports, technical manuals, and product specifications.

- *Calendar and track important deadlines*—such as the date by which a certain document must be filed with the court or the date by which the attorney must respond to a settlement offer.

- *Organize and maintain client files*—keep the documents in each client's file accessible.

- *Conduct legal research*—identify, analyze, and summarize the appropriate laws, court decisions, or regulations that apply to a client's case.

- *Draft legal documents*—such as legal correspondence, interoffice memos, contracts, wills, mortgages, and documents to be filed with the court.

- *File legal documents with courts*—including complaints, answers, and motions.

- *Summarize witness testimony*—such as when depositions (sworn testimony) are taken of individuals out of court or when the parties have given written statements.

- *Coordinate litigation proceedings*—communicate with opposing counsel, court personnel, and other government officials; prepare necessary documents for trial; and schedule witnesses.

- *Attend legal proceedings*—including trials, depositions, executions of wills, and court or administrative hearings.

- *Use computers and technology*—to perform many of the above tasks and help expand the social media presence of a firm.

No matter what task is being performed, paralegals have an obligation to meet high ethical standards. You will see an *Ethics Watch* feature in every chapter in the textbook, and ethical obligations will be reviewed in detail in Chapter 4. This chapter's *Ethics Watch* feature discusses the ethical balance between the role of paralegals and how to provide legal advice.

Paralegals' Duties Vary

The specific tasks that paralegals perform vary depending on the size of the office, the kind of law that the firm practices, and the expertise the paralegal has. If you work in a one-attorney office, for example, you may also perform secretarial functions. Tasks include conducting legal research and investigating the facts, copying documents, entering data into the computer, and answering the phone as needed.

If you work in a larger law firm, you usually have more support staff (secretaries, file clerks, and others) to whom you can delegate tasks. Your work may also be more specialized, so you may work on cases in only certain areas of law. If you work in a law firm's real estate department, for example, you may deal with legal matters only relating to that area.

Although paralegal duties vary, the tasks that paralegals report spending the most time performing are drafting legal documents, handling client relations, and conducting legal research.

ETHICS WATCH

PARALEGAL EXPERTISE AND LEGAL ADVICE

Paralegals often have deep knowledge in specific areas of law. If you specialize in environmental law, for example, you will become familiar with environmental claims. When working with a client on a matter involving an environmental agency, you might be tempted to advise the client on which type of action would be most favorable to him or her. Never do so. Only attorneys may give legal advice, and paralegals who give legal advice risk penalties for the unauthorized practice of law. Whatever legal advice is given to the client must come directly from the attorney.

If you speak to a client, the advice must reflect exactly (or nearly exactly) what the attorney said with no modification and must be communicated to the client as directed by the attorney. After consulting with your supervising attorney, for example, you can say

to the client that the attorney "advises that you do all that you can to settle the claim as soon as possible."

The rule prohibiting the unauthorized practice of law is stated in Section 1.8 of the NFPA *Model Code of Ethics and Professional Responsibility*: "A paralegal shall comply with the applicable legal authority governing the unauthorized practice of law in the jurisdiction in which the paralegal practices." It is also required by the NALA *Code of Ethics and Professional Responsibility*, Canon 4: "A paralegal must use discretion and professional judgment commensurate with knowledge and experience but must not render independent legal judgment in place of an attorney."

FEATURED CONTRIBUTOR

START TODAY

William McSorley

BIOGRAPHICAL NOTE

Bill McSorley received his B.A. degree in journalism and Juris Doctor degree from the University of South Carolina. He served as editor-in-chief for the past two editions of *The Paralegal Survival Guide: Facts and Forms*, a publication by the South Carolina Bar Continuing Legal Education Division. In addition, he was recently appointed by the South Carolina Supreme Court to a second term on the Board of Paralegal Certification for South Carolina.

McSorley is a faculty member and Paralegal Program Director at Midlands Tech in Columbia, South Carolina, where he has taught paralegal students for more than twenty-five years and served as director since 2002. He previously served a three-year term on the American Bar Association Approval Commission on Paralegal Education and continues to provide support to the commission.

For those seeking a new career in the legal field, the challenges are many. We are often frozen by uncertainty, and as a result, fail to move forward. So start moving. Start today!

Map out a strategy for yourself. Everyone has his or her own timetable and it's always subject to change, but let's put something down as an initial blueprint. Here is just a sample of a strategy for a full-time student in a two-year paralegal program.

> **"Map out a strategy for yourself."**

BEFORE YOU BEGIN: Educate yourself on this career path and do a self-assessment. What are the key skills and qualities needed in this profession? Where are the jobs? Ask yourself, "What are my strengths and weaknesses?" How can I improve on my weaknesses and align my skills with those needed for the profession? If you are not good at doing a self-assessment, ask somebody who will give you an honest answer.

Paralegals and Technology

Many paralegals have become the technology experts at law firms. Because lawyers are busy with the practice of law, paralegals are often in the best position to know the firm's working needs. Increasingly, paralegals take a leading role in reviewing and recommending specialized legal software programs and online databases.

Computer skills, technical knowledge, and, increasingly, the ability to use social media productively are highly valued. Paralegals use software packages for internal case management to organize client files, manage calendars, share research, record reference materials, and track the hours to be billed to clients. Attorneys and paralegals use time and billing software to manage expenses, generate bills, calculate accounts receivable, and produce financial reports. Legal databases available online allow paralegals to perform sophisticated legal research. When cases that involve many documents must be prepared for trial, litigation support software can help retrieve, categorize, and index

What do employers want in a new hire? They want somebody with strong communication skills, a working understanding of the law, a sense of integrity and professionalism, some technological skills, and a positive attitude. Is this you today? Can this be you by the time you graduate? How do you develop these skills?

SEMESTER ONE: Get good grades, get to know your program director and instructors, start making a list of contacts, and get working on a quality résumé. Full-time and adjunct faculty members often are the best place to start networking. They have strong ties to the legal community, appreciate students who do quality work, and are the source of many job placements. Think about developing a draft of a résumé and continue to add to this as you go along. Have it in just an outline form for now.

SEMESTER TWO: Join a local paralegal organization. Try to attend their regular meetings and make some contacts in this organization. The local paralegal organizations can be the best way to find out about job opportunities, learn about the profession, and expand your personal and professional network. I am always impressed by the kindness our local association shows toward student members. Working paralegals remember what it was like to be a student, and they are extremely supportive.

SEMESTER THREE: Work on securing an internship or doing volunteer work at a law office or other legal environment. If your school has a mandatory internship, now is the time to do it. Work on producing a professional résumé. It may be the only opportunity to separate you from a large stack of "applicants" seeking a job, so make yourself stand out from the crowd. My personal preference (though many disagree) is to include references as part of your résumé. In many areas, the legal and business communities are closely knit and having a "known reference" who can vouch for your good character could be what gets you the interview.

Check out your college's career services resources and discuss your résumé, interviewing skills, and placement opportunities with them. Reach out to your contacts for assistance in securing a position somewhere. Even if your school doesn't require an internship, getting some experience is key, even if you have to volunteer. One of my favorite stories involves a student who finished his volunteer internship, did good work, and asked if he could continue to volunteer since he was learning so much. They couldn't say "no" to free, quality help, so they let him stay on and after a couple of months they created a full-time job for him.

> **" . . . getting some experience is key . . . "**

SEMESTER FOUR: Make the final push to get that job you've worked so hard to obtain! At this point, you have a good-looking résumé, you have done a few mock (or real) interviews, and you have worked your network to help identify some potential job opportunities.

Recognizing the importance of strong interpersonal skills, you are getting better every day at being polite and friendly, using proper grammar, and learning to hold your tongue rather than saying something you'll regret later!

You have also developed your technology and research skills and are comfortable with Microsoft Office Suite or comparable products. You are familiar with the basics of calendaring, billing, and database management. Even if these skills aren't taught in your program, there's nothing stopping you from looking at all the free resources online. If a job comes down to you and another applicant, you want to make sure the "technology advantage" is on your side.

Your graduation may seem ages from now, but I promise it will be here before you know it. So make a plan, try to stick to it, and start today!

Source: William McSorley

the various materials for presentation. These technologies are discussed in appropriate chapters throughout this book.

Paralegal Education

The first paralegals were legal secretaries who learned on the job how to perform complex legal tasks given to them by attorneys. No formal paralegal education programs existed until the late 1960s. Once attorneys realized that using paralegals was cost-effective and benefited both the client and the firm, paralegal education programs began to expand. According to the ABA's Standing Committee on Paralegals, there are about a thousand paralegal training programs operating in the United States. Of course, your formal education is only part of becoming a successful legal professional, as the *Featured Contributor* article discusses above.

Educational Options

The role of formal paralegal education has become increasingly important in the growth and development of the profession. Many colleges offer programs. Generally, paralegal education programs fall into one of five categories:

- Two-year community college programs, leading to an associate of arts degree or a paralegal certificate. Programs often require the completion of about 60 semester hours and include some general education requirements.

- Four-year bachelor's degree programs with a major or minor in paralegal studies. A bachelor's degree in paralegal studies usually requires about 120 semester hours, with 50 to 60 of these hours spent on general education courses. A person may be able to select a minor field that enhances desirability in the job market. Conversely, a student who majors in another field—for example, nursing—and obtains a minor in paralegal studies will be very marketable to employers.

- Certificate programs offered by private institutions, usually three to eighteen months in length. Typically, these programs require a high school diploma or the equivalent for admission.

- Postgraduate certificate programs, usually three to twelve months in length, resulting in the award of a paralegal certificate. These programs require applicants to have already earned a bachelor's degree to be admitted; some require applicants to have achieved a certain grade-point average.

- Master's degree programs are offered by several universities, including an increasing number of online programs. These prepare students to work as paralegals, paralegal supervisors, or law office administrators. Some programs offer specific concentrations—for example, dispute resolution or intellectual property.

Because those seeking to become paralegals have diverse educational backgrounds, capabilities, and work experience, no one program is best for everyone. Deciding which program is most appropriate depends on personal needs and preferences.

Paralegal Curriculum—Substantive and Procedural Law

substantive law
Law that defines the rights and duties of individuals with respect to each other's conduct and property.

procedural law
Rules that define the manner in which the rights and duties of individuals are enforced.

A paralegal's education includes the study of both substantive law and procedural law. **Substantive law** includes laws that define, describe, regulate, and create legal rights and obligations. For example, a law prohibiting employment discrimination on the basis of age falls into the category of substantive law. **Procedural law** concerns the methods of enforcing the rights established by substantive law. Questions about what documents need to be filed to begin a lawsuit, when the documents must be filed, which court will hear a case, and which witnesses may be called are all procedural law questions. You will review aspects of both areas in this course and explore them in more detail in later courses.

The Role of the AAfPE and ABA in Paralegal Education

The American Association for Paralegal Education (AAfPE) was formed to promote high standards for paralegal education. The AAfPE and the ABA are the two major organizations responsible for developing standards and curriculum for paralegal education programs across the nation. California was the first state to require a paralegal to meet certain minimum educational requirements. Although most states do not have such requirements, many employers either require or prefer job candidates with a certain level of education. Some employers select only graduates from established programs. A list of schools offering paralegal programs is available at the AAfPE website, **aafpe.org**, in the "Find a Program" menu.

In 1974, the ABA established educational standards for paralegal training programs. The ABA guidelines have been revised over time to keep pace with changes in the profession. Paralegal schools are not required to be approved by the ABA. Rather, ABA approval is a voluntary process that gives extra credibility to the schools that successfully apply for it. A program that meets the ABA's quality standards is referred to as an **ABA-approved program**. Of the paralegal education programs in existence, about 260 have ABA approval (see the ABA website for a list of approved paralegal education programs).

Certification

Certification refers to formal recognition by a professional group or state agency that a person has met the standards of ability specified by the organization. Generally, this means passing an examination and meeting certain requirements with respect to education and/or experience. The term *certification*, as used here, does not refer to receiving a paralegal certificate. You may obtain a paralegal certificate after completing school, but you will not be considered a *certified paralegal* unless you complete the NALA, NFPA, NALS, AAPI, or state certification process. These programs are discussed next. No state requires paralegals to be certified. Although most employers do not require certification, earning a certificate from a professional society or the state can make one more competitive in the labor market and lead to a higher salary (see Chapter 2).

NALA and NFPA Certification

Paralegals who meet the background qualifications set by NALA (see **nala.org**) are eligible to take a comprehensive examination to become a **Certified Paralegal (CP®)**. According to NALA, salaries increase about $5,000 for those who become CPs. NALA also sponsors the **Advanced Paralegal Certification (APC)** program (before 2006, this was called the Certified Legal Assistant Specialty, or CLAS). The APC program provides a series of online courses composed of text lessons, slides, exercises, and interactive tests. NALA offers APC certification to those who are already CPs and want to show special competence in a particular field of law. Appendix E provides more detailed information on NALA certification and requirements.

Paralegals who have certain levels of education and experience can take the Paralegal Advanced Competency Exam (PACE®) through NFPA (see **paralegals. org** for details). The NFPA offers two credentialing exams. The first one, called the Paralegal CORE Competency Exam, covers general issues and ethics and provides designation as a Certified Registered Paralegal. Those who pass the exam may use the designation CRP after their name. Paralegals who pass the PACE exam can use the designation **Registered Paralegal (RP®)**, the highest level of designation offered by the NFPA.

ABA-approved program
A legal or paralegal educational program that satisfies the standards for paralegal training set forth by the American Bar Association.

certification
Formal recognition by a private group or a state agency that a person has satisfied the group's standards of ability, knowledge, and competence; ordinarily accomplished through the taking of an examination.

Certified Paralegal (CP®)
A paralegal whose legal competency has been certified by NALA: The Paralegal Association, following an examination that tests the paralegal's knowledge and skills.

Advanced Paralegal Certification (APC)
A credential awarded by NALA: The Paralegal Association to a Certified Paralegal (CP®) whose competency in a legal specialty has been certified based on an examination of the paralegal's knowledge and skills in the specialty area.

Registered Paralegal (RP®)
A paralegal whose competency has been certified by the National Federation of Paralegal Associations after successful completion of the Paralegal Advanced Competency Exam (PACE).

NALS and AAPI Certification

NALS ("the association for legal professionals") offers certification for paralegals who have five years of work experience or possess certain educational credentials. These paralegals take an examination to obtain Professional Paralegal (PP) certification.

In addition, the American Alliance of Paralegals, Inc. (AAPI), also provides a Paralegal Certification Program for paralegals who have met specific educational or practice requirements.

State Certification

Some states—including California, Florida, Louisiana, North Carolina, Ohio, and Texas—have implemented voluntary state certification programs. Details can be found online. Some state bar associations have information on certification as well. Generally, paralegal organizations (such as NALA) are in favor of *voluntary* certification and oppose *mandatory* (legally required) certification or state licensing (as you will read in Chapter 4).

Continuing Legal Education

continuing legal education (CLE) program
A course through which attorneys and other legal professionals extend their education beyond school.

Paralegals, like attorneys, often enhance their education by attending a **continuing legal education (CLE) program**. CLE courses, offered by state bar associations, commercial providers, law schools, and paralegal associations, are usually seminars and workshops that focus on specific topics or areas of law. Such programs are a good way to learn more about a specialized area of law or keep up to date on the latest developments in software and technology. Many employers encourage their paralegals to take CLE courses and may pay some or all of the costs involved.

Some paralegal organizations, such as NALA and the NFPA, require their members to complete a certain number of CLE hours per year as a condition of membership or certification status. The NFPA requires certified paralegals to complete twelve hours of CLE every two years. California requires a minimum number of CLE hours from all persons who work as paralegals. Paralegals in California are required to complete four CLE hours in legal ethics every three years and four CLE hours in substantive law every two years.[4]

Paralegal Skills and Attributes

As noted earlier, paralegals now perform many tasks that lawyers customarily performed. Thus, the demands on paralegals to be professional and efficient have increased. To be successful, a paralegal not only must possess specific legal knowledge but also should exhibit certain aptitudes and personality traits. For example, paralegals need to be able to think logically and to analyze complex issues of law and conflicting descriptions of fact. Some general characteristics that paralegals should have are discussed next.

Analytical Skills

Paralegals are often responsible for gathering and analyzing certain information. A corporate paralegal, for example, may be required to analyze new government regulations to see how they affect a corporation. A paralegal working for the Environmental Protection Agency may be responsible for collecting and studying data on toxic waste disposal and drafting a memo on the matter.

Legal professionals need to be able to break down theories and fact patterns into smaller, more easily understandable components. That is how lawyers formulate arguments and judges decide cases. The process of legal analysis is critical to a paralegal's duties, especially when engaged in factual investigation, trial preparation, and legal research and writing. Analytical reasoning will be discussed in greater depth in Chapters 7 and 9 of this text. For now, it is important that you focus on developing a step-by-step approach to tackling each new subject or task that you encounter. Making analytical thinking a habit will improve your proficiency as a paralegal.

Communication Skills

Good interpersonal skills are critical to people working in the legal area. The legal profession is a "communications profession" because effective legal representation depends to a great extent on how well a legal professional communicates with clients, witnesses, judges, juries, opposing attorneys, and others. Poor communication can damage a case, destroy a relationship with a client, and harm a professional's reputation. Good communication helps to win cases, clients, and sometimes promotions.

Communication skills involve more than speaking and listening; they include reading and writing. We look briefly at each of these here. Although we focus on communication skills in the law office setting, these skills are essential to success in any work environment.

Interpersonal Skills

Good listening skills are important in paralegal work. Instructions must be followed carefully. To understand instructions, you must listen to them carefully. Asking follow-up questions helps to clarify anything that you do not understand. In addition, repeating the instructions not only ensures that you understand them but also gives the attorney a chance to add anything that may have been forgotten.

Excellent reading skills are a plus in any profession, but they are especially important in the legal arena. As a paralegal, you must not only be able to read well, but also be able to interpret what you are reading, whether it be a statute, a court's decision, or a contract's provision. What other important skills should every paralegal acquire?

wavebreakmedia/Shutterstock.com.

Listening skills are particularly important when interviewing clients and other parties relevant to a legal matter. In Chapter 11, you will read about listening skills and techniques that will help you conduct effective interviews. If you can relate well to the person whom you are interviewing, your chances of obtaining useful information are increased. (See the accompanying *Developing Paralegal Skills* feature for more on client interviews.)

Similarly, there will be times when you have to deal with people in your office who are under a great deal of stress. You may have to deal with people you consider to be "difficult." The more effectively you can respond to these people in ways that promote positive working relationships, the more productive you will be as a member of a legal team.

Speaking Skills

Paralegals must be able to speak well. In addition to using correct grammar, be precise and clear in communicating ideas or facts to others. For example, when you discuss facts learned in an investigation with your supervising attorney, your oral report must explain exactly what you found, or it could mislead the attorney. A miscommunication in this context could have serious consequences if it leads the attorney to take an action that harms the client's interests.

Oral communication also has a nonverbal dimension—that is, we communicate our thoughts and feelings through gestures, facial expressions, and other "body language." For example, if your body language suggests you are uncomfortable with a client, the client will be less responsive to your questions.

Reading Skills

Reading skills involve more than just being able to understand the meaning of written letters and words. Reading skills also involve understanding the *meaning* of a sentence, paragraph, section, or page. As a legal professional, you need to be able to read and comprehend many different types of written materials, including statutes and court decisions. You need to be familiar with legal terminology and concepts so that you

DEVELOPING PARALEGAL SKILLS

INTERVIEWING A CLIENT

Brenda Lundquist is a paralegal in a small firm. Her responsibilities include interviewing divorce clients. Using a standard set of forms, Brenda meets with a prospective client and obtains information about the reasons for the divorce, finances and assets, and desired custody arrangements. This information is needed to assist the supervising attorney in determining whether to take the case. The information also helps Brenda to prepare documents to be filed with the court should the attorney represent the client. Brenda enjoys the work because she likes helping people, and often people who are getting divorced need both emotional and legal support.

Checklist for Client Interviews

- Plan the interview in advance.
- Print out forms and checklists to use during the interview.
- Introduce yourself as a paralegal.
- Explain the purpose of the interview to the client.
- Communicate your questions precisely.
- Listen carefully and be supportive, as necessary.
- Summarize the client's major concerns.
- Give the client a "timeline" for what will happen in the legal proceedings.

know the meaning of these legal writings. You also need to develop the ability to read documents carefully so that you do not miss important distinctions, such as the difference in meaning that can result from the use of *and* instead of *or*. The importance of proofreading as a reading skill is highlighted in the *Developing Paralegal Skills* feature below.

Writing Skills

Good writing skills are crucial to success. Paralegals draft letters, memoranda, and various legal documents. Letters to clients, witnesses, and court clerks must be clear and well organized, and must follow the rules of grammar and punctuation. Legal documents must also be free of errors. Lawyers are generally attentive to details, and they expect paralegals to be equally so. Remember, you represent your supervising attorney when you write. You will learn more about writing skills in Chapter 9.

Computer Skills

In all professional workplaces, computer skills are essential. At a minimum, you will be expected to have experience with document creation and to have data-entry skills. Paralegal specialists who know how to use sophisticated software, such as database-management systems, and how to adapt new technology, such as social media tools, to the workplace hold some of the best-paying positions.

DEVELOPING PARALEGAL SKILLS

PROOFREADING LEGAL DOCUMENTS

Geena Northrop, a paralegal, works for a solo practitioner (a one-attorney law firm). She handles some legal writing for the attorney, among other duties. Geena knows that when creating a legal document, writing it is only half the job. The rest is proofreading—and not just once. Geena has adopted the motto of one of the instructors in her paralegal program: "Proof, proof, and proof again!"

Today, she has set aside time to proofread carefully a last will and testament that her supervising attorney and she created for a client. Geena prints out a copy of the document for proofreading purposes, because she knows that it is difficult to proofread a document only on a computer screen. Moreover, style and formatting problems are often not as evident on a screen as they are on hard copy.

Her first step in proofreading the document is to make sure that the document reflects all of the relevant information from her notes. Geena reviews her notes point by point from the client interview and from her discussion with the attorney about the will. She compares the notes to the document.

All looks well in this respect, so she proceeds to her second step in proofreading: checking style and format. Are all of the headings in the correct size and font? Is the spacing between headings consistent? Are all paragraphs properly indented? She finds a few problems and marks her hard copy to make the appropriate changes. She then reads the document word for word to ensure that there are no grammatical problems, spelling errors, or typos. Finally, she revises the document on her computer, prints it out, and takes it to the attorney for review.

Checklist for Proofreading Legal Documents

- When you create a legal document, do not assume that one proofreading is sufficient to catch all problems or errors that the document may contain. Reading a document out loud can be an effective way to catch errors.

- Print out the document, and go through the contents line by line to make sure that it includes all required or relevant information. Many documents contain "boilerplate" that must be checked to be sure earlier entries for other clients are not retained.

- Read through the document again to make sure that the style and formatting elements are consistent throughout.

- Finally, read through the document word for word to ensure that it is free of grammatical errors, misspelled words, and typos.

We cannot stress enough that to become a successful paralegal, the best thing you can do during your training is to become as knowledgeable as possible about online communications. Throughout this book, you will read about how technology applies to all areas of legal practice. You will also learn how you can use technology to perform various paralegal tasks and to keep up to date on the law. (See this chapter's *Office Tech and Cybersecurity* feature for some online resources for paralegals.)

Organizational Skills

Being well organized is a plus. Law offices are busy. There are phone calls to be answered and returned, witnesses to get to court and to the witness stand on time, documents to be filed, and checklists and procedures to be followed. If you are able to organize files, create procedures and checklists, and keep things running smoothly, you will be a valued member of the legal team.

If organization comes naturally to you, you are ahead of the game. If not, now is the time to learn and practice organizational skills. You will find plenty of opportunities to do this as a paralegal student—by organizing your notebooks, devising an efficient tracking system for homework assignments, and creating a study or work schedule and following it. Other suggestions for organizing your time and work, both as a student and as a paralegal on the job, are included in the **Skill Prep: A Paralegal Skills Module** before Chapter 1.

OFFICE TECH AND CYBERSECURITY

ONLINE RESOURCES FOR PARALEGALS

Many career resources are available online. To keep your skills up to date and to stay on top of developments in the law, you should regularly check such resources.

Paralegal Associations

Many paralegals belong to NALA or to NFPA, discussed earlier. Both organizations offer excellent gateways for paralegal resources. NALA's website (**nala.org**) displays information on many professional certification and continuing education programs. It also provides links to state and local affiliated organizations. The NFPA website (**paralegals.org**) offers a continuing education calendar, a gateway to legal research sites, and a variety of career advice.

American Bar Association

The ABA is not just for lawyers. The Standing Committee on Paralegals (**americanbar.org/groups/paralegals/**) provides career information, continuing education, directories, a gateway to blogs by paralegals, and information on hundreds of paralegal education programs.

Bryan Garner's Legal Writing Site

America's most celebrated legal writing guru, law professor Bryan Garner, is best known for his books, which include *The Redbook: A Manual on Legal Style* and *Legal Writing in Plain English*. He is the editor of the famous *Black's Law Dictionary*. Garner's website, **lawprose.org**, offers a bibliography of articles on legal writing, a schedule of legal writing seminars, and other relevant links.

The Paralegal Gateway

Paralegal Gateway on Facebook focuses on job advice, examples of successful résumés and interviews, and networking tools such as LinkedIn. It also offers links to continuing education resources.

Legal News

Law firms produce a wide range of online newsletters and sites on specific areas of law. In addition, the LawProf blog network (**lawprofessorblogs.com**) provides many subject-specific blogs (known as *blawgs*) by law professors that offer commentary on new cases, statutes, and news from trustworthy sources. Using online resources will keep you up to date on relevant developments in law.

The Ability to Keep Information Confidential

Paralegals are required to have the ability to keep client information confidential. The ability to keep confidences is not just a desirable attribute in a paralegal, but a mandatory one.

As you will read in Chapter 4, attorneys are ethically and legally obligated to keep all information relating to the representation of a client strictly confidential unless the client consents to the disclosure of information. The attorney may disclose confidential information only to people who are also working on behalf of the client and who therefore need to know it. Paralegals share in this duty. If a paralegal reveals confidential client information to anyone outside the group working on the client's case, the lawyer (and the paralegal) may face consequences if the client suffers harm as a result. The law firm could be sued and the paralegal dismissed. Even if the client is not harmed, lack of confidence can be the end of a career.

Keeping client information confidential means that as a paralegal you cannot divulge such information even to your spouse, family members, or closest friends. You should not talk about a client's case in hallways, elevators, or wherever others may overhear your conversation. You must be careful when handling client documents that you do not expose them to outsiders. Keeping work-related information confidential is an essential part of being a responsible and reliable paralegal.

Professionalism

Paralegals should behave professionally at all times. That means being responsible and reliable to earn the respect and trust of the attorneys and clients with whom you work. It also means putting aside any personal bias or emotion that interferes with your representation of a client or assessment of a case. Paralegals must be honest and assertive in letting others know what things paralegals can and cannot do (for example, they cannot give legal advice). This is important because not everyone is sure what paralegals do.

As a paralegal, you are judged not only by your actions and words but also by your appearance, attitude, and other factors. When deadlines approach and the pace of office work becomes somewhat frantic, it can be difficult to meet the challenge of acting professionally. When the pressure is on, it is important to remain calm and focus on completing your task accurately to ensure quality work. If a client's call or another attorney interrupts you, be aware that the way you react is likely to affect whether others view you as professional. Be courteous and respectful during such interruptions, as outsiders have no idea about what else is occurring at the law firm. The paralegal must be detail oriented and accurate, even when working under pressure.

The Future of the Profession

The paralegal profession is an expanding field within the legal arena. Paralegals assume a growing range of duties in the nation's legal offices and perform many of the same tasks as lawyers. According to the Bureau of Labor Statistics, paralegal employment should grow "faster than average," and "formally trained paralegals with strong computer and database management skills should have the best employment opportunities." Growth is occurring because law firms and other employers with legal staffs are hiring more paralegals to lower the cost—and increase the availability and efficiency—of legal services.

Those entering the profession today find a broader range of career options than ever before. In addition, you have the opportunity to help chart the course the profession takes in the future. The paralegal profession has become a popular career choice, so the job market is competitive, but formally trained and skilled paralegals have excellent employment potential.

CHAPTER SUMMARY

TODAY'S PROFESSIONAL PARALEGAL

What Is a Paralegal?

The definition of *paralegal* varies within the legal community, but most definitions distinguish between the work of a paralegal and a legal assistant. Paralegals perform many of the tasks traditionally handled by attorneys. A paralegal is qualified by education, training, or work experience to be employed by a law office, corporation, governmental agency, or other entity. A paralegal performs delegated substantive legal work, for which a lawyer is responsible.

What Do Paralegals Do?

1. *Typical tasks*—Paralegals may perform the following duties: interviewing and maintaining contact with clients and witnesses, locating and interviewing witnesses, conducting legal investigations, calendaring and tracking deadlines, organizing and maintaining client files, conducting legal research, drafting legal documents, filing legal documents with courts, summarizing witness testimony, coordinating litigation proceedings, attending legal proceedings, and using technology.

2. *Duties often vary*—Paralegals perform different functions depending on where they work and on their abilities and experience. Duties vary according to the size of the law firm and the kind of law practiced by the firm. Paralegals commonly spend significant time performing document management, client relations, and research.

3. *Paralegals and technology*—Technology is the number-one area of expanding paralegal responsibility. Paralegals skilled in using technologies to assist them in performing their duties will excel.

Paralegal Education

Paralegal education programs have become increasingly important in the growth and development of the profession.

1. *Educational options*—Colleges offer a variety of programs to train paralegals, ranging in length from three months to four years.

2. *Curriculum*—Paralegal education includes coverage of substantive law and of procedural law, as paralegals are involved in most aspects of the legal process.

3. *ABA and AAfPE paralegal education*—The ABA sets voluntary educational standards for paralegal training programs. ABA-approved programs have volunteered to meet the ABA's standards. AAfPE and other paralegal associations, such as NALA, promote high standards in paralegal education.

4. *Certification*—Certification refers to recognition by a professional group or state agency that a person has met standards of proficiency specified by the group. Generally, this means passing an examination and meeting certain requirements with respect to education and/or experience. Paralegals may be certified by a paralegal association. No state requires paralegal certification, but employers see it as a sign of quality.

5. *Continuing legal education (CLE)*—Continuing legal education courses are offered by state bar associations and paralegal associations. These programs provide a way to learn more about a specialized area of law or keep up to date on developments in law and technology.

Paralegal Skills and Attributes

Because paralegals perform many of the tasks that lawyers used to perform, the demands on paralegals to be professional and efficient have increased.

1. *Analytical skills*—These include gathering and analyzing information relevant to legal matters.

2. *Communication skills*—The skills include the ability to communicate effectively with clients, witnesses, and others in the legal process. Understanding a legal matter and communicating about it involves reading, speaking, listening, and writing.

3. *Computer skills*—Most legal research is done online, and computers produce most legal documents. Familiarity with the tools available makes a paralegal more successful.

4. *Organizational skills*—Paralegals keep track of numerous legal documents and other matters related to cases and the functioning of a law office, so being well organized is a requirement of the profession.

5. *Keeping information confidential*—Because paralegals have knowledge of confidential legal matters and help represent clients, protecting information from exposure to others is a major requirement of the job.

6. *Professionalism*—In legal work, responsibility and trust are key. Legal professionals are judged on the basis of actions, words, and attitude.

The Future of the Profession

The role of paralegals in law continues to grow as the providers of legal services increasingly recognize the effectiveness of qualified non-attorney professionals.

KEY TERMS AND CONCEPTS

ABA-approved program   9

Advanced Paralegal Certification (APC)   9

American Association for Paralegal Education (AAfPE)   4

American Bar Association (ABA)   3

certification   9

Certified Paralegal (CP®)   9

continuing legal education (CLE) program   10

National Federation of Paralegal Associations (NFPA)   3

paralegal   3

procedural law   8

Registered Paralegal (RP®)   9

substantive law   8

The Paralegal Association (NALA)   3

QUESTIONS FOR REVIEW

1. What is a paralegal? Is there any difference between a paralegal and a legal assistant?

2. What types of educational programs and training are available to paralegals? Must a person meet specific educational requirements to work as a paralegal?

3. What role does the American Bar Association play in paralegal education?

4. What does *certification* mean?

5. List and describe the skills that are useful in paralegal practice. Do you have these skills?

6. Why is the paralegal profession an expanding field?

ETHICS QUESTION

1. Richard attends a six-month paralegal course and earns a certificate. In the West Coast city where he lives, certified paralegals—those with a CP designation—are in great demand in the job market. Richard responds to an online advertisement for a certified paralegal, indicating that he is one. Has Richard done anything unethical? What is the difference between a certificate and certification?

PRACTICE QUESTIONS AND ASSIGNMENTS

1. Using the material found in the chapter, identify which of the following employees are paralegals:

   a. Graciela works in the file room of a major law firm checking out and returning files as they are needed by attorneys.

   b. Maria does all of the typing, filing, and answering phones for two attorneys in a small law office.

   c. Tameko drafts legal documents, meets with clients, and assists her supervising attorney with trials.

   d. Majora, who has an MBA, supervises the day-to-day operations of a 250-attorney law firm.

2. Using the material in the chapter, identify which of the following laws are substantive laws and which are procedural laws:

   a. A law requiring a person to be sixteen years old to obtain a driver's license.

   b. A court rule requiring that an answer to a complaint be filed within twenty-one days of receipt of service of process.

   c. A law requiring a manufacturer of an automobile to replace the vehicle or refund the purchase price if it cannot be repaired.

   d. A law requiring civil lawsuits exceeding $25,000 to be filed with the circuit court.

3. Which national paralegal organizations offer paralegal certification exams, and what are the certifications called? Do states offer certifications for paralegals? Is a state certification a license to practice law? Explain your answer.

4. Tom and Sandy are having coffee after their paralegal class. The instructor discussed the recent change in the ABA definition of a *paralegal*, which no longer includes the term *legal assistant* as a synonymous term for a paralegal. Tom says he agrees with the ABA that the term *paralegal* is preferable because no one will confuse paralegals with legal secretaries. Sandy, who has worked as a legal secretary, is offended by Tom's remarks. What do you think of this change? Why is it important to distinguish between a paralegal and a legal assistant?

GROUP PROJECT

This project asks the group to review information on the websites of NALA (**nala.org**) and NFPA (**paralegals. org**) about the organizations' certification programs. The members of the group will do the following tasks to complete the project:

- Student one will determine and summarize the requirements of the NALA certification exams.

- Student two will determine and summarize the requirements of the NFPA certification exams.

- Student three will compile the results in a chart or graph in PowerPoint or Excel.

- Student four will present the results to the class.

CHAPTER 2

Career Opportunities

CHAPTER OBJECTIVES

After completing this chapter, you will be able to:

- Describe what types of firms and organizations hire paralegals, and the challenges and benefits of each.
- List and explain some areas of law in which paralegals specialize.
- Report how much paralegals can earn, and explain the variables that go into that determination.
- Explain how to prepare a career plan and pursue it.
- Describe how to search for an employer.
- Describe the steps involved in presenting yourself to prospective employers.
- Show how to use social media to promote your career.

©fizkes/Shutterstock.com

Introduction

Paralegals enjoy a wide range of employment opportunities in both the private and the public sectors. They are in demand especially at law firms because they help provide competent legal services at a lower cost to clients. Most paralegals work in law offices. However, almost any business that uses legal services, including large corporations, universities, insurance companies, banks, and real estate agencies, employ paralegals. In addition, the government has positions for paralegals at many agencies. Paralegals work in many court systems, county offices, and legal-services clinics across the nation.

This chapter provides you with a starting point for planning your career. In the pages that follow, you will read about where paralegals work and what compensation paralegals receive. You will also learn about the steps you will need to follow to plan your career, locate potential employers, present yourself in social media, and find a job.

Where Paralegals Work

A diverse array of employers hire paralegals. This section describes the general characteristics of each of the major types of working environments.

Law Firms

When paralegals first began to establish themselves in the legal community in the 1960s, they worked almost exclusively in law firms. Today, law firms continue to hire more paralegals than do any other organizations. Two-thirds of all paralegals work in law firms, but as was just noted, there are opportunities in a wide range of organizations. Law firms vary in size from the one-attorney office to the huge "megafirm" with hundreds of attorneys. Most paralegals work in firms that employ fewer than twenty-five attorneys.

Working for a Small Firm

Many paralegals begin their careers working for small law practices with just one or a few attorneys. One reason is that smaller law firms outnumber larger ones. Another reason relates to geographic location. For example, a paralegal who lives in a smaller community may find that the only option is a small legal practice. As Exhibit 2.1 indicates, salaries tend to rise by firm size. Note that most paralegals receive an end-of-year bonus. While that is often about $2,000, it is likely lower for new entrants.

The Size of the Firm Matters.   Working for a small firm offers many advantages to the beginning paralegal. If the firm is a general law practice, you have the opportunity to gain experience in many different aspects of the practice of law. You will learn whether you enjoy working in one area (such as family law) more than another (such as criminal defense work) in the event that you later decide to specialize. Some

EXHIBIT 2.1

Entry-Level Salary Averages by Firm Size

Source: Data from Internet Legal Research Group, www.ilrg.com.

Firm Size	Salary Range, 0–2 Years' Experience
Small Law Firm	$32,250–$36,750
Small/Midsize Law Firm	$33,500–$42,400
Midsize Law Firm	$35,500–$46,000
Large Law Firm	$37,250–$48,000

Paralegals who work for a large firm often need to research statutes, court cases, or regulations in the firm's law library. Notebook computers, tablet devices, and smartphones facilitate the ease with which paralegals can do research and communicate with attorneys, clients, and others. What are the pros and cons of working for a large law firm?

paralegals also prefer the more personal and less formal environment that usually exists in a small law office, as well as the variety of tasks and greater flexibility common in this setting.

Small size may also have disadvantages, however. Paralegals who work for small firms may have less support staff to assist them. This means that if you work in a small law office, your job may involve a substantial amount of secretarial or clerical work. In addition, if the small firm is a specialist, you will get less variety. It is worth asking plenty of questions during a job interview to figure out if a firm is a good match for your goals.

Think about Compensation Differentials.   Compensation is another topic of potential concern. Small firms pay, on average, lower salaries than do larger firms. Generally, the larger the firm, the higher paralegal salaries will be. Small firms also may provide fewer employee benefits, such as pension plans and health benefits. At the same time, however, a small firm may be in a convenient location, may not require an expensive wardrobe, and may provide free parking.

Working for a Large Firm

In contrast to the often more casual environment of smaller law offices, larger law firms usually are more formal. In a larger firm, your responsibilities will probably be limited to specific, well-defined tasks. For example, you may work for a department that handles (or for an attorney who handles) only certain types of cases, such as real estate transactions. Office procedures and employment policies will also be more clearly defined and may be set forth in a written employment manual.

The advantages of the large firm often include greater opportunities for promotions and career advancement, higher salaries and better benefits packages, more support staff for paralegals, and more sophisticated technology that affords greater access to research resources.

You may see certain characteristics of large law firms as either advantages or disadvantages, depending on your personality and preferences. For example, if you favor the more specialized duties and formal working environment of a large law firm, then you will view these characteristics as advantages. If you prefer to handle a greater variety of tasks and enjoy the more personal atmosphere of a small law office, then you might think the specialization and formality of a large law firm are disadvantages.

Corporations and Other Business Organizations

As already mentioned, many paralegals work outside of law firms. Almost any business that uses legal services may hire paralegals. An increasing number of paralegals work for corporate legal departments. In recent years, companies have been bringing more legal work "in house" rather than paying outside law firms for work, so this is a growth area for paralegal employment. Particularly for matters that a company handles frequently—leases for a real estate management company, for example—having in-house paralegals can save on legal bills and give the company greater quality control. Most large companies hire a large staff of in-house attorneys to handle corporate legal affairs. Paralegals who are employed by corporations usually work under the supervision of in-house attorneys.

Paralegals in a corporate setting perform a variety of functions, such as organizing meetings and maintaining necessary records, drafting employee contracts and benefit plans, and preparing financial and other reports for the corporation. Paralegals often help monitor government regulations to be sure the company operates within the law. When the firm is involved in a lawsuit, paralegals may be assigned duties related to that lawsuit. (For more information on the duties of corporate paralegals, see Chapter 18.)

About one-fifth of all paralegals work in corporate environments. Paralegals who are employed by corporations frequently receive higher salaries than those working for law firms. In addition, paralegals who are employed by corporations may work more regular hours. Unlike paralegals in law firms, corporate paralegals typically have not been required to generate a specific number of "billable hours" per year (hours billed to clients for paralegal services performed, to be discussed in Chapter 3).

Government

Paralegals employed by government agencies work in a variety of settings and often specialize in one aspect of the law. Agencies also usually provide excellent benefits and stable work environments, as budgets do not depend on client billing.

Administrative Agencies

Paralegals who work for federal or state government agencies may conduct legal research and analysis, investigate welfare eligibility or disability claims, assist in compliance reviews of private companies, examine documents (such as loan applications), and many other tasks. At the federal level, the U.S. Department of Justice employs the largest number of paralegals, followed by the Social Security Administration and the Department of the Treasury.

Paralegals who work for government agencies normally work regular hours and tend to work fewer total hours per year (have more vacation time) than paralegals in private law firms. Like paralegals in corporations, they may not have to worry about billable hours, although other measures of productivity are likely to be used. Additionally, paralegals who work for the government usually enjoy comprehensive employment benefits.

Legislative Offices

Legislators in the U.S. Congress and in some state legislatures typically have staff members to help them with their duties. Duties often include legal research and writing, and paralegals sometimes perform such services. For example, a senator who plans to propose an amendment to a certain law may ask a staff paralegal to research the legislative history of that law (to discern the legislature's intention when passing the law, as discussed in Chapters 5 and 7) and write up a summary of that history.

Law Enforcement Offices and Courts

Many paralegals work for government law enforcement offices and institutions. As you will read in Chapter 13, which discusses criminal law and procedures, a public prosecutor prosecutes a person accused of a crime. Public prosecutors (such as district attorneys, state attorneys general, and U.S. attorneys) are paid by the government. Accused persons may be defended by private attorneys or, if they cannot afford to hire a lawyer, by *public defenders*—attorneys paid for by the state to ensure that criminal defendants are not deprived of their constitutional right to be represented by counsel. Both public prosecutors and public defenders often rely on paralegals for assistance.

Paralegals also find work in other government settings, such as federal or state court administrative offices. Court administrative work ranges from recording and filing court documents (such as the documents filed during a lawsuit, described in Chapter 10) to working for a small claims court (a court that handles claims below a specified amount, covered in Chapter 6). Paralegals also work for bankruptcy courts (bankruptcy law and practice are discussed later in this chapter and in Chapter 19).

Legal Aid Offices

Legal aid offices provide legal services to those who find it difficult to pay for legal representation. Most legal aid is government funded, although some support comes from private foundations.

Many paralegals who work in this capacity find their jobs rewarding, even though they usually receive lower salaries than they would in other settings. In part, this is because of the nature of the work—helping people in need. Additionally, paralegals in legal aid offices generally assume a wider array of responsibilities than they would in a traditional law office. For example, some federal and state administrative agencies, including the Social Security Administration, allow paralegals to represent clients in agency hearings and judicial proceedings. As you will read in Chapter 4, paralegals normally are not allowed to represent clients—only attorneys can do so. Exceptions to this rule exist when a court or agency permits nonlawyers to represent others in court or in administrative agency hearings.

Freelance Paralegals

Some experienced paralegals operate as freelancers. A **freelance paralegal** (also called an *independent contractor* or a *contract paralegal*) owns his or her business and performs specific legal work for attorneys on a contract basis. Attorneys who need temporary legal assistance may contract with freelance paralegals to work on particular projects. In addition, attorneys who need legal assistance but cannot afford to hire full-time paralegals might hire freelancers to work on a part-time basis.

Freelancing has advantages and disadvantages. Because freelancers are their own bosses, they can set their own schedules. Thus, they enjoy a greater degree of work flexibility. In addition, depending on the nature of their projects, they may work at home or in attorneys' offices. With flexibility, however, comes added responsibility. A freelance paralegal's income depends on the ability to promote and maintain business. If there are no clients for a month, there is no income. Also, freelancers do not enjoy benefits such as employer-provided medical insurance.

Freelance paralegals work under attorney supervision. A freelancer is not to be confused with a **legal technician**—often called an **independent paralegal**—who does *not* work under the supervision of an attorney and who provide (sell) legal services directly to the public. These services include helping members of the public obtain and fill out forms for certain legal transactions, such as bankruptcy filings and divorce petitions. As we will see in Chapter 4, legal technicians run the risk of violating state

freelance paralegal

A paralegal who operates his or her own business and provides services to attorneys on a contract basis. A freelance paralegal works under the supervision of an attorney, who assumes responsibility for the paralegal's work product.

legal technician or **independent paralegal**

A paralegal who offers services directly to the public without attorney supervision. Independent paralegals assist consumers by supplying them with forms and procedural knowledge relating to simple or routine legal procedures.

statutes prohibiting the unauthorized practice of law, although some states (such as Washington state) have created "limited license legal technicians," who are authorized to practice in specific areas without attorney supervision.

Paralegal Specialties

While many paralegals perform a wide range of legal services, some find it satisfying to specialize in one area. Areas of law in which paralegals report that they work at least some of the time are litigation (52 percent), corporate law (9 percent), contract law (13 percent), and real estate law (11 percent). Here, we discuss a few of the areas in which paralegals may specialize.

Increasingly, in all practice settings, being able to use technology efficiently is a great asset. In particular, cybersecurity has become an essential part of any law practice, as this chapter's *Office Tech and Cybersecurity* feature discusses.

Litigation

litigation
The process of working a lawsuit through the court system.

litigation paralegal
A paralegal who specializes in assisting attorneys in the litigation process.

plaintiff
A party who initiates a lawsuit.

Working a lawsuit through the court system is called **litigation**. A paralegal who specializes in assisting attorneys in this process is called a **litigation paralegal**. Litigation paralegals work in general law practices, small litigation firms, litigation departments of larger law firms, and corporate legal departments. Litigation paralegals often specialize in a certain type of litigation, such as personal-injury litigation (discussed shortly) or product liability cases (which involve injuries caused by defective products).

Litigation paralegal work varies with the substantive law area being litigated. It also varies according to whether it is done on behalf of a **plaintiff** (who brings a

OFFICE TECH AND CYBERSECURITY

DEPLOYING CYBERSECURITY IN A LAW FIRM

Cybersecurity is increasingly important in all practice areas, as well as for the day-to-day operations of law firms of all sizes. As attorney Nicole Black noted, "Cybersecurity is an issue that is—or should be—on the minds of lawyers in firms big and small. This is because lawyers have an ethical obligation to preserve the confidentiality of client information. And as lawyers increasingly move their data into digital format, that obligation necessarily shifts to the firm's data stored online."[a]

As a new paralegal seeking employment, you can do three things to position yourself to take advantage of legal employers' increased interest in cybersecurity. First, be aware of the issues and solutions that will enable you to enhance a prospective employer's cybersecurity. You don't need to be a computer scientist to do this, but you do need to know what constitutes good digital "hygiene." For example, develop some familiarity with the use of virtual private networks as a means of accessing the Internet securely from public networks (VPNs), such as in airports or coffee shops.

Second, learn the basics of cybersecurity, either by taking a course in your paralegal program or by conducting independent research. Cybersecurity is more than using a password manager. For law firms (and so for you!), it also includes regulatory compliance with rapidly proliferating rules and regulations from multiple jurisdictions.

Third, keep up with the issues in the area, and be prepared to show that you are aware of the latest developments. Watch for local bar association talks or webinars on cyber issues, talk with friends working in technology fields, and look for low-cost and free training from information security associations such as the Center for Internet Security.

a. Nicole Black, "Lawyers and Cybersecurity in 2019: How Does Your Firm Compare?" www.abovethelaw.com.

lawsuit) or a **defendant** (against whom a lawsuit is brought). Variation exists because different types of cases follow different patterns. For example, personal injury litigation often involves multiple-fact witnesses, who describe what they saw at the time the injury occurred. In contrast, regulatory matters often focus on review of massive paper trails that document whether or not a firm is in compliance with the law. The paralegal's job will be quite different in these two scenarios. Some litigation paralegals investigate cases, review documents containing evidence, interview clients and witnesses, draft documents to file with the courts, and prepare for hearings and trials. You will read about litigation procedures and the important role played by paralegals in this process in Chapters 10 through 12.

defendant
A party against whom a lawsuit is brought.

Corporate Law

Corporate law consists of the laws that govern the formation, financing, structure, and termination of corporations, as well as the rights and duties of those who own and run corporations. Chapter 18 reviews the meaning of these functions and the tasks that corporate paralegals may perform.

corporate law
Law that governs the formation, financing, merger and acquisition, and termination of corporations, as well as the rights and duties of those who own and run the corporation.

Paralegals who specialize in corporate law may work in the legal department of a corporation or for a law firm that specializes in corporate law. Corporate paralegals often perform such tasks as preparing and filing documents with a state agency to setting up business entities, maintaining corporate records, and organizing and scheduling shareholders' meetings in accordance with state law. Organizing a business entity typically requires regular generation of records and filings with the state, with serious consequences for missed deadlines or mistakes, so paralegals can add a great deal of value by bringing comprehensive organizational skills to bear.

In general, corporate paralegals work at large firms in large cities and receive higher salaries than paralegals in other areas, such as those who focus on probate (wills) or real estate. Corporate paralegals who narrow their expertise to areas such as mergers are among the highest-paid paralegals.

Contract Law

Contract law work is common for many lawyers. As you will read in Chapter 15, a **contract** is an agreement (based on a promise or an exchange of promises) that can be enforced in court. Paralegals who specialize in contracts may work for a corporation's legal department, for a law firm, or for a government agency.

contract
An agreement (based on a promise or an exchange of promises) that can be enforced in court.

Paralegal work in contract law may involve preparing contracts and forms, and reviewing contracts to determine whether a party to a contract has complied with its terms. In a lawsuit for breach of contract, for example, a paralegal might be asked to look closely at the terms and do some factual investigation to find out whether the contract has been breached (broken). Contract specialists also may conduct research in the law governing contracts, before a contract is formed or during litigation concerning the contract. Because contracts are so common in our legal environment, many paralegals—not just contract specialists—are involved with work relating to contracts.

Real Estate Law

At law, **real estate**, or *real property*, consists of land and things attached to the land, such as houses, buildings, and trees. Because of the value of real estate (for most people, a home is the most expensive purchase they will ever make) and the complexities of the transaction, attorneys frequently assist parties that buy or sell real property to make sure that nothing important is overlooked. Regulatory issues are an increasing part of real estate practice as well, involving all levels of government, from local (zoning) to federal (environmental).

real estate
Land and things permanently attached to the land, such as houses, buildings, and trees.

Paralegals who specialize in real estate may find employment in a number of environments, including small law firms that specialize in real estate transactions, real estate departments in large law firms, other business firms that frequently buy or sell real property, banks (which finance real estate purchases), title companies, and real estate agencies. As we will discuss in Chapter 16, paralegals working in real estate law often draft contracts for the sale of real estate, draft mortgage agreements, draft and record deeds, and schedule closings on the sale of property.

Personal-Injury Law

Much litigation involves claims brought by persons who have been injured in automobile accidents or other incidents as a result of the negligence of others. *Negligence* is a **tort**, or civil wrong, that occurs when carelessness causes harm to another. Someone who has been injured as a result of another's negligence is entitled under tort law to attempt to obtain compensation from the wrongdoer. (Tort law, including negligence, will be discussed in Chapter 14.)

Paralegals who specialize in personal-injury litigation often work for law firms that concentrate in this field. Paralegals working in this capacity obtain and review medical and employment records to calculate the client's lost income. These items are needed to determine the plaintiff's damages in a personal-injury lawsuit. Personal-injury paralegals are also hired by insurance companies to investigate claims. Defendants in personal-injury cases are typically covered by insurance, and a defendant's insurance company has a duty to defend an insured customer who is sued.

Insurance Law

Insurance is a contract by which an insurance company (the insurer) promises to pay a sum or give something of value to another (either the insured or the beneficiary of the insurance policy) to compensate for a specified loss. Insurance may provide compensation for the injury or death of the insured or another, for damage to the insured's property, or for other losses, such as those resulting from lawsuits. Paralegals who specialize in insurance law may work for law firms that defend insurance companies in litigation brought against the companies. They may also work directly for insurance companies or for companies that buy large amounts of insurance or are self-insured, such as hospitals.

Paralegals may review insurance regulations and monitor an insurance firm's compliance with the regulations. They may also be asked to review insurance contracts, undertake factual and legal investigations relating to insurance claims, or provide litigation assistance in lawsuits involving the insurance company. Paralegals often help in litigation involving insurance. For example, a paralegal may be asked to provide investigative or litigation assistance for a client who is bringing a lawsuit or defending against personal-injury, malpractice, or other litigation in which insurance is a factor.

Employment and Labor Law

As will be discussed in Chapter 18, laws governing employment relationships are referred to collectively as *employment and labor law*. This body of law includes laws governing health and safety in the workplace, labor unions and union–management relations, employment discrimination, sexual harassment, wrongful termination, employee benefit plans, retirement and disability income, employee privacy rights, minimum wage, and overtime wages.

Some paralegals specialize in just one aspect of employment law, such as workers' compensation. Under **workers' compensation statutes**, employees who are injured on the job are compensated from state funds or insurance funds. Paralegals assist persons injured on the job in obtaining compensation from the state workers' compensation

tort
A civil wrong not arising from a breach of contract; a violation of a legal duty that causes harm to another.

insurance
A contract by which an insurance company (the insurer) promises to pay a sum of money or give something of value to another (either the insured or the beneficiary) to compensate for a specified loss.

workers' compensation statutes
State laws establishing an administrative procedure for compensating workers for injuries that arise in the course of their employment.

program. As mentioned earlier, some state workers' compensation boards allow paralegals to represent clients during agency hearings, which are conducted to settle disputes, or during negotiations with the agencies. There are similar jobs in other areas of employment and labor law, such as unemployment insurance, pension plan administration, Social Security disability insurance, and many more.

Frequently, working in employment law involves interacting with administrative agencies, such as the Occupational Safety and Health Administration and the Equal Employment Opportunity Commission. Each agency has its own rules and legal procedures. Paralegals who work in employment or labor law must be familiar with the relevant federal and state agencies, as well as with their specific roles in resolving disputes. We cover employment law in Chapter 18 and administrative agencies in Chapter 5.

Estate Planning and Probate Administration

Estate planning and probate administration have to do with the transfer of an owner's property, or *estate*, on the owner's death. Through **estate planning**, the owner decides, *before* death, how his or her property will be transferred to others. The owner may make a **will** to designate the persons to whom property is to be transferred. If someone contests the validity of the will, it must be proved through **probate**, which takes place in a **probate court**. Depending on the size and complexity of the estate, it may take months or longer for the probate court to approve the property distribution and for the property to be transferred to the rightful heirs.

Because the probate process is time consuming and expensive, many people engage in estate planning to try to avoid probate. For example, a person may establish a **trust** agreement, a legal arrangement in which the ownership of property is transferred to a third person (the *trustee*) to be used for the benefit of another (the *beneficiary*). Paralegals often are responsible for interviewing clients to obtain information necessary to draft wills and trust agreements, for gathering information on debts and assets, and for locating heirs if necessary (see Chapter 17). A paralegal who is sensitive and caring toward clients, yet professional in explaining and working out procedures, is well suited for this specialty.

Bankruptcy Law

Bankruptcy law allows debtors to obtain relief from their debts. Bankruptcy law is federal law, and bankruptcy proceedings take place in federal courts (see the discussion of the federal court system in Chapter 6). The goals of bankruptcy law are (1) to protect a debtor by giving him or her a fresh start and (2) to ensure that creditors who are competing for a debtor's assets are treated fairly. The bankruptcy process may provide several types of relief for individuals or business firms. Both large and small firms practice bankruptcy law and hire paralegals who specialize in this area.

Bankruptcy law, to be discussed in Chapter 19, imposes strict requirements, which means that paralegals working in this field may have detailed responsibilities. The process can involve complicated court filings about the debtor's assets and the claims against him or her. The paralegal might be responsible for interviewing debtors to obtain information about their income, assets, and debts. This often involves verifying the accuracy of information provided by debtors and ensuring that debtors have completed required credit counseling. The paralegal may also review the validity of creditors' claims and prepare documents that must be submitted to the bankruptcy court.

Intellectual Property Law

Intellectual property consists of the products of individuals' minds—products that result from creative processes. Those who create intellectual property acquire certain rights over the use of that property. Literary works, such as books, and artistic works,

estate planning
Arrangements made during a person's lifetime for the transfer of that person's property to others on the person's death. Estate planning often involves executing a will or establishing a trust fund.

will
A document directing how and to whom the maker's property and obligations are to be transferred on his or her death.

probate
The process of "proving" the validity of a will and ensuring that the instructions in a valid will are carried out.

probate court
A court that probates wills; usually a county court.

trust
An arrangement in which title to property is held by one person (a trustee) for the benefit of another (a beneficiary).

bankruptcy law
The body of federal law that governs bankruptcy proceedings. The twin goals of bankruptcy law are (1) to protect a debtor by giving him or her a fresh start and (2) to ensure that creditors competing for a debtor's assets are treated fairly.

intellectual property
Property that results from intellectual, creative processes. Copyrights, patents, and trademarks are examples of intellectual property.

such as songs, are protected by *copyright law*. *Trademark law* protects firms' distinctive marks or logos. Inventions are protected by *patent law*. Firms may also have *trade secrets*, such as the formula to make Coca-Cola. The owner of intellectual property rights may sell the rights to another, may collect royalties on the use of the property (such as a popular song) by others, and may prevent unauthorized publishers from reproducing the property without permission. Chapter 15 provides detail about laws governing intellectual property.

Some law firms (or departments of large law firms) specialize in intellectual property law. Other firms provide a variety of legal services, of which intellectual property law is a part. In addition, corporate legal departments may be responsible for registering copyrights, patents, or trademarks with the federal government.

Paralegals may specialize in intellectual property research regarding existing patents and trademarks. They also assist in compiling patent applications in accordance with detailed regulations, draft documents necessary to apply for trademark and copyright protection, and assist in litigating disputes. Because of the expertise required, paralegal intellectual property specialists are paid more than average. This is an especially good practice area for paralegals with a science background. In fact, anyone, including a paralegal, with three years of undergraduate science courses can apply to the U.S. Patent and Trademark Office to become a registered patent agent and thus be qualified to prepare patent applications.

Environmental Law

environmental law
All state and federal laws or regulations enacted or issued to protect the environment and preserve environmental resources.

Environmental law includes all state and federal laws or regulations that help to protect the environment. These involve the regulation of air and water pollution, protection of property from abuse, natural resource management, endangered species protection, proper hazardous waste disposal, the cleanup of hazardous waste sites, pesticide control, and nuclear power regulation.

Employers of paralegal specialists in environmental law include administrative agencies (such as the federal Environmental Protection Agency [EPA], state natural resource departments, and local zoning boards), environmental law departments of large law firms, law firms that specialize in environmental law, and corporations. For example, a company may employ a paralegal as an environmental coordinator to help maintain compliance with regulations, oversee company environmental programs, and obtain permits for certain kinds of land use. A familiarity with the terminology of biology, chemistry, and other sciences can help a paralegal working in this area.

Family Law

family law
Law relating to family matters, such as marriage, divorce, child support, and child custody.

Family law, as the term implies, deals with family matters, such as marriage, divorce, alimony, child support, and child custody. We will discuss it in detail in Chapter 17. State statutes govern family law, so if you specialize in this type of law, you will become familiar with your state's particular requirements.

As a family law specialist, you might work for a small law practice, for a family law department in a large law firm, or with a state or local agency, such as a community services agency that assists persons who need help with family-related legal problems. You might research and draft documents that are filed with the court in divorce and adoption proceedings. You might also perform investigations into assets and the grounds for divorce. Paralegals in this area often have extensive contact with clients and need to be skilled at extracting information from sometimes emotionally distraught persons. Those with a background or interest in social work or counseling are particularly well suited to this specialty.

Criminal Law

Law is sometimes classified into the two categories of civil law and criminal law. Civil law is concerned with the duties that exist between persons or between citizens and their governments, excluding criminal matters. Contract law, for example, is part of civil law. When the EPA demands that a company pay a fine for failure to comply with some aspect of environmental regulation, that is an area of civil law.

Criminal law, in contrast, is concerned with wrongs committed against the public. Criminal acts are prohibited by federal or state statutes (criminal law and procedures will be discussed in Chapter 13). In a criminal case, the government seeks to impose a penalty (which could include jail time) on a person who is alleged to have committed a crime. In contrast, in a civil case, one party tries to make the other party comply with a duty or pay for the damage caused by a failure to comply with a legal obligation.

Paralegals who specialize in criminal law may work for public prosecutors, public defenders (as discussed in the *Developing Paralegal Skills* feature below), or criminal defense attorneys. A paralegal working for the prosecutor's office, for example, might draft search or arrest warrants. A paralegal working for the defense attorney (public or private) might obtain police reports, conduct research, and draft documents to be filed with the court, such as a document arguing that the police violated the defendant's constitutional rights. Although criminal law and civil law are quite different, the trial process is comparable, and paralegals perform similar types of tasks (investigation, summarizing witness testimony, and so forth) in preparation for litigation.

Additional Specialty Areas

The listing of specialty areas is not exhaustive. Opportunities for paralegals exist in many other capacities. As the U.S. population ages, for example, more attorneys are focusing on serving the needs of older clients. **Elder law** is the term used to describe

civil law
Law dealing with the definition and enforcement of private rights, as opposed to criminal matters.

criminal law
Law that governs and defines those actions that are crimes and that subjects persons convicted of crimes to punishment imposed by the government (a fine or jail time).

elder law
A relatively new legal specialty that involves serving the needs of older clients, such as estate planning and making arrangements for long-term care.

DEVELOPING PARALEGAL SKILLS

WORKING FOR A PUBLIC DEFENDER

Michele Sanchez works as a paralegal for the public defender's office in her county. Today, she has been assigned to go to the county jail to meet with a new client, Geraldine Silverton. Silverton was arrested for child abuse after her child's school notified the police. According to school officials, the child had bruises all over his body. The child also told his teacher that his mother frequently "beat him up" for no reason at all.

The client, Silverton, is upset and tells Michele that "no way in the world would she harm her boy." Silverton claims that her son was hurt when he fell off the trampoline in their backyard and that he's just "making up" the abuse story to get attention.

Silverton demands to be released from jail immediately. Michele makes a note of Silverton's concerns and then explains the scheduling for the bail hearings.

Tips for Meeting with a New Client

• Review the police report before meeting with the client.

• During the interview with the client, ask the client for his or her side of the story.

• Listen carefully and supportively to the client, and communicate with empathy.

• Do not appear to judge the client.

this broad specialty. Paralegals who work in this practice area may be asked to assist in a variety of tasks, including those relating to estate planning, age-discrimination claims, financial arrangements for long-term care, Medicare and Medicaid, abuse suffered by elderly persons, and the visitation rights of grandparents.

Nurses have found profitable and challenging work as paralegals. A paralegal who is also a trained nurse is able to evaluate legal claims involving injuries, such as those involved in personal-injury, medical-malpractice, or product-liability lawsuits. A specialty area among nurses—and within the legal profession—is that of the **legal nurse consultant (LNC)**. LNCs usually work independently (offering their services on a contract basis) and are typically well paid for contract services. Some LNCs work for law firms, insurance companies, government offices, and risk management departments of companies as salaried employees. The American Association of Legal Nurse Consultants offers a certification program in which nurses who meet the eligibility criteria (including educational credentials and sufficient nursing experience) and pass an examination can become certified as LNCs.

legal nurse consultant (LNC)
A nurse who consults with legal professionals and others about medical aspects of legal claims or issues. Legal nurse consultants normally must have at least a bachelor's degree in nursing and significant nursing experience.

Paralegal Compensation

What do paralegals earn? This is an important question for anyone contemplating a career as a paralegal. You can obtain some idea of what paralegals make, on average, from paralegal compensation surveys. Following a discussion of these surveys, we look at some other components of paralegal compensation, including job benefits and compensation for overtime work. Note that the salaries reported by various sources vary significantly, so do not think of the numbers as a complete guide.

Compensation Surveys

Paralegal income is affected by a number of factors. We have already covered the effects of the size of the firm or legal department (see Exhibit 2.1 earlier in this chapter) and the specialty area in which the paralegal practices. Another income-determining factor is the paralegal's years of experience. Typically, as shown in Exhibit 2.2, more experienced paralegals enjoy higher rates of compensation. This is particularly noticeable when a paralegal has worked for the same employer for a long period of time.

Another major factor that affects paralegal compensation is geographical location. Exhibit 2.2 illustrates *national* averages. Exhibit 2.3, by contrast, shows averages in a few states. Remember, though, that these figures represent averages and can therefore be deceptive. For example, a paralegal working in San Francisco likely earns more than one doing a similar job in Chico, California.

Keep in mind, too, that salary statistics do not tell the whole story. Although paralegals earn more in California than in Texas, the cost of living and taxes are higher in California than in Texas. For example, a single person earning $75,000 in California

EXHIBIT 2.2

Average Paralegal Compensation by Experience Level

Position Classification	Years of Experience	Average Compensation + Bonus
Paralegal I	0–1	$56,659 + $2,332
Paralegal II	2–5	$65,571 + $2,695
Paralegal III	5–10	$77,885 + $3,164
Paralegal IV	15+	$88,134 + $6,895
Paralegal Supervisor	5–10	$76,120 + $12,568
Paralegal Manager	15+	$104,034 + $9,098

Source: Data from www.salary.com. See that website for definitions of the different paralegal positions and for job openings.

State	Average Salary
New York	$49,700
California	$45,150
New Mexico	$40,300
North Carolina	$35,300

EXHIBIT 2.3

Average Paralegal Salary in Law Firms by State

Source: Data from www.ZipRecruiter.com.

pays about 5% of that sum in state income tax in California but pays no such tax in Texas. This means that your real, after-tax income—the amount you can purchase with your income—may be the same despite the differences in gross salary. If you are comparing job offers in different cities, be sure to consider the cost of living and taxes as well as the pay being offered. Salary statistics also do not reveal another important component of compensation—job benefits.

Job Benefits

Part of your total compensation package as an employee will consist of job benefits. These benefits may include paid holidays, sick leave, group insurance coverage (life, disability, medical, dental), pension plans, and possibly others. Benefits packages vary from firm to firm. Most employers require employees to contribute part of the cost of insurance and retirement benefits. When evaluating any job offer, you need to consider the benefits that you will receive and what these benefits are worth to you. You will read more about the importance of job benefits later in this chapter in the context of evaluating a job offer.

Salaries versus Hourly Wages

Most paralegals are salaried employees. That is, they receive a specified annual salary. Others are paid an hourly wage rate for every hour worked. Paralegals are frequently asked to work overtime, and how they are compensated for overtime work usually depends on the employment status. Some firms compensate salaried paralegals for overtime work, diligence, or dedication to the firm through a year-end bonus. Bonuses may also depend on how well the firm is doing. Paralegals often receive annual bonuses that tend to rise with more years of experience. Some firms allow salaried employees to take compensatory time off work (for example, an hour off for every extra hour worked). Employees who are paid an hourly wage rate are normally paid overtime wages. In such cases, there may be no bonus or only a small one.

bonus
An end-of-the-year payment to a salaried employee in appreciation for that employee's overtime work, diligence, or dedication to the firm.

Planning Your Career

Career planning involves three key steps. The first step is defining your long-term goals. The second involves coming up with short-term goals and adjusting them to meet the realities of the job market. We look at these two steps in this section. (For some tips on how to succeed in your career, see this chapter's *Featured Contributor* article.) Later in this chapter, we discuss the third step: reevaluating your career after you have had some on-the-job experience as a paralegal.

Defining Your Long-Term Goals

You want to define, as clearly as possible, your career goals. This requires personal reflection and self-assessment. What are you looking for in a career? Why do you want to become a paralegal? Is income the most important factor? Is job satisfaction

FEATURED CONTRIBUTOR

TIPS TO JUMPSTART YOUR PARALEGAL CAREER

Antoinette France-Harris, J.D.

BIOGRAPHICAL NOTE

Antoinette France-Harris has been a licensed attorney since 1998. She began her legal career with a New York firm where she specialized in corporate and estate planning matters. After establishing herself as a successful transactional attorney, she decided to relocate to Georgia in 2002. Initially, she worked in-house for Fortune 1000 companies, and then, she became a solo practitioner. Her firm's areas of specialization included real estate, corporate, estate planning, and family law transactions.

In 2010, Professor Harris began teaching Paralegal Studies full time at Atlanta Technical College. In addition, she acted as department chair for two years before becoming assistant professor in Legal Studies at Clayton State University in August 2014. She is now an associate professor at Clayton State. Professor Harris has received a B.S. from Harvard University, an M.S.W. from Columbia University, and a J.D. from the University of Pennsylvania.

This is a great time to become a paralegal! Opportunities exist in various legal specialties, including bankruptcy, family, and environmental law. So, how does one get started? This article is designed to provide some useful strategies to launch a career in paralegalism. The list is by no means exhaustive, but it will give the reader a starting point on this exciting journey.

> " . . . continuously enhance your education. . . ."

Tip 1: Formal Education

Generally, people become paralegals either through on-the-job training or formal education. Many paralegal jobs require an associate's degree. For broader appeal, job seekers might pursue a bachelor's

degree. Others who already have a bachelor's in a different field might consider a post-baccalaureate certificate in paralegalism instead. Even paralegals who received on-the-job training report that obtaining a degree has opened doors to promotions and salary increases and makes it easier to transition from one employer to the next.

Tip 2: Never Stop Learning— Continuing Legal Education

In this perpetually changing and increasingly technological legal industry, it is important to continuously enhance your education and skills to keep pace. An easy way to do so is by attending

(doing the kind of work you like) the most important factor? Is the environment in which you work the most important factor? Asking yourself these and other broad questions about your personal preferences and values will help you define more clearly your overall professional goals.

Your Goals May Change

Do not be surprised to find that your long-term goals change over time. As you gain experience as a paralegal and your life circumstances alter, you may decide that your long-term goals are no longer appropriate. For example, the level of career involvement

timely classes, seminars, and workshops, which will equip you to optimize your usefulness to employers.

Tip 3: Get Certified

While they are not required to do so in many states, some paralegals are taking certification exams to distinguish themselves from other job seekers. The Paralegal Association (NALA) offers the entry-level Certified Legal Assistant/Certified Paralegal (CLA/CP) exam. The National Federation of Paralegal Associations (NFPA) offers the Paralegal Advanced Certification Exam (PACE) and the National Association of Legal Professionals (NALS) offers the Professional Paralegal (PP) exam, both of which require paralegal experience.

Tip 4: Improve Your Paralegal Résumé

Create a résumé that is tailored particularly for employment in this field. The paralegal résumé must highlight skills that every good paralegal should possess. Even if you have not worked as a paralegal, it is critical to accentuate any position that involved research and writing, organizational and communication skills, scheduling appointments or maintaining calendars, and multitasking. Your résumé should be a continual work in progress where trainings, achievements, associations, and the like are added regularly.

Tip 5: Network/Find a Mentor

It is essential for anyone seeking paralegal employment to meet people in the legal field. Most local bar associations have paralegal sections where you can attend events and network with experienced paralegals and attorneys. These individuals can provide unique insight and act as invaluable sources of information related to employment and advancement opportunities.

Tip 6: Become a Volunteer

One of the biggest complaints from job seekers is that most employers are seeking only candidates with legal experience.

> **"Your résumé should be a continual work in progress . . ."**

Once you have decided to become a paralegal, consider visiting a local law firm and offering your services voluntarily to gain experience. Who can resist free labor? The firm may not have an immediate paralegal opening, but if you make yourself invaluable, a job offer may come eventually. Be sure to add the volunteer experience to your résumé!

Tip 7: Take Other Jobs in the Legal Environment

Although you may not have paralegal experience, you undoubtedly have other work experience that a law firm or department may value and for which there is an opening. Once you have an "in" with the firm and the employer becomes more familiar with you, your skills, and your work ethic, eventually you may be considered for a paralegal position.

Tip 8: Keep Abreast of Hot Areas of the Law

As mentioned previously, the legal field is constantly evolving. Like any other business, it operates on the principles of supply and demand. Conduct thorough research in advance of your job search and consider choosing or changing your area of specialization based on where there is a projected need in the market.

In sum, launching a career as a paralegal will require extreme diligence, dedication, and determination. Setting and achieving short- and long-term goals and deadlines related to the job search will provide a sense of accomplishment throughout the process. To launch a career as a paralegal, you must be bold and willing to step outside of your comfort zone. In the end, your determination will yield great rewards.

This article was originally published in *The Paralegal Educator.*

---

that suits you as a single person may not be appropriate should you have children. Similarly, later in life, when your children leave home, you may have different goals with respect to work.

Explore New Challenges

At the outset of your career, you cannot know what opportunities might arise. Throughout your career as a paralegal, you will probably meet paralegals who have made career changes. Many paralegals, for example, decided on the field after several years of working in another profession, such as nursing, law enforcement, business administration, or accounting. Changes within the profession, your own experiences, and new opportunities affect the career choices before you. The realities you face during your career are likely to play a significant role in modifying your long-term goals.

Short-Term Goals and Job Realities

Long-term goals are just that—goals that we hope to achieve over many years or even a lifetime. Short-term goals are the steps we take to realize our long-term goals. When you are an entry-level paralegal, one short-term goal is to find a job.

Ideally, you will find a job that provides you with a salary consistent with your training and abilities, a level of responsibility that is comfortable (or challenging) for you, and good job benefits. The realities of the job market are not always what we wish them to be, however. You might not find the "right" employer or the "perfect" job when you first start. You may be lucky from the outset, but it may take several attempts before you find the employer and the job that best suit your needs, skills, and talents.

Remember that even if you do not find the perfect job right away, you gain valuable skills and experience in *any* job environment—skills and experience that can help you achieve long-term goals in the future. In fact, you might want to "try on" jobs at different-sized firms and in different specialty areas to see how they "fit" with your particular needs.

Locating Potential Employers

Looking for a job is time consuming and requires attention to detail, persistence, and creativity. Your paralegal education is preparing you, among other things, to do investigative research. The investigative skills that you will use on the job as a paralegal are the ones that you should apply when looking for a job.

Where do you begin your investigation? How can you find out what paralegal jobs are available in your area or elsewhere? How do you know which law firms practice the type of law that interests you? The following suggestions will help you answer these questions.

Networking

Career opportunities often go unpublished. Many firms post notices within their own organizations before publishing online. This opens doors to their own employees before the general public. It also spares employers from having to wade through many applications for a vacant position. If you have connections within an organization, you may be told that a position is opening up before other candidates are aware that an opportunity exists.

networking
Making personal connections and cultivating relationships with people in a certain field, profession, or area of interest.

More paralegals find employment through networking than through any other means. For paralegals, **networking** is the process of making personal connections with other paralegals, paralegal instructors, attorneys, and others who are involved in (or who know someone who is involved in) the paralegal or legal profession. Online networking, such as that provided by LinkedIn, has become popular as well. Professional organizations and internships offer important networking opportunities.

Join a Professional Association

Students can form a network of paralegal connections through affiliation with professional associations and student clubs. You have already learned about NALA and NFPA, the two largest national associations for paralegals. Other organizations of paralegals exist across the country. See if your local paralegal association allows students to be members. If it does, attend meetings and get to know other paralegals who may know of job opportunities in your area. Persons involved with other groups—such as the International Paralegal Management Association, or IPMA (an association of individuals who manage paralegals), and the **state bar association** (a state-level association of attorneys)—can also provide valuable inside knowledge of potential job openings.

Network during Internships

Many paralegal education programs include an internship in which students are placed temporarily in a law firm or other work setting. The people you meet in these settings often turn out to be beneficial to you in finding future employment. An intern who has performed well may be offered a full-time position after graduation. Even if you are not interested in working for the firm with which you do your internship, be careful not to "burn your bridges." The legal community is relatively small, and lawyers are more inclined to hire paralegals about whom their colleagues have made positive remarks. Many online social networks, such as Facebook and LinkedIn, are used by professionals to provide and obtain work-related information.

Volunteer

You can develop your skills and expand your professional network by volunteering with a local legal aid group or other organization that provides legal advice and assistance. Many attorneys volunteer for such work, so you may make a valuable connection while you help. You will also gain worthwhile experience and demonstrate to potential employers that you are willing and able to cooperate with other professionals in aiding others.

Finding Available Jobs

Your next effort should be to locate sources that list paralegal job openings. A **trade journal** or a similar publication, such as your local or state bar association's journal, newsletter, or website, may list openings for legal professionals. Increasingly, employers advertise job openings in online publications and turn to online databases to find prospective employees.

Identifying Possible Employers

You should identify firms and organizations for which you might like to work and submit an employment application to them. In a well-organized job search, you will locate and contact organizations that offer the benefits, salary, opportunities for advancement, work environment, and legal specialty of your choice. Even though these employers may not have vacancies in your field at the moment, you want your job application to be available when an opening occurs. Most firms, if they are interested in your qualifications, will keep your application on file for six months or so and may contact you if a position becomes available. As the following *Ethics Watch* feature discusses, be truthful about your background.

It is a good idea to begin compiling employer information for your job search while you are still completing your studies. Many of the resources you will need are available at the college you attend or through your paralegal program.

Legal Directories

Legal directories provide lists of attorneys, their locations, and their areas of practice. The *Martindale-Hubbell Law Directory*, which you can find online, lists the names, addresses, phone numbers, areas of legal practice, and other data for many lawyers and law firms. It is an excellent resource for paralegals interested in working for law firms or corporate legal departments. *West's Legal Directory* is another valuable source

state bar association
An association of attorneys within a state. In most states, an attorney must be a member of the state bar association to practice law in the state.

trade journal
A newsletter, magazine, or other periodical that provides a certain trade or profession with information (products, trends, or developments) relating to that trade or profession.

ETHICS WATCH

THE IMPORTANCE OF INTEGRITY

When looking for a job, be honest with others about your skills and experience. Even though you may want to impress a prospective employer, never give in to the temptation to exaggerate your qualifications. For example, suppose that you are working for a law firm during your internship and would really like to be hired by the firm in the future as a paralegal. In conversations with people in the firm, don't try to impress them by making misleading statements about your qualifications or skills. For instance, suppose you tell your supervisor that your GPA was 3.8 when in fact it was 3.4. This "little white lie" may come back to haunt you in the future. If the firm offers you a permanent job, it will likely check your credentials, including your college or professional school transcripts. Any

misrepresentation, no matter how minor it may seem, could doom your chances of being hired. Professional responsibility requires, among other things, that you be honest and pay close attention to detail—not only on the job but also when you are looking for a job.

This scenario is consistent with the NFPA *Model Code of Ethics and Professional Responsibility,* Section 1.3, "A paralegal shall maintain a high standard of professional conduct" and "A paralegal shall avoid impropriety and the appearance of impropriety and shall not engage in any conduct that would adversely affect his/her fitness to practice."

Reprinted by permission of the National Federation of Paralegal Associations, Inc. (NFPA®), www.paralegals.org.

of information (see **lawyers.findlaw.com**). It contains a listing of U.S. attorneys and law firms, state and federal attorneys and offices, and corporate legal departments and general counsel.

Job-Placement Services

Make full use of your school's placement service. Many colleges with paralegal programs provide job-placement services, and ABA-approved schools are required to provide ongoing placement services. Placement offices have personnel trained to assist you in finding a job, as well as in preparing job-search tools, such as your résumé and a list of potential employers. Some schools also offer practice interviews.

A growing trend is to use legal staffing or placement companies (also known as *recruiters*) to locate employment. Usually, the employer pays the fees for the placement company's services, and the company recruits candidates for the paralegal position and arranges interviews. Placement services can be located through paralegal program directors, local paralegal associations, and state bar associations, as well as on the Web.

Legal staffing companies place paralegal employees in both temporary (called "contract") and full-time (called "direct-hire") positions. Temporary contract employees are often used when a regular employee needs to take leave or when a special project requires additional paralegals, such as in large-scale litigation cases. Contract jobs can last from a few days to over a year. Long-term contract opportunities can provide valuable work experience in a particular specialty. Direct-hire positions typically provide long-term employment with salary and benefits, which are not provided in most temporary employment contracts.

Marketing Your Skills

Once you locate potential employers, the next step is to market your skills and yourself effectively. Marketing your skills involves three stages: the application process, interviewing for jobs, and following up on job interviews.

Keep in mind that each personal contact you make, whether it results in employment or not, has potential for your future. A firm may not hire you today because it has no openings, but it may hire you a year from now. Therefore, keep track of the contacts you make during your search, be patient, and be professional. A professional networking tool such as LinkedIn is especially helpful in doing so, since your contacts will update their contact information on it without your having to track their career moves.

The Application Process

When looking for paralegal employment, you need to assemble and present professional application materials. The basic materials you should create are a résumé, a cover letter, a list of professional references, and a portfolio. The following discussion explains each of these and gives some practical tips on how to create them.

The Résumé

For most job applications, you must submit a personal résumé that summarizes your employment and educational background. Your résumé is an advertisement, and you should invest the time to make it effective. Because human resource representatives in law firms, corporations, and government agencies may receive many résumés for each position they advertise, your résumé should create the best possible impression to gain a competitive edge over other job seekers.

Either generate your résumé yourself or work with a professional résumé-preparation service. Some school placement offices provide assistance. Format each page so that the reader is able to scan it quickly and catch the highlights. You might vary the type size, but never use a type size or style that is difficult to read.

What to Include in Your Résumé

Your name, address, telephone number, e-mail address, and website address, if you have one, belong in the heading of your résumé. The body of the résumé should be simple, brief, and clear. As a general rule, it should contain only information relevant to the job that you are seeking. A one-page résumé is usually sufficient, unless two pages are required to list relevant educational background and work experience. Exhibit 2.4 shows a sample résumé of a person with paralegal experience, and Exhibit 2.5 shows one of a person without such experience. Do not put your name and address in the upper left-hand corner, as that area is often stapled.

Provide Details. Divide your résumé into logical sections with headings as shown in the exhibits. Whenever you list dates, such as educational and employment dates, list them chronologically in reverse order. That is, list your most recent educational or work history first. When discussing your education, list the names and locations of the colleges you have attended and the degrees you have received. You may want to indicate your major and minor concentrations such as "Major: Paralegal Studies" or "Minor: Political Science." When listing work experience, specify your responsibilities in each position. Also include any relevant volunteer work that you have done. Substantive volunteer work is a major asset.

Scholarships or honors should also be indicated. If you have a high grade-point average (GPA), then include the GPA in your résumé. Under the heading "Selected Accomplishments," you might indicate your ability to speak more than one language, or note that you possess another special skill, such as expertise in online research.

No Work Experience? What if you are an entry-level paralegal and have no work experience to highlight? What can you include on your résumé to fill out the page? If you are facing this situation, add more information on your educational background

EXHIBIT 2.4

A Sample Résumé of a Person with
Paralegal Experience

ELENA LOPEZ

1131 North Shore Drive
Nita City, NI 48804
Telephone: (616) 555-0102 • E-mail: elopez@nitanet.net

EMPLOYMENT OBJECTIVE

A position as a paralegal in a private law firm that specializes in personal-injury practice.

EDUCATION

2017   Professional Training
        Midwestern Professional School for Paralegals, Green Bay, WI
        Focus: Litigation Procedures, Legal Investigation, Torts, Arbitration and Mediation, Case Preparation, and Trial. GPA 3.8.

2014   Bachelor of Arts degree
        University of Wisconsin, Madison, WI 53706. Political Science major. GPA 3.1.

PARALEGAL EXPERIENCE

- Caldwell Legal Clinic, Nita City, NI
  Paralegal: June 2017 to the present.
  Responsibilities: Legal research and document review; drafting discovery documents, including interrogatories, deposition summaries, and requests for admissions; and trial preparation in personal-injury cases.

- Legal Aid Society, Green Bay, WI
  Paralegal: June 2014 to May 2017.
  Responsibilities: Part-time assistance to legal aid attorneys in their representation of indigent clients in matters such as divorce, abuse, child custody, paternity, and landlord-tenant disputes.

- University of Wisconsin, Madison, WI
  Research Assistant: Political Science Department, January 2013 to May 2014.
  Responsibilities: Research on the effectiveness of federal welfare programs in reducing poverty in the United States.

AFFILIATIONS

Paralegal Association of Wisconsin
The Paralegal Association (NALA)

and experience. You can list specific courses that you took, student affiliations, or particular skills—such as computer competency in certain programs—that you acquired during your paralegal training.

Do Not Include Personal Data

Avoid including personal data (such as age, marital status, number of children, gender, or hobbies) in your résumé. Employers are prohibited by law from discriminating against employees or job candidates on the basis of race, color, gender, national origin, religion, age, or disability. You can help them fulfill this legal obligation by not including in your résumé any information that could serve as a basis for discrimination. For the same reason, you would be wise not to include a photograph of yourself with your résumé. It is to your advantage to list volunteer activities, but not hobbies or favorite leisure activities. You should also review your social media accounts before starting a

EXHIBIT 2.5

A Sample Résumé of a Person without Paralegal Experience

MARCUS BOHMAN

335 W. Alder Street
Gresham, CA 90650
Home Phone: (562) 555-6868 • Mobile: (562) 555-2468 • E-mail: mboh44@gresham.net

---

OBJECTIVE

To obtain a paralegal position in a firm that specializes in real estate transactions.

QUALIFICATIONS

I am a self-motivated, certified paralegal (CLA 2018) with knowledge and background in real estate and a strong academic record (3.7 GPA). In addition to the education listed below, I have completed several courses on real estate financing and possess excellent accounting skills.

EDUCATION

2021	*Bachelor of Arts Degree*—ABA-Approved Program
	University of La Verne, Legal Studies Program, La Verne, CA
	Major: Paralegal Studies; Minor: Business Management
	Emphasis on Real Property and Land-Use Planning, Legal Research and Writing.

EMPLOYMENT

2020–2021	*Intern, Hansen, Henault, Richmond & Shaw*
	Researched and drafted numerous real estate documents, including land sale contracts, commercial leases, and deeds. Scheduled meetings with clients. Participated in client interviews and several real estate closings. Filed documents with county.
2015–2020	*Office Assistant, Eastside Commercial Property*
	Maintained files and handled telephone inquiries at commercial real estate company. Coordinated land surveys and obtained property descriptions.
2014–2015	*Clerk, LandPro Title Company*
	Coordinated title searches and acted as a liaison among banks, mortgage companies, and the title company.
2012–2015	*Clerk, San Jose County Recorder's Office*
	Handled inquiries from the public and provided instruction to those seeking to look up records via microfiche.

---

job search, as many employers will conduct their own searches online. A Facebook feed of NSFW ("not safe for work") photos will not help your job prospects.

Proofread Your Results

Carefully proofread your résumé. Use the spelling checker and grammar checker on your computer, but do not totally rely on them. Have a friend or instructor review your résumé for punctuation, grammar, spelling, content, and visual appearance. If you find an error, you need to fix it. A mistake on your résumé tells the potential employer that you are a careless worker, a message that could ruin your chances of landing a job.

The Cover Letter

To encourage a recruiter to review your résumé, you need to capture her attention with a cover letter that accompanies the résumé. Because the cover letter is usually your first contact with an employer, it should be written carefully. It should be brief, perhaps only two or three paragraphs in length. Exhibit 2.6 shows a sample cover letter. When possible, you should learn the name of the person in charge of hiring (by phone or e-mail, if

EXHIBIT 2.6

A Sample Cover Letter

ELENA LOPEZ

1131 North Shore Drive
Nita City, NI 48804
Telephone: (616) 555-0102 • E-mail: elopez@nitanet.net

August 22, 2022

Allen P. Gilmore, Esq.
Jeffers, Gilmore & Dunn
553 Fifth Avenue, Suite 101
Nita City, NI 48801

Dear Mr. Gilmore:

I am responding to your advertisement in the Vegas Law Journal for a paralegal to assist you in personal-injury litigation. I am confident that I possess the skills and qualifications that you seek.

As you can see from the enclosed résumé, I received my paralegal certificate from Midwestern Professional School for Paralegals after obtaining a Bachelor of Arts degree from the University of Wisconsin. My paralegal courses included litigation procedures, legal research, legal investigation, and legal writing, and I graduated with a G.P.A. of 3.8.

After completing school, I obtained a position with a legal aid office, where I worked for several years and honed my legal research and writing skills. My current position with Caldwell Legal Clinic has provided me with valuable experience in preparing personal-injury cases for trial. I enjoy this area of law and hope to specialize in personal-injury litigation.

I am excited about the possibility of meeting with you to learn more about the position that you have available. A list of professional references is provided in my résumé, and a brief writing sample is attached for your perusal.

Please contact me to schedule an interview. You can contact me by phone after 3:00 p.m., Monday through Friday. I look forward to hearing from you.

Sincerely yours,

Elena Lopez

Elena Lopez

Enclosures

---

necessary) and direct your letter to that person. If you do not know that person's name, use a generic title, such as "Human Resources Manager" or "Paralegal Manager."

Content Is Key

Your cover letter should point out a few things about yourself and your qualifications for the position that might persuade a recruiter to examine your résumé. As a recently graduated paralegal, for example, you might draw attention to your academic standing at school, your eagerness to specialize in the same area of law as the employer (perhaps listing some courses relating to that specialty), and your willingness to relocate to the employer's city. Your job is to convince the recruiter that you are a close match to the mental picture that he or she has of the perfect candidate for the job. Make sure that the reader knows when and where you can be reached. Often, this is best indicated in the closing paragraph of the letter, as shown in Exhibit 2.6.

As with your résumé, read through your letter several times, and have someone else read it also to make sure that it is free from mistakes and easily understood. You should use the same type of paper for your cover letter as you use for your résumé.

Hard Copy Is Best

What about e-mailing your cover letter and résumé to prospective employers? This is a difficult question. On the one hand, e-mail is much faster than regular mail. On the other hand, an e-mail résumé does not look as nice. While some firms are accustomed to receiving applications by e-mail, others are not, and more senior attorneys often prefer traditional résumés. If the job you are applying for was advertised online or if the employer provided an e-mail address for interested job candidates to use, then e-mail is probably appropriate. Generally, though, job candidates who submit applications by e-mail should also send, by regular mail, printed copies of their letters and résumés.

List of Professional References

If a firm is interested in your application, you will probably be asked for a list of references—people the firm can contact to obtain information about you and your abilities. An instructor who has worked closely with you, an internship supervisor who has knowledge of your work, or a past employer who has observed your problem-solving ability would make excellent references. You should have at least three professionally relevant references, but more than five references are rarely necessary. Avoid using the names of family members, friends, or others who are clearly biased in your favor.

List your references on a separate sheet of paper, making sure to include your name, address, and telephone number at the top of the page, in the same format as on your résumé. For each person on the list, include current institutional affiliation or business firm, address, telephone number, fax number, and e-mail address. Make it easy for prospective employers to contact and communicate with your references.

Permission Is Required

When creating your list of references, always remember the following rule: never list a person's name as a reference unless you have that person's permission to do so. After all, it will not help you win the position you seek if one of your references is surprised by a call.

Obtaining permission from legal professionals to use them as references also gives you an opportunity to discuss your plans and goals with them, and they may be able to advise you and assist you in your networking. Additionally, it gives you a chance to discuss with them the kinds of experience and skills in which a prospective employer may be interested. You can also give them a few points that you want them to emphasize if they get a call. Afterward, you can get feedback from them about what those reference calls were like.

Build Your Contacts

Start building your list of possible references early in your studies. Dressing professionally in class, volunteering, arriving on time for class, being prepared, and turning in professional work for assignments are all ways to make a good impression on a professor. Keep in touch with those you want to use as references later. Use professional networking tools such as LinkedIn rather than social ones such as Facebook to keep track of them. The more they know about you, the more effective they will be as references.

Your Professional Portfolio

When a potential employer asks you for an interview, have your *professional portfolio* ready to give to the interviewer. The professional portfolio should contain another copy of your résumé, a list of references, letters of recommendation written by previous employers or instructors, samples of legal documents that you have composed, college or university transcripts, and any other relevant professional information, such as proof of professional certification or achievement. This collection of documents should be well organized and professionally presented. Depending on the size of your portfolio, a cover sheet, a table of contents, and a folder or commercial binder may be appropriate.

Show What You Can Do

The interviewer may be interested in your research and writing skills. Therefore, your professional portfolio should contain several samples of legal writing. If you are looking for your first legal position, go through your paralegal drafting assignments and pull out those that reflect your best work and that relate to the job skills you wish to demonstrate. Working with an instructor or other mentor, revise and improve those samples for inclusion in the portfolio. You might also use documents that you drafted while an intern or when working as a paralegal. These documents make excellent writing samples because they involve real-life circumstances. Be careful, however, and always remember, on any sample document, to completely black out (or "white out") any identifying reference to a client unless you have the client's permission to disclose his or her identity or if the information is not confidential.

Always include a résumé, as well as a list of references, in your professional portfolio, even though you already sent your résumé to the prospective employer with your cover letter. Interviewers may not have the résumé at hand at the time of the interview, and providing a second copy with your professional portfolio is a thoughtful gesture on your part.

Focus on Your Key Attribute

Some interviewers may examine your professional portfolio carefully. Others may keep it to examine later, after the interview. Still others may not be interested in it at all. If there is a particular item in your portfolio that you would like the interviewer to see, make sure you point it out before leaving the interview.

Digital Marketing

An important part of marketing yourself is ensuring that you have a presence online that helps potential employers evaluate your skills. We discuss the effective use of social media for career enhancement in the next section. Here we just note that your entire online presence needs to show that you are a professional who is able to handle the demands of a career that involves confidential information. Employers are likely to drop candidates from the pool of applicants when their social media presence reveals unprofessional photographs or focuses on parties.

As a paralegal, you will have access to personal information about your firm's clients, which can include valuable business information. Law firms and other employers want to be sure that they can rely on their staff to be professional. Your digital image must convey that you are competent, current, and organized.

The Interview

After an employer has reviewed your cover letter and résumé, the employer may contact you to schedule an interview. Interviews with potential employers may be the most challenging (and stressful) part of your search for employment.

Every interview will be different. Some will go well, but you will lose out to another candidate. Nonetheless, you have made a good contact, and you may be able to use this interviewer as a resource for information about other jobs. Remember what went right about the interview, and try to build on those positive aspects at the next one. While some interviews may go poorly despite your best efforts, lessons can still be learned from disappointing experiences.

Some interviewers are more skilled at interviewing than others. Some have a talent for getting applicants to open up, while others are confrontational and put a job candidate on the defensive. Still others may be unprepared. They may not have had time to compare applicants' qualifications with the job requirements, for example. Some employers now use a problem-focused interview technique to see how you would respond to a work situation.

As the person being interviewed, you have no control over who will interview you or what the style may be. You do, however, have control over your preparations for the interview. The following discussion will help you with these preparations.

Before the Interview

You can do many things prior to the interview to improve your chances of getting the job. First, do your "homework." Learn as much about the employer as possible. Check with your instructors or other legal professionals to find out if they are familiar with the firm or the interviewer. To see what you can learn about the firm and its members, check the employer's website and consult relevant directories, such as legal and company directories, as well as business publications. Then you can ask questions that indicate knowledge of the organization. Thorough preparation is appreciated and is a sign of professional diligence.

When you are called for an interview, learn the full name of the interviewer so that you will be able to address him or her by name during the interview and properly address a follow-up letter. During the interview, always use Mr. or Ms. in addressing the interviewer unless directed by the interviewer to be less formal.

Think about What May Be Asked

Anticipate and prepare answers for the questions you might be asked during the interview. You will benefit from rehearsing with a friend or with someone from your school's job placement center. For example, if you did not graduate from high school with your class but later received a general equivalency diploma (GED), you might be asked why you dropped out of school. If you have already prepared an answer for this question, it may save you the stress and embarrassment of having to decide, on the spot, how to reduce a complicated story to a brief sentence or two.

You should also prepare yourself to be interviewed by a "team" of legal professionals, such as an attorney, a paralegal, and perhaps others from the firm. Some prospective employers invite others who will be working with a new paralegal to participate in the interviewing process.

Promptness is extremely important. Plan to arrive for the interview at least ten minutes early, and allow plenty of extra time to get there. If the firm is located in an area that is unfamiliar to you, make sure that you know how to get there, how long it will take, and, if you are driving, whether parking is available nearby.

Look Professional

Personal appearance is important. Wear a relatively conservative suit or dress to the interview, and limit your use of jewelry and other accents, such as cologne or perfume. You can find further tips on how to prepare for a job interview by checking online career sites or by looking at books dealing with careers and job hunting.

At the Interview

During the interview, pay attention and listen closely. Interviewers ask questions to decide whether a candidate will fit comfortably into the firm, whether the candidate is organized and competent and will satisfactorily perform the job, and whether the candidate is reliable and will work hard to master the tasks presented. Your answers should be directly related to the questions. If you are unsure of what the interviewer means by a certain question, ask for clarification.

Interviewers use certain question formats to elicit certain types of responses. Four typical formats for questions are the following:

- *Closed-ended questions*—to elicit simple "Yes" or "No" answers.

- *Open-ended questions*—to invite you to discuss, in some detail, a specific topic or experience.

- *Hypothetical questions*—to learn how you might respond to situations that could arise during the course of your employment.

- *Pressure questions*—to see how you deal with uncomfortable situations or unpleasant discussions.

You will learn more about question formats in Chapter 11, where we discuss some techniques that paralegals use when interviewing clients.

Some Topics Are Not Appropriate

Certain questions are illegal or objectionable. These include questions about your marital status, family, religion, race, color, national origin, age, health or disability, or arrest record. You do not have to answer such questions unless you choose to do so. Exhibit 2.7 shows some examples of how you might respond to these types of questions. Note that because of record-keeping requirements imposed by the federal Equal Employment Opportunity Commission, an employer is likely to ask you to fill out a form that provides details regarding your race, age, and other personal facts. This information is needed for the record but is not to be discussed in the interview process.

Be Ready to Respond

As odd as it may seem, one of the most difficult moments is when the interviewer turns the inquiry around by asking, "Now then, do you have any questions?" Be prepared for this. Before the interview, take time to list your concerns. Bring the list to the interview

---

EXHIBIT 2.7

Objectionable or Illegal Interview Questions and Possible Responses

Q. Are you married?

A. If you are concerned that my social life will interfere with work, I can assure you that I keep the two very separate.

Q. Do you have any children yet?

A. That question leads me to believe that you would be concerned about my ability to prioritize my job and other responsibilities. Is that something that you are worried about?

Q. Are you or your husband a member of the Republican Party?

A. That is a private matter. Please realize that my family and political life will not interfere with my ability to do excellent work for your firm.

Q. You're quite a bit more mature than other applicants. Will you be thinking of retiring in the next ten years?

A. I don't understand how my age relates to my ability to perform this job.

with you. Questioning the interviewer gives you an opportunity to learn more about the firm and how it uses paralegal services. Questioning the interviewer also reveals how you might interview a client on behalf of the firm. Exhibit 2.8 lists some sample questions that you might ask the interviewer. You should not raise the issue of salary at the first interview unless you are offered the job. It is also not wise to ask early in the process about vacation time. The employer wants someone eager to work, not to take time off.

After the Interview

You should not expect to be hired as the result of one interview, although occasionally this does happen. Often, two or more interviews take place before you are offered a job. After leaving the interview, jot down a few notes to provide a refresher for your memory should you be called back for another interview. You will impress the interviewer if you are able to "pick up where you left off" from a discussion initiated several weeks earlier. Also, note the names and positions of the people you met during the interview process.

The Follow-up/Thank-You Letter

A day or two after the interview, but not longer than a week later, you should send a *follow-up letter* or e-mail to the interviewer. In this brief communication, you can mention again your availability and interest in the position, thank the interviewer for taking the time to interview you, and perhaps refer to a discussion that took place during the interview.

You may have left the interview with the impression that the meeting went poorly. But the interviewer may have a different sense of what happened. Interviewers have different styles, and what you interpreted to be a bad interview may just have been a reflection of that interviewer's style. You simply have no way of being certain, so follow through and make yourself available for the job or at least for another meeting. For an example of a follow-up letter, see Exhibit 2.9.

EXHIBIT 2.8

Questioning the Interviewer

Questions that you might want to ask the interviewer include the following:

- What method does the firm use to assign duties to paralegals?
- How do paralegals function within the organization?
- What clerical support is available for paralegals?
- Does the job involve travel? How will travel expenses be covered?
- What technology is used by the firm?
- Does the firm support paralegal continuing education and training programs?
- Will client contact be direct or indirect?
- Does the firm have an in-house library and access to computerized research services that paralegals can use?
- Will the paralegal be assigned work in a given specialty, such as real estate or family law?
- When does the job begin?
- What method is used to review and evaluate paralegal performance?
- How are paralegals supervised, and by whom?
- Are paralegals classified as exempt employees by this firm?
- Is there a written job description or employee policy manual for the job that I may review?

EXHIBIT 2.9
A Sample Follow-up Letter

ELENA LOPEZ
1131 North Shore Drive
Nita City, NI 48804
Telephone: (616) 555-0102 • E-mail: elopez@nitanet.net

September 3, 2022

Allen P. Gilmore, Esq.
Jeffers, Gilmore & Dunn
553 Fifth Avenue, Suite 101
Nita City, NI 48801

Dear Mr. Gilmore:

Thank you for taking time out of your busy schedule to meet with me last Thursday about your firm's paralegal position. I very much enjoyed our discussion, as well as the opportunity to meet some of your firm's employees.

I am extremely interested in the possibility of becoming a member of your legal team and look forward to the prospect of meeting with you again in the near future.

Sincerely yours,

Elena Lopez

Elena Lopez

Job-Hunting Files

In addition to keeping your professional portfolio materials up to date, you need to construct a filing system to stay on top of your job-search activities. Create a separate file for each potential employer, and keep copies of your letters, including e-mail messages, to that employer in your file, along with any responses. You might also want to keep lists or notes for addresses, telephone numbers, e-mail addresses, dates of contacts, advantages and disadvantages of employment with the various firms that you have contacted or by which you have been interviewed, topics discussed at interviews, and the like. Then, when you are called for an initial or repeat interview, you will have information on the firm at your fingertips. Always keep in mind that when looking for paralegal employment, your "job" is finding work as a paralegal—and it pays to be efficient.

Your files will also provide you with an excellent resource for networking even after you have a permanent position. The files may also provide useful information for a career change in the future.

Salary Negotiations

Sometimes a firm states a salary or a salary range in its advertisement for a paralegal. During a first interview, a prospective employer may offer that information as well. In other situations, an applicant does not know what the salary for a certain position will be until he or she is offered the job. You can prepare for the interview by checking salary information for the city where the job is located on the following websites:

salary.com, payscale.com, glassdoor.com, and paralegal411.com. In addition, you can access other paralegal salary survey sources, including NALA's *Facts and Findings* (subscription required), and of course, by keeping in touch with paralegal organizations in your city and state.

When you are offered a job, be prepared for the prospective employer to indicate a salary figure and ask if that figure is acceptable to you. If it is acceptable, then you have no problem. If you think it is too low, then the situation becomes more delicate. When you have no other job offer and really need a job, you may not want to foreclose this job opportunity by saying that the salary is too low. You might instead tell the prospective employer that the job interests you and that you will consider the offer seriously. Also, remember that salary is just one factor in deciding what a job is worth to you. In addition to salary, you need to consider job benefits and other factors, including those listed in Exhibit 2.10.

Gather Information Beforehand

Some prospective employers do not suggest a salary or a salary range but rather ask the job applicant what kind of salary he or she had in mind. You can prepare for this question by researching paralegal salaries in the area. You can find information on salaries by checking local, state, and national paralegal compensation surveys. Check first with your local paralegal association to see if it has collected data on local paralegal salaries. You might also find helpful information in your school's placement office.

EXHIBIT 2.10
Salary Negotiations: What Is This Job Worth to You?

BENEFITS

What benefits are included? • Will the benefits package include medical insurance? Life insurance? Disability insurance? Dental insurance? • What portion, if any, of the insurance premium will be deducted from your wages? • Is there an employee pension plan? • How many paid vacation days will you have? • Will the firm cover your paralegal association fees? • Will the firm assist you with tuition and other costs associated with continuing paralegal education? • Will the firm assist with day-care arrangements and/or costs? • Does the firm help with parking expenses (important in major cities)?

CAREER OPPORTUNITIES

Does the position offer you opportunities for advancement? You may be willing to accept a lower salary now if you know that it will increase as you move up the career ladder.

COMPENSATION

Will you receive an annual salary or be paid by the hour? • If you will receive an annual salary, will you receive annual bonuses? • How are bonuses determined? • Is the salary negotiable? (In some large firms and in government agencies, it may not be.)

COMPETITION

How stiff is the competition for this job? If you really want the job and are competing with numerous other candidates for the position, you might want to accept a lower salary just to land the job.

JOB DESCRIPTION

What are the paralegal's duties within the organization? Do you have sufficient training and experience to handle these duties? • Are you underqualified or overqualified for the job? • Will your skills as a paralegal be utilized effectively? • How much overtime work will likely be required? • How stressful will the job be?

JOB FLEXIBILITY

How flexible are the working hours? • If you work eight hours of overtime one week, can you take a (paid) day off the following week? • Can you take time off during periods when the workload is less?

LOCATION

Do you want to live in this community? • What is the cost of living in this area? Remember, a $50,000 salary in New York City, where housing and taxes are very expensive, may not give you as much real income as a $38,000 salary in a smaller community in the Midwest.

PERMANENCE

Is the job a permanent or a temporary position? Usually, hourly rates are higher for temporary assistance than for permanent employees.

TRAVEL

Will you be required to travel? • If so, how often or extensively? • How will travel expenses be handled? Will you pay them and then be reimbursed by the employer?

Suppose that you have found in your research that paralegals in the community usually start at $39,000 but that many with your education and training start at $46,000. If you ask for $48,000, then you may be unrealistically expensive—and the job offer may be lost. If you ask for $46,000, then you are still "in the ballpark"—and you may win the job.

Respond Carefully

Negotiating salaries can be difficult. On the one hand, you want to obtain a good salary and do not want to underprice your services. On the other hand, overpricing your services may extinguish an employment opportunity or eliminate the possibility of working for an otherwise suitable employer. Your best option might be to state a salary range that is acceptable to you. That way, you are not pinned down to a specific figure. Note, though, that if you indicate an acceptable salary range, you invite an offer of the lowest salary—so the low end of the salary range should be the threshold amount that you will accept.

Career Development

Once you have gained several years' experience working as a paralegal, you can undertake the third step in career planning: reevaluating your career goals and reassessing your abilities based on your accumulated experience. Paralegals who want to advance in their careers normally have three options: (1) You can be promoted within an organization, which may include transferring to another department or branch office of the firm. In a small firm, there may be no chance for upward movement, but if the position is satisfying and you receive salary increases, then that may not be an issue for you. (2) Even if you are happy at a firm, change, such as retirement of your supervising attorney, can force you to move to another firm, so you want to be sure you are always attractive to another employer. (3) After you have started working, you may consider going back to school for additional education. If you are interested in a particular specialty area, course work in that area may help you become more valuable to your current employer or land a job that can advance your career. Alternatively, you might decide to work toward an advanced degree, such as a master's in business administration (MBA), to create new opportunities. Some paralegals opt to go to law school and become attorneys. Whatever your decision, remember that the structure of law practice will continue to evolve, so expanded skills will be valuable.

Using Social Media Effectively

Social media can be a key factor in determining your success in your paralegal career. Yet many professionals don't use it effectively. Your online reputation, often called your *digital shadow*, will affect how employers, clients, opposing counsel, and others see you. You should assume that all your postings to Facebook, Twitter, LinkedIn, and other social media can be seen by everyone with whom you interact. As many people have learned, even Snapchat photos, which senders thought disappeared, can be online forever. Make sure that nothing you post diminishes your reputation.

Digital Shadow

You influence how people perceive your digital shadow. Think of it as online reputation management. Your reputation is not something that just happens to you or that you have no influence over. If you invest effort in creating an online reputation, you will see positive results. If you do not pay attention to what exists online and are careless in what you post, people will form their perceptions based on their searches.

You can invest in your digital shadow in these important ways:

1. Perhaps most important is what you do not do. Do not engage in heated arguments, post unprofessional photos, reveal personal information, suggest you do not work hard, or say negative things about any employer. A lawyer at a New York firm accidentally sent an e-mail message to his firm's entire practice group bragging about his two-hour sushi lunch and lack of productivity. Remember: Professionalism is a 24/7 commitment, not something that only occurs during working hours.

2. Post only about important professional events and accomplishments. When you do, accurately present the information without exaggeration. Your goal is to persuade people you are worth working with, recruiting to a new job, or networking with—not to massage your ego.

3. Keep your profiles on career sites such as LinkedIn and social sites such as Facebook consistent and up-to-date. While we often think of Facebook sites as personal—only for friends and family—they can be seen by anyone. Search firms can reveal posted information we thought was private or deleted long ago. If you presume that everything you send can be seen by anyone and can affect your employment future, you will exercise caution. Post only professional photos for your profile pictures on career-related sites such as LinkedIn. (It is often worth investing in a professional photo in business attire for such sites.)

4. Monitor your online presence. What you mean for others to think and know about you may not be the image being perceived by others.

5. Create online content that will give a positive impression of you. Write professionally and clearly, post regularly, and share useful information. Think of how a stranger will view your information, not how those who know you well will view it.

6. Use resources that professional networking sites make available. Many offer online training on how to effectively use their features. Invest time in learning how to get the most out of your digital shadow.

7. Invest fifteen minutes per week in managing your digital shadow. Review suggested connections on LinkedIn or other such sites; endorse your connections for their skills (which will often lead them to endorse you); and keep your profiles up to date.

By being proactive and managing your digital shadow, you can enhance your future career prospects and help ensure that those you deal with both online and offline have a positive impression of your professionalism, your abilities, and your work ethic. Remember, employers often look at Facebook and other social media seeking "digital dirt" to get ideas about a person before hiring someone. You control much about how others see you, so spend time cleaning up your profile before applying for jobs.

Social Media Skills Increase Your Value to Employers

Many law firms are just beginning to explore how to use social media in the practice of law. Industry leaders are focusing on increasing productivity within the firm through internal social networks and marketing their services through external social media such as Twitter and Facebook.

To succeed in your career, if you are knowledgeable about the latest social media tools, you can assist in your firm's efforts and, thereby, make yourself a more valued employee. While many attorneys are capable of writing useful content for a website or other media site for the firm, they may not have the time, interest, or ability to post effectively, so that is a role you can play. Smaller firms are unlikely to have a media specialist on the payroll, so social media–savvy paralegals can play a leadership role in this area. If your firm does not have a social media policy, volunteer to draft one.

Watching for Opportunities

Use Twitter and other social media to follow employers you might be interested in working for in the future. Many employers now use advertising links on Twitter to find candidates, so following your targeted employers can be helpful in learning about opportunities. Once you've got an interview, you can use your knowledge of the firm gleaned from watching its Twitter feed to ask questions that show you have real interest in the firm. Effective use of Twitter and other social media can help you promote yourself and maximize your chances of landing a good job, keeping a job, and moving to a better job.

CHAPTER SUMMARY

CAREER OPPORTUNITIES

Where Paralegals Work

1. *Law firms*—More than two-thirds of paralegals work in law firms—most of them in firms employing fewer than twenty-five attorneys. A small firm allows a paralegal to gain experience in a number of areas of law and to work in a less formal environment. Paralegals in small firms often earn less than those in large firms, however, and often must perform secretarial duties. Paralegals working for large firms tend to specialize in a few areas of law, enjoy better employee benefits, and have more support staff.

2. *Corporations and other businesses*—About one-fifth of paralegals work in corporations. Corporate legal departments may have hundreds of attorneys and paralegals on staff. Paralegals working for corporations work regular hours, do not have to be concerned with billable hours, and generally receive above-average salaries. They may specialize in certain aspects of corporate law. In addition, paralegals work in many other public and private institutions, such as insurance companies, banks, real estate companies, title

insurance companies, legal-software companies, and law schools.

3. *Government*—Paralegals work in many government administrative agencies, such as the Social Security Administration. Other employment opportunities exist with legislative offices, public prosecutors' offices, public defenders' offices, and federal and state courts.

4. *Legal aid offices*—Some paralegals find it rewarding to work in legal aid offices, which provide legal services to those who find it difficult to pay for legal representation. These offices are largely funded by the government, but some support comes from private foundations.

5. *Freelance paralegals*—Some experienced paralegals own their businesses and work for attorneys on a contract basis. This work can have more flexible working hours and often can be done from a home office. The success (and income) of a paralegal in this area depends on the person's skill, business sense, and motivation.

Paralegal Specialties

Many paralegals specialize in one or two areas of law, such as corporate law, contract law, real estate law, and personal-injury law. Other areas in which a paralegal can specialize include insurance law, employment and labor law, estate planning and probate administration, bankruptcy law, intellectual property law, environmental law, family law, criminal law, elder law, and legal nurse consulting.

Paralegal Compensation

Salaries and wage rates for paralegal employees vary. Factors affecting compensation include location, firm size, years of experience, and type of employer (law firm, corporation, or government agency). When evaluating a job, paralegals should consider not only salary or wages but also job benefits, such as insurance coverage, sick/vacation/holiday leave, and pension plans.

Planning Your Career

Career planning involves three steps: defining your long-term career goals, devising short-term goals and adjusting those goals to fit job realities, and reevaluating your career and career goals after you have had some on-the-job experience.

Locating Potential Employers

When looking for employment, paralegals should apply the investigative skills that they learned in their paralegal training.

1. *Networking*—Many jobs come through networking with other professionals. You can begin networking while you are a student. If your local paralegal association allows students to become members, join the association. Knowing others in the legal community is a great asset when looking for a job.

2. *Finding available jobs*—You can locate potential employers by reviewing published and posted information about law firms and other possible employers. Advertisements can be found in trade journals, in newspapers, on the Internet, and at your school's placement office. Check legal directories for lists of law offices.

3. *Job-placement services*—
   a. **SCHOOL PLACEMENT SERVICES**—Paralegals should stay in contact with their school's placement office, which is often staffed with personnel trained to assist paralegals with job hunting.
   b. **LEGAL STAFFING OR PRIVATE PLACEMENT COMPANIES**—Paralegals may locate employment through private placement companies. Usually, the employer pays the placement company's fees, and the company recruits candidates for the position and schedules interviews. Placements may be for temporary or long-term positions. Paralegals can find out about job-placement companies through school program directors, local paralegal associations, state bar associations, or the Web.

Marketing Your Skills

1. *The application process*—Prepare a professional résumé to outline your educational and work background. Do not include personal details. The cover letter that accompanies your résumé represents you, so draft it carefully. You should also have available a professional portfolio and a list of persons who have agreed to be professional references.

2. *The interview*—Do background research on a firm prior to your interview. Think through the answers you will give to likely questions, and be prepared to ask questions that indicate your interest and knowledge. After an interview, make notes of relevant issues so you can discuss them if called back.

3. *The follow-up/thank-you letter*—After an interview, send a personalized thank-you letter or e-mail expressing continued interest.

4. *Job-hunting files*—Keep your records organized as you look for work by creating a filing system for all your job-search activities.

5. *Salary negotiations*—Some employers will ask you to specify an acceptable salary. Be prepared to give a salary or a salary range, depending on the job requirements. Research information about the salaries paralegals earn in your area.

Using Social Media Effectively

Most people use social media routinely. It can help you in your job search, as employers often look at social media sites for evidence of personal behavior and professionalism. Manage your digital shadow by keeping in mind that your reputation is always on the line. Paralegals may increase their value to a firm by being able to contribute to the social media presence of the firm. Knowledge of effective use of social media tools can help your career in many ways.

KEY TERMS AND CONCEPTS

bankruptcy law   27

bonus   31

civil law   29

contract   25

corporate law   25

criminal law   29

defendant   25

elder law   29

environmental law   28

estate planning   27

family law   28

freelance paralegal   23

insurance   26

intellectual property   27

legal nurse consultant (LNC)   30

legal technician (independent
   paralegal)   23

litigation   24

litigation paralegal   24

networking   34

plaintiff   24

probate   27

probate court   27

real estate   25

state bar association   35

tort   26

trade journal   35

trust   27

will   27

workers' compensation statutes   26

QUESTIONS FOR REVIEW

1. List and describe the five types of organizations that hire paralegals.

2. List and briefly describe each of the paralegal specialties discussed in this chapter. Which specialty area or areas interest you the most? Why?

3. How can paralegals locate potential employers? How does networking help paralegals find jobs?

4. What are some of the factors that affect compensation for paralegals?

5. What are the three key steps involved in planning a career as a paralegal?

6. What is a digital shadow? List three ways a paralegal can increase his or her digital shadow.

ETHICS QUESTION

1. Sheila, a paralegal with twenty years of bankruptcy law experience, sets up a practice to provide bankruptcy forms and advice directly to the public. She advises a client to file for bankruptcy under Chapter 7, but due to the means test, he should have filed under Chapter 13. The wrong advice causes the client distress and added expense. What type of paralegal is Sheila working as? Is it permissible for a paralegal to provide legal services without attorney supervision? Should it be?

PRACTICE QUESTIONS AND ASSIGNMENTS

1. Where do most paralegals work? What are some advantages and disadvantages of working for a small law firm? For a large law firm? Which would you prefer to do? Why?

2. Using the material in the chapter, identify which kind of employer the paralegals in the following scenarios work for:

   a. Isabella works on a team of one attorney, three paralegals, and two secretaries. They defend product liability cases brought against their employer, a medical-device manufacturer.

   b. Ramon works as a case manager for a U.S. district court judge.

   c. Miranda works for a county legal aid office that provides low-cost legal services to elderly people in a large city.

   d. Anthony works for all of the attorneys in his firm. He has gained a variety of experience, as he does all of the clerical work as well as the paralegal work on the various cases his firm handles. He enjoys the casual environment of the office.

e. Felicia's practice is limited to discovery work in the commercial litigation department. The office environment is formal, but she is paid a high salary, along with good benefits, and has opportunities for promotion.

f. Michael provides paralegal services to attorneys in his local community on a contract basis. Most of his work involves support on litigation matters from discovery through trials.

3. What is the difference between a freelance paralegal and a legal technician (also called an independent paralegal)? How would working as a freelance paralegal compare to working for a law firm or other paralegal employer? How would working as a freelance paralegal compare to working as a legal technician?

4. Using the material in the chapter, identify each of the following types of questions (close-ended, open-ended, hypothetical, pressure) that an interviewer might ask during an interview:

a. Are you available to travel on weekends?

b. Please explain your work history.

c. What would you do in the following situation? Attorney Jones is in trial, and at 4 P.M., the judge assigns attorney Jones to research the rules of evidence and bring her findings to him in the morning

when the trial resumes. At 5 P.M., attorney Jones asks you to stay and help her do the research, indicating that it will "be a late night."

d. Thinking that you look like a polite person who is not assertive enough to work in a law firm, a human resources manager grabs your paperwork from you and says, "I'll complete that for you. You need to go to the lobby and wait for attorney Smith to interview you." There is clearly plenty of time for you to complete the paperwork.

5. Using the material in the chapter, determine which of the following are illegal questions that an interviewer might ask during a job interview:

a. Are you married?

b. How many children do you have?

c. How do you think that your prior work experience as a social worker will help you in this job as a family law paralegal?

d. You're quite a bit more mature than other applicants. Will you be thinking of retiring in the next ten years?

6. Draft a résumé for yourself using the samples in this chapter for guidance. Think of your strong traits that should be highlighted. Also, write a cover letter that introduces you in a favorable manner.

GROUP PROJECT

The group selects a legal specialty discussed in this chapter.

Students one and two find an article about the area from a paralegal publication or website. Each of them writes a one-page summary of the article, including the pros and cons of working in this specialty.

Student three interviews a paralegal who works in this practice area, and discusses the pros and cons of the specialty during the interview.

Student four summarizes the results of both the research and the interview and presents the results to the class.

The Inner Workings of the Law Office

CHAPTER OBJECTIVES

After completing this chapter, you will be able to:

- Explain how law firms are organized and managed, and how paralegal tasks in each differ.

- Describe the various personnel roles in law offices, including management roles.

- List and explain some typical policies and procedures governing paralegal employment.

- Explain the importance of an efficient filing system in legal practice and some typical filing procedures.

- Explain how clients are billed for legal services and how client funds are handled.

- Explain the importance of and best practices for effectively communicating with clients.

- Explain how law office culture and politics affect the paralegal's working environment.

Introduction

The diverse environments in which paralegals work make it impossible to predict exactly how the firm where you will work will be organized and operated. Typically, the way in which that firm operates will relate, at least in part, to the firm's form of business organization. Because most paralegals work for private law firms, this chapter focuses on the organization, management, and procedures of these firms.

First, we look at how the size and structure of a law firm affect the paralegal's working environment. For example, the working environment in a firm owned and operated by one attorney is significantly different from that in a large law firm with two hundred attorneys. Different still is the working climate of a large corporate enterprise or a government agency.

We then look at other aspects of the working environment of paralegals. Most law firms have specific policies and procedures relating to employment conditions, filing systems, billing and timekeeping practices, and financial procedures. Increasingly, firms make use of social media tools, and paralegals often have responsibilities in this area. We conclude the chapter with a brief discussion of law office culture and politics.

The Organizational Structure of Law Firms

Law firms range in size from one-attorney firms to megafirms with hundreds of attorneys. Regardless of size, law firms typically organize as sole proprietorships, partnerships, limited liability partnerships, professional corporations, or professional limited liability companies. How a business is organized affects the office environment, so we next look briefly at each of the major organizational forms of law firms. Organizational forms of businesses in general will be discussed in greater detail in Chapter 18.

Sole Proprietorships

The **sole proprietorship** is the simplest business form and is often used by attorneys when they first set up legal practices. In a sole proprietorship, one individual—the sole proprietor—owns the business. The sole proprietor is entitled to any profits made by the firm but is also personally liable for all of the firm's debts or obligations. **Personal liability** means that the owner's personal assets (such as savings and other property) may have to be sacrificed to pay business obligations if the business fails.

An attorney who practices law as a sole proprietor is often called a *sole (solo) practitioner*. To save on overhead expenses, a sole practitioner may share an office with other attorneys. A paralegal may split time among sole practitioners who share office space.

Working for a sole practitioner with a general practice is a good way for a paralegal to learn law office procedures because the paralegal will perform a wide variety of tasks. Many sole practitioners hire one person to act as a combined secretary, paralegal, administrator, and manager. Paralegals holding such multi-role positions handle many tasks. These might include receiving and date-stamping the mail, printing out e-mails, organizing and maintaining the filing system, interviewing clients and witnesses, bookkeeping (receiving payments from clients, preparing and sending bills to clients, and the like), conducting investigations and legal research, drafting and editing legal documents, assisting the attorney in trial preparation and perhaps in the courtroom, and other jobs, including office administration.

On the one hand, working for a sole practitioner is a good way to find out which area of law you most enjoy because you will learn about procedures relating to many areas. If you work for a sole practitioner who specializes in one area of law, you will have an opportunity to develop expertise in that area. On the other hand, you will

sole proprietorship
The simplest form of business organization, in which the owner is the business. Any individual who does business without creating a formal business entity has a sole proprietorship.

personal liability
An individual's personal responsibility for debts or obligations. The owners of sole proprietorships and partnerships are personally liable for the debts and obligations incurred by their businesses. If their firms go bankrupt or cannot meet debts, the owners will be personally responsible for the debts.

have fewer opportunities to learn from multiple supervisors and will likely work with fewer people on a day-to-day basis. In sum, working in a small law firm gives you an overview of law office procedures and legal practice that will help you throughout your career but may limit your in-firm contacts.

Partnerships

Many law firms with multiple attorneys are organized as partnerships. In a **partnership**, two or more people—each known as a **partner**—do business jointly. A partnership may consist of two or hundreds of attorneys. In a partnership, each partner owns a share of the business and shares in the firm's profits or losses.

In smaller partnerships, the partners may participate equally in managing the partnership. The partners meet to make decisions about clients, policies, procedures, and other matters important to the firm. In larger partnerships, managerial decisions are usually made by a committee of partners, one of whom may be designated as the **managing partner**.

Partnerships (and professional corporations, which are discussed below) frequently employ attorneys who are not partners and do not share in the profits. Typically, such an attorney is called an **associate attorney**. They usually are less experienced and may be invited to become partners after working for the firm for several years. Sometimes, firms will hire a **staff attorney**, who will not become a partner. Staff attorneys differ from *contract attorneys*, who provide services on a project basis. Many firms also will hire a **law clerk** or two—that is, a law student who works for the firm during the summer or part-time during the school year to gain practical legal experience. Law clerks who meet with the approval of the members of the firm may be offered positions as associates when they graduate and pass the bar exam.

Liability of Partners

Like sole proprietors, attorneys in a partnership are personally liable for the debts and obligations of the law firm if it fails. In addition, a partner can be held personally responsible for the misconduct or debts of another partner. For example, suppose a client sues a partner in the firm for malpractice and wins a large judgment. The firm carries malpractice insurance, but it is insufficient to pay the obligation. The court will order the attorney who committed the wrongful act to pay the balance due. Once the responsible attorney's personal assets are exhausted, the assets of the other partners can be used to pay the judgment even if they had nothing to do with the malpractice. The unlimited personal liability of partners is a major disadvantage for law firms organized as partnerships.

Limited Liability Partnerships (LLPs)

A form of partnership called the **limited liability partnership (LLP)** has become increasingly popular. The LLP normally allows professionals to avoid personal liability for the malpractice of other partners. The LLP is a business entity available only where a state legislature has passed a law allowing it. Although LLP statutes vary from state to state, generally state law limits the liability of partners in some way. For example, Delaware law protects each innocent partner from the "debts and obligations of the partnership arising from negligence, wrongful acts, or misconduct." You will read more about LLPs in Chapter 18.

Professional Corporations

A **professional corporation (PC)** is a corporation formed by licensed professionals, such as lawyers or physicians. Like other corporations, it is a "creature of

---

partnership
An association of two or more persons to carry on, as co-owners, a business for profit. Partners need not have explicitly agreed to be partners; so long as they meet the legal test by acting as partners, a court can decide that they have formed a partnership. In the United States, partnerships are governed by a mix of state common law and state statute law.

partner
A person who operates a business jointly with one or more others. Each partner is a co-owner of the business firm.

managing partner
The partner in a law firm who makes decisions relating to the firm's policies and procedures and who generally oversees the business operations of the firm.

associate attorney
An attorney working for a law firm who is not a partner and does not have an ownership interest in the firm. Associates are usually less experienced attorneys and may be invited to become partners after working for the firm for several years.

staff attorney
An attorney hired by a law firm as an employee. A staff attorney has no ownership rights in the firm and will not be invited to become a partner in the firm.

law clerk
A law student working as an apprentice with a law firm to gain practical experience.

limited liability partnership (LLP)
A business organizational form designed for professionals who normally do business as partners in a partnership. The LLP limits the personal liability of partners.

professional corporation (PC)
A corporation formed by licensed professionals, such as lawyers or physicians. The liability of shareholders is often limited to the amount of their investments.

statute"—that is, it is created by operation of state law—and is owned by share-holders. A **shareholder** is so called because he or she has purchased the corporation's stock, or shares, and thus owns a share of the business. The shareholders share in the profits and losses of the firm in proportion to how many shares they own. Their personal liability, unlike that of partners, may or may not be limited to the amount of their investments, depending on the circumstances and on state law. Limited personal liability is one of the key advantages of this corporate form of business.

> **shareholder**
> One who purchases corporate stock, or shares, and who thus becomes an owner of the corporation.

Most states allow attorneys to form a **professional limited liability company (PLLC)**. This is yet another state statute–based business organization. Depending on the state, the law firm may be required to receive permission from the state bar association. In such situations, the bar association will likely require that a licensed attorney or group of attorneys operate and own the PLLC. As with other organizational forms, the originating paperwork of the firm is on public file with the secretary of state in each state.

> **professional limited liability company (PLLC)**
> An organizational form law firms may use in most states to help limit personal liability by separating individuals from the legal entity, the firm.

In many respects, the PC or PLLC is run like a partnership, and the distinction among these forms of business organization can appear to be more of a legal formality than an operational reality. Because of this, attorneys who organize their business as a PC or PLLC are nonetheless sometimes referred to as partners. For simplicity, in this chapter we will refer to anyone who has ownership rights in a law firm as a partner. However, the business form used will determine which state statute governs the firm's operations. This typically is most important when a firm breaks up, or dissolves, or when there is a conflict among the partners or shareholders.

Law Office Management and Personnel

When you take a job as a paralegal, you will learn the relative status of the office personnel. Particularly, you want to know who has authority over you and to whom you are accountable. You also want to know who is accountable to you—whether you have an assistant or a secretary (or share an assistant or a secretary with another paralegal), for example. In a small firm, you will have no problem learning this information. If you work for a larger law firm, the lines of authority may be more difficult to perceive. Your supervisor will probably instruct you on the relative status of the firm's personnel. If you are not sure about who has authority over whom and what tasks are performed by different employees, ask your supervisor.

Law Office Organization

Regardless of formal lines of authority, it is important to be courteous and professional with everyone. You may outrank a partner's secretary on paper, but if the partner and secretary have a long history of working together, the partner is likely to pay close attention to the secretary's views.

The lines of authority and accountability vary from firm to firm, depending on the firm's size and management preferences. A sample organizational chart for a law partnership is shown in Exhibit 3.1. The partners at the top of the chart are the decision makers in the firm. Next in authority are the associate attorneys. Paralegals are supervised by both the attorneys (in regard to legal work) and the office manager (in regard to office procedural and paralegal-staffing matters). In larger firms, there may be a **paralegal manager** who coordinates paralegal staffing and programs relating to paralegal educational and professional development.

> **paralegal manager**
> An employee in a law firm who is responsible for overseeing the paralegal staff and paralegal professional development.

EXHIBIT 3.1

A Sample Organizational Chart for a Law Partnership

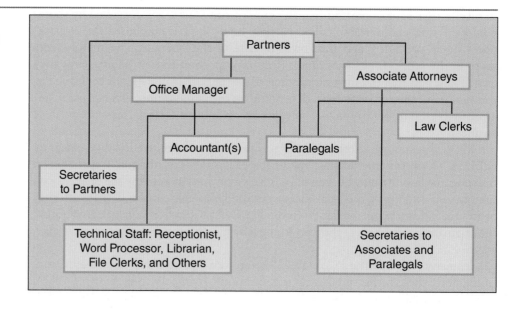

legal administrator

An administrative employee of a law firm who manages day-to-day operations. In smaller law firms, legal administrators are usually called office managers.

office manager

An administrative employee who manages the day-to-day operations of a firm. In larger law firms, office managers are usually called legal administrators.

support personnel

Employees who provide clerical, secretarial, or other support to the legal, paralegal, and administrative staff of a law firm.

Besides attorneys and paralegals, law firm employees include administrative personnel. In large firms, the partners may hire a **legal administrator** to run the business end of the firm. The legal administrator might delegate some authority to an office manager and other supervisory employees.

Variety of Support Staff

In medium-size firms, such as those represented in Exhibit 3.1, an office manager handles the administrative aspects of the firm. The legal administrator or office manager typically is in charge of docketing (calendaring) legal work undertaken by the attorneys; establishing and overseeing filing procedures; implementing new technology, such as new docketing software; ordering and monitoring supplies; and generally making sure that the office runs smoothly and that office procedures are established and followed. In a small firm, the office manager might handle client-billing procedures. The firm represented in Exhibit 3.1 has an accountant to perform this function.

The **support personnel** in a large law office may include secretaries, receptionists, bookkeepers, file clerks, messengers, and others. Depending on their functions and specific jobs, support personnel may fall under the supervision of any number of other personnel in the firm. In a small firm, just one person—the legal secretary, for example—may perform all of the above-mentioned functions. No matter the size of the office, the need for accuracy and organization is great. Increasingly, support for large volumes of routine documents may be provided by professionals in offshore locations, where wages are lower and educated professionals are available for reviewing documents or analyzing thousands of e-mails as part of discovery.

Employment Policies

employment manual

A firm's handbook or written statement that specifies the policies and procedures that govern the firm's employees and employer-employee relationships.

Employees of a law firm, which include all personnel other than the partners or those who work for the firm on a contract basis, are subject to the firm's employment policies. A firm's policies governing employment may be published in an **employment manual** in larger firms. In smaller firms, these policies are often unwritten. In either case, when you take a job as a paralegal, or perhaps before you accept a position, you will want to become familiar with the firm's conditions of employment.

There will be a policy, for example, on when you may take vacation time and how much you are entitled to take during the first year, second year, and so on. Other policies will govern which holidays are observed by the firm, how much sick leave you can take, when you are expected to arrive at work, and what serves as grounds for the employer to terminate your employment.

Employment policies vary from firm to firm. A leading concern of paralegals (and employees generally) is how much they will be paid, how they will be paid (whether they receive salaries or hourly wages), and what job benefits they will receive. These issues were discussed in Chapter 2, so we will not examine them here. Rather, we look at some other areas of concern to paralegals, including performance evaluations and termination procedures.

Performance Evaluations

Most law firms conduct periodic evaluations to give feedback on performance and to determine if employees will receive raises. Usually, performance is evaluated annually, but some firms conduct evaluations every six months, and some conduct them more often for new employees.

Know What Is Expected of You

Because paralegal responsibilities vary from firm to firm, no one evaluation checklist applies to every paralegal. Some of the factors that may be considered during a performance evaluation are indicated in Exhibit 3.2. Note, though, that performance evaluations may be much longer and more detailed than the list in the exhibit. For example, items in that list may have several subheadings. Normally, under each item is a series of options—ranging from "excellent" to "unsatisfactory" or something similar—for the supervisor or attorney to check. Often, written explanations for the rankings are given, especially to explain areas of weak performance.

When you begin work as a paralegal, you should learn at the outset exactly what your duties will be and what performance is expected of you. This way, you will be able to prepare for your first evaluation from the moment you begin working. You will not have to wait months before you learn that you were supposed to be doing something different.

---

1. RESPONSIBILITY
Making sure that all tasks are performed on time and following up on all pending matters.

2. EFFICIENCY
Obtaining good results in the least amount of time possible.

3. PRODUCTIVITY
Producing a sufficient quantity of work in a given time period.

4. COMPETENCE
Knowledge level and skills.

5. INITIATIVE
Taking responsibility for tasks, and making appropriate recommendations.

6. COOPERATION
Getting along well with others on the legal team.

7. PERSONAL FACTORS
Appearance, grooming habits, friendliness, and poise.

8. DEPENDABILITY
Arriving at work consistently on time, and being available when needed.

EXHIBIT 3.2

Factors That May Be Considered in a Performance Evaluation

Be Ready

Prepare for evaluations, and conduct yourself professionally at all times. Be your own advocate, but stay positive. Keep track of your accomplishments, such as the number of billable hours per week or month that you generate, so that you can point them out to your supervisor. If you were part of a team that worked many extra hours to win a big case for the firm, mention it during the evaluation. Make your supervisor aware of ways in which you save the firm money or contribute to the firm's success. If you master a new software program or pass the CP or PACE exam, tell your supervisor.

Get the Most from Your Performance Evaluation

Both paralegals and their employers can benefit from the discussions that take place during a performance evaluation. In the busy workplace, you may not have much time to talk with your supervisor about issues that do not relate to immediate work needs. Even if you do find a moment, you may feel awkward bringing up the topic of your performance or discussing a workplace problem. Performance evaluations are designed to allow both sides to exchange views on such matters.

During reviews, you will learn how the firm rates your performance. You can gain valuable feedback from your supervisor, learn more about your strengths and weaknesses, and identify the areas in which you need to improve your skills. Do not react negatively to criticisms of your work or conduct. Even during a performance review you are being evaluated. Keeping a positive outlook and showing that you appreciate constructive criticism will impress your supervisor. Discuss how you can make improvements that will enhance your value to the firm.

You can also use the evaluation to give your supervisor feedback on the workplace. This is especially useful if you believe you are capable of handling more complex tasks than you are being assigned. Attorneys sometimes underutilize paralegals because they do not know their capabilities. If you suggest ways in which your knowledge could be put to better use, you may earn more challenging and rewarding responsibilities. Also, if you and your supervising attorney never seem to have the time to meet face-to-face for an evaluation, consider writing up your own evaluation and presenting it to him or her for review.

The #MeToo era has raised sensitivity in many firms to issues of workplace harassment and discrimination. (#MeToo refers to a movement against sexual harassment and sexual assault. The phrase "Me Too" was initially used in this context on social media by a sexual harassment survivor and activist.) If you experience workplace harassment or discrimination, consult an appropriate supervisor as soon as possible. The firm should have guidelines explaining the appropriate channels for getting help posted in a breakroom or other common work area. If you work in a sole-practitioner office and the harasser is the sole practitioner, the local bar association or the federal Equal Employment Opportunity Commission (or equivalent state agency) may be able to help.

Employment Termination

Policy manuals almost always deal with the subject of employment termination. A policy handbook will likely specify what kind of conduct can serve as a basis for firing employees. For example, the manual might specify that if an employee is absent more than twelve days a year for two consecutive years, the employer has grounds to terminate the employment relationship. Be aware that most such lists are non exclusive—that is, the things listed are not the only reasons an employee can be terminated.

The manual will also probably describe termination procedures. For instance, the firm might require that it be notified one month in advance if an employee decides to leave the firm; if the employee fails to give such notice, he or she may lose accumulated vacation time or other benefits on termination. Leaving without notice will also make it harder to get a positive recommendation from the firm when you seek another position. Do not burn your bridges with an employer.

If you are considering moving to another firm, be sure to examine your employment agreement and employee handbook to determine if you are subject to a non compete agreement that restricts your ability to go to work for a competitor of your current firm. State laws on the validity of such agreements vary widely, so consulting an attorney specializing in employment law about any such clause will likely be necessary.

In the event that you believe you have been subject to discriminatory treatment in employment and were improperly dismissed, there may be a cause of action (see Chapter 18). In this situation, you will likely need to consult an attorney who specializes in employment law.

Filing Procedures

Every law firm has some kind of established filing procedures for office work. Efficient procedures are vital because the paperwork generated is substantial. Legal documents must be safeguarded yet be readily retrievable when needed. The need to protect client information is stressed in the *Developing Paralegal Skills* feature below. If a client file is misplaced or lost, the client may suffer costly harm.

Additionally, documents must be filed in such a way as to protect client confidentiality. The duty of confidentiality is discussed in Chapter 4 but is mentioned here because of the extent to which it frames all legal work and procedures. This is

DEVELOPING PARALEGAL SKILLS

CONFIDENTIALITY AND CLIENT INFORMATION

One of the most important professional obligations of a paralegal is to treat all of your clients' information as confidential. The obligation to treat information as confidential has been long recognized by the common law, and some jurisdictions even provide criminal sanctions for professionals who violate this duty.

As a general rule, never share *any* information about your clients—even the fact that they are clients—with anyone outside your firm. Don't share "war stories" from work with friends or relatives if doing so could reveal information about the client. Never leave *any* information about your clients where others might see it. In particular, be extremely careful about storing confidential information on your mobile devices.

To protect client confidentiality, you should:

- Keep all identifiable information about clients off the cover of files.
- Never leave a file unattended for even a short time in a publicly accessible location such as on a library table or in a courtroom.

- Make sure all client files are removed from internal workspaces where outsiders might be present, such as conference rooms.
- Do not allow outsiders access to computer systems or networks.
- Use only secure networks or encrypted communications systems for transmission of confidential information. Most wireless networks in airports or Internet cafés are *not* secure.
- Password protect all electronic devices on which confidential matters are stored, such as smartphones that receive e-mails.
- Secure your computer when you leave your desk.

The obligation to maintain confidentiality continues even after a file is closed. Your firm should have document-retention policies that detail how long closed files are kept and how they are to be destroyed. Be sure to follow your firm's policies carefully. Guides to such policies are available at **americanbar.org**; search "records retention" for a useful discussion.

particularly true of filing procedures. All information received from or about clients, including files and documents, is considered confidential. A breach of confidentiality by a paralegal or other employee can cause the law firm to incur liability as well as damage to its reputation.

If you work for a small firm, filing procedures may be informal, and you may need to assume the responsibility for organizing and developing an efficient and secure filing system. Larger firms normally have specific procedures concerning the creation, maintenance, use, and storage of office files. If you take a job with a large firm, a supervisor will probably train you in office procedures, including filing. Although the trend today, particularly in larger firms, is increasing computerization of filing systems, many firms create "hard copies" to ensure that files are not lost if computer systems crash.

Generally, law offices maintain several types of files. Typically, a law firm's filing system will include client files, work product files and reference materials, and forms files.

Client Files

To illustrate client-filing procedures, we present below the phases in the "life cycle" of a hypothetical client's file. The name of the client is Katherine Baranski. She has just retained (hired) one of your firm's attorneys to represent her in a lawsuit that she wants to bring against Tony Peretto. Because Baranski is initiating the lawsuit, she is referred to as the *plaintiff*. Peretto, because he has to defend against Baranski's claims, is the *defendant*. The name of the case is *Baranski v. Peretto*. Assume that you will be working on the case and that your supervising attorney, who has agreed to represent Baranski, has just asked you to open a new case file. (As the *Ethics Watch* feature below reminds us, backing up files is critical in law firms.) Assume that you have already verified, through a "conflicts check" (see Chapter 4), that no conflict of interest exists.

ETHICS WATCH

BACK UP YOUR WORK

When using computers regularly, we easily forget that a power failure or other problem can occur at any time. Should this happen, current work that has not been saved can be lost. Protect yourself and your firm by having backup copies of all your work, and have a contingency plan, such as a second computer available to use. File backup can be done both in the office on external hard drives and off-site through a service that automatically keeps your files secure should a catastrophe, such as a fire, destroy the office. Many automatic backup systems and cloud-based services are secure.

Backing up your work frequently is important and can "save the day" if the computer system crashes. Backups are also critical to protecting the firm from ransomware attacks, in which malicious hackers insert software onto a network that locks the owner out until a hefty monetary ransom is paid. If you routinely back up documents, you may save yourself valuable time that

could be required to recreate a document or file. You will also save yourself and the firm from the problem of deciding who pays—the client or the law firm—for the extra time spent recreating work. Moreover, with backups available, your employer will never be without a crucial document when needed. If your office computer system is connected to a server system, you will have online backup.

This practice is consistent with the NFPA *Model Code of Ethics and Professional Responsibility,* which we will discuss in Chapter 4. Section 1.3 of the code states: "A paralegal shall maintain a high standard of professional conduct." Section 1.5 states: "A paralegal shall preserve all confidential information provided by the client or acquired from other sources before, during, and after the course of the professional relationship." Be sure to learn and follow your firm's backup policy.

Opening a New Client File

The first step that you will take in opening a new file is to assign the case a file number. (A secretary may perform this step in some firms, depending on the proper procedure.) For reasons of efficiency and confidentiality, many firms identify their client files by numbers or some kind of numerical and/or alphabetical sequence instead of the clients' names. That is, the *Baranski v. Peretto* case file might be identified by the letters BAPE—the first two letters of the plaintiff's name followed by the first two letters of the defendant's name.

Most law firms use computerized databases to record and track case titles and files. Firms use file labels containing bar codes that contain attorney codes, subject-matter codes, the client's name and file number, and so forth. The databases are also used for contract and billing information.

Typically, law firms maintain a master client list on which clients' names are entered alphabetically and cross-referenced to the clients' case numbers. If file numbers consist of numerical sequences, there is also a master list on which the file numbers are listed in numerical order and cross-referenced to the clients' names.

Adding Subfiles

As work on the *Baranski* case progresses and more documents are generated or received, the file will expand. To ensure that documents will be easy to locate, you create subfiles. One subfile might be created for client documents (such as a contract, will, stock certificate, or photograph) that the firm needs for reference or for evidence at trial. As correspondence relating to the *Baranski* case is generated, you probably add a correspondence subfile. You will also want a subfile for your or the attorney's notes on the case, including research results.

As we will explore in Chapters 10 through 12, litigation involves several stages. As the *Baranski* litigation progresses through these stages, subfiles for documents relating to each stage will be added to the *Baranski* file. Many firms find it useful to color-code or add tabs to subfiles so that they can be readily identified. Often, in large files, an index of each subfile's contents is created and attached to the inside cover of the subfile.

Documents are typically filed within each subfile in reverse chronological order, with the most recently dated document on the top. Usually, to safeguard the documents, they are punched at the top with a two-hole puncher so they can be secured within the file with a clip. Note, though, that an original client document should not be punched or altered in any way. It should always be left loose within the file (or paper-clipped to a copy of the document that *is* punched and secured in the file). For example, if you were holding in the file a property deed belonging to a client, you would not want to alter that document in any way.

File Use and Storage

Often, files are stored in a file room or other specific area. Most firms have a procedure for employees to follow when removing files from the storage area. The office staff may be required to replace a removed file with an "out card" indicating the date, the name of the file, and the name or initials of the person who removed it.

Note that documents should not be removed from a client file or subfile. Rather, the entire file or subfile should be removed for use. This ensures that important documents will not be separated from the file and possibly mislaid, misfiled, or lost. Many paralegals make copies of documents in the file for their use. For example, if you are working on the *Baranski* case and need to review certain documents in the file, you might remove them from the file temporarily, copy them, and immediately return the original documents and the file to storage.

Increasingly, firms scan documents into computer files, but certain original paper documents must be retained for clients and to satisfy state law. To improve security of documents stored on computers and at on-site and off-site locations, a secure password policy is important. Complex passwords that are changed monthly are critical to help reduce hacker access to files. Large firms often have IT specialists, but in smaller firms, you can take a leadership role in helping to develop computer-security policies.

Files and the Cloud

An important information technology trend is cloud-based computing. That means files and programs are stored online and so are accessible from any computer, smartphone, or tablet connected to the Internet. Law firms are cautious about giving up physical control of confidential information, because they worry about protecting clients' rights to the attorney-client privilege. Be sure to clear any use of cloud storage on your personal devices such as smartphones, tablets, and laptops with your firm. Do not put business information in your iCloud-connected Apple device or on a cloud storage site such as Dropbox without discussing it with your firm.

Even the fact that your firm is representing a client may be something the client wants kept confidential. Storing something as simple as contact information in a mobile phone cloud app could result in revealing the fact of a relationship with the law firm. Be particularly cautious about leaving your portable devices logged on to cloud apps while using public wireless networks or in public places where electronic eavesdropping may occur. In general, be cautious about using personal equipment such as smartphones to conduct firm business. Be sure to know if your firm or supervising attorney has a policy about such equipment use.

Closing a File

Assume that the *Baranski* case has been settled out of court and that no further legal work on Baranski's behalf needs to be done. For a time, her file will be retained in the inactive files, but when it is fairly certain that no one will need to refer to it very often, if ever, it will be closed. Closed files are often stored in a separate area of the building or even off-site. Traditionally, many larger law firms stored the contents of old files on microfilm. Today, firms can use scanning technology to scan file contents for storage on hard drives at the firm and on secure off-site servers.

Procedures for closing files vary from firm to firm. Typically, when a case is closed, original documents provided by the client (for example, a deed to property) are returned to the client. Other materials, such as extra copies of documents or cover letters, are destroyed.

Destroying Old Files

Law firms do not have to retain client files forever, and at some point, the *Baranski* case file will be destroyed. Old files are normally destroyed by shredding so that confidentiality is ensured. Because shredded files can be pieced back together, and old computer and copier machine hard drives can be accessed, many firms hire companies that have equipment guaranteed to destroy such materials so that recovery is impossible. The National Association for Information Destruction (NAID) certifies firms that properly destroy files and hard drives. Law firms use great care when destroying client files because a court or government agency may impose a heavy fine on a law firm that destroys a file that should have been retained for a longer time. How long a particular file must be retained depends on many factors, including the nature of the client's legal matters and the governing statutes, such as the statute of limitations.

A statute of limitations limits the time period during which specific types of legal actions may be brought to court. Statutes of limitations for legal-malpractice actions vary from state to state—from six months to ten years after the attorney's last contact with the client. How long the statute of limitations runs in your state is an important factor in determining how long to retain a client file, because an attorney or law firm will need the information contained in the client's file to defend against a malpractice action. If the file has been destroyed, the firm will not be able to produce any documents or other evidence to refute the plaintiff's claim.

statute of limitations
A statute setting the maximum time period within which certain actions can be brought to court or rights enforced. After the period of time has run, no legal action can be brought.

Document Retention Policies

Your firm will have a document retention policy, and you should become familiar with it. Such policies set standards on retaining documents related to particular matters. Importantly, the policies include the retention of e-mails. Learn how your firm archives e-mails and what your responsibilities are with respect to maintaining those archives. In many cases, e-mails sent through the firm's computer systems (including smartphones provided by your firm) may be archived even if you delete them.

Not only must you be careful to comply with your firm's policies on retaining e-mails but any inappropriate use of a work-related e-mail account or device may leave evidence on servers or in archives. The law is clear that employers have the right to restrict use of company property, such as computers and smartphones given to employees, and can search e-mail files and other transmissions from company property.

Guidelines for e-mail professionalism are discussed in this chapter's *Office Tech and Cybersecurity* feature on the following pages.

Work Product Files and Reference Materials

Many law firms keep copies of research projects, legal memoranda, and various case-related documents prepared by the firm's attorneys and paralegals so that these documents can be referred to in future projects. That way, legal personnel do not have to start all over again when working on a claim similar to one dealt with in the past.

Traditionally, hard copies of work product files, or legal-information files, were filed in the firm's law library with other reference materials and publications. Today, work product documents and research materials are often generated on computers and stored on hard drives or networked data-storage devices. Often, in large firms, these materials are kept in a central data bank that is accessible by firm personnel.

Forms Files

Every law firm keeps on hand various forms that it commonly uses. These forms are usually stored in a forms file. A forms file might include forms for retainer agreements (to be discussed shortly), for filing lawsuits in specific courts, for bankruptcy petitions, for real estate matters, and for many other types of legal matters. Often, to save time, copies of documents relating to specific types of cases are kept for future reference. Then, when the attorney or paralegal works on a similar case, those documents can serve as models, or guides. As noted, these forms may also be kept in a work product file.

Forms files are almost always computerized. Computerized forms have simplified legal practice by allowing legal personnel to generate customized documents within minutes. Forms for many standard legal transactions are available from legal-software companies, as discussed in Chapter 8.

forms file
A reference file containing copies of the firm's commonly used legal documents and informational forms. The documents in the forms file serve as models for drafting new documents.

OFFICE TECH AND CYBERSECURITY

PROPER AND EFFECTIVE E-MAIL COMMUNICATIONS

E-mails have largely replaced the printed interoffice memos of the past as well as many letters. While convenience makes e-mail a powerful tool, the office environment demands different standards than most of us use in personal communications with family and friends.

E-mail's popularity relies on the fact that it is the perfect "one to many" communication tool. When you have the same message going to multiple recipients, it makes sense to use e-mail. However, e-mail messages can easily be misinterpreted because written communication has fewer social cues than other forms of communication and because of the high volume of e-mail messages we send and receive daily. The onus is on you, the author, to apply professional standards and to use proper formatting for all of your e-mail messages to prevent miscommunication.

Apply Professional Standards to E-Mail Communications

E-mail is *written communication.* In fact, next to letters, e-mail is the most formal way to communicate in writing. Nevertheless, when we use e-mail, we often adopt a casual, conversational tone and ignore grammatical rules of writing, such as sentence structure, spelling, and capitalization. Work e-mails should reflect the same professional tone and quality that you use in the firm's paper correspondence.

When you send an e-mail message to someone (especially a client), you need to use clear and effective language. Generally, you will want to include a call to action at the end. A call to action answers the question: What do you want the recipient to do as a result of reading your message? Including a call to action in an e-mail message increases the chance that the message will serve its purpose.

Your work e-mails, as mentioned, should also follow professional standards. Applying professional standards includes ensuring that you send an error-free message with correct formatting and that you follow proper etiquette. Typos, misspellings, and other errors detract from the message and reflect poorly on the professionalism of the firm. Some mistakes can be avoided by using a spelling and grammar checker. Make sure to proofread e-mails carefully, though, because these programs do not catch all errors. Sometimes, it helps to print a draft of an e-mail, let it sit for a while, and review the text from a fresh perspective or ask a colleague to review it. In addition, if you are sending the e-mail message to many recipients, you may ask a co-worker to review the message before you send it to ensure that there are no obvious mistakes.

Law Firms and Financial Procedures

In the business of law, the products are legal services that are sold to clients. A major concern of any law firm is to have a clear policy on fee arrangements and efficient procedures to ensure that each client is billed appropriately for the time and costs associated with serving that client. Efficient billing procedures require that attorneys and paralegals keep accurate records of the time they spend working on a given client's case or other legal matter.

Wide Range of Law Practices

Law firms differ in their fee structures. At the top are the elite law firms in the biggest cities such as New York and San Francisco. These firms focus primarily on complicated business transactions, international deals, and tax matters. The next tier consists of firms that dominate regional markets, such as in Cleveland or San Diego. These firms often work with large companies but are more likely to specialize, such as in insurance defense. There are also boutique firms handling specialized areas such as patents for high-end clients, as well as the many smaller firms serving smaller clients.

As Exhibit 3.3 illustrates, lawyers in larger firms have higher average incomes than solo practitioners. Similarly, those who practice in certain areas, such as medical malpractice, have higher average incomes than lawyers in areas such as family law. Female attorneys also report incomes about one-third lower than those earned by male attorneys.

Make sure that you use the same form as you would in a business letter. That is, your e-mail should include a salutation, a greeting, and your signature. You may also want to add your e-mail address below your name in the closing and the word *confidential* at the top (when appropriate). Many law firms have standard signature blocks that note that e-mails are confidential. Do not use quotes or pictures in your signature block. Those belong in personal e-mails, not in work e-mails.

Formatting E-Mail Messages

Because an e-mail message may look different on the recipient's device than it does on your screen, keep formatting simple. Use short sentences and short paragraphs, whenever possible. Bulleted or numbered lists can also break up your message and make it easier to read. Use double spacing between paragraphs rather than indenting with tabs, and do not underline or boldface text. Be particularly careful about how you identify the subject of the e-mail. For example, you could write, "Documents ready for signature" rather than "Bankruptcy petition ready to sign."

Send attachments as PDF files rather than Word files or files using other formats. That way, virtually any recipient will be able to open the attachment. Sending a PDF file also prevents a recipient from changing the content of the document.

Technology Tip

One advantage of e-mail is its permanence. If you need a written record of a conversation, e-mail is a better choice than face-to-face or telephone communication. Print a copy of each e-mail message to retain in the client's file so that a record exists. Be sure that any e-mail discloses your status as a paralegal (to avoid claims about the unauthorized practice of law).

Ask recipients to verify that important messages have been received, such as when you notify a person of a court date. If your e-mail system has this feature, request a "return receipt" to confirm that the message you sent was received. Respond to incoming e-mail promptly, within twenty-four hours, so the sender knows that you have received the e-mail.

Finally, make sure that you know the policies of your firm regarding confidential e-mail, particularly e-mail sent from your personal mobile devices. Used carefully, e-mail is an efficient way to fulfill your duties and communicate with clients. Used improperly, it can cause serious trouble.

Etiquette Issues

As stated earlier, one of the challenges of e-mail messages is giving each message the attention it deserves because of the high volume of messages we receive daily. Therefore, make sure you send e-mail messages only to recipients who need the information, carefully monitoring the cc: field. It is frustrating for employees to receive e-mail messages that do not concern them, or messages that they need to decipher to figure out how it pertains to them. Similarly, make sure you hit "reply" rather than "reply-all" to an e-mail message that is intended only for the recipient. Often, hitting "reply-all" is unnecessary and serves only to fill people's inboxes.

EXHIBIT 3.3

Legal Compensation Averages

Source: Data from: Martindale-Avvo, 2019 Attorney Compensation Report.

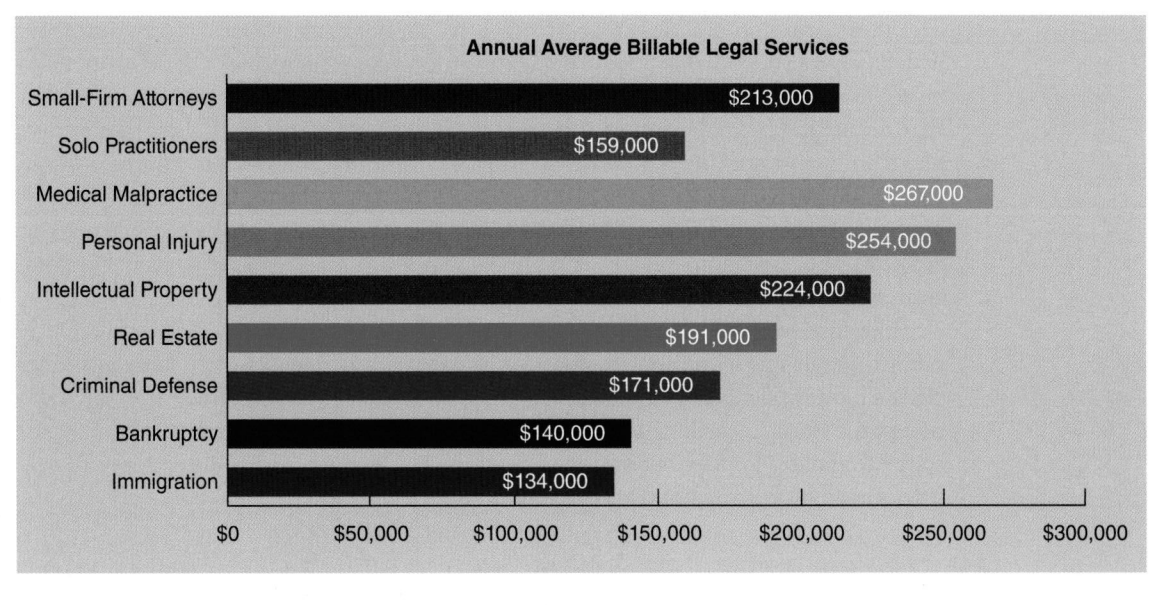

Annual Average Billable Legal Services

Small-Firm Attorneys	$213,000
Solo Practitioners	$159,000
Medical Malpractice	$267,000
Personal Injury	$254,000
Intellectual Property	$224,000
Real Estate	$191,000
Criminal Defense	$171,000
Bankruptcy	$140,000
Immigration	$134,000

Fee Arrangements

A major ethical concern of the legal profession has to do with the reasonableness of attorneys' fees and the ways in which clients are billed for legal services. State ethics codes governing attorneys require legal fees to be reasonable. The American Bar Association's *Model Rules of Professional Conduct* (to be discussed in Chapter 4) holds that the fees charged by lawyers must be reasonable. The rule then lists the factors that should be considered in determining the reasonableness of a fee. The factors include the time and labor required to perform the legal work, the fee customarily charged in the locality for similar legal services, and the experience and ability of the lawyer performing the services.

Normally, fee arrangements are discussed and agreed on at the outset of any attorney-client relationship. Most law firms require each client to agree to a fee arrangement in a signed writing called a **retainer agreement**, and some states require that fee arrangements be stated in writing. The agreement specifies that the client is retaining (hiring) the attorney and/or firm to represent the client in a legal matter and that the client agrees to the fee arrangements set forth in the agreement. Exhibit 3.4 shows a sample retainer agreement.

There are three main types of fee arrangements: fixed fees, hourly fees, and contingency fees. We examine next each of these types of fees, as well as some alternative fee arrangements. In addition, although the general American rule is that parties bear the costs of their own lawyers, some legal claims entitle the winning plaintiff to require the defendant to pay a reasonable attorney's fee to the plaintiff's lawyer. For example, many states provide for a losing defendant in a contracts case to pay the plaintiff's attorney's fees and costs. To collect under such statutes requires that the lawyer be able to document his or her time and expenses and that a court approve them as reasonable. (In the United Kingdom, the general rule is the loser pays the winner's legal fees. As a result, British plaintiffs think hard before suing, as they might have to pay the defendants' legal bills.)

Fixed Fees

The client may agree to pay a **fixed fee** for a specified legal service. Certain procedures, such as incorporation and simple divorce filings, are often handled on a fixed-fee basis because the attorney can reasonably estimate how much time will be involved in completing the work. Charging fixed fees is increasingly popular with clients who like knowing how much a matter will cost in advance.

Hourly Fees

The most common practice of law firms is to charge by the hour. Hourly rates vary widely from firm to firm. Some litigation firms charge high rates ($700 an hour or more) for services of senior partners because of their reputation for high-quality work that results in favorable settlements or court judgments for their clients. In contrast, an attorney just starting a practice as a sole practitioner will have to charge a lower, more competitive rate (perhaps $100 per hour) to attract clients. Experienced lawyers may charge more, but the total bill may be less because the experienced partner can deal with the issue more quickly. It is always important for clients to consider the total cost of the legal services, not just the hourly rate.

Law firms also bill clients for hourly rates for paralegal services. Because the hourly rate for paralegals is lower than that for attorneys, attorneys' use of paralegals saves clients money. Generally, the billing rate for paralegals depends on the size and location of the firm. According to various compensation surveys, billing rates for paralegals begin at about $60 per hour and may reach $245 per hour. Most billing for paralegal services ranges between $90 and $135 per hour.

retainer agreement
A signed document stating that the attorney or the law firm has been hired by the client to provide certain legal services and that the client agrees to pay for those services.

fixed fee
A fee paid to the attorney by his or her client for having provided a specified legal service, such as the creation of a simple will.

EXHIBIT 3.4
A Sample Retainer Agreement

RETAINER AGREEMENT

I, Katherine Baranski, agree to employ Allen P. Gilmore and his law firm, Jeffers, Gilmore & Dunn, as my attorneys to prosecute all claims for damages against Tony Peretto and all other persons or entities that may be liable on account of an automobile accident that caused me to sustain serious injuries. The accident occurred on August 4, 2016, at 7:45 A.M., when Tony Peretto ran a stop sign on Thirty-eighth Street at Mattis Avenue and, as a result, his car collided with mine.

I agree to pay my lawyers a fee that will be one-third (33 percent) of any sum recovered in this case, regardless of whether the sum is received through settlement, lawsuit, arbitration, or any other way. The fee will be calculated on the sum recovered, after costs and expenses have been deducted. The fee will be paid when any money is actually received in this case. I agree that Allen P. Gilmore and his law firm have an express attorney's lien on any recovery to ensure that their fee is paid.

I agree to pay all necessary costs and expenses, such as court filing fees, court reporter fees, expert witness fees and expenses, travel expenses, long-distance telephone and facsimile costs, and photocopying charges. I understand that these costs and expenses will be billed to me by my attorney on a monthly basis and that I am responsible for paying these costs and expenses, even if no recovery is received.

I agree that this agreement does not cover matters other than those described above. This agreement does not cover an appeal from any judgment entered, any efforts necessary to collect money due because of a judgment entered by a court, or any efforts necessary to obtain other benefits, such as insurance.

I agree to pay a carrying charge amounting to the greater of five dollars ($5.00) or four percent (4%) per month on the average daily balance of bills on my account that are thirty (30) days overdue. If my account is outstanding by more than sixty (60) days, all work by the attorney shall cease until the account is paid in full or a monthly payment plan is agreed on.

This contract is governed by the law of the state of Nita.

I AGREE TO THE TERMS AND CONDITIONS STATED ABOVE:

Date: 2 / 4 / 2022

Katherine Baranski
Katherine Baranski

I agree to represent Katherine Baranski in the matter described above. I will receive no fee unless a recovery is obtained. If a recovery is obtained, I will receive a fee as described above.

I agree to notify Katherine Baranski of all developments in this matter promptly, and I will make no settlement of this matter without her consent.

I AGREE TO THE TERMS AND CONDITIONS STATED ABOVE:

Date: 2 / 4 / 2022

Allen P. Gilmore
Allen P. Gilmore
Jeffers, Gilmore & Dunn
553 Fifth Avenue
Suite 101
Nita City, NI 48801

Note that although your services might be billed to the client at a certain hourly rate—say, $100—the firm will not pay you $100 an hour in wages. The billable rate for paralegal services, as for attorney services, takes into account the firm's expenses for overhead (rent, utilities, employee benefits, supplies, and other expenses).

Contingency Fees

contingency fee
A legal fee that consists of a specified percentage (such as 30 percent) of the amount the plaintiff recovers in a civil lawsuit. The fee is paid only if the plaintiff wins the lawsuit (recovers damages).

A common practice among litigation attorneys, especially those representing plaintiffs in certain types of cases (such as personal-injury or negligence cases) is to charge the client on a contingency-fee basis. A **contingency fee** is contingent (dependent) on the outcome of the case. If the plaintiff wins the lawsuit and recovers damages or settles out of court, the attorney is entitled to a percentage of the amount recovered (refer to Exhibit 3.4 for an example of a contingency-fee retainer agreement). If the plaintiff loses the lawsuit, the attorney gets nothing for the work and time invested in the case—although the client normally reimburses the attorney for the costs and expenses involved in preparing for trial (costs and expenses are discussed below, in regard to billing procedures). Contingency fees make legal services available to people who cannot afford to pay legal fees up front.

Fixed Percentage. Often, an attorney's contingency fee is one-fourth to one-third of the amount recovered. The agreement may provide for modification of the amount depending on how and when the dispute is settled. For example, an agreement that provides for a contingency fee of 33 percent of the amount recovered for a plaintiff may state that the amount will be reduced to a lower percentage if the case is settled out of court.

Limits on Fees. The law restricts the use of contingency-fee agreements to certain types of cases. An attorney can request a contingency fee only in civil matters, not in criminal cases. In a civil case, the plaintiff is often seeking monetary damages from the defendant to compensate the plaintiff for injuries suffered. In criminal cases, as you will read in Chapter 13, the government is seeking to punish the defendant for a wrongful act committed against society as a whole. If the defendant is found not guilty of the charges, he will not receive monetary damages that the attorney could share.

Attorneys are typically prohibited by state law from entering into contingency-fee agreements in divorce cases and probate cases (see Chapter 17) and in workers' compensation cases (see Chapter 18). States usually prohibit contingency fees in these cases because lawmakers have determined that allowing attorneys to share in the proceeds recovered would be contrary to public policy.

Client Trust Accounts

retainer
An advance payment made by a client to a law firm to cover part of the legal fees and/or costs that will be incurred on that client's behalf.

Law firms often require new clients to pay a **retainer**—an initial advance payment to the firm to cover part of the fee and costs that will be incurred on the client's behalf (such as travel expenses and the like). Some businesses keep an attorney on retainer by paying the attorney a fixed amount every month or year. The attorney handles all normal legal business that arises during that time. Retainer arrangements allow businesses to make legal costs more predictable over time.

trust account
A bank account in which one party (the trustee, such as an attorney) holds funds belonging to another person (such as a client); a bank account into which funds advanced to a law firm by a client are deposited. Also called an escrow account.

Funds received as retainers, as well as any funds received on behalf of a client (such as a payment to a client to settle a lawsuit), are placed in a special bank account. This account is usually referred to as a client **trust account** (or escrow account). The following *Developing Paralegal Skills* feature reviews the trust account procedure. It is extremely important that the funds held in a trust account be used *only* for expenses relating to the costs of serving that client's needs. Software programs designed for law offices simplify holding multiple accounts.

In many states, certain trust accounts come under the requirements of Interest on Lawyers' Trust Accounts (IOLTA) programs. All states have IOLTA programs, and most states' lawyers are required to participate. Client funds are deposited in an

DEVELOPING PARALEGAL SKILLS

CREATING A TRUST ACCOUNT

Louise Larson has been hired to work for Don Jones. Don is just starting his own solo practice of law after years of working with a medium-sized law firm in which he had nothing to do with the firm's financial management. Louise's first assignment is to establish a client trust accounting system.

Don and Louise review the ethical rules regarding client property and funds. These rules require that client funds not be commingled with the lawyer's funds. "It's too easy to 'borrow' from a client's funds when they are in the lawyer's own bank account," explains Don. "Therefore," he continues, "the first thing we need to do is open a checking account for client trust funds." Don and Louise then discuss what needs to be done in order to open the trust account and what other bookkeeping procedures will be involved in creating a client trust accounting system.

Checklist for Creating a Client Trust Account

- Obtain and prepare the necessary forms from the bank in which the account will be maintained.
- Devise a bookkeeping method for tracking all fees and expenses for a particular case and/or client.
- Retain all deposit slips and canceled checks.
- Keep a record of payments made to clients.
- Decide who will have access to the account.

IOLTA account when the amount is small or is to be held for a short time. In either case, the interest that could be earned for the client is less than the cost of maintaining a separate client account. The funds are instead placed in a single, pooled, interest-bearing trust account. Banks forward the interest earned on the account to the state IOLTA program, which uses the money to fund charitable causes, mostly to support legal assistance for the poor.

Misuse of client funds constitutes a major breach of the firm's duty to its client. An attorney's personal use of the funds, for example, can lead to disciplinary action and possible disbarment, as well as criminal penalties. *Commingling* (mixing together) a client's funds with the firm's funds also constitutes abuse and is one of the most common ways in which attorneys breach their professional obligations. If you handle a client's trust account, you should be especially careful to document your receipt and use of the funds to protect yourself and your firm against the serious problems that may arise if there are any problems with the account.

Billing and Timekeeping Procedures

As a general rule, a law firm bills its clients monthly. Each client's bill reflects the amount of time spent on the client's matter by the attorney or other legal personnel. Client billing serves an obvious financial function (collecting payment for services rendered). It also serves a communicative function (keeping the client informed of the work being done on a case), as discussed later in this chapter.

Client bills are usually prepared by a legal secretary or a bookkeeper or, in larger firms, by someone in the accounting department. The bills are based on the fee arrangements made with the client and the time slips collected from the firm's attorneys and paralegals. The time slips (discussed on the following page) indicate how many hours are to be charged to each client and at what hourly rate.

A paralegal keeps track of the time she spent in the law office library. Later, she will enter the information into her firm's computerized billing program. Why is accuracy in time tracking so important for both the paralegal and the law firm?

Billable Hours

The *legal fees* billed to clients are based on the number of billable hours generated for work requiring legal expertise. **Billable hours** are the hours or fractions of hours that attorneys and paralegals spend in client-related work that can be billed directly to clients. The *costs* billed to clients include expenses incurred on the client's behalf by the firm (such as court fees, travel expenses, express-delivery charges, and copying costs). If an attorney is retained on a contingency-fee basis, the client is not billed monthly for legal fees. The client is normally billed monthly for any costs incurred on the client's behalf.

billable hours
Hours or fractions of hours that attorneys and paralegals spend in work that requires legal expertise and that can be billed directly to clients.

Billing Programs

Typically, a preliminary draft of the client's bill is given to the attorney responsible for the client's account. After the attorney reviews and possibly modifies the bill, it is sent to the client. Exhibit 3.5 illustrates a sample client bill. Most law firms have computerized billing procedures and use time-and-billing software designed specifically for law offices. Time-and-billing software is based on traditional time-keeping and billing procedures. Familiarity with essential features of such programs, combined with knowledge of the basic principles and procedures involved in client billing, will help you understand whatever type of time-and-billing software your employer may use.

Documenting Time and Expenses

time slip
A record documenting, for billing purposes, the hours (or fractions of hours) that an attorney or a paralegal worked for each client, the date on which the work was done, and the type of work done.

Accurate timekeeping by attorneys and paralegals is crucial because clients cannot be billed for time spent on their behalf unless that time is documented. Traditionally, a **time slip** has been used to document time spent by attorneys and paralegals working for a client. Today, time slips are incorporated into timekeeping software programs. We look here at *Timeslips*, a commonly used time-and-billing software program created by Sage Software.

EXHIBIT 3.5

A Sample Client Bill

Jeffers, Gilmore & Dunn
553 Fifth Avenue
Suite 101
Nita City, NI 48801

BILLING DATE: February 28, 2022

Thomas Jones, M.D.
508 Oak Avenue
Nita City, NI 48801

RE: Medical-Malpractice Action Brought against Dr. Jones,
        File No. 15789

DATE	SERVICES RENDERED	PROVIDED BY	HOURS SPENT	TOTAL
1/30/22	Initial client consultation	APG (attorney)	1.00	$200.00
1/30/22	Client interview	EML (paralegal)	1.00	74.00
1/30/22	Document preparation	EML (paralegal)	1.00	74.00
2/5/22	Interview: Susanne Mathews (nurse)	EML (paralegal)	1.50	111.00
	TOTAL FOR LEGAL SERVICES			**$459.00**

DATE	EXPENSES			
2/5/22	Hospital charges for a copy of the medical documents			$75.00
	TOTAL FOR EXPENSES			$75.00
	TOTAL BILL TO CLIENT			**$534.00**

In the *Timeslips* entry form shown in Exhibit 3.6, the user enters his or her name, the task being billed for, the client for whom the work is being performed, the case referenced, and a description of the task. The user then either enters the time spent on the task or turns on an automated stopwatch timer—shown in Exhibit 3.7—to track the time spent on the task. Tasks can also be recorded as recurring, and rates can be adjusted according to any special agreements. Notice that in Exhibit 3.6 the time is noted to the minute. While we refer to "hourly billing," the time recorded in client bills should also be expressed in parts of hours, not rounded to whole hours.

Costs incurred on behalf of clients have traditionally been entered on an **expense slip**. Expenses are now usually entered into the billing program on a form similar to the *Timeslips* entry form shown in Exhibit 3.6. The form records a line-by-line description of each expense, along with the quantity and price of each item purchased on behalf of the client.

expense slip

A slip of paper on which any expense, or cost, that is incurred on behalf of a client (such as the payment of court fees or international telephone call charges) is recorded.

EXHIBIT 3.6

Timeslips Slip Entry

Source: Screen shots are reprinted with the permission of Sage Software, Inc. Timeslips is the registered trademark of Sage Software, Inc.

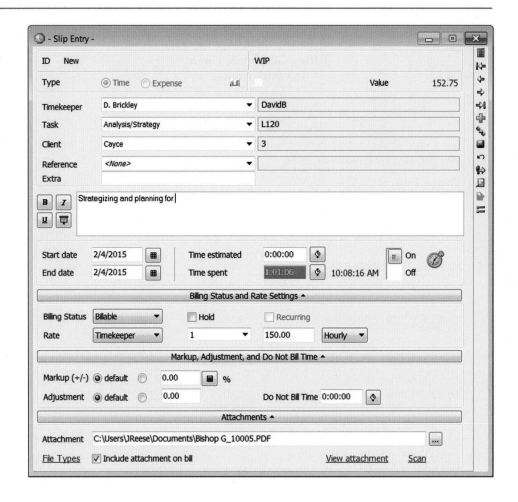

Billable versus Nonbillable Hours

The time recorded in timekeeping software is charged either to a client (billable hours) or to the firm (nonbillable hours). As mentioned, billable time generally includes the hours that attorneys and paralegals spend in client-related work that requires legal expertise. For example, the time you spend researching or investigating a client's claim is billable time. So is the time spent conferring with or about a client, drafting documents on behalf of a client, interviewing clients or witnesses, and traveling on a client's behalf, such as going to and from the courthouse to file documents.

Time spent on other tasks, such as administrative work, staff meetings, and performance reviews, is nonbillable time. For example, suppose that you spend thirty minutes photocopying forms for the forms file or a procedures manual for the office. That thirty minutes is not billable time. In *Timeslips*, the user designates whether the task being recorded is billable, as you can see in the "Billing status" box in Exhibit 3.6.

Law firms have a legitimate reason for wanting to maximize their billable hours: the financial well-being of a law firm depends to a great extent on how many billable hours are generated by its employees. Nonbillable time ultimately cuts into the firm's revenue used to pay salaries, rent, and other operating expenses. Therefore, the more billable hours generated by the firm's legal professionals, the more successful the firm will be.

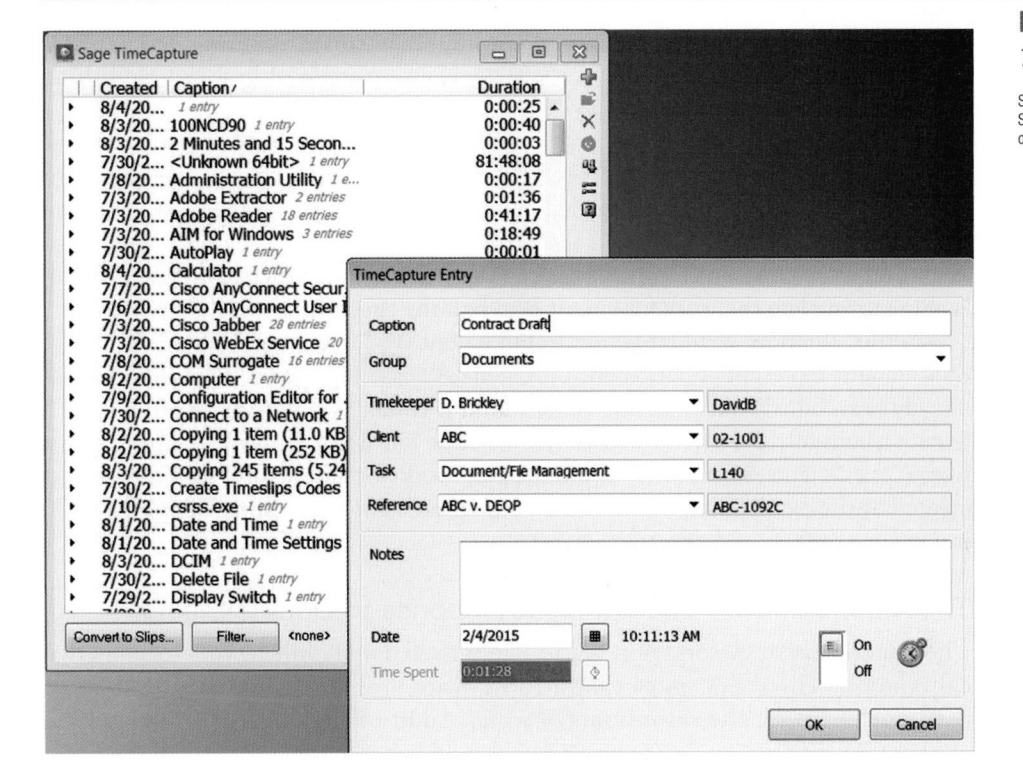

EXHIBIT 3.7

Timeslips TimeCapture

Source: Screen shots are reprinted with the permission of Sage Software, Inc. Timeslips is the registered trademark of Sage Software, Inc.

The Pressure to Generate Billable Hours

Attorneys and paralegals face pressure to produce billable hours for the firm. As a paralegal, you may be subject to this pressure and must learn how to handle it. Depending on the firm, a paralegal may be expected to generate between 800 and 2,000 billable hours per year. For example, suppose that your employer expects you to produce 1,800 billable hours per year. Discounting vacation time and holidays (assuming a two-week vacation and ten paid holidays), this equates to 37.5 hours per week. If you work 40 hours a week, you will have only 2.5 hours a week for such nonbillable activities as interoffice meetings, performance reviews, coffee breaks, reorganizing your work area, and chatting with others in the office.

Ethics and Client Billing Practices

Because attorneys have a duty to charge their clients "reasonable" fees, legal professionals must be careful in their billing practices. They must not "pad" their clients' bills by including more billable hours than actually worked on behalf of those clients. They also must avoid double billing—billing more than one client for the same time.

double billing
Billing more than one client for the same billable time period.

Double Billing

Sometimes, situations arise in which it is difficult to determine which client should be billed for a particular segment of time. For example, suppose that you are asked to travel to another city to interview a witness in a case for Client A. You spend three hours traveling in an airplane to get to that city. On the plane, you spend two hours summarizing a document relating to a case for Client B. Who should pay for those two hours, Client A, Client B, or both? In this situation, you could argue—as many attorneys do in similar circumstances—that you generated five billable hours, three on Client A's work, since travel time was required for Client A, and two on Client B's case. This is an example of how double billing can occur.

Double billing also occurs when a firm bills a new client for work that was done for a previous client. For example, suppose that an attorney is working on a case for Client B that is very similar to a case handled by the firm a year ago for Client A. The firm charged Client A $2,000 for the legal services. Because much of the research, writing, and other work done on Client A's case can transfer over to Client B's case, the firm is able to complete the work for Client B in half the time.

In this situation, would it be fair to bill Client B $2,000 also? After all, $1,000 of that amount represents hours spent on Client A's case (and for which Client A has already been billed). At the same time, would it be fair to Client A to bill Client B less for essentially the same services? Would it be fair not to allow the firm to profit from cost efficiencies generated by overlapping work? Could the firm split the savings created by the overlapping research ($1,000) with Client B by billing Client B $1,500 instead of $2,000?

The American Bar Association's Response to Double Billing

The American Bar Association (ABA) addressed double billing in a formal ethical opinion. The ABA states that attorneys are prohibited from charging more than one client for the same hours of work. Additionally, the ABA rejected the notion that the firm, and not the client, should benefit from cost efficiencies created by the firm's work for previous clients. "The lawyer who has agreed to bill solely on the basis of time spent is obliged to pass the benefit of these economies on to the client."

Although ABA opinions are not legally binding on attorneys unless they are adopted by the states as law, they carry significant weight in the legal community. Courts, for example, have tended to follow the ABA's position in resolving fee disputes. Typically, a court will not award attorneys' fees that it finds to be "excessive, redundant, or otherwise unnecessary." States will sanction or even disbar an attorney for double billing a client.

Communications and Social Media Tools

Excellent communication skills are a must for law firms to develop and retain clients, to function efficiently as a firm, and to help you develop as a paralegal. (See this chapter's *Featured Contributor* article on pages 78 and 79 for tips on effective communication.)

Traditional Communications

Sending monthly bills to clients helps keep attorney-client communication channels open, but billing may be inadequate to keep clients informed. The American Bar Association states that a part of professional conduct required of attorneys is to keep their clients reasonably informed about the status of legal matters. This means that attorneys, perhaps with the assistance of paralegals, should provide clients with adequate information so they understand the elements of legal matters being handled by the firm. The clients should also know about any legal proceedings that could come about as a result of a particular matter. Attorneys must also respond to inquiries from clients.

As a paralegal, you need to be aware that keeping clients reasonably informed about the progress being made on their cases goes beyond courtesy—it is a legal duty of attorneys. It also helps in building client loyalty to the firm. The meaning of "reasonably informed" varies depending on the client and on the nature of the work being done by the attorney. In some cases, a phone call every week or two will suffice to keep the client informed. In other cases, the attorney may ask the paralegal to draft a letter to a client explaining the status of the client's legal matter. Some firms send regular monthly mailings to update clients on the status of their cases. Generally, you should discuss with your supervising attorney how each client should be kept informed of the status of that client's case.

Copies of all letters and e-mails to a client should, of course, be placed in the client's file. The file should also contain a written record of each phone call made to or received from a client. That way, there is a "paper trail" in the event it is ever necessary to provide evidence of communication with the client. Indeed, this should be done for all phone calls relating to a client's matter. You will learn about the various forms of letters that attorneys send to clients in Chapter 9.

Communication by Social Media

The practice of law is an inherently collaborative environment. As a paralegal, you will be part of a team with your supervising attorney, other professionals, and clients. Social media tools help in facilitating collaboration. One of the most important uses of social media is for internal communication among employees. Some of the most constructive ways social media are being used in the legal environment include:

- Private client spaces created to keep clients up to date on case developments.

- An internal wiki where knowledge can be shared.

wiki
A Web page that can be added to and modified by anyone or by authorized users who share the site. The most famous example is Wikipedia.

- Collaborative spaces, secure behind firewalls, where a legal team can share documents.

- Internal community calendars to keep the legal team posted on where team members are and what they are doing, as well as progress on specific tasks.

- Firm-specific Twitter-like services for secure communication among members of the legal team.

- Firm Twitter feeds and other external social media that build the firm's digital shadow and help attract clients.

As a paralegal, you may be called on to play important roles in developing or implementing a social media strategy. This assignment can enable you to demonstrate your value to the firm.

Some firms have adopted social media strategies to bring in cases and build connections with clients. Showing familiarity with the latest developments in the law is a way for firms to demonstrate knowledge of various areas of the law. Social media contributors in law firms find that the discipline of regular blogging or posting on sites such as Twitter keeps their writing skills sharp and their knowledge up to date. Having a strategy is an important part of making a social media effort successful.

FEATURED CONTRIBUTOR

TIPS FOR EFFECTIVE COMMUNICATIONS

Robyn Ice

BIOGRAPHICAL NOTE

Robyn Ice, J.D., M.F.A., is a professor of practice and director of the General Legal Studies and Business and Leadership Programs at Tulane University's School of Professional Advancement. Before joining Tulane in 2014, Professor Ice practiced environmental and toxic tort law for more than twenty years in Atlanta and Manhattan, including twelve years as a Big Law partner. She also wrote and spoke widely on a variety of environmental topics, and developed and taught continuing legal education and litigation skills training programs. Professor Ice currently serves on the Approval Commission for the ABA's Standing Committee on Paralegals, is an active participant and regular presenter at AAfPE conferences, and has assisted in the development of the New Orleans Paralegal Association's Mentoring Program.

Professor Ice received her B.F.A. from West Virginia University, *magna cum laude;* M.F.A. from the University of Georgia; and J.D., *cum laude,* from Georgia State University College of Law*,* where she served as editor-in-chief of the *Georgia State University Law Review* and as research assistant to Professor David Maleski, with whom she authored two chapters of the treatise *Georgia Tort Law*.

Success in a legal career depends upon flawless oral and written communication skills, exhibited via a variety of live and technological channels. While simplifying our lives, phone and video options bring challenges. Thus, to help strengthen your oral communication skills and "maintain your professional image," both in the virtual world and in person, we offer the following tips.

1. **Prepare for phone or video conferences as thoroughly as if you were meeting in person.** Even before COVID-19 precautions introduced us to "social

> " **maintain your professional image. . ."**

distancing," many law firms and other businesses opted to conduct meetings and interviews via phone or video, rather than in person. While meeting remotely saves time and travel expenses, these electronic encounters can pose pitfalls for the unprepared or unwary. Knowing that a job interview or work meeting will occur in your own home may lead you to believe that the proceedings will be casual. Don't fall prey to this fallacy.

Every professional encounter, from the first interview through team meetings

Clear Policies

Establishing clear policies governing how the firm and its employees will use the Internet and social media tools is an important part of media strategy, just as with traditional communications. Any policy should be straightforward and concise. It should include "dos" as well as "don'ts" to encourage appropriate use of the tools. The policy should include specific instructions and examples so that those unfamiliar with social media can understand what is and is not permitted. Remember that client confidentiality is critically important in law firms, so any communication policy must address that issue.

with work colleagues, is an opportunity to shine—or not. Take steps to ensure a polished impression:

a. *Do your homework.* Review the agenda in advance and be prepared to discuss background materials. For interviews, re-read your résumé and dig into your research about the employer.

b. *Check your tech.* Download and practice on any software in advance. If possible, use your laptop, not your phone, for greater visibility and access to materials. Whatever the device, test the sound and camera in advance and make any necessary adjustments. Log in early to confirm a strong Internet connection and overcome any last-minute glitches.

c. *Mind your image.* Dress in a professional manner, sit up straight, make eye contact with the camera, and prepare to speak clearly and concisely.

2. **Observe video and phone conferencing etiquette.**

a. Find a space with good lighting, neutral décor and, if possible, a door to shut out noises or distractions.

b. Mute your microphone when entering the meeting and whenever you are not speaking.

c. Avoid speaking over others: listen and watch for verbal and physical cues indicating that speakers have finished.

d. Although multitasking seems efficient, undertaking a business conference while performing other tasks is distracting and wastes time.

e. Never, ever attempt to attend a virtual meeting while driving.

3. **Listen more than you speak: don't interrupt and don't filibuster or ramble.** Many current TV interviews devolve into shouting matches, with participants rudely interrupting and talking over one another. This chaos may be entertaining, but it has no place in a law office or courtroom. Even if you disagree with the speaker, courtesy and professionalism demand that you listen carefully and silently. Don't just wait for your turn: listen and comprehend the words, tone, and body language.

When the speaker finishes, state your position clearly and in complete sentences—then stop talking. Avoid the tendency to reword, restate, and ramble on. You need not fear or fill the silence that ensues while others consider what you have said.

4. **To be taken seriously, do not transform affirmative statements into questions.** Did you know that a spoken question typically ends with an upward inflection? Then you also know that a statement does not. Speaking in "question-nese" diminishes the power of your words.

5. **When highlighting a problem requiring action or correction, be prepared with a possible resolution.** In a law office, problems arise in a variety of contexts. Instead of complaining or asking what to do, prepare possible solutions before approaching your supervisor. Is a work-around available? Could another attorney cover the deposition? Can you reallocate work until a sick team member recovers? Even if your suggestions are not accepted, facing problems with a calm, analytical demeanor will strengthen your image as a legal professional.

> **" ensure a polished impression. . ."**

6. **Own your opinions**. Do not preface each affirmative statement with "I believe" or "I think." In legal documents, correspondence, or law office meetings, you should not make a statement unless you believe or have thought about it. Always cite properly to other sources, but if the words are yours, you need not equivocate.

7. **Maintain a professional tone when communicating via e-mail or text**. When writing to business colleagues via e-mail or text, use complete sentences and correct grammar, spelling, and punctuation. Avoid slang, emojis, and exclamation points. Proofread carefully and beware of autocorrect.

8. **Beware of reply-to-all.** Scary war stories abound. "Don't lose your job over a simple error."

9. **In meetings, put away your cell phone and silence your ringer**. Seriously.

Source: Robyn Ice.

Social media policies must comply with the law. The general counsel of the National Labor Relations Board (NLRB), the federal agency that oversees labor relations in private firms, issued a report addressing some of the restrictions imposed by law on social media policies. The report cautioned employers not to restrict employees from discussing wages or working conditions online, just as employers cannot restrict such discussions offline. However, employee comments that are not related to group efforts to address working conditions or wages may be restricted. Employers may restrict employees from pressuring others to "friend" or "like" them, since such behavior can sometimes stray into illegal discriminatory harassment.

Based on a review of lawsuits over social media policies, the book *Navigating Social Media Risks: Safeguarding Your Business* suggests that the key factors determining whether or not a policy is legal are:

- *WHEN* the social media post was done: During working hours or outside of work?

- *WHAT* the post discussed: Was it an effort to address working conditions, or was it about something unrelated? Was it an attempt to organize the employees or mere griping?

- *WHO* had access to the post? Co-workers or the public? Did co-workers respond (suggesting group action)?

Law Office Culture and Politics

As a paralegal, you will find that each law firm you work for is unique. Even though two firms may be the same size and may have similar organizational structures, they will have different cultures, or "personalities." The culture of a given legal workplace is ultimately determined by how the firm's owners (the partners, for example) define the goals of the firm.

Formality versus Reality

Each firm has an internal political structure that may have little to do with the lines of authority and accountability spelled out in the firm's employment manual or other policy statement. An up-and-coming young partner in the firm may, in reality, have more authority than one of the firm's senior partners near retirement. There may be rivalry among associate attorneys for promotion to partnership status, and you may be caught in the middle. In such cases, you may find yourself tempted to take sides, which could jeopardize your own future with the firm.

Unfortunately, paralegals have little way of knowing about the culture and politics of a given firm until they have worked for the firm awhile. Of course, if you know someone who works for the firm, you might gain some advance knowledge about its environment. Otherwise, when you start work, you will need to learn about interoffice politics. Listen carefully whenever a co-worker discusses the firm's staff. Ask questions to elicit information from co-workers about office politics and unwritten policies. This way, you can both prepare yourself to deal with these issues and protect your own interests. After you've worked for the firm for a time, you will be in a position to judge whether the company you have chosen is really the right firm for you.

Issues in Office Culture

Some of the things you should think about when investigating a law firm's culture include:

- Turnover—Because it is costly to train new employees, no firm wants to constantly replace staff. If a firm has high turnover, that may tell you that many employees are unsatisfied with the environment. Ask how long the average employee has been at the firm to get a sense of turnover.

- Competitive compensation—Are employees paid based on seniority, or are there rewards for exceptional performance?

- Special benefits—Does the firm offer more than the usual package of medical and retirement benefits? Is telecommuting or flextime possible? Are there provisions for emergency backup child care?

- Does the firm provide candid assessments of performance?

- How does the firm mentor new employees? Will you be assigned a mentor, or will you have to figure out on the job who can guide you?
- What is the firm's philosophy of management and its goals?
- What is the firm's vision and brand?
- What does it take to be successful at the firm?

You can ask about these issues in a job interview. You can also learn about many of them by looking at the firm's website, Twitter feed, or other online presence before your interview. Interviewers are often impressed by job applicants who have taken the time to research the firm before an interview, so be sure to learn as much as you can about the firm beforehand. Your career services office may be able to help with this, and legal directories are often good sources of information on law firms. Note also that a firm's culture does not remain constant. It changes over time as new employees are hired, older employees retire or move to new opportunities, and clients with different needs appear.

CHAPTER SUMMARY

THE INNER WORKINGS OF THE LAW OFFICE

The Organizational Structure of Law Firms

Law firms can be organized in the following ways:

1. *Sole proprietorship*—In a sole proprietorship, one attorney owns the business and is entitled to all the firm's profits. That individual also bears the burden of any losses and is personally liable for the firm's debts.

2. *Partnership*—In a partnership, two or more lawyers jointly own the firm and share in the firm's profits and losses. Attorneys who are employed by the firm but who are not partners (such as associates and staff attorneys) do not share in the profits and losses of the firm.

Generally, partners are subject to personal liability for all of the firm's debts or other obligations. In many states, firms can organize as *limited liability partnerships,* in which partners are not held personally liable for the malpractice of other partners in the firm.

3. *Professional corporation*—In a professional corporation (P.C.), two or more individuals jointly own the business as shareholders. The owner-shareholders of the corporation share the firm's profits and losses (as partners do) but are not personally liable for the firm's debts or obligations beyond the amount they invested in the P.C.

Law Office Management and Personnel

Each law firm has its own system of management and lines of authority. Generally, the owners of the firm (partners) oversee and manage the employees. Law firm personnel include associate attorneys; law clerks; paralegals; administrative personnel, who are supervised by the legal administrator or the office manager; and support personnel, including receptionists, secretaries, file clerks, and others.

Employment Policies

Employment policies relate to compensation and employee benefits, performance evaluations, employment termination, and other rules of the workplace, such as office hours. Frequently, especially in larger firms, the policies are spelled out in an employment manual or other writing. Paralegals must be sure to know their specific responsibilities. Most large firms have policies and procedures that apply to evaluation, promotion, and termination. The #MeToo era has raised sensitivity in many firms to issues of workplace harassment and discrimination. If you experience workplace harassment or discrimination, follow your firm's guidelines and consult an appropriate supervisor as soon as possible.

Filing Procedures

Every law firm follows certain filing procedures. In larger firms, these procedures may be written down. In smaller firms, procedures may be more casual and based on habit or tradition.

1. *Client files*—Confidentiality is a major concern and fundamental in every law firm. A breach of confidentiality by anyone in the law office can subject the firm to costly liability. The requirement of confidentiality shapes, to a significant extent, filing procedures. A typical law firm has client files, work product files and reference materials, forms files, and personnel files.

   Proper file maintenance is crucial to a smoothly functioning firm. An efficient filing system helps to ensure that important documents will not be misplaced and will be available when needed. Filing procedures must also maximize client confidentiality and the safekeeping of documents.

2. *Work product files*—Law firms often keep copies of all research materials, support materials related to cases, and legal memoranda. Maintenance of backup files is required.

3. *Forms files*—Firms often use standard forms files that may have been prepared internally or have been professionally prepared by a service.

Law Firms and Financial Procedures

A major concern of any law firm is to have a clear policy on fee arrangements and efficient billing procedures so that each client is billed appropriately.

1. *Wide range of law practices*—Top-level firms, which are generally full-service firms in major cities, usually have the highest billing rates, followed by major regional firms. Boutique firms and others fill the needs of different groups of clients.

2. *Fee arrangements*—Attorneys and clients may agree on fixed fees, hourly fees, or contingency fees. Clients who pay hourly fees are billed monthly for time spent by attorneys and other legal personnel on the clients' cases or projects, as well as other costs incurred on behalf of the clients.

3. *Client trust accounts*—Law firms are required to place all funds received from or for a client into a special account called a client trust account. This ensures that the client's money remains separate from the firm's money. The funds held in the trust account must be used only for expenses relating to the costs of serving the client's needs.

4. *Billing and timekeeping*—Firms require attorneys and paralegals to document their time use. Because the firm's income depends on billable hours produced by employees, firms usually require attorneys and paralegals to generate a certain number of billable hours per year. Double billing presents a major ethical problem for law firms.

Communications and Social Media Tools

Attorneys are obligated to keep clients informed. Paralegals should be aware that they play a role in meeting this legal duty. Sending billing statements to clients is one way to communicate; phone calls, letters, and e-mail messages also keep clients informed. Firms use a mix of traditional communications and social media to keep in touch with clients and to help generate new business. Firms need clear policies about communications within the firm and about how the firm presents itself to the outside world.

Law Office Culture and Politics

Each office has its own culture, or personality, which is largely shaped by the attitudes of the firm's owners and the qualities they look for when hiring employees. Office culture and politics, largely unknown to outsiders, make a great difference in terms of job satisfaction and comfort. Wise paralegals learn as soon as possible from co-workers about these aspects of the law office.

KEY TERMS AND CONCEPTS

associate attorney 56	double billing 75	fixed fee 68
billable hours 72	employment manual 58	forms file 65
contingency fee 70	expense slip 73	law clerk 56

legal administrator 58

limited liability partnership (LLP) 56

managing partner 56

office manager 58

paralegal manager 57

partner 56

partnership 56

personal liability 55

professional corporation (PC) 56

professional limited liability company (PLLC) 57

retainer 70

retainer agreement 68

shareholder 57

sole proprietorship 55

staff attorney 56

statute of limitations 65

support personnel 58

time slip 72

trust account 70

wiki 77

QUESTIONS FOR REVIEW

1. List and define the basic organizational structures of law firms discussed in the chapter. What is personal liability?

2. What is the difference between an associate and a partner? Are there attorneys in other roles in law firms? If so, what are their roles? Who supervises the work performed by paralegals?

3. What kinds of files do law firms maintain? What general procedures are typically followed in regard to client files?

4. List and define the different ways law firms bill their clients. What ethical obligations do attorneys have with respect to legal fees?

5. How do lawyers and paralegals keep track of their time? What is the difference between billable and nonbillable hours? What is a client trust account?

6. List some factors that may be considered in a paralegal's performance evaluation.

7. What are some of the things a paralegal should consider when investigating a law firm's culture?

ETHICS QUESTIONS

1. Sam Martin, an attorney, receives a settlement check for a client's case. It is made out jointly to Sam and his client. Sam endorses the check and instructs his paralegal to deposit it into his law firm's bank account, instead of the client's trust account, because he wants to take out his fee before he gives the client his portion of the money. Can Sam do this? Why or why not? What should Sam's paralegal do?

2. James Johnson is a sole practitioner. His office is about an hour's drive from the federal district court at which

he files many lawsuits. He used to talk on his cell phone to clients as he travelled the two hours to and from the courthouse. He would bill the client on whose behalf he was going to the courthouse for two hours and the clients with whom he talked on the phone for increments of the same two hours. When the American Bar Association issued its rule prohibiting double billing, he was concerned that the rule would drive him out of business due to the drop in income. Is what Johnson is doing ethical? Why or why not?

PRACTICE QUESTIONS AND ASSIGNMENTS

1. Using the material presented in the chapter on the organizational structures of law firms, identify the kind of law practices involved:

a. Rosa Suefentes practices immigration law. She owns her legal practice, the building, and the office furniture. She leases some office equipment. Rosa employs one secretary and one paralegal.

b. Mosabi Hamdei owns a general practice law firm with Hassam El-Khouri. They own equal interests in the firm, participate in the firm's management, and share in its profits and losses. Three associates, six secretaries, and three paralegals work for the firm.

c. Ajay Singh, Arun Patel, and Chandra Jindal need to limit their personal liability resulting from a potential legal malpractice claim against their partnership, not all of which will be covered by insurance. They file paperwork with the state to convert to an entity that, in most states, protects innocent partners from debts and obligations arising from negligence, which is the basis for a legal malpractice claim.

2. Using the material in the chapter, identify the following law office personnel:

   a. LaToya works as a paralegal in a large law firm. After twelve years with the firm, she was promoted and now oversees paralegal staffing, assignments, and professional development.

   b. Ani was hired by the partners of a large law firm to manage the day-to-day operations of the firm.

   c. Alicia is an attorney who works as an employee of Marsh & Martin, a law firm with 250 attorneys. She is not on the partnership track.

   d. Jamal is a file clerk for Wright & Goodman.

   e. Michael is a lawyer. He owns O'Dowd & O'Dowd LLP with his sister, Jane.

   f. Kathy is an attorney working on a document-review project in a mass tort litigation case for the BigLaw law firm. Her job will end when the project is completed.

3. Using the material in the chapter on fee arrangements, identify the type of billing that is being used in each of the following examples:

   a. The client is billed $200 per hour for a partner's time, $150 per hour for an associate attorney's time, and $125 per hour for a paralegal's time.

   b. The attorney's fee is one-third of the amount that the attorney recovers for the client, either through a pretrial settlement or through a trial.

   c. The attorney charges $250 to change the name of a client's business firm.

4. A law firm hired to represent a client in a paternity action withdrew from representation of the client while the case was pending, citing irreconcilable differences. In the retainer agreement, the client had agreed to pay hourly fees of $475 for the senior attorney, $425 for the junior attorney, $275 for any other attorney in the firm, and $150 for paralegal and law-clerk time. At the time the attorneys withdrew from representation, the client's total bill was $39,561, which she refused to pay. The law firm sued to recover its fee.

   a. What argument might the client make to get the fees reduced? Would it make a difference if the typical fee for a paternity case is usually less than $10,000?

   b. What argument would the law firm make to support its lawsuit for collecting its fee?

5. A lawyer representing indigent defendants as a court-appointed attorney billed the county courts for more than twenty-four hours a day on three different days and more than twenty hours a day five other times. On other occasions, she billed between fourteen and nineteen hours a day. The attorney did not keep detailed records of the hours that she worked, so she often guessed at how much time she had spent on a case. Using the material in the chapter on ethics and client billing practices, explain what this attorney did wrong.

6. Jose Hernandez hires Maria Alvarez, an attorney with the law firm of Alvarez, Banderos & Sedillo, located at 1000 Canyon Road, Phoenix, Arizona, to represent him in a divorce. He agrees to pay attorney Alvarez at a rate of $350 per hour and to pay a paralegal $150 per hour. He also agrees to pay all costs and expenses, such as filing fees, expert-witness fees, court-reporter fees, and other fees incurred in the course of her representation. Using Exhibit 3.4, *A Sample Retainer Agreement,* on page 69, draft a retainer agreement between Jose Hernandez and Maria Alvarez.

GROUP PROJECT

In this project, the group will research the use of social media by law firms and present its findings to the class. Student one will research for what purpose law firms use social media and what the pros and cons of using social media are. Student two will research statistics on how many law firms use social media. Student three will research statistics on which social media sites law firms use and what the trends are among law firms for using various sites. Student four will summarize and compile the results of the research and will present the group's findings to the class.

Ethics and Professional Responsibility

CHAPTER OBJECTIVES

After completing this chapter, you will be able to:

- Explain why and how legal professionals are regulated.

- Summarize some important ethical rules governing the conduct of attorneys, and explain what paralegals can do to comply with these rules.

- Explain how the rules governing attorneys affect paralegal practice, and explain the various rules developed to govern paralegal practice.

- List and describe the kinds of activities that paralegals are and are not legally permitted to perform.

- Explain some of the pros and cons of regulation, including the debate over paralegal licensing.

CHAPTER

4

Introduction

Paralegals preparing for a career in today's legal arena have many career options. Regardless of which path you follow, you should have a firm grasp of your state's ethical rules governing the legal profession. When you work under the supervision of an attorney, you and the attorney are team members. You work together on behalf of clients and share in the ethical and legal responsibilities arising as a result of the attorney-client relationship. As a paralegal, you must know what these responsibilities are, why they exist, and how they affect you.

Attorneys are subject to direct regulation by the state in which they practice. The first part of this chapter is devoted to the regulation of attorneys because the ethical duties imposed on attorneys affect paralegals as well. If a paralegal violates a rule that governs attorneys, that may result in serious consequences for the client, the attorney, and the paralegal.

Paralegals are subject to less regulation than attorneys, although states may impose more rules if believed desirable. Paralegals are regulated indirectly both by attorney ethical codes and by state laws that prohibit nonlawyers from practicing law. As the paralegal profession develops, professional paralegal organizations, the American Bar Association, and state bar associations continue to issue guidelines that impact paralegals.

The Regulation of Attorneys

Regulate can be defined as "to control or direct in agreement with a rule." To a significant extent, attorneys play critical roles in establishing most of the rules that govern their profession. One of the hallmarks of a profession is the establishment of minimum standards and levels of competence for its members. The accounting profession, for example, has established such standards, as have physicians, engineers, and members of other professions.

Attorneys are also regulated by the state, because the rules of behavior established by the legal profession are adopted and enforced by state authorities. First, by establishing educational and licensing requirements, state authorities ensure that anyone practicing law should be competent. Second, by defining specific ethical requirements for attorneys, the states protect the public against unethical attorney behavior that may affect clients' welfare. Because the rules limiting who can practice law are mostly written and enforced by lawyers, they also serve to assist lawyers by limiting competition from other groups, such as paralegals. We will discuss these requirements and rules shortly. Before we do, however, let's look at how these rules are created and enforced.

Who Are the Regulators?

Key participants in determining the rules that govern attorneys and the practice of law are bar associations, state supreme courts, state legislatures, and, in rare cases, the United States Supreme Court. Procedures for regulating attorneys vary, of course, from state to state. We next look at some of the key regulators.

Bar Associations

Lawyers determine the requirements for entering the legal profession and the rules of conduct that practicing attorneys will follow. Traditionally, lawyers have formed professional groups (bar associations) at the local, state, and national levels to discuss issues affecting the legal profession and to decide standards of professional conduct.

In all states, to be admitted to practice, a prospective attorney must pass the state bar examination. Although membership in local and national bar associations is voluntary, membership in the state bar association (called a "unified bar") is mandatory in many states. Many lawyers are also members of the American Bar Association (ABA), the voluntary national bar association discussed in Chapter 1. As you will see, the ABA plays a key role by proposing model (uniform) codes, or rules of conduct, for adoption by the states.

State Supreme Courts

Typically, the state's highest court, often called the state supreme court, is the ultimate regulatory authority in a state. That court decides what conditions must be met before an attorney can practice law within the state and when that privilege will be suspended or revoked. In most states, the state supreme court works with the state bar association. For example, the association may recommend rules and requirements to the court. If the court agrees, it can order the rules to become state law. Under the authority of the courts, state bar associations often handle regulatory functions, including disciplinary proceedings against attorneys who are accused of violating professional requirements.

State Legislatures

State legislatures also regulate the legal profession by passing laws affecting attorneys—such as statutes prohibiting the unauthorized practice of law and statutes concerning ethical conduct of licensed attorneys.

The United States Supreme Court

Occasionally, the United States Supreme Court decides issues relating to attorney conduct. At one time, state ethical codes, or rules governing attorney conduct, prohibited lawyers from advertising their services to the public. Restrictions on advertising were determined by the United States Supreme Court to be an unconstitutional limitation on attorneys' rights to free speech. Although there are still some restrictions on what attorneys can say in advertisements, legal ads on television, billboards, radio, and the Internet are common.

Licensing Requirements

The licensing of attorneys, which gives them the right to practice law, is accomplished at the state level.

licensing
A government's official act of granting permission to an individual, such as an attorney, to do something that would be illegal in the absence of such permission.

Basic Requirements

State licensing requirements may vary. Generally, though, an individual must meet three basic requirements to obtain a license:

1. In most states, a prospective attorney must have a bachelor's degree from a university or college and must have graduated from an accredited law school (in many states, the school must be accredited by the ABA), which requires an additional three years of study.

2. A prospective attorney must pass a state bar examination—a rigorous examination that tests the candidate's knowledge of the law. The examination covers both state law (law applicable to the particular state in which the attorney is taking the exam and wishes to practice) and multistate law (law applicable in most states, including federal law). In addition, most states require prospective lawyers to pass the Multistate Professional Responsibility Exam on the rules of ethics.

3. The candidate must pass an extensive personal background investigation to verify that he or she is a responsible individual and qualifies to engage in an ethical profession. An illegal act committed by the candidate in the past might disqualify the person from being permitted to practice law.

Only when these requirements have been met can a person be admitted to the state bar and practice law in the state. In addition, each federal court requires admission to practice before an attorney can appear in a case filed there. This generally requires a sponsor and an application, but no test.

Licensing and UPL

unauthorized practice of law (UPL)
The performance of actions defined by a legal authority, such as a state legislature, as constituting the "practice of law" without authorization to do so.

Licensing requirements for attorneys are part of a long history of restrictions on entry into the legal profession. Beginning in the 1850s, restrictions on who could (or could not) practice law were put in place by state statutes prohibiting the **unauthorized practice of law (UPL)**. Court decisions relating to unauthorized legal practice also date to this period. By the 1930s, almost all states had legislation prohibiting anyone but licensed attorneys from practicing law. Many of the regulatory issues facing the legal profession—and particularly paralegals—are directly related to these UPL statutes.

Ethical Codes and Rules

The legal profession is also regulated through ethical codes and rules adopted by each state—in most states, by the state supreme court. These codes of professional conduct evolved over time. A major step toward ethical regulation was taken in 1908, when the ABA approved its *Canons of Ethics*. The states adopted these canons as law. (Canons are generally accepted principles.)

Today's state ethical codes are based, for the most part, on later revisions of the ABA canons: the *Model Code of Professional Responsibility* (published in 1969) and the *Model Rules of Professional Conduct* (first published in 1983 to replace the *Model Code* and revised many times since then). Although most states have adopted laws based on the *Model Rules*, the *Model Code* is still in effect in some states. New York still uses the *Model Code*, for example, while California and Maine have developed their own rules. You should become familiar with rules that are in effect in your state, as rules may vary across the states. For example, the Vermont Supreme Court adopted a 2016 ABA *Model Rule* that prohibits lawyers from engaging in harassing or discriminatory conduct. The Supreme Court of South Carolina rejected it.

The *Model Code of Professional Responsibility*

The ABA *Model Code of Professional Responsibility*, often referred to simply as the *Model Code*, consists of nine canons. In the *Model Code*, each canon is followed by sections entitled "Ethical Considerations" (ECs) and "Disciplinary Rules" (DRs). The ethical considerations are "aspirational" in character—that is, they suggest ideal conduct, not necessarily behavior that is required by law. For example, Canon 6 ("A lawyer should represent a client competently") is followed by EC 6–1, which states (in part) that a lawyer "should strive to become and remain proficient in his practice." In contrast, disciplinary rules are mandatory in character—an attorney may be subject to disciplinary action for breaking a rule. DR 6–101 (which follows Canon 6) states that a lawyer "shall not … neglect a legal matter entrusted to him."

The *Model Rules* of Professional Conduct

The 1983 revision of the ABA *Model Code*—referred to as the *Model Rules of Professional Conduct* or simply the *Model Rules*—represented a major revision. The *Model*

Rules replaced the canons, ethical considerations, and disciplinary rules of the *Model Code* with a set of rules organized under eight general headings. Each rule is followed by comments shedding light on the rule's application and how the rule compares with the *Model Code*'s treatment of the same issue.

Because the 1983 *Model Rules* serve as models for the ethical codes of most states, we use the 1983 rules as the basis for our discussion. It is important to note, however, that the ABA's ethics commission periodically updates and revises the *Model Rules* as necessary in light of the realities of modern law practice. The ABA's ethics commission has revised the *Model Rules* to address new ethical concerns raised by technological developments (such as client confidentiality using e-mail), for example. To view the ABA *Model Rules of Professional Conduct*, go to the American Bar Association's website.

Sanctions for Violations

Attorneys who violate the rules governing professional conduct are subject to disciplinary proceedings brought by the state bar association, state supreme court, or state legislature—depending on the state's regulatory scheme. In most states, unethical attorney actions are reported by clients, other attorneys, or judges to the ethics committee of the state bar association, which is obligated to investigate each complaint. For serious violations, the state bar association or the court initiates disciplinary proceedings against the attorney.

Formal Sanctions

Sanctions imposed for violations range across the following:

1. A **reprimand** (a formal "scolding" of the attorney—the mildest sanction but one that can seriously damage an attorney's reputation and practice).

2. A **suspension** (a more serious sanction in which the attorney is prohibited from practicing law in the state for a period of time, such as one year).

3. A **disbarment** (revocation of the attorney's license to practice law in the state—the most serious sanction).

Civil Liability

In addition to these sanctions, attorneys may be subject to civil liability for negligence. As will be discussed in Chapter 14, *negligence* (called **malpractice** when committed by a professional, such as an attorney) is a tort (a wrongful act) that is committed when an individual fails to perform a legally recognized duty. Tort law allows one who is injured by another's wrongful or careless act to bring a civil lawsuit against the wrongdoer for **damages** (compensation in the form of money). A client may bring a lawsuit against an attorney if the client suffers harm because of the attorney's failure to perform a legal duty.

If a paralegal's breach of a professional duty causes a client to suffer substantial harm, the client may sue not only the attorney but also the paralegal. Although law firms' liability insurance policies typically cover paralegals as well as attorneys, these policies do not cover paralegals working on a contract (freelance) basis. Just one lawsuit could ruin a freelance paralegal financially—as well as destroy that paralegal's reputation in the legal community. Hence, obtaining liability insurance is important for freelance paralegals as well as for independent paralegals.

Attorneys and paralegals are also subject to potential criminal liability under federal and state criminal statutes prohibiting fraud, theft, and other crimes.

reprimand
A disciplinary sanction in which an attorney is rebuked for misbehavior. Although it is the mildest sanction for attorney misconduct, it is serious and may significantly damage the attorney's reputation in the legal community.

suspension
A serious disciplinary sanction in which an attorney who has violated an ethical rule or a law is prohibited from practicing law in the state for a specified or an indefinite period of time.

disbarment
A severe disciplinary sanction in which an attorney's license to practice law in the state is revoked because of unethical or illegal conduct.

malpractice
Professional misconduct or negligence—the failure to exercise due care—on the part of a professional, such as an attorney or a physician.

damages
Money awarded as a remedy for a civil wrong, such as a breach of contract or a tort (wrongful act).

Attorney Ethics and Paralegal Practice

Because the *Model Rules of Professional Conduct* guide most state codes, the rules discussed in this section are drawn from the *Model Rules*. Keep in mind, though, that your own state's code of conduct is the governing authority on attorney conduct in your state.

As a paralegal, you will need to carefully follow the rules in your state's ethical code. You will want to obtain a copy of your state's ethical code and be familiar with its contents. A good practice is to keep the code in your office. It is also helpful to develop a relationship with a trusted mentor at your firm for advice on such issues.

Professional duties—and the possibility of violating them—are involved in almost every task you will perform as a paralegal. Even if you memorize every rule governing the legal profession, you can still violate a rule unintentionally (few people breach professional duties intentionally). To minimize the chances that you violate a rule, you need to know not only what the rules are but also how they apply to the day-to-day realities of your job. In general, avoiding financial dealings and social relationships with clients helps you avoid violating ethical obligations. As this chapter's *Office Tech and Cybersecurity* feature discusses, electronic security is a major issue in protecting clients' interests—and yours.

OFFICE TECH AND CYBERSECURITY

E-COMMUNICATION AND CONFIDENTIALITY

It is not uncommon to send e-mail to the wrong recipient or accidentally click "reply to all" instead of just "reply," thus broadcasting a message to a larger group than intended. Law firm employees have sent inappropriate e-mails to partners and clients in this way. Similar problems can arise from personal pages, such as Facebook, where inappropriate content may be seen by employers, opposing parties, and clients.

Careless communications of these kinds can cause confidential information to be disclosed and privilege lost. That can damage the sender's career, the interests of the client, and the reputation of the firm. Here are four major issues for paralegals to consider when using electronic communications or social media at work and at home:

1. Is a work-related communication truly confidential, or could an opposing party discover it during litigation?
2. Is a communication an appropriate use of the employer's property?
3. What sort of information is appropriate to share with the world through Facebook, Twitter, and similar services?
4. Is the use of social media consistent with the firm's policies?

Confidentiality

Just labeling an e-mail or text message "confidential" does not mean that it will be treated as such. A firm should have a policy about when it is appropriate to send confidential information electronically and when it is not. Seek guidance from your supervising attorney if you have any doubt about the appropriateness of transmitting confidential information. Be careful with your phone, tablet, laptop, and home computer if you are accessing work-related materials on these devices. An unauthorized person may see privileged materials.

Personal Use of Business Systems

Many law firms provide employees with smartphones and laptops. Firms often allow some personal use of these devices but retain the right to monitor and audit the content of the e-mails, messages, and Web traffic on them. Be sure to check your employer's policies on appropriate use of the devices, such as for e-mail and text messages. Do not let family members or friends use these devices.

Technology Tip about Online Personal Information

Remember, when you post the details of your latest date or pictures of your vacation, your employer or clients may stumble across those postings simply by googling your name. Even if you change a Facebook page later, caching by search engines means that an embarrassing picture lingers in cyberspace for years. The bottom line: Don't post pictures or text online that you would feel uncomfortable showing to your boss. Assume employers and prospective employers will search your name online.

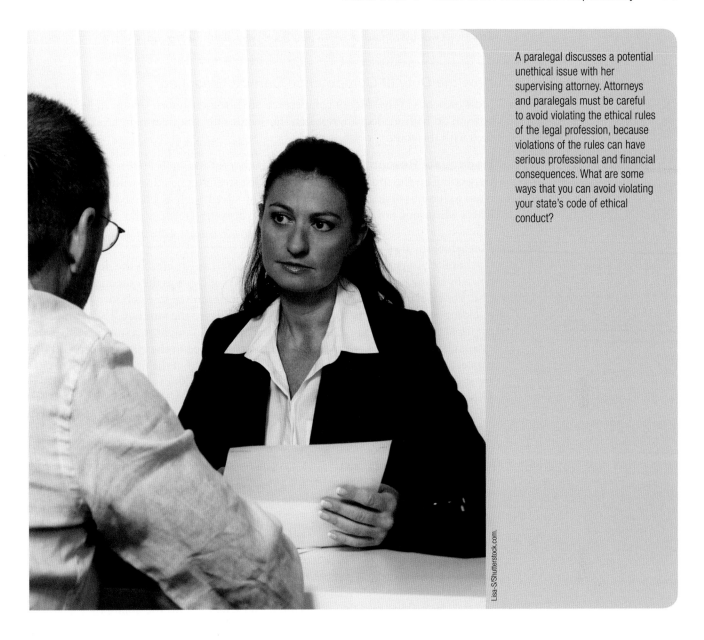

A paralegal discusses a potential unethical issue with her supervising attorney. Attorneys and paralegals must be careful to avoid violating the ethical rules of the legal profession, because violations of the rules can have serious professional and financial consequences. What are some ways that you can avoid violating your state's code of ethical conduct?

The rules relating to competence, confidentiality, and conflict of interest deserve special attention here because they can pose particularly difficult ethical problems for paralegals. Other important rules that affect paralegal performance—including the duty to charge reasonable fees, the duty to protect clients' property, and the duty to keep the client reasonably informed—will be discussed elsewhere in this text as they relate to special topics.

The Duty of Competence

Rule 1.1 of the *Model Rules* concerns a fundamental obligation of attorneys—the duty of competence. The ABA focuses on the requirement that attorneys provide able representation to their clients. Competency requires knowledge of the law, careful research to ensure being up to date, and proper preparation for representation. Most legal representation occurs out of court but requires the same knowledgeable approach. A **breach** (failure to perform) of this duty may subject attorneys to one or more of the

breach
To violate a legal duty by an act or a failure to act.

sanctions discussed earlier. As a paralegal, you share in this duty when you work on an attorney's behalf.

How the Duty of Competence Can Be Breached

Most breaches of the duty of competence are not intentional. Often, these breaches have to do with inadequate research, missed deadlines, or errors in legal documents filed with the court.

Inadequate Research.   Paralegals do both legal and factual research for attorneys. Depending on the situation, an attorney's first step after meeting with a new client is often to have a paralegal research the facts involved, such as who did what to whom, when, where, and how. If the paralegal fails to discover a relevant fact and the attorney relies on the paralegal's incomplete research in advising the client, the result could be a breach of the duty of competence.

Similarly, a paralegal conducting legal research might breach the duty of competence by failing to find or report a court decision that controls the outcome of a client's case. For example, suppose that a paralegal performs initial research into the law surrounding a particular dispute and reports the findings to the attorney. Then, while the paralegal is working on unrelated cases over the next few months, a state appeals court rules on a case with issues very similar to those involved in the client's dispute. If the paralegal or the attorney does not go back and confirm that the initial research results are still accurate, a ruling that would influence the client's case could be overlooked. This would breach the attorney's duty of competence.

Although attorneys are ultimately responsible for competent representation, paralegals play an important role in providing accurate information to their attorneys. If you are ever uncertain of the accuracy of your research results, make sure to let the attorney know of your doubts. Also, keep good notes recording each step you took in conducting research so that you know what was done and what still needs to be done. These measures help prevent accidental breaches of the duty of competence.

Missed Deadlines.   Paralegals often work on multiple cases at once. Keeping track of every deadline in every case can be difficult. Organization is the key to making sure that all deadlines are met. All dates relating to actions and events for every case or client should be entered on a calendar. Firms typically use computerized calendaring and "tickler" (reminder) systems.

Besides making sure that all deadlines are entered into the appropriate systems, you should also have your own personal calendar for tracking dates that are relevant to the cases on which you are working—and then make sure that you consistently use it. Check ahead regularly so that if a deadline arises while you are on leave, nothing is missed. Also, check frequently with your supervising attorney about deadlines.

Errors in Documents.   Breaches of the duty of competence can arise from errors in documents. That is, incorrect information might be included (or crucial information omitted) in a legal document to be filed with the court. If the attorney fails to notice the error before signing the document, and the document is delivered to the court, a breach of the duty of competence has occurred. Depending on its effect, this breach may expose the attorney to liability for negligence. To prevent such violations, be especially careful in drafting and proofreading documents.

Generally, if you are ever unsure about what to include in a document, when it must be completed or filed with the court, how extensively you should research a legal issue, or any other aspect of an assignment, ask your supervising attorney for clarification. Make sure that your work is adequately overseen by an attorney to reduce the chances that it contains costly errors.

Attorney's Duty to Supervise

Attorneys must adequately supervise paralegals' work to ensure that the duty of competence is not breached. Rule 5.3 of the *Model Rules* defines the responsibilities of attorneys to nonlawyer assistants. Attorneys must supervise their staff to ensure that they behave in accord with the standards of the profession. The rule also specifies the circumstances under which a lawyer is held responsible for conduct by a nonlawyer that violates an attorney's duty. The lawyer is responsible, for example, if she orders improper conduct or ratifies (approves of) it. Lawyers who have managerial authority in a law firm or have supervisory authority over a nonlawyer can also be held responsible for the nonlawyer's unethical conduct if they knew about it and failed to take action to prevent it.

This rule applies not only to lawyers who work in private law firms but also to lawyers in corporate legal departments, government agencies, and elsewhere. In addition, in the statements outlining attorneys' responsibilities toward nonlawyer employees in this area, the ABA commission changed the word *should* to *must*. Attorneys *must* both instruct and supervise nonlawyer employees concerning appropriate ethical conduct, as they can be held personally responsible for the ethical violations of their subordinates.

Inadequate Supervision

Because attorneys are legally responsible for staff work, it may seem logical to assume that attorneys will take time to direct that work carefully. In fact, paralegals may find it difficult to ensure that their work is adequately supervised. Most attorneys and paralegals are very busy. Making sure that all paralegals' tasks are properly overseen can be time consuming. At the same time, attorneys—especially if they know their paralegals are competent—often do not take the time to read every document the paralegals draft. Nonetheless, as a paralegal, you have a duty to assist your supervising attorney in fulfilling his or her ethical obligations, including the obligation to supervise your work.

If you ever believe that the attorney is not adequately supervising your work, there are several things you can do:

- Improve communications with the attorney—generally, the more you initiate communication with your supervising attorney, the more likely the attorney will take an active role in directing your activities.

- Ask the attorney for feedback on your work. Sometimes, it helps to place reminders on your calendar to discuss particular issues or questions with the attorney. When the opportunity to talk arises, these issues or questions will be fresh in your mind.

- Attach a note to a document that you have prepared for the attorney, requesting him or her to review the document (or revised sections of the document) carefully before signing it.

Ensuring proper supervision to protect yourself is highlighted in the *Developing Paralegal Skills* feature titled "Adequate Supervision" on the following page.

Confidentiality of Information

Rule 1.6 of the *Model Rules* concerns attorney-client confidentiality. The rule simply states that a lawyer may not reveal "information relating to representation of a client." This is one of the oldest and most important rules of the legal profession. It would be difficult for a lawyer to properly represent a client without such a rule. A client must be able to confide in the attorney so that the attorney can best represent the client's interest.

Because confidentiality is one of the easiest rules to violate, a thorough understanding of the rule is essential. The general rule of confidentiality is that all information relating to representation of a client must be kept confidential. There are exceptions to the rule, which we discuss shortly.

DEVELOPING PARALEGAL SKILLS

ADEQUATE SUPERVISION

Michael's supervising attorney, Muriel, asks him to prepare two complaints (documents filed with the court to initiate a lawsuit) and gives him information needed for the two different cases. Muriel is scheduled to attend a deposition (a pretrial procedure in which testimony is given under oath) in another matter this afternoon. She asks Michael to finish the complaints and file them with the court today. Muriel tells Michael to use a complaint from a previous client's case as a model for creating the new complaints, replacing that client's information as necessary.

Michael finishes the work at 3:00 P.M., while Muriel is attending the deposition in the conference room. Michael needs to file the complaints at the courthouse by 5:00 P.M. Knowing the adequate supervision rule, though, he does not want to file the documents before Muriel has reviewed them. He decides that he must interrupt the deposition so that Muriel can look over the complaints

before they are filed with the court. He flags a few passages that he is unsure about and proceeds into the conference room. Muriel asks the opposing counsel to take a short break so she can step out of the room.

Tips for Obtaining Adequate Supervision

- Always ask your supervising attorney to review your work.
- Use notes or ticklers as reminders to ask for a review.
- Make the review as convenient as possible for your supervising attorney, and mark anything that needs particular attention.
- Discuss any ethical concerns with the attorney.
- Be persistent.
- Complete your work in a timely fashion so the attorney can review it.

EXAMPLE 4.1 You know that a client is the president of a local company. Do you have to keep that information confidential? Suppose you tell a friend, "Mr. X is the president of XYZ Corporation." The fact that X is president is widely known. But in saying that, people are likely to presume that X is a client of your firm. Mr. X may not want it known that he is talking to a lawyer. People who learn that Mr. X has been at the law firm may think "something is up," which is likely true. Confidence has been breached.

Consider another example. Suppose that one evening you tell your spouse that you met Mr. X that day. Your spouse might reasonably assume that your firm was handling some legal matter involving Mr. X and might repeat that to other people. Because it may be difficult to decide what information is or is not confidential, a good rule of thumb is to regard all information about a client or a client's case as confidential.

Exceptions to the Confidentiality Rule

Rule 1.6, Confidentiality of Information, provides for certain exceptions to the confidentiality rule, which we look at here.

Client Gives Informed Consent to the Disclosure.   The rule indicates that an attorney can reveal confidential information if the client gives informed consent to the disclosure. The attorney must fully explain the risks and alternatives involved in the disclosure for consent to be informed.

EXAMPLE 4.2 Suppose an attorney is drawing up a will for a client. The client is leaving certain property to her son and not leaving a share of that property to her daughter. The daughter calls and wants to know how her mother's will reads. The attorney cannot divulge this confidential information because the client has not consented.

In this instance, the attorney may explain to the client that if her daughter does not learn about the provisions of the will until after her mother's death, it is more likely that she will contest it in court. After the attorney and client discuss the alternatives, the client can give informed consent to the attorney to disclose information to her daughter.

Impliedly Authorized Disclosures. The ABA rules allow attorneys to make disclosures of information that are presumed necessary to represent clients. This exception is clearly necessary. Legal representation of clients necessarily involves attorneys' paralegals who must have access to the confidential information to do their jobs. If a paralegal is working on the client's case, he or she must know what the client told the attorney about the matter and must have access to information in the client's file concerning the case.

Disclosures to Prevent Harm. The *Model Rules* recognize that there are certain circumstances in which an attorney should be allowed to disclose confidential information when it is necessary to prevent harm to persons or property. Rule 1.6 specifically lists four exceptions to the confidentiality rule for this purpose:

1. An attorney is allowed to reveal a client's information to prevent possible death or substantial bodily harm.

   EXAMPLE 4.3 A client confides to his attorney that he assaulted and nearly killed several people. The attorney is not allowed to disclose this information. If that client tells the attorney that he is going to attack a specific person in the future, however, the attorney can disclose this information to prevent likely bodily harm to the person.

   This issue is addressed further in the *Developing Paralegal Skills* feature below titled, "What If You Learn Your Client Is Planning to Commit a Crime?"

2. In certain situations, an attorney can disclose confidential information to prevent a client from committing a crime or fraud. The crime or fraud must be reasonably certain to result in significant injury to the financial interests or property of another. Also, the client must have used or be using the attorney's services to perpetrate the crime or fraud. If both these conditions are present, then the attorney can disclose information to the extent necessary to enable the affected person to contact the appropriate authorities.

DEVELOPING PARALEGAL SKILLS

WHAT IF YOU LEARN YOUR CLIENT IS PLANNING TO COMMIT A CRIME?

Communications between a client and an attorney, including those with the attorney's paralegal, are usually covered by the attorney-client privilege. Privileged statements may not be disclosed without the client's consent. When the client makes statements that suggest he or she is going to commit a crime, however, the privilege does not apply.

For example, in one criminal case, the defendant told his lawyer that he was going to attempt to bribe one or more witnesses against him and that if he was unable to do so, he would "whack" the witnesses.[a] Later, the defendant also threatened

the lawyer. The lawyer reported these threats to the district attorney and withdrew as the defendant's counsel. The defendant's new lawyer tried to have the first lawyer's testimony about the threats excluded but failed. Because the defendant had threatened criminal acts that could involve bodily harm or death, the California appeals court held that privilege did not apply.

State rules on privilege differ, and you should make sure that you understand the range of crimes covered by your state's laws. All states exempt threats of death or serious injury, and such statements should be reported immediately. In addition, some states require reporting of certain criminal acts.

a. *People v. Dang*, 93 Cal.App.4th 1293, 113 Cal.Rptr.2d 763 (2001).

3. If a client used the attorney to help commit a crime or fraud, and the crime or fraud will likely cause injury to the financial interests or property of another, the attorney can disclose confidential information to the extent necessary to prevent or reduce that injury.

4. An attorney can also disclose confidential information to establish a defense to a criminal charge in a controversy between the attorney and the client based on conduct involving the client. Similarly, the attorney may respond to allegations in proceedings regarding the attorney's representation of the client.

Disclosures to Ensure Compliance with *Model Rules*. If a lawyer is unsure what is required to comply with the *Model Rules of Professional Conduct* in a particular situation, the lawyer can seek legal advice from another lawyer without violating confidentiality.

> *EXAMPLE 4.4* An attorney representing a corporation becomes suspicious that the firm is engaged in fraud. The attorney is not sure what her professional responsibilities are in that particular situation, so she can seek confidential legal advice to assist her in complying with the *Model Rules*.

Defending against a Client's Legal Action. An attorney may also disclose confidential information if the information is necessary to establish a defense in an action brought by a client against the attorney.

> *EXAMPLE 4.5* A client sues his attorney for malpractice due to litigation that did not go well. The lawyer might need to reveal confidential information to prove that he was not negligent.

Note, though, that the attorney is permitted to disclose confidential information only to the extent that it is essential to defend the lawsuit.

Disclosures to Comply with a Court Order or Other Law. An attorney may also reveal information relating to the representation of a client if ordered to do so by a court or other governmental entity.

> *EXAMPLE 4.6* An attorney representing a client in a divorce case knows the client is hiding assets from his wife. In that situation, a court could require the attorney to reveal confidential information from the client related to the hidden assets. The attorney should first attempt to persuade the client to disclose the assets. The attorney can reveal as much information as is reasonable to satisfy the needs of the court or other governmental entity.

Violations of the Confidentiality Rule

Naturally, paralegals are tempted to discuss work with family members, co-workers, and friends. As a paralegal, a great temptation you will face is the desire to discuss an interesting case with someone you know.

You can deal with this temptation in two ways: you can decide never to discuss anything concerning legal matters at work, or you can limit your discussion to issues and comments that will not reveal the identity of clients. The latter approach is more realistic for most people, but it requires great care. Something you say may reveal a client's identity, even though you are not aware of it. (See this chapter's *Ethics Watch* feature.) Developing a reputation for being discreet will enhance your career by encouraging attorneys and clients to confide in you.

ETHICS WATCH

SOCIAL EVENTS AND CONFIDENTIALITY

You are at a party with some other paralegals. You tell a paralegal whom you know well of some startling news—that a client of your firm, a prominent city official, is being investigated for drug dealing. Although your friend promises to keep this information strictly confidential, she nonetheless tells her husband, who tells a coworker, who tells a friend, and so on. Soon, the news is in the open and the resulting media coverage harms the official's reputation in the community.

Revealing the juicy gossip breached your obligation to the client. If it can be proved that the harm is the result of your breach of the duty of confidentiality, the official could sue you and the attorney and the firm for whom you work for damages.

In this situation, you would have violated the NFPA *Model Code of Ethics and Professional Responsibility*, Section 1.5(f), which states: "A paralegal shall not engage in any indiscreet communications concerning clients." This behavior would also have violated the ABA *Model Guidelines for the Utilization of Paralegal Services*, Guideline 6: "Attorneys may utilize paralegals, but the attorneys must take proper steps to be sure that client confidentiality is protected." Finally, you would have violated the NALA *Code of Ethics and Professional Responsibility*, Canon 7: "A paralegal must protect the confidences of a client."

Reprinted by permission of the National Federation of Paralegal Associations, Inc. (NFPA®), paralegals.org. Copyright 1975; Adopted 1975; Revised 1979, 1988, 1995, 2007. Reprinted with permission of NALA, The Paralegal Association. Inquiries should be directed to NALA, 1516 S. Boston, #200, Tulsa, OK 74119, nala.org.

Conversations Overheard by Others.   Violations of the confidentiality rule can happen by oversight.

> **EXAMPLE 4.7** Suppose that you and a secretary in your office are working on the same case and continue, as you walk to the elevator, a conversation about the case. In the hall or coffee shop, your conversation could be overheard, and the confidential information revealed could have an adverse effect on your client's interests.

It is important to avoid the possibility of accidentally revealing confidential information. Therefore, never discuss confidential information when you are in common areas.

Electronic Communications and Confidentiality.   Whenever you talk to or about a client on the telephone, ensure that a **third party** does not overhear your conversation. You may be sitting in your private office, but if your door is open, someone may overhear the conversation. Even other employees of the firm should not hear information about cases they are not working on.

Paralegals should take special care when using cell phones. Although conversations on cell phones are difficult to intercept, there is still a security risk. No doubt you have overheard people talking on their phones as if other people could not hear. Some violations of confidentiality are low-tech, such as talking on the phone in the open. Others involve more sophisticated issues. This chapter's *Featured Contributor* article on the following pages provides more details about electronic security issues.

third party
A person or entity not directly involved in an agreement (such as a contract), legal proceeding (such as a lawsuit), or relationship (such as an attorney-client relationship).

Other Violations of the Confidentiality Rule.   There are many other ways in which you can reveal confidential information without intending to do so. A file or document sitting on your desk, if observed by a third party, may reveal the identity of a client or enough information to suggest the client's identity. A computer screen, if visible to those passing by your desk, could convey information to someone not authorized to know that information. You might be speaking to an expert witness about rescheduling a meeting and let something about the case slip out.

FEATURED CONTRIBUTOR

SECURING CLIENT INFORMATION IN THE DIGITAL AGE

Ceaser Espinoza

BIOGRAPHICAL NOTE

Professor Ceaser Espinoza is the director of the ABA-approved Paralegal Program at El Centro College in Dallas, Texas. A frequent speaker, he has made several academic and motivational presentations at various schools and organizations across the Dallas–Fort Worth Metroplex. Professor Espinoza has been honored with numerous awards recognizing his dedication to the classroom and the legal field. He still maintains a law and *pro bono* practice, advising on various legal issues. He earned his A.A.S. from Eastfield College, B.A. from the University of North Texas, and a J.D. from Oklahoma City University.

Our reliance on technology to improve our daily lives and our profession comes at a price. With all the information and data that we store and send virtually, we are susceptible more than ever to infiltrations and breaches. In this new millennium, we've witnessed several large corporate data breaches.[a] Unfortunately, the legal profession has not been immune. Recently, high-profile law firms have reported severe data breaches or piracy where their data was held for ransom.[b] This is a sign of what is to come.

Tag, You're It.

Regulations are nothing new to the legal profession. Although legal professionals understand that data protections must be enacted as a course of business, they may not be fully aware of the federally mandated cybersecurity measures. Take, for example, the following federal regulations that apply to law firms:

> ❝ **technology . . . comes at a price.** ❞

- The Health Insurance Portability and Availability Act (HIPAA) considers law firms "business associates."
- The Payment Card Industry Data Security Standard (PCI DSS) applies to law firms since they accept, store, and transmit cardholder data.
- The Federal Deposit Insurance Corporation (FDIC) also considers law firms "service providers" for maintaining and distributing funds.[c]

One thing is clear, attorneys and paralegals both have a duty and responsible to ensure client data are secure and protected.

Are you thinking, "What can I do? I don't own the firm. I'm not IT." Even though most paralegals do not control or implement most of the cybersecurity polices at a law firm or in-house legal department, we can play a significant role in securing client data.

With technology changing daily, so is our lexicon. Cyber Hygiene[d] describes the processes and practices that an individual

---

a. cnbc.com/2019/07/30/five-of-the-biggest-data-breaches-ever.html

b. abajournal.com/news/article/hacking-group-publishes-full-dump-of-law-firms-data-another-responds-to-cybersecurity-incident

c. zeguro.com/blog/law-firm-cybersecurity-protecting-attorney-client-privilege-in-a-digital-age

d. dictionary.cambridge.org/us/dictionary/english/cyber-hygiene

---

Alternatively, you might be friendly with a paralegal at an opposing attorney's office because the two attorneys have worked on cases together. You are on the phone trying to work out a date for an important meeting. This paralegal suggests a date, and you tell her that the attorney for whom you work is scheduled to be in court on a specific client's case that day. If you name the client, or indicate that the attorney will be arguing a particular type of motion in the case, you may breach the duty of confidentiality.

user implements to protect e-information. As legal practitioners, let's review some of our processes that we can improve.

Tip 1: Get Regular Checkups.

It is not uncommon in today's legal workplace for employers to allow employees to use their personal devices for work purposes. Bring-your-own-device (BYOD) policies are designed to provide the employer with a cost-saving measure and the employee with flexibility with remote access.

First, you need to make sure that your device (computer, tablet, smartphone, etc.) and all the applications have current updates/patches. Although each device is different, you should be able to search "update" on your device and get to the right place. Updates/patches are designed to correct flaws or security vulnerabilities that have been detected by the originator. These updates will ensure that you have established a baseline of security.

Tip 2: Take Your Vitamins.

Second, make sure that your devices have updated antivirus and malware software. This is one area where you can play a significant role in e-security. This requires some research to ensure which software works best for your applications and devices. I recommend that you have a conversation with your firm's IT department or consultant for recommendations. Although you'll notice that some software can be costly, there are several highly rated free versions available.

Tip 3: Free Comes at a Cost.

In the digital age, the new currency might as well be Internet speed. All of us have fallen victim to this new expectation of expediency. As we crave Internet speed, we start looking for a stronger Wi-Fi signal. By selecting an unsecure Wi-Fi signal or a fake "Starbucks_Wifi," for instance, you are bypassing some of the security measures you have already taken and essentially granting access to your system, your data, and your clients' data. Make sure you know your Wi-Fi source.

Tip 4: Avoid 1-2-3 Passwords.

Let's start by saying that, "Password1234" is not a good password. You may be thinking, "What does a good password look like?" How about XKr567%$2345@1? Is this password any better?

Unfortunately, it really isn't because hackers use the same algorithms as the ones used to generate these types of passwords.[e]

We need to move away from passwords and embrace passphrases. Personalized passphrases are proven to be more difficult to hack because they do not rely on logic. Here's how to create an effective passphrase. First, you want to think of a personalized phrase, such as "I like to watch Soccer." Second, manipulate it so that you replace letters with numbers and special characters such as "1like2watch$occer." This new passphrase now contains letters, numbers, and special characters that are unique and easy to remember.[f]

Tip 5: Don't Look and Click.

One of the biggest culprits to data breaches is human error by unintentionally providing access through e-mail phishing.[g] E-mail phishing is the use of a fraudulent e-mail from a familiar company or person to access a firm's or an individual's system or secure data.

When computer users click on a link or open an attachment in a compromised e-mail, they essentially allow the hacker to bypass the computer's security measures, thus granting unfettered access to the firm's and clients' data. Fortunately, some simple steps can prevent most of these infiltrations.

First, trust your spam filter. It will catch most of the e-mails that have irregularities. Even if you see an e-mail from someone you know in the spam filter, that account could have been compromised. If you're unsure, contact the person through another mechanism and confirm. Second, be wary if the e-mail asks you to click on a link in order to enter data or access additional information. Do not click on the link.

> **". . . know your Wi-Fi source."**

Technology has provided many tools and enhancements that will forever change the legal profession. We should embrace and not fear this technology and strive to maintain a level of technical competence to ensure our clients' data are secure.

---

e. zeguro.com/blog/five-tips-for-better-cyber-hygiene

f. Ibid.

g. us.norton.com/internetsecurity-online-scams-how-to-protect-against-phishing-scams.html

Source: Ceaser Espinoza

Confidentiality and the Attorney-Client Privilege

All information relating to a client's representation is considered confidential information. Some confidential information also qualifies as privileged information, or information subject to the **attorney-client privilege.**

The attorney-client privilege can be vitally important during litigation. As you will read in Chapter 10, prior to a trial each attorney is permitted to obtain information

attorney-client privilege
A rule of evidence requiring that confidential communications between a client and his or her attorney (relating to their professional relationship) be kept confidential, unless the client consents to disclosure.

relating to the case from the opposing attorney and other persons, such as witnesses. This means that attorneys must exchange certain information about their clients. An attorney need not provide privileged information, however—unless the client consents to the disclosure, or the court orders it. Similarly, if an attorney is called to the witness stand during a trial, the attorney may not disclose privileged information unless the court orders it.

What Kind of Information Is Privileged?

State statutes and court cases define what constitutes privileged information. Generally, any communications concerning a client's legal rights or problems fall under the attorney-client privilege. All information is confidential, but not all is privileged. For privilege to apply, the information must meet the four following criteria: (1) a communication (2) made between privileged persons (3) in confidence (4) and for the purpose of obtaining or providing legal advice.

> **EXAMPLE 4.8** Suppose that an attorney's client is a criminal defendant. The client tells the attorney that she was near the crime site at the time of the crime, but to her knowledge, no one saw her. This is privileged information that the attorney may disclose only with the client's consent or on a court's order to do so.

work product
An attorney's mental impressions, conclusions, and legal theories regarding a case being prepared on behalf of a client. Work product normally is regarded as privileged information.

Work Product.   Certain materials relating to an attorney's preparation of a client's case for trial are protected as privileged information under the **work product** doctrine. Usually, information concerning an attorney's legal strategy for conducting a case is classified as work product and, as such, may be subject to the attorney-client privilege. Legal strategy includes the legal theories that the attorney plans to use in support of the client's claim and how the attorney interprets the evidence relating to the claim.

Certain evidence gathered by the attorney to support the client's claim, however, will probably not be classified as work product. An example is financial statements relating to the client's business firm.

Caution Advised.   Because it is often difficult to tell what types of information (including work product) qualify as privileged, paralegals should consult with their supervising attorneys whenever issues arise that may require that such a distinction be made. You should be alert for accidental disclosures by opposing counsel or paralegals. If you think someone on the other side of a case has disclosed privileged information to you, immediately tell your supervising attorney. Also note that, like any other confidential information relating to a client's case, privileged information is subject to the exceptions to the confidentiality rule discussed previously.

When the Attorney-Client Privilege Arises

The attorney-client privilege comes into existence the moment a client communicates with an attorney concerning a legal matter. People sometimes mistakenly assume that an attorney has no duty to keep client information confidential until an agreement is signed. This is not so. The privilege—and thus the duty of confidentiality—arises even if the lawyer decides not to represent the client and even when the potential client is not charged a fee. Thus, mentioning to a friend that someone called your firm to discuss legal representation, and the firm declined to take the case, could violate the privilege.

Duration of the Privilege

The client is the holder, or "owner," of the privilege. Only the client can waive (set aside) the privilege. Unless waived by the client, the privilege lasts indefinitely. In other words, the privilege continues even though the attorney has completed the client's legal matter and is no longer working on the case.

Privileged information is confidential. If such information is disclosed to others, it is no longer confidential and can no longer be considered privileged. This is another reason why it is so important to guard against accidental violations of the confidentiality rule: if the rule is violated, information that otherwise might have been protected by the attorney-client privilege can be used against the client's interests.

> **EXAMPLE 4.9** By accident, a paralegal e-mails a confidential document to opposing counsel instead of to the client. The document, because it contained the attorney's analysis of confidential client information, might have been classified as privileged information under the work product doctrine. The disclosure of the information to the opposing counsel destroyed its confidential character.

Conflict of Interest

A **conflict of interest** arises when representing one client injures the interests of another client. *Model Rules* 1.7, 1.8, 1.9, 1.10, and 1.11 pertain to conflict-of-interest situations. The general rule is that an attorney should not represent a client if doing so would be adverse to another client. If there is a significant risk that the attorney's ability to consider, recommend, or carry out an appropriate course of action for the client would be materially (significantly) limited as a result of the attorney's other responsibilities or interests, a conflict of interest exists. A classic example is when an attorney represents two adverse parties in a legal proceeding. Clearly, in such a situation, the attorney's loyalties must be divided.

conflict of interest
A situation in which two or more duties or interests come into conflict, as when an attorney attempts to represent opposing parties in a legal dispute.

Simultaneous Representation

If an attorney reasonably believes that representing two parties in a legal proceeding will not adversely affect either party's interest, the attorney is permitted to do so—but only if both parties give informed consent. Normally, attorneys avoid this kind of situation because what might start out as an uncontested proceeding could evolve into a legal battle.

> **EXAMPLE 4.10** A couple seeking a divorce have agreed how to handle the matter and hire one attorney to represent them both. It is not uncommon for such matters to end up in a nasty dispute. The attorney then faces a conflict of interest: assisting one party could injure the interests of the other.

Because of the potential for a conflict of interest in divorce proceedings, some courts do not permit attorneys to represent both spouses.

Similar conflicts arise when an attorney is asked to handle a family matter and the family members eventually disagree on what the outcome should be. Suppose two adult children request the family lawyer to handle the procedures required to settle their deceased parents' estate. The will favors one child, and the other child decides to challenge the will's validity. The attorney cannot represent both sides without a conflict of interest.

Attorneys representing corporate clients may face conflicts of interest when corporate personnel become divided on an issue.

> **EXAMPLE 4.11** Finn, an attorney, represents ABC Corporation. Finn typically deals with the corporation's president, Johnson, when giving legal advice. At times, however, Finn deals with other personnel, including Harrison, the company's chief accountant. Harrison and Johnson disagree on some issues, and Johnson fires Harrison. Harrison wants attorney Finn to represent him in a lawsuit against the corporation for wrongful termination of his employment. Finn would have a conflict of interest if he represented Harrison. He can continue to represent Johnson and ABC, but he cannot represent Harrison.

Former Clients

The ABA rules call for caution when a lawyer may be in a position to represent a new client in a matter that would conflict with the interests of a former client. In such instances, at a minimum, the attorney must notify the former client of the matter and may need to obtain written consent. The rule regarding former clients is closely related to the rule on preserving the confidentiality of a client. The rationale behind the rule is that an attorney, in representing a client, is entrusted with certain information that may be unknown to others. That information should not be used against the client—even after the representation has ended.

Job Changes and Former Clients.   The rule concerning former clients does not prohibit an individual attorney or paralegal from working at a firm or agency that represents interests contrary to those of a former client. If that were the situation, many legal professionals would find it hard to change jobs. The rules depend on the specific circumstances. In some situations, when a conflict of interest results from a job change, the new employer can avoid violating the rules governing conflict of interest through the use of screening procedures. That is, the new employer can erect an **ethical wall** around the new employee so that person remains ignorant about the case that would give rise to the conflict of interest.

ethical wall
A screen erected around an attorney, a paralegal, or another member of a law firm to shield him or her from information about a case that would give rise to a conflict of interest.

Walling-off Procedures.   Law offices usually have procedures for "walling off" an attorney or a paralegal from a case when a conflict of interest exists. The firm may announce in a memo to all employees that a certain attorney or paralegal should not have access to specific files and may set out procedures to be followed to ensure that access to those files is restricted. Computer documents relating to the case may be protected by passwords or in some other way. Commonly, any hard-copy files relating to the case are flagged with a sticker to indicate that access to the files is restricted.

Firms normally take great care to establish and uphold such restrictions because if confidential information is used in a way harmful to a former client, the former client may sue the firm for damages. In defending against such a suit, the firm must show that it took reasonable precautions to protect that client's interests. The accompanying *Developing Paralegal Skills* feature summarizes how steps are taken to build an ethical wall.

Other Conflict-of-Interest Situations

Other situations may give rise to conflicts of interest. Gifts from clients may create conflicts of interest, because they tend to bias the judgment of the attorney or paralegal involved. Certain gifts are specifically prohibited. For example, the *Model Rules* prohibit an attorney from preparing documents (such as wills) for a client if the client gives the attorney or a member of the attorney's family a gift in the will. Note that as a paralegal, you may be offered gifts from appreciative clients at holidays. Generally, such gifts pose no ethical problems. If a client offers you a gift that has substantial value, however, you should discuss the issue with your supervising attorney.

Attorneys also need to be careful about taking on a client whose case may create an "issue conflict." Generally, an attorney cannot represent a client on a substantive legal issue if the client's position is contrary to that of another client being represented by the lawyer or the lawyer's firm.

Occasionally, conflicts of interest may arise when two family members who are both attorneys or paralegals are involved in the representation of adverse parties in

DEVELOPING PARALEGAL SKILLS

BUILDING AN ETHICAL WALL

Lana Smith, a paralegal, has been asked by her supervising attorney to set up an ethical wall because a new attorney, Chandra Piper, has been hired from the law firm of Nunn & Bush. While employed by Nunn & Bush, Piper represented a defendant, Seski Manufacturing, in an ongoing case in which Seski is being sued by Joseph Tymes. Smith's firm—and Piper's new employer—represents plaintiff Tymes in that case. Consequently, Piper's work for Nunn & Bush creates a conflict of interest, which Piper has acknowledged in a document signed under oath. Smith makes a list of the walling-off procedures to ensure that the firm does not violate the rules on conflict of interest.

Checklist for Building an Ethical Wall

- Prepare a memo to the office manager regarding the conflict and the need for special arrangements to ensure that Piper will have no involvement in the *Tymes* case.

- Prepare a memo to the team representing Tymes to inform them of the conflict of interest and the special procedures to be followed.

- Prepare a memo to the firm giving the case name, the nature of the conflict, the parties involved, and instructions to maintain a blanket of silence with respect to Piper.

- Arrange for Piper's office to be on a different floor from the offices of the team (if possible) to demonstrate, if necessary, that the firm took steps to separate Piper and the team and to prevent them from having access to one another's files.

- Arrange with the office manager for computer passwords to be issued to the team members so that only they have access to computer files on the *Tymes* case.

- Place "ACCESS RESTRICTED" stickers on the files for the *Tymes* case.

- Develop a security procedure for signing out and tracking the case files in the *Tymes* case to prevent inadvertent disclosure of the files to Piper or her staff members.

a legal proceeding. Because there is a risk that the family relationship will interfere with professional judgment, generally an attorney should not represent a client if an opposing party to the dispute is being represented by a member of the attorney's family (a spouse, parent, child, or sibling). If you, as a paralegal, are married to or living with another paralegal or an attorney, you should inform your firm of this fact if you ever suspect that a conflict of interest might result from your relationship. Similarly, if you discover that you may have a financial interest in the outcome of a lawsuit that your firm is handling (such as owning stock in a company involved in a lawsuit in which a party is represented by the firm), you should notify the attorney of the potential conflict.

Conflicts Checks

When a potential client consults with an attorney, the attorney will want to make sure that no potential conflict of interest exists before deciding whether to represent the client. Running a **conflicts check** is a standard procedure in every law office and one frequently undertaken by paralegals. Before you can run a conflicts check, you need to know the name of the prospective client, the other party or parties that may be involved in the client's legal matter, and the legal issues involved.

Normally, every law firm has some established procedure for conflicts checks, and in larger firms there is usually a database with the names of former clients and other information you need in checking for conflicts of interest.

conflicts check
A procedure for determining whether an agreement to represent a potential client will result in a conflict of interest.

The Indirect Regulation of Paralegals

Paralegals are regulated *indirectly* in several ways. Clearly, the ethical codes for attorneys just discussed indirectly regulate the conduct of paralegals. Additionally, paralegal conduct is evaluated on the basis of standards and guidelines created by paralegal professional groups that create best practices but do not have the force of law, as well as guidelines for the utilization of paralegals developed by the American Bar Association and various states.

Paralegal Ethical Codes

Paralegals are increasingly self-regulated. Three organizations discussed in Chapter 1—the National Federation of Paralegal Associations (NFPA), the National Association of Legal Professionals (NALS), and The Paralegal Association (NALA)—have adopted codes of ethics defining the ethical responsibilities of paralegals.

The NFPA's Code of Ethics

The NFPA's first code of ethics was called the *Affirmation of Responsibility*. It has been revised several times and, in 1993, was renamed the *Model Code of Ethics and Professional Responsibility*. In 1997, the NFPA revised the code and took the step of appending to its code a list of enforcement guidelines setting forth recommendations on how to discipline paralegals who violate ethical standards promulgated by the code. The full title of the NFPA's code is the *Model Code of Ethics and Professional Responsibility and Guidelines for Enforcement*.

Exhibit 4.1 presents the rules from Section 1 of the code, entitled "NFPA Model Disciplinary Rules and Ethical Considerations." For reasons of space, only the rules are included in the exhibit, not the ethical considerations that follow each rule. The ethical considerations are important to paralegals, however, because they explain what conduct the rule prohibits. The full text of the NFPA's code "can be found online."

NALS's *Code of Ethics and Professional Responsibility*

The oldest paralegal association, NALS, began almost a century ago to represent the professional interests of legal secretaries. Today, it is one of the major organizations that promote professionalism for paralegals. Appendix C presents the entire NALS *Code of Ethics and Professional Responsibility*. Exhibit 4.2 provides its Canons of Ethics.

EXHIBIT 4.1

Rules from Section 1 of the NFPA's *Model Code of Ethics and Professional Responsibility and Guidelines for Enforcement*

§1. NFPA MODEL DISCIPLINARY RULES AND ETHICAL CONSIDERATIONS

1.1 A paralegal shall achieve and maintain a high level of competence.

1.2 A paralegal shall maintain a high level of personal and professional integrity.

1.3 A paralegal shall maintain a high standard of professional conduct.

1.4 A paralegal shall serve the public interest by contributing to the improvement of the legal system and the delivery of quality legal services, including *pro bono publico* services.

1.5 A paralegal shall preserve all confidential information provided by the client or acquired from other sources before, during, and after the course of the professional relationship.

1.6 A paralegal shall avoid conflicts of interest and shall disclose any possible conflict to the employer or client, as well as to the prospective employers or clients.

1.7 A paralegal's title shall be fully disclosed.

1.8 A paralegal shall not engage in the unauthorized practice of law.

Reprinted by permission of the National Federation of Paralegal Associations, Inc. NFPA © paralegals.org.

EXHIBIT 4.2

NALS's *Code of Ethics and Professional Responsibility*

Members of NALS are bound by the objectives of this association and the standards of conduct required of the legal profession.

Every member shall:

- Encourage respect for the law and administration of justice
- Observe rules governing privileged communications and confidential information
- Promote and exemplify high standards of loyalty, cooperation, and courtesy
- Perform all duties of the profession with integrity and competence
- Pursue a high order of professional attainment

Integrity and high standards of conduct are fundamental to the success of our professional association. This Code is promulgated by NALS and accepted by its members to accomplish these ends.

Canon 1. Members of this association shall maintain a high degree of competency and integrity through continuing education to better assist the legal profession in fulfilling its duty to provide quality legal services to the public.

Canon 2. Members of this association shall maintain a high standard of ethical conduct and shall contribute to the integrity of the association and the legal profession.

Canon 3. Members of this association shall avoid a conflict of interest pertaining to a client matter.

Canon 4. Members of this association shall preserve and protect the confidences and privileged communications of a client.

Canon 5. Members of this association shall exercise care in using independent professional judgment and in determining the extent to which a client may be assisted without the presence of a lawyer and shall not act in matters involving professional legal judgment.

Canon 6. Members of this association shall not solicit legal business on behalf of a lawyer.

Canon 7. Members of this association, unless permitted by law, shall not perform legal functions except under the direct supervision of a lawyer and shall not advertise or contract with members of the general public for the performance of paralegal functions.

Canon 8. Members of this association, unless permitted by law, shall not perform any of the duties restricted to lawyers or do things which lawyers themselves may not do and shall assist in preventing the unauthorized practice of law.

Canon 9. Members of this association not licensed to practice law shall not engage in the practice of law as defined by statutes or court decisions.

Canon 10. Members of this association shall do all other things incidental, necessary, or expedient to enhance professional responsibility and participation in the administration of justice and public service in cooperation with the legal profession.

Reprinted by permission: https://nals.org/page/NALSCodeofEthics

NALA's Code of Ethics

In 1975, NALA issued its *Code of Ethics and Professional Responsibility,* which, like the NFPA's code, has since undergone several revisions. Exhibit 4.3 presents NALA's code in its entirety. Note that NALA's code, like the ABA *Model Code of Professional Responsibility* discussed earlier in this chapter, presents ethical precepts as a series of "canons."

Compliance with Paralegal Codes of Ethics

Paralegal codes of ethics express the ethical responsibilities of paralegals generally, and they particularly apply to members of paralegal organizations that adopted the codes. Any paralegal who is a member of an organization that has adopted one of the codes is expected to comply with the code's requirements. Compliance is not legally mandatory, however. If a paralegal does not abide by a particular ethical standard of a paralegal association's code of ethics, the association cannot initiate state-sanctioned disciplinary proceedings against the paralegal. The association can, however, expel the paralegal from the association, which may have significant implications for the paralegal's career.

EXHIBIT 4.3

NALA's *Code of Ethics and Professional Responsibility*

Preamble: A paralegal must adhere strictly to the accepted standards of legal ethics and to the general principles of proper conduct. The performance of the duties of the paralegal shall be governed by specific canons as defined herein so justice will be served and goals of the profession attained.

The canons of ethics set forth hereafter are adopted by [NALA, The Paralegal Association] as a general guide intended to aid paralegals and attorneys. The enumeration of these rules does not mean there are not others of equal importance although not specifically mentioned. Court rules, agency rules and statutes must be taken into consideration when interpreting the canons.

Definition: Legal assistants, also known as paralegals, are a distinguishable group of persons who assist attorneys in the delivery of legal services. Through formal education, training and experience, [paralegals] have knowledge and expertise regarding the legal system and substantive and procedural law which qualify them to do work of a legal nature under the supervision of an attorney.

CANON 1.

A paralegal must not perform any of the duties that attorneys only may perform nor take any actions that attorneys may not take.

CANON 2.

A paralegal may perform any task which is properly delegated and supervised by an attorney, as long as the attorney is ultimately responsible to the client, maintains a direct relationship with the client, and assumes professional responsibility for the work product.

CANON 3.

A paralegal must not:

(a) engage in, encourage, or contribute to any act which could constitute the unauthorized practice of law; and

(b) establish attorney-client relationships, set fees, give legal opinions or advice or represent a client before a court or agency unless so authorized by that court or agency; and

(c) engage in conduct or take any action which would assist or involve the attorney in a violation of professional ethics or give the appearance of professional impropriety.

CANON 4.

A paralegal must use discretion and professional judgment commensurate with knowledge and experience but must not render independent legal judgment in place of an attorney. The services of an attorney are essential in the public interest whenever such legal judgment is required.

CANON 5.

A paralegal must disclose his or her status as a [paralegal] at the outset of any professional relationship with a client, attorney, a court or administrative agency or personnel thereof, or a member of the general public. A paralegal must act prudently in determining the extent to which a client may be assisted without the presence of an attorney.

CANON 6.

A paralegal must strive to maintain integrity and a high degree of competency through education and training with respect to professional responsibility, local rules and practice, and through continuing education in substantive areas of law to better assist the legal profession in fulfilling its duty to provide legal service.

CANON 7.

A paralegal must protect the confidences of a client and must not violate any rule or statute now in effect or hereafter enacted controlling the doctrine of privileged communications between a client and an attorney.

CANON 8.

A paralegal must disclose to his or her employer or prospective employer any pre-existing clients or personal relationships that may conflict with the interests of the employer or prospective employer and/or their clients.

CANON 9.

A paralegal must do all other things incidental, necessary, or expedient for the attainment of the ethics and responsibilities as defined by statute or rule of court.

CANON 10.

A paralegal's conduct is guided by bar associations' codes of professional responsibility and rules of professional conduct.

Guidelines for the Utilization of Paralegals

As noted earlier, attorneys are regulated by the state to protect the public from the harms that could result from incompetent legal advice and representation. While licensing requirements may help to protect the public, they also give lawyers something of a monopoly over the delivery of legal services.

The increased use of paralegals stems, in part, from the legal profession's need to reduce the cost of legal services. The use of paralegals to do substantive legal work benefits clients because the hourly rate for paralegals is lower than that for attorneys. For this reason, bar associations (and courts, when approving fees) encourage attorneys to delegate work to paralegals to lower the costs of legal services—and thus provide the public with greater access to legal services.

NALA, the ABA, and many states have adopted guidelines for the utilization of paralegal services. These were created in response to questions that had arisen concerning the role and function of paralegals within the legal arena, including the following: What are paralegals? What kinds of tasks do they perform? What are their professional responsibilities? How can attorneys best utilize paralegal services? What responsibilities should attorneys assume with respect to their paralegals' work?

NALA's *Model Standards and Guidelines*

NALA's *Model Standards and Guidelines for the Utilization of Paralegals* provides guidance on several important issues. The document lists the minimum qualifications that paralegals should have and then, in a series of guidelines, indicates what they may and may not do. We will examine these guidelines in more detail shortly. (See Appendix B for the complete text of the annotated version of NALA's *Model Standards and Guidelines*.)

The ABA's *Model Guidelines*

The ABA adopted its *Model Guidelines for the Utilization of Legal Assistant Services* in 1991. The ABA Standing Committee on Paralegals revised these guidelines in 2003 and 2012 by basing them on the ABA's *Model Rules of Professional Conduct*. The document consists of ten guidelines, each followed by a lengthy comment on the origin, scope, and application of the guideline. The guidelines indicate, among other things, tasks that a lawyer may not delegate to a paralegal and, generally, the responsibilities of attorneys with respect to paralegal performance and compensation. For further detail on the revised guidelines, now entitled *Model Guidelines for the Utilization of Paralegal Services*, go to the American Bar Association website and search for "paralegal."

State Guidelines

Most states have adopted some form of guidelines concerning the use of paralegals by attorneys, the respective responsibilities of attorneys and paralegals in performing legal work, the tasks paralegals may perform, and other areas. Although the guidelines of some states reflect the influence of a paralegal association's standards and guidelines, they focus largely on state statutory definitions of the practice of law, state codes of ethics regulating the responsibilities of attorneys, and state court decisions. As a paralegal, make sure that you become familiar with your state's guidelines.

The Increasing Scope of Paralegal Responsibilities

The ethical standards and guidelines just discussed, as well as court decisions concerning paralegals, all support the goal of increasing the use of paralegals in the delivery of legal services. Today, paralegals can perform a wide array of legal tasks as long as the work is supervised by an attorney and does not constitute the unauthorized practice of law.

Paralegals working for attorneys may interview clients and witnesses, investigate legal claims, draft legal documents for attorneys' signatures, attend will executions (in some states), appear at real estate closings (in some states), and undertake other types of legal work, as long as they are supervised by attorneys. When state or federal law allows it, paralegals can also represent clients before government agencies. Paralegals may perform freelance services for attorneys and, depending on state law and the type of service, perform limited independent services for the public.

Paralegals may also give information to clients on many matters relating to a case or other legal concern. When arranging for client interviews, they let clients know what kind of information is needed and what documents to bring to the office. They inform clients about legal procedures and what clients should expect to experience during the progress of a legal proceeding. As a paralegal, you will be permitted to give clients all kinds of information. Nonetheless, you must make sure that you know where to draw the line between giving permissible advice and giving "legal advice" that only licensed attorneys may give.

The tasks that paralegals are legally permitted to undertake are described throughout this book. As stated in the ABA's guidelines, paralegals may not perform tasks that only attorneys can legally perform. If they do so, they risk liability for the unauthorized practice of law.

The Unauthorized Practice of Law

State statutes prohibit the unauthorized practice of law (UPL). Although the statutes vary, they all aim to prevent nonlawyers from providing legal counsel. These statutes apply to all persons—including paralegals, real estate agents, bankers, insurance agents, and accountants—who might provide services that are typically provided by licensed attorneys.

EXAMPLE 4.12 An insurance agent, talking to a client, offers advice about a possible personal-injury claim. The agent might be liable for UPL.

UPL statutes are not always clear about what constitutes the practice of law. Consequently, courts decide whether a person has engaged in UPL on a case-by-case basis. This may make it difficult to know exactly what activities constitute UPL. To avoid violating UPL laws, a person must be aware of the state courts' decisions on UPL.

Paralegals, of course, can also refer to the general guidelines for their profession provided by NALA. Guideline 2 in NALA's *Model Standards and Guidelines* prohibits a paralegal from engaging in any of the following activities:

- Establishing attorney-client relationships.

- Setting legal fees.

- Giving legal opinions or advice.

- Representing a client before a court, unless authorized to do so by the court.

- Engaging in, encouraging, or contributing to any act that could constitute the unauthorized practice of law.

State UPL Statutes

Because of the difficulty in predicting with certainty whether a court would consider a particular action to be UPL, some states have made efforts to clarify what is meant by the "practice of law." About half of the states have a formal definition of what constitutes the practice of law, established either by statute or by court ruling. For example, the Texas UPL statute provides, in part:

> the "practice of law" means the preparation of a pleading or other document incident to an action or special proceeding or the management of the action or proceeding on behalf of a client before a judge in court as well as a service rendered out of court, including the giving of advice or the rendering of any service requiring the use of legal skill or knowledge, such as preparing a will, contract, or other instrument, the legal effect of which under the facts and conclusions involved must be carefully determined.[1]

The Texas statute also states that this definition is not exclusive and that the state courts have the authority to determine that other activities, which are not listed, also constitute UPL. Other states' definitions focus on various factors, such as appearing in court or drafting legal papers, pleadings, or other documents in connection with a pending or prospective court proceeding. The enforcement of UPL statutes also varies widely among the states. In some states, the attorney general prosecutes violators; in others, a local or state prosecutor enforces UPL statutes, or the state bar association may be in charge of enforcement.

We next discuss some of the activities that are considered to constitute UPL in most states. But it must be emphasized that paralegals should know the details of the UPL statute in the state in which they work. Avoiding UPL problems is also discussed in the *Developing Paralegal Skills* feature below.

DEVELOPING PARALEGAL SKILLS

THE DANGERS OF THE UNAUTHORIZED PRACTICE OF LAW

Every state restricts the "practice of law" to licensed attorneys. State bar associations take this restriction seriously, and they aggressively enforce UPL rules against anyone the bar suspects is infringing on attorneys' control of the practice of law.

Unfortunately, the definition of the "practice of law" is unclear, making it a trap for the unwary. The ABA defines it as "the rendition of services for others that call for the professional judgment of a lawyer." In essence, "practicing" law includes giving legal advice, preparing legal documents, and representing a client in court.

Of course, paralegals routinely do the first two of these. Each is perfectly legal as long as these activities are done under the supervision of a licensed attorney. For example, you will often have to relay legal advice from the attorney to the client. To protect yourself, you must make clear that the advice comes from the lawyer, not you. You can avoid unauthorized practice problems by:

1. Being clear that everyone understands you are a paralegal in all communications and meetings by:

   - Including your title when signing letters, e-mails, and other documents and on your business cards.

   - Introducing yourself with your title in meetings.

   - Disclosing your status when communicating with a court.

2. Ensuring that activities that might be construed to be the "practice of law" are supervised by a licensed attorney by:

   - Making sure that an attorney reviews and signs off on all legal documents you prepare.

   - Explicitly stating that the attorney is the source of any legal advice when relaying advice to a client by stating, "I asked Attorney Smith about that and she said. …"

3. Informing yourself about your state's unauthorized practice rules by:

   - Researching court decisions, regulations, and state bar opinions on the topic.

   - Contacting your state paralegal associations and state bar for information and publications on the topic.

Taking care to follow such guidelines protects the law firm you work for and protects you, your career, and your firm's clients. Also, be careful offering opinions about legal issues on social media sites so that you do not stray into offering legal advice.

The Prohibition against Fee Splitting

An important ethical rule related to the unauthorized practice of law is Rule 5.4 of the *Model Rules of Professional Conduct.* For an attorney or a law firm to split legal fees with a nonlawyer is prohibited. For this reason, paralegals cannot be partners in a law partnership (because the partners share the firm's income), nor can they have a fee-sharing arrangement with attorneys.

One of the reasons for this rule is that it protects the attorney's independent judgment concerning legal matters.

> *EXAMPLE 4.13* An attorney shares office space with two CPAs (accountants), and the three of them work for some of the same clients. The three form a partnership. Is there a problem? Yes, in this situation, a conflict might arise between the interests of the partnership and the attorney's duty to exercise independent professional judgment about a client's case.

The rule against fee splitting also protects against the possibility that nonlawyers would indirectly, through attorneys, be able to engage in the practice of law.

Giving Legal Opinions and Advice

Giving legal advice goes to the essence of legal practice. After all, a person would not seek out a legal expert if he or she did not want legal advice on some matter. Although a paralegal can communicate an attorney's legal advice to a client, a paralegal cannot independently give legal advice.

The Need for Caution

You need to be careful to avoid giving legal advice even when discussing matters with friends and relatives. Although other nonlawyers often give advice affecting others' legal rights or obligations, paralegals should not do so. For example, when a person gets a speeding ticket, a friend or relative who is a nonlawyer might suggest that the person should argue the case before a judge and explain his side of the story. When a paralegal gives such advice, however, she may be accused of engaging in the unauthorized practice of law. Paralegals are prohibited from giving even simple, common-sense advice because of the greater weight the recipient might give to the advice of someone who has legal training.

Similarly, you need to be cautious in the workplace. Although you may develop expertise in a certain area of law, you must refrain from advising clients with respect to their legal obligations or rights.

> *EXAMPLE 4.14* Suppose you are a bankruptcy specialist and know that a client who wants to file for bankruptcy has two options to pursue under bankruptcy law. Should you tell the client about these options and their consequences? No. Advising someone of legal options is dangerously close to advising a person of his legal rights and may therefore constitute the unauthorized practice of law. Even though you may tell the client that he needs to check with an attorney, this does not alter the fact that you are giving advice on which the client might rely.

Be on the Safe Side

What constitutes the giving of legal advice can be difficult to pin down. Paralegals are permitted to advise clients on certain matters, so drawing the line between permissible and impermissible advice may be difficult. To be on the safe side—and avoid potential liability for the unauthorized practice of law—never advise anyone regarding any matter if the advice may alter that person's legal position or legal rights.

Whenever you are pressured to render legal advice—as you surely will be at one time or another by your firm's clients or friends—say that you cannot give legal advice because it is against the law to do so. Paralegals usually find that a frank and honest approach provides the best solution to the problem.

Representing Clients in Court

The rule that only attorneys can represent others in legal matters has a long history. There are two limited exceptions to this rule. First, the United States Supreme Court has held that people have a constitutional right to represent themselves in court.[2] Second, paralegals are allowed to represent clients before some federal and state government agencies, such as the federal Social Security Administration. Hence, as a paralegal, you should know that you are not allowed to appear in court on behalf of your supervising attorney—although local courts in some states have made exceptions to this rule for limited purposes.

Disclosure of Paralegal Status

Because of the close working relationship between an attorney and a paralegal, a client may have difficulty perceiving that the paralegal is not an attorney.

> **EXAMPLE 4.15** A client calls an attorney's office and is transferred to the attorney's paralegal. The paralegal talks with the client about a legal matter and advises the client that the attorney will be in touch. The client may assume that the paralegal is an attorney and may make inferences based on the paralegal's comments that result in actions with harmful consequences—in which event the paralegal might be charged with the unauthorized practice of law.

To avoid problems, make sure that clients or potential clients know that you are a paralegal and, as such, are not permitted to give legal advice.

Similarly, in correspondence with clients or others, you should indicate your non-attorney status by adding "Paralegal" after your name. If you have printed business cards, or if your name is included in the firm's letterhead or other literature, also make sure that your status is clearly indicated.

Guideline 1 of NALA's *Model Standards and Guidelines* emphasizes the importance of disclosing paralegal status by stating that all paralegals have an ethical responsibility to "disclose their status as legal assistants at the outset of any professional relationship with a client, other attorneys, a court or administrative agency or personnel thereof, or members of the general public." Disciplinary Rule 1.7 of the NFPA's *Model Code of Ethics and Professional Responsibility* also stresses the importance of disclosing paralegal status. Guideline 4 of the ABA's *Model Guidelines* gives attorneys the responsibility for disclosing the nonattorney status of paralegals.

Attorneys are responsible for the work product of their offices, including the work done by paralegals. Hence, attorneys are required to ensure that clients and other relevant parties, including other attorneys and the courts, know when work has been performed by a paralegal.

Paralegals Freelancing for Attorneys

Some paralegals work on a freelance basis. The New Jersey Supreme Court held years ago that freelance paralegals could be as adequately supervised by the attorneys for whom they worked as are paralegals working inside attorneys' offices. Since that decision, courts in other states, and ethical opinions issued by various state bar associations, have held that freelance paralegals who are adequately supervised by attorneys are not engaging in the unauthorized practice of law.

Legal Technicians (Independent Paralegals) and UPL

Legal technicians (also called independent paralegals) provide "self-help" legal services directly to the public. The courts have had to wrestle with questions such as the following: If an independent paralegal advises a client on what forms are necessary to obtain a simple uncontested divorce, how to file those forms with the court, how to schedule a court hearing, and the like, do those activities constitute the practice of law?

Generally, the mere dissemination of legal information does not constitute the unauthorized practice of law. There is a fine line, however, between disseminating legal information (by providing legal forms to a customer, for example) and giving legal advice (which may consist of merely selecting the forms that best suit the customer's needs), and the courts do not always agree on just where this line should be drawn.

An Ongoing Problem

Legal technicians continue to face UPL allegations brought against them primarily by UPL committees and state bar associations. In one case, an Oregon appellate court upheld the conviction of Robin Smith for engaging in UPL. The bar association complained that Smith had provided consumers with various legal forms, advised them on which forms to use, and assisted them in completing the documents. The court reasoned that by drafting and selecting documents and giving advice with regard to their legal effect, Smith was practicing law.[3]

Some legal technicians faced UPL charges in California when the legislature authorized nonlawyers to provide certain types of legal services directly to the public. Under that law, a person who qualifies and registers with the county as a "legal document assistant" (LDA) may assist clients in filling out legal forms but cannot advise clients which forms to use.[4]

The Controversy over Legal Software

Even publishers of self-help law books and computer software programs have come under attack for the unauthorized practice of law. For example, a Texas Court held that the legal software program *Quicken Family Lawyer* violated Texas's UPL statute.[5] The program provided a hundred different legal forms (including contracts, real estate leases, and wills), along with instructions on how to fill out these forms.

The Texas legislature then amended the UPL statute to reverse the court's ruling. The new law explicitly authorizes the sale of legal self-help software, books, forms, and similar products to the public.[6] Note, however, that the Texas law authorizes these products to be used only for "self-help." The law does not permit persons who are not licensed to practice law to use these programs to give legal advice to others.

Do Paralegals Who Operate as Legal Technicians Engage in UPL?

Debate continues as to whether it is legal, in some situations, for legal technicians to operate without a lawyer's supervision. Generally, unless a state statute or rule specifically allows paralegals to assist the public directly without the supervision of an attorney, paralegals would be wise not to engage in such practices. Most state courts are much more likely to find that a paralegal is engaging in UPL than that a publisher of legal software is doing so. The consequences of violating state UPL statutes can be serious. Any paralegal who contemplates working as a legal technician (independent paralegal) must investigate the relevant state laws and court decisions on UPL before offering any services directly to the public and must abide by the letter of the law.

Should Paralegals Be Licensed?

A major issue facing legal professionals is whether paralegals should be subject to direct regulation by the state through licensing requirements. Unlike certification, discussed in Chapter 1, licensing involves direct and mandatory regulation by the state of an occupational or professional group. When licensing requirements are established for a professional group, such as for attorneys, a member of the group must have a license to practice his or her profession.

Movements toward regulation of paralegals have been motivated in large part by the activities of legal technicians or independent paralegals—those who provide legal services directly to the public without attorney supervision. Many legal technicians call themselves paralegals even though they may have little legal training or experience. At the same time, those who cannot afford to hire an attorney can benefit from the self-help services provided by legal technicians who have training and experience.

General Licensing

Some states have considered implementing a **general licensing** program that would require all paralegals to meet certain educational requirements and other specified criteria before being allowed to practice.

For example, the New Jersey Supreme Court Committee on Paralegal Education and Regulation recommended that paralegals be licensed. The committee's report proposed that paralegals be subject to state licensure based on educational requirements and knowledge of the ethical rules governing the legal profession. The New Jersey Supreme Court, however, declined to follow the committee's recommendations. The court concluded that direct oversight of paralegals is best accomplished through attorney supervision rather than through a state-mandated licensing system.

general licensing
Licensing in which all individuals within a specific profession or group (such as paralegals) must meet licensing requirements imposed by the state in order to legally practice their profession.

Paralegal Registration

In Florida, any paralegal who wishes to become a Florida Registered Paralegal (FRP) must register with the state. (Other states, including Indiana, Oregon, Utah, and Washington, have similar programs.) Initially, experienced paralegals in Florida were allowed to register without meeting an educational requirement. Since 2011, applicants who wish to be registered must provide proof of educational qualification and must meet certain personal requirements, such as not having engaged in the unauthorized practice of law. All FRPs are listed on the Florida Bar website.

FRPs must meet the continuing education (CE) requirement of thirty hours every three-year reporting cycle. At least five of the hours must be in ethics or professionalism. Failure to complete the CE requirement means loss of FRP status. CE courses specifically authorized are provided by NALA, the NFPA, and the Florida Bar.

In 2020, the Florida Bar Board of Governors reviewed a proposal to recognize Advanced Registered Paralegals. To gain this distinction, paralegals would be required to have more education and work experience than what is required to be a Florida Registered Paralegal. Additionally, paralegals would also be required to be aware of "lawyer's protocols" in performing authorized services. Advanced Registered Paralegals could engage in the limited practice of law *under a lawyer's supervision* in the areas of family law, landlord-tenant law, guardianship law, wills, advance directives, and debt collection defense.

Education and Certification

The law in California defines a paralegal as someone who works under the supervision of an attorney, meets certain educational criteria, and completes specified continuing education requirements. Paralegals do not have to register, but an independent paralegal not working under the supervision of an attorney cannot be called a paralegal in California. Independent paralegals can register with the state as legal document assistants (LDAs). LDAs prepare documents at the direction of their clients and assist clients in a wide range of areas, from family law to incorporation of businesses. They cannot provide legal advice.

The Louisiana Certified Paralegal Program illustrates another approach. Paralegals who successfully complete NALA's certification exam and the Louisiana Certified

Paralegal (LCP) exam are certified as Louisiana Certified Paralegals. Certification exams offered by paralegal associations allow you to demonstrate general knowledge of law and the judicial system, and knowledge of specific areas of law. The LCP exam focuses on the Louisiana legal and judicial system, ethics, civil procedure, and four areas of substantive Louisiana law.

Direct Regulation—The Pros and Cons

A significant part of the debate over direct regulation has to do with the issue of who should do the regulating. State bar associations and government authorities would have a major say in the matter. Paralegal organizations and educators, such as the NFPA, NALA, and the American Association for Paralegal Education (AAfPE), also want to play a leading role in developing the educational requirements, ethical standards, and disciplinary procedures required by a licensing program should one be implemented.

The NFPA's Position

The NFPA endorses the regulation of the paralegal profession on a state-by-state basis. The NFPA asserts that wide-scale regulation of paralegals would improve consumers' access to high-quality legal services by lowering costs. The NFPA's role would be primarily to educate decision makers about paralegal requirements. It promotes strong educational requirements and competency exams, such as PACE.

NALA's Position

NALA supports voluntary certification (**self-regulation**). Paralegals can demonstrate their ability through completion of the Certified Paralegal (CP) program, discussed previously, offered by NALA.

The AAfPE's Position

The American Association for Paralegal Education (AAfPE) does not take a position on paralegal licensing. The AAfPE contends that paralegals, through professional associations, and paralegal educators should present a united front in influencing licensing proposals.

Other Considerations

Other groups have expressed additional considerations. For example, one of the concerns of lawyers is that if legal technicians are licensed—through limited licensing programs—to deliver low-cost services directly to the public, the business (and profits) of law firms would suffer. Many lawyers are also concerned that if paralegals are subject to mandatory licensing requirements, law firms will not be able to hire and train persons of their choice to work as paralegals.

The Ethical Paralegal

Perhaps the most important point to remember as you embark on a paralegal career is that you need to think and act in an ethical, professionally responsible manner. Although this takes time and practice, in the legal arena there is little room for learning ethics by "trial and error." Therefore, you need to be especially attentive to the ethical rules governing attorneys and paralegal practice discussed in this chapter. Ethical behavior is required by law, but it is also mandatory if you want other professionals to place their trust and confidence in you.

The *Ethics Watch* features throughout this book offer insights into some ethical problems that arise in various areas of paralegal performance. Understanding how violations can occur will help you anticipate and guard against them as you begin your career. On the job, you can protect the ethics of legal practice by asking questions whenever you are in doubt and by making sure that your work is adequately supervised.

self-regulation
The regulation of the conduct of a professional group by members of the group. Self-regulation involves establishing ethical or professional standards of behavior with which members of the group must comply.

CHAPTER SUMMARY

ETHICS AND PROFESSIONAL RESPONSIBILITY

The Regulation of Attorneys

Attorneys are regulated by licensing requirements and by the ethics rules of their state. The purpose of regulation is to protect the public against incompetent legal professionals and unethical attorney behavior.

1. *Who are the regulators?*—Lawyers establish the majority of rules governing their profession through state bar associations and the American Bar Association (ABA), which has established *Model Rules* and guidelines relating to professional conduct. Other key participants in the regulation of attorneys are state supreme courts, state legislatures, and (occasionally) the United States Supreme Court.

2. *Licensing requirements*—Licensed attorneys generally must be graduates of a law school and must have passed a state bar examination and an extensive personal background check.

Attorney Ethics and Paralegal Practice

Some of the ethical rules governing attorney behavior pose difficult problems for paralegals, so paralegals should consult their state's ethical code to learn the specific rules for which they will be accountable. The following rules apply in most states.

1. *Duty of competence*—This duty is violated whenever a client suffers harm as a result of the attorney's (or paralegal's) incompetent action or inaction.

    a. Breaching the duty of competence may lead to a lawsuit against the attorney (and perhaps against the paralegal) for negligence. This may arise from faulty research, missed deadlines, or mistakes in documents.

    b. Attorneys must adequately supervise a paralegal's work to ensure that this duty is not breached.

2. *Confidentiality of information*—All information relating to a client's representation must be kept in confidence and not revealed to third parties who are not authorized to know the information.

    a. Paralegals should be careful on and off the job not to discuss client information with third parties. Breaches of confidentiality can include unauthorized persons overhearing telephone conversations or personal comments, or e-mails being sent to parties not intended to see them.

    b. Client confidences can be revealed only in certain circumstances, such as when a client gives

3. *Ethical codes and rules*—Most states have adopted a version of either the 1969 *Model Code of Professional Responsibility* or the 1983 revision of the *Model Code*, called the *Model Rules of Professional Conduct*, published by the ABA. The *Model Rules*, which have been adopted in most states, are often amended by the ABA to keep up-to-date with the realities of modern law practice.

4. *Sanctions for violations*—The *Model Code* and *Model Rules* spell out the ethical and professional duties governing attorneys and the practice of law. Attorneys who violate these duties may be subject to reprimand, suspension, or disbarment. Additionally, attorneys (and paralegals) face potential liability for malpractice or for violations of criminal statutes.

informed consent to the disclosure, when disclosure is necessary to represent a client or to prevent harm to persons or property, or when a court orders an attorney to reveal the information.

    c. *Confidentiality and the attorney-client privilege*—Some client information is regarded as privileged information under the rules of evidence and receives even greater protection by attorneys and paralegals subject to rules of confidentiality.

3. *Conflict of interest*—This occurs when representing a client injures the interests of another client.

    a. An attorney may represent both sides in a legal proceeding only if the attorney believes that neither party's rights will be injured and only if both clients are aware of the conflict and have given informed consent to the representation. Paralegals also fall under this rule.

    b. When a firm is handling a case and one of the firm's attorneys or paralegals cannot work on the case because of a conflict of interest, that attorney or paralegal must be "walled off" from the case—that is, prevented from having access to files or other information relating to the case.

    c. Normally, whenever a prospective client consults with an attorney, a conflicts check is done to ensure that if the attorney or firm accepts the case, no conflict of interest will arise.

The Indirect Regulation of Paralegals

Paralegals are regulated indirectly by attorney ethical rules, by ethical codes created by the NFPA, NALA, and NALS, and by guidelines on the utilization of paralegals, which define the status and function of paralegals and the scope of their authorized activities. The ABA and some states have adopted guidelines on the utilization of paralegals. These codes and guidelines provide paralegals, attorneys, and the courts with guidance on the paralegal's role in the practice of law. The general rule is that paralegals can perform almost any legal task that attorneys can (other than represent a client in court) as long as they work under an attorney's supervision.

The Unauthorized Practice of Law

State laws prohibit nonlawyers from engaging in the unauthorized practice of law (UPL). Violations of these laws can have serious consequences.

1. *State UPL statutes*—Determining what constitutes UPL is complicated by the fact that many state laws give vague or broad definitions. Court decisions in this area of law may provide guidance.

2. *The prohibition against fee splitting*—Paralegals working for attorneys as well as legal technicians (independent paralegals) need to be careful not to engage in activities that the state will consider UPL, such as a fee-sharing arrangement with an attorney.

3. *Prohibited acts*—The consensus is that paralegals should not engage in the following acts:

   a. Establish an attorney-client relationship.
   b. Set legal fees.
   c. Give legal advice or opinions.
   d. Represent a client in court (unless authorized to do so by the court).
   e. Encourage or contribute to any act that could constitute UPL.

4. *Paralegal status*—Paralegals should always make clear their professional status so clients will not be confused.

5. *Freelance and independent paralegals*—Freelance paralegals work under the supervision of attorneys, just as full-time employees of attorneys do. The position of independent paralegals (legal technicians) is more problematic.

Should Paralegals Be Licensed?

An issue for legal professionals is whether paralegals should be directly regulated by the state through licensing requirements.

1. *General licensing*—General licensing would establish minimum standards that every paralegal would have to meet in order to practice as a paralegal in the state.

2. *Registration*—Some states, such as Florida, offer registration of paralegals. While not mandated, it does provide more visibility and professional recognition. Other states, such as California, have educational requirements that must be met to be a paralegal.

3. *Direct regulation*—The pros and cons of direct regulation through licensing are being debated vigorously by the leading paralegal and paralegal education associations, state bar associations, state courts, state legislatures, and public-interest groups.

KEY TERMS AND CONCEPTS

attorney-client privilege 99
breach 91
conflict of interest 101
conflicts check 103
damages 89
disbarment 89

ethical wall 102
general licensing 113
licensing 87
malpractice 89
reprimand 89
self-regulation 114

suspension 89
third party 97
unauthorized practice of law (UPL) 88
work product 100

QUESTIONS FOR REVIEW

1. Why is the legal profession regulated? Who are the regulators? How is regulation accomplished?

2. How is the paralegal profession regulated by attorney ethical codes? How is it regulated by paralegal codes of ethics?

3. What does the duty of competence involve? How can violations of the duty of competence be avoided?

4. What is the duty of confidentiality? What is the attorney-client privilege? What is the relationship between the duty of confidentiality and the attorney-client privilege? What are some potential consequences of violating the confidentiality rule?

5. How is the practice of law defined? The unauthorized practice of law (UPL)? How might paralegals violate state statutes prohibiting UPL? What types of tasks can legally be performed by paralegals?

6. Explain the difference between licensing and certification. What are the positions of the NFPA, NALA, and the AAfPE on the issue of licensing for paralegals? Do you think paralegals should be licensed?

ETHICS QUESTIONS

1. Norma Sollers works as a paralegal for a small law firm. She is a trusted, experienced employee who has worked for the firm for twelve years. One morning, Linda Lowenstein, one of the attorneys, calls from her home and asks Norma to sign Linda's name to a document that must be filed with the court that day. Norma has just prepared the final draft of the document and placed it on Linda's desk for her review and signature. Linda explains to Norma that because her child is sick, she does not want to leave home to come into the office. Norma knows that she should not sign Linda's name—only the client's attorney can sign the document. She mentions this to Linda, but Linda says, "Don't worry. No one will ever know that you signed it instead of me." How should Norma handle this situation?

2. The law firm of Dover, Cleary, and Harper decides to store all of its data in the cloud and enters into a contract with Cloud Service Provider for data storage. The firm does not mention its conversion to cloud storage to any of its clients. Six months later, an employee of the Cloud Service Provider notices that one of the firm's clients, a local celebrity, has serious financial problems and broadcasts this fact on Facebook, causing significant embarrassment to the client. The client is able to track the disclosure of her confidential information on Facebook to Cloud Service Provider, which obtained the client's file from Dover, Cleary, and Harper. Is the law firm guilty of an ethical violation?

PRACTICE QUESTIONS AND ASSIGNMENTS

1. In which of the following instances may confidential client information be disclosed?

   a. The client in a divorce case threatens to hire a hit man to kill her husband because she believes that killing her husband is the only way that she can stop him from stalking her. It is clear that the client intends to do this.

   b. A former client sues her attorney for legal malpractice in the handling of a breach-of-contract case involving her cosmetics home-sale business. The attorney discloses that the client is having an affair with her next-door neighbor, a fact that is unrelated to the malpractice case or the breach-of-contract case.

2. Using the material presented in the chapter on conflicts of interest, determine which type of conflict of interest is presented in the following situations:

   a. A lawyer has a case pending before the state supreme court, advocating that a divorced parent must obtain court permission to move a child more than three hundred miles from the other parent. The same lawyer takes a case for a client who wants to move seven hundred miles from the other parent, and in this case he argues that no court permission is needed. This case will likely end up before the state supreme court.

b. Melissa is an attorney with a criminal law practice. She has a big case in which her client was convicted of violating the state's recently enacted medical marijuana law, and she is appealing his conviction to the state supreme court. Tom, her husband, is a paralegal who works for the state attorney's office. He has been assigned to gather research opposing the brief that Melissa filed on behalf of her client.

c. Attorney Sam prepares a will for a client; the will leaves the client's vacation home to Sam.

d. A new client brings a case to attorney Mark and asks Mark to represent him. The case would require Mark to sue a former client whom he previously defended on the same issue.

3. Which of the following actions should you take as a paralegal to avoid charges of engaging in the practice of law?

a. Include the title "paralegal" when signing letters and e-mails.

b. Introduce yourself without using your title in meetings with clients.

c. Include the title "paralegal" on your business cards.

d. Disclose your status as a paralegal when communicating with a court.

4. Matthew Hinson is a legal technician. He provides divorce forms and typing and filing services to the public at very low rates. Samantha Eggleston uses his services. She presents him with her completed forms, but she has one question: How much will she be entitled to receive in monthly child-support payments? How may Matthew legally respond to this question?

5. A paralegal experienced in employment discrimination law was hired by an attorney to develop a practice requiring appearances before both the state discrimination agency and the Equal Employment Opportunity Commission (EEOC). The paralegal had previously advocated for clients before this state agency as permitted by state law. The attorney had no experience with employment discrimination cases. The attorney's clients were charged contingency fees, with the attorney receiving two-thirds of the fees and the paralegal one-third. The paralegal solicited clients and handled their cases without supervision, to the extent of having more than forty cases pending before the state agency. The paralegal also removed cases from the agencies and refiled them in the courts using the attorney's name and bar license without seeking the attorney's approval for doing so. Using the material in the chapter, what ethical violations did the paralegal commit? Did the attorney violate any ethical duties?

6. According to this chapter's text, which of the following tasks can a paralegal legally perform?

a. Provide legal advice to clients in the course of helping them prepare divorce pleadings.

b. Interview a witness to a car accident.

c. Represent a client in court.

d. Set legal fees.

e. Work as a freelance paralegal for attorneys.

f. Work as a legal technician providing legal services directly to the public.

GROUP PROJECT

This project involves the review of your state's version of one of the ethical rules of competence, conflict of interest, or client confidentiality as assigned by your instructor.

Students one, two, and three will locate your state's version of the rule using online sources, your school's library, or a local law library. They will also summarize the assigned sections of the rule and will determine which rule is the law in your state.

Student four will compare the summarized sections of the state rule to the ABA *Model Rule* discussed in this chapter and will present the comparison to the class.

©fizkes/Shutterstock.com

Sources of American Law

CHAPTER

5

CHAPTER OBJECTIVES

After completing this chapter, you will be able to:

- Define *law*, and list sources of primary and secondary law.

- Describe how English law influenced the development of the American legal system.

- Explain what the common law tradition is and how it evolved.

- Discuss the difference between remedies at law and equitable remedies.

- Define and explain some of the terms that are commonly found in case law.

- Explain the meaning and relative importance in the American legal system of constitutional law.

- Explain the meaning and relative importance in the American legal system of statutory law.

- Explain the meaning and relative importance in the American legal system of administrative law.

- Describe how national law and international law differ and why these bodies of law sometimes guide judicial decision making in U.S. courts.

Introduction

European colonists brought laws and legal traditions with them to the New World, and the American legal system absorbed ideas from the English, French, Scottish, and Spanish legal systems as the country grew. The English legal system had the greatest influence, and most American states passed statutes formally adopting English common law as part of their own legal systems. For example, New York's 1777 Constitution adopted English common law as of April 19, 1775. Over time, American law developed its own unique characteristics as a blend of these different legal traditions.

We open this chapter with a discussion of the nature of law and then examine traditional law and its significance in the American legal system. Next, we focus on other sources of American law, including constitutional, statutory, and administrative law. We also explain how the laws of other countries and international law affect decision making in U.S. courts. Another major part of the American legal structure—the court system—will be examined in Chapter 6.

The Framework of American Law

The law means different things to different people. Before beginning your study of American law, it is useful to have an understanding of what law is and some of the different approaches to law that influence courts' decisions. These topics are covered in the following subsections.

What Is the Law?

law
A body of rules of conduct established and enforced by the controlling authority (the government) of a society.

How a person defines *law* frequently depends on the person's views on morality, ethics, and truth. Generally, we define **law** as a body of rules of conduct established and enforced by the government of a society. These "rules of conduct" may consist of written principles of behavior, such as those established by ancient societies. They may be set forth in a comprehensive code, as used in many European nations. They may consist of a combination of legislatively enacted statutes, administrative regulations, and court decisions, as in the United States. Regardless of how the rules are created, they establish rights, duties, and privileges for the citizens they govern.

One of the most important functions of law in any society is to provide stability, predictability, and continuity so that people can arrange their affairs. If a legal system is to be credible, citizens must be able to determine what is legally permissible and what is not.

> **EXAMPLE 5.1** Citizens must know what penalties will be imposed on them if they commit wrongful acts. If people suffer harm as a result of others' wrongful acts, they need to know whether and how they can receive compensation for their injuries.

By setting forth the rights, obligations, and privileges of citizens, the law enables people to go about their business and personal lives with confidence and a certain degree of predictability.

Primary Sources of American Law

primary source of law
In legal research, a document that establishes the law on a particular issue, such as a case decision, legislative act, or administrative rule.

American law has numerous sources. A source that establishes the law on a particular issue is called a **primary source of law.** Primary sources include the following:

1. Case law and common law doctrines.
2. The U.S. Constitution and the constitutions of the various states.

3. Statutes—including laws passed by Congress, state legislatures, and local governing bodies.

4. Regulations created by administrative agencies, such as the U.S. Food and Drug Administration (FDA) or state insurance commissions.

We describe each of these important sources of law in the following discussion. Note that treaties with other nations are also a primary source of law, although most legal practitioners do not deal with them directly but instead retain a specialist in international law to assist them. We will discuss international law near the end of this chapter.

A **secondary source of law** is a book or article that summarizes, synthesizes, or explains a primary source of law. Examples include legal encyclopedias, treatises, articles in law reviews, and compilations of law, such as the *Restatements of the Law* (to be discussed later in this chapter). Courts often refer to secondary sources of law for guidance in interpreting the primary sources of law discussed here. They are also useful research tools that aid in locating primary sources. Secondary sources can be persuasive authorities, particularly if the authors are widely respected. For example, courts often cite the treatise *Prosser & Keeton on Torts*, which was originally written by two famous tort law scholars, William Prosser and Paige Keeton.

Case Law and the Common Law Tradition

An important source of law consists of the opinions issued by judges in cases that come before the courts. Lawyers call this **case law.** As mentioned earlier, because of our colonial heritage, much American law is based on the English legal system. Our reliance on reported court decisions is a key part of our English heritage, as legal systems not derived from Britain's put much less weight on judicial opinions.

The English **common law** is a body of general rules applied by the courts. In deciding common law cases, judges attempt to be consistent by basing decisions on principles from earlier cases. By doing this, they seek to ensure that they decide similar cases in similar ways. Each decision becomes part of the law on the subject and serves as a legal **precedent.** Later cases that involve similar legal principles or facts are decided with reference to precedents. An important part of legal research involves finding relevant court opinions.

The Doctrine of *Stare Decisis*

The practice of deciding new cases with reference to former decisions, or precedents, is a cornerstone of the English and American judicial systems. It forms a doctrine called *stare decisis* ("to stand by things decided"). Under this doctrine, judges are obligated to follow the precedents established by their own courts or by higher courts in their *jurisdictions* (the areas over which they have authority). These controlling precedents are referred to as binding authorities.

A **binding authority** is a source of law that a court must follow when deciding a case. Binding authorities include constitutions, statutes, and regulations that govern an issue being decided, as well as court decisions that are controlling precedents within the jurisdiction. When no binding authority exists, courts will often review a **persuasive precedent**, which includes precedents decided in similar cases in other jurisdictions, treatises, scholarly articles, and other secondary sources. The court may either follow or reject persuasive precedents.

The doctrine of *stare decisis* helps the courts be more efficient because if other courts have carefully reasoned through similar cases, their legal reasoning and opinions

secondary source of law
In legal research, any publication that indexes, summarizes, or interprets the law, such as a legal encyclopedia, a treatise, or an article in a law review.

case law
Rules of law announced in court decisions.

common law
A body of law developed from custom or earlier judicial decisions in English and U.S. courts and not by a legislature.

precedent
A court decision that furnishes authority for deciding later cases in which similar facts are presented.

stare decisis
The doctrine of precedent, under which a court is obligated to follow earlier decisions of that court or higher courts within the same jurisdiction. This is a major characteristic of the common law system.

binding authority
Any source of law that a court must follow when deciding a case. Binding authorities include constitutions, statutes, and regulations that govern the issue being decided, as well as court decisions that are controlling precedents within the jurisdiction.

persuasive precedent
A precedent that a court may either follow or reject. Such precedents include precedents decided in similar cases in other jurisdictions, treatises, scholarly articles, and other secondary sources.

can serve as guides. *Stare decisis* also makes the law more stable and predictable. If the law on a given subject is well settled and there are numerous precedents, someone wishing to bring a case is likely to be told by an attorney how the law will likely resolve the matter.

Departures from Precedent

Sometimes a court will depart from the rule of precedent. If a court decides that a precedent is wrong or that technological or social changes have made the precedent inappropriate, the court might overrule the precedent. These cases often receive a great deal of publicity.

> *EXAMPLE 5.2* In *Brown v. Board of Education of Topeka*,[1] decided in 1954, the United States Supreme Court expressly overturned prior precedent when it held that separate schools for whites and African Americans—which had been upheld as constitutional in previous cases—were in violation of the U.S. Constitution. The Court's departure from precedent in *Brown* received tremendous publicity as people began to realize the impact of this change in the law. It helped encourage the civil rights movement, which included legal challenges to laws that imposed racial segregation.

Cases of First Impression

Sometimes, there is no precedent on which to base a decision, as when a case involves a new technology.

> *EXAMPLE 5.3* A New Jersey court had to decide whether a surrogate-parenting contract should be enforced against the wishes of the surrogate parent (the birth mother).[2] This was the first such case to reach the courts, and there was no precedent involving surrogates in any jurisdiction to which the court could look for guidance. (Note: The court invalidated the contract but upheld the original agreement by treating the case as a child custody case and awarding custody to the parents who hired the surrogate.)

case of first impression
A case presenting a legal issue that has not yet been addressed by a court in a particular jurisdiction.

public policy
A governmental policy based on widely held societal values.

remedy
The means by which a right is enforced or the violation of a right is compensated for.

court of law
A court in which the only remedies were money and property. Historically, in England, a court of law was different from a court of equity.

remedies at law
Remedies available in a court of law. Monetary damages and property are awarded as remedies at law.

A case with no precedents is called a **case of first impression.** In these cases or when precedents conflict, courts may consider a number of factors, including legal principles and policies underlying previous court decisions or existing statutes, fairness, social values and customs, **public policy** (a governmental policy based on widely held societal values), and data and concepts drawn from the social sciences. Which of these sources receives the greatest emphasis will depend on the nature of the case being considered and the particular judge hearing the case.

Judges try to be free of personal bias in deciding cases. Each judge, however, has a unique personality, values or philosophical leanings, personal history, and intellectual attributes—all of which frame the decision-making process.

Remedies at Law versus Remedies in Equity

A **remedy** is the means given to a party to enforce a right or to compensate for the violation of a right. The early English courts could grant only specific and limited remedies. If one person wronged another in some way, the court could award property or money as compensation. The court that awarded such compensation became known as a **court of law,** and the two remedies awarded by these courts became known as **remedies at law.** These early English courts also required plaintiffs to follow highly specific legal forms in making their cases, and even a small mistake could cause a plaintiff to lose a case.

This system helped to standardize the ways in which disputes were settled, but parties who wanted a remedy other than economic compensation—or whose lawyers had not performed every step exactly right—could not be helped. Sometimes, these parties petitioned the king for relief. Most petitions were decided by an adviser to the king, called a *chancellor,* who was said to be the "keeper of the king's conscience." When the chancellor thought that the claim was a fair one for which there was no adequate remedy at law, he would fashion a different remedy, called a **remedy in equity.** In this way, a new body of rules and remedies came into being and eventually led to the establishment of formal courts of chancery, or a **court of equity.**

remedy in equity
A remedy allowed by courts in situations where remedies at law are not appropriate. Remedies in equity are based on rules of fairness, justice, and honesty.

Equity is founded on what might be described as notions of justice and fair dealing, and seeks to supply a remedy when there is no adequate remedy available at law. Once the courts of equity were established, plaintiffs could bring claims in either courts of law (if they sought monetary damages) or courts of equity (if they sought equitable remedies). Plaintiffs had to specify whether they were bringing an "action at law" or an "action in equity," and they chose their courts accordingly. Only one remedy could be granted for a particular wrong. Today, most states have combined the separate courts, and both types of remedies can be sought in a single case from the same court. (See Exhibit 5.1.) Whether a claim is based on law or equity still matters, however, since the distinction determines whether a jury trial is available (legal claims) or whether the judge will decide both law and fact (equitable claims).

court of equity
A court that decides controversies and administers justice according to the rules, principles, and precedents of equity.

Equitable Principles and Maxims

Since most courts in the United States can award both legal and equitable remedies, plaintiffs may request both equitable and legal relief in the same case. Whenever a court orders a party to do or not do something as part of a remedy, such as to stop a discriminatory practice, it is providing an equitable remedy. In deciding whether to grant equitable remedies, judges continue to be guided by **equitable principles and maxims.** *Maxims* are propositions or general statements of rules of law that courts often use in arriving at a decision. Some of the most influential maxims of equity are:

equitable principles and maxims
Propositions or general statements of rules of law that are frequently involved in equity jurisdiction.

- Whoever seeks equity must do equity. (Anyone who wishes to be treated fairly must treat others fairly.)

- Equity requires clean hands. (The plaintiff must have acted fairly and honestly.)

- Equity will not suffer a right to exist without a remedy. (Equitable relief will be awarded when there is a right to relief and there is no adequate legal remedy.)

- Equity values substance over form. (It is more concerned with fairness and justice than with legal technicalities.)

- Equity aids the vigilant, not those who sleep on their rights. (Individuals who fail to assert their legal rights within a reasonable time will not be helped.)

Additionally, as a historical accident, California codified a large number of "Maxims of Jurisprudence," which you can find in the California Civil Code Sections 3509–3548. These include "The greater contains the less" and "Interpretation must be reasonable."

Procedure	Action at Law	Action in Equity
Decision	By judge or jury	By judge (no jury)
Result	Judgment	Decree
Remedy	Monetary damages	Injunction or decree of specific performance

EXHIBIT 5.1
Procedural Differences between an Action at Law and an Action in Equity

Doctrine of Laches

The equitable doctrine of **laches** encourages people to bring lawsuits while the evidence is still fresh. The idea is that if a party waits too long, the party has "slept on his rights" and lost the ability to bring a claim. What constitutes a reasonable time depends on the circumstances of the case. The reason for this doctrine is that a long delay could prejudice the defendant by making evidence hard to find.

> **EXAMPLE 5.4** The Nature Conservancy (TNC) contracted to buy land from Wilder Corporation. Wilder promised that there were no storage tanks on the property. Six years later, having discovered such tanks, TNC sued. Wilder claimed that laches barred the suit—TNC had waited too long to sue. The appeals court held that laches did not apply, as there was no unreasonable delay by TNC in bringing the litigation.[3]

The time period for pursuing a particular claim against another party is now usually fixed by a statute of limitations. After the time allowed under the statute of limitations has expired, further action on that claim is barred. (See this chapter's *Ethics Watch* feature.)

For civil wrongs (torts), the statute of limitations varies, typically ranging from two to five years. For contracts involving the sale of goods, it is normally four years. Statutes of limitations may be "tolled" (put on hold) if a defendant has acted to conceal the facts or it would have been impossible for the plaintiff to discover the existence of the claim.

For criminal prosecutions, the duration is related to the seriousness of the offense. For example, the statute of limitations for petty theft (the theft of an item of insignificant value) may be a year, while the statute of limitations for armed robbery might be twenty years. For the most serious crimes involving first degree murder, there is no statute of limitations.

Equitable Remedies

As mentioned previously, equitable remedies are normally granted only if the court concludes that the remedy at law (monetary damages) is inadequate. No jury is used in deciding an equitable claim—the trial judge will decide both the facts and the law. The most important equitable remedies—specific performance and injunction—are discussed here and will be discussed further in Chapter 15.

Specific Performance. A judge's decree of **specific performance** is an order to do what was promised. This remedy was, and still is, generally only available in the United States when the dispute before the court concerns a contractual transaction involving something unique for which monetary damages are inadequate. By contrast, many European countries routinely allow a decree of specific performance. The parties to complex contracts also regularly include provisions in their contracts allowing each party to seek it against the other in case of breach.

Contracts for the sale of goods that are readily available on the market rarely qualify for specific performance. Monetary damages ordinarily are adequate in such situations because substantially identical goods can be bought or sold in the market.

If the goods are unique, however, a court of equity may grant specific performance. For example, paintings, sculptures, and rare books and coins are so unique that monetary damages will not enable a buyer to obtain substantially identical substitutes in the market. Similarly, it is sometimes allowed in cases involving the sale of a business. The same principle applies to disputes relating to interests in land because each parcel is unique.

ETHICS WATCH

THE STATUTE OF LIMITATIONS AND THE DUTY OF COMPETENCE

The duty of competence requires, among other things, that attorneys and paralegals be aware of the statute of limitations governing a client's legal matter. For example, if a client of your firm, a restaurant owner, wanted to sue a restaurant-supply company for breaking a contract for the sale of dishes, the first thing you should check is your state's statute of limitations covering contracts for the sale of goods. If the time period is about to expire, then you and your supervising attorney need to act quickly to make sure that the complaint (the document that initiates a lawsuit) is filed before the claim is time barred.

Of course, the attorney is responsible to the client, but it is normal for an attorney to rely on a paralegal to check such details. This example reflects the NFPA *Model Code of Ethics and Professional Responsibility*, Section 1.1(a), "A paralegal shall achieve competency through education, training, and work experience," and Section 1.1(c), "A paralegal shall perform all assignments promptly and efficiently."

Reprinted by permission of the National Federation of Paralegal Associations, Inc. (NFPA®), paralegals.org.

EXAMPLE 5.5 A party agreed to sell a piece of land to a buyer, who hired engineers and architects to design a building suited for the particular piece of land. Right before the transaction was to be completed, and for no clear reason, the seller refused to go through with the property transfer. The buyer may sue for specific performance, asking the court to require the sale to proceed, due to the time and expense in planning for the unique use of that particular piece of property.

Specific performance is rarely granted in cases involving personal services, but see the *Developing Paralegal Skills* feature below for a practical example of how the issue arises.

DEVELOPING PARALEGAL SKILLS

REQUIREMENTS FOR SPECIFIC PERFORMANCE

Louise Lassen, a wealthy heiress, buys a painting from an artist in New York for $275,000. The artist agrees to ship the painting to Louise's home in Chicago within two weeks. After Louise returns home, she learns from the artist that he has changed his mind—he is no longer interested in selling the painting and is returning her payment.

Louise contacts the firm of Murdoch & Larson to have the contract enforced. Kevin Murdoch, one of the firm's partners, asks paralegal Lars Humboldt to assist him in determining whether the remedy of specific performance, which would require the artist to provide the painting, can be sought. Lars is to research case law on specific performance and prepare a research memorandum summarizing his results. Lars lets the

attorney know that he will have the memorandum on the attorney's desk by the next morning.

Checklist for Analyzing a Legal Problem

- Gather the facts involved in the problem.
- Determine whether unique or rare articles are involved.
- Find out what type of remedy the client wants.
- Determine whether a remedy at law, such as monetary damages, will compensate the client.
- Apply the law to the client's facts to reach a conclusion regarding the appropriate remedy.

injunction
A court decree ordering a person to do or to refrain from doing a certain act.

Injunction.   An injunction is a court order directing the defendant to do or, more commonly, to refrain from doing a particular act. An injunction may be obtained to stop a neighbor from burning trash in his yard or to prevent an estranged husband from coming near his wife.

> **EXAMPLE 5.6** Jacqueline Kennedy Onassis, the widow of U.S. President John F. Kennedy, asked a court to stop a photographer from pulling stunts—such as throwing a firecracker near her or getting someone to scream at her—so he could get an unusual photograph to sell at a high price. The court agreed that money was not the issue and ordered the photographer to keep his distance and not to play any more tricks.

Persons who violate injunctions may be held in contempt of court and punished with a jail sentence or a fine.

The Common Law Today

The common law—which consists of the rules of law announced in previous court decisions—plays a significant role in the United States. The rules governing contracts, property, and tort law (civil wrongs) are largely common law. Even where there is a statute, court decisions often play an important role by clarifying ambiguous statutory language. Federal and state courts frequently must interpret and enforce constitutional provisions, statutes enacted by legislatures, and regulations created by administrative agencies.

To summarize and clarify common law rules and principles, the American Law Institute (ALI) has published a number of *Restatements of the Law*. The ALI, which was formed in the 1920s, is a group of highly regarded practicing attorneys, legal scholars, and judges. The *Restatements* generally summarize and explain the common law rules that are followed in most states with regard to a particular area of law, such as contracts or torts. Although the *Restatements* do not have the force of law unless adopted by a state's highest court, they are important secondary sources of legal analysis on which judges often rely in making their decisions. The *Restatements* are an excellent tool for quickly getting an overview of an area of the law and will likely be helpful to you in your career as a paralegal. (You will read more about the *Restatements of the Law* in Chapter 7, in the context of legal research.)

The Terminology of Case Law

Throughout this text, you will encounter terms traditionally used to describe parties to lawsuits, case titles, and the types of decisions that judges write. At this point, it is worthwhile to explain some of the terminology when researching case law.

Case Titles

The title of a case, or the *case name*, indicates the names of the parties to the lawsuit. A case title, such as *Baranski v. Peretto*, includes only the parties' surnames, not their first names. The *v.* in the case title stands for *versus*, which means "against." In the trial court (the court in which a lawsuit is first brought and tried), Baranski is the plaintiff, so Baranski's name appears first in the case title.

If the case is appealed to a higher court for review, the appeals court sometimes places the name of the party appealing the decision first, so that on appeal the case may be called *Peretto v. Baranski*. Because some appeals courts retain the trial court order of names, it is often impossible to distinguish the plaintiff from the defendant just by looking at the title of a reported decision. You must read the facts of the case to identify the parties.

When attorneys or paralegals refer to a court decision, they give the title of the case and the case citation. The **citation** indicates the reports or reporters in which the case can be found (reports and reporters are volumes in which cases are published, or "reported").

> **EXAMPLE 5.7** A citation to 251 Kan. 728 following a case name (*Tongish v. Thomas*) indicates that the opinion (the court's decision) can be found in Volume 251 of the Kansas state court reports on page 728. Other common law countries, such as England, have similar systems, but you should consult an appropriate reference work before dealing with a system of case reporting with which you are unfamiliar.

The Parties to a Lawsuit

One **party** to a lawsuit is called the *plaintiff*, who initiates (files) the lawsuit. The other party is called the *defendant*, against whom the lawsuit is brought. Lawsuits frequently involve multiple parties—that is, more than one plaintiff or defendant. In addition, sometimes the parties bring claims against each other.

> **EXAMPLE 5.8** A consumer named Aiken, claiming to be injured by a product made by Toshiba that he purchased at Target, may sue both Toshiba and Target (the manufacturer and the retailer) to try to obtain compensation for injuries alleged to be caused by the product. The manufacturer and the retailer would be *co-defendants*. On appeal, the party asking for review is often called the *appellant*, and the other party is called the *appellee*.

Judges and Justices

The terms *judge* and *justice* usually mean the same and represent two designations given to judges in various U.S. courts. All members of the United States Supreme Court are referred to as justices. Justice is also the formal title usually given to judges of appeals courts, although this is not always the case. Different states use different terms. Justice

citation
A reference that indicates where a particular constitutional provision, statute, reported case, or article can be found.

party
With respect to lawsuits, the plaintiff or the defendant. Some cases involve multiple parties (more than one plaintiff or defendant).

Why is the common law important even in areas that are primarily governed by statutory law?

is commonly abbreviated as J., justices as JJ., and Chief Justice as C.J. A Supreme Court case might refer to Justice Sotomayor as Sotomayor, J., or to Chief Justice Roberts as Roberts, C.J.

In a trial court, one judge hears a case. In an appeals court, normally a panel of three or more judges (or justices) sits on the bench to hear the appeal. Decisions reached by appeals courts are often explained in written court opinions.

Decisions and Opinions

opinion
A statement by the court setting forth the applicable law and the reasons for its decision in a case.

In U.S. jurisdictions, the **opinion** typically contains a brief procedural history of the case, a summary of the relevant facts, the court's reasons for its decision, the rules of law that apply, and the judgment. Foreign court opinions have their own unique structures. For example, English court opinions are typically much longer than U.S. court opinions, number the paragraphs for reference, and have a more conversational style, since they are often read from the bench as well as published.

There are several types of opinions. When all judges or justices agree on an opinion, the opinion is written for the entire court and is called a *unanimous opinion*. When there is not a unanimous opinion, a *majority opinion* is written, explaining the views of the majority of the judges deciding the case. Sometimes, a majority agrees on the result but not on the reasoning. The opinion joined by the largest number of judges, but less than a majority, is called a *plurality opinion*. Additionally, a court occasionally issues a per curiam *opinion* (*per curiam* is Latin for "of the court"), which does not indicate which judge wrote the opinion.

A judge who feels strongly about making or emphasizing a point that was not made in the majority opinion writes a *concurring opinion*. In that opinion, the judge agrees (concurs) with the decision given in the majority opinion but for different reasons. When an opinion is not unanimous, a judge who does not agree with the majority may write a *dissenting opinion*. The dissenting opinion may be important, as it may form the basis of arguments used in the future to modify the law or even overrule the current majority opinion.

The Adversarial System of Justice

adversarial system of justice
A legal system in which the parties to a lawsuit are opponents, or adversaries, and present their cases in the light most favorable to themselves. The impartial decision maker (the judge or jury) determines who wins based on an application of the law to the evidence presented.

U.S. courts follow the **adversarial system of justice,** in which the parties act as adversaries, or opponents. Parties to a lawsuit come before the court as contestants, both sides presenting the facts of their cases in the light most favorable to themselves, in an attempt to win. The parties do not come to the courtroom with the idea of working out a compromise solution to their problems or of looking at the dispute from each other's point of view. Rather, they take sides, present their best case to the judge or jury, and hope that the decision maker rules in their favor. Because both sides' positions are tested at trial, in theory the strongest case wins. In the adversarial system, the judge serves as a neutral party.

Constitutional Law

constitutional law
Law based on the U.S. Constitution and the constitutions of the states.

We turn next to other primary sources of law. The federal government and the states have separate written constitutions that set forth the general organization, powers, and limits of their respective governments. In the United States, **constitutional law** is made up of the text of a constitution and court decisions interpreting that text. Not every country has a written constitution, however. The United Kingdom's constitution, for example, is unwritten and consists of custom, precedent, and some written documents like the Magna Carta (written in 1215).

The Federal Constitution

The U.S. Constitution is often called the nation's highest law. This principle is set forth in Article VI of the Constitution, which states that the Constitution, laws, and treaties of the United States are "the supreme Law of the Land." This provision is commonly referred to as the **supremacy clause.** A law in conflict with the Constitution (including its amendments), no matter what its source, will be declared unconstitutional when challenged.

supremacy clause

The provision in Article VI of the U.S. Constitution that declares the Constitution, laws, and treaties of the United States "the supreme Law of the Land."

> **EXAMPLE 5.9** Congress is authorized by the Constitution to regulate trade with foreign nations. If a state passes a law to prohibit the import into the state of products from a particular country, or imposes taxes on imports, the state law will be unconstitutional, as it conflicts with the Constitution's allocation of that power to the federal government.

The U.S. Constitution consists of seven articles. These articles, which are summarized in Exhibit 5.2, set forth the powers of the three branches of government and the relationships among the three branches.

Constitutional Rights

Soon after the Constitution was ratified by the states, the first Congress of the United States submitted amendments to the Constitution to the states for approval.

Bill of Rights.   The first ten amendments, commonly known as the **Bill of Rights,** were adopted in 1791 and provide protections for individuals—and in some cases, business entities—against various types of government interference. Summarized below are the protections mentioned by the Bill of Rights. The full text of the U.S. Constitution, including its amendments (there are now twenty-seven), is presented in Appendix F.

Bill of Rights

The first ten amendments to the U.S. Constitution.

1. The First Amendment guarantees individuals the freedoms of religion, speech, and the press and the rights to assemble peaceably and to petition the government.

2. The Second Amendment guarantees individuals' right to keep and bear arms.

EXHIBIT 5.2

The Articles of the U.S. Constitution

Article I creates and empowers the legislature. It provides that Congress is to consist of a Senate and a House of Representatives and fixes the composition of each house and the election procedures, qualifications, and compensation for senators and representatives. Article I also establishes the procedures for enacting legislation and the areas of law in which Congress has the power to legislate.

Article II establishes the executive branch, the process for electing and removing a president from office, the qualifications to be president, and the powers of the president.

Article III creates the judicial branch and authorizes the appointment, compensation, and removal of judges. It also sets forth the jurisdiction of the courts and defines *treason*.

Article IV requires that all states respect one another's laws. It requires each state to give citizens of other states the same rights and privileges it gives its own citizens. It requires that persons accused of crimes be returned to the state in which the crime was committed.

Article V governs the process for amending the Constitution.

Article VI establishes the Constitution as the supreme law of the land. It requires that every federal and state official take an oath of office promising to support the Constitution. It specifies that religion is not a required qualification to serve in any federal office.

Article VII requires the consent of nine of the original thirteen states to ratify the Constitution.

3. The Third Amendment prohibits, in peacetime, the lodging of soldiers in any house without the owner's consent.

4. The Fourth Amendment prohibits unreasonable searches and seizures of persons or property.

5. The Fifth Amendment guarantees the rights to indictment by grand jury and to due process of law and prohibits compulsory self-incrimination and double jeopardy. (This will be discussed in Chapter 13, which deals with criminal law and procedures.) The Fifth Amendment also prohibits the taking of private property for public use without just compensation.

6. The Sixth Amendment guarantees the accused in a criminal case the right to a speedy and public trial by an impartial jury and the right to counsel. The accused has the right to cross-examine opposing witnesses and to solicit testimony from favorable witnesses.

7. The Seventh Amendment guarantees the right to a trial by jury in a civil case involving at least twenty dollars.

8. The Eighth Amendment prohibits excessive bail and fines, as well as cruel and unusual punishment.

9. The Ninth Amendment establishes that the people have rights in addition to those specified in the Constitution.

10. The Tenth Amendment establishes that powers neither delegated to the federal government nor denied to the states are reserved for the states.

Application to State Governments.   Originally, the Bill of Rights limited only the powers of the national government. That changed after the adoption of the Fourteenth Amendment to the Constitution. That amendment, passed in 1868 after the Civil War, provides in part: "No State shall … deprive any person of life, liberty, or property, without due process of law." The Supreme Court defines various rights and liberties guaranteed in the national Constitution as "due process of law," which is required of state governments under the Fourteenth Amendment. Today, most of the rights in the Bill of Rights—such as the freedoms of speech and religion guaranteed by the First Amendment—apply to state governments as well as to the national government. This is referred to as the "incorporation" of the First Amendment into the Fourteenth Amendment.

The Courts and Constitutional Law

The rights secured by the Bill of Rights are not absolute. The principles outlined in the Constitution are given form and substance by the courts. Courts often have to balance the rights and freedoms stated in the Bill of Rights against other rights, such as the right to be free from the harmful actions of others. Ultimately, it is the United States Supreme Court, as the final interpreter of the Constitution, which gives meaning to constitutional rights and determines their boundaries.

Courts Balance the Right to Free Speech.   An instance of how the courts must balance the rights and freedoms set out in the Constitution can be found by looking at our right to free speech. Even though the First Amendment guarantees the right to free speech, we are not, in fact, free to say anything we want.

EXAMPLE 5.10 In interpreting the meaning of the First Amendment, the United States Supreme Court has been clear that certain speech will not be protected. Speech that harms the good reputation of another, for instance, is commonly considered to be a tort, or civil wrong. If the speaker is sued, she may be ordered by a court to pay damages to the harmed person (see Chapter 14).

Free Speech and the Internet.   The Internet raised new issues for the courts in determining how to apply the protections conferred by the Constitution, particularly with respect to free speech. For example, the Supreme Court ruled that obscene speech, though difficult to define, is not entitled to complete First Amendment protection. Regulating obscene online speech has proved to be difficult.

> *EXAMPLE 5.11* Congress attempted to prohibit online obscenity in the Communications Decency Act (CDA), which made it a crime to make available to minors online any "obscene or indecent" message.[4] Civil rights groups claimed the CDA was an unconstitutional restraint on speech. The Supreme Court held that portions of the act were unconstitutional in *Reno v. American Civil Liberties Union*.[5] Congress then passed the Child Online Protection Act (COPA).[6] That law was struck down by a federal appeals court as being unconstitutional because it was too vague.[7] The Supreme Court agreed with that ruling.[8]

State Constitutions

Each state has a constitution that sets forth the general organization, powers, and limits of the state government. State constitutions tend to be much more specific and detailed than the federal constitution. As a result, they also tend to be much longer. The longest state constitution (that of Alabama) is forty times longer than the U.S. Constitution.

The Tenth Amendment to the U.S. Constitution, which defines the powers and limitations of the federal government, reserves all powers not granted to the federal government to the states. Unless they conflict with the U.S. Constitution, state constitutions are supreme within the states' borders, so they are important sources of law.

Statutory Law

A **statute** is a law enacted by a legislative body at any level of government. Statutes make up a major source of law. The body of written laws created by the legislature is generally referred to as **statutory law.**

statute
A written law enacted by a legislature under its constitutional lawmaking authority.

statutory law
The body of written laws enacted by the legislature.

Federal Statutes

Federal statutes are laws enacted by the U.S. Congress. As mentioned, any law—including a federal statute—that violates the U.S. Constitution will be struck down. Areas of federal statutory law include protection of intellectual property rights (see Chapter 15), regulation of the purchase and sale of corporate stock (see Chapter 18), prohibition of employment discrimination (see Chapter 18), protection of the environment (see Chapter 19), and protection of consumers (see Chapter 14). As is discussed in this chapter's *Featured Contributor* article on the following pages, paralegals must know how to use a variety of legal sources to research federal, state, and local statutes pertaining to a given case.

The Federal Government's Constitutional Authority to Enact Laws

In the **federal system** of government established by the Constitution, the national government (usually called the federal government) and the state governments *share* sovereign power. The Constitution specifies, however, that certain powers can be exercised only by the national government. For example, the national government is authorized to regulate domestic and foreign commerce (trade).

federal system
The system of government established by the Constitution, in which the national government and the state governments share sovereign power.

FEATURED CONTRIBUTOR

SOURCES OF LAW

John D. DeLeo, Jr.

BIOGRAPHICAL NOTE

John D. DeLeo, Jr., earned a B.A. from Penn State University and a law degree from Loyola of New Orleans College of Law. He is licensed to practice law in Louisiana and Pennsylvania. For the past thirty years, DeLeo has served as a professor and director of the Legal Studies Program at Central Penn College in Summerdale, Pennsylvania, where he was Faculty Member of the Year for 1990, 1993, and 2005.

He is the author of *The Student's Guide to Understanding Constitutional Law*; *Administrative Law;* and co-author of *The Pennsylvania Paralegal*, published by Delmar Cengage Learning.

As a paralegal, you will be asked to conduct legal research. You will learn the mechanics of doing research and finding sources of law in your legal research classes. For now, let's take a look at the *kinds* of legal sources that can give you answers.

The U.S. Constitution

The U.S. Constitution is the supreme law of the land, and all federal, state, and local officials must operate within its bounds. The Constitution consists of seven articles that comprise the original text, in addition to the Bill of Rights (the first ten amendments) plus seventeen other amendments. The Constitution is the source of many rights such as freedom of speech, due process, and equal protection. All states also have their own constitutions.

> **The U.S. Constitution is the supreme law of the land . . . "**

Statutes

Congress and state governments pass statutes that may add to the rights found in the Constitution and state constitutions. The Civil Rights Act of 1964, which outlawed discrimination based on race and national origin, is one example. States pass statutes that control within state borders.

Judicial Rulings/ Common Law

Courts from the United States Supreme Court on down to state courts interpret statutes and base their rulings on a body of common law known as judge-made law. For example, the law related to contracts has been developed by judges in the process of deciding cases.

The president of the United States is the nation's chief executive and commander in chief of the armed forces. And, as already noted, the Constitution makes clear that laws made by the national government take priority over conflicting state laws. At the same time, the Constitution provides for certain states' rights, including the right to control commerce within state borders and to exercise powers to protect public health, safety, morals, and general welfare.

To protect citizens from the national government using its power arbitrarily, the Constitution divided the national government's powers among three branches:

- The legislative branch, or Congress, which makes the laws.
- The executive branch, which enforces the laws.
- The judicial branch, which interprets the laws.

Executive Orders

An executive order is issued by the president or governor directing an agency to follow a certain policy. Such orders do not require legislative approval.

Rules or Regulations

Federal and state agencies issue regulations—policies that implement and enforce a statute. For example, in the area of environmental law, Congress might pass a statute that directs the Environmental Protection Agency (EPA) in general terms to "clean up the air." The EPA then issues regulations that ban or limit various emissions.

Legal Sources for Research

Imagine that authorities have quarantined one of your firm's clients because it is alleged that he or she was exposed to Ebola and thus poses a health risk to the public. What can be done? You are asked to do the legal research and draft a memo that gives the attorney options in assisting the client. Now, let's look at how legal sources could be useful to you in researching the issue at hand.

A Quarantine and the Constitution

A government may only quarantine individuals within the bounds of the Constitution and the constitution of the respective state. Individuals who are detained can file a writ of *habeas corpus* under Article I, Section 9 of the Constitution to challenge the legality of their detention. States have primary authority for containing infectious diseases within their borders based on state "police power" derived from the Tenth Amendment to the Constitution.

A Quarantine and Statutes

Congress passed the Public Health Service Act to prevent the entry and spread of communicable diseases from foreign countries into the United States and between states. States also pass laws designed to protect citizens from communicable diseases. An example of a state statute is one passed by Maine to deal with disease outbreaks

[22 M.R.S. Section 811(3)]. This statute authorizes a court to "make such orders as it deems necessary to protect other individuals from the dangers of infection."

A Quarantine and Judicial Rulings/Common Law

An American nurse treated patients with Ebola in West Africa. She then returned to New Jersey, where she was quarantined for three days before returning to her home in Maine. A state judge in Maine, pursuant to 22 M.R.S. Section 811(3), issued an order specifying the limits on her activity during the twenty-one-day incubation period. The United States Supreme Court has recognized the power of states to quarantine individuals to prevent the spread of infectious diseases.

A Quarantine and Executive Orders

Federal Executive Order 13295 lists the communicable diseases for which individuals can be subject to quarantine. These diseases are cholera, diphtheria, infectious tuberculosis, plague, smallpox, yellow fever, viral hemorrhagic fevers (including Ebola), SARS, and influenza viruses.

A Quarantine and Rules or Regulations

The Public Health Service Act grants the secretary of Health and Human Services the authority to make and enforce regulations "to prevent the introduction, transmission, or spread of communicable diseases from foreign countries into the States or possessions, or from one State or possession into any other State or possession." The authority for carrying out these functions on a daily basis has been delegated to the Centers for Disease Control and Prevention. State health agencies also issue regulations to control the spread of infectious diseases.

As this quarantine example shows, you need to be familiar with many legal sources to be an effective researcher. By knowing where to look and casting a wide net in your research, you will be in a position to provide answers and serve the best interests of the firm's client.

> " . . . you need to be familiar with many legal sources to be an effective researcher."

Each branch performs a separate function, and no branch may exercise the authority of another branch. Each branch has some power to limit the actions of the other branches. Congress, for example, can enact legislation relating to spending and commerce, but the president can veto that legislation. The executive branch is responsible for foreign affairs, but treaties with foreign governments require approval by the Senate. Although Congress determines the jurisdiction of the federal courts, the federal courts have the power to hold acts of the other branches of the federal government unconstitutional. With this system of **checks and balances,** the framers of the U.S. Constitution intended to ensure that no one branch of government would accumulate too much power, even if this made the federal government less efficient and slower to act than a government lacking those checks and balances.

checks and balances
A system in which each of the three branches of the national government—executive, legislative, and judicial—exercises a check on the actions of the other two branches.

The Federal Lawmaking Process

Each law passed by Congress begins as a *bill*, which may be introduced either in the House of Representatives or in the Senate. (Look up the 1970s *Schoolhouse Rock!* public education video titled "I'm Just a Bill" on YouTube.) Often, similar bills are introduced in both chambers of Congress. In either the House or the Senate, the bill is referred to a committee and its subcommittees for study, discussion, hearings, and rewriting. If the committee does not approve the bill, it "dies" and goes no further. If approved by the committee, it is scheduled for debate by the full House or Senate. Finally, a vote is taken, and the bill is passed or defeated. If the two chambers pass similar, but not identical, bills, a *conference committee* is formed to write a compromise bill, which must then be approved by both chambers before it is sent to the president to sign. Once the president signs the bill, it becomes law.

During the legislative process, bills are identified by a number. A bill in the House of Representatives is identified by a number preceded by "HR" (such as HR 212). In the Senate, the bill's number is preceded by an "S" (such as S 212). When both chambers pass the bill and it is signed into law by the president, the statute is initially published in the form of a *slip law*. The slip law is assigned a **public law number,** or P.L. number (such as P.L. 5030).

At the end of the two-year congressional term, or session, the statute is published in the term's *session laws*, which are collections of statutes contained in volumes and arranged by year or legislative session. The statute is included in the *United States Code,* or U.S. Code, in which all federal laws are codified (systematized, or arranged in topical order). You may need to locate a statute by bill number, public law number, or U.S. Code section number in the course of your research.

public law number
An identification number assigned to a statute.

State Statutes

State statutes are laws enacted by state legislatures. Any state law that is found by a court to conflict with the U.S. Constitution or with the state's constitution will be deemed unconstitutional. State statutes include state laws governing real property and insurance (see Chapter 16), estates and family law (discussed in Chapter 17), the formation of corporations and other business entities (see Chapter 18), and certain crimes (see Chapter 13), along with state versions of the Uniform Commercial Code (see Chapter 15).

Conflicts between Federal and State Laws

If a state statute conflicts with a federal statute, the state law is invalid. Because some powers are shared, however, it is often necessary to determine which law governs in a particular circumstance. *Concurrent powers* are those shared by the federal government and the states, such as the power to impose taxes or to establish courts.

Preemption occurs when Congress chooses to act exclusively in a concurrent area. In this circumstance, a valid federal law or regulation in the preempted area takes precedence over a conflicting state or local law. Often, it is not clear whether Congress, in passing a law, intended to preempt an entire area of law. In these situations, the courts must determine Congress's intention. No single factor determines whether a court will find preemption. Congress has recognized that the states regulate some areas of business, such as insurance. In those areas, Congress generally does not preempt state law. As the accompanying *Developing Paralegal Skills* feature discusses, federal preemption of state law can be a critical issue.

preemption
A doctrine under which a federal law preempts, or takes precedence over, conflicting state and local laws.

The State Lawmaking Process

When passing laws, state legislatures follow procedures similar to those followed in Congress. All of the states except one have bicameral (two-chamber) legislatures (Nebraska has a unicameral, or one-chamber, legislature). Bills may be introduced

DEVELOPING PARALEGAL SKILLS

STATE VERSUS FEDERAL REGULATION

Stephanie Wilson works as a paralegal in the legal department of National Pipeline, Inc., whose business is transporting natural gas to local utilities, factories, and other sites around the country. Last month, one of National's pipelines, which ran under a residential street in Minneapolis, Minnesota, exploded, resulting in several injuries and one death.

The federal government has regulated pipeline safety and maintenance since 1968, under the Natural Gas Pipeline Safety Act. As a result of the explosion, the state of Minnesota wants to regulate pipeline safety as well. Stephanie's boss, the general counsel of the company, and several other executives believe that the federal act preempts this field of law, preventing the state from enacting another layer of safety legislation. Stephanie is assigned the task of researching the statute and relevant case law to determine if the federal law does in fact preempt the state's regulation.

Tips for Determining Federal Preemption

- Read through the statute to see if it expressly states that Congress intended to preempt (or not) the relevant field (in this case, pipeline safety).

- If there is no express provision, look for indications that Congress has impliedly occupied the field: Is the federal regulatory scheme pervasive? Is federal occupation of the field necessitated by the need for national uniformity? Is there a danger of conflict between state laws and the administration of the federal program?

- Locate and read cases discussing the issue of federal preemption in this area.

---

in either chamber, or both chambers, of the legislature. As in the U.S. Congress, if the two chambers pass bills that differ from one another in any respect, a conference committee works out a compromise, which must then be approved by both chambers before being sent to the state's governor to sign into law. State constitutions often impose additional restrictions on state legislatures beyond what the federal constitution imposes on Congress. For example, many state legislatures operate under a state constitutional "single subject rule" which requires that each piece of legislation address only one subject, while Congress is free to combine multiple topics within a single bill.

Local Ordinances

Statutory law also includes local governments' ordinances. An **ordinance** is an order, rule, or law passed by a city, county, or special district government to govern matters not covered by federal or state law. Because state governments create local governments, ordinances may not violate the state constitution or the federal Constitution, or go beyond what is allowed by state law. Local ordinances often have to do with land use (zoning ordinances), building and safety codes, construction and appearance of housing, and other matters affecting a local area. Persons who violate ordinances may be fined, jailed, or both.

ordinance
An order, rule, or law enacted by a municipal or county government to govern a local matter as allowed by state or federal legislation.

Uniform Laws

Many areas of state law vary from state to state. The differences were particularly notable in the 1800s, when conflicting statutes created problems for the rapidly developing trade among the states. To counter these problems, representatives of many of the states formed the National Conference of Commissioners on Uniform State Laws (NCCUSL) in 1892 to draft proposed uniform statutes for adoption by the states. The NCCUSL continues to issue uniform statutes, sometimes in conjunction with the American Law Institute.

Adoption of uniform laws is a state matter, and a state may reject all or part of proposed uniform laws or rewrite them as the state legislature wishes. Hence, even when a uniform law is adopted in many states, the laws may not be entirely "uniform." Once adopted by a state legislature, a uniform act becomes a part of the statutory law of that state. Many uniform laws deal with areas in which having similar rules across the states makes the law simpler. For example, the Uniform Simultaneous Death Act covers how to handle wills when people who have left each other portions of their estates (such as spouses) die within 120 hours of each other.

> **EXAMPLE 5.12** One uniform law that has been adopted (at least in part) by all states is the Uniform Commercial Code (UCC). First published in 1952, it provides a set of rules governing commercial transactions and sales contracts. It helps harmonize terms of sales across state lines and sets rules for bank checks and other standard financial instruments. If you work in business law, you will become quite familiar with the UCC during your career as a paralegal.

Administrative Law

administrative law
A body of law created by administrative agencies in the form of rules, regulations, orders, and decisions in order to carry out their duties and responsibilities.

administrative agency
A federal or state government agency established to perform a specific function. Administrative agencies are authorized by legislative acts to make and enforce rules relating to the purpose for which they were established.

Another important source of American law is **administrative law.** It consists of the rules, orders, and decisions of administrative agencies and the rules governing how these agencies operate. An **administrative agency** is a federal, state, or local government agency established to perform a specific function, such as the regulation of food sold to consumers. Rules issued by administrative agencies affect most aspects of a business's operation, including the firm's financing, its hiring and firing procedures, its relations with employees and unions, and the way it manufactures and markets its products.

At the federal level there are many administrative agencies with a variety of missions.

> **EXAMPLE 5.13** The federal Environmental Protection Agency (EPA) enforces federal environmental laws and oversees state environmental regulations. The states are authorized to customize regulations and enforce them at the state level. The Securities and Exchange Commission (SEC) regulates purchases and sales of securities (corporate stocks and bonds). Congress has limited the ability of the state courts to handle many aspects of federal securities laws.

Some state administrative agencies work with a federal agency to regulate an area. State environmental agencies, as noted, play important roles in implementing regulations issued by the federal EPA. Other state agencies, such as those dealing with workers' compensation, mostly operate under state law. Just as federal statutes take precedence over conflicting state statutes, so do federal agency regulations take precedence over conflicting state regulations. Because the rules of state and local agencies vary widely, we focus here exclusively on federal administrative law.

Agency Creation

enabling legislation
A statute enacted by a legislature that authorizes the creation of an administrative agency and specifies the name, purpose, composition, and powers of the agency being created.

Because Congress cannot possibly oversee the implementation of all the laws it enacts, it delegates such tasks to others, particularly when the issues relate to technical areas, such as air and water pollution. Congress creates an administrative agency by passing **enabling legislation,** which specifies the name, composition, purpose, and powers of the agency being created.

EXAMPLE 5.14 The Federal Trade Commission (FTC) was created in 1914 by the Federal Trade Commission Act. This act prohibits unfair and deceptive trade practices. It also describes the procedures the agency must follow to charge persons or organizations with violations of the act, and it provides for judicial review (review by the courts) of agency orders. The act also grants the agency powers to "make rules and regulations for the purpose of carrying out the Act," to conduct investigations of business practices, to obtain reports from interstate corporations concerning their business practices, to investigate possible violations of the act, to publish findings of its investigations, and to recommend new legislation. The act empowers the FTC to hold trial-like hearings and to **adjudicate** certain kinds of trade disputes that involve FTC regulations.

adjudicate
To resolve a dispute using a neutral decision maker.

Note that the FTC's grant of power incorporates functions associated with the legislative branch of government (rulemaking), the executive branch (investigation and enforcement), and the judicial branch (adjudication). Taken together, these functions constitute the *administrative process*.

Rulemaking

One of the major functions of an administrative agency is **rulemaking**—creating or modifying rules or regulations. The Administrative Procedure Act imposes procedural requirements that federal agencies must follow in their rulemaking and other functions.

rulemaking
The actions undertaken by administrative agencies when formally adopting new regulations or amending old ones.

The most common rulemaking procedure involves three steps:

1. The agency must give public notice of the proposed rulemaking proceedings, must announce where public hearings will be held, and must convey the subject matter of the proposed rule. The notice must be published in the *Federal Register*, a daily online publication of the U.S. government.

2. Following this notice, the agency must allow time for interested parties to comment in writing on the proposed rule. After the comments have been reviewed, the agency takes them into consideration when drafting the final version of the regulation.

3. The last step is the writing of the final rule and its publication in the *Federal Register*.

Most states have similar statutes governing how state agencies operate.

Investigation and Enforcement

Many agencies have both investigatory and prosecutorial powers. When conducting an investigation, an agency can request that individuals or organizations hand over specific papers, files, or other documents. Firms subject to regulations often must file reports on a regular basis, including reports of violations. Agencies may also conduct on-site inspections. Sometimes, a search of a home, an office, or a factory is the only way to obtain evidence needed to prove a regulatory violation.

EXAMPLE 5.15 The Environmental Protection Agency employs special agents, authorized to carry firearms, who investigate environmental crimes such as illegal dumping of untreated wastewater into a sewer system or disposal of toxic wastes in a municipal landfill.

After investigating a suspected rule violation, an agency may take administrative action against an individual or a business. Most actions are resolved through negotiated settlements, without the need for formal adjudication. If a settlement cannot be reached, the agency may issue a formal complaint against the suspected violator, and the case may proceed to adjudication.

Adjudication

Agency adjudication usually involves a trial-like hearing before an **administrative law judge (ALJ).** The ALJ presides over the hearing and has the power to administer oaths, take testimony, rule on questions of evidence, and make determinations of fact. Although the ALJ works for the agency prosecuting the case, he or she is required by law to be an unbiased adjudicator (judge). Hearing procedures vary from agency to agency. They may be informal meetings conducted at a table in a conference room, or they may be formal hearings resembling trials. Some agencies allow paralegals to represent clients at these hearings.

After the hearing, the ALJ issues a decision. The ALJ may compel the charged party to pay a fine or may prohibit the party from carrying on a certain activity. Either side may appeal the ALJ's decision through an internal agency review process. Once the agency has completed its procedures, but not before, a dissatisfied party may appeal to a federal court. If no party appeals the case, or if the commission and the court decline to review the case, the ALJ's decision becomes final.

National and International Law

Because business and other activities are increasingly global in scope, many cases now brought before U.S. courts relate to issues involving foreign parties or governments. The laws of other nations and international doctrines or agreements may affect the outcome of these cases. Many paralegals, particularly those who work for law firms with clients operating in foreign countries, may need to become familiar with the legal systems of other nations during the course of their careers.

For example, if you work in a firm in Arizona, California, New Mexico, or Texas, you are likely to have cases involving the representation of clients who are citizens of Mexico, as well as clients who are U.S. citizens or firms conducting business or other activities across the border. In this situation, you will want to have some familiarity with Mexican law and any international agreements that regulate U.S.-Mexican relations, such as the United States–Mexico–Canada Agreement (USMCA).

National Law

The law of a particular nation is referred to as **national law.** Broadly speaking, however, there are three general types of legal systems used by the various countries of the world. We have already discussed one of these systems—the common law system of England and the United States. Generally, countries that were once colonies of Great Britain retained parts of their English common law heritage after they achieved their independence.

In contrast to the common law countries, most continental European nations base their legal systems on *civil law,* or "code law." This system has its origins in both the law of the Roman Empire and the French codification of the law under Emperor Napoleon, who then imposed versions of the French system across the continent as he conquered large portions of it. (Even after other European countries threw out Napoleon and the French occupiers, most kept the French-based legal system because of its high quality.)

The term *civil law,* as used here, refers not to civil as opposed to criminal law but to *codified law*—which is an ordered grouping of legal principles enacted into law by a legislature or governing body. In a **civil law system,** the primary source of law is a comprehensive statutory code, and case precedents usually are not judicially binding, as they normally are in a common law system.

This is not to say that precedents are unimportant in a civil law system. Judges in such systems do refer to previous decisions as sources of legal guidance. The difference is that judges in a civil law system are not obligated to follow precedent to the extent that judges in a common law system are; in other words, the doctrine of *stare decisis* does not apply. As this chapter's *Office Tech and Cybersecurity* feature discusses, tracing relevant law in other nations is becoming an ever-increasing requirement.

Today, the civil law system is followed in most of the continental European countries, as well as in the Latin American, African, and Asian countries that were once colonies of the continental European nations. China, Japan, and Thailand also have civil law systems. In the United States, the state of Louisiana, because of its historical ties to France, has in part a civil law system. The legal systems of Puerto Rico, Québec, and Scotland also have elements of the civil law system.

Another legal system is the **Islamic law system**, or *sharia*, which is based on the Koran and on hundreds of years of jurisprudence by religious scholars. It covers a wide range of subjects, and countries differ in which areas it governs. *Sharia* is adopted in predominantly Muslim countries, such as Saudi Arabia, and is having an increasing international influence, as its principles are shaping Islamic finance. For example, *sharia* prohibits the payment of interest and so requires that banking, mortgages, and business finance be conducted quite differently than under common law or civil law. Because many Islamic countries are significant economic centers, this has led to an explosion in *sharia-compliant* financial products that avoid using interest payments.

Islamic law system
A system of law, based on the teachings of the Koran and the prophet Mohammed and on social and legal traditions, prescribing both religious and secular duties.

International Law

Relationships among countries are regulated to an extent by international law. **International law** can be defined as a body of written and unwritten laws observed by independent nations and governing the acts of individuals as well as governments. The key difference between national law and international law is the fact that national law can be enforced by government authorities, whereas international law is enforced primarily for reasons of courtesy or expediency. There is no single body that determines or enforces international law. Rather, international law comes from a variety of multinational bodies (such as the World Trade Organization), treaties, traditions, and customs.

international law
The law that governs relations among nations. International customs and treaties are generally considered to be two of the most important sources of international law.

OFFICE TECH AND CYBERSECURITY

CYBER ISSUES AND SOURCES OF LAW

Technology has broadened the sources of applicable law in many areas. For example, the European Union (EU) created the General Data Protection Regulation (GDPR) in 2016. It governs data protection and privacy for EU citizens. It also covers the transfer of personal data outside the EU. This can be relevant for U.S. businesses with EU customers, because any data that a U.S. business stores concerning its EU customers must be kept in compliance with the GDPR (even if the U.S. business has no physical presence in the European Union). Google offers one example of a U.S. business fined under the GDPR. The French Data Protection Authority fined Google 50 million euros in 2019 for violating the GDPR because of how its Android-operating system created Google accounts when configuring mobile phones. You can find a record of enforcement actions under the GDPR at **enforcementtracker.com**.

China also strictly regulates the Internet, and its regulations differ from both U.S. and EU regulatory regimes. For example, China requires every website owner to have a license. The government blocks noncompliant Internet services, such as Google and its e-mail service, and it restricts transfer of data outside of China. China's government also insists that businesses respect its views on China's boundaries. Taiwan cannot be labeled as a separate country, for example, so U.S. airlines flying to the area must change the maps in their inflight magazines to list destinations in Taiwan only by the city name.

The cyber issues may be important to you as a paralegal. Even if you work for a U.S. law firm in an office in the United States, you may need to find information on foreign legal requirements for a U.S. client if the client's business has a cyber component.

In essence, international law is the result of attempts to reconcile the need of each nation to be the final authority over its own affairs with the desire of nations to benefit economically from trade and good relations with one another. Although no independent nation can be compelled to obey a law external to itself, nations can and do voluntarily agree to be governed in certain respects by international law for the purpose of facilitating international trade and commerce and civilized discourse.

Treaties

treaty
An agreement, or compact, formed between two independent nations.

Traditional sources of international law include the customs that have been historically observed by nations in their dealings with one another. Other sources are treaties and international organizations and conferences. A **treaty** is an agreement between two or more nations that creates rights and duties binding on the parties to the treaty, just as a private contract may be used to create rights and duties binding on the parties to the contract. To give effect to a treaty, the supreme power of each nation that is a party to the treaty must ratify it. For example, the U.S. Constitution requires approval by two-thirds of the Senate before a treaty executed by the president will be binding on the U.S. government.

Bilateral agreements, as their name implies, occur when two nations form an agreement that will govern their relations with each other. *Multilateral agreements* are formed by several nations. The European Union, for example, which regulates commercial activities among its European member nations, is the result of a multilateral treaty. Other multilateral agreements have led to the formation of regional trade associations.

> **EXAMPLE 5.16** In 1993, Congress approved the North American Free Trade Agreement (NAFTA), which included Canada, Mexico, and the United States. It gradually eliminated many of the trade barriers among those nations. In 2019, the three countries adopted a revised agreement known as the United States–Mexico–Canada Agreement (USMCA). Like NAFTA, the USMCA includes dispute resolution procedures by which panels of experts will interpret the text of the agreement when there are differences of opinion between the signatories.

International Organizations

International organizations play an important role in the international legal arena. They adopt resolutions, declarations, and other types of standards that often require a particular behavior of nations. The General Assembly of the United Nations, for example, has adopted numerous resolutions and declarations that embody principles of international law and has sponsored conferences that have led to the formation of international agreements. The United States is a member of more than one hundred multilateral and bilateral organizations, including at least twenty through the United Nations.

CHAPTER SUMMARY

SOURCES OF AMERICAN LAW

The Framework of American Law

1. *What is the law?*—The law has been defined in many ways, but all definitions rest on the assumption that law consists of a body of rules of conduct established and enforced by the controlling authority (the government) of a society.

2. *Primary sources of American law*—There are four primary sources of American law: the common law doctrines developed in cases; the U.S. Constitution and the constitutions of various states; statutory law, including laws passed by Congress, state legislatures, and local governing bodies; and regulations created by administrative agencies.

Case Law and the Common Law Tradition

Case law consists of the decisions issued by judges in cases that come before the court. Case law evolved through the common law tradition, which originated in England and was adopted in America during the colonial era.

1. *The doctrine of* stare decisis—*Stare decisis* means "to stand by things decided" and is the doctrine of precedent, which is a major characteristic of the common law system. Under this doctrine, judges must follow the earlier decisions of their courts or a higher court within their jurisdiction if the same points arise again in litigation.

   a. A court will depart from precedent if the court decides that the precedent should no longer be followed because the earlier ruling was incorrect or does not apply in view of changes in the social or technological environment.

   b. If no precedent exists, the court considers the matter as a case of first impression and looks to other areas of law and public policy for guidance.

2. *Remedies at law versus remedies in equity*—Historically in England, two types of courts emerged: courts of law and courts of equity. Courts of law granted remedies at law (such as monetary damages). Courts of equity arose in response to the need for other types of relief. In the United States today, the same court can typically grant either legal or equitable remedies.

3. *Remedies in equity*—Remedies in equity, which are normally available only when the remedy at law (money or property) is inadequate, include the following:

   a. **SPECIFIC PERFORMANCE**—A court decree ordering a party to perform a contractual promise.

   b. **INJUNCTION**—A court order directing someone to do or refrain from doing a particular act.

4. *The common law today*—The common law governs all areas of law not covered by statutory law. As the body of statutory law grows to meet different needs, the common law covers fewer areas. Even if an area is governed by a statutory law, however, the common law plays an important role because statutes are interpreted and applied by the courts, and court decisions may become precedents that must be followed by lower courts within the jurisdiction.

5. *The terminology of case law*—

   a. **CASE TITLES**—A case title consists of the surnames of the parties, such as *Baranski v. Peretto.* The citation itself (such as 12 P.3d 385) indicates the volume and page number of the reporter in which the case can be found.

   b. **PARTIES**—The plaintiff or the defendant. Some cases involve multiple parties—that is, more than one plaintiff or defendant.

   c. **JUDGES AND JUSTICES**—These terms are often used synonymously. Usage of the terms varies among courts. The term *justice* is traditionally used to designate judges who sit on the bench of a supreme court.

   d. **DECISIONS AND OPINIONS**—A document containing the court's reasons for its decision, the rules of law that apply, and the judgment. If the opinion is not unanimous, a majority opinion—reflecting the view of the majority of judges or justices—will be written. Concurring and dissenting opinions may also be written.

6. *The adversarial system of justice*—American courts, like English courts, follow a system of justice in which the parties to a lawsuit are opponents, or adversaries, and present their cases in the light most favorable to themselves. The impartial decision maker (the judge or jury) then determines who wins and who loses based on the evidence presented.

Constitutional Law

Constitutional law is based on the provisions in the U.S. Constitution and the state constitutions. The U.S. Constitution creates and empowers the three branches of government, sets forth the relationship between the states and the federal government, and establishes procedures for amending the Constitution.

1. *The federal Constitution*—The U.S. Constitution is the supreme law of the land. A law in violation of the Constitution or one of its amendments, no matter what its source, will be declared unconstitutional and will not be enforced. A state constitution, so long as it does not conflict with the U.S. Constitution, is the supreme law within the state's borders.

2. *Constitutional rights*—The first ten amendments to the federal Constitution are known as the Bill of Rights. These amendments embody a series of protections for individuals—and in some instances, business entities—against certain government actions. The Bill of Rights initially limited only the powers of the federal government. After the Fourteenth Amendment was passed, the Supreme Court applied the protections of the Bill of Rights against state government actions.

3. *The courts and constitutional law*—The rights secured by the Constitution are interpreted and defined by the courts, especially the United States Supreme Court.

Statutory Law

Statutory law consists of all laws enacted by the federal Congress, a state legislature, a municipality, or some other governing body.

1. *Federal statutes*—Laws passed by Congress are *statutes.* Congress has power over areas declared in the Constitution to be within federal jurisdiction. The power of Congress is subject to checks and balances as the judicial branch interprets the laws and the executive branch helps to enforce the laws. Public laws must pass both branches of Congress and then be signed by the president to become part of the U.S. Code.

Administrative Law

Administrative law consists of the rules, regulations, and decisions of administrative agencies at all levels of government.

1. *Agency creation*—Congress creates administrative agencies by passing enabling legislation, which specifies the name, function, and powers of the agency created.

2. *Administrative process*—Administrative agencies exercise three basic functions:

   a. **RULEMAKING**—Agencies make rules governing activities within the areas of their authority. Typically, rulemaking procedure involves publishing notice of the proposed rulemaking, allowing a comment period, and then drafting the final rule.

National and International Law

1. *National law*—The law of a particular nation. National law differs from nation to nation because each country's laws have evolved from that nation's unique customs and traditions. Most countries have one of the following types of legal systems:

   a. **THE COMMON LAW SYSTEM**—Great Britain was the originator of common law. Countries that were once colonies of Great Britain retained at least part of their English common law heritage after achieving independence. Under the common law, case precedents are judicially binding.

   b. **THE CIVIL LAW SYSTEM**—Many of the continental European countries and the nations that were formerly their colonies have civil law systems. Civil law (or code law) is a grouping of legal principles

4. *State constitutions*—Each state has a constitution that defines and limits the powers of state government. Most state constitutions are much more detailed than the U.S. Constitution.

2. *State statutes*—Laws enacted by state legislatures under the powers granted by the state constitution. If a state statute conflicts with federal law, it will be stricken as unconstitutional, as federal law preempts state law.

3. *Local ordinances*—Laws passed by local governing units (cities and counties) are called *ordinances.* Such laws may not violate either the federal or state constitution or conflict with laws at the state or federal levels.

4. *Uniform laws*—While laws vary in detail from state to state, many states have adopted uniform statutes, such as the Uniform Commercial Code, to reduce confusion as businesses operate across state lines.

   b. **INVESTIGATION AND ENFORCEMENT**—Agencies conduct investigations of regulated entities to gather information and to monitor compliance with agency rules. When an entity fails to comply with agency rules, the agency can take administrative action. Most violations are resolved by negotiated settlements.

   c. **ADJUDICATION**—If a settlement cannot be reached, the agency may issue a formal complaint, and an administrative law judge (ALJ) conducts a hearing and decides the issue. Either party can appeal the ALJ's order to the board or commission that governs the agency if dissatisfied. Most agency decisions can also then be appealed to a court.

enacted into law by a governing body. The primary source of law is a statutory code. Although important, case precedents are not judicially binding. Judges focus on the code.

   c. **THE ISLAMIC LEGAL SYSTEM**—Many predominantly Muslim nations rely on religious law for their legal systems. *Sharia* is based on the Koran and sayings of the prophet Mohammed, as well as religious scholars' jurisprudence.

2. *International law*—A body of laws that governs relationships among nations. International law allows nations to enjoy good relations with one another and to benefit economically from international trade. Sources include international customs developed over time, treaties among nations, and international organizations.

KEY TERMS AND CONCEPTS

adjudicate 137
administrative agency 136
administrative law 136
administrative law judge (ALJ) 138
adversarial system of justice 128
bill of rights 129
binding authority 121
case law 121
case of first impression 122
checks and balances 133
citation 127
civil law system 138
common law 121
constitutional law 128
court of equity 123

court of law 122
enabling legislation 136
equitable principles and maxims 123
federal system 131
injunction 126
international law 139
islamic law system 139
laches 124
law 120
national law 138
opinion 128
ordinance 135
party 127
persuasive precedent 121
precedent 121

preemption 134
primary source of law 120
public law number 134
public policy 122
remedies at law 122
remedy 122
remedy in equity 123
rulemaking 137
secondary source of law 121
specific performance 124
stare decisis 121
statute 131
statutory law 131
supremacy clause 129
treaty 140

QUESTIONS FOR REVIEW

1. Define *law*. What are the primary sources of American law?

2. Why is the doctrine of *stare decisis* the cornerstone of American common law, and what is its relationship to binding authority? May courts depart from precedent? What is a case of first impression?

3. What remedies were originally available from courts of law? Courts of equity? How did courts of equity evolve? Are the courts of law and equity still separate?

4. What is a statute? How is statutory law created? What is the difference between a statute and an ordinance? What happens when a state statute conflicts with a federal statute?

5. What is the supremacy clause, and where is it located? Briefly summarize each article of the Constitution. What is the Bill of Rights?

6. What is national law? What is international law? Explain the three types of legal systems that most countries have.

ETHICS QUESTION

1. Paralegal Carlos is asked by his supervising attorney to do some research. Carlos is to review a new state statute exempting ill persons certified to use medical marijuana from prosecution. His job to find out what the requirements are for becoming a certified medical marijuana user. Carlos looks up the relevant state statute and finds the requirements. He conveys this information to John, his supervising attorney. Carlos has neglected to research the federal drug laws and fails to tell the attorney that there is not an exemption for the medical use of marijuana under federal law. The attorney, relying on Carlos's conclusion, advises the client that once she is a certified medical user, she will be exempt from prosecution. Have John and Carlos violated any ethical rules? Explain.

PRACTICE QUESTIONS AND ASSIGNMENTS

1. In the following hypothetical situations, identify the remedy being sought and whether it is a remedy at law or a remedy in equity:

   a. Brianna files a petition with the court. She is seeking compensation from Travis, who failed to deliver new furniture as promised.

   b. Juan sues Bob, seeking to be compensated for the cost of replacing several new trees that Bob's dog destroyed.

   c. Laurie seeks to have a contract enforced for the sale of an antique Mercedes automobile.

   d. Sam files a petition seeking to prevent the electric company from cutting down a large tree on his property.

2. Identify the type of law (common law, constitutional law, statutory law, or administrative law) that applies in each of the following scenarios:

   a. LaToya strongly disagrees with the U.S. government's decision to declare war on a foreign country. She places an antiwar sign in the window of her home. The city passes an ordinance that bans all such signs.

   b. An official of the state department of natural resources learns that the Ferris Widget Company has violated the state's Hazardous Waste Management Act. The official issues a complaint against the company for not properly handling and labeling its toxic waste.

   c. Mrs. Samson was walking down a busy street when two teenagers on skateboards crashed into her because they were racing and not watching where they were going. As a result of the teenagers' conduct, Mrs. Samson broke her hip, and according to her doctor, she will never walk normally again. Mrs. Samson's attorney files suit against the teenagers for damages.

   d. Joseph Barnes is arrested and charged with the crime of murder.

3. Look at the U.S. Constitution in Appendix F of this text. Identify the amendment and quote the relevant language in the Bill of Rights that gives U.S. citizens the following rights and protections:

   a. The right to freedom of the press.

   b. Protection from excessive bail and fines.

   c. Protection against self-incrimination.

   d. The right to counsel in criminal prosecutions.

   e. The right to keep and bear arms.

4. Identify the constitutional amendment being violated in the following hypothetical situations:

   a. A state imposes the death penalty on a seventeen-year-old.

   b. The federal government suppresses political speech based on the speaker's identity as a corporation.

   c. The police decide that because a house is located in a poor neighborhood, it must be a crack house. The police burst in, tear the house apart looking for drugs, and find nothing.

   d. A local government bans handgun possession in the home.

5. Unhappy with her attorney's services, Ashley decided to sue him. The Arkansas Supreme Court issued an opinion in the case, and the citation to that opinion is *Ashley v. Eisele*, 247 Ark. 281 (1969). In this citation:

   a. Who is the appellant?

   b. Who is the appellee?

   c. In what volume of the *Arkansas Reports* can this case be located? At what page number?

   d. What year was the case decided?

   e. Why would an attorney or a judge be interested in reading a case this old?

GROUP PROJECT

This chapter describes uniform laws that were created to alleviate conflicting laws that hindered rapidly developing trade among the states. One such uniform law was the Uniform Commercial Code (UCC), a core provision of which regulates the sales of goods. Trade problems also arise among nations. For this project, the group should search the Internet to locate a uniform international law similar to the UCC. Student One will research the source of law to determine what entity created it and what form the law takes (such as case law, statutory law, or a treaty). Student Two will research the law and provide an overview of its main provisions. Student Three will research the role of the U.S. government and U.S.-based businesses: how they are (or are not) governed by this law, and why. Student Four will prepare a two-page written summary of this particular law on behalf of the group and submit it to the instructor.

CHAPTER

6

The Court System and Alternative Dispute Resolution

CHAPTER OBJECTIVES

After completing this chapter, you will be able to:

- List and explain the requirements that must be met before a lawsuit can be brought in a particular court by a particular party.

- Explain the difference between jurisdiction and venue.

- Describe the types of courts that make up a typical state court system, and compare the different functions of trial courts and appellate courts.

- Explain the organization of the federal court system and the relationship between state and federal jurisdiction.

- Explain how cases reach the United States Supreme Court.

- List and explain the ways in which disputes can be resolved outside the court system.

Introduction

American law is based on the case decisions and legal principles that form the common law, the federal and state constitutions, statutes passed by federal and state legislatures, administrative law, and, in some instances, the laws of other nations and international law.

Paralegals need to understand the different types of courts in the American system. There are fifty-two court systems—one for each of the fifty states, one for the District of Columbia, and the federal system. There are many similarities among these systems, but there are differences as well.

In the first part of this chapter, we examine the structure of the American courts. In addition to the federal and state public courts, there is also a system of private dispute resolution mechanisms. Because of the costs, in time and money, and the publicity that can come from court trials, many parties use these alternative methods of dispute resolution to resolve disputes outside of court. In some cases, parties are required by the courts to try to resolve their disputes by one of these methods. In the second part of this chapter, we provide an overview of these alternative methods of dispute resolution and the role that attorneys and paralegals play in facilitating them.

Judicial Requirements

Before a lawsuit can be brought before a court, certain requirements must be met. We begin with these important requirements and some of the key features of the American system of justice.

Standing to Sue

standing to sue
A sufficient stake in a controversy to justify bringing a lawsuit. To have standing to sue, the plaintiff must demonstrate an injury or a threat of injury.

To bring a lawsuit before a court, a party must have **standing to sue**—a sufficient "stake" in a matter to justify seeking relief through the court system. In other words, a party must have a legally protected, genuine interest at stake in the litigation to have standing. The party bringing the lawsuit must have suffered a legally recognized harm as a result of the action about which he or she has complained.

> **EXAMPLE 6.1** Assume that a friend of one of your firm's clients was injured in a car accident caused by defective brakes. The client's friend would have standing to sue the automobile manufacturer for damages. Your firm's client, who feels horrible about the accident and is angry about it, would not have standing, because the client was not injured and has no legally recognizable stake in the controversy.

Note that in some situations, a person does have standing to sue on behalf of another person. A court will allow a person to bring a lawsuit on behalf of a child or an incapacitated adult as an *ad litem* guardian (*ad litem* means "for purposes of the litigation only").

> **EXAMPLE 6.2** Suppose that five-year-old Emma suffers serious injuries as a result of a defectively manufactured toy. Because Emma is a minor, her parent or legal guardian could bring a lawsuit on her behalf.

justiciable controversy
A controversy that is real and substantial, as opposed to hypothetical or academic.

Standing to sue also requires that the controversy at issue be justiciable. A **justiciable controversy** is one that is real and substantial, as opposed to hypothetical.

EXAMPLE 6.3 Suppose a child's parents learned through news reports that a toy they purchased was defective and had injured some children. The parents could not sue on the ground that they feared the toy could cause injury. The issue would become justiciable only if their child had actually been injured due to a defect in the toy. The parents could not ask the court to determine what damages might be obtained if their child were to be injured, because that would be a hypothetical question.

Types of Jurisdiction

In Latin, *juris* means "law," and *diction* means "to speak." Thus, "the power to speak the law" is the literal meaning of the term **jurisdiction**. Before any court can hear a case, it must have jurisdiction over the person against whom the suit is brought or over the property involved in the suit as well as over the subject matter.

jurisdiction
The authority of a court to hear and decide a specific case.

Jurisdiction over Persons

Generally, a court can exercise personal jurisdiction (*in personam* jurisdiction) over residents of a certain geographic area. A state trial court, for example, normally has jurisdictional authority over residents within the state or within a particular area of the state, such as a county or district. A state's highest court (often called the state supreme court) has jurisdictional authority over all residents within the state.

Under the authority of a **long arm statute**, a state court can exercise personal jurisdiction over nonresident defendants based on activities that took place within the state. Before a court can exercise jurisdiction over a nonresident under a long arm statute, though, it must be demonstrated that the nonresident had sufficient contacts (*minimum contacts*) with the state to justify the jurisdiction.

long arm statute
A state statute that permits a state to obtain jurisdiction over nonresidents. The nonresidents must have certain "minimum contacts" with that state for the statute to apply.

EXAMPLE 6.4 If a California citizen causes an injury in a car accident in Arizona, an Arizona state court usually can exercise jurisdiction over the California citizen in a suit by the Arizona victim. Similarly, a state may exercise personal jurisdiction over a nonresident defendant who is sued for breaching a contract that was formed within that state.

For corporations, the minimum-contacts requirement boils down to whether the corporation does business in the state. If the corporation has an office or physical presence in a state, it clearly has minimum contacts. If the corporation intentionally does business by mail, such as Amazon does, it is also likely to be subject to the jurisdiction of state courts.

EXAMPLE 6.5 A Maine corporation that has a branch office or warehouse in Georgia has sufficient minimum contacts with the state to allow a Georgia court to exercise jurisdiction over the Maine corporation. If, however, someone from Georgia is injured while on a guided fishing trip in Maine and claims that personnel from the Maine fishing company caused the injury, suit cannot be brought in a Georgia court if the Maine company has no business presence in Georgia. A Georgia court cannot exercise jurisdiction in this situation.

A state court may also be able to exercise jurisdiction over a corporation in another country if it can be demonstrated that the alien (foreign) corporation has met the minimum-contacts test.

EXAMPLE 6.6 A Chinese corporation markets its products through an American distributor. Because the corporation knew its products would be distributed throughout the United States, it could be sued in any state by a plaintiff injured by one of the products.

Jurisdiction over Property

in rem jurisdiction
The power a court has to determine the legal status of property (a thing) even if the court does not have jurisdiction over persons with interests in the property.

A court can also exercise jurisdiction over property that is located within its boundaries even if the parties involved in the suit do not. This kind of jurisdiction is known as *in rem* jurisdiction, or "jurisdiction over the thing."

> **EXAMPLE 6.7** A dispute arises over ownership of a boat docked in Fort Lauderdale, Florida. Ownership is claimed by residents of both Ohio and Nebraska. A Florida court normally cannot exercise personal jurisdiction, but in this situation, a lawsuit concerning the boat can be brought in a Florida state court on the basis of the court's *in rem* jurisdiction.

Jurisdiction over Subject Matter

subject-matter jurisdiction
The authority of a court to hear cases concerning certain matters of law.

probate court
A state court with limited jurisdiction that has the power to control proceedings concerning the settlement of a person's estate.

bankruptcy court
A federal court of limited jurisdiction that hears only bankruptcy proceedings.

Subject-matter jurisdiction concerns the kinds of cases a certain court can hear. In both the state and the federal court systems, there are courts of *general jurisdiction* and courts of *limited jurisdiction*. The basis for the difference is the subject matter of cases heard. A **probate court**—a state court that handles only matters relating to the transfer of a person's assets and obligations on that person's death—is a court with limited subject-matter jurisdiction. A federal court of limited subject-matter jurisdiction is a **bankruptcy court**, which handles only proceedings governed by bankruptcy law (see Chapter 19). In contrast, a court of general jurisdiction can decide a wide array of cases.

The subject-matter jurisdiction of a court is usually defined in the statute creating the court. In both the state and the federal court systems, a court's subject-matter jurisdiction can be limited not only by the subject of the lawsuit but also by the amount in controversy, by whether the case is a felony (serious crime) or a misdemeanor (less serious crime), or by whether the proceeding is a trial or an appeal.

Original and Appellate Jurisdiction

original jurisdiction
The power of a court to take a case, try it, and decide it.

trial court
A court in which cases begin and in which questions of fact are examined.

The distinction between courts of original jurisdiction and courts of appellate jurisdiction normally lies in whether the case is being heard for the first time or not. A court having **original jurisdiction** is called a court of the first instance and is usually a **trial court**—that is, a court in which lawsuits begin, trials take place, evidence is presented, and a decision is rendered.

In the federal court system, the *district courts* are trial courts. In a few instances, such as appeals of agency rules, the court of original jurisdiction is a federal court of appeals. There are a few rare instances in which cases begin in the United States Supreme Court. In the state court systems, the trial courts are known by different names for historical reasons. For example, New York's trial courts are confusingly known as the "Supreme Court," and its highest court as the "Court of Appeals."

appellate jurisdiction
The power of a court to hear and decide an appeal; the authority of a court to review cases that have already been tried in a lower court and to make decisions about them without holding a trial.

appellate court
A court that reviews decisions made by lower courts, such as trial courts; a court of appeals.

A court having **appellate jurisdiction** acts as a reviewing court, or an **appellate court** (court of appeal). In general, cases can be brought to appellate courts only on appeal from an order or a judgment of a trial court or other lower court.

Jurisdiction of the Federal Courts

Because the federal government is a government of limited powers, the jurisdiction of the federal courts is also limited. Article III of the U.S. Constitution establishes the boundaries of federal judicial power. Section 2 of Article III states that "the judicial Power shall extend to all Cases, in Law and Equity, arising under this Constitution, the Laws of the United States, and Treaties made, or which shall be made, under their Authority."

Federal Questions

Whenever a plaintiff's cause of action is based, at least in part, on the U.S. Constitution, a treaty, or a federal law, then a **federal question** arises, and the federal courts have subject-matter jurisdiction. Any lawsuit involving a federal question can originate in a federal district (trial) court.

> **EXAMPLE 6.8** J-H Computers, a California company, sues Ball Computers, a Texas company, for patent infringement. J-H claims that some parts Ball used in its new computers are based on J-H inventions. J-H contends that Ball has used its protected patents without permission. Because patent law is federal law and the federal courts have exclusive jurisdiction over such suits, J-H must file suit against Ball in federal court.

federal question
A question that pertains to the U.S. Constitution, acts of Congress, or treaties. It provides a basis for jurisdiction by the federal courts as authorized by Article III, Section 2, of the Constitution.

Diversity Jurisdiction

Federal district courts can also exercise original jurisdiction over cases involving **diversity of citizenship**. Such cases may arise between (1) citizens of different states, (2) a foreign country and citizens of a state or of different states, or (3) citizens of a state and citizens or subjects of a foreign country. The amount in controversy must be more than $75,000 before a federal court can take jurisdiction. For purposes of diversity-of-citizenship jurisdiction, a corporation is a citizen of the state in which it is incorporated and of the state in which its principal place of business is located.

> **EXAMPLE 6.9** Helen Ramirez, a Florida citizen, was walking along a street in Miami when a box fell off a truck and hit and seriously injured her. She incurred medical expenses and could not work for six months. She wants to sue the trucking firm for $500,000 in damages. The firm's headquarters are in Georgia, but the company does business in Florida. Ramirez could bring suit in a Florida court because she is a resident of Florida, the trucking firm does business in Florida, and that is where the accident occurred. She could also bring suit in a Georgia court, because a Georgia court could exercise jurisdiction over the trucking firm, which is headquartered in that state. She could also sue in a federal court because the requirements of diversity jurisdiction have been met—the lawsuit involves parties from different states, and the amount in controversy (the damages Ramirez is seeking) exceeds $75,000.

diversity of citizenship
Under the U.S. Constitution, a basis for federal district court jurisdiction over a lawsuit between (1) citizens of different states, (2) a foreign country and citizens of a state or states, or (3) citizens of a state and citizens of a foreign country. The amount in controversy must be more than $75,000 before a federal court can exercise jurisdiction in such cases.

When a case is based on a federal question, a federal court will apply federal law. In a case based on diversity of citizenship, however, a federal court will normally apply state law. This is because cases based on diversity of citizenship generally do not involve claims based on federal law.

Exclusive versus Concurrent Jurisdiction

When both federal and state courts have the power to hear a case, as is true in suits involving diversity of citizenship (such as Ramirez's case, described in *Example 6.9*), **concurrent jurisdiction** exists. When cases can be tried only in one or the other, **exclusive jurisdiction** exists. Federal courts have exclusive jurisdiction in cases involving federal crimes, bankruptcy, patents, trademarks, and copyrights; in most class-action lawsuits; and in suits against the United States. States also have exclusive jurisdiction in certain subject matters—for example, in divorce and adoptions.

The concepts of concurrent and exclusive jurisdiction are illustrated in Exhibit 6.1. Some matters, such as bankruptcy law, are under the exclusive jurisdiction of the federal courts. Other matters, such as banking regulation, can fall under state or federal jurisdiction, whereas corporate law falls under state jurisdiction.

concurrent jurisdiction
Jurisdiction that exists when two different courts have the power to hear a case. For example, some cases can be heard in either a federal or a state court.

exclusive jurisdiction
Jurisdiction that exists when a case can be heard only in a particular court, such as a federal court.

EXHIBIT 6.1

Exclusive and Concurrent Jurisdiction
in Business Law

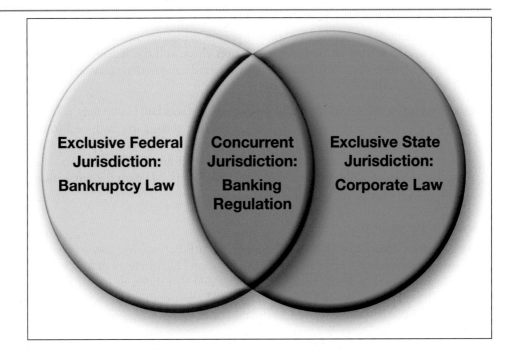

Exclusive Federal
Jurisdiction:

Bankruptcy Law

Concurrent
Jurisdiction:

Banking
Regulation

Exclusive State
Jurisdiction:

Corporate Law

docket

The list of cases entered on a court's
calendar and scheduled to be heard
by the court.

When concurrent jurisdiction exists, a party has a choice of whether to bring a suit in a federal or a state court. As described in the accompanying *Developing Paralegal Skills* feature, the party's lawyer will consider several factors in counseling the party. The lawyer may prefer to litigate the case in a state court, perhaps because of familiarity with the state court's procedures, or in a federal court, because the **docket** is known to be less crowded. Other considerations include the law in an available jurisdiction, how that law has been applied in the jurisdiction's courts, and what the results have been in that jurisdiction.

Jurisdiction in Cyberspace

The Internet makes it easier to interact across jurisdictions. As discussed, for a court to compel a defendant to come before it, there must be at least minimum contacts with the jurisdiction within which the court sits—such as the presence of a company's salesperson within the state. Are there sufficient minimum contacts if the only connection to a jurisdiction is an ad on the Web originating from a remote location?

> **EXAMPLE 6.10** Tom, who lives in Idaho, orders $20,000 worth of merchandise from Juanita's Carpets, an online New Mexico company. After paying for and receiving the merchandise, Tom claims Juanita's goods are not of the quality described on the company's website. Tom sues Juanita's in an Idaho state court. Does the Idaho state court have jurisdiction over the matter? Yes. Juanita's Carpets offers to sell goods around the country, and it made a sale to Tom, so it has sufficient contacts with Idaho to give Idaho courts jurisdiction.

The "Sliding-Scale" Standard

To cope with the challenges to jurisdictional analysis posed by business conducted over the Internet, the courts use a "sliding-scale" standard for determining when the exercise of jurisdiction over an out-of-state party is proper. The courts have identified three types of Internet business contacts: (1) substantial business conducted over the Internet (with contracts or sales, for example), (2) some interactivity through a website, and (3) passive advertising. Jurisdiction is proper for the first category, is improper for the third. In *Example 6.10*, the court would have jurisdiction due to the online sale, not from advertising on the website.

International Jurisdictional Issues

Because the Internet is global, international jurisdictional issues arise. What seems to be emerging is a standard that echoes the requirement of minimum contacts applied by the U.S. courts. Courts in many nations indicate that minimum contacts—such as doing business within the jurisdiction—are enough to compel a defendant to appear and that the defendant's physical presence is not required for the court to exercise jurisdiction. The effect is that a company may have to comply with the laws of any jurisdiction in which it has Internet-based customers. This has been a problem for online auction sites such as eBay, because countries have different rules on what may be offered for sale. Germany, for example, prohibits advertising Nazi memorabilia.

EXAMPLE 6.11 A Minneapolis company requested bids from smartphone makers. A firm in Singapore won the bid to supply the phones. Discussions between the companies took place by e-mail, telephone, and online video conferencing. The Singapore supplier delivered the goods to the buyer at the port in Singapore for shipment. When the phones arrived in Minneapolis, the buyer claimed they did not meet the terms of the contract and sued the Singapore firm. Did the federal court in Minnesota have jurisdiction over the Singapore company? No. The Singapore supplier sold the goods to the Minneapolis company *in Singapore* over the Internet; it had no business presence in the United States. The Minneapolis company would have to file a lawsuit in a Singapore court.

DEVELOPING PARALEGAL SKILLS

CHOICE OF COURTS: STATE OR FEDERAL?

Susan Radtke, a lawyer specializing in employment discrimination, and her paralegal, Joan Dunbar, meet with a new client who wants to sue her former employer for gender discrimination. The client complained to her employer when she was passed over for a promotion. She was fired, she claims, in retaliation for her complaint. The client appears to have a strong case, because several of her former co-workers have agreed to testify that they heard the employer say that he would never promote a woman to a managerial position.

Because both state and federal laws prohibit gender discrimination, the case could be brought in either state or federal court. The client wants Susan to decide whether the case should be filed in a state or federal court. Joan will be drafting the complaint, so Susan and Joan discuss the pros and cons of filing the case in each court. Joan and Susan review a list of considerations for which court to choose.

Tips for Choosing a Court

- Review the jurisdiction of each court.
- Evaluate the strengths and weaknesses of the case.
- Evaluate the remedy sought.
- Evaluate the population from which the jury will be selected in each court.
- Evaluate the likelihood of winning in each court.
- Evaluate the length of time it will take each court to decide the case.
- Review the costs and procedural rules involved in filing in each court.
- Evaluate the types of discovery available in each court.
- Evaluate the personalities and records of the judges sitting in each court.

Venue

venue

The geographic district in which an action is tried and from which the jury is selected.

While jurisdiction has to do with whether a court has authority to hear a case, **venue** is concerned with the most appropriate location for a trial. The concept of venue reflects the policy that a court trying a suit should be in the geographic area in which the parties involved reside or in which the incident leading to the lawsuit occurred. Pretrial publicity may require a change of venue to another community, especially in criminal cases in which the defendant's right to a fair and impartial jury has been impaired.

> **EXAMPLE 6.12** In 1995, Timothy McVeigh was indicted in connection with the bombing of a federal building in Oklahoma City that killed 168 persons and injured many others. The defense attorneys argued—and the court agreed—that McVeigh could not receive a fair trial in Oklahoma because an impartial jury could not be chosen. The court ordered a change of venue to a federal court in Denver for trial.

Judicial Procedures

From beginning to end, litigation follows specifically designated procedural rules. As this chapter's *Office Tech and Cybersecurity* feature discusses, courts are increasingly moving to fulfill procedural processes electronically.

OFFICE TECH AND CYBERSECURITY

COURTS IN THE INTERNET AGE

E-filing systems for handling documents are growing more common within court systems. For example, New York uses the New York State Courts Electronic Filing (NYSCEF) system for the New York State Unified Court system. Cases can be initiated and documents filed twenty-four hours a day. The system provides e-mailed notices of filing. Attorneys must consent to use e-filing in nonmandatory cases.

Once a party agrees to the use of the e-filing system for a case, hard copies may not be filed except in unusual circumstances. Attorneys may authorize paralegals to e-file a document using the attorney's login and password, but the attorney remains the filer of record. If the system breaks down, hard-copy filing is allowed, and many deadlines are extended. Filing fees are paid by credit card.

Texas has a different system. Its eFiling for Courts system requires use of an approved Electronic Filing Service Provider. The service provider e-mails receipts of filings. Once a court accepts a document, a confirmation message and file-stamped copy are e-mailed to the filing attorney. Texas also allows "eService" of documents for cases in which parties have consented to it. The average cost is about ten dollars per document.

Systems such as those used in Texas and New York are becoming increasingly common as courts move to more efficient document-handling procedures. Paralegals need to be familiar with software such as Adobe Acrobat that produces PDF files suitable for e-filing.

Court Structures

Each state's court system is unique. The National Center for State Courts (NCSC) shows the structure of each state court system at **ncsc.org**. You can find links to state court websites, state court statistics, and articles about state court trends. Many state judicial systems have centralized websites with links to circuit and trial courts' websites. For example, the Michigan courts' website offers a directory of all courts and their holdings at **courts.michigan.gov**.

Technology Tip

Paralegals should become comfortable gathering court information online. It is easy to find websites for courts in your area, review various courts' rules, examine court dockets, and check out what digital forms are available.

A paralegal should develop skills in finding, filling out, and submitting court forms online. Click on "Forms & Rules" from the menu at the top of the California Courts home page at **courts.ca.gov**, read the instructions, choose a form, and fill it out. Then search for the procedures required for filing the documents with the court. You will find valuable court information through such exercises and be on the road to becoming the technology expert of your legal team.

The general procedural rules for federal civil court cases are set forth in the Federal Rules of Civil Procedure. For criminal cases, they are presented in the Federal Rules of Criminal Procedure. Each federal court also has its own local rules. State rules, which are often similar to the federal rules, vary from state to state, and even from court to court within a given state. Rules of procedure also differ in criminal and civil cases. Paralegals who work for trial lawyers need to be familiar with the procedural rules of the relevant courts. Because judicial procedures will be examined in detail in Chapters 10 through 13, we do not discuss them here.

State Court Systems

Each state has its own system of courts, and no two state systems are the same. As Exhibit 6.2 indicates, there may be several levels, or tiers, of courts within a state court system:

1. State trial courts of general jurisdiction and limited jurisdiction.

2. State appellate courts.

3. The state's highest court (often called the state supreme court).

Judges in the state court system are sometimes elected by the voters for a specified term; in other states, they are appointed.

EXHIBIT 6.2

Levels in a State Court System

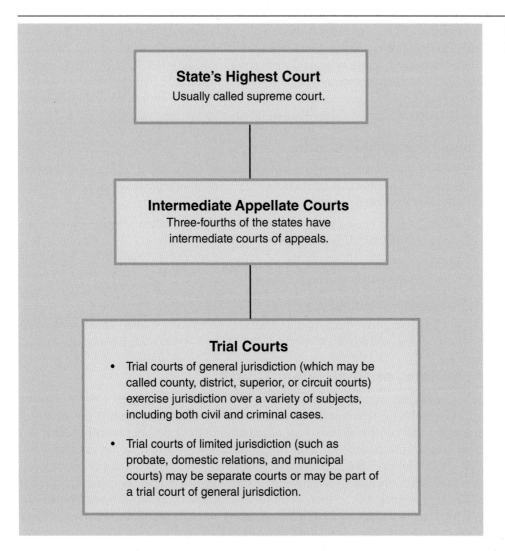

State's Highest Court
Usually called supreme court.

Intermediate Appellate Courts
Three-fourths of the states have intermediate courts of appeals.

Trial Courts
- Trial courts of general jurisdiction (which may be called county, district, superior, or circuit courts) exercise jurisdiction over a variety of subjects, including both civil and criminal cases.

- Trial courts of limited jurisdiction (such as probate, domestic relations, and municipal courts) may be separate courts or may be part of a trial court of general jurisdiction.

Generally, any person who is a party to a lawsuit has the opportunity to plead the case before a trial court and then, if she loses, appeal to at least one level of appellate court. Finally, if a federal statute or federal constitutional issue is involved in the decision of a state supreme court, that decision may be further appealed to the United States Supreme Court.

Trial Courts

Trial courts are what their name implies—courts in which trials are held and testimony taken. You will read about trial procedures in Chapter 12, where we follow a hypothetical case through the various stages of a trial.

Briefly, a trial court is presided over by a judge, who controls the proceedings and issues a decision on the matter before the court. If the trial is a jury trial (many are held without juries), the jury decides the outcome of factual disputes, and the judge issues a judgment based on the jury's conclusion. During the trial, the attorney for each side introduces evidence (such as relevant documents, exhibits, and testimony of witnesses) in support of his or her client's position. Each attorney is given an opportunity to cross-examine witnesses and challenge evidence offered by the opposing party.

General Jurisdiction Courts

State trial courts have either general or limited jurisdiction. Trial courts that have general jurisdiction as to subject matter may be called county, district, superior, or circuit courts. State trial courts of general jurisdiction have jurisdiction over a wide variety of subjects, including both civil disputes (such as landlord-tenant matters or contract claims) and criminal prosecutions. In some states, trial courts of general jurisdiction may hear appeals from courts of limited jurisdiction.

Limited Jurisdiction Courts

Courts with limited subject-matter jurisdiction are often called "inferior" trial courts or minor courts as they may be under the jurisdiction of a general trial court. Courts of limited jurisdiction include:

- Small claims courts, which hear only civil cases involving claims of less than a certain amount, such as $5,000.

- Domestic relations courts, which handle only divorce actions, paternity suits, and child-custody and support cases.

- Municipal courts, which mainly handle traffic violations.

- Probate courts, which handle the administration of wills, estate-settlement problems, and related matters.

Appellate, or Reviewing, Courts

After a trial, the parties have the right to file an appeal to a higher court if they are unsatisfied with the trial court's ruling. In practice, parties are unlikely to file an appeal unless the trial court may have committed a reversible error. A **reversible error** is a legal error at the trial court level that is significant enough to have affected the outcome of the case. For example, the judge may have given improper instructions about the law to the jury. Usually, appellate courts do not look at questions of *fact* (such as whether a party did, in fact, commit a certain action) but at questions of *law* (whether the trial judge applied the law properly to the facts established at trial). Only a judge, not a jury, can rule on questions of law.

reversible error
A legal error at the trial court level that is significant enough to have affected the outcome of the case. It is grounds for reversal of the judgment on appeal.

Appellate courts normally defer to a trial court's findings on questions of fact because the trial court judge and jury were in a better position to evaluate testimony by directly observing witnesses' gestures, demeanor, and nonverbal behavior during the trial. When a case is appealed, an appellate panel of three or more judges reviews the record, including the written transcript of the trial.

Intermediate Appellate Courts

A majority of states have intermediate appellate courts or courts of appeals. The subject-matter jurisdiction of these courts is limited to hearing appeals. Usually, appellate courts review the records, read appellate briefs, and listen to the oral arguments presented by the parties' attorneys. Then the panel of judges renders (issues) a decision. If a party is unsatisfied with the appellate ruling, that party can appeal to the highest state court. Review by the high court is often discretionary, so writs of appeals may be rejected.

Highest State Courts

The highest appellate court in a state is usually called the supreme court but may be called by some other name. For example, both Maryland and New York refer to the highest state court as the court of appeals. Texas and Oklahoma have two high courts, one for civil cases and one for criminal cases. The decisions of each state's highest court on all questions of state law are final. Only when issues of federal law are involved can a decision made by a state's highest court be reviewed by the United States Supreme Court.

The Federal Court System

The federal court system is basically a three-level model consisting of (1) U.S. district courts (trial courts of general jurisdiction) and various courts of limited jurisdiction, (2) U.S. courts of appeals (intermediate courts of appeals), and (3) the United States Supreme Court. Exhibit 6.3 shows the organization of the federal court system.

EXHIBIT 6.3
The Organization of the Federal Court System

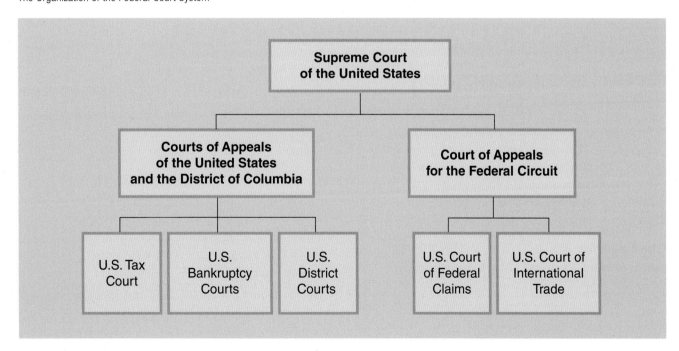

According to Article III of the U.S. Constitution, there is only one federal Supreme Court. All other courts in the federal system are considered "inferior." Congress has the power to create inferior courts. The courts that Congress has created include the district courts and courts of limited jurisdiction, as well as the U.S. courts of appeals.

Unlike state court judges, who are often elected, federal court judges—including the justices of the United States Supreme Court—are appointed by the president of the United States and confirmed by the U.S. Senate. Federal judges receive lifetime appointments (because under Article III they "hold their Offices during good Behavior").

U.S. District Courts

At the federal level, the trial court of general jurisdiction is the district court. There is at least one federal district court in every state. The number of judicial districts varies over time, owing to population changes and caseloads. Currently, there are ninety-four judicial districts.

U.S. district courts have original jurisdiction in matters of federal law. There are other trial courts with original but special (or limited) jurisdiction, such as the federal bankruptcy courts and others shown in Exhibit 6.3. The *Developing Paralegal Skills* feature below discusses some considerations in federal jurisdiction.

U.S. Courts of Appeals

As seen in Exhibit 6.4, in the federal court system, there are thirteen U.S. courts of appeals—also referred to as U.S. circuit courts of appeals. The federal courts of appeals for twelve of the circuits (including the District of Columbia Circuit) hear appeals from the federal district courts located within their respective judicial circuits. The court of appeals for the thirteenth circuit, called the Federal Circuit, has national appellate jurisdiction over certain types of cases, such as cases involving patent law and cases involving contract claims against the U.S. government.

DEVELOPING PARALEGAL SKILLS

FEDERAL COURT JURISDICTION

Mona, a new client, comes to the law offices of Henry, Jacobs & Miller in Detroit, Michigan. She wants to file a lawsuit against a New York hospital where she had emergency gallbladder surgery. Mona contracted an infection after the surgery and nearly died. She was so sick that she missed several months of work and lost wages of $28,000. She also has medical expenses exceeding $60,000. Jane Doyle, a paralegal, is asked to review the case to determine if it can be filed in federal court.

Checklist for Determining Federal Court Jurisdiction

- Is the case based, at least in part, on the U.S. Constitution, a treaty, or other question of federal law?

- If the case does not involve a question of federal law, does it involve more than $75,000 and citizens of different states?

- If the case does not involve a question of federal law, does it involve more than $75,000 and a foreign country and citizens of a state or different state?

- If the case does not involve a question of federal law, does it involve more than $75,000 and citizens of a state and citizens or subjects of a foreign country?

If the case involves more than $75,000 and one of the citizenship requirements above, then diversity jurisdiction exists.

A party who is dissatisfied with a federal district court's decision on an issue may appeal that decision to the relevant federal circuit court of appeals. The judges on the court review decisions made by trial courts for any errors of law. The judges generally defer to a district court's findings of fact. The decisions of the circuit courts of appeals are final in most cases, but review by the United States Supreme Court is possible.

The United States Supreme Court

The highest level of the federal court system is the United States Supreme Court, traditionally composed of nine justices. Although the Supreme Court has original, or trial, jurisdiction in rare instances (set forth in Article III, Section 2, of the Constitution—see Appendix F), most of its work is as an appeals court. The Supreme Court can review any case decided by any of the federal courts of appeals, and it also has appellate authority over some cases decided in the state courts.

EXHIBIT 6.4

Boundaries of the U.S. Courts of Appeals and U.S. District Courts

Source: Administrative Office of the United States Courts.

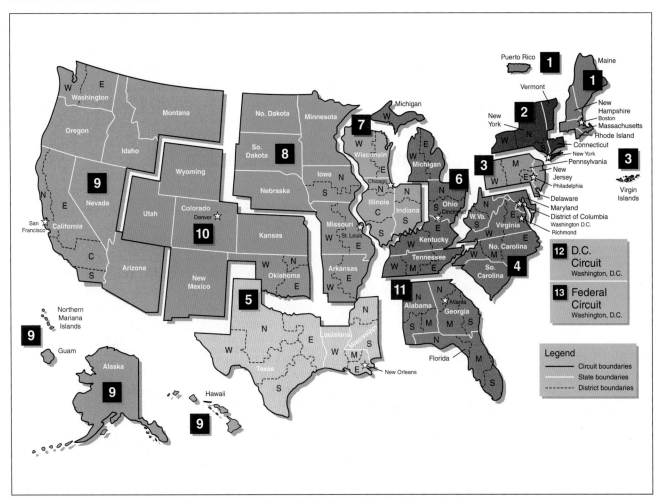

How Cases Reach the Supreme Court

There is no absolute right of appeal to the United States Supreme Court. Thousands of cases are filed with the Supreme Court each year, but it hears only about eighty cases each year.

To bring a case before the Supreme Court, a party requests the Court to issue a writ of *certiorari*. A **writ of *certiorari*** is an order issued by the Supreme Court to a lower court requiring it to send the record of the case for review. The Court will issue a writ only if at least four of the nine justices vote to do so. The vast majority of petitions for writs are denied. A denial is not a decision on the merits of a case, nor does it indicate agreement with the lower court's opinion. It simply means that the Supreme Court declines to grant the request (petition) for appeal.

writ of *certiorari*

A writ from a higher court asking a lower court to send it the record of a case for review. The United States Supreme Court uses *certiorari* to review most of the cases it decides to hear.

Types of Cases Reviewed by the Supreme Court

Typically, petitions are granted by the Court in cases that raise constitutional questions or where lower court decisions conflict with other state or federal courts' decisions. Similarly, if federal appellate courts issue inconsistent opinions on an issue, the Supreme Court may review a case involving that issue and generate a decision to settle the issue.

> **EXAMPLE 6.13** An employer fires an employee who refuses to work on Saturdays for religious reasons. The fired employee applies for unemployment benefits from the state unemployment agency. The agency concludes that the employer had good reason to fire the employee, and so it denies unemployment benefits. The fired employee sues the agency on the ground that the employee's right to free exercise of religion—a constitutional right—was violated. The case is ultimately appealed to a state supreme court, which decides the issue in a way contrary to several recent federal appellate courts' interpretations of freedom of religion in the employment context. If the losing party petitions the Supreme Court for a writ of *certiorari*, the Court is more likely to grant the petition and review the case than if all lower court decisions were consistent.

Alternative Dispute Resolution

Litigation is expensive, adversarial, and time consuming. For these and other reasons, more and more individuals are turning to **alternative dispute resolution (ADR)** as a means of settling their disputes.

alternative dispute resolution (ADR)

The resolution of disputes in ways other than those involved in the traditional judicial process. Negotiation, mediation, and arbitration are forms of ADR.

Methods of ADR range from neighbors sitting down over a cup of coffee in an attempt to work out their differences to multinational corporations agreeing to resolve a dispute through a formal hearing before a panel of experts. The great advantage of ADR is its flexibility. Normally, the parties themselves decide the method that will be used to settle the dispute, what procedures will be used, and whether the decision reached (either by themselves or by a neutral third party) will be legally binding.

About 95 percent of cases filed with the courts are settled before trial, often through some form of ADR. Indeed, about half the states either require or encourage parties to undertake ADR (usually mediation) prior to trial. Several federal courts have instituted ADR programs as well. Here, we examine various forms of ADR. Keep in mind that new methods of ADR—and variations of existing methods—are being devised. Additionally, ADR services are now being offered via the Internet. Paralegals who develop expertise in the area of ADR can expand their career opportunities (by becoming mediators, for example). Paralegals can also help attorneys to clarify the issues for clients who must decide whether to take a case to court or choose ADR, as described in the accompanying *Developing Paralegal Skills* feature.

DEVELOPING PARALEGAL SKILLS

TO SUE OR NOT TO SUE

Millie Burke, a paralegal, works for a sole practitioner, Jim Wilcox. She has been asked by Wilcox to draw up a checklist consisting of questions that clients should consider before initiating a lawsuit. Wilcox wants to have the checklist on hand when he first interviews clients who come to him for advice on whether to bring a lawsuit or to settle a dispute by some alternative means. Burke drafts a checklist for Wilcox's review.

Checklist for Deciding Whether to Sue

- Now that you have a rough idea of what it might cost to litigate your dispute, are you still interested in pursuing a trial? If so, you will need to pay a retainer now from which I will draw the initial filing fees and court costs. You will also need to sign an agreement that you will pay me hourly rates if the costs exceed the amount of the retainer.

- What is your goal for the litigation? What do you want to accomplish? What could the other party do to settle the case now?

- Do you have the time and patience to follow a court case through the judicial system, even if it takes several years?

- Is there a way to settle your grievance without going to court? Even if the settlement is less than you think you are owed, you may be better off settling now for the smaller figure. An early settlement will save the cost of litigation and prevent the time loss and frustration associated with litigation.

- Can you use some form of alternative dispute resolution (negotiation, mediation, or arbitration) to settle the dispute? Before you say no, let's review these dispute-settlement methods and discuss the pros and cons of each alternative.

Negotiation

Negotiation is one alternative means of resolving disputes. Attorneys frequently advise their clients to try to negotiate a settlement of their disputes voluntarily before they proceed to trial. During pretrial negotiation, the parties and/or their attorneys may meet to see if a mutually satisfactory agreement can be reached.

> **EXAMPLE 6.14** Assume that Katherine Baranski is suing Tony Peretto. He ran a stop sign and crashed into Baranski's car, causing her to suffer injuries and damages exceeding $100,000. After pretrial investigations, both parties realize that Baranski will likely win a suit. Peretto's attorney may make a settlement offer on behalf of Peretto. Baranski may be willing to accept a settlement offer for an amount lower than the amount of damages claimed in her complaint to avoid the time, trouble, expense, and uncertainty involved in taking the case to trial.
>
> To facilitate an out-of-court settlement, Baranski's attorney may ask his paralegal to draft a letter to Baranski pointing out the strengths and weaknesses of her case against Peretto, the ADR options for settling the case before trial, and the advantages and disadvantages associated with each ADR option. Additionally, the paralegal may be asked to draft a letter to Peretto's attorney indicating the strengths of Baranski's case against him and the advantages to Peretto of settling the dispute out of court.

As a result of pretrial negotiations such as those just described, a settlement agreement may be reached. In a **settlement agreement**, one party gives up the right to initiate or continue litigation in return for a sum to be paid by the other party. Exhibit 6.5 shows an example of a settlement agreement. Settlements must usually be approved by the court, and if a party does not live up to the agreement, that can be the basis for a lawsuit to enforce the settlement.

negotiation
A process in which parties attempt to settle their dispute voluntarily, with or without attorneys to represent them.

settlement agreement
An out-of-court resolution to a legal dispute, which is agreed to by the parties in writing. A settlement agreement may be reached at any time prior to or during a trial.

EXHIBIT 6.5
A Sample Settlement Agreement

SETTLEMENT AGREEMENT

THIS AGREEMENT is entered into this twelfth day of May, 2022, between Katherine Baranski and Tony Peretto.

WITNESSETH

WHEREAS, there is now pending in the U.S. District Court for the District of Nita an action entitled *Baranski v. Peretto,* hereinafter referred to as "action."

WHEREAS, the parties hereto desire to record their agreement to settle all matters relating to said action without the necessity of further litigation.

NOW, THEREFORE, in consideration of the covenants and agreements contained herein, the sufficiency of which is hereby mutually acknowledged, and intending to be legally bound hereby, the parties agree as follows:

1. Katherine Baranski agrees to accept the sum of seventy-five thousand dollars ($75,000) in full satisfaction of all claims against Tony Peretto as set forth in the complaint filed in this action.

2. Tony Peretto agrees to pay Katherine Baranski the above-stated amount, in a lump-sum cash payment, on or before the first day of July, 2022.

3. Upon execution of this agreement and payment of the sum required under this agreement, the parties shall cause the action to be dismissed with prejudice.

4. When the sum required under this agreement is paid in full, Katherine Baranski will execute and deliver to Tony Peretto a release of all claims set forth in the complaint filed in the said action.

Katherine Baranski
Katherine Baranski

Tony Peretto
Tony Peretto

Sworn and subscribed before me this twelfth day of May, 2022.

Leela M. Shay
Leela M. Shay
Notary Public
District of Nita

---

mediation
A method of settling disputes outside of court by using the services of a neutral third party, who acts as a communicating agent between the parties; mediation is less formal than arbitration.

Mediation

Another alternative to a trial is mediation. In the **mediation** process, the parties attempt to negotiate an agreement with the assistance of a neutral third party, a mediator. In mediation, the mediator typically talks with the parties separately and often

A paralegal mediates a dispute by emphasizing the common ground shared by the parties as she proposes possible solutions. Is mediation binding on both parties? Why or why not?

talks with them jointly. The mediator emphasizes points of agreement, helps the parties evaluate their positions, and proposes solutions. The mediator, however, does not make a binding decision on the matter being disputed.

The parties may select a mediator on the basis of expertise in a particular field or a reputation for fairness and impartiality. The mediator need not be a lawyer. The mediator may be one person, such as a paralegal, an attorney, or a volunteer from the community, or a panel of mediators may be used. Usually, a mediator charges a fee, which can be split between the parties. Many state and federal courts require that parties mediate disputes before being allowed to resolve the disputes through trials. In this situation, the mediators may be appointed by the court.

A Nonadversarial Forum

Mediation is not adversarial in nature, as lawsuits are. In litigation, the parties "do battle" with each other in the courtroom, while the judge serves as the neutral referee. The adversarial nature of the trial process may inflame tensions between the parties. Because of its nonadversarial nature, the mediation process tends to reduce the hostility between the parties and may allow them to resume their former relationship. For this reason, mediation is often the preferred form of ADR for disputes involving businesses, family members, or other long-term relationships.

EXAMPLE 6.15 Suppose two business partners have a dispute over how the profits of their firm should be distributed. If the dispute is litigated, the parties will be adversaries, and their attorneys will emphasize how the parties' positions differ, not what they have in common. In contrast, if the dispute is mediated, the mediator emphasizes common ground shared by the partners and helps them work toward agreement. If the partners wish to do business together after the case is over, mediation will be preferred to litigation.

Paralegals as Mediators

Because a mediator need not be a lawyer, this field is open to paralegals who acquire appropriate training and expertise. If you are interested in becoming a mediator, check with paralegal associations to find out how you can pursue this career goal. You can

FEATURED CONTRIBUTOR

WHY MEDIATION MAY BE THE BEST LEGAL ALTERNATIVE

P. Darrel Harrison

BIOGRAPHICAL NOTE

P. Darrel Harrison is a trained mediator who holds an M.B.A. in organizational development and a J.D. degree. He is an instructor and the program director for the ABA-approved paralegal program at San Diego Miramar College in San Diego, California. Mr. Harrison is also vice president and chief grievance/arbitration officer for the San Diego Chapter of the American Federation of Teachers (AFT), Local 1931. He currently serves as a board member of the San Diego County Law Enforcement Review Board, which reviews citizen complaints filed against the San Diego County Sheriff's Department.

Litigated cases can be costly. Mediation is a cost-effective method of resolving many disputes because it avoids the expense of going to court. Mediation is satisfying because it allows a client the ability to negotiate an outcome based on compromise rather than a simple win or loss in court.

Mediation is a process for resolving conflicts, in which a neutral, skilled mediator assists the parties to discuss and negotiate their issues and reach a mutually acceptable resolution.

Because many state and federal courts around the United States have provided alternative dispute resolution services,

> " **. . . mediation basics are universally applied."**

various forms of mediation specialties have developed over the years, such as parent/teen mediation, family mediation, business mediation, employment mediation, elder care mediation, and guardianship mediation, to name a few.

The Mediation Process

Despite the specialty areas, mediation basics are universally applied. First, there must be willing participants. The commitment to mediation creates an atmosphere of good faith and the positive momentum that leads to a negotiated conclusion.

also check with a county, state, or federal court in your area to see how to qualify as a mediator for court-referred mediation (to be discussed shortly).

Generally, any paralegal aspiring to work as a mediator must have excellent communication skills. This is because, as a mediator, it will be your job to listen carefully to each party's complaints and communicate possible solutions to a dispute in a way that is not offensive to either party. (See this chapter's *Featured Contributor* article for further details on the functions performed by mediators and the role paralegals play in the mediation process.)

Arbitration

A more formal method of ADR is arbitration, in which an arbitrator hears a dispute and determines the outcome. The key difference between arbitration and the forms of ADR just discussed is that in arbitration, the third party hearing the dispute makes the

arbitration
A method of settling disputes in which a dispute is submitted to a disinterested third party (other than a court), who issues a decision that may or may not be legally binding.

Once the parties have joined the process, it is essential that the mediator—the neutral third party—have the ability to engage the parties and help navigate them through the issues to come to a common solution. Unlike arbitration, where the intermediary listens to the arguments of both sides and makes a decision for the disputants, a mediator assists the parties to develop a solution themselves.

Although mediators may provide ideas or even formal proposals for settlement, the mediator is primarily a "process person." The mediator helps the parties define the agenda, identify and reframe the issues, communicate more effectively, find areas of common ground, negotiate fairly, and reach an agreement. A successful mediation has an outcome that is accepted and owned by the parties themselves.

The Mediator's Skills

No license is required to be a mediator, but nonprofit organizations and universities offer certificates and degrees for mediation training. The National Conflict Resolution Center (NCRC) headquartered in San Diego, California, provides a training program for paralegals, attorneys, mental health professionals, managers, educators, law enforcement professionals, and others who want to complete the certification or credentialing process.

Below is a list of the characteristics of a successful mediator.

- A good listener.
- Possesses the discipline to resist taking sides.
- Comprehends facts and repeats them accurately.

- Engages the parties diligently at all times.
- Possesses the writing skills needed to draft the final agreement.

Additionally, mediators must be diplomatic and use persuasion to get people to soften hard-line positions. Although many mediators are highly trained and experienced, many are not full-time mediators. They work in a variety of professions.

When and How to Engage a Mediator

If your firm's client is engaged in a dispute with another party and is considering litigation, consider the following tips:

- It may help to give the other party information about mediation. Provide a link to a mediator's website for information about the process.
- Consider asking the other party to suggest a mediator to help resolve the dispute.
- Some mediators will call the other side, explain mediation to them, and encourage them to mediate the dispute.
- You can ask the other side to mediate your dispute *before* or *after* a case is filed.

Preparing for mediation is a lot like preparing to go to a court hearing. Identify and organize the facts relevant to the dispute and make sure you know the facts that support the other side, too. If the parties are willing, and the mediator provides good facilitation skills, the benefits of the process and outcome can far outweigh the cost and stress of litigation.

Source: P. Darrel Harrison.

> " ... the mediator is primarily a 'process person.' "

decision for the parties—a decision that usually will be legally binding. In negotiation and mediation, in contrast, the parties decide for themselves, although a third party assists them. In a sense, the arbitrator acts as a private judge, even though the arbitrator is not required to be a lawyer. In some instances, a panel of experts arbitrates disputes.

Arbitration can resemble a trial, although the procedural rules are much less restrictive than those governing litigation. In the typical format, the parties present facts and arguments to the arbitrator and describe the outcome they want. Witnesses may be called, but the format is less formal than in court. The arbitrator then issues a decision.

Depending on the parties' circumstances and preferences, the arbitrator's decision may or may not be legally binding on the parties. In nonbinding arbitration, the parties submit their dispute to a third party but remain free to reject the third party's decision. Nonbinding arbitration is more similar to mediation than to binding arbitration. As will be discussed later in this chapter, ADR mandated by the courts is not binding on the parties. If, after mandated arbitration, the parties are not satisfied with the results, they may insist on litigation in court. It is rare to be able to appeal the results of binding arbitration.

Arbitration Clauses and Statutes

Commercial matters are often submitted to arbitration both for speed and because the parties may wish to preserve their relationship. When a dispute arises, parties can agree to settle their differences through binding arbitration rather than through the court system.

> *EXAMPLE 6.16* A building is being constructed for $20 million. As construction proceeds, issues arise that are not covered in the details of the original plans. Extra expense will be incurred. Rather than stop work and negotiate a change to the contract, it is common for the parties to have agreed in the original contract to resolve such issues through binding arbitration when the job is done. The arbitrator is likely be an experienced contractor who understands construction processes and expenses.

Contractual Obligation.   Disputes are often arbitrated because of an arbitration clause in a contract agreed to before the dispute arose. For example, contracts to open checking accounts generally include an arbitration clause. An **arbitration clause** provides that any disputes arising under the contract will be resolved by arbitration and usually explains how the arbitration will be handled. For example, an arbitration clause in a contract for the sale of goods might provide that "any controversy or claim arising under this contract will be referred to arbitration before the American Arbitration Association." Most international business contracts require arbitration, often in an international business center such as London or Stockholm.

arbitration clause
A clause in a contract providing that, in case of a dispute, the parties will determine their rights through arbitration rather than the judicial system.

Statutory Backing.   Most states have statutes (often based on the Uniform Arbitration Act) under which arbitration clauses will be enforced, and some state statutes compel arbitration of certain disputes, such as those involving public employees. At the federal level, the Federal Arbitration Act (FAA) enforces arbitration clauses in contracts involving interstate commerce. Agreements involving business transactions usually fall under the FAA.

The FAA does not establish a set arbitration procedure. The parties must agree on the manner of resolving their disputes. The FAA provides only that if the parties have agreed to arbitrate disputes arising in relation to their contract, through an arbitration clause, the arbitration clause will be enforced by the courts. In other words, arbitration must take place. There is no right to file suit in court. The Supreme Court has vigorously enforced the presumption in favor of arbitration clauses, fending off efforts by some states to limit their application.

The Arbitration Process

The arbitration process generally consists of a submission agreement, a hearing, and an award.

The Submission Agreement.   The first step in the arbitration process is the **submission agreement**, in which the parties agree to submit their dispute for arbitration. If an arbitration clause was included in a contract, the clause serves this function so the complaining party can file with the arbitrator to begin the process. Once a submission agreement has been filed, going to court is no longer an option, unless both parties agree to do so. Most states require that an agreement to submit a dispute to arbitration must be in writing. The submission agreement typically identifies the

submission agreement
A written agreement to submit a legal dispute to an arbitrator or arbitrating panel for resolution.

parties, the nature of the dispute, the monetary amounts in the dispute, the place of arbitration, and the powers that the arbitrator will exercise. Frequently, the agreement includes a signed statement that the parties intend to be bound by the arbitrator's decision.

The Hearing. The next step in the process is the *hearing*. Normally, the parties agree prior to arbitration—in an arbitration clause or a submission-to-arbitration agreement—on the procedural rules that will govern the proceedings, including the method of selecting an arbitrator or a panel of arbitrators. In a typical hearing, the parties begin as they would at a trial by presenting opening arguments and stating what remedies should or should not be granted. In some cases, the matter is handled entirely by submitting documents online and by phone calls. No in-person contact with the arbitrator may be needed.

After the opening positions are established, evidence is presented. Witnesses may be called and examined by both sides. Once all evidence has been presented, the parties give their closing arguments. Although arbitration is in some ways similar to a trial, the rules (such as those regarding what kinds of evidence may be introduced) are usually much less restrictive, and lead to a quicker resolution, than those involved in formal litigation.

The Award. After each side has had an opportunity to present its case, the arbitrator reaches a decision. The decision of the arbitrator is called an **award**, even if no monetary award is conferred as a result of the proceedings. The award is usually announced within thirty days of the close of the hearing. In most instances, the arbitrator does not give a written explanation for the decision. The award is like a court decision, so it is enforceable in court if the losing party does not comply.

award
In the context of ADR, the decision rendered by an arbitrator. It is enforceable in court.

A paralegal may become involved in preparations for arbitration, just as in preparing for a trial. The paralegal will assist in obtaining and organizing evidence relating to the dispute, may interview witnesses and prepare them for the hearing, and generally will help with other tasks commonly undertaken prior to a trial (see Chapter 10).

The Role of the Courts in Prearbitration

The role of the courts in arbitration is limited. One important role is at the prearbitration stage. When a dispute arises as to whether the parties have agreed in an arbitration clause to submit a particular matter to arbitration, one party may file suit to force arbitration. The court before which the suit is brought will not decide the underlying substantive controversy but must decide whether the dispute is *arbitrable*—that is, whether the matter is one capable of being resolved through arbitration and whether the parties actually agreed to the arbitration.

> *EXAMPLE 6.17* Suppose that a dispute involves a claim of employment discrimination on the basis of age. If the issue of arbitrability reaches a court, the court will have to decide whether the Age Discrimination in Employment Act (which protects persons forty years of age and older against employment discrimination on the basis of age) permits claims brought under the act to be arbitrated.

Compelled Arbitration. If the court finds that the subject matter in controversy is covered by an arbitration agreement, then a party is almost always compelled to arbitrate the dispute. Even when a claim involves a violation of a statute passed to protect a certain class of people, such as a statute prohibiting age discrimination against employees in the workplace, a court will likely determine that the parties must nonetheless abide by their agreement to arbitrate the dispute.

EXAMPLE 6.18 In the employment discrimination claim discussed in *Example 6.17*, suppose that the "agreement to arbitrate" is a paragraph in a three-hundred-page employee handbook. The court will have to decide whether there was actually an agreement between the parties to arbitrate their disputes. Generally, courts expect arbitration agreements to be clearly stated. If an "agreement to arbitrate" is buried in fine print or unclearly stated, it is unlikely to be enforceable.

Usually, a court will allow the claim to be arbitrated if the court, in interpreting the statute, can find no legislative intent to the contrary and the parties clearly agreed to arbitration.

Fairness Issue.   The courts will not compel arbitration if the arbitration rules and procedures are inherently unfair to one of the parties.

EXAMPLE 6.19 Suppose that an employer's arbitration agreement with an employee states that the employer establishes the rules for the arbitration and that each side must pay half the cost of arbitration. In this situation, the court is likely to conclude that the rules are unfair and thus refuse to enforce the arbitration agreement.

Note, though, that a properly drafted arbitration clause generally will stand.

The Postarbitration Role of the Courts

Courts may play a role at the postarbitration stage. After arbitration produces an award, one party may appeal the award or may seek a court order compelling the other party to comply with the award. The general view is that because the parties were free to frame the issues and set the powers of the arbitrator at the outset, they cannot complain about the result. An arbitration award may be set aside if the award resulted from the arbitrator's misconduct or "bad faith," or if the arbitrator exceeded his or her powers in arbitrating the dispute. Setting aside an award does not happen very often. Courts generally enforce arbitration awards and will order payment to be made if the losing party fails to pay.

Other ADR Forms

The three forms of ADR just discussed have been the most commonly used forms to date. In recent years, a variety of new types of ADR have emerged. Some combine elements of mediation and arbitration. For example, in **binding mediation**, a neutral mediator tries to facilitate agreement between the parties, but if no agreement is reached, the mediator issues a legally binding decision on the matter. In one version of this approach, known as mediation arbitration (med-arb), an arbitrator first attempts to help the parties reach an agreement, just as a mediator would. If no agreement is reached, then formal arbitration is undertaken, and the arbitrator issues a legally binding decision.

Another ADR form is referred to as "assisted negotiation" because it involves a third party in what is essentially a negotiation process. For example, in **early neutral case evaluation**, the parties select a neutral third party (generally an expert in the subject matter of the dispute) to evaluate their respective positions. The parties explain their positions to the case evaluator however they wish. The case evaluator then assesses the strengths and weaknesses of the parties' positions, and this evaluation forms the basis for negotiating a settlement.

The mini-trial is a form of assisted negotiation that is often used by business parties. In a **mini-trial**, each party's attorney briefly argues the party's case before representatives of each firm who have the authority to settle the dispute. Typically, a

binding mediation
A form of ADR in which a mediator attempts to facilitate agreement between the parties but then issues a legally binding decision if no agreement is reached.

early neutral case evaluation
A form of ADR in which a neutral third party evaluates the strengths and weaknesses of the disputing parties' positions; the evaluator's opinion forms the basis for negotiating a settlement.

mini-trial
A private proceeding that assists disputing parties in determining whether to take their case to court. Each party's attorney briefly argues the party's case before the other party and (usually) a neutral third party, who acts as an adviser. If the parties fail to reach an agreement, the adviser issues an opinion as to how a court would likely decide the issue.

neutral third party (usually an expert in the area being disputed) acts as an adviser. If the parties fail to reach an agreement, the adviser renders an opinion as to how a court would likely decide the issue. The proceeding assists the parties in determining whether they should negotiate a settlement of the dispute or take it to court. It is a useful way for the parties to assess the strength of each side's case.

Collaborative Law

Still another method of resolving disputes is the collaborative law approach, which is increasingly being used during marital separation procedures. In *collaborative law*, both parties, their attorneys, and any professionals working with the parties agree to meet to resolve all of their issues without litigation. (Sometimes a single attorney handles the matter for both sides.) The lawyers act as negotiators and communication moderators while advising their clients about their legal rights, entitlements, and obligations. Both parties promise to take a reasoned stand on every issue, to keep discovery cooperative and informal, and to work together to craft an agreement. Any abusive communications are identified, discussed, and eliminated.

Because the attorneys agree not to take part in any litigation that may occur if an agreement is not reached, the attorneys focus only on settlement rather than on preparing documents or presentations for court. If either party seeks court intervention, all attorneys must withdraw from representation. The Uniform Collaborative Law Act, written by the Uniform Law Commission, has been adopted in eighteen states as of 2020.

Court-Referred ADR

Today, most states require or encourage parties to undergo mediation or arbitration prior to trial. Generally, when a trial court refers a case for arbitration, the arbitrator's decision is not binding on the parties. If the parties do not agree with the arbitrator's decision, they can go forward with the lawsuit.

The types of court-related ADR programs in use vary widely. In some states, such as Missouri, ADR is completely voluntary. In other states, such as Minnesota, parties are required to undertake ADR before a court will hear their cases. Some states offer a menu of options. Other states, including Florida (which has a statewide, comprehensive mediation program), offer only one alternative.

Courts experiment with a variety of ADR alternatives to speed up justice and reduce its cost. Some federal and state courts hold summary jury trials. In a **summary jury trial (SJT)**, the parties present their arguments and supporting evidence (other than witness testimony—witnesses are not called in an SJT). The jury then renders a verdict, but unlike the verdict in an actual trial, the jury's verdict is not binding. The verdict acts as a guide to both sides in reaching an agreement during mandatory negotiations that immediately follow the SJT. If no settlement is reached, both sides have the right to a full trial later.

Other alternatives being employed by the courts include summary procedures for commercial litigation and the appointment of special masters to assist judges in deciding complex issues.

summary jury trial (SJT)
A settlement method in which a trial is held but the jury's verdict is not binding. The verdict acts as a guide to both sides in reaching an agreement during mandatory negotiations that follow the trial. If a settlement is not reached, both sides have the right to a full trial later.

Providers of ADR Services

ADR services are provided by both government agencies and private organizations. A major provider of ADR services is the **American Arbitration Association (AAA)**. Most of the nation's largest law firms are members of this nonprofit association. Hundreds of thousands of disputes are submitted to the AAA for resolution each year in the United States and internationally. Cases brought to the AAA are heard by an

American Arbitration Association (AAA)
The major organization offering arbitration services in the United States.

expert or a panel of experts in the area relating to the dispute and are usually settled quickly. Generally, about half of the panel members are lawyers. To cover its costs, the AAA charges a fee, paid by the party filing the claim. In addition, each party to the dispute pays a specified amount for each hearing day. An additional fee is charged for cases involving personal injuries or property loss.

Various for-profit firms around the country also provide ADR services. Some firms hire retired judges to conduct arbitration hearings or assist parties in settling their disputes. ADR firms normally allow the parties to decide on the date of the hearing, the presiding judge, whether the judge's decision will be legally binding, and the site of the hearing—which may be a conference room, a law school office, or a leased courtroom. The judges follow procedures similar to those of the federal courts and use similar rules. Usually, each party to the dispute pays a filing fee and a designated fee for a hearing session or conference.

As mentioned, courts also have ADR programs, in which disputes are resolved by court-appointed attorneys or paralegals who are qualified to act as arbitrators or mediators in certain types of disputes. Paralegals have found that becoming a mediator or an arbitrator is an especially rewarding career option. See this chapter's *Ethics Watch* feature regarding the paralegal's role in ensuring that the arbitration process is proper.

Online Dispute Resolution

online dispute resolution (ODR)
The resolution of disputes with the assistance of an organization that offers dispute resolution services via the Internet.

A number of organizations offer **online dispute resolution (ODR)**. Disputes resolved in online forums often involve disagreements over the right to use a certain website address or disputes involving online sales. Those who do business online (and the attorneys who represent them) should be aware of this ADR option.

Most online forums do not automatically apply the law of a specific jurisdiction but use general, universal legal principles. As with traditional methods of dispute resolution, a party normally may appeal to a court at any time. Negotiation, mediation, and arbitration services are all available to disputants over the Internet.

ETHICS WATCH

POTENTIAL ARBITRATION PROBLEMS

When individuals and businesses prefer to arbitrate disputes rather than take them to court, they include arbitration clauses in their contracts. These clauses specify who or what organization will arbitrate the dispute, where the arbitration will take place, and what law will apply.

To safeguard a client's interests when drafting and reviewing arbitration clauses in contracts, the careful paralegal will be alert to the possibility that those who arbitrate the dispute might not truly be neutral or that the designated place of arbitration may pose a great inconvenience and expense for the client. As a paralegal, you should call any such problems to your supervising attorney's attention. The attorney can then discuss the problem with the client and help the client negotiate a more favorable arbitration clause.

This level of care is necessary to be consistent with the NFPA *Model Code of Ethics and Professional Responsibility*, Section 1.6(a): "A paralegal shall act within the bounds of the law, solely for the benefit of the client." It is also consistent with the ABA *Model Guidelines for the Utilization of Paralegal Services*. The *Guidelines* state that lawyers may assign legal work to paralegals, but the lawyers remain responsible for the work product. Hence, be sure your work is reviewed by supervising attorneys. You may not perform work for attorneys that may only be performed by licensed attorneys by the rules of a court, the bar association, a statute, or other controlling authority.

Reprinted by permission of the National Federation of Paralegal Associations, Inc. (NFPA®), paralegals.org.

Several firms offer online forums for negotiating monetary settlements. Typically, one party files a complaint, and the other party is notified by e-mail. Password-protected access to the online forum site is made available. Fees are generally low (often 2 to 4 percent, or less, of the disputed amount). The parties can drop the negotiations at any time. For example, the online firm Smartsettle offers a unique blind-bidding system to help resolve disputes. Given the rapid advances in online services, more creative, lower-cost dispute resolution methods will be devised.

CHAPTER SUMMARY

THE COURT SYSTEM AND ALTERNATIVE DISPUTE RESOLUTION

Judicial Requirements

1. *Standing to sue*—A legally protected and real interest in a matter sufficient to justify seeking relief through the court system. The controversy at issue must also be a justiciable controversy—one that is real and substantial, not hypothetical.

2. *Types of jurisdiction*—Before a court can hear a case, it must have jurisdiction over the person against whom the suit is brought (*in personam* jurisdiction) or the property involved in the suit (*in rem* jurisdiction), as well as jurisdiction over the subject matter.

   a. **JURISDICTION OVER PERSONS AND PROPERTY**—Courts have jurisdiction over persons, including businesses, who reside in the geographic area of the court. Businesses that have a certain level of minimum contacts in a state will be subject to court jurisdiction under a long arm statute. Courts also have jurisdiction over property located within the boundaries of the court.

   b. **JURISDICTION OVER SUBJECT MATTER**—Limited jurisdiction exists when a court is limited to a specific subject matter, such as probate or divorce. General jurisdiction exists when a court can hear any kind of case. State and federal statutes often define the power of courts to hear matters relating to statutory law.

   c. **ORIGINAL AND APPELLATE JURISDICTION**—Courts that have authority to hear a case for the first time (trial courts) have original jurisdiction. Courts of appeals, or reviewing courts, have appellate jurisdiction; generally, these courts do not have original jurisdiction.

3. *Jurisdiction of federal courts*—Is limited to powers of the national government that arise from the Constitution.

   a. **FEDERAL QUESTIONS**—Jurisdiction exists in federal court when a federal question is involved (when the plaintiff's cause of action is based, at least in part, on the U.S. Constitution, a treaty, or a federal law).

   b. **DIVERSITY JURISDICTION**—May arise for a federal court when a case involves diversity of citizenship (as in disputes between citizens of different states, between a foreign country and citizens of a state or states, or between citizens of a state and citizens of a foreign country) and the amount in controversy exceeds $75,000.

   c. **EXCLUSIVE VERSUS CONCURRENT JURISDICTION**—Concurrent jurisdiction exists when two different courts have authority to hear the same case. Exclusive jurisdiction exists when only state courts or only federal courts have authority to hear a case.

4. *Jurisdiction in cyberspace*—Because the Internet does not have physical boundaries, traditional jurisdictional concepts are applied to develop standards to determine when jurisdiction over a website owner or operator in another state is proper.

5. *Venue*—Venue has to do with the most appropriate location for a trial, which is usually the geographic area where the event leading to the dispute took place or where the parties reside.

6. *Judicial procedures*—Rules of procedure prescribe the way in which disputes are handled in the courts. The Federal Rules of Civil Procedure govern all civil litigation in federal courts. Each state has its own procedural rules (often similar to the federal rules), and each court within a state has specific court rules that must be followed.

State Court Systems

1. *Trial courts*—Courts of original jurisdiction, in which legal actions are initiated. State trial courts have either general jurisdiction or limited jurisdiction.

2. *Appellate, or reviewing, courts*—After a trial, there is a right of appeal in the federal and state court systems. The focus on appeal is for reversible errors in law at trial.

   a. **INTERMEDIATE APPELLATE COURTS**—Many states have intermediate appellate courts that review the proceedings of the trial courts; generally, these courts do not have original jurisdiction. Appellate courts ordinarily examine questions of law and procedure while deferring to the trial court's findings of fact.

   b. **HIGHEST STATE COURTS**—Each state has a supreme court, although it may be called by some other name. Decisions of the state's highest court are final on all questions of state law. If a federal question is at issue, the case may be appealed to the United States Supreme Court.

The Federal Court System

1. *U.S. district courts*—The federal district court is the equivalent of the state trial court. The district court exercises general jurisdiction over claims arising under federal law or based on diversity of citizenship. Federal courts of limited jurisdiction include the U.S. Tax Court, the U.S. Bankruptcy Court, and the U.S. Court of Federal Claims.

2. *U.S. courts of appeals*—There are thirteen intermediate courts of appeals (or circuit courts of appeals) in the federal court system. Twelve of the courts hear appeals from the district courts within their circuits. The thirteenth court has national appellate jurisdiction over certain cases, such as those involving patent law and those in which the U.S. government is a defendant.

3. *United States Supreme Court*—The United States Supreme Court is the highest court in the land and the final arbiter of the Constitution and federal law. There is no absolute right of appeal to the Supreme Court, and only a fraction of the cases filed with the Court each year are heard.

   a. **HOW CASES REACH THE UNITED STATES SUPREME COURT**—The Supreme Court has original jurisdiction in a few cases, but it functions primarily as an appellate court. A party wishing to appeal to the Court requests that the Court issue a writ of *certiorari*. At least four justices must agree to issue the writ, or the request will be rejected. Only a tiny fraction of appeals are accepted.

   b. **TYPES OF CASES REVIEWED**—As a rule, only petitions that raise constitutional questions are granted. The Court may also review matters where the lower courts are split in their interpretation of a legal issue.

Alternative Dispute Resolution

The costs and time-consuming character of litigation, as well as the public nature of court proceedings, have caused many to turn to various forms of alternative dispute resolution (ADR) for settling disagreements. The methods of ADR include the following:

1. *Negotiation*—The simplest form of ADR, in which the parties come together, with or without attorneys to represent them, and try to reach a settlement without the involvement of a third party.

2. *Mediation*—A form of ADR in which the parties reach an agreement with the help of a neutral third party, called a mediator, who proposes solutions and emphasizes areas of agreement.

3. *Arbitration*—The most formal method of ADR, in which the parties submit their dispute to a neutral third party, the arbitrator (or panel of arbitrators), who issues a decision. The decision may or may not be legally binding, depending on the circumstances.

   a. **ARBITRATION CLAUSES AND STATUTES**—Arbitration clauses that are agreed on in contracts require the parties to resolve their disputes in arbitration (rather than in court). Federal and state laws encourage the courts to uphold arbitration agreements.

   b. **THE ARBITRATION PROCESS**—A submission agreement is given to the arbitrator to outline the dispute. A hearing is held before a single arbitrator or a panel so both sides may present facts and arguments. After proceedings less formal than those in a court, an award is issued to declare the results of the matter.

   c. **ROLE OF THE COURTS IN PREARBITRATION**—A court may be asked to determine if a matter is, in fact, subject to arbitration rather than a court proceeding.

   d. **POSTARBITRATION ROLE OF THE COURTS**—Awards, even when binding, may be appealed to the courts for review. The court's review is much more restricted than an appellate court's review of a trial court record.

4. *Other ADR forms*—These include binding mediation, mediation arbitration, early neutral case evaluation, and mini-trials; generally, these are forms of "assisted negotiation."

5. *Collaborative law*—A form of ADR in which both parties, their attorneys, and any professionals working with the parties meet to resolve their issues without litigation. The lawyers act as negotiators and communication moderators while advising their clients about their legal rights, entitlements, and obligations. If either party seeks court intervention, both attorneys must withdraw from representation.

6. *Court-referred ADR*—In some jurisdictions, courts require parties to undergo some form of ADR so as to help resolve disputes prior to trial. One form for more complicated matters is the summary jury trial, where a jury hears a shortened form of a full trial and issues a nonbinding verdict.

7. *Providers of ADR services*—The leading nonprofit provider of ADR services is the American Arbitration Association. Many for-profit firms also provide ADR services domestically and internationally.

8. *Online dispute resolution*—A number of organizations and firms offer negotiation and arbitration services through online forums. These forums have been a practical alternative for the resolution of disputes over the right to use a certain website address or the quality of goods purchased over the Internet.

KEY TERMS AND CONCEPTS

alternative dispute resolution (ADR) 158
American Arbitration Association (AAA) 167
appellate court 148
appellate jurisdiction 148
arbitration 162
arbitration clause 164
award 165
bankruptcy court 148
binding mediation 166
concurrent jurisdiction 149

diversity of citizenship 149
docket 150
early neutral case evaluation 166
exclusive jurisdiction 149
federal question 149
in rem jurisdiction 148
jurisdiction 147
justiciable controversy 146
long arm statute 147
mediation 160
mini-trial 166
negotiation 159

online dispute resolution (ODR) 168
original jurisdiction 148
probate court 148
reversible error 154
settlement agreement 159
standing to sue 146
subject-matter jurisdiction 148
submission agreement 164
summary jury trial (SJT) 167
trial court 148
venue 152
writ of *certiorari* 158

QUESTIONS FOR REVIEW

1. Define *jurisdiction*. Define *venue*. What is the difference between personal jurisdiction and subject-matter jurisdiction? What is a long arm statute?

2. Describe the types of cases over which federal courts exercise jurisdiction.

3. How do original and appellate jurisdictions differ? The relationship between state and federal jurisdiction is an example of what type of jurisdiction?

4. How do the functions of a trial court differ from the functions of an appellate court?

5. Describe the procedure for cases to reach the United States Supreme Court.

6. Describe the various methods of alternative dispute resolution.

ETHICS QUESTION

1. Aaron is a paralegal with a law firm that specializes in intellectual property law. Aaron's supervising attorney asks him to e-mail a letter to the client that the attorney has prepared. The letter and its attachments discuss a patent application and contain drawings and plans for a heated steering wheel that the client plans to sell to automobile manufacturers. Aaron does so without encrypting the letter or the attachments, which contain confidential information. A temporary employee working at the client's office accesses the unencrypted e-mail and steals the information. Have any ethical rules been violated by Aaron or by his supervising attorney? If so, which rules? What could Aaron and his supervising attorney have done differently to better protect the client's interests? The client's best friend is enraged that this happened and wants to sue the firm. Can the friend sue?

PRACTICE QUESTIONS AND ASSIGNMENTS

1. Identify each of the following courts. If not indicated, specify whether it is a state or federal court.

a. This state court has general jurisdiction over civil and criminal cases and takes testimony from witnesses and receives evidence.

b. This court has appellate jurisdiction and is part of a court system that is divided into geographic units called *circuits*.

c. This state court hears only issues related to divorce and custody matters. It has original jurisdiction.

d. This court can exercise jurisdiction in matters involving federal questions and diversity of citizenship. It receives testimony and other evidence.

e. The decisions of this state court are usually final. It is the highest appellate court within its court system.

f. This federal court has nine justices. It has original jurisdiction over several types of cases but functions primarily as an appellate court. There is no automatic right to appeal to this court.

2. Look at Exhibit 6.4 and answer these questions:

- How many federal circuits are there?
- In which federal circuit is your state located?
- How many federal judicial districts are located in your state? In which federal district is your community located?

3. Marcella, who is from Toledo, Ohio, drives to Troy, Michigan, and shops at a popular mall. When leaving the parking lot, Marcella runs a red light while texting and causes an accident resulting in personal injuries to the driver of the other vehicle. On what basis could a Michigan court obtain jurisdiction over Marcella? If the damages in the lawsuit exceed $75,000, could a federal court in Michigan have jurisdiction over this case? On what jurisdictional basis? What type of jurisdiction would exist if both the courts of the state of Michigan and the federal court have jurisdiction over this case? Discuss the other types of jurisdiction the court may have in this case (such as *in personam* jurisdiction, *in rem* jurisdiction, subject-matter jurisdiction, limited jurisdiction, general jurisdiction, original jurisdiction, appellate jurisdiction, concurrent jurisdiction, and exclusive jurisdiction).

4. Using the materials presented in the chapter, identify the following methods of alternative dispute resolution:

a. The parties to a divorce meet with a neutral third party who emphasizes points of agreement and proposes solutions to resolve their dispute. After several hours, the parties reach a compromise.

b. The parties to a contract dispute submit it to a neutral third party for a legally binding resolution. The neutral third party is not a court.

c. The plaintiff and defense attorneys in a personal-injury case propose settlement figures to one another and their clients in an effort to resolve the lawsuit voluntarily.

d. The attorneys from the personal-injury example above are able to reach an acceptable settlement figure of $100,000. They draft an agreement whereby the plaintiff gives up her right to sue in exchange for a payment of $100,000 by the defendant.

e. A commercial dispute involving $95,000 in damages is filed in a federal court. The judge requires the parties' attorneys to present their arguments and supporting evidence, excluding witnesses, to the jury. The jury then renders a nonbinding verdict. Once the nonbinding verdict is rendered, the parties reach a settlement.

GROUP PROJECT

As a group, diagram your state court system by going to the National Center for State Courts website at **ncsc.org/information-and-resources/state-court-websites**. Use the "Alphabetical Quick Jump" link to locate your state. The jurisdiction of each court may be accessed by clicking on the "Court Structure Chart."

Students one and two will locate the state's trial courts and describe the jurisdiction of each one. Courts of limited jurisdiction, such as probate and divorce courts, should be included, along with the trial courts of general jurisdiction. Students will create a diagram showing the various levels of trial courts, as well as the subject-matter jurisdiction of each one.

Student three will describe the state's intermediate appellate court and the types of appeals it hears. This information should be added to the diagram created by students one and two.

Student four will research the state's highest appellate court, list the types of appeals it accepts, and outline the basic procedure for filing an appeal with this court. This information should be added to the diagram created by the other students.

Each group will submit its court diagram to the instructor.

PART 2
Legal Procedures and Paralegal Skills

fizkes/ShutterStock.com

Legal Research and Analysis

CHAPTER OBJECTIVES

After completing this chapter, you will be able to:

- Explain how to define the issue and to determine your research goals.

- Compare primary and secondary sources of law, and describe how to use each of these types of sources in the research process.

- Describe how court decisions are published, and explain how to read case citations.

- Demonstrate how to analyze case law and summarize, or brief, cases.

- Explain how federal statutes and regulations are published and the major sources of statutory law.

- List rules for statutory interpretation, and explain the kinds of resources available for researching the legislative history of a statute.

- Explain how federal regulations are published and the major sources of administrative law.

175

Introduction

Legal research is a central and fascinating part of paralegal work. It is interesting to read the actual words of a court's opinion on a legal question or the text of a statute. Additionally, by conducting legal research, paralegals acquire firsthand knowledge of the law and how it applies to people and events. The ability to conduct research thoroughly yet efficiently enhances a paralegal's value to the legal team.

You may be asked to perform a variety of research tasks. Some tasks will be simple, such as locating and printing a court case. Other tasks may take days or weeks to complete. In all but the simplest tasks, legal research overlaps with legal analysis. To find relevant case law, you need to be able to analyze the cases you find to ensure that they are on point and remain good law. As this chapter's *Featured Contributor* article discusses, you will want to think carefully about the questions to be addressed in approaching a case.

FEATURED CONTRIBUTOR

LEGAL ANALYSIS: IS THE GLASS HALF FULL?

Judith Mathers Maloney

BIOGRAPHICAL NOTE

Judith Mathers Maloney is an attorney licensed in New York State. Her practice focuses on contracts, alternative dispute resolution, and civil litigation. She is director of paralegal studies, an adjunct professor, and advisor to the moot court team at Molloy College in Rockville Centre, New York. She is a member of the American Bar Association, the Nassau County Bar Association, and the board of the American Association for Paralegal Education (AAfPE), serving as director of the northeast region.

Mathers Maloney has been involved in the legal education field at the undergraduate and graduate levels for two decades. She co-authored a publication on litigation practice under New York State law and reviews texts and manuscripts on paralegal studies topics. She has developed courses for both the traditional and hybrid classroom.

Legal analysis connects the research you engage in with the written documents you produce, but it can also be a stumbling block. Analysis forces an objective interpretation of facts and requires the ability to support the chosen argument with primary law. For many, it is often difficult to move from "I think" to "the law states." A simple way to focus yourself on the concept is to look at the problem in context and determine which facts are significant. Arguments

> **". . . in legal analysis, words matter."**

need to be properly constructed and thoroughly supported.

Ask the question: "Is that glass of water half full or half empty?" It seems simple and elicits an easy answer. Depending on your point of view, the answer can go either way and still be "right." However, if we subject this seemingly simple question and answer to the type of rigorous legal analysis that we require of legal professionals, the results can be less obvious.

Many paralegals conduct research without entering a law library. Westlaw, Lexis, and Bloomberg Law are the leading providers of online research services for legal professionals needing access to legal documents. Many free sources also can be located via Google and other search engines. (See Chapter 8 for a discussion of online legal research.) Regardless of how or where you conduct legal research, it is essential to know what sources to consult for different types of information.

Researching Case Law—The Preliminary Steps

To illustrate how to research case law, we use a hypothetical case. One of your firm's clients, Trent Hoffman, is suing Better Homes Store for negligence. During the initial client interview, Hoffman explained to your supervising attorney and you that he had gone to the store to buy a large mirror. As he was leaving the store through a side

The Factual Question

The first step in legal research and analysis, before we ever get to the "answer," is to sort through the facts and analyze the question. In our example, we would determine what information is critical to the analysis. For example:

- Is the question about materials? If so, we need to determine if the "glass" is really glass, or is it plastic, acrylic, or some other transparent substance.

- Is the question about what is in the glass? If so, we need to determine if the "water" is water or some other clear liquid.

- Is the question about measurement? Do we need to measure the volume of the glass and the amount of water in it to determine if it is filled exactly halfway?

To answer those factual questions, we need to test the materials and determine the composition or measurement through established scientific practice. You can follow this example, understanding that the first steps in analysis are to identify the salient facts of a client's case and research the primary law assumed to be applicable.

The Answer

When, and only when, all factual questions have been fully analyzed do we move toward the answer. We have gathered all of the information we can. That is, we know that the volume of liquid in the container is exactly half of the volume of the container, the liquid is water, and the container is made of acrylic. Now we look at the context in which the answer is required and translate it into legal form.

For example:

- In a pleading, the answer could be to admit that the glass is half full and deny knowledge or information as to any other part of the allegation.

- At a deposition, the answer to the question about whether the glass is half full or half empty could be "both" or an even more disingenuous "yes."

The point of this exercise is to show that in legal analysis, words matter. A huge difference exists between a statute that imposes strict liability and one that imposes liability for only "knowing" violations. For the defendant, it may be the difference between incarceration and freedom.

> **Legal analysis, done right, is a team sport."**

It is critical for every member of the legal team to understand the importance of precise expression. Legal analysis, done right, is a team sport. A clear, precise question will result in a more focused and useful answer—one that responds to the exact issues that exist in the particular case. Take time to focus on the factual question. Do we care if the glass is glass, or the water is water, or is the focus only on the amount in the glass? The team can then concentrate on what is important and use the right tools—a measuring cup if volume is important, or a microscope if we must determine composite materials.

Ensuring precision of expression in questions and answers is an everyday part of the legal team's analysis. It has a considerable effect on the likelihood that, at the conclusion of the case, the client's glass will be objectively full.

Source: Judith Mathers Maloney

entrance, carrying the mirror, he ran into a large pole just outside the door. He did not see the pole because the mirror blocked his view. When he hit the pole, the mirror broke, and a piece of glass went into his left eye, causing permanent loss of eyesight. Hoffman claims that the store was negligent in placing a pole so close to the door and wants to sue the store for millions of dollars in damages.

You have done a preliminary investigation and have obtained evidence supporting Hoffman's account of the facts. Your supervising attorney now asks you to research case law to find other cases with similar fact patterns and see what the courts decided. Before you begin, however, you need to (1) define the issue to be researched and (2) determine your research goals. We look now at these two preliminary steps in researching case law.

Defining the Issue

In defining the legal issue that you need to research, your first task is to examine the facts of Hoffman's case to determine the nature of the legal issue involved. (An example is provided in the *Developing Paralegal Skills* feature below.) Based on his description of the circumstances (verified through your preliminary investigation) and on his allegation that Better Homes Store should not have placed a pole just outside one of the store's entrances, you know that the legal issue relates to the tort of negligence and premises liability. As a starting point, you should therefore review what you know about negligence theory.

This is one crossroads at which knowledge of the law helps to make a paralegal's job easier. The more you know about negligence law, the easier it will be to define the issues presented by your case and select the topics of your research queries. For example, a paralegal with strong knowledge of the law might already know whether the state where the accident took place follows a contributory or comparative negligence

DEVELOPING PARALEGAL SKILLS

DEFINING THE ISSUES TO BE RESEARCHED

Federal agents observed David Berriman in his parked car talking on his cell phone. Other cars were seen driving up to Berriman's car and stopping. The drivers received brown paper bags in exchange for money. The agents then questioned Berriman, and his car was searched. Cocaine was found in the car. He was arrested for transporting and distributing cocaine, and the police took his car and cell phone. His lawyer is arguing that the government agents did not have the authority to seize the car and cell phone and force Berriman to forfeit this property.

Natalie Chen, a paralegal with the U.S. attorney's office, has been assigned to research the federal statutes and cases on this issue. Natalie can begin her research project only if she first frames the issues critical to the case. She must thoroughly review the case to determine what specific issues need to be researched. Using a checklist method, she breaks the facts of the case down into five categories and fills in the relevant facts. Now Natalie is ready to begin her research.

Checklist for Defining Research Issues

- **Parties:** Who are the people involved in the action or lawsuit?

- **Places and things:** Where did the events take place, and what items are involved in the action or lawsuit?

- **Basis of action or issue:** What is the legal claim or issue involved in the action or lawsuit?

- **Defenses:** What legal justification did the police have for seizing Berriman's car and cell phone? Will this justification still exist if Berriman is found not guilty of the underlying charges, or will the police be required to return the forfeited property?

- **Relief sought:** What is the legal remedy or penalty sought in the case?

regime (discussed in Chapter 14). This will help in narrowing the scope of research and selecting the terms to include in a legal database search.

Background Research

If you are unfamiliar with negligence law or premises liability for merchants, you can start by doing background research to familiarize yourself with the topic, as described in the section on legal encyclopedias later in this chapter.

The tort of negligence (see Chapter 14) is defined as the failure to exercise reasonable care. To succeed in a negligence action, a plaintiff must establish four elements:

1. **Duty:** The defendant owed a duty of care to the plaintiff.
2. **Breach:** The defendant breached that duty.
3. **Injury:** The plaintiff suffered a legally recognizable injury.
4. **Causation:** The injury was caused by the defendant's breach of the duty of care.

Focus on the Legal Issues

These elements help you determine the issue that needs to be researched. There is little doubt that the third requirement has been met—Hoffman's loss of sight is a legally recognizable injury for which he can be compensated. However, he must still succeed in proving the other three elements of negligence. The fourth element, causation, depends largely on proving the first two elements—duty and breach. You will therefore focus your research on the first two elements. Specifically, you need to answer the following questions:

- Did Better Homes Store owe a duty of care to its customer, Hoffman? You might phrase this question in more general terms: Does a business owner owe a duty of care to a **business invitee**—someone, such as a customer or client, invited onto the business premises?

- If so, what is the extent of that duty, and how is it measured? In other words, are business owners always liable when customers are injured on their premises, or must some condition be met before merchants are liable? Must a customer's injury be a *foreseeable* consequence of a condition on the premises, such as the pole right outside the store's door, for the merchant to be liable for the injury?

- If the injury must be a foreseeable consequence of a condition, would a court find that Hoffman's injury in this case was a foreseeable consequence of the pole's placement just outside the store's door?

These are the issues you need to research. Notice that there is more than one issue. This is common in legal research—only rarely will you be researching a single legal issue.

Determining Your Research Goals

Once you have defined the issues to be researched, you will be in a better position to determine your research goals. Remember that you are working on behalf of a client, who is paying for your services. Your overall goal is to find legal support for Hoffman's claim, but you must also locate legal authority that could be a problem for his claim. To do so, you want to find cases on point and cases that are binding authority. Depending on what you find, you may also need to look for persuasive authorities.

Cases on Point

One goal is to find cases on point in which the court held for the plaintiff. A **case on point** is one involving fact patterns and legal issues similar to those in the case you are researching. For Hoffman's negligence claim, a case on point would be one in which the plaintiff alleged that he was injured while on a store's premises because of a dangerous condition on the premises.

business invitee
A person, such as a customer or client, who is invited onto business premises by the owner of those premises for business purposes.

case on point
A case involving factual circumstances and issues that are similar to those in the case being researched.

The ideal case on point would be one in which all four elements (the parties, the circumstances, the legal issues involved, and the remedies sought by the plaintiff) are as similar as possible to those in your case. Such a case is called a case on "all fours." Here, a **case on "all fours"** would be a case in which the plaintiff-customer did not expect a condition (such as an obstacle in her path) to exist and was prevented from seeing the condition by some action that a customer would reasonably undertake (such as carrying an item out of a store). The parties and the circumstances of the case would thus be similar to those in Hoffman's case. In addition, the plaintiff would have sustained a permanent injury, as Hoffman did, and sought damages for negligence.

case on "all fours"
A case in which all four elements (the parties, the circumstances, the legal issues involved, and the remedies sought) are very similar to those in the case being researched.

Binding Authorities

Another research goal is to find cases that are binding authorities. As discussed in Chapter 5, a *binding authority* is one that the court must follow in deciding an issue. A binding authority may be a statute, regulation, or constitution that governs the issue, or it may be a previously decided court case that is controlling in your jurisdiction.

Although today most legal research is carried out using online resources, some paralegals still consult printed legal volumes when conducting legal research. How could you use printed resources to confirm some of your online research results?

Blend Images/Shutterstock.com

Be on Point.   For a case to serve as a binding authority, it must be on point and must have been decided by a higher court (or the same court) in the same jurisdiction.

The Source of a Precedent.   A lower court is bound to follow the decisions of a higher court in the same jurisdiction. An appellate court's decision in a case involving facts and issues similar to a case brought in a trial court in the same jurisdiction would thus be a binding authority. A higher court is not required to follow an opinion written by a lower court in the same jurisdiction. When you are performing research, as in the Hoffman case, look for cases on point decided by the highest court in your jurisdiction, because those cases carry the most weight.

State courts generally have the final say on state law, and federal courts have the final say on federal law. Thus, except in deciding an issue that involves federal law, state courts do not have to follow the decisions of federal courts. In deciding issues that involve federal law, state courts must abide by the decisions of the United States Supreme Court or the U.S. Courts of Appeals if the Supreme Court has not ruled on the matter. In diversity cases, federal courts must follow the relevant state case law.

Published and Unpublished Opinions

Some court opinions are "published," while others, despite being available in commercial databases such as Westlaw, Lexis, and Bloomberg Law, may be "unpublished." This distinction is important. A published decision has been declared, by the court that issued it, to be binding precedent. For example, California defines published opinions as those that are "certified for publication or ordered published" and that "may be cited or relied on by courts and parties." A published decision appears in the official **reporter**.

Decisions of the Supreme Court of California, for example, are published in *California Reports (Cal.)*, and decisions of the California Courts of Appeal are published in *California Appellate Reports (Cal. App.)*. Other "unofficial" reporters, such as West's *California Reporter (Cal. Rptr.)*, publish decisions from both supreme and appellate courts. West's *Pacific Reporter (P.)* publishes only California Supreme Court decisions. Note that half the states do not publish official reporters, so the West reporters, although "unofficial," are relied on in those states.

reporter
A book in which court cases are published, or reported.

Unpublished Opinions May Be Cited.   In general, an unpublished decision is *not* binding precedent, but it may be both persuasive to a court and indicative of how a court is likely to rule in the future. Note that the distinction between published and unpublished can be confusing. Opinions that appear in West's *Federal Appendix* reporter are considered unpublished and are often not citable as precedent, but they do appear in a reporter that lawyers and paralegals can cite.

Slip Opinions and Unofficial Reporters.   Often, a court will issue an opinion and publish it online before the opinion is compiled with others in an official reporter. This opinion, called a **slip opinion**, is subject to further editing and revision by the court that issued it before it is added to an official reporter. Thus, before citing a slip opinion, a paralegal or lawyer should take care to make sure there is not an official version of the opinion. Additionally, it should be noted that the opinion is a slip opinion.

slip opinion
A recent judicial opinion by a court that is subject to revision before being recorded in an official reporter.

Some court opinions appear in official reporters, such as those published by West and Lexis, and also in unofficial reporters, such as the *Supreme Court Reporter* or Westlaw's electronic database. The benefit of reporters like these is that they publish more frequently than the official databases, making it easier to cite important court opinions before they are entered into the relevant court's official reporter. Care should be taken, however, to cite the court's official reporter whenever that option is available.

Look for a Statement by the Court.   Sometimes, unpublished opinions include a statement noting that they are not formally published. For example, the federal Second

Circuit Court of Appeals provides that its unpublished "summary disposition" opinions "shall not be cited or otherwise used before this or any other court." In contrast, the federal District of Columbia Circuit Court of Appeals allows citation of its unpublished opinions.

Many courts issue large numbers of unpublished decisions. Each court has its own rules about the citation of unpublished decisions. Some courts forbid citing these decisions. Others require that an attorney citing an unpublished opinion note that it is not published, or perhaps provide the court and opposing counsel with a copy of the opinion. Be sure to check the rules of the jurisdiction in which a legal document is going to be filed to ensure that any reference to an unpublished decision is done properly.

For example, California defines unpublished opinions as "opinions not certified for inclusion in the Official Reports that are not generally citable as precedent." California also has a practice of "depublishing" appellate court opinions that its supreme court dislikes. When citing California appellate decisions, it is thus important to verify that they have not been depublished.

Persuasive Authorities

persuasive authority
Any legal authority, or source of law, that a court may look to for guidance but on which it need not rely in making its decision. Persuasive authorities include cases from other jurisdictions, discussions in legal periodicals, and so forth.

A **persuasive authority** is not binding on a court. In other words, the court is not required to follow that authority in making its decisions. Examples of persuasive authorities include:

- Persuasive precedents—previous court opinions from other jurisdictions.
- Legal periodicals, such as law reviews, in which the issue at hand is discussed by legal scholars.
- Encyclopedias summarizing legal principles or concepts relating to a particular issue.
- Legal dictionaries that describe how the law has been applied in the past.
- Treatises published by scholars synthesizing rules of law for a particular topic.

Often, a court refers to persuasive authorities when deciding a *case of first impression,* which is a case involving an issue that has never been specifically addressed by that court before. For example, if in researching Hoffman's claim you find that no similar cases have ever reached a higher court in your jurisdiction, you will look for similar cases decided by courts in other jurisdictions. Decisions by these courts may help guide the court deciding Hoffman's case. Your supervising attorney will want to know about these persuasive authorities so that she can present them to the court for consideration.

Finding Relevant Cases

When conducting legal research, you must distinguish between two basic categories of legal sources: primary sources and secondary sources. As discussed in Chapter 5, *primary sources of law* include court decisions, statutes enacted by legislative bodies, rules and regulations created by administrative agencies, presidential orders, and generally any documents that *establish* the law. *Secondary sources of law* consist of books and articles that summarize, systematize, compile, explain, and interpret the law.

Generally, when beginning research projects, paralegals use secondary sources of law to help them find relevant primary sources and to educate themselves on topics of law with which they are unfamiliar. For this reason, secondary sources of law are often referred to as *finding tools.* For the Hoffman claim, how can you find cases on point and binding authorities on this issue? American case law consists of millions of court decisions, and more than forty thousand new decisions are added each year. Finding relevant precedents would be a terrible task if not for secondary sources of law that classify decisions according to subject. Two important finding tools that are helpful in researching case law are legal encyclopedias and case digests, which we describe next. We also look at some other secondary sources that may be helpful.

Legal Encyclopedias

In researching Hoffman's claim, you might look first at a legal encyclopedia to learn more about negligence and the duty of care that businesses owe to business invitees. A popular legal encyclopedia is *American Jurisprudence, Second Edition*, commonly referred to as *American Jurisprudence 2d* or, more briefly, as *Am. Jur. 2d*. (An excerpt from this encyclopedia is shown in Exhibit 7.1. It is also available online from Westlaw and Lexis.)

EXHIBIT 7.1

Excerpt from *American Jurisprudence 2d*

PREMISES LIABILITY
by
Irwin J. Schiffres, J.D. and Sheila A. Skojec, J.D.

Scope of topic: This article discusses the principles and rules of law applicable to and governing the liability of owners or occupants of real property for negligence causing injury to persons or property by reason of defects therein or hazards created by the activities of such owners or occupants or their agents and employees. Treated in detail are the classification of persons injured as invitees, licensees, or trespassers, and the duty owed them, as well as the rules applicable in those jurisdictions where such status distinctions are no longer determinative of the duty owed the entrant; the effect of "recreational use" statutes on the duty owed persons using the property for such purposes; the greater measure of duty owed by the owner to children as compared to adult licensees and trespassers, including the attractive nuisance doctrine; and the specific duties and liabilities of owners and occupants of premises used for business or residential purposes. Also considered is the effect of the injured person's negligence on the plaintiff's right to recover under principles of contributory or comparative negligence.

Federal aspects: One injured on premises owned or operated by the United States may seek to recover under general principles of premises liability discussed in this article. Insofar as recovery is sought under the Federal Torts Claims Act, see 35 Am Jur 2d, FEDERAL TORTS CLAIMS ACT § 73.

Treated elsewhere:
Mutual obligations and liabilities of adjoining landowners with respect to injuries arising from their acts or omissions, see 1 Am Jur 2d, ADJOINING LANDOWNERS AND PROPERTIES §§ 10, 11, 28 et seq., 37 et seq.

Liability for the acts or omissions of the owners or occupants of premises abutting on a street or highway which cause injury to those using the way, see 39 Am Jur 2d, HIGHWAYS, STREETS, AND BRIDGES §§ 517 et seq.

Liability for violation of building regulations, see 13 Am Jur 2d, BUILDINGS §§ 32 et seq.

Liability of employer for injuries caused employees on the employer's premises, see 53 Am Jur 2d, MASTER AND SERVANT §§ 139 et seq.

Liability for injuries caused by defective products on the premises, see 63 Am Jur 2d, PRODUCTS LIABILITY

Respective rights and liabilities of a landlord and tenant where one is responsible for an injury suffered by the other, or by a third person, on leased premises or on premises provided for the common use of tenants, see 49 Am Jur 2d, LANDLORD AND TENANT §§ 761 et seq.

Liability of a receiver placed in charge of property for an injury sustained thereby or thereon by someone other than the persons directly interested in the estate, see 66 Am Jur 2d, RECEIVERS § 364

Duties and liabilities of occupiers of premises used for various particular types of businesses or activities, see 4 Am Jur 2d, AMUSEMENTS AND EXHIBITIONS §§ 51 et seq.; 14 Am Jur 2d, CARRIERS §§ 964 et seq.; 38 Am Jur 2d, GARAGES, AND FILLING AND PARKING STATIONS §§ 81 et seq.; 40 Am Jur 2d, HOSPITALS AND ASYLUMS § 31; 40 Am Jur 2d, HOTELS, MOTELS, AND RESTAURANTS §§ 81 et seq.; 50 Am Jur 2d, LAUNDRIES, DYERS, AND DRY CLEANERS §§ 21, 22; 54 Am Jur 2d, MOBILE HOMES, TRAILER PARKS, AND TOURIST CAMPS § 17; 57 Am Jur 2d, MUNICIPAL, COUNTY, SCHOOL, AND STATE TORT LIABILITY; AND 59 AM JUR 2D, PARKS, SQUARES, AND PLAYGROUNDS §§ 43 et seq.

Duties and liabilities with respect to injuries caused by particular agencies, such as

317

Reprinted from *American Jurisprudence 2e* with permission of Thomson Reuters.

Major Legal Encyclopedias

American Jurisprudence 2d covers hundreds of topics in more than 140 volumes. The topics are presented alphabetically, and each topic is divided into subtopics describing rules of law that have emerged from generations of court decisions. The encyclopedia also provides cross-references to specific court cases, statutory law, and relevant secondary sources of law. Additionally, each volume includes an index; a separate index covers the entire encyclopedia.

Traditional printed volumes are kept current through supplements called a **pocket part**. Pocket parts, so named because they slip into a pocket (sleeve) in the front or back of the volume, contain changes and additions to various topics and subtopics. Updates to the online services are added regularly. Online services such as Westlaw and Lexis include the date of the most recent update of particular statutory and regulatory provisions. When a legislature or Congress is in session, it is necessary to check more than one online database to get the most up-to-date information on a statutory provision.

A similar encyclopedia is *Corpus Juris Secundum*, or C.J.S. This encyclopedia also provides detailed information on most areas of the law and includes indexes for each volume as well as for the entire set. Its 164 volumes (plus five index volumes and eleven table-of-cases volumes) cover 433 topics, which are presented alphabetically and divided into subtopics. Like *American Jurisprudence 2d*, this encyclopedia is available on Westlaw.

Other Sources

Another tool is *Words and Phrases*, which offers definitions and interpretations of legal terms and phrases. Each term or phrase in this 132-volume set is followed by brief summary statements from federal or state court decisions in which the word or phrase has been interpreted or defined. The summary statements also indicate the names of the cases and the reporters in which they can be located. As mentioned, reporters are publications containing the actual text of court cases, and we will discuss them later.

When beginning your research into the Hoffman claim, you could use any of these secondary sources to familiarize yourself with the topic of premises liability and lead you to the primary sources (cases) that you need to read and analyze. You can also search some free online sources, such as FindLaw (**findlaw.com**) and Justia US Law (**justia.com**) for ideas. Sources may be searched for such terms as *premises liability*, *business invitees*, and *duty of care*. Remember, though, that legal encyclopedias do not include state-specific rules of law, which you will need to locate for your state.

Case Digests

In researching Hoffman's case, you might want to check a case digest as well as a legal encyclopedia for references to relevant case law. A **digest** is a helpful research tool because it provides indexes to case law—from the earliest recorded cases through the most current opinions. Case digests arrange topics alphabetically and provide information to help you locate referenced cases, although they do not offer the detail found in legal encyclopedias.

Collected under each topic heading in a case digest are annotations. An **annotation** is a comment, an explanatory note, or a case summary. In case digests, annotations consist of very short statements of relevant points of law in reported cases.

Case digests are produced by various publishers and are available both in hard copy and online. The online versions are usually included in legal databases such as Westlaw and Lexis. There are also some free online digests that may be worth searching.

---

pocket part
A pamphlet containing recent cases or changes in the law that is used to update legal encyclopedias and other legal authorities. It is called a "pocket part" because it slips into a pocket, or sleeve, in the front or back binder of the volume.

digest
A compilation in which brief summaries of court cases are arranged by subject and subdivided by jurisdiction and court.

annotation
A brief comment, an explanation of a legal point, or a case summary found in a case digest or other legal source.

One example of a digest is *American Law Reports*, which compiles information on a wide variety of legal topics and questions, providing summaries of court opinions from every jurisdiction on a particular topic. The digests published by West offer the most comprehensive system for locating cases by subject matter. Exhibit 7.2 shows some excerpts from one of West's federal digests on the standard of care that is owed to an invitee.

The West Key Number System

West's Key Number system has simplified the task of researching case law. The system divides all areas of American law into specific categories, or topics, arranged in alphabetical order. The topics are further divided into many subtopics, each designated by a **Key Number**, which is accompanied by the West key symbol: ⚷. You can see the use of this key symbol in Exhibit 7.2. Exhibit 7.3 on page 187 shows some of the Key Numbers used for other subtopics under the general topic of negligence.

Using Key Numbers.   The Key Number system organizes millions of case summaries under specific topics and subtopics. In researching the Hoffman claim, suppose you locate a negligence case on point decided by a court in your state five years ago. Your goal is to find related—and perhaps more recent—cases that support Hoffman's claim. Here is how the Key Number system can help. When you read through any case in a West's case reporter, you will find a series of headnotes preceding the court's actual opinion. Each **headnote** summarizes one aspect of the opinion. West editors create each headnote and assign it to a particular topic with a Key Number.

Finding What You Need.   Key Numbers correlate the headnotes in cases to the topics in digests and can be useful in finding cases on a particular subject. Once you find the Key Number in a case that discusses the issue you are researching, you can find every other case in your state that discusses the same issue. You go to the West case digest and locate the particular Key Number and topic. Beneath the Key Number, the digest provides case summaries, titles, and citations to cases discussing the issue in the area covered by the digest. When you find a case that seems on point, you know where to find it because you have the citation. (In the next chapter, we will see how this works using *KeyCite*, offered by West, and *Shepard's*, offered by Lexis.)

Types of Digests

As mentioned, West offers a comprehensive system of digests. West publishes digests of both federal court opinions and state court opinions, as well as regional digests and digests that correspond with its reporters covering specialized areas, such as bankruptcy. For example, the *Supreme Court Digest* corresponds to decisions published in West's *Supreme Court Reporter*.

Other sources, available online and sometimes free, publish various digests (for example, **lawdigest.uslegal.com**). Some digests are specific to individual states. Note that other publishers' digests do not use the Key Number system.

Annotations: *American Law Reports*

The *American Law Reports* (ALR) and *American Law Reports Federal* (ALR Fed), published by West, are also useful resources for legal researchers. They are helpful in finding cases from jurisdictions around the country with similar facts and legal issues.

There have been seven different series of ALR covering case law since 1919. The first and second series contain separate digests that provide references to cases and also have word indexes to assist the researcher in locating specific areas.

Key Number
A number (accompanied by the symbol of a key) corresponding to a specific legal topic within West's Key Number system to facilitate legal research of case law.

headnote
A note, usually a paragraph long, near the beginning of a reported case summarizing the court's ruling on an issue.

EXHIBIT 7.2

Excerpt from *West's Federal Practice Digest 4th* on Negligence

---

77A F P D 4th—173

NEGLIGENCE ☞ 1037(4)

For references to other topics, see Descriptive-Word Index

E.D.Mich. 1998. Under Michigan law, a property owner is not an absolute insurer of the safety of invitees.

Meyers v. Wal-Mart Stores, East, Inc., 29 F.Supp.2d 780.

E.D.Mich. 1995. under Michigan law, property owner is not insurer of safety of invitees.

Bunch v. Long John Silvers, Inc., 878 F.Supp. 1044.

E.D.Mich. 1994. Under Michigan law, property owner is not insurer of safety of invitees.

Dose v. Equitable Life Assur. Soc., 864 F.Supp. 682.

E.D.N.C. 1993. Premises owner does not automatically insure safety of invitees and is not liable in absence of negligence.

Faircloth v. U.S., 837 F.Supp. 123.

E.D.Va. 1999. Under Virginia law, owner of premises is not insurer of his invitees safety; rather, owner must use ordinary care to render premises reasonably safe for invitee's visit.

Sandow-Pajewski v. Busch Entertainment Corp., 55 F.Supp.2d 422.

☞ **1037(4). Care required in general.**

C.A.7 (Ill.) 1986. Under Illinois law, landowner is liable for physical harm to his invitees caused by condition on his land: where landowner could by exercise of reasonable care have discovered condition; where landowner should realize that condition involves unreasonable risk to harm to invitees; where landowner should expect that invitees will not discover danger or will fail to protect against it; and where landowner fails to exercise reasonable care to protect invitees.

Higgins v. White Sox Baseball Club, Inc., 787 F.2d 1125.

C.A.7 (Ind.) 1994. Under Indiana law, landowner's duty to invitee while that invitee is on premises is that of reasonable care.

Salima v. Scherwood South, Inc., 38 F.3d 929.

Under indiana law, landowner is liable for harm caused to invitee by condition on land only if landowner knows of or through exercise of reasonable care would discover condition and realize that it involves unreasonable risk of harm to such invitees, should expect the invitee will fail to discover or realize danger or fail to protect against it, and fails to exercise reasonable care in protecting invitee against danger.

Salima v. Scherwood South, Inc., 38 F. 3d 929.

Under Indiana law, landowner is not liable for harm caused to invitees by conditions whose

For cited U.S.C.A. sections and legislative

danger is known or obvious unless landowner could anticipate harm despite obviousness.

Salima v. Scherwood South, Inc., 38 F.3d 929.

C.A.6 (Mich.) 1998. Under Michigan law, where invitor has reason to expect that, despite

---

NEGLIGENCE

77A F P D 4th—542

XVI. DEFENSES AND MITIGATING CIRCUMSTANCES.—Continued.

570. _____ Pofessional rescuers; "firefighter's rule."
575. Imputed contributory negligence.

XVII. PREMISES LIABILITY.

(A) IN GENERAL.
☞ 1000. Nature.
1001. Elements in general.
1002. Constitutional, statutory and regulatory provisions.
1003. What law governs.
1004. Preemption.

(B) NECESSITY AND EXISTENCE OF DUTY.
☞ 1010. In general.
1011. Ownership, custody and control.
1012. Conditions known or obvious in general.
1013. Conditions created or known by defendant.
1014. Foreseeability.
1015. Duty as to children.
1016. _____ In general.
1017. _____ Trespassing children.
1018. Duty to inspect or discover.
1019. Protection against acts of third persons in general.
1020. Duty to warn.
1021. Duty of store and business proprietors.
1022. _____ In general.
1023. _____ Duty to inspect.
1024. _____ Protection against acts of third persons.
1025. Duty based on statute or other regulation.

(C) STANDARD OF CARE.
☞ 1030. In general.
1031. Not insurer or guarantor.
1032. Reasonable or ordinary care in general.
1033. Reasonably safe or unreasonably dangerous conditions.
1034. Status of entrant.
1035. _____ In general.
1036. _____ Care dependent on status.
1037. _____ Invitees.
(1). In general.
(2). Who are invitees.
(3). Not insurer as to invitees.
(4). Care required in general.
(5). Public invitees in general.
(6). Implied invitation.
(7). Persons working on property.
(8). Delivery persons and haulers.
1040. _____ Licensees.
(1). In general.
(2). Who are licensees.

EXHIBIT 7.3

Subtopics and Key Numbers
in a West Digest

NEGLIGENCE

SUBJECTS INCLUDED

General civil negligence law and premises liability, including duty, standards of care, breach of duty, proximate cause, injury, defenses, and comparative fault, whether based on the common law or statute, as well as procedural aspects of such actions

General civil liabilities for gross negligence, recklessness, willful or wanton conduct, strict liability and ultrahazardous instrumentalities and activities

Negligence liabilities relating to the construction, demolition and repair of buildings and other structures, whether based on the common law or statute

General criminal negligence offenses and prosecutions

SUBJECTS EXCLUDED AND COVERED BY OTHER TOPICS

Accountants or auditors, negligence of, see ACCOUNTANTS ⛘ 8,9

Aircraft, accidents involving, see AVIATION ⛘ 141–153

Attorney's malpractice liability, see ATTORNEY AND CLIENT ⛘ 105–129.5

Banks, liabilities of, see BANKS AND BANKING ⛘ 100

Brokers, securities and real estate, liabilities of, see BROKERS

Car and highway accidents, see AUTOMOBILES

Common carriers, liabilities to passengers, see CARRIERS

Domestic animals, injuries by or to, see ANIMALS

Dram Shop liability and other liabilities for serving alcohol, see INTOXICATING LIQUORS ⛘ 282–324

*   *   *   *

For detailed references to other topics, see Descriptive-Word Index

---

Analysis

   I. **IN GENERAL,** ⛘ 200–205.

  II. **NECESSITY AND EXISTENCE OF DUTY,** ⛘ 210–222.

 III. **STANDARD OF CARE,** ⛘ 230–239.

 IV. **BREACH OF DUTY,** ⛘ 250–259.

  V. **HEIGHTENED DEGREES OF NEGLIGENCE,** ⛘ 272–276.

 VI. **VULNERABLE AND ENDANGERED PERSONS; RESCUES,** ⛘ 281–285.

VII. **SUDDEN EMERGENCY DOCTRINE,** ⛘ 291–295.

VIII. **DANGEROUS SITUATIONS AND STRICT LIABILITY,** ⛘ 301–307.

The remaining sets of ALR volumes use a different approach, called a *Quick Index*, which lets the user access cases and information on a particular topic. In electronic databases, such as Westlaw, these reports contain many links that are helpful in jumping from one topic or case to another. The cases in the reports also include annotations—references to articles that explain or comment on the specific issues involved in the cases.

ALR can be a good source to turn to for an overview of a specific area of law or current trend in the law. When using any of the volumes of ALR, be sure to update your results. ALR annotations are periodically updated by the addition of relevant cases.

Other Secondary Sources

A number of other secondary sources are useful in legal research. We look here at three of these sources: treatises, *Restatements of the Law*, and legal periodicals. Like other secondary sources of law, these sources do not establish the law. Nevertheless, they are important sources of legal analysis and opinion and are often cited as persuasive authorities.

Treatises

treatise
In legal research, a work that provides a systematic, detailed, and scholarly review of a particular legal subject.

hornbook
A single-volume scholarly discussion, or treatise, on a particular legal subject.

A **treatise** is a scholarly work by a law professor or other legal professional that treats a particular subject systematically and in detail. Some treatises are published in multivolume sets, such as Wayne Lafave's *Search and Seizure*, while others are contained in a single book, such as *Farnsworth on Contracts*.

A single-volume treatise that synthesizes the basic principles of a given legal area is known as a **hornbook**. Some hornbooks are available online. These texts are useful to paralegals to familiarize themselves with a particular area of the law, such as torts or contracts. For example, in researching the issues in Hoffman's negligence case, you might want to locate the treatise entitled *Prosser and Keeton on the Law of Torts*, Fifth Edition, which is included in West's *Hornbook Series*, and read the sections on negligence. (Exhibit 7.4 shows the book open to the chapter on defenses to negligence.) Hornbooks—such as *Prosser and Keeton on the Law of Torts*—present many examples of case law and references to cases that may be helpful to a researcher.

Restatements of the Law

The *Restatements of the Law*, published by the American Law Institute, are also a helpful resource, and one on which judges often rely as a persuasive authority when making decisions. They are available on Lexis and Westlaw. There are *Restatements* in the areas of contracts, torts, agency, trusts, property, restitution, security, judgments, and conflict of laws. Each section in the *Restatements* contains a statement of the principles of law that are generally accepted by the courts or embodied in statutes, followed by a discussion of those principles. The discussions present cases as examples and also discuss variations.

Be aware that some editions of treatises are more highly regarded and widely accepted by the courts than others. For example, the *Restatement (Second) of Contracts* is generally more accepted as a persuasive authority than the *Restatement (Third) of Contracts*.

Legal Periodicals

Legal periodicals, such as law reviews and law journals, are secondary sources that can be helpful. If an article in a legal periodical deals with the specific area that you are researching, the article will likely include footnotes citing cases relating to the topic. These references can save you hours of research time in finding relevant case law.

Many law review and journal articles are freely available through law school institutional repositories and can be found through a Google Scholar search (**scholar.google.com**). Other articles can be found by searching JSTOR (**jstor.org**) or SSRN (**ssrn.com**). Many legal scholars post their work on SSRN, including articles separately published by scholarly journals.

EXHIBIT 7.4

A Page from the
Hornbook on the Law of Torts

Chapter 11

NEGLIGENCE: DEFENSES

§ 65. Contributory Negligence

The two most common defenses in a negligence action are contributory negligence and assumption of risk. Since both developed at a comparatively late date in the development of the common law,[1] and since both clearly operate to the advantage of the defendant, they are commonly regarded as defenses to a tort which would otherwise be established. All courts now hold that the burden of plead-

ing and proof of the contributory negligence of the plaintiff is on the defendant.[2]

Contributory negligence is conduct on the part of the plaintiff, contributing as a legal cause to the harm he has suffered, which falls below the standard to which he is required to conform for his own protection.[3] Unlike assumption of risk, the defense does not rest upon the idea that the defendant is relieved of any duty toward the plaintiff. Rather, although the defendant has violated his duty, has been negligent, and would oth-

---

§ 65

1. The earliest contributory negligence case is Butterfield v. Forrester, 1809, 11 East 60, 103 Eng.Rep. 926. The first American case appears to have been Smith v. Smith, 1824, 19 Mass. (2 Pick.) 621. Assumption of risk first appears in a negligence case in 1799. See infra, § 68 n. 1.

2. E.g., Wilkinson v. Hartford Accident & Indemnity Co., La.1982, 411 So.2d 22; Moodie v. Santoni, 1982, 292 Md. 582, 441 A.2d 323; Addair v. Bryant, 1981, ___ W.Va. ___, 284 S.E.2d 374; Pickett v. Parks, 1981, 208 Neb. 310, 303 N.W.2d 296; Hatton v. Chem-Haulers, Inc., Ala.1980, 393 So.2d 950; Sampson v. W. F. Enterprises, Inc., Mo.App.1980, 611 S.W.2d 333; Howard v. Howard, Ky.App.1980, 607 S.W.2d 119; cf. Reuter v. United States, W.D.Pa.1982, 534 F.Supp. 731 (presumption that person killed or suffering loss of memory was acting with due care).

Illinois and certain other jurisdictions held to the contrary for some time. See West Chicago Street Railroad Co. v. Liderman, 1900, 187 Ill. 463, 58 N.E. 367; Kotler v. Lalley, 1930, 112 Conn. 86, 151 A. 433; Dreier v. McDermott, 1913, 157 Iowa 726, 141 N.W. 315. See Green, Illinois Negligence Law II, 1944, 39 Ill.L.Rev. 116, 125–130.

3. Second Restatement of Torts, § 463. See generally, Malone, The Formative Era of Contributory Negligence, 1946, 41 Ill.L.Rev. 151; James, Contributory Negligence, 1953, 62 Yale L.J. 691; Bohlen, Contributory Negligence, 1908, 21 Harv.L.Rev. 233; Lowndes, Contributory Negligence, 1934, 22 Geo.L.J. 674; Malone, Some Ruminations on Contributory Negligence, 1981, 65 Utah L.Rev. 91; Schwartz, Contributory and Comparative Negligence: A Reappraisal, 1978, 87 Yale L.J. 697; Note, 1979, 39 La.L.Rev. 637.

451

From Dan B. Dobbs, *The Law on Torts*. Reprinted with permission of West Academic.

Using Judicial Opinions for Research

Often, it can be difficult to find a binding precedent on point. Keyword searches and secondary resources might not illuminate any landmark decisions that inform your legal research question. This does not, however, mean that those decisions do not exist—perhaps they use different terminology than you expect. Finding lower-court decisions considering your legal question can be helpful not only so that you can cite those cases as persuasive authorities, but also because those opinions often contain citations to cases that are binding authorities on point with your research question.

Finding one case might also lead to another case, which can lead to further cases and research that will support your firm's legal argument. Some trial-level or intermediate appellate court opinions review extensive primary and secondary sources that can be helpful in answering your research question, even if the opinion in which you found it is not a binding authority. Even unpublished lower-court opinions can be helpful in this way.

The Case Reporting System

The primary sources of case law are the cases themselves. Once you have learned which cases are relevant to the issue you are researching, you need to find the cases and examine the court opinions.

Assume, for example, that in researching Hoffman's case, you learn that your state's supreme court issued a decision a few years ago on a case with a similar fact pattern. In that case, the state supreme court upheld a lower court's judgment that a retail business owner had to pay damages to a customer who was injured on the store's premises when carrying a large item. You know that the state supreme court's decision is a binding authority, and, to your knowledge, the decision has not been overruled or modified. Therefore, the case will likely provide weighty support to your attorney's arguments in support of Hoffman's claim.

At this point, however, you have only read about the case in secondary sources. To locate the case itself and make sure it is applicable (this chapter's *Ethics Watch* feature explains why this is important), you must understand the case reporting system and the legal "shorthand" employed in referencing court cases.

State Court Decisions and Reporters

Written decisions of state appellate courts are published chronologically in volumes called *reports* or *reporters*, which are numbered consecutively. State appellate court decisions are found in the state reporters of that particular state. The reporters may be either "official" reporters, designated as such by the state legislature or the state's highest court, or "unofficial" reporters, published by West. Although some states still

ETHICS WATCH

USING SECONDARY SOURCES

When rushing to meet a deadline, you may be tempted to avoid a critical step in the research process—checking primary sources. For example, suppose a firm's client complains that a publisher of his novels is now publishing the novels online, as e-books. The client wants to know if online publication is copyright infringement. At issue is whether the publisher, which has the right to publish the printed texts, also has the right to publish the books online. An attorney for the firm asks Sarah, a paralegal, to research case law to see how the courts have dealt with this issue.

Sarah has just read an article in a law journal about a similar case recently decided by the United States Supreme Court. Without taking the time to read the case itself, she relies on the author's conclusions in the article. She prepares a memo to the attorney presenting her "research" results.

Based on Sarah's memo, the attorney advises the client that the publisher had no right to publish the client's works online. The client decides to sue the publisher. Later, during more extensive pretrial research, Sarah reads the case. Unfortunately for her (and the client and the attorney), the author of the article did not discuss an important qualification made by the Court in its ruling relating to the terms of the publishing contract. The Court's decision does not apply to the client's situation because of that important qualification.

While the attorney is responsible for the work product for the client, Sarah's failure to rely on primary sources is likely seen as a failure to produce competent work. Such a failure could injure the position of the client and violate the NFPA Model Disciplinary Rule 1.1, "A paralegal shall achieve and maintain a high level of competence."[a]

a. Reprinted by permission of the National Federation of Paralegal Associations, Inc. (NFPA®), paralegals.org.

have official reporters (and a few states, such as New York and California, have more than one official reporter), many states have eliminated their own official reporters in favor of West's National Reporter System, discussed next. Most state trial court decisions are not published.

Regional Reporters

State court opinions also appear in regional units of West's National Reporter System. Many lawyers and libraries have the West reporters because they report cases more quickly and are distributed more widely than the state-published reports.

West's National Reporter System divides the states into the following geographic areas: *Atlantic* (A., A.2d, or A.3d), *South Eastern* (S.E. or S.E.2d), *North Eastern* (N.E. or N.E.2d), *North Western* (N.W. or N.W.2d), *Pacific* (P., P.2d, or P.3d), *South Western* (S.W., S.W.2d, or S.W.3d), and *Southern* (So., So. 2d, or So. 3d). The *2d* and *3d* in the abbreviations refer to *Second Series* and *Third Series*. The states included in each of these regional divisions are shown in Exhibit 7.5 on the following page, which illustrates West's National Reporter System.

The names of the areas may not be the same as what we commonly think of as a geographic region. For example, the *North Western Reporter* does not include the Pacific Northwest but includes Iowa, which people do not think of as being in the Northwest. Similarly, Oklahoma is in the *Pacific Reporter*.

Citation Format

To locate a case, you must know where to look. After a decision has been published, it is normally referred to (cited) by the name of the case, the volume number and the abbreviated name of the book in which the case is located, the page number on which the case begins, and the year. In other words, there are five parts to a standard citation:

Case name	Volume number	Name of book	Page number	(Year)

This format is used for every citation regardless of whether the case is published in an official state reporter or a regional reporter (or both). When more than one reporter is cited for the same case, each reference is called a **parallel citation** and is separated from the next citation by a comma. The first citation is to the state's official reporter (if there is one), although the text of the court's opinion will be the same (parallel) at all of the listed locations.

An Example. To illustrate how to find case law from citations, suppose you want to find the following case: *Goldstein v. Lackard*, 81 Mass. App. Ct. 1112, 961 N.E.2d 163 (2012). You can see that the opinion in this case can be found in Volume 81 of the official *Massachusetts Appellate Court Reports*, beginning on page 1112. The parallel citation is to Volume 961 of the *North Eastern Reporter, Second Series*, at page 163. In some cases, additional information may appear in parentheses at the end of a citation, usually indicating the court that heard the case (if that information is not clear from the citation alone). Exhibit 7.6 on pages 194–195 further illustrates how to read case citations.

Proper Form. When conducting legal research, you should write down the citations to the cases or other legal sources that you have consulted, quoted, or want to refer to in a written summary of your research results. Several guides have been published on how to cite legal sources.

Traditionally, the most widely used guide has been *The Bluebook: A Uniform System of Citation*, published by the Harvard Law Review Association. This book explains the proper format for citing cases, statutes, constitutions, regulations, and

---

citation
In case law, a reference to a case by the name of the case, the volume number and name of the reporter in which the case can be found, the page number on which the case begins, and the year. In statutory and administrative law, a reference to the title number, name, and section of the code in which a statute or regulation can be found.

parallel citation
A second (or third) citation for a given case. When a case is published in more than one reporter, each citation is a parallel citation to the other(s).

EXHIBIT 7.5
West's National Reporter System—Regional and Federal

Regional Reporters	Coverage Beginning	Coverage
Atlantic Reporter (A., A.2d, or A.3d)	1885	Connecticut, Delaware, Maine, Maryland, New Hampshire, New Jersey, Pennsylvania, Rhode Island, Vermont, and District of Columbia.
North Eastern Reporter (N.E., N.E.2d, or N.E.3d)	1885	Illinois, Indiana, Massachusetts, New York, and Ohio.
North Western Reporter (N.W. or N.W.2d)	1879	Iowa, Michigan, Minnesota, Nebraska, North Dakota, South Dakota, and Wisconsin.
Pacific Reporter (P., P.2d, or P.3d)	1883	Alaska, Arizona, California, Colorado, Hawaii, Idaho, Kansas, Montana, Nevada, New Mexico, Oklahoma, Oregon, Utah, Washington, and Wyoming.
South Eastern Reporter (S.E. or S.E.2d)	1887	Georgia, North Carolina, South Carolina, Virginia, and West Virginia.
South Western Reporter (S.W., S.W.2d, or S.W.3d)	1886	Arkansas, Kentucky, Missouri, Tennessee, and Texas.
Southern Reporter (So., So.2d, or So.3d)	1887	Alabama, Florida, Louisiana, and Mississippi.

Federal Reporters

Federal Reporter (F., F.2d, or F.3d)	1880	U.S. Circuit Court from 1880 to 1912; U.S. Commerce Court from 1911 to 1913; U.S. District Courts from 1880 to 1932; U.S. Court of Claims (now called U.S. Court of Federal Claims) from 1929 to 1932 and since 1960; U.S. Court of Appeals since 1891; U.S. Court of Customs and Patent Appeals since 1929; and U.S. Emergency Court of Appeals since 1943.
Federal Supplement (F.Supp., F.Supp.2d, or Ft.Supp.3d)	1932	U.S. Court of Claims from 1932 to 1960; U.S. District Courts since 1932; and U.S. Customs Court since 1956.
Federal Rules Decisions (F.R.D.)	1939	U.S. District Courts involving the Federal Rules of Civil Procedure since 1939 and Federal Rules of Criminal Procedure since 1946.
Supreme Court Reporter (S.Ct.)	1882	U.S. Supreme Court since the October term of 1882.
Bankruptcy Reporter (Bankr.)	1980	Bankruptcy decisions of U.S. Bankruptcy Courts, U.S. District Courts, U.S. Courts of Appeals, and U.S. Supreme Court.
Military Justice Reporter (M.J.)	1978	U.S. Court of Military Appeals and Courts of Military Review for the Army, Navy, Air Force, and Coast Guard.

NATIONAL REPORTER SYSTEM MAP

other legal sources. It is a good idea to memorize the basic format for citations to cases and statutory law because these legal sources are frequently cited in legal writing. This information can be found in Rules 10 and 11 in *The Bluebook*.

An alternative guide is a booklet entitled *ALWD Citation Manual: A Professional System of Citation*, which is published by the Association of Legal Writing Directors. Legal practitioners should check the rules of their jurisdiction for guidelines on the proper format for citations in documents submitted to a court.

Federal Court Decisions

Court decisions from the U.S. district courts (federal trial courts) are published in West's *Federal Supplement* (*F. Supp.*, *F. Supp. 2d*, *or F. Supp. 3d*), and opinions from the courts of appeals are reported in West's *Federal Reporter* (*F.*, *F.2d*, or *F.3d*). These are both unofficial reporters (there are no official reporters for these courts). Both the *Federal Reporter* and the *Federal Supplement* incorporate decisions from specialized federal courts. West also publishes separate reporters, such as its *Bankruptcy Reporter*, that contain decisions in certain specialized fields under federal law. All of these reporters are published online.

United States Supreme Court Decisions

Opinions from the United States Supreme Court are published in several reporters, including the *United States Reports*, West's *Supreme Court Reporter*, and the *Lawyers' Edition of the Supreme Court Reports*, each of which we discuss here. A sample citation to a Supreme Court case is also included in Exhibit 7.6. Note that there is free access to Supreme Court materials at the Court's website and also at the Oyez website.

The *United States Reports*

The *United States Reports* (U.S.) is the official edition of decisions of the United States Supreme Court for which there are written opinions. Published by the federal government, the series includes reports of Supreme Court cases dating from the August term of 1791. Soon after the Supreme Court issues a decision, the U.S. Government Publishing Office publishes the official slip opinion. (It is published online more quickly at the Supreme Court's website. Go to **supremecourt.gov**, and select "Opinions," then "Opinions of the Court.") The slip opinion is the first authoritative text of the opinion and is later printed in what the Supreme Court notes is the official version. The full text of all opinions is on the Court's website.

After a number of slip opinions have been issued, the advance sheets of the official *United States Reports* appear. These are issued in pamphlet form to provide a temporary resource until the official bound volume is finally published.

The *Supreme Court Reporter*

Supreme Court cases are also published in West's *Supreme Court Reporter* (S. Ct.), which is an unofficial edition of Supreme Court opinions dating from the Court's term in October 1882. In this reporter, the case report—the formal court opinion—is preceded by a **syllabus** (summary of the case) and headnotes with Key Numbers (used throughout the West reporters and digests) prepared by West editors. This reporter, like the others, can be accessed through online legal search services, as discussed later in the chapter.

The syllabus to a legal opinion can be a useful tool for conducting research. When you are searching a legal database for a case on point, a case syllabus can give you an idea about the major issues addressed in a judicial opinion so that you can either move on (when the case seems to involve legal issues or distinguishing features that separate it from your case) or mark the case for further inspection.

syllabus
A brief summary of the holding and legal principles involved in a reported case, which is followed by the court's official opinion.

EXHIBIT 7.6
How to Read Citations

STATE COURTS

304 Neb. 848, 937 N.W. 2d 190 (2020)[a]

N.W. is the abbreviation for the publication of state court decisions rendered in the *North Western Reporter* of West's National Reporter System. *2d* indicates that this case was included in the *Second Series* of that reporter.

Neb. is an abbreviation for *Nebraska Reports*, Nebraska's official reports of the decisions of its highest court, the Nebaraska Supreme Court.

44 Cal. App. 5th 437, 257 Cal. Rptr. 3d 671 (2020)

Cal. Rptr. is the abbreviation for the unofficial reports—titled *California Reporter*—of the decisions of California courts.

179 A.D.3d 1476, 117 N.Y.S.3d 408 (2020)

N.Y.S. is the abbreviation for the unofficial reports—titled *New York Supplement*—of the decisions of New York courts.

A.D. is the abbreviation for *Appellate Division*, which hears appeals from the New York Supreme Court—the state's general trial court. The New York Court of Appeals is the state's highest court, analogous to other states' supreme courts.

71 Va. App. 385, 837 S.E.2d 54 (2020)

Va. App. is the abbreviation for *Georgia Virginia Court of Appeals Reports*, Virginia's official reports of the decisions of its court of appeals.

FEDERAL COURTS

__ U.S. __, 140 S. Ct. 582, 205 L. Ed. 2d 419 (2020)

L. Ed. is an abbreviation for *Lawyers' Edition of the Supreme Court Reports*, an unofficial edition of decisions of the United States Supreme Court.

S. Ct. is the abbreviation for West's unofficial reports—titled *Supreme Court Reporter*—of decisions of the United States Supreme Court.

U.S. is the abbreviation for *United States Reports*, the official edition of the decisions of the United States Supreme Court. The blank lines in this citation (or any other citation) indicate that the appropriate volume of the case reporter has not yet been published and nopage number is available.

a. The case names have been deleted from these citations to emphasize the publications. It should be kept in mind, however, that the name of a case is as important as the specific page numbers in the volumes in which it is found. If a citation is incorrect, the correct citation may be found in a publication's index of case names. In addition to providing a check on errors in citations, the date of a case is important because the value of a recent case as an authority is likely to be greater than that of older cases from the same court.

EXHIBIT 7.6

How to Read Citations—Continued

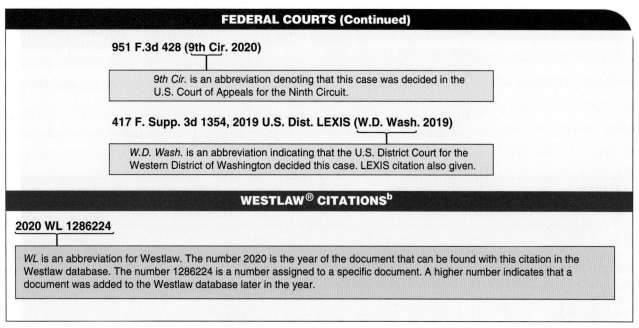

FEDERAL COURTS (Continued)

951 F.3d 428 (9th Cir. 2020)

> *9th Cir.* is an abbreviation denoting that this case was decided in the U.S. Court of Appeals for the Ninth Circuit.

417 F. Supp. 3d 1354, 2019 U.S. Dist. LEXIS (W.D. Wash. 2019)

> *W.D. Wash.* is an abbreviation indicating that the U.S. District Court for the Western District of Washington decided this case. LEXIS citation also given.

WESTLAW® CITATIONS[b]

2020 WL 1286224

> *WL* is an abbreviation for Westlaw. The number 2020 is the year of the document that can be found with this citation in the Westlaw database. The number 1286224 is a number assigned to a specific document. A higher number indicates that a document was added to the Westlaw database later in the year.

b. Many court decisions that are not yet published or that are not intended for publication can be accessed through Westlaw and Lexis, two online legal databases.

The *Lawyers' Edition of the Supreme Court Reports*

The *Lawyers' Edition of the Supreme Court Reports* (*L. Ed.* or *L. Ed. 2d*) is an unofficial edition of the entire series of the Supreme Court reports containing many decisions not reported in early official volumes. It is published by LexisNexis. The advantage offered to the legal researcher by the *Lawyers' Edition* is its research tools. In its second series, it precedes each case report with a summary of the case and discusses in detail selected cases of special interest to the legal profession. Also, the *Lawyers' Edition* is the only reporter of Supreme Court opinions that provides summaries of the briefs presented by counsel.

Analyzing Case Law

Attorneys often rely heavily on case law to support a position or argument. One of the difficulties all legal professionals face in analyzing case law is the length and complexity of many court opinions. While some opinions may be only two or three pages long, others can be a hundred pages. Understanding the components of a case—that is, the basic format in which cases are presented—can simplify your task of reading and analyzing case law. Over time, as you acquire experience, case analysis becomes easier. This section focuses on how to read and analyze cases, as well as how to summarize, or *brief*, a case.

The Components of a Case

Reported cases have different parts, and you should know why each part is there and what information it communicates. To illustrate the various components of a case, we present an annotated sample court case in Exhibit 7.7 on the following pages. This exhibit shows an actual case that was decided by a California court of appeal.

Important sections, terms, and phrases in the case are defined or explained in the margins. You will also note that triple asterisks (* * *) may appear in the exhibit. The triple asterisks indicate that we have deleted a few words or sentences from the opinion for the sake of readability or brevity. If the asterisks appear between paragraphs, then one or more paragraphs have been deleted. Also, when the opinion cites another case or legal source, the citation to the referenced case or source has been omitted to save space and to improve readability.

Following Exhibit 7.7, we discuss the various parts of a case. As you read through the descriptions of these parts, refer to the exhibit, which illustrates most of them. Remember, though, that the excerpt presented in Exhibit 7.7, because it has been pared down for illustration, may be much easier to read than many court opinions that you will encounter.

EXHIBIT 7.7

A Sample Court Case

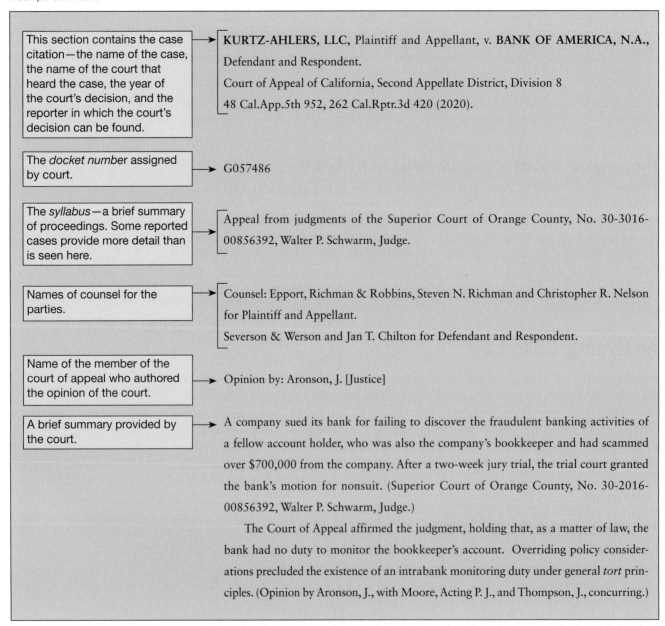

This section contains the case citation—the name of the case, the name of the court that heard the case, the year of the court's decision, and the reporter in which the court's decision can be found.

KURTZ-AHLERS, LLC, Plaintiff and Appellant, v. **BANK OF AMERICA, N.A.,** Defendant and Respondent.

Court of Appeal of California, Second Appellate District, Division 8

48 Cal.App.5th 952, 262 Cal.Rptr.3d 420 (2020).

The *docket number* assigned by court.

G057486

The *syllabus*—a brief summary of proceedings. Some reported cases provide more detail than is seen here.

Appeal from judgments of the Superior Court of Orange County, No. 30-3016-00856392, Walter P. Schwarm, Judge.

Names of counsel for the parties.

Counsel: Epport, Richman & Robbins, Steven N. Richman and Christopher R. Nelson for Plaintiff and Appellant.

Severson & Werson and Jan T. Chilton for Defendant and Respondent.

Name of the member of the court of appeal who authored the opinion of the court.

Opinion by: Aronson, J. [Justice]

A brief summary provided by the court.

A company sued its bank for failing to discover the fraudulent banking activities of a fellow account holder, who was also the company's bookkeeper and had scammed over $700,000 from the company. After a two-week jury trial, the trial court granted the bank's motion for nonsuit. (Superior Court of Orange County, No. 30-2016-00856392, Walter P. Schwarm, Judge.)

The Court of Appeal affirmed the judgment, holding that, as a matter of law, the bank had no duty to monitor the bookkeeper's account. Overriding policy considerations precluded the existence of an intrabank monitoring duty under general *tort* principles. (Opinion by Aronson, J., with Moore, Acting P. J., and Thompson, J., concurring.)

EXHIBIT 7.7

A Sample Court Case—Continued

> The court divides the opinion into parts, beginning with the Background. It covers the facts developed at trial and the ruling of the lower courts.

BACKGROUND

Freelance bookkeeper Elizabeth Mulder perpetrated a nearly five-year fraud against her client, plaintiff Kurtz-Ahlers, LLC. Both Kurtz-Ahlers and Mulder coincidentally had their checking accounts at defendant Bank of America, N.A. (the Bank). Mulder ran her scam through her account at the Bank.

Mulder's scam consisted of the following acts: First, she added the fictitious business name (or "dba") "Income Tax Payments" to her existing checking account at the Bank. Then Mulder instructed Kurtz-Ahlers to write its checks for quarterly state and federal income tax payments to "Income Tax Payments" rather than to the Internal Revenue Service or Franchise Tax Board, and to give the checks to Mulder for mailing. After laying that groundwork, Mulder began depositing Kurtz-Ahlers's tax payment checks drawn from the Bank directly into her personal account at the Bank. Over a period of nearly five years, Mulder swindled Kurtz-Ahlers out of more than $700,000. Eventually, Mulder pleaded guilty to several federal crimes and is currently in federal prison.

After discovering the fraud, Kurtz-Ahlers notified the Bank and made a claim for its losses. The Bank denied the claim and Kurtz-Ahlers sued the Bank for *negligence*. The complaint alleged the Bank acted negligently in failing to monitor Mulder's account for fraudulent activity after permitting her to add the "inherently suspicious" name "Income Tax Payments" to the account.

After a two-week jury trial, the trial court granted the Bank's motion for nonsuit (Code Civ. Proc., § 581c), essentially holding the Bank owed Kurtz-Ahlers no duty to investigate or monitor Mulder's account.

> The Discussion section reviews the issues raised on appeal and explains the reasoning of the court for its decision. More complex cases often have more sections.

DISCUSSION

Standard of Review

Recovery in a <u>negligence</u> action depends as a threshold matter on whether the defendant had 'a duty to use due care toward an interest of [the plaintiff's] that enjoys legal protection against unintentional invasion. We review de novo whether this '"essential prerequisite"' to recovery is satisfied. We also independently review a trial court's grant of nonsuit.

The Trial Court Properly Granted Nonsuit for the Bank

Kurtz-Ahlers argues two grounds for finding the trial court erred in granting the Bank's motion for nonsuit. First, Kurtz-Ahlers argues the court erred in taking from the jury the disputed issue of whether the dba "Income Tax Payments" was so suspicious it triggered a duty on the part of the Bank to investigate possible fraudulent activity in Mulder's account. Second, Kurtz-Ahlers contends the court wrongly concluded as a

Continued

EXHIBIT 7.7

A Sample Court Case—Continued

matter of law banks owe no duty to depositors to monitor other depositors' accounts for fraud. In regard to the latter contention, Kurtz-Ahlers argues existing case law supports finding the Bank had a duty of inquiry. Alternatively, Kurtz-Ahlers argues we should recognize a new duty of inquiry owed by banks to depositors.

For the reasons set forth below, the trial court correctly ruled as a matter of law the Bank had no duty to monitor Mulder's account. That conclusion renders moot the dispute over whether Mulder's dba "Income Tax Payments" was a highly suspicious "red flag" triggering an inquiry into possible fraud. Consequently, we conclude the court properly granted nonsuit for the Bank.

Banks Have No Common Law Duty to Monitor Deposit Accounts

There is a wealth of case law defining the duties a bank owes to account holders. Those duties do not include "policing" other depositors' accounts for fraud.

The relationship between a bank and its depositor is not fiduciary in character but, rather, 'founded on contract,' which is ordinarily memorialized by a signature card that the depositor signs upon opening the account. Nevertheless, it is well established that a bank has 'a duty to act with reasonable care in its transactions with its depositors … .' The duty is an implied term in the contract between the bank and its depositor.

Case law reflects the narrow scope of a bank's duties under the deposit agreement. Such duties include the duty to honor checks properly payable from the depositor's account; the duty to *dishonor* checks lacking required signatures; and the duty "to render faithful and accurate accounts under the contract of deposit."

The parties have not cited, and we have not found, any published case involving the issue of whether a bank owes a depositor a duty to investigate and disclose possible fraudulent activity in another depositor's account. A legion of cases, however, rejects the notion banks owe such a duty to nondepositors. In *Casey v. U.S. Bank Nat. Assn.* (*Casey*), another panel of this court presented a "primer on California banking law" and pronounced the following blanket rule: "Under California law, a bank owes no duty to nondepositors to investigate or disclose suspicious activities on the part of an account holder."

Casey cited numerous cases which refused to recognize a bank's duty to third parties to "police" a depositor's account. * * *

The court in *Software Design* expressed this conclusion perfectly: "The burden on banks, if we were to recognize a duty of inquiry and detection in the circumstances of appellants' complaint, is out of proportion to the potential harm averted by such a result. Scrutiny into the financial and business affairs of prospective customers for the

EXHIBIT 7.7

A Sample Court Case—Continued

express purpose of ferreting out the faithless fiduciary and divining illegal conduits for embezzled funds would be intrusive for the citizenry and add to the cost of financial transactions, both in terms of time and money. Better that the one contemplating the services of a financial advisor do the background check and then monitor the services rendered. It is that person who has the most control and the most to win or lose, and with whom the investigative tasks should rest."

In sum, we conclude "'overriding policy considerations'" preclude the existence of an "intra-bank" monitoring duty under general tort principles. Consequently, we find the trial court properly granted nonsuit for the Bank.

| The Disposition is the conclusion of the court of appeal. | → | **DISPOSITION** |

DISPOSITION

The judgment is affirmed. Respondent is entitled to its costs on appeal.

Moore, Acting P. J., and Thompson, J., concurred.

Case Title

The title of a case indicates the names of the parties to the lawsuit, and the *v.* in the case title means *versus*, or "against." This is often referred to as the "style" of the case and can communicate, among other things, whether the case is civil or criminal. Two last names, one on either side of the "*v.*," usually indicate a civil lawsuit. The word "People," "State," or "Commonwealth" on one side of the "*v.*" likely indicates a criminal case.

In the trial court, the plaintiff's last name appears first in the case title, and the second name is the defendant's. If the case is appealed, however, the appellate court will sometimes place the name of the party appealing the decision first, so the parties' names may be reversed. You must carefully read the facts of each case to identify the roles of the parties.

Case Citation

Typically, the citation to the case is found just above or just below the case title (and often at the tops of consecutive printed or online pages). If the citation appears on Westlaw and one of the parallel citations is not yet available, the citation may include underlined spaces for the volume and page numbers to be filled in once they become available (such as "___ U.S. ___").

Docket Number

The docket number immediately follows the case title. The court clerk assigns a docket number when a case is initially filed. The number serves as an identifier for all papers submitted in connection with the case. A case published in a reporter should not be cited by its docket number, but the number may serve as a tool in obtaining background information on the case.

Cases appearing in slip-opinion form (decisions that have been decided but not yet published in a reporter) are usually identified, filed, and cited by docket number. After publication of the decision, the docket number may continue to serve as an identifier for appellate records and briefs (appellate briefs will be discussed in Chapter 9). There may be changes to correct typographical mistakes made between the initial slip opinion and the reported decision, or the court may change its mind on a matter of substance and withdraw the opinion. Always check to see whether there is a later, reported version of a slip opinion you find during your research to ensure you are citing the correct version of the opinion.

Dates Argued and Decided

An important component of a case is the date on which the court decided it. Usually, the date of the decision immediately follows the docket number. In addition to the date of the court's decision on the matter, the date on which the case was argued before the court (in appellate court cases) may also be included.

Syllabus

Following the docket number is the *syllabus*—a brief synopsis of the facts of the case, the issues analyzed by the court, and the court's conclusion. In official reporters, the courts usually prepare the syllabi. In unofficial reporters, the publishers of the reporters usually prepare them. The syllabus is often a helpful research tool. It provides an overview of the case and points out legal issues discussed by the court. In a few states, such as Ohio, the official syllabus has precedential value. In most states, the syllabus is not binding. In all cases, keep in mind that reading the syllabus is not a substitute for reading the case if the case is relevant.

Headnotes

Unofficial reporters, such as those published by West, often make extensive use of case *headnotes*. As discussed earlier, headnotes are short paragraphs that highlight and summarize specific rules of law mentioned in the case. In reporters published by West, they are correlated to the comprehensive West Key Number system. In Exhibit 7.7, the headnotes were deleted for reasons of space.

Names of Counsel

The published report of the case usually contains the names of the lawyers (counsel) representing the parties. The attorneys' names are typically found just following the syllabus (and headnotes, if any).

Name of Judge or Justice Authoring the Opinion

The name of the judge or justice who authored the opinion in the case will also be included in the published report of the case, just before the court's opinion. In some cases, instead of the name of a judge or justice, the decision will be authored *per curiam* (Latin for "by the court"), which means that the opinion is that of the whole court, or the majority of the court, and not the opinion of any one judge or justice. Sometimes, the phrase is used to indicate that the chief justice or presiding judge wrote the opinion. The phrase also may be used for an announcement of a court's disposition of a case that is not accompanied by a written opinion.

Opinion

The term *opinion* is often used loosely to refer to a court case or decision. In fact, the term has a precise meaning. The opinion of the court contains the analysis and decision of the judge or judges who heard and decided the case. Most opinions contain a brief statement of the facts of the case, a summary of the legal issues raised by the facts, and the remedies sought by the parties.

In appellate court cases, the court summarizes the errors of the lower court, if any, and the impact of these errors on the case's outcome. The main body of the opinion is the application of the law to the particular facts. The court often mentions case precedents, relevant statutes, and administrative rules to support its reasoning. Additionally, court opinions may contain discussions of policy and other factors that clarify the reason for the court's decision. The various kinds of opinions that may be issued by an appellate court are explained in Exhibit 7.8.

The Court's Conclusion

In the opinion, the judges indicate their conclusion, or decision, on the issue or issues before the court. If several issues are involved, as often happens, there may be a conclusion at the end of the discussion of each issue. Often, at the end of the opinion, the conclusions are briefly summarized.

An appellate court also specifies what the *disposition* of a case should be. If the court agrees with a lower court's decision, it will *affirm* that decision, which means that the decision of the lower court remains unchanged. If the appellate court concludes that the lower court erred in its interpretation of the law, the court may *reverse* the lower court's ruling.

Sometimes an appellate court concludes that further factual findings are necessary or that a case should be retried and a decision made that is consistent with the appellate court's conclusions of law. Then, the appellate court will *remand* the case to the lower court for further proceedings consistent with its opinion.

Analyzing Cases

When you are researching case law, your main focus should be on the opinion—the words of the court itself. Some opinions are easier to understand than others. Some judges write more clearly than others. You may need to reread a case (or a portion of a case) to understand what is being said, why it is being said at that point in the case, and what the judge's legal reasoning is.

EXHIBIT 7.8

Types of Appellate Court Opinions

CONCURRING When one or more judges agree with the decision of the majority, but not necessarily the reasoning of the majority, they may wish to explain their own reasons for supporting the decision or may wish to emphasize a particular point.

DISSENTING When one or more judges disagree with the decision of the majority, the dissenters may write an explanation of why the result should have been different. These opinions can be important as persuasive authority later should the holding in the case be limited or overturned. They are also important as signals that the law in a particular area may not be completely settled.

MAJORITY An opinion that represents the views of the majority of the judges who decide a case, either affirming or reversing the decision of the lower court.

MEMORANDUM An opinion in a case that does not create precedent.

PLURALITY When no single opinion receives the support of a majority of the judges on a court, the plurality is the opinion receiving the most votes. This often happens when a majority agrees on the outcome but for incompatible reasons.

UNANIMOUS When all judges on a court (or the panel of judges assigned to hear an appeal) agree on the legal reasoning and decision. This is sometimes referred to as a *per curiam* opinion.

EN BANC When every judge on an appellate court participates in deciding a case, rather than a limited panel of judges. This term applies to the case rather than an individual opinion but is important because it can give a majority or plurality opinion more weight.

Some cases contain several pages describing facts and issues of previous cases and how those cases relate to the one being decided by the court. You might want to reread these discussions several times to distinguish among comments made in the previous cases and comments that are being made about the case at bar (before the court).

Look for Guideposts in the Opinion

Often, the judge writing the opinion provides some guideposts, perhaps by indicating sections and subsections within the opinion by numbers, letters, or subtitles. Note that in Exhibit 7.7, subheadings are used to divide the opinion into basic sections. Scanning through the opinion for these types of indicators can help orient you to the opinion's format.

In cases that involve dissenting or concurring opinions, make sure that you identify these opinions so that you do not mistake one of them for the majority opinion. You can scan through the case a time or two to identify its components and then read the case (or sections of the case) until you understand the facts and procedural history of the case, the issues involved, the applicable law, the legal reasoning of the court, and how the reasoning led to the court's conclusion on the issues.

Distinguish the Court's Holding from *Dicta*

When analyzing cases, you should determine which statements of the court are legally binding and which are not. Only the **holding** (the legal principle to be drawn from the court's decision) is binding. Other views expressed in the opinion are referred to as *dicta* and are not binding.

Dicta is the plural of *dictum*. *Dictum* is an abbreviated form of the Latin term *obiter dictum*, which means "a remark by the way." *Dicta* are statements made in a decision that go beyond the facts of the case or that do not directly relate to the facts or to the resolution of the issue being addressed. If you think of a court's reasoning as comprising a metal chain, *dicta* are not links that connect two other links in that chain. Instead, they are appendages that perform no function logically necessary to the disposition of the case.

Dicta include comments used by the court to illustrate an example and statements concerning a rule of law not essential to the case. You can probably assume that statements are *dicta* if they begin with "If the facts were different" or "If the plaintiff had" or some other "if/then" phrase.

Summarizing and Briefing Cases

After you have read and analyzed a case, you may decide that it is on point and that you want to include a reference to it in your research findings. If so, you will summarize in your notes the important facts and issues in the case, as well as the court's decision, or holding, and the reasoning used by the court. This is called **briefing a case**.

There is a fairly standard procedure for briefing court cases. First, read the case opinion carefully. When you feel you understand the case, begin to prepare the brief. Typically, a brief presents the essentials of the case under headings such as those listed below. Many researchers conclude their briefs with an additional section in which they note their own comments or conclusions about the case.

1. **Citation.** Give the full citation for the case, including the name of the case, the date it was decided, and the court that decided it.

2. **Facts.** Briefly indicate (a) the reasons for the lawsuit (who did what to whom) and (b) the identity and arguments of the plaintiff(s) and defendant(s).

3. **Procedure.** Indicate the procedural history of the case in a sentence or two. What was the lower court's decision? What did the appellate court do (affirm, reverse, remand)? How did the matter arrive before the present court?

holding
The binding legal principle, or precedent, that is drawn from the court's decision in a case.

dicta
A Latin term referring to nonbinding (nonprecedential) judicial statements that are not directly related to the facts or issues presented in the case and thus are not essential to the holding.

briefing a case
Summarizing a case. A case brief gives the full citation, the factual background and procedural history, the issue or issues raised, the court's decision, the court's holding, and the legal reasoning on which the court based its decision. It may also include conclusions or notes concerning the case made by the individual briefing it.

4. **Issue**. State, in the form of a question, the essential issue before the court. If more than one issue is involved, you may have two—or even more—questions.

5. **Decision**. Indicate here—with a "yes" or "no," if possible—the court's answer to the question (or questions) that you noted in the *Issue* section.

6. **Reasoning**. Summarize as briefly as possible the reasons given by the court for its decision (or decisions) and the case or statutory law relied on by the court in arriving at its decision.

7. **Holding**. State the rule of law for which the case stands.

Exhibit 7.9 presents a briefed version of the sample court case presented in Exhibit 7.7. This brief illustrates the typical format used in briefing cases.

IRAC: A Method for Briefing Cases

Besides the example just provided, another standard format for briefing cases is called the *IRAC method*, referring to *issue, rule, application,* and *conclusion*. This method, which will be discussed further in Chapter 9, involves the following steps:

1. First, decide what legal *issues* are involved in the case. The case brief in Exhibit 7.9 uses the heading "Issue" to identify this matter for the sample case in Exhibit 7.7.

2. Next, determine the *rule of law* that applies to the issues. In Exhibit 7.9, the rule of law is discussed under "Reasoning."

3. After identifying the applicable law, determine the *application* of the law to the facts of the case. In Exhibit 7.9, the "Holding" section deals with the court's application of the law.

4. Finally, draw a *conclusion*. Exhibit 7.9 calls that the "Decision." It is the determination of the court after it has applied the law to the case.

EXHIBIT 7.9

A Briefed Version of the Sample Court Case

KURTZ-AHLERS, LLC v. BANK OF AMERICA, N.A.

48 Cal.App.5th 952, 262 Cal.Rptr.3d 420 (2020).

FACTS For five years, bookkeeper Mulder engaged in fraud against her client Kurtz-Ahlers. Mulder wrote checks on the Kurtz-Ahlers account at Bank of America to make it appear she was making payments to federal and state tax authorities when she was, in fact, moving funds to her own account. After the $700,000 fraud was discovered, Mulder was sent to prison.

PROCEDURE Kurtz-Ahlers sued Bank of America for not discovering the fraud, contending that it was negligent for the bank not to notice checks with large amounts that were made out to unusual recipients, such as "Income Tax Payment." The bank moved to have the lawsuit dismissed, but the matter went to a jury that held the bank was not negligent. Plaintiffs appealed.

ISSUE Did the bank have a common law or statutory obligation to monitor clients' checking accounts for improper activity?

DECISION The appeals court held that there was no basis in common law or statute for a bank to oversee the use of funds in accounts.

REASONING A bank is not in a fiduciary relationship where it monitors the use of funds in checking accounts. Rather, the bank is in a contractual relationship that requires it to honor checks properly payable from a depositor's account. Banks are required to make sure parties have authority to write checks; they are not responsible to see if the recipient is proper.

HOLDING Affirmed. The court held that the trial court decision for the bank was consistent with precedent from a number of similar cases.

Different lawyers and law offices have different preferences for the format to be used in briefing cases. What is most important is accuracy in explaining the key facts, the issues under consideration, the rule of law or legal reasoning used by the court, the application of the law, and the conclusion resulting from that application.

Researching Constitutional and Statutory Law

To this point, we have been discussing case law, which is sometimes called *judge-made* law because it is made by the judges in the state and federal court systems. Judge-made law is also known as the common law, as explained in Chapter 5. Another primary source of law is *statutory law*—the statutes and ordinances enacted by legislative bodies, such as the U.S. Congress, state legislatures, and town governments.

Congress draws its authority to enact federal legislation from the U.S. Constitution. A state legislature draws its authority from the state constitution. In some legal disputes, the constitutionality of a statute or government action may be an issue. In such instances, you may have to go behind the statutes to the relevant constitution, so we look at constitutional law before going into detail about statutes.

Finding Constitutional Law

The federal government and all states have constitutions describing the powers, responsibilities, and limitations of the branches of government. Constitutions, especially state constitutions, are amended over time. All are available online.

A key source of federal constitutional law is *The Constitution of the United States of America*, published under the authority of the U.S. Senate and available through the Library of Congress (available at **congress.gov**). It includes the U.S. Constitution, annotations concerning United States Supreme Court decisions interpreting the Constitution, and a discussion of each provision, including background information on its history and interpretation.

Additional constitutional sources are found in the *United States Code Annotated* and the *United States Code Service*, which contain the text of the Constitution and its amendments as well as citations to cases discussing particular constitutional provisions. We discuss these publications shortly, and they are available online. Annotated state codes provide a similar service for state constitutions. State constitutions are usually included in the publications containing state statutes.

Finding Statutory Law

Some statutes supplement the common law, while other statutes replace it. State legislatures and the U.S. Congress have broad powers to establish law. If a common law principle conflicts with a statutory provision, the statute will normally take precedence. Additionally, a legislature may create statutes that deal with issues, such as age discrimination, that are not covered by the common law. Statutes—for example, the statutes of a particular state—are often published in a compilation called a code, which arranges materials by topic.

Note that, when you find a statute that seems relevant, you will need to investigate whether the statute has been amended. Online legal research services such as Westlaw and Lexis include notes about how up-to-date their coverage is. Printed services are also available.

code
A systematic and topically organized presentation of laws, rules, or regulations.

Federal Statutes

Federal statutes are contained in the *United States Code*, or U.S.C. This official compilation of federal statutes is published by the U.S. government and is updated annually.

The U.S.C. is divided into titles (topics) as seen in Exhibit 7.10. For example, laws relating to commerce and trade are in Title 15. Laws concerning the judiciary and judicial procedures are in Title 28.

Titles are divided into chapters (sections) and subchapters. A citation to the U.S.C. includes title and section numbers. Thus, a reference to "28 U.S.C. Section 1346" means that the statute can be found in Section 1346 of Title 28. "Section" may also be designated by the symbol §, and "Sections" by §§.

Names of Statutes.   Statutes are listed in the U.S.C. by their official names. Many legislative bills enacted into law are commonly known by a popular name, however. Some have descriptive titles reflecting their purpose. Others are named after their sponsors.

Sometimes a researcher may know the popular name of a legislative act but not its official name. In this situation, the researcher can consult the U.S.C. volume entitled *Popular Name Table*, which lists statutes by their popular names. For example, suppose

EXHIBIT 7.10

Titles in the *United States Code*

*1. General Provisions.
2. The Congress.
*3. The President.
*4. Flag and Seal, Seat of Government, and the States.
*5. Government Organization and Employees; and Appendix.
†6. [Surety Bonds.]
7. Agriculture.
8. Aliens and Nationality.
*9. Arbitration.
*10. Armed Forces; and Appendix.
*11. Bankruptcy; and Appendix.
12. Banks and Banking.
*13. Census.
*14. Coast Guard.
15. Commerce and Trade.
16. Conservation.
*17. Copyrights.
*18. Crimes and Criminal Procedure; and Appendix.
19. Customs Duties.
20. Education.
21. Food and Drugs.
22. Foreign Relations and Intercourse.
*23. Highways.
24. Hospitals and Asylums.
25. Indians.
26. Internal Revenue Code.
27. Intoxicating Liquors.

*28. Judiciary and Judicial Procedure; and Appendix.
29. Labor.
30. Mineral Lands and Mining.
*31. Money and Finance.
*32. National Guard.
33. Navigation and Navigable Waters.
‡34. [Navy.]
*35. Patents.
36. Patriotic Societies and Observances.
*37. Pay and Allowances of the Uniformed Services.
*38. Veterans' Benefits.
*39. Postal Service.
40. Public Buildings, Property, and Works.
41. Public Contracts.
42. The Public Health and Welfare.
43. Public Lands.
*44. Public Printing and Documents.
45. Railroads.
*46. Shipping; and Appendix.
47. Telegraphs, Telephones, and Radiotelegraphs.
48. Territories and Insular Possessions.
*49. Transportation; and Appendix.
50. War and National Defense; and Appendix.
51. National and Commercial Space Programs
52. Voting and Elections
53. [reserved]
54. National Park Service and Related Programs

*This title has been enacted as law. However, any Appendix to this title has not been enacted as law.
†This title was enacted as law and has been repealed by the enactment of Title 31.
‡This title has been eliminated by the enactment of Title 10.

Page III

Source: *The United States Code.*

you have learned that the Landrum-Griffin Act governs an issue that you are researching. This is the popular name for the act, not the official name. You can consult the *Popular Name Table* to find the act's official title, which is the Labor-Management Reporting and Disclosure Act of 1959. In online searches, you would want to use both names. The U.S.C. is available online at **govinfo.gov/app/collection/uscode.**

When using a database such as Lexis or Westlaw, you can perform a search of secondary sources and case law by using the popular name. Chances are, a court or law review article using the popular name will also contain a citation to the specific act itself in the U.S.C., sometimes in the form of a hyperlink that will take you to the page for that statute in the database.

Unofficial Versions of the U.S.C. There are also two unofficial versions of the federal code, each of which contains additional information that is helpful to researchers. West's *United States Code Annotated* (U.S.C.A.) contains the full text of the U.S.C., the U.S. Constitution, the Federal Rules of Evidence, and other rules, including the Rules of Civil Procedure and the Rules of Criminal Procedure. This set of approximately two hundred volumes includes historical notes relating to the text of each statute, along with amendments to the act. Annotations offer additional assistance by listing cases that have analyzed, discussed, or interpreted the statute.

The other unofficial version of the code is the *United States Code Service* (U.S.C.S.), published by LexisNexis. The U.S.C.S. and the U.S.C.A. provide somewhat different research tools. For example, the U.S.C.S. contains references and citations to some sources, such as legal periodicals and the legal encyclopedia *American Jurisprudence*, that are not included in the U.S.C.A. The U.S.C.A. is available on Westlaw, while the U.S.C.S. is available on Lexis. With access to an electronic legal database such as Westlaw, Lexis, or Bloomberg Law, you can search any of these compilations by keyword.

State Statutes

State codes follow the U.S.C. pattern of arranging statutes by subject. Depending on the state, they may be called codes, revisions, compilations, consolidations, general statutes, public laws, or statutes.

In some codes, subjects are designated by number. In others, they are designated by name. For example, "13 Pennsylvania Consolidated Statutes Section 1101" means that the statute can be found in Section 1101 of Title 13 of the Pennsylvania code. "California Commercial Code Section 1101" means that the statute can be found in Section 1101 under the heading "Commercial" in the California Code. Abbreviations may be used. For example, "13 Pennsylvania Consolidated Statutes Section 1101" may be abbreviated to "13 Pa. Cons. Stat. § 1101," and "California Commercial Code Section 1101" may be abbreviated to "Cal. Com. Code § 1101."

In many states, official codes are supplemented by annotated codes published by private publishers. Annotated codes follow the numbering scheme set forth in the official state code but provide outlines, explanations, and indexes to assist in locating information. These codes also provide references to case law, legislative history sources, and other documents in which the statute has been considered or discussed.

Analyzing Statutory Law

Because of the tremendous growth in statutory and regulatory law in the last century, statutes and administrative agency regulations often govern the legal issues dealt with by attorneys. Paralegals must understand how to interpret and analyze this body of law. Although we use the terms *statute* and *statutory law* in this section, the following discussion also applies to regulations issued by administrative agencies.

Two Steps in Statutory Analysis

The first step in statutory analysis is to read the language of the statute. As with court cases, some statutes are more difficult to read than others. Some are extremely wordy, lengthy, or difficult to understand for some other reason. By carefully reading a statute, however, you can usually determine:

- The reasons for the statute's enactment.
- The date on which it became effective.
- The class of parties to which the statute applies.
- The kind of conduct regulated by the statute.
- The circumstances in which that conduct is prohibited, required, or permitted.

You can also learn whether the statute allows for exceptions and, if so, in what circumstances.

The second step in statutory analysis is to interpret the meaning of the statute. Generally, when trying to understand the meaning of statutes, you should do as the courts do. We now look at some of the techniques used by courts when faced with the task of interpreting the meaning of a given statute or statutory provision. Some practical tips for reading statutes are provided in the *Developing Paralegal Skills* feature below.

DEVELOPING PARALEGAL SKILLS

READING STATUTORY LAW

Statutes are a major source of law at both the state and federal level. Being able to read statutes properly is a crucial skill for paralegals. Reading and understanding a statute, however, is not the same as reading a court decision. It takes application of special techniques (called principles of statutory interpretation) to properly interpret a statute. Here are four of the most important principles:

1. **The Plain Meaning Rule.** If the language of a statute is clear, the court applies the language as written. While this rule seems obvious and easy to employ, it is not, because courts and agencies often stumble over how to interpret particular words in a statute.

2. **Read a Statute as a Whole.** Provisions in different parts of a statute should be interpreted to fit together, not conflict. As a result, to understand a statute, you must look at all of the statute, not just a single section. A good first step is to skim the statute quickly, noting the organizational structure, location of definition sections, and other key elements.

3. **Statutory Definitions Govern.** When a statute includes a specific definition, that meaning will be used in interpreting the statute. Dictionary definitions are guides when there is no statutory definition, but dictionaries differ, and the meaning of a word can shift over time.

The United States Supreme Court has relied on dictionaries in hundreds of cases. You should check to see if a particular dictionary is recognized as authoritative by the court involved and should use an edition of the dictionary that was current at the time legislation was drafted. *Just doing an Internet search of a word is not an acceptable research technique.*

4. **Distinguish between "and" and "or."** When a list of requirements in a statute uses "and," all of the things in the list must be satisfied. When the list in a statute uses "or," only one of the items in a list must be satisfied.

Learning how to interpret statutes takes practice and effort. The most important concept to remember is that you must read statutes carefully and look at the entire statute, not just one provision. A statute generally includes a section defining important terms in the statute. Some of these definitions sections include guides for interpreting and applying some of the rules of construction mentioned above. In researching a statute, study not only the code itself but also any relevant definitions sections associated with the statute.

Bear in mind, however, that although understanding the language of a statute is necessary, that language will not control in every case. Constitutional law is superior to statutory law, and language in statutes has often been invalidated as unconstitutional by the courts. Furthermore, because legislatures are slow to amend and repeal laws, many statutes still on the books are wholly or partially unconstitutional.

For example, many criminal laws are unconstitutional in whole or in part because they violate the First Amendment right to free speech or the Fourth Amendment right to freedom from unreasonable searches and seizures. For these reasons, a research inquiry involving a statute should never end with the words of the statute itself.

Previous Judicial Interpretation

Researching statutory law means researching case law to see how the courts have interpreted and applied statutory provisions. As discussed, courts are obligated to follow the precedents set by higher courts in their jurisdictions. A statutory interpretation made by a higher court must be accepted as binding by lower courts in the same jurisdiction. You can find citations to court cases relating to specific statutes by referring to annotated versions of state or federal statutory codes, such as the U.S.C.A., in print and online.

Legislative Intent

Another factor in statutory interpretation is learning the intent of the legislature. A court determines the meaning of the statute by attempting to find out why the legislators chose to word the statute as they did or, more generally, what the legislators sought to accomplish by enacting the statute. To learn the intent of the legislators who wrote a particular law, it is often necessary to investigate the legislative history of the statute. This can be done by researching such sources as committee reports and records of official hearings and other proceedings.

Committee Reports

Committee reports are the most important source of legislative history. Congressional committees produce reports for each bill, and these reports often contain the full text of the bill, a description of its purpose, and the committee's recommendations. Several tables are also included to set out dates for certain actions. The dates help the researcher locate floor debates and committee testimony in the *Congressional Record* and other publications. Committee reports are published according to a numerical series and are available through the U.S. Government Publishing Office, which is accessible online at **govinfo.gov**.

Other Sources of Legislative History

The two tools most frequently used in conducting research on legislative history are the *United States Code Congressional and Administrative News* (U.S.C.C.A.N.) and the **congress.gov** website.

The U.S.C.C.A.N., a West publication, contains reprints of statutes and sections describing the statutes' legislative history, including committee reports. Statutes in the U.S.C.A. are followed by notations directing the researcher to the corresponding legislative history in the U.S.C.C.A.N. The website **congress.gov** provides access to committee reports, the text of Congressional bills, and the *Congressional Record*, which is published daily while Congress is in session. This publication contains the text of congressional debates and proceedings.

While our focus here has been on existing statutes and related materials, there are times when we need to know what may be coming. Resources devoted to new developments are reviewed in this chapter's *Office Tech and Cybersecurity* feature.

OFFICE TECH AND CYBERSECURITY

LOOKING AHEAD

Every day, it seems, legislatures propose or pass new laws, administrative agencies propose or issue new regulations, and new cases begin to work their way through the court system. A few of these may reach the nation's highest court. As a paralegal, you can perform a valuable service for your supervising attorney by keeping up with new developments in the legal arena or in your specialty area.

What New Federal Statutes Are Likely to Be Enacted?

You can keep up to date on what bills are pending in Congress by subscribing to e-newsletters published by law firms, think tanks, and interest groups. Washington-based think tanks, for example, often follow specific areas, and their e-newsletters and blogs include useful information on the progress of pending legislation. There are no guarantees that the information on such sites is up to date or accurate, so be careful to read the actual legislation rather than relying on a third-party account.

Law firms with specific practice areas also monitor legislation. Use a legal directory to identify major Washington firms in the practice area you are interested in and then explore the firms' websites for free newsletters. The Library of Congress's website also tracks pending legislation. Finally, Web searches can help you spot the mention of legislative proposals in the news media.

Are Any New Uniform Laws Being Developed?

To find out about new uniform laws being developed by the National Conference of Commissioners on Uniform State Laws (NCCUSL), you can visit its website at **uniformlaws.org**. There, you will find the text of all uniform acts, including every draft of the final uniform act. You can also find out which states have adopted an act and which states have legislation pending, as well as the status of the legislation.

Technology Tip

You can find out what cases are pending before the Supreme Court from online sources. For example, at **oyez.org**, you will find a list of cases that the Supreme Court has heard recently or is scheduled to hear in the current term. **SCOTUSblog.com** likewise tracks pending cases, in addition to petitions submitted to the Supreme Court.

If you are interested in a particular case pending before the Court or want to search for cases on a particular issue, you can find the case name and a brief description at these sites. All details of cases, including briefs, can be found at **supremecourt.gov**, as well as through online research services, including Westlaw and Lexis.

Researching Administrative Law

Administrative rules and regulations constitute a growing source of American law. As discussed in Chapter 5, Congress frequently delegates authority to administrative agencies through enabling legislation. For example, in 1914 Congress passed the Federal Trade Commission Act, which established the Federal Trade Commission, or FTC. The act gave the FTC the authority to issue and enforce rules and regulations relating to unfair and deceptive trade practices in the United States. Of course, there are many other federal administrative agencies. The orders, regulations, and decisions of such agencies are legally binding and, as such, are primary sources of law.

The *Code of Federal Regulations*

The *Code of Federal Regulations* (C.F.R.) is a government publication containing all federal administrative agency regulations. The regulations are compiled from the *Federal Register*, a daily government publication consisting of executive orders and administrative regulations, in which regulations are first published.

The C.F.R. uses the same titles as the *United States Code*. This subject-matter organization allows the researcher to determine the section in the C.F.R. in which a regulation will appear. Each title of the C.F.R. is divided into chapters, subchapters, parts, and sections.

The C.F.R. is revised and formally republished four times a year. Recent regulations appear in the *Federal Register* until they are incorporated into the C.F.R. The online version is updated continuously and is available at **govinfo.gov/app/collection/CFR**.

Administrative Guidance Documents

Many administrative agencies, such as the Environmental Protection Agency, issue guidance documents that outline how the agency interprets the rules that it has promulgated. While these documents do not constitute binding law since they are not regulations or legislation, they can be helpful as persuasive and informative sources. Judges grant varying degrees of deference to these documents, and in recent years, there has been an effort to make these documents more widely available on administrative agencies' websites.

CHAPTER SUMMARY

LEGAL RESEARCH AND ANALYSIS

Researching Case Law—The Preliminary Steps

1. *Defining the issue*—The first step in research is to identify the legal question, or issue, to be researched. Often, more than one issue is involved.

2. *Determining your research goals*—In researching case law, the goal is to find cases that are on point and are binding authorities. Binding authorities are all legal authorities (statutes, regulations, constitutions, and cases) that courts must follow in making their decisions. Courts are not bound to follow persuasive authorities (such as cases decided in other jurisdictions), although courts often consider such authorities, particularly when deciding cases of first impression.

Finding Relevant Cases

Primary sources of law include all documents that establish the law, including court decisions, statutes, regulations, constitutions, and presidential orders. *Secondary sources of law* are publications written about the law, such as legal encyclopedias, digests, treatises, and periodicals.

1. *Legal encyclopedias*—Legal encyclopedias provide detailed summaries of legal rules and concepts and are useful for finding background information on issues being researched. These books arrange topics alphabetically and contain citations to cases and statutes relating to the topic. Two popular legal encyclopedias are *American Jurisprudence, Second Edition (Am. Jur. 2d),* and *Corpus Juris Secundum (C.J.S.).* A third encyclopedia, *Words and Phrases,* covers legal terms and phrases and cites cases in which the terms or phrases are defined.

2. *Case digests*—Digests are compilations in which brief summaries of court cases are arranged by subject and subdivided by jurisdiction and court. They are major secondary sources of law and helpful finding tools. Digests using the West system of topic classification and Key Numbers provide cross-references to other West publications. Digests arrange topics alphabetically with annotations to cases on each topic but are not as detailed as encyclopedias.

3. *Annotations: American Law Reports*—The *American Law Reports* present annotations of leading cases that discuss the key issues in the cases and that refer the researcher to other sources on the issues.

4. *Other secondary sources*—Treatises are scholarly publications that summarize, evaluate, or interpret specific areas of law, either in a single volume or in multivolume sets. Hornbooks are single-volume

treatises. *Restatements of the Law* are respected scholarly compilations of the common law that present

The Case Reporting System

The primary sources of case law are the cases themselves. Cases are published in various case reporters.

1. *State court decisions and reporters* — Most state trial court decisions are not published in printed volumes. Opinions of state appellate courts (including state supreme courts) normally are published in official state reporters. Online official reports are also available. Many states eliminated their own reporters in favor of West's National Reporter System, which reports state cases in its regional reporters. To locate a case in a reporter, you use the case citation. There are five parts: the case name, the volume number, the abbreviated name of the book (volume), the page

Analyzing Case Law

Case law is often relied on to support positions taken in court.

1. *Components of a case* — Typically, case formats include the following components:
   - The case title (usually plaintiff versus defendant).
   - The name of the court that decided the case.
   - The case citation.
   - The docket number assigned by the court.
   - The dates on which the case was argued and decided.
   - The syllabus (a brief summary of the facts, issues, and ruling).
   - The headnotes (short paragraphs that summarize the rules of law discussed in the case; in West's reporters, headnotes correlate with the Key Number system).

Researching Constitutional and Statutory Law

Statutory and constitutional law are primary sources of law. Statutes are based on the constitutional authority of a legislature to enact laws.

1. *Finding constitutional law* — The U.S. Constitution can be found in a number of publications, including *The Constitution of the United States of America.* Annotated versions of state constitutions are also available.

2. *Finding statutory law* — Bills and ordinances passed by legislative bodies (federal, state, and local) become statutory law. Statutes are eventually published in codes, which are available online. Federal laws are

particular cases as examples. Legal periodicals, such as law reviews, contain articles on specific areas of law.

number on which the decision begins, and the year the case was decided. A parallel citation may appear after the first citation when the case is reported in more than one reporter.

2. *Federal court decisions* — Federal trial court opinions are published unofficially in West's *Federal Supplement,* and opinions from the federal circuit courts of appeals are published in West's *Federal Reporter.*

3. *United States Supreme Court decisions* — Supreme Court opinions are published officially in the *United States Reports,* published by the federal government, and unofficially in West's *Supreme Court Reporter* and the *Lawyers' Edition of the Supreme Court Reports.*

- The names of counsel.
- The name of the judge who authored the opinion.
- The opinion (the court's own words on the matter).
- The conclusion (holding, ruling).

2. *Analyzing cases* — Legal professionals often brief, or summarize, the cases they research. Knowing how to read, analyze, and summarize cases makes it easier to compare cases and bring together research results accurately and efficiently. One must distinguish holdings from *dicta.*

3. *Summarizing and briefing cases* — Although the format of briefs varies, the following headings are typical: citation, facts, procedure, issues, decision, reasoning, and holding.

4. *IRAC: A method for briefing cases* — Another format for briefing cases is IRAC, which refers to issue, rule, application, and conclusion.

published officially in the *United States Code* (U.S.C.). The U.S.C. organizes statutes into subjects, or titles, and divides titles into chapters (sections) and subchapters. The *United States Code Annotated (U.S.C.A.)* and the *United States Code Service (U.S.C.S.)* are unofficial publications of federal statutes. They are useful because they provide annotations and citations to other resources. State codes follow the U.S.C. pattern of arranging statutes by subject. They may be called codes, revisions, compilations, general statutes, or statutes. In many states, official codes are supplemented by annotated codes published by private publishers.

Analyzing Statutory Law

Statutory law may be difficult to understand, so careful reading and rereading are often required.

1. *Previous judicial interpretation*—How courts have interpreted a statute in the past offers helpful guidelines.

2. *Legislative intent*—The legislative history of a statute can reveal what the legislature intended the statute to accomplish. Sources of legislative history include transcripts of committee reports and hearings, transcripts of congressional proceedings, and the wording of statutes.

Researching Administrative Law

Regulations issued by federal administrative agencies are primary sources of law. Agency regulations are published in the *Code of Federal Regulations* (C.F.R.). The C.F.R. follows a format similar to that of the *United States Code* (U.S.C.), and the subject classifications (titles) of the C.F.R. correspond to the titles in the U.S.C. Many administrative agencies issue guidance documents that outline how the agency interprets the rules that it has promulgated.

KEY TERMS AND CONCEPTS

annotation   184
briefing a case   202
business invitee   179
case on "all fours"   180
case on point   179
citation   191
code   204

dicta   202
digest   184
headnote   185
holding   202
hornbook   188
Key Number   185
parallel citation   191

persuasive authority   182
pocket part   184
reporter   181
slip opinion   181
syllabus   193
treatise   188

QUESTIONS FOR REVIEW

1. What is binding authority? Persuasive authority?

2. What is the difference between a case on point and a case on "all fours"? Why is finding either of these important when researching case law?

3. What is the definition of a primary source of law? A secondary source of law? How are these sources of law used in legal research?

4. List and identify the various parts of a case citation. How do citations help you locate a case?

5. List and briefly describe the components of a reported case. Which part should you focus on when analyzing a case? How do you brief a case? What is the purpose of briefing a case? What should be included in a case brief?

6. Describe how statutes are published. What is the name of the official code containing the statutes of the U.S. government? What are the parts of a statute's citation?

7. What are principles of statutory interpretation? List four principles of statutory interpretation. What is the plain meaning rule?

8. Where are administrative agency regulations first published? Where are they codified? Where can you find these sources online?

ETHICS QUESTION

1. Krystee Connolly, a paralegal in a litigation firm, has finished reading a brief that the opposing side submitted to the court in support of a motion for summary judgment. In the brief, she notices a citation to a state supreme court case of which she is unaware. Krystee is experienced in the field and keeps current with new cases as they are decided. She wants to look at the case because it gives the other side a winning edge, so she checks in case digests and state encyclopedias, as well as on Westlaw. Krystee also checks the state supreme court's website and sees no record of such a case. She asks the paralegal for the opposing counsel to give her a copy of the case. When she does not receive it, she decides that the case is probably fictional. What should Krystee do?

PRACTICE QUESTIONS AND ASSIGNMENTS

1. Identify the case name, volume number, reporter abbreviation, page number, and year of decision for each of the following case citations, including the parallel citations:

   a. *Towe v. Sacagawea, Inc.*, 246 Or. App. 26, 264 P.3d 184 (2011).

   b. *Miranda v. Arizona*, 384 U.S. 436, 86 S. Ct. 1602, 16 L. Ed. 2d 694 (1966).

2. Identify the title number, code abbreviation, and section number for the following statutory citations:

   a. 42 U.S.C. § 1161(a).

   b. 20 C.F.R. § 404.101(a).

3. Ana returns home from a business trip to find that her house has been ransacked. Her former boyfriend, Jason, had a key, but when they broke up he returned it. Ana's neighbors tell her that someone matching Jason's description stayed at Ana's house while she was away and had a loud party one night. Ana's food has been taken, several pieces of her furniture have been broken, her bed was slept in, and the house is such a mess that it will require professional cleaning. Ana has come to your firm for legal advice on pursuing a claim against Jason. Using the *Developing Paralegal Skills* feature "Defining the Issues to Be Researched," create a checklist for defining the research issues for the case of *Ana v. Jason*.

4. Ms. Consumer bought a weight-loss tea, advertised as "the dieter's secret weapon," that guaranteed weight loss of seventeen pounds in just twelve weeks without diet or exercise. This offer was appealing because Ms. Consumer's job and family commitments left her with no time to exercise. In addition, her doctor was concerned about her cholesterol and blood sugar levels and told her she needed to lose twenty-five pounds. Ms. Consumer learned about the product, Healthtea, on a national TV show. While being interviewed, the owner of the company claimed that his product was backed by clinical studies. Ms. Consumer decided to purchase the required minimum six-month supply at a cost of one hundred dollars a month. After using the tea for six months, Ms. Consumer had lost only three pounds. She sought legal counsel because she felt she had been taken advantage of and wanted to prevent Healthtea from continuing to make false claims. She also wanted to get her money back, but that was not her primary concern.

   The federal government and many states have laws and agencies that protect consumers from unfair and deceptive business practices. In this assignment, you will review a secondary source pertaining to consumer protection laws and government agencies to see how they could help Ms. Consumer.

   a. Begin by analyzing the facts. Make a list of relevant legal terms to look up in an index.

   b. Select a secondary legal resource—such as *American Jurisprudence*, *Corpus Juris Secundum*, or *American Law Reports*—to use in your research. Record the name of the source. Consult the general index volumes.

   c. List the index topics and citations from the general index volumes under which you found relevant information. (If you have difficulty locating relevant information, try checking the topic indexes in the individual volumes.) Many primary and secondary sources include tables of abbreviations that you can consult about the meaning of abbreviations.

d. Look up these citations in the individual volumes of the secondary sources to find an answer to Ms. Consumer's legal issues. According to the secondary source, what rights does Ms. Consumer have against Healthtea? What action(s) can Ms. Consumer take to stop Healthtea from selling its product? Can Ms. Consumer recover any money?

e. List the citations to the volumes, topics, and sections where you found the possible answers. Be sure to check the pocket part for the most current citations if you use printed resources.

5. After you have analyzed the facts of Ms. Consumer's legal dilemma, made a list of legally and factually relevant terms, and reviewed a secondary source, can you find a citation to the federal law governing this topic? If so, locate the volume needed in the federal statutes. If not, use an index to an annotated version of the federal statutes in order to look up the relevant terms that will help you locate the statute volume. Then do the following:

a. Go to the volume of the statute containing the cited sections and read those sections. Have you located any additional information in the statute to help resolve Ms. Consumer's legal problem?

b. Does your research on relevant federal statutes lead you to the same conclusions you arrived at by using the secondary source? If not, how did your results differ? Under what topics did you look in each phase of your research?

6. Using the annotated version of the federal statutes, look for relevant case law annotations on Ms. Consumer's legal problem in the notes of decisions following the relevant statutory section. If there is not an annotated version of the federal statutes in your library, if no cases appear there, or if you want to learn to use another source, use a federal digest. Once you find relevant case annotations, you will want to locate the cases that interpret the statute and are as similar to Ms. Consumer's situation as possible.

a. Write down the citations to no more than three relevant cases. Now look up those cases in the case reporters.

b. Read through the summary and headnotes of each case. Do the cases still appear to be relevant? If not, go back to the annotated statute or digest and look for more relevant cases.

c. What did you find? Did the courts' application of the statute change your answer to the legal problem facing Ms. Consumer?

d. How would you update the case law that you located to make sure that it was still current law?

7. If you concluded that Ms. Consumer should pursue a state law remedy, research the answer to Ms. Consumer's problem in your state's law. Provide the citations to the relevant state statute sections and no more than three cases explaining Ms. Consumer's legal rights and the action she should take under state law to prevent Healthtea from selling its product. Based on your findings, is Ms. Consumer likely to recover any money?

GROUP PROJECT

This project will involve creating a case brief of the *Kurtz-Ahlers, LLC v. Bank of America* case in Exhibit 7.7.

Student one will write the facts section of the case brief. Student two will write the procedure section of the case brief. Student three will write the issues and answers section and the holding. Student four will write the reasoning section.

The group members will then compare the brief that they have prepared to the sample case brief in Exhibit 7.9 and critique their brief by making a list of the differences between their case brief and the sample case brief.

CHAPTER
8

Online Legal Research

CHAPTER OBJECTIVES

After completing this chapter, you will be able to:

- Demonstrate how to find some of the best legal resources available on the Internet.

- Describe the advantages of the major fee-based online programs.

- List and describe the features of lower-cost alternative legal research sources.

- Explain strategies for planning and conducting research on the Internet.

- Demonstrate how to find people and investigate companies using Internet search tools.

Introduction

Online services and databases have improved the ability of paralegals to do high-quality legal research. As you learned in Chapter 7, thorough and up-to-date legal research requires access to a huge volume of source materials, including state and federal court decisions, statutory law, and regulatory codes. Attorneys and paralegals can access most of these materials online.

An obvious advantage of online research is that you can locate, download, and print court cases, statutory provisions, and other legal documents quickly without leaving your desk. For those with subscriptions to online databases, these documents can even be highlighted and annotated digitally or sorted into online folders. Another advantage is that new case decisions and changes in statutory law are normally entered quickly into certain online legal databases, especially Westlaw and Lexis. This means that you can find out quickly whether a case decided two years ago is still "good law" today.

In this chapter, we describe various forms of online research. By the time you read the chapter, some of what we say will have changed, particularly with respect to Internet resources. Some of these resources may have improved, others may have been removed, and new ones may have been added. The general approach to conducting research online will not have altered, however. If you master the basic principles of online research discussed in this chapter, you will be able to conduct research on the Internet no matter how much its content changes. The fee-based Lexis and Westlaw services are the dominant legal research resources on the Internet, and we discuss them later in the chapter. First, we consider some free online services.

Free Legal Resources on the Internet

Most public documents, such as statutes and cases, are available to the public. Many of these documents are on the Internet, accessible through various websites, but some sites have evolved to maintain lead positions in legal research. Here, we look at leading free legal information sites. Later, we look at subscription-based sites.

Expanded online access to legal resources has changed the nature of legal research. Today, paralegals conduct most of their legal research online. How does online legal research benefit your clients?

StockLite/Shutterstock.com

As a general rule, you must know that case law sources are reliable. Commercial databases, such as Westlaw and Lexis, have their content verified but can be expensive, so free sources are important to save your and your clients' resources. But you must be sure the sites you use for legal analysis are trustworthy. The *Developing Paralegal Skills* feature below suggests ways to check the accuracy and currency of websites used in legal research.

General Legal Resources

There are several commonly used legal sites for those who are not using fee-based services. The Justia site (**justia.com**) and FindLaw for Legal Professionals (**findlaw.com**) provide access to a massive amount of legal information, such as case law, codes, law reviews, and other legal materials broken down by topics of legal practice areas. The Legal Information Institute (LII) at Cornell University Law School (**law.cornell.edu**) is another major legal resource site. Besides legal documents, this site provides other useful information, such as a guide to legal citations (**law.cornell.edu/citation**), a legal encyclopedia (a good place to start a project), and a dictionary of legal terms (**law.cornell.edu/wex**).

The Washburn University Law School maintains a popular site at **washlaw.edu**. As you will see, it has a plain, no-nonsense menu that provides easy access to certain categories of legal information. Another helpful research portal is **lawhelp.org**. This site is particularly useful when searching for legal information for a specific state. For example, **texaslawhelp.org** provides a sample landlord-tenant agreement for the state of Texas. See this chapter's *Ethics Watch* feature on finding ethics opinions online.

DEVELOPING PARALEGAL SKILLS

INTERNET-BASED RESEARCH

Many legal materials are available on the Internet, with both fee-based (Westlaw, Lexis, Fastcase, Casemaker, VersusLaw) and free (Cornell Law School's Legal Information Institute, Google Scholar) services providing court opinions, statutes, and agency materials. Courts, legislatures, and agencies also operate their own websites, which are often useful resources. Interest groups and law firms maintain specialized collections of key materials as well.

With all that information at your fingertips, often the most important problem is winnowing it down to what is really useful. Here are five questions you should ask about any legal resource you find on the Internet.

- **Who created it, and why did they post it on the Internet?** Does the information come from a neutral source or an interest group? From someone with experience and credentials or a fraud? Before you rely on the results of a Web search, check to make sure your results have a legitimate pedigree.

- **Is it accurate?** Joe's Legal Blog may be fun to read, but has Joe accurately reproduced a court opinion or statute? It is always best to check unofficial materials against either an official Web resource or a commercial service that certifies the accuracy of its

materials. A medical study on cancer from a respected hospital's site may be more reliable than a similar report you find on a blog.

- **Is it up to date?** Last year's brilliant website on employment law in Illinois might be wrong or incomplete if there has been a new statute, regulation, or case since it was last updated. Attorneys are always concerned with the currency of the information they're reading.

- **Is it easy to use?** Many court websites are harder to use than commercial services such as Westlaw. It may save your client a few dollars in search costs, but if it takes you twice as long to find the information, the total bill won't be any less.

- **What is the coverage?** Does the resource cover material only up to a certain date? Can you tell easily? How can you get the most up-to-date information? Your clients are paying for your expertise in research. You must be able to deliver a comprehensive answer to them.

One of the most important skills you must have as a paralegal is the ability to do quality legal research. Your clients and your employer deserve your best efforts, so always make sure you use the best research tools to obtain the most accurate information.

ETHICS WATCH

FINDING ETHICS OPINIONS ON THE WEB

Suppose that your supervising attorney is defending a client in court, and the attorney learns that the client has given testimony that the attorney knows is false. What is the attorney's ethical responsibility in this situation? Should the attorney disclose the client's perjury to the court? Would this be a violation of the attorney-client privilege? Or suppose the attorney learns that the client intends to testify falsely in court. Must the attorney inform the court of the client's intention?

In such situations, the attorney may ask you to find out if the state bar association or the American Bar Association (ABA) has issued an ethical opinion on this issue. You can find this information by accessing **americanbar.org**, where the ABA posts summaries of its ethical opinions. The ABA also posts ethical opinions issued by state bar associations on its website.

Specific Legal Resources

Besides the sites just mentioned, which offer access to a broad range of resources, other websites provide legal information within specific areas. We discuss just a sampling here.

Secondary Sources of Law

The savvy legal researcher realizes that consulting a relevant secondary source at the beginning of a research project may save time and effort, as the source should provide a good overview of the law in an area and point to leading cases and issues. Many secondary sources, such as commercially published legal encyclopedias and treatises, are not likely to be found online for free. However, an increasing number of law review articles are published free online by the law review's institution.

Individual law review articles are not organized by topic. One volume of a law journal may include articles on topics ranging from changes in the laws of bankruptcy litigation to the theoretical property laws of space. Therefore, without a citation to a specific law review article, you must search by topic to find articles on point.

Google Scholar. Google Scholar (**scholar.google.com**) indexes the content of databases that make themselves available to Google. Although not comprehensive, Google Scholar is easy to use and free. Selecting "Articles" under the search box will enable you to search by key words, author, publisher, and date.

Google Scholar also provides multiple ways to build on an initial search. If an article looks relevant to the original search query, the "Cited By" and "Related Articles" hyperlinks beneath the article can be useful in leading you to other sources. The "Cited By" option provides a function similar to Lexis's *Shepard's* citator and West's *KeyCite* (discussed later). This function allows you to scan article footnotes to find the sources from which the author derived his or her information. "Cited By" helps you discover relevant articles that were written after the publication of the current search result.

The SSRN. The SSRN, formerly known as the Social Science Research Network, is another online location (**ssrn.com**) for finding secondary authorities. Many legal scholars publish (or republish) their work on this website. Access to the website is free after registering an account, and it contains tags and abstracts that simplify the search process. Similarly, many universities have "digital commons" where legal faculty members publish (or republish) their work.

Court Opinions

More than a century's worth of United States Supreme Court opinions are available on FindLaw (**findlaw.com**), and several decades' worth are available through LII at Cornell Law School. You can also find the Supreme Court's opinions on its website (**supremecourt.gov**). Archived audio recordings and text of Supreme Court oral arguments from 1955 onward are found on the Oyez Project (**oyez.org**), along with brief summaries of the facts, issues, and decisions of the Court. Federal appeals courts began to place opinions on the Internet in the early 1990s. For information about federal courts and the cases they release, see **uscourts.gov**. FindLaw also provides access to federal district courts, as well as to state courts and other state bodies. (See this chapter's *Featured Contributor* article on the following pages for tips on conducting research online.)

We have already discussed Google Scholar's article-search capability. Google Scholar has built a vast, although incomplete, collection of federal and state case law. Again, the "Cited By" hyperlink provides a similar function to *Shepard's* or *KeyCite*. While Google Scholar's citation function is not as complete or easy to navigate as Lexis's or commercial citators, Google provides a free and easy-to-use starting point for researching unfamiliar areas of the law. Regardless of which search tool you use, remember the rules covered in this chapter's *Office Tech and Cybersecurity* feature on page 222.

Dockets

Justia (**dockets.justia.com**) provides a way to search for information included in case dockets of lawsuits recently filed in federal court. State court dockets are usually located on each state court's website. For example, if you are looking for a recent motion filed in the Florida Supreme Court, you can search the dockets on Florida's state court website, **flcourts.org**.

Federal Law Starting Points

The website **usa.gov** is the official portal to U.S. government information. The A–Z Index of U.S. Government Departments and Agencies on that site provides an exhaustive list of links to every branch of the federal government. The U.S. Government Publishing Office's collection of government information online (**govinfo.gov**) provides links to the *Code of Federal Regulations*, the *Congressional Record*, the *Federal Register*, all bills introduced in Congress, the *United States Code*, and other government publications. The Library of Congress's website, **congress.gov**, provides a daily congressional digest, a link to the Law Library of Congress, and the full text of laws passed by Congress, as well as summaries of bills. This website is a good place to find information about the status of a bill before Congress. Finally, the U.S. Department of Justice (**justice.gov**) provides information on federal criminal prosecutions and the enforcement of the federal laws of civil rights, employment discrimination, and immigration.

Federal Legislative Home Pages

The U.S. House of Representatives website at **house.gov** provides links to representatives' roll-call votes, the Congressional schedule, current debates on the House floor, and websites of representatives. The U.S. Senate site (**senate.gov**) hosts a Virtual Reference Desk with links to more than sixty topics pertaining to the Senate's history and operations. The site also displays roll-call votes, information about recent legislative activity, and links to sites of senators.

FEATURED CONTRIBUTOR

TIPS FOR DOING ONLINE LEGAL RESEARCH

Matt Cornick

BIOGRAPHICAL NOTE

Matthew S. Cornick is a graduate of SUNY at Buffalo and the Emory University School of Law. He has been teaching legal research, law office technology, and introduction to law and ethics to paralegal students for more than twenty-five years. He frequently speaks to paralegal associations and law firms on the topic of technology in the law office. Cornick has served on the Approval Commission to the American Bar Association's Standing Committee on Paralegals. He is the author of *Using Computers in the Law Office*, Eighth Edition (Cengage Learning).

Online legal research can make research easier, more efficient, and more thorough. But for some students, and some practicing legal professionals, online legal research offers the prospect of the inherent difficulties of legal research combined with the frustration of working with computers. I have been in your shoes, and I can assure you that everything is going to be all right. In that spirit, here is some advice for completing your online legal research with a minimum of hassle and distress.

Tip 1: Think Before You Begin the Research.

Much of the frustration that students feel when researching online is due to the lack of proper preparation. Make sure you know precisely which terms you will use in your search query. Prepare a list of alternative terms. For example, if you are researching an issue relating to divorce, it might be found under "Divorce" or "Dissolution" or "Marriage, Termination of" or "Husband and Wife."

Business Information

The U.S. Department of Commerce (**commerce.gov**) provides a wealth of business and economic statistical data and other information. The U.S. Patent and Trademark Office provides many resources regarding patents and trademarks at **uspto.gov**. Information on copyrights and a searchable database of copyright records is provided by the U.S. Copyright Office at **copyright.gov**. The Equal Employment Opportunity Commission (EEOC) posts information on employment discrimination, EEOC regulations, and enforcement at **eeoc.gov**.

Numerous resources to help in forming, financing, and operating small businesses are offered by the Small Business Administration at **sba.gov**. The Securities and Exchange Commission maintains public companies' electronic filings at **sec.gov** (see the Filings menu for a link to its EDGAR database, which will be described later in this chapter). **The website usa.gov/statistics** provides access to the statistical information compiled by federal agencies, including information about population, crime, and income.

Other Resources

Many law libraries create research guides on various topics of law. Georgetown University Law Library maintains an extensive collection of up-to-date research guides (**guides. ll.georgetown.edu/home**). These guides provide a comprehensive overview of sources

Tip 2: There Is No Need to Reinvent the Wheel.

By searching in legal encyclopedias, law journals, treatises, and the like, you can tap into a world of useful information. This is especially true if you review the footnotes. This is where you will find specific references to cases, statutes, and administrative regulations.

Tip 3: Both Westlaw and Lexis Offer Online Training Lessons.

Westlaw offers a free certification program (it does not require access to Westlaw) at **training.west-law.com/paralegal**.

Tip 4: Utilize a Variety of Online Legal Research Websites.

For example, Google now offers the ability to research case law using Google Scholar (**scholar.google.com**).

Tip 5: Use Time Wisely to Avoid Extra Costs.

Know whether the tool you plan to use permits unlimited use or charges by the minute. While in paralegal school, you may have free access to Westlaw or Lexis. Rest assured, in the real world, there is no "free access." Make sure you have permission to use Westlaw or Lexis and keep an eye on the clock. Do not use $500 worth of time to solve a $100 problem.

Tip 6: Keep Your Skills Current.

Westlaw is now Westlaw Edge; Lexis is now Lexis Advance. These new versions make online legal research even more intuitive.

Tip 7: Keep Track of Your Research.

Making mistakes during legal research is unavoidable. Making the same mistakes twice (or more) is completely avoidable. Making a list of all the cases, statutes, articles, and other sources you have reviewed will save time and aggravation.

Tip 8: Develop the Ability to Cite Check Primary Authorities.

Take the time in school to gain the expertise employers will value. Here is an online resource you may find useful: **law.cornell. edu/citation**.

Tip 9: Know When to Walk Away.

Once you start seeing the same cases and statutes over and over again, you have probably found everything worth finding.

Tip 10: Don't Worry.

You are not going to break the Internet. Make mistakes, but learn from them.

Source: Matt Cornick

> " Make mistakes, but learn from them."

to consult in your research. Each guide lists relevant primary and secondary sources, books, Internet resources, and electronic resources that the school's library can access.

A state library's research guide is a great place to find an extensive list of state resources. For example, the New York State Library has a useful guide for researching legislative history for New York law. The School of Law at Indiana University maintains a site that provides links to legislative materials for all states, as well as information on many other legal topics.

Lexis and Westlaw

Most legal researchers use Lexis and Westlaw (Lexis is part of LexisNexis Group and is supplemented by Lexis Advance; Westlaw, owned by Thomson Reuters, was replaced by Westlaw Edge, and we use the respective terms interchangeably). They are the dominant fee-based providers in the legal research business. The services are comprehensive, and once you become familiar with them, they are user friendly. Subscribers pay for the use of these services, and they are expensive. Different law firms pay different rates depending on their contracts with the providers.

Both Westlaw and Lexis include searchable versions of federal and state cases, statutes, and regulations. Additionally, they both contain many law reviews, treatises,

OFFICE TECH AND CYBERSECURITY

STAY AHEAD OF THE CURVE

You can quickly find a long list of cases through online databases. But research requires more than turning on a computer, connecting to Lexis or Westlaw, and pressing "print." Your attorneys need the *most relevant* cases, and it takes skill to winnow a list of search results down to the important cases. Moreover, technical problems can disrupt even a careful research strategy, and there are budget constraints to consider. Here are some tips to help deal with the realities of life as a legal researcher.

Rule 1: Never put off research to the last minute. What seems like a simple research question can be complicated. Your server may fail at a crucial time, for instance. Be prepared—if your firm's Internet connection goes out, don't panic. Know how to switch your research to a smartphone or tablet Internet connection. Nearby alternative locations are often available, from libraries to coffee shops. And always start your research early enough to allow for being thorough, as well as following up on unexpected leads you discover.

Rule 2: Be familiar with low-cost and free alternatives to commercial legal research databases. Westlaw and Lexis are great tools, but sometimes clients cannot afford the cost of their use. Many websites provide free access to court rules and forms as well as links to useful sources of legal information on the Web. As mentioned in the text, for example, Cornell Law School's Legal Information Institute (LII) offers free and reliable access to court opinions, statutes, and more. Google Scholar (**scholar.google.com**) allows researchers to run key-word searches for cases and legal articles. These resources can help you get research done inexpensively. But keep in mind that "cheap" is not always less expensive. If you use twice as much research time on a free site as you would on a paid site, the "free" one may be more expensive overall.

Rule 3: Have a backup system and use it. Make sure you regularly archive your research on a server or other location. Your firm likely has a backup system for computers. Find out how it works and what steps you need to take to keep your research files secure and backed up. Many firms use a cloud backup service to ensure that key materials are also stored off-site—but the cloud service must offer adequate security. Be equally sure you are not putting sensitive materials on portable media, such as a flash drive, that could be lost.

Rule 4: Download and archive. Don't rely on being able to find a crucial document you saw on the Web again. Websites vanish, are reorganized, and change content. Download and store crucial information on your computer or print it out, but make sure you can find what you need quickly. Tools such as X1 (**x1.com**), Copernic (**copernic.com/en/**), and Instant File Find (**popusoft. com/instant-file-find/**) make finding files stored on your computer quick and easy. Free-form databases, such as DEVONthink (for Macs) and askSam (for both PCs and Macs), allow you to create sets of information of varied materials for quick retrieval. Free browser extensions such as Zotero (**zotero.org**) and Evernote (**evernote.com**) allow you to save documents and Web clippings to a cloud-based personal account accessible from any computer. Find a tool that works for you and master it.

Rule 5: Plan ahead. As you plan your work on a case, think about what resources you must have to accomplish each task. What documents will you need so you can keep working on the project if your office is closed? Are there any things that cannot be done securely off-site? Do you have all the relevant passwords and login information needed to access websites to continue researching off-site? Which deadlines are coming up? A missed deadline can mean that your client loses the case.

legal encyclopedias, legal forms, public records, newspapers and magazines, and other sources. Both services are particularly popular for their *KeyCite* and *Shepard's* citator services (discussed below). Westlaw's Key Number service, which arranges the issues in case law into categories, is a fundamental part of many legal research projects, as we discussed in the previous chapter. *KeyCite* builds upon that service.

Accessing Westlaw or Lexis

A subscriber can access Westlaw (WestlawNext) and Lexis (Lexis Advance) via **westlaw.com** and **advance.lexis.com**, respectively. The opening pages are seen in Exhibit 8.1 and Exhibit 8.2. To use most of the legal research tools offered by these services, you must subscribe to them and obtain a password. Once you have a password,

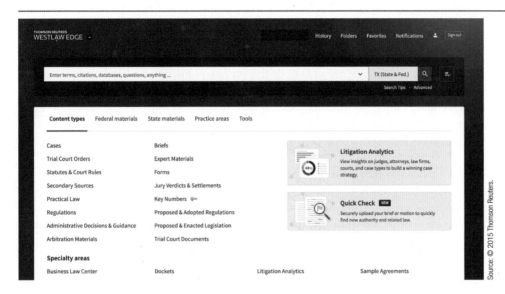

Source: © 2015 Thomson Reuters.

EXHIBIT 8.1

Opening Screen of Westlaw Edge

when you sign on to the service, a welcome page is displayed. You can then begin your research. You can conduct a search, check citations, review documents related to a case or topic, set up alerts, and track previous research trails. Documents can also be saved to project-specific research folders, highlighted, and annotated digitally. Printing options will allow for your notes to be included within the documents.

Conducting a Search

Veteran users of either Westlaw or Lexis know how much the look of both databases has changed over the past decade. With the rise in Google's popularity, many databases have simplified their user interfaces to incorporate a single, Google-like search box.

Regardless of the change in appearance, Westlaw and Lexis still allow subscribers to locate documents using various search-and-browse methods. If you have the citation for a document, such as a court case or statute, you can enter the number and quickly call up the document. If you do not know the citation number, you can search according to legal topic, by case or party name, or by publication.

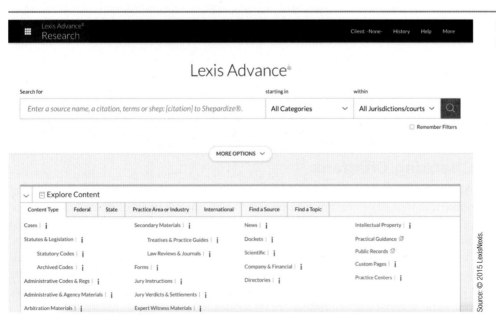

Source: © 2015 LexisNexis.

EXHIBIT 8.2

Opening Screen of Lexis Advance

Although a single search box looks easy to use, this type of searching comes with its own advantages and disadvantages. Simply typing a few key words in the search box will yield results from all databases your firm can access. Casting a wide search net can be helpful when you are unsure of the precise phrasing of a legal term or simply want to see what kinds of cases or secondary sources discuss a particular legal concept. A disadvantage of this approach is that unless you narrow your search to only a few databases, searches conducted through the main search bar can easily turn up thousands of documents. Not only does wading through a long list of results become overwhelming and time consuming, but it can also rack up hefty charges for a firm that does not pay a flat-rate subscription for either Westlaw or Lexis.

Additionally, both Westlaw and Lexis have the single search box set to interpret your query as a natural language search, which means you can type a phrase, sentence, or question to indicate what you are looking for. This method contrasts with the more traditional Boolean searching approach, in which key words are joined by "operator words" such as *and, not,* and *or* that serve to tailor the results. Natural language searching uses the database's own unique algorithm, which ranks document relevance on factors such as the frequency with which your search terms appear in a document.

The natural language method of searching is ideal when you know only a few basic search terms or need general information. When initiating a natural language search query, you use the same terms that you would if you were describing this topic to another person. For example, if you are researching whether a client in Louisiana is responsible when his dog bites another dog, you may search for the terms "dog bite liability Louisiana." Note that a researcher could enter a search query at the initial screen, and then narrow down the results that appear on the left side of the screen by jurisdiction, date, damages, and so forth.

Alternatively, Boolean searching, sometimes referred to as "terms-and-connector" searching, allows the user to construct sophisticated searches with less chance of including irrelevant documents. Boolean searches can often resemble complicated math equations. This is because Boolean searching uses symbols and shortcuts to control a search.

Following the dog bite example above, you can craft a specific Boolean search for the same query to weed out irrelevant results. A Boolean search for "(("dog bite" & liability) /p Louisiana) & DA(aft 12-31-1990)" means that you are searching for any variation of the phrase "dog bite." This includes "dog bites," "dog biting," and so forth. Additionally, results must include the words "dog bite" and "liability" within the same paragraph as "Louisiana." These results are further narrowed down by defining the date range. Adding "DA" to the query shows that you only want results dated after December 31, 1990. Notice how this form of tailored searching provides much more control over initial search results.

To craft Boolean searches, find the advanced search button located on both Lexis's and Westlaw's homepage (see Exhibit 8.3 for a Westlaw Boolean search). There, you will find lists of shortcuts to assist you in crafting your search. You will find another description of searching styles under "Search Methods" later in this chapter.

Checking Citations

citator

A book or online service that provides the history and interpretation of a statute, regulation, or court decision and a list of the cases, statutes, and regulations that have interpreted, applied, or modified a statute or regulation.

All paralegals should become familiar with **citators**. A *citator* provides a list of legal references that have cited or interpreted a case, statute, or regulation. A *case citator* provides, in addition, a history of the case. The primary purpose of a case citator is to determine the validity of a case. Secondarily, the purpose is to locate additional sources. A case decided a year or two ago may now be "bad law" if it has been reversed or modified on appeal. A statute may have been amended or held unconstitutional after its passage by a legislature. So whether you are looking at cases, regulations, or statutes, you want to know if your findings are up to date and considered "good law."

EXHIBIT 8.3
Westlaw Advanced Search Screen Shot

The tools provided by *KeyCite* and *Shepard's* allow you to access updated law within seconds. As emphasized in Chapter 7, a crucial part of legal research is making sure your findings are accurate and up to date. If your supervising attorney is preparing for trial, for example, the attorney will want to base a legal argument on current authorities. A precedential case that may have been good law last month may not remain so today.

Both Westlaw and Lexis provide online citators. In Lexis, the primary citator is *Shepard's*. Westlaw provides a similar service, *KeyCite*. For practical purposes, you can think of *Shepard's* and *KeyCite* as performing much the same functions. The *Developing Paralegal Skills* feature on the following page discusses some extra points about *KeyCite*.

Note that *Shepard's Citations* is available in print as well as online. However, most libraries and law firms no longer subscribe to the print citators because most attorneys prefer to use the online version.

Information Provided by *Shepard's* and *KeyCite*

Paralegals use *Shepard's* and *KeyCite* citators to accomplish several research objectives:

- **Parallel citations**—On occasion, a court's opinion may be published in several different sets of books. Cases that have multiple citations are referred to as having parallel citations. Both *Shepard's* and *KeyCite* list those parallel citations.

- **Other cases**—When you check a case or other law in a citator, you will find a list of cases. These are citing cases; that is, they are cases that cite the case you looked up in the citator ("the cited case"). Because they cite the case you are researching, these cases may deal with the same issue and may therefore may be of interest to an attorney.

- **References to periodicals, treatises, and *American Law Reports* annotations**—If you are researching a case on point, *Shepard's* and *KeyCite* may include references to periodicals and treatises that cite that case. A book or article that references the cited case may provide a valuable discussion of the issues in the cited case, as well as referring to other, related cases.

- **Case history**—As mentioned, the citators provide a history of the cited case. For example, they will tell you if the decision in your case on point has been overturned on appeal (or if any further action has been taken).

KeyCite
An online citator on Westlaw that can trace case history, retrieve secondary sources, categorize legal citations by legal issue, and perform other functions.

Shepard's
An online citator on Lexis that provides a list of all the authorities citing a particular case, statute, or other legal authority.

citing cases
Cases listed in a citator that cite the case being researched.

DEVELOPING PARALEGAL SKILLS

CITE CHECKING ON WESTLAW

Katia, a paralegal, needs to check a citation quickly for a case from the court of appeals to see if it is still good law. Her supervising attorney wants to use the case in a brief that must be filed within a few hours. Katia accesses Westlaw. She enters her password and client-identifying information. Once she has gained access, she enters the case citation in the main search box. The search turns up a red flag in the top left corner, which means that at least part of the case has been reversed or overruled and is no longer good law.

Katia clicks on the red flag, which takes her to the decision in which the previous decision was reversed or overruled. It turns out that part of the decision was reversed on grounds that were not related to the rule of law for which her supervising attorney wants to cite the case. Katia and her supervisor can use the case in their brief after all, because the issue they are researching is still good law.

Tips for Using *KeyCite*

- A red flag means that a decision has been reversed or overruled for at least one point of law and must be reviewed.
- A yellow flag means that a decision has been questioned or criticized and should be checked.
- A blue-striped flag means that the case has been appealed to the U.S. Court of Appeals or the U.S. Supreme Court.
- Never cite a case without verifying that it is still good law.
- Always read a citing case (discussed shortly) to find out why your case has a flag and to determine what issue has been questioned, reversed, or overruled. A red flag doesn't always mean that the entire opinion has been reversed. The case may still provide the support you need for a particular issue. Similarly, a yellow flag may not be limiting, particularly if the court that questioned the reasoning used in the case is in a jurisdiction irrelevant to your litigation.

Use of Symbols

Shepard's uses an elaborate abbreviation system to provide information on how the cited case has been used or treated in the citing case. See Exhibit 8.4 for a list of the abbreviations. For example, the symbol *f* indicates that a citing case "followed" the reasoning of a cited case. Thus, if a paralegal is "Shepardizing" a state appellate court opinion (the cited case) and finds an *f* before a citation to a subsequent appellate court opinion (the citing case), then the citing case has followed the opinion in the cited case.

Both online citators use a series of color-coded symbols to indicate a law's status. Red stop signs or flags next to a case name, for instance, indicate that the case is no longer good law for at least one of its points. A yellow stop sign or flag indicates that a case has been questioned, distinguished, or criticized by a later court decision. Online user guides that explain more about the symbols used in *KeyCite* and *Shepard's* are available from Westlaw and Lexis.

You can use *Shepard's* or *KeyCite* for almost any legal citation. If you have a regulation, a law review article, or a code section, you can always use a citator to try to find other materials that cite it. If, for instance, you are trying to interpret a code section, you might want to look at the materials that cite it in order to get an idea of how courts have interpreted the code. Similarly, if you are aware of a landmark United States Supreme Court case establishing an important principle of law related to your case, you might search through the citing references and filter them for your jurisdiction to see how those courts have interpreted and applied that principle. This approach is often a fruitful starting point for research.

EXHIBIT 8.4
Abbreviations Used in *Shepard's*

ABBREVIATIONS—ANALYSIS

History of Case

a	(affirmed)	Same case affirmed on rehearing.
cc	(connected case)	Different case from case cited but arising out of same subject matter or intimately connected there with.
m	(modified)	Same case modified on rehearing.
r	(reversed)	Same case reversed on rehearing.
s	(same case)	Same case as case cited.
S	(superseded)	Substitution for former opinion.
v	(vacated)	Same case vacated.
US cert den		*Certiorari* denied by U.S. Supreme Court.
US cert dis		*Certiorari* dismissed by U.S. Supreme Court.
US reh den		Rehearing denied by U.S. Supreme Court.
US reh dis		Rehearing dismissed by U.S. Supreme Court.

Treatment of Case

c	(criticized)	Soundness of decision or reasoning in cited case criticized for reasons given.
d	(distinguished)	Case at bar different either in law or fact from case cited for reasons given.
e	(explained)	Statement of import of decision in cited case. Not merely a restatement of the facts.
f	(followed)	Cited as controlling.
h	(harmonized)	Apparent inconsistency explained and shown not to exist.
j	(dissenting opinion)	Citation in dissenting option.
L	(limited)	Refusal to extend decision of cited case beyond precise issues involved.
o	(overruled)	Ruling in cited case expressly overruled.
p	(parallel)	Citing case substantially alike or on all fours with cited case in its law or facts.
q	(questioned)	Soundness of decision or reasoning in cited case questioned.

Source: LexisNexis.

Selecting Databases

The legal research materials available through Westlaw and Lexis draw from thousands of databases. As discussed earlier, searching in the main search box on Lexis's or Westlaw's homepage yields results from every one of these databases. Instead, paralegals often need to limit their searches to specified databases. On Westlaw, you can find specific databases in multiple ways. The first is simply searching for that database in the main search bar. For example, if you enter "tax" into the search bar, a dropdown menu will reveal suggestions of databases. If you would rather drill down further, you can browse databases by federal and state material, practice areas of law, and tools.

Note that Westlaw recognizes database identifiers, which are a common shortcut used to direct searches into a particular database. For example, you can start your search by trying "ca-cs" to direct Westlaw to search all California cases. However, with the move toward natural language searching, you can also use key words to find recommended databases.

Lexis functions similarly to Westlaw when navigating through databases. You can search for the database in the main search box, as well as browse databases by content type, jurisdiction, topics, and sources in the Explore Content box. (See Exhibit 8.5.)

EXHIBIT 8.5

Lexis Advance Explore Content Browse

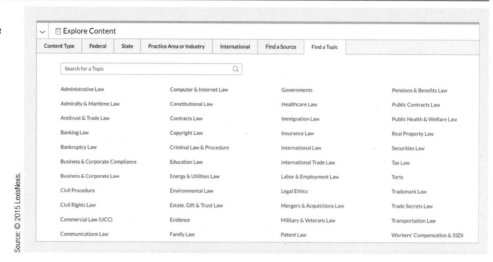

For example, suppose your supervising attorney has asked you to research case law on the liability of tobacco-product manufacturers for cancer caused by the use of tobacco products. To investigate, you need to search the databases containing decisions from all state courts, as well as from all federal courts. By working your way through the "Explore Content" box on Lexis, or conducting a similar search in Westlaw, you will be able to find the databases containing decisions from all state and federal courts.

Search Methods

As discussed previously, Lexus and Westlaw use two basic search methods: Boolean and natural language. Generally, when drafting a search query, make sure the query is not too broad. If you entered just the term *liability*, for example, your search would be futile because so many thousands of documents contain that term. At the same time, you do not want your search to be so narrow that no cases will be retrieved.

Boolean Searches

A search employing terms and connectors, or a Boolean search, uses numerical and grammatical connectors to specify the relationships of the terms. For example, to find cases on the liability of tobacco products manufacturers for cancer caused by the use of the products, you could type the following terms and connectors in the query box:

> liability /p cancer /s tobacco

This would retrieve all cases in which the term *liability* is in the same paragraph ("/p") as the term *cancer*, with the term *cancer* in the same sentence ("/s") as the term *tobacco*. To restrict the scope of your search, you can add a field restriction. For example, you might want to retrieve only court opinions rendered after 2016. If you are using Westlaw, you could add the following to your query to restrict the search results to cases decided after 2016:

> & DA (12/31/2016)

Many other grammatical and numerical connectors can be used to efficiently search a database. These are listed in the instructions provided to Lexis and Westlaw subscribers.

The Natural Language Method

The natural language method allows you to type a description of an issue without the use of terms and connectors in order to retrieve the most relevant documents.

In searching for cases relating to the topic in the previous example, your query might read as follows:

Is a tobacco manufacturer liable for cancer caused by the use of its products?

This query would retrieve the documents most closely matching your description. You could also write a query that consisted only of the most important key words:

tobacco manufacturer liable cancer products

Including synonyms in the search may sometimes be necessary to produce more comprehensive results.

Searching within Results

Often, once you have retrieved your search results, you would like to quickly locate certain key information. For example, suppose that your search resulted in a list of twenty cases relevant to your topic. At this point, Westlaw's "Search within Results" tool allows you to scan the documents in your search result for terms that were not included in your query.

Assume that your original request was, in natural language, "Is a tobacco manufacturer liable for cancer caused by the use of its products?" If you want to know whether "death" is discussed in any of your search-result documents, you can use the "Search within Results" tool on either Westlaw or Lexis.

When browsing through your search results, remember that the time you spend using the service online is costly. Although different electronic database service providers, such as Westlaw, Lexis, and Bloomberg, structure their pricing differently (for example, by search, by click, or by time), remember that the hours you spend researching one item is time you are not researching a second topic, drafting a memorandum, or assisting with other important work for the firm. If you have found cases that appear to be on point, you can download them for further study. Check with your supervisor before you print out or download materials so you know how charges are incurred for research materials.

Advanced Technology Services

As computer algorithms and data management technologies continue to advance, more intuitive user interfaces are developing. One example of this is Westlaw's "Research Recommendations" tab. During each research session, this Westlaw service will learn from the searches you perform, the documents you click on, and those you do not click on. It will use this information to compile a list of sources that fit the research question it believes you are attempting to answer, including providing some sources you may have missed in your research thus far. More services of this kind are becoming available in the research world and will likely continue to become more effective over the years.

Is Lexis or Westlaw Better?

Because Lexis and Westlaw compete head-on, they provide similar services. The formats are somewhat different, and there are differences in the specialty publications offered. Some users prefer one to the other, but that may be largely a matter of which program they have learned to use. Often, when asked which database is the best, the answer is always whichever service you can access.

In one survey, respondents said that legal researchers could switch between the systems and use *KeyCite* or *Shepard's* to accomplish the same tasks. So while Westlaw may have pulled ahead of Lexis as the dominant seller of premier online services, both do the task well. Respondents to the survey also noted that it is desirable to learn about other, less costly programs. We now turn to some of those offerings.

Alternative Legal Research Sources

Although Lexis and Westlaw control a majority of the market for subscription-based online legal research services, several other fee-based online programs offer more limited but less expensive services. All take advantage of public-access databases, such as those for federal cases. Some have extra search features, usually for higher subscription fees. None is as comprehensive as Westlaw and Lexis, but each provides a lower-cost alternative that can fulfill many research needs.

Bloomberg Law

Bloomberg Law offers primary legal content, court dockets, legal filings, and reports just like Westlaw and Lexis. However, Bloomberg Law also provides unique content, such as the popular Bureau of National Affairs (BNA) law reports. Additionally, because Bloomberg Law is currently an underdog in the market, the service is priced more favorably than Lexis or Westlaw services.

PACER

Public Access to Court Electronic Records (PACER) (**pacer.gov**) is an Internet service that allows users to obtain federal court cases and docket information from federal circuit, district, and bankruptcy courts. While PACER contains court opinions, its chief purpose is to provide a site where attorneys and other court personnel can view documents filed in federal litigation. A user might access PACER to view a complaint filed in a lawsuit in federal court, for example.

Fastcase

Fastcase (**fastcase.com**) provides access to all Supreme Court decisions, federal appeals decisions back to 1924, and federal district court decisions back to 1932. For most research, that is adequate. Fastcase also has bankruptcy court decisions, as well as decisions of state supreme courts and appeals courts back to 1950. All federal and state statutes, constitutions, and administrative codes are included. A unique feature of Fastcase is "BadLawBot," which provides red flags for possible bad law. Fastcase's opening screen is shown in Exhibit 8.6.

Annual and monthly subscription fees for Fastcase are lower than those for Lexis and Westlaw, which has enhanced the system's popularity. Many state bar associations, such as those in Illinois and Ohio, have arranged for members to have access to Fastcase as part of membership, so it is becoming more widely used.

Casemaker

Similar to Fastcase, Casemaker (**public.casemakerlegal.net**), which includes Casemaker Legal Research and CasemakerPRO, is provided by many state bar associations to their members as a part of bar membership. Casemaker provides essentially the same set of federal and state case reports, statutes, and regulations as most other services. In some states, it provides state-specific documents, such as opinions of attorneys general, jury instructions, links to court forms, local federal court rules, and other helpful materials. Casemaker has been expanding its services, so it is worth reviewing its latest capabilities.

VersusLaw

VersusLaw (**versuslaw.com**) is a low-cost service that includes Supreme Court and U.S. Court of Appeals cases and current federal district court cases, as well as state appellate court cases and cases of some specialized courts. A higher-level subscription plan includes federal district court opinions back to about 1950, along with state

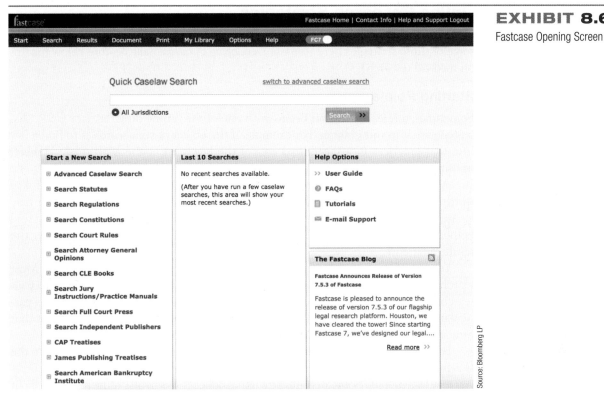

Source: Bloomberg LP

EXHIBIT 8.6

Fastcase Opening Screen

statutes and regulations. The highest-level plan includes the *United States Code* and the *Code of Federal Regulations* and provides added search features. VersusLaw has limited access to publications that are not in the public domain, so it primarily offers a reasonably priced means to access reported court cases and federal regulatory materials.

Conducting Online Research

As we have seen, the Internet dominates how paralegals gather information while doing legal research. In addition to investigating the applicability of case law to clients' cases, paralegals often research other matters as well. They may need to locate people, gather information about companies, or conduct other practical, fact-based research into matters not directly related to legal issues. There are numerous online databases that make it possible to perform such research quickly and efficiently.

Your goal when conducting any online research is to find accurate, up-to-date information on the topic you are researching in a minimum amount of time. As anyone who has used the Internet knows, it is possible to spend hours navigating through cyberspace looking for specific information. Planning your research in advance and using a variety of research strategies, such as those discussed in this section, can help you achieve your goal of conducting thorough online research efficiently.

Plan Ahead—
Analyze the Facts and Identify the Issues

Once you have been given a particular research project, you should plan your research steps before going online. The first step is to know what you are seeking. To avoid wasting time and money, outline your objectives clearly and be sure you understand your goals. To narrow the scope of your research, you may need to know the reason for the research or how the results will be used.

Online Research Strategies

Once online, you can use many strategies to find what you are looking for. We discuss some of those strategies here (see the *Developing Paralegal Skills* feature below for tips on medical research).

Starting Points

Sometimes, a research session begins with one of the online directories or guides discussed earlier in this chapter. For example, if the object of your search is to find a law firm that practices in a specialized area of the law, start at the Martindale-Hubbell website (**martindale.com**).

A search engine can be used to compile a list of websites containing certain key words. Keep in mind the limitations of search engines, however. Your search may locate many irrelevant sources and may not lead you to every site that you would find helpful. In addition, different search engines will yield different results or order the results differently.

You may have to try several searches before you get to the right websites. Most search engines contain an advanced search feature that will help you refine your search. For instance, Google's advanced search will let you limit your search to particular phrases, eliminate unwanted words from your results, or find Web pages that were added to the Web after a particular date.

From the preliminary results of a general search, you can click on the links to the sites and determine which are useful. Many sites include their own links to other sources you may find helpful. Some websites attempt to collect links to all online resources about particular topics. These sites include directories, which were discussed earlier, as well as other sites, such as **usa.gov**, which provides links to federal offices and agencies.

Discovering Available Resources

Despite your best intentions and attempts to focus your research, you may have to approach a project without a clear objective regarding what you need to find. Your initial research goal may be to discover the extent of resources available online, with your ultimate goal being to obtain more precise results.

DEVELOPING PARALEGAL SKILLS

MEDICAL RESEARCH ON THE INTERNET

Thom Shannon needs to locate information on bipolar disorder. Thom's supervising attorney is trying to prove that the defendant in a case has this mental condition. Thom runs a Google search on "bipolar disorder" and finds a reference to the Mayo Clinic's website (**mayoclinic.org**). He searches within the Mayo Clinic's site for articles describing this disorder. Thom finds several citations to articles, along with summaries of the articles, but the full text of the articles is not online. He goes to the library at the local medical school to obtain the full text of the articles he cannot find by using Google Scholar or other search services.

Tips for Performing Medical Research Online

- Become familiar with medical terminology.
- Search the appropriate medical categories on the website.
- Locate appropriate articles and summaries.
- If the full text of the articles is not available online, go to the nearest medical school's library to obtain the articles.
- Make sure that your information is taken from a reputable website.

Check the Law Libraries.   Keep in mind that there are several different approaches you can take to find legal resources on the Web. As noted before, many law school libraries provide online subject guides to legal issues. These subject guides typically discuss the basic sources used for research in a particular field, and on occasion provide information about the best approaches for researching particular issues. For instance, Georgetown Law Library has an extensive list of the major books available for a particular legal field in its online legal treatise finder (**guides. ll.georgetown.edu/home/treatise-finders**). Most law schools provide a guide to searching Google or another search engine for words, such as *tax law treatise* or *tax law research*, that will retrieve a list of relevant websites.

Many libraries provide access to their catalogs online (see, for example, the New York Public Library's website at **catalog.nypl.org** or Yale Law School's catalog at **morris.law.yale.edu**). You can search these catalogs on the Internet just as you would search them in the library, saving you the time that you otherwise might spend traveling to the library. Often, you can arrange to have source material from a distant library delivered to a closer library or directly to you.

Usually, state university, courthouse, or state law libraries are open to the public. You may think the only value of entering a library to conduct research is the opportunity to look through printed materials. However, there are many benefits to researching within the confines of a library. The first is the ability to communicate your research needs to a reference librarian. Law librarians have expertise in navigating legal information and can quickly point out the best resource for your needs. Furthermore, many universities provide public access to their database subscriptions. If a pay wall blocks a resource you are looking for, it can be beneficial to check with your local library to see if you can access that resource on one of the library computers. Additionally, many public universities offer patrons limited access to databases in Westlaw and Lexis.

Blogs.   Another way to find out what resources are available is to begin with a blog, which is essentially an online journal. Millions of people generate blogs on a regular basis, and they can be used to update your research. Some blogs are well established, while others disappear as the authors tire of them. The American Bar Association's *ABA Journal* website maintains a list of legal blogs (**abajournal.com/blawgs**).

Browsing the Links

As you browse through the links that could be useful for your research, you will need to keep track of the websites you visit. Marking a site as a "Favorite" (Internet Explorer) or adding a "Bookmark" (Firefox, Safari, or Chrome) for the site is an electronic substitute for keeping a book on your desk. With these, you can create an automatic link to any point on the Web. Once you have added a bookmark, you can return to that site again without searching for it. For example, you might want an automatic link to the site at which you begin your research: a directory, a search engine, or a site that has many links that relate to what you need.

Narrowing Your Focus

Once you find a website that could be useful, you will probably need to zero in on specific data within that site. One way to do this, of course, is to use the links within the site.

Remember that your browser also has the ability to search a Web page that you are viewing. This can be particularly helpful when you are attempting to review a long document on the Web for a particular word or phrase. Assume that you found the text of a bill being considered by Congress at the Library of Congress's site (**congress.gov**). Your browser's "Find" tool (ctrl+f or cmd+f) will let you search through that bill—which might be very lengthy—for a particular phrase. You might also use your find tool to search a company's document in the Electronic Data Gathering, Analysis, and Retrieval (EDGAR) database of the Securities and Exchange Commission (SEC) (go to **sec.gov/edgar.shtml** and select "Filings"). EDGAR is an indexed collection of documents and forms that public companies are required to file with the SEC. The "Find" tool is also helpful for searching through cases in Lexis, Westlaw, and other services for particular phrases, such as "assumption of the risk" or "contributory negligence."

Evaluating What You Find

After you have found what appears to be exactly what you are looking for, you need to consider its reliability and credibility. Ask yourself whether the source of the information is a primary, a secondary, or a tertiary source. Primary sources include company websites, experts, and persons with firsthand knowledge. For example, the inventor of a product would be a primary source for information about the invention.

Publicly filed documents are also primary sources. For example, the legal forms that companies are required to file with the Securities and Exchange Commission are good primary sources for the information that they contain (see the discussion of company investigations later in this chapter).

Secondary sources include books and periodicals (such as law journals, newspapers, and magazines) and their online equivalents, which contain "secondhand" information.

Tertiary sources are any other sources that might be used in research (*tertiary* means "third" or "thirdhand"). It is always a good idea to find and interpret primary sources yourself before forming conclusions based on secondary or tertiary sources, though those sources might help you to find the primary sources to begin with.

A researcher also needs to be aware of whether a source is reputable. A reputable source might be an organization that has established itself in a particular field. A less reputable source might be a personal, self-serving home page. Was the information placed on the Web by an organization that may be biased in a certain way? Some people providing information on the Internet may not even be who they represent themselves to be. Online resources are available to help you evaluate websites, including *Georgetown University Library's Guide to Evaluating Internet Resources* **at library. georgetown.edu/tutorials/research-guides/evaluating-internet-content.**

Updating Your Results

Staying current with events in the law and in other areas that relate to your research is important. One way to confirm whether your research results represent the most recent data available is by going online. News sites abound on the Internet. There are general sites sponsored by news organizations, as well as sources such as Google's news search feature (**news.google.com**). Corporate press releases—both current and from archives—can be reviewed at PRNewswire's site, **prnewswire.com**. You can also subscribe to e-mailed newsletters and bulletins from various sites. FindLaw offers many free legal news e-mail services at **newsletters.findlaw.com**. Cornell Law School's Legal Information Institute will e-mail subscribers bulletins about Supreme Court cases and arguments.

It is very difficult to keep track of every new blog post published on a particular topic. Without subscribing to a listserv or RSS feed, staying up-to-date with current blogs or finding new blogs would require constant Internet searching. One way to keep on top of blogs and news about particular legal topics is to set up a Google Alert, (**google.com/alerts**), seen in Exhibit 8.7. To set up an alert, it is best to have a Google account already. Using your e-mail address, you can then set up alerts for important key

Source: © 2015 Google.

EXHIBIT 8.7
Google Alert Screenshot

words, and you will be notified by e-mail when the service finds new results that match those words. For example, if you set up alerts for "property law" and "takings clause," you will receive regular e-mail with all new websites or blogs that mention those terms.

As discussed earlier, regular searches can also be conducted within Westlaw or Lexis, filtered by date to show the most recent judicial decisions first. Both of these services post opinions relatively soon after their initial date of publication. Additionally, both providers allow for subscribers to set up alerts similar to the Google Alerts just described.

Locating People and Investigating Companies

Paralegals often need to locate people or find information about specific companies, and the Internet can be especially useful in searching for this type of information. There are numerous search services. The comprehensive services charge for their searches.

Finding People

A paralegal may need to find a particular person for various reasons: to assist a lawyer in collecting a debt, administering an estate, serving a summons, or preparing a case for court, for example. (We will discuss this topic more in Chapter 11.) Not all public-record information can be found on the Internet, but search engines such as Instant Checkmate can be helpful. Conducting searches online can be more effective and faster than going to a government office. Sometimes, using a commercial locator service or database can also be less costly than a trip out of the office to the local courthouse or state archives. Some versions of Lexis include limited personal background information services.

Broad Searches.   Online, a researcher can run a broad search with a general search engine such as Google. A researcher might narrow the focus of a search to, say, all U.S. telephone books. There are several phone book websites, such as **whitepages. com**. Some sites provide business listings (for example, **superpages.com**). Some can conduct a reverse lookup search with a telephone number or an e-mail address to reveal a name and a street address (for example, **ZabaSearch.com**).

Narrow Searches. If you know something about a person, such as an employer or a profession, you can use that information to narrow the search. If you are looking for an attorney, you can link to the *West Legal Directory* in Westlaw, a comprehensive compilation of lawyers in the United States, or conduct a search on **lawyers.findlaw.com**. The Martindale-Hubbell directory also provides attorneys' contact information.

If you are looking for a professor at a particular university or an employee at a certain company, you can often search the staff directory of the school or business firm online. LinkedIn, a site for networking professionals, is also a great tool to find personal profiles.

Specialty Search Tools. With the right database, you can verify a person's business license, access information about a federal prison inmate, and find a military member or veteran. (For the latter, see **gisearch.com**.) Information can also be obtained about persons who contribute to federal election campaigns (see Political Money Line at **politicalmoneyline.com**). Adoptees and their birth parents can be located through databases such as **adoption.com** and **omnitrace.com**. For genealogy searches, there are huge databases of facts about family trees and historical events (see, for example, **ancestry.com**). Most local tax assessors' databases (see the Mobile, Alabama, County Revenue Office's website at **mobilecopropertytax.com**) provide information about local property owners and property values.

Fee-Based Searches. Some commercial services provide access to their information for a fee. For example, possible aliases, home value and property ownership, bankruptcies, tax liens, and small claims civil judgments can be searched through US Search at **ussearch.com**. Through a service with access to states' incorporation data and other information, people can be located based on their ownership interests in business organizations. Real property records, bankruptcy filings, and documents relating to court dockets, lawsuits, and judgments can be searched through such sites as KnowX at **knowx.com**.

Social Security numbers can also be verified through the Veris database at **veris.info**. Similarly, the public records databases on Westlaw and Lexis can provide a great deal of background information, such as past addresses, marriage and divorce records, criminal history and arrest records, professional licenses, and other such information. Social Security numbers can be verified through these sites as well.

Investigating Companies

Lawyers often need to know about companies involved in their clients' cases. For example, if a client has suffered an injury caused by a defectively designed product, a lawyer will need to identify the defendant manufacturer, find out whether the manufacturer is a subsidiary of a larger company, and learn the defendant's address. If a client wants to acquire or invest in a particular business firm, research into the firm's background may be vital. A client company's competitors may also be of interest. There are many ways to find some of this information on the Web.

Finding Company Names and Addresses. A researcher can run a search using a telephone number to find a company's name and address (for example, see **superpages.com**). Without a telephone number, a company's name and address can be found with the help of a directory that searches by industry and state (see **whitepages.com**, for example). A search with such a directory can also help determine whether a specific firm name is in use anywhere in the United States. You can find out who owns a domain name by using the domain lookup tool at **whois.com** and other such service providers.

Uncovering Detailed Information about Companies. You can find more detailed company information on company websites, which may contain annual reports, press releases, and price lists. Some companies put their staff directories online.

Information about publicly held companies may be available through the sites of government agencies. For example, the Securities and Exchange Commission (SEC) regulates public companies and requires them to file documents and forms reporting certain information. This material can be accessed through the SEC's EDGAR database, as already mentioned.

Other information about public companies can be found at free sites as well as fee-based sites. Some free sites provide data on the companies and links to the companies' home pages and other sources of information, such as news articles. The *Wall Street Journal*, at **wsj.com**, often includes archives of information that may span decades and may cover companies in other countries. Some of this information is free; some must be purchased. Another source of both free and for-a-fee information on public companies is **corporateinformation.com**. In addition, the newspaper databases on Westlaw and Lexis are good sources of information about companies featured in the media.

Although Lexis and Westlaw tend to have more comprehensive databases than their smaller competitors, Bloomberg Law has compiled a vast trove of company documents and financial records. This material is useful in researching a company's structure, the identity of its principal officers, and basic information on its tax filings and major assets (depending on whether the company is held publicly or privately).

Data on privately held companies is more difficult to find because these firms are not subject to the SEC's disclosure requirements. Much of the information available includes only what the companies want to reveal. There are a few sites that compile some data on private companies, associations, and nonprofit organizations. For example, Hoover's **(hoovers.com)**, a Dun & Bradstreet company, provides brief profiles of many companies, with links to other sites, including search engines. For a fee, Hoover's will provide expanded profiles. Many of Hoover's databases are available through Lexis.

Many guides to online business research are available on the Web. A search on Google for a phrase such as *business research guide online* will retrieve many of them.

Associations and Organizations

When gathering information about a person or a company, you may find it useful to check various professional organizations and associations. The Internet Public Library provides lists of associations by category at **ipl.org** (select "Special Collections" and then "Associations on the Net"). Access to lists of many nonprofit organizations can be found at **idealist.org**.

CHAPTER SUMMARY

ONLINE LEGAL RESEARCH

Free Legal Resources on the Internet

A great deal of legal information, especially public documents such as statutes and cases, is accessible through free Internet sites.

1. *General legal resources*—Some free legal sites act as portals, giving access to a broad range of free information. Major sites include FindLaw and Justia. Another is the Legal Information Institute at Cornell University Law School. Other law schools also provide research source assistance.

2. *Specific legal resources*—Secondary sources are generally not found at free sites. However, an increasing number of law review articles are available. One can also find court opinions and various other legal resources at free sites.

3. *Federal law starting points*—All federal government organizations have Internet sites.

Lexis and Westlaw

For serious legal research, legal professionals often use online commercial legal research services, particularly Lexis and Westlaw.

1. *Accessing Westlaw or Lexis*—Subscribers to these fee-based services can access the services' databases, which include extensive collections of legal, business, and other resources. Using these services, paralegals can access specific documents, update the law, and search hundreds of databases.

2. *Conducting a search*—Both Lexis and Westlaw allow users to search databases with queries using the Boolean (terms-and-connectors) method or the natural language method.

3. *Checking citations*—For citation checking, Lexis provides *Shepard's Citations* and Westlaw provides

KeyCite. Both services enable researchers to make sure their research results are still valid.

4. *Selecting databases*—Because of the mass of data found in many searches, researchers learn to restrict searches to specific databases to perform searches that are more efficient and precise.

5. *Search methods*—Within a given Westlaw or Lexis database, researchers can use natural language searching or Boolean (terms-and-connectors) searching. Researchers can also conduct searches within their initial search results to further refine their searches.

6. *Is Lexis or Westlaw better?*—Both services offer similar features; researchers tend to develop personal preferences.

Alternative Legal Research Sources

Since Westlaw and Lexis are costly to use, less expensive and less comprehensive alternatives have become more popular. Examples include Bloomberg Law, PACER,

Fastcase, Casemaker, VersusLaw, and Google Scholar. Such services may be adequate for some projects and may also be used for preliminary research.

Conducting Online Research

Searching can be costly in time and access fees, so paralegals must become proficient in conducting extensive research as efficiently as possible. The following tips will help you as you learn to make full use of Internet resources:

1. *Plan ahead by analyzing the facts and identifying the issues*—To avoid wasting time, define what you are seeking and determine which sources are most likely to lead you to the desired results.

2. *Develop online research strategies*—Once online, you can use various search tools and other resources (such as listservs, newsgroups, and blogs) to locate information relevant to your topic. Often, researchers need to "browse the links" for a time before finding a site that is particularly relevant. Once you find a useful site, you can use your browser or the site's internal search tool to look for specific information within the site.

3. *Evaluate what you find*—In evaluating your research results, it is especially important to consider the

reliability of any information obtained online. Discriminate among primary sources, secondary sources, and tertiary sources.

4. *Update your results*—To update results, you can access online news sites to look for articles or press releases concerning recent developments in the area you are researching.

5. *Locate people and investigate companies*—Paralegals often engage in online research to locate people and obtain their contact information, and to gather data about companies. Sometimes, a person can be located through a broad search of the Web using a search engine such as Google. Narrow searches can be conducted by accessing—for free or for a fee—specialized databases, such as compilations of physicians, lawyers, or expert witnesses. Searches for persons may also be conducted based on defining characteristics such as place of employment. Numerous online sites contain information about both private and public companies.

KEY TERMS AND CONCEPTS

citator 224   citing cases 225   *KeyCite* 225   *Shepard's* 225

QUESTIONS FOR REVIEW

1. What questions should you ask yourself before going online to perform legal research?

2. List five free legal resources that can be accessed via the Internet.

3. What kinds of legal resources can be accessed at various government sites?

4. What is *KeyCite?* How can Westlaw be used to stay current on the law? Does Lexis have an online citator? Describe two ways in which you can search databases on Lexis and Westlaw.

5. List and briefly describe the dominant fee-based online legal research database services. Do the same for the alternative online legal research databases.

ETHICS QUESTION

1. Tony is doing research for his supervising attorney to include in a brief that has to be filed with the court of appeals by 5 P.M. today. He finds a case that is on point and provides the exact support needed for their argument. In his haste to summarize the case and get it into the brief, Tony fails to update the case using *Shepard's* or *KeyCite.* As a result, he does not inform the attorney that the case was reversed on appeal and is no longer good law. What ethical rule has Tony violated? What impact might Tony's neglect have on the client's case? On Tony's supervising attorney?

PRACTICE QUESTIONS AND ASSIGNMENTS

1. Go to **usa.gov** and locate the website for the Federal Trade Commission (FTC). Click on the link to the FTC site. Answer the following questions:

   a. What is the URL for the Federal Trade Commission?

   b. Where would you go to file an online complaint with the FTC about a weight-loss product? Paste the Web link to the complaint form into your assignment.

   c. To file a complaint about a weight-loss product, what category would you choose? Does the FTC website provide information on what consumers can expect once a consumer complaint has been filed?

2. If you did one of the research assignments in the Chapter 7 *Practice Questions and Assignments* (Question 6 or Question 7), Shepardize one of the cases that you found, using *Shepard's* in print. Is the case still good law, or has it been reversed or overruled? How can you tell? How many citing cases are there? If you have access to Westlaw, Lexis, or any of the alternative legal research sites, update the same case using one of the online sources. Print out the results. Explain the differences between *Shepard's* print and online versions.

3. Do a Google Scholar search for articles about tobacco-products manufacturers' liability when cancer results from the use of their products. How many items did your search retrieve? Print the first two pages of your result to submit to your instructor.

4. You are working as a paralegal for a probate and estate planning law firm. One of the firm's clients died, and now you have to locate all of the heirs. One is a twenty-eight-year-old nephew, whose last known address is a college dorm, according to the records that you have. This nephew was orphaned at the age of seventeen when his parents died in a car accident, so there are no close relatives to help you find him. You reach an aunt who tells you that she believes the nephew is in graduate school in Chicago. Using the material on finding people, which websites would you use in your search to locate the missing nephew? If the free websites do not return any contact information for him, would you use fee-based sites? If so, which ones would you consult?

5. Visit the Martindale-Hubbell website (**martindale.com**). Search for an attorney in your city who does personal injury law. How many results did you find?

GROUP PROJECT

This project has you investigate the alternative legal research databases. Students one, two, and three will go online and find information about what state and federal case and statutory law databases, forms databases, citators, and other services are offered by either Casemaker, VersusLaw, or Fastcase. Each student should write a summary of what is offered and describe the strengths and weaknesses for doing research with that database. Student four will collect and organize the summaries and present them to the class.

©lizkes/Shutterstock.com

CHAPTER
9

Legal Writing:
Form and Substance

CHAPTER OBJECTIVES

After completing this chapter, you will be able to:

- List and explain what a paralegal should consider when accepting a writing assignment.

- Discuss what to consider when drafting a legal document.

- Demonstrate some techniques for improving writing effectiveness.

- List and explain some guidelines for drafting effective paragraphs and sentences.

- Identify whether documents submitted to courts are persuasive or objective, and explain the importance of reading court rules before drafting pleadings.

- Describe the format for legal correspondence and the most common kinds of letters.

- Write a legal memorandum.

Introduction

As a paralegal, you will likely draft a variety of documents, including letters, internal legal memoranda, and pleadings and motions. Legal writing is often closely related to legal research and analysis. Once your research identifies the law that governs an issue, you need to understand the law and, through legal analysis, determine how it applies to a client's case. If your supervising attorney asks you to draft a memorandum, you will need to explicitly summarize your research and analysis in writing. Of course, many writing assignments are not directly related to legal research. For example, you would not need to do any research to write a letter to a client recapping recent developments in her or his case.

Many of the same writing principles apply regardless of the kinds of documents you draft. This chapter discusses (1) what to consider when receiving a writing assignment, (2) how to present a well-written product, and (3) what kinds of documents are commonly prepared by paralegals.

Receiving a Writing Assignment

First, we need to consider what you should do when you receive a writing assignment. When a supervising attorney gives you a writing assignment, you must learn the nature of the assignment, when it needs to be completed, and what kind of writing approach it calls for. We consider each in turn.

Understanding the Assignment

The practice of law can be hectic, and paralegals are often expected to research and write about issues within a short time. When you receive a writing assignment, make sure you understand its exact nature so that you can work as efficiently as possible. If you do not understand the assignment, you will likely waste time doing unnecessary work. Each project is a little different, and your approach will vary depending on the kind of document you are drafting, the complexity of the subject matter, and the reader's needs. If you are uncertain about any aspect of the assignment, ask questions until the assignment is clear in your mind. As the old saying goes, there is no such thing as a stupid question.

Much of a paralegal's work involves legal writing, whether it be a research memorandum, a letter to a client, or a pleading or motion to be filed with a court. Excellent writing skills are a must for the professional paralegal. Assess your own writing skills. Think of ways that you can become a better writer, and start putting them into practice now.

eurobanks/Shutterstock.com

Time Constraints and Flexibility

Knowing the deadline for a writing assignment and adhering to it are essential. Clients and supervising attorneys often need quick answers to questions, and you may need to file a document with a court by a specific date. Missing deadlines could have serious consequences.

Paralegals must be flexible and prepared to deal with changing circumstances. For example, you may discover an important issue in the middle of a trial or when a transaction is being finalized. Similarly, your supervising attorney may change an assignment because the client has charted a new course of action. If possible, budget extra time for the unexpected. Always begin a writing assignment immediately, especially if it involves the participation of others. You will be in a better position to take your work in new directions if necessary.

Writing Approaches

When you get an assignment, you must also determine its purpose. Does it call for objective or persuasive analysis? Some documents call for objective analysis, meaning that you should present a balanced discussion of an issue or a neutral summary of facts. For a persuasive document, you need to advocate for the client by presenting the law, issues, and facts in a favorable light.

Consider a situation in which your supervising attorney asks you to determine whether certain clauses in two lease agreements create different legal obligations. Your assignment is not to argue that one agreement is better. Rather, you need to compare the documents objectively, pointing out which clauses lead to what obligations.

Objective analysis may also be required when a document will help an attorney advise a client. Clients often rely on their attorney to advise them as to whether they have claims that justify filing suit. In such situations, the attorney may ask you to research the issue and draft a memorandum summarizing your analysis. Although you may be tempted to advocate for the client's position, it would be better to present an unbiased discussion. If the client has a weak claim, he or she should learn that before spending time and money on a hopeless lawsuit. You would not do the client any favors by predicting a favorable outcome that is ultimately unlikely.

If you are advocating for a client, in contrast, you need to write persuasively. For example, persuasive analysis is essential if you are drafting a motion asking a court to exclude certain evidence from a trial. When writing persuasively, you should present an analysis that clearly favors the client without misrepresenting the facts or the law.

Writing Well

Law is a communication-intensive profession, so writing is particularly important. For paralegals and attorneys, good writing skills go hand in hand with successful job performance. See the *Developing Paralegal Skills* feature on the following page for tips on creating high-quality documents.

Tools for Writers

As you embark on your career, consider collecting a dictionary, a thesaurus, a style manual (such as *The Chicago Manual of Style*), and a book on proper English use (such as Strunk and White's *Elements of Style*). Those are tools common to all writers. Good legal writing benefits from using tools relevant to such work:

1. Legal writing requires accurate use of legal terminology. Words such as "trusts" or "consideration" have specific meanings that are not necessarily

DEVELOPING PARALEGAL SKILLS

CREATING A USER-FRIENDLY DOCUMENT

Rianna Barnes works as a paralegal for a large law firm. A partner of the firm asks her to draft a policy on sexual harassment for a corporate client. The attorney gives Rianna several sheets of handwritten instructions and some notes on what the document should include. Rianna writes a draft and begins to proofread it.

She realizes that although she used plain English when possible and followed the principles of good writing, the document is somewhat daunting in its appearance. She decides to add a series of headings and subheadings to break up the "fine print" and make the document more visually inviting to readers.

Tips for Creating a User-Friendly Document

- Format the document attractively. For example, add enough margin space to make the text more open and inviting.

- Divide the document into sections with headings to make the organization immediately clear to the reader.

- Add subheadings to further divide large blocks of text. If you use subheadings, always create at least two.

- Make sure the relationships between sections and subsections are clear. You can often do this by drafting an introduction or using transitional sentences at the beginning of each section or subsection.

- Use short sentences, but do not overdo it. Too many short sentences in a row can make the writing choppy and interrupt the flow of the text.

- Use short paragraphs, and group similar ideas together.

- Use the active voice unless the situation calls for a passive construction (discussed later in this chapter).

- Use plain English whenever appropriate, especially when writing for readers who lack legal training.

- Be stylistically consistent. For example, do not hyphenate a phrase in one place but not others, and be sure to use the same line spacing between paragraphs throughout the document.

---

the same as their meaning in ordinary speech. Use a legal dictionary regularly to ensure that you have the right word. *Black's Law Dictionary* is the standard reference.

2. Legal writing has specific rules about how to refer to sources. These citation rules are quite complex, specifying everything from typeface to specific punctuation rules. The rules are set out in *The Bluebook: A Uniform System of Citation* (**legalbluebook.com**) and the *ALWD Guide to Legal Citation* (**alwd.org**).

3. Legal writing requires clarity and organization. Legal writing guru (and editor of *Black's Law Dictionary*) Bryan Garner publishes *The Redbook: A Manual on Legal Style*. The manual provides detailed writing tips and numerous examples of model documents. One of Garner's tips is to read good writing (he recommends *The New Yorker* magazine, for example).

4. Legal writing requires specific organizational features. Some courts have explicit formats that must be followed, so you must learn any particular rules that apply. In general, appellate briefs must include a table of authorities, listing all sources cited and the page on which they are cited. Fortunately, electronic tools can both relieve the tedium of creating these reference lists and improve accuracy. Document-creation programs include tools to assist with citations. Specialized programs, such as Best Authority, can help.

Next, we consider elements needed to produce high-quality legal documents.

Choice of Format

A legal document's formatting can often be quite important. Rather than simply using your document-creation program's default settings for margin widths, paragraph indentations, line spacing, and so forth, you need to confirm that you are using the right formatting for the kind of document you are drafting. If you are drafting a document to be filed in court, you need to check the court's formatting rules, which are often available online. Your employer will probably also have special formats and even templates for certain documents, such as letters and legal memoranda.

Write for Your Reader

Paralegals write for an audience. When you draft a legal document, you are writing for a judge, an attorney, a client, or a witness. To communicate information or ideas effectively, write with the reader's needs in mind. For example, you may use legal terms and concepts in a letter to an attorney, but those terms and concepts may confuse someone who lacks legal training. Similarly, a motion filed in court need not explain legal concepts in detail because your primary reader is the judge or the judge's clerk. A judge knows to follow a governing statute or a binding precedent of a higher court. Adding unnecessary background writing in such a document could distract or even annoy the judge, which will be unfavorable to your client's case.

In addition to the reader's legal knowledge, a paralegal should consider the reader's understanding of the subject matter. You cannot assume that the reader knows as much as you do, especially in cases involving complicated issues. You should normally assume that the reader lacks expertise in the area and is unfamiliar with the key facts and concepts. To help the reader, make the document understandable on its own terms. Be explicit about how everything fits together, leading the reader from Point A to Point B, from Point B to Point C, and so on. Write in a way that would have made sense to you before you began working on the matter.

Outline the Material

Once you know what you want to demonstrate, discuss, or prove to your reader, you must decide how to organize the material. Organization is essential to effective legal writing, so you should have a framework in mind before you begin writing. Most people find that writing is easier if they have an outline. For a simple writing assignment, you may need only to sketch an outline on a notepad. If you are drafting a complicated analysis of a legal issue, on the other hand, you may use a document creator to develop a detailed outline, complete with numbers, letters, and bullet points. An outline helps you write more effectively and efficiently. Your first draft will be better organized, and you will spend less time moving material around.

When creating an outline, your first task is to decide the sequence in which topics should be discussed. Your goal is to organize the points you want to make in a logical fashion. Similar topics should be addressed together, and different topics should generally be addressed separately. Lawyers also often begin with their best points, especially when making arguments. As a matter of logic, however, you may need to work your way up to your best point by first establishing other things. As you outline, think about the advantages and disadvantages of different ways of organizing your information, paying special attention to the document's purpose and the reader's needs.

Organize the Material Logically

Once you begin writing, you need to divide the document into manageable blocks of information. As in an outline, similar topics should generally be addressed together. Also, when analyzing a topic that consists of several elements that must be proved, it is a good idea to address each element in the order in which the elements must be proved.

For example, to have a valid contract, there must be (1) an offer, (2) an acceptance, (3) an exchange of consideration, (4) legal subject matter, and (5) contractual capacity. Thus, it would be logical to organize the material by first listing the elements to be proved and then analyzing each element in the order listed.

Purpose of a Paragraph

The most basic device for organizing ideas in a document is the paragraph. A paragraph is a group of sentences that develops a particular idea. A well-written paragraph often begins with a topic sentence that indicates what the paragraph is about. The paragraph's remaining sentences help develop the topic, leading the reader from one point to another. If a sentence does not relate to the topic of the paragraph, consider moving it to another paragraph or simply deleting it.

When you write, be conscious of why and when you begin new paragraphs. In general, you should start a new paragraph whenever you begin discussing a new topic. If possible, however, you should also keep paragraphs relatively short. Long paragraphs are often hard to follow, and some topics are complicated enough that they deserve multiple paragraphs. As with outlining, you might try using different approaches to organization, seeing what works best given your writing objectives.

Be sure to take your reader with you as you move from one paragraph to another. Although the connections between paragraphs may be clear to you, they may not be clear to your reader. In places, you will need to provide transitional words and phrases to show the reader how different paragraphs relate to each other. Exhibit 9.1 gives some examples of words and phrases that you can use to establish smooth transitions.

Use of Headings

In a long document, you may lead the reader through the discussion by adding descriptive headings and subheadings for different parts of the text. For example, if you are writing about a complex legal research project involving several issues, you may devote a separate section to each issue. You may make the document more reader friendly by providing an introductory "road map" that orients the reader by briefly identifying the issues. In places, you might also use bulleted or numbered lists to highlight key points or make complicated material more approachable. Try to write with the reader's needs in mind.

EXHIBIT 9.1

Examples of Transitional Words
and Phrases

1. **Indicating a series of ideas**
   first, second, third, next, then, finally
2. **Indicating a continuation of an idea**
   also, moreover, further, additionally
3. **Indicating a causal relationship**
   thus, therefore, hence, as a result, so, because
4. **Indicating a sequence of events**
   before, earlier, meanwhile, at the same time, next, later, then, afterward, eventually
5. **Indicating a contrast**
   although, however, nevertheless, in contrast, though
6. **Indicating a similarity**
   similarly, likewise, for the same reason
7. **Indicating a conclusion**
   in summary, in conclusion, to conclude, finally, in short

Proper Sequence

If your document discusses various events, it may help to arrange them chronologically—that is, in a time sequence. A chronologically structured discussion is often clearest, especially when you are describing a factual background leading to a lawsuit. You may also use chronological organization when discussing legal issues. For example, you will probably need to structure a discussion chronologically if you are writing about how a particular rule has developed over time.

chronologically

In a time sequence; chronological organization names or list events in the time order in which they occurred.

Write Effective Sentences

Most good writers prefer short, concrete sentences because they are easier to understand. Good writers write forcefully by using active verbs in place of nominalizations, which are verbs that have been transformed into nouns. For example, it is better to say "the plaintiff decided to settle" than "the plaintiff made a decision to settle." Similarly, you could change "make a statement" to "state," "take into consideration" to "consider," and "reach an agreement" to "agree." Strive to write concisely in every writing project. Wordy writing often obscures your points. Concise writing is clearer, more forceful, and more persuasive. See Exhibit 9.2 for additional examples of how to write more concisely.

Active versus Passive Voice

When constructing a sentence, using the active voice rather than the passive voice generally makes for better sentences. In an active-voice sentence, the subject is a person or thing that is *performing an action*—for example, "The plaintiff filed a motion to exclude evidence." In contrast, the subject of a passive-voice sentence is a person or thing that is *being acted upon*—for example, "A motion to exclude evidence was filed by the plaintiff." Using fewer words, the active voice is more direct and concise, and it energizes your writing by emphasizing who did what.

In some situations, you may need to use the passive voice. For instance, you may want to avoid referring to something inappropriate that your client may have done. Thus, if your firm represents a defendant who has been accused of stealing a car, you may say "the car was stolen" instead of "the defendant allegedly stole the car."

Wordy	Concise
a period of five years	five years
as well as	and
at that point in time	then
due to the fact that	because
for the purpose of	for
in order to	to
in spite of the fact that	although
in the event that	if
it may be argued that	arguably
it seems probable that	probably
take into consideration	consider
whether or not	whether

EXHIBIT 9.2
Writing Concisely

Write Neatly

Finally, it should go without saying: be sure to write neatly. Typographical errors and punctuation mistakes reflect poorly on you, your employer, and the client. Here are some examples:

- *Incorrect:* The plaintiff should *of* told the defendant.
- *Correct:* The plaintiff should *have* told the defendant.
- *Incorrect:* *You're* hearing will be on December 15.
- *Correct:* *Your* hearing will be on December 15.
- *Incorrect:* The *plaintiffs* allegations are vague.
- *Correct:* The *plaintiff's* allegations are vague.

When proofreading, set aside time to check for basic writing mistakes. You must avoid them to produce acceptable, professional work.

Limit Legalese: Use Plain English

legalese
Legal language that is hard for the general public to understand.

As discussed earlier, write with the reader's needs in mind. If you are writing for a person without legal training, minimize **legalese**, which consists of legal terms and phrases that may be unfamiliar to laypeople. Some novice legal writers assume that using legalese will impress the reader, but plain English will generally impress the reader more. When writing to someone without legal training, you should either define legal terms or avoid them altogether. For instance, you may refer to "*voir dire*" as simply "jury selection." You should generally avoid outdated words like "hereof," "therein," and "thereto."

Legal documents, especially contracts, also often contain unnecessary language. Consider a contractual provision that applies when a borrower makes a representation that is "false or erroneous or incorrect." What is the difference between being "false," being "erroneous," and being "incorrect"? These terms are interchangeable—it is hard to imagine that something could be false without also being erroneous and incorrect. The contractual provision would achieve its intended purpose by referring only to false misrepresentations.

Although you should minimize legalese, you must also be careful to convey the right meaning. If you do not understand the purpose of specific language in a contract or pleading, ask your supervising attorney. For more information about writing in plain English, see this chapter's *Office Tech and Cybersecurity* feature.

Do Not Quote Heavily

Just as you should minimize legalese, you should limit quotations. Quotations can be effective if you use them sparingly, but numerous quotations create stylistic problems and rob a document of your voice and ideas.

When writing about the law, use quotations for the language that matters most and put everything else into your own words. If there is a statute on point, for example, you should probably quote it because its precise language matters. Similarly, you might quote a court's requirements for a claim or defense. But if the language itself does not matter, you should probably paraphrase it. Even when quoting an important rule, you usually need not quote the entire sentence. Instead, quote only the phrase or word that you want to emphasize, and weave it into your own sentence.

Avoid Sexist Language

Traditionally, legal writing has used masculine pronouns to refer to both males and females, but a definite trend toward using gender-neutral language has emerged in recent years.

OFFICE TECH AND CYBERSECURITY

ONLINE "PLAIN ENGLISH" GUIDELINES

The ability to write clearly and effectively is a valuable asset, because almost every paralegal's job requires writing. As mentioned elsewhere, clear and effective writing means keeping legalese—legal terminology typically understood only by legal professionals—to a minimum or even eliminating it entirely. The problem is how to convert traditional legal language into clear and understandable prose. Today's paralegals can find helpful instruction at many online locations on the art of writing in plain English.

Government Publications

The U.S. government publishes some of the best online plain English guides. *A Plain English Handbook,* produced by the Securities and Exchange Commission (SEC), is available at **sec.gov/pdf/handbook.pdf**. Although the handbook was intended to help individuals create clearer and more informative SEC disclosure documents, the booklet's guidelines apply generally. For guidelines on legal writing, see the Office of the Federal Register's booklet *Drafting Legal Documents, Principles of Clear Writing,* which is available online at **archives .gov/federal-register/write/legal-docs/clear-writing.html**. The U.S. government has an official website dedicated to the use of plain language (**plainlanguage.gov**) where you can find *Federal Plain Language Guidelines* and other helpful information.

Global Campaign for Clarity

The plain English movement, which is fighting to have public information (such as laws) written in plain English, has received worldwide attention. A British organization called the Plain English Campaign is one of the most prominent groups in this movement. The Plain English Campaign has worked to promote the use of plain English in many nations, including the United States. You can find several helpful guides and online instruction at its website (**plainenglishcampaign.com**). As businesses and the movement of people become ever more global, the ability to communicate clearly with non-native English speakers is critical in legal processes.

Technology Tip

Paralegals interested in improving their plain English writing skills have many online resources, including programs that suggest how to clarify and simplify writing. In addition, paralegals can take online writing courses and use software programs to help edit their writing. Employers value such skills.

In addition, take special care to avoid sexist language in your own writing. For example, if you see a word with "man" or "men" in it (such as "policeman," "fireman," or "workmen's compensation"), use a gender-neutral substitute (such as "police officer," "firefighter," or "workers' compensation"). Over time, writers have devised various ways to avoid sexist language, including the following:

- Use "he or she" rather than "he."
- Alternate between masculine and feminine pronouns.
- Make the noun plural so that a gender-neutral plural pronoun ("they," "their," or "them") can be used.
- Repeat the noun rather than using a pronoun.

Edit and Proofread Your Document

When you receive a writing assignment, budget time for editing and proofreading. Accuracy and precision are important for paralegal work, and a writer rarely turns out an error-free document on the first try. Proofreading helps you discover typographical errors, improve your document's organization, and confirm that the document says what it should. Do not expect your document-creation program's spell checker and grammar checker to catch everything. There is no substitute for printing out hard copies and reviewing them several times.

Writing is a process, and good writers go through several drafts before filing a document in court or sending a letter to a client. The purpose of a first draft is primarily to get your ideas down. Second and subsequent drafts help you fix important details. When reviewing drafts, look for gaps in content. Confirm that points are fully developed and well organized, and ask yourself whether the document says what you intended. It is often helpful to read the document aloud or solicit feedback from someone who is unfamiliar with the case or topic. Another technique is to take a break and work on another project, then come back to review the document with fresh eyes.

When editing later drafts, pay attention to paragraph construction, sentence formation, word choice, and so forth. You might find it helpful to prepare a checklist to remind you of specific things to do or avoid—particularly if there is a required format for the kind of document you are drafting. Creating a polished product takes time, so spend time proofreading and revising. (Additional editing tips are offered in the *Developing Paralegal Skills* feature below and in this chapter's *Featured Contributor* article on pages 252 and 253.)

Take Advantage of Research and Writing Tools

Tools that assist in effective legal writing are continually coming on the market to improve accuracy and productivity. For example, Lexis for Microsoft Office is a legal drafting and review tool that runs within Word and Outlook. This tool is downloadable through **Lexisnexis.com** as an extension to Microsoft products. It requires a Lexis Advance subscription. Once the tool is installed, a LexisNexis ribbon appears in Word and Outlook.

DEVELOPING PARALEGAL SKILLS

EFFECTIVE EDITING

A supervising attorney asks paralegal Dixie Guiliano to draft a letter to an insurance company demanding that it settle a dispute with a client. The client, Nora Ferguson, is an eighty-year-old woman who will never walk again because of a failed hip-replacement operation involving alleged malpractice by her surgeon. The attorney wants to settle the case out of court because of Nora's age and declining health.

Dixie creates the first draft using a settlement letter from another case as a sample. She then uses her document-creation program's spell-check and grammar-check features to look for errors. Dixie knows, however, that using these features is only a preliminary step in proofreading the document. Careful editing will improve the quality and persuasiveness of her letter.

Tips for Editing

- Always edit from a printed copy of the document. It is much easier to proofread and revise on paper than on a computer screen.

- If you use another document as a sample or if you cut and paste text from another document, double-check that you have changed the names, dates, and other information accurately.

- Allow some time (a day or so) to pass before you edit the first draft so that you can review your writing more critically. Examine each draft in its entirety.

- Edit the content first. Ensure that the document is complete and says what you intended. Look for gaps in your reasoning. Make sure you have discussed all the points that you planned to discuss (including cases or statutes). Confirm that the document is well organized and progresses logically from one idea to another.

- Next, review for stylistic issues. Make sure the document is aimed at the appropriate audience and that you have omitted unnecessary words. Change passive voice to active voice, if possible. Make sure that the document is stylistically consistent.

- Check your grammar and spelling. For all sentences, confirm that verbs agree with subjects and that you use proper verb tenses. Check for punctuation problems with plurals, possessives, and commas.

The various buttons on the ribbon are useful when reading legal documents and also when drafting legal documents. The "Get Cited Docs" button allows you to access all of the cited documents in a brief or memo, for example, and save them in virtual stacks as printable PDFs. You can also access *Shepard's* citation service to check the status of the cited laws and cases. Furthermore, this program gives you an efficient way to check *Bluebook* citations, automatically create a table of authorities, and check the accuracy of quotations. You should use great care in relying on computer-generated citations, however, as they may not conform exactly to the local rules of the court where the document being drafted will be filed.

Pleadings, Discovery, and Motions

Many paralegal writing tasks involve forms that must be submitted to courts or opposing counsel in connection with lawsuits or criminal prosecutions. These documents are covered in Chapters 10, 12, and 13. You can see those chapters for explanations and illustrations of specific pretrial forms (pleadings, discovery procedures, and pretrial motions) and for motions made during trials. Keep in mind that most documents submitted to courts should be written persuasively because they directly advocate for clients.

You should always know the rules of the specific court in which a document is being filed. If you cannot find a copy of a court's rules, ask your supervising attorney for help. It is critical that you use the correct formats and include all the right information.

General Legal Correspondence

Paralegals often draft letters to clients, witnesses, opposing counsel, and other parties. Even when a message has already been conveyed orally to a party by phone or in person, you may write a letter confirming the discussion in writing. In fact, paralegals and lawyers often document communications. A letter helps prevent future problems by confirming that the conversation took place and resolving any ambiguities.

Most law firms and legal departments have official letterhead and stationery. The letterhead contains basic information about the firm or department, including its name, address, phone and fax numbers, and an e-mail address. Some law firms have more detailed letterhead that includes the names of partners or the locations of various offices. Always use your firm's or department's letterhead when representing your organization or writing a letter for an attorney. Put the correspondence's first page on letterhead paper and additional pages on plain, matching, and numbered sheets.

In this section, you will read about some common formats and types of legal correspondence. Keep in mind, though, that your employer will probably have its own forms, procedures, and requirements to follow.

General Format for Legal Correspondence

There are many types of legal correspondence, but most include the components discussed next. See Exhibit 9.3 on page 254 for a labeled example.

Date

Legal correspondence must be dated. The date appears below the official letterhead, and it should also be part of the file name on your computer. Typing the wrong date could have serious consequences, so make sure the date is right.

FEATURED CONTRIBUTOR

TIPS FOR MAKING LEGAL WRITING EASIER

William Putman

BIOGRAPHICAL NOTE

William Putman received his J.D. degree from the University of New Mexico School of Law and has been a member of the New Mexico Bar since 1975. For ten years, he was an instructor in the Paralegal Studies programs at Central New Mexico Community College in Albuquerque, New Mexico, and Santa Fe Community College in Santa Fe, New Mexico.

Putman is the author of the *Pocket Guide to Legal Writing* and the *Pocket Guide to Legal Research.* He also wrote the textbooks *Legal Analysis and Writing; Legal Research, Analysis, and Writing;* and *Legal Research.* He authored the legal writing column and some articles in *Legal Assistant Today.*

A legal writing assignment may seem to be a daunting task. All writing assignments are made easier, however, if you answer some preliminary questions before you begin to conduct research or start writing.

What Is the Assignment's Purpose?

An important step in the writing process is to be sure that you understand the task you have been assigned. If you have any questions concerning the general nature or specifics of the assignment, ask. Most attorneys welcome inquiries and prefer that a paralegal ask questions rather than proceed in a wrong direction. Misunderstanding the assignment can result in wasting a great deal of time performing the wrong task or addressing the wrong issue.

What Type of Legal Writing Is Required?

Before you begin, determine what type of legal writing the assignment requires—a legal research memorandum, correspondence, the rough draft of a court brief, and so on. This is important because each type of legal writing serves a different function and has its own required elements and format.

Who Is the Audience?

When assessing the requirements of an assignment, identify the intended audience. The intended reader may be a judge, an attorney, or a client. You should ensure that the writing meets the needs of that reader. A legal writing designed to inform a client or other layperson of the legal analysis of an issue is drafted differently than a writing designed to convey the same information to an attorney.

What Are the Constraints?

Most assignments have time and length constraints. Assignments usually have a time deadline. Typically, they should not exceed a certain number of pages. These constraints govern the amount of research you will conduct and require that you allocate sufficient time for both research and writing.

Dates serve important functions in legal matters. For example, the date of a letter may be critical to establish that someone had legal notice of a particular event. Additionally, legal correspondence is normally filed chronologically. Without any record of the date, accurately filing a letter would be difficult if not impossible. As a general rule, place a date on every written item you create, including telephone messages, memos to file, and personal reminders.

What Format Should You Be Using?

Most law offices have rules or guidelines that govern the organization and format of most types of legal writing, such as case briefs, office memoranda, and correspondence. Courts have formal rules governing the format and style of briefs and other documents submitted for filing. Because the assignment must be drafted within the constraints of the required format, identify the format at the beginning of the process.

These preliminary questions are often overlooked or not given sufficient attention by beginning writers, resulting in headaches later. The task is made easier if you answer these questions and implement the following writing tips:

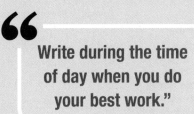

"Write during the time of day when you do your best work."

Tip 1: Select the Right Time and Place.

Write during the time of day when you do your best work. For example, if you are a "morning person," write in the morning and save other tasks for later in the day. Also, make sure that the work environment is pleasant and physically comfortable. Have available all of the resources you will need—writing paper, a computer, research materials, and so on. Legal writing requires focus and concentration. Therefore, select a writing time and an environment that allow you to be as free from interruptions and distractions as possible.

Tip 2: Do Not Procrastinate.

Often, one of the most difficult steps in writing is starting to write. Do not put it off. The longer you put it off, the harder it will become to start your writing project. Start writing anything that has to do with the project. Do not expect what you start with to be great—just start. Once you begin writing, it will get easier.

Tip 3: Start with the Easiest Part.

You do not have to write in the sequence of the outline. Write the easiest material first, especially if you are having trouble starting.

Tip 4: The First Draft Is Not the Final Draft.

The goal of the first draft should be to translate the research and analysis into organized paragraphs and sentences, not to produce a finished product. Just write the information in rough form. It is much easier to polish a rough draft than to try to make the first draft a finished product.

Tip 5: Be Prepared before You Begin.

Do all the research and analysis before you begin to write. It is much easier to write a rough draft if you have completed the research and if the research is thorough.

Tip 6: When You Get Stuck, Move on.

If you are stuck on a particular section, leave it. The mind continues to work on a problem when you are unaware of it. That is why solutions to problems often seem to appear in the morning. Let the subconscious work on the problem while you move on. The solution to the difficulty may become apparent when you return to the problem.

Tip 7: Establish a Timetable.

Break the project into logical units and allocate your time accordingly. This helps you avoid spending too much time on one section of the writing and running out of time. Do not become fanatical about the time schedule, however. You created the timetable, and you can break it. It is there as a guide to keep you on track and alert you to the overall time constraints.

Address Block and Method of Delivery

Below the date, you should include an **address block**. It indicates the name of the person to whom the letter is addressed. The address block should contain the person's name and title, and the name and address of the person's firm or place of business. If the letter is sent other than by U.S. mail, you should indicate the method of delivery in the line above the address block. If the letter is to be sent by FedEx, the line should read "Via FedEx."

address block
The part of a letter that indicates to whom the letter is addressed. The address block is placed in the upper left-hand portion of the letter, above the salutation (and reference line, if one is included).

EXHIBIT 9.3

Components of a Legal Letter

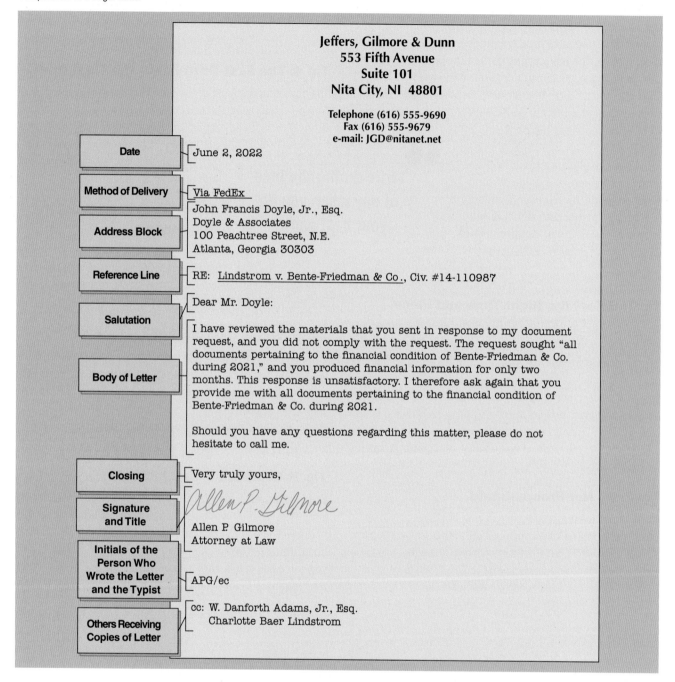

Similarly, hand-delivered correspondence should say "By Hand Delivery," and fax communications can use the words "By Fax" or "By Facsimile." (Fax machines are still used more in law offices than in many other places.) If a copy is sent as an attachment by e-mail, the communication should be in Portable Document Format (PDF) so it cannot be altered.

Reference Line and Salutation

Following the address block, a writer may include a **reference line** identifying the matter discussed in the letter. In a letter regarding a pending lawsuit, the reference line may contain the name of the case, its case file (or docket) number, and a brief notation

reference line

The portion of the letter that indicates the matter to be discussed. The reference line is placed just below the address block and above the salutation.

about the nature of the dispute. Many attorneys also include the firm's file number for the case. In an informative letter (discussed below), the reference line may take the form of a title. For example, for a letter concerning the closing procedures for a financing transaction, the reference line may read "RE: Closing Procedures for ABC Company's $4,000,000 Financing Package."

Immediately below the reference line, you should place the **salutation**, which is a greeting to the addressee. Because legal correspondence is a professional means of communication, you should generally call the person "Mr." or "Ms.," followed by the person's last name and a colon. Of course, it may be appropriate to address the person by his or her first name if you are writing to a friend or close acquaintance. Use your discretion to determine the appropriate level of formality. It is best to err on the side of being too formal.

salutation

In a letter, the formal greeting to the addressee. The salutation is placed just below the reference line.

Body, Closing, and Signature

The main part of the letter is the body. The body's content varies depending on the letter's purpose, but it should always be written formally and communicate information effectively. If, for example, you are asking the recipient of your letter to respond in some way, be sure you are clear about what is expected and when a response is needed. A paralegal must carefully proofread all outgoing correspondence and confirm that it is accurate, well written, and free of grammatical and spelling errors. A carelessly written letter or e-mail reflects poorly on your employer and you.

The last part of the body typically consists of one or two concluding sentences. Final sentences are usually courteous statements, such as "Thank you for your time and attention to this matter" or "Should you have any questions or comments, please do not hesitate to contact me."

The last substantive part of a letter is the **closing**, which is followed by the writer's signature, name, and title. Closings in legal correspondence should be formal—for example, "Sincerely" or "Very truly yours." When you write a letter using your own signature, you should always include your title ("Paralegal") immediately after your name. Similarly, you may include a line saying "Attorney at Law" when you write a letter to be signed by an attorney.

closing

In a letter, an ending word or phrase placed above the signature, such as "Sincerely" or "Very truly yours."

Types of Legal Letters

There are several types of legal correspondence, and each one serves a different purpose. The types of legal letters that you should be familiar with include informative letters, confirmation letters, opinion (or advisory) letters, and demand letters.

Informative Letters

An **informative letter** conveys information to another party. As a paralegal, you will likely write many such letters, and many will be to clients. You might write an informative letter to advise a client about recent developments in a case, to tell about an upcoming meeting or filing, to provide general background on a legal issue, or simply to break down the firm's bill. Write an informative letter so it is understandable to the client, given his or her education and experience.

Informative letters are also sent to opposing counsel and other parties. For example, law firms often send scheduling information to opposing counsel, witnesses, and other people involved in trials. Exhibit 9.4 is a sample letter to a witness in an arbitration proceeding. An informative letter may also serve as a cover letter when you send someone documents.

informative letter

A letter that conveys information to a client, a witness, an adversary's counsel, or some other person regarding a legal matter (such as the date, time, place, and purpose of a meeting) or a cover letter that accompanies other documents being sent to a person or court.

EXHIBIT 9.4
A Sample Informative Letter

Jeffers, Gilmore & Dunn
553 Fifth Avenue
Suite 101
Nita City, NI 48801

Telephone (616) 555-9690
Fax (616) 555-9679
e-mail: JGD@nitanet.net

June 25, 2022

Bernadette P. Williams
149 Snowflake Drive
Irving, TX 75062

RE: Kempf/Joseph Arbitration Proceedings

Dear Ms. Williams:

The arbitration will resume on Wednesday, August 6, 2022. Please arrive at the offices of the American Arbitration Association (the AAA) before 8:30 A.M. The offices of the AAA are located at 400 West Ferry Boulevard in Dallas. You will be called as a witness sometime before 12:00 noon.

Should you have any questions or concerns regarding your responsibilities as a witness, please do not hesitate to contact me.

Sincerely,

Elena Lopez

Elena Lopez
Paralegal

Confirmation Letters

confirmation letter
A letter that summarizes an oral conversation to provide a permanent record of the discussion.

A paralegal also may be called upon to write a **confirmation letter** to communicate certain information. Confirmation letters differ from informative letters in that they generally summarize oral conversations that have already occurred. By providing attorneys with permanent records of conversations, confirmation letters safeguard against any misinterpretation or misunderstanding of what was said. If there is any disagreement about a conversation's details, an attorney can use a confirmation letter to support his or her account. See Exhibit 9.5 for a sample confirmation letter.

Opinion Letters

opinion (advisory) letter
A letter from an attorney to a client containing a legal opinion on an issue raised by the client's question or legal claim. The opinion is based on a detailed analysis of the law.

The purpose of an **opinion (advisory) letter** is to provide information and advice. Unlike an informative letter, an opinion letter actually gives a legal opinion about the matter discussed. An attorney sending an opinion letter is required to provide an analysis of the law and to bring the analysis to a definite conclusion that states a formal opinion.

An opinion letter may also advise a client about the legality of a course of action. An example appears in Exhibit 9.6 on page 258. For example, a company planning to establish operations in a foreign country may seek a lawyer's opinion on whether certain conduct would be permissible. The attorney (or a paralegal) will research the issue and then draft an advisory letter to the client. Opinion letters are commonly quite long and include detailed explanations of how the law applies to the client. Sometimes,

EXHIBIT 9.5
A Sample Confirmation Letter

Jeffers, Gilmore & Dunn
553 Fifth Avenue
Suite 101
Nita City, NI 48801

Telephone (616) 555-9690
Fax (616) 555-9679
e-mail: JGD@nitanet.net

August 4, 2022

Pauline C. Dunbar
President
Minute-Magic Corporation
7689 Industrial Boulevard
San Francisco, CA 80021

RE: Purchase of real estate from C. C. Barnes, Inc.

Dear Ms. Dunbar:

As we discussed on the phone today, the Minute-Magic Corporation will purchase real estate located at 2683 Millwood Ave., Nita City, NI, from C. C. Barnes for $800,000. The purchase will be financed by a mortgage with Citiwide Bank at an interest rate of 5.5 percent.

I look forward to seeing you next week. If you have any questions or comments before then, please give me a call.

Very truly yours,

Allen P. Gilmore
Attorney at Law

APG/ec

the attorney simply summarizes his or her conclusion in the opinion letter and attaches a detailed legal memorandum explaining the supporting law and analysis.

A firm's opinion letter reflects legal expertise and advice on which a client can rely. As discussed in this chapter's *Ethics Watch* feature on page 260, an attorney must sign an opinion letter. Should a client suffer a loss in a legal matter due to poor-quality legal advice or improper action by an attorney, the client may sue the firm for malpractice. An attorney's signature represents acceptance of responsibility for the document's content.

Demand Letters

Another basic type of letter is the demand letter. In a **demand letter**, one party explains its legal position in a dispute and demands that the recipient take some action. Typically, an attorney will send a demand letter before filing a lawsuit against a person or company. In fact, sending a demand letter may be required legal process, such as in many cases involving consumer-protection violations. Suppose your supervising attorney asks you to draft a letter demanding that a company pay a debt it owes to your firm's client. Your demand letter would summarize the relevant facts, demand payment by a certain date, and say that the client will sue if the company does not pay the debt.

demand letter
A letter in which one party explains its legal position in a dispute and demands that the recipient take some action, such as paying money owed.

EXHIBIT 9.6

A Sample Opinion Letter

Jeffers, Gilmore & Dunn
553 Fifth Avenue
Suite 101
Nita City, NI 48801

Telephone (616) 555-9690
Fax (616) 555-9679
e-mail: JGD@nitanet.com

December 10, 2022

J. D. Joslyn
President and Chief Executive Officer
Joslyn Footwear, Inc.
700 Kings Avenue, Suite 4000
New City, NI 48023

Dear Ms. Joslyn:

After careful consideration, I have concluded that Joslyn Footwear, Inc., would risk significant liability by expanding into Latin American markets. The biggest problem concerns the proposed shoe-manufacturing plants. Due to their size, the plants would violate industrial regulations in Mexico, Uruguay, and Argentina.

The enclosed legal memorandum explains in detail how the law applies to your situation and the reasons for my conclusion. Please call me if you have any questions.

Very truly yours,

Allen P. Gilmore

Allen P. Gilmore
Attorney at Law

APG/ec

Enclosure

Although a demand letter should be insistent and adversarial, it should not come across as unreasonable or harassing. After all, it seeks to accomplish something. For a sample demand letter, see Exhibit 9.7. It covers the common situation of demanding that an adversarial party respond to a settlement offer in a lawsuit.

E-Mail Correspondence

Increasingly, legal professionals communicate by e-mail rather than by letter or telephone. E-mail often may be used for the same purposes as traditional correspondence with less formal content. For example, you might use e-mail to tell a client about recent case developments, to send copies of documents to a witness, or to confirm the details of a conversation. Nevertheless, it is still generally better to send hard copies of more formal legal documents, such as demand letters to opposing parties and formal opinion letters to clients. As always, follow your supervising attorney's preferences, and be sure to include a standard confidentiality notice if your employer has one.

Most e-mails from a law office should be written formally. E-mails represent your employer and you to the outside world, and it should be presumed that they never

EXHIBIT 9.7

A Sample Demand Letter

Jeffers, Gilmore & Dunn
553 Fifth Avenue
Suite 101
Nita City, NI 48801

Telephone (616) 555-9690
Fax (616) 555-9679
e-mail: JGD@nitanet.com

June 3, 2022

Christopher P. Nelson, Esq.
Nelson, Johnson, Callan & Sietz
200 Way Bridge
Philadelphia, PA 40022

RE: *Fuentes v. Thompson*

Dear Mr. Nelson:

This morning, I met with my clients, Eduardo and Myrna Fuentes, the plaintiffs in the lawsuit against your client, Laura Thompson. Mr. and Mrs. Fuentes expressed a desire to withdraw their complaint and settle with Ms. Thompson. The Fuentes' settlement demand is $50,000, payable by certified check no later than July 15, 2022. We think that you and Ms. Thompson will find this offer quite reasonable. After all, given the strength of the Fuentes' claims, a jury award exceeding $200,000 is quite possible.

If you plan to take advantage of the Fuentes' settlement offer, please contact me by the close of business on Friday, June 20, 2022. If we do not hear from you by that date, we will assume that you have rejected our demand and we will proceed with litigation.

Very truly yours,

Allen P. Gilmore

Allen P. Gilmore
Attorney at Law

APG/ec

disappear. You should generally follow the same writing conventions that you would when drafting a letter. The salutation, for example, should generally address the recipient as "Mr." or "Ms.," and you should also write formally in the subject line, body, and closing. No matter how short the e-mail, always proofread before clicking "send." As with letters, professionalism is highly important. Refer back to Chapter 3 for the extended discussion of e-mail use in the *Office Tech and Cybersecurity* feature.

Also, before clicking on "send," reconfirm that the recipients are truly the ones who are supposed to receive the e-mail. It's easy to have added an incorrect recipient in the "To" line and in the "Cc" line (which comes from "carbon copy") or the "Bcc" line (which comes from "blind carbon copy").

The Legal Memorandum

A legal memorandum is prepared for internal use within a law firm, legal department, or other organization. Generally, a memo presents a thorough analysis of one or more specific legal issues.

ETHICS WATCH

LETTERS AND THE UNAUTHORIZED PRACTICE OF LAW

Engaging in the unauthorized practice of law is unlawful and unethical. To avoid liability for the unauthorized practice of law, never sign opinion or advisory letters with your own name, and when you sign other types of letters, always indicate your status as a paralegal.

Even, if you are sending a letter to a person who knows you well and knows that you are a paralegal, indicate your status on the letter itself. By doing so, you will prevent both potential confusion and potential legal liability. In addition, if your name and status are included in the letterhead, as some state laws allow, always type your title below your name as a precaution. Here are some relevant rules and guidelines to remember once you start your paralegal career.

- NALA *Code of Ethics,* Canon 3:

  "A paralegal must not … give legal opinions or advice."

- NALA *Code of Ethics,* Canon 5:

  "A paralegal must disclose his or her status as a paralegal at the outset of any professional relationship with a client, an attorney, a court or administrative agency or personnel thereof, or a member of the general public."

- The ABA *Model Guidelines* state that attorneys may not grant paralegals the authority to give legal opinions to clients. The guidelines also make clear that attorneys have a duty ensure that clients and any other relevant parties, such as other lawyers, know that paralegals working with attorneys are not authorized to practice law.

- The NFPA *Model Code of Ethics,* EC 1.7(a):

  "A paralegal's title shall clearly indicate the individual's status and shall be disclosed in all business and professional communications to avoid misunderstandings and misconceptions about the paralegal's role and responsibilities."

Reprinted by permission of the National Federation of Paralegal Associations, Inc. (NFPA®), www.paralegals.org.; Copyright 1975; Adopted 1975; Revised 1979, 1988, 1995, 2007. Reprinted with permission of NALA, The Paralegal Association. Inquiries should be directed to NALA, 1516 S. Boston, #200, Tulsa, OK 74119, www.nala.org.

As a paralegal, you may be asked to draft a legal memorandum for your supervising attorney. The attorney may need the memo for a number of reasons. For example, the attorney may be preparing an opinion letter or brief, either of which would require detailed legal analysis. To help your supervising attorney represent or advise a client more effectively, a memo should be thorough, well reasoned, and clearly written. Your primary reader is an attorney, so you need not explain basic legal concepts or define common legal terms. Instead, assume that your reader has general knowledge of the law but lacks expertise in the specific area you are discussing.

As with all legal documents, attention to detail is important. A memo must be accurate and neat. As the accompanying *Developing Paralegal Skills* feature notes, you may be able to help improve the quality of documents drafted by attorneys.

Format

A legal memorandum must be well organized. There is no "right" way to structure a legal memo, but most are divided into sections that serve different purposes. The following sections are very common:

- A heading.
- A statement of the facts.
- The question or questions presented.
- Brief answers to the question or questions presented.
- A discussion of how the law applies to the facts.
- A conclusion.

DEVELOPING PARALEGAL SKILLS

REVIEWING ATTORNEY-GENERATED DOCUMENTS

Ashana Carroll works as a paralegal for Jeremy O'Connell, a sole practitioner in general practice. Jeremy frequently drafts motions and other legal documents because Ashana has her hands full with other writing tasks and general legal work. Typically, Jeremy e-mails his documents to Ashana, instructing her to send letters to recipients and file pleadings and motions in court. Ashana usually takes time to quickly review Jeremy's documents. Even though Jeremy has practiced law for years, Ashana occasionally finds errors in his documents, which could have serious consequences.

Tips for Reviewing an Attorney's Documents

- Confirm that all names and addresses are current and correct. The attorney may have forgotten that a client recently moved, for example, and mistakenly used an old address.

- If you are filing a document with a court, confirm that you have the most recent version of the court's rules. Court rules change, and it is important to ensure that the correct court rules are referenced in the document filed.

- Confirm that a document to be filed with a court complies with the court's rules concerning format, style, content, and deadlines. Also confirm that the document complies with the specific judge's preferences if you have them on file.

- Check with your supervising attorney if you have any question about how a particular document should be delivered.

Of course, if your employer or supervising attorney prefers a particular format, you should follow it. Similarly, check for sample documents that your firm uses so that you can make use of them in preparing new memos.

Heading

The heading of a legal memorandum contains four types of information:

- The date on which the memo is submitted.
- The name of the person for whom the memo was prepared.
- The name of the person submitting the memo.
- A brief description of the matter, usually in the form of a reference line.

Exhibit 9.8 illustrates a sample heading for a legal memorandum.

Statement of Facts

The statement of facts provides a factual background for the reader, focusing primarily on the facts that are relevant to the legal issues discussed in the rest of the memo. Facts are relevant if they have a bearing on your analysis, which will appear in the memo's discussion section. Therefore, you may consider writing the statement of facts after drafting the discussion section, even though the statement of facts will appear earlier in the final document. See which facts are important for your analysis, and then use them as a starting point for drafting the statement of facts. That approach also ensures that the statement of facts is thorough, so that the reader does not learn new details about the facts later in the memo. An example appears in Exhibit 9.9 on the following page.

Stay Objective. Like other parts of the memo, the statement of facts should be objective. This section should not present an argument for the client. Rather, it gives an objective, dispassionate summary of the key facts. You should never omit facts that are unfavorable to the client's case. To help the client, your supervising attorney needs to know everything.

EXHIBIT 9.8

Legal Memorandum—Sample Heading

MEMORANDUM

DATE: August 6, 2022

TO: Allen P. Gilmore, Partner

FROM: Elena Lopez, Paralegal

RE: Neely, Raquel: Emotional Distress—File No. 00-2146
           Neely, Raquel, and D'andrea: Emotional Distress—File No. 00-2147

Importance of Organization. The statement of facts must also be well organized. For example, you can help orient the reader by providing an introductory paragraph that briefly explains the client's issue, as in the sample statement of facts in Exhibit 9.9. After a short introductory paragraph, you should explain the key facts in a logical order. For many memos, a chronological organization will work well, especially if the facts are relatively simple. If the facts are complicated, you might try a more topical organization that devotes separate paragraphs to various kinds of facts. Feel free to experiment with different ways of organizing and see what works best, given the subject matter and the reader's needs.

Questions Presented

The questions-presented section identifies the main legal issues discussed in the memorandum. Depending on how complicated the memo is, you may present one simple question or several more complicated questions. Often, a supervising attorney will identify the issues for you when asking you to write a memorandum. If so, you can use the attorney's request as a starting point for drafting this section of the memo.

EXHIBIT 9.9

Legal Memorandum—Sample Statement of Facts

STATEMENT OF FACTS

Raquel Neely ("Neely") and her 11-year-old daughter, D'andrea Neely ("D'andrea"), seek advice in connection with possible emotional distress claims against Miles Thompson.

In October 2020, Neely and D'andrea moved from San Francisco to Union City, where Neely began working for an investment firm. At the firm, Neely worked for Thompson, and the two initially had a friendly, professional relationship. After about six months, however, their relationship soured when Thompson expressed romantic interest in Neely.

On April 1, 2022, Thompson visited Neely's house. D'andrea was home alone because Neely had gone to the grocery store, and Thompson invited D'andrea for a ride in his Corvette. Not knowing about her mother's problems with Thompson, D'andrea said yes. When Neely soon returned home to find D'andrea missing, she panicked and called the police.

Thompson drove D'andrea around Union City for approximately thirty minutes. During the drive, Thompson told D'andrea that her mother was a "selfish woman," that she did not care about her, and that she would leave her "once the right man comes along." As Thompson made his way back to Neely's house, an oncoming vehicle hit the car at the corner of Oak Street and Maple Road, where the Neelys live. According to the police report, Thompson had a high blood-alcohol level, indicating that he was drunk.

Neely heard the crash, ran outside, and approached Thompson's car. Neely then saw D'andrea bleeding profusely from head injuries, causing Neely to faint. She had to spend a day in Union City Hospital for extreme anxiety and trauma.

D'andrea spent two days in Union City Hospital, where she was kept under observation for possible internal injuries. D'andrea is also undergoing psychiatric therapy because of Thompson's comments. She is severely depressed and emotionally unstable, and she suffers from frequent nightmares.

EXHIBIT 9.10

Legal Memorandum—Sample
Questions Presented

QUESTIONS PRESENTED

I. Under California common law, may Raquel Neely recover for negligent infliction of emotional distress when she witnessed injuries to her daughter, D'andrea Neely, but was not herself hurt by the car accident that caused the injuries?

II. Under California common law, may D'andrea Neely recover against Miles Thompson for intentional infliction of emotional distress because he made statements to her that have made her emotionally unstable and have caused severe depression?

Questions presented help bring the main issues into focus. They should be case specific and based on the facts. Each question should identify the governing law, briefly identify the issue, and explain the most important facts for that issue. See Exhibit 9.10 for some examples.

Brief Answers

Brief answers respond to the questions presented, and they should follow the same order. An answer's length will depend on the issue's complexity, but each answer should probably be only a few sentences long. Try to begin with a one- or two-word answer to the question, like "yes," "no," "probably," or "probably not." After giving a short answer, explain your reasoning in one to three sentences. Your goal is to give an overview of the discussion section, which will examine the issue in greater detail. See Exhibit 9.11 for sample answers to the questions presented in Exhibit 9.10.

Discussion

The discussion section presents the writer's detailed analysis of how the law applies to the facts. Some memos address only one main issue, but many address multiple issues. If a memo discusses more than one issue, you may need to divide the discussion section into subsections. For example, if a memo discusses a client's potential claims for both negligent and intentional infliction of emotional distress, you may devote a separate subsection to each cause of action, providing a descriptive heading for each.

To be consistent, you should follow the discussion section's organization in other sections of the memo. Thus, if you address negligent infliction first in the discussion section, you should also address it first in the questions presented, brief answers, statement of facts, and conclusion sections.

EXHIBIT 9.11

Legal Memorandum—Sample
Brief Answers

BRIEF ANSWERS

I. Probably not. California courts require someone not injured physically to have been present at the scene of the injury-producing event at the time of the event. In this case, Neely did not witness the accident itself, merely the aftermath.

II. Probably. To recover for intentional infliction of emotional distress, a plaintiff must prove that the defendant (1) intended to cause emotional distress or was substantially certain it would result, (2) in fact caused severe emotional distress, and (3) engaged in outrageous conduct. In this case, all three requirements are probably satisfied.

The Heart of the Memorandum

The discussion section is the heart of a legal memorandum, and it should explicitly summarize both your research and your analysis. A good memorandum should answer the following kinds of questions for each issue:

- What is the probability that the client will succeed? For example, does the client have a claim or defense?

- What law governs the issue?

- Is there a statute on point? If so, how does it apply to the client's case? Are the statute's requirements satisfied?

- Are there any cases on point? If so, how do they apply to the client's case? Are the court's rules satisfied? How is the client's case similar to the precedents? How does it differ?

Your analysis should be objective because the memo's purpose is to help an attorney represent or advise a client. The discussion section should candidly evaluate both the strengths and the weaknesses of the client's position. If there is a problem with the client's position, you should address it. After all, the supervising attorney can deal with the problem much more effectively if he or she knows about it early on. Remember that your goal is to help the attorney.

The IRAC Method

Like other kinds of legal writing, the discussion section must be well organized. You can keep the discussion clear by using the IRAC method, which stands for *issue, rule, application, conclusion*. As discussed in Chapter 7, IRAC is an organizational device that helps you present your analysis in a logical order. If you analyze multiple issues or rules of law, you should probably present multiple IRACs for each rule you analyze. For each IRAC:

1. Identify the *issue*.

2. Explain the governing *rule*, which may come from statutory provisions, cases on point, or administrative agency regulations.

3. *Apply* the rule to the facts of the client's case.

4. State your *conclusion*.

Then repeat the process until all of the rules from various sources have been applied to the client's case.

Exhibit 9.12 presents an excerpt from a simple discussion section that uses IRAC. The exhibit identifies the elements of IRAC for illustration purposes, but you would omit them from a memorandum to a supervising attorney. Also note that the sample discussion provides citations to legal authorities for various points of law. As mentioned in Chapter 7, there are citation guides, including *The Bluebook: A Uniform System of Citation* and the *ALWD Guide to Legal Citation*. You should use the one that your supervising attorney prefers.

Conclusion

The conclusion is the culmination of the legal memo. The discussion section has examined the issues in detail, evaluating the strengths and weaknesses of the client's position. The conclusion is your opinion of how to resolve the issues. Exhibit 9.13 gives an example.

The conclusion may acknowledge that research into a particular area bore little fruit. For example, there may be no cases on point addressing one of the issues. The

EXHIBIT 9.12

Legal Memorandum—Sample
Discussion (Excerpt Using the
IRAC Method)

DISCUSSION (Excerpt)

I. Negligent Infliction of Emotional Distress

Issue   The first issue is whether Neely can recover for negligent infliction of emotional distress because she witnessed injuries to her daughter D'andrea.

Rule   All relevant events occurred in California, so California law governs this case. There is no statute on point. The California Supreme Court, however, did reject the "impact rule" that prevents a party from recovering when a plaintiff alleges emotional distress caused by merely witnessing a third party's injuries in *Thing v. La Chusa,* 771 P.2d 814, 830 (Cal. 1989). The case concerned a claim brought by a woman whose child was struck by a car. The mother did not see the accident but saw her injured child unconscious and bleeding on the road when she arrived on the scene. *Id.* at 815.

The Court stated: "The merely negligent actor does not owe a duty the law will recognize to make monetary amends to all persons who have suffered emotional distress on viewing or learning about the injurious consequences of his conduct." *Id.* at 830.

Under California's approach, a plaintiff must satisfy three elements to recover for negligent infliction of emotional distress based on injury to another person: (1) the plaintiff must be closely related to the victim; (2) the plaintiff must be present at the scene of the injury-producing event at the time it occurs and be contemporaneously aware that the injury is being caused; and (3) the plaintiff must suffer serious emotional distress as a result. *Id.* at 829-30.

The California rule limits the circumstances under which a negligent infliction claim could be brought. The concern is that an expanding "circle of liability" would result unless the law restricted who could bring such claims. *Morton v. Thousand Oaks Surgical Hosp.*, 114 Cal. Rptr. 3d 661, 667 (Cal. Ct. App. 2010).

Application   In this case, Neely did not witness the car crash that injured D'andrea. Rather, she was inside her house when the accident occurred. The facts of her case are thus almost exactly identical to those in which the California Supreme Court rejected an analogous claim. Moreover, recent California court decisions cite approvingly and do not suggest any movement to relax the rule announced.

Conclusion   Because Neely did not witness the accident, she probably cannot recover for negligent infliction of emotional distress. The law is well settled in this area, and Neely is unlikely to prevail on that claim.

conclusion may also inform the attorney that more facts are needed or suggest that a certain issue needs to be explored more fully. Finally, this section gives you an opportunity to make strategic suggestions. Paralegals should feel comfortable in recommending specific courses of action, especially after conducting a careful analysis. Your judgment will be helpful to your supervising attorney.

EXHIBIT 9.13

Legal Memorandum—Sample
Conclusion

CONCLUSION

Neely probably does not have a cause of action against Thompson for negligent infliction of emotional distress because she did not witness the accident that caused D'andrea's injuries. However, D'andrea probably has a cause of action for intentional infliction of emotional distress based on Thompson's convincing her to ride in a car he was driving while drunk and then making outrageous comments to her about her mother.

Neely might also pursue, on her own behalf, a claim that Thompson intentionally inflicted emotional distress on her by taking D'andrea from her home and making outrageous statements about Neely. I recommend that we talk to Neely about how Thompson's statements affected her. If it can be shown that Thompson intentionally or recklessly caused her emotional distress, there may be a claim for Neely.

CHAPTER SUMMARY

LEGAL WRITING: FORM AND SUBSTANCE

Receiving a Writing Assignment

When receiving a writing assignment, a paralegal should learn the nature of the assignment, when the assignment is due, and what kind of writing approach should be used.

1. *Understanding the assignment*—Getting clear direction about an assignment is important so that you do not waste time working needlessly on something or taking the wrong approach because you did not receive clear direction about what was required.

2. *Time constraints and flexibility*—Knowing and adhering to deadlines is essential. Some matters, such as those arising during a trial, will have to be addressed very quickly.

3. *Writing approaches*—Some documents, such as pretrial motions, are persuasive and require you to advocate for a particular position. Other documents call for objective analysis, meaning that you should present a balanced discussion of an issue or a neutral summary of facts.

Writing Well

Good writing skills are essential for preparing legal documents. With experience and practice, you will improve your writing.

1. *Choice of format*—The document should be well organized and in the appropriate format. Most firms use specific templates, and courts often require certain formats in documents submitted to them.

2. *Write for your reader*—Tailor your writing to the intended reader. Documents written for a supervising attorney, a judge, and a client will have different styles and writing levels.

3. *Outline the material*—Create an outline before you begin writing. To help the reader follow the discussion, write effective paragraphs and provide transitions between ideas.

4. *Organize the material logically*—Large assignments should be broken into manageable blocks that can be

organized in logical paragraphs. There should be headings between groups of paragraphs to help frame the presentation in an orderly sequence.

5. *Write effective sentences*—Draft short, concrete sentences with active verbs. Generally use the active voice, in which the sentence's subject is the actor, rather than the passive voice, in which the subject is being acted upon. Limit legalese—it is usually better to use plain English so the reader understands what is being said. Do not quote heavily, and use gender-neutral language.

6. *Edit and proofread your document*—Creating a polished product takes time, and you should spend much of that time proofreading and revising both on the computer and on hard copy. Confirm that the document is thorough, well organized, and neat.

Pleadings, Discovery, and Motions

Paralegals often help draft litigation documents, which should almost always be persuasive in tone. When drafting a document for court, always follow the court's rules concerning formatting and other issues.

General Legal Correspondence

Paralegals frequently draft letters to clients, witnesses, opposing counsel, and others.

1. *Format*—Most firms and legal departments have preferred formats for legal correspondence. The first page of a letter is typically printed on the firm's letterhead. Letters should generally be formal in tone and include the following:

   a. The date.

   b. The address block and the method of delivery.

   c. The reference line (including case or file numbers when appropriate) and the salutation.

   d. The body of the letter, the closing, and the signature.

2. *Types of letters*—Paralegals commonly draft the following types of letters:

   a. Informative letters notify clients or others about something, or serve as cover letters to accompany other documents.

   b. Confirmation letters summarize oral conversations.

   c. Opinion letters convey a formal legal opinion about an issue or give formal advice. Only an attorney can sign an opinion letter.

   d. A demand letter explains a party's legal position in a dispute and demands that the recipient take some action, such as paying money owed.

The Legal Memorandum

A legal memorandum is a thoroughly researched analysis of one or more legal issues. A memo's purpose is to inform a supervising attorney about the strengths and weaknesses of a client's position.

1. *Format*—Generally, a legal memo includes the following sections:

   a. Heading

   b. Statement of facts

   c. Questions presented

   d. Brief answers

   e. Discussion and conclusion

2. *The heart of the memorandum*—The discussion section will clearly state your research and analysis objectively, summarizing the strengths and weaknesses of a case and the relevant law.

3. *IRAC method*— method You can make your analysis of an issue clear by using the IRAC method, which stands for *issue, rule, application, conclusion*.

4. *Conclusion*—The conclusion is the culmination of the legal memo. In it, you offer your opinion of how to resolve the issues.

KEY TERMS AND CONCEPTS

address block 253
chronologically 247
closing 255
confirmation letter 256

demand letter 257
informative letter 255
legalese 248
opinion (advisory) letter 256

reference line 254
salutation 255

QUESTIONS FOR REVIEW

1. What are the three things you should consider when receiving a legal writing assignment?

2. Why is it important for paralegals to have good writing skills? What is the active voice? What is the passive voice? Why is it better to use the active voice in your legal writing?

3. List the components of a typical legal letter. What are the four types of letters discussed in this chapter? What is each letter's purpose?

4. How is a legal memorandum organized? List and describe its components. What is the IRAC method? How is it used in a legal memorandum?

5. Should a memorandum be objective or persuasive? Explain your answer.

6. Should documents submitted to the court be objective or persuasive? Explain your answer.

ETHICS QUESTION

1. A lawyer filed a badly drafted complaint with a court. After giving the lawyer an additional opportunity to correct and refile it, the court dismissed the complaint with prejudice (meaning that the complaint could not be revised and refiled). One sentence in the complaint contained 345 words, and many other sentences contained over 100 words and were unintelligible. On appeal, the appellate court affirmed dismissal of the complaint with prejudice, issued an order to show cause to the attorney instructing him to explain to the court why he should not be barred from practicing law before the court, and directed the court clerk to send its opinion to the state ethics board. What ethics rules did the attorney violate? Would it make a difference if the attorney's writing problems were caused by a serious illness?

PRACTICE QUESTIONS AND ASSIGNMENTS

1. Proofread the following paragraph, circling all of the mistakes. Then rewrite the paragraph.

    The defendent was arested and charge with drunk driving. Blood alcohol level of .15. He refused to take a breahalyzer test at first. After the police explained to him that he would loose his lisense if he did not take it, he concented. He also has ablood test to verify the results of the breathalyzer.

2. Prepare an informative letter to a client using the following facts:

    The client, Dr. Brown, is being sued for medical malpractice and is going to be deposed on January 15, 2022, at 1:00 P.M. The deposition will take place at the law offices of Callaghan & Young. The law office address is 151 East Jefferson Avenue, Cincinnati, Ohio. Ask Dr. Brown to call you to set up an appointment, so that you and your supervising attorney, Jeffrey Brilliant, can prepare Dr. Brown for the deposition.

3. Summarize the following hypothetical by applying the IRAC method:

    Mr. Damien was a teacher at the Wabash Academy, a private boarding school. He had a twenty-one-year-old son, Dave, with bipolar affective disorder, formerly called manic depression, a mood disorder. While visiting Mr. Damien, Dave repeatedly threatened members of the school community. On one occasion, Dave abducted the headmaster's sixteen-year-old daughter and attempted to have her admitted to a psychiatric hospital. Dave also made threatening phone calls to the headmaster. In one call, he claimed to have drained several quarts of his own blood from his body because he was not permitted to communicate with the headmaster's daughter. Mr. and Mrs. Damien refused to prevent their son from visiting their home on the school's campus. As a result, the school fired Mr. Damien. He claimed that the termination of his employment violated the Americans with Disabilities Act (ADA) of 1990.

    The ADA prohibits an employer from discriminating against a person because he or she is related to a person with disabilities. Under case law interpreting the ADA, however, employment is not protected if a disabled relative poses a direct threat to the health and safety of others.

4. If you did the research required by the *Practice Questions and Assignments* at the end of Chapter 7, prepare a legal memorandum summarizing Ms. Consumer's legal problem and her options for resolution. Be sure to use the IRAC method and include the statutory provisions and cases on point from your research.

GROUP PROJECT

In this assignment, students will document the benefits of using plain English in legal writing. To complete the assignment, refer to the Securities and Exchange Commission's *A Plain English Handbook* at **sec.gov/pdf/handbook.pdf**. (If you do not know what the Securities and Exchange Commission does, conduct an Internet search before doing this assignment.)

Student one will review the preface and describe the "unoriginal but useful" writing tip given by the author.

Student two will review Chapter 1 of the handbook and write a definition of a plain English document.

Student three will provide two pairs of "before" and "after" examples from Chapter 6 of the handbook showing how plain English improved sentences in SEC disclosure documents.

Student four will summarize the information found by students one, two, and three, using their examples to describe the benefits of using plain English in legal documents.

©fizkes/Shutterstock.com

10

Civil Litigation: Before the Trial

CHAPTER OBJECTIVES

After completing this chapter, you will be able to:

- List the basic steps involved in the civil litigation process and the types of tasks that may be required of paralegals during each step of the pretrial phase.

- Explain what a litigation file is, what it contains, and how it is organized, maintained, and reviewed.

- Describe how a lawsuit is initiated and what documents and motions are filed during the pleadings stage of the civil litigation process.

- Explain what discovery is and what kinds of information attorneys and their paralegals obtain from parties to the lawsuit and from witnesses when preparing for trial.

- Explain the disclosure requirements of FRCP 26.

- Explain the importance of and requirements for discovery of electronic evidence.

- Discuss the concerns involved in creating an effective records management system.

- Describe the kinds of motions parties may file before trial.

Introduction

Every paralegal should be acquainted with the basic phases of civil litigation and the forms and terminology commonly used in the process. The paralegal plays an important role in helping the trial attorney prepare for and conduct a civil trial. Preparation involves a variety of tasks, including:

- Carefully researching relevant law.
- Gathering and documenting evidence.
- Creating and organizing the litigation file.
- Meeting procedural requirements and deadlines for filing documents with the court.
- Preparing a **witness**—a person asked to testify at trial—in advance and making sure that individual is available to testify during the trial.
- Preparing trial exhibits, such as charts, photographs, and video recordings.
- Making arrangements to have any necessary equipment, such as a video player, laptop, and projector, available for use at the trial.

Paralegals' efforts are critically important in preparing for trial, and attorneys usually rely on paralegals to ensure that nothing has been overlooked.

witness
A person who is asked to testify under oath at a trial.

FEATURED CONTRIBUTOR

PRETRIAL PREPARATION

Thomas McClure

BIOGRAPHICAL NOTE

After Thomas McClure graduated from the DePaul University Law School, he clerked for an appellate judge for two years. Following his clerkship, he was in general practice for twenty-eight years, where he focused on litigation and appellate work. In 2007, he became the director of Legal Studies at Illinois State University. He has served as the chair of the American Bar Association's Standing Committee on Paralegals Approval Commission since 2017. Professor McClure has co-authored a criminal law paralegal textbook, written social science and law journal articles, and contributed chapters to books featuring legal topics.

Personal injury (PI) was one of my specialties in private practice. I relied on paralegals to assist me in these cases. They were involved in most aspects of pretrial preparation. Some of the considerations encompassed in a PI paralegal's role apply to other types of cases as well.

Pretrial preparation begins when the client first gets in touch with the office. If you are involved at this point of contact, you will likely inform prospective clients to bring certain documents to their initial interview. In a PI case, you might request police reports, medical bills, and pay stubs or other earnings documentation. In a dissolution of marriage case, you could ask for tax returns and other financial information. Always check with your supervising attorney to find out what is needed. Lawyers are a diverse group. Don't be surprised if attorneys in the same office treat cases in different ways.

The need for accuracy at even a simple civil trial requires that the paralegal be familiar with the litigation process and courtroom procedures. While we discuss the major elements of that process here, expertise can be acquired only through hands-on experience. Attorneys may request that their paralegals assist them during the trial as well. In the courtroom, a paralegal performs numerous tasks. For example, the paralegal can locate documents or exhibits as they are needed. The paralegal can also observe jurors' reactions to statements made by attorneys or witnesses, check to see if a witness's testimony is consistent with sworn statements made by the witness before the trial, and give witnesses last-minute instructions outside the courtroom before they are called to testify.

In this chapter, you learn about the pretrial stages of a civil lawsuit, from the initial attorney-client meeting to the time of the trial. In the next chapter, you will read about conducting investigations and interviews prior to trial. This chapter's *Featured Contributor* article provides ideas about pretrial preparation.

Civil Litigation—A Bird's-Eye View

Although civil trials vary greatly in terms of complexity, cost, and detail, they share similar structural characteristics. They begin with an event that gives rise to the legal action, and (provided the case is not settled by the parties at some point during the

Establish a Professional Relationship

Establish a professional rapport when you meet with clients. Be courteous, but not overly friendly. Display a nonjudgmental attitude, showing respect for the client's point of view. By adopting these qualities, you will build trust. This approach not only encourages clients to share their story but also lays the groundwork for open communication as the case progresses.

Be a Careful Listener

Although you may be tempted to tune out facts that seemingly occur in every case, train yourself to listen for the nuances presented in each client's situation. Don't limit yourself to the specific information requested in a standard questionnaire when you complete it. An intake form is merely a tool to help you gather relevant information; you don't have to follow it verbatim.

Organize the Discovery Process

Once the client hires your firm, you probably will be involved in informal discovery. In a simple PI case, paralegals routinely order traffic crash reports, as well as request client medical and employment records. Your supervising attorney may direct you to interview witnesses, retain an investigator, or hire a photographer. In other cases, your role may be to collect and organize commercial

" ... stay current and organized..."

documents. Whether you are working with paper or electronic documents, it is important to stay current and organized as you gather information.

Be Prepared to Write and Rewrite

Paralegals often draft the documents needed to initiate a civil lawsuit, such as complaints, summonses, and disclosure statements. Litigation paralegals also prepare written discovery directed to opposing parties and draft the responses to discovery served on clients.

Don't be discouraged if your supervisor changes your work product. Treat these editorial changes as an opportunity to improve your writing skills. Compare the final product with your initial draft to see what text was changed. There is more than one approach to preparing a document. Modify your technique to fit your supervising attorney's style. Bear in mind that you may need to adapt your style again when you work for someone else.

Always collaborate in the spirit of cooperation to find out what was expected. There is no reason to argue or defend what you drafted. Remember, you and your supervisor both want you to produce the best work, so make a sincere effort to learn from your mistakes.

Source: Thomas McClure

judgment
The court's final decision regarding the rights and claims of the parties to a lawsuit.

litigation process—as most cases are) they end with the issuance of a **judgment**, the court's decision on the matter. In the process, the litigation itself may involve many twists and turns. Even though each case has its own "story line," most civil lawsuits follow some version of the course charted in Exhibit 10.1.

Pretrial Settlements

In most cases, the parties reach a *settlement*—an out-of-court resolution of the dispute—before the case goes to trial. Lawsuits are costly in both time and money, and it is usually in the interest of both parties to settle the case out of court. Throughout the pretrial stage of litigation, the attorney will therefore attempt to help the parties reach a settlement. At the same time, the attorney and the paralegal must operate under the assumption that the case will go to trial, because all pretrial preparation must be completed prior to the trial date.

Procedural Requirements

Understanding and meeting procedural requirements are essential in the litigation process. These requirements are set out in the procedural rules of the court in which a lawsuit is brought. Civil trials held in federal district courts are governed by the

EXHIBIT 10.1

A Typical Case Flowchart

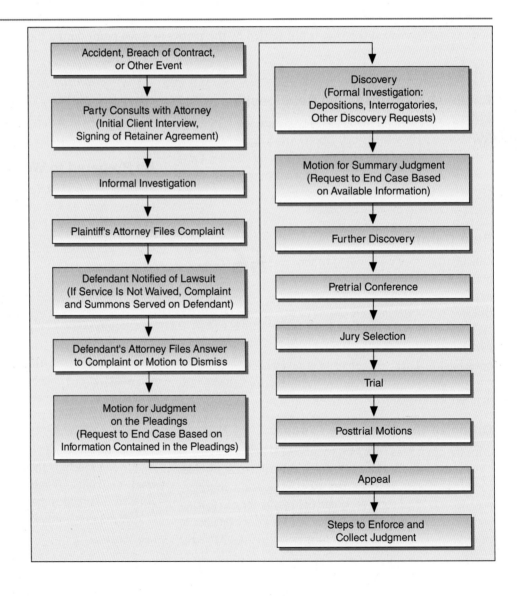

Federal Rules of Civil Procedure (FRCP). These rules specify what must be done during the various stages of the federal civil litigation process. For example, Rule 4 of the FRCP describes the procedures that must be followed in notifying the defendant of the lawsuit.

Each state also has its own rules of civil procedure (which in many states are similar to the FRCP). In addition, many courts have their own rules of procedure that supplement the federal or state rules. The attorney and the paralegal must comply with all of the rules of procedure that apply to the court in which the trial will take place. Local rules are easily overlooked but are important to know. They often set out requirements for fonts, page limits, timing, and form for certain court filings.

Federal Rules of Civil Procedure (FRCP)
The rules controlling all procedural matters in civil trials brought before the federal district courts.

A Hypothetical Lawsuit

To illustrate the procedures involved in litigation, consider a hypothetical civil lawsuit. The case involves an automobile accident in which a car driven by Tony Peretto collided with a car driven by Katherine Baranski. Baranski suffered injuries and incurred substantial medical and hospital costs. She also lost wages for the five months during which she was unable to work. Baranski has decided to sue Peretto for damages. Because Baranski is the person bringing the lawsuit, she is the plaintiff. Peretto, because he must defend against Baranski's claims, is the defendant. The plaintiff and the defendant are referred to as the *parties* to the lawsuit, as discussed in Chapter 5. (Some cases involve several plaintiffs and/or defendants.)

The attorney for the plaintiff (Baranski) is Allen P. Gilmore. Gilmore is assisted by paralegal Elena Lopez. The attorney for the defendant (Peretto) is Elizabeth A. Cameron. Cameron is assisted by paralegal Gordon McVay.

The Preliminaries

Katherine Baranski arranges to meet with Allen Gilmore, an attorney with the law firm of Jeffers, Gilmore & Dunn, to see if Gilmore will represent her in the lawsuit. Gilmore asks paralegal Elena Lopez to prepare the usual forms and information sheets, including a retainer agreement and a statement of the firm's billing procedures, and to bring them to the initial interview with Baranski. Gilmore also asks Lopez to run a *conflicts check* (see Chapter 4) to ensure that representing Baranski in this action will not create a conflict of interest.

The Initial Client Interview

Most often, the attorney—for several reasons—conducts an initial client interview. First, if attorney Gilmore is interested in taking on a new client, he will want to explain to the client the value of his services and those of his firm. Second, only an attorney can agree to represent a client. Third, only an attorney can set fees, and if Gilmore takes Baranski on as a client, fee arrangements will be discussed, and possibly agreed on, during the initial client interview. Finally, only an attorney can give legal advice, and the initial client interview may involve advising Baranski of her legal rights and options. In short, what transpires during the initial client interview normally falls under the umbrella of "the practice of law," and, as we have emphasized, only attorneys are permitted to practice law.

Because attorney Gilmore and paralegal Lopez will be working together on the case, Gilmore asks Lopez to sit in on the interview. Gilmore wants Lopez to meet Baranski, become familiar with Baranski's claim, and perhaps make arrangements for follow-up interviews with Baranski should Gilmore take the case.

Note that while the initial client interview is typically handled by a licensed attorney, a paralegal may exchange certain communications with a prospective client before this meeting. For example, many public interest and legal-aid firms use screening procedures to determine whether a prospective client's legal claim matches the firm's mission, or whether the person qualifies for legal services that can be billed to a public or private grant of funds. Because paralegals sometimes perform this screening function, they need to be familiar with the criteria used by their firm to identify cases and clients that its attorneys would or should consider taking on.

Collecting Facts

During the initial client interview, Katherine Baranski explains to attorney Gilmore and paralegal Lopez the facts of her case, as she perceives them. Baranski tells them that Tony Peretto, who was driving a Dodge van, ran a stop sign and crashed into the driver's side of her Ford Fusion as she was driving through the intersection of Mattis Avenue and Thirty-eighth Street in Nita City, Nita. The accident occurred at 7:45 A.M. on August 4, 2021. Baranski has misplaced Peretto's address, but she knows that he lives in another state, the state of Zero. Baranski claims that as a result of the accident, she has been unable to work for five months and has lost about $20,000 in wages. Her medical and hospital expenses total $95,000, and the damage to her car is estimated to be $15,000. Throughout the initial interview, Lopez takes notes to record the details of the case as relayed by Baranski.

Release Forms

Gilmore agrees to represent Baranski in the lawsuit against Peretto. He explains the fee structure to Baranski, and she signs the retainer agreement. Gilmore has Baranski sign forms authorizing him to obtain relevant medical, employment, and other records relating to the claim. (These *release forms* will be discussed in Chapter 11.) At the end of the interview, Gilmore asks Lopez to schedule a follow-up interview with Baranski. Lopez conducts that interview and obtains more details from Baranski about the accident and its consequences.

Preliminary Investigation

After Baranski leaves the office, attorney Gilmore asks paralegal Lopez to undertake a preliminary investigation to get as much information as possible concerning the facts of Baranski's accident. Sources of this information will include the police report of the accident, medical records, employment data, and eyewitness accounts of the accident.

You will read in Chapter 11 about the steps in investigating the facts of a client's case, so we will not discuss investigation here. Bear in mind that at this point in the pretrial process, the paralegal may engage in extensive investigation of the facts. Investigation is a key part of pretrial work, and facts discovered (or not discovered) by the investigator may play an important role in determining the outcome of the lawsuit.

Creating the Litigation File

Attorney Gilmore also asks paralegal Lopez to create a litigation file for the case. As the litigation progresses, Lopez will carefully maintain the file to make sure that such items as correspondence, bills, research and investigation results, and all documents and exhibits relating to the litigation are in the file and arranged in an organized manner.

Much of a paralegal's work involves legal writing, whether it be a research memorandum, a letter to a client, or a pleading or motion to be filed with a court. Excellent writing skills are a must for the professional paralegal. Assess your own writing skills. Think of ways that you can become a better writer and start putting them into practice now.

Organization

Each law firm or legal department has its own organizational scheme to follow when creating and maintaining client files. Recall from Chapter 3 that there are three goals of any law office filing system:

1. To preserve confidentiality.

2. To safeguard legal documents.

3. To ensure that the contents of files can be easily and quickly retrieved when needed.

Usually it is the paralegal's responsibility to make sure that the litigation file is properly created and maintained.

As a case progresses through the litigation process, subfiles may be created for documents relating to the various stages. For example, at this point in the *Baranski* case, the litigation file contains notes taken during the initial client interview, the signed retainer agreement, and information and documents gathered by Lopez during her preliminary investigation of the claim. As the lawsuit progresses, Lopez will make sure that subfiles are created for documents relating to the pleadings and discovery stages (to be discussed shortly). Depending on the office filing system, the file folders for these subfiles may be color-coded or numbered so that each subfile can be readily recognized and retrieved.

Many firms also scan documents and create electronic copies of the files. Lopez also prepares an index for each subfile to indicate the documents included. The index is placed at the front of the folder for easy reference.

Litigation Files

A properly created and maintained litigation file provides a comprehensive record of the case so that others in the firm can quickly acquaint themselves with the progress of the proceedings. Because well-organized files are critical to the success of any case, Lopez should take special care to properly maintain the file. The *Developing Paralegal Skills* feature on the following page discusses file organization in more depth.

DEVELOPING PARALEGAL SKILLS

FILE WORKUP

Once a litigation file has been created, the paralegal typically "works up" the file. In the *Baranski* case, after paralegal Lopez has completed her initial investigation into Baranski's claim, she reviews and summarizes the information she has amassed so far. This includes the information gathered through the initial and subsequent client interviews and any investigation that she has conducted.

Lopez also identifies areas that might require testimony of an expert witness. For example, if Baranski claimed that as a result of the accident she would always walk with a limp, Gilmore would want a medical specialist to give expert testimony to support the claim. (How to locate expert witnesses will be discussed in later chapters.) Lopez would prepare a list of potential experts for Gilmore to review.

Once Lopez has worked up the file, she prepares a memo to Gilmore summarizing the file. This memo provides him with factual information to decide which legal remedy or strategy to pursue, what legal issues need to be researched, and generally how to proceed with the case.

Tips for Preparing a File Workup Memo

- Summarize the information that has been obtained about the case.
- Suggest a plan for further investigation in the case (reviewed in Chapter 11).
- Suggest additional information that might be obtained during discovery (discussed later in this chapter).
- Include a list of expert witnesses to contact, explaining which witnesses might be preferable, and why.

The Pleadings

complaint

The pleading made by a plaintiff or a charge made by the state alleging wrongdoing on the part of the defendant.

pleadings

Statements by the plaintiff and the defendant that detail the facts, charges, and defenses involved in the litigation.

The next step is for plaintiff Baranski's attorney, Gilmore, to file a complaint in the appropriate court. The **complaint** (called a *petition* in some courts) is a document that states the claims the plaintiff is making against the defendant. The complaint also contains a statement regarding the court's jurisdiction over the dispute and a demand for a remedy (such as monetary damages) or an injunction.

The filing of the complaint is the step that begins the formal legal action against the defendant, Peretto. The complaint is one of the **pleadings**, which inform each party of the claims made by the other and specify the issues (disputed questions) involved in the case. We examine here two basic pleadings—the plaintiff's complaint and the defendant's answer.

The complaint must be filed within the period of time allowed by law for bringing legal actions. The allowable period is fixed by state statutes of limitations (discussed in Chapter 5), and this period varies for different types of claims. For example, actions concerning breaches of sales contracts must usually be brought within four years. After the time allowed under a statute of limitations has expired, normally no action can be brought, no matter how strong the case was originally. For instance, if the statute of limitations covering the auto-negligence lawsuit that plaintiff Baranski is bringing against defendant Peretto allows two years for bringing an action, Baranski normally must initiate the lawsuit within that time or give up the possibility of suing Peretto for damages caused by the car accident.

Drafting the Complaint

The complaint itself may be no more than a few paragraphs long, or it may be many pages in length, depending on the complexity of the case. In the *Baranski* case, the complaint will probably be only a few pages long unless special circumstances require additional details. The complaint will include the following sections, each of which we discuss below:

- Caption.
- Jurisdictional allegations.
- General allegations (the body of the complaint).
- Prayer for relief.
- Signature.
- Demand for a jury trial.

Exhibit 10.2 shows a sample complaint.

Baranski's case is filed in a federal court, so the Federal Rules of Civil Procedure (FRCP) apply. If the case were filed in a state court, paralegal Lopez would need to review the appropriate state rules of civil procedure. The rules for drafting pleadings in state courts may differ from the FRCP. The rules may also differ from state to state and even from court to court within the same state. Lopez could obtain pleading forms from "form books" available in the law firm's files or library (or online) or from pleadings drafted previously in similar cases litigated by the firm. Firms often keep a digital file folder with form motions, pleadings, subpoenas, and other legal documents used in litigation.

The Caption

All documents submitted to the court or other parties during the litigation process begin with a caption. The caption is the heading, which identifies the name of the court, the title of the action, the names of the parties, the type of document, and the court's file number. Note that the court's file number may also be referred to as the case number or *docket number,* depending on the jurisdiction. (A **docket** is the official schedule of proceedings in lawsuits pending before a court.)

A client might be a listed party in multiple pending lawsuits, some of which might have the same names on both sides of the "v." It is critical in these cases to be certain that a document is being filed in the correct case by checking to see that the docket number is correct. This is particularly important for family law litigation.

The caption for a complaint leaves a space for the court to insert the number that it assigns to the case. Courts typically assign the case a number when the complaint is filed. Any document subsequently filed with the court in the case will list the file, case, or docket number on the front page of the document. Exhibit 10.2 shows how the caption will read in the case of *Baranski v. Peretto.*

Jurisdictional Allegations

Because attorney Gilmore is filing the lawsuit in a federal district court, he must include in the complaint an allegation that the federal court has jurisdiction to hear the dispute. (An **allegation** is an assertion, claim, or statement made by one party in a pleading that sets out what the party expects to prove to the court.) Recall from Chapter 6 that federal courts can exercise jurisdiction over disputes involving either a *federal question* or *diversity of citizenship.*

A federal question arises whenever a claim in a civil lawsuit relates to a federal law, the U.S. Constitution, or a treaty executed by the U.S. government. Diversity of citizenship exists when the parties involved in the lawsuit are citizens of different states and the amount in controversy exceeds $75,000. Because Baranski and Peretto are citizens of different states (fictitious Nita and Zero, respectively) and because the amount in controversy exceeds $75,000, the case meets the requirements for

docket
The list of cases entered on a court's calendar and thus scheduled to be heard by the court.

allegation
A party's statement, claim, or assertion made in a pleading to the court. The allegation sets forth the issue that the party expects to prove.

EXHIBIT 10.2

The Complaint

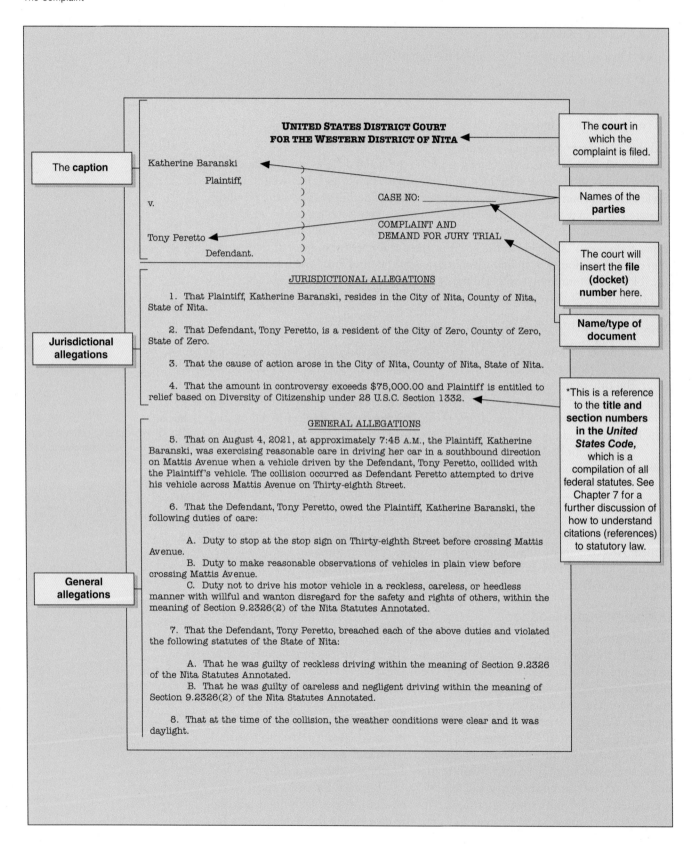

The **caption**

UNITED STATES DISTRICT COURT
FOR THE WESTERN DISTRICT OF NITA

The **court** in which the complaint is filed.

Katherine Baranski

Plaintiff,

v.

Tony Peretto

Defendant.

CASE NO: _____

COMPLAINT AND
DEMAND FOR JURY TRIAL

Names of the **parties**

The court will insert the **file (docket) number** here.

Name/type of document

Jurisdictional allegations

JURISDICTIONAL ALLEGATIONS

1. That Plaintiff, Katherine Baranski, resides in the City of Nita, County of Nita, State of Nita.

2. That Defendant, Tony Peretto, is a resident of the City of Zero, County of Zero, State of Zero.

3. That the cause of action arose in the City of Nita, County of Nita, State of Nita.

4. That the amount in controversy exceeds $75,000.00 and Plaintiff is entitled to relief based on Diversity of Citizenship under 28 U.S.C. Section 1332.

*This is a reference to the **title and section numbers in the** *United States Code,* which is a compilation of all federal statutes. See Chapter 7 for a further discussion of how to understand citations (references) to statutory law.

General allegations

GENERAL ALLEGATIONS

5. That on August 4, 2021, at approximately 7:45 A.M., the Plaintiff, Katherine Baranski, was exercising reasonable care in driving her car in a southbound direction on Mattis Avenue when a vehicle driven by the Defendant, Tony Peretto, collided with the Plaintiff's vehicle. The collision occurred as Defendant Peretto attempted to drive his vehicle across Mattis Avenue on Thirty-eighth Street.

6. That the Defendant, Tony Peretto, owed the Plaintiff, Katherine Baranski, the following duties of care:

   A. Duty to stop at the stop sign on Thirty-eighth Street before crossing Mattis Avenue.
   B. Duty to make reasonable observations of vehicles in plain view before crossing Mattis Avenue.
   C. Duty not to drive his motor vehicle in a reckless, careless, or heedless manner with willful and wanton disregard for the safety and rights of others, within the meaning of Section 9.2326(2) of the Nita Statutes Annotated.

7. That the Defendant, Tony Peretto, breached each of the above duties and violated the following statutes of the State of Nita:

   A. That he was guilty of reckless driving within the meaning of Section 9.2326 of the Nita Statutes Annotated.
   B. That he was guilty of careless and negligent driving within the meaning of Section 9.2326(2) of the Nita Statutes Annotated.

8. That at the time of the collision, the weather conditions were clear and it was daylight.

EXHIBIT 10.2
The Complaint—Continued

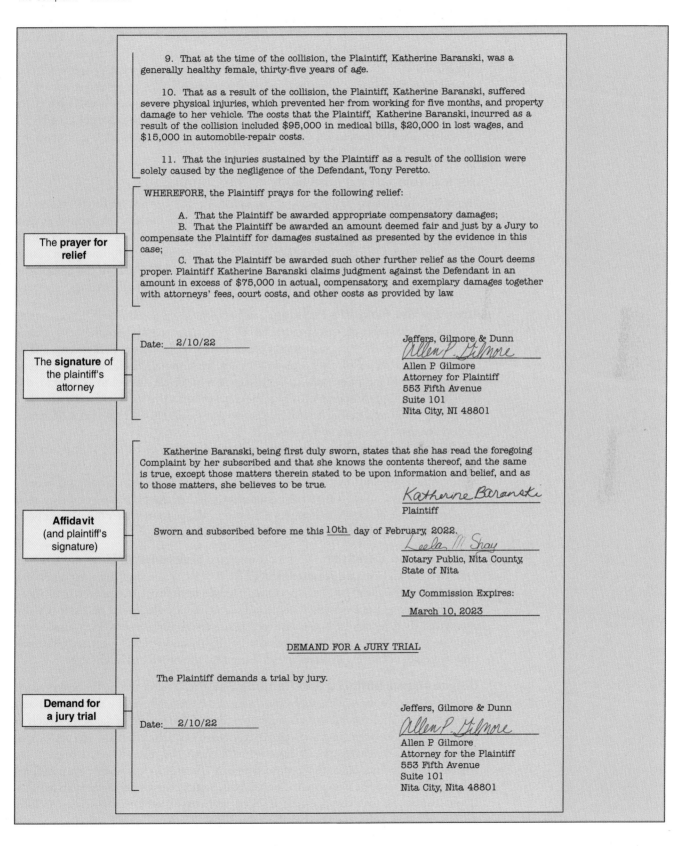

9. That at the time of the collision, the Plaintiff, Katherine Baranski, was a generally healthy female, thirty-five years of age.

10. That as a result of the collision, the Plaintiff, Katherine Baranski, suffered severe physical injuries, which prevented her from working for five months, and property damage to her vehicle. The costs that the Plaintiff, Katherine Baranski, incurred as a result of the collision included $95,000 in medical bills, $20,000 in lost wages, and $15,000 in automobile-repair costs.

11. That the injuries sustained by the Plaintiff as a result of the collision were solely caused by the negligence of the Defendant, Tony Peretto.

The prayer for relief

WHEREFORE, the Plaintiff prays for the following relief:

A. That the Plaintiff be awarded appropriate compensatory damages;
B. That the Plaintiff be awarded an amount deemed fair and just by a Jury to compensate the Plaintiff for damages sustained as presented by the evidence in this case;
C. That the Plaintiff be awarded such other further relief as the Court deems proper. Plaintiff Katherine Baranski claims judgment against the Defendant in an amount in excess of $75,000 in actual, compensatory, and exemplary damages together with attorneys' fees, court costs, and other costs as provided by law.

The signature of the plaintiff's attorney

Date: 2/10/22

Jeffers, Gilmore & Dunn

Allen P. Gilmore
Allen P Gilmore
Attorney for Plaintiff
553 Fifth Avenue
Suite 101
Nita City, NI 48801

Affidavit (and plaintiff's signature)

Katherine Baranski, being first duly sworn, states that she has read the foregoing Complaint by her subscribed and that she knows the contents thereof, and the same is true, except those matters therein stated to be upon information and belief, and as to those matters, she believes to be true.

Katherine Baranski
Plaintiff

Sworn and subscribed before me this 10th day of February, 2022.

Leela M Shay
Notary Public, Nita County,
State of Nita

My Commission Expires:

March 10, 2023

Demand for a jury trial

DEMAND FOR A JURY TRIAL

The Plaintiff demands a trial by jury.

Jeffers, Gilmore & Dunn

Date: 2/10/22

Allen P. Gilmore
Allen P Gilmore
Attorney for the Plaintiff
553 Fifth Avenue
Suite 101
Nita City, Nita 48801

diversity-of-citizenship jurisdiction. Gilmore thus asserts that the federal court has jurisdiction on this basis, as illustrated in Exhibit 10.2.

Certain cases, including those involving diversity of citizenship, may be brought in either a state court or a federal court. (This was discussed in the *Developing Paralegal Skills* feature entitled "Choice of Courts: State or Federal?" in Chapter 6.) Thus, an attorney in Gilmore's position can advise the client that there is a choice. Gilmore probably considered several factors when advising Baranski on which court would be preferable for her lawsuit. One issue is how long it would take to get the case to trial. Many courts are overburdened by their caseloads, and sometimes it can take years before a court will be able to hear a case. If Gilmore knows that the case could be heard two years earlier in the federal court than in the state court, that fact is an important factor to consider.

General Allegations (The Body of the Complaint)

The body of the complaint contains a series of allegations that set forth a claim for relief. In plaintiff Baranski's complaint, the allegations outline the factual events that gave rise to Baranski's claims. The events are described in a series of chronologically arranged, numbered allegations so that the reader can follow them easily. As Exhibit 10.2 shows, the numbers of the paragraphs in the body of the complaint continue the sequence begun in the section on jurisdictional allegations.

Advocate the Plaintiff's Position. When drafting the complaint, Lopez acts as an advocate. She must present the facts forcefully to support and strengthen the client's claim. The recitation of the facts must demonstrate that defendant Peretto engaged in conduct that entitles plaintiff Baranski to relief. Even though Lopez wants to present the facts in a light most favorable to Baranski, she must be careful not to exaggerate the facts or make false statements. Rather, she must present the facts in such a way that the reader could reasonably infer that Peretto was negligent and that his negligence caused Baranski's injuries and losses.

What if her research into the case gave Lopez reason to believe that a fact was probably true even though she could not verify it? She could still include the statement in the complaint by prefacing it with the phrase "on information and belief." This language would indicate to the court that plaintiff Baranski has good reason to believe the truth of the statement, but that the evidence for it either has not yet been obtained or might not hold up under close scrutiny.

Be Clear and Concise. The most effective complaints are clear and concise. Brevity and simplicity are required under FRCP 8(a). When drafting the complaint, Lopez should use clear language and favor simple and direct statements over more complex wording. Lopez should include only facts that are absolutely necessary for the complaint. By reducing the body of the complaint to the simplest possible terms, Lopez achieves greater clarity and minimizes the possibility of divulging attorney Gilmore's trial strategies or hinting at a possible defense that the opponent might use.

Outline Harms Suffered and Remedy Sought. After telling Baranski's story, Lopez adds one or more paragraphs outlining the harms suffered by the plaintiff and the remedy sought. In general, it is preferable that all allegations of damages—such as hospital costs, lost wages, and auto-repair expenses—be included in a single paragraph, as in Exhibit 10.2, Paragraph 10. Lopez should check the relevant court rules to see whether the court requires that certain damages (Baranski's lost wages, for example) be alleged in a separate paragraph. Additionally, some forms of damages, such as emotional distress, are not compensable in every state and therefore should be carefully examined before being included in the complaint.

Prayer for Relief

Paralegal Lopez includes a paragraph at the end of the complaint, as shown in Exhibit 10.2, asking that judgment be entered for the plaintiff and appropriate relief be granted. This **prayer for relief** will indicate that plaintiff Baranski is seeking money damages to compensate her for the harms that she suffered. Without this paragraph, the complaint is functionless, because it does not call upon the court to actually *do* anything.

prayer for relief
A statement at the end of the complaint requesting that the court grant relief to the plaintiff.

Signature

In federal practice, the signature following the prayer for relief certifies that the plaintiff's attorney (or the plaintiff, if not represented by an attorney) has read the complaint and that the facts alleged are true to the best of his or her knowledge. In addition, some state courts require an affidavit signed by the plaintiff verifying that the complaint is true to the best of the plaintiff's knowledge. An **affidavit** is a sworn statement attesting to the existence of certain facts. Affidavits are acknowledged by a notary public or another official authorized to administer such oaths or affirmations. Exhibit 10.2 illustrates an affidavit for the Baranski complaint.

affidavit
A written statement of facts, confirmed by the oath or affirmation of the party making it and sworn before a person having the authority to administer the oath or affirmation.

Demand for a Jury Trial

The Seventh Amendment to the U.S. Constitution guarantees the right to a jury trial in federal courts in all "suits at common law" when the amount in controversy exceeds $20 (the equivalent of forty days' salary at that time). Most states have similar guarantees in their own constitutions, although many states put a higher minimum dollar restriction on the guarantee (for example, in Maryland the minimum amount is $10,000). If this threshold requirement is met, either party may request a jury trial.

The right to a trial by jury does not have to be exercised, and many cases are tried without one, with the judge making the findings of fact. In most states and in federal courts, one of the parties must request a jury trial, or the right is presumed waived (that is, the court will presume that neither party wants a jury trial). The decision to exercise the right to a jury trial usually depends on what legal theory the party is using and which judge is assigned to the trial. In the *Baranski* case, Gilmore may advise Baranski to demand a jury trial if he believes that a jury would be sympathetic to her position. If Baranski wants a jury trial, Gilmore will ask Lopez to include a demand for a jury trial (as in Point B of the prayer for relief in Exhibit 10.2) with the complaint. More tips for drafting a complaint are presented in the *Developing Paralegal Skills* feature on the next page.

Filing the Complaint

Once the complaint has been prepared, checked for accuracy, and signed by attorney Gilmore, paralegal Lopez files the complaint with the court in which the action is being brought.

Traditional Method of Filing

Traditionally, a person filing a complaint personally delivers the complaint to the clerk of the court, together with a specified number of copies of the complaint and a check payable to the court in the amount of the required filing fee. Usually, a summons (discussed shortly) is also attached. If Lopez uses this method of filing, she can either deliver the complaint to the court clerk or have someone deliver it for her. If she is not aware of the court's procedures for filing the complaint, she needs to contact the court to verify the filing fee and how many copies of the complaint need to be filed.

DEVELOPING PARALEGAL SKILLS

A CHECKLIST FOR DRAFTING A COMPLAINT IN A FEDERAL CIVIL CASE

Civil cases begin when a complaint is filed in court. To draft a complaint, you need to know the facts your client alleges and the law that supports your client's claim for relief. You need to review notes from client interviews and meetings with the attorneys, factual materials (e.g., police or hospital reports), and preliminary research. It is a good idea to review complaints from similar cases handled by your firm in the past. They can give you a feel for the appropriate writing style. Form books also provide guidance on how to draft particular claims. It is also critical to check the appropriate court's rules for local requirements.

For civil suits in federal court, FRCP 8 sets out the required elements. State rules have equivalent provisions. Generally, local rules will cover the typeface, type and size of paper, and other such matters.

A well-drafted complaint contains the information needed to answer the following questions:

- Who is the plaintiff? Use the plaintiff's legal name and include a statement of the jurisdiction where the plaintiff is a legal resident. If the plaintiff is suing as the representative of someone else, identify the relationship.

- Who is the defendant? It is critical to use the defendant's correct legal name so that you sue the proper person or firm. You also need to provide the defendant's legal residence.

- Why is the suit being filed in this court? How does the court have jurisdiction over the case? List the specific statutes involved. For example, list 28 U.S.C. § 1331 for federal question jurisdiction, 28 U.S.C. § 1332 for diversity-of-citizenship jurisdiction, or 42 U.S.C. § 1983 for civil rights violations. Remember, the court must have jurisdiction over both the cause of action and the defendants.

- Did any administrative prerequisites have to be satisfied prior to filing the lawsuit? If so, how were they satisfied?

- Is the claim timely filed (within the relevant statute of limitations)?

- What are the facts that make up the plaintiff's case? State these accurately, clearly, and briefly. Give names and dates where known.

- What are the legal claims made by the plaintiff? Draft each claim in a separate "count" in the complaint.

- Are there special pleadings requirements for particular claims (e.g., fraud)? How has the plaintiff satisfied them?

- What is the plaintiff asking for? Clearly describe the relief the plaintiff wants. Is it monetary damages? An injunction? Declaratory relief? Attorneys' fees and costs? Prejudgment interest? Postjudgment interest? Are special damages requested (such as statutory damages or punitive damages)?

- Who is the attorney filing the suit? Include an appropriate signature block for the lawyer to sign, certifying that the attorney has conducted a reasonable inquiry into the facts that support the claim.

- Is a jury requested? Check to see if the claim is one for which a jury is available. Find out whether the attorney overseeing the case wants to request a jury. If so, you need to include the appropriate language demanding a jury trial.

All parts of the complaint should be written in clear, direct English. Professionalism is appreciated by a court.

Typically, the original (signed) complaint is filed with at least two copies (the court keeps the original, and the plaintiff and defendant receive a copy). Additional copies may be required, particularly if there are multiple plaintiffs or defendants.

The court clerk files the complaint by doing the following:

- Stamping the date on the first page of all the documents (original and copies).

- Assigning the case a file number, or docket number.

- Assigning the case to a particular judge.

(In some state courts, the file number or judge may not be assigned until later.) The clerk then returns the date-stamped copies to the person who delivered the documents for service on the defendant (to be discussed shortly).

E-Filing

Instead of delivering a paper document to the court, Lopez may be able to file the complaint electronically. Electronic filing is becoming more common. Because of the reduced time and paperwork involved, electronic filing can result in savings for attorneys, clients, and the courts. With an **electronic filing (e-filing) system**, registered attorneys can file case documents over the Internet at any time right up to the filing deadline. (Go to **pacer.gov** to see the service for the federal court system.)

The security of the e-filing process is important. Only registered parties may access a court's e-filing system. As with most secure electronic communications, the registered party has a user ID and a password. An attorney may give a paralegal authority to use the system on the attorney's behalf. Consent of the parties to use e-filing may be required. Once parties agree to e-filing, the court assigns a docket number to the case. From that point forward, all documents filed by consenting parties must use the system. Often, documents must be formatted as secure PDF files so that they cannot be altered. The parties must provide e-mail addresses for notification of service of documents.

A party to an action being handled by e-filing may have the right to request hard copies of documents. When hard copies are used, they are to include a notice that they have been filed electronically. Special steps are taken to protect private information, such as Social Security numbers, credit-card information, a minor child's name, or trade secrets. Fees for documents filed are paid electronically. Therefore, in many cases, all paperwork and communications between the parties and the court are electronic.

> **electronic filing (e-filing) system**
> An online system that enables attorneys to file case documents with courts twenty-four hours a day, seven days a week.

Service of Process

Before the court can exercise jurisdiction over the defendant, the court must have proof that the defendant was notified of the lawsuit. Serving the summons and complaint—that is, officially delivering these documents to the defendant in a lawsuit—is referred to as **service of process**.

The Summons

The **summons** identifies the parties to the lawsuit, as well as the court in which the case will be heard, and directs the defendant to respond to the complaint within a specified period of time. In the *Baranski* case, paralegal Lopez will prepare a summons by filling out a form similar to that shown in Exhibit 10.3 on the following page. Lopez also prepares a cover sheet for the case (a preprinted form), as is required in federal courts and in most state courts.

If the case were being brought in a state court, Lopez would deliver the summons to the court clerk at the same time she delivers the complaint. In federal court cases, the complaint may already have been filed under the FRCP provisions relating to waiver of notice.

After the clerk files the complaint and signs, seals, and issues the summons, attorney Gilmore is responsible for making sure that the summons and complaint are served on defendant Peretto. The service of the complaint and summons must happen within a specific time—120 days under FRCP 4(m)—after the complaint has been filed.

> **service of process**
> The delivery of the summons and the complaint to a defendant.
>
> **summons**
> A document served on a defendant in a lawsuit informing the defendant that a legal action has been commenced against him or her and that the defendant must appear in court or respond to the plaintiff's complaint within a specified period of time.

Serving the Complaint and Summons

How service of process occurs depends on the rules of the court or jurisdiction in which the lawsuit is brought. Under FRCP 4(c)(2), service of process in federal court cases may be effected "by any person who is not a party and who is at least 18 years of age." Paralegal Lopez, for example, could serve the summons and complaint by personally delivering it to defendant Peretto. Alternatively, she could make arrangements for someone else to do so, subject to approval of attorney Gilmore.

Most law firms contract with independent companies that provide process service in the local area. In some cases, the attorney might request that the court have a U.S. marshal

EXHIBIT 10.3

A Summons in a Civil Action

UNITED STATES DISTRICT COURT
FOR THE WESTERN DISTRICT OF NITA

Katherine Baranski)
                Plaintiff,)
V.)
)
Tony Peretto)
               Defendant.)

Civil Action, File Number 14-14335-NI

Summons

To the above-named Defendant:

You are hereby summoned and required to serve upon A. P. Gilmore, Jeffers, Gilmore & Dunn, plaintiff's attorney, whose address is 553 Fifth Avenue, Suite 101, Nita City, NI 48801, an answer to the complaint which is herewith served upon you, within 20 days after service of this summons upon you, exclusive of the day of service. If you fail to do so, judgment by default will be taken against you for the relief demanded in the complaint.

C. H. Hynek _____   February 10, 2022 _____
CLERK   DATE

John Dolan
BY DEPUTY CLERK

---

or other federal official serve the summons. See the U.S. Marshals Service website (**usmarshals.gov**) for a discussion of their services and the service requirements. For a list of process methods in each state, see that website and search for "Service of Process."

Under FRCP 4(e)(1), service of process in federal court cases may be performed "pursuant to the law of the state in which the district court is located." Some state courts require that a public officer, such as a sheriff, serve the complaint and summons.

Alternative Service Methods. Although the most common way to serve process on a defendant is through personal service, as described above, other methods are permissible at times, depending on the jurisdiction. *Substituted service*, such as service by certified mail or e-mail, is allowed, although it generally is not favored. Posting—a form of service allowed in some jurisdictions—entails affixing the summons or complaint to the front door of the defendant's last known address when personal service has not been successful. The paralegal and attorney need to know the types of service authorized by the laws in the relevant state.

Proof of Service. Regardless of how the summons is served, attorney Gilmore will need proof that defendant Peretto actually received the summons. In federal court cases, unless service is made by a U.S. marshal or another official, the process server fills out and signs a form similar to the **return-of-service form** shown in Exhibit 10.4. This form is then submitted to the court as proof of service.

return-of-service form
A document signed by a process server and submitted to the court to prove that a defendant received a summons.

Jurisdictions Vary. Paralegal Lopez must be careful to comply with the service requirements of the court in which plaintiff Baranski's suit has been filed. If service is not properly made, defendant Peretto has legal grounds for asking the court to dismiss the case against him. The court cannot exercise jurisdiction over Peretto until he has been properly notified of the lawsuit being brought against him.

EXHIBIT 10.4

A Return-of-Service Form

RETURN OF SERVICE

Service of the Summons and Complaint was made by me	DATE 2/11/22
NAME OF SERVER Elena Lopez	TITLE Paralegal

Check one box below to indicate appropriate method of service

[X] Served personally upon the defendant. Place where served: Defendant Peretto's Home: 1708 Johnston Drive, Zero City, Zero 59806

[ ] Left copies thereof at the defendant's dwelling house or usual place of abode with a person of suitable age and discretion then residing therein.
Name of person with whom the summons and complaint were left: _____

[ ] Returned unexecuted: _____

[ ] Other (specify): _____

DECLARATION OF SERVER

I declare under penalty of perjury under the laws of the United States of America that the foregoing information contained in the Return of Service and Statement of Service Fees is true and correct.

Executed on ___2/11/22___   *Elena Lopez*
            Date   *Signature of Server*

308 University Avenue, Nita City, Nita 48804
            Address of Server

Serving Corporate Defendants

In cases involving corporate defendants, the summons and complaint may be served on an officer or a *registered agent* (representative) of the corporation. The name of a corporation's registered agent and its business address can usually be obtained from the secretary of state's office in the state in which the company is incorporated or in any state in which it does business. Often, this information is available online. Many states operate websites with searchable databases of licensed entities that contain such details.

Finding the Defendant

Because some defendants may be difficult to locate, paralegals sometimes have to search for a defendant so that process can be served. Information sources include telephone directories, banks, former business partners or fellow workers, credit bureaus, Social Security offices, insurance companies, landlords, state and county tax rolls, utility companies, automobile-registration bureaus, bureaus of vital statistics, and the post office. (Chapter 11 discusses these and other sources that the paralegal might consult when trying to locate parties or witnesses in lawsuits.) In addition, social media should not be underestimated as a tool for tracking down a witness or defendant.

The Defendant Can Waive Formal Service

Often, the plaintiff's attorney contacts the defendant before process is served and indicates that a complaint will be filed. The attorney can request the defendant to *waive* (give up) the right to be formally served with a summons. FRCP 4(d) sets forth the procedure by which a plaintiff's attorney can request the defendant to accept service of the documents through the mail or "other reliable means." Most states have similar rules.

The aim of FRCP 4(d) is to reduce the costs associated with service of process. As an incentive, defendants who agree to waive formal service of process under the federal rules receive additional time to respond to the complaint (sixty days, compared with the twenty-one days that a defendant normally has to respond to the complaint under FRCP 12). Some state rules of civil procedure provide other incentives, such as requiring that a party who will not agree to waive service pay for reasonable expenses thereafter incurred in serving or attempting to serve the party.

The Defendant's Response

default judgment

A judgment entered by a clerk or court against a party who has failed to appear in court to answer or defend against a claim that has been brought against him or her by another party.

Once a defendant receives the plaintiff's complaint, the defendant must respond to the complaint within a specified time (typically twenty-one days). If the defendant fails to respond within that time, the plaintiff can ask the court to enter a **default judgment** against the defendant. The defendant will then be liable for all damages the plaintiff is claiming and loses the opportunity to defend against the claim in court.

In the *Baranski* case, assume that defendant Peretto consults with an attorney, Elizabeth Cameron, to decide on a course of action. Before Cameron advises Peretto on the matter, she will investigate plaintiff Baranski's claim and obtain evidence of what happened at the time of the accident. She may ask her paralegal, Gordon McVay, to call anyone who may have witnessed the accident and any police officers who were at the scene. Cameron will also ask McVay to gather relevant documents, including the traffic ticket Peretto received at the time of the accident and any reports filed by the police. If all goes well, Cameron and McVay will complete their investigation in a few days and then assess the results.

Most cases are dropped by the plaintiff or settled out of court before they go to trial. But even if Peretto's attorney suspects that an out-of-court settlement might be preferable to a trial, she will draft a response to Baranski's claim. She knows that if Peretto does not respond to the complaint within the proper time period, the court could enter a default judgment against him.

The Answer

answer

A defendant's response to a plaintiff's complaint.

A defendant's **answer** must respond to each allegation in the plaintiff's complaint. FRCP 8(b) permits the defendant to admit or deny the truth of each allegation. Peretto's attorney may advise him to admit to some of the allegations in Baranski's complaint, because doing so narrows the number of issues in dispute. Allegations not denied by the defendant are deemed to have been admitted.

If Peretto does not know whether a particular allegation is true or false, Cameron may indicate that in the answer. This puts the burden of proving the allegation on Baranski. It is not necessary for Peretto's attorney to include in the answer any of the reasons for the denial of particular allegations in Baranski's complaint. These reasons may be revealed during the discovery phase of the litigation process (discussed later in this chapter).

Exhibit 10.5 illustrates the responses that Peretto might make in his answer. Like the complaint, the answer begins with a caption and ends with the attorney's signature. It may also include an affidavit signed by the defendant and/or a demand for a jury trial.

affirmative defense

A response to a plaintiff's claim that does not deny the plaintiff's facts but attacks the plaintiff's legal right to bring an action.

Answer and Affirmative Defenses.   A defendant may assert in the answer a reason why he or she should not be held liable for the plaintiff's injuries even if the facts, as alleged by the plaintiff, are true. This is called raising an **affirmative defense**.

For example, Peretto's attorney might raise the defense of *contributory negligence*. That is, she could argue that even though Peretto's car collided with Baranski's, Baranski was also negligent because she was exceeding the speed limit when the accident occurred. The plaintiff's role in contributing to the accident could result in reduced or no damages for her. Although affirmative defenses are directed toward the plaintiff, the plaintiff is not required to file additional pleadings in response to these defenses.

EXHIBIT 10.5

The Answer

UNITED STATES DISTRICT COURT
FOR THE WESTERN DISTRICT OF NITA

Katherine Baranski)	CASE NO. 14-14335-NI
Plaintiff,)	Honorable Harley M. Larue
)	
v.)	
)	ANSWER AND
Tony Peretto)	DEMAND FOR JURY TRIAL
Defendant.)	

JURISDICTIONAL ALLEGATIONS

1. Defendant lacks sufficient information to form a belief as to the truth of the allegations contained in paragraph 1 of Plaintiff's Complaint.

2. Defendant admits the allegations contained in paragraph 2 of Plaintiff's Complaint.

3. Defendant admits the allegations contained in paragraph 3 of Plaintiff's Complaint.

4. Defendant lacks sufficient information to form a belief as to the truth of the allegations contained in paragraph 4 of Plaintiff's Complaint.

GENERAL ALLEGATIONS

5. Defendant admits the allegations contained in paragraph 5 of Plaintiff's Complaint.

6. Defendant admits the allegations contained in paragraph 6 of Plaintiff's Complaint.

7. Defendant contends that he was operating his vehicle properly and denies the allegations contained in paragraph 7 of Plaintiff's Complaint for the reason that the allegations are untrue.

8. Defendant admits the allegation contained in paragraph 8 of Plaintiff's Complaint.

9. Defendant lacks sufficient information to form a belief as to the truth of the allegation contained in paragraph 9 of Plaintiff's Complaint.

10. Defendant lacks sufficient information on the proximate cause of Plaintiff's injuries to form a belief as to the truth of the averments contained in paragraph 10 of Plaintiff's Complaint.

11. Defendant denies the allegation of negligence contained in paragraph 11 of Plaintiff's Complaint.

Continued

EXHIBIT 10.5

The Answer—Continued

<u>NEW MATTER AND AFFIRMATIVE DEFENSES</u>

Although denying that the Plaintiff is entitled to the relief prayed for in the Plaintiff's Complaint, Defendant further states that the Plaintiff is barred from recovery hereunder by reason of the following:

1. That the Plaintiff's injuries were proximately caused by her own contributory negligence and want of due care under the circumstances prevailing at the time of the accident.

2. That the Plaintiff was exceeding the posted speed limit at the time and place of the accident and therefore was guilty of careless and negligent driving within the meaning of Section 9.2325(1) of the Nita Statutes Annotated.

3. That the Plaintiff failed to exercise that standard of care that a reasonably prudent person would have exercised under the same or similar conditions for her own safety and that her own negligence, contributory negligence, and/or comparative negligence caused or was a contributing factor to the incident out of which the Plaintiff's cause of action arises.

4. The Defendant reserves the right, by an appropriate Motion, to move the Court to amend the Defendant's Answer to the Plaintiff's Complaint, to allege other New Matters and Affirmative Defenses as may be revealed by discovery yet to be had and completed in this case.

WHEREFORE, the Defendant prays for a judgment of no cause of action with costs and attorneys' fees to be paid by the Plaintiff.

Cameron & Strauss, P.C.

Elizabeth A. Cameron

Date: _2/25/22_

Elizabeth A. Cameron
Attorney for the Defendant
310 Lake Drive
Zero City, ZE 59802

Tony Peretto, being first duly sworn, states that he has read the foregoing Answer by him subscribed and that he knows the contents thereof, and the same is true, except those matters therein stated to be upon information and belief, and as to those matters, he believes to be true.

Tony Peretto

Defendant

Sworn and subscribed before me this _25th_ day of February, 2022.

Laura Curtis

Notary Public, Zero County,
State of Zero

My Commission Expires:
December 8, 2023

<u>DEMAND FOR A JURY TRIAL</u>

The Defendant demands a trial by jury.

Cameron & Strauss, P.C.

Elizabeth A. Cameron

Date: _2/25/22_

Elizabeth A. Cameron
Attorney for the Defendant
310 Lake Drive
Zero City, Zero 59802

Answer and Counterclaim. Peretto's attorney may assert one or more counterclaims. A **counterclaim** is like a reverse lawsuit. The defendant asserts a claim against the plaintiff for injuries the defendant suffered from the same incident. For example, Peretto might contend that Baranski lost control of her car and skidded into Peretto's car, causing him to be injured. This allegation would be a counterclaim. The plaintiff is required to reply to any counterclaims made by the defendant.

Cross-Claim. If a complaint names multiple defendants, the answer filed by one defendant might be followed by a **cross-claim**, in which the defendant asserts a claim against another defendant. (Note that cross-claims may also be filed by one plaintiff against another plaintiff in the same case.) For example, suppose that plaintiff Baranski had been struck by two vehicles, one belonging to defendant Peretto and one belonging to Leon Balfour. If Peretto and Balfour had been named as co-defendants in Baranski's complaint, Peretto's attorney might have filed an answer to Baranski's complaint that included a cross-claim against Balfour. The party against whom the cross-claim is brought is required to reply to (answer) the claim.

Under the federal rules, a defendant who has a claim against the plaintiff related to the same incident is normally required to file a counterclaim within the defendant's pleading. A party who fails to do so may lose the possibility of asserting the claim at a later date. This requirement is intended to prevent multiple lawsuits between the same parties from dragging on interminably and creating excess expense for the court and the parties. Reasoning of this kind is often referred to in legal rules and policies as **judicial economy**.

Filing a Motion

A **motion** is a request submitted to the court by an attorney on behalf of the attorney's client. When one party files a motion with the court, that party must also send to, or serve on, the opposing party a *notice of motion*. The notice informs the opposing party that the motion has been filed and indicates when the court will hear the motion. The notice gives the opposing party an opportunity to prepare for the hearing. Note that motions are often filed at a date and time agreed on by the parties before the filing takes place. Other times, the parties might agree on a date for a motion to be filed while in court during a separate hearing before the judge.

The **motion to dismiss**, as the phrase implies, requests the court to dismiss the case for reasons provided in the motion. Defendant Peretto's attorney, for example, could file a motion to dismiss if she believed that Peretto had not been properly served, that the complaint had been filed in the wrong court, that the statute of limitations for that type of lawsuit had expired, or that the complaint did not state a claim for which relief (a remedy) could be granted. See Exhibit 10.6 for an example of a motion to dismiss. This kind of motion to dismiss is sometimes referred to as a "12(b)(6) motion," named for the FRCP that makes such motions possible.

If Peretto's attorney decides to file a motion to dismiss Baranski's claim, she may want to attach supporting affidavits. A **supporting affidavit** is a sworn statement as to certain facts that may contradict allegations made in the complaint. Peretto's attorney may also have her paralegal draft a **memorandum of law** (which is called a *brief* in some states) to be submitted along with the motion to dismiss and the accompanying affidavits. The memorandum of law presents the legal basis for the motion, citing any statutes and cases that support it. A supporting affidavit gives factual support to the motion to dismiss, while the memorandum of law provides the legal grounds for the dismissal of the claim.

Lawyers may be reluctant to file a memorandum of law if one is not requested because they may not wish to inform the other side of the particulars of their argument before the hearing in which the judge will rule on the motion. In some cases, however, the memorandum gives an attorney the ability to advise the court on a complex area

counterclaim
A claim made by a defendant in a civil lawsuit against the plaintiff; in effect, a counterclaiming defendant is suing the plaintiff.

cross-claim
A claim asserted by a defendant in a civil lawsuit against another defendant or by a plaintiff against another plaintiff.

judicial economy
Efficiency in the administration of the courts.

motion
A procedural request or application presented by an attorney to the court on behalf of a client.

motion to dismiss
A motion filed by the defendant in which the defendant asks the court to dismiss the case for a specified reason, such as improper service, lack of personal jurisdiction, or the plaintiff's failure to state a claim for which relief can be granted.

supporting affidavit
An affidavit accompanying a motion that is filed by an attorney on behalf of his or her client. The sworn statements in the affidavit provide a factual basis for the motion.

memorandum of law
A document (known as a *brief* in some states) that delineates the legal theories, statutes, and cases on which a motion is based.

EXHIBIT 10.6
A Motion to Dismiss

UNITED STATES DISTRICT COURT
FOR THE WESTERN DISTRICT OF NITA

Katherine Baranski   )
                    Plaintiff,)   CASE NO. 14-14335-NI
)   Honorable Harley M. Larue
v.   )
)
)   MOTION TO DISMISS
Tony Peretto   )
                    Defendant.)

The Defendant, Tony Peretto, by his attorney, moves the court to dismiss the above-named action because the statute of limitations governing the Plaintiff's claim has expired, as demonstrated in the memorandum of law that is being submitted with this motion. The Plaintiff therefore has no cause of action against the Defendant.

Cameron & Strauss, P.C.

Elizabeth A. Cameron

Date: 2/20/22

Elizabeth A. Cameron
Attorney for the Defendant
310 Lake Drive
Zero City, ZE 59802

that he or she might not otherwise have the time to detail during the oral arguments at the motion hearing. While a motion should state the laws and facts on which it is based, a memorandum of law allows the attorney to provide greater detail, complexity, and nuance.

The Scheduling Conference

After the complaint and answer have been filed, the court typically schedules a conference to consult with the attorneys for both sides. (A party not represented by an attorney attends the conference himself or herself.) Following this meeting, the judge enters a *scheduling order* that sets out the time limits within which pretrial events (such as the pleadings, the discovery, and the final pretrial conference) must be completed, as well as the date of the trial. Under FRCP 16(b), the scheduling order should be entered "as soon as practicable but in any event within 90 days after the appearance of a defendant and within 120 days after the complaint has been served on a defendant." The purpose of this meeting is to enable the court to manage the case and establish time restrictions given the nature of the case.

Traditional Discovery Tools

discovery
Formal investigation prior to trial. Opposing parties use various methods, such as interrogatories and depositions, to obtain information from each other and from witnesses to prepare for trial.

Before a trial begins, the parties can use a number of procedural devices to obtain information and gather evidence about the case. Baranski's attorney, for example, will want to know how fast Peretto was driving, whether he had been drinking, and whether he saw the stop sign. The process of obtaining information from the opposing party or from other witnesses is known as **discovery**.

Purpose of Discovery

Discovery serves several purposes. It preserves evidence from witnesses who might not be available at the time of the trial or whose memories will fade as time passes. It can lead to an out-of-court settlement if one party decides that the opponent's case is too strong to challenge. If the case does go to trial, discovery prevents surprises by giving parties access to evidence that might otherwise be hidden. This allows both parties to learn as much as they can about what to expect at a trial before they reach the courtroom. It also serves to narrow the issues so the trial focuses on the main questions in the case.

The FRCP and similar rules in the states set forth the guidelines for discovery activity. Discovery is intended to give the parties access to witnesses, documents, records, and other evidence that the opposing side has. The rules governing discovery are also designed to make sure that a witness or a party is not unduly harassed, that **privileged information** (communications that ordinarily may not be disclosed in court) is safeguarded, and that only matters relevant to the case at hand are discoverable. Courts generally allow broad discovery so that there are fewer surprises at trial. Typically, a lawyer may request anything that would even tend to lead to discoverable evidence. The information sought during the discovery process does not necessarily need to be admissible in court under the rules of evidence.

Discovery methods include interrogatories, depositions, requests for production and physical examination, and requests for admission. Remember, as with most legal matters, you have an obligation to keep all such information confidential, as discussed in this chapter's *Ethics Watch* feature.

privileged information
Confidential communications between certain individuals, such as an attorney and his or her client, that are protected from disclosure except under court order.

Interrogatories

Interrogatories are written questions that must be answered, in writing, by the parties to the lawsuit and then signed by the parties under oath. In the *Baranski* case, attorney Gilmore may ask paralegal Lopez to draft interrogatories to be sent to defendant Peretto.

interrogatories
A series of written questions for which written answers are prepared and then signed under oath by a party to a lawsuit (the plaintiff or the defendant).

Drafting Interrogatories

All discovery documents, including interrogatories, normally begin with a caption similar to the complaint caption illustrated earlier in this chapter. Following the caption, Lopez adds the name of the party who must answer the interrogatories, instructions to be followed by the party, and definitions of certain terms used in the interrogatories. The body of the document is the interrogatories themselves—that is, the questions that the opposing party must answer. Interrogatories end with a signature line for the attorney, followed by the attorney's name and address.

Review the File. Before drafting the questions, Lopez carefully reviews the case file (including the pleadings and the evidence and other information she obtained during her preliminary investigation into Baranski's claim). She will consult with Gilmore on the litigation strategy he believes should be pursued as the case moves forward. For further guidance, she might consult form books containing sample interrogatories. Some of these forms may be found in digital legal databases, and a paralegal might be asked to locate a suitable form. Additionally, the firm might have an internal bank of examples, forms, and interrogatories used in prior cases.

Courts May Limit the Number of Interrogatories. Depending on the complexity of the case, interrogatories may be few or may number in the hundreds. Exhibit 10.7 illustrates the types of interrogatories that have traditionally been used in cases similar to the *Baranski* case.

ETHICS WATCH

KEEPING CLIENT INFORMATION CONFIDENTIAL

As it happens, attorney Gilmore's paralegal, Lopez, is a friend of plaintiff Baranski's sister. Lopez learns from the results of Baranski's medical examination that Baranski has a serious illness. Lopez is sure that the sister, who quarreled with Baranski two months ago and hasn't spoken to her since, is unaware of the illness and would probably be hurt if she learned that Lopez knew of it and didn't tell her so that she could make amends with Baranski.

Should Lopez tell her friend about the illness? No. This is confidential information at this point, which Lopez only became aware of by virtue of her job. Should the information be revealed publicly during the course of the trial, Lopez would be free to disclose it to her friend if the friend still remained unaware of it. In the meantime, Lopez is ethically (and legally) obligated to protect the information from anyone who is not working on the case, including her friend.

This behavior is consistent with the NFPA *Model Disciplinary Rules and Ethical Considerations*, Section EC-1.5(f): "A paralegal shall not engage in any indiscreet communications concerning clients."

Reprinted by permission of the National Federation of Paralegal Associations, Inc. (NFPA®), www.paralegals.org.

Many state courts limit the number of interrogatories that can be used. FRCP 33 limits the number in federal court cases to twenty-five (unless a greater number is allowed by stipulation of the parties or by court order). Before drafting interrogatories, the paralegal should check the rules of the court in which an action is filed to find out if there are limits.

Answering Interrogatories

After receiving the interrogatories, Peretto must answer them within a specified time (thirty days under FRCP 33) in writing and under oath. Depending on the rules of the court, answers to interrogatories can often be handled electronically. Peretto will likely have substantial guidance from his attorney and his attorney's paralegal in forming his answers. He must answer each question truthfully, because he is under oath. His attorney will counsel him, though, on how to phrase his answers so that they are truthful and strategically sound. For example, she will advise him on how to limit his answers to prevent disclosing more information than necessary.

Depositions

deposition

A pretrial question-and-answer proceeding, usually conducted orally, in which a party or witness answers an attorney's questions. The answers are given under oath, and the session is recorded.

deponent

A party or witness who testifies under oath during a deposition.

Like an interrogatory, a **deposition** is given under oath. However, depositions are usually conducted orally (except in rare circumstances when the party cannot be deposed in person or by telephone or videoconference). Furthermore, unlike interrogatories, depositions may be taken from witnesses as well as parties to the court proceedings.

In a deposition, the attorney is able to question the person being deposed (the **deponent**) *in person* and follows up with new questions that come to mind. The attorney is not limited in the number of questions asked in a deposition, whereas most courts limit the number of interrogatory questions. Moreover, because the questioning is often done in person, the deponent must answer without asking an attorney how to respond.

When both the defendant and the plaintiff are located in the same jurisdiction, the site of the deposition is usually the offices of the attorney requesting the deposition. When the parties are in different jurisdictions, other arrangements may be made. In the *Baranski* case, attorney Gilmore may go to Peretto's city and depose Peretto in the office of Peretto's attorney, Cameron. Or the parties may agree to a videoconference or phone call for the deposition.

Procedure for Taking Depositions

The attorney wishing to depose a party or witness must give reasonable notice in writing to all other parties in the case and to the deposed. This is done by serving the opposing attorney (or attorneys) with a notice of the time and place of the deposition and the name of the person being examined (see Exhibit 10.8).

If the person scheduled to be deposed will not attend voluntarily, a paralegal may need to prepare a subpoena for deposition and submit it to the clerk of the court for

---

EXHIBIT 10.7

Sample Interrogatories

UNITED STATES DISTRICT COURT
FOR THE WESTERN DISTRICT OF NITA

Katherine Baranski)
          Plaintiff,)
)
v.)
)
Tony Peretto)
          Defendant.)

CASE NO. 14-14335-NI
Honorable Harley M. Larue

PLAINTIFF'S FIRST
INTERROGATORIES
TO DEFENDANT

    PLEASE TAKE NOTICE that the following Interrogatories are directed to you under the provisions of Rule 26(a)(5) and Rule 33 of the Federal Rules of Civil Procedure. You are requested to answer these Interrogatories and to furnish such information in answer to the Interrogatories as is available to you.

    You are required to serve integrated Interrogatories and Answers to these Interrogatories under oath, within thirty (30) days after service of them upon you. The original answers are to be retained in your attorney's possession, and a copy of the answers is to be served upon Plaintiff's counsel.

    The answers should be signed and sworn to by the person making answer to the Interrogatories.

    When used in these Interrogatories the term "Defendant," or any synonym thereof, is intended to and shall embrace and include, in addition to said Defendant, all agents, servants and employees, representatives, attorneys, private investigators, or others who are in possession of or who may have obtained information for or on behalf of the Defendant.

    These Interrogatories shall be deemed continuing, and supplemental answers shall be required immediately upon receipt thereof if Defendant, directly or indirectly, obtains further or different information from the time answers are served until the time of trial.

1. Were you the driver of an automobile involved in an accident with Plaintiff on August 4, 2021, at about 7:45 A.M. at the intersection of Mattis Avenue and Thirty-eighth Street, in Nita City, Nita? If so, please state:

    (a) Your name;
    (b) Every name you have used in the past;
    (c) The dates you used each name;
    (d) The date and place of your birth.

2. Please list your current residence and all residences you occupied in the five years preceding your move to your current residence, including complete addresses, dates of residence, and names of owners or managers.

3. Please indicate where you are presently employed and where you were employed during the five years preceding the beginning of your current employment. In so doing, please indicate the following:

    (a) The names, addresses, and telephone numbers of each employer or place of business, including the dates during which you worked there;
    (b) How many hours you worked, on average, per week;
    (c) The names, addresses, and telephone numbers of your supervisors (or owners of the business);
    (d) The nature of the work that you performed.

Continued

EXHIBIT 10.7

Sample Interrogatories—Continued

4. At the time of the incident, were you acting as an agent or employee for any person? If so, state:

   (a) The name, address, and telephone number of that person;
   (b) A description of your duties.

5. At the time of the incident, did you have a driver's license? If so, state:

   (a) The state or other issuing entity;
   (b) The license number and type;
   (c) The date of issuance and expiration;
   (d) Any violations, offenses, or restrictions against your license.

6. Indicate whether you have ever had your driver's license suspended, revoked, or canceled and whether you have ever been denied the issuance of a driver's license for mental or physical reasons. If you have, please indicate the date and state of such occurrence as well as the reasons for it.

7. At the time of the incident, did you or any other person have any physical, emotional, or mental disability or condition that may have contributed to the occurrence of the incident? If so, for each person state:

   (a) The name, address, and telephone number;
   (b) The nature of the disability or condition;
   (c) The name, address, and telephone number of any qualified person who treated or diagnosed the condition and the dates of such treatment;
   (d) The manner in which the disability or condition contributed to the occurrence of the incident.

8. Within twenty-four hours before the incident, did you or any person involved in the incident use or take any of the following substances: alcoholic beverage, marijuana, or other drug or medication of any kind (prescription or not)? If so, for each person state:

   (a) The name, address, and telephone number;
   (b) The nature or description of each substance;
   (c) The quantity of each substance used or taken;
   (d) The date and time of day when each substance was used or taken;
   (e) The address where each substance was used or taken;
   (f) The name, address, and telephone number of each person who was present when each substance was used or taken;
   (g) The name, address, and telephone number of any health-care provider that prescribed or furnished the substance and the condition for which it was prescribed or furnished.

9. For each time you have had your vision checked within the last five years, please indicate the following:

   (a) The date and reason for the vision examination;
   (b) The name, address, and telephone number of the examiner;
   (c) The results and/or actions taken.

10. For each time you have had your hearing checked within the last five years, please indicate the following:

    (a) The date and reason for the hearing examination;
    (b) The name, address, and telephone number of the examiner;
    (c) The results and/or actions taken.

[Additional questions would be asked relating to the accident, including questions concerning road conditions and surface, posted speed limits, shoulders and curbs on the road, general character of the neighborhood, when the defendant noticed the plaintiff's vehicle, where it was located and the speed at which the plaintiff was traveling, whether there were other vehicles between the plaintiff's and the defendant's vehicles, and so forth.]

Dated: 2/15/22 _____

_____
Allen P. Gilmore
Attorney for Plaintiff

EXHIBIT 10.8
Notice of Taking Deposition

**UNITED STATES DISTRICT COURT
FOR THE WESTERN DISTRICT OF NITA**

Katherine Baranski)
       Plaintiff,)
)
v.)
)
Tony Peretto)
       Defendant.)

CASE NO. 14-14335-NI
Honorable Harley M. Larue

NOTICE OF TAKING
DEPOSITION

TO: Elizabeth A. Cameron
     Cameron & Strauss, P.C.
     310 Lake Drive
     Zero City, ZE 59802

    PLEASE TAKE NOTICE that Katherine Baranski, by and through her attorneys, Jeffers, Gilmore & Dunn, will take the deposition of Tony Peretto on Wednesday, April 16, 2022, at 1:30 P.M., at the law offices of Cameron & Strauss, P.C., 310 Lake Drive, Zero City, ZE 59802, pursuant to the Federal Rules of Civil Procedure, before a duly authorized and qualified notary and stenographer.

Dated: March 20, 2022

Jeffers, Gilmore & Dunn

Allen P Gilmore
Allen P Gilmore
Attorney for Katherine Baranski
553 Fifth Avenue, Suite 101
Nita City, NI 48801

---

signature. Generally, a **subpoena** is an order issued by the court clerk directing a party to appear and to testify at trial, as will be discussed in Chapter 12. A *subpoena for deposition* orders the person to appear at a deposition rather than in a court proceeding. A subpoena should also be prepared if the attorney wants the deponent to bring certain documents or tangible things to the deposition (this is called a *subpoena duces tecum*). Court rules differ on how subpoenas may be issued. Attorneys are often allowed to issue them in the name of the court.

    Under FRCP 30 and 31, court permission is required for depositions to be taken before the parties have made the initial disclosures required by Rule 26 (discussed later in this chapter). Also, court approval may be required if either party wants to take more than one deposition from the same person or more than a total of ten depositions in the case. Always check the relevant court rules when planning discovery strategy.

Drafting Deposition Questions

Depositions are conducted by attorneys. Paralegals may attend depositions but do not ask questions. Deposition questions are often drafted by paralegals, however. In the *Baranski* case, for example, Gilmore might ask Lopez to draft questions for a deposition of defendant Peretto or someone else, such as an eyewitness to the accident. For Peretto's deposition, Lopez might draft questions similar to those presented in Exhibit 10.9. Gilmore can then use Lopez's questions as a checklist during the deposition.

    Note, though, that Gilmore's questions are not limited to the questions in the list. Unforeseen questions may arise as Gilmore learns new information during the

subpoena
A document commanding a person to appear at a certain time and place to give testimony concerning a certain matter.

EXHIBIT 10.9

Sample Deposition Questions

DEPOSITION QUESTIONS

1. Please state your full name and address for the record.
2. Please state your age, birth date, and Social Security number.
3. What is your educational level, and what employment position do you hold?
4. Do you have a criminal record, and if so, for what?
5. Have you been involved in previous automobile accidents? What driving violations have you had? Has your driver's license ever been suspended?
6. What is your medical history? Have you ever had health problems? Are you in perfect health? Were you in perfect health at the time of the accident?
7. Do you wear glasses or contact lenses? If so, for what condition? Were you wearing your glasses or contacts at the time the accident occurred?
8. Do you take medication of any kind?
9. Do you have any similar lawsuits or any claims pending against you?
10. Who is your automobile insurer? What are your policy limits?
11. Were there any passengers in your vehicle at the time of the accident?
12. Describe your vehicle. What was the mechanical condition of your vehicle at the time of the accident? Do you do your own mechanical work? If so, what training do you have in maintaining and repairing automobiles? Had you taken your vehicle to a professional mechanic's shop prior to the accident?
13. Please state the date on which the accident occurred.
14. Where were you prior to the accident, for at least the six hours preceding the accident?
15. Where were you going when the accident occurred, and for what purpose?
16. What were you doing during the last few moments before the accident? Were you smoking, eating, drinking, or chewing gum?
17. What were you thinking about just before the accident occurred?
18. What route did you take to reach your destination, and why did you take this particular route?
19. Describe the weather conditions at the time of the accident.
20. Please recite the facts of how the accident occurred.
21. Please describe the area in which the accident occurred. Were there many cars and pedestrians on the streets? Were there traffic controls, obstructions, or the like?
22. What was your location, and in what direction were you going?
23. When did you see the plaintiff's automobile approaching?
24. How far away were you when you first saw the auto? What was your rate of speed?
25. Did your vehicle move forward or was it pushed backward by the impact?
26. When did you first apply your brakes? Were your brakes functioning properly?
27. Did you attempt to avoid the accident? If so, how?
28. Did you receive a traffic ticket as a result of the accident?
29. Do you own the vehicle that you were driving at the time of the accident?
30. Were you acting within the scope of your employment when the accident occurred?
31. What were the conditions of the parties affected by the accident just after the accident occurred?
32. Did you attempt to provide first aid to any party?
33. How did the plaintiff leave the scene, and what was the plaintiff's physical condition?
34. What was the damage to your vehicle, and has it been repaired?

deposition. Also, the deponent's answer to one question may reveal the answer to another, so not all the questions on the checklist will need to be asked.

Preparing the Client for a Deposition

No attorney can predict a deponent's answers beforehand. Spontaneous and sometimes contradictory statements can seriously damage the deponent's case. For this reason, the deposed parties and their lawyers prepare for depositions by formulating answers to likely questions. For example, if defendant Peretto's attorney plans to depose plaintiff Baranski, attorney Gilmore might have Baranski come to the office for a run-through of possible questions that Peretto's attorney might ask her.

This preparation does not mean that the lawyer tells the deponent what to say. Instead, the lawyer offers suggestions as to how the answers to certain questions should be phrased. The answers must be truthful, but the truth can be presented in many ways.

A practice deposition can also help laypeople become accustomed to the unfamiliar format and can reduce stress. That lessens the chances that the witness will make an error during the deposition due to nervousness. For example, Gilmore would caution Baranski to limit her responses to the questions and not engage in speculative answers. If Baranski was asked whether she had ever been involved in an automobile accident before, for example, Gilmore would probably caution her to give a simple (but truthful) "yes" or "no" answer. Gilmore normally would permit Baranski to provide additional information only in response to precisely phrased questions.

The Role of the Deponent's Attorney

The deponent's attorney attends the deposition, but the attorney's role is limited. Under FRCP 30, the attorney may instruct a deponent not to answer a question only when necessary to preserve a privilege, to enforce a limitation directed by the court, or to present a motion to terminate the deposition. In other words, if Baranski is deposed by Peretto's attorney, Cameron, she will have to answer Cameron's questions even if the questions are not clearly relevant to the issues of the case—unless the court has previously limited this line of questioning. The deponent's attorney, Gilmore, can object only to questions that call for privileged information to be disclosed. Under Rule 30, the attorney is required to state objections concisely, in a nonargumentative and nonsuggestive manner.

These rules differ significantly from the rules of evidence at trial, which limit questioning in many additional and more restrictive ways. As a result, much testimony from depositions will never become admissible at the trial. A good legal tactician will craft a line of questioning and select witnesses in such a way that the helpful statements from depositions will *become* admissible under the rules of evidence at trial.

The deponent's attorney or the other party's attorney may also ask questions during the deposition to clarify a point or to establish facts needed for a motion. These questions are asked after the attorney conducting the deposition has finished. After the deponent's attorney has asked questions, the attorney conducting the deposition has another chance to ask questions. This process continues until everyone is done.

As will be discussed shortly, deposition proceedings are recorded. If both attorneys agree, they can go "off the record" to clarify a point or discuss a disputed issue. Depositions are stressful, and tempers often flare. In the event that the deposition cannot be conducted in an orderly fashion, the attorney conducting the deposition may have to terminate it.

The Deposition Transcript

Every utterance made during a deposition is recorded. A court reporter usually records the deposition proceedings and creates an official **deposition transcript**. Methods of recording a deposition include stenographic recording (a traditional method that involves the use of a shorthand machine or written shorthand), digital audio recording, digital video recording, or some combination of these methods. Rule 30(b)(2) of the FRCP states that unless the court orders otherwise, a deposition "may be recorded by sound, sound-and-visual, or stenographic means."

Either party may use the deposition transcript during the trial to prove a particular point or to **impeach** (call into question) the credibility of a witness who says something during the trial that is different from what that witness stated during the deposition. For example, a witness in the *Baranski* case might state during the deposition that Peretto *did not* stop at the stop sign before crossing Mattis Avenue. If, at trial, the witness states that Peretto *did* stop at the stop sign, Baranski's attorney could challenge the witness's

deposition transcript
The official transcription of the recording taken during a deposition.

impeach
To call into question the credibility of a witness by challenging the truth or accuracy of his or her trial statement.

credibility on the basis of the deposition transcript. Exhibit 10.10 shows a page from a transcript of a deposition conducted by Gilmore in the case. The deponent was Julia Williams, an eyewitness to the accident. On the transcript, the letter "Q" precedes each question asked by Gilmore, and "A" precedes each of Williams's answers.

Summarizing and Indexing the Deposition Transcript

Typically, the paralegal summarizes the deposition transcript. The summary, which along with the transcript will become part of the litigation file, allows members of the litigation team to review the information obtained from deponents during depositions. It is important for paralegals to have a strong grasp of what is legally relevant to the trial issues so that they will know what to include in their summaries.

If Lopez summarizes the deposition transcript of Julia Williams, the transcript is likely summarized sequentially—that is, in the order in which it was given during the deposition—as shown in Exhibit 10.11. Notice that the summary includes the page and line numbers in the deposition transcript where the full text of the information can be found.

Often, in addition to summarizing the transcript, the paralegal provides an index. It is a list of topics (such as education, employment status, injuries, and medical costs) followed by the relevant page and line numbers of the deposition transcript. Together,

---

EXHIBIT 10.10

A Deposition Transcript (Excerpt)

67	Q: Where were you at the time of the accident?
68	A: I was on the southwest corner of the intersection.
69	Q: Are you referring to the intersection where Thirty-eighth Street crosses Mattis Avenue?
70	A: Yes.
71	Q: Why were you there at the time of the accident?
72	A: Well, I was on my way to work. I usually walk down Mattis Avenue to the hospital.
73	Q: So you were walking to work down Mattis Avenue and you saw the accident?
74	A: Yes.
75	Q: What did you see?
76	A: Well, as I was about to cross the street, a dark green van passed within three feet of me and ran the
77	stop sign and crashed into another car.
78	Q: Can you remember if the driver of the van was a male or a female?
79	A: Yes. It was a man.
80	Q: I am showing you a picture. Can you identify the man in the picture?
81	A: Yes. That is the man who was driving the van.
82	Q: Do you wear glasses?
83	A: I need glasses only for reading. I have excellent distance vision.
84	Q: How long has it been since your last eye exam with a doctor?
85	A: Oh, just a month ago, with Dr. Sullivan.

page 4

EXHIBIT 10.11

A Deposition Summary (Excerpt)

Case:	Baranski v. Peretto	Attorney:	Allen P. Gilmore
	Plaintiff 15773	Paralegal:	Elena Lopez

Deponent:	Julia Williams	Date: March 17, 2022
	3801 Mattis Avenue	
	Nita City, Nita 48800	

Page	Line(s)	

* * * *

4	72–77	Williams stated that she was on the way to work at the time of the accident. She was about to cross the street when Peretto's car ("a dark green van") passed within three feet of her, ran the stop sign, and crashed into Baranski's car.
4	80–81	When shown a picture of Peretto, she identified him as the driver of the green van.
4	82–83	Williams has excellent distance vision and does not require corrective lenses. She does need reading glasses for close work.

* * * *

the summary and the index allow anyone involved in the case to locate information quickly. More tips for summarizing a deposition are provided in the accompanying *Developing Paralegal Skills* feature on the following page.

Requests for Production and Physical Examination

Another form of discovery is a request for the production of documents or tangible things or for permission to enter property for inspection and other purposes. FRCP 34 authorizes each party to request evidence from any other party. If the item requested is large or cannot be "produced" for some reason (Peretto's van, for example), then the party can request permission to enter on the other party's land to inspect, test, sample, and photograph the item. In federal courts, the duty of disclosure under FRCP 26, discussed shortly, has greatly decreased the need to file such production requests.

When the mental or physical condition of a party is in controversy, the opposing party may request the court to order the party to submit to a physical or mental examination by a licensed examiner. For example, if Peretto claims that Baranski's injuries were the result of a preexisting medical condition rather than the collision, defense attorney Cameron may file a request to have Baranski examined by a physician. Because the existence, nature, and extent of Baranski's injuries are important in calculating the damages that she might be able to recover from Peretto, the court may grant the request.

Requests for Admission

During discovery, a party can also request that the opposing party admit the truth of matters relating to the case. For example, Baranski's attorney can request that Peretto admit that he owned the car involved in the accident. Such admissions save time at trial because the parties do not spend time proving admitted facts. Any matter admitted under such a request is established as true for the trial. FRCP 36 permits requests for

DEVELOPING PARALEGAL SKILLS

DEPOSITION SUMMARIES

After a deposition is taken, each attorney orders a copy of the deposition transcript. Copies may be obtained in printed form or in an electronic file. When the transcript is received, the paralegal's job is to prepare a summary of the testimony that was given. The summary is typically only a few pages in length.

The paralegal must be very familiar with the lawsuit and the legal theories that are being pursued so that he or she can point out possible inconsistencies in the testimony or between the testimony and the pleadings. The paralegal might also give special emphasis to any testimony that will help to prove the client's case in court.

After the deposition summary has been created, the paralegal places the summary in the litigation file, usually in a special discovery folder or binder within the larger file. The deposition summary will be used to prepare for future depositions, to prepare pretrial motions, and to impeach witnesses at the trial, should they give contradictory testimony.

Tips for Summarizing a Deposition

- Find out how the deposition is to be summarized—by chronology, by legal issue, by factual issues, or otherwise.
- Read through the deposition transcript and mark important pages.
- Be sure to include a reference to the page and line that is being summarized.
- Take advantage of software that can assist in summarizing the deposition transcript.

admission but requires that a request cannot be made, without the court's permission, before the pre-discovery meeting of the attorneys.

The Duty to Disclose under FRCP 26

Each party has a duty to disclose to the other party specified types of information prior to the discovery stage of litigation. Under FRCP Rule 26(f), once a lawsuit is brought, the parties (the plaintiff and defendant and/or their attorneys) must schedule a pre-discovery meeting to discuss the nature of the lawsuit, any defenses that may be raised against the claims being brought, and possibilities for promptly settling or otherwise resolving the dispute. The meeting should take place as soon as practicable but at least fourteen days before a scheduling conference is held or a scheduling order issued.

Either at this meeting or within ten days after it, the parties must also make the initial disclosures described next and submit to the court a plan for discovery. As the trial date approaches, the attorneys must make subsequent disclosures relating to witnesses, documents, and other relevant information.

These rules do not replace the methods of discovery discussed in the preceding section. Rather, they impose a duty on attorneys to disclose specified information to opposing counsel early in the litigation process so that discovery time and costs can be reduced. Attorneys use discovery tools (such as depositions and interrogatories) to obtain information, but they cannot do so until the pre-discovery meeting has been held and initial disclosures have been made.

Initial Disclosures

FRCP 26(a)(1) requires each party to disclose the following information to the other party at an initial meeting of the parties or within ten days of the meeting:

- The name, address, and telephone number of any person likely to have "discoverable information" and the nature of that information.

- A copy or "description by category and location" of all documents, data, and other "things in the possession, custody, or control of the party" relevant to the dispute.

- A computation of the damages claimed by the disclosing party. The party must make the documents on which the computation is based available to the other party for inspection and copying.

- Copies of any insurance policies that cover the injuries or harms alleged in the lawsuit and that may pay part or all of a judgment resulting from the dispute.

In the *Baranski* case, Gilmore and Lopez must quickly assemble all relevant information, documents, and other evidence gathered during client interviews and preliminary investigation. Lopez prepares copies of the documents—or a description of them—for Gilmore's review and signature. These will be filed with the court and sent to Peretto's attorney. In the information disclosed, Gilmore and Lopez must include even information that might damage Baranski's position. They need not disclose *privileged information*, however, such as confidential discussions between Baranski and Gilmore.

Failure to Disclose

A party is not excused from disclosing relevant information simply because that party has not yet completed an investigation into the case or because the other party has not yet made disclosures. FRCP 37(c) makes clear that the failure to make initial disclosures can result in serious sanctions.

If a party fails to make required disclosures, that party will not be able to use the information as evidence at trial. In addition, the court may impose other sanctions, such as ordering the party to pay reasonable expenses, including attorneys' fees, created by the failure to disclose. In sum, Gilmore and Lopez need to make sure that all relevant information (that is not privileged) is disclosed, or Gilmore will not be able to use it in court (and may face other sanctions).

Discovery Plan

As mentioned above, at the initial meeting of the parties, the attorneys must work out a **discovery plan** and submit a report describing the plan to the court within ten days of the meeting. The type of information to be included in the discovery plan is illustrated in Exhibit 10.12, which shows Form 35, a form created for this purpose. As indicated by the form, Rule 26(f) allows the attorneys room to negotiate details of discovery, including time schedules to be followed.

In the *Baranski* case, paralegal Lopez will make sure that attorney Gilmore takes a copy of Form 35 with him to the initial pre-discovery meeting of the parties to use as a checklist, along with tentative dates for completion of discovery. After the attorneys decide on the details of the plan to be proposed to the court, Gilmore may have Lopez draft a final version of the plan for his review and signature.

discovery plan
A plan formed by the attorneys litigating a lawsuit, on behalf of their clients, that indicates the types of information that each party will disclose to the other prior to trial, the testimony and evidence that each party will or may introduce at trial, and the general schedule for pretrial disclosures and events.

Subsequent Disclosures

In addition to the initial disclosures just discussed, each party must make other disclosures prior to trial. All subsequent disclosures must also be in writing, signed by the attorneys, and filed with the court. These include information relating to expert witnesses, other witnesses, and exhibits that may be used at trial.

Expert Witnesses

Under FRCP 26(a)(2), parties must disclose to other parties the names of expert witnesses who may be called to testify during the trial. Additionally, the following

EXHIBIT 10.12

Form 35—Report of Parties' Planning Meeting (Discovery Plan)

[Caption and Names of Parties]

1. Pursuant to Fed. R. Civ. P. 26(f), a meeting was held on ____(date)____ at ____(place)____ and was attended by:

____(name)____ for plaintiff(s) ____(party name)____
____(name)____ for defendant(s) ____(party name)____
____(name)____ for defendant(s) ____(party name)____

2. Pre-Discovery Disclosures. The parties [have exchanged] [will exchange by ____(date)____] the information required by [Fed. R. Civ. P. 26(a)(1)] [(local rule _____)].

3. Discovery Plan. The parties jointly propose to the court the following discovery plan: [Use separate paragraphs or subparagraphs as necessary if parties disagree.]

Discovery will be needed on the following subjects:
_____(brief description of subjects on which discovery will be needed)_____
All discovery commenced in time to be completed by __(date)__. [Discovery on__(issue for early discovery)____
to be completed by _____(date)_____.]
Maximum of ____ interrogatories by each party to any other party. [Responses due ____ days after service.]
Maximum of ____ requests for admission by each party to any other party. [Responses due ____ days after service.]
Maximum of ____ depositions by plaintiff(s) and ____ by defendant(s).
Each deposition [other than of _____] limited to maximum of ____ hours unless extended by agreement of parties.
Reports from retained experts under Rule 26(a)(2) due:
    from plaintiff(s) by _____(date)_____.
    from defendant(s) by _____(date)_____.
Supplementations under Rule 26(e) due (time(s) or intervals(s)).

4. Other Items. [Use separate paragraphs or subparagraphs as necessary if parties disagree.]

The parties [request] [do not request] a conference with the court before entry of the scheduling order.
The parties request a pretrial conference in____(month and year)____.
Plaintiff(s) should be allowed until __(date)__ to join additional parties and until ____(date)____ to amend the pleadings.
Defendant(s) should be allowed until ___(date)___ to join additional parties and until ____(date)____ to amend the pleadings.
All potentially dispositive motions should be filed by__(date)__.
Settlement [is likely] [is unlikely] [cannot be evaluated prior to ____(date)____] [may be enhanced by use of the following alternative
    dispute resolution procedure: _____].
Final lists of witnesses and exhibits under Rule 26(a)(3) should be due
    from plaintiff(s) by __(date)__.
    from defendant(s) by __(date)__.
Parties should have _____ days after service of final lists of witnesses and exhibits to list objections under Rule 26(a)(3).
The case should be ready for trial by ____(date)____ [and at the time is expected to take approximately ____(length of time)____].
[Other matters.]

Date: _____

information about each expert must be disclosed in a report signed by the expert witness:

- A statement by the expert indicating the opinions that will be expressed, the basis for the opinions, and the data or information the witness considered when forming the opinions.

- Exhibits that will be used to summarize or support the opinions.

- The qualifications of the expert witness, including a list of all publications authored by the witness in the last ten years.

- The compensation to be paid to the expert witness.

- A list of other cases in which the witness has testified as an expert at trial or by deposition in the preceding four years.

These disclosures must be made at times set by the court. If the court does not indicate any times, then they must be made at least ninety days before the trial date.

Other Pretrial Disclosures

Under FRCP 26(a)(3), each party must also disclose to the other party the following information:

- A list of the names, addresses, and telephone numbers of other witnesses who may be called during the trial to give testimony. The list must indicate whether the witness "will" or "may" be called.

- A list of witnesses whose deposition testimony may be offered during the trial and a written transcript of the relevant sections of the deposition testimony.

- A list of exhibits that indicates which exhibits will be offered and which may be offered.

These disclosures must be made at least thirty days before trial, unless the court orders otherwise. Once disclosures have been made, the opposing party has fourteen days to file objections to the use of any deposition or exhibit with the court. If objections are not made, they are presumed to be waived (unless a party can show good cause why he or she failed to object to the disclosures previously).

An attorney's duty to disclose relevant information is ongoing throughout the pretrial stage. Any time an attorney learns new, relevant supplemental information concerning statements or responses made earlier, that information must be disclosed to the other party. An important task for many paralegals is keeping track of the opposing parties' discovery requests so the attorney can be alerted if a supplemental filing is necessary.

Discovery of Electronic Evidence

Electronic evidence, or e-evidence, consists of computer-generated and electronically recorded information. Examples include e-mail, voice mail, blog posts, and posts on social media sites such as Facebook, Instagram, and Twitter, as well as documents and other data saved on a cloud server. E-evidence has become increasingly important because it can reveal facts found only in electronic format. The FRCP and state rules specifically allow discovery of electronic "data compilations." As in other areas of the practice of law, electronic tools are playing a growing part in discovery.

The Advantages of Electronic Evidence

Most information stored on computers is never printed on paper. When a person works on a computer, information is recorded on a hard drive even if not "saved" by the user. This information, called **metadata**, is the hidden data kept by the computer about a file, including location, path, creator, date created, date last accessed, earlier versions, passwords, and formatting. It reveals information about how, when, and by whom a file was created, accessed, modified, and transmitted. This information can only be obtained from the file in its electronic format.

metadata
Embedded electronic data recorded by a computer in association with a particular file, including location, path, creator, date created, date last accessed, hidden notes, earlier versions, passwords, and formatting. Metadata reveal information about how, when, and by whom a document was created, accessed, modified, and transmitted.

E-Mail Communications

Billions of e-mails are sent annually. E-mail has become fertile ground for evidence in litigation and has been the "smoking gun" in some cases. Many people converse casually in e-mail communications, as if talking to a friend. This makes e-mail believable and compelling evidence—which can be damaging if discovered by outsiders.

In addition, in its electronic form, e-mail contains information that provides links to other e-mails, e-mail attachments, erased files, and metadata. Metadata reveal the identity of any person who received copies of an e-mail message (even "blind" copies). Thus, e-evidence can be used to trace a message to its true originator, reconstruct an e-mail conversation, and establish a timeline of the events in dispute (who knew what, and when). Attorneys also use it to verify clients' claims or discredit the claims of the opposition.

Deleted Files Can Be Retrieved

A major advantage of e-evidence is that even deleted files can often be retrieved. Deleting a file does not destroy the data but simply makes the space occupied by the file available to be overwritten by new information. Until that space is actually used for new data (which may never occur), experts can retrieve the deleted record.

The use of backup drives and cloud storage makes it even less likely that simply erasing a file actually deletes it. Online storage servers are often themselves backed up, so it is possible to locate copies of files deleted from individual computers. Postings on blogs or other websites may be accessed using backups of a Web-hosting service. Never assume that a file from a computer connected to a network is gone just because it was erased from that computer.

The same is true of e-mails and other messages. Many people think that when they delete an e-mail message and empty the "trash," the message is gone. As just described, however, deleted data remain on the computer until overwritten by new data (or wiped out by utility software) and usually remain in a central server as well. Similarly, tweets may have been "re-tweeted," blog posts may have been distributed through networks of servers, and so forth.

Experts have even been able to retrieve data, in whole or in part, from computers that have been damaged by water, fire, or severe impact. Therefore, do not assume that e-evidence is not available just because a file was deleted, a computer was damaged, or a utility program was run.

The Sources of Electronic Evidence

The key to conducting electronic discovery is developing an understanding of the kinds of information it can provide so you know where to look for particular information. Generally, data can be located in active files, in backup files, or as residual data. Active files are currently accessible on the computer (documents and e-mail, for example). Backup files have been copied to other locations such as flash drives or to remote servers. Residual data appear to be gone but are still recoverable from somewhere on the computer system by special software.

Backup Data

Backup files can be a hidden treasure for the legal team. Reviewing backup copies of documents and e-mail provides useful information about how a particular matter progressed over several weeks or months. Because the location of the data depends on the backup practice used, you need to find out what the backup policy is as soon as you can during discovery. See the accompanying *Developing Paralegal Skills* feature for more tips on e-discovery.

DEVELOPING PARALEGAL SKILLS

ELECTRONIC DISCOVERY

Paralegals must be prepared to deal with electronic discovery. This means not only formulating electronic discovery plans but also making sure to preserve the integrity of any electronic evidence acquired. It is important, too, to remember that e-evidence is fragile. Although—as discussed in the chapter—it may be difficult to permanently delete files from a computer system, it is not impossible. Every time a user enters new data, downloads new software, or performs routine maintenance procedures, the data on the computer are permanently altered. Just booting up a computer can change dates and times on numerous files.

Tips for Conducting E-Discovery

• Immediately write a preservation-of-evidence letter to all parties involved, including your client, at the outset of the case. This letter informs the parties that they have a duty to take immediate action to preserve any potential electronic evidence.

• Use interrogatories to gather information about the opposing party's computer system so that you can learn about the various technologies used by that party.

• Follow up with depositions. Once you know the names of the parties who oversee the system or have special knowledge of it, take depositions from them.

• After you have found out the details of where electronic evidence is located, draft a request for production of the evidence.

• When the e-evidence is acquired, determine how best to manage, review, and interpret the data, which may involve using the services of an outside company that specializes in this field. Special software can help manage files of millions of e-mails or large amounts of other e-evidence.

Backup files contain not only e-mail messages and word-processing documents, but also other embedded information that can be useful. When computers are networked, audit trails that keep track of network usage may be available. An audit trail will tell you who accessed the system, when it was accessed, and whether those who accessed the system copied, downloaded, modified, or deleted any files. Some word-processing software allows users to insert hidden comments or track changes while drafting and revising documents. These comments and revisions can also be accessed from the electronic version of the backup file.

Other Sources of E-Evidence

Electronic evidence is not limited to the data on computer systems. It includes *all* electronically recorded information, such as voice mail, video, electronic calendars, and phone logs on smartphones, iPads, tablets, laptops, and other devices that digitally store data. You can use traditional discovery tactics (such as interrogatories and depositions) to find out about other sources of potential e-evidence. Be sure to consider all possible sources that might prove fruitful, but remember that such requests must be reasonable and made in good faith.

The Special Requirements of Electronic Evidence

While courts allow discovery of electronic evidence, judges know that electronic evidence can be manipulated. To ensure that the evidence obtained during discovery will be admissible, you must do two things. First, make sure that you obtain an exact *image copy* of the electronic evidence. Second, make sure you can prove that nothing has been changed from the time the image copy was made. Keeping a backup copy of the material as received from the other party is one way to do this. Your law firm will likely have policies on how to handle e-evidence.

Acquiring an Image Copy

To use any evidence, you must convince the court that it is authentic. In the case of electronic evidence, you must show that the electronic version is the same as the version that was present on the target system. The way to do this is to have an image copy made. As this chapter's *Office Tech and Cybersecurity* feature examines, electronic discovery can be very costly, so it must be approached carefully.

OFFICE TECH AND CYBERSECURITY

THE COSTS OF ELECTRONIC DISCOVERY

Traditionally, the party responding to a discovery request pays the expenses involved in obtaining requested materials. If compliance would be too costly, however, the judge could limit the scope of the request or shift some or all of the costs to the requesting party. How do these traditional rules governing discovery apply to requests for electronic evidence?

Why Courts Shift the Costs of Electronic Discovery

Electronic discovery has dramatically increased the costs of complying with some discovery requests. It is no longer simply a matter of photocopying paper documents. Now the responding party may need to hire computer forensics experts to make image copies of document on desktop, laptop, and server hard drives, as well as removable storage media (such as flash drives), backup drives, and server-based systems, voice mail, smartphones, and other forms of digitally stored data.

In cases involving multiple parties or large corporations, the electronic discovery process can easily run into hundreds of thousands of dollars.

Costly Discovery

For example, Viacom sued YouTube, owned by Google, for more than $1 billion. Viacom claimed that YouTube had committed copyright violations by allowing clips from Viacom's television shows to be posted on YouTube without permission. Viacom hired BayTSP, which specializes in searching for online content, to search for possible violations on YouTube. BayTSP identified more than 150,000 clips posted on YouTube. Viacom claimed losses from each such posting.

YouTube demanded to see evidence of the violations. BayTSP estimated that it had gathered more than a million documents, all electronic, related to the clip postings. It protested to the court that the document request was unreasonable. BayTSP then spent months searching and reviewing the documents and eventually narrowed the list to 650,000 potentially relevant documents. The court allowed YouTube's request for these documents to go forward. Given the amount at stake in the litigation, YouTube was within its rights, and BayTSP had to provide the records. The cost of document production would be borne by BayTSP or, the court noted, by Viacom, which had hired BayTSP.

What Factors Do Courts Consider in Deciding to Shift Costs?

When is it appropriate for a court to shift costs from one party to another in discovery? The FRCP advisory committee lists seven factors:

1. The specificity of the discovery request.
2. The quantity of information available from other and more easily accessed sources.
3. The failure to produce relevant information that seems likely to have existed but is no longer available on more easily accessed sources.
4. The likelihood of finding relevant responsive information that cannot be obtained from other, more easily accessed sources.
5. Predictions as to the importance and usefulness of the further information.
6. The importance of the issues at stake in the litigation.
7. The parties' resources.

Technology Tip

Paralegals should keep in mind not only the high costs of some electronic discovery requests but also the possibility that the court may shift some costs. Suppose you are assisting a corporate defendant in a product liability lawsuit brought by a plaintiff claiming harm from one of the defendant's products. If the plaintiff requests extensive electronic evidence during discovery, the defendant corporation may be required to cover a significant portion of the costs.

Suppose the target system is a computer hard drive. Making an image copy involves creating an electronic image of the drive being copied. The copy would capture all data, including residual data. This process is different from the usual file-by-file copying method. An image copy of a computer drive should be made by an expert in computer forensics. These experts collect, preserve, and analyze electronic evidence and testify in court if needed.

Preserving the Chain of Custody

Once you have acquired an exact copy of the electronic evidence, you must establish and maintain a chain of custody to avoid any claims that the evidence has been tampered with. The phrase **chain of custody** refers to the movement and location of evidence from the time it is obtained to the time it is presented in court.

It is crucial when dealing with electronic evidence to track the evidence from its original source to its submission to the court. Tracking provides the court assurance that nothing has been added, changed, or deleted. The original image copy should be protected so it is tamperproof, labeled as the original, and kept in a secure location. Typically, a forensic specialist copies the original data to ensure security. You may need to review the evidence only on a secure computer not connected to the Internet to protect data integrity.

chain of custody
A series describing the movement and location of evidence from the time it is obtained to the time it is presented in court. The court requires that evidence be preserved in the condition in which it was obtained if it is to be admitted into evidence at trial.

Federal Rule of Evidence 502

The use of electronic evidence can result in a huge number of documents being made available to an opposing party. This availability has increased the number of documents accidentally released. In many cases, for example, a party had the right to access e-mails of the opposing party relating to a particular matter. While attempts are made to filter out nonrelevant e-mail messages, some messages that should have been protected by attorney-client confidentiality rules have been accidentally included among the thousands of e-mails seen by the opposing party.

To deal with this problem, Congress changed Federal Rule of Evidence 502. Under it, if there is an accidental release of material that should have been protected, the court may rule that protection was not waived by accidental disclosure. Courts consider the following factors in deciding if a privileged document has been lost to the opposing party or is still protected:

1. The reasonableness of precautions taken to prevent inadvertent disclosure in view of the extent of document production.

2. The number of inadvertent disclosures.

3. The extent of the disclosures.

4. The promptness of steps taken to remedy the disclosure.

5. Whether interests of justice would be served by relieving the party of its error of disclosing a protected document.

Paralegals often play a key role in organizing documents, so they must be alert to such issues. In complex cases involving a huge number of electronic documents, firms that are experts in such matters can be hired to help filter and sort documents.

Maintenance of Electronic Records

To this point, we have considered the collection of electronic matter. A related issue for all firms is the need to put in place a records-management system before litigation arises to minimize the burden of responding to discovery requests. Because litigation is a virtual certainty for many businesses, the up-front investment is often worthwhile. Most corporate legal departments use a records-management system that covers everything from data preservation to production of documents.

Do Not Keep What Is Not Needed

The key to an e-discovery-ready records-management system is to ensure that records are properly categorized and stored. Records not required for business or legal purposes are destroyed and "scrubbed" from computers by programs that ensure actual deletion of the material.

Cost and Risk Controls

Important issues for clients are controlling costs and reducing risks. Among the most costly aspects of document production is review for relevance and privilege, a process that may consume more than half of a litigation budget. Automated processes can help reduce costs by excluding documents based on criteria such as file type, dates, storage location, and the presence or absence of key words.

Risk control refers to the measures used to identify, preserve, and organize documents. Errors can lead to fines or other penalties. Among the most difficult issues to address is how to handle e-mail and calendar archives. It is necessary to save not only the e-mails themselves but also the metadata about the e-mails, such as storage location, creation dates and times, path information, and so on.

Paralegals working in the corporate setting find proper record maintenance a key part of document control. Records—both paper and electronic—that the company is no longer legally required to maintain are destroyed. This helps prevent a party in litigation from going on a "fishing" expedition into documents that may date back in time beyond what is required. When records are not well monitored, a court is more likely to allow open access to electronic media. Similarly, law firms should be proactive in careful record organization and maintenance to protect the firm and its clients.

Pretrial Motions

As we discussed earlier in the chapter, and as shown in Exhibit 10.13, there are a number of motions that may be made before trial. In Chapter 6, we noted that many conflicts are settled by some form of alternative dispute resolution before trial. When that happens, and the parties reach a settlement agreement, the court is informed and, after reviewing the agreement, usually approves it and dismisses the case.

Summary Judgment

motion for summary judgment
A motion that may be filed by either party in which the party asks the court to enter judgment in his or her favor without a trial. A motion for summary judgment can be supported by evidence outside the pleadings, such as witnesses' affidavits, answers to interrogatories, and other evidence obtained prior to or during discovery.

If there is no settlement, one of the last substantive motions likely to be filed before trial is a **motion for summary judgment**. The party filing the motion is asking the court to grant a judgment in his or her favor without a trial because there is no real disagreement about the relevant facts. Once discovery is complete, the parties can argue that no material (relevant) facts are in dispute and the only question is how the law applies to undisputed facts. Because legal questions are the province of judges, no jury is necessary. Nor must the judge hear evidence beyond the pleadings and filed documents in order to find facts.

Considerations by the Court

When the court considers a motion for summary judgment, it considers the evidence the parties have gathered for trial. To support the motion, a party submits evidence obtained, such as depositions and interrogatories, and argues that, given the facts, the

EXHIBIT 10.13
Pretrial Motions

MOTION TO DISMISS

A motion filed by the defendant in which the defendant asks the court to dismiss the case for a specified reason, such as improper service, lack of personal jurisdiction, or the plaintiff's failure to state a claim for which relief can be granted. A plaintiff would file a motion to dismiss against a counterclaim or cross-claim.

MOTION TO STRIKE

A motion filed by a party in which the party asks the court to strike (delete) material from another party's filing. Motions to strike help to clarify the underlying issues by removing paragraphs that are redundant or irrelevant to the action.

MOTION TO MAKE MORE DEFINITE AND CERTAIN

A motion filed by the defendant to compel the plaintiff to clarify the basis of the plaintiff's cause of action. The motion is filed when the defendant believes that the complaint is too vague or ambiguous for the defendant to respond to it in a meaningful way. Similarly, a plaintiff might file such a motion about a counterclaim or cross-claim.

MOTION TO COMPEL DISCOVERY

A motion that may be filed by either party in which the party asks the court to compel the other party to comply with a discovery request. If a party refuses to allow the opponent to inspect and copy certain documents, for example, the party requesting the documents may make a motion to compel production of the documents.

MOTION FOR JUDGMENT ON THE PLEADINGS

After all pleadings have been filed, either party may file this motion. It may be used when there are no facts in dispute, only a question of how the law will apply to the undisputed facts.

MOTION FOR SUMMARY JUDGMENT

A motion that may be filed by either party in which the party asks the court to enter judgment in his or her favor without a trial. Unlike a motion for judgment on the pleadings, a motion for summary judgment can be supported by evidence outside the pleadings, such as witnesses' affidavits, answers to interrogatories, and other evidence obtained prior to or during discovery.

---

other party cannot prevail at trial. The court reviews the evidence in the light most favorable to the nonmoving party. That is, the court must be satisfied that it has drawn all permissible inferences in that party's favor in interpreting the evidence. This motion is more likely to be successfully used by the defendant, but in about a quarter of cases in which the motion is used, it is successful for the plaintiff.

Note that in any litigation where a government agent or entity is a defendant, the plaintiff should be prepared for the defense's motion for summary judgment on the grounds of **sovereign immunity**. The doctrine of sovereign immunity is also used as a basis for motions to dismiss (discussed earlier).

sovereign immunity
A doctrine that immunizes foreign nations from the jurisdiction of U.S. courts when certain conditions are satisfied.

Motion by Defendant

In the *Baranski* case, suppose it is established that Peretto was in another state at the time of the accident. Peretto's attorney could make a motion for summary judgment in Peretto's favor and attach to the motion a witness's sworn statement that Peretto was in the other state when the accident occurred. Unless Baranski's attorney could bring in other evidence to show that Peretto was at the scene of the accident, Peretto's motion for summary judgment would be granted.

A motion for summary judgment would also be appropriate if Baranski had previously signed a release waiving her right to sue Peretto on the claim. In that situation, attorney Cameron would attach a copy of the release to the motion before filing the motion with the court. Cameron would also prepare a memorandum of law in support of the motion. When the court heard the motion, Cameron would argue that execution of the waiver barred Baranski from pursuing her claim against Peretto.

Burden of Proof

The burden would then shift to Gilmore to show that the release was invalid or otherwise not binding on Baranski. If the judge believed that Baranski had signed the release involuntarily, then the judge would grant the motion. If Gilmore convinced the judge that there was an issue concerning the validity of the release, such as evidence that the release signed by Baranski had been procured by fraud, then the judge would deny the motion for summary judgment and permit the case to go to trial. The validity of the release would then be determined at trial by the fact finder.

CHAPTER SUMMARY

CIVIL LITIGATION: BEFORE THE TRIAL

Civil Litigation—A Bird's-Eye View

1. *Pretrial settlements*—Throughout the pretrial stage of litigation, the attorney and paralegal attempt to help the parties reach a settlement at the same time as they are preparing the case for trial.

2. *Procedural requirements*—Although civil lawsuits vary from case to case in terms of complexity, cost, and detail, all civil litigation involves similar procedural steps, as described in Exhibit 10.1.

The Federal Rules of Civil Procedure (FRCP) govern civil cases in federal courts and set forth what must be done during various stages of litigation. Each state has adopted its own rules of civil procedure, which are often similar to the FRCP. Many courts also have (local) rules of procedure that supplement the federal or state rules.

The Preliminaries

1. *The initial client interview*—The first step occurs when an attorney meets with a client who wishes to bring a lawsuit against another party. Before the meeting, the paralegal checks to ensure that representing the client would not create a conflict of interest. The attorney normally conducts the initial client interview, although the paralegal often attends and may make arrangements for subsequent meetings.

2. *Preliminary investigation*—Once the attorney agrees to represent the client in the lawsuit and the client has

signed the retainer agreement, the attorney and paralegal undertake a preliminary investigation to determine the facts alleged by the client and gain other information relating to the case.

3. *Creating the litigation file*—A litigation file is created to hold all documents and records pertaining to the lawsuit. Each law firm or legal department has procedures for organizing and maintaining litigation files. Generally, the file expands as the case progresses to include subfiles for the pleadings, discovery, and other documents relating to the litigation.

The Pleadings

The pleadings inform each party of the claims of the other and detail the facts, charges, and defenses involved in the litigation. Pleadings typically consist of the plaintiff's complaint, the defendant's answer, and any counterclaim or cross-claim.

1. *Drafting the complaint*—A complaint states the claim(s) that plaintiff is making against the defendant. A lawsuit is initiated by filing a complaint with the clerk of the appropriate court.

   a. The complaint includes a caption, jurisdictional allegations, general allegations (body of the complaint) detailing the cause of action, a prayer for relief, a signature, and, if appropriate, a demand for a jury trial.

   b. A complaint can be filed either by personal delivery of the papers to the court clerk or, if the court permits, by electronic filing. The procedural requirements of courts that allow electronic filing vary and must be followed carefully.

2. *Filing the complaint*—The document is filed on paper or electronically. E-filing is becoming more common; some states have statewide systems, and some courts require e-filing.

3. *Service of process*—Typically, the defendant is notified of a lawsuit by delivery of the complaint and a summons (called service of process). The summons identifies the parties to the suit, identifies the court in which the case has been filed, and directs the defendant to respond to the complaint within a specified time period.

   a. Although often the complaint and summons are personally delivered to the defendant, other methods of service are allowed in some situations.

   b. In federal cases and in many states, the defendant can waive, or give up, the right to be personally served with the summons and complaint (and accept service by mail, for example).

   c. Under FRCP 4, if the defendant waives service of process, the defendant receives additional time to respond to the complaint.

4. *The defendant's response*—On receiving the complaint, the defendant has several options.

   a. The defendant may submit an answer that denies wrongdoing or asserts an affirmative defense against the plaintiff's claim, such as the plaintiff's contributory negligence. The answer may be followed by a counterclaim, in which the defendant asserts a claim against the plaintiff arising out of the same incident; or it may be followed by a cross-claim, in which the defendant makes claims against another defendant named in the complaint.

   b. The defendant may make a motion to dismiss the case. It asserts that, even assuming that the facts of the complaint are true, the plaintiff has failed to state a cause of action or there are other grounds for dismissal of the suit.

5. *The scheduling conference*—The court may hold a conference to consult attorneys on both sides for case management purposes.

Traditional Discovery Tools

Before trial, the attorney for each party undertakes a formal investigative process called discovery to obtain evidence helpful to the client's case.

1. *Interrogatories*—Interrogatories are written questions that the parties to the lawsuit must answer, in writing and under oath. The FRCP and some states' rules limit the number of questions that may be asked and the number of interrogatories that may be filed.

2. *Depositions*—Depositions are given under oath, but unlike interrogatories, they may be taken from witnesses as well as from the parties to the lawsuit. Also, the attorney is able to question the deponent (the person being deposed) in person. There is no limit on the number of questions that may be asked. Usually, a court reporter records the official transcript of the deposition.

3. *Requests for production and physical examination*—During discovery, the attorney for either side may request that another party produce documents or other tangible things, or allow the attorney access to them for inspection. When the mental or physical condition of a party is in controversy, the opposing party may request the court to order the party to submit to an examination.

4. *Requests for admission*—A party can request that the opposing party admit the truth of matters relating to the case. Such admissions save time at trial because the parties do not have to spend time proving facts on which they agree.

The Duty to Disclose under FRCP 26

In federal court, FRCP 26 requires that attorneys cooperate in forming a discovery plan early in litigation. It also requires attorneys to disclose relevant information *automatically.* Only after initial disclosures have been made can attorneys resort to the use of traditional discovery tools. An attorney's duty to disclose relevant information continues throughout the pretrial stage.

1. *Initial disclosures*—Each party must disclose information about persons likely to have discoverable information, any information relevant to the dispute, information about the damages requested, and information about insurance that may apply.

2. *Failure to disclose*—Should a party fail to disclose relevant information, court sanctions may be imposed.

3. *Discovery plan*—Must be reported within ten days of the initial meeting of the attorneys.

4. *Subsequent disclosures*—After the initial disclosure, parties in civil litigation must tell each other before trial about expert witnesses to be used, the names of witnesses, and the evidence to be presented at trial.

Discovery of Electronic Evidence

Electronic evidence includes computer-generated and electronically recorded information, such as e-mail, voice mail, spreadsheets, electronically stored documents, and Internet postings. Federal and state rules allow discovery of evidence in electronic form.

1. *Advantages of e-evidence*—Electronic evidence often provides more information than paper discovery, because it can reveal facts found only in electronic format. In addition, the computer contains hidden data (metadata) about documents and e-mail that can be useful. Even files deleted by the user can be retrieved from residual data in the computer.

2. *Sources of e-evidence*—E-evidence may be located in computers, in the backup data copied to removable media or remote servers, or in deleted files. Other sources for e-evidence include voice mail, social media, phone logs, and so forth.

3. *Special requirements of e-evidence*—Preserving the integrity of e-evidence is essential for it to be admissible. Key steps include making an exact image of the original data and preserving the chain of custody until trial.

Maintenance of Electronic Records

Firms should have proactive policies to organize all documents. When discovery occurs, documents from previous cases are more likely to be protected if clearly organized and shown to not be relevant to the current litigation. Many firms also destroy all copies of records no longer required by law to be maintained so as to prevent their resurrection in future litigation.

Pretrial Motions

Various motions may be filed by either party during or after the discovery stage of litigation. A motion for summary judgment is common. It asks the court to enter judgment without a trial and can be supported by evidence outside the pleadings (including affidavits, depositions, and interrogatories). The motion is not granted if key facts are in dispute.

KEY TERMS AND CONCEPTS

affidavit 281

affirmative defense 286

allegation 277

answer 286

chain of custody 307

complaint 276

counterclaim 289

cross-claim 289

default judgment 286

deponent 292

deposition 292

deposition transcript 297

discovery 290

discovery plan 301

docket 277

QUESTIONS FOR REVIEW

1. What rules govern civil trials in federal court? Who are the parties to a lawsuit?

2. Describe what takes place during the initial client interview. Who conducts this interview, the attorney or the paralegal? Why?

3. Describe the pleadings in a civil lawsuit. How does each type of pleading affect the litigation? If a defendant fails to respond to the plaintiff's complaint within a specified time period, what can happen?

4. What is service of process? What are the methods of serving a complaint on a defendant in a federal court lawsuit? What happens if the defendant is not properly served?

5. When does discovery take place, and what does it involve? List three traditional discovery devices that can be used to obtain information prior to trial. Is electronic evidence discoverable?

6. What is the duty to disclose under FRCP 26? What happens if there is a failure to disclose?

7. What is risk control? Why is it important in electronic discovery?

8. What pretrial motions are discussed in this chapter? What is the purpose of each motion?

ETHICS QUESTION

1. A client who is suing her employer for employment discrimination calls paralegal DeShawn from her employer-issued smartphone to discuss her case against her employer. Later, from her office computer, the client e-mails documents to DeShawn that may be used as evidence in her upcoming trial. What ethical issues do the client's actions raise? What are DeShawn's ethical obligations in this situation? The law firm's obligations?

PRACTICE QUESTIONS AND ASSIGNMENTS

1. Assume that you work for attorney Tara Jolans of Adams & Tate, 1000 Town Center, Suite 500, White Tower, Michigan. Jolans has decided to represent Sandra Nelson in her lawsuit against David Namisch. Based on the following information and the material in the chapter, draft a complaint to be filed in the U.S. District Court for the Eastern District of Michigan.

    Sandra Nelson is the plaintiff in a lawsuit resulting from an automobile accident. Sandra was turning left at a traffic light at the intersection of Jefferson and Mack Streets while the left-turn arrow was green. In the intersection, she was hit from the side by a 2014 Toyota Camry driven by David Namisch, who failed to stop at the light. The accident occurred on June 3, 2021, at 11:30 P.M. David lives in New York, was visiting his family in Michigan, and just prior to the accident had been out drinking with his brothers. Several witnesses saw the accident. One of the witnesses called the police.

    Sandra was not wearing her seat belt at the time of the accident, and she was thrown against the windshield, sustaining massive head injuries. When the police and ambulance arrived, they did not think that she would make it to the hospital alive, but she survived. She wants to claim damages of $500,000 for medical expenses, $65,000 for lost wages, and $75,000 for property damage to her Mercedes. The accident was reported in the local newspaper, complete with photographs.

2. Using Exhibit 10.3, A Summons in a Civil Action, draft a summons to accompany the complaint against David Namisch. David's address is 1000 Main Street, Apartment 63, New York, New York 10009. The court clerk's name is David T. Brown.

3. Review Exhibit 10.7, Sample Interrogatories. Draft the first ten questions for a set of interrogatories to be directed to the plaintiff, Sandra Nelson, based on the facts given in Question 1 above. How do the interrogatories for Sandra Nelson differ from those in the sample?

4. In an employment discrimination lawsuit, the plaintiff printed more than 400 e-mail messages related to her discrimination claim. Her former employer produced only 120 e-mail messages in response to a discovery request for e-mails between management and human resources. The employer claimed that additional e-mails were stored on backup tapes and would be extremely costly to produce. What would the judge consider in determining whether to order the employer to produce additional e-mails?

5. Open a saved Word document. Find the properties tab and open it. The document properties contain the document's metadata. Find and write down the document's author, its creation date, the date it was last revised, and the name of the person who revised it. What is one way in which metadata could be used in a trial?

GROUP PROJECT

This project addresses the issue of the discoverability of social networking information.

Student one will do an Internet search on whether information on social networking sites, such as Facebook, is discoverable.

Student two will assume it is discoverable, and will research who has to provide it—the user of a social networking account, or the social networking site itself.

Student three will research whether penalties apply if the postings on a social networking site are removed (known as spoliation of evidence) after a lawsuit begins. If the information is removed, is the removal permanent?

Student four will present the group's findings in a one-page paper.

CHAPTER
11

CHAPTER OUTLINE

Conducting Interviews and Investigations

CHAPTER OBJECTIVES

After completing this chapter, you will be able to:

- Explain how to prepare for an interview.
- Describe the kinds of skills employed during the interviewing process.
- Explain the common types of client interviews paralegals may conduct.
- Explain the kinds of witnesses paralegals may need to interview during a preliminary investigation.
- Create an investigation plan.
- Identify the variety of sources available to locate information or witnesses.
- List the rules governing the types of evidence that are admissible in court.
- Summarize investigation results.

Introduction

Paralegals frequently interview clients and witnesses. After the initial interview (which is usually conducted by the supervising attorney), the paralegal may conduct additional interviews to obtain detailed information. How well the paralegal relates to a witness has an important effect on the witness's attitude toward the attorney or legal team handling the case.

Learning how to conduct interviews and investigations is thus an important part of preparing for your career as a paralegal. In this chapter, you will read about the basic skills and concepts used when interviewing clients or witnesses and conducting investigations.

Planning the Interview

Planning an interview involves organizing many details. As a paralegal, you may be responsible for locating a witness, scheduling the interview, determining where the interview should take place, arranging for the use of one of the firm's conference rooms or other office space for the interview, and managing additional details. Thorough preparation is crucial to the success of any interview.

Know What Information You Want

interviewee
The person who is being interviewed.

Before any interview, you should have clearly in mind the information you want to obtain from the client or witness being interviewed—the **interviewee**. If possible, discuss with your supervising attorney the goal of the interview and the type of information the attorney hopes to obtain. This will ensure that you and the attorney share an understanding of what topics need to be covered in the interview. Once you know the questions that you want to ask, prepare a checklist or outline in advance so that you can refer to it during the interview. As the accompanying *Developing Paralegal Skills* feature explains, it is most productive to think through what may happen in an investigation before proceeding.

Review Relevant Legal Topics

It may be necessary to review the legal topics involved in the case with the supervising attorney before preparing for the interview. At times, information that a layperson might dismiss as irrelevant can play an important role in the litigation. For example, a sound understanding of the elements of negligence is critical for a paralegal who is about to interview a witness for a personal injury case involving a traffic accident. Likewise, a paralegal interviewing a witness for a case involving disorderly conduct would need to know what conduct the state considers "disorderly" before drafting a list of questions.

Remember Digital Shadows

When planning an interview, do not neglect the "digital shadow" of the person being interviewed. Part of your preparation for any interview, whether of a client or a potential witness, should include investigating their online presence. Look for information about the person being interviewed and what the person may have posted about events related to the case. For example, a witness to a car accident may have sent a tweet about the crash or posted a photo or video. The timeline of events provided by an interviewee may be confirmed or contradicted by social media posts.

Frequent social media users may not recall having used social media to discuss a topic unless you prompt them. "Did you post anything about this to Facebook, Twitter, or Instagram?" should be added to your standard set of interview questions.

DEVELOPING PARALEGAL SKILLS

THINKING THROUGH A FRAUD INVESTIGATION

As a paralegal, you may be asked to help conduct an internal investigation in which someone suspects that fraud has occurred in a business. Suppose a client is concerned that an employee may have taken sensitive documents. Here are some key questions that need to be considered:

- **Is an internal investigation the appropriate step?** In some cases, an internal investigative report may simply serve as a road map for a later investigation by law enforcement agencies. The main reasons to conduct an internal review are to send a clear signal that fraud is not tolerated and to stop the fraud.

- **Who is being defrauded?** If the harm is to someone not working for the company, outside legal advice is usually advised, and a key question will be whether the company could be liable for fraud committed by an employee.

- **What steps are being taken to avoid defaming individuals accused of fraud?** A costly defamation suit (discussed in Chapter 14) is possible if an individual is falsely accused.

- **Should an employee suspected of fraud have known that his conduct was fraudulent or against company policy?** Answering this question will require reviewing company policies and education and training procedures.

- **How will the investigation be documented?** Usually, the investigating paralegal will take notes and, with permission, record the interview. You should sign and date your notes. An attorney may also ask an interviewee to prepare a written statement.

- **How will the results be evaluated?** Any report should be solidly based on the facts uncovered during the investigation, not on speculation or assumptions.

- **What statutes are relevant to the possible fraud?** Regulations from state and federal governments increasingly dominate many businesses.

Preparing for an investigation by thinking through all major issues that could arise, sometimes unexpectedly, means the investigation will be more thorough and helpful to the legal team responsible for the matter.

Interviewees' digital shadows may also tell you a great deal about their potential reliability as witnesses. A person with multiple photos of drinking contests may not be as reliable a witness as someone whose online profile focuses on her interest in accounting. By preparing in advance, you can avoid surprises later if such information comes out.

Standardized Interview Forms

Many law firms have preprinted or computerized forms indicating the kinds of information that should be gathered during client interviews relating to particular types of claims. Firms that frequently handle personal-injury claims, for example, often use a personal-injury intake sheet such as the one shown in Exhibit 11.1 on pages 319 and 320. Client intake forms are also available as part of many legal software programs and from a variety of online sources. They may be completed electronically. Using standardized forms helps to ensure that all essential information will be addressed in the interview.

In some cases, the information needed is clear from the legal forms or documents that may eventually be filed with the court. For example, a paralegal interviewing a client who is petitioning for bankruptcy or divorce can look at the bankruptcy or divorce court forms during the interview to make sure all required information is obtained.

Remain Flexible

The prepared questions and preprinted forms should only be used as guidelines during the interview. Do not just read the questions mechanically word for word from a prepared list or adhere rigidly to a planned outline of topics. If you do, you lose an opportunity to interact with the interviewee and gain the interviewee's trust, and he or she will probably not disclose information other than what is specifically asked for.

The interviewer should be flexible, listen carefully to the interviewee's responses, and let those responses guide the questioning. Remember that you can always ask the interviewee to return to a certain topic later on in the interview. In fact, it is often fruitful to return to the topics discussed earlier in the interview after the person being interviewed becomes more comfortable.

Avoid focusing too much on your own role and on what your next question will be. Focus instead on what the client or witness is saying. Never forget that you are speaking with a person, not merely an information source. Make sure that you listen to the interviewee's responses and modify your questions accordingly.

Plan to Ask Follow-up Questions

An important point to remember is to ask for details and clarification after the interviewee has made a statement. Find out who, what, when, where, and how. If an interviewee says, for example, that he saw someone hit Jane in the face, you will need to ask for more specifics, such as:

- How far away was the interviewee at the time?
- What exactly did he see?
- How many times was Jane hit, and with what (open hand, fist, weapon)?
- Who else was present?
- Was it light or dark? Inside or outside?
- From what angle did the interviewee view the incident?
- Does he know Jane or her assailant? How?
- What were Jane and the assailant doing before and after the incident?
- What was the witness doing before the incident?

While legal professionals are taught to place events in chronological order, people often do not tell stories that way. You should expect an interviewee to skip around. Therefore, you might need to interject occasionally by asking "Did this happen before or after [some other event]?" Another common hazard during interviews of clients and witnesses is the use of pronouns. Often, an interviewee will say "he" or "she" did something when there are multiple actors in the story to whom those pronouns could refer. A good interviewer will seek clarification of the names of the people involved. Sometimes, this requires insisting on the use of only proper names instead of pronouns.

Although you should read the case file thoroughly before the interview, try to set aside what you have read or heard about the case. Let the interviewee tell you the story from his perspective and avoid preconceived notions about what he will say.

One approach is to pretend that you know nothing about the case. Let the interviewee tell you his version of the facts. Then, as the interview unfolds, think about what the person is saying from the perspective of your opponent—why should anyone believe that story? Ask follow-up questions aimed at establishing what makes the person's story more or less believable. If a witness says a car was going sixty miles per hour, for example, ask how she could tell the speed. If it turns out the witness has been racing cars for the past ten years, this fact can be used to help make the witness's testimony more credible.

Recording the Interview

Some interviewers record their interviews. Before you record an interview, get permission to do so from both your supervising attorney and the person being interviewed. When you record an interview, state or include at the beginning the following identifying information:

- The name of the person being interviewed and any other relevant information about the interviewee.
- The name of the person conducting the interview.
- The names of other persons present at the interview, if any.
- The date, time, and place of the interview.
- On the record, the interviewee's consent to having the interview recorded.

EXHIBIT 11.1

Personal-Injury Intake Sheet

PERSONAL-INJURY INTAKE SHEET

**Prepared for Clients of
Jeffers, Gilmore & Dunn**

1. Client Information:

Name: Katherine Baranski

Address: 335 Natural Blvd.

Nita City, NI   48802

Social Security No.: 206-15-9858

Marital Status: Married   Years Married: 3

Spouse's Name: Peter Baranski

Children: None

Phone Numbers: Cell (616) 555-2211   Work (616) 555-4849

Employer: Nita State University
Mathematics Department

Position: Associate Professor of Mathematics

Responsibilities: Teaching

Salary: $64,000

2. Related Information:

Client at Scene: Yes

Lost Work Time: 5 months

Client's Habits: Normally drives south on Mattis Avenue on way to university each morning at about the same time.

Continued

EXHIBIT 11.1

Personal-Injury Intake Sheet
—Continued

3. **Incident/Accident:**

Date: August 4, 2021   Time: 7:45 A.M.

Place: Mattis Avenue and 38th Street, Nita City, Nita

Description: Mrs. Baranski was driving south on Mattis Avenue
when a car driven by Tony Peretto, who was
attempting to cross Mattis at 38th Street, collided
with Mrs. Baranski's vehicle.

Witnesses: None known by Mrs. Baranski

Defendant: Tony Peretto

Police: Nita City

Action Taken: Mrs. Baranski was taken to City Hospital
by ambulance (Nita City Ambulance Co.).

4. **Injuries Sustained:**

Nature: Multiple fractures to left hip and leg; lacerations
to left eye and left side of face; multiple contusions
and abrasions

Medical History: No significant medical problems prior to the
accident

Treating Hospital: Nita City Hospital

Treating Physician: Dr. Swanson

Hospital Stay: August 4, 2021   to September 20, 2021

Insurance: Southwestern Insurance Co. of America

Policy No: 00631150962-B

Interview Conducted by:

Allen P. Gilmore   January 30, 2022
Attorney   Date

Elena Lopez   January 30, 2022
Paralegal/Witness   Date

Benefits of Recording

There are several advantages to recording an interview. Having an audio record of the interview reduces the need to take extensive notes during the interview. You can either have the audio file transcribed for future reference or listen to it later (when creating an interview summary, for example) to refresh your memory of how the interviewee responded to certain questions.

You may want to have other members of the legal team read the transcript or listen to the file. Sometimes, what seemed insignificant to you may seem significant to someone else working on the case. Also, as a case progresses, a remark made by an interviewee that did not seem important at the time of the interview may take on added significance in view of evidence gathered later.

The Downside of Recording

There are some disadvantages to recording interviews. If clients and witnesses know everything they are saying is being recorded, they may feel uncomfortable and be less willing to disclose information freely. Such reluctance is understandable in view of the fact that the interviewee does not know what exactly will happen during the interview or how the recording may later be used.

When asking an interviewee for permission to record an interview, you should evaluate how the interviewee responds to this question. Depending on the interviewee's response, you might consider taking notes instead of recording the session. Another option is to go through the questions you will ask with the interviewee once before asking permission to turn on the recorder. Additionally, clarifying the limited uses to which the recording will be put might place the interviewee's mind at ease. In other words, by simply explaining that recording the interview may lead to a more accurate record could be enough to convince a reluctant interviewee to agree.

Interviewing Skills

Interviewing skills include interpersonal and communication skills that help you to conduct a successful interview. In this section, you will learn how the use of such skills can help you establish a comfortable relationship with the interviewee. Then, you will read about specific questioning and listening techniques that can help you control the interview and elicit information.

Interpersonal Skills

In conducting an interview, your primary goal is to obtain information. Although some people share information readily, others need prompting and encouragement. If people feel comfortable in your presence and in the interviewing environment, they will generally be more willing to disclose information.

Remember that the interviewee may be nervous or uncomfortable. While you may have conducted many interviews of this nature, your interviewee may be involved in the legal process for the first time. Help put the person at ease as quickly as possible. A few minutes chatting casually is time well spent. Also, saying or doing something that shows your concern for the interviewee's physical comfort helps to make the interviewee feel more relaxed. You might offer a coffee or another beverage, for example.

Using language that the interviewee understands is essential in establishing a good relationship. If you are interviewing a client with only a grade-school education, for example, do not use the phrase "facial lacerations" when talking about "cuts on the face." If you are interviewing a witness who does not speak English well, and you are not fluent in the witness's language, have an interpreter present. Because most clients and witnesses are not familiar with legal terminology, avoid using legal terms that will not be clearly understood. If you must use a legal term, be sure that you define the term clearly. After defining the term, be sure that your definition is understood.

Questioning Skills

When questioning witnesses or clients, remain objective at all times and gather as much relevant information as possible. Sometimes, you may find it hard to remain objective when questioning witnesses because you sympathize with the client and may not want to hear about facts contrary to the client's position. But you need to uncover details that could weaken the client's case as well as those that support it. Indeed, your supervising attorney must know *all* of the facts, especially any that might damage the client's case. Explaining *why* it is important to know these facts might help the interviewee be more forthcoming.

Mask Your Emotions

In some situations, it may be difficult to remain objective not because of your sympathy *for* the client but because of your own personal biases *against* the client, the witness, or the case. Interviewers must be careful to evaluate their feelings prior to conducting an interview. If you feel a person's conduct has been morally wrong, you may unintentionally convey those feelings during the interview. We often communicate feelings nonverbally through unspoken gestures and facial expressions. If an interviewee senses your disapproval, she is likely to limit the information disclosed.

Suppose you are interviewing Sandra, a client who is trying to regain custody of her children. The state removed Sandra's children because she abused drugs and failed to properly care for the children. You have read the file and strongly disapprove of Sandra's past conduct and have doubts about whether she has recovered from her drug problem. If you do not set aside your personal feelings before meeting with Sandra, they may affect your interaction and limit the success of the interview.

The experienced legal interviewer uses various questioning techniques to prompt interviewees to communicate. Types of questions include open-ended, closed-ended, leading, and hypothetical questions. Exhibit 11.2 provides some examples of the types of questions discussed in the following subsections.

EXHIBIT 11.2

Types of Interview Questions

Type of Question	Open-Ended Question	Closed-Ended Question	Leading Question	Hypothetical Question
Definition	A broad, exploratory question that may elicit a lengthy response.	A question phrased in such a way that it elicits a "yes" or "no" response.	A question phrased in such a way that it suggests the desired answer.	A question that asks the interviewee to assume certain facts in forming an answer.
Typical Uses	Mostly with friendly witnesses and clients.	To clarify an interviewee's statement or to keep the interviewee on track. With adverse or reluctant witnesses.	At times, with adverse witnesses in interviews. By attorneys to cross-examine witnesses at trial (see Chapter 12).	Primarily with expert witnesses in interviews and during trial.
Examples	• Describe the morning of the accident. What did you do that morning? • What did you see before entering the intersection? • When did you first see the defendant's car, and where was it? • How fast was the defendant going at the time of the accident?	• Were you late for work that morning? • Was there anyone in the car with you at the time? • Were you already in the intersection at the time you first saw the plaintiff's car? • Were you exceeding the speed limit at the time the accident occurred?	• You were running late for work that morning, correct? • You saw that the light had turned red before you entered the intersection, didn't you? • Isn't it true that you were driving over the speed limit at the time of the accident? • Isn't it true that you had been out drinking at a bar until late on the night before the accident?	• If a full-sized van is going sixty miles per hour, how far before reaching an intersection must the driver apply the brakes in order to stop the vehicle at the intersection? • If a two-hundred-pound man drank fourteen beers in six hours, how long would it take before the alcohol was out of his system so that it would not affect his ability to drive?

Open-Ended Questions

The **open-ended question** is a broad, exploratory question that invites any number of responses. It can be used when you want to give the interviewee an opportunity to talk at length about a given subject. "What happened on the night of October 28—the night of the robbery?" and "What did you see as you approached the intersection?" are open-ended questions. When you ask this kind of question, be prepared for a lengthy response. If a witness has difficulty narrating the events he observed, or if a lull develops during the explanation, you will need to encourage the witness to continue by using prompting responses (which will be discussed shortly).

Open-ended questions are useful in interviewing clients or friendly witnesses (witnesses who favor the client's position). These interviewees are usually forthcoming, and you will be able to gain information from them by indicating in broad terms what you want them to describe. Open-ended questions are also a good way for the interviewer to evaluate whether the interviewee's behavior and overall effectiveness would make her a good witness at trial. Someone who speaks clearly and confidently is likely to be a more persuasive witness than someone who hems and haws.

open-ended question
A question phrased in such a way that it elicits a relatively unguided and lengthy narrative response.

Closed-Ended Questions

The **closed-ended question** is intended to elicit a "yes" or "no" response. "Did you see the gun?" is an example of a closed-ended question. Although closed-ended questions tend to limit communication, they can be useful. For example, if an interviewee tends to wander from the topic being discussed, closed-ended questions can help keep him on track. Closed-ended questions, because they invite specific answers, also may be useful to clarify the interviewee's previous response and to relax the interviewee in preparation for more difficult questions that follow. In addition, closed-ended questions may help to draw information from adverse witnesses (those not favorable to the client's position), who may be reluctant to volunteer information.

closed-ended question
A question phrased in such a way that it elicits a simple "yes" or "no" answer.

Leading Questions

A **leading question** is one that suggests to the listener the answer to the question. "Isn't it true that you were only ten feet away from where the murder took place?" is a leading question. Leading questions can be effective for drawing information out of eyewitnesses or clients, particularly when they are reluctant to disclose information. They can be useful for interviewing adverse witnesses who are hesitant to communicate information that may be helpful to the client's position. They are the primary method of questioning used by attorneys when cross-examining witnesses at trial, as you will read in Chapter 12.

When used with a client or friendly witnesses, however, leading questions have a major drawback. They may lead to distorted answers because the client or witness may tailor the answer to fit her perception of what the interviewer wants to know. For this reason, leading questions should be used cautiously in interviews and only when the interviewer is aware of the possible distortions that might result.

leading question
A question that suggests, or "leads to," a desired answer. Interviewers may use leading questions to elicit responses from witnesses who otherwise would not be forthcoming.

Hypothetical Questions

You may be asked to interview an expert witness to gather information about a case or to evaluate whether that person would be an effective expert witness at trial (expert witnesses are discussed later in this chapter). The **hypothetical question** is frequently used with expert witnesses. Hypothetical questions allow you to obtain an answer to an important question without giving away the facts (and confidences) of a client's case. For example, you might invent a hypothetical situation involving a knee injury (the same injury sustained by a client) and ask an orthopedic surgeon what kind of follow-up care would ordinarily be needed for that injury.

hypothetical question
A question based on hypothesis, conjecture, or fiction.

Listening Skills

The interviewer's ability to listen is one of the most important communication skills. When conducting an interview, you want to absorb the interviewee's verbal answers *and* any nonverbal messages. Before the interview, make sure that the room in which it is to be held will be free of phone calls, visitors, and other distractions. Put your cell phone on silent and ask the witness to do the same. During the interview, you can use several listening techniques to maximize communication and guide the interviewee toward full disclosure.

Passive Listening

As noted, the interviewer should listen attentively to the interviewee. It is critical that the client or witness knows that the interviewer is interested in what she is saying. If the interviewee pauses briefly or there is a lull in the conversation, the interviewer can use passive listening techniques, which are verbal or nonverbal cues that encourage the speaker to continue. For example, the interviewer might say, "Please go on" or "And what happened then?" A nonverbal cue can be a facial expression or body language that shows you are interested in what is being said. Nodding positively, for example, is an effective way to convey your interest. Maintaining eye contact is another nonverbal cue to indicate interest.

Active Listening

For communication to be interactive, the listener must engage in active listening. Active listening involves paying close attention to what the speaker is saying and providing appropriate feedback to show that you understand and may have sympathy for what is being said. Because people do not always say what they mean to say—or what they think they are saying—active listening is key to a productive interview. It allows the interviewer to clarify and confirm the interviewee's statements throughout the interview.

Reflecting Back.   One effective active listening technique is for the interviewer to "reflect back," or "mirror," what the interviewee has already said. For example, after the interviewee has expressed his thoughts on a topic, you might say, "Let me see if I understand you correctly" and summarize your impression of what was said. If your interpretation is incorrect, the interviewee has the opportunity to make you understand what he meant to say. This technique is useful for clarifying the person's statement. In addition, it reinforces the idea that you are listening carefully and are interested.

Controlling the Flow of the Interview.   Active listening enables the interviewer to put the person's statements into the context of the larger picture and facilitates smooth transitions between interview topics. Suppose you are interviewing a client who is suing her former employer. After telling you about the rude and offensive behavior of her co-workers, she says she just couldn't go back to work and starts to cry. By restating what she has told you, you can make the client feel you support and identify with her: "I understand that you did not return to work because of the hostility of your co-workers." You might then move into a discussion of damages by saying, "It sounds as if you've been through a lot. Did you go see a counselor or get help from anyone during that time?"

The interviewer who engages in active listening can direct the flow of the interview according to the reactions and responses of the person being interviewed. As this chapter's *Featured Contributor* article on pages 326 and 327 notes, effective techniques increase the amount and quality of information you gain through interviews.

passive listening
The act of listening attentively to the speaker's message and responding to the speaker by providing verbal or nonverbal cues that encourage the speaker to continue—in effect, saying, "I'm listening, please go on."

active listening
The act of listening attentively to the speaker's message and responding by giving appropriate feedback to show that you understand what the speaker is saying; restating the speaker's message in your own words to confirm that you accurately interpreted what was said.

Interviewing Clients

Here, we first look at client interviews and then discuss witness interviews. The types of client interviews include the initial interview, subsequent interviews to obtain further information, and informational interviews, or meetings, to inform the client of the case's status and to prepare the client for various legal proceedings.

The Initial Client Interview

As discussed in previous chapters, when a client seeks legal advice from an attorney, the attorney normally holds an initial interview with the client. During this interview, the client explains his problem so that the attorney can advise him on possible legal options and potential legal fees. The client and the attorney will agree on the terms of the representation, if the attorney decides to take the case.

Paralegals often attend initial client interviews, although the attorney normally conducts the first interview. Usually, you observe the client and take notes on what the client says. You also provide the client with forms, statements explaining the firm's fees, and other prepared information normally given to new clients. Following the interview, you and the attorney may compare impressions of the client and of what the client said during the interview.

Introduce All Parties Clearly

All people present at an interview should be introduced to the client, their titles given, and the reason for their presence made known. In introducing you to the potential client, the attorney will probably stress that you are not a lawyer and cannot give legal advice. If your supervising attorney does not indicate your nonattorney status to the client, you should do so. If a firm takes a client's case, the client should be introduced to all members of the legal team working on the case.

A follow-up letter, such as the one shown in Exhibit 11.3, will be sent or e-mailed to the client after the interview. The letter states whether the attorney has decided to accept the case or, if the attorney orally agreed during the initial client interview to represent the client, confirms the oral agreement in writing.

Intake and Screening Procedures

Note that while the initial interview with an attorney is often a paralegal's first contact with a client, this is not always the case. Certain law firms—such as public interest, high-profile, and legal aid firms—have a separate intake and screening procedure. This procedure entails having paralegals and other office staff evaluate applicants who request a meeting with an attorney by phone, by e-mail, or as walk-ins.

Typically, an intake form is generated for each applicant including contact information, a summary of the legal claim, and other information that helps the firm to decide whether to take on the applicant as a client. In this way, clients who do not fit within the firm's practice area, objectives, or funding specifications can be screened out before the firm expends time and resources on an initial sit-down interview.

Some applicants will seek quick legal advice over the phone, via e-mail, or in person during this initial screening. Again, it is important for paralegals to explain to these prospective clients that they are not attorneys and cannot provide any legal advice.

Handling Client Documents

Clients frequently give paralegals important documents during initial and subsequent interviews. States impose strict requirements on attorneys about safekeeping clients' property, including documents.

FEATURED CONTRIBUTOR

TEN STRATEGIES FOR EFFECTIVE INTERVIEWS AND INVESTIGATIONS

John Bell

BIOGRAPHICAL NOTE

John Bell graduated *magna cum laude* from Central Michigan University in 1987. He spent several years managing small businesses before attending law school. Bell graduated *cum laude* with a J.D. from the University of South, Carolina School of Law, where he served on the editorial board of the law review and was honored with membership in the Order of the Wig and Robe and the Order of the Coif.

Bell has been licensed to practice law in South Carolina since 2004. He began his legal career at a boutique defense law firm in Greenville, South Carolina, representing some of the nation's biggest corporations in civil litigation. He later owned a small general practice, where he primarily represented individuals in civil and domestic litigation.

He is a certified family and civil court mediator and maintains a mediation practice. In 2011, Bell joined the faculty of the ABA-approved paralegal program at Greenville Technical College, where he is an associate professor and previously served as the paralegal program director.

The investigator is one of the valuable roles that paralegals play in delivering legal services to clients. As an investigator, paralegals are often called on to interview clients, witnesses, and experts as a first step in gathering the information and evidence necessary to build the cases in which they are involved. Here are ten strategies to make your investigations and interviews effective and efficient.

Make a Plan.

An investigation should begin with a written plan that includes the information that you are seeking and the possible sources of the information as well as a plan for how the information will be obtained from each source. The client interview is usually the best initial source of information.

Prepare for Interviews.

Be thoughtful and conscientious in scheduling interviews. Select an appropriate time and location for the interview in consultation with the client or witness. Make sure to arrange for any special needs (e.g., interpreter). Confirm the date, time, and location of the interview in writing by letter or e-mail.

You should never rely on memory when it comes to client documents. Immediately after the conclusion of an interview, record the receipt of any documents or other items received from the client. The information may be recorded in an evidence log (discussed later) or as required by the procedures established by your firm to govern the receipt and storage of such property. In addition, paper documents should be scanned into electronic case files so that backup copies exist.

Whenever it is not necessary for a law firm to keep an original document provided by a client, it is a best practice (employed at many firms) to make a copy of the document and return the original before the client departs from the interview. This minimizes legal risks associated with the duty to safeguard clients' possessions.

Subsequent Client Interviews

Paralegals are often asked to conduct additional client interviews once cases are accepted. Assume that a client seeks a divorce. After the initial interview, your supervising attorney may ask you to arrange for an interview to get the information necessary

Determine the Details for the Interview.

Efficiency is a key part of an effective investigation. Anticipate information and documents the client or witness should bring to the interview that will assist in investigating and evaluating the case, as well as responding to discovery from the other side. Communicate in writing the information the client or witness should bring to the interview.

Put the Interviewee at Ease.

Before beginning the interview, introduce yourself and try to establish some rapport with the interviewee. Professional small talk and refreshment offerings can often make the interviewee more comfortable when you eventually have to begin asking sensitive questions. Start the interview by explaining your role and the purpose of the interview.

Prepare an Interview Outline.

Most law firms have template interview outlines and checklists. A best practice in using these template forms is to add specific questions unique to the case you are working on.

Also, a good checklist or template outline is no substitute for listening carefully and asking appropriate follow-up questions.

Take Note of Facts and Verify Them.

The focus of your interview and your investigation should be finding facts important to your case. Make careful notes of the factual information obtained from interviewees and then verify those facts from other sources, if possible.

Efficiency is a key part of an effective investigation."

Keep a Poker Face.

A good interview requires the client or witness to feel comfortable being entirely honest and forthcoming. The interviewee must feel heard and not judged. While gathering information, demonstrate empathy, compassion, and impartiality while maintaining appropriate professional boundaries. Choose your words carefully, and be aware of your body language during interviews.

Explain the Duty of Confidentiality.

Your legal team must know the good, the bad, and the ugly about your client's case. Encourage the client to be entirely forthcoming by assuring them that everything they tell you or someone on your legal team will be kept confidential.

Refine Your Interview Skills.

Best practices include asking open-ended questions, listening actively and confirming understanding, avoiding distractions, avoiding antagonizing the interviewee with judgmental statements, staying focused, and not becoming emotional.

Demonstrate Cultural and Gender Sensitivity.

You need to be gender and culturally sensitive about how a client's unique background and belief systems influence his or her behavior. Clients from different backgrounds, for example, will have different attitudes about eye contact, body language, and physical contact. Take the time to inform yourself about these potential differences.

Source: John Bell

---

to prepare the divorce pleadings. When scheduling the interview, you should tell the client what kinds of documents to bring to the interview. Then send the client a letter and an e-mail message confirming the date and time of the interview and the items you want the client to bring. During the interview, you will fill out the form that the firm uses to record client information in divorce cases.

As always, when conducting a client interview, the paralegal should disclose his or her nonlawyer status if this fact was not made clear earlier. To protect yourself against potential claims that you have engaged in the unauthorized practice of law, clearly state that you are not an attorney and cannot give legal advice.

The Informational Interview

The informational interview, or meeting, is an interview in which the client is brought in to discuss legal proceedings. Most clients know little about the procedures involved in litigation, and firms often have paralegals explain procedures and help prepare

EXHIBIT 11.3

A Sample Follow-up Letter
E-Mailed to a Client

From: Allen P. Gilmore, Attorney at Law <allen.p.gilmore@jgd.com>
To: Ms. Katherine Baranski <k.baran@nitamail.net>
Cc: Ms. Elena Lopez <elena.lopez@jgd.com>
Subject: Case Involving Tony Peretto

February 2, 2022
Ms. Katherine Baranski
335 Natural Blvd.
Nita City, Nita 48802

Dear Ms. Baranksi:

It was a pleasure to meet and talk with you on January 30. Jeffers, Gilmore & Dunn will be pleased to act as your representative in your action against Tony Peretto to obtain compensation for your injuries.

Attached is a copy of a fee agreement for your review. A copy of this letter and the agreement are being sent to you by mail. The mailing will contain a self-addressed, stamped envelope for your convenience. As soon as I receive the completed agreement, we will begin investigating your case.

As I advised during our meeting, to protect your rights, please refrain from speaking with the driver of the vehicle, Mr. Peretto; his lawyer; or his insurance company. If they attempt to contact you, simply tell them that you have retained counsel and refer them to me. I will handle any questions that they may have.

If you have any questions, please do not hesitate to call me or my paralegal, Ms. Elena Lopez.

Sincerely,

Allen P. Gilmore, Attorney at Law
Jeffers, Gilmore & Dunn
553 Fifth Avenue, Suite 101
Nita City, NI 48801
Telephone: (616) 555-9690
Fax: (616) 555-9679

1 Attachment
Baranski Agreement.doc
194K View as HTML Download

The preceding e-mail message (including any attachments) contains information that may be confidential, be protected by the attorney-client or other applicable privileges, or constitute nonpublic information. It is intended to be conveyed only to the designated recipient(s). If you are not an intended recipient of this message, please notify the sender by replying to this message and then delete it from your system. Use, dissemination, distribution, or reproduction of this message by unintended recipients is not authorized and may be unlawful.

clients for trial. The paralegal can describe to clients what takes place during the trial, how they should dress and conduct themselves appropriately for trial, where they should look when they testify, and so forth. The informational interview helps clients understand why proceedings are taking place and their role in those proceedings.

Summarizing the Interview

The interviewing process does not end with the close of the interview. A crucial step in the process involves summarizing the results of the interview for the legal team working on the case. As a paralegal, you are likely to create an intake memorandum following each initial client interview. If the firm has a prepared intake form for particular types of cases—such as the personal-injury intake sheet referred to earlier and illustrated in Exhibit 11.1—the completed form might serve as the interview summary. Information obtained during subsequent interviews with a client should be summarized in a memo for your supervising attorney or other team members to review and for inclusion in the client's file.

Do It Now

Your interview summary should be created immediately after the interview, while the session is fresh in your mind. When summarizing an interview, review your notes and, if the session was recorded, review the recording. Never rely only on your memory of the statements made during the interview. It is easy to forget the client's specific words, and it may be important later to know exactly how the client phrased a response. Relying on memory is also risky because a statement that seemed irrelevant at the time may turn out to be important to the case. Make sure that the facts are accurately recorded. Also note your impressions of the client and the client's nonverbal behaviors.

Visual Evidence

Depending on the nature of the legal claim being made by the client, you may want to include a visual element or two in your summary. For example, if the claim concerns an automobile accident, you might consider creating a graphic depiction of the accident to attach to the summary. (For a further discussion of the value of visual communications, see this chapter's *Office Tech and Cybersecurity* feature.)

Interviewing Witnesses

Witnesses play a key role in establishing the facts of an event. As an investigator, your goal is to elicit as much relevant and reliable information as possible from each witness about the event that you are investigating. Interviewing witnesses is similar to interviewing clients, and many of the interviewing skills that we have already discussed also apply. A major difference is that witnesses may not always be friendly to the client's position. Here we describe the types of witnesses, as well as some skills and principles relevant to investigative interviews.

Types of Witnesses

Witnesses include expert witnesses, lay witnesses, and eyewitnesses. Witnesses are also sometimes classified as friendly witnesses or hostile (adverse) witnesses.

Expert Witnesses

An **expert witness** has professional training, advanced knowledge, or substantial experience in a specialized area, such as medicine, computer technology, ballistics, or construction techniques. Paralegals often arrange to hire expert witnesses to testify in court or to render an opinion on some matter relating to the client's case. Expert witnesses are often used in cases involving medical malpractice and product liability to establish the duty, or standard of care, that the defendant owed to the plaintiff. For example, if a client is suing a physician for malpractice, your supervising attorney might arrange to have another physician testify as to the standard of care owed by a physician to a patient in similar circumstances.

An expert witness need not be a scientific professional with scholarly credentials. In fact, mechanics are often necessary or useful witnesses in litigation concerning the operation of vehicles. Accountants and electricians can likewise serve as expert witnesses in cases where their experience or expertise is helpful.

expert witness
A witness with professional training or substantial experience qualifying him or her to testify as to his or her opinion on a particular subject.

OFFICE TECH AND CYBERSECURITY

COMMUNICATING THROUGH GRAPHICS

If a picture is worth a thousand words, a bad picture can do as much damage as a thousand badly chosen words. Information may be easier to convey through a chart or diagram than in a narrative. Unfortunately, it is also easy to confuse people with cluttered graphics and badly designed diagrams. Learning to communicate graphically is an important skill for paralegals, because they may be called upon to design courtroom graphics and use graphic skills in developing the facts.

Diagrams and Interviews

Diagrams can help you when you are interviewing witnesses. For example, if you are talking to a car-accident victim or witness, sketching the scene can help the person you are interviewing remember crucial details. Creating an accurate diagram of the accident scene can help you uncover potential contradictions in witnesses' testimony or discover missing information. Diagrams may be critical to communicating information to a jury about your case. In an accident case, a diagram can show the jury where the witnesses and parties were, helping the jury members to understand the testimony.

It is important to remember that this process need not start with freehand drawings. Google Maps is a great resource. Many attorneys like to have a large map on an easel that they can point to or have a witness draw on during trial.

Graphics Software

There are many graphics packages to help you produce diagrams and charts. SmartDraw Legal Edition provides business graphics as well as templates for crime scene diagrams, accident reconstruction diagrams, patent drawings, and other graphics. Many other programs (such as High Impact) help produce accident or crime-scene reconstructions and other useful graphics. Skills in graphics will give you an edge in creating value for a law firm.

Design Principles

One of the best resources for visual display of information is the work of statistician and artist Edward Tufte, dubbed the "Leonardo da Vinci of data" by the *New York Times*. Tufte's books (including *Beautiful Evidence*) have been cited as influencing products such as the iPhone. Tufte regularly offers seminars on presenting information at various locations around the country (**edwardtufte.com**).

An example of the impact of the misleading nature of some visual presentations occurred in NASA's PowerPoint™ presentation to senior management after the Space Shuttle *Columbia* sustained damage during liftoff that could have been avoided. Tufte's critique of the presentation was included in the final report of the Columbia Accident Investigation Board as part of its explanation of why NASA made the bad decisions that led to *Columbia's* explosion.

Technology Tip

If you want to develop your graphic skills, watch director Errol Morris's award-winning documentary film *The Thin Blue Line*, which shows a crime scene repeatedly, based on different witnesses' testimony in a criminal trial. The film pioneered modern methods of crime scene reconstruction. To improve your graphic skills, make crime scene diagrams based on each witness's testimony as you listen to each one, and then use your diagrams to illustrate the inconsistencies among the testimonies.

Lay Witnesses

lay witness
A witness who can truthfully and accurately testify on a fact in question without having specialized training or knowledge; an ordinary witness.

Most witnesses in court are lay witnesses. In contrast to an expert witness, a **lay witness** does not possess any particular skill or expertise relating to the matter before the court. Lay witnesses are people who happened to observe or have factual knowledge about an event. A physician involved in a financial fraud case, for example, might give testimony about the fraud as a lay witness but not as an expert witness.

Eyewitnesses

eyewitness
A witness who testifies about an event that he or she observed or experienced firsthand.

An eyewitness is a lay witness who may testify in court about an event he or she observed or experienced firsthand. The term *eyewitness* is deceiving. A better term might be "sense" witness. This is because an eyewitness's firsthand knowledge of an event need not have been derived from actually seeing the event. An eyewitness may be someone who heard a telephone conversation between an accused murderer and an accomplice, for example. A blind man may have been an eyewitness to a car crash, because he heard it.

In interviews, eyewitnesses are ordinarily asked to describe an event in their own words and as they recall it. Eyewitness accounts may be lengthy, and the paralegal may want to record the interview session to ensure accuracy. You may also find that different eyewitnesses to the same event give contradictory accounts of what took place because people's perceptions differ. You will deal with many kinds of witnesses and clients and, as this chapter's *Ethics Watch* feature reminds us, caution is always in order. Asking witnesses *how sure* they are about observations that conflict with other witnesses' statements will help you to reconcile differing accounts.

Friendly Witnesses

Some witnesses to an event may be the client's family members, friends, or co-workers who want to be helpful in volunteering information. Such a witness is regarded as a **friendly witness**. You may think that friendly witnesses are the best kind to interview, and they often are. They may also be biased in the client's favor, however, so the paralegal should look closely for the actual facts (and not the witness's favorable interpretation of the facts) when interviewing friendly witnesses.

Friendly witnesses (and clients) often make statements involving conclusions that they have drawn and present them as fact. This is a normal tendency, but it is critical to know whether a witness is speaking from personal observation or is giving a conclusion reached from second-hand evidence or assumptions. One example is a witness who arrived at the scene of an assault and battery after the physical altercation ended.

friendly witness
A witness who is biased against your client's adversary or sympathetic toward your client in a lawsuit or other legal proceeding.

ETHICS WATCH

INTERVIEWING CLIENTS AND THE UNAUTHORIZED PRACTICE OF LAW

Paralegals must be especially careful not to give legal advice when interviewing clients. Suppose that you are interviewing a client, Collins, who was injured in a car accident and is suing the other driver for negligence. Collins previously told your supervising attorney and you that the accident was the result of the other driver's negligence. During your follow-up interview, however, Collins says to you, "What would happen, in a lawsuit such as mine, if the plaintiff was looking in the backseat to see why her baby was crying? Could the plaintiff still expect to win in court?"

You know that under the laws of your state, contributory negligence on the part of the plaintiff (discussed in Chapter 14) could bar recovery of damages. Should you explain this to Collins? No. Even though the question is phrased as a hypothetical, it is possible that your answer could affect Collins's actions. Tell Collins that you are not permitted to give legal advice and that you will relay the "hypothetical" question to your supervising attorney.

This action would be consistent with the following codes and guidelines:

- The NFPA *Model Code of Ethics and Professional Responsibility*, Section EC-1.8: "A paralegal shall comply with the applicable legal authority governing the unauthorized practice of law in the jurisdiction in which the paralegal practices."

- The *ABA Model Guidelines for the Utilization of Paralegal Services* advises that it is improper for attorneys to allow paralegals to take responsibility for giving legal opinions to clients.

- NALA's *Code of Ethics and Professional Responsibility*, Canon 4: "A paralegal must use discretion and professional judgment commensurate with knowledge and experience but must not render independent legal judgment in place of an attorney."

The witness might tell you that the defendant punched his wife, but suppose the witness only "knows" that because the wife, who is a friend of hers, *told* her that was what happened. Such information is important to have.

Hostile Witnesses

hostile witness
A witness who is biased against your client or friendly toward your client's adversary in a lawsuit or other legal proceeding; an adverse witness.

A witness who may be prejudiced against your client or friendly to your client's adversary are regarded as a **hostile witness** (or *adverse witness*). Interviewing a hostile witness can be challenging. Sometimes the witness has an interest in the outcome of the case and would be in a better position if your client lost in court. For example, if the client is a tenant who refuses to pay rent until the landlord repairs the roof, then the paralegal interviewing the landlord's building manager should be prepared to deal with that person as a potentially hostile witness.

Some hostile witnesses refuse to be interviewed. On learning that the alternative might be a subpoena, however, a hostile witness may consent to at least a limited interview. If you plan to interview hostile witnesses, contact and interview them early in your investigation. The longer you wait, the greater the chance that they may be influenced by the opposing party's attorney or the opinions of persons sympathetic to the opposing party.

When interviewing hostile witnesses, be careful to be objective, fair, and unbiased in your approach. This does not mean that you ignore your client's interests. On the contrary, you will best serve those interests by doing all you can to keep from further alienating a witness whose information might ultimately help your client's case. Be careful not to disclose information that the hostile witness might report back to the opposing attorney.

Questioning Witnesses

When you are asking questions as a legal investigator, you should phrase your questions so that they lead to the most complete answer possible. Investigative questions should thus be open ended. Compare, for example, the following two questions:

1. "Did you see the driver of the green van run the stop sign?"
2. "What did you see at the time of the accident?"

The first question calls for a "yes" or "no" answer. The second question, in contrast, invites the witness to explain fully what she actually saw. Something else that the witness saw could be important to the case—but unless you allow room for the witness's full description, you will not learn this information.

Notice that the first question also assumes a fact—that the driver of the green van ran the stop sign. The second question makes no assumptions and conveys no information to the witness that may influence the answer. Generally, the less the witness knows about other witnesses' descriptions, the better, because other descriptions could influence the witness's perception. You want to find out exactly what the witness observed, in her own words.

Checking a Witness's Qualifications

When interviewing a witness during the course of an investigation, you often will not know whether the testimony of that witness will be needed in court or even whether the claim you are investigating will be litigated. Nonetheless, you should operate under the assumption that each witness is a potential court witness. Make sure that the witness is competent to testify, and is reliable and credible.

Competence

Under the Federal Rules of Evidence, a person is competent to be a lay witness as long as she has personal knowledge of the matter. Thus, only if a potential witness did not actually see, hear, or perceive in some way information relevant to

As part of a factual investigation into a client's legal claim, a paralegal may contact witnesses or other sources for information. Although a restaurant is not an ideal setting for discussing confidential information, sometimes it is not possible to meet a witness or other information source in an office environment. What are the benefits of meeting in a public location? What are some potential problems with such a meeting place?

the trial issues will she be judged not competent to testify. Although state rules of evidence vary, most states also define competence for lay witnesses broadly. Expert witnesses are qualified only if they possess special knowledge, skill, experience, or education.

Credibility

Because it is easy to establish competence for most witnesses, the primary issue is generally not whether a witness can testify but whether the testimony will be credible, or believable. The parties to a lawsuit can attack the credibility of an opponent's witness and try to show that the witness is not telling the truth or is unreliable. In federal courts and most state courts, the credibility or reliability of a witness's testimony can be called into question by evidence that points to the witness's character for truthfulness or untruthfulness. Thus, the paralegal investigating the case should inquire into any matters that tend to show whether the witness is honest.

For example, does the witness abuse drugs or have a reputation in the community as a troublemaker? Has the witness been convicted of a crime? If so, was it a felony, or did it involve any dishonesty or false statement? How long ago was the conviction? Under the federal rules, a witness's credibility can be attacked by evidence of a conviction for a felony or a conviction for any crime involving dishonesty or false statements that occurred within the last ten years. Attorneys call these **crimes of moral turpitude.**

Bias

The paralegal should investigate possible bias on the part of the witness. Does the witness have an interest in the claim being investigated that would tend to make his testimony less credible? Is the witness a relative or close friend of someone (including another witness or a party) involved in the claim? Does the witness hold a grudge against someone involved? If the answer to any of these questions is yes, the witness's testimony may be discredited in court and will probably not be as convincing as testimony given by an unbiased witness.

crimes of moral turpitude
Criminal offenses involving false statements or dishonesty, such as larceny, fraud, and perjury.

Winding up the Interview

At the conclusion of an interview, the paralegal should ask if there is anything else the witness would like to add. This gives the witness the opportunity to expand on areas not previously discussed or explain an answer previously given. The paralegal should verify the witness's mailing address, physical address, e-mail address, and phone number and should find out if the witness has a website or a Facebook, Instagram, or Twitter account. It is also a good idea to get the name and phone number of a friend or relative living in the area whom you can contact to locate the witness if he moves before the trial.

Whenever you interview a witness, take thorough and accurate notes and prepare a memo to your supervising attorney. Include in the memo your evaluation of the witness's credibility and a description of any nonverbal communication that you thought was relevant. For example, did the witness seem uncomfortable with some aspect of the interview or become nervous when asked questions about a particular topic?

Witness Statements

witness statement
The written record of the statements made by a witness during an interview, signed by the witness.

You may also prepare a formal witness statement. Check with your supervising attorney before preparing such a statement, because formal witness statements may have to be given to the opposing party under applicable discovery rules (discussed in Chapter 10). A **witness statement** is a written document setting forth what the witness said during the interview. The witness is given an opportunity to review the contents of the statement and then signs the statement to verify its contents. Exhibit 11.4 shows the type of information normally contained in a witness statement, and Exhibit 11.5 presents excerpts from a sample witness statement.

EXHIBIT 11.4

Information Contained in a Witness Statement

1. **Information about the Witness**
   —Name, address, and phone number.
   —Name, address, and phone number of the witness's employer or place of business.
   —Interest, if any, in the outcome of the claim being investigated.

2. **Information about the Interview**
   —Name of the interviewer.
   —Name of the attorney or law firm for which the claim is being investigated.
   —Date, time, and place of the interview.

3. **Identification of the Event Witnessed**
   —Nature of the action or event observed by the witness.
   —Date of the action or event.

4. **Witness's Description of the Event**

5. **Attestation Clause**
   —Provision or clause at the end of the statement affirming the truth of the witness's description as written in the statement.

[Witness's Signature]

_____

EXHIBIT 11.5
A Sample Witness Statement (Excerpt)

STATEMENT OF JULIA WILLIAMS

I, Julia Williams, am a thirty-five-year-old female. I reside at 3765 Mattis Avenue, Nita City, Nita 48800, and my cell phone is (616) 555-8989. I work as a nurse at the Nita City Hospital & Clinic, 412 Hospital Way, Nita City, Nita 48802. My work telephone number is (408) 555-9898. I am making this statement in my home on the afternoon of February 8, 2022. The statement is being made to Elena Lopez, a paralegal with the law firm of Jeffers, Gilmore & Dunn.

In regard to the accident on the corner of Mattis Avenue and Thirty-eighth Street on August 4, 2021, at approximately 7:45 A.M. on that date, I was standing at the southwest corner of that intersection, waiting to cross the street, when I observed . . .

* * * *

I affirm that the information given in this statement is accurate and true to the best of my knowledge.

Julia Williams
Julia Williams

Statutes and court rules vary as to the value of witness statements as evidence. Usually, statements made by witnesses during interviews cannot be introduced as evidence in court to prove the truth of what the witness said, but can be used for other purposes. For example, if a hostile witness's testimony in court contradicts something he said during your interview, the witness statement may be used to impeach the witness—that is, to call into question his testimony or demonstrate that he is unreliable. Witness statements also can be used to refresh a witness's memory at trial or in depositions.

Planning and Conducting Investigations

Because the facts are often crucial to the outcome of a legal issue, investigation is an important part of legal work. Attorneys often rely on paralegals to conduct investigations, and you should be prepared to accept the responsibility for making sure that an investigation is conducted professionally. In the following pages, you will read about the basics of legal investigation—how to plan and undertake an investigation, how the rules of evidence shape the investigative process, and how important it is to carefully document the results of your investigation. Of course, much of the investigation will be done online, searching for the sources recommended in this discussion.

You have already read about one aspect of investigations—interviewing witnesses. A preliminary investigation, however, can involve much more. For one thing, before witnesses can be interviewed, they must be located. Information relating to the case may also have to be obtained from a police department, weather bureau, or other source.

Where Do You Start?

Assume that you work for Allen Gilmore, the attorney representing the plaintiff in the hypothetical case discussed in Chapter 10. Recall that the plaintiff in that case, Katherine Baranski, is suing Tony Peretto for negligence. She claims that Peretto ran a stop sign at an intersection and his car collided with hers. Further assume that the case is still in its initial stages. Gilmore has just met with Baranski for the initial client interview. You sat in on the interview, listened to Baranski's description of the accident and of the damages she sustained as a result (medical expenses, lost wages, and so on), and took notes.

After the interview, Gilmore asks you to do a preliminary investigation into Baranski's claim. It is now your responsibility to find the answers to a number of questions. Did the accident really occur in the way perceived by Baranski? Exactly where and when did it happen? (See the *Developing Paralegal Skills* feature below.) How does the police report describe the accident? Were there witnesses? Was Peretto insured, and if so, by what company? What other circumstances (such as weather) are relevant? Your supervising attorney will want to know the answers to such questions before advising Baranski as to what legal action should be pursued.

As in any legal investigation, your point of departure is the information you already have about the matter. Begin with the statements made by Baranski during the initial client interview and summarized in your notes. She described what she remembered about the accident, including when it occurred. She said she thought that the police investigator had the names of some people who had witnessed the accident. Baranski also stated that she was employed as an associate professor teaching math at Nita State University, earning about $64,000 a year. Using this information, you can map out an investigation plan.

DEVELOPING PARALEGAL SKILLS

CHECKING THE ACCIDENT SCENE

Gina Hubbard, a paralegal, and her supervising attorney, Juan Calpert, have just concluded an intake interview with a new client. The client was involved in an automobile accident, and the driver of the other car, who sustained serious injuries, is suing the client for damages. The client maintains that he was not at fault and has asked Calpert to defend him in the lawsuit. The attorney asks Gina to obtain a copy of the police report on the accident to verify the exact location of the accident, along with other pertinent information, such as photographs taken by police officers. Then Gina will go to the accident site to learn what she can about the site.

Both Gina and the attorney know that this case may be settled early on, and therefore it may be too soon to hire a private investigator to investigate the accident scene. Even if the case is not settled before trial and an investigator is hired later, months may pass, and the scene may change. Road repairs may alter the area, new signs may be installed, or the street may be widened. It is therefore important that Gina visit the site right away. She makes a list of the equipment she needs to take with her to use when checking the site.

Tips for Checking an Accident Scene

- Take a digital or smartphone camera with you at all times so you can include the photos in the file.

- Take a camcorder and audio recorder as well. You may want to dictate notes about your observations or record an interview with an eyewitness should you encounter someone at the site who saw the accident.

- Use an iPad, laptop, or smartphone so you can create a Google map of the location.

- Take a pencil and pad of paper to create sketches of the area. Be sure to include in the sketches any obstacles that could interfere with visibility.

- Include a tape measure in the tool kit as well. This will allow you to obtain precise measurements so that you can create a scale for your photographs and sketches.

Creating an Investigation Plan

An **investigation plan** is a step-by-step list of the tasks that you must complete to verify factual information relating to a legal problem. In the *Baranski* case, the steps in your investigation plan would include those summarized in Exhibit 11.6 and discussed next. Make sure your supervising attorney approves the investigation plan. Throughout the investigation, keep in touch with your supervising attorney about your progress.

investigation plan
A plan that lists each step involved in obtaining and verifying facts and information relevant to the legal problem being investigated.

Contacting the Police Department

The initial step in your plan should be to contact the police department. You want to look at a copy of the police report of the accident, view any photographs taken at the scene, get the names of persons who may have witnessed the accident, find out which officer responded, and, if possible, talk to the investigating officer.

Contacting and Interviewing Witnesses

Next, you want to contact and interview any known witnesses and document their descriptions of what took place at the time of the accident. Known witnesses include the driver (Peretto) of the vehicle that hit Baranski, the police officer at the scene, and the witnesses noted in the police investigation report. If Peretto is aware of

Continued

EXHIBIT 11.6

An Investigation Plan

INVESTIGATION PLAN
File No. 15773

	Date Requested	Date Received
1. Contact Police Department		
—To obtain police report	_____	_____
—To ask for photographs of accident scene	_____	_____
—To talk with investigating officer	_____	_____
—SOURCE: Nita City Police Dept.		
—METHOD: Request in person or by mail		
2. Contact Known Witnesses		
—Tony Peretto, van driver	_____	_____
—Michael Young, police officer at accident scene	_____	_____
—Julia Williams, witness at accident scene	_____	_____
—Dwight Kelly, witness at accident scene	_____	_____
—SOURCE: Police report		
—METHOD: Contact witnesses by initial phone call and personal interview when possible		
3. Obtain Employment Records		
—To learn Baranski's employment status and income	_____	_____
—SOURCE: Nita State University		
—METHOD: Written request by mail with Baranski's release enclosed		
4. Obtain Hospital Records		
—To learn necessary information about Baranski's medical treatment and costs	_____	_____
—SOURCE: Nita City Hospital		
—METHOD: Written request by mail with Baranski's release enclosed		

EXHIBIT 11.6

An Investigation Plan—Continued

	Date Requested	Date Received
5. Contact National Weather Service —To learn what the weather conditions were on the day of the accident	_____	_____
—SOURCE: National Weather Service and Internet —METHOD: Phone call or online search		
6. Obtain Vehicle Title and Registration Records —To verify Peretto's ownership of the vehicle	_____	_____
—SOURCE: Department of Motor Vehicles —METHOD: Order by mail		
7. Contact Peretto's Insurance Company —To find out about insurance coverage —To check liability limits	_____ _____	_____ _____
—SOURCE: Insurance company —METHOD: Written request by mail		

8. Use a Professional Investigator
—To contact such witnesses as
  –ambulance attendants
  –doctors
  –residents in neighborhood of accident scene
—To inspect vehicle
—To take photos of accident site
—To investigate accident scene, and so on
	_____
	
	_____
	_____
	_____
		_____
		
		_____
		_____
		_____

—SOURCE: Regular law firm investigator —METHOD: In person		

Baranski's intention to sue, he will probably have retained an attorney. If he has, you are not permitted to contact him directly—you may communicate with him only through his attorney.

Additional witnesses might be discovered from canvassing the area of the accident. For example, if the collision occurred in a populated area near shops or restaurants, one or more of the owners or employees might have heard or seen something. Perhaps the client or defendant went into a nearby store after the accident and said something to a cashier or waiter.

Verbal statements might not be the only evidence this investigation uncovers. Many stores and restaurants have cameras trained on the sidewalks and streets nearby that might have caught footage of the collision. Discovering this evidence early is important because some stores keep these records for only two or three weeks before erasing the data. Convenience stores are a common source of surveillance footage.

Obtaining Medical and Employment Records

To justify a claim for damages, you need to determine the nature of the injuries suffered by Baranski as a result of the accident, the medical expenses that she incurred, and her income (because she lost income as a result of the accident). To get this information, you need copies of her medical and employment records.

The institutions holding these records will not release them to you unless Baranski authorizes them to do so. Therefore, you need to arrange with Baranski to sign release forms to include with your requests for copies. (A sample authorization form to release medical records is shown in Exhibit 11.7. Law firms typically use general medical information release forms; however, some hospitals and medical service providers have their own specialized forms that must be filled out before they will release any documents or information. Gathering these specialized forms ahead of time can speed up the authorization process.)

If possible, make sure that Baranski signs the necessary forms before she leaves the office after the initial interview. Waiting for her to return the signed forms may delay your investigation. In addition to obtaining medical records, you may be asked to do some research on the types of injuries suffered by Baranski and related information. Typically, this requires consulting medical texts and specialized resources on medicine for lawyers.

Contacting the National Weather Service

Weather conditions at the time of the accident may be consequential. If it was raining, for example, Peretto's attorney may argue that water on the road prevented Peretto from stopping. You can determine what the weather conditions were at the time of the accident by contacting the National Weather Service and consulting other records. When you interview eyewitnesses, ask them about weather conditions at the time of the accident.

EXHIBIT 11.7

Authorization to Release
Medical Records

RELEASE OF MEDICAL RECORDS

TO: Nita City Hospital & Clinic
Nita City, NI 48802

PATIENT: Katherine Baranski
335 Natural Boulevard
Nita City, NI 48802

You are hereby authorized to furnish and release to my attorney, Allen P. Gilmore of Jeffers, Gilmore & Dunn, all information and records relating to my treatment for injuries incurred on August 4, 2021. Please do not disclose information to insurance adjusters or to other persons without written authority from me. The foregoing authority shall continue in force until revoked by me in writing, but for no longer than one year following the date given below.

Date: January 30, 2022   *Katherine Baranski*
Katherine Baranski

Please attach your invoice for any fee or photostatic costs and send it with the information requested above to my office.

Thank you,

Allen P. Gilmore
Allen P. Gilmore
Jeffers, Gilmore & Dunn
Attorneys at Law
553 Fifth Avenue
Suite 101
Nita City, NI 48801

Helena Moritz
Helena Moritz
Notary Public State of Nita
Nita County
My Commission Expires: November 12, 2023

Obtaining Vehicle Title and Registration Records

To verify that Peretto owns the vehicle that he was driving at the time of the accident, you need to obtain title and registration records. Usually, these can be acquired from the state department of motor vehicles, although in some states the secretary of state's office handles such records. The requirements for obtaining such information vary from state to state and may include the submission of special forms and fees. It may be possible to conduct this search online.

Contacting the Insurance Company

Once you learn the name of Peretto's insurance company from Baranski or from the police report, contact that company to find out what insurance coverage Peretto has and the limits of his liability under the insurance policy. Insurance companies usually are reluctant to give this information to anyone other than the policyholder. They sometimes cooperate with such requests, however, because they know that if they do not, the information can be obtained during discovery, should a lawsuit be initiated.

Using a Professional Investigator's Services

Depending on the circumstances, your supervising attorney may decide to use a professional investigator for certain tasks, including those just described. An experienced investigator often has useful contacts with law enforcement officers, subject-matter experts, and other sources. These contacts can speed up the investigation and may give the investigator access to information that others could not easily get. In addition, access to some government and private databases is restricted to government agents and licensed investigators. Attorneys may hire professional licensed investigators to obtain facts omitted from police reports, search public records, serve subpoenas, evaluate trial presentations, and conduct surveillance on parties important to the case.

You may work with the investigator. For example, your supervising attorney may ask you to arrange for the investigator to inspect and take photographs of the accident scene. You may also work with the investigator to determine the credibility and effectiveness of certain witnesses. In addition, you may meet with the investigator to review discovery documents to provide additional insight or generate investigative leads.

Locating witnesses can be difficult and time consuming, and attorneys sometimes use investigators for this task. As discussed next, however, paralegals today can find people online much more easily than was once possible, potentially reducing the need for outside assistance.

Locating Witnesses

A challenging task for a legal investigator can be locating a witness whose address is unknown. Suppose, for example, that in the *Baranski* case the police investigation report lists the name, address, and phone number of Edna Ball, a witness to the accident. When you call her number, you learn that the phone has been disconnected. You go to her address, and the house is vacant. What is your next step? A good starting point is to visit other homes in the neighborhood. Perhaps someone living nearby knows Edna Ball and can give you some leads as to where she is. Other sources are discussed below.

Finding People on the Internet

One important role paralegals play in many law practices is locating witnesses and other relevant people. The Internet is an essential source of information for paralegals conducting such investigations, but Internet tools both simplify and complicate searches. On the one hand, these tools allow fast searches of large databases. On the other hand, they add complexity, because the results may include information about multiple people with the same or similar names. With practice, you will develop online search methods that will aid you greatly in locating people.

Services.   Many paralegals use Internet people-finding services to locate witnesses (and witnesses' assets, if needed). Some online services charge a fee for each search, depending on the type of report requested (simple address record, background check, e-mail address, assets). The services check public records, telephone directories, court and criminal records, and a variety of other sources and provide results quickly and efficiently. (For an example, go to **whitepages.com**.) Both of the largest online legal research services (Westlaw and Lexis, discussed in Chapter 8) offer people-finding services as well.

Social Media Search Engines.   There are also important search engines that focus on social media sites and so-called "deep Web" information from Web pages not indexed by search engines like Google. For example, Spokeo looks for data across social media sites and seeks information from e-mails as well. It can find personal photos or profile data on Facebook and other postings. Another approach is taken by services such as PeekYou, which finds associations between people and Web addresses. While it uses the same information as Google, it packages the data in a way that is more useful for finding out about a person. Try these tools out using your own name to get an idea of how they work.

Other Information Sources

Other sources of information about people include:

- Media reports (newspaper articles and television videos covering the event).
- Court records (probate proceedings, lawsuits, and the like).
- Deeds to property (usually located in the county courthouse).
- Birth, marriage, and death certificates and voter-registration lists.
- The post office (at which a witness may have left a forwarding address).
- Consumer reporting agencies.
- The tax assessor's office.
- Utilities, such as the electric or water company.

Professional organizations may be useful sources as well. For example, if you have learned from one of Edna Ball's neighbors that she is a paralegal, you can check with state and local paralegal associations to see if they have current information on her. You might also check with federal, state, or local governmental agencies (discussed in the following section) to see if information contained in public records will be helpful in locating her.

Accessing Government Information

Records and files acquired and stored by government offices and agencies can be a key resource for the legal investigator. Public records are available at local government buildings or offices (such as the county courthouse), as mentioned above. You can also often find these records on the website of the agency that maintains them. Additionally, it is possible to obtain information from federal agencies, such as the Social Security Administration, and from state agencies, such as the state revenue department or the secretary of state's office.

If you wish to obtain information from any government files or records, check with the specific agency or department to see what rules apply. The *Developing Paralegal Skills* feature below provides more tips on obtaining public information.

The Freedom of Information Act (FOIA) requires the federal government to disclose certain records to any person on request. A request that complies with the FOIA procedures need only contain a reasonable description of the information sought. The FOIA exempts some information from the disclosure requirement, including classified information, confidential material dealing with trade secrets, government personnel rules, and medical files. Requesting information through the FOIA is usually slow and should be used only when there is no other choice.

Investigation and the Rules of Evidence

Because an investigation is conducted to obtain information and verify facts that may be introduced as evidence at trial, you should know what kind of evidence will be admissible in court before undertaking your investigation.

evidence
Anything that is used to prove the existence or nonexistence of a fact.

Evidence is anything that is used to prove the existence or nonexistence of a fact. Whether evidence can be used in court is determined by the **rules of evidence**—rules that explain what types of evidence are admissible and how to have evidence admitted. The Federal Rules of Evidence govern the admissibility of evidence in federal courts. State rules of evidence apply in state courts. (Many states have adopted evidence rules patterned on the federal rules.) You do not need to become an expert in evidentiary rules, but a basic knowledge of how evidence is classified and what types of evidence are admissible in court will greatly assist your investigative efforts. For you to know something is not enough. You must have admissible evidence to prove the fact in court. Having a strong grasp of whether, when, and how certain types of evidence could become admissible makes a paralegal a much more effective and efficient investigator.

rules of evidence
Rules governing the admissibility of evidence in trial courts.

DEVELOPING PARALEGAL SKILLS

ACCESSING GOVERNMENT INFORMATION

Ellen Simmons works for Smith & Case, a law firm that handles environmental cases (see Chapter 19). Ellen is to request copies of documents from the Environmental Protection Agency (EPA). She needs to determine if the EPA has the waste-in/waste-out report that gives the total volume of hazardous waste at a particular site and lists the potentially responsible parties.

Tips for Working with Government Agencies

- Before you call the agency, review the file to familiarize yourself with the case, and go online to the agency website to search for as much background information as possible.

- Review the agency's regulations to ascertain which documents the agency prepares in specific types of cases, such as Superfund cases.

- Make a list of the various documents.

- Determine in advance (from the list) which documents you will be requesting.

- Develop a list of alternatives to use in the event that the documents you request have not been prepared or are not available.

- Make reasonable requests from the agency.

As is true in all areas of law practice, developing good working relationships with agency staff members can result in getting more cooperation, more quickly, than might otherwise occur. Being organized and knowledgeable about document requests will produce a better response.

Direct versus Circumstantial Evidence

Two types of evidence may be brought into court—direct evidence and circumstantial evidence. **Direct evidence** is any evidence that, if believed, establishes the truth of the fact in question. Bullets found in the body of a shooting victim provide direct evidence of the type of gun that fired them. **Circumstantial evidence** is indirect evidence that, even if believed, does not establish the fact in question but is meant to establish the degree of likelihood of the fact. That is, circumstantial evidence can create an inference that a fact exists.

Suppose your firm's client owns the type of gun that shot the bullets found in the victim's body. This circumstantial evidence does not establish that the client shot the victim. Combined with other circumstantial evidence, however, it could help to convince a jury that the client committed the crime. For instance, if other circumstantial evidence indicates that your firm's client had a motive for harming the victim, that the client was at the scene of the crime at the time the crime was committed, and had recently fired his gun, a jury might conclude that the client committed the crime even if there were no witnesses.

direct evidence
Evidence directly establishing the existence of a fact.

circumstantial evidence
Indirect evidence offered to establish, by inference, the likelihood of a fact that is in question.

Relevance

Evidence will not be admitted in court unless it is relevant. **Relevant evidence** is evidence that tends to prove or disprove the fact in question. For example, evidence that the gun belonging to your firm's client was with another person when the victim was shot would be relevant, because it would tend to prove that the client did not shoot the victim.

Even relevant evidence may not be admitted in court if its probative (proving) value is substantially outweighed by other important considerations. For example, even though evidence is relevant, it may not be necessary—the fact at issue may have been sufficiently proved or disproved by previous evidence. In that situation, the introduction of further evidence would be a waste of time and would cause undue delay in the trial proceedings. Relevant evidence may also be excluded if it would tend to distract the jury from the main issues of the case, mislead the jury, or cause the jury to decide the issue on an emotional basis. Gruesome photos of a murder victim are sometimes excluded on this basis.

A witness's credibility is *always* relevant. Suppose the defendant in a negligence lawsuit has a previous conviction for fraud. If the defendant testifies at trial, then his fraud conviction will be admissible. Even though it has nothing to do with whether he committed negligence, it is relevant to whether he is telling the truth on the stand. In contrast, if the defendant does *not* testify, evidence of his fraud conviction is not relevant and therefore cannot be presented to the court.

relevant evidence
Evidence tending to prove or disprove the fact in question. Only relevant evidence is admissible in court.

Authentication of Evidence

At trial, an attorney must lay the proper foundation for the introduction of certain evidence, such as documents, exhibits, and other objects, and must demonstrate to the court that the evidence is what the attorney claims it is. The process by which this is accomplished is referred to as **authentication**. The authentication requirement relates to relevance, because something offered in evidence becomes relevant to the case only if it is authentic, or genuine. As a legal investigator, make sure the evidence you obtain is not only relevant but also capable of being authenticated if introduced at trial.

Commonly, evidence is authenticated by the testimony of witnesses. For example, if an attorney wants to introduce an autopsy report as evidence in a case, she can have the report authenticated by the testimony of the medical examiner who signed it. Generally, an attorney must offer enough proof of authenticity to convince the court that the evidence is, in fact, what it seems to be.

authentication
The process of establishing the genuineness of an item that is to be introduced as evidence in a trial.

The Federal Rules of Evidence provide for the self-authentication of specific types of evidence. In other words, certain documents or records need not be authenticated by testimony. Certified copies of public records, for example, are automatically deemed authentic. Other self-authenticating evidentiary documents include official publications (such as a report issued by the federal EPA), documents containing a notary public's seal or the seal of a public official, and manufacturers' trademarks.

Hearsay

When interviewing a witness, keep in mind that the witness's testimony *in court* must generally not be based on **hearsay**—that is, on out-of-court statements they heard, read, or made previously. Hearsay generally is not admissible in court when offered to prove the truth of the matter asserted.

Hearsay is generally not allowed because the person who made the out-of-court statement was neither under oath nor subject to cross-examination at the time the statement was made. Also, the witness reporting the statement may have misunderstood what the person was saying. Although it appears simple on its face, the rule against hearsay is one of the most complicated components of evidence law, partly because it is riddled with exceptions. Never assume that an out-of-court statement will be inadmissible or that any particular exception to the rule will apply.

Personal Observation.   As an example of the hearsay rule, a witness in the *Baranski* case cannot testify in court that she heard an observer say, "That van was going ninety miles per hour"—even if the other observer was a police officer. Such testimony would be inadmissible under the hearsay rule. The witness can only testify about what she personally observed regarding the accident. Of course, during the investigation, witnesses often tell you what other people said (and you should not discourage them from doing so). If you wish to use information obtained this way as evidence in court, however, you need to find an alternative method of proving it (such as by the testimony of the people who made the original statements).

Exceptions.   The hearsay rule provides exceptions in specific circumstances, often for statements made in situations that indicate a high degree of reliability. For example, a witness is usually allowed to testify about what a dying person said concerning the cause or circumstances of his or her impending death. The courts have concluded that a dying person usually does not lie about who or what caused the death.

Similarly, if a person makes an excited statement at the time of a stressful or startling event (such as "Oh no! That woman just threw her baby out the window!"), a witness can usually testify as to that statement in court. If one of the parties to a lawsuit makes an out-of-court admission (for example, if defendant Peretto in the *Baranski* case admits to friends that he was driving too fast at the time of the accident), a witness's testimony about what the party said may be admissible, although the rules on out-of-court admissions vary among jurisdictions. Exhibit 11.8 describes some of the traditional exceptions to the hearsay rule.

Summarizing Your Results

The final step in any investigation is summarizing the results. Your investigation report should provide an overall summary of your findings, a summary of the facts and information gathered from each source that you investigated, and your conclusions and recommendations based on the information obtained.

hearsay
Testimony from a witness who is repeating an out-of-court statement offered to prove the truth of the matter asserted. Hearsay generally is not admissible as evidence.

EXHIBIT 11.8
Some Exceptions to the Hearsay Rule

Statements by a Party Opponent—A statement made by a party to the litigation can be offered into evidence by an opponent of that party [FRE* 801(d)(2)]. *Example: The defendant makes the statement, "I blew past that stop sign because I was in a hurry," and the plaintiff then offers it in evidence.*

Present Sense Impression—A statement describing an event or condition made at the time the declarer perceived the event or condition or immediately thereafter [FRE 803(1)]. *Example: "I smell smoke."*

Excited Utterance—A statement relating to a startling event or condition made while the declarer was under the stress or excitement caused by the startling event or condition [FRE 803(2)]. *Example: "Oh no! The brakes aren't working!"*

State of Mind—A statement of the declarer's then-existing state of mind, emotion, sensation, or physical condition (such as intent, plan, motive, design, mental feeling, pain, or bodily health). Such statements are considered trustworthy because of their spontaneity [FRE 803(3)]. *Example: "My leg is bleeding and hurts terribly."*

Recorded Recollection—A memorandum or record indicating a witness's previous statements concerning a matter that the witness cannot now remember with sufficient accuracy to testify fully about the matter. If admitted in court, the memorandum or record may be read into evidence but may not itself be received as an exhibit unless offered by an adverse party [FRE 803(5)]. *Example: An employer's memo to one of his or her employees in which the employer responds to the employee's complaint about safety violations in the workplace.*

Former Testimony—Testimony that was given at another hearing or deposition by a witness who is now unavailable, if the party against whom the testimony is now offered was a predecessor in interest and had an opportunity to examine the witness in court during the previous hearing or deposition [FRE 804(b)(1)]. *Example: An employee's testimony about her employer that was introduced at a trial brought by the employee's co-worker against that employer for sexual harassment. The employer is now being sued by another employee for sexual harassment, and the employee who testified in the previous trial is out of the country. The employee's testimony in the previous trial may be admissible.*

Business Records—A document or compilation of data made in the course of a regularly conducted business activity, unless the source of the information or the method or circumstances of the document's preparation indicate that it is not trustworthy as evidence. The source of information must be from a person with firsthand knowledge, although this person need not be the person who actually made the entry or created the document [FRE 803(6)]. *Example: Financial statement of a business firm.*

Dying Declarations—In a prosecution for homicide or in a civil proceeding, a statement made by a person who believes that his death is impending about the cause or circumstances of his impending death [FRE 804(b)(2)]. *Example: Derek said just before he died, "Jethro stabbed me."*

Statement against Interest—A statement that was made by someone who is now unavailable and that was, at the time of its making, so far contrary to the declarer's financial, legal, or other interests that a reasonable person in the declarer's position would not have made the statement unless he or she believed it to be true [FRE 804(b)(3)]. *Example: Sanchez says that Jackson, who is now missing, made the following statement to Sanchez just before leaving town: "I committed the perfect crime!"*

Miscellaneous Exceptions—Miscellaneous exceptions include records of vital statistics [FRE 803(9)]; records of religious organizations [FRE 803(11)]; marriage, baptismal, or similar certificates [FRE 803(12)]; family records (including charts, engravings on rings, inscriptions on family portraits, and engravings on tombstones) [FRE 803(13)]; and statements offered as evidence of a material fact that are trustworthy because of the circumstances in which they were uttered [FRE 804(b)(5) and FRE 803(24)].

*Federal Rules of Evidence.

Overall Summary

The overall summary should thoroughly describe all of the facts you have gathered. It should be written so that someone not familiar with the case could read it and become adequately informed about the case's factual background.

Source-by-Source Summaries

Create a list of your information sources, including witnesses, and summarize the facts gleaned from each of these sources. Each "source section" should contain all information gathered from that source, including direct quotes from witnesses.

Each source section should also contain a subsection giving your comments on that particular source. You might comment on a witness's demeanor, for example, or on whether the witness's version of the facts was consistent or inconsistent with the versions of other witnesses. Your impressions of the witness's competence or reliability could be noted. If the witness provided you with further leads to explore, this should also be included.

Conclusions and Recommendations

In the final section, you present your overall conclusions about the investigation, as well as suggestions that you have on the development of the case. Attorneys rely on investigators' impressions of witnesses and evaluations of investigative results because the investigators have firsthand knowledge of the sources. Your impression of a potentially important witness, for example, may help the attorney decide whether to arrange for a follow-up interview with the witness. Usually, the attorney will want to interview only the most promising witnesses, and your impressions and comments serve as a screening device. Based on your findings during the investigation, you might also suggest to the attorney what further information can be obtained during discovery, if necessary, and what additional research needs to be done.

CHAPTER SUMMARY

CONDUCTING INTERVIEWS AND INVESTIGATIONS

Planning the Interview

Paralegals often interview clients and witnesses.

1. *Know what information you want*—The interviewer should have in mind the kind of information being sought from the interviewee.

2. *Standardized interview forms*—Preprinted interview forms provide helpful guidelines, but the interviewer should remain flexible during the interview, tailor questions to the interviewee's responses, and ask follow-up questions.

3. *Recording the interview*—Some paralegals record their interviews for future reference. If you do, make sure to obtain permission from your supervising attorney and the person being interviewed before recording. Keep in mind that some clients and witnesses will be less willing to disclose information freely when being recorded. If the interviewee appears hesitant, consider taking notes instead.

Interviewing Skills

Interviewing skills include interpersonal skills, questioning skills, and communication skills, particularly listening skills.

1. *Interpersonal skills*—The interviewer should put the interviewee at ease, use language that the person will understand, and avoid using legal terms.

2. *Questioning skills*—Types of questions used during the interviewing process include open-ended, closed-ended, leading, and hypothetical questions. The questioning technique will depend on the person being interviewed and the type of information sought.

3. *Listening skills*—Passive listening involves listening attentively to the speaker and using either verbal or nonverbal cues to encourage the speaker to continue. Active listening involves giving feedback to indicate that you understand what the speaker is saying. The interviewer may "reflect back," or restate, what the interviewee has said. This gives the speaker an opportunity to clarify previous statements. Active listening helps the interviewer control the flow of the interview. It also put the interviewee's statements into the larger context and facilitates transitions between topics.

Interviewing Clients

There are three basic types of client interviews: initial, subsequent, and informational. Interviews are often summarized. The paralegal may play a role in all phases.

1. *Initial client interview*—In setting up an interview, the paralegal should tell the client what documents to bring and follow up with a confirmation letter giving the date and time of the interview and listing the items the client is to bring.

2. *Subsequent client interviews*—Paralegals often conduct interviews after the initial interview, which is more likely to be conducted by the attorney. Always specify that you are not an attorney.

3. *Informational interview*—This kind of interview brings the client up to date on progress in a legal matter and prepares the client for further steps in the process.

4. *Summarizing the interview*—Soon after an interview is concluded, the paralegal should summarize in a written memorandum the information gathered in the interview. The memorandum should include impressions of the client's statements and nonverbal behaviors.

Interviewing Witnesses

1. *Types of witnesses*—Witnesses include expert witnesses (who have specialized training that qualifies them to testify as to their opinion in a given area), lay witnesses (ordinary witnesses who have factual information about the matter being investigated), eyewitnesses (who have firsthand knowledge of an event), friendly witnesses (who are favorable to the client's position), and hostile witnesses (who are biased against the client, are friendly to the opponent, or resent being interviewed).

2. *Questioning witnesses*—Investigative questions should be open ended to elicit the most complete answers.

3. *Witness qualifications*—Additional questions should ascertain whether the witness is competent, credible, and reliable and whether the witness is biased about the case.

4. *Winding up the interview*—The paralegal should ask the witness at the end of the interview if the witness would like to add anything to her or his statement. This gives the witness an opportunity to explain an answer or expand on the areas discussed.

5. *Witness statements*—Following an interview, the paralegal should prepare a memo to the supervising attorney relating what the witness said and asking if the attorney wants a formal witness statement prepared. That statement identifies the witness, discloses what was discovered during the interview, and is signed by the witness.

Planning and Conducting Investigations

Factual evidence is crucial to the outcome of a legal problem, and paralegals are often asked to conduct investigations to discover any factual evidence that supports (or contradicts) a client's claims.

1. *Where do you start?*—Before starting an investigation, the paralegal should outline an investigation plan—a step-by-step list of which sources will be investigated to obtain specific types of information.

2. *Creating an investigation plan*—A plan will note sources that need to be contacted for key information (police reports, medical and employment records, insurance companies, and so forth). The paralegal should discuss the plan with the supervising attorney before embarking on the investigation.

3. *Locating witnesses*—Sources of information regarding witnesses include directories; online people finders; media reports; court records; utility companies; professional organizations; and information recorded, compiled, or prepared by federal, state, and local government entities. Much of this information is available online.

4. *Accessing government information*—Some government records are public and are available in local offices or online. The Freedom of Information Act requires federal agencies to disclose certain records on request. Obtaining such records is usually a slow process.

5. *Investigation and rules of evidence*—Evidence is anything that is used to prove the existence or nonexistence of a fact. Rules of evidence established by the federal and state courts spell out what types of evidence may or may not be admitted in court.

   a. Direct evidence is any evidence that, if believed, establishes the truth of the fact in question.

   b. Circumstantial evidence is evidence that does not directly establish the fact in question but that establishes, by inference, the likelihood of the fact.

c. Only relevant evidence, which tends to prove or disprove a fact in question, is admissible as evidence in court.

d. For evidence to be admitted at trial, the attorney must prove to the court that the evidence is what it purports to be. This is called *authentication.*

e. Hearsay is testimony from a witness who is repeating an out-of-court statement offered to prove the truth of the matter asserted. Generally, hearsay evidence is not admissible in court. Exceptions are made in circumstances that indicate a high degree of reliability.

6. *Summarizing your results*—When the investigation is complete, the paralegal should summarize the results. This report should include an overall summary, source-by-source summaries, and a final section giving conclusions and recommendations.

KEY TERMS AND CONCEPTS

active listening 324

authentication 343

circumstantial evidence 343

closed-ended question 323

crimes of moral turpitude 333

direct evidence 343

evidence 342

expert witness 329

eyewitness 330

friendly witness 331

hearsay 344

hostile witness 332

hypothetical question 323

interviewee 316

investigation plan 337

lay witness 330

leading question 323

open-ended question 323

passive listening 324

relevant evidence 343

rules of evidence 342

witness statement 334

QUESTIONS FOR REVIEW

1. What types of questions described in the chapter can be used in an interview? Explain when you would use each type.

2. What types of interviews are described in this chapter? What is the purpose of each? What is the paralegal's role in each type of interview?

3. List the various types of witnesses discussed in the chapter. Describe the type of testimony each witness might give. Do any of these categories overlap—that is, could one witness fall into more than one of the categories? Explain.

4. Describe how you would locate a witness. Give five sources you would consult. Which would be the most useful? Which would be the least useful? Explain why.

5. Define and give examples of the following types of evidence: direct evidence, circumstantial evidence, relevant evidence, authenticated evidence, and hearsay.

6. What should be included in an investigative report?

ETHICS QUESTION

1. Paralegal Leah's boss has asked her to arrange for a private investigator to place a GPS tracking device, the size of a deck of cards, on the company car of a salesperson of one of the firm's clients. The client suspects the salesperson of playing golf instead of working and wants to investigate his whereabouts. Is it legal? Ethical? Do an Internet search to find support for your answer.

PRACTICE QUESTIONS AND ASSIGNMENTS

1. Review the Baranski-Peretto hypothetical case discussed in Chapter 10. Write sample questions that you would ask when interviewing eyewitnesses to the accident. Phrase at least one question in each of the question formats discussed in this chapter.

2. Using the information in this chapter on questioning skills, identify the following types of questions:

   a. "Did you go on a cruise in the Bahamas with a woman who was not your wife, Mr. Johnson?"

   b. "Isn't it true, Mr. Johnson, that a woman other than your wife accompanied you on a cruise in the Bahamas?"

   c. "Mr. Johnson, please describe where you were between January 10 and January 17, 2021."

3. Paralegal Malik is assigned to do a follow-up interview with a client to get details about the client's employment-discrimination claim. Malik is instructed to record the interview so that the attorney, who is involved in a trial with another client, can listen to the interview later. How should Malik proceed with the client when she comes to the office for the interview? What are the advantages and disadvantages of recording a client interview?

4. Determine whether each of the following statements is a statement of fact or a statement of opinion, and explain why:

   a. "I am sure that the driver was drunk because he pulled up next to me at the stoplight, then threw the car into reverse and backed a quarter of a mile down the one-way street."

   b. "The driver who was arrested for drunk driving ran a stop sign, then made a U-turn so that he could enter the highway. When he was arrested for erratic driving, his Breathalyzer reading was 0.19."

5. Kirsten works as an in-house paralegal for a debt-collection agency. She has been given a list of people who have defaulted on their car loans and cannot be located. Kirsten has been told by her supervising attorney to try to locate the debtors using Facebook. What should Kirsten do? Is this ethical? Is it legal? Review the Federal Trade Commission's summary of the Fair Debt Collection Practices Act at **consumer.ftc.gov/blog/facing-debt-collection-know-your-rights**.

6. Assume that a witness is being questioned about statements she heard a third party make. Which of the following statements would qualify as exceptions to the hearsay rule? Identify the reason for each exception.

   a. The third party exclaimed, "Watch out, he's not stopping at the red light!"

   b. Following a car accident, the third party apologized to the driver of the vehicle she hit, saying, "Are you all right? I am so sorry. I didn't mean to hurt you."

   c. Just before he died, the third party said, "Make sure you find Joe. He is the one who shot me. Tom didn't have anything to do with this."

   d. The third party stated, "I smell gas fumes!"

GROUP PROJECT

Working in groups of three, role-play the initial client interview described in Chapter 10 between Katherine Baranski and the legal team—attorney Allen Gilmore and paralegal Elena Lopez. The group should work together to draft the questions that attorney Gilmore will ask during the interview. Include questions in each format discussed in the chapter. Paralegal Lopez will remind attorney Gilmore of any questions he may have missed at the end of the interview. Lopez will also take interview notes, provide the retainer agreement and release forms, and schedule the follow-up interview. Change roles if time allows.

fizkes/Shutterstock.com

Trial Procedures

CHAPTER OBJECTIVES

After completing this chapter, you will be able to:

- Explain how attorneys prepare for trial and how paralegals assist in this task.

- Explain the purpose of a pretrial conference and a motion *in limine*.

- Describe how jurors are selected and the roles of attorneys and their paralegals in the selection process.

- Identify the various phases of a trial and trial-related tasks that paralegals often perform.

- Explain the options available to the losing party after the verdict is in.

- Discuss how a case is appealed to a higher court for review.

- Explain the options available for enforcing a judgment.

Introduction

Trials cost time and money, so parties to lawsuits often try to avoid going to trial. Pretrial negotiations between the parties through their attorneys often lead to out-of-court settlements. Using the pretrial motions discussed in Chapter 10, the parties may try to end the litigation after the pleadings are filed or while discovery takes place. In many cases, parties opt for alternative dispute resolution (ADR), such as mediation or arbitration. Recall from Chapter 6 that ADR is not always optional. Some state and federal courts *mandate* that a dispute be mediated before the parties are permitted to bring the dispute before a court. If the parties fail to settle their dispute, the case will go to trial.

To illustrate how attorneys and paralegals prepare for trial, we continue using the hypothetical scenario developed in Chapter 10, in which Katherine Baranski (the plaintiff) is suing Tony Peretto (the defendant) for negligence. In the Baranski-Peretto case, Allen Gilmore is the attorney for plaintiff Baranski, and Gilmore's paralegal is Elena Lopez. Defendant Peretto's attorney is Elizabeth Cameron, and Cameron's paralegal is Gordon McVay. In preparing for trial, paralegals use a wide range of evolving skills, as discussed in the *Developing Paralegal Skills* feature below.

Preparing for Trial

As the trial date approaches, the attorneys for the plaintiff and the defendant and their paralegals complete trial preparations. The paralegals collect and organize the documents and other evidence relating to the dispute. They may create a trial-preparation

DEVELOPING PARALEGAL SKILLS

NEW TOOLS IN TRIAL PREPARATION

Attorneys' trial tactics are evolving to include more sophisticated presentations, creating a greater need for paralegals with design and technology skills. Exhibits are no longer simply copies of documents blown up to larger sizes but may include elaborate video presentations.

In addition, technology is changing how litigation is being conducted outside the courtroom. Web research on opposing witnesses may uncover valuable information to use in discrediting them. However, you must also do thorough Internet-based research about *your* witnesses before you present them. Otherwise, opposing counsel may reveal some facts about your witnesses that you do not know, because they did not tell you embarrassing information.

Some of the less sophisticated work formerly done by paralegals is now automated, creating a demand for paralegals with higher skill levels. For example, electronic indexing makes document retrieval faster and more accurate, enhancing cross-examination. Some courtrooms even allow for real-time transmission of

transcribed testimony outside the courtroom, allowing paralegals back in the office to be scouring a witness's testimony for inconsistencies as they occur.

One of the impacts of these changes is a need for paralegals reviewing electronic evidence to be familiar with the programs used to create records. This knowledge enables them to explore issues such as documents' *metadata* (electronic data tracking document creation and revision—see Chapter 10), which might provide additional evidence beyond the text of the document itself. For instance, documents created with programs such as Microsoft Word include records showing who created it, when it was created, and when it was altered. Such information can be crucial in cases where the parties disagree about the sequence of events. Some metadata is easier to discover than other metadata. Therefore, being proficient in the technical functions of productivity software—such as Microsoft Office Suite, Adobe PDF readers and editors, the Windows operating system, and the Mac operating system—is a valuable skill set for a paralegal.

checklist similar to the one in Exhibit 12.1. Settlement negotiations often continue before and throughout the trial; however, both sides must assume that the trial court will decide the issue. Hence, they must be prepared for trial.

At this point in the litigation, plaintiff Baranski's attorney, Gilmore, focuses on legal strategy and how he can best use the information learned during the pleadings and discovery stages when presenting Baranski's case to the court. He will meet with his client and with his key witnesses to make last-minute preparations for trial. He might also meet with defendant Peretto's attorney to try to settle the dispute. Gilmore's paralegal, Elena Lopez, notifies witnesses of the trial date and helps Gilmore prepare for trial. For example, she makes sure that all exhibits to be used during the trial are ready and verifies that the trial notebook (discussed shortly) is in order.

Contacting and Preparing Witnesses

Typically, the paralegal is responsible for ensuring that witnesses are available and in court on the day of the trial. As mentioned before, a witness is any person asked to testify at trial. The person may be an eyewitness, an official witness (such as a police officer), an expert witness, or anyone with knowledge relevant to the lawsuit.

EXHIBIT 12.1

Trial-Preparation Checklist

TWO MONTHS BEFORE THE TRIAL

____ Review the status of the case and inform the attorney of any depositions, interrogatories, or other discovery procedures that need to be completed before trial.
____ Interview witnesses, and prepare witness statements
____ Review deposition transcripts/summaries, answers to interrogatories, witness statements, and other information obtained about the case. Inform the attorney of any further discovery that should be undertaken prior to trial.
____ Begin preparing the trial notebook.

ONE MONTH BEFORE THE TRIAL

____ Make a list of the witnesses who will testify at the trial for the trial notebook.
____ Prepare a subpoena for each witness, and arrange to have the subpoenas served.
____ Prepare any exhibits that will be used at trial, and reserve any special equipment (such as for a PowerPoint presentation) that will be needed at the trial.
____ Draft *voir dire* (jury selection) questions, and perhaps prepare a jury profile.
____ Prepare motions and memoranda.
____ Continue assembling the trial notebook.

ONE WEEK BEFORE THE TRIAL

____ Check the calendar and call the court clerk to confirm the trial date.
____ Complete the trial notebook. Keep electronic copies of everything.
____ Make sure that all subpoenas have been served.
____ Prepare the client and witnesses for trial.
____ Make the final arrangements (housing, transportation, and the like) for the client and witnesses, as necessary.
____ Check with the attorney to verify how witnesses should be paid (for lost wages, travel expenses, and the like).
____ Make final arrangements to have all equipment, documents, and other items in the courtroom on the trial date.

ONE DAY BEFORE THE TRIAL

____ Meet with others on the trial team to coordinate last-minute efforts.
____ Have a final pretrial meeting with the client.

Several types of negligence lawsuits require expert witnesses. As discussed in the preceding chapter, an expert witness has specialized knowledge in a particular field. Such witnesses are often called to testify in negligence cases, because one element to be proved in a negligence case is the reasonableness of the defendant's actions. In medical-malpractice cases, for example, it takes someone with specialized knowledge in the defendant physician's area of practice to establish the reasonableness of the defendant's actions.

Issuing Subpoenas

In the *Baranski* case, attorney Gilmore and paralegal Lopez have lined up witnesses to testify on behalf of their client. Lopez informs the witnesses that the trial date is set and that they will be expected to appear at the trial to testify. A *subpoena* (an order issued by the court clerk directing a person to appear in court) is served on each of the witnesses to ensure the witness's presence in court. A subpoena to appear in a federal court is shown in Exhibit 12.2. Although not shown here, a return-of-service form—similar to the one illustrated in Chapter 10—will be attached to the subpoena to verify that the witness received it.

Unless already familiar with the court's requirements, Lopez checks with the court clerk to learn what fees and documents she needs to take to court to obtain the subpoena. In some court systems, attorneys, as officers of the court, may issue subpoenas. The subpoena is then served on the witness. Paralegals may serve subpoenas, but they are commonly served by a process server. Local and state rules often govern who and what can be subject to a subpoena.

When contacting *friendly* witnesses (those favorable to Baranski's position), Lopez should take care to explain that all witnesses are served with subpoenas, as a precaution, and to tell all witnesses when they can expect the subpoenas. Otherwise, a friendly witness might believe that Gilmore and Lopez did not trust him to keep a promise to appear in court and might be offended.

Preparing Witnesses for Trial

No prudent attorney puts a nonhostile witness on the stand unless the attorney has discussed the testimony beforehand with that person. Advance preparation makes a big difference to the testimony that a witness provides. The time devoted to preparing a witness varies depending on the size of the case, the importance of the witness's testimony, and whether the attorney believes the witness will communicate clearly and effectively in court. Additional time is needed to prepare witnesses who are relatively inexperienced, are not very articulate, or are especially nervous about testifying.

Tell Witnesses What to Expect. Prior to trial, Gilmore and Lopez will meet with each witness to prepare her or him for trial. Gilmore will discuss the types of questions that he intends to ask the witness in court and the questions that he expects the opposing attorney to ask. He will also tell the witness that during cross-examination opposing counsel will ask leading questions and may try to confuse the witness or attack the witness's statements. Gilmore may recommend that the witness answer the opponent's questions in as few words as possible while not appearing to be overly defensive. The attorney may not, of course, tell the witness what to say in response to questions.

Gilmore also reviews with the witness any statements the witness made about the case, particularly if the statements were given under oath (such as during a deposition). It is important that a witness understand that during the trial, he may be asked about inconsistencies between statements previously given or between trial testimony and prior statements. Additionally, Gilmore may review the substantive legal issues involved in the case and discuss how the witness's testimony will affect the outcome of those issues.

EXHIBIT 12.2

A Subpoena

AO 88 (Rev. 2/06) Subpoena in a Civil Case

Issued by the
UNITED STATES DISTRICT COURT

— WESTERN DISTRICT OF NITA —

Katherine Baranski

V.

Tony Peretto

SUBPOENA IN A CIVIL CASE

CASE NUMBER   14-14335-NI

TO: Julia Williams
3765 Mattis Avenue
Nita City, NI 48800

[X] YOU ARE COMMANDED to appear in the United States District Court at the place, date, and time specified below to testify in the above case.

PLACE OF TESTIMONY	COURT ROOM
4th and Main Nita City, NI	B
	DATE AND TIME 8/4/22 10:00 A.M.

[ ] YOU ARE COMMANDED to appear at the place, date, and time specified below to testify at the taking of a deposition in the above case.

PLACE OF DEPOSITION	DATE AND TIME

[ ] YOU ARE COMMANDED to produce and permit inspection and copying of the following documents or objects at the place, date, and time specified below (list documents or objects):

PLACE	DATE AND TIME

[ ] YOU ARE COMMANDED to permit inspection of the following premises at the date and time specified below.

PREMISES	DATE AND TIME

Any organization not a party to this suit that is subpoenaed for the taking of a deposition shall designate one or more officers, directors, or managing agents, or other persons who consent to testify on its behalf, and may set forth, for each person designated, the matters on which the person will testify. Federal Rules of Civil Procedure, 30(b)(6).

ISSUING OFFICER SIGNATURE AND TITLE (INDICATE IF ATTORNEY FOR PLAINTIFF OR DEFENDANT)	DATE
Allen P. Gilmore, Attorney for the Plaintiff	July 13, 2022

ISSUING OFFICER'S NAME, ADDRESS AND PHONE NUMBER
Allen P. Gilmore, Jeffers, Gilmore & Dunn,
553 Fifth Avenue, Suite 101, Nita City, NI 48801   (616) 555-9690

(See Rule 45, Federal Rules of Civil Procedure, Parts C & D on Reverse)
If action is pending in district other than district of issuance, state district under case number.

Role-Playing. If a witness needs additional preparation, Gilmore or Lopez may engage in role-playing with the witness. Such rehearsal is often valuable in helping the witness to understand more fully how questioning will proceed and what tactics may be involved in the opposing attorney's questions. It also may alleviate some of the witness's fears. In addition, Lopez might take the witness to the courtroom in which the trial will take place to familiarize her with the trial setting. As testifying is often stressful, anything that the paralegal can do to reduce a witness's discomfort will help the witness to better control her responses when testifying and thus will benefit the client.

Numerous Details. Paralegals are often responsible for handling the details in preparing witnesses for court. For example, Lopez might recommend appropriate clothing and grooming or tell the witness where to look and how to remain calm and composed when speaking to the court. If the witness will be asked about any exhibits or evidence (such as photographs or documents), Lopez will show these items to the witness. Lopez will also update the witness as to when she will probably be called to testify.

Exhibits and Displays

Paralegals frequently prepare exhibits or displays to present at trial. Gilmore may wish to show the court a photograph of plaintiff Baranski's car taken after the accident occurred, a diagram of the intersection, an enlarged document (such as a police report), or other relevant evidence. Lopez will be responsible for making sure that exhibits are properly prepared and ready for trial. If any exhibits require special equipment, such as an easel, projector, or laptop, Lopez must also make sure that these will be available in the courtroom and properly set up when needed.

Even within the same courthouse, some courtrooms might be better equipped for the presentation of electronic evidence and media than others. Often, the courtroom number, floor, and judge can be determined in advance. If Lopez is not sure whether the courtroom is properly equipped for the evidence and exhibits to be used, a call to the clerk's office should provide the necessary information. Lopez must also be prepared for the equipment to malfunction. Although the courtroom might have audio playback capabilities, she should bring an alternative device to perform audio playbacks in case the equipment is not functioning, as well as additional cables for various ports, such as HDMI (video and sound), AV (video), USB (data), and AUX (sound).

The Trial Notebook

To present Baranski's case effectively, Gilmore needs to have all relevant documents in the courtroom. He also needs to be able to locate them quickly. To accomplish these goals, Lopez prepares a trial notebook and sets up computer files. Traditionally, the **trial notebook** has been a binder containing trial-related materials separated by tabbed divider sheets. Most lawyers today rely primarily on documents kept in computers, but paper copies are still common. The discussion here applies to both.

trial notebook
Traditionally, a binder that contains copies of all the documents and information that an attorney will need to have at hand during the trial.

Key Materials

Lopez meets with Gilmore to discuss what he wants to include in the trial notebook for Baranski's case and how the notebook should be organized. Gilmore tells Lopez that the organization of the notebook should make it possible to find quickly whatever documents they may need during the trial. Lopez should include the following materials in the notebook:

- Copies of the pleadings.
- Interrogatories.

- Deposition transcripts and summaries.
- Pretrial motions and any recent rulings on them.
- A list of exhibits and a case outline indicating when they will be used.
- A witness list, the order in which witnesses will testify, and the questions to be asked of each witness.
- Relevant cases or statutes that Gilmore plans to cite.
- Additional documents important to have close at hand during the trial.

Note that many of the above materials will be scanned and saved in files on a laptop or elsewhere.

Lopez will create a general index to the notebook or computer file's contents and place this index at the front of the notebook. She may also create an index for each section of the binder or computer file and place an index at the beginning of each section. Paralegals sometimes use a notebook computer and a software retrieval system to help them quickly locate documents, especially in complicated cases involving thousands of documents. Careful, consistent organization of computer files is critical. Most software packages today allow you to add "tags" to documents so that they can be more easily sorted into categories.

Original Documents

When preparing a traditional trial notebook, remember that the notebook should not contain the original documents but rather scanned copies. The original documents (unless needed as evidence at trial) should remain in the firm's files, for security (should the trial notebook be misplaced) and for access by staff in the office during trial.

Lopez will not wait until the last minute to prepare the trial notebook and electronic files. At the outset of the lawsuit, she makes copies of the pleadings and other documents as they are generated to include in the notebook. That way, just before the trial, she is free to attend to other pressing needs. As discussed in this chapter, high-tech presentations are changing trial-preparation tasks (see this chapter's *Office Tech and Cybersecurity* feature).

Confidential Information

Many of the materials related to cases are confidential. To protect the interests of clients, help make sure information is not exposed to visitors to the office or to other employees who do not need to know information related to a particular case.

To protect confidential information, put away materials when you are not working on them. Because most work is done on computers, close files on your computer whenever you leave your desk. Computers can be easily locked. Entering your password generally returns you to the same point, so you do not have to close all files. While your computer is locked, its contents should be encrypted and therefore inaccessible without your password.

Be particularly careful with laptops, iPads, and flash drives outside of the office. Losing a computer or drive with confidential documents can be disastrous for reasons of practicality, ethics, and legal liability. Make sure all devices with files are password protected.

Note, too, that many people talk on the phone as if no one around them is listening. Be cautious when talking about legal matters, especially on a cell phone out of the office. In a courthouse, vacant conference rooms are often available that can be used to take a sensitive phone call or speak to a client or witness privately.

OFFICE TECH AND CYBERSECURITY

TAKE ADVANTAGE OF THE LATEST TOOLS

Cases can involve huge document files and extensive preparation of motions and other court documents. Programs exist to help keep documents organized, provide details related to trials, remind you of schedules, and assist in making sure research is comprehensive. A few are discussed here.

Trial-Related Programs and Apps

A number of apps can help you in various ways.

- An easy-to-use iPad app, *Trialpad*, is designed to assist in trial preparation. Users are able to organize and create polished displays of trial exhibits. (**itunes.apple.com/us/app/trialpad-organize-present/id828542236?mt=8**)

- *IJuror* is a jury-selection app that provides a seating chart and allows entry of information on each prospective juror. (**itunes.apple.com/us/app/ijuror/id372486285?mt=8**)

- *Deadline Assistant* uses Microsoft Outlook to keep track of litigation-related dates based on court rules governing a case. (**legal.thomsonreuters.com/en/products/deadline-assistant**)

- Like *Deadline Assistant*, the *Court Days Pro* app lets the user calculate dates and deadlines based on a customizable database of court rules and statutes. (**itunes.apple.com/us/app/court-days-pro-rules-based/id419708480?mt=8**)

- *MyCase* manages calendaring, legal billing, document organization, and file sharing. (**www.mycase.com**)

Browser Tools

- *Bestlaw* is a browser extension, available to download free, that enhances usability of Westlaw Edge and Lexis Advance. This product allows the user to copy *Bluebook* citations, open documents in free sources before opening them on Westlaw, and instantly look up case information on platforms such as Google Scholar, Wikipedia, and Cornell LII. (**bestlaw.io**)

- For frequent users of PACER (discussed in Chapter 8), *Recap-thelaw* (**free.law/recap**) is a browser extension that allows users to add to a free, open repository of public court records. Whenever a document is purchased from PACER, this feature automatically places the document in a public repository hosted by the Internet archive. The extension alerts users when a document they are searching for has already been uploaded to the public repository and is now accessible for free.

- Powered by Cornell Legal Information Institute, *Jureeka!* (**jureeka.blogspot.com**) turns legal citations found in Web pages into hyperlinks.

Technology Tip

Technology can make a litigation paralegal's job easier, especially in cases that involve extensive documentation. All programs have their limitations, so be sure you fully understand how a program works—what it does and what it does not do—so you do not miss critical information.

Pretrial Conference

Before the trial begins, the attorneys usually meet with the trial judge in a **pretrial conference** to explore the possibility of resolving the case and, if a settlement is not possible, to determine how the trial will be conducted. In particular, the court or the parties may attempt to clarify the issues in dispute and establish ground rules to restrict such matters as the admissibility of certain types of evidence. For example, Gilmore might have Lopez draft a **motion** *in limine* (a motion to limit evidence) to submit to the judge at this time. The motion requests the judge to order that certain evidence not be brought out at trial.

To illustrate: Suppose Baranski was arrested in the past for illegal drug possession. Gilmore knows that the arrest, if introduced by the defense at trial, might prejudice the jury against Baranski. Because the arrest is not relevant to the case and is potentially prejudicial, Gilmore might submit a motion *in limine* to keep the defense from presenting evidence of the arrest. Exhibit 12.3 presents a sample motion *in limine*.

pretrial conference
A conference prior to trial in which the judge and the attorneys litigating the suit discuss settlement possibilities, clarify the issues in dispute, and schedule forthcoming trial-related events.

motion *in limine*
A motion requesting that certain evidence not be brought out at the trial, such as prejudicial, irrelevant, or legally inadmissible evidence.

EXHIBIT 12.3

A Sample Motion *in Limine*

A. P. Gilmore
Jeffers, Gilmore & Dunn
553 Fifth Avenue
Suite 101
Nita City, NI 48801
(616) 555-9690

Attorney for Plaintiff

UNITED STATES DISTRICT COURT
FOR THE WESTERN DISTRICT OF NITA

Katherine Baranski	)	
Plaintiff,	)	CASE NO. 17-14335-NI
	)	Honorable Harley M. Larue
v.	)	
	)	MOTION IN LIMINE
Tony Peretto	)	
Defendant.	)	

The Plaintiff respectfully moves the Court to prohibit counsel for the Defendant from directly or indirectly introducing or making any reference during the trial to the Plaintiff's arrest in 2018 for the possession of illegal drugs.

The grounds on which this motion is based are stated in the accompanying affidavits and memorandum.

Date: 6/18/22

Allen P. Gilmore
Allen P. Gilmore
Attorney for the Plaintiff

With the motion, Gilmore would include affidavits and/or a memorandum of law (a brief)—documents discussed in Chapter 10—to convince the judge why the motion should be granted. The judge may order oral arguments to be held on the motion before rendering a decision.

Once the pretrial conference has concluded, both parties turn their attention to the trial itself. Assuming that a jury will hear the trial, one more step is necessary before the trial begins: selecting the jurors who will hear the trial and render a verdict on the dispute.

Jury Selection

Before the trial gets under way, a panel of potential jurors must be assembled. The clerk of the court usually notifies local residents by mail that they have been selected for jury duty. How prospective jurors are chosen varies, depending on the court, but often they are randomly selected from lists of registered voters or licensed drivers.

The prospective jurors report to the courthouse on the date specified (unless they are granted exceptions or waivers). At the court, they are gathered into a pool of potential jurors, and the process of selecting the jurors who will actually hear the case begins. Although some trials require twelve-person juries, civil matters can be heard by a jury of as few as six persons in many states. Many courts also select one or two alternate jurors. They will sit with the rest of the jury and hear evidence throughout the trial but will take part in deliberations only if one or more selected jurors cannot participate because of illness or some other unforeseen reason.

Federal court juries are usually chosen from a wider geographic area than are state court juries. The different demographics are a reason an attorney might prefer one court rather than the other.

Voir Dire

Both the plaintiff's attorney and the defendant's attorney have some input into the ultimate makeup of the jury. Each attorney usually questions prospective jurors in a proceeding known as *voir dire*. Litigators know the importance of the *voir dire* process. It helps to pick the right jury, but it also is a time for attorneys to introduce themselves and their clients to the jury before the trial begins. Attorneys may also craft questions in subtle ways so as to expose the jury pool to the themes and arguments they will be presenting in the trial to come.

> **voir dire**
> A proceeding in which attorneys for the plaintiff and the defendant ask prospective jurors questions to determine whether any potential juror is biased or has any connection or conflict of interest with a party to the action or a prospective witness.

Paralegals may work with their attorneys to write questions to ask jurors during *voir dire*. Because the jurors will have filled out forms giving basic information about themselves, the questions can be tailored accordingly. The idea is to uncover biases on the part of prospective jurors and to find persons who might identify with the plights of their respective clients.

Typically, the legal team for each side has already developed an idea of what kind of person would be most sympathetic toward or most likely to vote in favor of its client, but the focus is typically on which jurors to *exclude* rather than which to *include*. In complex cases, experts may be hired to help create a juror profile.

Jury selection may last an hour or days, depending on the complexity of the case and the rules and preferences of the particular court or judge. In some courts, the judge questions prospective jurors using queries prepared and submitted by the attorneys. In other courts, the judge has each juror answer a list of standard questions and gives each attorney a small amount of time to ask follow-up questions. When large numbers of prospective jurors are involved, the attorneys (or the judge) may direct their questions to groups of jurors as opposed to individual jurors to reduce the time spent choosing a jury.

At some point during the questioning, the judge might allow or insist on the questioning of a juror separately from the rest of the pool. This allows the judge and attorneys to get answers about sensitive topics the juror might not be comfortable discussing before a larger audience. It also prevents any strong language, inadmissible information, or bias on the part of the juror from being heard by the rest of the pool.

Jury Selection Experts and Tools

Picking a jury is a critical step in a trial. The famous litigator Clarence Darrow claimed "almost every case is won or lost when the jury is sworn." Experienced trial lawyers gauge whether a juror is likely to be sympathetic to their clients based on gut reactions, on stereotypes about marital status, race, religion, occupation, or on other factors. Today, jury selection is a big business when the stakes are high. Significant sums are spent on jury consultants who use data science to help lawyers pick a jury.

By using online search tools, paralegals and assisting attorneys can discover valuable information about prospective jurors from their online "digital shadows." A prospective juror may appear in court dressed professionally, but his Facebook profile may feature wild partying. Spotting such information may help a lawyer defending a DWI case decide to keep the party animal on the jury, reasoning that he is more likely to sympathize with the defendant. As the amount of information available online about people increases, having the skills to quickly find revealing information is ever more valuable for the paralegal.

Challenges during *Voir Dire*

During *voir dire*, the attorney for each side decides if there are any individuals he or she would like to prevent from serving as jurors in the case. The attorney may exercise a **challenge** to exclude a particular person from the jury. Two types of challenges are available to both sides in a lawsuit: challenges for cause and peremptory challenges.

Challenges for Cause

The attorney can exercise a **challenge for cause** if the prospective juror is biased against the client or case for some reason. For example, if a juror indicates during *voir dire* that she dislikes immigrants and the client is foreign born, the attorney can exercise a challenge for cause. Each side can exercise an *unlimited* number of challenges for cause. Because most people are not forthcoming about their biases, the attorney must be able to prove sufficiently to the court that the person cannot be an objective juror in the case. Often, the judge will ask the challenged juror follow-up questions and then determine if the juror can likely be objective.

Peremptory Challenges

Either attorney may exercise a **peremptory challenge** without giving any reason to the court as to the nature of the objection to the particular juror. The number of peremptory challenges is limited. In most cases, peremptory challenges are the only challenges exercised (because there is often no proof that any juror is biased). A juror may be excused from serving on the jury for any reason, including her facial expressions or nonverbal behavior during the questioning. Peremptory challenges based on race or sex, however, are illegal.

Because the number of peremptory challenges is limited (a court may allow only three, for example), attorneys must exercise peremptory challenges carefully. Litigators conserve their peremptory challenges to eliminate the prospective jurors who appear the most hostile to their client's case.

Procedure for Challenges

Typically, *voir dire* takes place in the courtroom, and the attorneys question the six to twelve prospective jurors who are seated in the jury box. Other prospective jurors may be seated in the courtroom, so that as one person is excused, another person can take his place in the jury box. The procedure varies depending on the jurisdiction.

Often, rather than making challenges orally in front of the jury, the attorneys write down on a piece of paper which juror they wish to challenge, and the paper is given to the judge. The judge thanks and dismisses the prospective juror, and the process starts over with the next individual. Then the remaining prospective jurors do not know which side dismissed a person and so are less likely to guess why.

The Paralegal's Role during *Voir Dire*

As mentioned, paralegals help develop a jury profile and draft questions asked during *voir dire*. In addition, a paralegal can assist an attorney by providing another pair of eyes and ears during the jury selection process. Attorneys frequently rely on the observations of other members of the legal team who are present during the questioning.

If paralegal Lopez attends *voir dire* with attorney Gilmore in the *Baranski* case, she will watch all jurors as the attorneys question them. Because Lopez is not participating in the questioning, she is free to observe the prospective jurors. She can report any verbal or nonverbal actions she observed that Gilmore might not have noticed. Suppose that as Gilmore is questioning one juror, another juror is frowning with disapproval at Baranski. Gilmore might not notice this, and Lopez can bring it to his attention. As this chapter's *Ethics Watch* feature notes, paralegals must limit their contact with jurors.

---

challenge
An attorney's objection, during *voir dire*, to the inclusion of a particular person on the jury.

challenge for cause
A *voir dire* challenge to exclude a potential juror from serving on the jury for a reason specified by an attorney in the case that disqualifies the juror.

peremptory challenge
A *voir dire* challenge to exclude a potential juror from serving on the jury without any supporting reason or cause. Peremptory challenges based on racial or gender are illegal.

ETHICS WATCH

COMMUNICATING WITH JURORS

Suppose that you are the paralegal working on the *Baranski* case and you run into one of the jurors in the grocery store. The juror approaches you and says, "You know, I didn't really understand what that witness, Williams, was saying. Did she really see the accident? Also, is it true that Mrs. Baranski will never be able to walk normally again?" You know the answers to these questions, and you would like the juror to know the truth. You also know that it would enhance Baranski's chances of winning the case if this juror were as familiar with the factual background as you are. What should you do?

1. Explain to the juror that neither you nor a juror is permitted to discuss a case they are hearing with anyone.
2. Inform the juror that as a paralegal, you have an ethical duty to abide by the professional rules of conduct governing the legal profession. One of these rules prohibits *ex parte* (private) communications with jurors about a case being tried.

3. Report the conversation to attorney Gilmore, who may decide to tell the judge about it.

These actions are consistent with the NFPA's *Model Code of Ethics and Professional Responsibility*, Section EC-1.2(a), "A paralegal shall not engage in any *ex parte* communications involving the courts or any other adjudicatory body [a person or panel that makes a legal decision] in an attempt to exert undue influence or to obtain advantage or the benefit of only one party," and Section EC-1.5(f), "A paralegal shall not engage in any indiscreet communications concerning clients."

They are also consistent with NALA's *Code of Ethics*, Canon 9, "A paralegal must do all other things incidental, necessary, or expedient for the attainment of the ethics and responsibilities as defined by statute or rule of court."

Reprinted by permission of the National Federation of Paralegal Associations, Inc. (NFPA®), www.paralegals.org; Copyright 1975; Adopted 1975; Revised 1979, 1988, 1995, 2007. Reprinted with permission of NALA, The Paralegal Association. Inquiries should be directed to NALA, 1516 S. Boston, #200, Tulsa, OK 74119, www.nala.org.

Alternate Jurors

As mentioned, because unforeseeable circumstances or illness may necessitate that one or more of the sitting jurors be dismissed, the court often seats alternate jurors. Depending on the rules of the particular jurisdiction, a court might have two or three alternate jurors present throughout the trial. If a juror has to be excused during the trial, then an alternate can take his place without disrupting the proceedings. Unless they replace jurors, alternates do not participate in jury deliberations at the end of the trial.

The Trial

Once the jury members are seated, the judge swears in the jury, and the trial begins. During the trial, the attorneys present their cases to the jury. While the attorneys concentrate on the trial, their paralegals can coordinate the logistical aspects of the trial and observe the trial proceedings. Because Lopez is thoroughly familiar with the case and Gilmore's legal strategy, she will be a valuable ally during the trial. She will anticipate Gilmore's needs and provide appropriate reminders or documents.

The Paralegal's Duties

Prior to each trial day, Lopez assembles the documents and materials needed and makes sure that Gilmore has within reach any documents or exhibits he needs for questioning parties or witnesses. At the end of the day, Lopez organizes the materials, decides what will be needed for the next day, and files the documents that can remain in the office.

Lopez also monitors each witness's testimony to ensure that it is consistent with previous statements made by the witness. She has the relevant deposition transcript (and summary) at hand when a witness takes the stand. She follows the deposition transcript (or summary) of each witness during testimony. This way, she can pass a note to Gilmore if he misses any inconsistencies in the testimony.

Lopez also observes how the jury responds to witnesses and their testimony or to the attorneys. She will take notes during the trial on these observations as well as on the points being stressed and the evidence introduced by opposing counsel. At the end of the day, Lopez and Gilmore may review the day's events, and Lopez's "trial journal" provides a ready reference to what happened in the courtroom.

Opening Statements

opening statement
An attorney's statement to the jury at the beginning of the trial. The attorney outlines the evidence that will be offered during the trial and the legal theory that will be pursued.

The trial both opens and closes with attorneys' statements to the jury. In the **opening statement**, each attorney gives a brief version of the facts and the supporting evidence to be used during the trial. Because some trials can take weeks or even months, it is helpful for jurors to hear a summary of the story that will unfold during the trial.

The opening statement is a kind of "road map" that describes the destination that each attorney hopes to reach and outlines how he or she plans to reach it. Plaintiff Baranski's attorney, Gilmore, focuses on such things as his client's lack of fault and the injuries she sustained when she was hit by defendant Peretto's car. Peretto's attorney, Cameron, highlights the points that weaken Baranski's claim (Cameron might point out that Baranski was speeding) or otherwise suggest that Peretto did not commit a wrongful act. Note that the defendant's attorney has the right to reserve her opening statement until after the plaintiff's case has been presented.

The Plaintiff's Case

Once the opening statements have been made, Gilmore will present the plaintiff's case first. Because he is the plaintiff's attorney, he has the burden of proving that defendant Peretto was negligent.

Direct Examination

direct examination
The examination of a witness by the attorney who calls the witness to the stand to testify on behalf of the attorney's client.

Gilmore will call eyewitnesses to the stand and ask them to tell the court about the events that led to the accident. This questioning is known as **direct examination**. For example, Gilmore will call Julia Williams, an eyewitness who saw the accident, and ask her questions such as those presented in Exhibit 12.4. He will also call other witnesses, including the police officer and ambulance driver who were summoned to the accident. Gilmore will try to elicit responses from these witnesses that strengthen Baranski's case—or at least that do not weaken it.

During direct examination, attorney Gilmore usually will not be permitted to ask *leading questions*, which are questions that lead the witness to a particular desired response (see Chapter 11). A leading question might be something like the following: "So, Mrs. Williams, you noticed that the defendant ran the stop sign, right?" If Mrs. Williams answers "yes," she has, in effect, been "led" to this answer by Gilmore's leading question. Leading questions discourage witnesses from telling their stories in their own words.

When Gilmore is dealing with *hostile witnesses* (uncooperative witnesses or those testifying on behalf of the other party), however, he is normally permitted to ask leading questions. This is because hostile witnesses may be uncommunicative and unwilling to describe the events they witnessed. If Gilmore asked a hostile witness what she observed on the morning of August 4 at 7:45 A.M., for example, the witness might respond, "I saw two trucks driving down Mattis Avenue." That answer might be

ATTORNEY:	Mrs. Williams, please explain how you came to be at the scene of the accident.
WITNESS:	Well, I was walking north on Mattis Avenue toward Nita City Hospital, where I work as a nurse.
ATTORNEY:	Please describe for the court, in your own words, exactly what you observed when you reached the intersection of Mattis Avenue and Thirty-eighth Street.
WITNESS:	I was approaching the intersection when I saw the defendant run the stop sign on Thirty-eighth Street and crash into the plaintiff's car.
ATTORNEY:	Did you notice any change in the speed at which the defendant was driving as he approached the stop sign?
WITNESS:	No. He didn't slow down at all.
ATTORNEY:	Mrs. Williams, are you generally in good health?
WITNESS:	Yes.
ATTORNEY:	Have you ever had any problems with your vision?
WITNESS:	No. I wear reading glasses for close work, but I see well in the distance.
ATTORNEY:	And how long has it been since your last eye examination?
WITNESS:	About a month or so ago, I went to Dr. Sullivan for an examination. He told me that I needed reading glasses but that my distance vision was excellent.

EXHIBIT 12.4

Direct Examination—Sample Questions

true, but it has nothing to do with the Baranski-Peretto accident. Therefore, to elicit relevant information from this witness, Gilmore would be permitted to use leading questions to force the witness to respond to the question at issue.

Typically, an attorney will request permission from the judge to treat a witness as hostile at the appropriate time. Opposing counsel will then have an opportunity to object, and the judge may hear arguments from both sides on whether the witness should be declared hostile.

Cross-Examination

After Gilmore has finished questioning a witness on direct examination, Peretto's attorney, Cameron, begins her **cross-examination** of that witness. During her cross-examination, Cameron is primarily concerned with reducing the witness's credibility in the eyes of the jury and the judge. Attorneys typically use leading questions during cross-examination. Generally, experienced trial attorneys ask only questions to which they know the answers—otherwise a question might elicit testimony from the witness that further supports the opponent's case.

cross-examination
The questioning of an opposing witness during the trial.

Make Questions Relevant. Cameron formulates questions for Gilmore's witnesses based on the witnesses' answers in depositions and interrogatories. Discovery usually provides attorneys with a good idea as to what areas of questioning may prove fruitful. If a witness's testimony on the witness stand differs materially from the answers previously given, or contradicts some other item of evidence (physical evidence or testimony of another witness), the attorney can use this discrepancy to attack the witness's credibility.

Focus on Credibility.   The defendant's attorney must generally confine her cross-examination to matters that were brought up during direct examination or that relate to a witness's credibility. This restriction is not followed in all states, however, and ultimately both the nature and the extent of the cross-examination are subject to the discretion of the trial judge. In any event, Cameron's interrogation may not extend to matters unrelated to the case. She normally may not introduce evidence that a witness for the plaintiff is a smoker or dislikes children, for example, unless she can demonstrate that such facts are relevant to the case.

In general, Cameron may try to uncover relevant physical infirmities of the plaintiff's witnesses (poor eyesight or hearing), as well as any evidence of bias (such as a witness's habit of playing golf with Baranski every Saturday). Some questions that Cameron might ask Julia Williams, Gilmore's eyewitness, are presented in Exhibit 12.5.

Redirect and Recross

After defendant Peretto's attorney has finished cross-examining each witness, plaintiff Baranski's attorney will try to repair any damage done to the credibility of the witness's testimony—or to the case itself. Gilmore does this by again questioning the witness and allowing the witness to explain her answer. This is known as **redirect examination**.

If Cameron's cross-examination revealed that one of Gilmore's eyewitnesses to the accident had vision problems, for example, Gilmore could ask the witness whether she was wearing glasses or contact lenses at the time of the accident. Gilmore might have the witness demonstrate to the court that she has adequate

redirect examination
The questioning of a witness following the adverse party's cross-examination.

EXHIBIT 12.5
Cross-Examination—Sample Questions

ATTORNEY:	You have just testified that you were approaching the intersection when the accident occurred. Isn't it true that you stated earlier, under oath, that you were at the intersection at the time of the accident?
WITNESS:	Well, I might have, but I think I said that I was close to the intersection.
ATTORNEY:	In fact, you said that you were at the intersection. Now, you say that you were approaching it. Which is it?
WITNESS:	I was approaching it, I suppose.
ATTORNEY:	Okay. Exactly where were you when the accident occurred?
WITNESS:	I think that I was just in front of the Dairy Queen when the accident happened.
ATTORNEY:	Mrs. Williams, the Dairy Queen on Mattis Avenue is at least seventy-five yards from the intersection of Mattis Avenue and Thirty-eighth Street. Is it your testimony today that you noticed the defendant's car from seventy-five yards away as it was approaching the intersection on Mattis Avenue?
WITNESS:	Well, no, I guess not.
ATTORNEY:	Isn't it true that there were a lot of other cars driving on the road that morning?
WITNESS:	Yes.
ATTORNEY:	And you had no reason to be paying particular attention to the defendant's car, did you?
WITNESS:	Not really.
ATTORNEY:	In fact, you did not see the defendant's car until after the collision occurred, did you, Mrs. Williams?

vision by having her identify an object at the far end of the courtroom. Because redirect examination is primarily used to improve the credibility of cross-examined witnesses, it is limited to matters raised during cross-examination. (If Cameron chooses not to cross-examine a particular witness, then there can be no redirect examination by Gilmore.)

Following Gilmore's redirect examination, Cameron is given an opportunity for **recross-examination**. Gilmore would then have another opportunity for more direct examination and so on until both sides are done. When both attorneys have finished with the first witness, Gilmore calls succeeding witnesses in Baranski's case. Each will be subject to cross-examination (and redirect and recross, if necessary).

Motion for a Directed Verdict

After attorney Gilmore has presented his case for Baranski, then Cameron, as counsel for defendant Peretto, may make a **motion for a directed verdict** (known as a *motion for judgment as a matter of law* in federal courts). Cameron will be arguing to the court that the plaintiff's attorney has not offered enough evidence to support a claim against Peretto. If the judge agrees and grants the motion, then judgment is entered for Peretto, the case is dismissed, and the trial is over. A sample motion for judgment as a matter of law is shown in Exhibit 12.6.

The motion for a directed verdict (judgment as a matter of law) is not common because only cases that involve genuine factual disputes proceed to trial in the first place. If the judge had believed that Baranski's case was flawed before the trial started, then the judge would probably have granted a pretrial motion to dismiss the case, thereby avoiding the expense of a trial. Occasionally, however, the witnesses' testimony unexpectedly leaves a crucial element unproven. In that event, the court may grant the defendant's motion for a directed verdict.

The Defendant's Case

Assuming the court denies the motion for a directed verdict, the two attorneys now reverse their roles. Cameron presents evidence demonstrating the weaknesses of plaintiff Baranski's claims against defendant Peretto. She essentially follows the same procedure used by Gilmore when he presented Baranski's side of the story. Cameron calls witnesses to the stand and questions them. After her direct examination of each witness, the witnesses are subject to possible cross-examination by Gilmore, redirect examination by Cameron, recross-examination by Gilmore, and so on.

In her presentation of the defendant's case, Cameron attempts to counter the points made by Gilmore. Cameron and her paralegal, McVay, may have to prepare new exhibits and memoranda of law in addition to those originally prepared. The need to prepare additional exhibits and memoranda may arise when the plaintiff's attorney pursues a strategy different from the one anticipated by the defense team. Depending on Cameron's strategy, she may choose to begin by exposing weaknesses in the plaintiff's case (by asserting that Baranski was speeding, for example) or by presenting Peretto's version of the accident. In either case, McVay, like Lopez, keeps track of the materials brought to court each day.

Once Cameron has finished presenting her case, Gilmore will offer evidence to *rebut* (refute) evidence introduced by Cameron on Peretto's behalf. After Gilmore's rebuttal, if any, both attorneys make their closing arguments to the jury.

Closing Arguments

In the **closing argument**, each attorney summarizes his or her presentation and argues in his or her client's favor. A closing argument should include all major points that support the client's case. It should also emphasize the shortcomings of the opposing

---

recross-examination
The questioning of an opposing witness following the adverse party's redirect examination.

motion for a directed verdict
A motion (known as a *motion for judgment as a matter of law* in the federal courts) requesting that the court grant a judgment in favor of the party making the motion on the ground that the other party has not produced sufficient evidence to support his or her claim. In some jurisdictions, and especially in criminal cases, this is called a *motion to strike* or *motion to strike out all the evidence*.

closing argument
The argument made by each side's attorney after the cases for the plaintiff and defendant have been presented. Closing arguments are made prior to the jury charge.

EXHIBIT 12.6

A Sample of a Motion for Judgment as a Matter of Law

Elizabeth A. Cameron
Cameron & Strauss, P.C.
310 Lake Drive
Zero City, ZE 59802
(616) 955-6234

Attorney for Defendant

UNITED STATES DISTRICT COURT
FOR THE WESTERN DISTRICT OF NITA

Katherine Baranski) 　　　　　Plaintiff,) 　　　　　　　　　) v. 　　　　　　　　　) 　　　　　　　　　) Tony Peretto 　　　) 　　　　　Defendant.)	CASE NO. 17-14335-NI Honorable Harley M. Larue MOTION FOR JUDGMENT AS A MATTER OF LAW

The Defendant, Tony Peretto, at the close of the Plaintiff's case, moves the court to withdraw the evidence from the consideration of the jury and to find the Defendant not liable.

As grounds for this motion, Defendant Peretto states that:

(1) No evidence has been offered or received during the trial of the above-entitled cause of action to sustain the allegations of negligence contained in Plaintiff Baranski's complaint.

(2) No evidence has been offered or received during the trial proving or tending to prove that Defendant Peretto was guilty of any negligence.

(3) The proximate cause of Plaintiff Baranski's injuries was not due to any negligence on the part of Defendant Peretto.

(4) By the uncontroverted evidence, Plaintiff Baranski was guilty of contributory negligence, which was the sole cause of the Plaintiff's injuries.

Date: _7/21/22_

Elizabeth A Cameron
Elizabeth A. Cameron
Attorney for the Defendant

party's case. Jurors view a closing argument with some skepticism if it merely recites the central points of a party's claim or defense without also responding to the unfavorable facts or issues raised by the other side. Of course, neither attorney wants to focus too much on the other side's position, but the elements of the opposing position need to be acknowledged and their flaws highlighted.

Both attorneys will organize their presentations so they can explain their arguments and show the jury how their arguments are supported by the evidence. Once both attorneys have completed their remarks, the case will be submitted to the jury, and the attorneys' role in the trial will be finished.

At trial, attorneys and paralegals must have close at hand all of the documents and information that they may need to refer to during the proceedings. Typically, these materials are contained in the trial notebook, which may consist of several binders. Increasingly, for complex litigation, attorneys and paralegals retrieve necessary documents from offline or online databases using laptop computers. When might it be preferable to have physical documents rather than scanned documents in a digital file?

Edler von Rabenstein/Shutterstock.com

Jury Instructions

Before the jurors begin deliberations, the judge gives the jury a **charge**. The judge sums up the case and instructs the jurors on the rules of law that apply. (In some courts, jury instructions are given prior to closing arguments and may even be given at some other point during trial proceedings.) These often include definitions of legal terms relevant to the case and standard instructions on deliberations. In addition, the charge usually contains a request for findings of fact, typically phrased in an "if, then" format.

For example, in the portion of the charge presented in Exhibit 12.7, the jury is first asked to decide if the defendant was negligent. *If* the jury decides that the defendant was negligent, *then* the jury must decide whether the defendant's negligence caused the plaintiff's injuries. This format helps to channel the jurors' deliberations.

Each side typically submits a proposed charge to the court before the trial begins, and an attorney's trial strategy will likely be linked to the charges. The paralegal may draft proposed instructions for the attorney's review. There are standard form charges in most jurisdictions. Court opinions and your firm's case files may have helpful examples of language from similar cases. Because errors in the charge can lead an appellate court to reverse a judgment, it is critical to get the charge right. The judge, however, has the final decision as to what instructions are submitted to the jury.

charge
The judge's instruction to the jury setting forth the rules of law that the jury must apply in reaching its decision, or verdict.

The Verdict

Following its receipt of the charge, the jury begins deliberations. Once it has reached a decision, the jury issues a **verdict** in favor of one of the parties. Typically, the jury foreperson will announce the verdict, but the party against whom the verdict was entered may request to *poll the jury*, which means that each juror will state independently how he or she voted.

verdict
A formal decision made by a jury.

EXHIBIT 12.7

Jury Charge—Request for Findings of Fact

The jury is requested to answer the following questions:

(1) Do you find by a preponderance of the evidence that the defendant was negligent?

Answer: (yes or no) _____

If your answer to question (1) is "yes," go on to question (2).
If your answer to question (1) is "no," stop here.

(2) Do you find by a preponderance of the evidence that the defendant's negligence was a proximate (direct) cause of the plaintiff's injuries?

Answer: (yes or no) _____

If your answer to question (2) is "yes," go on to question (3).
If your answer to question (2) is "no," stop here.

(3) Do you find that the plaintiff was negligent?

Answer: (yes or no) _____

If your answer to question (3) is "yes," go on to question (4).
If your answer to question (3) is "no," then skip down to question (6).

(4) Do you find that the plaintiff's negligence was a proximate (direct) cause of the accident and injuries that she suffered?

Answer: (yes or no) _____

If your answer is "yes," go on to question (5).
If your answer is "no," skip to question (6).

(5) Taking 100% as the total fault causing the accident and injuries, what percentage of the total fault causing the accident and injuries do you attribute to:

the defendant _____

the plaintiff _____

(If you find that a party has no fault in causing the accident, then attribute 0% of the fault to that party.)

(6) Disregarding any negligence or fault on the part of the plaintiff, what sum of money would reasonably compensate the plaintiff for her claimed injury and damage?

Answer: $ _____

If the jury finds that a party owes damages on a claim or counterclaim, the jury specifies the amount to be paid to the other party. Following the announcement of the verdict, the jurors are discharged. Usually, immediately after the verdict has been announced and the jurors discharged, the party in whose favor the verdict was issued makes a motion asking the judge to issue a *judgment*—the court's final word on the matter—consistent with the jury's verdict. If the jury in the *Baranski* case finds that Peretto was negligent and awards Baranski damages of $85,000, the judge will order Peretto to pay the plaintiff that amount.

Posttrial Motions and Procedures

Every trial must have a winner and a loser. Although civil litigation is an expensive and cumbersome process, the losing party may wish to pursue the matter further after the verdict.

Assume that Baranski wins at trial and is awarded $85,000 in damages. Cameron, as defendant Peretto's attorney, may file a posttrial motion or appeal the decision to a higher court. Note that even though Baranski won the case, she could also appeal the judgment. For example, she might appeal the case on the ground that she should have received $170,000 in damages instead of $85,000, arguing that the latter amount inadequately compensates her for the harms that she suffered as a result of Peretto's negligence.

Motions after the Trial

Assume that Cameron believes that the verdict for Baranski is not supported by the evidence. She may file a **motion for judgment notwithstanding the verdict** (known as a *motion for judgment as a matter of law* in federal courts). By filing this motion, Cameron asks the judge to enter a judgment in favor of Peretto on the ground (basis) that the jury verdict in favor of Baranski was unreasonable and erroneous. Cameron may file this motion only if she previously filed a motion for a directed verdict during the trial. She must generally file the motion within ten days following the entry of judgment against Peretto, although the procedure and time period for filing such a motion varies among the states.

Similar to most motions in federal court, this motion must be accompanied by a supporting affidavit or a memorandum of law, or brief (discussed in Chapter 10). The judge then determines whether the jury's verdict was proper in view of the evidence presented at trial. Such motions are rarely granted.

Rule 50 of the Federal Rules of Civil Procedure permits either party to file a **motion for a new trial**. Such a motion may be submitted along with a motion for judgment notwithstanding the verdict. A motion for a new trial is a far more drastic tactic because it asserts that the trial was so pervaded by error or so fundamentally flawed that a new trial should be held. For a motion for a new trial to have a reasonable chance of being granted, the motion must allege serious problems such as jury misconduct, prejudicial jury instructions, excessive or inadequate damages, or the existence of newly discovered evidence (but not if the evidence could have been discovered earlier through the use of reasonable care).

Similar to other posttrial motions in federal courts, the motion for a new trial must generally be filed within ten days following the entry of the judgment. Exhibit 12.8 illustrates a motion for judgment as a matter of law or, in the alternative, for a new trial.

Appealing the Verdict

If Cameron's posttrial motions are unsuccessful or if she decides not to file them, she may still file an **appeal**. The purpose of an appeal is to have the trial court's decision reversed or modified by an appellate court. As discussed in Chapter 6, appellate courts, or courts of appeals, are *reviewing* courts, not trial courts. No new evidence is presented to the appellate court, and there is no jury.

The appellate court reviews the trial court's proceedings to decide whether the trial court erred in applying the law to the facts of the case, in instructing the jury, in ruling on a motion, or in administering the trial generally. Appellate courts rarely tamper with a trial

motion for judgment notwithstanding the verdict
A motion (referred to as a *motion for judgment as a matter of law* in federal courts) requesting that the court grant judgment in favor of the party making the motion on the ground that the jury verdict against him or her was unreasonable or erroneous.

motion for a new trial
A motion asserting that the trial was so fundamentally flawed (because of error, newly discovered evidence, prejudice, or other major reason) that a new trial is needed to prevent a miscarriage of justice.

appeal
A challenge seeking a higher court's review of a lower court's decision for the purpose of correcting or changing the lower court's judgment or decision.

EXHIBIT 12.8

A Sample of a Motion for Judgment as a Matter of Law or for a New Trial

Elizabeth A. Cameron
Cameron & Strauss, P.C.
310 Lake Drive
Zero City, ZE 59802
(616) 955-6234

Attorney for Defendant

UNITED STATES DISTRICT COURT
FOR THE WESTERN DISTRICT OF NITA

Katherine Baranski	)	CASE NO. 17-14335-NI
Plaintiff,	)	Honorable Harley M. Larue
	)	
v.	)	MOTION FOR JUDGMENT AS
	)	A MATTER OF LAW OR, IN
	)	THE ALTERNATIVE,
Tony Peretto	)	MOTION FOR A NEW TRIAL
Defendant.	)	

The Defendant, Tony Peretto, moves this Court, pursuant to Rule 50(b) of the Federal Rules of Civil Procedure, to set aside the verdict and judgment entered on August 15, 2022, and to enter instead a judgment for the Defendant as a matter of law. In the alternative, and in the event the Defendant's motion for judgment as a matter of law is denied, the Defendant moves the Court to order a new trial.

The grounds for this motion are set forth in the attached memorandum.

Date: ___8/18/22___

Elizabeth A. Cameron
Elizabeth A. Cameron
Attorney for the Defendant

---

appellant

The party who takes an appeal from one court to another; sometimes referred to as the *petitioner*.

appellee

The party against whom an appeal is taken—that is, the party who opposes setting aside or reversing the judgment; sometimes referred to as the *respondent*.

record on appeal

The items submitted during the trial (pleadings, motions, briefs, and exhibits) and the transcript of the trial proceedings, which are forwarded to the appellate court for review when a case is appealed.

court's findings of fact because the judge and jury were in a better position than the appellate court to evaluate the credibility of witnesses, the nature of the evidence, and the like.

As grounds for the appeal, Cameron might argue that the trial court erred in one of the ways mentioned in the preceding paragraph. Unless she believes that a reversal of the judgment is likely, however, she will probably advise Peretto not to appeal the case, as an appeal adds to the costs already incurred by Peretto in defending against Baranski's claim.

Notice of Appeal

When the appeal involves a federal district court decision, the **appellant** (the party appealing the decision) must file a notice of appeal with the district court that rendered the judgment. The clerk of the court then notifies the **appellee** (the party against whom the appeal is taken) as well as the court of appeals. The clerk forwards to the appellate court a transcript of the trial court proceedings, along with related pleadings and exhibits. These materials constitute the **record on appeal**.

The Appellate Brief and Oral Arguments

When a case is appealed, the attorneys for both parties submit written *briefs* that present their positions on the issues to be reviewed by the appellate court. The briefs outline each party's view of the proper application of the law to the facts. In preparing the briefs, the attorneys cite relevant pages of the court records. Paralegals often index and summarize the record to assist in the brief writing. These tasks are similar to the organization and summarizing of discovery materials before trial.

After the appellate court has reviewed the briefs, the court usually sets a time for both attorneys to argue their positions before the panel of judges. The attorneys then present their arguments and answer any questions the judges might have. Generally, the attorneys' arguments before an appellate court are limited in the time allowed for argument and the scope of the argument. Following oral arguments, the judges decide the matter and issue a formal written opinion, which normally is published in the relevant reporter (see Chapter 7).

The Appellate Court's Options

Once they have reviewed the record and heard oral arguments, if any, the judges have several options. In the *Baranski* case, if the appellate court decided to uphold the trial court's decision, then it would **affirm** the judgment for Baranski. If the judges decided to **reverse** the trial court's decision, then Peretto would no longer be obligated to pay the damages awarded to Baranski by the trial court. The court might also affirm or reverse a decision *in part*. For example, the judges might affirm the jury's finding that Peretto was negligent but **remand** the case—that is, send it back to the trial court—for further proceedings on another issue (such as the extent of Baranski's damages). An appellate court can also *modify* a lower court's decision. If, for example, the appellate court decided that the jury awarded an excessive amount in damages, the appellate court might reduce the award.

The decision of the appellate court may sometimes be appealed further. A state intermediate appellate court's decision may be appealed to the state supreme court. A federal appellate court's decision may be appealed to the United States Supreme Court. The higher courts decide whether or not they will review the case. These courts normally are not *required* to review cases. Recall from Chapter 6 that although thousands of cases are submitted to the United States Supreme Court each year, it hears fewer than ninety. An action decided in a state court has a somewhat greater chance of being reviewed by the state supreme court.

Note that it is also possible to appeal certain trial court rulings even before the trial is held. This is called an **interlocutory appeal**. Such an appeal is common for rulings on motions for preliminary injunctions, which are requests to prevent another party from doing some act that is part of the basis for the lawsuit while the case is pending.

affirm
To uphold the judgment of a lower court.

reverse
To overturn the judgment of a lower court.

remand
To send a case back to a lower court for further proceedings.

interlocutory appeal
An appeal from a trial court's ruling on a specific motion or argument before a judgment on the merits of the case is entered.

Enforcing the Judgment

The uncertainties of the litigation process are compounded by the lack of guarantees that a judgment will be enforceable. Indeed, the difficulty of enforcing court judgments, coupled with the high costs accompanying litigation (including attorneys' fees, court costs, and the litigants' time costs), are reasons why most disputes are settled out of court, before or during the trial.

The *Developing Paralegal Skills* feature on the following page discusses the practical problems of enforcing judgments. It is one thing to have a court enter a judgment in your favor; it is another to collect the funds to which you are entitled from the opposing party. Even if the jury awarded Baranski the full amount of damages requested

($170,000), for example, she might not, in fact, "win" anything. Peretto's auto insurance coverage might have expired before the accident, in which event it would not cover damages. Alternatively, Peretto's insurance coverage might be limited to $30,000, meaning that Peretto would have to pay the remaining $140,000 personally.

writ of execution
A writ that puts in force a court's decree or judgment.

If Peretto did not have that amount or he simply refused to pay, then Baranski would need to go back to court and request that it issue a **writ of execution**—an order, usually issued by the clerk of the court, directing the sheriff to seize (take temporary ownership of) Peretto's assets. Assets may have to be sold. The proceeds would be used to pay the damages owed to Baranski. Any excess proceeds of the sale would go back to Peretto.

Judgment Creditor

judgment creditor
A creditor who is legally entitled, by a court's judgment, to collect the amount of the judgment from a debtor.

Even as a **judgment creditor** (one who has obtained a court judgment against a debtor), Baranski may not be able to obtain the full amount of the judgment from Peretto. Laws protecting debtors provide that certain property (such as a debtor's home up to a specific value and tools used by the debtor in his trade) is *exempt* from seizure. Exempt property cannot be seized and sold to pay debts owed to judgment creditors.

Similar exemptions would apply if Peretto declared bankruptcy. Thus, even though Baranski won at trial, she, like many others who are awarded damages, might not be able to collect what she is owed. However, judgments constitute liens (legal claims) for significant time periods. If the financial circumstances of the debtor—such as Peretto—improve in the future, recovery may be possible. There are many roles for paralegals in collecting judgments, including researching defendants' assets, filing liens, and so on. Many of the skills used in pretrial investigations are useful here.

DEVELOPING PARALEGAL SKILLS

LOCATING ASSETS

Paralegal Myra Cullen works for a firm that represented Jennifer Roth in a lawsuit brought against Best Eatery, a restaurant. Roth won $500,000 in a lawsuit for damages she suffered when she fell and broke her leg in the restaurant's lobby on a rainy morning. Best Eatery's liability insurance will pay only a portion of Roth's award.

Myra has been assigned to investigate Best Eatery's assets to determine how the judgment might be collected. She knows from pretrial discovery that John Dobman owns Best Eatery as a sole proprietor, which means that he is personally liable for the debts of the business. Myra contacts the county register of deeds to research the value of the property on which Best Eatery is located and any other property owned by John Dobman. The county clerk's deed records can be searched online. Myra knows, however, that after conducting a search she will need to verify the information obtained. She writes down the document numbers provided online so that she can quickly access the information at the clerk's office.

Myra determines that Dobman's equity (market value minus mortgage outstanding) in the property on which Best Eatery is located is at least $700,000, which could cover any shortfall in the damages. Because the equity in the restaurant is sufficient to cover the award, Myra simply notes the record number of Dobman's other real property (his house) in the client's file.

Tips for Locating Assets

- Ask what property the defendant owns during discovery, such as in interrogatories.
- Locate the address of the property (you can do this on the Internet).
- Go to the register of deeds (usually online) to learn about any liens filed against the property and the amount of any mortgage loan.
- Check with a real estate agent or an appraiser as to the market value of the property. Tax appraisal values can be accessed online.
- Deduct the liens and the mortgage debt from the market value to determine the defendant's equity.

Social Media Tools at Work

Enforcing judgments is another area where a paralegal's social media skills can pay dividends. Search engines and other tools can be used to look for social media postings that give evidence of valuable assets. Does a judgment debtor have pictures on his Facebook page showing a new boat or vacation home? People often reveal important clues about their lifestyles in social settings that can help locate assets that could be used to satisfy a judgment.

Judgment debtors' digital shadows may be a useful source of information for developing questions that can be used in a post-verdict deposition taken in the search for assets. Be sure to check out spouses, children, and other relatives as well. If a husband or wife tweets about the generous gift he or she received just before trial, the asset may be able to be recaptured through collection proceedings against the defendant.

Finally, this chapter's *Featured Contributor* article reminds us of the roles the paralegal plays in the litigation process.

CHAPTER SUMMARY

TRIAL PROCEDURES

Preparing for Trial

Before trial, attorneys for both sides and their paralegals gather and organize evidence, documents, and other materials relating to the case. A comprehensive checklist ensures that nothing is overlooked during this stage.

1. *Contacting and preparing witnesses*—Paralegals often assist in contacting and issuing subpoenas to witnesses, as well as in preparing witnesses for trial.

2. *Exhibits and displays*—Paralegals assume responsibility for making sure that all exhibits and displays are ready by trial; technology in this area is changing rapidly.

3. *Trial notebook*—A comprehensive trial notebook is critical when preparing for trial and at trial, and often afterward. Paralegals may be responsible for obtaining and organizing copies of all relevant documents.

Pretrial Conference

Before trial, the attorneys for both sides meet with the trial judge in a pretrial conference to decide whether a settlement is possible or, if not, to decide how the trial will be conducted and what types of evidence will be admissible. It is not uncommon for one or both of the attorneys to make a motion *in limine*, which asks the court to keep certain evidence from being offered at the trial.

Jury Selection

1. Voir dire—During the *voir dire* process, attorneys for both sides question potential jurors to determine whether any potential jurors should be excluded from the jury.

2. *Online searches*—Online searches for information about prospective jurors may provide helpful information in the selection process. Consultants may be employed in complex cases.

3. *Challenges during* voir dire—Attorneys for both sides can exercise an unlimited number of challenges for cause on the basis of prospective jurors' bias against the client or case. Attorneys can exercise a limited number of peremptory challenges without giving any reason to the court for excluding a potential juror.

4. *Paralegals' role during* voir dire—Paralegals may help prepare jury profiles and observe prospective jurors to gain insights into the potential jurors' views of the case.

5. *Alternate jurors*—In case of illness or other problem during a trial, an alternate juror may be called to step in so the trial may proceed.

Continues

FEATURED CONTRIBUTOR

THE COMPLEX ROLES IN LITIGATION

Regina C. Graziani, Esq.

BIOGRAPHICAL NOTE

Regina C. Graziani serves the Paralegal Studies Program at the University of Hartford in Connecticut as both program director and instructor. She received her law degree from Villanova University. She is the co-chair of the Paralegals Section of the Connecticut Bar Association and a past member of the Connecticut Bar Association's House of Delegates. She also is co-chair of the Hartford County Bar Association's Paralegal Committee.

Attorney Graziani has been a member of the greater Hartford legal community for more than twenty years, beginning her career as a litigation paralegal in a major Hartford law firm, where she specialized in large-case management. As an attorney, she focuses on the representation of regulated industrial, financial, and commercial establishments, as well as a small number of citizen plaintiffs in state and federal court, especially in environmental law.

While litigators are often viewed poorly, litigation plays an important role in our society. It is the method by which disputes are settled in a civilized manner.

When parties cannot resolve a dispute on their own, they take it to the courthouse. A trier of fact (jury) and a trier of law (judge) apply precedent to the facts of the matter and reach a decision that is consistent with prior decisions that are similar unless there is a substantive reason for not applying precedent. As citizens and practitioners, we know (or

are able to determine) what the law is—what the consequence for a specified behavior is or what the compensation is for an injury.

Initial Strategies in Civil Litigation

Civil litigation requires patience, an appreciation of strategy, and attention to detail. The litigation process is about strategy—that is, which parties will be sued, in which court, and under which causes of action. Each of those decisions is strategic. The plaintiff must

The Trial

Once the jury has been selected and seated, the trial begins.

1. *Paralegal duties*—Paralegals who attend the trial may coordinate witnesses' appearances, track the testimony of witnesses and compare it with sworn statements that the witnesses made before the trial, and provide the attorneys with reminders or documents when necessary.

2. *Opening statements*—The trial begins with opening statements in which the attorneys briefly outline their versions of the facts of the case and the evidence they will offer to support their views.

3. *Plaintiff's case*—Following the opening statements, the plaintiff's attorney presents evidence supporting the claims, including the testimony of witnesses.

   a. In direct examination, the attorney questions witnesses who are called to testify.

   b. Following direct examination by the plaintiff's attorney, the defendant's attorney may cross-examine the witness.

   c. If the witness was cross-examined, the plaintiff's attorney may question the witness on

determine whether to file the complaint in state court or federal court, and must analyze the benefits and detriments of filing in each court, and ultimately select the one that is most beneficial to the matter.

Discovery Tools

Once discovery is entered, consideration is given as to which discovery tools will be used. Tools are selected on the basis of which will yield the most valuable results. Cost may also be a criterion. Depositions are expensive, and a client may not be able to afford them. As a result we must determine how else to best obtain the information needed. When faced with a request to produce documents, for instance, the scale of the request must be determined, as it possibly could range from millions of pages to a single document.

> **Discovery is like a large puzzle."**

The Art of Drafting Documents

There is an art to drafting interrogatories, requests for production, and requests for admission. The key is what information is needed to prove the plaintiff's cause of action, or to break down the plaintiff's case (as a defendant). All reports, statements, tests, and documents must be reviewed to ascertain what facts are known and what evidence is needed to meet the burden of proof. Once that determination is made, the interrogatories, requests for production, or requests for admission are crafted narrowly and precisely to elicit the necessary information.

Discovery is like a large puzzle. Each party has some pieces but needs more to determine what the picture is. As the picture is developed, a party may realize that its case is not as strong as it first appeared, and settlement may be desirable.

Trial Preparation and Duties

Preparing for trial can be daunting. A good paralegal has the ability to organize the documents and create a trial notebook for the attorney's use during trial. The notebook contains the important documents and pleadings that have been filed during the course of the litigation, among other documents.

A paralegal plays a significant role during the trial as well and may operate electronic media that are used to present exhibits to the jury. Most likely, the paralegal created the product that is viewed by the jury. The days of bringing a trifold display or an enlarged copy of a document are gone; we use electronic methods.

A paralegal may also be charged with note taking during the testimony of witnesses, in preparation for cross-examination or rebuttal. The paralegal may also watch jurors during testimony to try to read their expressions.

Paralegal's Role

A successful litigation paralegal is highly motivated, pays attention to detail, possesses strong written and oral skills, is curious, and is competent with technology.

The litigation paralegal is invaluable to the attorney. One may undertake many tasks under the supervision of an attorney. With the exception of providing legal advice to the client, signing documents that require an attorney's signature, appearing in court, and asking questions at a deposition, the paralegal can do most any other litigation task. From conducting research on the causes of action to drafting the complaint to assembling the trial notebook, the paralegal is an important and invaluable member of the litigation team.

Source: Regina C. Graziani

redirect examination, after which the defendant's attorney may question the witness on recross-examination.

4. *Motion for a directed verdict*—After the plaintiff's attorney has presented the client's case, the defendant's attorney may make a motion for a directed verdict (a motion for judgment as a matter of law). It asserts that the plaintiff has not offered enough evidence to support the claim against the defendant. If the judge grants the motion, the case is dismissed.

5. *Defendant's case*—The attorneys reverse roles, and the defendant's attorney presents evidence and testimony to refute the plaintiff's claims. Witnesses called to the stand by the defendant's attorney are subject to direct examination by that attorney, cross-examination by the plaintiff's attorney, and possible redirect examination and recross-examination.

6. *Closing arguments*—After the attorneys have finished their presentations, both attorneys give closing arguments. The arguments summarize the major points that support the client's case and emphasize shortcomings in the opposing party's case.

7. *Jury instructions*—Following the attorneys' closing arguments (or, in some courts, at some other point),

Continues

the judge instructs the jury in a charge—a document that includes statements of the applicable law and a review of the facts as presented during the trial. The jury must not disregard the judge's instructions as to what the applicable law is and how it should be applied to the facts of the case as interpreted by the jury.

8. *Verdict*—Once the jury reaches a decision, it issues a verdict in favor of one of the parties and is discharged. The court then enters a judgment.

Posttrial Motions and Procedures

After the verdict has been pronounced and the trial concluded, the losing party's attorney may file a posttrial motion or an appeal.

1. *Posttrial motions*—A motion for judgment notwithstanding the verdict (a motion for judgment as a matter of law) asks the judge to enter a judgment in favor of the losing party in spite of the verdict because the verdict was not supported by the evidence or was otherwise in error. A motion for a new trial asserts that the trial was so flawed—by juror misconduct or other pervasive errors—that a new trial should be held.

2. *Appealing the verdict*—The attorney may, depending on the client's wishes, appeal the decision to an appellate court for review. Appeals are usually filed only when the attorney believes there is a good chance of reversal.

   a. In an appeal, the appellant must file a notice of appeal with the court that rendered the judgment. The clerk forwards the trial record to the reviewing court.

   b. The parties then file appellate briefs arguing their positions. Later, they are given the opportunity to present oral arguments before the appellate panel.

   c. The appellate court decides whether to affirm, reverse, remand, or modify the trial court's judgment.

   d. The appellate court's decision may sometimes be appealed further (to the state supreme court, for example).

Enforcing the Judgment

Even though a plaintiff wins a lawsuit for damages, it may be difficult to enforce the judgment against the defendant, particularly if the defendant has few assets. The paralegal is often involved in locating assets so the attorney can request a writ of execution (a court order to seize property) to try to collect the amount the client is owed.

KEY TERMS AND CONCEPTS

QUESTIONS FOR REVIEW

1. What role does the paralegal play in pretrial preparation of witnesses, exhibits, and displays for trial? How are the trial notebooks prepared?

2. What are the goals of a pretrial conference? Who attends a pretrial conference?

3. Describe the juror selection process. What is the difference between a peremptory challenge and a challenge for cause?

4. What are the different phases of a trial? List the process steps in attorneys' questioning of witnesses. What is the difference between direct examination and cross-examination?

5. Describe the procedure for filing an appeal. What factors does an attorney consider when deciding whether a case should be appealed? Can the jury decide matters of law?

6. What is a writ of execution? What is a judgment creditor?

ETHICS QUESTION

1. During the course of a products liability trial, a juror consulted the website **howstuffworks.com** to better understand components in the piece of equipment involved in the case. Aaron, a paralegal for the defense attorney, overheard two jurors discussing the information as they left the jury box. The information that the juror had learned would be beneficial to the defendant, whom Aaron's boss is defending in the case. What should Aaron do in this situation?

PRACTICE QUESTIONS AND ASSIGNMENTS

1. Using the material from this chapter, identify the different phases of a trial (opening statement, direct examination, cross-examination, motion for directed verdict, closing statement, verdict) in the hypothetical situations below:

   a. The plaintiff's attorney asks the witness, "Mrs. Wong, could you explain what you observed at the scene of the accident on January 17, 2021?"

   b. The defense attorney makes a motion saying that the plaintiff's attorney has not offered enough evidence to support a claim against the defendant.

   c. The defense attorney asks the plaintiff's witness, "Mr. Bashara, isn't it true that you were drinking alcohol immediately before you were involved in the car accident?"

   d. The plaintiff's attorney gives her version of the facts and the supporting evidence that she will use to prove her case during the trial.

2. Using the material presented in the chapter, identify the motion that would be filed in each of the following situations:

   a. A plaintiff's attorney loses a case, and she believes that her loss is due to prejudicial jury instructions given by the judge.

   b. The defendant's key witness died during trial, and there was no way to obtain the testimony he would have provided. As a result, key evidence was not presented, and the defendant was unable to prove his case.

   c. In the same case (see Question 2b above), the plaintiff's attorney made an appropriate motion, which was not granted, and ultimately lost the lawsuit. Thus, according to the plaintiff's attorney, the judgment was not supported by the evidence.

   d. The defense attorney sees the grisly photographs of an accident that the plaintiff's attorney has in her file. The defense attorney is concerned that these photographs would unfairly prejudice a jury against the defendant during the trial.

3. During jury selection for a medical malpractice trial, three employees of the insurance company that carried the malpractice insurance for the doctor and hospital being sued were members of the jury pool. Should employees of an insurance company be allowed to serve on the jury? If not, discuss the challenges that the plaintiff's attorney could raise to have them removed.

4. Attorney Johnson calls witness Roberta Looper to the stand to testify. When the judge asks Roberta to raise her hand to be sworn in, Roberta refuses, saying that she is an atheist and cannot swear an oath to God on the Bible. Given the material on the First Amendment covered in Chapter 5, can the judge make Roberta take the oath? Can the judge refuse to let her testify? What alternative might there be for Roberta to swear to tell the truth?

5. Indicate what action the appellate court has taken in each hypothetical below (affirmed, modified, or reversed the trial court's decision or remanded the case for further proceedings):

   a. A trial court finds for the plaintiff in the amount of $150,000 in a case in which the plaintiff slipped and fell in a grocery store. The court of appeals finds that while the plaintiff is entitled to damages, the damages awarded by the jury are excessive. The appellate court sends the case back to the trial court for reevaluation of the amount of damages awarded.

   b. A trial court finds that the plaintiff was slandered by the defendant. On appeal, the court of appeals finds that the trial court admitted evidence that it should not have allowed and holds that without this evidence, there was no slander.

   c. A trial court finds that the defendant breached a contract and owes the plaintiff $1,000,000 in damages. The defendant appeals, claiming that the damages are not supported by the evidence. The court of appeals agrees with the trial court's decision.

6. Using Exhibit 12.2, draft a subpoena for a friendly witness using the following facts:

   Simon Kolstad, whose address is 100 Schoolcraft Road, Del Mar, California, is a witness to be subpoenaed in *Sumner v. Hayes*, a civil lawsuit filed in the U.S. District Court for the Eastern District of Michigan, case number 15–123492. He is being subpoenaed by the plaintiff's attorney, Marvin W. Green, whose office is located at 300 Penobscot Building, 705 Premier Ave., Detroit, Michigan. Kolstad is to appear in Room 6 of the courthouse, which is located at 231 Lafayette Boulevard, Detroit, Michigan, at 2:30 P.M. on January 10, 2022.

GROUP PROJECT

The group should research how a paralegal might use social media sites to find information about jurors.

Student one will use online sources (and library sources, if necessary) to find out what kinds of information are available online about potential jurors. Student one should summarize how this information could be used during *voir dire*.

Students two and three will research whether investigation of this nature is ethical, and if so, under what circumstances it might become unethical.

Student four will create a presentation to share the group's results with the rest of the class.

CHAPTER
13

Criminal Law and Procedures

CHAPTER OBJECTIVES

After completing this chapter, you will be able to:

- Explain the difference between crimes and other wrongful acts.

- Identify the two elements required for criminal liability and some of the most common defenses that are raised in defending against criminal charges.

- List the major categories of crimes and some common types of crimes.

- Define *cyber crime*, and describe various forms of cyber crime.

- Describe the importance of social media to the criminal justice system.

- Summarize the constitutional rights of anyone accused of crimes.

- Explain the basic steps involved in criminal procedure, from the time a crime is reported to the resolution of the case.

- Explain how and why criminal litigation procedures differ from civil litigation procedures.

- Describe the criminal trial and appeal process.

Introduction

Each year, more than 10 million people are arrested on criminal charges and enter the criminal justice system. Therefore, it is no wonder that many attorneys and paralegals work on criminal law cases. In fact, about one in every five paralegals spends most of her or his work time on criminal law.

A **public prosecutor** is employed by the government to prosecute criminal cases. The chief public prosecutor in federal criminal cases is called a U.S. attorney. Assistant U.S. attorneys conduct most trials for those cases. In cases tried in state or local courts, the public prosecutor may be referred to as a *prosecuting attorney, state prosecutor, district attorney, county attorney, commonwealth attorney,* or *city attorney.*

Note, however, that sometimes a minor crime is prosecuted by a **complaining witness**. Complaining witnesses are members of the community who believe that they witnessed a crime, were injured by one, or both. Many police officers act as complaining witnesses in minor crimes not prosecuted by a public prosecutor, such as certain traffic offenses or disturbances of the peace. Loss prevention officers or

public prosecutor

An individual, acting as a trial lawyer, who initiates and conducts criminal cases in the government's name and on behalf of the people.

complaining witness

A person who claims to be the victim of a crime or who reports an apparent violation of the law to enforcement authorities.

FEATURED CONTRIBUTOR

PARALEGALS AND CRIMINAL LITIGATION

Steven C. Kempisty

BIOGRAPHICAL NOTE

Steven Kempisty is a graduate of the State University of New York at Fredonia and the Massachusetts School of Law at Andover. A licensed attorney, he joined Bryant & Stratton College in 1999 and has served as program director for the two-year paralegal program at the Liverpool, New York, campus since 2009. Kempisty also is a member of the Financial Industry Regulatory Authority (FINRA), where he is an arbitration panelist. His main fields of interest are contract and corporations work.

One of the most important things I tell new students is *"Law & Order* is a nice program; please understand that it is fiction. The practice of law, especially criminal law and procedure, is not how Hollywood portrays it."

The U.S. legal system can be very complex and cumbersome. The criminal court system often has "log-jammed" dockets. Criminal law professionals are often overworked and may have more cases than can be handled by even the most skilled individual. Three important rules for anyone who wishes to become a part of the legal profession are be available, be organized, and be prepared.

Be Available

Criminal law provides vital protections to the accused. Government officials take their jobs seriously, and skilled defense attorneys are just as committed as they represent their clients. Being available could mean doing anything from:

1. Reviewing files.
2. Reading over old affidavits and looking at all pertinent information.
3. Reading and organizing deposition statements.
4. Looking over police reports.
5. Looking over many different records that may be germane to a case, ranging from old tax records to old indictments.

store clerks might prosecute shoplifting as complaining witnesses, just as property owners might prosecute trespassers.

Defendants in criminal cases may hire private attorneys to defend them. If a defendant cannot afford to hire an attorney, the court will appoint one. Everyone accused of a crime that may result in a jail sentence has a right to counsel, and court-appointed attorneys ensure this right. Some court-appointed defense lawyers work for organizations funded by the state. Such a lawyer is usually called a **public defender**. Other defenders are private attorneys appointed to represent a particular defendant.

In this chapter, we provide an overview of criminal law and procedure. We begin by explaining the nature of crime and the key differences between criminal law and civil law. We then discuss the elements of criminal liability and some of the many types of crime. We emphasize the constitutional protections that come into play when a person is accused of a crime, and focus on how and why criminal procedures differ from civil procedures. As this chapter's *Featured Contributor* article highlights, paralegals need certain talents to be effective in the criminal justice arena.

public defender
Court-appointed defense counsel; a lawyer appointed by the court to represent a criminal defendant who is unable to pay to hire private counsel.

6. Answering the phone.
7. Rereading the initial interview of a client.
8. Reviewing numerous pages of statutes, cases, and footnotes.
9. Researching on Westlaw or Lexis.
10. Being skilled and capable in storing, managing, and organizing many forms of electronically stored information (ESI).

Some of these tasks may seem mundane, but finding information that is helpful to a case, whether for a prosecutor or defense counsel, is important.

Being available to weed through and organize endless paperwork is hugely valuable to a legal team. It needs to be done. Being available to complete this task, although it appears thankless, will be valued and appreciated.

Be Organized

Organization is never overrated. Every legal textbook will mention the importance of discovery, document production, and information organization. Becoming organized is especially important for deposition testimony, for material evidence that may be challenged under hearsay rules, and for keeping the order of your case flowing logically so as to best represent your side in an issue.

Colleagues have told me more than once that they missed an opportunity at some point in a case simply because they were not organized on a particular issue of evidence or procedure. To help avoid confusion, team members should work together on the case's organization as well as its file. The fundamental importance of organization is that it enables everyone on a legal team to understand the system and the legal team's goals.

> **The practice of law, especially criminal law and procedure, is not how Hollywood portrays it."**

Be Prepared

Be prepared for the unexpected, because you must "expect the unexpected." With evidentiary disclosure, there should never be any surprises or cliff-hanging elements of a case that magically appear the day of trial. However, witnesses get cold feet, unorganized people lose important documents, and subpoenas are defied.

During the many hours that a legal team puts into a case, there can be shifts. When a curveball is thrown, you must seek assistance or seek a continuance or adjournment, but remain calm and carry on. There is no such thing as the perfect plan in law, but being prepared for all problems means they can be handled properly. Panicking will not get the job done.

Conclusion

In my very first case, I had a client who did not speak English. I had to hire an interpreter for myself and for court appearances with the client. One time, the interpreter was late, and I started to panic. A veteran colleague of mine was in court and talked me through the problem. I had forgotten that the client could read and write some in English, so we could progress. My interpreter eventually showed up, and we proceeded. My colleague taught me a valuable lesson: remain focused and calm. To do so, paralegals must be organized and prepared with all relevant information to assist the clients properly.

Source: Steven C. Kempisty

Defining Crime

What is a crime? To answer, we begin by distinguishing crimes from other wrongs, such as torts—and, hence, criminal law from tort, or civil, law. Major differences between civil law and criminal law are summarized in Exhibit 13.1. After discussing the differences, we explain how one act can qualify as both a crime and a tort. We then describe classifications of crimes and jurisdiction over criminal acts.

Key Differences between Civil Law and Criminal Law

crime

A broad term for violations of law that are punishable by the state and are codified by legislatures. The objective of criminal law is to protect the public.

A **crime** can be distinguished from other wrongful acts, such as torts, in that a crime is an *offense against society as a whole*. Criminal defendants usually are prosecuted by public officials on behalf of the state, as mentioned above, not by their victims or other private parties. (In practice, however, cooperation of the victim is important. In some instances, the prosecutor can file criminal charges even if the victim does not wish to cooperate, but that makes a successful prosecution less likely.) In addition, those who have committed crimes are subject to penalties, including fines, imprisonment, and, in rare cases, death.

Remedies

As will be discussed in Chapter 14, tort remedies—remedies for civil wrongs—are generally intended to compensate the injured party (by awarding money damages, for example). Criminal law, however, is concerned with punishing the wrongdoer in an attempt to deter others from similar actions. Proponents of a robust criminal justice system might also point to the ability of the law to provide restitution or retribution to victims or society, as well as to the hoped-for rehabilitation of criminals into productive members of society.

Statutory Basis

Another factor distinguishing criminal law from tort law is that criminal law is primarily statutory law. Essentially, a crime is whatever a legislature has declared to be a crime. Although the U.S. Congress defines federal crimes, most crimes are defined by state legislatures and by regulatory agencies.

Standards of Proof

The burden of proof required in criminal and civil cases is another difference. Because the state has extensive resources at its disposal when prosecuting criminal cases, there are procedural safeguards to protect the rights of defendants. One safeguard is the higher burden of proof in a criminal case. In a civil case, the plaintiff usually must prove a case by a *preponderance of the evidence*. Under this standard, the plaintiff must

EXHIBIT 13.1

A Comparison between Civil Law and Criminal Law

Issue	Under Civil Law	Under Criminal Law
Area of Concern	Rights and duties between individuals and between persons and government	Offenses against society as a whole
Wrongful Act	Harm to a person or to a person's property	Violation of a statute that prohibits a certain activity
Party who Brings Suit	Person who suffered harm	The state
Standard of Proof	Preponderance of the evidence	Beyond a reasonable doubt
Remedy	Damages to compensate for the harm or a decree to achieve an equitable result	Punishment (fine, removal from public office, imprisonment, or death)

convince the court that, based on the evidence presented by both parties, it is more likely than not that the plaintiff's allegation is true.

In a criminal case, in contrast, the state must prove its case beyond a reasonable doubt—that is, every juror in a criminal case normally must be convinced, beyond a reasonable doubt, of the defendant's guilt. Judges often describe this burden to a jury by instructing them that the evidence they heard must rule out every reasonable hypothesis of innocence. The higher standard of proof in criminal cases reflects a fundamental social value—a belief that it is worse to convict an innocent individual than to let a guilty person go free. We will look at other safeguards later in the chapter, in the context of criminal procedure.

Victimless Crimes

Yet another factor that distinguishes criminal law from tort law is the fact that a criminal act does not necessarily involve a victim, in the sense that the act directly and physically harms another. If Marissa grows marijuana in her backyard for her personal use, she may not be physically or directly harming another's interests, but she is nonetheless committing a crime (in many states and under federal law). Why? Because she is violating a rule of society that has been enacted into law by elected representatives of the people.

Civil Liability for Criminal Acts

Note that a person who commits a crime may be subject to both civil and criminal liability. Suppose Joe is walking down the street, minding his own business, when suddenly an attacker stabs and injures him. A police officer arrests the wrongdoer. In separate legal actions, the attacker may be subject both to criminal prosecution by the state and to a tort (civil) lawsuit brought by Joe. Exhibit 13.2 illustrates how the same act can result in both a tort action and a criminal action against the wrongdoer.

Because the burden of proof is higher in criminal prosecutions than in civil cases, it is possible that a defendant will be acquitted by a jury in the criminal case but subject to liability for damages in the civil case. The prosecution in the 1990s of O.J. Simpson—a former National Football League star accused of murdering his wife—is a well-known example of criminal and civil prosecution for the same act.

Classifications of Crimes

Generally, crimes are divided into two broad classifications: felonies and misdemeanors. Most states, however, have subcategories of both classifications that prescribe the maximum and minimum penalties for certain classes and subclasses of crimes.

Felonies

A felony is a serious crime that may be punished by imprisonment for more than one year. In some states, certain felonies are punishable by death. Examples of felonies include murder, rape, robbery, arson, and grand larceny. (You will read more about these and other crimes later in the chapter.)

Felonies are commonly classified by degree. For example, the Model Penal Code, promulgated by the American Law Institute,[1] provides for four degrees of felony:

1. *Capital offenses*, for which the maximum penalty is death.
2. *First degree felonies*, punishable by a maximum penalty of life imprisonment.
3. *Second degree felonies*, punishable by a maximum of ten years' imprisonment.
4. *Third degree felonies*, punishable by up to five years' imprisonment.

beyond a reasonable doubt
The standard used to determine the guilt or innocence of a person charged with a crime. To be guilty of a crime, a suspect must be proved guilty "beyond and to the exclusion of every reasonable doubt."

felony
A crime—such as arson, murder, assault, or robbery—that carries the most severe sanctions. Sanctions range from one year in a state or federal prison to life imprisonment or (in some states) the death penalty.

EXHIBIT 13.2

Tort (Civil) Lawsuit and Criminal Prosecution for the Same Act

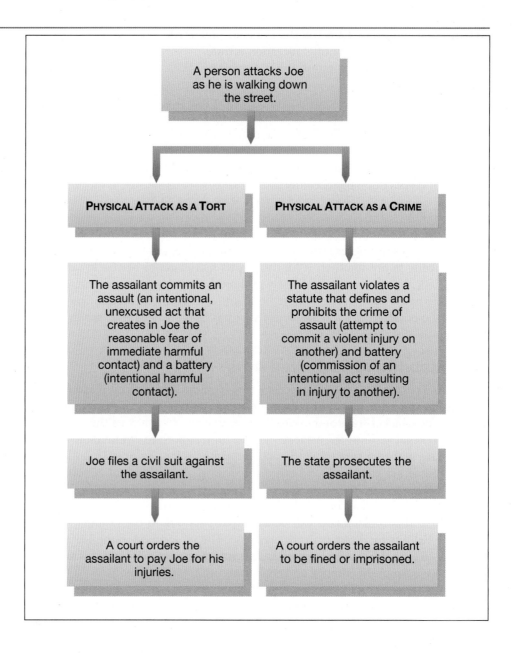

Misdemeanors

misdemeanor

A crime less serious than a felony, punishable by a fine or incarceration for up to one year in jail (not in a state or federal penitentiary).

A **misdemeanor** is a crime that may be punished by incarceration of not more than one year. If incarcerated, the guilty party goes to a local jail instead of to prison. A misdemeanor, by definition, is not a serious crime. Under federal law and in most states, a misdemeanor is any crime that is not defined by statute as a felony. State legislatures specify what crimes are classified as felonies or misdemeanors and what the potential punishment for each type of criminal act may be. Examples of misdemeanors include prostitution, disturbing the peace, and public intoxication.

Petty Offenses

petty offenses

In criminal law, the least serious kind of wrong, such as traffic or building-code violations.

Certain criminal or quasi-criminal actions, such as violations of building codes, are termed **petty offenses**, or *infractions*. Many traffic violations fall within this category. In most jurisdictions, such actions are considered a subset of misdemeanors. Some states, however, classify them separately.

CHAPTER 13 Criminal Law and Procedures **385**

Jurisdiction over Crimes

Most crimes are defined in state statutes, and the states have jurisdiction in cases involving these crimes. Federal jurisdiction extends to thousands of crimes. If a federal law defines a certain action as a crime, federal jurisdiction exists. Generally, federal criminal jurisdiction applies to the following types of crimes:

1. Crimes that occur outside the jurisdiction of a state.

2. Crimes that involve interstate commerce or communications.

3. Crimes that interfere with the operation of the federal government or its agents.

4. Crimes directed at citizens or property located outside the United States.

Consider just one example: Burning down a person's home in Dallas is arson under Texas law. Burning down a Dallas post office, which is federal property, is a federal crime. Burning down a warehouse used by Amazon—a building used in interstate commerce—is a federal crime but may be prosecuted under state law.

A challenging legal issue today concerns how a state or the federal government can exercise jurisdiction over criminal acts that are committed via the Internet, which knows no geographical borders. Often either the state or the federal government may prosecute such a matter.

Elements of Criminal Liability

For a person to be convicted of a crime, two elements must normally exist: (1) the performance of a criminal act and (2) a specified state of mind, or intent. This section describes these two elements of criminal liability and some of the defenses that can be used to avoid liability for crimes.

The Criminal Act

A criminal act is known as the *actus reus*, or guilty act. Most crimes require an act of *commission*. That is, a person must *do* something to be accused of a crime. In some cases, an act of *omission* can be a crime, but only when a person has a legal duty to perform the omitted act. Failure to file a tax return or care properly for a child is an example of an omission that can be treated as a crime.

The guilty-act requirement is based on one of the premises of criminal law—that a person is punished for harm done to society. Thinking about stealing a car may be wrong, but the thought does no harm unless translated into action. Of course, a person can be punished for *attempting* to commit a crime, but normally only if substantial steps toward the criminal objective have been taken.

actus reus
A guilty (prohibited) act. The commission of a prohibited act is one of the two essential elements required for criminal liability.

State of Mind

An act that harms society is not legally a crime unless the court finds that the second element—the required state of mind—was present. Usually a wrongful mental state, or *mens rea*, is as necessary as a wrongful act in establishing criminal liability.

What constitutes such a mental state varies according to the wrongful action. For murder, the criminal act is the taking of a life, and the mental state is the intent to take a life. For theft, the guilty act is the taking of another person's property, and the mental state involves both the knowledge that the property belongs to another and the intent to steal that property. Without the mental state required by law for a particular crime, there is generally no crime.

The same criminal act can result from varying mental states, and how a crime is defined and punished depends on the degree of "wrongfulness" of the defendant's state

mens rea
A wrongful mental state, or intent. A wrongful mental state is a requirement for criminal liability. What constitutes a wrongful mental state varies according to the nature of the crime.

of mind. For example, taking another's life is *homicide*, a criminal act. The act can be committed coldly, after premeditation; this is *murder in the first degree*, which carries the most severe criminal penalty. The act can be committed in the heat of passion; this is *voluntary manslaughter*, which carries a less severe penalty than murder. Or the act can be committed as a result of criminal negligence (reckless driving, for example); this is *involuntary manslaughter*. In each of these situations, the law recognizes a different degree of wrongfulness, and the harshness of the punishment depends on the degree to which the act of killing another was an *intentional* act. Mental states in criminal law are often described as a sliding scale between purposeful and negligent, with knowing and reckless falling at different points in between the extremes.

Corporate Criminal Liability

A corporation may be held liable for crimes committed by its agents and employees within the course and scope of their employment. Obviously, corporations cannot be imprisoned, but they can be fined or denied certain legal privileges.

Corporate directors and officers are personally liable for the crimes they commit, regardless of whether the crimes were committed for their personal benefit or on the corporation's behalf. Additionally, corporate directors and officers may be held liable for the actions of employees under their supervision. Under what has become known as the **responsible corporate officer doctrine**, a court may impose criminal liability on a corporate officer regardless of whether she or he participated in, directed, or even knew about a given criminal violation.

For example, in one case the chief executive officer of a supermarket chain was held personally liable for sanitation violations in corporate warehouses where rodents had contaminated food. The case was eventually heard by the United States Supreme Court, which held that the corporate officer was personally liable not because he intended to commit the crime or even knew about it, but because he was in a "responsible relationship" to the corporation and had the power to prevent the violation.[2] Courts have used similar reasoning to impose criminal liability on corporate managers who allowed harm to the environment in violation of federal law, such as the Clean Water Act (see Chapter 19).

Defenses to Criminal Liability

A person accused of a crime will typically offer a **defense**—a reason why he or she should not be found guilty. Asserting that a defendant lacked the required criminal intent for a specific crime is one way of defending against criminal liability. This defense and others are discussed below.

No one charged with a crime is obligated to offer a defense. The government must prove guilt beyond a reasonable doubt even if the defendant does not offer any particular defense but simply tries, at trial, to point out defects in government claims and evidence. In fact, partway through a criminal trial, after the prosecution rests its case, if the evidence provided is insufficient to prove the crime charged, a defendant may be acquitted by the judge following a motion and an argument by the defendant's attorney.

The Required Mental State Is Lacking

Proving that a defendant did or did not possess the required mental state for a given crime is difficult because a person's state of mind cannot be known. For example, assume that Jackson shot and killed Avery. Jackson is arrested and charged with the crime of murder. Jackson contends that he did not commit murder because he was too high on drugs to know what he was doing and thus lacked the required mental state for murder—intent to kill. Jackson claims that, at most, he committed the crime of

---

responsible corporate officer doctrine
A common law doctrine under which the court may impose criminal liability on a corporate officer for actions of employees under her or his supervision regardless of whether she or he participated in, directed, or even knew about those actions.

defense
The evidence and arguments presented in the defendant's support in a criminal action or lawsuit.

involuntary manslaughter. There will have to be facts in evidence tending to show that Jackson was indeed so under the influence of drugs that he could not have intended to kill Avery.

Criminal defendants may assert that they lacked the required degree of criminal intent for other reasons, including:

- *Insanity* (the inability to distinguish between right and wrong due to diminished mental capacity).

- *Duress* (which exists when someone is forced to commit a specific act).

- *Mistake* (for example, taking someone else's property, as when a person picks up an iPad, thinking that it is her own).

Protection of Persons or Property

We all have the right to protect ourselves from physical attacks by others. This is the right of **self-defense**. In most states, the force we use to protect ourselves must be reasonable under the circumstances. The force used must be necessary based on the degree of threat posed in a given situation. If someone is about to take your life, the use of *deadly force* (shooting that person with a gun, for example) might be deemed reasonable. If, however, someone in a shopping mall tries to steal a bag you are carrying, you normally do not have a right to shoot the thief, because there was no physical threat to your person.

self-defense
The legally recognized privilege to protect oneself or one's property against injury by another. The privilege of self-defense protects only acts that are reasonably necessary to protect oneself or one's property.

Defense of Others.   Similarly, we have the right to use force in **defense of others** if they are threatened with imminent harm. If you and a friend are walking down a city street one night and someone attacks and threatens to kill your friend, you are justified in responding with reasonable force to protect your friend. As with self-defense, the reasonableness of the force used is judged in view of the nature of the threat.

defense of others
The use of reasonable force to protect others from harm.

Defense of Property.   We also have the right to use reasonable force in the **defense of property**. In particular, if someone is trespassing on our property or is stealing our property, we have the right to use force to stop the trespassing or prevent the theft. Again, the amount of force used must be reasonable. Because human life has a higher value than property, deadly force is normally not allowed in the protection of property unless the thief or trespasser poses a threat to human life.

defense of property
The use of reasonable force to protect one's property from harm threatened by another. The use of deadly force in defending one's property is seldom justified.

Depending on the situation, the *castle* (or *stand your ground*) *doctrine* may come into play. This doctrine is based on the common law concept that you have a right to defend your home (your castle), yourself, your property, or an innocent person from the illegal acts of another. In general, if an intruder is in a home, the legal residents of the home do not have a *duty to retreat*. Rather, they have an express right to *stand their ground*. About half the states have expressed this principle in legislation, but the details of how the principle is applied vary across the states.

Statutes of Limitations

With some exceptions, such as for the crime of murder, statutes of limitations apply to crimes. In other words, criminal cases must be prosecuted within a certain number of years. If a criminal action is brought after the statutory time period has expired, the accused can raise the statute of limitations as a defense.

Other Defenses

Another defense is *mistaken identity*, in which a defendant claims to have been incorrectly identified by witnesses to the crime. A defendant may also offer an *alibi* (proof that the defendant was somewhere else at the time of the crime, for example).

Because criminal law brings the force of the state to bear against the individual, law enforcement authorities must abide by the letter of procedural law when arresting and prosecuting a person accused of a crime. If they do not, the defendant may be able to use the prosecution's violations of procedural laws as a defense, depending on the nature of the right that was violated and the degree of violation.

Types of Crimes

The number of acts that are categorized as criminal is nearly endless. Federal, state, and local laws provide for the classification and punishment of thousands of different criminal acts. Traditionally, though, crimes have been grouped into five broad categories, or types: violent crime, property crime, public order crime, white-collar crime, and organized crime.

Violent Crime

Crimes against persons, because they cause others to suffer harm or death, are referred to as *violent crimes*. Murder is a violent crime. So are sexual assault, rape, and assault and battery (discussed further in Chapter 14). **Robbery**—the taking of money, personal property, or any other article of value from a person by means of force or fear—is another violent crime. Typically, states have more severe penalties for *aggravated robbery*—robbery with the use of a deadly weapon—than for simple robbery. Many crimes carry greater penalties if a deadly weapon is involved.

Each violent crime is further classified by degree, depending on the circumstances surrounding the criminal act. These include the intent of the person committing the crime, whether a weapon was used, and the level of pain and suffering experienced by the victim. For example, traditionally, killing another human being could result in one of three different offenses, depending on the defendant's intent: murder (if the killing was intentional), voluntary manslaughter (if intentional but provoked), or involuntary manslaughter (if the killing was unintentional but resulted from criminal negligence or an unlawful act, such as from drunk driving).

Most states follow these basic classifications of homicide but add degrees of murder to provide penalties of different severity. For example, deliberate and premeditated killing is usually first degree murder (a *capital offense*—a crime possibly punishable by death). First degree murder may also include killings committed during certain types of felonies, such as arson, burglary, rape, or robbery. When a person is killed during other types of felonies, the charge is likely to be second degree murder, which is typically not punishable by death. Some jurisdictions will hold a defendant criminally responsible for the death of another during the commission of a felony even if that defendant did not cause the death. This is known as the *felony murder rule*.

Property Crime

The most common type of criminal activity is property crime—a crime in which the goal of the offender is some form of economic gain or damage to property. Robbery is a form of property crime, as well as a violent crime, because the offender seeks to gain the property of another by use of force or the threat of force (which creates fear). Other property crimes are discussed next.

Burglary

Burglary usually involves breaking and entering onto the property of another with the intent to commit a felony. A burglary does not necessarily involve theft. The defendant may have intended to commit some other felony and still be guilty of burglary.

robbery
The taking of money, personal property, or any other article of value from a person by means of force or fear.

burglary
Breaking and entering onto the property of another with the intent to commit a felony.

Breaking and entering is a common form of burglary that requires the prosecution to prove the intent to commit a larceny, or theft, inside another's home or property. The "breaking" element of this offense does not refer to physically forcing a door or window, but instead to breaking the "plane," an invisible barrier that separates a person's property from the outside world.

Larceny

Any person who wrongfully or fraudulently takes and carries away another person's personal property is guilty of **larceny**. In other words, larceny is "stealing." To be guilty of larceny, the accused must have intended to deprive the owner permanently of the property. Larceny does not involve force or fear (as in robbery) or breaking into a building (as in burglary). Taking company products and supplies home for personal use, if one is not authorized to do so, is larceny. Many states have expanded the definition of larceny to include thefts of computer files, computer time, and electricity.

larceny
The wrongful or fraudulent taking and carrying away of another person's personal property with the intent to deprive the person permanently of the property.

Obtaining Goods by False Pretenses

It is a criminal act to obtain goods by means of false pretenses—for example, buying groceries with a check knowing that there are insufficient funds to cover it. Using counterfeit currency is also an example of this offense. Statutes dealing with such illegal activities vary from state to state.

Receiving Stolen Goods

It is a crime to receive stolen goods. The recipient of such goods need not know the true identity of the owner or the thief. All that is necessary is that the recipient knew or *should have known* that the goods were stolen (which implies the intent to deprive the owner of those goods). In other words, if someone sells you a new laptop for fifty dollars from the back of a truck full of laptops, you may be guilty of receiving stolen property.

Arson

The willful and malicious burning of a building (and, in some states, personal property) owned by another is the crime of **arson**. Every state also has a special statute that covers burning a building for the purpose of collecting insurance.

arson
The willful and malicious burning of a building (and, in some states, personal property) owned by another. Arson statutes have been extended to cover the intentional destruction of any building, regardless of ownership, by fire or explosion.

Forgery

The fraudulent making or altering of any writing in a way that changes the legal rights and liabilities of another is **forgery**. If, without authorization, Tyler signs Ben's name to the back of a check made out to Ben, Tyler is committing forgery. Forgery also includes changing trademarks, falsifying public records, counterfeiting, and altering a legal document.

forgery
The fraudulent making or altering of any writing in a way that changes the legal rights and liabilities of another.

Public Order Crime

Societies outlaw activities considered to be contrary to public values and morals. Today, the most common public order crimes include public drunkenness, gambling, illegal drug use, and disorderly conduct. These are sometimes referred to as victimless crimes because they potentially harm only the offender. Nevertheless, legislatures have deemed these acts to be detrimental to society because they may create an environment that gives rise to property crimes and violent crimes.

Laws in this area may criminalize conduct ordinarily protected by the First Amendment, including free speech and peaceful assembly. Some states with such laws on the books enforce them only in particular contexts. For example, courts generally have limited the application of laws criminalizing "disorderly conduct" to the use of "fighting words" that would tend to draw a violent response from the intended recipient.

Some public order crimes can result in property forfeitures. For example, someone who transports illegal drugs in his car may lose the car to the government as well as suffer a prison term.

White-Collar Crime

white-collar crime

A crime that typically occurs in a business context; popularly used to refer to an illegal act or series of acts committed by a person or business entity using nonviolent means.

A crime that typically occurs in the business context is commonly referred to as a **white-collar crime**. A famous white-collar criminal is Bernard Madoff, who pleaded guilty to defrauding clients of billions of dollars through an investment scam. Although there is no official definition of white-collar crime, the term is popularly used to mean an illegal act or series of acts committed by a person or business entity using some nonviolent means. Usually, this kind of crime is committed in relationship to a legitimate occupation. Many, but not all, corporate crimes fall into this category.

Embezzlement

embezzlement

The fraudulent appropriation of the property or money of another by a person entrusted with that property or money.

When a person entrusted with another person's property fraudulently takes it, **embezzlement** occurs. Typically, embezzlement involves an employee who steals funds. Banks face this problem, and so do businesses in which officers or accountants "cook" the books to cover up the taking of funds for their own benefit. Embezzlement is not larceny, because the wrongdoer does not physically take the property from the possession of another, and it is not robbery, because neither force nor fear is used.

Mail and Wire Fraud

One of the most potent weapons against white-collar criminals is the Mail Fraud Act. Under this act, it is a federal crime (mail fraud) to use the mails, including e-mail, to defraud the public. Illegal use of the mails must involve (1) mailing or causing someone else to mail (or e-mail) something written, printed, or photocopied for the purpose of executing a scheme to defraud and (2) a contemplated or an organized scheme to defraud by false pretenses. If, for example, Johnson advertises by mail the sale of a cure for cancer that she knows has no medical validity, she can be prosecuted for fraudulent use of the mails.

Federal law also makes it a crime (called *wire fraud*) to use the telephone to defraud. Under the same statute, it is a crime to use almost any means of public communication, such as radio, television, or the Internet, to defraud.

Bribery

Basically, three types of bribery are considered crimes: bribery of public officials, commercial bribery, and bribery of foreign officials. The attempt to influence a public official to act in a way that serves a private interest is a crime. As an element of this crime, intent must be proved. The bribe can be anything the recipient considers to be valuable. Realize that *the crime of bribery occurs when the bribe is offered*. It does not matter whether the bribe is accepted. *Accepting a bribe* is a separate crime.

Typically, people make commercial bribes to obtain information, cover up an inferior product, or secure new business. For example, a person in one business may offer an employee in a competing business some type of payoff in exchange for trade secrets or pricing schedules. A *kickback,* or payoff for special favors, is commercial bribery in some situations, as when a company's purchasing agent is secretly paid to order goods from a particular supplier. Bribing foreign officials to obtain favorable business contracts is also a crime under U.S. law even though the payment takes place in another country.

Bankruptcy Fraud

Federal bankruptcy law allows many individuals and businesses to be relieved of oppressive debt through bankruptcy proceedings, as explained in Chapter 19. Criminal violations may occur during various stages of bankruptcy. A creditor, for example, may file a false claim against a debtor, which is a crime. Also, a debtor may fraudulently transfer assets to favored parties before or after the petition for bankruptcy is filed. For example, an automobile may be "sold" at a bargain price to a trusted friend or relative. It is also a crime for the debtor to fraudulently conceal property during bankruptcy, such as by hiding gold coins.

Theft of Trade Secrets

As will be discussed in Chapter 15, trade secrets are a form of intellectual property that is extremely valuable for many businesses. The Economic Espionage Act made the theft of trade secrets a federal crime. The act also made it a federal crime to buy or possess trade secrets, knowing that the trade secrets were stolen or otherwise acquired without the owner's authorization. Conviction can result in a prison sentence and a large fine.

Additionally, the law provides that any property acquired as a result of the violation, and any property used in the commission of the violation, are subject to criminal *forfeiture*—meaning that the government can take the property. A theft of trade secrets conducted via the Internet, for example, could result in the forfeiture of every computer or other device used to facilitate the violation.

Insider Trading

A person who obtains "inside information" about the plans or financial status of a corporation with publicly traded stock can make a profit by using the information to guide decisions about the purchase or sale of the stock. **Insider trading** is a violation of securities law that subjects the violator to criminal penalties. Someone who possesses inside information and who has a duty not to disclose it to outsiders may not profit from the purchase or sale of securities based on that information until the information is public. Thus, a paralegal who knows that a client of the law firm is about to announce a merger—which will increase the price of the company's stock—cannot buy the stock before the announcement.

insider trading
Trading in the stock of a publicly listed corporation based on inside information. One who possesses inside information and has a duty not to disclose it to outsiders may not profit from the purchase or sale of securities based on that information until the information is available to the public.

Organized Crime

As mentioned, white-collar crime takes place within the confines of the legitimate business world. *Organized crime*, in contrast, operates illegitimately by, among other things, providing illegal goods and services. For organized crime, the traditional preferred markets are gambling, prostitution, illegal narcotics, and loan sharking (lending funds at very high interest rates), along with more recent ventures into counterfeiting, credit-card scams, and hacking computers for financial data.

Money Laundering

The profits from illegal activities, particularly illegal drug transactions, are tens of billions of dollars a year. Under federal law, banks and other financial institutions are required to report currency transactions that involve more than $10,000 or that are otherwise suspicious. Consequently, those who engage in illegal activities face difficulties in depositing their cash profits from illegal transactions.

As an alternative to simply storing cash from illegal transactions in a safe-deposit box, wrongdoers and racketeers have invented ways to launder "dirty" money to make it "clean." This **money laundering** is done through legitimate businesses. Suppose

money laundering
Falsely reporting income that has been obtained through criminal activity, such as illegal drug transactions, as income obtained through a legitimate business enterprise to make the "dirty" money "clean."

Matt, a successful drug dealer, becomes a partner with a restaurant owner. Little by little, the restaurant shows increasing revenue because Matt falsely reports income obtained through drug dealing as restaurant income. As a partner in the restaurant, Matt is able to report the "profit" as legitimate income on which he pays federal and state taxes. He can then spend that after-tax income without worrying that his lifestyle may exceed the level possible with his reported income.

The Racketeer Influenced and Corrupt Organizations Act (RICO)

To curb the entry of organized crime into the legitimate business world, Congress passed the Racketeer Influenced and Corrupt Organizations Act (RICO). The act makes it a federal crime to (1) use income obtained from racketeering activity to purchase any interest in an enterprise, (2) acquire or maintain an interest in an enterprise through racketeering activity, (3) conduct or participate in the affairs of an enterprise through racketeering activity, or (4) conspire to do any of the preceding activities. In practice, RICO is used more often to attack white-collar crime than organized crime.

Racketeering activity is not a new type of crime created by RICO. Rather, RICO incorporates by reference many federal crimes and state felonies and declares that a person who commits *two* of these offenses is guilty of "racketeering activity."

Any person found guilty of a violation is subject to a fine of up to $25,000 per violation, imprisonment for up to twenty years, or both. Additionally, the statute provides that those who violate RICO may be required to forfeit any assets, in the form of property or cash, that were acquired as a result of the alleged illegal activity or that were "involved in" or an "instrumentality of" the activity.

Cyber Crimes

cyber crime
A crime that occurs online, in the virtual community of the Internet, as opposed to the physical world.

Many crimes are committed in cyberspace. These crimes fall under the broad label of **cyber crime**. Most cyber crimes are not "new" crimes. Rather, they are existing crimes in which the Internet is the instrument of wrongdoing. The challenge for law enforcement is to apply traditional laws—which were designed to protect persons from physical harm or to safeguard their physical property—to new methods of committing crime.

Cyber Theft

In cyberspace, thieves are not subject to the physical limitations of the "real" world. A thief with Internet access could, in theory, steal data stored in a networked computer anywhere on earth.

Financial Crimes

Computer networks provide opportunities for employees to commit crimes that involve serious economic losses. For example, employees of a company's accounting department can transfer funds among accounts with little effort and often with less risk than is involved in paper transactions. Businesses' dependence on computer operations has left many companies vulnerable to sabotage, fraud, embezzlement, and the theft of proprietary data.

Identity Theft

identity theft
The theft of a form of identification, such as a name, date of birth, and Social Security number, which is then used to access the victim's financial resources.

A form of cyber theft that causes serious trouble is **identity theft**. It occurs when the wrongdoer steals identification information—such as name, date of birth, and Social Security number—and uses that to access the victim's financial resources or get credit in the victim's name. The Internet provides not only a way to steal personal information but also a way to use stolen items such as credit-card numbers while protected by anonymity.

Cyberstalking

California passed the first antistalking law in 1990, in response to the murders of six women by stalkers. The law made it a crime to harass or follow a person while making a "credible threat" that puts the person in reasonable fear for his or her safety or the safety of his or her immediate family. Most states and the federal government followed with similar antistalking legislation.

Later, it became clear that these laws, which required a "physical act" such as following the victim, were insufficient. They could not protect persons against **cyberstalking**, in which the perpetrator harasses the victim using the Internet, e-mail, Facebook, Twitter, or some other electronic communication. Federal and state laws now include threats made through electronic communication devices.

Hacking

A **hacker** who breaks into computers without authorization often does so to commit cyber theft. Sometimes, however, the principal aim of a hacker is to cause random data errors on others' computers or otherwise disrupt the target's business.

It is difficult to know how frequently hackers succeed in breaking into databases across the United States. The FBI reports that only a minority of security breaches are reported to a law enforcement agency. Admitting to a breach would be admitting to a certain degree of incompetence, which could damage reputations.

Prosecuting Cyber Crimes

The Internet has raised new issues in the investigation of crimes and the prosecution of offenders. As discussed in Chapter 6, the issue of jurisdiction presents difficulties in cyberspace. Identifying the wrongdoers can be very difficult. Cyber criminals do not leave physical traces, such as fingerprints, as evidence of their crimes. Electronic "footprints" can be hard to find and follow, and many are in foreign countries. Even when cyber criminals can be traced, uncertainty surrounding how the U.S. Constitution protects digital information presents a further obstacle to investigating, prosecuting, and defending cybercrimes.

A significant federal statute specifically addressing cyber crime is the Counterfeit Access Device and Computer Fraud and Abuse Act. It provides, among other things, that a person who accesses or attempts to access a computer online, without authority, to obtain classified, restricted, or protected data is subject to criminal prosecution. Such data could include financial and credit records, medical records, legal files, national security files, and other confidential information in government or private computers.

The crime has two elements: accessing a computer without authority and taking the data. This theft is a felony if it is committed for a commercial purpose or for private financial gain or if the value of the stolen data (or computer time) exceeds $5,000. Penalties include fines and imprisonment for up to twenty years. In addition, a victim of computer theft can bring a civil suit against the violator to obtain damages, an injunction, and other relief.

Social Media and Criminal Justice

Both law enforcement officers and criminals use social media tools, and paralegals working regularly in criminal law need to keep up with the latest developments. Some law enforcement social media are open only to police department employees. Other sites are open to anyone interested in keeping up with developments in social media and criminal law.

cyberstalking
The crime of stalking in cyberspace. The cyberstalker usually finds the victim through Internet chat rooms, newsgroups, bulletin boards, or e-mail and proceeds to harass that person or put the person in reasonable fear for his or her safety or the safety of his or her immediate family.

hacker
A person who uses one computer to break into another.

Uses of Social Media

Criminals use social media to seek out victims and to organize group criminal activity. Flash mobs have been organized via Twitter to create opportunities to "grab and snatch" items from stores. As a result, law enforcement officials are taking more interest in obtaining records from smartphones and social media sites as part of their investigations.

Law enforcement agencies are expanding their use of social media in solving crimes. For example, the FBI has created a popular YouTube channel featuring videos describing wanted criminals. The FBI's YouTube video on former mob boss and fugitive James "Whitey" Bulger was part of a social media campaign that ultimately led to the tip that Bulger was living in an apartment in California. Thanks to the tip, Bulger was captured after a twenty-year manhunt.

Similarly, police in Tacoma, Washington, used social media evidence to confirm that victims and suspects in a triple homicide knew each other. Utah police discovered photos on a convicted sex offender's social media account that showed forbidden contact with two youths. A Colorado detective created a photo lineup from social networking profile photos, helping victims to identify the suspects.

Protection of Social Media Information

Paralegals assisting in criminal defenses should determine whether their clients have a presence on social media sites and, if so, whether the information about them can be protected from police investigators. The law in this area is not settled. The courts consider the following factors, in addition to the usual requirements of relevance and reliability, in determining if evidence from social media sites deserves privacy protection:

1. Did a password or other form of privacy protection exist to protect the information?

2. Did the affected party have a reasonable expectation of privacy even if no password protection was used (e.g., was the material accessible to outsiders)?

3. Did the police have a reasonable suspicion or probable cause to investigate the social networking site, or were they simply engaged in a "fishing expedition"?

4. Is there a reason to believe the evidence is a reliable representation of what the person posted, or might it have been hacked?

Other Social Media Issues

Social media also impact the courtroom. A juror in a Pennsylvania criminal case posted updates on the case on Twitter and Facebook. In a Florida criminal case, several jurors used Google to look up definitions of terms and to learn about evidence excluded by the judge. That led to a mistrial. An alert paralegal watches the jury for signs of use of smartphones or tablets during trial and checks open jury-member sites on social media, because such activities can be highly prejudicial to either side.

Paralegals working in both criminal defense and criminal prosecution need to keep up to date on the latest developments in social media technology. Not only do they need this knowledge to do their own jobs, but it will also help them to anticipate what the other side in the case is going to do next.

Constitutional Safeguards

From the time a crime is reported until the trial concludes, law enforcement officers and prosecutors must follow specific procedures that protect an accused person's constitutional rights. Before allowing a case to go to trial, the prosecutor and paralegals assigned to the case review pretrial events closely to make sure that requirements have been properly observed. Defense attorneys and their paralegals investigate and review the actions of arresting and investigating police officers in an attempt to obtain grounds for a dismissal of the charges against their clients.

The Bill of Rights

The U.S. Constitution provides specific procedural safeguards to protect persons accused of crimes against potentially arbitrary or unjust use of government power. Safeguards are spelled out in the amendments to the U.S. Constitution and are summarized below. (The full text of the Constitution is presented in Appendix F.)

1. The Fourth Amendment prohibits unreasonable searches and seizures and requires a showing of probable cause (discussed shortly) before a search or an arrest warrant may be issued.

2. The Fifth Amendment requires that no one shall be deprived of "life, liberty, or property without due process of law." **Due process of law** means that the government must follow a set of reasonable, fair, and standard procedures (that is, criminal procedural law) in any action against a citizen.

3. The Fifth Amendment prohibits **double jeopardy** (trying someone twice for the same criminal offense).

4. The Fifth Amendment guarantees that no person shall be "compelled in any criminal case to be a witness against himself." This is known as the privilege against compulsory **self-incrimination**.

5. The Sixth Amendment guarantees a speedy and public trial, a trial by jury, the right to confront witnesses, and the right to a lawyer at various stages in some proceedings.

6. The Eighth Amendment prohibits excessive bail and fines, as well as cruel and unusual punishment.

The Exclusionary Rule

Under what is known as the **exclusionary rule**, evidence obtained in violation of the rights spelled out in the Fourth, Fifth, and Sixth Amendments normally is excluded from trial, along with evidence derived from the improperly obtained evidence. Evidence derived from illegally obtained evidence is known as the "fruit of the poisonous tree." For example, if drugs are discovered during an illegal search, the search is "the poisonous tree," and the drugs are the "fruit," which normally will be excluded from evidence if the case is brought to trial. As the *Developing Paralegal Skills* feature on the following page notes, rapid advances in the ability to detect evidence means that paralegals must keep on top of new technology to understand possible pitfalls.

The purpose of the exclusionary rule is to deter police from conducting warrantless searches and engaging in other misconduct. The rule is sometimes criticized because it can lead to injustice. Some defendants have "gotten off on a technicality" because law enforcement personnel failed to observe procedural requirements. Even though a defendant may be obviously guilty, if the evidence of that guilt was obtained improperly, it normally cannot be used against the defendant in court. Often, the outcome of a case is decided on the basis of whether evidence is excluded. This is common in prosecutions for possession of controlled substances.

due process of law
Fair, reasonable, and standard procedures that must be used by the government in any legal action against a citizen. The Fifth Amendment to the U.S. Constitution prohibits the deprivation of "life, liberty, or property without due process of law."

double jeopardy
To place at risk (jeopardize) a person's life or liberty twice for the same offense. The Fifth Amendment to the Constitution prohibits double jeopardy.

self-incrimination
The act of giving testimony that implicates oneself in criminal wrongdoing. The Fifth Amendment to the Constitution states that no person "shall be compelled in any criminal case to be a witness against himself."

exclusionary rule
In criminal procedure, a rule under which any evidence obtained in violation of the accused's constitutional rights, as well as any evidence derived from illegally obtained evidence, will not be admissible in court.

DEVELOPING PARALEGAL SKILLS

EVOLVING DISCOVERY TECHNOLOGY

Technology is revolutionizing criminal law practice by enhancing what police can discover when investigating crimes. Criminal prosecutions often involve evidence collected with the latest scientific techniques. Paralegals working in criminal law need to educate themselves on how these technologies work so they can prepare arguments for and against admissibility of high-tech evidence.

Technologies moving from science fiction to reality include the following:

- Facial recognition software facilitates identification of suspects outside of traditional police line-ups. It bases recognition on underlying bone structure, so cosmetic changes to hairstyles or beards will not fool it.

- Hand-held spectrometers allow investigators in the field to detect drug residues and other substances at levels invisible to the naked eye.

- Fluorescent dyes and special lights react to blood and can reveal even tiny droplets of blood that are otherwise invisible. Once blood-spatter data are collected, simulations can suggest the type of weapon used, how a wound was inflicted, and whether the assailant was left- or right-handed.

- Portable lasers allow crime scene investigators to locate tiny bits of evidence, such as a fragment from a strand of hair.

- 3-D scanning allows instant re-creation of crime scenes on laptops at the scene, giving police faster access to important information.

- Firearms databases allow police to distinguish bullets fired from different guns as accurately as they use fingerprints to distinguish individual people.

All of these technologies can help solve crimes, but they can also be misused by police or prosecutors. Paralegals on both sides of a case need to understand the technologies to effectively argue their relevance and admissibility in individual cases.

Miranda rights

Certain constitutional rights of accused persons taken into custody by law enforcement officials, such as the right to remain silent and the right to counsel, as established by the United States Supreme Court's decision in *Miranda v. Arizona*.

The *Miranda* Rule

In *Miranda v. Arizona*,[3] a case decided in 1966, the United States Supreme Court established the rule that individuals who are arrested must be informed of certain constitutional rights, including their Fifth Amendment right to remain silent and their Sixth Amendment right to counsel. These rights, called *Miranda* rights, are listed in Exhibit 13.3.

EXHIBIT 13.3

The *Miranda* Rights

> On taking a criminal suspect into custody and before any interrogation takes place, law enforcement officers are required to communicate the following rights and facts to the suspect:
>
> 1. **The right to remain silent.**
> 2. **That any statements made may be used against the person in a court of law.**
> 3. **The right to talk to a lawyer and to have a lawyer present while being questioned.**
> 4. **If the person cannot afford to hire a lawyer, the right to have a lawyer provided.**
>
> In addition to being advised of these rights, the suspect must be asked if he or she understands the rights and whether he or she wishes to exercise the rights or waive (not exercise) the rights.

Miranda rights come into play when a suspect is (1) placed in custody and (2) subjected to interrogation. If the arresting officers fail to inform a criminal suspect of these constitutional rights, any statements the suspect makes normally are not admissible in court. Note that police officers are not required to give *Miranda* warnings until the individual is placed in custody. Thus, if a person who is not in custody makes voluntary admissions to an officer, these statements are admissible. Additionally, the *Miranda* rule applies only to interrogation. A suspect in custody who makes spontaneous statements that are not in reaction to questioning or interrogation will not receive *Miranda* protection for those statements.

The exact meaning of the *Miranda* rule is subject to frequent tests in the courts. The Supreme Court has held that a confession need not be excluded even though the police failed to inform a suspect in custody that his attorney had tried to reach him by telephone. Furthermore, the Court has stated that a suspect's conviction will not be overturned solely on the ground that law enforcement personnel coerced the suspect into making a confession if other, legally obtained evidence admitted at trial is enough to justify the conviction without the confession.

A suspect in custody must unequivocally invoke the right to counsel or the privilege against self-incrimination to cut off interrogation. Law enforcement officers are bound to honor this request by immediately ceasing all questioning. Note, however, that the request must be made clearly. For example, the United States Supreme Court found that a suspect did not properly invoke his right to counsel under *Miranda* when he said "lawyer, dog" in response to custodial interrogation.

Criminal Procedures Prior to Prosecution

Although the Constitution guarantees due process of law to persons accused of committing crimes, the steps in bringing a criminal action vary across jurisdictions and type of crime. In this section, we provide an overview of the basic procedures that take place before an individual is prosecuted for a crime. Exhibit 13.4 illustrates a general outline of criminal procedure in both federal and state cases. Because of the procedural variations, however, a paralegal involved in a criminal case must learn the specific requirements that apply to the case.

Arrest and Booking

An **arrest** occurs when the police take a person into custody and charge that person with a crime. (Often the interaction with the police is captured on video.) After the arrest and a search, the police typically take the suspect to a *holding facility* (usually at the police station or a jail), where booking occurs. **Booking** is the process of entering a suspect's name, the offense for which the suspect is being held, and the time of arrival into the police log (or blotter). The suspect is fingerprinted and photographed, told the reason for the arrest, and allowed to make a phone call. The questions asked during the booking process are not subject to the *Miranda* rule.

If the crime is not serious, the officer may then release the suspect on personal recognizance—that is, on the suspect's promise to appear before a court at a later date. Otherwise, the suspect may be held in custody pending an initial appearance in court (usually within a few days).

Law enforcement personnel are in control of the arrest and booking of suspects. Paralegals and attorneys usually are not involved until after an arrest has been made. The defense will, however, look closely to see that the proper procedure was followed in the arrest of the client. Often, an officer can legally arrest a person with or without a warrant if the officer has probable cause to believe that the person committed a crime

arrest
To take into custody a person suspected of criminal activity.

booking
The process of entering a suspect's name, offense, and arrival time into the police log (blotter) following his or her arrest.

EXHIBIT 13.4

Major Procedural Steps
in a Criminal Case

ARREST

Police officer takes suspect into custody Most arrests are made without a warrant. After the arrest, the officer searches the suspect, who is then taken to the police station.

↓

BOOKING

At the police station, the suspect is searched again, photographed, fingerprinted, and allowed at least one telephone call. After the booking, charges are reviewed, and if they are not dropped, a complaint is filed and a magistrate reviews the case for probable cause.

↓

INITIAL APPEARANCE

The suspect appears before the magistrate, who informs the suspect of the charges and of his or her rights. If the suspect requires a lawyer, one is appointed. The magistrate sets bail (conditions under which a suspect can obtain release pending disposition of the case).

GRAND JURY	**PRELIMINARY HEARING**
A grand jury determines if there is probable cause to believe that the defendant committed the crime. The federal government and about half of the states require grand jury indictments for at least some felonies.	In a court proceeding, a prosecutor presents evidence, and the judge determines if there is probable cause to hold the defendant over for trial

↓ ↔ ↓

INDICTMENT	**INFORMATION**
The grand jury formally charges a criminal suspect by issuing an indictment.	The prosecutor formally charges a criminal suspect by filing an information, or criminal complaint.

↓

ARRAIGNMENT

The suspect is brought before the trial court, informed of the charges, and asked to enter a plea.

↓

PLEA BARGAIN

The prosecutor may offer a plea bargain. A plea bargain is a prosecutor's promise to make concessions (or promise to seek concessions) in return for a suspect's guilty plea. Concessions may include a reduced charge or a lesser sentence.

↓

GUILTY PLEA	**TRIAL**
In most jurisdictions, most cases that reach the arraignment stage do not go to trial but are resolved by a guilty plea, often as a result of a plea bargain. The judge sets the case for sentencing.	Generally, most felony trials are jury trials, and most misdemeanor trials are bench trials (trials before judges). If the verdict is "guilty" the judge sets the case for sentencing. Everyone convicted of a crime has the right to an appeal.

(discussed shortly). Most states have statutes detailing when and how an arrest can be made with or without a warrant. Before an officer questions a suspect who has been arrested, the officer must give the *Miranda* warning.

Detention Is Not an Arrest

An arrest differs from a *stop* or *detention*, such as a traffic stop. Police officers have a right to stop and detain a person if they have a *reasonable suspicion* that the person committed, or is about to commit, a crime. Reasonable suspicion is a lower standard than probable cause—because a stop is much less invasive than an arrest. It means, for example, that based on reasonable suspicion an officer can stop a person who seems to match the description of an assailant in the neighborhood. The officer can even "frisk" the person being detained (pat down the person's clothes) to make sure the person is not carrying a weapon, but only if there is reason to believe that the suspect is armed and dangerous. There can be no arrest, however, without probable cause.

Probable Cause

The requirement of **probable cause** is a key factor that is assessed repeatedly throughout the stages of criminal proceedings. The first stage, arrest, requires probable cause. In an arrest, probable cause exists if there is a substantial likelihood that a crime was committed and that the suspect committed the crime. Probable cause involves a *likelihood*—not just a possibility—that the suspect committed the crime. The probable cause requirement comes from the Fourth Amendment, which prohibits unreasonable searches and seizures.

Typically, a search or seizure is considered unreasonable, and therefore unconstitutional under the Fourth Amendment, if it occurs before a warrant is acquired. Warrantless arrests, however, are one of many exceptions to this rule if the officer saw the crime committed, prevented the crime from being committed, or has probable cause to believe that the suspect committed a felony, even if the officer did *not* observe the felony.

If a crime is reported to the police, the police must decide whether there is enough information about the alleged wrongdoer's likely guilt to establish probable cause to arrest. What is considered probable cause varies across jurisdictions. Usually, if the suspect is at home at the time of the arrest, the police need to obtain an arrest warrant unless the police chased the suspect into the home or some other emergency circumstance exists.

Warrants

Often, the police try to gather information to help them determine whether a suspect should be arrested. If, after investigating the matter, the police decide to arrest the suspect, they must obtain an **arrest warrant**, which is typically issued by a judge. To obtain the warrant, the police must convince the official, usually through supporting affidavits, that probable cause exists. The warrant process is discussed further in the *Developing Paralegal Skills* feature on the following page.

Search Warrants.   Probable cause is also required to obtain a **search warrant**. A search warrant authorizes police officers or other investigators to search specifically named persons or property for evidence and to seize evidence if they find it. Probable cause requires law enforcement officials to have trustworthy evidence that would convince a reasonable person that the proposed search or seizure is more likely justified than not. The Fourth Amendment prohibits general warrants. It requires a description of what will be searched or seized. The search cannot extend beyond what is described in the warrant.

probable cause
Reasonable grounds to believe the existence of facts warranting certain actions, such as the search or arrest of a person.

arrest warrant
A written order, based on probable cause and typically issued by a judge, commanding that the person named on the warrant be arrested by the police.

search warrant
A written order based on probable cause and issued by a judge or public official (magistrate) commanding that police officers or criminal investigators search a specific person, place, or property to obtain evidence.

DEVELOPING PARALEGAL SKILLS

THE PROSECUTOR'S OFFICE—WARRANT DIVISION

Kathy Perello works as a paralegal in the warrant division of the county prosecutor's office. Officer McCarthy gives her the paperwork from the prosecutor that authorizes the arrest of a burglary suspect and requests that Kathy prepare an arrest warrant. Officer McCarthy will take the warrant to the court, swear to the truth of its contents, and ask the judge to sign the warrant so that he can make the arrest.

Checklist for Preparing a Warrant

- Obtain written authorization from a prosecutor before initiating the warrant procedure.

- Obtain a copy of the suspect's criminal history.

- Prepare the warrant.

- Verify that the police record matches that of the suspect.

- Make sure that the crime and the suspect are both specifically described.

- Review the typed warrant to ensure that it includes any other required terms.

- Call the officer to pick up the warrant and take it to a judge for a determination of probable cause.

When a Warrant Is Not Needed. There are exceptions to the requirement for a search warrant. For example, if an officer is arresting a person (with either an arrest warrant or sufficient probable cause) and sees drug paraphernalia "in plain view," no warrant is required to seize that evidence. Exceptions also exist when it is likely that the items sought will be removed or destroyed before a warrant can be obtained or when an officer is in pursuit of a suspect.

Investigation after the Arrest

The police often must find and interview witnesses and conduct searches (of the suspect's home or car, for example) to collect evidence. Witnesses may view the suspect in a *lineup*, in which the suspect appears with a group of several others. In more serious cases, detectives may take charge of the investigation.

As the police review the evidence, they may conclude that there is not enough evidence to justify recommending the case for prosecution. If so, the suspect is released, and no charges are filed. The police can still recommend prosecution later if more evidence is obtained. Or the police may decide to change the offense with which the suspect is being charged. The police may also decide to release the suspect with a warning or a referral to a social-service agency. Unless the suspect is released at this point in the criminal process, control over the case usually moves from the police to the public prosecutor.

The Prosecution Begins

Prosecution of a criminal case begins when the police inform the public prosecutor of the alleged crime, provide the reports written by the arresting and investigating officers, and turn over their evidence. The prosecutor may investigate the case further by interviewing the suspect, the officers, and witnesses, and by gathering other evidence. The prosecutor's paralegals often participate in these tasks. Based on a review of the police file or an investigation, the prosecutor decides whether to take the case to trial or to drop the case and allow the suspect to be released. Major reasons for releasing the suspect include insufficient evidence and unreliable witnesses.

Prosecutorial Discretion

Prosecutors have broad discretion. If they decide to pursue a case, they decide what charges to file. Because prosecutions are expensive and resources are limited, most prosecutors do not go forward with a case unless they are confident that they can prove the case in court. Typically, a prosecutor who decides to file a case alleges as many criminal offenses as the facts appear to support. If the defendant is facing numerous charges, the likelihood is greater that the prosecutor will get a conviction on at least one. The chances are also greater that the defendant will plead guilty to one or more of the offenses in exchange for having other charges dropped.

If the decision is made to prosecute, the prosecutor must initiate the procedures necessary to formally charge the person before the court. Procedures vary depending on the jurisdiction and the type of case. Often, misdemeanor charges are handled differently than felony charges. Some prosecutors may file complaints involving misdemeanor charges. A grand jury indictment (discussed shortly) is used for felony charges in some jurisdictions, but in most cases, a grand jury is not used. Instead, the prosecutor files an information. The way a criminal case is initiated is one area of criminal procedure that varies substantially among the states. Keep this in mind as you read the following subsections.

Complaint and Initial Appearance

The criminal litigation process may begin with the filing of a *complaint* (see Exhibit 13.5). The complaint includes a statement of the charges that are being brought against the suspect, who now becomes a criminal defendant. Because the defendant is in the court system, prosecutors must show that they have legal grounds to proceed. They must show probable cause that the defendant committed a crime.

Initial Appearance

In most jurisdictions, defendants are taken before a judge or magistrate soon after arrest. During this *initial appearance*, the judge makes sure that the person appearing is the person named in the complaint, informs the defendant of the charges made in the complaint, and advises the defendant of the right to counsel and the right to remain silent. If a defendant cannot afford to hire an attorney, a public defender or member of the private bar may be appointed to represent the defendant (the defendant may be asked to fill out an application for appointed counsel).

Bail

The judge must decide whether to set bail or release the defendant until the next court date. **Bail** is an amount paid by the defendant to the court as insurance that the defendant will show up for future court appearances. If the defendant shows up as promised, the court returns the funds. Courts often use standard bail schedules, which set the bail for specific kinds of cases, and may deny bail for more serious crimes. The Eighth Amendment prohibits "excessive bail," and a defendant can request a hearing to seek a reduction in bail.

If the court sets bail in an amount that the defendant is unable to pay, the defendant (or the defendant's attorney or paralegal) can arrange with a *bail bondsperson* to post a bail bond on the defendant's behalf. The bail bondsperson promises to pay the bail amount to the court if the defendant fails to return for further proceedings. In return, the bail bondsperson receives a payment from the defendant, usually 10 percent of the bail amount.

bail
The amount of money or conditions set by the court to ensure that an individual accused of a crime will appear for further criminal proceedings. If the accused person provides bail, whether in cash or by means of a bail bond, the person is released from jail.

EXHIBIT 13.5

A Sample of a Complaint

AO 91 (Rev. 11/11)   Criminal Complaint

UNITED STATES DISTRICT COURT
for the

United States of America)
v.)
)   Case No.
)
)
)
_____)

Defendant(s)

CRIMINAL COMPLAINT

       I, the complainant in this case, state that the following is true to the best of my knowledge and belief.

On or about the date(s) of _____ in the county of _____ in the

_____ District of _____ , the defendant(s) violated:

          Code Section   *Offense Description*

      This criminal complaint is based on these facts:

     ❒ Continued on the attached sheet.

_____

Complainant's Signature

_____

Printed Name and Title

Sworn to before me and signed in my presence.

Date: _____

_____

Judge's Signature

City and State: _____

_____

Printed Name and Title

Preliminary Hearing

The defendant again appears before a magistrate or judge at a **preliminary hearing**. During this hearing, the judge determines whether the evidence presented is sufficient to establish probable cause to believe that the defendant committed the crime as charged. This may be the first adversarial proceeding in which both sides are represented by counsel. Paralegals may become involved in the process at this point by assisting in preparation for the hearing.

The prosecutor may present witnesses, who may be cross-examined by defense counsel (the defense rarely presents its witnesses prior to trial). A defendant who intends to plead guilty usually waives the right to a preliminary hearing to help move things along more quickly. In many jurisdictions, however, the preliminary hearing is required in certain felony cases.

If the judge or magistrate finds the evidence insufficient to establish probable cause, either the charge is reduced to a lesser one or charges are dropped and the defendant is released. If the magistrate believes there is sufficient evidence to establish probable cause, the prosecutor issues an information. The **information** (which may also be called an accusation or complaint) is the formal charge against the defendant and binds over the defendant for further proceedings. Usually, the defendant is arraigned and the case proceeds to trial.

preliminary hearing
An initial hearing in which a judge or magistrate decides whether there is probable cause to believe that the defendant committed the crime with which he or she is charged.

information
A formal criminal charge made by a prosecutor without a grand jury indictment.

Grand Jury Review

In many felony cases, the federal government and about half of the states use a grand jury—not a prosecutor—to make the decision as to whether a case should go to trial. In other words, a grand jury's indictment is an alternative to a prosecutor's information to initiate the criminal litigation process.

A **grand jury** is a group of citizens called to decide whether there is probable cause to believe that the defendant committed the crime charged and therefore should go to trial. Even in cases in which grand jury review is not used and an information is submitted, the prosecutor may call a grand jury to evaluate the evidence against a suspect, which will indicate to the prosecutor the relative strength or weakness of the case.

grand jury
A group of citizens called to decide whether probable cause exists to believe that a suspect committed the crime with which he or she has been charged and thus should stand trial.

At a preliminary hearing, a judge or a magistrate evaluates the evidence against the defendant. If the evidence is sufficient to establish probable cause (reasonable grounds to believe that the defendant committed the crime with which he or she is charged), the prosecutor issues an information, and the defendant is bound over for further proceedings. Paralegals often assist either the defendant or the prosecutor in preparing for preliminary hearings. What might be some of the duties of a paralegal?

wavebreakmedia/Shutterstock.com

The grand jury sits in closed session and hears only evidence presented by the prosecutor—the defendant cannot present evidence at this hearing. Normally, the defendant and the defendant's attorney are not allowed to attend grand jury proceedings, although in some cases the prosecutor calls the defendant as a witness. The prosecutor presents to the grand jury the evidence the state has against the defendant, including photographs, documents, tangible items, test results, and the testimony of witnesses.

If the grand jury finds that probable cause exists, it issues an **indictment** against the defendant called a *true bill*. An overwhelming majority of the cases that prosecutors bring to grand juries result in an indictment. The indictment (or information, if that is used instead) is filed with the trial court and becomes the formal charge against the defendant. An example of an indictment is shown in Exhibit 13.6.

Arraignment

At the **arraignment**, the defendant is informed of the charges and must respond to the charges by entering a plea: guilty, not guilty, or **nolo contendere**, which is Latin for "I will not contest it" and is often called a no-contest plea. A plea of no contest is neither an admission of guilt nor a denial of guilt, but it operates like a guilty plea in that the defendant is convicted.

The primary reason for pleading no contest is so that the plea cannot later be used against the defendant in a civil trial. For example, if a defendant pleads guilty to assault, the admission of guilt can be used to impose civil liability, whereas with a no-contest plea, the plaintiff in the civil suit must prove that the defendant committed the assault. No-contest pleas are thus useful for the defendant who could be sued in a civil action for damages caused to a person or property.

At the arraignment, the defendant can move to have the charges dismissed, which happens in a fair number of cases. The defendant may claim, for example, that the case should be dismissed because the statute of limitations for the crime in question has

---

indictment
A charge or written accusation, issued by a grand jury, that probable cause exists to believe that a person has committed a crime for which he or she should stand trial.

arraignment
A court proceeding in which the suspect is formally charged with the criminal offense stated in the indictment. The suspect then enters a plea (guilty, not guilty, or *nolo contendere*) in response.

nolo contendere
Latin for "I will not contest it." A criminal defendant's plea in which he or she chooses not to challenge, or contest, the charges brought by the government. Although the defendant will still be convicted and sentenced, the plea neither admits nor denies guilt.

EXHIBIT 13.6
A Sample of an Indictment

[Title of Court and Cause]

The Grand Jury charges that:

On or about _____ , 20__ , at _____ , _____ , in the _____ District of _____ , _____ , having been convicted of knowingly acquiring and possessing a SNAP/Food Stamp EBT card in a manner not authorized by the provisions of Chapter 51, Title 7, United States Code, and the regulations issued pursuant to said chapter, a felony conviction, in the federal district court for the _____ District of _____ , and sentenced on _____ , 20__ , did knowingly possess a firearm that had been transported in and affecting commerce, to wit: an OMC Pistol, Back Up 380 Caliber, serial number _____ ; all in violation of Section 1202(a)(1) of Title 18, United States Code, Appendix.

A True Bill

_____ ,
Foreperson.

_____ ,
United States Attorney.

lapsed. Most frequently, the defendant pleads guilty to the charge or to a lesser charge that has been agreed on through **plea bargaining** between the prosecutor and the defendant. If the defendant pleads guilty, no trial is necessary, and either the defendant is sentenced based on the plea or a separate sentencing hearing is scheduled. If the defendant pleads not guilty, the case is set for trial.

Pretrial Motions

Defense attorneys and their paralegals search for and are alert to any violation of the defendant's rights. Many pretrial motions are based on possible violations of the defendant's rights as provided by the Constitution and criminal procedural law. We discuss here a few of the most common motions filed in a criminal case.

The specific requirements for pretrial motions vary by jurisdiction. Not every jurisdiction allows every type of pretrial motion, and the standards used by judges to evaluate motions may differ as well. A motion is generally accompanied by a pleading that sets forth the legal argument in support of the motion. A memorandum of law, a brief, affidavits, or supporting points and authorities may be filed to support a pleading.

Motions to Suppress

One of the most common motions made by defense attorneys is the **motion to suppress evidence**. A motion to suppress asserts that the evidence against the defendant was illegally obtained and should be excluded (inadmissible). Typically, this motion is filed when an officer performs a search without probable cause, seizes evidence, and then arrests the defendant based on that evidence.

Suppose an officer stops the defendant's vehicle because his taillight is out and then searches the defendant's trunk, finding illegal narcotics. The defendant is charged with possession. A motion to suppress would be appropriate here (and probably successful) because the officer did not have probable cause to search the trunk when carrying out the traffic stop.

The defense attorney normally prepares the motion and submits a brief in support of the motion. (These motions and memoranda may be drafted by paralegals.) Exhibit 13.7 shows a sample memorandum. Often, the attorney requests the court to allow oral argument on the motion, although in some jurisdictions it is automatic. If the court conducts a hearing on the motion, the attorneys for both sides may call witnesses (police officers and others who were present) to testify, and the judge makes a ruling. If the judge grants the motion to exclude evidence, the prosecution may not be able to prove its case against the defendant and may drop the charges.

Motions to Dismiss

A motion can be filed to dismiss charges pending against the defendant. Motions to dismiss in criminal cases often assert that the defendant's constitutional rights—or required criminal procedures—have been violated. The defense might argue that the prosecution waited too long to prosecute the case in violation of the Sixth Amendment right to a speedy and public trial (sometimes called a *speedy trial motion*). The defense files the motion with a supporting memorandum, which may argue that the defendant has been prejudiced by the delay, that witnesses are no longer available, and that a fair trial cannot be had. If the judge agrees, the case is dismissed.

Because it may eliminate charges against a client without subjecting the client to the risks of a jury trial, the motion to dismiss is one of the most useful motions for the defense to file. A paralegal who becomes skilled at writing persuasive motions to dismiss will be a valuable asset to the defense team.

plea bargaining
The process by which the accused and the prosecutor in a criminal case work out a mutually satisfactory disposition of the case, subject to court approval. Usually, plea bargaining involves the defendant's pleading guilty to a lesser offense in return for a lighter sentence.

motion to suppress evidence
A motion requesting that certain evidence be excluded from consideration during the trial.

EXHIBIT 13.7

A Sample of a Memorandum in Support of a Motion to Suppress

[Attorney for Defendant]

SUPERIOR COURT OF THE STATE OF NITA
FOR THE COUNTY OF NITA

THE PEOPLE OF THE STATE OF NITA,	)	Case No.: C45778
Plaintiff,	)	D.A. No.: A39996
	)	
v.	)	**MEMORANDUM OF LAW IN SUPPORT**
	)	**OF MOTION TO SUPPRESS**
	)	
	)	DATE: 10-27-22
Eduardo Jose Mendez,	)	TIME: 1:15
Defendant.	)	Estimated Time: 45 min.
	)	No. of Witnesses: 1

Defendant, Eduardo Jose Mendez, by and through his attorney the Public Defender of the County of Nita, respectfully submits the following memorandum of law in support of his motion to Suppress.

STATEMENT OF FACTS

On or about September 23, 2022, at approximately 02:15, Officer Ramirez observed Mr. Mendez riding his bicycle in the area of 1300 Elm St. and 500 C St. It was drizzling, and few people walked the streets. Officer Ramirez indicated that the area is known for narcotic activity and that he believed Mr. Mendez had been participating or was about to participate in narcotic activity.

Mr. Mendez was on his bicycle at the corner of Elm and C St. when Officer Ramirez approached him. He indicated that Mr. Mendez appeared to be nervous and was sweating profusely. He asked Mr. Mendez what he was doing, and Mr. Mendez responded that he was waiting for his girlfriend. Officer Ramirez conducted a pat-down search for weapons. He felt several hard objects inside Mr. Mendez's pants pockets and asked Mr. Mendez if he had a knife in his pocket. Mr. Mendez consented to a search of his pockets, and Officer Ramirez found only a wooden pencil.

Without asking for permission, and without notice, Officer Ramirez reached for and grabbed Mr. Mendez's baseball cap. The officer took the cap off of Mr. Mendez's head. He felt the outside of the cap and with his fingers manipulated a small soft lump in Mr. Mendez's cap. He went through the cap and moved the side material of the cap. He found a small plastic package burnt on one end. He opened the package. Officer Ramirez found a small amount of an off-white powder substance inside the package.

ARGUMENT

I. MR. MENDEZ'S FOURTH AMENDMENT RIGHT TO PRIVACY WAS VIOLATED BECAUSE THE OFFICER'S DETENTION OF MR. MENDEZ WAS NOT JUSTIFIED BY REASONABLE SUSPICION

A person has been seized within the meaning of the Fourth Amendment if, in view of all the circumstances surrounding the incident, a reasonable person would have believed that he was not free to leave. *United States v. Mendenhall,* 446 U.S. 544, 554 (1980). Here, Officer Ramirez seized Mr. Mendez when he stopped to question him. Mr. Mendez submitted to Officer Ramirez's show of authority when he responded to the questioning. Mr. Mendez's belief that he was not free to leave is evidenced by his actions during the seizure. He appeared nervous and kept looking around in all directions as if looking for someone to help him. A reasonable person such as Mr. Mendez, in view of all of the circumstances, would have believed and in fact did believe he was not free to leave. Therefore, the officer's initial stop was a seizure.

* * * *

EXHIBIT 13.7

A Sample of a Memorandum in Support of a Motion to Suppress —Continued

Officer Ramirez did not have reasonable suspicion to stop Mr. Mendez. He fails to point to specific facts causing him to suspect criminal activity was afoot. Officer Ramirez notes in his police report that he "felt" that defendant "had been participating or was about to participate in narcotic activity." The officer also indicated that he believed the area was known for narcotic activity. However, "Persons may not be subjected to invasions of privacy merely because they are in or are passing through a high-crime area." *McCally-Bey v. Kirner,* 24 F.Supp.3d 389 (N.D. Nita 2002).

These observations taken as a whole and Officer Ramirez's explanation do not rise to the requisite level of reasonable suspicion necessary to invade the privacy of a citizen.

II. OFFICER RAMIREZ'S PAT-DOWN SEARCH EXCEEDED ITS SCOPE WHEN HE SEARCHED THE BASEBALL CAP AND MANIPULATED ITS CONTENTS

Under the *Terry* doctrine, a search is referred to as a "frisk." *Terry v. Ohio,* 392 U.S. 1 (1968). A *frisk* is justified only if the officer reasonably believes that the person is armed and dangerous. A frisk is a pat-down of a person's outer clothing. It is limited in scope to its purpose, which is to search for weapons. Even slightly lingering over a package because it feels like it contains drugs exceeds the scope of the search. *Minnesota v. Dickerson,* 508 U.S. 366 (1993). An officer cannot manipulate a package or a substance that is clearly not a weapon through an individual's clothing during a *Terry* pat-down search.

* * * *

III. OFFICER RAMIREZ DID NOT HAVE PROBABLE CAUSE TO CONDUCT A WARRANTLESS SEARCH OF MR. MENDEZ

* * * *

IV. ALL EVIDENCE OBTAINED AS A RESULT OF AN UNLAWFUL DETENTION MUST BE SUPPRESSED AS TAINTED EVIDENCE; FRUIT OF THE POISONOUS TREE

* * * *

* * * *

As discussed above, the detention of Mr. Mendez did not meet constitutionally established standards of reasonableness. Hence, all evidence obtained as a result of such unlawful detention is inadmissible. In addition, all evidence seized as a result of the arrest that followed from his unlawful detention is inadmissible as fruit of the poisonous tree.

* * * *

For the above-mentioned reasons, all evidence obtained as a result of Mr. Mendez's detention, illegal search, and subsequent arrest in this case must be suppressed.

Dated:

Respectfully Submitted,

_____

Attorney for Defendant

Other Common Motions

Just as in civil cases, attorneys in criminal cases may file motions *in limine* (discussed in Chapter 12) to keep certain evidence out of the trial. A defense attorney whose client has prior criminal convictions may file a motion *in limine* requesting the court to prevent any evidence of these convictions from being offered by the prosecution. The prosecutor may also file such motions to keep possibly prejudicial evidence from being admitted (such as evidence concerning a victim's reputation).

In some circumstances, defense attorneys may file the following motions:

motion for a change of venue
A motion requesting that a trial be moved to a different location to ensure a fair and impartial proceeding, for the convenience of the parties, or for some other acceptable reason.

- When there is a good deal of pretrial publicity, the defense may make a **motion for a change of venue**, asking the court to relocate the trial.

- When the judge has publicly displayed bias or personally knows a party or witnesses in a case, the defense may file a **motion to recuse**, asking the trial judge to remove himself from the case. If the motion is granted, a different judge will hear the case.

motion to recuse
A motion to remove a particular judge from a case.

- When a case involves more than one defendant, the defense counsel may file a **motion to sever** (separate) the cases for purposes of trial.

motion to sever
A motion to try multiple defendants separately.

Various other motions—including motions to reduce the charges against the defendant, to obtain evidence during discovery, or to extend the trial date—may also be made prior to the trial. As with motions made during the civil litigation process, each motion must be accompanied by supporting affidavits and/or legal memoranda.

Discovery

In preparing for trial, public prosecutors, defense attorneys, and paralegals engage in discovery (including depositions and interrogatories), interview and subpoena witnesses, prepare exhibits and a trial notebook, examine documents and evidence, and do other tasks necessary to effectively prosecute or defend the defendant. Although similar to civil litigation in these respects, criminal discovery is generally more limited, and the time constraints are different. The *Developing Paralegal Skills* feature below gives some useful tips for discovery in criminal cases.

During discovery, defendants generally are entitled to obtain certain evidence defined by statute that is in the possession of the prosecutor, often including statements previously made by the defendant, objects, documents, and reports of tests and examinations. The prosecutor *must* hand over evidence that tends to show the defendant's innocence. Some rules governing discovery come from court cases, others from state laws, and still more from arrangements between local prosecutors' offices, courts, and defense attorneys, sometimes including public defenders' offices.

DEVELOPING PARALEGAL SKILLS

DISCOVERY IN THE CRIMINAL CASE

A law firm is defending Taylor Rogers in an attempted murder case. He allegedly shot a person in a drive-by shooting.

Lee Soloman, a paralegal, is working on the case. Today, as the result of a successful discovery motion his supervising attorney received from the court, Lee has obtained copies of all evidence that the prosecuting attorney has in his file.

Lee's job is to create the discovery file and then work with the material in the file to prepare the case.

Tips for Criminal Discovery

- Create a discovery file containing sections for the defendant's statements, witnesses' statements, police reports, tests, and other evidence.
- Review the evidence and prepare a memo summarizing it.
- Review the memo and/or evidence with your supervising attorney.
- If the supervising attorney agrees, contact witnesses and obtain statements.
- Interview police officers who were involved in the arrest or who were at the crime scene.

Some state statutes allow the prosecutor access to materials that the defense intends to introduce as evidence in the trial. In some jurisdictions, when the defense attorney requests discovery of case materials from the prosecutor, the defense is required to disclose similar materials to the prosecutor in return. In the absence of such statutes, courts have generally refused discovery to the prosecution. This judicial restraint is intended to protect the defendant from self-incrimination, as guaranteed by the Fifth Amendment to the U.S. Constitution (see Appendix F).

The Trial

Only a small fraction of the criminal cases brought by the state go to trial. Some defendants are released without charges, or the charges against them are dropped. Most defendants plead guilty to the offense or to a lesser offense prior to trial. Plea bargaining often occurs in criminal proceedings, from the arraignment to the date of trial or even during a trial. Because a trial is expensive and the outcome is uncertain, both sides have an incentive to negotiate a plea.

Although some criminal trials go on for weeks and are highly publicized, most criminal trials last less than one week (often only a few days). In the case of a misdemeanor, a trial may last less than one hour. The trial is conducted in much the same way as a civil trial. The prosecutor and the defense attorney make opening statements, examine and cross-examine witnesses, and summarize positions in closing arguments. Graphics may be used for illustration (see the *Developing Paralegal Skills* feature below, as well as this chapter's *Ethics Watch* feature below). Following closing arguments, the jury is instructed

DEVELOPING PARALEGAL SKILLS

PREPARING GRAPHIC PRESENTATIONS

Melanie Hofstadter, a paralegal who is about to retire from her job, is training her replacement. Melanie works for a law firm that specializes in criminal law and has assisted the attorneys many times with trial preparations. Now she is instructing the new paralegal, Keera Mason, on how to prepare graphic presentations for the attorneys' courtroom use.

Melanie explains that trial graphics are classified into three main types: fact graphics, concept graphics, and case graphics.

1. Fact graphics show only the facts on which both parties agree—for example, a timeline indicating the order in which events occurred.
2. Concept graphics are used to educate the judge and jury about ideas with which they may not be familiar, such as the general procedures involved in DNA fingerprinting.
3. Case graphics, or analytical graphics, illustrate the basis of the defense or allegation; for example, a flowchart could be used to show how certain facts are related and how they lead to a specific conclusion.

Melanie gives Keera a list of tips and suggestions that Keera should keep in mind when preparing trial graphics.

Tips for Preparing a Graphic Presentation

- Remember that less can be more. A good graphic presentation should be simple and straightforward. Trim excess words and punctuation from charts, lists, and diagrams; using incomplete sentences and simple phrases is acceptable in graphic presentations.

- Use boldfaced text and easy-to-read fonts.

- Keep plenty of "white space" in the graphic displays.

- Know what you want the reader to focus on, and eliminate all distractions.

- Remember that it is your job to make it easy for the jury to see, read, and understand your points. Don't overburden the graphic displays with too much information or detail.

- Keep in mind that the main purpose of trial graphics is to focus attention on the points that you want to emphasize or highlight, not to focus attention on the actual presentation or display.

ETHICS WATCH

THE IMPORTANCE OF ACCURACY

In preparing exhibits for trial, especially when creating an exhibit from raw data, it is important that the paralegal ensure that the exhibit is accurate and not misleading. If erroneous evidence is introduced in court and challenged by opposing counsel, the paralegal's supervising attorney may face serious consequences.

By preparing an inaccurate exhibit (for example, by miscalculating a column of figures), the paralegal may jeopardize the attorney's professional reputation by causing the attorney to breach a professional duty.

This paralegal responsibility comes from the following codes:

- NALA's *Code of Ethics*, Canon 10:

  "A paralegal's conduct is guided by bar associations' codes of professional responsibility and rules of professional conduct."

- The NFPA *Model Code of Ethics and Professional Responsibility*, Section EC-1.3:

  "A paralegal shall maintain a high standard of professional conduct."

Reprinted by permission of the National Federation of Paralegal Associations, Inc. (NFPA®), www.paralegals.org; Copyright 1975; Adopted 1975; Revised 1979, 1988, 1995, 2007. Reprinted with permission of NALA, The Paralegal Association. Inquiries should be directed to NALA, 1516 S. Boston, #200, Tulsa, OK 74119, www.nala.org.

and sent to deliberate. When the jury renders a verdict, the trial comes to an end. In spite of the similarities, there are major procedural differences between criminal trials and civil trials, as discussed next.

The Presumption of Innocence

In criminal trials, the defendant is innocent until proved guilty. The prosecutor bears the burden of proving the defendant guilty as charged. Defendants do not have to prove their innocence. In fact, they are not required to present any evidence to counter the state's accusations (although it is usually in their best interests to do so). Even a defendant who actually committed the crime is innocent at law unless the prosecutor presents sufficient evidence to convince the jury or judge of guilt.

Not only does the state bear the burden of proving the defendant guilty, but it also is held to a high standard of proof. The prosecution must prove its case *beyond a reasonable doubt*. It is not enough for the jury (or judge) to think that the defendant is probably guilty. The members of the jury must be firmly convinced of guilt. The jurors receive instructions such as "If you think there is a real possibility that he is not guilty, you *must* give him the benefit of the doubt and find him not guilty."

The Privilege against Self-Incrimination

The Fifth Amendment to the Constitution states that no person can be forced to give testimony that might be self-incriminating. Therefore, a defendant does not have to testify at trial. Witnesses may also refuse to testify on this ground. For example, suppose a witness is asked a question on the stand which, if answered, would reveal her own criminal wrongdoing. The witness may "take the Fifth" and refuse to testify on the ground that the testimony may incriminate her. The privilege against self-incrimination does not prevent defendants from being required to provide physical samples (such as blood); submit to fingerprinting, photography, or measurements; write or speak for identification purposes; appear in court; or make a gesture or assume a particular position.

The Right to a Speedy Trial

The Sixth Amendment requires a speedy and public trial for criminal prosecutions but does not specify what is meant by "speedy." The federal Speedy Trial Act (18 U.S.C. § 3161-3174) sets time limits. Federal Rule of Criminal Procedure 48 also gives courts discretion to dismiss cases not brought to trial promptly. Most states have similar statutes and rules.

Generally, criminal cases are brought to trial much more quickly than civil cases. A defendant who remains in custody prior to trial, for example, may be tried within thirty to forty-five days from the date of arraignment. If the defendant (or the defendant's attorney) needs more time to prepare a defense, the defendant may give up the right to be tried as quickly but typically will still go to trial within a few months.

As noted in Chapter 5, the Sixth Amendment also guarantees accused persons the right to confront and cross-examine witnesses against them.

The Requirement for a Unanimous Verdict

Of the criminal cases that go to trial, most are tried by a jury. In most jurisdictions, jury verdicts in criminal cases must be *unanimous* for **acquittal** or conviction. In other words, all twelve jurors (some states allow smaller juries) must agree that the defendant is either guilty or not guilty.

If the jury cannot reach unanimous agreement on whether to acquit or convict the defendant, the result is a **hung jury**. When the jury is hung, the defendant may be tried again, but often the case is not retried. The requirement for unanimity is important because if even one juror is not convinced of the defendant's guilt, the defendant is not convicted. Thus, the prosecuting attorney must make as strong a case as possible, while the defense attorney can aim at persuading some jurors to have doubts. As in all litigation, throughout a trial, a law firm must take steps to maintain the security of its information, as discussed in this chapter's *Office Tech and Cybersecurity* feature.

acquittal
A certification or declaration following a trial that the individual accused of a crime is innocent, or free from guilt, in the eyes of the law and is thus absolved of the charges.

hung jury
A jury whose members are so irreconcilably divided in their opinions that they cannot reach a verdict. The judge in this situation may order a new trial.

Sentencing

When a defendant is found guilty by a trial court (or pleads guilty to an offense without a trial), the judge will pronounce a **sentence**, which is the penalty imposed on anyone convicted of a crime. Often, the sentence is pronounced in a separate proceeding.

sentence
The punishment, or penalty, ordered by the court to be inflicted on a person convicted of a crime.

Limited Role of Jury

Unless the prosecutor is seeking the death penalty, the jury normally is not involved in sentencing the defendant. Jurors are dismissed after they return a verdict, and the judge either sentences the defendant on the spot or schedules a future appearance for sentencing. In some jurisdictions, the jury recommends a sentence that the judge may reduce within his or her discretion. At the sentencing hearing, the judge usually listens to arguments from both attorneys concerning the factors in "aggravation and mitigation" (that is, why the defendant's punishment should be harsh or lenient).

Range of Penalties

Most criminal statutes set forth a maximum and minimum penalty that should be imposed for a violation. Thus, judges often have some discretion in sentencing defendants. The judge typically sentences the offender to one or more of the following:

- Incarceration in a jail or a prison.
- Probation (formal or informal).
- Fines or other financial penalties.
- Public work service (for less serious offenses).

- Class attendance (for offenses such as domestic violence and alcohol- or drug-related crimes).
- Death (in some states).

In federal and many state cases, the defense and prosecuting attorneys prepare sentencing memoranda arguing for particular sentences. For more serious crimes, the federal courts use the Federal Sentencing Guidelines (which can be found online) to help determine sentences. Paralegals are often involved in helping to draft sentencing memoranda and organize supporting documents, such as letters of support for the defendant or statements from the victim for a prosecutor. In some states, victims have the right to address the court and may have an attorney or paralegal assist them in preparing their statements.

Incarceration

Defendants sentenced to incarceration will go to a county jail for less serious offenses (involving sentences of less than one year) or a state or federal prison for serious crimes (involving sentences of more than one year).

The judge may consider alternatives to jail time. Defendants may be placed on house arrest and wear an electronic device that notifies authorities if they leave a

OFFICE TECH AND CYBERSECURITY

EVOLVING SECURITY AND FORENSIC TOOLS

Technologies used in law offices change frequently, and paralegals should be aware of developments that affect their offices' functioning. Technology can pose threats to the security of information as well as offer new opportunities in the collection and evaluation of evidence.

Protecting Security

New technology can mean that documents believed to be secure are not. For example, members of the media were able to read parts of a confidential settlement that had been redacted (blacked out) in the settlement of a lawsuit involving Facebook and ConnectU. The computer codes that supposedly hid some information from public view were bypassed in electronic copies of documents released to the press, allowing reporters to see the private information. The lawyers for ConnectU claimed to have received $65 million from Facebook in the settlement, but the press could see that the amount was actually $31 million. ConnectU fired the law firm that made the mistake.

Knowing Where People Are or Were

Global positioning system (GPS) devices are built into many vehicles. Information collected by these devices may allow investigators to determine the location of a vehicle (and therefore a suspect) at a given point in time, which can help in criminal investigations.

Federal rules require cell phones to support GPS information so that 911 emergency calls can be pinpointed by location. This can be important in criminal investigations, because it enables an investigator to find out the location of persons and their cell phones, even if they did not call 911.

Using Digital Forensic Experts

The use of digital forensic experts in litigation is increasing. Professionals can assist in the evaluation of digital material and identify when it has been compromised and is no longer trustworthy. Just as the use of DNA evidence has helped to convict some people accused of crimes and free others falsely accused, digital evidence is playing an increasing role in helping to establish guilt or innocence.

Technology Tip

The rapid evolution of technology means that law firms must watch for possibilities not envisioned before. Various websites provide information about innovations affecting law and about how to find experts when needed. Paralegals should use such resources to keep up to date with evolving technologies.

designated area. Defendants who have alcohol or drug problems may sometimes be allowed to satisfy the incarceration portion of a sentence in an inpatient rehabilitation program. In some states, defendants may be allowed to satisfy short periods of custody time (ten to thirty days) by checking into the jail on weekends only or by participating in a supervised release program, which enables them to stay employed.

Probation

A part of many sentences is **probation**. Typically, defendants are sentenced to less than the maximum penalty and placed on probation with certain conditions for a set time. In such cases, the sentence imposed is said to be *suspended*. If the person fails to meet the conditions of probation, probation may be revoked, and the person may be sentenced to custody time up to the maximum for the offense.

probation
Action by which a convicted defendant is released from confinement but is still under court supervision for a period of time.

Combination of Penalties.   A combination of penalties may be imposed for the same offense. If convicted of driving while under the influence, for example, a defendant might be sentenced to two days in jail, three years of informal probation, a fine of $3,000, and ten days of public work service (picking up roadside trash, for example). The court could also require the defendant to attend a first-offenders program (meeting twice a week for six to eight weeks and costing several thousand dollars). If the defendant does not do all of these things, the court could revoke probation and sentence the person to spend up to a year in jail.

Types of Probation.   Probation can be either formal or informal. In formal probation, which is typical in felony cases, the defendant is required to meet regularly with a probation officer. The defendant may be required to submit to drug and alcohol testing, to possess no firearms, and to avoid socializing with those who might be engaging in criminal activity, for example.

Defendants on informal probation do not have a probation officer, but they may be required to comply with certain conditions. This could include paying a fine, performing public work service, staying in a certain geographic area, participating in specified programs (such as attending Alcoholics Anonymous meetings or anger management classes), and not violating the law.

Diversion

In many states, defendants charged with certain offenses may be able to participate in a **diversion program**. Diversion is an alternative to prosecution. Generally, these programs suspend criminal prosecution for a certain period of time and require that the defendant complete specified conditions—such as attending special classes and not getting in trouble with the police—during that time. If the person fulfills the diversion requirements, the case will be dismissed. If the defendant fails to complete the diversion satisfactorily, the criminal prosecution springs back to life, and the defendant is prosecuted for the crime.

diversion program
In some jurisdictions, an alternative to prosecution that is offered to certain felony suspects to deter them from future unlawful acts.

The objective is to deter the defendant from further wrongdoing by offering an incentive—namely, a way to avoid any record of conviction. Diversion is a good option for defendants who want to avoid having convictions on their records. Most defendants who are eligible for diversion choose that option and thus do not proceed to trial.

Appeal

Persons convicted of crimes have a right of appeal. Most felony convictions are appealed to an intermediate court of appeal. In some states, there is no intermediate court of appeal, so the appeal goes directly to the state's highest appellate court, usually called the supreme court. Most convictions that result in supervised release or fines are not appealed, but a high percentage of the convictions that result in prison sentences are appealed. About 10 percent of such convictions are reversed on appeal. The most common reason for reversal is that the trial court admitted improper evidence, such as evidence obtained by a search that did not meet constitutional requirements.

If a conviction is overturned on appeal, the defendant may or may not be tried again, depending on the reason for the reversal and on whether the case was reversed with or without prejudice. A decision reversed "with prejudice" means that no further action can be taken on the claim or cause. A decision reversed "without prejudice" means the case may be tried again.

CHAPTER SUMMARY

CRIMINAL LAW AND PROCEDURES

Defining Crime

1. *Key differences between civil and criminal law*—Crimes are distinguished from civil wrongs, such as torts, in several ways:

   a. Crimes are deemed to be offenses against society as a whole.

   b. Tort (civil) litigation involves lawsuits between private parties; criminal litigation involves the state's prosecution of a wrongdoer.

   c. Crimes are defined as such by state legislatures or the federal government.

   d. In criminal cases, the state must prove the defendant's guilt beyond a reasonable doubt. In civil cases, the plaintiff proves a case by a preponderance of the evidence.

   e. A criminal act need not involve a victim.

2. *Civil liability for criminal acts*—Those who commit crimes may be subject to both criminal and civil liability (such as when a person commits an assault), but the legal actions are separate matters.

3. *Classifications of crimes*—Crimes fall into two basic classifications: felonies and misdemeanors.

   a. Felonies are more serious crimes (such as murder, rape, and robbery) for which penalties may range from imprisonment for a year or longer to (in some states) death.

   b. Misdemeanors are less serious crimes (such as prostitution, disturbing the peace, and public intoxication) for which penalties may include imprisonment for up to a year. Petty offenses, or infractions, such as violations of building codes, are usually a subset of misdemeanors.

4. *Jurisdiction over crimes*—Most crimes fall under state statutes and state prosecution, but there are many federal criminal acts as well.

Elements of Criminal Liability

For criminal liability to exist, the state must meet certain standards of proof:

1. *The criminal act*—Most crimes require that the defendant be shown to have committed or attempted to commit a guilty act, or *actus reus*.

2. *State of mind*—The defendant must also have had the required intent to do a criminal act, or *mens rea*.

3. *Corporate criminal liability*—Corporations may be held liable for crimes. Corporate officers and directors may be held personally liable for the crimes of the corporation.

4. *Defenses to criminal liability*—Criminal liability may be avoided if the state of mind required for the crime was lacking or another defense against liability can be raised. Defenses include self-defense, defense of others, defense of property, and the running of a statute of limitations.

Types of Crimes

Many acts are defined as criminal by federal and state laws. The five traditional major categories of crimes are as follows:

1. *Violent crime*—Crimes that cause another person to suffer harm or death, such as murder, rape, robbery, and assault and battery.

2. *Property crime*—Crimes in which the offender takes or damages the property of another. Property crimes include burglary, larceny (stealing), obtaining goods by false pretenses, receiving stolen goods, arson, and forgery.

3. *Public order crime*—Crimes involving behavior society has deemed inappropriate, such as public drunkenness and illegal drug use.

4. *White-collar crime*—Illegal acts committed by individuals or business entities in the course of legitimate business—for example, embezzlement, mail or wire fraud, bribery, theft of trade secrets, and insider trading.

5. *Organized crime*—The criminal enterprises that provide illegal goods and services such as gambling, prostitution, and illegal narcotics. Money from such activities can be made to appear legitimate through money laundering. The Racketeer Influenced and Corrupt Organizations Act (RICO) was designed to discourage organized crime but is applied to a wide range of activities.

Cyber Crimes

Cyber crimes are committed with computers, typically by using the Internet to achieve illegal ends. Cyber crimes include theft of money or data, identity theft, cyberstalking, and hacking. Prosecuting cyber crimes presents new challenges to law enforcement and the courts.

Social Media and Criminal Justice

Social media tools are used by law enforcement authorities, so legal providers must know the boundaries of such use when defending clients.

1. *Uses of social media*—Criminals are making greater use of social media to exploit victims, and law enforcement is responding by monitoring transmissions and gathering records of transmissions.

2. *Protection of social media information*—In defending those accused of crimes, lawyers (and paralegals) check to see if clients' rights have been violated by investigators' collection of evidence on social media.

Constitutional Safeguards

Specific procedures must be followed in arresting and prosecuting a criminal suspect to safeguard constitutional rights.

1. *The Bill of Rights*—Persons accused of crimes have rights, including protection against unreasonable searches and seizures, the right to due process of law, protection against double jeopardy, protection against self-incrimination (the right to remain silent), the right to a speedy and public trial, the right to confront witnesses and be represented by an attorney, and protection against excessive bail and cruel and unusual punishment.

2. *The Exclusionary rule*—Evidence obtained in violation of a defendant's constitutional rights normally must be excluded from trial, along with evidence derived from illegally obtained evidence.

3. The Miranda *rule*—At the time a criminal suspect is taken into custody, the arresting officers must inform the suspect of his or her rights by reading the *Miranda* warnings. Evidence or confession obtained in violation of the suspect's rights will normally not be admissible in court. The Supreme Court has made exceptions to the *Miranda* rule.

Criminal Procedures Prior to Prosecution

The initial procedure undertaken by the police after a crime is reported or observed includes steps that must be followed properly for a case to proceed.

1. *Arrest and booking*—Officers take a person into custody and charge the person with a crime. The suspect is usually taken to a holding facility (jail), where the person is detained while being booked (entered into the police log). Police must show probable cause for the accusation and, in many cases, must have an arrest warrant issued by a judge.

2. *Investigation after the arrest*—Police may need to interview witnesses, collect evidence, execute search warrants, and take other steps in making the case that a suspect should be prosecuted.

The Prosecution Begins

Police make a report of the alleged crime to a public prosecutor.

1. *Prosecutorial discretion*—The prosecutor decides, based on a review of the evidence, if the case should proceed or if the accusations should be dropped.

2. *Complaint and initial appearance*—A complaint against an accused person includes a statement of charges; upon being served with a complaint, the person formally becomes a defendant. The defendant makes an initial appearance before a judge or magistrate, after which the defendant ordinarily is released on personal recognizance or required to post bail.

3. *Preliminary hearing*—Appearance before a judge will determine if there is sufficient evidence to show probable cause so as to allow the matter to proceed.

The Trial

Most criminal cases are settled before they get to trial through plea bargaining. Most criminal trials last less than one week and differ from civil trials in a few major ways.

1. *The presumption of innocence*—The defendant is innocent until the prosecutor proves the defendant's guilt to the jury (or judge) beyond a reasonable doubt. The defendant is not required to present any evidence at the trial.

2. *The privilege against self-incrimination*—The defendant and witnesses cannot be forced to testify if such testimony would be self-incriminating.

3. *The right to a speedy trial*—Defendants have a right to a speedy and public trial. Even if they waive that right, criminal cases usually go to trial more quickly than civil cases.

4. *Grand jury review*—The federal government and many states use a grand jury to obtain an indictment in certain felony cases; only with such an indictment will the case go to trial. In other cases, the prosecutor issues an information allowing the prosecution to proceed.

5. *Arraignment*—The defendant is formally charged in court and enters a plea. Often, the parties have agreed to a plea bargain that will terminate proceedings at this point.

6. *Pretrial motions*—If the case proceeds, various motions may be entered, often by the defense, such as a motion to suppress evidence or a motion to dismiss the case.

7. *Discovery*—In criminal cases, the defendant is entitled to obtain any evidence relating to the case possessed by the prosecution, including documents, statements previously made by the defendant, objects, reports of tests or examinations, and other evidence.

4. *The requirement for a unanimous verdict*—Most criminal cases are tried by juries. Generally, all jurors must reach agreement to acquit or convict the defendant.

5. *Sentencing*—The judge sentences a defendant who has been found guilty (or who pleads guilty or no contest), often in a separate proceeding. Most criminal statutes set forth a range of penalties that can be imposed, and judges are free to select the appropriate penalty within that range. Typically, sentences involve fines, imprisonment, and/or probation.

6. *Diversion*—A defendant may be sentenced to a diversion program, which results in dismissal of the case provided the defendant complies with the requirements of diversion (which vary by state).

7. *Appeal*—If the defendant loses at trial, he or she may appeal the case to a higher court. A small percentage of criminal cases are reversed on appeal.

KEY TERMS AND CONCEPTS

QUESTIONS FOR REVIEW

1. What are the key differences between civil and criminal law?

2. What two elements are required for criminal liability?

3. What are the five traditional types of crime? What defenses can be raised against criminal liability?

4. What are cyber crimes? What role has social media played in these crimes? What factors determine whether social media evidence deserves privacy protection?

5. Which constitutional amendments provide rights to a person accused of a crime, and what rights are provided? What are *Miranda* rights, and which amendments provide the basis for *Miranda* rights?

6. List and explain the basic steps involved in criminal procedure from the time a crime is reported to the resolution of the case.

7. Explain what happens during sentencing. Describe the various types of penalties and alternatives. What happens during an appeal?

ETHICS QUESTION

1. A man who was not a lawyer opened a law office and filled out a court registration form using the Social Security number, birth date, law school credential, and last name of a real lawyer—information he had obtained online. He filed a lawsuit in federal court unbeknownst to the supposed plaintiffs in the case. When visited by undercover FBI agents purportedly seeking legal representation, the man told the agents that he would represent them for a $5,000 retainer and would charge $400 an hour. What crime did he commit? What state regulatory statute related to the practice of law was violated?

PRACTICE QUESTIONS AND ASSIGNMENTS

1. Identify each of the following crimes by its classification (petty offense, misdemeanor, felony):

a. Jerry refuses to put his trash out at the curb for the weekly trash pickup. Instead, he lets it collect at the side of his garage, where it is an eyesore and attracts rats to the neighborhood. The police department receives complaints from his neighbors and gives Jerry a citation for violating the trash ordinance.

b. Neehan is arrested for being under the influence of drugs in public. She faces a possible jail sentence of six months.

c. Susanna is arrested for forging Martha's name on the back of a check made out to Martha and then depositing the check into her own bank account. The penalty includes confinement for more than one year in prison on conviction.

2. Using the material presented in the chapter on state of mind, identify the type of homicide (involuntary manslaughter, voluntary manslaughter, or first degree murder) committed in each of the following situations:

   a. David, while driving in an intoxicated state, crashes into another car and kills its occupants.

   b. David, after pulling up next to his wife at a stoplight and observing her passionately kissing another man, smashes into her car and kills her.

   c. David, who is angry with his boss for firing him, plans to kill his boss by smashing his car into his boss's car, killing his boss and making it look like a car accident. David carries out his plan, kills his boss, and survives the accident.

3. Identify the following criminal procedures:

   a. Ani is charged with the crime of arson. She pleads not guilty and is bound over for trial in the district court.

   b. Reyna is taken to the police station, searched, photographed, fingerprinted, and allowed to make one telephone call.

   c. A jury of Barbara's peers reviews the evidence against her and determines whether probable cause exists for the prosecutor to proceed to trial for manslaughter.

   d. Police officers stop Miguel on the street because his description matches that of a reported gas-station robber. He is three blocks from the gas station when they stop him. They question him, search him, and find that he has a pocketful of $20 and $50 bills—the same denominations that the gas-station attendant reported stolen. The police read Miguel his rights and take him to the police station.

   e. Andrew is taken before a magistrate, where the charges against him are read and counsel is appointed. His request to be set free on bail is denied.

   f. In exchange for a guilty plea to manslaughter, the prosecutor agrees to drop the more serious murder charges against Desmond.

4. Mona was laid off from her accounting job three years ago. Her unemployment compensation has run out, as has her severance package, and she has few prospects for finding work. Mona learns that a former co-worker has died. Using records she has in her possession from her former accounting position, Mona decides to use the co-worker's name and Social Security number to collect a tax refund. In January 2022, Mona files the tax return in the deceased's name. She receives a refund check. Mona decides that this is a quick and easy way to make money, so she continues to take names and Social Security numbers from the documents in her possession and file more false tax returns until she has collected more than $100,000. What crimes has Mona committed?

5. The police pick up Larry and take him to the station for questioning in a local murder case. They detain him for three days. After two days of questioning, Larry says, "I want an attorney. You haven't let me call my attorney." It is late, and Larry's attorney does not answer the phone, but she receives the message first thing in the morning on the third day that Larry is in custody and heads directly to the police station, where she secures Larry's release. She confirms that the police failed to tell Larry that he had the right to have an attorney present and did not give him any of his other *Miranda* rights. What will be the result if the information Larry gave to the police is used against him in court?

6. After answering a few background questions regarding his name and title, a government official took the Fifth Amendment eighty-two times during the course of a hearing on corruption charges. What does taking the Fifth Amendment eighty-two times say about guilt or innocence? Does taking the Fifth Amendment protect the official from self-incrimination?

7. A women's clothing boutique posted information on Facebook about a leopard-print dress with hot-pink and lime-green accents that was stolen from the store. The theft was captured on security video. Shortly after the store's posting, a Facebook selfie of a woman wearing the dress, captioned "Love my new dress," was forwarded to the store owner. The owner contacted the police, who arrested the woman pictured in the selfie for theft. What factors would the court consider in determining whether the Facebook selfie was admissible?

8. During a criminal trial involving child pornography charges, the defendant's lawyer returned late from the lunch recess. The trial resumed, and the defendant had no lawyer present for seven minutes. During that time, prosecutors introduced incriminating evidence. When the lawyer returned from lunch, he did not object to the testimony that had been presented while he was absent. The defendant was convicted and sentenced to life in prison. Which of the defendant's rights were violated? Can an argument be made that his conviction should be overturned?

GROUP PROJECT

This project involves researching CryptoWall ransomeware.

Student one will locate the *New York Times* article, "How My Mom Got Hacked" and provide a summary of the facts and legal issues.

Student two will locate and summarize an article discussing the CryptoWall cyber attack on the Dickson County, Tennessee, Sheriff's Office.

Student three will locate the online Internet Crime Complaint Center and provide information on how to file a complaint with the agency.

Student four will locate and summarize an article on **abajournal.com** about a lawyer who clicked on an e-mail link and lost $289,000.

The group will make a recommendation on how law offices can avoid becoming victims of cyber crimes and how to respond if they do.

PART 3

Key Elements of the Law

CHAPTER 14

Tort Law, Product Liability, and Consumer Law

CHAPTER OBJECTIVES

After completing this chapter, you will be able to:

- Define *tort*.

- Explain the purpose of tort law and the basic categories of torts.

- State two categories of intentional torts, and list and explain the torts in each category.

- Identify the elements of and defenses to negligence, define *damages*, and discuss special negligence doctrines.

- Discuss issues related to online defamation.

- Define strict liability and what it applies to.

- State the underlying policy for imposing strict product liability, and explain what defenses can be raised in product liability actions.

- Explain some of the ways in which the government protects consumers against unfair business practices and harmful products.

Introduction

tort

A civil wrong not arising from a breach of contract; a breach of a legal duty that causes harm or injury to another.

A **tort** is a wrongful action. In fact, the word *tort* is French for "wrong." Through tort law, society seeks to compensate those who have suffered injuries as a result of the wrongful conduct of others. Although many torts, such as trespass and negligence, originated in the English common law, the field of tort law continues to expand. As evolving technologies provide new ways to commit wrongs—such as the use of the Internet to commit wrongful acts—the principles of tort law expand to cover them.

Here, we discuss some of the primary concepts of tort law and how they are being applied today. We also consider *product liability*, which is a major area of tort law under which sellers can be held liable for defective products. In the final pages of the chapter, we look at a growing body of law designed to protect the health and safety and the credit of consumers.

The Basis of Tort Law

Two notions serve as the basis of torts: wrongs and compensation. Tort law recognizes that some acts are wrong because they cause injuries to others. In a tort action, one person or group brings suit against another person or group to obtain compensation (monetary damages) or other relief for the harm suffered.

Because tort suits involve *private* wrongs, they are distinguishable from criminal actions, which involve *public* wrongs. A government prosecutor brings criminal actions against individuals who are accused of committing acts that are wrongs against society (crimes are usually defined by statutes).

Some acts may result in both a tort lawsuit and a criminal prosecution. For example, if Ted punches Robert in the nose, the state may prosecute Ted for striking Robert, and Robert may sue Ted for the tort of *battery* (discussed shortly). Although both legal actions involve the same facts and the same defendant (Ted), they involve different parties (the state and Robert) and different legal theories (criminal law and tort law). Note that Robert does not have to agree to the state's prosecution of Ted (although he will likely be an important witness), but only Robert can initiate the tort action against Ted.

The purpose of tort law is to provide remedies for the invasion of protected interests or rights—such as people's interests in physical safety, privacy, freedom of movement, and reputation—that society seeks to protect. We first discuss two broad categories of torts: *intentional torts* and *negligence*. The classification of a particular tort depends largely on how it occurs (intentionally or unintentionally) and the circumstances. We then examine the concept of *strict liability*, a doctrine under which a defendant may be held liable for harm or injury to another regardless of intention or fault.

elements

The issues and facts that the plaintiff must prove to succeed in a tort claim.

When thinking about torts, it is important to focus on the **elements** of the tort. A plaintiff must prove the elements to succeed in a tort claim. These are important to know, as they will affect your work. In analyzing a client's tort claim, you will check to make sure there is evidence to prove each element of the tort.

Intentional Torts

intentional tort

A wrongful act knowingly committed.

tortfeasor

One who commits a tort.

An **intentional tort**, as the term implies, requires *intent*. Hence, intent is an element of intentional torts. In tort law, intent does not necessarily mean that the person accused (who may be called the **tortfeasor**) intended to harm someone. Rather, it means that the actor intended the consequences of an act or knew, or should have known, that certain consequences would result from an act. Thus, pushing another person—even if done in fun and without any bad intent—is an intentional tort if an injury is the result. We should know that if we shove someone, it is possible that he will fall.

There are two categories of intentional torts: intentional torts against persons and intentional torts against property. We look at both categories.

Intentional Torts against Persons

Intentional torts against persons include assault and battery, false imprisonment, intentional infliction of emotional distress, defamation, invasion of the right to privacy, appropriation, misrepresentation, and wrongful interference.

Assault

An **assault** is any communication or action intended to make another person fearful of immediate physical harm. In other words, an assault is a threat that a reasonable person would believe. The tort law of assault protects our interest in freedom from fear of harmful or offensive contact. The occurrence of apprehension is enough to justify compensation. The elements of assault are:

assault
Any word or action intended to make another person apprehensive or fearful of immediate physical harm; a reasonably believable threat.

1. An act intended to cause an apprehension of harmful or offensive contact.

2. An act that causes fear of imminent bodily harm.

Battery

The *completion* of the threat, if it results in harm to the plaintiff, is a **battery**, which is defined as harmful or offensive physical contact *intentionally* performed. Note, however, that no threat (assault) need be made prior to a battery. If someone was struck from behind, unaware that an attack was coming, a battery occurred. (Remember that assault and battery can be criminal acts as well as torts and that the definition of the terms varies somewhat across states.)

battery
The intentional and offensive touching of another without lawful justification.

> *EXAMPLE 14.1* Suppose Ivan threatens Jean with a gun, then shoots her. Pointing the gun at Jean is an assault. Firing the gun (if the bullet hits Jean) is a battery.

Tort law for battery protects our right to personal security and safety. The contact can be physically harmful, or it can be merely offensive (such as an unwelcome kiss). The contact can involve any part of the body or anything attached to it—for example, an item of clothing or a purse. Whether the contact is offensive or not is determined by the *reasonable person standard* (discussed later). The contact can be made by the defendant or by some force the defendant sets in motion—for example, a rock that is thrown or food that is poisoned. The elements of battery are:

1. An intent to cause an unwanted contact.

2. Unwanted, offensive, and harmful contact.

Compensation.   If the plaintiff shows that there was offensive contact, or fear of such contact, and the jury agrees, the plaintiff has a right to compensation. There is no need to show that the defendant acted out of malice. The underlying motive does not matter, only the intent to bring about the harmful or offensive contact to the plaintiff. Proving a motive is not necessary but is often relevant and makes a case stronger.

Defenses to Assault and Battery.   A number of legally recognized defenses, or reasons why plaintiffs should not obtain compensation they are seeking, can be raised by defendants in tort actions. Later, we review defenses that can be raised in a broad range of tort cases. The following defenses may be used by a defendant who is sued for assault, battery, or both:

- *Consent.* When a person gives permission to the act that damages her, there is generally no liability (legal responsibility) for the damage done. For instance, if Suzi and Bryan are playing football, Bryan can raise this as a defense if Suzi sues for battery after he tackles her while she has the ball.

- *Self-defense.* A person defending her life or physical well-being can claim self-defense. In situations of both *real* and *apparent* danger, a person may use whatever force is *reasonably* necessary to prevent harmful contact. Thus, if Simon assaults Linda with a knife, she can claim this defense if Simon sues her for hitting him with a baseball bat.

- *Defense of others.* A person can act in a reasonable manner to protect others who are in real or apparent danger. If Fred offensively grabs Ray's child and Ray hits Fred, Ray can raise this as a defense if Fred tries to sue him for battery.

- *Defense of property.* People can use reasonable force in attempting to remove intruders from their homes. Generally, force that is likely to cause death or great bodily injury should not be used to protect property. However, if you catch someone in the act of breaking into your garage, you can use nondeadly force to stop that person without being liable for battery.

The defendant bears the burden of proving the facts necessary to rely on these defenses. The plaintiff must, of course, respond to such defenses when they are raised.

False Imprisonment

false imprisonment
The intentional confinement or restraint of a person against his or her will.

False imprisonment is the intentional confinement or restraint of another person's activities without justification. The elements of false imprisonment are:

1. Intent to confine or restrain a person.
2. Actual confinement in boundaries not of the plaintiff's choosing.

False imprisonment interferes with the freedom to move without restraint. The confinement can be accomplished through the use of physical barriers, restraint, or threats of physical force. It is essential that the person being restrained not comply with the restraint willingly, but a person does not have to resist physically to be subject to restraint.

Stores are sometimes sued for false imprisonment after they have attempted to confine a suspected shoplifter for questioning. (An example is provided in the accompanying *Developing Paralegal Skills* feature.) Under the "privilege to detain" granted to merchants in some states, a merchant could use the defense of *probable cause* to justify delaying a suspected shoplifter. Probable cause exists when the evidence to support the belief that a person may be guilty outweighs the evidence against that belief. Although laws governing false imprisonment vary from state to state, generally they require that any detention be conducted in a *reasonable* manner and for only a *reasonable* length of time.

Intentional Infliction of Emotional Distress

intentional infliction of emotional distress
Intentional, extreme, and outrageous conduct resulting in severe emotional distress to another.

The tort of **intentional infliction of emotional distress** (or mental distress) involves these elements:

1. Outrageous conduct by the defendant.
2. Intent to commit the act or conduct involved.
3. Causation.
4. Severe emotional distress in the plaintiff.

DEVELOPING PARALEGAL SKILLS

A CLAIM OF FALSE IMPRISONMENT

Julie Waterman works for a small law firm. She is interviewing a new client who detained a customer in his store for suspected shoplifting. Now he is facing a lawsuit brought by the customer for false imprisonment. Julie will gather as much information as she can about the incident and summarize what she learns in a memorandum for the attorney to review later. Before the interview, Julie checks the relevant state law governing false imprisonment. During the interview, Julie makes sure that she covers the topics on her checklist for determining false imprisonment.

Checklist for Determining False Imprisonment

- Did the client have cause to believe that the customer was shoplifting? What made the client suspect that the customer took merchandise without paying for it?

- Did the customer resist the detention?

- How long did the client detain the customer? Fifteen minutes? An hour? Was the duration of the detention reasonable?

- Was the customer in a reasonably comfortable environment during the detention?

- Was he prevented from leaving the store?

- Was the customer subjected to abusive or accusatory words or to indignity while being confined?

- Were all procedures used to detain the customer reasonable?

- Were the police called? How soon were they called after the detention began?

Focusing on legal standards for such incidents helps the attorney determine the likely outcome of litigation in this contentious area.

EXAMPLE 14.2 Suppose that a prankster calls Erica and says that Erica's husband has just been killed in a horrible accident. As a result, Erica suffers intense mental pain. The caller's behavior is extreme and outrageous conduct that exceeds the bounds of decency accepted by society and is therefore **actionable** (serving as the basis for a lawsuit).

Courts in some jurisdictions require that the emotional distress be evidenced by some physical symptom, illness, or emotional disturbance that can be documented by a psychiatric consultant or other medical professional.

actionable
Capable of serving as the basis of a lawsuit. An actionable claim can be pursued in a lawsuit or other legal action.

Defamation

Wrongfully harming a person's good reputation is the tort of **defamation**. The law imposes a general duty on all persons to refrain from making false, damaging statements about others. Breaching this duty orally involves the tort of **slander**. Breaching it in writing involves the tort of **libel**. The tort of defamation also arises when a false statement is made about a person's product, business, or title to property.

The common law defines four types of false statements that are considered defamation *per se* (meaning that no proof of injury or harm is required for these false statements to be actionable):

- That a person has a loathsome communicable disease.

- That a person committed improprieties while engaging in a profession.

- That a person has committed or has been imprisoned for a serious crime.

- That an unmarried woman is unchaste.

defamation
Anything published or publicly spoken that causes injury to another's good name, reputation, or character.

slander
Defamation in oral form.

libel
Defamation in writing or other published form (such as video).

The Publication Requirement.   The tort of defamation requires the publication of a statement or statements that hold an individual up to contempt, ridicule, or hatred. Publication here means that the defamatory statements are communicated to third parties.

> **EXAMPLE 14.3** If Crystal writes Andrew a private letter accusing him of embezzling funds, the action does not constitute libel. If Juan calls Rita dishonest and incompetent when no one else is around, the action does not constitute slander. In neither case was the message communicated to a third party. This is true even if the statements were completely false.

If a third party overhears defamatory statements by chance, the courts usually hold that this constitutes publication. Defamatory statements made on the Internet are actionable as well. Anyone who republishes or repeats defamatory statements, knowing them to be false, is liable even if that person reveals the source of the statements.

Defenses against Defamation.   Truth normally is an absolute defense against a defamation charge. In other words, if the defendant in a defamation suit can prove that his allegedly defamatory statements were true, the defendant will not be liable.

Another defense that is sometimes raised is **privilege**. If the statements were privileged communications, the defendant is immune from liability. Privileged communications are of two types: absolute and qualified. Only in judicial proceedings and certain legislative proceedings is an *absolute* privilege granted. For example, statements made in the courtroom by attorneys and judges during a trial are absolutely privileged, as are statements made by legislators during debate in a legislature. A *qualified*, or *conditional*, privilege applies when a statement is related to a matter of public interest or when the statement is necessary to protect a person's private interest and is made to another person with an interest in the same subject matter.

In general, false and defamatory statements that are made about *public figures* (public officials and other figures who are in the public eye) and that are published in the media are privileged if they are made without **actual malice**. To be made with actual malice, a statement must be made *with either knowledge of falsity or a reckless disregard of the truth*. Statements made about public figures, especially when they are made through the media, are usually related to matters of general public interest. Furthermore, public figures usually have access to the media to respond to defamatory statements. Hence, public figures have a greater burden of proof in defamation cases (they must prove actual malice) than do private individuals.

privilege
In tort law, the ability to act contrary to another person's right without that person's having legal redress for such acts. Privilege may be raised as a defense to defamation.

actual malice
Real and demonstrated evil intent. In a defamation suit, a statement made about a public figure normally must be made with actual malice (with either knowledge of its falsity or a reckless disregard of the truth) for liability to be incurred.

Invasion of the Right to Privacy

A person has a right to solitude and freedom from prying public eyes—in other words, to privacy. The Supreme Court has held that a fundamental right to privacy is implied by various amendments to the U.S. Constitution. Some state constitutions explicitly provide for privacy rights. In addition, a number of federal and state statutes protect individual rights in specific areas. Tort law also safeguards these rights through the tort of *invasion of privacy*. Four acts qualify as an invasion of privacy:

- *The use of a person's name, picture, or other likeness for commercial purposes without permission.* This tort, which is usually referred to as appropriation, will be examined shortly.

- *Intrusion into a person's affairs or seclusion.* For example, invading someone's home or snooping in someone's briefcase is an invasion of privacy. The tort has been held to extend to eavesdropping by wiretap, hacking into a computer, the unauthorized viewing of a bank account, and window peeping.

- *Publication of information that places a person in a false light.* This could be a story attributing to the person ideas not held or actions not taken. (Publishing such a story could involve the tort of defamation as well.)

- *Public disclosure of private facts about an individual that an ordinary person would find objectionable.* A newspaper account of a private citizen's sex life or financial affairs could be an actionable invasion of privacy.

The Electronic Privacy Information Center (EPIC) website (**epic.org**) is a good resource on privacy issues.

Appropriation

The use by one person of another person's name or likeness without permission and for the benefit of the user is the tort of **appropriation**. A person's right to privacy normally includes the right to the exclusive use of his or her identity.

> **EXAMPLE 14.4** Vanna White, the hostess of the television game show *Wheel of Fortune*, sued Samsung Electronics for appropriation. Without White's permission, Samsung included in an advertisement for its video recorders a depiction of a robot dressed in a wig, gown, and jewelry, posed in a scene that resembled the *Wheel of Fortune* set. The court held in White's favor, holding that the tort of appropriation does not require the use of a celebrity's name or exact likeness. Samsung's robot ad left "little doubt" as to the identity of the celebrity whom the ad was meant to depict.

appropriation
In tort law, the use by one person of another person's name, likeness, or other identifying characteristic without permission and for the benefit of the user.

Misrepresentation (Fraud)

Misrepresentation leads someone to believe in a condition that is different from the condition that actually exists. This is often accomplished through a false or an incorrect statement. The tort of **fraudulent misrepresentation**, or fraud, involves intentional deceit for personal gain—not misrepresentations innocently made by someone who is unaware of the facts.

fraudulent misrepresentation
Any misrepresentation, either by misstatement or omission of a material fact, knowingly made with the intention of deceiving another and on which a reasonable person would and does rely to his or her detriment.

Elements of Fraud.   The tort of fraudulent misrepresentation includes several elements:

- Misrepresentation of facts or conditions with knowledge that the information is false or with reckless disregard for the truth.

- Intent to induce another to rely on the misrepresentation.

- Justifiable reliance by the deceived party.

- Causal connection between the misrepresentation and the harm suffered.

- Damages suffered as a result of the reliance that justify monetary compensation.

Fraud exists when a person presents as a fact something he knows is untrue. It is fraud to claim that a roof does not leak if you know it does. Facts can be objectively determined, unlike *seller's talk*, or hype.

> **EXAMPLE 14.5** If Harry says, "I am the best accountant in town," that is seller's talk, not fraud. The speaker is not trying to represent something as fact, because the term *best* is subjective (open to interpretation) and because a "reasonable person" would not rely on Harry's statement.

Fact versus Opinion.   Normally, the tort of misrepresentation or fraud occurs only when there is reliance on a *statement of fact*. Sometimes, however, reliance on a *statement of opinion* may involve the tort of misrepresentation if the person making the statement of opinion has a superior knowledge of the subject matter.

> *EXAMPLE 14.6* When a lawyer makes a statement of opinion to a client about the law in a state in which the lawyer is licensed to practice, a court would hold reliance on such a statement to be equivalent to reliance on a statement of fact.

Wrongful Interference

Some lawsuits involve situations in which a person or business is accused of wrongfully interfering with the business of another. A **business tort** is generally divided into two categories: wrongful interference with a contractual relationship and wrongful interference with a business relationship.

business tort
Involving wrongful interference with another's business rights.

Wrongful Interference with a Contractual Relationship.
The area of tort law relating to intentional interference with a contractual relationship has expanded in recent years. Three elements are necessary to establish the tort of wrongful interference with a contractual relationship:

1. A valid, enforceable contract exists between two parties.
2. A third party knows that this contract exists.
3. The third party *intentionally* causes either of the two parties to breach the contract.

The contract may be between a firm and its employees or a firm and its customers. Sometimes a competitor of a firm draws away one of the firm's key employees. If the original employer can show (1) that the competitor induced the employee to leave in breach of a contract and (2) that the employee would not otherwise have broken the contract, then the employer may be entitled to compensation from the competitor.

Wrongful Interference with a Business Relationship.
Wrongful interference with a business relationship occurs when a party unreasonably interferes with another's business in an attempt to gain a larger share of the market. The elements of a wrongful interference with a business relationship are:

1. The defendant knew or had reason to know that a third party and the plaintiff were in a business relationship or were considering doing business together.
2. The defendant intentionally interfered in the relationship.

predatory behavior
Business behavior that is undertaken with the intention of unlawfully driving competitors out of the market.

There is a difference between competitive methods that do not give rise to tort liability and **predatory behavior**—actions undertaken with the intention of unlawfully driving competitors completely out of the market. The distinction usually depends on whether a business is attempting to attract customers in general or to target customers who have shown an interest in a similar product or service of a specific competitor.

> *EXAMPLE 14.7* If a shopping center contains two shoe stores, an employee of Store A cannot be sent to the entrance of Store B to divert customers to Store A. Such activity constitutes the tort of wrongful interference with a business relationship, commonly considered to be an unfair trade practice.

Defenses to Wrongful Interference.
A party will not be liable for the tort of wrongful interference with a contractual or business relationship if it can be shown that the interference was justified, or permissible. Good faith competitive behavior is a permissible interference even if it results in the breaking of a contract.

> *EXAMPLE 14.8* Antonio's Meat Supply advertises so effectively that Beverly's Supermarket breaks its contract with Otis Meat Supply Company. Otis Meat will be unable to recover against Antonio's Meats for lost profits on a wrongful interference theory. Public policy favors free competition through honest advertising and competition for business.

Intentional Torts against Property

Intentional torts against property include trespass to land, trespass to personal property, and conversion. These torts are wrongful actions that interfere with legally recognized rights to land or personal property. The law distinguishes real property from personal property (see Chapter 16). *Real property* is land and things "permanently" attached to the land. *Personal property* consists of movable items. Thus, a house is real property, whereas the furniture inside the house is personal property. Money and stocks and bonds are also personal property. (See this chapter's *Office Tech and Cybersecurity* feature for a discussion of how spamming can constitute the tort of interference with personal property.)

Trespass to Land

A **trespass to land** occurs whenever a person, without permission, enters onto land that is owned by another, causes anything to enter onto the land, remains on the land, or permits anything to remain on it. The elements are:

1. Lawful possession of the property by the plaintiff at the time of the trespass.

2. Unauthorized entry by the defendant.

3. Damage suffered by the plaintiff.

Actual harm to the land is not an essential element of this tort because the tort is designed to protect the right of owners to exclusively possess their property. Common trespasses include walking or driving on the land, shooting a gun over the land, throwing rocks at a building that belongs to someone else, causing water to back up on someone else's land, and placing part of a building or fence on an adjoining landowner's property.

Trespass Criteria, Rights, and Duties.　The owner of the real property must show that a person is a trespasser. For example, a person who ignores "private property" signs and enters, uninvited, onto the property is clearly a trespasser. A guest in your home is an invitee, not a trespasser—unless she has been asked to leave but refuses. Any person who enters onto your property to commit an illegal act (such as a thief) is a trespasser, with or without posted signs. Normally, a trespasser must pay for any damage caused to the property and can be removed from the premises through the use of reasonable force without the owner being liable for assault and battery.

Further, a property owner owes no duty of care to a trespasser. If a trespasser sneaks across your backyard and breaks a leg when he steps in a hole in the lawn, he cannot sue you for having a hole in the lawn. The trespasser should not have been in your yard.

Defenses against Trespass to Land.　The most common defense to trespass is that the trespass was justified. For example, when a trespasser enters to assist someone in danger, a defense exists. Another defense exists when the trespasser can show that he had permission to come onto the land for a specified purpose, such as to deliver a package. Note that the property owner can revoke such permission. If the property owner asks the person delivering the package to leave and the person refuses, the person becomes a trespasser.

Trespass to Personal Property

Whenever any individual unlawfully harms the personal property of another or otherwise interferes with the owner's right to exclusively possess that personal property, **trespass to personal property** occurs. The elements of trespass to personal property are:

1. Lawful possession of the property by the plaintiff.

2. Unauthorized entry onto or use of the property by the defendant.

trespass to land
The entry onto, above, or below the surface of land owned by another without the owner's permission.

trespass to personal property
The unlawful taking or harming of another's personal property; interference with another's right to the exclusive possession of his or her personal property.

OFFICE TECH AND CYBERSECURITY

IDENTITY THEFT, SPAM, AND RELATED LEGAL ISSUES

The Internet is plagued with deceptive and destructive practices, and these practices are constantly evolving. As a paralegal, you should be aware of the problems, efforts to control them, and resources that can provide assistance.

Identity Theft

Identity theft causes grief and tens of billions of dollars in financial losses annually. We hear horror stories about people having their accounts drained and their credit ruined. The largest losses, however, fall on businesses victimized by the use of stolen financial information and other valuable data.

One type of identity theft involves *phishing*. A perpetrator "fishes" for financial data and passwords by posing as a legitimate bank, the IRS, a credit-card company, or some other reputable source. The *phisher* sends an official-looking e-mail asking the recipient to "update" or "confirm" vital information. Once those data are received, the phisher quickly drains accounts.

Various government agencies provide information about identity theft and advice about preventing it or dealing with its effects:

- The Federal Trade Commission offers information at **ftc.gov**. Enter "Identity Theft" in the search box.

- At the Department of Justice website, **justice.gov**, enter "Identity Theft" in the search box.

- The Social Security Administration offers advice about stolen Social Security numbers at **ssa.gov**.

Private sources include the Identity Theft Resources Center at **idtheftcenter.org** and the Privacy Rights Clearinghouse at **privacyrights.org**.

To guard against identity theft, only give out personal information such as credit-card or bank account numbers—for yourself or your employer—after verifying the identity of the person you are speaking with or confirming that the website you are using is secure. Remember that e-mail requests for personal or sensitive information usually are scams disguised to look official.

The Federal Can-Spam Act

Bulk, unsolicited e-mail, or *spam*, imposes a burden on e-mail recipients. No doubt you know that spam accounts for a high percentage of all e-mail. When dealing with clients who market goods or services through commercial e-mails, paralegals need to understand laws regulating spam. An important federal law in this area is the Controlling the Assault of Non-Solicited Pornography and Marketing (CAN-SPAM) Act. You can find information about the act, including some FTC regulations, at the Federal Trade Commission's website at **ftc.gov**. Enter "CAN-SPAM" in the search box.

Spamming as a Tort

Spamming may be a tort if it interferes with a computer system's functioning. A number of plaintiffs have sued, under tort law, when spam impaired their businesses' computer systems. In these cases, spamming was held to constitute unauthorized interference with the use of the personal property of another, which is a trespass to personal property. Because a great deal of spam comes from other countries, however, tort actions are limited in their effectiveness.

An example of how spamming can interfere with a business's computer system is a distributed denial of service (DDoS) attack, which occurs when outside computers flood a server with requests, making it inaccessible to others. Such an attack is analogous to flooding the door to a store with a crowd so large that it prevents customers from entering the store. DDoS attacks are becoming more common and can strike businesses of all sizes.

Technology Tip

Paralegals in consumer law need to keep up to date on issues, such as identity theft, to protect the firm's clients and assets. Paralegals should also be familiar with the resources available to those who have complaints and with laws regulating spam and hacking.

EXAMPLE 14.9 Suppose a student takes another student's paralegal book as a practical joke and hides it so that the owner is unable to find it for a week before the final exam. In this situation, the student has engaged in a trespass to personal property.

If it can be shown that trespass to personal property was warranted, then a defense exists. Most states, for example, allow vehicle repair shops to hold a customer's car (under what is called an *artisan's* or *mechanic's lien*) when the customer does not pay for repairs already completed. Not all service providers can do this, however. Veterinarians are generally not permitted to keep a pet until the bill owed for pet treatment has been paid.

Conversion

Whenever personal property is wrongfully taken from its owner, the act of **conversion** occurs. The elements of conversion are:

conversion
The act of wrongfully taking or retaining a person's personal property and placing it in the service of another.

1. The plaintiff has rightful possession of personal property.

2. The defendant intentionally interferes with that right.

3. The interference deprives the plaintiff of the possession or use of the property.

Conversion is any act depriving an owner of personal property without that owner's permission and without just cause. When conversion occurs, the lesser offense of trespass to personal property usually occurs as well. If the initial taking of the property is unlawful, there is trespass. Keeping the property is conversion. Even if the owner permitted the initial taking of the property, failure to return it may be conversion. Conversion is the civil side of crimes related to theft. A store employee who steals merchandise from the store commits a crime and engages in the tort of conversion at the same time. Even if a person mistakenly believed that she was entitled to the goods, conversion may occur.

EXAMPLE 14.10 Someone who buys stolen goods may be guilty of conversion even if she did not know that the goods were stolen. If the true owner brings a tort action against the buyer, the buyer, despite having paid the thief, must return the property to the owner or pay the rightful owner the value of the property.

Negligence

The second major category of torts is **negligence**. This tort occurs when someone suffers injury because of another's failure to meet a required *duty of care*. The elements of the tort of negligence are:

negligence
The failure to exercise the standard of care that a reasonable person would exercise in similar circumstances.

1. The defendant owed a duty of care to the plaintiff.

2. The defendant breached that duty.

3. The plaintiff suffered a legally recognizable injury.

4. The defendant's breach caused the injury suffered.

In contrast to intentional torts, in torts involving negligence, the one committing the tort did not intend to commit the initial act or to bring about the consequences of the act. Rather, the actor's careless conduct creates a *risk* of such consequences. If no risk is created, there is no negligence. The risk must be foreseeable—that is, it must be such that a reasonable person engaging in the same activity would anticipate the risk and guard against it.

Many of the actions discussed in the section on intentional torts constitute negligence if the element of intent is missing.

EXAMPLE 14.11 If Juan intentionally shoves Naomi, who falls and breaks an arm as a result, Juan will have committed the intentional tort of battery. If Juan carelessly bumps into Naomi on the stairway because he is running down the stairs, and she falls and breaks an arm as a result, Juan's action will constitute negligence. In either situation, Juan has committed a tort.

Next, we elaborate on each of the four elements of negligence.

The Duty of Care and Its Breach

Central to the tort of negligence is the concept of a **duty of care**. This concept arises from the belief that for people to live together in society some actions can be tolerated and some cannot. Some actions are right, and some are wrong. Some actions are reasonable, and some are not. The basic principle underlying the duty of care is that people are free to act as they please so long as their actions do not infringe on the protected interests of others.

Reasonable Person Standard

The law of torts defines and measures the duty of care by the **reasonable person standard**. In determining whether a duty of care has been breached, the courts ask how a reasonable person would act in the same circumstances. This standard is not necessarily how a particular person would act. Rather, it is how a judge or jury thinks a person of ordinary sense should have acted under circumstances similar to those in the matter in question. That we must exercise a reasonable standard of care in our activities is a pervasive concept in the law.

In negligence cases, the degree of care to be exercised depends on the defendant's occupation or profession, relationship with the plaintiff, and other factors. Generally, a breach of the duty of care is determined on a case-by-case basis. The outcome depends on how the trial court judge (or jury) decides a reasonable person in the defendant's position would have acted in the circumstances of the case. Next, we examine the degree of care typically expected of property owners and professionals.

The Duty of Property Owners

Property owners are expected to exercise reasonable care to protect invited persons coming onto their property from harm. Owners who rent or lease property to tenants are expected to exercise reasonable care to ensure that the tenants and their guests are not harmed in common areas, such as stairways and laundry rooms, by keeping them in safe condition.

Duty to Business Invitees.   Retailers and other businesses that invite persons to come onto their premises have a duty to exercise reasonable care to protect those persons, each of whom are considered a **business invitee**. Any business open to the public is assumed to "invite" people to enter the business's premises, whether they intend to buy something or not.

> *EXAMPLE 14.12* If you entered a supermarket, slipped on a wet floor from a spilled product, and suffered injuries, the owner of the supermarket could be liable for negligence and required to pay damages. Liability could be imposed if, when you slipped, there was no sign warning that the floor was wet, and this condition had existed for some time. A court could hold that the business owner failed to exercise a reasonable degree of care in protecting the store's customers against foreseeable risks about which the owner knew or *should have known*. That a patron might slip on the wet floor and be injured as a result was a foreseeable risk, and the owner should have taken care to avoid this risk or to warn customers of it.

The owner also has a duty to discover and remove any hidden dangers that might injure a customer or other invitee.

Open and Obvious Risks.   Some risks, of course, are so obvious that the owner need not warn of them. For instance, a business owner does not need to warn customers to open a door before attempting to walk through it. Other risks, however, even though they may seem obvious to a business owner, may not be so in the eyes of another, such as a child.

EXAMPLE 14.13 A hardware store owner may not think it is necessary to warn customers that a stepladder leaning against the back wall of the store could fall down and harm them. It is possible, though, that a child could tip the ladder over or climb on it and be hurt as a result. In that case, the store could be held liable for leaving the ladder in an accessible area.

The Duty of Professionals

If a person has special knowledge or skill, the person's conduct must be consistent with that knowledge or skill. Professionals—including physicians, architects, engineers, accountants, contractors, lawyers, and others—are required to have the standard knowledge and ability expected of members of the profession. In determining what is reasonable care for professionals, their training, the standards of the profession, and their expertise are taken into account. In other words, an accountant cannot defend against a lawsuit for negligence by stating, "I was not familiar with the technical rules of accounting." Furthermore, a business is held to the standard of care expected of knowledgeable people in that line of work. Thus, an auto repair shop cannot deny knowledge of the proper procedures for an oil change.

If a professional violates the duty of care toward a client, the professional may be sued for malpractice. For example, a patient might sue a physician for *medical malpractice*. Thus, a surgeon who did not follow standard procedures and thereby injured a patient would have negligently committed medical malpractice. Similarly, a client might sue an attorney for *legal malpractice* (see Chapter 4) for failure to demonstrate the knowledge expected of a competent member of the bar.

The Injury Requirement and Damages

To recover damages (receive compensation), the plaintiff in a tort lawsuit must prove that she or he suffered a *legally recognizable* injury—some loss, harm, wrong, or invasion of a legally protected interest. This is generally true in lawsuits for intentional torts as well as lawsuits for negligence.

Essentially, the purpose of tort law is to compensate for legally recognized injuries resulting from wrongful acts. If no harm or injury results from a given negligent action, there is nothing to compensate.

EXAMPLE 14.14 If you carelessly bump into a passerby, who stumbles and falls as a result, you may be liable in tort if the passerby is injured in the fall. If the person is unharmed, however, there normally can be no suit for damages, because no injury was suffered.

Compensatory Damages

The purpose of tort law is to compensate injured parties for damages suffered, not to punish people for the wrongs that they commit. **Compensatory damages** are intended to compensate, or reimburse, a plaintiff for actual losses—to make the plaintiff "whole." Occasionally, however, punitive damages are also awarded in tort lawsuits.

compensatory damages
A money award equivalent to the actual value of injuries or damages sustained by the aggrieved party.

Punitive Damages

To punish the wrongdoer and deter others from similar wrongdoing, a court may award **punitive damages**. Such damages are rarely awarded in lawsuits for ordinary negligence. They are more likely to be awarded in cases involving intentional torts. If the defendant's negligent conduct was particularly reckless or willful, a plaintiff has a greater chance of prevailing. In 1989, for example, the *Exxon Valdez*, an oil tanker owned by Exxon Shipping Company, struck a reef in Alaska's Prince William Sound and spilled more than 10 million gallons of oil into the pristine waters. Afterward, a jury awarded

punitive damages
Monetary damages awarded to a plaintiff to punish the defendant and deter future similar conduct.

$5 billion in punitive damages against Exxon in addition to $287 million in actual damages. (This award was later reduced to $507.5 million on appeal.)

Causation

Another element necessary to a tort is *causation*. If a person fails in a duty of care and someone suffers injury, the wrongful activity must have caused the harm for a tort to have been committed. In deciding whether there is causation, the court must address two questions:

- *Is there causation in fact?* Did the injury occur because of the defendant's act, or would it have occurred anyway? If an injury would not have occurred without the defendant's act, then there is causation in fact. **Causation in fact** usually can be determined by the use of the *but for* test: "but for" the wrongful act, the injury would not have occurred.

> **causation in fact**
> Causation brought about by an act or omission without which an event would not have occurred.

EXAMPLE 14.15 Annie runs a red light and runs into Joe's car. The accident would not have occurred but for Annie's running the red light, so she is liable. Causation is clear.

- *Was the act the proximate cause of the injury?* **Proximate cause**, or legal cause, exists when the connection between an act and an injury is strong enough to justify imposing liability.

> **proximate cause**
> Legal cause; exists when the connection between an act and an injury is strong enough to justify imposing liability.

EXAMPLE 14.16 Arnie runs a red light and hits Nicki's car. Her car has explosives in the trunk, and they explode when the car is hit. The explosion hurts bystanders. The injured bystanders cannot sue Arnie. His negligence was the cause in fact of the accident, but it was not the proximate cause of the bystanders' injuries. The likelihood of that incident was so remote that Arnie could not reasonably have foreseen its occurrence. The bystanders may be able to sue Nicki, however, because it is not reasonable to transport explosives in the trunk of a car.

Both questions must be answered in the affirmative for liability in tort to arise. If a defendant's action constitutes causation in fact but a court decides that the action was not the proximate cause of the plaintiff's injury, the causation requirement has not been met—and the defendant normally will not be liable to the plaintiff.

Paralegals who work in the area of tort law often assist in litigation involving automobile accidents. Investigating the facts of the accident and preparing graphics are usually an important aspect of the paralegal's job. What is the relationship between fact investigation and preparation of graphics for trial?

bikeriderlondon/Shutterstock.com

Notice that detailed information is required in the evaluation of negligence claims. This chapter's *Featured Contributor* article on the following pages discusses the kind of research that may be required in a liability case.

Defenses to Negligence

Defendants often defend against negligence claims by asserting that the plaintiffs have failed to prove the existence of one or more of the required elements for negligence. Additionally, there are three basic *affirmative* defenses to negligence claims that defendants can raise to avoid or reduce their liability even if the facts are as the plaintiff claims: (1) assumption of risk, (2) superseding cause, and (3) contributory or comparative negligence.

Assumption of Risk

A plaintiff who voluntarily enters into a risky situation, knowing the risk involved, will not be allowed to recover. This is the defense of **assumption of risk**. The requirements of this defense are (1) knowledge of the risk and (2) voluntary assumption of the risk. Remember, the defendant has the burden of proof of establishing these conditions.

The risk can be assumed by express agreement, or the assumption of risk can be implied by the plaintiff's knowledge of the risk and subsequent conduct.

EXAMPLE 14.17 Bob, a race-car driver, enters a NASCAR race. Because he knows there is a risk of being killed or injured in a crash, he is unlikely to succeed in a liability suit against another driver in case of an accident.

Of course, the plaintiff does not assume a risk different from or greater than the risk normally carried by the activity. In the scenario just mentioned, the race driver does not assume the risk that the operators of the raceway will do nothing about an oil slick on the track.

In emergency situations, risks are not considered assumed. Neither are they assumed when a statute protects a class of people from harm and a member of the class is injured by the harm.

Today, employers are under a statutory duty to provide a safe workplace to their employees, who therefore do not assume all risks associated with the workplace. In the nineteenth century, this employer duty was not the standard, however, and many courts held that employees assumed the risk of working in a dangerous factory. One result of this situation was workers' compensation laws—some of which explicitly bar the assumption of risk defense for employers who fail to secure workers' compensation insurance. Workers' compensation statutes also generally bar tort claims against employers who have the required insurance (to be discussed in Chapter 18).

Superseding Cause

An unforeseeable intervening event may break the connection between a wrongful act and an injury to another. If so, it acts as a *superseding cause*—that is, it relieves a defendant of liability for injuries caused by the intervening event.

EXAMPLE 14.18 Suppose Derrick keeps a plastic bottle of gasoline in the trunk of his car. Carrying the gasoline creates a foreseeable risk and so is negligent. If Derrick's car crashes into a tree, causing the bottle filled with gasoline to explode, Derrick will be liable for injuries sustained by passing pedestrians because of his negligence. If lightning striking the car causes the explosion, however, the lightning supersedes Derrick's original negligence as a cause of the damage. The lightning strike was so unlikely that it was not foreseeable.

assumption of risk
Voluntarily taking on a known risk; a defense against negligence that can be used when the plaintiff has knowledge and understanding of a danger and voluntarily exposes himself or herself to the danger.

FEATURED CONTRIBUTOR

IN-DEPTH RESEARCH AND ATTENTION TO DETAIL

Kenneth O'Neil Salyer

BIOGRAPHICAL NOTE

Kenneth O'Neil Salyer earned his undergraduate, J.D., and Master of Arts in Teaching degrees at the University of Louisville. He is licensed to practice law in the state of Kentucky and has litigated tort, product liability, and real estate matters. He has served as chair of the legal studies department at a college in Louisville. Mr. Salyer consults with colleges across the country about online education and remains active in the legal community. He is the head coach for the University of Louisville undergraduate moot court teams.

"Neil," said the managing partner, "I need you to go with Laura to research the history of asbestos-insulation installation in Kentucky buildings prior to 1965." I received this directive during my third year of law school while clerking at a personal-injury defense firm that specialized in mass torts and product liability cases. Without any construction or engineering experience, I was severely overwhelmed and woefully underprepared to execute this task successfully. I knew the firm was defending certain businesses in mesothelioma litigation, but had no idea why the history of asbestos insulation was so important, and worse, no idea how to find the answer.

The aforementioned "Laura" was the managing partner's lead paralegal; she had worked on asbestos and mesothelioma cases for longer than I had been with the firm. Without hesitation, she

Contributory and Comparative Negligence

People are expected to exercise a reasonable degree of care in looking out for themselves. In a few jurisdictions, recovery for injury resulting from negligence is prevented if the plaintiff was also negligent. This is the defense of **contributory negligence**. Under the common law doctrine of contributory negligence, any negligence by the plaintiff means that the plaintiff will not recover damages.

Today, most states apply the doctrine of **comparative negligence**. Here, the plaintiff's negligence and the defendant's negligence are compared and the liability for damages distributed accordingly. Some jurisdictions have adopted a "pure" form of comparative negligence that allows the plaintiff to recover even if his fault is greater than that of the defendant. For example, if the plaintiff was 80 percent at fault and the defendant 20 percent at fault, the plaintiff may recover 20 percent of her damages. Many states' comparative negligence statutes, however, contain a "50 percent" rule by which the plaintiff recovers nothing if he was more than 50 percent at fault.

Special Negligence Doctrines and Statutes

There are a number of special doctrines and statutes relating to negligence. We examine only a few of them here.

contributory negligence
A theory in tort law under which a complaining party's own negligence contributed to his or her injuries. Contributory negligence is an absolute bar to recovery in some jurisdictions.

comparative negligence
A theory in tort law under which the liability for injuries resulting from negligent acts is shared by all persons who were guilty of negligence (including the injured party) on the basis of each person's proportionate carelessness.

took me under her wing and quickly taught me what it takes to be a topflight legal professional in the competitive world of tort and products liability litigation.

We logged countless hours traveling across the state to every library with an engineering or construction section housing historical records. We found engineering specs from the 1950s, scoured old building codes, and located regional "best practices," all in an effort to better equip our attorneys in their upcoming mass tort litigation.

Once all the information had been gathered, Laura explained how to piece it together like a jigsaw puzzle. We had to determine the questions and then formulate the answers to provide the managing partner with the necessary knowledge to become an expert in this nonlegal field. I quickly learned that exceptionally good attorneys are not just experts at the law; they also become experts in the fields in which they litigate. This expertise comes not only from personal research and knowledge, but also from the research performed by their trusted paralegals.

For this case, the attorney needed to know and understand the common practices at the time the buildings in question were built, as well as asbestos research that was readily available at the time. Both of these would help determine liability of the business and the builder.

> **" Good attorneys become experts in the fields in which they litigate."**

Laura taught me many things about success in the legal field: extreme attention to detail, thinking outside the box when presented with complex questions, and most importantly, going above and beyond what was necessary to ensure success for a client. Our days of traversing the state and sitting in dark, damp libraries flipping through moldy records helped the clients prove to the jury that they acted in good faith by following standard procedures of the time.

After law school, and throughout my years as a litigator, I always made sure a competent, trustworthy paralegal was by my side. I never walked into trial without feeling I knew more about the subject at hand than opposing counsel. Simply stated, this would have been impossible without the help of knowledgeable, driven, and exceptional paralegals.

When I began teaching students how to be effective paralegals, Laura's early lessons never left my mind. An intimate understanding of the law is important, but it is not the only skill one needs to be an effective, high-performing paralegal. Your attention to detail and ability to think outside the box when addressing in-class questions, homework, and more will be key to success when you enter the highly specialized and stressful world of a legal professional.

Negligence *Per Se*

Certain conduct, whether it consists of an action or a failure to act, may be treated as **negligence *per se*** (*per se* means "in or of itself"). Negligence *per se* may occur if an individual violates a statute or an ordinance providing for a criminal penalty and that violation causes another to be injured. The injured person must prove:

negligence *per se*
An action or failure to act in violation of a statutory requirement.

1. That the statute sets out what standard of conduct is expected, when and where it is expected, and of whom it is expected.

2. That the injured person is in the class intended to be protected by the statute.

3. That the statute was designed to prevent the type of injury that was suffered.

The standard of conduct required by the statute is the duty that the defendant owes to the plaintiff, and a violation of the statute is the breach of that duty.

> **EXAMPLE 14.19** A statute requires property owners to keep buildings in safe condition and may subject owners to a criminal penalty, such as a fine, if the building is not kept safe. The statute is meant to protect those who are rightfully in the building. Thus, if an owner, without sufficient excuse, violates the statute and a tenant is injured as a result, then courts will likely hold that the owner's unexcused violation of the statute establishes a breach of a duty of care—the owner's violation is negligence *per se*.

Good Samaritan statutes
State statutes stipulating that persons who provide emergency services to others in peril—unless they do so recklessly, thus causing further harm—cannot be sued for negligence.

dram shop acts
State statutes that impose liability on the owners of bars, as well as those who serve alcoholic drinks to the public, for injuries resulting from accidents caused by intoxicated persons when the sellers or servers of alcoholic drinks contributed to the intoxication.

cyber tort
A tort committed by use of the Internet.

Special Negligence Statutes

Many states have enacted statutes prescribing responsibilities in certain circumstances. Most states have what are called **Good Samaritan statutes**. Under these statutes, persons who receive voluntary aid from others cannot turn around and sue the persons providing assistance (the "Good Samaritans") for negligence. These laws were passed largely to protect medical personnel who volunteer their services in emergency situations to those in need, such as people hurt in car accidents.

Many states have enacted **dram shop acts**. A bar owner or bartender may be held liable for injuries caused by a person who became intoxicated while drinking at the bar or who was already intoxicated when served by the bartender. In some states, statutes impose liability on *social hosts* (persons hosting parties) for injuries caused by guests who became intoxicated at the hosts' homes. For liability to be imposed, it is unnecessary to prove that the bar owner, bartender, or social host was negligent.

Cyber Torts: Defamation Online

Who should be held liable for a **cyber tort**? For example, who should be held liable when someone posts a defamatory message online? Should an Internet service provider (ISP) be liable for the remark?

Cyber torts (like cyber crimes, discussed in Chapter 13) are not new torts as much as they are new ways of committing torts that present special issues of proof. How, for example, can it be proved that an online defamatory remark was "published," which requires that a third party see or hear it? How can the identity of the person who made the remark be discovered?

Liability of Internet Service Providers

Online forums allow anyone—customers, employees, or crackpots—to complain about a business firm's personnel, policies, practices, or products. Regardless of whether the complaint is justified, it might have an impact on the business. One question that initially created problems for the courts was whether providers of such forums could be held liable for defamatory statements. Congress responded with the Communications Decency Act, which states that Internet service providers, or "interactive computer service providers," are not liable for such material.[1] Some European countries impose much greater liability on ISPs and other service providers.

Piercing the Veil of Anonymity

A problem for anyone who seeks to sue for online defamation is discovering the identity of the person who posted the defamatory message. In general, ISPs can disclose personal information about their customers only when ordered to do so by a court. Because of this, businesses and individuals have resorted to lawsuits against unidentified "John Does." Then, if the courts approve, they might obtain from the ISPs the identities of the persons responsible for the messages.

> ***EXAMPLE 14.20*** Eric Hvide, the former chief executive of a company called Hvide Marine, sued a number of "John Does" who had posted allegedly defamatory statements about him and his company online. Hvide sued the John Does for libel in a Florida court. The court ruled that the ISPs had to reveal the identities of the defendant Does. Hvide was then able to amend his complaint to substitute the names of the actual individuals for the John Does listed in his original complaint.

In some cases, the rights of plaintiffs in such situations have been balanced against the defendants' rights to free speech. Some courts have concluded that more than a bare allegation of defamation is required to outweigh an individual's right to anonymity in the exercise of free speech.

Strict Liability

Intentional torts and torts of negligence involve acts that depart from a reasonable standard of care and cause injuries. Under the doctrine of **strict liability**, liability for injury is imposed for reasons other than fault. Traditionally, strict liability was imposed for damages proximately caused by an abnormally dangerous or exceptional activity.

Abnormally dangerous activities have three characteristics. The activities:

1. Involve potential harm, of a serious nature, to persons or property.

2. Involve a high degree of risk that cannot be completely guarded against by the exercise of reasonable care.

3. Are not commonly performed in the community or area.

The primary basis of liability is the creation of an extraordinary risk. Even if blasting with explosives is performed with all reasonable care, for instance, there is still a risk of injury. Because of the potential for harm, the person who is engaged in an abnormally dangerous activity is responsible for paying for any injuries caused by that activity. Knowing that they will be liable for injuries, those engaged in such activities have strong incentives to use extreme caution.

The most significant application of strict liability is in the area of *product liability*—liability of manufacturers and sellers for harmful or defective products. This is a newer application of the doctrine of strict liability.

strict liability
Liability regardless of fault. In tort law, strict liability may be imposed on a merchant who introduces into commerce a good that is so defective as to be unreasonably dangerous.

Product Liability

Those who manufacture or sell goods can be held liable for injuries and damages caused by defects under the law of **product liability**. Liability is based on the notion that manufacturers are better able to bear the cost of injury than innocent victims. In addition, requiring producers to pay for injuries caused by their products encourages them to make safer products. The kinds of issues that arise for paralegals who work in this area of law are discussed in the *Developing Paralegal Skills* feature on the following page.

product liability
The legal liability of manufacturers, sellers, and lessors of goods to consumers, users, and bystanders for injuries or damages that are caused by the goods.

Theories of Product Liability

A party who is injured by a defective product can bring a suit against the product's seller or manufacturer under several theories. These theories include negligence, misrepresentation, and strict product liability.

Product Liability Based on Negligence

If a manufacturer fails to exercise due care to make a product safe, *any person* who is injured by the product can sue the manufacturer for negligence. The plaintiff does not have to be the person who purchased the product. The manufacturer must use due care in designing the product, selecting the materials, producing and assembling the product, testing and inspecting the product for safety, and placing adequate warnings on the label to inform users of dangers.

DEVELOPING PARALEGAL SKILLS

HANDLING PRODUCT-RELATED CLAIMS

Product liability cases account for about 7 percent of personal injury cases in the United States. These cases affect products used in every American home, from cars to toys. For example, there are more than 200,000 toy-related injuries annually. Product-related injuries can be caused by anything from a child's choking on a small part in a toy to an electric vehicle's battery catching fire.

If a client brings a product liability case to your firm, there are important steps to take in the course of investigating the claim. You must attempt to locate and preserve the product that allegedly caused the injury. This may require quick action. If an individual is injured in a car accident that you suspect may have been caused by a product defect, you will need to contact the owner (if different from your client), garage, towing company, or police impound lot that has possession of the vehicle and ask that party to refrain from any work on or disposal of the vehicle. You will also want to inspect it as soon as possible. You will need photographs, a secure chain of custody for the product, and an expert inspection.

If an injury led to an ambulance or police call, you will want to secure authenticated copies of any tapes of the calls or records created. If anyone saw a doctor as a result of the product's malfunction, you will need the doctor's medical records. If someone died, you will want the death certificate and autopsy report (if any). Getting these records and any witness statements quickly is important to your supervising attorney's evaluation of the case.

Product liability cases often involve considerable technical evidence. Knowing the scientific and engineering terms and being able to interact with experts in these areas will make you a more effective paralegal.

Product Liability Based on Misrepresentation

When a manufacturer or seller misrepresents the quality, nature, or appropriate use of a product, and the user is injured as a result, the basis of liability may be the tort of fraud. Generally, the misrepresentation must have been made knowingly or with reckless disregard for the facts, and the party must have intended the user to rely on the statement.

Strict Product Liability

Under the doctrine of strict liability, a manufacturer that has exercised reasonable care can still be held liable if a product is defective and injures someone. Strict product liability reflects the general principle that the law should protect consumers from dangerous products. The rule of strict liability is also applicable to the suppliers of component parts that are used in the final product.

In general, strict liability will be imposed if the plaintiff can establish the following six requirements:

1. The product must be in a defective condition when the defendant sells it.

2. The defendant must normally be engaged in the business of selling the product (that is, not someone selling old equipment at a garage sale).

3. The product must be unreasonably dangerous to the user or consumer because of its defective condition.

4. The plaintiff must incur physical harm to self or property by use or consumption of the product.

5. The defective condition must be the proximate cause of the injury or damage.

6. The goods must not have been substantially changed from the time the product was sold to the time the injury was sustained.[2]

Note that the plaintiff is not required to show why or how the product became defective. The plaintiff must only prove that the **unreasonably dangerous product** caused the injury and that the condition of the product was essentially the same as when it was sold. A product may be unreasonably dangerous due to a flaw in the manufacturing process, a design defect, or an inadequate warning.

unreasonably dangerous product
A product that is defective such that it threatens a consumer's health and safety. A product is considered unreasonably dangerous if it is dangerous beyond the expectation of the ordinary consumer or if a less dangerous alternative was economically feasible for the manufacturer but was not used.

Manufacturing Defects.   A product that departs from its intended design, even though all possible care was exercised in the preparation and marketing of the product, has a manufacturing defect. Liability is imposed on the manufacturer (and possibly on the wholesaler and retailer) regardless of whether the manufacturer acted "reasonably."

Design Defects.   A product has a design defect if the foreseeable risks of harm posed by the product could have been reduced or avoided by adopting an economically feasible, reasonable alternative design. This chapter's *Ethics Watch* feature discusses how work and personal life can conflict in this area of law.

Warning Defects.   A product may also be deemed defective because of inadequate instructions or warnings in situations in which the risk of harm was foreseeable and could have been avoided if a proper warning had been given.

In evaluating the adequacy of warnings, courts consider the risks of the product and whether the content of the warning was understandable to the expected user.[3] For example, children would likely respond better to bright, bold, simple warning labels, whereas adults may benefit from more detailed information.

Sellers must warn those who purchase their products of harms that can result from the *foreseeable misuse* of the product. The key is the foreseeability of the misuse. Sellers are not required to take precautions against every possible unusual use of their products.

ETHICS WATCH

CONFIDENTIALITY AND PRODUCT LIABILITY

Paralegals who work in the area of product liability may find themselves in a sticky situation. For example, suppose your firm represents a particular toy manufacturer. The toy firm sells a toy that is popular for young children. The toy, however, is apparently defective and has injured some children. It has not been recalled. Everything you know about this toy you have learned from the work you have done on the case.

Should you talk to your attorney about the possibility of discussing with the client the possibility of a voluntary recall? Suppose some of your friends have children around that age. Can you warn your friends about the defective toy? If you tell one person, you may violate the ethical rule of confidentiality. What if you don't warn someone and that person's child is injured?

This is just one example of ethical dilemmas that may arise for paralegals who work in the area of product liability. In circumstances such as these, it is advisable to consult your supervising attorney for direction.

The issue discussed here is related to NALA's *Code of Ethics and Professional Responsibility*, Canon 4: "A paralegal must use discretion and professional judgment commensurate with knowledge and experience but must not render independent legal judgment in place of an attorney."

It is also related to the NFPA's *Model Code of Ethics*, Section EC 1.5: "A paralegal shall preserve all confidential information provided by the client or acquired from other sources before, during, and after the course of the professional relationship."

Defenses to Product Liability

There is no duty to warn about risks that are obvious or commonly known. Gas stations do not have to warn consumers to avoid drinking gasoline. Knives are supposed to be sharp. Warnings about *obvious risks* do not add to the safety of a product and could even detract from it by making other warnings seem less significant.

To avoid liability, the defendant in a product liability case can show that there is no basis for the plaintiff's claim or that the plaintiff has not met the requirements for liability. For example, if the suit alleges a product caused an injury and the defendant proves that the product did not cause the plaintiff's injury, the defendant will not be liable. Defendants may also assert the affirmative defenses discussed next.

Assumption of Risk

The obviousness of a risk and a user's decision to proceed in the face of that risk may be a defense in a product liability suit. For example, if a buyer ignored a product recall by the seller, a court might conclude that the buyer had assumed the risk. To establish this defense, the defendant must show that:

1. The plaintiff knew and appreciated the risk created by the product defect.
2. The plaintiff voluntarily assumed the risk, even though it was unreasonable to do so.

Product Misuse

Defendants can also claim that the plaintiff misused the product. This defense is similar to claiming that the plaintiff assumed the risk. Here, however, the use was not one for which the product was designed. If the misuse is reasonably foreseeable, the seller must take measures to guard against it, such as by warning consumers, but if a consumer does something obviously dangerous, such as using a chain saw to trim toenails, the chainsaw maker is not liable.

Comparative Negligence

Developments in the area of comparative negligence (discussed earlier in this chapter) have affected the doctrine of strict liability. Most jurisdictions consider the negligent or intentional actions of both the plaintiff and the defendant when apportioning liability and damages.

Consumer Law

consumer
A person who buys products and services for personal or household use.

Since the 1960s, many laws have been passed to protect the health and safety of consumers. A **consumer** is a person who purchases, for private use, goods or services from business firms. Sources of consumer protection exist at all levels of government. Exhibit 14.1 indicates some of the areas of consumer law regulated by statutes and by associated regulations. Many federal agencies have an office of consumer affairs, and most states have one or more offices, including the offices of state attorneys general, to assist consumers.

consumer law
Statutes, agency rules, and judicial decisions protecting consumers of goods and services.

All statutes, agency rules, and common law judicial decisions that serve to protect the interests of consumers are classified as **consumer law**. Because of the wide variation among state consumer protection laws, our primary focus here is on federal legislation—specifically, on legislation governing advertising, labeling and packaging, sales, health protection, product safety, and credit protection.

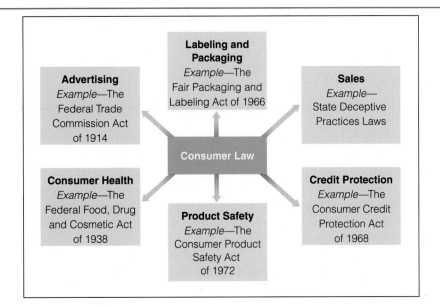

EXHIBIT 14.1

Selected Areas of Consumer Law Regulated by Statutes

Deceptive Sales Practices

Under the common law, if a seller misrepresented the quality, price, or availability of a certain product, the consumer's recourse was to sue the seller for fraud or for breach of contract. Fraud requires proof of *intent* to misrepresent the product's usefulness to the buyer. Frequently, the burden of having to prove intent was too great, and consumers were left with little or no legal recourse against deceptive practices. Furthermore, because litigation is costly, consumers rarely pursued actions involving relatively small losses, even if they would have been likely to win the cases.

Today, various agencies, both federal and state, are empowered to protect consumers from deceptive business practices. At the federal level, the most important agency is the Federal Trade Commission (FTC). The Federal Trade Commission Act authorizes the FTC to determine what constitutes a deceptive practice. The FTC policy on deception holds that a practice is deceptive and subject to agency action if:

1. There is misrepresentation or omission of information in a communication to consumers.

2. The deception is likely to mislead a reasonable consumer.

3. The deception is material—it is likely to be misleading to the detriment of consumers.

This broad definition allows the FTC to attack a wide variety of business practices, as do statutes such as the California Civil Code, Chapter 3, which concerns deceptive practices. Besides such general regulations, there are more specific areas of regulation, as described next.

Deceptive Advertising

Over the past several decades, consumers have received increased protection against **deceptive advertising**. Deception comes in many forms. It may arise from a false statement or claim about a company's own products or a competitor's products. Some advertisements contain "half-truths," meaning that the information presented is true but incomplete, leading consumers to a false conclusion.

deception
In consumer law, a material misrepresentation or omission in information that is likely to mislead a reasonable consumer to his or her detriment.

deceptive advertising
Advertising that misleads consumers, either through unjustified claims concerning a product's performance or through failure to disclose relevant information concerning the product's composition or performance.

> **EXAMPLE 14.21** The makers of Campbell's soups advertised that most Campbell's soups were low in fat and cholesterol and thus were helpful in fighting heart disease. The ads did not say that Campbell's soups are high in sodium and that high-sodium diets may increase the risk of heart disease. The FTC ruled that Campbell's claims were thus deceptive.

Generally the test for whether an ad is deceptive is *whether a reasonable consumer would be deceived by the ad*.

If the FTC believes that an advertisement is deceptive, it drafts a formal complaint and sends it to the alleged offender. The company may agree to settle the complaint without further proceedings. If the company does not agree to a settlement, the FTC can conduct a hearing, at which the company can present its defense. If the FTC succeeds in proving that a business practice, such as an advertisement, is deceptive, it usually issues a **cease-and-desist order** requiring that the challenged practice or advertising be stopped.

cease-and-desist order
An administrative or judicial order prohibiting a person or business firm from conducting activities that an agency or court has deemed illegal.

Labeling and Packaging Laws

A number of federal and state laws deal with the information on labels and packages. In general, labels must be accurate and must use words that are easily understood by the ordinary consumer. For instance, a box of cereal cannot be labeled "giant" if that would exaggerate the amount of cereal in the box. In some instances, labels must specify the raw materials used in the product, such as the percentage of cotton or other fiber used in clothing. In other instances, the product must carry a warning. Cigarette packages must include warnings about the health hazards of smoking, for example.

Food products must bear labels detailing nutritional content, including how much fat the food contains and what kind of fat it is. The federal Food and Drug Administration (FDA) has guidelines to standardize nutritional information on packaged foods, and the FTC plays a key role in enforcing the restrictions. The Nutrition Labeling and Education Act requires standard nutrition facts on food labels; regulates the use of such terms as *fresh*, *low fat*, and *organic*; and, subject to FDA approval, authorizes certain health claims.

Sales Transactions

Many laws that protect consumers require the disclosure of terms in sales transactions and provide rules governing certain sales, such as door-to-door sales, mail-order sales, and the receipt of unsolicited merchandise. One FTC regulation, for example, requires sellers to give consumers three days to cancel any door-to-door sale. In addition, the FTC requires that consumers be notified in Spanish of this right if the oral negotiations for the sale were in Spanish. The FTC also has rules requiring sellers of some goods and services (such as used cars and funeral services) to disclose particular information to consumers. Most states have enacted laws specifically governing consumer sales transactions that apply to a wide range of practices.

Consumer Health and Safety

Regulating the labeling and packaging of products helps to promote consumer health and safety. But there is a difference between regulating information about a product and regulating the content of the product.

> **EXAMPLE 14.22** Most tobacco products have not been banned despite their known hazards. Rather, regulations require producers to warn consumers about the hazards of tobacco. If people choose to use tobacco products with knowledge of the risks to their health, that is their choice.

We now look at several laws that regulate the actual products made available to consumers.

In 1906, Congress passed the Pure Food and Drug Act, which was the first legislation aimed at protecting consumers against impure and misbranded food and drug products. In 1938, the Federal Food, Drug and Cosmetic Act was passed to strengthen the 1906 law. These acts and later amendments established standards for foods, specified safe levels of food additives, and regulated some aspects of food advertising. They also required that drugs must be proved effective as well as safe before they could receive permission to be sold. The Food and Drug Administration enforces most of the statutes involving food and drugs, but the Department of Agriculture has jurisdiction over some food products.

Still other statutes, categorized as product-safety acts, regulate the distribution of hazardous or defective products. One example is the Consumer Product Safety Act, enacted to protect consumers from dangerous products. The Consumer Product Safety Commission, which was created by the act, conducts research on the safety of products and maintains a clearinghouse on the risks associated with various products. The commission sets standards for consumer products and bans the sale of products it deems hazardous to consumers. Products banned include unsafe fireworks, cribs, and toys, as well as many products containing asbestos, lead, or vinyl chloride.

Consumer Credit Protection

Because of the extensive use of credit by American consumers, credit protection has become an important area of consumer protection legislation.

Truth-in-Lending Act (TILA)

One of the most significant statutes regulating the credit and credit-card industry is the Truth-in-Lending Act (TILA), the name commonly given to Title 1 of the Consumer Credit Protection Act, passed by Congress in 1968 and greatly expanded since then. TILA, which is administered by the Consumer Financial Protection Bureau, is basically a *disclosure law*.

TILA requires sellers and lenders to disclose credit terms or loan terms so that borrowers can shop around for the best financing arrangements. TILA requirements apply only to entities that, in the ordinary course of business, lend money, sell on credit, or arrange for the extension of credit. Sales or loans made between two consumers do not come under the act. Additionally, the act protects only persons (not businesses).

Under TILA, terms of a credit instrument must be clearly and conspicuously (obviously) disclosed and must follow regulations. The law provides that a consumer can cancel a contract if a creditor fails to follow exactly the required procedures.

Equal Opportunity.   The Equal Credit Opportunity Act (ECOA) amended TILA in 1974. It prohibits the denial of credit solely on the basis of race, religion, national origin, color, gender, marital status, age, or whether the credit applicant receives public-assistance benefits. Creditors may not collect information about any of these characteristics from an applicant and may not require the signature of an applicant's spouse, other than as a joint applicant.

Credit Cards.   The TILA also contains provisions regarding credit cards. One provision limits the liability of a cardholder to $50 per card for unauthorized charges made before the card issuer is notified that the card has been lost. Another provision prohibits a credit-card company from billing a consumer for any unauthorized charges on a credit card that was improperly issued by the company. Further provisions of the act concern billing disputes related to credit-card purchases. The act outlines specific procedures and time deadlines for both the consumer and the credit-card company to follow in settling a dispute. Note that these protections generally do not apply to *debit cards*, an important distinction.

The Credit Card Accountability Responsibility and Disclosure (CARD) Act of 2009 also provides protection for credit-card holders. It limits the fees credit-card companies can charge for various services, thereby reducing the average cost of possessing a credit card. The main impact is not on the interest rate charged but on such charges as fees for late payments, fees for exceeding the approved credit limit, and unexpected rate increases. The CARD Act focuses on the provision of transparent information in plain language by card issuers. The Consumer Financial Protection Bureau is responsible for implementing the statute.

Fair Credit Reporting Act

Lenders use *credit reports* to decide whether and how much to lend to prospective borrowers. To protect consumers against inaccurate credit reporting, Congress enacted the Fair Credit Reporting Act. It provides that consumer credit reporting agencies—such as Equifax, TransUnion, and Experian—may issue credit reports only for specified purposes. Such purposes include the extension of credit, the issuance of insurance policies, and compliance with a court order. A report may also be issued in response to a consumer's request for a copy of her own credit report. When a consumer is denied credit or insurance on the basis of a credit report, the consumer must be notified of that fact and of the name and address of the credit-reporting agency that issued the credit report.

Under the act, consumers may request the source of any information being given out by a credit agency, as well as the identity of any party that received an agency's report. Consumers also have access to the information contained about them in a credit reporting agency's files. If a consumer discovers that these files contain inaccurate information, the agency, on the consumer's written request, must investigate. If the investigation reveals that the information is unverifiable or inaccurate, the agency must delete it within a reasonable period of time.

Fair and Accurate Credit Transactions Act

To help combat identity theft, Congress passed the Fair and Accurate Credit Transactions (FACT) Act. It established a fraud alert system so that consumers who suspect that they have been victimized by identity theft can place an alert on their credit files. The act also requires the major credit reporting agencies to provide consumers with free copies of their own credit reports every twelve months. The act requires financial institutions to work with the FTC to identify "red flag" indicators of identity theft and to develop rules on how to dispose of sensitive credit information.

The FACT Act gives consumers who have been victimized by identity theft some assistance in rebuilding their credit reputations. For example, credit reporting agencies must stop reporting allegedly fraudulent account information once the consumer establishes that identify theft has occurred. Business owners and creditors are required to provide consumers with copies of any records that can help the consumers prove that a particular account or transaction is fraudulent (a forged signature, for example).

Fair Debt Collection Practices Act

The Fair Debt Collection Practices Act (FDCPA) was enacted to curb abuses by collection agencies. The act applies to debt-collection agencies that regularly attempt to collect debts on behalf of someone else.

The act prohibits contacting consumers at their place of employment if the employers object, contacting consumers at inconvenient times, and contacting consumers if attorneys represent them. The act also prohibits debt-collection agencies from contacting most third parties about a debt unless authorized to do so by a court, using harassment and intimidation (such as abusive language), using false or misleading information, and communicating with the consumer after receipt of a notice that the consumer is refusing to pay the debt except to advise the consumer of legal action being taken by the agency.

> *EXAMPLE 14.23* West Asset Management, a debt collector, was sued for harassment under the FDCPA for repeatedly calling a widow and trying to convince her to pay a debt owed by her deceased husband to Bank of America. The widow had no obligation to repay the debt, as Bank of America and the debt collector knew. A Florida court held both Bank of America and the debt collector liable for improper debt-collection tactics.

Garnishment Proceedings

Creditors have numerous remedies available to them when consumers fail to pay their debts. Among these remedies is garnishment. **Garnishment** occurs when a creditor, after complying with procedures mandated by state law, legally seizes a portion of a debtor's property (usually wages) in the possession of a third party (such as an employer). To gain access to the property, the creditor must obtain an *order of garnishment* from the court. Laws governing garnishment vary considerably from state to state.

Both federal and state laws limit the amount that can be taken from a debtor's take-home pay. The federal Consumer Credit Protection Act provides that a debtor can keep either 75 percent of the net earnings per week or a sum equivalent to the pay for thirty hours of work at federal minimum wage rates, whichever is greater. State laws also provide dollar exemptions, and these amounts are often larger than those provided by federal law.

Employers dislike garnishment proceedings. Such proceedings impose time costs on employers (possible appearance at court hearings, record-keeping costs, and the like). To protect the job security of employees whose wages are subject to garnishment, federal law provides that garnishment of an employee's wages usually cannot be grounds for that employee's dismissal. The *Developing Paralegal Skills* feature below discusses this issue with respect to the role that may be played by a paralegal.

garnishment
A proceeding in which a creditor legally seizes a portion of a debtor's property (such as wages) that is in the possession of a third party (such as an employer).

DEVELOPING PARALEGAL SKILLS

DISCHARGED FOR GARNISHMENT

Eva White works as a paralegal for a firm that specializes in employment law. A business client has called Eva's supervising attorney to ask for advice concerning garnishment. Basically, the client wants to know if he can fire an employee so that he can avoid having to comply with garnishment proceedings that have been initiated against the employee. The attorney has asked Eva to research recent case law and current statutes and regulations on the question of whether an employer may fire an employee for this reason.

Eva goes online to research garnishment and locates a case in which an employee was fired two days after his employer received notice of garnishment. The case turned on whether the employer had notice that the garnishment proceedings had already been initiated against the employee. She reads the case

and finds a citation to the statute. Eva's next step is to check the statute itself to ensure that she has up-to-date knowledge of how the statute is being applied.

Checklist for Legal Research

- Locate statutes and regulations issued under the statutes.

- Locate case law to see how the statute and regulations have been interpreted and applied and whether the statute has been found to be unconstitutional.

- Update your case law findings by checking a citator (see Chapter 8) to make sure that the holding in the case is still good law.

- Update the statute by checking the pocket part or using a citator to see if the statute has been amended or repealed.

CHAPTER SUMMARY

TORT LAW, PRODUCT LIABILITY, AND CONSUMER LAW

The Basis of Tort Law

Two notions serve as the basis of all torts: wrongs and compensation. Tort law recognizes that some acts are wrong because they cause injuries to others. A *tort* is a civil wrong. In a tort action, one party brings a personal-injury suit against another party to obtain compensation (monetary damages) or other relief for the harm suffered. Tort law provides remedies for the invasion of protected interests, such as physical security, privacy, freedom of movement, and reputation. Torts fall into two broad classifications: *intentional torts* and *negligence.*

Intentional Torts

Intentional torts occur when the actor intended to perform an act that resulted in an injury to a protected right of another party.

1. *Intentional torts against persons*—Intentional acts that violate protected interests under the common law.

    a. An assault is an intentional act that causes another person to be apprehensive or fearful of immediate harm. A battery is an assault that results in physical contact. Defenses to such actions include consent, self-defense, and the defense of others and of property.

    b. False imprisonment is the intentional confinement or restraint of another person's movement without justification.

    c. Intentional, extreme, and outrageous conduct that results in severe emotional distress to another can be the basis of a suit for intentional infliction of emotional (mental) distress.

    d. A false statement, not made under privilege, that is communicated to a third person and that causes damage to a person's reputation may constitute defamation. If spoken, it is slander; if in print, it is libel. Defenses include the privilege to relay the information, such as in news coverage, or to protect another interest.

    e. Invasion of the right to privacy may involve the use of a person's name or likeness for commercial purposes without permission, wrongful intrusion into a person's private activities, publication of information that places a person in a false light, or disclosure of private facts that an ordinary person would find objectionable.

    f. The use of another person's name, likeness, or other identifying characteristic without permission and for the benefit of the user is the intentional tort of appropriation.

    g. Misrepresentation or fraud is a false representation made by one party with the intent of deceiving another, and on which the other reasonably relies to his or her detriment, thereby suffering a loss.

    h. The tort of wrongful interference occurs when a third party intentionally interferes with an enforceable contractual relationship or an established business relationship between other parties for the purpose of advancing the economic interests of the third party.

2. *Intentional torts against property*—Intentional acts that interfere with a person's legally protected rights to his or her property.

    a. Trespass to land is the invasion of another's real property without consent or privilege.

    b. Unlawfully damaging or interfering with the owner's right to use, possess, or enjoy personal property is the tort of trespass to personal property.

    c. Conversion is a tort in which personal property is taken from its rightful owner.

Negligence

Negligence is the careless performance of a legally required duty or the failure to perform a legally required act. Elements that must be proved are that a legal duty of care existed to another party, that the defendant breached that duty, and that the breach caused damage or injury to another.

1. *The duty of care and its breach*—Negligence involves the failure to exercise the duty of care expected of a reasonable person under the circumstances. For businesses, this means an obligation to provide safe premises for clients. Professionals must meet the standards expected of knowledgeable members of their profession.

2. *The injury requirement and damages*—A plaintiff in a negligence suit must have sustained an injury that produced legally recognized damages. Most commonly, plaintiffs receive compensatory damages, but when the actions of a defendant are particularly offensive, punitive damages may be added.

3. *Causation*—The injury must be logically attributable to the violation of a protected interest by the defendant. Both causation in fact and proximate cause must be present for liability to arise.

Cyber Torts: Defamation Online

General tort principles are extended to cover cyber torts, or torts that occur in cyberspace, such as online defamation. Federal and state statutes may also apply to certain forms of cyber torts.

1. *Liability of Internet service providers*—ISPs are generally protected from liability when they have been the means

Strict Liability

Under the doctrine of strict liability, a person or company may be held liable, regardless of the degree of care exercised, for damages or injuries caused by an abnormally dangerous activity or a harmful or defective product.

1. *Abnormally dangerous activities*—Strict liability applies to parties engaged in particularly dangerous activities, such as activities involving toxic chemicals

Product Liability

The makers of products can be liable in tort for injuries and damages caused by harmful or defective products.

1. *Theories of product liability*—Suits for product liability may be based on negligence, misrepresentation, or strict product liability. Negligence arises when the manufacturer did not use due care in designing, producing, or testing the product or failed to place adequate warnings on the product. Misrepresentation occurs when the seller misrepresents the quality, nature, or appropriate use of the product, and the user is injured as a result. Strict product liability covers situations in which a manufacturer exercised reasonable care, but the product was

Consumer Law

Statutes, agency rules, and common law judicial decisions that serve to protect the interests of consumers are classified as consumer law. There are many federal consumer protection statutes, including the ones listed here. States also provide similar consumer protection statutes.

4. *Defenses to negligence*—A defendant may plead an affirmative defense in negligence cases. Affirmative defenses include assumption of risk, superseding cause, and contributory negligence.

5. *Special negligence doctrines and statutes*—Negligence *per se* is a type of negligence occurs that when a person violates a statute or an ordinance providing for a criminal penalty and the violation causes another to be injured. Many states have special negligence statutes, such as dram shop acts and Good Samaritan statutes, which prescribe duties and responsibilities in certain circumstances.

of transmitting damaging information, as long as they have taken reasonable steps to protect against abuse of their services.

2. *Piercing the veil of anonymity*—ISPs may be required to provide the names of clients who have been accused of torts. The law is still evolving on this point.

or explosives. These parties will be held liable for any injuries related to the dangerous activities, so they have strong incentives to protect others against injury by exercising great care.

2. *Other applications of strict liability*—The most important application of the doctrine of strict liability is in the area of harmful or defective products.

defective, and injury resulted. A product may be unreasonably dangerous due to a flaw in the manufacturing process, a design defect, or an inadequate warning.

2. *Defenses to product liability*—If sued, a producer can offer several defenses: assumption of risk—the user or consumer knew of the risk of harm and voluntarily assumed it; product misuse—the user or consumer misused the product in a way unforeseeable by the manufacturer; comparative negligence—the plaintiff's misuse of the product contributed to the risk of injury; and commonly known dangers—dangers that are obvious, such as the danger associated with using a sharp knife.

1. *Deceptive sales practices*—The Federal Trade Commission (FTC) has authority to investigate and sue firms engaged in deceptive business practices that could injure consumers. The agency also issues regulations to define certain deceptive practices.

2. *Deceptive advertising*—The FTC prohibits advertising that misleads consumers or that is based on false claims. Generally, the test for whether an ad is deceptive is whether a reasonable consumer would be deceived by the ad. The FTC can require the advertiser to stop the challenged advertising, often by getting a court to issue a cease-and-desist order.

3. *Labeling and packaging*—Manufacturers must comply with labeling and packaging requirements for their specific products. In general, labels must be accurate and not misleading. Food products must bear labels detailing their nutritional content, and standards must be met before producers can use terms like *fresh* and *organic* on labels.

4. *Sales transactions*—Many federal laws regulate the disclosure of terms to consumers in sales transactions, particularly in door-to-door and mail-order sales. The FTC conducts most of the federal regulation of sales.

5. *Consumer health and safety*—Laws protecting the health and safety of consumers regulate the content of a food, drug, or other item. The Federal Food, Drug and Cosmetic Act protects consumers against impure and misbranded foods and drugs. The act establishes food standards, specifies safe levels of food additives, and regulates some aspects of food advertising. The Consumer Product Safety Act seeks to protect consumers from risk of injury from hazardous products. The Consumer Product Safety Commission may ban the sale of hazardous products.

6. *Consumer credit protection*—Credit protection has become an important area regulated by federal consumer protection legislation. Among the most important is the Truth-in-Lending Act (TILA). It is a disclosure law requiring sellers and lenders to disclose credit terms or loan terms so that individuals can shop around to compare terms. This law also provides for the following:

a. *Equal credit opportunity*—Prohibits creditors from discriminating on the basis of race, religion, national origin, color, gender, marital status, or age.

b. *Credit-card protection*—Limits the liability of cardholders for unauthorized charges made on unsolicited credit cards. The CARD Act limits fees for various actions by credit-card holders and requires issuers to provide clear information about card pricing.

c. *Credit-card rules*—TILA provides detailed rules that apply in case of a dispute between a credit-card holder and the bank that issued the card.

The Fair Credit Reporting Act protects consumers against inaccurate credit reporting and provides that credit reports can only be issued for certain purposes. Consumers are entitled to receive a copy of their credit report on request and to be notified any time they are denied credit or insurance based on the report. The reporting agency must conduct an investigation if the consumer contests any information on the credit report.

The Fair and Accurate Credit Transactions (FACT) Act helps protect against identity theft by establishing a national fraud-alert system for credit users; by requiring major credit-reporting agencies to provide consumers with free copies of their credit reports every twelve months; and by assisting victims of identity theft in reestablishing their credit reputations.

The Fair Debt Collection Practices Act (FDCPA) prohibits debt collectors from using unfair debt-collection practices, such as contacting debtors at their place of employment if their employers object, contacting debtors at unreasonable times, contacting third parties about the debt unless authorized to do so by a court, and harassing debtors.

Garnishment occurs when a creditor has the right to seize a portion of the debtor's property (such as wages) in the possession of a third party (such as an employer) to satisfy a debt. The creditor must comply with specific procedures mandated by state law.

KEY TERMS AND CONCEPTS

actionable 425

actual malice 426

appropriation 427

assault 423

assumption of risk 435

battery 423

business invitee 432

business tort 428

causation in fact 434

cease-and-desist order 444

comparative negligence 436

compensatory damages 433

consumer 442

consumer law 442

contributory negligence 436

conversion 431

cyber tort 438

deception 443

deceptive advertising 443

defamation 425

dram shop acts 438

duty of care 432

elements 422

false imprisonment 424

QUESTIONS FOR REVIEW

1. Define *tort*. What is the purpose of tort law? What are the main categories of torts?

2. Define *intentional tort*. List the elements of assault, battery, intentional infliction of emotional distress, and defamation. How do intentional torts against persons differ from cyber torts?

3. List and define the four elements of negligence. Why is the duty of care of professionals different from the duty of an ordinary person? What are the defenses to a negligence action?

4. What is product liability? What are the three legal theories for product liability suits? List and define the affirmative defenses to a product liability suit.

5. List and describe the six areas of federal consumer law discussed in the chapter. Do states have consumer protection laws? If so, what level of consumer protection do state laws provide?

6. What are the three characteristics of abnormally dangerous activities?

ETHICS QUESTION

1. Chloe is a new paralegal interviewing a client who wants to sue the manufacturer of an allegedly defective elliptical-training machine. The client claims that while he was using the machine, it stopped suddenly, causing him to fall off and seriously injure his hip. Near the end of the interview, the client asks Chloe whether she thinks he has a good case. Chloe responds, "Well, as you know, I'm a paralegal, and I cannot give legal advice. Personally, though, I think that you do have a good case." Has Chloe violated her ethical duties? How would you have handled the situation?

PRACTICE QUESTIONS AND ASSIGNMENTS

1. Bob is driving to work for his morning shift at the plant when he encounters strikers who are picketing and blocking the entrance to the factory. Bob cannot afford to lose his job, so he decides to cross the picket line. When he attempts to drive through, the picketers surround his car and begin to rock and push it. Bob's car is spun around and ends up in oncoming traffic. Bob suffers a panic attack, and his anxiety disorder is aggravated so that he cannot work. Does Bob have a tort claim against the picketers? If so, which torts were committed?

2. During the Ebola crisis, hospitals throughout the United States set up protocols for handling Ebola patients, including providing an Ebola checklist for use by emergency room staff. When the first Ebola patient was initially seen at a Texas hospital's emergency room, he reported a fever and flu-like symptoms (classic symptoms of the Ebola virus) and told the emergency room staff that he had just come from Liberia, a country with a severe Ebola outbreak. The patient was treated for the flu, given antibiotics, and sent home. Despite the presence of Ebola symptoms and his recent arrival from Liberia, his illness was not reported to any authorities. The man returned three days later by ambulance, deathly ill. He was admitted to the hospital, was diagnosed with Ebola, and died within a few days. On which tort law theory discussed in the chapter might the hospital be liable?

3. Two middle-school girls labeled a male gym teacher a "perv" and "creeper." They spread false rumors that he inappropriately touched students and peeked into the girls' locker room. The girls' parents shared these falsehoods about the teacher with their friends. The teacher was cleared of allegations of criminal behavior and filed a lawsuit against the parents for spreading false rumors about his behavior. Under which tort theory would the teacher file a suit?

4. A law school has an open admissions policy, and because of an antiquated state law, it accepts students with the equivalent of an associate's degree. Once admitted, students must earn a grade of "C" or better in all courses to stay enrolled. Many students flunk out. Several disgruntled students start a blog where they complain about the law school's policies. Over time, more students post on the blog, and some of the statements are untrue. The law school sues for online defamation, naming the defendants as John Does. Will the Internet service provider (ISP) have to reveal the identities of the defendant Does? How do the rights of the plaintiff balance against the defendants' First Amendment rights to free speech? Can the ISP be held liable for defamation?

5. Carmen buys a television set manufactured by AKI Electronics. She is going on vacation, so she takes the set to her mother's house for her mother to use. Because the set is defective, it explodes, causing considerable damage to her mother's house. Carmen's mother sues AKI for the damage to her house. Discuss the product liability theories under which Carmen's mother can recover from AKI.

GROUP PROJECT

This project asks you to research the ignition-switch recall by General Motors (GM) in 2014.

Student one will locate and summarize articles describing the problem with ignition switches on GM vehicles, when and how the problem was discovered, and what injuries or deaths resulted from the defective ignition switches.

Student two will locate and summarize articles on why product-liability lawsuits against GM were not a viable alternative in 2014.

Student three will locate and summarize articles on the Congressional testimony of GM's executives on the ignition-switch issue and describe what remedies resulted for persons who were injured or for the families of those who died.

Student four will compile the summaries and present them to the class.

CHAPTER
15

Contracts and Intellectual Property Law

CHAPTER OBJECTIVES

After completing this chapter, you will be able to:

- List and explain the requirements for forming a valid contract.

- Explain the circumstances under which contracts are not enforceable.

- Describe how the Uniform Commercial Code (UCC) applies to the sale of goods and what warranties it provides.

- Define *performance* and *specific performance*, and describe the remedies available when a contract is breached or broken.

- Explain the nature of online contracting and the legal validity of an electronic signature.

- Identify the nature and forms of intellectual property.

- Describe what conduct gives rise to a violation of intellectual property rights.

Introduction

The law governs most activities. Simple, everyday transactions—such as buying a gallon of milk at a convenience store or installing a new app on your smartphone—are subject to laws that define the rights and duties of the parties involved. This chapter covers two of the most important areas of law—contracts and sales. Paralegals routinely help attorneys deal with disputes involving contract and sales law. Because such disputes often deal with complicated issues, paralegals need to understand the principles of these areas.

Another field of law that has become increasingly important involves intellectual property, such as patents, trademarks, and copyrights. As you will learn later in the chapter, the value of intellectual property has increased because of the massive flow of ideas and innovations. Attorneys and their paralegals are frequently called on to help clients register and protect various forms of intellectual property.

Requirements to Form a Valid Contract

promise
An assurance that a party will or will not do something in the future.

Contract law deals with, among other things, the keeping of promises. A **promise** is an assurance that a party will or will not do something in the future. As mentioned in Chapter 2, a *contract* is any agreement based on a promise or an exchange of promises that can be enforced in court.

Note that the principles discussed in the first part of this chapter come from the common law of contracts. These principles still govern many contracts, but as you will see later in the chapter, contracts for the sale of goods are governed by statutory law—the Uniform Commercial Code (UCC).

Bilateral and Unilateral Contracts

Contracts may be *bilateral* or *unilateral*. Both types of contracts are valid.

Most contracts are bilateral. The exchange of a promise for a promise creates a bilateral contract.

> **EXAMPLE 15.1**   Yvonne offers to sell Sean her car for $10,000, and he accepts, saying he will have the money tomorrow. Yvonne and Sean have formed a bilateral contract.

When people make a unilateral contract, they exchange a promise for an act.

> **EXAMPLE 15.2**   Yvonne tells Devon she will pay him $100 if he will detail her car. He says nothing but then details the car. Because he completed the requested act, Yvonne owes him $100.

Contracts may be referred to by different names in different states. Some states do not use the term *unilateral contract.*

Contract Validity

If a client alleges that a party has breached (failed to perform) a contract, the first issue that your supervising attorney and you need to examine is whether a *valid contract* (a contract that will be enforced by a court) was ever formed. To form a valid contract, four basic requirements must be met:

- **Agreement.**   An agreement includes an offer and an acceptance. One party must offer to enter into a legal agreement, and another party must accept the terms of the offer.

- **Consideration.**   Promises made by parties must be supported by legally sufficient and bargained-for consideration (something of value that is received or promised to convince a person to make a deal, as discussed shortly).

- **Contractual capacity.** Both parties entering into the contract must have the contractual capacity to do so. The law must recognize them as qualified, competent parties.

- **Legality.** The contract's purpose must be to accomplish some goal that is legal and not against public policy.

If any of these elements is lacking, no contract was formed. We look more closely at these requirements in the following subsections.

Agreement

A contract is an **agreement** between two or more parties. If the parties fail to reach an agreement on the essential terms of the contract, no contract exists. Just what constitutes the *essential terms* may vary with the facts surrounding potential contract claims. In particular, as discussed later in this chapter, sales contracts are subject to special rules concerning some contract terms.

Ordinarily, agreement is evidenced by two events: an *offer* and an *acceptance*. One party offers a certain bargain to another party, who then accepts that bargain. When contracts are drafted with the assistance of an attorney, both parties to the agreement may want to use the same attorney. That scenario raises special issues, as noted in this chapter's *Ethics Watch* feature.

agreement
A meeting of the minds; a requirement for a valid contract. Agreement involves two distinct events: an offer to form a contract and the acceptance of that offer by the offeree.

Offer

An **offer** is a promise or commitment to do or not do some specified thing in the future. Three elements are necessary for an offer to be effective:

- The **offeror** (the party making the offer) must have the *intent to be bound* by the offer.

offer
A promise or commitment to do or refrain from doing some specified thing in the future.

offeror
The party making the offer.

ETHICS WATCH

POTENTIAL CONFLICTS OF INTEREST

It is not uncommon for two parties to want an attorney to write a contract that represents an agreement between the parties, such as an agreement to build an apartment building together. This situation raises a conflict-of-interest issue. Can the attorney represent both parties in a contract? Rules governing conflicts of interest prevent an attorney from simultaneously representing adverse parties in a legal proceeding. Should a dispute arise over the contract, assisting either party would necessarily be adverse to the other.

In a state that has adopted the 2002 Revision of the *Model Rules of Professional Conduct* for lawyers (discussed in Chapter 4), an attorney must obtain the informed consent of each party in writing. This means that the attorney must explain the risks of having one attorney draw up a contract for two people and also must discuss the alternatives. If the two parties then decide to have the attorney draw up the contract, they must sign a consent form.

Paralegals often have a role to play in these situations, such as conducting an initial interview with the parties. The position of a paralegal in such circumstances is covered by NALA's *Code of Ethics and Professional Responsibility,* Canon 2: "A paralegal may perform any task which is properly designated and supervised by an attorney, as long as the attorney is ultimately responsible to the client, maintains a direct relationship with the client, and assumes professional responsibility for the work product."

- The terms of the offer must be *reasonably certain,* or *definite,* so that the parties and the court can determine the terms of the contract. (In contracts for the sale of goods, which will be discussed later, the requirement of definiteness is relaxed somewhat so that a contract can exist even if certain terms are left "open," or unspecified.)

offeree
The party to whom the offer is made.

- The offer must be communicated to the **offeree** (the party to whom the offer is made).

Offers made in jest, in undue excitement, or in obvious anger do not meet the intent requirement.

> **EXAMPLE 15.3** Al and Sue ride to work together each day in Sue's car, which she bought for $18,000 six months ago. One cold morning, Al and Sue get into the car, but Sue cannot get it started. Angry, she yells, "I'll sell you this stupid car for $100!" Al writes Sue a check for $100. Has a contract to sell the car been formed? If Al consulted with your supervising attorney, claiming that Sue had breached a contract because she had refused to give him the car, what would the attorney say? The attorney would tell Al that a reasonable person would have recognized under the circumstances that Sue's offer was not serious—she did not intend to be bound but was simply frustrated. Therefore, no valid contract was formed.

Similarly, an offer will not be effective if it is too ambiguous in its terms.

> **EXAMPLE 15.4** Kim wants to sell her set of legal encyclopedias but has not mentioned a price. Jamal says to Kim, "I'll buy your encyclopedias and pay for them next week." In this situation, no contract results, because no price was set.

Note that when considering a dispute, the courts evaluate it from the standpoint of a reasonable person.

> **EXAMPLE 15.5** Jeff has been attempting to buy some land from Raul for months. One night, while drinking together at a bar, Jeff offers Raul $20,000 for the land. Raul agrees, and the two sign a simple agreement while in the bar. Raul later claims that he did not mean it and refuses to sell. Because a reasonable person would think this was an agreement to sell, Raul has agreed to sell despite his mental reservation.

Advertisements

Advertisements generally are not offers but are invitations to make an offer. When an ad is "clear, definite, and explicit" and leaves nothing open for negotiation, however, it may be an offer.

> **EXAMPLE 15.6** A Pepsi ad encouraged consumers to accumulate "Pepsi Points" by buying Pepsi products. The ad showed many items, from sunglasses to hats, that the consumer could acquire. The final item was a military fighter jet, listed for 7 million points. When someone earned the points and demanded the jet, Pepsi refused to deliver it, and the consumer sued. The court ruled that the advertisement was not an offer because an objective, reasonable person would not have considered it to be an offer. (You can find the commercial on YouTube by searching for "Pepsi Harrier Jet." There are two versions—one from before the lawsuit and one from after it.)

Termination of the Offer

Once an offer has been communicated, the party to whom the offer was made can accept the offer, reject the offer, or make a counteroffer. If a party accepts the offer, a contract is formed (provided the other requirements to form a contract are met). If

A real estate paralegal reviews the terms of a purchase offer with a potential home buyer to ensure that all of the contract's terms are clear. What is the role of the paralegal during real estate transactions?

the party rejects the offer, the offer is terminated. That is, the offer no longer stands (and the offeree cannot later take the offeror up on the offer). The offeree also has the option of rejecting the offer and simultaneously making an offer called a counteroffer.

Counteroffer.   In a counteroffer, the offeree becomes the offeror—offering to form a contract with different terms.

> *EXAMPLE 15.7* Dilan offers to work for Wayne for $50,000 a year. Wayne responds, "Your price is too high. I'll hire you for $40,000." Wayne's response is a counteroffer that terminates Dilan's offer and creates a new offer by Wayne.

Both a rejection of the offer and the making of a counteroffer terminate the original offer. The original offer can also be terminated if the party making the offer withdraws the offer before it has been accepted (called *revoking* the offer). If the offer has already been accepted, however, then both parties are bound in contract.

Other Bases for Termination.   An offer also terminates automatically in some circumstances, such as when the subject matter of the offer is destroyed, one of the parties dies or becomes incompetent, or a new law is passed that makes the contract illegal. Additionally, an offer ends if a period of time is specified in the offer and the offer is not accepted within that period. If no time for acceptance is specified in the offer, the offer expires when a *reasonable* period of time has passed. What constitutes a reasonable period in the eyes of the court varies, depending on the circumstances.

Acceptance

A party's **acceptance** of the offer results in a legally binding contract if the other elements of a valid contract are present. The acceptance must be *unequivocal*—that is, the terms of the offer must be accepted exactly as stated by the offeror. This principle of contract law is known as the **mirror image rule**—the terms of the acceptance must be the same as ("mirror") the terms of the offer. If the acceptance is subject to new conditions or if the terms of the acceptance materially change the original offer, the acceptance may be deemed a counteroffer that implicitly rejects the original offer.

acceptance
In contract law, the offeree's indication to the offeror that the offeree agrees to be bound by the terms of the offeror's offer, or proposal to form a contract.

mirror image rule
A common law rule that requires that the terms of the offeree's acceptance adhere exactly to the terms of the offeror's offer for a valid contract to be formed.

EXAMPLE 15.8 Sara agrees to sell her house to Thomas for $271,000. When he signs the contract, Thomas adds a note that he wants Sara to leave her furniture in the living room. That is not a valid acceptance; it is a counteroffer, because Thomas has added a new condition. Unless Sara wants to accept the revised terms, there is no contract, and she is free to sell to someone else.

Proper Communication.   Another requirement, for most types of contracts, is that the acceptance must be communicated to the offeror. An issue in contract formation has to do with the timeliness of acceptances. The general rule is that acceptance of an offer is timely if it is made before the offer is terminated.

Problems arise, however, when the parties involved are not dealing face to face. In such cases, acceptance takes effect at the time the acceptance is communicated via the mode expressly or impliedly authorized by the offeror. This is the **mailbox rule.** Under this rule, if the offer states that it may be accepted by mail, the acceptance becomes valid the moment it is deposited in the mail or sent by e-mail.

Reasonableness Standard.   Often, the party making an offer does not indicate how acceptance is to be made. In those cases, acceptance may be made in any manner that is *reasonable under the circumstances*. Several factors determine whether the acceptance is reasonable: the nature of the circumstances at the time the offer was made, the means used to transmit the offer, and the reliability of the offer's delivery.

EXAMPLE 15.9 An offer is sent by FedEx overnight because an acceptance is urgently required. In this situation, the offeree's acceptance by fax or e-mail will be deemed reasonable.

In contracts formed on the Internet, the issues of timeliness and method of acceptance usually do not arise. This is because persons often accept online offers simply by clicking on the box "I agree" or "I accept." Such an agreement is called a **click-on agreement** and is widely used in the formation of contracts online (as discussed later).

Consideration

Another requirement under U.S. law for a valid contract is **consideration**, which is usually defined as something of value—such as money or the performance of an action not otherwise required—that is given in exchange for a promise. Promises are generally not enforceable without consideration. (Civil law systems—discussed in Chapter 4—generally do not require consideration, an important difference if you are working on a cross-border contract.)

EXAMPLE 15.10 You give your friend $1,000 in exchange for her promise to take care of your house and garden for six months. This promise normally will be enforceable, because consideration has been given. Your consideration is $1,000. Your friend's consideration is the assumption of an obligation (taking care of the house and garden) that she otherwise would not assume.

Both parties to the contract must give consideration for the contract to be enforceable. Many disputes arise when one party argues lack of consideration.

Elements of Consideration

Often, consideration is divided into two parts: (1) something of *legal value* must be given in exchange for the promise, and (2) there must be a *bargained-for* exchange. The "something of legal value" may consist of a return promise that is bargained for. It may also consist of performance, which may be an act, a forbearance, or the creation, modification, or destruction of a legal relationship. Forbearance involves not doing something one has a legal right to do.

mailbox rule
A rule providing that an acceptance of an offer takes effect at the time it is communicated via the mode expressly or impliedly authorized by the offeror, rather than at the time it is actually received by the offeror. If acceptance is to be by mail, for example, it becomes effective the moment it is placed in the mailbox.

click-on agreement
An agreement that arises when buyers, engaging in a transaction on a computer, indicate assent to be bound by the terms of an offer by clicking on a button that says, for example, "I agree."

consideration
Something of value, such as money or the performance of an action not otherwise required, that motivates the formation of a contract. Each party must give consideration for the contract to be binding.

EXAMPLE 15.11 When you are twenty-one, your grandfather promises to pay you $10,000 if you agree not to smoke any cigarettes before the age of twenty-five. The consideration for your performance in this situation is his promise to pay, and your consideration for his performance is refraining from smoking cigarettes.

Contract Change Requires New Consideration

Once a contract has been formed, the general common law rule is that the terms of a contract cannot be modified without further consideration. For instance, after making the deal in the example just given, your grandfather cannot modify the terms by requiring you not to drink alcohol before age twenty-five for the same $10,000—you would have to receive additional consideration for this new agreement.

Legal Sufficiency of Consideration

For a binding contract to be created, consideration must be *legally sufficient*. To be legally sufficient, consideration for a promise must be either *legally detrimental to the promisee* or *legally beneficial to the promisor*. A party can incur legal detriment either by promising to give legal value (such as the payment of money) or by a forbearance or a promise of forbearance.

The requirement of consideration is what distinguishes contracts from gifts.

EXAMPLE 15.12 You promise to give your friend $1,000 as a gift, and she says she will be very happy to receive your gift. In this situation, no contract results, because your friend has given no legally sufficient consideration.

Adequacy of Consideration

Adequacy of consideration refers to the fairness of the bargain. In general, a court will not question the adequacy of consideration if the consideration is legally sufficient. Parties are normally free to bargain as they wish. If people could sue merely because they had entered into a bargain they later regret, the courts would be overloaded with frivolous suits.

EXAMPLE 15.13 Alonzo sells his 2019 Mercedes Benz, which is in excellent condition, to Herb for $3,000, even though the car is worth much more. Later, Alonzo says he wants the car back and argues that there was insufficient consideration because the car was worth much more. The court will not invalidate the contract as long as it was made freely by a person with legal capacity to contract, even if one party got a very good deal at the expense of the other. Courts generally are not in the business of ensuring that deals are based on fair market value.

A court may sometimes consider the adequacy of consideration in terms of value because inadequate consideration may indicate fraud, duress, undue influence, or a lack of bargained-for exchange. It may also reflect a party's incompetence (for example, an individual might have been too mentally incompetent to make a contract).

Promissory Estoppel

In some circumstances, contracts will be enforced even though consideration is lacking. Under the doctrine of **promissory estoppel**, a person who has reasonably and substantially relied on the promise of another may obtain some measure of recovery. The following elements are required:

- There must be a clear and definite promise.
- The promisee must justifiably rely on the promise.
- The reliance normally must be of a substantial and reasonable character.
- Justice will be better served by enforcement of the promise.

promissory estoppel
A doctrine under which a promise is binding if the promise is clear and definite, the promisee justifiably relies on the promise, the reliance is reasonable and substantial, and justice will be better served by enforcement of the promise.

If these requirements are met, a promise may be enforced even though it is not supported by consideration. In essence, the promisor will be *estopped* (prevented) from asserting the lack of consideration as a defense.

> *EXAMPLE 15.14* Your uncle tells you, "I'll pay you $500 a week so you won't have to work while you are in college." In reliance on your uncle's promise, you quit your job. Your uncle then refuses to pay you, putting you in financial difficulty. Under the doctrine of promissory estoppel, you may be able to enforce such a promise.

Contractual Capacity

contractual capacity
The threshold mental capacity required by law for a party who enters into a contract to be bound by that contract.

For a contract to be deemed valid, the parties to the contract must have **contractual capacity**—the legal ability or competence to enter into a contractual relationship. Courts generally presume the existence of contractual capacity, but there are some situations in which capacity is lacking or questionable. In many instances, a party may have the capacity to enter into a valid contract but also have the right to avoid liability under it.

Minors

Minors usually are not legally bound by contracts. Subject to certain exceptions, the contracts entered into by a minor are *voidable* (they can be canceled, or avoided) at the option of that minor. The minor has the option of *disaffirming* (renouncing) the contract and setting aside the contract and all legal obligations arising from it. An adult who enters into a contract with a minor, however, cannot avoid his contractual duties on the ground that the minor can do so. Unless the minor exercises the option to set aside the contract, the adult party is bound by it.

Intoxication and Mental Capacity

Intoxication is a condition in which a person's normal capacity to act or think is inhibited by alcohol or some other drug. Under the common law rule, if the person was sufficiently intoxicated to lack mental capacity, the transaction is voidable at the option of the intoxicated person even if the intoxication was purely voluntary. In spite of the common law rule, most courts rarely permit contracts to be avoided on this basis.

If a person has been adjudged mentally incompetent by a court of law and a guardian has been appointed, any contract made by the mentally incompetent person is *void*—no contract exists. Only the guardian can enter into binding legal duties on the incompetent person's behalf. Even if the court has not previously ruled that the person is mentally incompetent, the contract may be avoided if incompetence is proved.

> *EXAMPLE 15.15* Rita, who suffers from Alzheimer's disease, signs a contract to buy ten new vacuum cleaners. If the contract is challenged and it can be proved that Rita did not understand what she was doing at the time she signed the contract, the contract will not be valid.

The issue of contractual capacity is discussed further in the accompanying *Developing Paralegal Skills* feature.

Legality

A contract to do something that is prohibited by federal or state statutory law is illegal and, as such, void from the outset and unenforceable. For example, a contract to buy a liver from another person is void because it is illegal. No court would enforce the contract if a lawsuit were brought for breach of contract. Any contract to commit an illegal act is unenforceable.

DEVELOPING PARALEGAL SKILLS

ASSESSING CONTRACTUAL CAPACITY

You are a paralegal for Jeff Barlow. He asks you to draft a contract for Margaret Klaus, a seventy-nine-year-old widow. In the contract, Margaret will transfer all of her shares in NAPO Corporation to her nephew Jeremy. In return, Jeremy promises to take care of Margaret for the rest of her life. Barlow is leaving on vacation and asks you to have the document completed and to arrange for a meeting with the client and her nephew to sign the contract when he returns.

You learn that the stock being conveyed is worth millions. More importantly, you begin to have doubts about Margaret's mental status. You have talked to her several times a week for three weeks. She often calls you by different names, repeats herself, and does not remember what you just told her. Although Jeremy has been living with Margaret for the past six months, whenever Margaret calls, she is alone and often frightened. Now that you have finished the contract, you wonder if Margaret is capable of genuine consent and whether Jeremy has too much influence over her. What should you do?

Tips for Dealing with Suspicions of Incompetence

- Document everything. Keep a record of all the conversations you had with the client that led you to suspect a lack of contractual capacity, as well as any other facts that contributed to your suspicions (if you discovered the person was taking medication for mental illness, for example).

- Do not discuss your suspicions with *anyone* except your supervising attorney. Making such statements about a person can damage her reputation, and you may even be held liable for defamation.

- Remember, it is the attorney's job to take into consideration the client's contractual capacity, not yours. You just want to make Barlow aware of the situation in an effort to protect the client's best interests.

In some instances, the subject matter of the contract is not illegal, but one of the parties is not legally authorized to perform the contract. For example, all states require that members of certain occupations—including physicians, lawyers, real estate brokers, architects, electricians, contractors, and stockbrokers—obtain licenses allowing them to practice. When a person enters into a contract with an unlicensed individual for services that should be performed by a licensed professional, the contract may not be enforceable, depending on the nature of the licensing statute.

Some states expressly provide that the lack of a license in certain occupations bars the enforcement of work-related contracts. If there is no express provision, it is necessary to look to the underlying purpose of the licensing requirements for a particular occupation. If the purpose is to protect the public from unauthorized practitioners, a contract involving an unlicensed individual normally is unenforceable. If the underlying purpose of the statute is to raise government revenues, however, a contract entered into with an unlicensed practitioner generally is enforceable—although the unlicensed person may be fined.

Additionally, some contracts are not enforced because the court deems them to be contrary to public policy. For example, contracts that restrain trade (anticompetitive contracts) and contracts that are so oppressive to innocent parties that they are deemed *unconscionable* (unconscionable contracts will be discussed shortly) are not enforceable owing to the negative impact they would have on society.

Defenses to Contract Enforceability

Two competent parties enter into a contract for a legal purpose. The agreement is supported by consideration. The contract thus meets the four requirements for a valid contract. Nonetheless, the contract may be unenforceable if the parties have not genuinely assented (agreed) to its terms, if the contract is so oppressive to one of the parties that a court will refuse to enforce it, or if the contract is not in the proper form—such as in writing, if the law requires it to be in writing.

As this chapter's *Office Tech and Cybersecurity* feature discusses, specific clauses may be required in certain kinds of contracts to satisfy government requirements.

Genuineness of Assent

genuineness of assent
Knowing and voluntary assent to the contract terms. If a contract is formed as a result of mistake, misrepresentation, undue influence, or duress, genuineness of assent is lacking, and the contract will be voidable.

Lack of **genuineness of assent** can be used as a defense to the contract's enforceability. Genuineness of assent may be lacking because of a mistake, fraudulent misrepresentation, undue influence, or duress.

Mistake

It is important to distinguish between *mistakes of fact* and *mistakes of value or quality*. If a mistake concerns the future market value or quality of the object of the contract, the mistake is one of *value*, and either party normally can enforce the contract. Each party is considered to have assumed the risk that the value would change or prove to be different from what he or she thought. Without this rule, almost any party who did not receive what he or she considered a fair bargain could argue mistake. Only a mistake of fact allows a contract to be avoided.

unilateral mistake
Mistake as to a material fact on the part of only one party to a contract. In this situation, the contract is normally enforceable against the mistaken party, with some exceptions.

material fact
A fact that is important to the subject matter of the contract.

Mistake of Fact.   Mistakes of fact occur in two forms—*unilateral* and *mutual (bilateral)*. A **unilateral mistake** occurs when one party to the contract makes a mistake as to some **material fact**—that is, a fact important to the subject matter of the contract. A unilateral mistake generally does not give the mistaken party any right to relief from the contract. There are some exceptions, however.

rescission
A remedy in which the contract is canceled and the parties are returned to the positions they occupied before the contract was made.

> **EXAMPLE 15.16** A contractor's written bid to remodel a house was $10,000, substantially lower than it should have been, because he made a mistake in totaling the estimated costs. In this situation, the contractor may be able to rescind the contract resulting from the bid. (**Rescission** is the act of canceling, or nullifying, a contract.)

mutual mistake
Mistake as to the same material fact on the part of both parties to a contract. In this situation, either party can cancel the contract.

Mutual Mistake.   When *both* of the parties are mistaken about the same material fact, a **mutual mistake** has occurred. In this situation, because both parties are mistaken about the same material fact, either party can cancel the contract.

OFFICE TECH AND CYBERSECURITY

CYBERSECURITY AND GOVERNMENT CONTRACTING

The federal government requires those signing its contracts to comply with cybersecurity requirements. Failing to do so can lead to major penalties. For example, a vendor who sold video surveillance manager software to the government, knowing that it allowed unauthorized access to government information, paid $8.6 million in damages in a 2019 settlement. The law firm of Baker Donelson recommends that those with government contracts:

- Review contracts for cybersecurity compliance.
- Have cybersecurity professionals audit cybersecurity procedures to ensure compliance with government standards.
- Create a culture of compliance by including cybersecurity policies in the contractor's Code of Business Conduct.

EXAMPLE 15.17 At Perez's art gallery, Diana buys a painting of a landscape. Both Diana and Perez believe that the painting is by the famous artist Vincent van Gogh. A month later, Diana discovers that the painting is a fake. Because neither Perez nor Diana was aware of this material fact when they made their deal, Diana can rescind (cancel) the contract and recover the purchase price of the painting. In contrast, if the painting had been listed as "by an unknown artist," but Diana bought it thinking it might be a van Gogh, she would not be able to undo the deal if the painting turned out to have been done by someone else.

Fraudulent Misrepresentation

When an innocent party is fraudulently induced to enter into a contract, the contract usually can be avoided because that party has not *voluntarily* consented to its terms. Normally, the innocent party can either rescind the contract and be restored to her original position or enforce the contract and seek damages for any injuries resulting from the fraud.

You read about the tort of fraud in Chapter 14. In the context of contract law, fraudulent misrepresentation occurs when one party to a contract misrepresents a material fact to the other party, with the intention of deceiving the other party, and the other party justifiably relies on the misrepresentation. To collect damages, a party must also have been injured. A party may be able to avoid the contract in some states without proving that she was injured by the fraud, however.

Note that the misrepresentation may be based on conduct as well as oral or written statements.

EXAMPLE 15.18 Gene is contracting to buy Rachelle's horse. While showing Gene the horse, Rachelle skillfully keeps the horse's head turned one way so that Gene does not see that the horse is blind in one eye. Rachelle's conduct constitutes fraud.

Undue Influence

Undue influence arises from special kinds of relationships in which one party can greatly influence another party, thus overcoming that party's free will. For example, caretakers may unduly influence elderly people. In addition, attorneys may unduly influence clients, and parents may unduly influence children. The essential feature of undue influence is that the party being taken advantage of does not exercise free will in entering into a contract. A contract entered into under excessive or undue influence lacks genuine assent and is voidable.

Duress

Assent to the terms of a contract is not genuine if one of the parties is *forced* into the agreement. Forcing a party to do something, including entering into a contract, through fear created by threats is legally defined as *duress*. In addition, blackmail or extortion to induce consent to a contract constitutes duress. Duress is both a defense to the enforcement of a contract and a ground for the rescission of a contract.

Unconscionable Contracts

Ordinarily, a court does not look at the fairness or equity of a contract. For example, a court normally will not inquire into the adequacy of consideration. Persons are assumed to be reasonably intelligent, and the court does not come to their aid just because they have made unwise or foolish bargains.

unconscionable contract
A contract that is so oppressive to one of the parties that the court will refuse to enforce the contract.

adhesion contract
A contract drafted by the dominant party and then presented to the other—the adhering party—on a take-it-or-leave-it basis.

Statute of Frauds
A state statute that requires certain types of contracts to be in writing to be enforceable.

In certain circumstances, a bargain is so oppressive to one of the parties that the court will refuse to enforce the contract. Such a contract is called an **unconscionable contract**. For example, contracts entered into because of one party's vastly superior bargaining power may be deemed unconscionable. These situations usually involve an **adhesion contract**, which is a contract drafted by the dominant party and then presented to the other—the adhering party—on a take-it-or-leave-it basis.

The Statute of Frauds

An otherwise valid contract may be unenforceable if it is not in the proper form. To ensure that there is reliable proof of the agreement, certain contracts are required to be in writing. If a contract is required by law to be in writing and there is no written evidence of the contract, it may not be enforceable.

Every state has a statute that specifies what types of contracts must be in writing or be evidenced by a written document. This is commonly referred to as the **Statute of Frauds**. Although the statutes vary slightly, the following contracts are normally required to be in writing:

- Contracts involving interests in land or anything attached to land, such as buildings, minerals, or timber.

- Contracts that cannot be performed within one year after formation.

- Collateral, or secondary, contracts, such as promises to be responsible for the debts of another.

- Promises made in consideration of marriage, such as *prenuptial agreements* (see Chapter 17).

- Contracts for the sale of goods for $500 or more. (This is under the Uniform Commercial Code, not the common law.)

Note that the test for determining whether an oral contract is enforceable under the "one-year rule" is not whether an agreement is *likely* to be performed within one year but whether performance is *possible* within one year. Exhibit 15.1 below illustrates the one-year rule.

EXHIBIT 15.1
The One-Year Rule

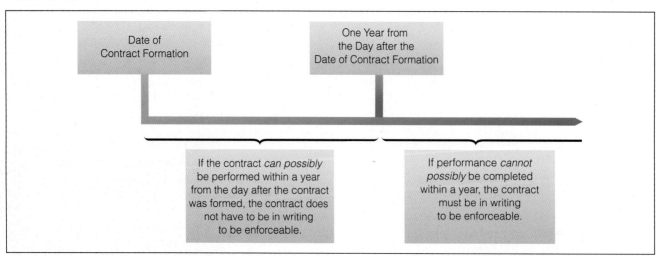

Sales Contracts and Warranties

As mentioned, the principles discussed in the first part of this chapter come from the common law of contracts. Recall from Chapter 5 that legislatures can pass laws that replace common law principles. That is what happened in the case of the **Uniform Commercial Code (UCC)**. A **sales contract**—or, more specifically, a contract for the sale of goods—is governed by state statutes based on Article 2 of the UCC.

The UCC is one of many uniform laws created by the American Law Institute and the National Conference of Commissioners on Uniform State Laws. It has been revised multiple times to reflect the changing customs and needs of business. The UCC was first enacted (by Pennsylvania) in 1954 and has been adopted, in whole or in part, by all states. State codes are not necessarily called the Uniform Commercial Code. In Ohio, for example, UCC provisions are part of the Ohio Commercial Code.

Researching matters involving the sale of goods usually requires using specialized legal resources because UCC provisions are generally the same (uniform) across states. Decisions from other states are more of a persuasive authority than is the case in other areas of law. Commentary by the Uniform Law Commission on the UCC provisions is also important.

Uniform Commercial Code (UCC)
Statutes adopted by all states, in part or in whole, that contain uniform laws governing business transactions as defined in the code.

sales contract
A contract for the sale of goods, as opposed to contracts for the sale of services, real property, or intangible property. Governed by Article 2 of the Uniform Commercial Code.

The Scope of UCC Article 2

Two factors should be kept in mind about Article 2 of the UCC. First, it deals with the sale of *goods*, not real property (real estate), services, or intangible property (such as a patent). Second, the rules may vary depending on whether the buyer or seller is a merchant. You should always note the subject matter of a contract dispute. If the subject is goods, then the UCC likely governs. If it is real estate or services, then the common law principles apply.

As under the common law, the parties to sales contracts are free to fashion the terms as they wish. The UCC normally comes into play only when a dispute arises over ambiguous or missing terms. Note that the UCC does not replace the common law of contracts. A contract for the sale of goods is also subject to the common law requirements of agreement, consideration, contractual capacity, and legality. Similarly, the common law defenses against contract formation or enforceability also apply to sales contracts. If the UCC has not modified a common law principle, then the common law governs. In other words, the general rule is that when the UCC addresses a particular matter, the UCC governs. When the UCC is silent, then the common law of contracts applies.

Warranties under the UCC

The UCC provides that a **warranty** of title arises in any sale of goods—that is, a seller automatically warrants (promises) to a buyer that the seller has good title to (legitimate ownership rights in) the goods being sold and transfers good title to the buyer. If the goods turn out to be stolen, for example, and the buyer has to return the goods to the real owner, the seller is liable to the buyer for the value of the goods.

warranty
An express or implied promise by a seller that specific goods to be sold meet certain criteria, or standards of performance, on which the buyer may rely.

Express Warranty

The UCC also contains provisions on express and implied warranties as to the quality or nature of the goods being sold. An *express warranty* is an oral or written promise made by a seller concerning the nature of the goods being sold.

> **EXAMPLE 15.19** The statement, "This is a new Toro lawn mower" is an express warranty, or promise, that the mower is indeed a Toro lawn mower and that it is new. If you buy the mower and learn that it is used or a different brand, the seller has breached an express warranty.

Implied Warranties

Under the UCC, every merchant makes an *implied warranty of merchantability* when goods are sold. The goods must be merchantable—that is, they must be "reasonably fit for the ordinary purposes for which such goods are used." Examples of unmerchantable goods are a light bulb that explodes when switched on, hamburger meat that contains bits of glass, and a new boat that leaks. Note that an implied warranty of merchantability applies only against merchants. If you buy something from a co-worker who is not in the business of selling such goods, the implied warranty of merchantability does not apply.

Goods sold by merchants must also be fit for the particular purpose for which they are sold. For the *implied warranty of fitness for a particular purpose* to arise, the buyer must rely on the seller's skill or judgment in selecting suitable goods.

> **EXAMPLE 15.20** Suppose Kathleen indicated to the sellers of a horse who were professional horse dealers that she planned to use the horse for breeding. In this case, the horse was to be used for a particular, non-ordinary purpose. When Kathleen later discovered the horse was incapable of reproducing, she could rely on the implied warranty of fitness to recover the purchase price.

Disclaimers

The UCC permits express and implied warranties to be disclaimed, provided the buyer is made aware of the disclaimers at the time the contract is formed. To disclaim an implied warranty of fitness for a particular purpose, the disclaimer must be in writing and be conspicuous (printed in larger or contrasting type or in a different color, for example).

Generally speaking, unless circumstances indicate otherwise, the implied warranties are disclaimed by the expression "as is," "with all faults," or similar language that is commonly understood by both parties as meaning that there are no implied or express warranties. An example of the application of these issues in the practice of contract law is presented in the *Developing Paralegal Skills* feature below.

DEVELOPING PARALEGAL SKILLS

CONTRACT REVIEW

Sam Thompson works as a paralegal for a corporation. One of his jobs is to review contracts between the firm and outside vendors. He is reviewing a contract for the corporation's purchase of fifty new tablet devices from an outside vendor.

The contract, which is a preprinted form contract, was submitted by the vendor and consists of thirty paragraphs of "fine print." The vendor has filled in the blanks in the form for terms such as price and quantity. As Sam reads the contract, he comes across a warranty disclaimer provision. Sam realizes that this contract provision means that there will be no warranty of merchantability or fitness for a particular purpose for the new tablet devices. They are taken "as is." He makes a note to tell his supervising attorney about this provision. The attorney will want to inform management of this limitation on warranties.

Tips for Reviewing a Contract

- Find out which contract provisions are acceptable to the client.

- Obtain the original copy of the contract.

- Read each provision carefully.

- Be certain you understand the meaning of each provision. If you are uncertain, find out what a provision means. Do not rely on the formulaic language in standard contract forms.

- Prepare a memo explaining the client's rights and liabilities under the contract.

- In the memo, mention any contract terms and provisions that the client might find objectionable.

Contract Performance and Remedies

A party's contractual duties, under a common law contract or a contract formed under the UCC, can be terminated in several ways. The most common way to terminate contractual duties is by the **performance** of those duties. Failure to perform contractual duties as promised results in a **breach of contract**. When one party breaches a contract, the other party (the nonbreaching party) can seek remedies.

Contract Performance

Conditions expressly stated in a contract must be fully satisfied for complete performance to take place. A party who in good faith performs substantially all terms of a contract can usually enforce the contract against the other party under the doctrine of *substantial performance*. Generally, performance that provides a party with the important and essential benefits of a contract, in spite of any omission or deviation from the terms, is substantial performance. Because substantial performance is not perfect, the other party is entitled to damages to compensate for the part of the contract not completed.

Impossibility of Performance

After a contract has been made, performance may become impossible in an objective sense ("it can't be done," rather than "I can't do it").

> *EXAMPLE 15.21* Colter promises to sell his car to Janine the next day for $4,500. Colter is in an accident in the car later that day. Because the car has been damaged, Colter cannot deliver the car that was promised, and Janine does not have to accept the damaged vehicle even if Colter has it repaired.

Similarly, a party to a contract may die prior to performance, or performance may become illegal because of a change in the law. In these situations, the law excuses parties from their contractual performance duties under the doctrine of *impossibility of performance*.

Commercial Impracticability

Under the doctrine of *commercial impracticability*, courts may excuse parties from their obligations when the performance becomes much more difficult or expensive than contemplated at the time the contract was formed. For someone to invoke this doctrine, however, anticipated performance must become *extremely* difficult or costly.

> *EXAMPLE 15.22* Delbert's Trucking agreed to carry a load of freight each day for a year from Molly's Factory to a train station four miles away. Delbert's and Molly's agreed that the price would be $400 per day. Two months later, the road Delbert's used to get to the train station was torn out by highway crews for reconstruction work expected to take six months. As a result, Delbert's must travel thirty miles to get to the station. Molly's cannot expect Delbert's to fulfill the contract at the original price. Unexpected cost conditions have arisen, making fulfillment of the contract impracticable.

Contract Remedies

A *remedy* is the relief provided for a party when the other party has breached the contract. It is the means employed to enforce a right or to redress an injury. The most common remedies available to a nonbreaching party include damages, rescission, restitution, reformation, and specific performance.

performance
In contract law, the fulfillment of duties arising under a contract; the normal way of discharging contractual obligations.

breach of contract
The failure, without legal excuse, of a contractual party to perform the obligations assumed in a contract.

Damages

A breach of contract entitles the nonbreaching party to sue for monetary damages (see Chapter 4). Damages are designed to compensate a party for the loss of the bargain. Generally, innocent parties are to be placed in the position they would have occupied had the contract been fully performed.

Compensatory Damages.   Damages compensating the nonbreaching party for the loss of the bargain are known as *compensatory damages*. These damages compensate the injured party only for damages actually sustained and proved to have arisen directly from the loss of the bargain caused by the breach of contract. They simply replace what was lost because of the breach.

Compensatory damages are the difference between the value of the breaching party's promised performance and the value of actual performance. This amount is reduced by any loss that the injured party has avoided. In addition, the injured party may be able to recover *incidental damages*—expenses resulting directly from the breach of contract, such as those incurred to obtain performance from another source.

> *EXAMPLE 15.23* You are hired to perform certain services during August for $3,000, but the employer breaches the contract, and you find another job that pays only $500. You can recover $2,500 as compensatory damages. In addition, as incidental damages, you can recover any expenses you incurred in finding the other job.

Damages in contract cases must be reasonably certain, not based on speculation. This often comes up in cases where the plaintiff alleges that the defendant's breach caused lost profits for the plaintiff. Lost future profits may be established based on past profits, which raises difficulties for new businesses that have no track record.

Consequential Damages.   *Consequential damages*, or *special damages*, are a type of compensatory damages. Consequential damages are caused by circumstances beyond the contract itself. They flow from the results of a breach. For consequential damages to be awarded, the breaching party must have known (or have had reason to know) that circumstances would cause the nonbreaching party to suffer additional losses.

> *EXAMPLE 15.24* Glenda contracts with Eric to ship an item she needs to repair her printing press. The contract clearly states that Glenda must receive the item by Monday or she will not be able to print advertising posters for a customer and will lose $10,000. If Eric is late in shipping, Glenda normally can recover the consequential damages caused by the delay (that is, the $10,000 in losses).

Liquidated Damages.   Parties may specify an amount to be paid in the event of a future breach of the contract. This amount, called *liquidated damages*, must be reasonably related to the damages that may be suffered if the contract is not fulfilled. Liquidated damages are a form of compensatory damages. They may not be designed to serve as a *penalty* to deter a party from breaching a contract.

> *EXAMPLE 15.25* Shandy is planning to open a new store in a shopping center on June 1. The owner of the center assures her the store space will be ready. But what if it is not? Shandy will be stuck with inventory that she will have to put in storage, employees who cannot work, and so forth. The parties may agree that if the store space is not ready when promised, the shopping center will pay Shandy $500 a day in liquidated damages to compensate her for her expenses. That would be a reasonable amount. In contrast, damages of $50,000 a day would be a penalty that could not be enforced, because the amount is not reasonably related to the loss suffered.

Punitive Damages. *Punitive damages* are not available in an action for breach of contract. They are intended to punish guilty parties, and contract law is not concerned with punishing guilt. Its purpose is to compensate a party for the loss of a bargain, no more and no less. However, if a tort such as fraud or negligence is involved, punitive damages may be appropriate. In such situations, a tort claim may be added.

Rescission, Restitution, and Reformation

As already discussed, *rescission* is essentially an action to undo, or terminate, a contract—to return the contracting parties to the positions they occupied prior to the transaction. When fraud, a mistake, duress, undue influence, misrepresentation, or lack of contractual capacity is present, rescission is available. The failure of one party to perform entitles the other party to rescind the contract.

Generally, to rescind a contract, the parties must make **restitution** to each other by returning goods, property, or funds previously conveyed. If physical property or goods can be returned, they must be. If the property or goods have been consumed, the restitution must be made in an equivalent dollar amount.

When the parties have imperfectly expressed their agreement in writing, the equitable remedy of **reformation** may also be available. In breach of contract cases, this remedy occurs when the court revises a contract to reflect the true intention of the parties—if a mutual mistake occurred, for example.

Specific Performance

The equitable remedy of **specific performance** calls for the performance of the act promised in the contract. Normally, specific performance is not granted unless the party's legal remedy (monetary damages) is inadequate. For this reason, contracts for the sale of goods rarely qualify for specific performance—substantially identical goods can be bought or sold in the market. If the contract involves unique goods, however, such as a painting or a rare book, a court will grant specific performance.

Generally, courts refuse to grant specific performance of contracts for personal services—contracts that require one party to work personally for another party. Public policy discourages involuntary servitude, and ordering one party to perform personal services against her will amounts to a type of servitude. Moreover, the courts do not want to monitor personal-service contracts.

> **EXAMPLE 15.26** If you contract with a famous artist to paint your portrait and the artist later refuses to perform, the court will not compel the artist to perform. The court cannot assure meaningful performance in such situations.

Remedies for Breach of Sales Contracts

Remedies for breach of a contract for the sale of goods are designed to put the aggrieved party in as good a position as if the other party had fully performed. The seller's remedies for breach include the right to stop or withhold delivery of the goods and the right to recover damages or the purchase price of the goods from the buyer.

The buyer's remedies include:

1. The right to reject *nonconforming goods* (goods that do not conform to those specifically agreed on in the contract) or improperly delivered goods.

2. The right to *cover* (buy goods elsewhere and recover from the seller the extra cost of obtaining the substitute goods).

3. The right to recover damages.

4. In certain circumstances, the right to obtain specific performance of the sales contract.

---

restitution
An equitable remedy under which a person is restored to his or her original position prior to loss or injury.

reformation
An equitable remedy granted by a court to correct, or "reform," a written contract so that it reflects the true intentions of the parties.

specific performance
An equitable remedy requiring exactly the performance that was specified in a contract; usually granted only when monetary damages would be an inadequate remedy and the subject matter of the contract is unique (for example, real property).

Online Contracting and Electronic Signatures

Today, many contracts are formed online. In general, the courts apply the traditional principles of contract law in cyberspace. Many disputes concerning contracts formed online tend to center on the specific terms of the contract and whether the parties voluntarily agreed to those terms.

Online Offers and Acceptances

Generally, the terms of an online offer should be as comprehensive as the terms in an offer made in a written (paper) document. Possible contingencies should be anticipated and provided for in the offer. Because jurisdictional issues often arise with online transactions, dispute-settlement provisions, such as arbitration clauses, are frequently used. The offer should be displayed on the screen so as to be easily readable and clear. An online offer should also include some mechanism, such as providing an "I agree" or "I accept" box, by which a customer accepts the offer.

Click-On Agreements

As described earlier, a click-on agreement arises when a buyer, completing a transaction on a computer, indicates assent to be bound by the terms of an offer by clicking on a button that says "I agree" or "I accept." The terms may be contained on a website through which the buyer is obtaining goods or services, or they may appear when software is loaded. The courts normally enforce click-on agreements.

> **EXAMPLE 15.27** Aaron is downloading a new program. A message pops up on the screen with a window in which Aaron can read the licensing agreement. (Note that a contract involving software usually grants a license giving a party the right to use the software rather than ownership of the software.) If Aaron clicks on the "I agree" box below the window without reading the terms, he will nonetheless be bound by the terms of that agreement.

Shrink-Wrap Agreements

shrink-wrap agreement
An agreement whose terms are expressed in a document located inside the box in which the goods (usually software) are packaged.

A **shrink-wrap agreement** is an agreement whose terms are expressed inside the box in which the goods are packaged. *Shrink-wrap* refers to the plastic that may cover the box. Usually, the party who opens the box is told that he agrees to the terms by keeping whatever is in the box.

> **EXAMPLE 15.28** Abdul orders a new computer that is sent via FedEx. When he receives the computer, he finds that the box also contains an agreement setting forth the terms of the sale, including what remedies are available. The document states that Abdul's use of the computer for more than thirty days is construed as an acceptance of the terms.

In many cases, a shrink-wrap agreement is between the manufacturer of the hardware or software and the ultimate buyer-user of the product, although it may be between a retailer and a buyer. Thus, the terms typically concern warranties, remedies, and other issues associated with the use of the product.

Generally, the courts have enforced the terms of shrink-wrap agreements with one exception: If a court finds that the buyer learned of the shrink-wrap terms *after* the parties entered into a contract, the court may conclude that those terms were proposals for additional terms and were not part of the contract unless the buyer expressly agreed to them.

EXAMPLE 15.29 When Abdul entered into the contract to purchase the computer, he was not informed in the online materials that he would have to pay a monthly license fee to maintain the operating system for the computer. If this term is contested, the court may find that it was not part of the expected contract.

E-Signatures

In some instances, a contract cannot be enforced unless it is signed by the party against whom enforcement is sought. An issue in online transactions has to do with how an electronic signature, or **e-signature**, can be created and verified on e-contracts.

In the days when many people could not write, documents were often signed with an "X." Then handwritten signatures became common, followed by typed signatures, printed signatures, and, most recently, digital signatures, which are transmitted electronically. In the evolution of signature technology, the question of what constitutes a valid signature is a major issue—without consensus on what constitutes a valid signature, little business could be accomplished.

Today, several technologies allow electronic documents to be signed. The use of trusted programs such as Adobe Sign and DocuSign eSignature help ensure that signatures are valid. Because paralegals are frequently responsible for obtaining the necessary signatures on legal documents, some knowledge of digital signatures and alternative technologies is useful.

> **e-signature**
> An electronic sound, symbol, or process attached to or logically associated with a record and executed or adopted by a person with the intent to sign the record, according to the Uniform Electronic Transactions Act.

State Laws Governing E-Signatures

Most states have laws governing e-signatures. In an attempt to create uniformity among these laws, the National Conference of Commissioners on Uniform State Laws and the American Law Institute issued the Uniform Electronic Transactions Act (UETA). It has been adopted, at least in part, by forty-seven states and the District of Columbia (the other three states have other laws to recognize such signatures). The UETA states that a signature or a contract may not be denied legal effect or enforceability solely because it is in electronic form.

Under the UETA, an e-signature is broadly defined as "an electronic sound, symbol, or process attached to or logically associated with a record and executed or adopted by a person with the intent to sign the record." In other words, the signature does not have to be created by any specific technology and can be simply a person's name typed at the end of an e-mail message. The parties do have to agree to conduct business electronically for the UETA provisions to apply. Also, the UETA states that it does not apply to (or change) the provisions of the UCC and does not apply to wills and trusts.

Federal Law on E-Signatures and E-Documents

The Electronic Signatures in Global and National Commerce Act (E-SIGN Act) provides that no contract, record, or signature may be "denied legal effect" solely because it is in an electronic form. In other words, an electronic signature is as valid as a signature on paper, and an electronic document can be as enforceable as a paper one. For an e-signature to be enforceable, the contracting parties must have agreed to use e-signatures. For an e-document to be valid, it must be in a form that can be retained and accurately reproduced.

The E-SIGN Act does not apply to every document. Contracts and documents that are exempt include court papers, divorce decrees, evictions, foreclosures, health-insurance terminations, prenuptial agreements, and wills.

Intellectual Property Law

intellectual property
Property resulting from intellectual, creative processes.

Contract law had its origins hundreds of years ago. Now we move to an area of law that, although it has existed for some time, has rapidly grown in importance in recent years. Most people think of wealth in terms of houses, land, cars, stocks, and bonds. Wealth, however, also includes **intellectual property**, the products that result from intellectual, creative processes. As the *Developing Paralegal Skills* feature below notes, complex strategic issues involving intellectual property (IP) are becoming more important in law practice.

Although it is an abstract term, intellectual property is familiar to virtually everyone. *Trademarks, copyrights, trade secrets,* and *patents* are all forms of intellectual property. This book is copyrighted. If you drink a Coke™ you consume a product with a trademarked name, made by a formula that is a trade secret, advertised using copyrighted material, and manufactured with patented equipment. The apps you use, the movies you see, and the music you listen to are all forms of intellectual property, as is this book.

The need to protect creative works was voiced by the framers of the U.S. Constitution more than two hundred years ago: Article I, Section 8, of the Constitution authorized Congress "[t]o promote the Progress of Science and useful Arts, by securing for limited Times to Authors and Inventors the exclusive Right to their respective Writings and Discoveries." Laws protecting patents, trademarks, and copyrights are designed to protect and reward inventive and artistic creativity. Exhibit 15.2 summarizes the forms of intellectual property, how they are acquired, and what remedies are available for *infringement,* or unauthorized use.

DEVELOPING PARALEGAL SKILLS

NEW STRATEGIES IN INTELLECTUAL PROPERTY

A growing area of practice in intellectual property (IP) law involves licensing agreements made by owners of patents, copyrights, and trademarks. IP owners often license rights to other businesses. In addition, strategies to reduce taxes often lead firms to put their collection of IP rights in a subsidiary. For example, the band U2 moved the IP rights to its music to the Netherlands to reduce taxes on royalties. Similarly, Google used what is called the "double Irish" strategy. It licensed the European rights to its search and advertising business to Google Ireland Holdings, based in Bermuda, where taxes are low. It operates the business through Google Ireland Limited, which passes the revenue to the Bermuda-based company.

A key part of any licensing or IP-based tax strategy is proper valuation of the intellectual property rights involved. Paralegals are often involved in documenting the value of the IP rights, which must be done with great care. For patents, you might be asked to research the following:

- Is the patent in force in the relevant jurisdiction, and have all fees been paid?
- Are there related patents listed in the foreign or domestic patent applications? If so, who owns them?
- What is the scope of the patent claim? Were there any amendments that narrow or broaden the scope made during the application process?
- Is there any past or pending litigation involving the patent?
- Are there any "blocking" patents—that is, patents on which this patent infringes?
- Is the patent protected in relevant foreign jurisdictions?

By researching these types of questions and documenting the answers, a paralegal can assist in establishing a fair valuation for IP rights that will enable firms to negotiate the licensing of rights or to claim appropriate tax benefits.

EXHIBIT 15.2

Forms of Intellectual Property

Type	Definition	How Acquired	Duration	Remedy for Infringement
Patent	A grant from the government that gives an inventor exclusive rights to an invention.	By filing a patent application with the U.S. Patent and Trademark Office and receiving its approval.	For inventions, 20 years from the date of application; for design patents, 14 years from the date of application.	Monetary damages, including royalties and lost profits, *plus* attorneys' fees. Damages may be tripled for intentional infringements.
Copyright	The right of an author or a creator of a literary or artistic work or other production (such as a computer program) to have the exclusive use of that work for a given period of time.	Automatic (once the work or creation is put in tangible form). Only the *expression* of an idea (and not the idea itself) can be protected by copyright.	For authors: the life of the author plus 70 years. For publishers: 95 years after the date of publication or 120 years after creation.	Actual damages plus profits received by the party who infringed or statutory damages under the Copyright Act, *plus* costs and attorneys' fees in either situation.
Trademark	A distinctive word, name, symbol, or device that an entity uses to distinguish its goods or services from those of others. The owner has the exclusive right to use that mark.	1. At common law, created by use of the mark. 2. Registration with the U.S. Patent and Trademark Office; mark must already be in use or be placed in use within the following six months.	1. Unlimited, as long as the mark is in use. To continue notice by registration, holder must renew between the fifth and sixth years and, thereafter, every ten years.	1. Injunction prohibiting future use of mark. 2. Actual damages plus profits received by the party who infringed. 3. Destruction of articles that infringed. 4. *Plus* costs and attorneys' fees.
Trade Secret	A business secret that makes a company or product unique and that would be of value to a competitor. Trade secrets include customer lists, plans, and research and development.	Through the development of the information and processes that constitute the business secret.	Unlimited, so long as not revealed to others (once a trade secret is revealed to others, it is no longer secret).	Monetary damages for misappropriation (the Uniform Trade Secrets Act also permits punitive damages if willful), *plus* costs and attorneys' fees.

Growing Value of Intellectual Property

The study of intellectual property law is important because intellectual property has taken on increasing significance. In the digital age, the value of the world's intellectual property exceeds the value of physical property, such as machines and houses. Ownership rights in intangible intellectual property are more important to the prosperity of U.S. companies than are their tangible assets. Because of the importance of obtaining and protecting intellectual property rights, attorneys and paralegals with specialized knowledge in this area are in great demand in law firms and in corporations.

Patents

A **patent** is a grant from the government that gives an inventor the exclusive right to make, use, and sell an invention for a period of twenty years from the date of filing the application for a patent. Patents for designs, as opposed to inventions, are given for a

patent
A government grant that gives an inventor the exclusive right or privilege to make, use, or sell an invention for a limited time period.

fourteen-year period. To secure a patent, the applicant must demonstrate to the satisfaction of examiners at the U.S. Patent and Trademark Office (USPTO) that the invention, discovery, process, or design is genuine, novel, useful, and not obvious in light of current technology. In case of a race to invent and protect, the law protects the first to file for a patent, not the first to invent. A patent holder gives notice to all that an article or design is patented by placing on it the word *Patent* or *Pat.* and the patent number.

Patent Application

Filing patents is complicated and is a specialized area of law. Often, patents must be filed in multiple nations, so the expense of dealing with the different requirements in Europe and Japan can be considerable. Inventors can employ the services of professionals to apply for patents. A *patent agent* is a professional licensed by the USPTO to assist with patent applications. Patent agents must pass the patent bar examination but need not have a law degree. Patent agents who do have law degrees are known as *patent attorneys*. Both patent agents and patent attorneys must have technical degrees.

Patent Infringement

If a firm makes, uses, or sells another's patented design, product, or process without permission, it commits the tort of patent infringement. Patent infringement may exist even though the patent owner has not put the patented product in commerce. Patent infringement may also occur even though not all features or parts of an invention are copied. With respect to a patented process, however, all steps or their equivalent must be copied for infringement to exist.

Copyrights

copyright

The exclusive right of an author (or other creator) to publish, print, or sell an intellectual production for a statutory period of time.

Literary or artistic productions (including computer software) are protected under copyright law. A **copyright** gives the creator of a work the right to the exclusive use of that work for a given period of time. The Copyright Act of 1976, as amended, governs copyrights. Works are automatically given statutory copyright protection for the life of the author plus 70 years. For works by more than one author, the copyright expires 70 years after the death of the last surviving author. For copyrights owned by publishing houses, the copyright expires 95 years from the date of publication or 120 years from the date of creation, whichever is first.

Copyrights can be registered with the U.S. Copyright Office in Washington, D.C. (but registration is not required). Registration is a simple and inexpensive process. A copyright owner also need not place a © or *Copyright* on the work to have the work protected against infringement. Chances are that if somebody created it, somebody owns it.

What Can Be Copyrighted?

It is not possible to copyright an *idea*. Others may freely use the ideas embodied in a work. What is copyrightable is how an idea is *expressed*. When an idea and an expression are inseparable, the expression cannot be copyrighted. Generally, anything that is not an original expression of an idea does not qualify for copyright protection. Facts widely known to the public are not copyrightable. Page numbers normally are not copyrightable because they follow a sequence known to everyone. Mathematical calculations are not copyrightable. The key requirement to obtain copyright protection is originality, but the work need not have market value.

Copyright Infringement

When the form or expression of an idea is copied, an infringement of copyright occurs. The reproduction does not have to be exactly the same as the original, nor does it have to reproduce the original in its entirety.

Penalties and Remedies.   Penalties or remedies can be imposed on those who infringe copyrights. These range from actual damages (damages based on the actual harm caused to the copyright holder by the infringement) to statutory damages. Damages provided for under the Copyright Act for willful infringement are up to $150,000 per work. In most instances, damages are $750 to $30,000 per work at the discretion of the court. When many copyrighted songs have been downloaded and improperly distributed, the total damages can be huge.

The Fair-Use Exception.   An exception to liability for copyright infringement is made under the "fair use" doctrine. Under the Copyright Act, a person or organization can in certain situations reproduce copyrighted material without paying *royalties* (fees paid to the copyright holder for the privilege of reproducing the copyrighted material). Generally, the courts determine whether a particular use is fair on a case-by-case basis.

In determining whether the use of a work in a particular case is a fair use, a court takes several factors into account. The purpose of the use is considered, along with the nature of the copyrighted work and how much of it is copied. The most important factor is the effect of the use on the market for the copyrighted work. One of the most common examples of the fair-use exception is making copies of copyrighted material for use in education settings, because most often the act does not affect the marketing value of the copyrighted work.

Open Access and Copyrights

Some content creators do not want to charge for the use of particular content. Various *open access* regimes have developed to enable them to allow others to use their work with few restrictions. For example, some scientific journals are free to anyone to copy, so long as the original source is acknowledged in any use.

Other content creators provide *open source* content. For example, the Linux operating system for computers is open source software. Anyone is free to copy and use it, but people other than the creators cannot charge for the source code. Linux software is covered by the *GNU General Public License* (GPL) (sometimes called a "copyleft" license to distinguish it from copyright). The GPL allows people to make money distributing and modifying Linux but forbids them from restricting the right of others to also distribute the software. Any work derived from the original computer code must be covered by the GPL as well. (Companies that sell Linux make their money by providing services such as installation programs and support services.)

Open source programmer Richard Stallings explains the distinction as "free as in free speech, not free as in free beer." Rather than being motivated by pay, the programmers who work on Linux are rewarded by respect within the programming community, which can lead to paid consulting or other employment as well as fame among other programmers.

Trademarks and Related Property

A **trademark** is a distinctive mark, motto, or emblem that a manufacturer stamps, prints, or otherwise affixes to the goods it produces so they can be distinguished from the goods of other manufacturers and merchants. Examples of trademarks are brand-name labels on jeans, luggage, shoes, and other products. Generally, to be protected under trademark law, a mark must be distinctive. A distinctive mark might consist of an uncommon or invented word (such as *Xerox*, *Exxon*, or *Google*) or words used in an uncommon or fanciful way (such as *English Leather* for an aftershave lotion rather than for leather processed in England).

At common law, the person who used a symbol or mark to identify a business or product was protected in the use of that trademark. Today, trademarks are usually registered with the federal government. The registration process is easy, and the Trademark Office website allows you to search existing marks. A mark can be registered with the Trademark Office (1) if it is already in commerce or (2) if the applicant intends to put it into commerce within six months.

A person need not have registered a trademark in order to sue for trademark infringement, but registration furnishes proof of the date the owner began using the trademark. Only those trademarks that are deemed sufficiently distinctive from competing trademarks will be protected. Trademarks must be protected in each country separately.

Trade dress is an extension of trademark. It applies to the look and feel of a product or service. For example, Home Depot stores have orange signage. Because the company has invested in developing that distinctive look, and it is well recognized by consumers, other home supply stores cannot imitate the orange motif claimed by Home Depot. Similarly, Owens Corning insulation is colored pink. The company has spent large sums in advertisements featuring the pink product. The color is not functional; it is distinctive to the product, so other insulation makers cannot use it.

Trade Names

Trademarks apply to *products*. The term **trade name** is used to indicate part or all of a business's name, such as McDonald's. Unless the trade name is also used as a trademark (as with Coca-Cola, for example), the name is not protected under federal trademark law. Trade names are protected under the common law, however. Holiday Inns, Inc., which does business as Holiday Inn, for example, could sue a motel owner who used that name or a portion of it (such as "Holiday Motels") without permission. Like trademarks, trade names must actually be used to receive protection.

Trademark Infringement

Registration of a trademark gives notice that the trademark belongs to the registrant. The registrant is allowed to use the symbol ® to indicate that the mark has been registered. Whenever that trademark is copied partly or in whole by another party (intentionally or unintentionally), the trademark has been infringed, and the owner can sue. The extent of protection depends on real use and recognition of the mark in the market. Marks are limited to specific goods or services in the areas in which a firm actually operates. If a mark is truly famous, such as Nike, then it receives protection in all markets.

---

trademark

A distinctive mark, motto, or emblem that a manufacturer stamps, prints, or otherwise affixes to the goods it produces so that they can be identified on the market and their origins made known. Once a trademark is established (under the common law or through registration), the owner is entitled to its exclusive use.

trade name

A term that is used to indicate part or all of a business's name and that is directly related to the business's reputation and goodwill. Trade names are protected under the common law (and under trademark law, if the business's name is the same as its trademark).

Trademark Dilution

Historically, federal trademark law prohibited the unauthorized use of the same mark on competing or "related" goods or services only when such use would be likely to confuse consumers. The federal Trademark Dilution Act extends that protection.

Trademark *dilution* occurs when a trademark is used, without authorization, in a way that diminishes the distinctive quality of the mark. Unlike trademark infringement, a dilution cause of action does not require proof that consumers are likely to be confused by a connection between the unauthorized use and the mark. For this reason, the products (or services) involved do not have to be similar. In addition, a famous mark may be diluted not only by the use of an *identical* mark but also by the use of a *similar* mark.

Trade Secrets

Business processes and information that are not (or cannot be) patented, copyrighted, or trademarked may be protected against appropriation by a competitor as trade secrets. A **trade secret** consists of customer lists, plans, research and development, pricing information, marketing techniques, production techniques, and generally anything that is in fact not known outside the company and that would have value to a competitor.

trade secret
Information or process that gives a business an advantage over competitors who do not know the information or process.

Protecting Trade Secrets

Unlike copyright and trademark protection, protection of trade secrets extends both to ideas and to their expression. Of course, the secret formula, method, or other information must be disclosed to some persons, particularly to key employees. Businesses must actively protect their trade secrets. The owner of the secret must restrict access to the knowledge. Commonly, all employees who use the process or information agree, by a signed confidentiality agreement, never to divulge or use the information outside of the company.

To protect intellectual property, a firm must know what assets it possesses. See this chapter's *Featured Contributor* article on pages 478 and 479 for a discussion on intellectual property audits.

Misappropriation of Trade Secrets

Someone who discloses or uses another's trade secret, without a privilege to do so, is liable to the other if (1) he or she discovered the secret by improper means or (2) the disclosure or use constitutes a breach of confidence. The theft of confidential business data through industrial espionage, such as when a business taps into a competitor's computer, is a theft of trade secrets and is actionable. Claims also often arise when a departing employee takes trade secrets from his former employer to use when working for his new employer.

At one time, nearly every law with respect to trade secrets was common law. In an effort to reduce the unpredictability of the law in this area, the Uniform Trade Secrets Act (UTSA) was proposed. Today, it has been adopted in forty-seven states. New York and Massachusetts have not adopted it; North Carolina has a statute similar to the UTSA. Under the UTSA, a plaintiff can recover punitive damages for willful misappropriation of business secrets.

A federal statute, the Economic Espionage Act, also addresses trade secret theft. While its focus is on the theft of trade secrets that are sold to foreign entities, it also applies to domestic theft. Violations of the statute can result in a prison term and significant fines.

FEATURED CONTRIBUTOR

STRATEGIES FOR PROTECTING INTELLECTUAL PROPERTY: THE INTELLECTUAL PROPERTY AUDIT

Deborah E. Bouchoux

BIOGRAPHICAL NOTE

Deborah E. Bouchoux is an attorney licensed to practice in the District of Columbia. She has been involved in paralegal education for more than twenty years. Bouchoux teaches in the Paralegal Studies Program at Georgetown University in Washington, D.C., and serves as a member of the advisory board for the program.

Ms. Bouchoux is a frequent lecturer for the National Capital Area Paralegal Association and is the author of *Intellectual Property: The Law of Trademarks, Copyrights, Patents, and Trade Secrets*, as well as *Protecting Your Company's Intellectual Property: A Practical Guide to Trademarks, Copyrights, Patents, and Trade Secrets*.

Because clients are often unaware of the value of their intangible assets or intellectual property, many law firms conduct intellectual property audits. These audits specify the clients' intellectual property and outline strategies to protect and exploit that property. These types of audits are also conducted when a company sells its assets or merges with another entity so the buyers know what intellectual property is involved in the purchase.

Without an audit, valuable intellectual property rights may be lost. Once companies realize what intellectual property they own and its value, they can use that intellectual property to create revenue. Trademarks, copyrights, patents, and trade secrets can all be licensed to others for fees to generate a continuing revenue stream for the company. For example, IBM reportedly earns more than $1 billion annually from licensing and sales of its intellectual property.

In addition, routinely conducted audits also save clients time. In the event a client wishes to borrow money from a bank, for instance, it will have an accurate and up-to-date list of its intellectual property assets that can then be pledged as collateral to ensure repayment of the loan.

Here are several steps in conducting a successful intellectual property audit.

> **"Without protection, valuable rights may be lost."**

Step 1: Designate the Team.

The law firm should designate an attorney and paralegal to serve as representatives of the firm, and the company should select an individual who will serve as the company's team leader. Together, these individuals will be primarily responsible for conducting the audit and can answer any questions that may arise in the course of the audit. The team should have a preliminary meeting to discuss the scope and nature of the audit.

For example, the client will need to determine whether only U.S. materials will be reviewed or whether consideration will be given to seeking protection in foreign countries for certain trademarks and patents. The involvement of legal counsel ensures that any matters discussed are subject to the attorney-client privilege and remain confidential.

Step 2: Prepare the Audit Questionnaire.

The legal team should prepare a worksheet or questionnaire for the client that is designed to elicit information about its intellectual property assets. Paralegals play a significant role in drafting the audit questionnaire. The audit questionnaire will typically ask the following:

- Does the client use any specific names, logos, or slogans in advertising its products and services?

- Are any written materials used in marketing (such as brochures, newspaper or Web-based advertisements, and materials used for presentations)?

- Has the client developed any inventions, products, software, or processes?

- Does the client use any software or products owned by another entity?

- Does the client use any confidential methods or processes in developing and marketing its products and services, including financial forecasts, marketing plans, and customer lists?

- Has the company ever been sued for or accused of infringing another party's intellectual property rights?

- How does the company control access to its valuable and proprietary materials to protect against inadvertent disclosure or misappropriation of these materials?

- Do employment, confidentiality, nondisclosure, and noncompete contracts exist to protect proprietary materials?

> "Paralegals play a significant role in drafting the audit questionnaire."

Step 3: Conduct the Audit.

On receiving the questionnaire, the client should begin gathering the materials that are responsive to the questionnaire. The legal team will then review the materials that the client has assembled to determine which materials can be protected under intellectual property law. If the client has a website, it should be carefully reviewed to ensure not only that the site is protected under copyright law but also that it does not infringe on the rights of another party by, for example, using another's copyrighted music or artwork.

Paralegals often coordinate the time and manner of the audit by scheduling the audit date, arranging for a conference room, and ensuring that a photocopy machine is available to copy documents that are responsive to the questionnaire. Generally, the audit is conducted at the client's office because this is where the pertinent materials and documents are located.

Step 4: Write the Audit Report.

The report identifies all of the intellectual property owned by the client and makes recommendations for its continued protection and maintenance. For example, the audit may disclose that the client uses a distinctive slogan in its advertising materials or that title to some of the intellectual property assets is unclear or out of date. The legal team will then recommend that the slogan be registered as a trademark and that the chain of title be corrected to reflect current ownership of the intellectual property.

Step 5: Complete Post-Audit Activity.

After the audit is complete, the legal team, and particularly the paralegal, will begin preparing applications to register trademarks, copyrights, and patents and will develop written policies to protect the client's trade secrets.

Other post-audit tasks include the following:

- Check that the U.S. Patent and Trademark and Copyright Office records accurately indicate the client's ownership of trademarks, patents, and copyrights.

- Draft contracts that the client can use when it hires independent contractors to develop certain products.

- Write agreements to allow clients to license their intellectual property to others.

- Define online and social use policies that state the confidentiality of the client's intellectual property to its employees and vendors.

- Ensure the client reviews all materials to know when competitors infringe on its rights and what actions to take.

- Implement a docketing system to ensure the client's intellectual property rights are maintained, such as creating a calendar of important dates and deadlines.

- Schedule the next intellectual property audit.

CHAPTER SUMMARY

CONTRACTS AND INTELLECTUAL PROPERTY LAW

Requirements to Form a Valid Contract

A contract is any agreement (based on a promise or an exchange of promises) that can be enforced in court. To form a valid contract, four basic requirements must be met.

1. *Agreement*—An agreement includes an offer and an acceptance. One party must offer to enter into a legal agreement, and another party must accept the terms of the offer.

   a. An offer is a promise to do or to refrain from doing some specified thing in the future.

   b. The offeror must have the intent to be bound, the terms must be reasonably certain or definite, and the offer must be communicated to the offeree.

   c. Both a rejection of the offer and the making of a counteroffer terminate the original offer. The offer is also terminated if the party making the offer withdraws the offer before it has been accepted. Otherwise, the offer expires after a reasonable period of time has passed.

   d. An offer may automatically terminate by law if the subject matter is destroyed, one party dies or becomes incompetent, or the contract becomes illegal.

   e. The terms of the acceptance must be the same as ("mirror") the terms of the offer.

   f. Acceptance of an offer is timely if it is made before the offer is terminated. Acceptance takes effect at the time the acceptance is communicated via the mode expressly or impliedly authorized by the offeror. This is called the *mailbox rule*.

   g. If the contract does not specify the method of acceptance, an offer may be accepted by any means that is reasonable under the circumstances.

2. *Consideration*—Consideration is usually defined as "something of value"—such as money or the performance of an action—given in exchange for a promise.

   a. To be legally sufficient, consideration must involve a legal detriment to the promisee, a legal benefit to the promisor, or both.

   b. In general, a court will not question the adequacy of consideration (fairness of the bargain). Courts will inquire into the adequacy of consideration only when fraud, undue influence, duress, or incompetence is involved.

   c. Some contracts may be enforced (or partially enforced) under the doctrine of promissory estoppel even though consideration is lacking.

3. *Contractual capacity*—The parties to the contract must have the legal ability to enter into a contractual relationship. Courts generally presume contractual capacity unless one party is a minor, intoxicated, or mentally incompetent.

4. *Legality*—A contract to do something that is prohibited by federal or state statutory law is illegal and, as such, void from the outset and thus unenforceable.

   a. Contracts entered into by persons who do not have a license, when one is required by statute, may not be enforceable.

   b. Some contracts are not enforced because the court deems them to be contrary to public policy.

Defenses to Contract Enforceability

A contract that meets all the specified requirements may not be enforceable if (1) the parties have not genuinely assented (agreed) to its terms, (2) the contract is so oppressive to one of the parties that a court will refuse to enforce it, or (3) the contract is not in the proper form.

1. *Genuineness of assent*—A contract can be avoided if there was a lack of real consent. This may be due to mistake of material fact (not value) when both parties are mistaken (mutual mistake). Lack of consent may also be based on fraudulent misrepresentation, undue influence, or duress.

2. *Unconscionable contracts*—When a contract is so oppressive to one of the parties that a court will refuse to enforce it, the oppressed party will be excused from performance. These situations usually involve an adhesion contract, which is a contract drafted by the dominant party and presented on a take-it-or-leave-it basis.

3. *Statute of Frauds*—Every state has a Statute of Frauds, which is a statute that specifies what types of contracts must be in writing (or be evidenced by a written document). The following types of contracts are normally required to be in writing:

   a. Contracts involving interests in land.

   b. Contracts that cannot by their terms be performed within one year from the day after the date of formation.

   c. Collateral, or secondary, contracts, such as promises to answer for the debt or duty of another.

   d. Promises made in consideration of marriage.

   e. Under the UCC, contracts for the sale of goods priced at $500 or more.

Sales Contracts and Warranties

States have statutes to replace common law contracts in certain areas of commerce.

1. *The scope of UCC Article 2*—The Uniform Commercial Code (UCC) governs contracts for the sale of goods (as opposed to real property or services). The UCC primarily comes into play when disputes arise over ambiguous or missing terms and when the buyer or seller is a merchant.

2. *Warranties under the UCC*—The UCC contains provisions on express and implied warranties that arise when goods are sold. For example, under the UCC, every merchant warrants that the goods are reasonably fit for the ordinary purpose for which such goods are used.

Contract Performance and Remedies

The most common way to terminate contractual duties under a common law contract or UCC-based contract is by the performance of those duties. Failure to perform contractual duties as promised results in a breach of the contract.

1. *Contract performance*—Performance that provides a party with the essential benefits of the contract, in spite of deviations from the terms, is substantial performance. Because substantial performance is not in full compliance with the contract, the other party is entitled to damages to compensate for the deviations. Performance may be excused if it becomes objectively impossible or, in some instances, commercially impracticable.

2. *Contract remedies*—When there is a breach, remedies can include the following:

   a. Monetary damages are a legal remedy designed to compensate a party for the loss of the bargain.

   (1) Compensatory damages compensate the injured party for damages actually sustained. Incidental damages compensate the injured party for expenses caused directly by a breach of contract, such as the cost of obtaining performance from another source.

   (2) Consequential damages flow from the breach and must have been foreseeable at the time the contract was formed.

   (3) Liquidated damages are an amount specified in the contract to be paid in case of a failure to perform.

   b. The following equitable remedies are available only in limited circumstances:

   (1) Rescission is an action to undo, or cancel, the contract. When a contract is rescinded, restitution must be made.

   (2) Reformation is an action in which the court rewrites the contract to reflect the parties' true agreement.

   (3) Specific performance, which requires a party to perform the contract, is available when monetary damages are an inadequate remedy.

3. *Remedies for breach of sales contracts*—The UCC may provide additional remedies to buyers and sellers (such as the buyer's right to reject nonconforming goods).

Online Contracting and Electronic Signatures

Many contracts are formed online. How the courts apply the traditional rules of contract law to online contracts is an increasingly important issue. Generally, the terms of the offer should be as comprehensive as in written documents. The method of acceptance should also be specified.

1. *Online offers and acceptances*—As with regular contracts, it is best to have clear terms to reduce grounds for later disputes.

   a. *Click-on agreements*—The buyer accepts an online offer by clicking, for example, "I agree." The courts enforce these agreements.

b. *Shrink-wrap agreements*—The terms are expressed inside or on the box in which the goods are packaged, and the buyer accepts by keeping the goods. Courts enforce such agreements unless the buyer learned of the terms after entering the contract.

2. *E-signatures*—Digital signatures verify the identity of parties to a contract. Several technologies allow electronic documents to be signed.

3. *State laws governing e-signatures*—The Uniform Electronic Transactions Act (UETA), which governs e-signatures, has been adopted, at least in part, by forty-seven states and the District of Columbia.

4. *Federal law on e-signatures and e-documents*—The Electronic Signatures in Global and National Commerce (E-SIGN) Act gives validity to e-signatures by providing that no contract, record, or signature may be "denied legal effect" solely because it is in electronic form.

Intellectual Property Law

Intellectual property—The products that result from intellectual, creative processes are becoming increasingly valuable. The following are the four basic types of intellectual property rights. If a party infringes on these rights, the owner of the property can file a suit and possibly obtain damages.

1. *Patent*—A grant from the government that gives an inventor the exclusive right to make, use, and sell an invention.

2. *Copyright*—The right of an author or a creator of a literary or artistic work or other production (such as a computer program) to have the exclusive use of that work for a given period of time.

3. *Trademarks and related property*—A trademark is a distinctive mark or motto that a manufacturer stamps, prints, or affixes to goods so that its products are distinguishable from those of others. Whereas trademarks apply to products, trade names apply to business names. Infringements and dilution of marks are bases for suits for unauthorized use of the property.

4. *Trade secret*—A business secret that makes a particular company or product unique and that would be of value to a competitor (such as customer lists, plans, and research and development).

KEY TERMS AND CONCEPTS

acceptance 457
adhesion contract 464
agreement 455
breach of contract 467
click-on agreement 458
consideration 458
contractual capacity 460
copyright 474
e-signature 471
genuineness of assent 462
intellectual property 472
mailbox rule 458

material fact 462
mirror image rule 457
mutual mistake 462
offer 455
offeree 456
offeror 455
patent 473
performance 467
promise 454
promissory estoppel 459
reformation 469
rescission 462

restitution 469
sales contract 465
shrink-wrap agreement 470
specific performance 469
Statute of Frauds 464
trade name 476
trade secret 477
trademark 476
unconscionable contract 464
Uniform Commercial Code (UCC) 465
unilateral mistake 462
warranty 465

QUESTIONS FOR REVIEW

1. What are the four basic requirements for forming a valid contract? Are there any circumstances in which the court will enforce the parties' agreement even though it lacks consideration? What defenses can be used against a claim of breach of contract?

2. Consideration, a requirement for a valid contract, is defined as *something of value*. What items, other than money, meet this definition? Explain how consideration distinguishes a contract from a gift.

3. What is the Uniform Commercial Code (UCC), and to what types of contracts does it apply? How does the UCC affect the common law of contracts? What warranties exist under the UCC?

4. Describe the remedies that are available when a contract is breached. What is specific performance, and in what circumstances is it available?

5. What kinds of electronic contracts do the courts enforce? What constitutes an electronic signature, and what makes it valid? What state and federal laws govern electronic signatures and contracts?

6. List the four major forms of intellectual property and describe what intellectual property is. Why is it significant in the law today?

ETHICS QUESTION

1. Shayna is a paralegal at a bank. She reviews a package of loan documents for a complex commercial transaction that has been submitted by the lawyers for the borrower. She does not fully understand one provision in the documents that eliminates the need for a guarantor. A guarantor promises that the loan will be repaid in the event that the borrower fails to do so, an important protection for the bank. Shayna does not include this provision in her summary to her supervising attorney, and the loan goes through without the guarantee. Later the borrower defaults on the loan, and the bank is out several million dollars. What ethics rules have been violated? What might be the outcome for Shayna? For her supervising attorney?

PRACTICE QUESTIONS AND ASSIGNMENTS

1. Using the material on contract law in this chapter, identify which contract below is a bilateral contract and which is a unilateral contract:

   a. Juanita offers to sell Mier her laptop for $200. Mier agrees and tells her he will meet her in the cafeteria at noon the next day with cash.

   b. Jonah e-mails Michael and offers Michael $5,000 to paint his house green during the first week of June. Michael does not respond to Jonah's e-mail, but arrives at Jonah's house on June 1 and begins painting it green.

2. Bernie, the sole owner of a small business, has a large piece of used farm equipment for sale. He offers to sell the equipment to Hank for $10,000. Discuss what happens to the offer in the following situations:

   a. Bernie dies prior to Hank's acceptance; at the time he accepts, Hank is unaware of Bernie's death.

   b. The night before Hank accepts, a fire destroys the equipment.

3. Using the material on acceptances presented in this chapter, identify which situation below will result in a contract:

   a. Kelly offers to sell her used algebra textbook to Patrick for $50. He responds, "Maybe—if I have enough money once I get my book refund later this week."

   b. Kirk offers Kristina $50 for her textbook. Kristina says, "Sure. I'll drop it off in the morning."

4. Using the material on contract law presented in this chapter, identify which defenses the defendants in the following hypothetical cases might use in an action for breach of contract:

   a. Mrs. Martinez, a Spanish-speaking immigrant, buys a washing machine and signs a financing agreement that allows her to pay for it in monthly installments. The agreement contains a clause that allows the store to repossess the appliance if she misses a payment. Mrs. Martinez misses the next-to-last payment. The store notifies Mrs. Martinez that she has breached her contract and that it intends to repossess the washing machine. How might Mrs. Martinez defend against the store's action?

   b. Sally orally agrees to purchase a farm from her lifelong friend, Fred. She promises to pay Fred $120,000 for the farm. She trusts Fred, so she does not put the deal in writing. A few days later, Fred sells the same property to Nell for $140,000. Fred and Nell put their agreement in writing. When Sally learns of Fred's contract with Nell, she sues Fred for breach of contract. What is Fred's defense?

c. Rob enters into a contract with Tom to sell Tom fifty sweaters in Christmas colors and featuring Christmas designs. The first shipment of sweaters is due on October 1, 2021. When the sweaters are not delivered, Tom calls Rob and learns that the factory where the sweaters were to be produced has burned down. Tom, who is upset because he needed the sweaters for his Christmas catalog sales, sues Rob for breach of contract. What is Rob's defense?

5. Joel goes to an expensive restaurant in New York for lunch. He orders the special, pasta with white truffles. The price is not given, and he does not ask the waiter how much it costs. When the bill arrives at the end of the meal, Joel is flabbergasted—he was charged $175 for his entrée. Does a dinner meet the definition of a sale of goods under the UCC?

6. Using the requirements for an offer that were stated in the chapter, draft a simple offer to purchase a used iPad from a classmate. Make sure that the offer is definite and certain. Next, write an explanation (in one or two paragraphs) of how you would communicate the offer to the person, how long the offer would remain open, and what method of acceptance you would prefer.

7. Based on the material on intellectual property law presented in the chapter, in which of the following situations would a court likely hold Maruta liable for copyright or trademark infringement?

a. At the library, Maruta photocopies ten pages from a scholarly journal relating to a topic on which she is writing a term paper.

b. Maruta makes leather handbags and sells them in her small leather shop. She advertises her handbags as "Vutton handbags," hoping that customers might mistakenly assume that they were made by Vuitton, the well-known maker of high-quality luggage and handbags.

c. Maruta owns a video game store. She buys a copy of the latest games from various developers. She makes copies to rent or sell to her customers.

8. Rosalia, a very experienced paralegal, works in a firm specializing in appellate law practice. She prepares many legal briefs along with her supervising attorney, and sometimes her supervising attorney just reviews, signs, and files the briefs. Recently, it has come to the firm's attention that several fee-based online legal research databases have been reproducing the firm's legal briefs in their databases and selling access to them. Rosalia's supervising attorney has obtained copyright registration over many of their briefs and is considering suing for copyright infringement. Explain whether Rosalia and her supervising attorney have a case, or whether the reproduction of the briefs represents fair use.

GROUP PROJECT

In this project, each group will analyze advertisements to determine if they can be offers.

Students one and two will review the Pepsi Harrier Jet commercials (numbers one and two) on **YouTube.com** to determine the differences between the two ads. (These ads are discussed in *Example 15.6.*)

Student three will locate the U.S. Second Circuit Court of Appeals opinion in this case and create a list of the reasons the court gave for finding that the first ad was not enforceable.

Student four will play the two commercials for the class, explaining how they differ and offering support for the court's opinion that no legal offer was made.

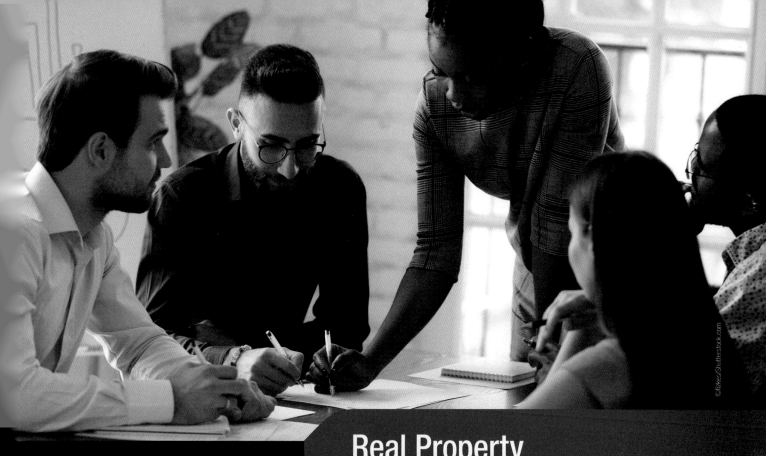

CHAPTER
16

Real Property and Insurance Law

CHAPTER OBJECTIVES

After completing this chapter, you will be able to:

- Compare real property and personal property.

- Explain how one acquires, holds, and transfers ownership or possessory rights in property and what procedures are involved in the sale of real estate.

- Define the terminology used in insurance contracts and the various classifications of insurance.

- Define *insurable interest*.

- Identify the provisions typically included in an insurance contract and the rights and duties of the parties under insurance contracts.

- Describe tasks that paralegals working for an insurance company may perform.

Introduction

As you study the major areas of substantive law, remember that although the topics are covered separately, as if they existed in isolation from one another, there is in fact a great deal of overlap among them. For example, in tort and product liability cases, covered in Chapter 14, the defendant's insurance coverage—or lack of it—is often an important factor in how litigation proceeds. Property owners also depend on insurance to protect themselves from liability, because torts or crimes could occur on their property for which they could be held responsible.

The first part of this chapter investigates property law. Approximately one-quarter of all paralegals work in this area. After that, we look at insurance law, another area of specialization for many paralegals. While these are distinct areas of law, they are connected in practice. Most property owners insure their property against possible losses due to fires, accidents, or other perils. Further, mortgage companies and banks that make loans to finance property purchases require that the property be covered by insurance.

Real Property

real property

Immovable property consisting of land and the buildings and plant life thereon.

For centuries, the law has divided property into two classifications: real property and personal property. **Real property**, or *real estate*, is land and things attached to the land, such as trees and buildings, as well as the minerals below the surface of the land and the air above the land.

personal property

Any property that is not real property. Generally, any property that is movable or intangible is classified as personal property.

Personal property is all other property. Personal property can be either tangible or intangible. *Tangible* personal property, such as an iPhone, jewelry, or a car, has physical substance. *Intangible* personal property represents a set of rights and interests but has no real physical existence. Stocks, bonds, and intellectual property rights (discussed in Chapter 15) are examples of intangible personal property.

Ownership Rights in Property

fee simple absolute

Ownership rights entitling the holder to use, possess, or dispose of the property however he or she chooses during his or her lifetime.

Property ownership is often viewed as a "bundle of rights." A person who owns the entire bundle—who has ownership rights to the greatest degree possible—is said to own the property in **fee simple absolute**. Owners in fee simple absolute (sometimes just called fee simple) are entitled to use, possess, or dispose of the real or personal property (by sale or gift) however they choose during their lifetime. On their death, the interests in the property descend to their heirs.

Government Restrictions on Property

eminent domain

The power of a government to take land for public use from private citizens for just compensation.

Even those who own real property in fee simple absolute are subject to restrictions on their right to use the property as they choose. For example, zoning laws may prohibit an owner of property in a given area from conducting certain activities (such as running a business) on the property. Also, under its power of **eminent domain**, the government has a right to take private property for public use (for a highway, for example), as long as the government fairly compensates the owner for the value of the land taken.

Easements

easement

The right to make limited use of another's real property.

Property owned in fee simple absolute may be subject to an **easement**, which is the right of another to use the owner's land for a limited purpose. Easements are said to "run with the land." That is, they usually pass with title to real property as its ownership changes over time. There are many kinds of easements:

- An easement may allow utility companies to maintain underground gas pipelines and electricity wires that cross above the property.

- A right-of-way easement may allow people to cross the property to get to other property.

- A solar easement may be granted to a neighbor to guarantee that trees will not be allowed to grow to block sunlight from hitting solar panels on the neighbor's roof.

- A historic preservation easement (also called a covenant) may require that the appearance of a house will not be changed.

Concurrent Ownership

Persons who share the bundle of ownership rights to property are said to be concurrent owners. There are two principal types of concurrent ownership: tenancy in common and joint tenancy (this should not be confused with renters of property, who may be called tenants).

Tenancy in Common. A tenancy in common is a form of co-ownership in which two or more persons own *undivided* interests in certain property. The interest is undivided because each tenant has rights in the whole property. Although the ownership is in common, tenants may have equal or unequal shares.

> **EXAMPLE 16.1** Rosa and Chao own a rare stamp collection as tenants in common. This does not mean that Rosa owns certain stamps and Chao others. Rather, it means that each has rights in the entire collection. (If Rosa owned some of the stamps and Chao owned others, then the interest would be divided.)

When a tenant in common dies, the tenant's ownership rights pass to his heirs.

Joint Tenancy. A joint tenancy is a form of co-ownership in which two or more persons own undivided interests in property. The key feature of a joint tenancy is the "right of survivorship." When a joint tenant dies, that tenant's interest passes to the surviving joint tenant or tenants and not to the deceased tenant's heirs, as it would with a tenancy in common.

> **EXAMPLE 16.2** Suppose that Rosa and Chao from the previous example held their stamp collection in a joint tenancy. If Rosa died before Chao, the entire collection would become the property of Chao. Rosa's heirs would receive no interest in the collection.

If a joint tenant transfers her interest in the property, the transfer terminates the joint tenancy. The new co-owner (the one to whom the rights were transferred) and the other tenant or tenants become tenants in common.

Other Tenancies. Two other types of concurrent ownership are tenancy by the entirety and community property. A *tenancy by the entirety* is a form of co-ownership by husbands and wives that is similar to a joint tenancy, except that the spouses cannot separately transfer their interests in the property during their lifetimes. Not all states recognize tenancies by the entirety. In ten states, husbands and wives generally hold property as *community property*. In those states, community property is all property acquired during the marriage. Each spouse technically owns an undivided interest in the property. Usually each owns one-half, but courts may decide otherwise when there is a divorce.

Life Estates

A *life estate* is an interest in real property that is transferred to another for the life of that individual. A conveyance of a house "to Allison for her life" creates a life estate. In a life estate, the life tenant cannot do anything to the property that would reduce its value for the owner of the future interest in it. Often, the life tenant lives

tenancy in common
A form of co-ownership of property in which each party owns an undivided interest that passes to his or her heirs at death.

joint tenancy
The joint ownership of property by two or more co-owners in which each co-owner owns an undivided portion of the property. On the death of one of the joint tenants, his or her interest automatically passes to the surviving joint tenant or tenants.

in the house, but she does not have to occupy the property. She may use it for rental income during her life.

Future Interests

When someone who owns real property in fee simple conveys the property to another conditionally or for a limited time, the original owner still retains an interest in the land. This interest is called a *future interest* because it will arise in the future. The holder of a future interest may transfer it to another during his or her lifetime. If the interest is not transferred, it will pass to the owner's heirs on his or her death. The law has complex rules governing future interests that vary from state to state.

The Transfer and Sale of Real Property

The ownership of property, or the right to use it, can be transferred in many ways. Property can be given as a gift, transferred by inheritance, leased, or sold. Most commonly, property is transferred by sale. The sale of tangible personal property (goods) is covered by the common law of contracts, as modified by Article 2 of the Uniform Commercial Code (UCC), which we discussed in Chapter 15. Rights in certain types of intangible property (such as checks and money orders) are covered by other articles of the UCC. The sale of real property, such as a house, is governed by the common law of contracts as well as state (and, to a limited extent, federal) statutory law.

Here, we look at some of the basic steps and procedures involved in the sale of real estate. These steps and procedures are summarized in Exhibit 16.1.

EXHIBIT 16.1

Steps Involved in the Sale of Real Estate

BUYER'S PURCHASE OFFER

Buyer offers to purchase seller's property. The offer may be conditioned on buyer's ability to obtain financing, on satisfactory inspections of the premises, and so on. Included with the offer is earnest money.

SELLER'S RESPONSE

If seller accepts buyer's offer, then a contract is formed. Seller can also reject the offer or make a counteroffer that modifies buyer's terms. Buyer may accept or reject seller's counteroffer or make a counteroffer that modifies seller's terms.

PURCHASE AND SALE AGREEMENT

Once an offer or a counteroffer is accepted, a purchase and sale agreement is formed.

TITLE EXAMINATION AND INSURANCE

Title examiner investigates and verifies seller's rights in the property and discloses any claims or interests held by others. Buyer (and/or seller) may purchase title insurance to protect against a defect in title.

CLOSING

After financing is obtained and all inspections have been completed, the closing takes place. The escrow agent (such as a title company or a bank) transfers the deed to buyer and the proceeds of the sale to seller. The proceeds are the purchase price less any amount already paid by buyer and any closing costs to be paid by seller. Included in the closing costs are fees charged for services performed by the lender, escrow agent, and title examiner. The purchase and sale of the property is complete.

Contract Formation for Property—Offer and Acceptance

The common law contractual requirements discussed in Chapter 15 apply to real estate contracts. Because the Statute of Frauds applies to contracts for the sale of real property, these contracts must be in writing.

A buyer who wishes to purchase real estate submits an offer to the seller. The offer specifies the key terms of the proposed contract—a description of the property, the price, and other conditions that the buyer wishes to include. Often, a buyer conditions the offer on the buyer's ability to obtain financing. The offer might also specify which party will bear the cost of any repairs that need to be made. Typical provisions included in a real estate sales agreement are illustrated in Exhibit 16.2. When signed by the buyer and the seller, the offer constitutes a contract for the sale of land that is binding on the parties.

Earnest Money.   The buyer normally puts up a sum of money, called *earnest money*, along with the offer to buy the property. By paying earnest money, the buyer indicates that the offer is serious. Normally, the offer provides that if the seller accepts the offer (and forms a contract with the buyer), the buyer will forfeit this money if the buyer then breaches the contract. Other damages for breach might also be specified in the agreement. If the deal goes through, the earnest money is usually applied to the purchase price of the real estate.

Responding to an Offer.   Once the offer is submitted to the seller, the seller has three options: accept the offer, reject it, or modify its terms—thus creating a counteroffer. The buyer, in turn, can then accept, reject, or modify the terms of the counteroffer—thus creating yet another counteroffer for the seller to consider. In real estate transactions, bargaining over price and other conditions of the sale frequently involves the exchange of one or more counteroffers.

- Names of parties and/or real estate agents.
- Date of agreement and how long seller has to accept the agreement.
- Legal description of the property's location and size.
- Amount of the purchase offer.
- Amount of cash to be paid at the time of sale.
- Amount of earnest money deposit.
- Type of loan or financing the buyer plans to use.
- Whether the sale is contingent on the buyer's obtaining financing.
- Condition of the title and debt that buyer will assume.
- Warranties of title (restrictions, rights, or limitations).
- Condition of property and zoning or use rights.
- Dividing (prorating) taxes, insurance, or other obligations to the portion of the year property is owned by one party or the other.
- Description of any fixtures, appliances, and furnishings that will be included in the sale and any warranty as to the condition of such items.
- Inspection rights given to the buyer, who will pay the costs of inspections, and whether the sale is contingent on inspectors' approval. (Inspections may include, for example, water, well, mechanical, structural, electrical, and termite inspections.)
- Statement of who will bear the cost for such items as transfer fees, abstracts of title, and closing costs.
- Conditions under which the offer may be canceled.

EXHIBIT 16.2

Typical Provisions in Real Estate Sales Agreements

When one of the parties accepts an offer or counteroffer, a contract is formed by which both parties normally must abide. As this chapter's *Ethics Watch* feature discusses, paralegals must be sure real estate paperwork is accurate.

The Role of the Escrow Agent

The sale of real property normally involves three parties: the seller, the buyer, and the escrow agent. Frequently, real estate agents, attorneys, and paralegals assist both the buyer and the seller. The *escrow agent*, which may be a title company, a bank, or an escrow company, acts as a neutral party in the transaction and facilitates the sale by allowing the buyer and the seller to complete the transaction without having to exchange documents and funds directly with each other.

To understand the vital role played by the escrow agent, consider the problems that might otherwise arise. Essentially, in the sale of property, the buyer gives the seller funds, and the seller conveys (transfers) to the buyer a deed, representing ownership rights in the property (deeds will be discussed shortly). Neither the buyer nor the seller wishes to part with the funds or the deed until all conditions of the sale and purchase have been met.

The solution is the use of an escrow agent. The agent holds the deed until the buyer pays the seller for the property at the *closing* (the final step in the sale of real estate). The escrow agent also holds any funds paid by the buyer, including the earnest money mentioned earlier, until the sale is completed. At the closing, the escrow agent receives funds from the buyer, the buyer is given the deed, and the seller is given the money. The triangular relationship among the buyer, the seller, and the escrow agent is depicted in Exhibit 16.3.

Financing

mortgage
A written instrument giving a creditor an interest in the debtor's property as security for a debt.

Because few buyers pay cash for real property, buyers generally need to secure financing. Commonly, a buyer of real property finances the purchase by obtaining a loan (a **mortgage**) from a bank, a mortgage company, or some other party. When a buyer obtains a mortgage, the lender takes a *security interest* in the property—that is, the lender secures the right to claim ownership of the property if the buyer fails to make scheduled payments.

ETHICS WATCH

ACCURATE PAPERWORK AND REAL ESTATE TRANSACTIONS

Arlie Song, a paralegal, drafted a real estate offer for one of the firm's clients. Instead of entering $90,000 as the amount being offered for a piece of land, he accidentally entered $900,000. The document was sent to the seller, who recognized the mistake and returned the paperwork unsigned. Before the paperwork could be redone, another buyer offered the seller $100,000, and that offer was accepted. The client who made the original offer then bought a similar piece of property for $105,000 and sued Song's supervising attorney for $15,000 in damages. The chance to buy the property for $90,000 had been missed due to the mistake. As with all legal documents, a paralegal must be sure that real estate transaction documents are accurate, because the law firm could be liable for errors.

The duty to use care in preparing work products arises from NALA's *Code of Ethics*, Canon 2: "A paralegal may perform any task which is properly delegated and supervised by an attorney, as long as the attorney is ultimately responsible to the client . . . and assumes professional responsibility for the work product."

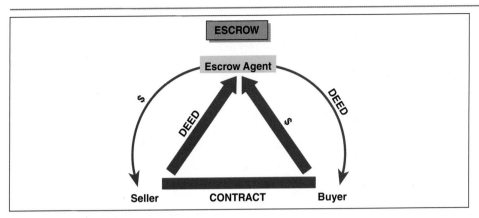

EXHIBIT 16.3

The Concept of Escrow

This exhibit illustrates the triangular relationship among the escrow agent, the seller, and the buyer in a transfer of real estate. The seller gives the escrow agent the deed to hold, the buyer gives the escrow agent the funds to hold, and at the time of the closing, the escrow agent gives the seller the funds and the buyer the deed.

Inspection of the Premises

In addition to obtaining financing, buyers usually have the premises inspected to see if there are any major electrical or plumbing problems, structural defects, termite or insect infestations, or other concerns. Often, the contract of sale is conditioned on the outcome of these inspections. If problems surface during the inspections, the buyer and seller may negotiate (or may have included in the contract) arrangements specifying which party will pay what portion of the costs of any necessary repairs.

Title Examination

Whenever **title** to property is transferred from one party to another, the transfer is recorded at the county recording office. The title is the right of legal ownership of the property. The *deed* is the document that conveys title.

The *title examination* is an important task done before the purchase of real estate. The examination is conducted to make sure the seller is actually the owner of the property described in the purchase offer and to determine whether claims (such as for overdue taxes) on the property exist that were not disclosed by the seller. Most of this work is done online, but visits to a county courthouse may be required in some instances. The title examination may be undertaken by the buyer or the buyer's attorney (paralegals frequently assume this responsibility) or by the lending institution, a title insurance company, or another party.

Normally, the history of past ownership and transfers of the property has already been summarized in a document called an *abstract*, which may be in the possession of the seller (or the holder of the seller's mortgage or other company or institution). After examining the abstract, the title examiner gives an opinion as to the validity of the title. Title examinations are not foolproof, and buyers of real property often buy title insurance to protect their interests in the event that some defect in the title was not discovered and ownership of the property is not secure.

title
The right of ownership of property, which includes a certain bundle of rights. A deed is the most common form of conveyance of a title.

Commercial Property Title Issues

Because of the wide range of uses of commercial properties, title examination may be more complex than in a residential real estate deal. Approval of local government zoning authorities may be needed, or an environmental regulator may need to sign off on the use. Careful investigation of previous property uses is necessary if there is any possibility of environmental contamination from earlier occupants. Paralegals are often involved in tracing the history of a commercial or industrial site, including identifying previous owners and tenants.

Armed with such a list, the paralegal may need to consult industry publications and do research to learn what sorts of chemicals may have been used on the property. Years ago, it was not uncommon for floor drains to simply discharge into the ground. If machinery was used in a room with such a drain, there may be ground contamination that is costly to remedy. As a result of such possibilities, the contract should take into account all approvals needed for the buyer to make use of the property and how costs will be handled in case environmental remediation is required.

The Closing

One of the terms specified in the contract is when the closing will take place. The closing—also called the *settlement* or the closing of escrow—is coordinated by the escrow agent. At the closing, several events are likely to happen at once:

- The buyer signs the mortgage note (if the purchase was financed by a mortgage).
- The buyer obtains title insurance.
- The seller receives the proceeds of the sale (the purchase price less the amount previously paid by the buyer and less closing costs).
- The buyer receives the deed to the property.

deed
A document by which title to property is transferred from one party to another.

Deeds. A deed is the instrument of conveyance (transfer) of real property. As indicated on the sample deed in Exhibit 16.4, a deed gives the names of the seller (*grantor*) and buyer (*grantee*), describes the property being transferred, evidences the seller's intent to convey (for example, "I hereby bargain, sell, grant, or give") the property, and contains the seller's signature.

Closing Costs. *Closing costs* comprise fees for services, including those performed by the lender, escrow agent, and title company. These costs can range from hundreds to thousands of dollars, depending on the amount of the mortgage loan and other conditions of the sale, and must be paid at the closing.

Under the federal Real Estate Settlement Procedures Act, lending institutions must notify—within a specified time period—each mortgage loan applicant of the precise costs that must be paid at the closing. Paralegals are often involved in this process, as illustrated in the *Developing Paralegal Skills* feature on page 494.

Leases

lease
In real property law, a contract by which the owner of real property (the landlord) grants to a person (the tenant) an exclusive right to use and possess the property, usually for a specified period of time, in return for rent or some other form of payment.

An owner of either personal or real property can usually lease, or rent, the property to another person or a business. A **lease** is a contractual agreement under which a property owner (the *lessor*) agrees to rent property to another (the *lessee*) for a specific time period. Leases of personal property (such as cars) are covered by the Uniform Commercial Code, which spells out the rights and duties of lessors and lessees.

Leases of real property are governed by the common law of contracts and by state statutory law. Although under the common law an oral lease is valid, a party who seeks to enforce an oral lease may have difficulty proving its existence. In most states, the Statute of Frauds mandates that leases exceeding one year's duration must be in writing. When real property is leased, the lessor (landlord) retains ownership rights to the property, but the lessee (tenant) obtains the right to the exclusive possession of the property. Most leases give the landlord the right to come onto the property for certain purposes, such as to make repairs.

Paralegals frequently draft or review lease agreements for clients or for corporate employers. You should therefore be familiar with the terms typically included in a lease. Normally, a lease contract specifies the names of the lessor and lessee, the location of the premises being leased, the amount of rent to be paid by the lessee, the duration of the lease, and the respective rights and duties of the parties in regard

EXHIBIT 16.4

A Sample Deed

Date: May 31, 2022

Grantor: RAYMOND A. GRANT AND WIFE, JOANN H. GRANT

Grantor's Mailing Address (including county):
          4106 North Loop Drive
          Austin, Travis County, Texas
Grantee: DAVID F. HOGAN AND WIFE, RUTH E. HOGAN, AS
          JOINT TENANTS WITH RIGHT OF SURVIVORSHIP
Grantee's Mailing Address (including county):
          5929 Fuller Drive
          Austin, Travis County, Texas

Consideration:
For and in consideration of the sum of Ten and No/100 Dollars ($10.00) and other
valuable consideration to the undersigned paid by the grantees herein named, the receipt
of which is hereby acknowledged, and for which no lien is retained, either express or
implied.

Property (including any improvements):
Lot 23, Block "A", Northwest Hills, Green Acres Addition, Phase 4, Travis County, Texas,
according to the map or plat of record in volume 22, pages 331-336, of the Plat Records
of Travis County, Texas.

Reservations from and Exceptions to Conveyance and Warranty:

This conveyance with its warranty is expressly made subject to the following:
Easements and restrictions of record in volume 7863, page 53, volume 8430, page 35,
volume 8133, page 152, of the Real Property Records of Travis County, Texas; and to
any other restrictions and easements affecting said property which are of record in
Travis County, Texas.

    Grantor, for the consideration and subject to the reservations from and exceptions to conveyance and
warranty, grants, sells, and conveys to Grantee the property, together with all and singular the rights and
appurtenances thereto in any wise belonging, to have and hold it to Grantee, Grantee's heirs, executors,
administrators, successors, or assigns forever. Grantor binds Grantor and Grantor's heirs, executors,
administrators, and successors to warrant and forever defend all and singular the property to Grantee and
Grantee's heirs, executors, administrators, successors, and assigns against every person whomsoever
lawfully claiming or to claim the same or any part thereof, except as to the reservations from and exceptions
to conveyance and warranty.

When the context requires, singular nouns and pronouns include the plural.

                    BY: _Raymond A Grant_
                         Raymond A. Grant
                    BY: _JoAnn H Grant_
                         JoAnn H. Grant

STATE OF TEXAS
COUNTY OF TRAVIS
    This instrument was acknowledged before me on the   31st   day of   May 2022
by   Raymond A. and JoAnn H. Grant

                    Rosemary Potter
                    Notary Public, State of Texas
                    Notary's name (printed): ROSEMARY POTTER

Notary Seal   Notary's commission expires: 1/31/2023

DEVELOPING PARALEGAL SKILLS

REVIEWING THE CLOSING PACKAGE

Addie Casmir, a paralegal, is reviewing a closing package for her supervising attorney. Addie's job is to request the closing package from the lender and review it before the closing takes place. The closing package consists of the purchaser's requirements, closing statement, settlement statement, deed, bill of sale, mortgage documents, and title insurance policy. Addie needs to make sure that there are no mistakes in the closing documents.

Checklist for Reviewing a Closing Package

- Order the closing package as far in advance as possible.
- Set aside uninterrupted time for reviewing the closing package.

- Review for accuracy the address and legal description of the property in the mortgage note and the deed.
- Using a calculator, review the purchaser's requirements sheet, the closing statement, the bill of sale, and the mortgage documents to make sure that there are no numerical errors.
- Review each document to make sure that the parties' names are listed and spelled correctly.
- Review the deed to ensure that the ownership rights are listed accurately and that the names are correct.
- Inform the client of the items that must be brought to the closing.

to the use and maintenance of the leased premises. Exhibit 16.5 illustrates the kinds of provisions that are commonly included in lease agreements.

Commercial Leases

Leases for commercial or business property are usually longer and much more detailed than residential leases, so special expertise is needed. State statutes set background rules for residential leases, which is not the case for commercial leases—almost everything needs to be spelled out in a commercial lease.

Commercial leases include specific discussion of common areas and responsibilities for them. Such leases also often discuss inspection rights, what signage will be allowed, liability waivers, damage provisions, how alterations are to be handled, responsibility for repairs, and other issues usually peculiar to commercial property. In addition, the terminology in commercial leases generally follows industry practices and uses terms of the Building Owners and Managers Association International (BOMA)—for example, *gross leasable footage* and *net leasable square footage*. Paralegals working this area must therefore be familiar with BOMA definitions.

Property Law and the Paralegal

Paralegals frequently perform tasks that require an understanding of the law governing real property. If you work in a small legal practice, your work may involve assisting a supervising attorney in handling real estate transactions. If you work for a law firm (or a department within a law firm) that specializes in real estate transactions, you will have extensive contact with buyers and sellers of real property, as well as with real estate agents, title companies, banking institutions that finance real estate purchases, and the legal professionals who work on behalf of parties in real estate transactions. See this chapter's *Featured Contributor* article on pages 496 and 497 for a discussion of the role of a legal due-diligence team in purchases of real estate.

Here are just some of the types of tasks that you might perform as a real estate paralegal working for a law firm:

- Interview a client who wants to buy or sell property, and identify potential issues regarding the property and financing.

EXHIBIT 16.5

Typical Lease Terms

Term of lease: Indicates the duration of the lease, including the beginning and ending dates.

Rental: Indicates the amount of the rent payments and the intervals (monthly or yearly, for example) at which rent will be paid.

Maintenance and use of leased premises: Describes which areas will be repaired and maintained by the landlord and which by the tenant.

Utilities: Stipulates which utilities (electricity, water, and so forth) will be paid by the landlord and which by the tenant.

Alterations: Normally states that no structural alterations to the property will be made by the tenant without the landlord's consent.

Assignment: States whether the tenant's rights in the lease can be assigned (transferred) by the tenant to a third party.

Insurance: Indicates whether the landlord or the tenant will insure the premises against damage. (Normally, the landlord secures insurance coverage for the building, and the tenant obtains a "renter's policy" for his or her own personal property—furniture and other possessions—that will be housed in the building.)

Taxes: Designates which party will be liable for taxes or special assessments on the property. (Normally, the landlord assumes this responsibility, but in some commercial leases, the tenant agrees to take on this obligation.)

Destruction: States what will happen in the event that the premises are totally destroyed by fire or other casualty.

Quiet enjoyment: A covenant (promise) by the landlord that the tenant shall possess and enjoy the premises without interference by any third party.

Termination: Usually specifies that the tenant's right to possession of the premises ends when the lease expires.

Renewal: Indicates that the tenant has an option to renew the lease if the landlord is notified of the intent to renew within a certain period of time (such as one month or three months) before the lease expires.

- Assist the client with the preliminary negotiations (offers and counteroffers) leading up to the purchase contract.

- Draft the offers and counteroffers, as well as other documents necessary to the sale.

- Conduct a title examination by going online, or perhaps to the county courthouse, to examine records of previous property transfers.

- Obtain or create a title abstract.

- Contact the title company to arrange for the closing.

- Handle the escrow account.

- Attend the closing. (In some states, paralegals are allowed to represent clients at closings.)

Corporations also buy and sell property, and some larger firms have real estate groups within their legal departments. If you work for a business that buys and sells a significant amount of property, your employer will be the "client," and you will perform similar tasks on the corporation's behalf.

FEATURED CONTRIBUTOR

PROTECTING THE REAL ESTATE PURCHASER: THE LEGAL DUE-DILIGENCE TEAM

Daniel F. Hinkel

BIOGRAPHICAL NOTE

Daniel F. Hinkel earned a J.D. degree from the University of Illinois School of Law and a B.S. from Eastern Illinois University. He is vice president and corporate counsel for ING Investment Management, LLC, in Atlanta, Georgia.

Mr. Hinkel has taught in paralegal programs for years. He is also the author of a number of books, including *Practical Real Estate Law* and *Essentials of Practical Real Estate Law*, both published by Delmar Cengage Learning.

Home ownership is highly desired by many families, and commercial real estate is a preferred asset for many investors. Whether the purchaser is acquiring a home for a residence or purchasing a shopping center as an investment, the transaction will be governed by the common law doctrine of *caveat emptor*, "let the buyer beware." This doctrine provides that a seller, absent an express warranty, is not liable to a buyer for any existing defects regarding the title to the land or any physical defects in the improvements located on the land. Even misrepresentations made by a seller concerning the property are generally not recoverable in an action for fraud if the purchaser could have discovered the truth from proper due diligence, such as a thorough inspection of the home or a title examination.

The Legal Due-Diligence Team

A legal due-diligence team can save a real estate purchaser money and future headaches. Paralegals are important members of the legal due-diligence team. The extent of the team's work will depend on the nature of the property being purchased. A home may require only a title and survey review. An investment property may require a review of title, survey, government regulations, leases, and other contracts that affect the use of the property.

Title Due Diligence

One of the main responsibilities of the legal due-diligence team is to determine that the purchaser will have good title of ownership to the real property when the sale has been completed. The legal due-diligence team should require that the public real property title records be examined and the examination carefully reviewed to determine the title's marketability.

Local government title registry offices are using electronic data technology for their deed and title records. A title search of the title indices can now be conducted from a computer, and recorded instruments can be viewed online. Many local governments also have Web pages where, for a reasonable fee, a person can access the real property records online. A title search is possible in some instances without a trip to the courthouse.

It is common in many communities for a title insurance company to examine the public records and provide the legal due-diligence team with a title report or commitment to issue title insurance and copies of all the recorded documents listed in the title report. The

Insurance Law

risk

A prediction concerning potential loss based on known and unknown factors.

As mentioned in Chapter 2, *insurance* is a contract in which the insurance company (the *insurer*), in return for consideration, promises to pay a sum of money to another (the *insured* or the *beneficiary*) if the insured suffers harm or loss from stated perils. Insurance is an arrangement for *transferring and allocating risk*. In many instances, **risk** is a prediction concerning potential loss based on known and unknown factors.

team's paralegal will review this report and, in consultation with the team's attorney, determine if the title matters affect the marketability and the purchaser's proposed use of the property. The legal due-diligence team will also arrange for a title insurance policy insuring the purchaser's ownership to be issued at the time of purchase.

Survey Due Diligence

The legal due-diligence team should require a survey of the property. Most surveys are "as built," meaning the survey locates all physical improvements on the land in relation to the boundary lines of the land. The surveyor will locate all fences, walls, driveways, pavements, building structures, and natural features, such as streams and ponds. The survey will also indicate if the property is in a flood hazard area, which may require flood insurance.

The team's paralegal may review the survey. A survey is usually reviewed in conjunction with the title commitment. This review will determine that all matters that would have a physical presence on the property, such as easements or building setback lines, are shown on the survey. The review will confirm that the description of the real property matches the description offered by the seller and that the description can be insured by the title insurance company. If there are differences between the description shown on the survey and in the title report, the legal due-diligence team will investigate the matter and determine why the differences exist and how they can be resolved.

In addition, the survey reviewer will note the location of improvements on the property and look for encroachments onto (or by) the property, or encroachments of buildings over easements. The reviewer will also determine if there is proper access to the property from a public street and if the necessary utilities, such as electricity, gas, and water, are available.

Government Regulation Due Diligence

For an investment property, the legal due-diligence team will inquire into government regulations that affect the property. The team will obtain confirmation of the property's zoning status and determine if the purchaser's use or intended use of the property will comply with the uses permitted by zoning regulations.

Lease Review

The legal due-diligence team may review leases in connection with an investment property. The leases provide income to the purchaser, and the price of the property may be based on assumptions regarding the rental income contained in the leases. The team's paralegal may review the leases and prepare an abstract, or summary, of the leases. The summary review will verify the terms of the lease, such as rental terms, the duration of the lease, and the various obligations and responsibilities of both the landlord and the tenant. A lease will also be reviewed to determine if the tenant has an option to purchase the property. If the lease contains an option to purchase, the team attorney will carefully discuss the option with the purchaser to verify that it is acceptable.

The legal due-diligence team may prepare and require each tenant to sign an estoppel certificate. An estoppel certificate signed by the tenant generally confirms the basic facts regarding the lease, such as rental terms and duration and payment of security deposits. Also, it will state that there is no default under the lease and that the tenant has no defenses, setoffs, recoupments, claims, or counterclaims of any nature against the landlord.

The Legal Due-Diligence Team Provides Value

A legal due-diligence team made up of attorneys and paralegals performs an important role in protecting a purchaser from the harsh effects of the *caveat emptor* rule. A legal team's thorough investigation and competent review and analysis of supporting documents provide good value for the real property purchaser-client.

> **One of the main responsibilities of the legal due-diligence team is to determine that when the sale has been completed, the purchaser will have good title of ownership to the real property."**

Risk management normally involves the transfer of certain risks from the insured party to the insurance company by contract. The insurance contract and its provisions will be examined later in this section. First, however, we look at the different types of insurance that can be obtained, insurance terminology, and the concept of insurable interest.

Classifications of Insurance

Insurance is classified according to the nature of the risk involved. For instance, fire insurance, automobile insurance, and life insurance apply to different types of risk

risk management
Planning undertaken to reduce the risk of loss from known and unknown events. In the context of insurance, risk management involves transferring certain risks from the insured to the insurance company.

and protect against different types of loss. Exhibit 16.6 lists and describes a number of insurance classifications.

Insurance Terminology

policy
In insurance law, a contract for insurance coverage. The policy spells out the precise terms and conditions as to what will and will not be covered under the contract.

premium
In insurance law, the price paid by the insured for insurance protection for a specified period of time.

underwriter
In insurance law, the insurer, or the one assuming a risk in return for the payment of a premium.

An insurance contract is called a **policy**, the consideration paid to the insurer is called a **premium**, and the insurance company is sometimes called an **underwriter**. The parties to an insurance policy are the insurer (the insurance company) and the insured (the person covered by its provisions or the holder of the policy).

Insurance contracts are usually obtained through an *agent*, who works for the insurance company, or through a *broker*, who is usually an *independent contractor*. When a broker deals with an applicant for insurance, the broker may be the applicant's agent and not an agent of the insurance company. In contrast, an insurance agent is an agent of the insurance company, not of the applicant. As a general rule, the insurance company is bound by the acts of its insurance agents when they act within the agency relationship (agency relationships are discussed in Chapter 18). In most situations, state law determines the status of all parties writing or obtaining insurance.

EXHIBIT 16.6

Selected Insurance Classifications

Type of Insurance	Coverage
Automobile	May cover damage to automobiles resulting from specified hazards or occurrences (such as fire, vandalism, theft, or collision); normally provides protection against liability for personal injuries and property damage resulting from the operation of the vehicle.
Casualty	Protects against losses incurred by the insured as a result of being held liable due to negligence for personal injuries or property damage sustained by others.
Fidelity or Guaranty	Provides indemnity against losses in trade or losses caused by the dishonesty of employees, the insolvency of debtors, or breaches of contract. May also be called a *surety bond*.
Fire	Covers losses incurred by the insured as a result of fire.
Group	Provides individual life, medical, or disability insurance coverage but is obtainable through a group of persons, usually employees; the policy premium is paid either fully by the employer or partially by the employer and partially by the employee.
Health	Covers expenses incurred by the insured as a result of physical injury or illness and other expenses relating to health and life maintenance.
Homeowners'	Protects homeowners against some or all risks of loss to their residence and the residence's contents or liability arising from the use of the property.
Key Person	Protects a business in the event of the death or disability of a key employee.
Liability	Protects against liability imposed on the insured as a result of injuries to the person or property of another. May also cover product liability actions.
Life	Covers the death of the policyholder. On the death of the insured, an amount specified in the policy is paid by the insurer to the insured's beneficiary.
Malpractice	Protects professionals (physicians, lawyers, and others) against malpractice claims brought against them by their patients or clients; a form of liability insurance.
Mortgage	Covers a mortgage loan; the insurer pays the balance of the mortgage to the creditor on the death or disability of the debtor.
Title	Protects against any defects in title to real property and any losses incurred as a result of existing claims against or liens on the property at the time of purchase.
Umbrella	Provides additional coverage beyond other policies. It is a means of protecting against catastrophic losses.

Insurable Interest

People can insure anything in which they have an **insurable interest**. Without an insurable interest, there can be no enforceable contract. For real and personal property, an insurable interest exists when the insured derives a pecuniary (monetary) benefit from the continued existence of the property, such as a car, a home, business premises, or computer data. Put another way, a person has an insurable interest in property when that person would sustain a financial loss from its damage or destruction. For life insurance, a person must have a reasonable expectation of benefit from the continued life of another to have an insurable interest in that person's life.

insurable interest
An interest either in a person's life or well-being or in property that is sufficiently substantial to justify insuring against injury to or death of the person or damage to the property.

The Insurance Contract

An insurance contract is governed by the general principles of contract law. However, the insurance industry is regulated by each state and, in some areas, such as health insurance, by federal law as well. Here, we consider several aspects of the insurance contract: the application for insurance, the date when the contract takes effect, and some important provisions typically found in insurance contracts. We also discuss the cancellation of an insurance policy and defenses that insurance companies can raise against payment on a policy.

Application

The filled-in application form for insurance is usually attached to the policy and made a part of the insurance contract. Because the insurance company evaluates the risk factors based on the information included in the insurance application, misstatements or misrepresentations can void a policy, especially if the insurance company can show that it would not have extended insurance if it had known the true facts. In some instances, there can be a criminal prosecution for fraud.

Effective Date

The effective date of an insurance contract—the date on which the insurance coverage begins—is important. In some instances, the insurance applicant is not protected until a formal policy is issued. In other situations, the applicant is protected between the time the application is received and the time the insurance company either accepts or rejects it. The following facts should be kept in mind:

- A broker is usually the agent of an applicant. Therefore, until the broker obtains a policy from the insurer, the applicant normally is not insured.

- A person who seeks insurance from an insurance company's agent is usually protected from the moment the application is taken by the agent, provided that some premium has been paid. From the time the application is received and is rejected or accepted, the applicant is covered. Usually, the agent writes a memorandum, or **binder**, indicating that a policy is pending and stating its essential terms.

binder
A written, temporary insurance policy anticipating issuance of the regular policy.

- If the parties agree that the policy will be issued and delivered later, the contract is not effective until the policy is issued and delivered or sent to the applicant, depending on the agreement. Thus, any loss sustained between the time of application and the delivery of the policy is not covered.

- The parties may agree that a life insurance policy will be binding at the time the insured pays the first premium or that the policy may be expressly contingent on the applicant's passing a physical examination. If the applicant pays the premium and passes the examination, the policy coverage is in effect. If the applicant pays the premium but dies before having the physical examination, then to collect, the applicant's estate must show that the applicant *would have passed* the examination.

Executives of a newly formed corporation consult with an attorney concerning the types of insurance they should purchase for the business. Many paralegals work in the area of insurance law and assist with tasks relating to insurance claims. What types of claims arise in an insurance context?

Pressmaster/Shutterstock.com

Coinsurance Clauses

Often, when taking out fire insurance policies, property owners insure their property for less than full value because most fires do not result in a total loss. To encourage owners to insure their property for an amount close to full value, fire insurance policies commonly include a coinsurance clause. Typically, a *coinsurance clause* provides that if owners insure the property up to a specified percentage of its replacement value—often 80 percent—they will be fully reimbursed for any loss. If the insurance is for less than the required percentage, the owners are responsible for a proportionate share of the loss.

> **EXAMPLE 16.3** Assume that a property is valued at $100,000 and the owner insures this property for $80,000, satisfying the insurer's 80 percent coinsurance requirement. When the property suffers $50,000 in fire damages, the owner recovers the full $50,000. If the owner had insured the same property for only $40,000—half of the usual 80 percent ($80,000) coinsurance requirement—then the owner would have recovered only half of the $50,000 in fire damages, or $25,000.

Indemnity Clauses

The term *indemnity* refers to a duty to make good on any loss, damage, or liability claims incurred by another. The term is used frequently in insurance contracts because it involves the duty to compensate for loss. Under the principle of indemnity, indemnified parties are restored to the financial position they were in before the loss or accident. Indemnity clauses are frequently found in rental contracts.

> **EXAMPLE 16.4** Martinez is seeking to lease a building that is suitable for a dry-cleaning business. Commercial Property, Inc., a rental agency, has such a building for rent in the area Martinez likes. Martinez signs a lease agreement with Commercial that contains an indemnity clause. Under the indemnity clause, an employee who is injured while using the dry-cleaning equipment cannot sue Commercial Property. In effect, Martinez has agreed to hold the rental agency harmless for any damages caused by use of the equipment.

Because indemnity clauses protect specified parties from suffering financial loss due to lawsuits, they are sometimes referred to as *hold-harmless clauses*.

Corporations often indemnify their directors and officers for any legal costs and fees that they might incur if they become involved in lawsuits by virtue of their positions (to be discussed in Chapter 18.)

> **EXAMPLE 16.5** Patricia Harding files a product liability lawsuit against Repp, Inc., and its chief executive officer, James Kerr. If Kerr's employment contract includes an indemnity clause, Repp will assume responsibility for any costs that Kerr incurs in defending himself against this lawsuit.

Subrogation Clauses

The right to pursue another party's claim is called *subrogation*. In insurance, subrogation deals with the right of the insurer to be put in the position of the insured to pursue recovery from a third party who is legally responsible to the insured for a loss paid by the insurer to the insured. If the insurance company has compensated the insured for a loss sustained and then later receives recovery from a third party in the name of the insured, the company can ask a court to order reimbursement from the proceeds.

> **EXAMPLE 16.6** Greta owns an insured building that she leases out to several businesses. A third party negligently causes a fire, which burns down the building. Greta is fully compensated for the damages by her fire insurance company. Although Greta can sue the third party for damages, she fails to do so. Under a subrogation clause, the insurance company can step into Greta's shoes and file a negligence claim against the third party on Greta's behalf. If the lawsuit is successful, the insurer is entitled to be reimbursed from litigation proceeds in the amount it paid to Greta to cover her loss under the insurance policy.

Most insurance contracts contain explicit subrogation clauses. They usually require the insured party to cooperate with the insurance company by providing documents, records, and whatever else is necessary for the company to pursue claims on behalf of the insured. Even if the contract does not contain a subrogation clause or does not use the word *subrogation*, however, courts have held that insurance companies have a right to subrogation unless this right is explicitly waived (given up).

Other Provisions and Clauses

Some other important provisions and clauses in insurance contracts are defined in Exhibit 16.7. The courts are aware that most people do not have the training necessary

EXHIBIT 16.7
Insurance Contract Provisions and Clauses

Type of Clause	Description
Incontestability Clause	An incontestability clause provides that after a policy has been in force for a specified length of time—usually two or three years—the insurer cannot contest statements made in the application.
Appraisal Clause	Insurance policies frequently provide that if the parties cannot agree on the amount of a loss covered under the policy or the value of the property lost, an appraisal, or estimate, by an impartial and qualified third party can be demanded.
Arbitration Clause	Many insurance policies include clauses that call for arbitration of disputes that may arise between the insurer and the insured concerning the settlement of claims.
Antilapse Clause	A provision that the policy will not automatically lapse if no payment is made on the date due. Ordinarily, the insured has a *grace period* of thirty or thirty-one days within which to pay an overdue premium before the policy is canceled.
Multiple Insurance Clause	Many insurance policies include a clause providing that if the insured has multiple insurance policies that cover the same property and the amount of coverage exceeds the loss, the loss will be shared proportionately by the insurance companies.

to understand the special terminology used in insurance policies. Thus, the words used in an insurance contract have their ordinary meanings, not technical meanings specific only to insurance. The courts interpret them in light of the nature of the coverage involved.

(For some online sources relating to policy interpretation and analysis, as well as sources relating to other aspects of insurance-related legal work, see this chapter's *Office Tech and Cybersecurity* feature.)

When there is an ambiguity in the policy, the provision generally is interpreted against the insurance company. Also, when it is unclear whether an insurance contract actually exists because the written policy has not been delivered, the uncertainty normally is resolved against the insurance company. The court presumes that the policy is in effect unless the company can show otherwise. Similarly, an insurer must notify the insured of any change in coverage under an existing policy.

Cancellation

The insured can cancel a policy at any time, and the insurer can cancel under certain circumstances. When an insurance company can cancel its insurance contract, the

OFFICE TECH AND CYBERSECURITY

ONLINE RESOURCES CONCERNING INSURANCE CLAIMS

When a dispute arises between an insurance company and a policyholder regarding an insurance claim, attorneys are often consulted. In these situations, paralegals fulfill functions for both sides, including analyzing insurance policies, researching the facts involved in the claim, and locating experts.

General insurance law resources can be found at **law.cornell.edu/wex/insurance** and **hg.org/insurance.html**. The University of Connecticut School of Law also provides specialized information on insurance law at **ilc.law.uconn.edu**.

Analyzing Clauses in Insurance Policies

Insurance policies are sometimes written in terms that laypersons do not understand. A glossary of insurance terms is offered by the Insurance Information Institute at **iii.org**.

Insurance Complaints and Insurance Fraud

A paralegal assisting a client with an insurance claim may need to research related complaints against the client's insurance company. The website of the National Association of Insurance Commissioners (NAIC) offers a good starting point for such research. NAIC's home page, at **naic.org**, furnishes an online fraud-reporting system and links to state insurance department websites.

To assist in the prevention and discovery of fraudulent insurance claims, the Coalition Against Insurance Fraud (CAIF) presents many resources at **insurancefraud.org**. Through CAIF's website,

you can access state regulations related to insurance fraud and links to many antifraud associations, state fraud bureaus, and investigation tools. CAIF also posts many reports related to insurance fraud offenses.

Locating Adjusters and Appraisers

When a policyholder files a claim, the insurance company may use an insurance adjuster. The adjuster inspects the damaged property, analyzes the insurance policy, and estimates the amount of loss. Paralegals sometimes assist attorneys in locating adjusters. The National Association of Independent Insurance Adjusters (NAIIA) represents independently owned claims-adjusting companies approved by insurance carriers. Through the NAIIA's website, **naiia.com**, a claim can be assigned to an NAIIA adjuster in your area.

Another resource is the National Association of Public Insurance Adjusters (NAPIA), **napia.com**. It accredits public insurance adjusters, who are hired to assist consumers. The NAPIA website offers a search engine to locate local public insurance adjusters.

In the case of an automobile insurance claim, it may be beneficial to use the online appraiser locator available through the Independent Automotive Damage Appraisers (IADA) website at **iada.org**. IADA is an association of automotive appraisers organized to protect insurance consumers from overpaying for auto body repairs.

policy or a state statute usually requires that the insurer give advance written notice of the cancellation to the insured. This also applies when only part of a policy is canceled. Any premium paid in advance may be refundable on the policy's cancellation. The insured may also be entitled to a life insurance policy's cash surrender value.

The insurer can cancel an insurance policy for various reasons, depending on the type of insurance.

> **EXAMPLE 16.7** Automobile insurance can be canceled for nonpayment of premiums or suspension of the insured's driver's license. Property insurance can be canceled for nonpayment of premiums or for other reasons, including the insured's fraud or misrepresentation, conviction for a crime that increases the hazard insured against, or gross negligence that increases the hazard insured against. Life and health policies can be canceled because of false statements made by the insured in the application, but cancellation can only take place before the effective date of an incontestability clause. An insurance company can also decide to quit participating in a particular insurance market in a given state.

An insurer cannot cancel—or refuse to renew—a policy for discriminatory reasons or other reasons that violate public policy or because the insured has appeared as a witness in a case against the company.

Good Faith Obligations

Both parties to an insurance contract are responsible for the obligations that they assume under the contract. In addition, both the insured and the insurer have an implied duty to act in good faith. Good faith requires the party who is applying for insurance to reveal things necessary for the insurer to evaluate the risk. The applicant must disclose all material facts, including facts that an insurer would consider in determining whether to charge a higher premium or to refuse to issue a policy. Once the insurer has accepted the risk, and some event occurs that gives rise to a claim, the insurer has a duty to investigate to determine the facts.

When a policy provides insurance against third party claims, the insurer is obligated to make reasonable efforts to settle such a claim. If a settlement cannot be reached, then regardless of the claim's merit, the insurer must defend any suit against the insured. Usually, a policy provides that in this situation the insured must cooperate. A policy provision may expressly require the insured to attend hearings and trials, to help in obtaining evidence and witnesses, and to assist in reaching a settlement.

Defenses against Payment

If an insurance company can show that a policy was obtained by fraud, it may have a valid defense for not paying on a claim. A defense also exists if the insurer can show that the insured lacked an insurable interest—thus rendering the policy void from the beginning. Improper actions, such as those that are against public policy or are otherwise illegal, can also give the insurance company a defense against the payment of a claim or allow it to rescind the contract.

An insurance company can be prevented from asserting some defenses that are normally available, however.

> **EXAMPLE 16.8** Suppose a company tells an insured that information requested on a form is optional, but the insured provides it anyway. The company cannot use the information to avoid its contractual obligation under the insurance contract. Similarly, an insurance company normally cannot escape payment on the death of an insured on the ground that the person's age was stated incorrectly on the application.

Self-Insurance

Sometimes firms and individuals *self-insure* against risks. That means they set aside money to cover risks rather than buy insurance. For example, some large employers can predict their employees' total health care costs even if they cannot predict which individual employees will need benefits. Rather than pay an insurance company, the company sets aside the amount of money necessary to pay the claims it predicts will occur. Paralegals are often involved in administering self-insurance plans on behalf of corporate legal departments. Note that since a company that self-insures is engaged in an insurance function, it may need to follow certain insurance laws.

Captive Insurance

Increasingly, companies with large insurance needs are considering establishing their own insurance companies, called *captive insurers*. When a company owns its own insurance company, it has three advantages.

1. It can determine the type of coverage it will carry. Instead of being limited to insurance policies available in the marketplace, it can design its own coverage.

2. It can deduct the premiums it pays its captive insurer from its profits before paying taxes, a significant advantage over self-insurance.

3. It can control the investment policy the captive insurer uses for its reserves.

Most captive insurance companies in the United States are registered in Vermont, which has special laws making it easier to run a captive insurance company. Many hospitals and other medical firms use captive insurance based in the Cayman Islands, which also has such laws. Paralegals at companies using captives are often involved in administration of the captives.

The Paralegal and Insurance

A paralegal working for an insurance company may be asked to assist in drafting insurance policies or amendments to policies and to investigate the facts behind claims filed by policyholders. A paralegal working for a real estate investment firm may analyze insurance policies related to commercial property investments. Additionally, a paralegal might work for a state insurance regulatory agency. In this context, a paralegal may assist in drafting administrative procedures, investigating insurance fraud and licensing issues, and responding to consumers' insurance claims and questions—such as claims for *workers' compensation* (discussed in Chapter 18).

Paralegals who assist in insurance-related litigation involving torts will likely be involved in many of the same types of work that are required in the area of tort law (discussed in Chapter 14). Here is just a sampling of tasks related to insurance law that paralegals commonly manage:

- Research insurance clauses in relation to specific claims.

- Interact with experts, witnesses, and clients to obtain factual information about events giving rise to insurance claims.

- Obtain medical records concerning a client who needs assistance in obtaining payment from the insurer. (This involves issues covered in the accompanying *Developing Paralegal Skills* feature.)

- Create, review, or prepare insurance application forms or insurance policies.

- Schedule medical appointments for health-insurance claimants.

DEVELOPING PARALEGAL SKILLS

MEDICAL RECORDS

Derek Busset is a paralegal for a small personal-injury firm. Attorney McNair is handling a case in which Rosenthal's car was struck by an automobile driven by Gomez, who is insured by Reliable Insurance. The police report indicates that at the time of the accident, Gomez was speeding through a yellow/red light at the intersection when his car collided with Rosenthal's 2019 Hyundai, which had just entered the intersection on a green light.

Reliable has compensated Rosenthal for the damage to her vehicle but disputes the amount she is claiming for medical expenses. The insurance company believes that Rosenthal's back injury was a preexisting condition. That is, it was not caused by the accident. After speaking with a representative from the insurance company, McNair asks Busset to contact Rosenthal and acquire medical records to support her claims. McNair also wants Busset to write a summary of what the records show.

Tips for Obtaining and Evaluating Medical Records

- Obtain a list from the client of all of the physicians who treated the client and the hospitals or other facilities in which the client received medical care.
- Prepare—and have the client sign—medical release forms, which authorize the treating physicians to provide the patient's medical records directly to the law firm.
- Keep a log of the records as they are received.
- If a claim involves the possibility of a preexisting condition, make certain to request the client's complete medical history (from before the injury as well as after it). These records will be needed to determine whether a preexisting condition might have caused or contributed to the plaintiff's injury.
- Use a medical dictionary or reference book so that you can decipher the terminology and abbreviations frequently used by medical personnel in charts and records.

CHAPTER SUMMARY

REAL PROPERTY AND INSURANCE LAW

Real Property

Real property (also called real estate or realty) includes land and things attached to the land such as buildings and plants, as well as subsurface and air rights. Other types of property, both tangible and intangible, are personal property.

1. *Ownership rights in property*—Fee simple absolute is the most complete form of ownership, entitling the holder to use, possess, or dispose of the property however he or she chooses during his or her lifetime. Restrictions on property use can be imposed by easements, which grant others limited rights to use property. In addition, the government has the right to use the power of eminent domain to take property with compensation and to impose use limits on property through zoning rules. Co-ownership rights include tenancy in common, in which each party owns an undivided interest in the

property that passes to the party's heirs at death, and joint tenancy, in which each party owns an undivided interest in the property that automatically passes to the surviving joint tenant(s) on the death of one of them.

2. *The transfer and sale of real property*—Real property can be transferred as a gift, by inheritance, by lease, or by sale. Usually, real property is transferred by sale, which typically involves the following steps.

   a. The buyer makes a purchase offer, often conditioned on obtaining financing, and pays an earnest money deposit.

   b. If the seller accepts the offer, a contract is formed. Real estate agents may assist the buyer and the seller in negotiating the terms.

c. An escrow agent acts as a neutral party in the transaction, holding the deed and any money paid by the buyer until the sale is completed.

d. Most buyers obtain a mortgage loan to finance the purchase. The holder of the mortgage then has a security interest in the property.

e. Often, the sale is contingent on certain inspections of the property.

f. A title examination is performed to ensure that the seller is actually the owner of the property and that no liens exist of which the buyer was not aware.

g. At the closing, the buyer signs the mortgage note (if the sale is financed) and obtains title insurance, the seller is paid the purchase price (less any closing costs), and the buyer is given the deed to the property.

3. *Leases*—The owner of real property (the lessor) may agree (contract) to rent the property out to another (the lessee) for a specified period of time. The lessee has the exclusive right to use the property. Leases are governed by contract law and by state statutes. Leases are usually in writing and must be written if the lease period exceeds one year.

4. *Commercial leases* are usually much more detailed than residential leases and contain more specialized terminology.

Insurance Law

1. *Classifications*—See Exhibit 16.6.

2. *Terminology*—

   a. *Policy*—The insurance contract.

   b. *Premium*—The consideration paid to the insurer for the policy.

   c. *Underwriter*—The insurance company.

   d. *Insurer*—The insurance company.

   e. *Insured*—The person or property covered by the insurance.

   f. *Insurance agent*—A representative of the insurance company.

   g. *Insurance broker*—Ordinarily, an independent contractor.

   h. *Beneficiary*—A person to receive payment under the policy.

3. *Insurable interest*—An insurable interest exists whenever an individual or entity benefits from the preservation of the property to be insured or the continued health or life of the person to be insured.

4. *The insurance contract*—The general principles of contract law are applied; the insurance industry is also regulated by the states.

   a. An insurance applicant is bound by any false statements made in the application (subject to certain exceptions), as the application is part of the insurance contract.

   b. Misrepresentations may be grounds for voiding the policy.

   c. Coverage on an insurance policy can begin when a binder (a written memorandum indicating that a formal policy is pending and stating its essential terms) is written; when the policy is issued; at the time of contract formation; or, depending on the terms of the contract or specific state law, when certain conditions are met.

   d. See Exhibit 16.7 for a review of major provisions in insurance contracts. Words are given their ordinary meanings. Ambiguity in the policy is interpreted against the insurance company. When it is unclear whether an insurance contract actually exists, the uncertainty generally is resolved against the insurance company. The court presumes that the policy is in effect unless the company can show otherwise.

   e. Defenses against payment to an insured include fraud, lack of an insurable interest, and improper actions on the part of the insured.

5. *Self-insurance*—Some parties prefer to self-insure against risk of loss by setting aside funds for such possibilities.

6. *Captive insurance*—Sometimes employed by large companies that form their own insurance companies to handle insurance needs.

KEY TERMS AND CONCEPTS

binder   499

deed   492

easement   486

eminent domain   486

fee simple absolute   486

insurable interest   499

joint tenancy   487

lease   492

mortgage   490

personal property   486

policy   498

premium   498

real property   486

risk   496

risk management   497

tenancy in common   487

title   491

underwriter   498

QUESTIONS FOR REVIEW

1. Explain the difference between real property and personal property. What is a fee simple? List and define the other ways in which ownership rights in property can be held.

2. Explain what law governs the sale of real property. Describe the basic steps involved in the sale of real estate. What role does an escrow agent play?

3. What are the various classifications of insurance?

4. Define an insurable interest. How does an insurable interest arise in property? In another's life?

5. What is the difference between an insurance agent and an insurance broker? Why is this difference significant for people seeking insurance coverage?

6. What are some of the tasks a paralegal who assists in insurance-related litigation might perform?

ETHICS QUESTION

1. Joanne Dorman works as a paralegal in the claims department of an automobile insurance company. She is asked to review a claim brought by Derek Farmer, her nephew. Derek is a college student with few financial resources. Joanne's sister (Derek's mother) told Joanne that Derek broke his windshield recently when he accidentally ran into a mailbox beside the road leading to their rural home. In the claim that she is reviewing, however, Derek states that a rock hit his windshield. Joanne understands immediately what Derek is trying to do. Derek's policy states that his collision coverage (which would apply to the mailbox accident) has a $500 deductible. His comprehensive coverage (which would apply if a rock hit his windshield) has a deductible of only $50. Derek is obviously trying to avoid having to pay the full $500 deductible, which he can ill afford. In contrast, the insurance company could easily absorb the extra cost. What should Joanne do in this situation?

PRACTICE QUESTIONS AND ASSIGNMENTS

1. Assume that John submits an offer to Lisa to purchase Lisa's home for $150,000. Lisa responds to John's offer with a counteroffer: she will sell John her home for $175,000. John then offers to purchase the home for $165,000, so long as he can obtain a mortgage and the house does not have termites. Lisa accepts the offer. In each of these transactions, who is the offeror, and who is the offeree? At what point is a contract for the sale of the home formed?

2. Using the material presented in Exhibit 16.4, *A Sample Deed*, and the following facts, draft a deed to real property.
   - At a closing on January 22, 2022, Roberto Alvarez and Paloma Alvarez, husband and wife, of 987 Packard Street, Galveston, Texas, transfer their beachfront condo to Javier and Eduardo Gomez, brothers, for consideration of $250,000 cash. Javier Gomez lives at 10101 Summit Place, New City, Texas. Eduardo Gomez's address is 99901 Hill

Street, Casper, Texas. The Gomez brothers will own the condo as tenants in common.

- The legal description of the property is Lot 91 of Whiteacre Subdivision, Galveston County, Texas, according to the plat map contained in volume 89, pages 123–129, of the Plat Records of Galveston County, Texas.

- The conveyance with a warranty is expressly made subject to the Easements and Restrictions of Record in volume 7877, page 456, and volume 9988, page 431, of the Real Property Records of Galveston County, Texas, and to any other restrictions and easements affecting the property that are of record in Galveston County, Texas.

- The notary public who will acknowledge the deed is Rosemary Potter, and her commission expires January 31, 2023.

3. Identify the types of ownership rights described in the following statements.

    a. John and Linda, a brother and a sister, jointly own a cottage that they inherited from their mother. They have rights of survivorship.

    b. Janet conveys her townhouse to her mother for as long as her mother lives. On her mother's death, the property is to go to Janet's daughter.

    c. Alya owns her home, and she can use, possess, or dispose of it as she pleases. On Alya's death, the property will descend to her heirs.

    d. John Tully and Sam Marsh jointly own a large farm in Iowa. If either of them dies, the heirs of the deceased owner will inherit that owner's share of the farm.

4. Identify the following steps in a real estate sales transaction:

    a. An offer or counteroffer is accepted.

    b. Title to the property is reviewed to determine the seller's ownership interest and to determine if any liens against the property exist.

    c. The buyer applies for financing at a bank or mortgage company.

    d. A house is inspected to see if it needs repairs exceeding $1,000, such as roof repairs or basement waterproofing.

    e. The buyer tenders a sum of money along with an offer.

5. John's Used Cars, Inc., sold Willie a 2018 Cadillac in return for $5,500 and what turned out to be a stolen 2014 Cadillac. (Willie provided a fraudulent title for the stolen car.) Hank bought the 2014 Cadillac from John's Used Cars without knowing that the title was fraudulent or that the car had been stolen. He insured it against theft and damage. Hank's Cadillac was stolen from him about three weeks later. His insurance company refused to pay Hank for the loss, claiming that he did not have an insurable interest in the vehicle because it had been stolen at the time he bought it. Using the definition of *insurable interest* in the chapter text, analyze whether Hank has an insurable interest in the car. Would it make a difference if Hank knew the car had been stolen at the time he purchased it? Can Hank make a claim against John's Used Cars for selling him a stolen car?

GROUP PROJECT

This project requires students to review leases of real property, such as houses or apartments. Students one, two, and three should each select a lease to examine. They may find a lease online, buy one at a local office supply store, or use their own lease if they prefer. The leases should contain state-specific provisions. Each student will summarize the provisions in the lease he or she selected. Student four will create a chart comparing the provisions of the three leases and present it to the class.

CHAPTER
17

Family Law and Estates

CHAPTER OBJECTIVES

After completing this chapter, you will be able to:

- Explain the requirements for a valid marriage and the duties spouses owe to one another, including the duty to refrain from spousal abuse.

- Discuss the legal rights and obligations of parents and children.

- Explain the adoption process.

- Explain how marriages may be terminated.

- Discuss the factors involved in deciding child-custody and child-support issues.

- Explain how marital property and debts are divided when a marriage is dissolved.

- Define *estate planning*, list various tools for estate planning, and discuss the tasks involved in estate administration.

- Summarize the requirements for a valid will and the laws that govern property distribution when a person dies without a valid will.

- Define *trusts*, and list various kinds of trusts.

Introduction

Family law, the subject of the first part of this chapter, governs the legal relationships of people within a family. Family law describes such matters as how we create families, who can create a family, and the legal obligations owed to family members. It also governs the dissolution of families through divorce.

Marital law, including divorce law, is a major area of work for paralegals. There is property to be distributed at the end of a marriage. Issues regarding child custody, child support, and alimony can further complicate matters. Such complications can lead to ongoing conflicts that involve legal support.

Whether property is distributed before or during a marriage, or when one ends, property must be transferred when a person dies. For that reason, the laws governing the succession of property are a necessary extension to the laws concerning the ownership of property. Later in the chapter, we examine various legal devices, including wills and trusts, that are often used to transfer a person's property, or *estate*, after death.

Family Law

Marriage, divorce, adoption, child support and custody, child and spousal abuse, and parental rights and duties are all areas of family law. Much of the legal work relating to family law has to do with marriage dissolution. Marriage is a status conferred by state law. Thus, when a marriage ends, the state, through the court system, must become involved. Because of the complexity of unraveling a family's legal and financial affairs, many attorneys and paralegals deal with divorce cases. Such cases may include child-support and child-custody issues. In addition, the property owned by a divorcing couple must be divided between the spouses. (As a result, wealthier families are increasingly creating *family offices* to manage their legal affairs, and there is considerable work for paralegals and lawyers in supporting these offices.)

In this section, you will read about some important legal concepts and doctrines governing family matters, including the matters surrounding marriage dissolution. (For a discussion of the important role that paralegals can play in the area of family law, see this chapter's *Featured Contributor* article on pages 512 and 513.)

Marriage Requirements

Despite the fact that many couples today live together (cohabit) without marrying, most American adults marry at least once during their lifetimes. Marriage confers certain legal and practical advantages. The marriage establishes the rights and duties of the spouses, as well as of any children born during the marriage. Married couples may also have an easier time obtaining insurance and credit and adopting children. Additionally, some employers offer health insurance to spouses but not to unmarried partners.

Age Requirements

States place some limitations on who can marry. The betrothed (those intending to marry) must be currently unmarried, not closely related by blood, and over a certain age—usually eighteen years. State laws vary, and some states prohibit marriage between those who are closely related even if the relation is only by marriage. Persons who are under the required age can marry with parental consent or if they are emancipated from their parents. **Emancipation** normally occurs when children leave home to support themselves. Below a certain age, such as fourteen or sixteen, marriage may be absolutely prohibited by state law except with court approval.

emancipation

The legal relinquishment by a child's parents or guardian of the legal right to exercise control over the child. Usually, children who move out of their parents' home and support themselves are considered emancipated.

Procedural Requirements

Certain procedures are generally required for a legally recognized marriage to take place. The parties must obtain a *marriage license* from the state government, usually through the county clerk's office. About half of the states also require a *blood test* to check for certain diseases. Some states require couples to go through a short *waiting period* before getting the license or between the time of acquiring the license and getting married.

In most states, some form of *marriage ceremony* is also required. The parties must present the license to someone authorized by the state to perform marriages, such as a justice of the peace, a judge, or a member of the clergy. The marriage ceremony must involve a public statement of the agreement to marry. After the ceremony, the *marriage license must be recorded* with the proper government office. That provides notice to those who deal with the couple that they are indeed married. Because marriage can affect property rights and the ability to pay debts, this is an important role of the law.

Common Law Marriages

A common law marriage is one in which the parties become married solely by mutual consent and without a license or ceremony. At one time, common law marriages were frequent. Today, only certain states recognize common law marriage, and even in those states obtaining recognition of the marriage is not simple.

There are four general requirements for a common law marriage. The parties:

1. Must be eligible to marry.
2. Must have a present and continuing intention and implied agreement to be a couple.
3. Must live together as a couple.
4. Must hold themselves out to the public as a couple.

Note that cohabitation alone does not normally produce a common law marriage. The parties must additionally hold themselves out to others as a married couple.

Once a couple is legally regarded as married by common law, they have all of the rights and obligations of a traditionally married couple—including the obligation to support each other and their children. In addition, if a couple is regarded as married by common law, they must obtain a court decree to dissolve the marriage. There is no legal meaning to the notion of a "common law divorce." Many people not trained in law do not understand common law marriages. Hence, it is important for paralegals to ask questions in situations in which one may exist so that the supervising attorney can properly advise the client.

common law marriage
A marriage that is formed by mutual consent and without a marriage license or ceremony. The couple must be eligible to marry, have a present and continuing agreement to be a couple, live together as a couple, and hold themselves out to the public as a couple. Many states do not recognize common law marriages.

Marital Duties

In the old days, marriages were arranged between families through private contracts. Part of the contractual arrangement was that the husband would support and provide for his wife and children. The wife, in turn, had certain duties in the home. Although we still hear the term *marriage contract*, in fact, marriage represents a special type of contract that is governed not by contract law but by the state. In the United States, each state has laws that govern marriage and divorce and establish the spousal obligations of married partners and their obligations toward any children.

Financial Support

Generally, spouses are allowed to arrange their own affairs however they see fit. Nonetheless, the law still holds that each spouse has a duty to support the other spouse and the couple's children financially by providing such basics as food, shelter, and medical

FEATURED CONTRIBUTOR

A CHANGING, CHALLENGING, AND CARING AREA OF LEGAL PRACTICE

Janis Walter

BIOGRAPHICAL NOTE

Janis Walter has coordinated the paralegal program at the University of Cincinnati for thirty years. She is an author and frequent speaker at national and statewide forums. Professor Walter is an active member of the American Association for Paralegal Education and has served as editor of *The Paralegal Educator*.

She has also served on the ABA's Standing Committee on Paralegals and currently presides over the American Bar Association's Approval Commission on Paralegals. In this capacity, she has chaired site visits of paralegal programs across the United States. Professor Walter is also a partner in the Wright Law Group.

I have focused my practice on advocating for the individual. The areas of family law and estate administration allow us to assist clients grieving the loss of their family and help them protect the family unit.

Changes in Society

These areas of law are challenging because they are constantly evolving, as is the characterization of what constitutes a family. Changes in marriage, divorce, and fertility mean that family structures are changing and becoming more diverse. Recent decades have seen a dramatic rise in divorce, cohabitation rather than marriage, civil unions, blended families of both gay and heterosexual design, and nonmarital children.

Changes in Technology

The advancement of technology has also played a major role in changing what constitutes a family. The ability to freeze sperm and conceive children posthumously through a surrogate affects issues such as

care—insofar as the spouses are able to do so. In many states, this duty lasts throughout the marriage, even if the spouses are living apart. Failure to provide support for a child may be a criminal violation. States are particularly insistent on child support, as it helps them avoid having to provide public support to children who might be impoverished by a divorce. Additional duties may be created by a separate agreement between the spouses.

Spousal Abuse

Each state creates its own definition of domestic violence through legislation and court decisions. In all states, however, it is a criminal act to batter a spouse. Unlawful abuse has been extended to include extreme cases of harassment (such as stalking) and threats of physical beating or confinement. In some cases, an emergency restraining order may be necessary. A **restraining order** is a court order that requires one person (such as an abusive spouse) to stay away from another (such as the victim of abuse). Shelters are available in many cities to assist abused spouses and their children. As professionals who interact with individuals who might be the victims of spousal abuse, paralegals should be aware of the signs of abuse and alert their supervising attorney if they suspect a client may be a victim of abuse.

restraining order
A court order that requires one person (such as an abusive spouse) to stay away from another (such as an abused spouse).

custody and inheritance rights. While there are many forms of family structures, the family itself is not disappearing. Indeed, the issues in family law and estate administration are diverse and numerous.

Technology has also had an impact on estate planning and administration. Digital assets have essentially replaced tangible ones in today's world. People need to carefully plan the fate of their online presence after their death. For example, many people use direct deposit and automatic monthly payments that need to be terminated when they die. Other aspects of one's digital presence may include e-mail accounts, photos, music, client lists, social media accounts, domain names, online manuscripts or blogs, computer code, online gaming avatars, and bitcoins. Often, user names and passwords are not provided to survivors, and current federal privacy laws restrict disclosure of private electronic communications.

Changing Rules in the Digital Age

States are responding to these issues by enacting laws on fiduciary authority regarding digital assets following death. The Uniform Fiduciary Access to Digital Assets Act (UFADAA), which is being adopted by many states, vests fiduciaries with the authority to manage, distribute, copy, and access digital assets. For the benefit of survivors, provisions should be made during the estate planning process to attend to various digital assets. Doing so will protect the estate against economic losses and will preserve prized mementos and memories of the decedent.

> " ... today's paralegal must be knowledgeable yet flexible. ... "

The Paralegal and Family Law

Because paralegals who practice in family law and estate administration play such an integral role in the delivery of legal services to clients, perhaps more than in most areas of law, it is essential that they stay current with changing and evolving developments. Such competency requires substantive legal knowledge and interpersonal skills that enable the paralegal to work with clients about sensitive personal issues.

Family law paralegals must be able to thrive in a fast-paced work environment with constant deadlines. Those in estate administration must pay close attention to detail while working independently. In both, the legal team works with emotionally charged clients. A paralegal can be extremely valuable not only in assisting the attorney in handling the legal work and tending to the client's needs, but also in being cost-effective. Through close contact with the client and by understanding his or her struggles and desires, the paralegal is often able to assess the situation and offer practical resolutions to the client's issues. Each case involves unique issues, just as each client is unique.

One day, the paralegal may be interviewing a client, filing documents with the court, or completing an investigation. The next day may be spent preparing legal documents, analyzing discovery requests, or organizing trial exhibits. As a result, today's paralegal must be knowledgeable yet flexible in order to deliver quality legal services.

Domestic Abuse

Domestic abuse often remains unrecognized in family relationships. Injurious behavior takes many forms and may not be only physical. American law started taking greater notice of domestic abuse only in recent decades, so it is a relatively "new" area of law. Paralegals should therefore expect as many legal questions as answers when they encounter domestic abuse situations.

Domestic abuse is a complex topic and one for which paralegals with social work training often are particularly valuable. Among the issues that victims of domestic abuse encounter are problems of threats, financial abuse, fear of losing custody of children, isolation, mental illness, shame and embarrassment, and prior negative experiences with the courts or police. Law firms are not equipped to handle all the problems surrounding domestic abuse, but paralegals who may encounter such situations can help clients with referrals to social service agencies such as The National Domestic Violence Hotline (**thehotline.org**).

Parental Rights and Obligations

Legally, a child is defined as an unmarried minor (under the age of eighteen) who is not emancipated. Prior to a child's emancipation, parents have certain rights of control over the child. Parents can direct the upbringing of their children and control where they live, what school they attend, and even what religion they practice. Parents also generally control the medical care to be given, although a parent's refusal to provide for such care in life-threatening situations (for religious reasons, for example) can be a crime. Parents have broad legal authority to control the behavior of their children and even physically punish them—so long as the punishment does not constitute child abuse (to be discussed shortly).

Parents also have obligations toward their children. Parents must provide food, shelter, clothing, medical care, and other necessities. They must also ensure that their children attend school (normally until the age of sixteen or eighteen). Parents can be criminally liable in some states if their children miss too much school. For example, under California's truancy laws, the state can bring criminal charges against parents if their children (ages six to eighteen) miss three or more days of school, are absent for more than thirty minutes three or more times, are tardy three or more times, or any combination of those things. A California parent convicted of "failing to supervise a child's attendance" in school can be fined up to $2,500 and/or imprisoned for up to one year.

If a couple is married, the law presumes that the husband fathered any newborn child, and the husband must support the child unless he can prove that he is not the biological father. Although parental duties to a child generally end when the child reaches the age of eighteen, these duties may continue for a longer period if the child is seriously disabled.

Liability for Children's Wrongful Acts

Parents are sometimes held liable for the wrongful actions of their children. Although state laws vary considerably, parents are most likely to be held liable when they have knowledge of prior, similar behavior by the child. They may also be liable if they improperly assisted a child in procuring a driver's license or provided the child with a vehicle when the child should not be driving. Parents have been held liable for giving their children access to firearms, as well as when their children have vandalized property.

In some states, greater liability is provided by statute. In California, for example, parents can be liable for up to $25,000 per incident of property defacement, while Illinois provides for liability of $2,500 for willful and malicious acts by children.

EXAMPLE 17.1 Vanessa Casado permits her fourteen-year-old son, Jeremy, to drive the family car to the grocery store by himself, without supervision, although he has no driver's license. En route to the store, Jeremy causes an accident in which Thomas Boone, a passenger in the other car, is seriously injured. Boone would probably succeed in a negligence suit against Vanessa Casado in this situation.

Child Abuse and Neglect

All states allow parents to physically punish their children within reason. A parent, for example, may slap or spank a child without violating the laws prohibiting child abuse. Some states allow corporal (physical) punishment in the schools (under the doctrine of *in loco parentis*, or "in the place of the parents"). In all states, however, laws prohibit sexual molestation and extreme punishment of children by anyone. For punishment to constitute physical child abuse, the punishment normally must result in injuries—such as broken skin or bones, excessive bruising, or swelling.

Child neglect is also a form of child abuse. Child neglect occurs when parents or legal guardians fail to provide for a child's basic needs, such as food, shelter, clothing, and medical treatment. Child abuse may even extend to emotional abuse, as when a person publicly humiliates a child in an extreme way.

Children Born out of Wedlock

A large number of children are born to unmarried parents. The law provides rights and protections for these children. One important right is the right of the child to be supported by the biological father. The biological father has a legal obligation to contribute to the support of the child that is identical to that of a married father. The obligation usually lasts until the child is no longer a minor. The mother's subsequent marriage to another person does not necessarily extinguish the obligation of the biological father to support the child.

In most states, the eventual marriage of the parents of a child born outside of marriage "legitimizes" the child. Unmarried men can also take legal responsibility for their children by formally acknowledging paternity.

Paternity Suits. An unmarried mother may file a **paternity suit** to establish that a certain person is the biological father of her child. If the unwed mother is on public-welfare assistance, the government may file a paternity suit on the mother's behalf to obtain reimbursement for welfare payments given to the mother, even if the mother objects to the suit. Fathers may also file paternity actions in order to obtain visitation rights or custody of a child. In addition, grandparents may seek to prove a child's paternity to gain visitation rights in some states. The paternity of a child can be proved scientifically. DNA testing or comparable procedures that check for genetic factors can determine, with almost 100 percent accuracy, whether a person parented a particular child.

With the widespread availability of inexpensive DNA testing kits, some men are discovering that they are not the biological fathers of children they believed to be theirs. Such test results can lead to complications in determining paternity disputes. Some of these complicated cases end up in court.

Inheritance Rights. Under the common law, a child born out of wedlock (an illegitimate child) had no right to inherit. Today, inheritance laws governing illegitimate children vary from state to state. Generally, an illegitimate child is treated as the child of the mother and can inherit from her and her relatives. The child is usually not regarded as the legal child of the father unless paternity is established through a legal proceeding.

Many state statutes permit the illegitimate child to inherit from the father if paternity has been established prior to the father's death. Even if paternity has been established, however, the illegitimate child will not necessarily have inheritance rights identical to those of legitimate children. Generally, the courts have upheld state probate statutes that discriminate between legitimate and illegitimate children for valid state purposes.

> **EXAMPLE 17.2** Civil law jurisdictions often require that a particular share of a parent's estate go to a particular child. For example, France requires a parent to leave a single child 50 percent of his or her estate. If there are two children, each is to get 33 percent, and if there are three or more, they are to get 75 percent, divided equally.
>
> When the French pop superstar Johnny Hallyday, known as the "French Elvis," died in California, he left his entire estate to his last wife, Laëtitia Hallyday. His two older children, Laura Smet and David Hallyday, received nothing. The French courts ruled that Hallyday's estate was governed by French law. As a result, the court ruled that Hallyday's two older children (Laura and David), the two children he and Laëtitia had adopted, and Laëtitia herself would all share in the estate.

Adoption

In contrast to children born out of wedlock, today adopted children normally have the same legal rights as the biological children of a married couple, including the right to inherit property from their adoptive parents on the parents' deaths. (In the past, that

paternity suit
A lawsuit brought by an unmarried mother to establish that a certain person is the biological father of her child. DNA testing or a comparable procedure is often used to determine paternity.

was not always the case.) **Adoption** is a procedure in which persons become the legal parents of a child who is not their biological child.

Once an adoption is formally completed, the adoptive parents have all the responsibilities of biological parents. Should they divorce, each adoptive parent has all the child-support obligations of a biological parent. Note that adoption is not the same as **foster care**, which is a temporary arrangement in which a family is paid by the state to care for a child for a limited period of time, often pending adoption.

Requirements for Adoptions

State laws govern adoptions, and these laws vary from state to state. Generally, there are three minimum requirements for an adoption to be legal. First, the child's biological parents must give up their legal rights (either by consent, by death, or by order of the court). Second, the adopting parents must follow all procedures required by the state in which the adoption occurs. Finally, a judge must formally approve the adoption. There may be additional requirements in specific circumstances. For example, adopting a child above a certain age generally requires the child's official consent.

All states permit single persons to adopt children, but married couples are generally preferred. Although some courts have approved adoptions by same-sex couples, generally such couples have found it more difficult to adopt children, but the law on this is changing to create fewer restrictions.

Agency Adoptions

Adoption is often carried out through social-service agencies licensed by the state to place children for adoption. The biological parents terminate their parental rights, essentially giving up these rights to the agency and authorizing the agency to find legal parents for their child. In the past, in agency adoptions, the identities of the biological and the adoptive parents were kept confidential. Increasingly, state laws allow for the disclosure of this information in certain circumstances. In some states, for instance, if an adopted child wants to meet with a birth parent or vice versa, the court will contact the child or parent to see if that person will agree to a meeting. Over-the-counter genetic testing now connects some adoptees with their biological parents, sometimes unexpectedly.

Independent Adoptions

Prospective adoptive parents may also pursue independent adoption. An **independent adoption** is one that is arranged privately, as when a physician, lawyer, or other person puts a couple seeking to adopt a child in contact with a pregnant woman who has decided to give up her child for adoption. These parties make their own private arrangements. Usually, the adopting parents pay for the legal and medical expenses associated with the childbirth and adoption. The intermediary may also receive a fee. Because this method of adoption has the potential for abuse, it is prohibited by most states.

Stepparent Adoptions

Many adoptions today are stepparent adoptions, which occur when a married partner adopts his or her spouse's children from a former marriage or relationship. Usually, in such adoptions, the parental rights of the children's other biological parent are terminated either by consent or through a court proceeding.

Surrogacy and Other Fertility Treatments

Couples having difficulty conceiving a child sometimes use a surrogate mother or other advanced fertility treatments to have a child. These options, however, can raise a variety of legal issues. A *surrogate* is a woman who carries an embryo implanted into her womb and has contracted to give the child to someone else after its birth. The child is then adopted by the people who hired the surrogate. Surrogacy contracts are heavily regulated by the states, and requirements vary considerably. Problems can arise when a surrogate has second thoughts and wants to keep the child. Courts have also been thrust into divorce disputes over the custody of frozen embryos stored for future implantation in either a surrogate or a wife. The frontiers of science are advancing faster than the law in this area.

Court Approval and Probation

All adoptions must be approved in court. The primary standard for approving an adoption is the "best interests of the child." Because this standard is so vague, the courts have a great deal of leeway in deciding whether to place children with prospective adoptive parents. The court considers the financial resources of the adopting parents, their family stability and home environment, their ages, their religious and racial compatibility, and other factors relevant to the child's future health and welfare.

After the adoption, many states place the new parents on "probation" for a time—usually from six months to one year. The agency or court appoints an individual to monitor developments in the home to ensure that the adoptive parents are caring appropriately for the child's well-being. If not, the child may be removed and returned to an agency for placement in another home.

Marriage Termination

A marriage can only be terminated by the state. In other words, even though partners want to end their marriage, and even though they separate and live apart, they continue to have the rights and obligations of spouses until their marriage is legally terminated. There are two ways in which a marriage can be terminated: by annulment or by divorce.

Annulment

An **annulment** is a court decree that invalidates (nullifies) a marriage. This means that the marriage never took legal effect in the first place. Annulments are not common. Many seeking annulments do so because their religion does not condone divorce. In such situations, an annulment allows a subsequent marriage to be recognized as valid in the eyes of religious authorities.

An annulment may be granted on various grounds. For example, lack of genuine consent, fraud, and bigamy may be grounds for annulment. **Bigamy** is the act of marrying one person while already legally married to another.

Even though a marriage is deemed invalid through annulment, children born during the marriage are legitimate in the eyes of the law. Also, as in a divorce, when a marriage is annulled, issues involving child support, spousal support, child custody, and property settlement must be decided by the couple or by the court.

Note that some religious entities provide religious annulments for couples who want religious affirmation of a divorce. For example, the Roman Catholic Church has an extensive body of canon law, which is practiced by canon lawyers in church tribunals and governs religious annulments for Catholics also seeking civil divorces. Coordination between the lawyers handling the state court proceeding and the canon lawyers handling the canon law proceedings is thus necessary.

Divorce

The most common way to end a marriage is divorce. A **divorce** is a formal court proceeding that legally dissolves a marriage. Divorce laws vary among the states, with some states having simpler divorce procedures than others. Paralegals involved in

annulment
A court decree that invalidates (nullifies) a marriage. Although the marriage itself is deemed nonexistent, children of a marriage that is annulled are deemed legitimate.

bigamy
The act of entering into marriage with one person while legally married to another.

divorce
A formal court proceeding that legally dissolves a marriage.

family law practice have an important role to play in gathering accurate information on a divorcing client's finances. The other spouse may be affecting the client by disposing of joint assets or by continuing to incur debt for which the client may be liable in part.

Fault-Based versus No-Fault Divorces.

Until the 1960s, to obtain a divorce, a petitioning party had to allege reasons for the divorce. Adultery, desertion, cruelty, and abuse were among the acceptable grounds for divorce under state law. This system is called *fault-based divorce*. Unless the petitioning party could prove that his or her partner was "at fault" for the breakdown of the marriage in one of these ways, a divorce would not be granted. Changing economic and social conditions in America led to new attitudes toward divorce, which resulted in less stringent requirements for divorce. Thus arose the **no-fault divorce**—a divorce in which neither party is deemed to be legally at fault for the breakdown of the marriage.

Today, all states allow no-fault divorces. Generally, a no-fault divorce may be based on one of three grounds:

- Irreconcilable differences (the most common ground).
- Living separately for a period of time specified by state statute (ranging from six months to three years).
- Incompatibility.

No-fault divorces effectively make it impossible for one spouse to prevent a divorce desired by the other. Even in no-fault divorces, however, fault may be taken into consideration by the court in determining a couple's property settlement or spousal support arrangements.

The majority of the states permit both fault-based and no-fault divorces. Sometimes, a party may seek a fault-based divorce in an attempt to gain a more favorable property settlement (to be discussed shortly) than could be obtained in a no-fault divorce.

Divorce Procedures.

The first step in obtaining a divorce is to file a **petition for divorce** with the appropriate state court. Although the form and content of the petition vary, generally the petition includes:

- The names and addresses of both spouses.
- The date and place of their marriage.
- The names and addresses of any minor children and whether the wife is currently pregnant.
- The reasons for the divorce.
- A summary of arrangements made by the divorcing couple as to support, custody, or visitation.
- The relief sought.

The petition is served on the other spouse, who must file an answer to the petition within the time specified by state law. If the couple cannot agree on certain matters while the divorce is pending—such as who obtains custody of the children or who pays the mortgage—the court will hold a hearing to decide which partner should temporarily assume what responsibilities. Unless the case is settled through mediation or negotiation, a trial will be conducted, and the judge will decide the terms of the parties' final divorce decree.

As noted, religious couples may seek a marriage dissolution or annulment from religious authorities in addition to a legal divorce. Because such proceedings insisted upon by one party can affect the other, civil law practitioners need to be alert to

no-fault divorce
A divorce in which neither party is deemed to be legally at fault for the breakdown of the marriage.

petition for divorce
The document filed with the court to initiate divorce proceedings. The requirements governing a divorce petition vary from state to state.

possible issues that can complicate matters. Working on divorce matters is, of course, sensitive and requires great discretion on the part of attorneys and paralegals.

Negotiation and Mediation.   Few divorces actually go to trial. Usually, the parties settle their differences prior to trial—often after lengthy negotiations that are facilitated by their attorneys. If the parties agree to a settlement concerning contested issues, the agreement is put in writing and presented to the court for approval.

Divorcing spouses increasingly use mediation to settle disagreements, and in many states mediation is mandatory in divorce cases. The mediator typically meets with the parties in the absence of lawyers and tries to guide the parties into agreeing on a mutually satisfactory settlement. As we noted in Chapter 6, some paralegals are trained mediators and conduct mediation proceedings.

Child Custody

In many divorces, the issue of child custody—the right to live with and care for the children on an everyday basis—is the most contentious issue to be resolved. In some cases, a court may appoint a guardian *ad litem* for the child. A **guardian *ad litem*** is a person appointed by the court (often an attorney) to represent the interests of a child or a mentally incompetent person before the court.

guardian *ad litem*
A person appointed by the court to represent the interests of a child or a mentally incompetent person before the court.

Factors Considered in Determining Child Custody

Traditionally, the mother almost always received child custody. Mothers still usually receive primary custody. However, courts now explicitly consider a number of factors when awarding custody, including the following:

- The nature of the relationship and emotional ties with each parent.
- The ability of each parent to provide for the child's needs and education, and each parent's interest in doing so.
- The ability of each parent to provide a stable environment for the child.
- The mental and physical health of each parent.
- The wishes of the child—especially older children.

In determining custody, courts may also consider other relevant factors, such as whether one parent is a drug user. Custodial arrangements are not permanent and may be changed by a court in view of the parents' changing circumstances.

Types of Custodial Arrangements

The parent who has **legal custody** of a child has the right to make major decisions about the child's life without consulting the other parent. Usually, the parent who has legal custody also has physical custody.

Many states now provide for **joint custody**—shared custody—of the children of divorcing parents. Joint *legal custody* means that both parents together make major decisions about the child. Some procedures, such as mediation, are usually available in the event of disagreement. In some states, including California, mediation is mandatory in child-custody disputes.

Joint legal custody may also involve joint *physical* custody, in which both parents maintain a home for the child and have physical custody of the child for specific time periods. Joint physical custody usually works best if both parents live in the same school district or if the child attends a private school to which both parents have access.

Divorced parents may take turns living in a home where the child resides, moving out when it is the other parent's turn to have physical custody. Courts consider creative arrangements such as this to provide the child with the best environment.

legal custody
Custody of a child that confers on the parent the right to make major decisions about the child's life without consulting the other parent.

joint custody
Custody of a child shared by the parents following the termination of a marriage.

A divorcing couple meets with a mediator in an attempt to resolve their dispute over child-custody arrangements. Couples are often required to mediate their disputes before being allowed to litigate them in court. What are the benefits of such mediation?

Paralegals involved with family law will need expertise ranging from social work and psychology to property law and tax law to assist in such cases.

Grandparents can petition the court to obtain custody of their grandchildren as well. In some situations, such as when a parent is disabled or when parents are not taking proper care of their children, a court may decide that grandparents should be granted custody.

Visitation Rights

visitation rights

The right of a noncustodial parent to have contact with his or her child. Grandparents and stepparents may also be given visitation rights.

Typically, the noncustodial parent receives **visitation rights**—the right to have contact with the child. The parent may get to spend weekends, holidays, or other time periods with the child. The times and duration of the noncustodial parent's visits are often stated in the divorce settlement, and state statutes may set standards. In some situations, the court may order supervised visitation to ensure the child's safety. This means that the noncustodial parent's visits will take place in the presence of a third party. Only in extreme situations—such as when child abuse is involved—will a court completely deny visitation rights to the noncustodial parent.

In most states, courts can grant visitation rights to grandparents, although these laws vary from state to state. Such laws require the visitation to be in the best interest of the child and may require the grandparent to have an established relationship with the child. If the state's requirements are met, a court may set a schedule specifying the time that grandchildren are to spend with their grandparents.

Child Support

child support

The financial support necessary to provide for a child's needs. Commonly, when a marriage is terminated, the noncustodial spouse is required by the court to make child-support payments to the custodial spouse.

Regardless of the custody arrangements, a court must make some provision for **child support**—the financial support necessary to provide for the child's needs. States have official, standardized guidelines determining child-support duties. These guidelines are often percentage formulas based on parental income. Judges must follow the guidelines, unless special circumstances justify a departure from them or the parents agree to a different arrangement. A child with a disability, for example, likely requires more support than provided for under the guidelines.

Child-support orders may be revised and adjusted according to the changing needs of the child and incomes of the parents. When a parent fails to make child-support payments, the other parent or the court can take action. Paralegals assisting with such cases will find many of the skills necessary to collect judgments or locate assets (discussed in Chapter 12) to be useful.

Withholding Payment

It is a common misconception that if one former spouse fails to meet an obligation under a divorce settlement or other court order (such as by withholding visitation rights), the other party can withhold payment of child support. Child support is a court order—it cannot be withheld because a former spouse does something that the other former spouse does not like. Similarly, a parent cannot withhold visitation rights because the other parent did not pay support. An obligation to the child and to the state is involved, not an obligation to the other parent.

Interstate Enforcement of Child Support Decrees

We discussed uniform laws in Chapter 5. One such law, the Uniform Interstate Family Support Act, has been adopted by every state to help deal with the problem of nonpayment of child support by a parent who has moved to another state. Every state agrees to respect and enforce child-support orders entered by the court of the child's home state. Only the law of the state in which the child and the parent have been living will govern issues regarding child support, so a parent cannot escape obligations by moving to a state with more lenient rules. The act also allows the parent who is supposed to receive the child-support payments to obligate the employer of the other parent to withhold payments from the other parent's paycheck for the benefit of the child.

Spousal Support

In some situations, a divorce decree may require that one spouse provide for the other spouse's support. Alimony (sometimes called *maintenance*) is financial support paid to a former spouse. Historically, the husband was the only wage earner and was expected to pay alimony to his former wife so that she could maintain her standard of living. Today, the law governing alimony has changed significantly, largely because so many couples are dual income earners.

alimony
Financial support paid to a former spouse after a marriage has been terminated. The alimony may be permanent or temporary (rehabilitative).

Alimony may be permanent or temporary. If a court orders one spouse to pay *permanent alimony* to the other, the alimony must be paid until the recipient remarries or dies (unless the court modifies the order for some reason). A more common form of alimony is temporary. This *rehabilitative alimony* is designed to provide ex-spouses with the education, training, or job experience necessary to support themselves. In deciding whether rehabilitative alimony is appropriate, a court usually considers the recipient's prospects of developing a new career.

> *EXAMPLE 17.3* Rather than seek more education, Janeen worked long hours to help put her husband, Nguyen, through medical school. Soon after finishing school, he filed for divorce. Janeen may be entitled to the resources necessary to help her develop her own skills through more education.

If the recipient is relatively advanced in age, and so has poor prospects for beginning a career, the court may grant permanent rather than rehabilitative alimony.

The amount of alimony awarded usually depends on the specific circumstances of the parties—their age, education, and incomes, for example. In about half the states, courts may also consider the reason for the divorce. If one party was more responsible than the other for the breakdown of the marriage, the alimony paid by that spouse might be higher than it would otherwise have been. Courts will also consider whether one spouse supported the other through college or graduate school in determining alimony awards.

In some states, even if two people who have been living together never married, one of the partners may be awarded support payments, sometimes called *palimony*, after the couple breaks up.

Property Division

property settlement
The division of property between spouses on the termination of a marriage.

When a marriage is terminated, the property owned by the couple (as well as their debts) must be divided. **Property settlement**—the division of property on divorce—is often a main area of disagreement. Although most divorcing couples eventually settle their financial disputes, the settlement reached is colored by the requirements of state law. As the *Developing Paralegal Skills* feature below indicates, property-settlement cases often involve significant detail work.

DEVELOPING PARALEGAL SKILLS

PREPARING FOR PROPERTY-SETTLEMENT NEGOTIATIONS

Lea, a paralegal, works for a small law firm that specializes in family law matters. One of the firm's clients, Mrs. Clark, is seeking a divorce. Tomorrow, her husband and his attorney will meet with Mrs. Clark and Lea's supervising attorney to negotiate a property settlement. Lea is preparing a settlement-agreement checklist for the attorney to take to the settlement meeting.

Lea makes a list of all of the property owned by the Clarks, along with the approximate value of each item and outstanding liens (which are legal claims, such as to satisfy debts) on the property. She also leaves blanks after "H" for husband and "W" for wife. After the parties agree to how they will divide the property, the attorney can fill in the appropriate amounts. Lea also includes a list of the debts owed by the Clarks. Again, she leaves blanks so that the attorney can write in how much of each debt will be paid by each spouse.

Lea goes over the checklist carefully to make sure that all of the Clarks' property and debts are included and that the amounts are accurate. Once she is satisfied that the checklist is accurate and complete, she takes it to her supervising attorney for review.

Property	Value	Amount Owed	Disposition	
Home	$500,000	$200,000	H _____	W _____
Cottage	$193,000	$50,000	H _____	W _____
BMW	$52,000	$27,500	H _____	W _____
Savings Account	$9,500	_____	H _____	W _____
Retirement (H)	$2,000,000	_____	H _____	W _____
IRA (H)	$800,000	_____	H _____	W _____
Life Insurance (H)	$1,000,000	_____	H _____	W _____
Debts		Amount Owed	Disposition	
Visa		$7,300	H _____	W _____
MasterCard		$2,500	H _____	W _____
Current Taxes (Due)		$9,456	H _____	W _____
Next Year's Taxes (Estimated)		$13,180	H _____	W _____

Marital Property

The way in which any court divides a couple's property depends largely on whether the property is considered marital property or separate property. **Marital property** is all property acquired during the course of a marriage (apart from inheritances and gifts received by one of the spouses). **Separate property** is property that a spouse owned before the marriage, plus inheritances and gifts acquired during the marriage. This property belongs to the spouse personally and not to the marital unit. On dissolution of the marriage, separate property is not divided but is retained by the owner.

The ownership right in separate property may be lost, however, if the property is combined with marital property.

> **EXAMPLE 17.4** Hannah owns property in Bangor, Maine. Hannah marries Richard, and they decide to build a house together. Hannah sells her property, and the couple uses a combination of the proceeds of the sale and their salaries to build a new house. By commingling the proceeds of the sale with their salaries (thus creating marital property), Hannah has lost her separate property rights in the sale proceeds.

Merely renovating separately held property (sprucing up a vacation home, for instance) may transform the separate property into joint property. Placing separate property (money) into a jointly held bank account may also transform the money into joint property.

Pension Benefits

Dividing pension benefits can be particularly complicated. Suppose one spouse served for twenty years in the military. She is entitled to future personal benefits that must be taken into account in a property division, even though no benefits are being collected at the present time. (Note that military pensions are governed by federal law rather than state law.)

Protecting Property Interests

The legal team representing a client in a divorce action must, of course, work to protect the client's property interests as the case progresses. It is sometimes important to determine if action may be needed immediately to protect those interests.

> **EXAMPLE 17.5** Suppose Maria tells you that she and her husband, Julio, who are divorcing, own some property as *joint tenants* (see Chapter 16). If Maria were to die before the divorce was final, the joint tenancy would be severed, and Julio would acquire title to the property. Action to sever the joint tenancy immediately would be necessary, such as by converting the ownership to a *tenancy in common* (see Chapter 16) while the divorce is pending.

Community Property

As discussed in Chapter 16, in some states, mostly in the West, husbands and wives hold property as community property. In those states, **community property** is all property acquired during the marriage (not including inheritances or gifts received by either party during the marriage). Even if only one party supplied all of the income and assets during the marriage, both spouses share equally (half and half) in the ownership of that property. Property owned by either partner before the marriage—and inheritances or gifts that partner received during the marriage—remain the property of that individual, or separate property.

Complex accounting issues appear when community and separate property are commingled, such as when one spouse deposits money she or he inherited into a joint bank account. Particularly tricky issues arise when couples move from a community property state to a common law property state (discussed next), or vice versa. Paralegals

marital property
All property acquired during the course of a marriage, apart from inheritances and gifts made to one or the other of the spouses.

separate property
Property that a spouse owned before the marriage, plus inheritances and gifts acquired by the spouse during the marriage.

community property
In certain states, all property acquired during a marriage, except for inheritances or gifts received during the marriage by either marital partner. Each spouse has a one-half ownership interest in community property.

need to be alert as to where a couple has lived so they can check for such potential complications.

Common Law Marital Property

Common law property states provide for the *equitable distribution* (fair distribution) of property to the divorcing spouses—that is, the marital property is divided according to the equities of the case (not necessarily split evenly). In some of these states, only the marital property is subject to distribution. In other states, all of the property owned by the couple, including separate property, may be factored into the property distribution.

While in most settlements, separate property remains with the owner, the courts exercise substantial discretion in deciding which person should receive what property. In deciding how to divide property between divorcing spouses, the courts consider a number of factors, including the following:

- The duration of the marriage.
- The health of the parties.
- The individuals' occupations and vocational skills.
- The individuals' relative wealth and income.
- The standard of living during the marriage.
- The relative contributions to the marriage (both financial and homemaker contributions).
- The needs and concerns of any children.
- Tax and inheritance considerations.

A typical property controversy in divorce cases concerns rights to the marital residence. If there are minor children, the house is usually given to the parent with custody of the children. It may be difficult to balance the grant of the house with other property (many families have few substantial assets other than their homes). Once the children are grown, the court may order the house to be sold and the proceeds divided to ensure that the property distribution is equitable.

Prenuptial Agreements

prenuptial agreement
A contract formed between two persons who are contemplating marriage to provide for the disposition of property in the event of a divorce or the death of one of the spouses after they have married.

Increasingly, couples use prenuptial agreements to avoid problems over property division that may arise in the future. A **prenuptial agreement** (also known as an *antenuptial agreement*) is a contract between the parties that is entered into before marriage and that provides for the disposition of property in the event of a divorce or the death of one of the spouses. Prenuptial agreements must be in writing to be enforceable.

Most states generally uphold prenuptial agreements, even if the agreements eliminate financial support in the event of divorce. More than half of the states have adopted the Uniform Premarital Agreement Act. This act helps to standardize the legal framework governing prenuptial agreements around the country, so there is less confusion when parties are from different states. Courts look closely at prenuptial agreements for evidence of unfairness. Courts may find a prenuptial agreement unfair if the parties did not retain independent counsel prior to signing the agreement. To enforce a prenuptial agreement, a party must also show that the agreement was made voluntarily and without threats or unfair pressure.

Family Law and the Paralegal

The opportunities for paralegals in the area of family law are extensive. Many paralegals work for law practices that specialize in legal work related to divorces, such as child-custody arrangements and property settlements. However, divorce is just one specialty within the broad area of family law. Paralegals often work in other areas of family law, such as adoption law, state welfare departments, publicly sponsored legal aid foundations, or groups that assist low-income persons with family-related legal problems.

Because the area of family law involves many special legal areas, paralegals working in family law perform many different types of work. Here are some examples of the kinds of tasks you might perform if you work in this specialty:

- Interview a client who is seeking a divorce to obtain information about the married couple, their property and debts, the reasons for the marriage breakdown, and their children, if any.

- Draft a petition for divorce and file divorce-related documents with the court.

- Assist in pretrial divorce proceedings, negotiations, and mediation.

- Assist in preparing a divorcing client for trial and in other trial-preparation matters.

- Draft a settlement agreement or prenuptial agreement.

- Assist in making arrangements for a private adoption.

- Research state laws governing marriage requirements, divorce procedures, child-custody arrangements, property settlements, and other matters.

- Help battered spouses obtain protection from their abusing spouses.

- Assist in preparing tax documents for a client getting a divorce.

- Help victims of child abuse obtain assistance.

Wills, Trusts, and Estates

As mentioned previously, a person's real and personal property will be transferred to others when the person dies. People must undertake *estate planning* if they wish to control how their property will be transferred. *Wills* and *trusts* are two basic devices used in the estate-planning process. We look at these devices, as well as others, in this section. We also discuss the process of *estate administration*, which involves collecting and transferring a decedent's (deceased person's) property.

Wills

As we noted in Chapter 2, a *will* is the final declaration of how a person wishes to have his or her property disposed of after death. The maker of a will is also called a **testator** (from the Latin *testari*, "to make a will"). A will is referred to as a *testamentary disposition* of property, and a person who dies after having made a valid will is said to have died **testate**. If no valid will has been executed, a decedent is said to have died **intestate**. When a person dies intestate, state **intestacy laws** govern the distribution of the property among heirs or next of kin. For example, in the state of New York, a surviving spouse of a person who dies with no will and no surviving children will inherit everything.

A will can serve other purposes besides the distribution of property. It can appoint a guardian for minor children or incapacitated adults. It can also appoint a *personal representative* to settle the affairs of the deceased. An **executor** (traditionally called an *executrix* if a woman, because of the word's Latin roots) is a personal representative named in a will. An **administrator** is a personal representative appointed by the court for a decedent who died without a will, who made a will but failed to name an executor for the estate, or whose executor is unable to serve.

Executors and administrators are fiduciaries (discussed in Chapter 18), which means they are held to the highest standard of trust imposed by law. As the Ohio Revised Code (2109.01) states: "Fiduciary . . . means any person . . . appointed by and accountable

testator
One who makes a valid will.

testate
The condition of having died with a valid will.

intestate
The condition of having died without a valid will.

intestacy laws
State statutes that specify how property will be distributed when a person dies intestate.

executor
A person appointed by a testator to serve as a personal representative on the testator's death.

administrator
A person appointed by a court to serve as a personal representative for a person who died intestate, who made a will but failed to name an executor, or whose executor cannot serve.

to the probate court and acting in a fiduciary capacity for any person, or charged with duties in relation to any property, interest, trust, or estate for the benefit of another."

Under a will, an executor distributes the property of the estate according to the terms of the will. When a person dies intestate, the value of having paid a lawyer to prepare a will becomes clear. Because there is no will, the court appoints an administrator, who may not be the person the deceased would have chosen. The property is divided according to a schedule created by state law, usually giving it to close relatives or, if none can be found, to the state. The process is usually more costly than it would have been had a will existed, and the property of the estate may not be distributed the way the decedent would have preferred. Over half of all people die without a will, leaving an additional burden on their families.

Paralegals often play major roles in preparing wills and must be cautious to follow ethical guidelines, as noted in this chapter's *Ethics Watch* feature.

Laws Governing Wills

probate

To prove and validate a will; the process of proving and validating a will and settling matters pertaining to the administration of a decedent's estate, guardianship of a decedent's children, and similar matters.

The laws governing wills come into play when a will is probated. To **probate** (prove) a will means to establish its validity and carry the administration of the estate through a process supervised by a *probate court*. When drafting wills for clients, attorneys and paralegals must make sure that the wills meet the specific requirements imposed by state statute.

Probate laws vary from state to state. The National Conference of Commissioners on Uniform State Laws has approved the Uniform Probate Code (UPC), which has been adopted in part or in whole by one-third of the states. The UPC codifies general principles and procedures for the resolution of conflicts in settling estates and relaxes some of the requirements for a valid will contained in earlier state laws.

Probate laws vary widely among states, and paralegals should always check the particular laws of the state involved. If your clients own property in several states or in foreign countries, you will need to research the other states' or countries' laws as well when assisting with an estate plan or the administration of an estate.

ETHICS WATCH

WILLS AND PARALEGAL SUPERVISION

Wills should accurately reflect the testator's wishes, so special care must be exercised in preparing a client's will. After all, unless the will is modified or revoked, it is the "final word" on how the testator intends property to be distributed. You will rest easier if you make sure that your supervising attorney reviews carefully any will that you draft, any subsequent modifications that are made, and particularly the final document. Attorneys have a duty to supervise paralegals' work. If necessary, you should remind your supervising attorney of this duty.

Proper supervision by an attorney is required by the NALA *Code of Ethics*, Canon 2: "A paralegal may perform any task which is properly delegated and supervised by an attorney, as long as the attorney is ultimately responsible to the client, maintains a direct relationship with the client, and assumes professional responsibility for the work product."

Supervision is also required by the ABA *Model Guidelines for the Utilization of Paralegal Services*. According to the ABA, attorneys responsible for a work product may assign certain tasks to paralegals that the attorneys would normally perform. However, attorneys may not delegate work that must be performed by lawyers. That would include tasks specifically required to be performed by attorneys as stipulated by statute, court rule, rules of professional conduct, or another legal authority.

As noted in *Example 17.2*, civil law countries require that a specific portion of the estate be left to the surviving spouse and/or children of the deceased, regardless of what any will might provide. Knowing if any of the client's assets are located in a civil law jurisdiction is thus critical information in an estate plan. A paralegal assisting with developing such a plan must be sure to investigate where assets are located.

Requirements for a Valid Will

A will must comply with state statutory requirements and formalities. If it does not, it will be declared void, and the decedent's property will be distributed according to state intestacy laws. Generally, most states uphold the following basic requirements for executing a will:

- *The testator must have testamentary capacity.* In other words, the testator must be of legal age (usually eighteen) and sound mind at the time the will is made.

- *Generally, a will must be in writing.* A will can be handwritten (called a *holographic will*). In some states, *nuncupative* wills (oral "deathbed" wills made before witnesses) that dispose of certain types of property are permitted.

- *A will must be signed by the testator.* The signature is generally at the end of the document.

- *A will must be witnessed.* The number of witnesses (often two, sometimes three), their qualifications, and the manner in which the witnessing must be done are generally determined by state law. Law firm employees are often called on to witness wills. Generally, you should not witness a will you helped to prepare.

- *In some states, a will must be published.* A will is "published" by an oral declaration by the maker to the witnesses that the document they are about to sign is the maker's "last will and testament."

Paralegals can often help in ensuring that wills comply with relevant requirements, as illustrated in the *Developing Paralegal Skills* feature below.

DEVELOPING PARALEGAL SKILLS

DRAFTING A CLIENT'S WILL

Mr. Perkins has come to the law firm of Smith & Hardy to have his will prepared. He has previously met with attorney Jennifer Hardy, who has been assisting him in estate planning.

Today, Perkins meets with Hardy's paralegal, James Reese, who will review the information needed to prepare the will. After the meeting, James returns to his office and begins drafting Perkins's will.

Later in the week, after going over the will with his supervising attorney, Hardy, James will meet with Perkins again. At that second meeting, Perkins can review and sign the will.

Checklist for Drafting a Will

- Start with a computerized standard will form.
- Review each provision, or clause, in the standard form.
- Input the client's name, address, and other information.
- Modify the clauses as necessary to fit the client's needs.
- Detail the assets the client wishes to leave to specific heirs.
- Number each page and clause of the will.
- Print out the document and carefully proofread it.
- Prepare the final copy to be reviewed by your supervising attorney.

The Probate Process

Probate procedures may vary depending on the size of the decedent's estate. For smaller estates, most state statutes provide for the distribution of assets without formal probate proceedings. Faster and less expensive methods are then used. The intent to transfer property to an heir may be established by *affidavit*, which is a statement of facts written down and sworn to voluntarily in the presence of an official authorized to affirm it. In addition, some state statutes provide that title to cars, savings and checking accounts, and certain other property can be passed to heirs merely by filling out forms. Property held by joint tenants or tenants by the entirety (see Chapter 16) does not go through probate but passes automatically to the other tenants or tenant.

Family Settlement Agreements.   Most states allow *family settlement agreements,* which are private agreements among the beneficiaries. Once a will is admitted to probate, the family members can agree to settle among themselves the distribution of the decedent's assets. Although a family settlement agreement speeds the settlement process, a court order is still needed to protect the estate from future creditors and to clear title to the assets involved. The use of these and other types of summary procedures in estate administration can save time and money.

Larger Estates.   For larger estates, formal probate proceedings are normally undertaken, and the probate court supervises the settlement of the decedent's estate. Additionally, in some situations—such as when a guardian for minor children or for an incompetent person must be appointed and a trust has been created to protect the minor or the incompetent person—more formal probate procedures cannot be avoided. Formal probate proceedings may take several months to complete. As a result, a sizable portion of the decedent's assets may go toward payment of fees charged by attorneys and personal representatives, as well as court costs.

Trusts

Trusts are important estate-planning devices that are being increasingly utilized to avoid the costs associated with probating a will. A **trust** involves any arrangement by which legal title to property is transferred from one person (called the *settlor* or *grantor*) to be administered by another (the trustee) for the benefit of still another party (the *beneficiary*).

trust
An arrangement in which property is transferred by one person (the grantor, or settlor) to another (the trustee) for the benefit of a third party (the beneficiary).

> *EXAMPLE 17.6* If Mendel conveys (transfers) his farm to Western Bank to be held for the benefit of his daughters, Mendel has created a trust. Mendel is the *settlor* or *grantor*. Western Bank is the *trustee*. Mendel's daughters are the *beneficiaries*. (Exhibit 17.1 illustrates this trust arrangement.)

There are many kinds of trusts, each with its own special characteristics. Increasingly, trusts are used for family businesses to handle issues relating to ownership and control. Trusts are also used for planning purposes to protect assets from creditors and to reduce estate taxes. Trusts enable grantors to avoid intestacy statutes, as well as any laws that might restrict the content of wills. Remembering that the use of trusts is flexible, we now look at some of the most common types of trusts.

Living Trusts

inter vivos trust
A trust created by the grantor (settlor) and effective during the grantor's lifetime—that is, a trust not established by a will.

A living trust—or *inter vivos* **trust** (*inter vivos* is Latin for "between or among the living")—is a trust executed by a grantor during her lifetime. A living trust may be a good estate-planning option because living trusts are not included in the property of a probated estate.

EXHIBIT 17.1

A Trust Arrangement

In a trust, there is a separation of interests in the trust property. The trustee takes *legal* title, which appears to be complete ownership and possession but does not include the right to receive any benefits from the property. The beneficiary takes *equitable* title, which is the right to receive all benefits from the property. This exhibit illustrates the trust arrangement from *Example 17.6*.

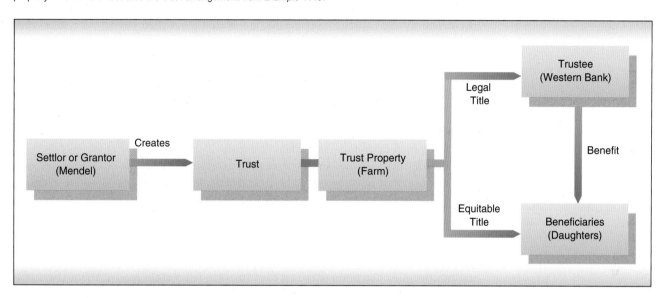

Revocable or Irrevocable.

Living trusts can be irrevocable or revocable. The distinction between these two types of living trusts is an important one for estate planners. In an *irrevocable* living trust, the grantor permanently gives up control over the property. In a *revocable* living trust, in contrast, the grantor retains control over the trust property during his lifetime.

Trust Administration.

To establish an irrevocable living trust, the grantor executes a trust deed, and legal title to the trust property passes to the named trustee. The trustee has a duty to administer the property as directed by the grantor for the benefit and in the interest of the beneficiaries. The trustee must preserve the trust property by not engaging in speculative schemes with the trust assets. The focus is on investments that are prudent and generate revenue over time. If required by the terms of the trust agreement, the trustee must pay income to the beneficiaries, all in accordance with the terms of the trust. Once an irrevocable *inter vivos* trust has been created, the grantor has, in effect, given over the property for the benefit of the beneficiaries.

To establish a revocable living trust, the grantor deeds the property to the trust but retains the power to amend, alter, or revoke the trust during his lifetime. The grantor may also arrange to receive income earned by the trust assets during his lifetime. Unless the trust is revoked, the principal of the trust is transferred to the trust beneficiary on the grantor's death.

Testamentary Trusts

A trust created by will to come into existence on the settlor's death is called a **testamentary trust**. Although a testamentary trust has a trustee who maintains legal title to the trust property, actions of the trustee are subject to judicial approval. This trustee may be named in the will or appointed by the court. Thus, a testamentary trust does not fail because a trustee has not been named in the will. The legal responsibilities of the trustee are the same as in an *inter vivos* trust.

testamentary trust
A trust that is created by will and that does not take effect until the death of the testator.

If a will that establishes a testamentary trust is invalid, then the trust will also be invalid. The property that was supposed to be in the trust will then pass according to intestacy laws, not according to the terms of the trust.

Special Types of Trusts

There are many kinds of special trusts. So long as such trusts do not violate state law, their creators can construct any arrangements that meet their needs.

Life Insurance Trust. In a *life insurance trust*, the trust owns a life insurance policy, which usually covers the life of the grantor of the trust. When the insured party dies, the life insurance proceeds go into the trust and are used in the manner provided for by the grantor's instructions.

Charitable Trust. A trust designed for the benefit of a segment of the public or the public in general is called a *charitable trust*. It differs from other types of trusts in that the identities of the beneficiaries are uncertain. Usually, to be deemed a charitable trust, a trust must be created for charitable, educational, religious, or scientific purposes.

Asset Protection Trust. In an *asset protection trust*, a person concerned with potential liability risks may put his or her assets into a trust to keep them away from potential creditors. For example, some surgeons worried about the high cost of medical malpractice judgments use these types of trusts to deter suits against them. Typically, such trusts are formed in jurisdictions that specifically authorize them. Almost half of the states specifically authorize "Domestic Asset Protection Trusts."

Spendthrift Trust. In a *spendthrift trust*, the beneficiary has limited right of access to money in the trust. This type of trust is used to protect beneficiaries (for example, compulsive gamblers) from themselves. The trustee who oversees the trust usually has authority to decide how much money goes to the beneficiary at any given time. Most states allow spendthrift trust provisions to prohibit creditors from attaching such trusts. A divorced spouse or a minor child of the beneficiary may be permitted to obtain alimony or child-support payments, however.

Other Estate-Planning Devices

Commonly, beneficiaries under a will must wait until the probate process is complete—which can take months if formal probate proceedings are undertaken—to have access to funds or other assets received under the will. For this and other reasons, some persons arrange to have property transferred in ways other than by will and outside the probate process.

One method of avoiding probate is by establishing a trust, as has already been discussed. A person can also arrange to hold title to certain real or personal property as a joint tenant with a spouse or other person. Remember from Chapter 16 that, in a joint tenancy, when one joint tenant dies, the other joint tenant or tenants automatically inherit the deceased tenant's share of the property. (This is true even if the deceased tenant has provided otherwise in a will.)

Yet another way someone can transfer property outside the probate process is by making gifts to children or others while the transferor is still living. Note that if a person makes a large gift (under current U.S. law, a gift of more than $15,000 in a year), the giver must pay a gift tax. In other words, a gift of less than $15,000 is exempt from the tax. The lifetime exemption is much higher than this annual exemption.

Finally, to make sure that a spouse, child, or some other dependent is provided for, many people take out life insurance policies. On the death of the policyholder, the proceeds of the policy go directly to the beneficiary and are not involved in the probate process.

The role that a paralegal might play in the estate-planning process in general is discussed in the accompanying *Developing Paralegal Skills* feature.

Estate Administration

Estate administration is the process of collecting a decedent's assets, settling his or her debts, and distributing all remaining assets. The decedent's personal representative undertakes these tasks. In some states, a probate court oversees the administration of decedents' estates. The rights of both creditors and beneficiaries must be protected during the estate-administration proceedings.

The decedent's assets may, of course, include real and personal property, as well as funds. Assets, however, can also be complicated or novel, as discussed in this chapter's *Office Tech and Cybersecurity* feature.

estate administration
The process in which a decedent's personal representative settles the affairs of the decedent's estate (collects assets, pays debts and taxes, and distributes the remaining assets to heirs); the process is usually overseen by a probate court.

Executor

If a will exists, it likely names a personal representative (executor) to administer the estate. If there is no will, if the will fails to name a personal representative, or if the personal representative named in the will cannot serve, then the court must appoint one (an administrator). The personal representative must inventory and collect the assets of the decedent and, if necessary, have them appraised to determine

DEVELOPING PARALEGAL SKILLS

HELPING CLIENTS WITH ESTATE PLANNING

Being an estate-planning paralegal can be particularly satisfying if you enjoy helping people. Unlike litigation, estate planning rarely involves adversarial work. Instead, it takes place in a cooperative atmosphere in which the lawyer and paralegal assist the client in creating a plan that satisfies the requirements of tax law and state law to accomplish the client's goals.

Clients generally have three different objectives in creating an estate plan.

1. **They want to ensure that they have adequately provided for their own future needs.** Because end-of-life medical care can be particularly costly, elderly clients in particular worry about preserving their assets in case of an emergency. You may find yourself working with a financial adviser to address these needs.

2. **They want to minimize their estate-tax bills and provide their heirs with as much money and assets as possible.** In many cases, estate planning involves sophisticated plans to minimize the tax burden, using trusts, insurance policies, and

other techniques for this purpose. For clients who own small businesses or farms, estate taxes can be substantial if proper planning is not done. You can have a satisfying experience helping to pass a family business or farm from one generation to the next.

3. **They seek to distribute their assets to provide for loved ones now rather than after death.** A reason for this may be so that their assets are not exhausted in paying for medical expenses in old age. If the assets have been given to others, Medicare will have to cover more of the givers' medical costs. A paralegal may be called upon to create legal documents that ensure a particular gift is used for the purpose the client wishes, such as to fund a grandchild's education or to pay for a specific charitable activity.

Using a mixture of drafting skills, interviewing skills, and legal research skills, you can help people achieve peace of mind about their own financial situations, as well as give them the satisfaction of knowing their heirs will be provided for.

OFFICE TECH AND CYBERSECURITY

CYBERSECURITY AND DIGITAL ASSETS

As digital assets such as Bitcoin and other cryptocurrencies continue to develop and as blockchain-based distributed asset registers become more common, the practice of law must adapt. As a paralegal working in estate planning, where the identification and disposition of assets are critical parts of what law firms do, you will need to be familiar with these technologies so that you can identify potential problems for your clients.

Digital assets like Bitcoin have no physical presence. They only exist electronically, and ownership is recorded in a blockchain-based register incorporated into the digital representation of the asset. If a party in a divorce has thirty bitcoins, for example, there are no physical "coins" but merely a digital record of ownership. These assets are often "stored" in a "digital wallet," and the owner must use a cryptographic key (something like a particularly complex password) to access the asset. If the key is lost, so is the asset. If the digital wallet turns out to have been a fraud, the assets are also gone.

One victim of a Bitcoin fraud scheme, who lost £1.5 million at the time of the theft from the Mt. Gox Bitcoin exchange in Japan, has been trying since 2011 to recover his bitcoins and has organized creditors of the exchange to seek relief in the Japanese courts. He advises Bitcoin owners "to print your bitcoin key on a piece of paper. Delete it from your computer, then hide the paper in your jewelry box" rather than trust an online digital wallet.

For estate-planning clients with digital assets, you will need to work with your supervising attorney to ensure that the necessary information to access those assets does not die with your client. For clients in a divorce, once you identify digital assets, you will need to help your supervising attorney ensure that the court retains jurisdiction over those assets and that digital wallets are not drained of their contents by the other party. These are steps you would also take for conventional bank accounts, but the digital nature of the assets adds new challenges.

their value. In addition, the personal representative is responsible for managing the assets of the estate during the administration period and for preventing them from being wasted or unnecessarily depleted.

> *EXAMPLE 17.7* The estate of Barney includes a farm where crops have been planted. The representative would need to arrange for the crops to be harvested and sold so as to make good use of estate assets.

Duties of Personal Representative

The personal representative pays debts owed by the decedent and also arranges for the estate to pay taxes. For larger estates, a federal tax is levied on the value of the estate after debts and expenses for administration have been deducted and after various exemptions have been allowed. The tax is on the estate itself rather than on the beneficiaries. In some states, a state inheritance tax is imposed on the recipient of a decedent's property rather than on the estate. Some states also have a state estate tax similar to the federal estate tax.

In general, inheritance tax rates are graduated according to the type of relationship between the beneficiary and the decedent. The lowest rates and largest exemptions are applied to a surviving spouse and the children of the decedent.

When the ultimate distribution of assets to the beneficiaries is determined, the personal representative is responsible for distributing the estate pursuant to the court order. Once the assets have been distributed, an accounting is rendered to the court, the estate is closed, and the personal representative is relieved of any further responsibility or liability for the estate.

Wills, Trusts, and Estates and the Paralegal

Paralegals are often involved in legal work relating to wills, trusts, other estate-planning devices, and estate administration. If you work for a general law practice, you may assist in handling tasks relating to all of these areas at one time or another. If you specialize in estate planning and administration, you may be employed by a law firm or a probate court and work extensively with probate proceedings. Among other things, you might be responsible for coordinating the efforts of the personal representative with those of the probate court. An increasing number of paralegals specialize in trust law and find career opportunities in trust departments of banking institutions.

Here is a sampling of the tasks paralegals perform in the areas of wills, trusts, and estates:

- Interview clients to obtain information about their assets and liabilities for estate-planning purposes.

- Draft a will for a client.

- Create the necessary documents to establish a trust for a client.

- Monitor a trust fund's investments to ensure that the funds are not unnecessarily depleted.

- Locate beneficiaries named in a will or the next of kin of a person who died intestate.

- File a will with the probate court to initiate probate procedures.

- Research laws governing estate and inheritance taxes to determine how they apply to a decedent's estate.

- Research state laws governing wills and probate procedures.

- Perform asset appraisals.

CHAPTER SUMMARY

FAMILY LAW AND ESTATES

Family Law

1. *Marriage requirements*—Marriage is a status conferred by state law that establishes the rights and duties of spouses to one another and to any children born to them.

   a. Traditionally, the couple being married had to be a man and a woman, currently unmarried, not closely related by blood, and at least eighteen (unless they had parental consent or were emancipated). The traditional rules have changed to allow same-sex couples to marry.

   b. Certain procedures may be required by the state for a marriage to be legally recognized, including a marriage license, a blood test, a waiting period, and a marriage ceremony, after which the license must be recorded.

2. *Common law marriage*—A minority of states allow parties who hold themselves out to the world as married to be married without a ceremony or license.

3. *Marital duties*—Spouses have the duty to support the other spouse and children financially by providing basic necessities. Abusing one's spouse is illegal in all states.

4. *Parental rights and obligations*—Parents have the legal right to control the upbringing of their minor children and to punish them within reason. They also provide for the children's necessities and ensure that the children attend school (until a certain age).

   a. Generally, parents are not liable for the wrongful actions of their children unless the actions result from the parents' negligence.

b. Child abuse and neglect are prohibited in all states.

c. The biological father of a child born out of wedlock is obligated to support the child once paternity is established. An illegitimate child can usually inherit from the mother but not from the father unless paternity has been established. Even when paternity has been established, an illegitimate child may not have the same inheritance rights as legitimate children.

5. *Adoption*—Adoption is a procedure by which persons become the legal parents of a child who is not their biological child. An adopted child normally has the same legal rights as the biological children of a married couple, including inheritance rights. State law governs adoption, and procedures vary. The court must approve all adoptions.

   a. Agency adoptions are done through state-licensed social-service agencies.

   b. Independent adoptions are arranged privately, often through lawyers or doctors.

   c. Stepparent adoptions are those in which a married partner adopts his or her spouse's children from a prior marriage.

   d. A child may be carried by a surrogate mother and then adopted by the parents who sponsored the surrogacy. Strict state regulations apply.

6. *Marriage termination*—A marriage can only be terminated by the state, through annulment or divorce.

   a. Annulment is a court order invalidating a marriage; it is no longer common.

   b. Divorce is the most common way to end a marriage. Divorce laws vary across states and may provide for fault-based or no-fault divorces. In a fault-based divorce, the petitioner must prove certain grounds for the divorce, such as adultery, cruelty, or abuse. A party may seek a fault-based divorce in the hope of gaining a more favorable property settlement. No-fault divorces are based on the grounds that the partners have irreconcilable differences, have been living separately for the length of time required by state statute, or are incompatible.

   c. The first step in obtaining a divorce is to file a petition for divorce with the appropriate state court. The petition is served on the other spouse. If the parties cannot agree on certain matters (child custody, finances) in the interim, the court may hold a hearing to assign temporary responsibility for those matters. Many states require parties to attend mediation before trial.

7. *Child custody*—Which parent the child will live with is often contested in a divorce. The court sometimes appoints a guardian *ad litem* to protect the interests of the child. The court considers a number of factors when deciding custody.

   a. Parents granted joint legal custody make major decisions about the child together. Parents with joint physical custody have physical custody of the child for specific time periods. Many states now provide for joint custodial arrangements.

   b. Usually, one parent is awarded legal custody of the child and can make major decisions without consulting the other parent. The noncustodial parent receives visitation rights, which are normally stated in divorce settlements.

8. *Child support*—The noncustodial parent will likely be required to pay a certain sum monthly as support for the child. States have official, standardized guidelines determining child-support duties, though judges may depart from them under certain circumstances.

9. *Spousal support*—In some situations, one of the spouses is ordered to pay support (alimony) to the other. Alimony can be temporary (rehabilitative) or permanent.

10. *Property division*—

   a. Marital property is property acquired during the marriage. It is divided on divorce. Separate property is anything that a spouse owned prior to the marriage, plus inheritances and gifts received during the marriage. Separate property is usually not divided.

   b. In some states, all property acquired during the marriage is considered community property, even if only one party supplied all of the income and assets during the marriage. Each spouse has a one-half ownership interest in community property.

   c. Other states divide the divorcing couple's property by equitable (fair) distribution. The court decides how much of the marital property each spouse should receive given the circumstances of the parties and does not necessarily divide the property equally. In some states, only the marital property is divided; in others, separate property may also be included.

11. *Prenuptial agreements*—Agreements (contracts) made before marriage to provide for division of property in the event of divorce or death. Prenuptial agreements must be in writing. Most states enforce such agreements unless they are clearly unfair.

Wills, Trusts, and Estates

A will is the final declaration of how a person wishes to have his or her property disposed of after death.

1. *Laws governing wills*—A person who dies without leaving a will is said to have died intestate, and the decedent's property is distributed under state intestacy statutes. A person who makes a will is called a testator. A personal representative named in a will to settle the affairs of the decedent is called an executor. A personal representative appointed by a court is called an administrator.

2. *Requirements for a valid will*—A will must comply with state statutory requirements, which usually involve the following:

   a. The testator must have testamentary capacity (be of sound mind at the time the will is made).

   b. The will generally must be in writing.

   c. The testator must sign the will.

   d. The will must be witnessed by a specified number of persons (usually two or three).

   e. In some states, the will must be published.

3. *Probate process*—To probate a will means to establish its validity and administer the estate through a court process. Probate laws vary from state to state. Procedures may be formal or informal, depending on the size of the estate and other factors, such as whether a guardian for minor children must be appointed.

4. *Trusts*—A trust is an arrangement by which property is transferred from one person (the grantor, or settlor) to be administered by another (the trustee) for the benefit of a third party (the beneficiary).

   a. A living *(inter vivos)* trust is executed during the grantor's lifetime and can be revocable or irrevocable.

   b. A testamentary trust is created by will and comes into existence on the grantor's death.

   c. Special types of trusts include life insurance trusts, charitable trusts, and spendthrift trusts.

5. *Other estate-planning devices*—Several other strategies may be used to transfer property. These include owning property as joint tenants, giving gifts to children or others during one's lifetime, and purchasing life insurance policies.

6. *Estate administration*—The process of collecting a decedent's assets, settling debts, and distributing remaining assets that is carried out by the executor or representative of the estate under probate court supervision.

KEY TERMS AND CONCEPTS

administrator 525
adoption 516
alimony 521
annulment 517
bigamy 517
child support 520
common law marriage 511
community property 523
divorce 517
emancipation 510
estate administration 531
executor 525

foster care 516
guardian *ad litem* 519
independent adoption 516
inter vivos trust 528
intestacy laws 525
intestate 525
joint custody 519
legal custody 519
marital property 523
no-fault divorce 518
paternity suit 515
petition for divorce 518

prenuptial agreement 524
probate 526
property settlement 522
restraining order 512
separate property 523
testamentary trust 529
testate 525
testator 525
trust 528
visitation rights 520

QUESTIONS FOR REVIEW

1. What are the rights and duties of parents with respect to their children? What are the legal obligations of parents to children born out of wedlock and to adopted children?

2. What are the requirements for a valid marriage? On the termination of a marriage, how is property divided? What is separate property? Community property?

3. List the requirements of a valid will. Why is it important to check the laws of your state for the requirements of a will? What laws govern the distribution of the estate of a person who dies without a valid will?

4. Why and how are wills probated? What are the duties of a personal representative?

5. What is a trust? List and describe the various types of trusts discussed in this chapter. What are some other estate-planning devices?

ETHICS QUESTIONS

1. James Simpson, an attorney, has represented Miss Morgan for forty years. She is now eighty-three years old and is revising her will. She has a sizeable estate. Miss Morgan instructs her attorney to include a bequest in the will to James Simpson in the amount of $50,000. Can Simpson prepare the will with this bequest in it? Why or why not?

2. Cynthia Warner works as a paralegal for a sole practitioner, Samuel Weingarten. Weingarten's practice consists mainly of estate planning and probate. Today, Weingarten has received a check for $100,000 from the sale of real property that was in an estate that he is probating. Weingarten instructs Cynthia to deposit the check in the firm's bank account—not the client trust account—because he has some bills to pay. Is this ethical? Explain your answer.

PRACTICE QUESTIONS AND ASSIGNMENTS

1. Matthew, an eleven-year-old boy with mild autism, was regularly bullied at school by another boy. In one instance, the bully pushed Matthew down on the playground, resulting in stitches. Most recently, the bully beat Matthew badly enough that he required hospitalization for a broken arm and a broken nose. Matthew's parents decide that suing the parents of the bully might help the situation. Using the material in the chapter on the liability of parents for their children's actions, can Matthew's parents sue? Discuss what the likely outcome will be.

2. Using the no-fault divorce material discussed in the chapter, which of the following are grounds for a no-fault divorce?

   a. Irreconcilable differences.

   b. Cruelty.

   c. Living separately for a period of time specified by state statute (ranging from six months to three years).

   d. Adultery.

3. A woman agrees that in exchange for $10,000, she will be artificially inseminated, carry the child to term, and surrender the baby at birth to the biological father and his wife. The agreement states that the surrogate mother will terminate her parental rights, and the father's wife will adopt the child. If the surrogate mother breaches the contract and refuses to give up the baby, how might a court use existing custody laws to resolve the dispute?

4. Identify each of the following types of trusts:

   a. Barbara inserts a trust provision in her will requiring that all of her property be held in trust for her children until they reach the age of thirty.

b. Steve, who is seventy years old, transfers his home into a trust for the benefit of his children and their spouses.

c. Kathy creates a trust in her will for cancer research.

5. Identify which of the following types of estate-planning devices allow property to be transferred outside the probate process:

a. Living trusts.

b. Life insurance.

c. Testamentary trusts.

d. Holding property as joint tenants with rights of survivorship.

e. Gifts to children.

GROUP PROJECT

This project requires the group to review the status of grandparents' visitation as a result of the United States Supreme Court decision in *Troxel v. Granville*, 530 U.S. 57, 120 S.Ct. 2054, 147 L.Ed.2d 49 (2000).

Student one will explain the legal issue addressed in *Troxel v. Granville* and outline the facts of the case.

Student two will summarize the decisions of all courts that heard the case.

Student three will describe the influence of *Troxel v. Granville* on state statutes regulating grandparent visitation rights, by locating an online article discussing the effect that the *Troxel* decision had on the future of grandparent visitation rights.

Student four will sum up how grandparents can try to obtain visitation rights and then compile the group's answers for submission.

Business Organizations and Employment Law

CHAPTER OBJECTIVES

After completing this chapter, you will be able to:

- Identify the major forms of business organizations, and describe how each is created and operated.

- Explain how profits and liabilities are distributed in different forms of business organizations.

- Define *agency relationship*, and explain the significance of agency law for business.

- Describe how the government regulates employer-employee relationships.

Introduction

Paralegals usually are employees of business entities, and their work often involves businesspersons. Consequently, law firms' clients frequently need help forming and operating various business entities. Knowledge of the legal forms used by businesses is helpful in understanding the legal issues that arise.

In this chapter, we first review how different business organizations are formed and some of the key features of the various legal structures. Then we turn to agency law, a part of the common law that plays a role in most business relationships, including employment. Because a key part of operating a business is employing people, we investigate that subject in the final part of this chapter.

Forms of Business Organization

Traditionally, there were three basic forms of business organization: the sole proprietorship, the partnership, and the corporation. Today, added to these are some newer business organizational forms known as limited liability companies (LLCs), limited liability partnerships (LLPs), and professional corporations (PCs).

Each type of business entity involves different relationships, rights, obligations, and regulatory schemes. As a paralegal, you will want to know what rights and duties are associated with each of these entities when you work on behalf of clients.

> **EXAMPLE 18.1** Your firm represents a person injured in a traffic accident involving a delivery van. You will need to determine the type of business entity that owns the van in order to file suit. A sign on the van may say "Smith Produce," but the van may be owned by "Smith Bros., LLC," which is likely to be the defendant in an action.

Different business entities may be appropriate for different purposes. Businesses may be a collection of related entities. A limited partnership may own a building, an LLC may run a business located in the building, and a corporation may hold intellectual property rights related to the enterprise. Paralegals must often do careful investigative work to help unravel the web of entities that may be involved in a case.

Sole Proprietorships

Remember from Chapter 3 that the simplest form of business is the *sole proprietorship*, in which one person—the sole proprietor—owns the business. The sole proprietor is entitled to the business's profits and bears personal responsibility for the business's debts and other obligations. Sole proprietors can own and manage a wide range of businesses, from a home-office undertaking to a large restaurant or construction firm.

There are millions of sole proprietorships in the United States. In fact, they constitute more than two-thirds of all American businesses. They are usually small enterprises—only about 1 percent of sole proprietorships earn more than $1 million per year.

Formation of a Sole Proprietorship

The sole proprietorship is easier and less costly to start than any other kind of business, as few legal formalities are involved. No partnership agreement need be devised, because there are no partners. No papers need be filed with the state to establish the business. At most, minor paperwork will be required, depending on the law of the city in which the business is located. In the majority of states, if retail sales are involved, the proprietor will need a tax number to report and remit sales taxes.

Because it is the simplest business form to create, a person first starting up a business often chooses to operate a sole proprietorship, converting to another form later. An attorney or a freelance paralegal might begin doing business as a sole proprietor.

Advantages of Sole Proprietorships

An advantage of the sole proprietorship is that the sole proprietor is entitled to all the profits made by the firm (because the sole proprietor takes all the risk). The sole proprietor is also free to make all decisions concerning the business—whom to hire, when to take a vacation, what kind of business to pursue, and the like. Additionally, sole proprietors are allowed to establish tax-exempt retirement accounts.

Disadvantages of Sole Proprietorships

A major disadvantage of the sole proprietorship is that the proprietor alone, as the firm's sole owner, is personally liable for any losses, debts, and obligations incurred by the business enterprise. As discussed in Chapter 3, *personal liability* means that the personal assets of the business owner (such as a home, savings, and other tangible or intangible property) may be subject to creditors' claims if the business fails or is sued in tort or for breach of contract.

As a paralegal, if you are asked to do a preliminary investigation of a client's claim against a business entity, one of the first things you should check is the form of the business.

> *EXAMPLE 18.2* Your law firm's client wants to sue a business for damages. If you learn that the firm is a sole proprietorship, then you will know that if the firm itself has insufficient assets to pay damages to the client (should the client win in court), the firm's owner will be personally liable for the damages. Depending on what you learn about the firm's financial condition, you may want to investigate the owner's personal financial position as well as the firm's assets, since the two are legally one.

Another disadvantage of the sole proprietorship is that it may be difficult to obtain capital for expansion. The sole proprietor is dependent on personal resources and loans made by lending institutions and others. For this reason, sole proprietors sometimes decide to take on partners who will contribute capital to the business, or they may incorporate and sell ownership (equity) shares in the business to raise funds.

Taxation and Sole Proprietorships

A sole proprietor must pay income taxes on business profits but does not have to file a separate tax return in the name of the business. Rather, the profits are reported on the sole proprietor's personal tax return, usually on Schedule C of the federal tax return, and taxed as personal income.

Termination of the Sole Proprietorship

In a sole proprietorship, the owner is the business. For that reason, when the owner dies, the business is automatically dissolved. If the business is transferred to family members or other heirs, a new entity is created. Similarly, if the proprietor sells the business, whoever buys it must establish either a new sole proprietorship or some other business form, such as a partnership or a corporation.

> *EXAMPLE 18.3* A client inherited her father's business assets, which include a clothing store. If the business was a sole proprietorship, you will need to help her change the title on all real estate and any vehicles owned by the business, as well as the names on all licenses used by the business. If the business was organized as a corporation, however, these things may not need to be changed.

The sole proprietor on the right has so much business she has decided to form a partnership with her friend on the left. Will the new partner face the same liabilities that were faced by the sole proprietor?

Partnerships

As discussed in Chapter 3, some law firms are organized in the form of a *partnership*, which arises when two or more individuals decide to do business together. Each partner owns a portion of the business and shares jointly in the firm's profits or losses. Partners are personally liable for all debts and obligations of the business if the business fails, just as sole proprietors are. Each partner has decision-making authority involving partnership assets, unless the partners have agreed otherwise and proper legal formalities have been observed.

The Uniform Partnership Act (UPA) or the Revised Uniform Partnership Act (RUPA)—depending on which law a state has adopted—governs the operation of partnerships *unless the partners have expressly agreed otherwise*. Like the Uniform Commercial Code (UCC), the UPA is a model that becomes law when adopted by a state legislature. The earliest version of the UPA was issued in 1914. The most recent version, the RUPA, was issued in 1997, and a majority of the states have adopted it; however, the UPA is most commonly referred to for purposes of simplicity.

Partnership Formation

To create a partnership, two or more persons interested in establishing a profit-making business agree to do so as partners. The partnership agreement can be expressed orally or in writing, or it can be implied by conduct. To satisfy the Statute of Frauds (see Chapter 15), if the partnership is to continue for over a year, the agreement must be evidenced by a writing. It is always better for the partners to create a written partnership agreement.

Rights and Duties of Partners

When two or more persons agree to do business as partners, legally they enter into a special relationship with one another. This relationship involves various rights and duties that arise from the partners' agreement, in which they agree to place some or all of their money or other assets, labor, and skill in a business with the understanding that profits and losses will be shared in some proportion.

EXHIBIT 18.1

Rights of Partners

> **PARTNERS HAVE THE RIGHT:**
>
> - To hold an ownership interest in the firm and to receive a share of the profits.
> - To inspect partnership books and records.
> - To an accounting of partnership assets and profits (for example, to determine the value of each partner's share in the partnership). An accounting can be performed voluntarily or can be compelled by a court order. Formal accounting occurs by right when a partnership is dissolved.
> - To participate in the management of the business operation unless the partnership agreement specifies otherwise.

Default Rules.   The rights of partners are often written into the partnership agreement. If the agreement does not specify these rights, then the UPA comes into play (the state's version of the UPA, as adopted). Some of the important rights of partners are listed in Exhibit 18.1.

If two or more people are engaged in a common business enterprise and they do not form a separate legal entity, by default the law will treat them as having formed a partnership. The partners may not realize they have formed a partnership and may never have used the words "partner" or "partnership" to describe their relationship.

> **EXAMPLE 18.4** Tyrel and Maria decide to open a coffee shop together. They do not consult a lawyer or take any other steps to form a separate business entity. Maria signs a contract to buy six espresso machines at $12,000 each. Should Maria not make the payments, Tyrel will be liable on the contract as Maria's partner despite not having signed the contract or even knowing that she made the agreement. Likewise, if Tyrel negligently spills a hot espresso on a customer, causing severe burns, Maria will also be liable for the customer's injuries.

Obligation to Partners.   All partners owe each other a *fiduciary duty*, the highest level of obligation imposed by the law. (We discuss this concept later in this chapter under the topic of *agency*.) This means that partners must put the interests of the partnership ahead of their own personal interests in any matters related to the purpose of the enterprise.

> **EXAMPLE 18.5** A partner in a real estate investment partnership sees an excellent opportunity to buy a piece of property. She cannot buy it for herself without first giving the partnership the opportunity to buy the property.

Liability of Partners

Most states recognize the partnership as a legal entity that can sue or be sued and collect judgments in the partnership's name.

Joint Liability.   A distinguishing feature of the partnership, and one that is considered a disadvantage, is the potentially extensive personal liability faced by partners for partnership obligations and for the actions of the other partners. Partners have **joint liability,** or shared liability. In other words, partners may be held personally liable not only for their own actions and those of the partnership as an entity but also for the actions of other partners.

Joint and Several Liability.   Partners may also be subject to **joint and several liability.** Several liability is *individual* liability. Joint and several liability means that a third party may sue all of the partners (jointly) or one or more of the partners

joint liability
Shared liability. In partnership law, partners incur joint liability for partnership obligations and debts.

joint and several liability
Shared and individual liability. In partnership law, the term means that a third party may sue all of the partners (jointly) or one or more of the partners separately (severally). This is true even if one of the partners sued did not participate in, ratify, or know about whatever gave rise to the cause of action.

separately (severally). This is true even if one of the partners sued did not participate in, ratify, or know about whatever gave rise to the cause of action. In fact, that partner could be liable for the entire matter if the other partners have no assets. A partner who is sued has the right to bring in other partners who may not be named in the litigation.

> **EXAMPLE 18.6** Suppose a plaintiff wants to recover for damages allegedly caused by a physician's negligence (medical malpractice). The physician is one of four partners in a medical practice partnership. Because partners are jointly and severally liable, the plaintiff could sue either the physician who allegedly caused the harm, the partnership, one of the other physicians (even if that physician had nothing to do with the plaintiff's treatment), or all of the physicians to recover damages.

The liability faced by partners is a major reason for the rapid growth of a new form of partnership, the limited liability partnership, as well as the professional corporation. Both will be discussed later.

Taxation of Partnerships

The partnership itself, as an entity, does not pay federal income taxes. The partnership files an information return with the Internal Revenue Service on which the income received by the partnership is reported. The partners declare their shares of the partnership's profits on their personal income tax returns and pay taxes accordingly. For this reason, a partnership is referred to as a "pass-through" entity. The profits "pass through" to the partners. Avoiding a separate layer of taxation on the business is a major advantage of a partnership.

Partnership Termination

In general, a partnership can be ended by a partner at any time. (This makes sense, as you would not want to be in business with someone you no longer trusted, especially since that person could expose you to unlimited liability.) However, a partnership agreement may specify the duration of the partnership by indicating that the partnership will end on a certain date or on the occurrence of a certain event. In those situations, it would be a breach of the partnership agreement for one partner to withdraw from the partnership before the specified date arrived or the specified event occurred. The withdrawing partner would be liable to the remaining partners for any related losses.

Dissolution. When an agreement does not specify the duration of the partnership, a partner is free to withdraw at any time without incurring liability to the remaining partners. Under an older version of the UPA, still in effect in some states, withdrawal by a partner results in the **dissolution** (the formal disbanding) of the partnership (although a new partnership may arise among those who stay with the enterprise). Under the RUPA, in effect in most states, the withdrawal of a partner causes a partnership to be dissolved only if the withdrawal results in the breakup of the partnership itself and the business cannot continue. The occurrence of certain other events, such as the death or bankruptcy of a partner, results in a process similar to the withdrawal of a partner.

dissolution
The formal disbanding of a partnership or a corporation.

Winding Up. Partnership termination is a two-step process. Dissolution is the first step in the process. The second step is the **winding up** of partnership affairs (collecting and distributing the firm's assets). Once the firm is dissolved, it continues to exist legally until the process of winding up all business affairs is complete.

winding up
The process of ending all business affairs (collecting and distributing the firm's assets) after a partnership or corporation has been dissolved.

Limited Partnerships

limited partnership
A partnership consisting of one or more general partners and one or more limited partners.

Ordinary partnerships, such as those just discussed, are often referred to as *general partnerships*. The **limited partnership**, in contrast, is a special form of partnership involving two different types of partners—general partners and limited partners. There must be at least one **general partner**. General partners manage the business and have the same rights and liabilities as partners in a general partnership. A **limited partner** is only an investor in the business.

general partner
A partner who participates in managing the business of a partnership and has all the rights and liabilities that arise under traditional partnership law.

Investment funds are typically limited partnerships. A limited partnership may be formed, for example, to purchase and develop real estate, oil and gas wells, intellectual property, or other assets. The limited partners play a passive role. Their funds help to finance the venture, and they receive a share of the profits in return.

Unlike general partners, who are personally liable for partnership obligations, limited partners are liable only up to the amounts that they have invested. In other words, if the partnership goes bankrupt, they will lose their investments but cannot be held liable for partnership debts beyond that amount. Note, though, that the limited partners may lose this limited liability protection if they participate in the management of the partnership.

limited partner
A partner who invests in a limited partnership but who cannot play an active role in managing the operation of the business. Unlike general partners, limited partners are liable for partnership debts only up to the amounts that they have invested.

In contrast to the informal, private, and voluntary agreement that may create a general partnership, the formation of a limited partnership is a public and formal proceeding that must follow state statutory requirements. The partners must sign a *certificate of limited partnership*. To do so, the partners must submit information similar to that found in a corporate charter. The certificate must be filed with the proper state official (usually, the secretary of state). In this respect, the limited partnership resembles the corporation. The formal steps put potential creditors on notice of the limitations on the liabilities of the limited partners. Usually the limited partnership's name must include the initials "L.P." or some other indication of its status.

Corporations

Paralegals frequently help clients form corporations. Paralegals also work on behalf of corporate clients or on legal matters involving corporations. An increasing number of paralegals work for corporate employers. As a paralegal, you should thus have a basic knowledge of how corporations are formed and operated.

shareholder
One who has an ownership (equity) interests in a corporation through the purchase of corporate shares (stock).

You should also be familiar with the basic rights and responsibilities of corporate participants. These include the **shareholder** (the owner of the business and called shareholder because that person purchases a corporate **share**, or stock), the **director** (a person elected by the shareholders to direct corporate affairs), and the **officer** (a person hired by the directors to manage the day-to-day operations of the corporation). Corporate officers include the corporate president, vice president, secretary, treasurer, and possibly others, such as a chief financial officer and chief executive officer. Corporate officers are employees of the corporation and subject to employment contracts.

share
A unit of stock; a measure of ownership interest in a corporation.

Entity Status

director
A person elected by the shareholders to direct corporate affairs.

Although individuals or other businesses own it, the corporation is a separate legal entity that is created and recognized by law. In the United States, corporations are formed under state law, not federal law. In the eyes of the law, a corporation is a *legal person* that enjoys many of the rights and privileges that U.S. citizens enjoy, such as the right of access to the courts as an entity that can sue or be sued. A corporation also has, among other rights, the right to due process of law and the right to freedom from unreasonable searches and seizures.

officer
A person hired by corporate directors to assist in the management of the day-to-day operations of the corporation.

The Model Business Corporation Act (MBCA) is a codification of modern corporation law that has been influential in the codification of corporation statutes. Today, most state statutes are guided by the revised version of the MBCA, known as the Revised Model Business Corporation Act (RMBCA). There is, however, considerable variation among the statutes of the states that have based their statutes on the MBCA or the RMBCA, and several states do not follow either act. Because of this, as a paralegal you will need to rely on individual state corporation laws rather than the model statutes.

A corporation may be incorporated in one state but do business elsewhere. For example, many large corporations are incorporated in Delaware. This state has highly regarded corporate law and judges who are experts in corporate legal matters. Similarly, some companies are legally organized in foreign countries, sometimes for tax reasons and sometimes to take advantage of unique features of a particular jurisdiction's corporate law. For example, many insurance firms doing business in the United States incorporate in Bermuda because Bermuda has developed significant regulatory expertise and legal precedents in the area of insurance.

Corporate Formation

Generally, forming a corporation involves two steps. The first consists of preliminary organizational and promotional undertakings—particularly, obtaining capital for the future business. Before a corporation becomes a reality, people may invest in the proposed corporation as subscribers. The subscribers become the shareholder-owners of the corporation when the corporation becomes a legal entity. Thus, even before the corporation legally exists, work must be done on its behalf.

The second step in forming a corporation is the process of incorporation. Exact procedures for incorporation differ among states, but the basic requirements are similar. The primary document needed to begin the incorporation process is called the **articles of incorporation** (see Exhibit 18.2 for sample articles of incorporation for a small corporation). The articles include basic information about the corporation and serve as a source of authority for its future organization and business functions. The articles normally are relatively short; the details are spelled out in the bylaws, discussed shortly. Once the articles have been filed in the appropriate state office, they become a public record.

articles of incorporation
The document filed with the appropriate state official, usually the secretary of state, when a business is incorporated. State statutes usually prescribe what kind of information must be contained in the articles of incorporation.

Paralegals frequently assist their supervising attorneys in preparing incorporation papers and filing them with the appropriate state office. In most instances, standard forms are used, and filing to create the legal entity is done online. (See the *Developing Paralegal Skills* feature on page 547 for an illustration of another way in which paralegals can help with incorporation tasks.) Also, as a paralegal, you may need to obtain information about a corporation—for example, when you are conducting an investigation. For these reasons, you should know what information is generally included in the articles of incorporation. Exhibit 18.3 lists on page 548 and describes this information.

After the articles of incorporation have been prepared, signed, and authenticated by the incorporators, they are sent to the appropriate state official, usually the secretary of state, along with the appropriate filing fee. In many states, the secretary of state then issues a **certificate of incorporation** representing the state's authorization for the corporation to conduct business. (This may be called the *corporate charter*.) This is largely a matter of form—if the filing requirements are met, the certificate or charter will be issued. The certificate and a copy of the articles are returned to the incorporators, who then hold the initial organizational meeting that completes the details of incorporation.

certificate of incorporation
The document issued by a state official, usually the secretary of state, granting a corporation legal existence and the right to function. Also called a corporate charter.

At this first organizational meeting, the corporation adopts a set of rules to govern the management of the corporation, called the **bylaws**. The bylaws grant or restrict the powers of the corporation. They usually outline the details of the organization of a company—the structure of the board of directors, rights of shareholders, and other key

bylaws
A set of governing rules adopted by a corporation or other association.

EXHIBIT 18.2

A Sample Articles of Incorporation

Filed with Secretary of State
_____, 20_____

SHORT FORM
ARTICLES OF INCORPORATION
OF
_____ Hiram, Inc. _____

ARTICLE I

The name of this corporation _____ Hiram, Inc. _____

ARTICLE II

The purpose of this corporation is to engage in any lawful act or activity for which a corporation may be organized under the General Corporation Law of New Pacum other than the banking business, the trust company business, or the practice of a profession permitted to be incorporated by the New Pacum Corporation Code.

ARTICLE III

The name and address in the State of New Pacum of this corporation's initial agent for service of process is: _____ Hiram Galliard, _____
8934 Rathburn Avenue, North Bend, New Pacum 98754

ARTICLE IV

The corporation is authorized to issue only one class of shares of stock; and the total number of shares that this corporation is authorized to issue is _____ 10,000 _____.

ARTICLE V

The corporation is a close corporation. All the corporation's issued shares of stock shall be held of record by not more than ten (10) persons.

DATED: ___ June 3, 2022 _____

Hiram Galliard   *Martha Bonnell*
_____   _____
[Signature(s) of Incorporator/Directors(s)]

I (we) hereby declare that I (we) am (are) the person(s) who executed the foregoing Articles of Incorporation, which execution is my (our) act and deed.

Hiram Galliard   *Martha Bonnell*

---

matters that were not dealt with in such detail in the articles of incorporation. The bylaws are not filed with the state, and they may contain confidential information. As this chapter's *Office Tech and Cybersecurity* feature discusses on page 549, attention to security is a major responsibility of a law firm.

Classifications of Corporations

How a corporation is classified depends on its purpose, ownership characteristics, and location. A *private corporation* is, as the term indicates, a corporation that is privately owned. A *public corporation* is formed by the government for a political or governmental purpose, as when a town incorporates. Note that a public corporation is not the same as a publicly held corporation. A **publicly held corporation** is a corporation with shares

publicly held corporation
A corporation whose shares are eligible to be publicly traded in securities markets, such as the New York Stock Exchange and NASDAQ.

DEVELOPING PARALEGAL SKILLS

RESERVING A CORPORATE NAME

Jon is a paralegal at a law firm. A local building contractor, Thiess Brown, comes to the law firm for assistance. He believes that his firm is going to grow and that he should incorporate. In a discussion with Jon and his supervising attorney, Brown asks about calling his new corporation Thiess Construction. The attorney says that the availability of the name will be investigated. Jon is assigned to look into the naming issue.

Jon knows that, as in most states, he must contact the secretary of state's office to check on the availability of names for corporations. In Jon's state, the secretary of state's Department of Business Services maintains the database of registered corporate names in the state. A search of the department's website reveals that the names Thiess Construction and Thiess Corporation are not in use. Either name could be reserved for Brown's firm. Jon also checks a list of available domain names at Network Solutions to find out whether Brown can buy the domain name thiessconstruction.com should he want to establish a website. He should also check alternative domains such as .biz and .net. Then Jon goes to the website of the U.S. Patent and Trademark Office to check the availability of names for possible trademark use.

Tips for Claiming a Corporate Name, Domain Name, and Trademark

- Determine if the preferred name and several possible alternatives are available.
- Check on the possibility of registering the company name, or a part of it, as a trademark mark. This is especially valuable should the company grow larger.
- Check on the availability of domain names for the client to use today or in the future for a website. Buying a domain name and similarly spelled domain names before a firm becomes well known is good strategy.
- Provide the lists of possibilities to your supervising attorney for the client's consideration.
- Once the client has decided what to do, file the appropriate forms.

that are or could be publicly traded in securities markets, such as the New York Stock Exchange and NASDAQ.

For-Profit or Not-for-Profit. Corporations may also be classified as either *for-profit corporations* or *not-for-profit (nonprofit) corporations*. A not-for-profit corporation may be formed by a group—such as a charitable association, a hospital, or a religious organization—to conduct its business without exposing the individual owners to personal liability.

Close Corporations. A corporation owned by a small group of shareholders, such as family members, is called a **close corporation**. Unlike publicly held corporations, close corporations cannot sell their shares on public securities markets and usually place restrictions on the transfer of corporate shares—to keep the business in the family, for example. State laws may provide more flexibility for close corporations than for publicly held corporations, such as by reducing the statutory formalities that must be observed.

Certain close corporations are permitted to elect a special corporate tax status under Subchapter S of the Internal Revenue Code. These corporations are called *S corporations* and will be discussed shortly.

A significant problem for close corporations is ensuring that appropriate records are kept, meetings are held, and formalities are observed so that corporate status can be maintained. As a paralegal, one of your roles may be helping to keep track of such

close corporation
A corporation owned by a small group of shareholders, often family members. Shares in close corporations cannot be publicly traded. Restrictions on stock transfers may apply.

EXHIBIT 18.3

Information Generally Included
in the Articles of Incorporation

THE NAME OF THE CORPORATION

- The choice of a corporate name is subject to state approval to ensure against duplication or deception. State statutes usually require that the secretary of state run a check on the proposed name in the state of incorporation. Once cleared, a name can be reserved for a short time, for a fee, pending the completion of the articles of incorporation.

THE NATURE AND PURPOSE OF THE CORPORATION

- The intended business activities of the corporation must be specified in the articles, and, naturally, they must be lawful. Stating a general corporate purpose (for example, "to engage in lawful business") is usually sufficient to give rise to all of the powers necessary or convenient for the purpose of the organization. There is no need to give specific details of the planned business.

THE DURATION OF THE CORPORATION

- A corporation can have perpetual existence under most state corporation statutes. A few states, however, prescribe a maximum duration, after which the corporation must formally renew its existence.

THE CAPITAL STRUCTURE OF THE CORPORATION

- The capital structure of the corporation may be set forth in the articles. A few state statutes require a small capital investment (for example, $1,000) for ordinary business corporations but a greater capital investment for those engaged in insurance or banking. The number of shares of stock authorized for issuance, their valuation, the various types or classes of stock authorized for issuance, and other relevant information concerning equity, capital, and credit must be outlined in the articles.

THE INTERNAL ORGANIZATION OF THE CORPORATION

- Whatever the internal management structure of the corporation, it should be described in the articles, although it can be included in bylaws adopted after the corporation is formed.

THE REGISTERED OFFICE AND AGENT OF THE CORPORATION

- The corporation must indicate the location and address of its registered office within the state. The registered office is likely the principal office of the corporation. The corporation must give the name and address of a specific person who has been designated as an agent (often the corporate attorney) and who can receive legal documents (including service of process) on behalf of the corporation.

THE NAMES AND ADDRESSES OF THE INCORPORATORS

- Each incorporator must be listed by name and must indicate an address. An incorporator is a person—often the corporate promoter—who applies to the state on behalf of the corporation to obtain its corporate charter. States vary on the required minimum number of incorporators. It can be as few as one or as many as three. Incorporators are required to sign the articles of incorporation when they are submitted to the state. Often, this is their only duty. In some states, they participate in the first organizational meeting of the corporation.

matters, reminding clients of the need to hold corporate board meetings, file papers, and create records.

Professional Corporations.   Lawyers, physicians, accountants, architects, engineers, and other professionals sometimes incorporate as *professional corporations*. We discuss these organizations later in the chapter.

Directors and Officers

Corporations legally separate ownership and control. The shareholders own the corporation, but the directors have legal control. The separation of ownership and control allows shares to be widely dispersed among many shareholders without overly complicating the decision-making arrangement. The articles of incorporation name the initial board of directors, which is appointed by the incorporators. Thereafter, the board of directors is elected by the shareholders. The board holds formal meetings and records the minutes (formal notes of what transpired at the meetings). Each director has one vote, and generally the majority rules unless the articles provide otherwise.

OFFICE TECH AND CYBERSECURITY

CORPORATE DATA SECURITY

The security of electronic corporate records maintained by law firms is a developing issue. You may have read about the Panama Papers, a massive data leak of more than 11.5 million documents and 2.6 terabytes of information from the Panamanian law firm of Mossack Fonseca. An anonymous source provided electronic records to the German newspaper *Süddeutsche Zeitung*, which then shared them with the International Consortium of Investigative Journalists. The papers revealed an extraordinary amount of private information on Mossack Fonseca's clients. While this was an unusually large leak of such information, there have been others involving other law firms and service providers.

While no one knows who leaked the Panama Papers, cybersecurity experts have concluded that the attack on the law firm's data was "dead simple" and the weaknesses of the firm's data policies "appallingly common." It appears that the records were obtained from the firm's servers through outdated versions of the popular WordPress website software. An analysis of the firm's website after the leak showed its WordPress software was three months out of date and another key security program was two years out of date. The problem was simply that the law firm had not updated its software. WordPress had corrected the problem

long before the hack occurred. Moreover, the Web server was not protected by a firewall but was hosted on the same computer network as the company's e-mail.

Experts offer four key takeaways from the Panama Papers leak for protecting electronic client records:

- Update security software regularly.
- Segment your computer systems, isolating e-mail and data from Web pages.
- Test any software or updates in a separate testing environment before installing them on the main system.
- Pay attention to *data lineage,* which refers to who has access to data, where the data are located, and how the data are secured.

The key lesson of the Panama Papers leak for paralegals is to be vigilant in protecting clients' digital records. Just as you would not leave sensitive documents exposed in a coffee shop, you should not expose digital records on the Internet. Talk with your firm's IT department to make sure you understand the procedures it follows to protect confidential information. Small firms without IT departments should hire a consultant to help design a safe system and instruct firm personnel on maintaining proper practices.

Rights and Responsibilities. The directors' rights include the right to participate in board meetings and the right to inspect corporate books and records. The directors' responsibilities to the corporation and its shareholders include declaring and paying a **dividend** (a payment to shareholders representing their share of corporate profits), appointing and removing officers, and making significant policy decisions.

The board of directors appoints the corporate officers who manage the day-to-day operations of the firm. As previously mentioned, the officers are employees of the corporation and are subject to employment contracts. Officers are also agents of the corporation. (We discuss agency later in this chapter.)

Directors and officers have fiduciary duties to the corporation and its shareholder-owners, including the duty of loyalty and the duty to exercise care when conducting corporate business. The duty of loyalty is breached when an officer or director uses corporate funds or confidences for personal gain, such as when an officer discloses a company secret (such as a proposed merger) to an outsider. The duty of care is breached when a director's or an officer's negligence results in harmful consequences for the corporate entity.

Potential Liability. Corporate directors and officers can face criminal penalties for their actions or for the actions of employees under their supervision. In addition, a corporation may be held financially liable for any criminal acts or torts committed by its agents or officers within the course and scope of their employment.

dividend
A distribution of profits to corporate shareholders, paid in proportion to the number of shares held unless an agreement provides otherwise.

The federal Sarbanes-Oxley Act imposes numerous disclosure requirements on corporate directors and officers of publicly held companies. Chief corporate executives—and the lawyers and accountants who work for them—must take legal responsibility for the accuracy of their financial statements and reports or risk severe penalties for violating the act.

Shareholders

Any person who purchases a share in a corporation becomes an owner of the corporation. Through shareholders' meetings, the shareholders play a role in the corporate entity—they elect the directors who control the corporation, and they have a right to vote on some decisions that significantly affect the corporation, such as whether to sell the company. They also have a right to share in corporate profits as defined in the articles, most often based on the number of shares they hold.

Shareholders do not manage the daily affairs of the corporation, nor are they liable for corporate debts or other obligations beyond the amounts of their investments. Shareholders thus have *limited liability*—a key advantage of the corporate form of business.

An Exception to Limited Liability: Piercing the Corporate Veil

On rare occasions, courts may ignore the corporate structure ("pierce the corporate veil") to expose the shareholders to personal liability when it is required to achieve justice. If the managers or owners of a corporation abuse its form, fail to follow the proper formalities, or treat the company's assets as personal assets, a court may be willing to put aside the corporation's legal status and allow creditors to reach the owners' personal assets. Piercing the corporate veil most commonly happens with close corporations.

> **EXAMPLE 18.7** Roger and his wife formed a series of roofing companies, abandoning each company when it ran out of money. Roger and his wife were the only shareholders and directors of the companies. Each time they formed a new roofing business, they used the same corporate address, phone number, and vehicles. Roger's most recent company, Two Dog Roofing, paid out most of its income as "rent" for properties he owned personally and as "salaries" to his wife and himself. Two Dog also bought supplies on credit from Andy's Hardware. When Two Dog became insolvent due to the rent and salary payments, the corporation refused to pay Andy's.

Here, a court will most likely "pierce the corporate veil" of Two Dog and hold Roger and his wife personally liable for the corporate debt to Andy's because they used the corporate entity to commit fraud by paying themselves all income earned.

Corporate Taxation

The corporation as an entity pays income taxes on corporate profits. Then, when the profits are distributed to the shareholders in the form of dividends, the shareholders pay personal income taxes on the income they receive out of the already-taxed profits. This so-called double-taxation feature of the corporate form of business is one of its major disadvantages, because it means that income earned by corporations is more heavily taxed than income earned by partnerships or sole proprietorships.

Some small corporations avoid the double taxation of corporate profits by electing S corporation status under Subchapter S of the Internal Revenue Code. An S corporation, like a partnership, is a "pass-through" entity for tax purposes. This means that the corporation files an information return only, as a partnership does, indicating the S corporation's net profits. The S corporation shareholders declare their shares of the corporation's net income on their personal tax returns and pay taxes on that income.

Types of Stock

Corporations may issue different types of stock, each of which grants the owner a different set of rights. Some stock may carry extra voting rights. This is often used in family corporations to preserve family control. *Preferred stock* has greater rights to receive dividends or payments if the company liquidates compared to *common stock*, which typically carries greater voting rights than preferred stock. Some corporations have different classes of stock, which hold different voting and profit participation rights.

> **EXAMPLE 18.8** Facebook has two classes of stock. Most shareholders own Class A shares, which get one vote per share. Each Class B share, however, gets ten votes. Founder Mark Zuckerberg and a group of company insiders own the B shares. This ownership gives Zuckerberg an estimated 60 percent of the voting power.

Corporate Termination

Like partnership termination, corporate termination involves two steps. The first step, dissolution, extinguishes the legal existence of the corporation. The second step, liquidation, involves the winding up of the corporation's business affairs. After creditors have been paid, all remaining assets are distributed to the shareholders. The secretary of state of the appropriate state is notified that the corporation no longer exists.

Corporations can be terminated at a time specified in the articles of incorporation or by the agreement of the shareholders and the board of directors. In certain circumstances, a court may dissolve a corporation. For example, a corporation may be terminated by law if it fails to meet certain statutory requirements, such as the payment of taxes or annual fees.

liquidation
For corporations, the process by which corporate assets are converted into cash and distributed among creditors and shareholders according to specific rules of preference.

Limited Liability Organizations

Recall that one of the major tax advantages of a partnership is that its income passes through to the partners as personal income. Consequently, partners avoid the double taxation of the corporate form of business. But there is a price to pay for this tax advantage: partners face unlimited personal liability. The partners normally can avoid unlimited personal liability by incorporating their business, because corporate owners (shareholders) have limited liability. But again, there is a price to pay: the double taxation of profits characteristic of the corporate form of business.

As mentioned, one way to achieve both goals—limited liability and single taxation of profits—is to elect S corporation status. Not every business can do so, however. Certain requirements must be met before a corporation can qualify for S corporation status. One requirement is that the corporation must have one hundred or fewer shareholders, thus excluding large firms. Another requirement is that an S corporation may have only one class of stock (meaning that there is little flexibility in how corporate profits are distributed). Additionally, certain entities (such as partnerships) cannot be shareholders in an S corporation.

Several forms of organization have developed to address these problems. They include the limited liability company, the limited liability partnership, and the professional corporation. The use of these business forms has spread quickly because of the advantages they offer to businesspersons.

Limited Liability Companies

The **limited liability company (LLC)** is a hybrid form of business enterprise that combines the pass-through tax benefits of S corporations and partnerships with the limited liability of limited partners and corporate shareholders. Like the limited partnership and the corporation, an LLC must be formed and operated in compliance with state law. To form an LLC, *articles of organization* must be filed with a central state agency,

limited liability company (LLC)
A form of business organization authorized by a state that gives the owners of the business limited liability. Taxes on profits are passed through the business entity to the owners.

usually the secretary of state's office. The business's name must include the words "Limited Liability Company" or the initials "L.L.C."

Advantages of an LLC.   A major advantage of the LLC is that, as indicated, it does not pay taxes as an entity. Rather, as in a partnership, profits are "passed through" the LLC, and taxes are paid personally by the owners of the company, who are called *members* instead of shareholders. Another key advantage is that the liability of members is limited to the amounts of their investments. In an LLC, members are also allowed to participate in management activities, and under some state statutes, the firm's managers need not be members of the LLC.

Yet another advantage is that corporations and partnerships, as well as foreign investors, can be LLC members. Additionally, in contrast to S corporations, there is no limit on the number of members of the LLC. Finally, part of the LLC's attractiveness to businesspersons is the flexibility it offers. The members themselves can decide how to operate the various aspects of the business through a simple document called the *operating agreement*.

Disadvantages of an LLC.   The disadvantages of the LLC are relatively few, so this form of organization has become popular particularly for smaller, privately held companies. Just as Delaware is the premier state for corporate charters, Nevada has become a frequent choice of jurisdiction for LLC formation. Nevada offers special courts to handle LLC disputes, so the judges are LLC experts and tend to handle the disputes rather quickly.

One disadvantage of LLCs is a lack of precedent, making it harder to predict how courts will handle disputes among members. If you are researching the law concerning LLCs, you will likely have to rely more on persuasive precedents from other jurisdictions than you would if you were researching a similar question of corporate law. (See Chapter 5 for a discussion of different types of precedent.)

Limited Liability Partnerships

limited liability partnership (LLP)
A form of business organization authorized by a state that allows professionals to enjoy the tax benefits of a partnership while limiting the joint and several liability of partners.

The **limited liability partnership (LLP)** is similar to the LLC. The difference is that the LLP is designed for professionals, such as attorneys, who normally do business as partners in a partnership. Like LLCs, LLPs must be formed and operated in compliance with state statutes. The appropriate form must be filed with a central state agency, usually the secretary of state, and the business's name must include either "Limited Liability Partnership" or the initials "L.L.P."

The major advantage of the LLP is that it allows a partnership to function as a pass-through entity for tax purposes but limits the personal liability of the partners for partnership tort liability. Although LLP statutes vary from state to state, generally each state statute limits in some way the liability of partners. In most states, it is relatively easy to convert a traditional partnership into an LLP because the firm's basic organizational structure remains the same. Additionally, all of the laws governing partnerships still apply (apart from those modified by the LLP statute). Normally, an LLP statute is simply an amendment to a state's already existing partnership law.

Some states provide for a specific type of limited partnership called a *limited liability limited partnership* (LLLP). In an LLLP, the liability of all partners is limited to the amounts of their investments in the firm.

Professional Corporations

professional corporation (PC)
A corporation formed by professionals, such as attorneys or accountants. Each member of the firm is liable for his or her own malpractice but is generally otherwise protected by limited liability.

Professionals in practice together, such as a group of physicians or lawyers, traditionally formed partnerships or limited partnerships. An alternative to those forms of organization that is used in many states is the **professional corporation (PC)**. While the rules vary from state to state, in general, a PC may only be formed by licensed professionals, such as a group of dentists.

A practicing professional can be held personally liable for malpractice, but the existence of the professional corporation limits the liability of the other members.

> **EXAMPLE 18.9** A group of physicians form and own a PC through which they offer medical services. The physicians share office space and staff. If one physician in the group is found liable for monetary damages due to medical malpractice, the other physicians in the PC are not likely to be personally liable for that judgment. The physician who lost the malpractice suit will be personally liable, but other members of the medical practice will be protected, and the practice can continue in operation.

In general, only the professionals involved in the PC can be owners. In other words, there cannot be outside investors. Only members of the practice can be shareholders in the firm, and all members of the firm must be licensed members of the same profession. So that people who deal with the firm are aware of its legal status, state law requires that the name be followed by the letters "P.C."

The Paralegal and Business Organizations

The discussion in this chapter touches on the many ways in which paralegals benefit from knowledge of business organizations. Because so much legal work has to do with business clients, it is impossible to summarize the diverse tasks involving business organizations that paralegals carry out. (See this chapter's *Featured Contributor* article for further discussion.) The following list, however, will give you an idea of some of the types of work that paralegals frequently perform in this area:

- Reserve a corporate name for an incorporator.
- Draft a partnership agreement.
- Draft the documents necessary to form a limited partnership or limited liability company and file the required papers with the appropriate state office.
- Prepare a limited partnership agreement, LLC operating agreement, or articles of incorporation and file them with the appropriate state office.
- Prepare minutes of corporate meetings and maintain a binder of the meeting minutes.
- Review or prepare documents relating to the sale of corporate securities (stocks and bonds) and assist a supervising attorney in making sure that federal and state requirements relating to the sale of corporate securities are met.
- Assist in the dissolution of a partnership, LLC, corporation, or other entity.
- Assist in litigation relating to a corporation or other form of business.
- Monitor deadlines to ensure regulatory filings are up to date.

Agency Law

The common law of agency involves concepts and principles with which all paralegals should be familiar. An **agency relationship** exists when one party, called the **agent**, agrees to represent or act for another party, called the **principal**. If you are working as a paralegal employee, in essence you are an agent of your employer. Attorneys, because they represent and act for their clients, are agents of those clients. All forms of business organizations involve agents.

Indeed, a business world without agents is hard to imagine. The owner of a large company, for example, could hardly design, produce, and sell all of the company's output. Obviously, other people are appointed to fill in—act as agents—for the owners of businesses—the principals.

agency relationship
A relationship between two persons in which one person (the agent) represents or acts in the place of the other (the principal).

agent
A person who is authorized to act for or in the place of another person (the principal).

principal
In agency law, a person who, by agreement or otherwise, authorizes another person (the agent) to act on the principal's behalf in such a way that the acts of the agent are binding on the principal.

FEATURED CONTRIBUTOR

GOING CORPORATE

Angela Schneeman

BIOGRAPHICAL NOTE

Angela Schneeman is a freelance paralegal and author who specializes in corporate law. She has been a paralegal since 1984, when she received her legal assistant certificate from the University of Minnesota. She also earned her B.S. in business and legal studies from the University of Minnesota. Schneeman has worked as a paralegal for a sole proprietor, law firms, the legal departments of publicly held corporations, and a major accounting firm. She is the author of several textbooks for paralegals, including *The Law of Corporations and Other Business Organizations*, Sixth Edition, and *The Pocket Guide to Legal Ethics*.

If you are contemplating a career as a paralegal, or perhaps desire a new focus in your current paralegal employment, you may want to explore a career as a corporate paralegal. Corporate paralegals may work in-house in a corporation's legal department, or they may work for a law firm and specialize in corporate law.

Paralegals and Corporate Legal Departments

Roughly 20 percent of all paralegals work in-house for corporations. Generally, the paralegals who work in corporate legal departments have relatively high job satisfaction. Often, they receive better-than-average salaries and benefits, work less overtime, and are not subject to the billing requirements imposed on their counterparts in law firms.

Many paralegals who work for law firms, however, will tell you they wouldn't consider trading the fast-paced atmosphere of the

> **"...paralegals who work in corporate legal departments have relatively high job satisfaction."**

law firm for an in-house position. Most corporate paralegals who work in law firms assist one or more attorneys who represent a number of corporate clients and often limited liability companies (LLCs). These paralegals are usually required to work at least forty hours per week and meet established billing requirements. Most corporate paralegals have regular contact with the firm's corporate clients and may meet with them either at the law firm or at the client's office. Typically, these paralegals report that they enjoy the variety of their work and like working for an array of corporate clients.

What You Will Need to Know

Corporate paralegals must be familiar with the business corporation act of the state in which they work and with federal law concerning corporations. Corporate paralegals in law firms that represent

Employees and Independent Contractors

Normally, all employees who deal with third parties are deemed to be agents.

> **EXAMPLE 18.10** A salesperson in a department store is an agent of the store's owner (the principal) and acts on the owner's behalf. Any sale of goods made by the salesperson to a customer in the ordinary course of business is binding on the principal. Similarly, most representations of fact made by the salesperson with respect to the goods sold are binding on the principal.

LLCs and other limited-liability entities must also be familiar with the pertinent state law governing those types of organizations. In addition, paralegals must have an understanding of the procedures of the state office, such as the secretary of state, that creates and regulates corporations and other business organizations.

Duties of Corporate Paralegals

The work of corporate paralegals is diverse, and it's difficult to generalize about their duties. Paralegals who work in law firms are often responsible for maintaining the corporate minute books of all corporate and LLC clients, as well as reviewing those books periodically to make sure annual minutes are prepared and all documents are kept up to date.

In-house paralegals may assist the corporate secretary in keeping the corporate record books up to date for the corporation and any subsidiaries. Corporate paralegals may also perform the following types of duties:

- Draft contracts and corporate documents of all types.
- Assist with incorporation and dissolution of corporations.
- Assist with the formation and dissolution of LLCs and other limited-liability entities.
- Research state and federal law pertaining to corporations and limited-liability entities.
- Assist with mergers and acquisitions.
- Assist with completing and filing periodic reports with the Securities and Exchange Commission and stock exchanges.

Corporate Specialties

Because of the complexities of modern corporate law and transactions, most corporate attorneys and paralegals specialize within this field. One popular corporate paralegal specialty is the area of mergers and acquisitions. Paralegals are essential members of most merger and acquisition teams and are often responsible

> **Because of the complexities of modern corporate law and transactions, most corporate ... paralegals specialize."**

for much of the related due-diligence work. Due-diligence work involves investigating the financial risks of a merger or acquisition. Large transactions can include on-site inspections of facilities and inventory, as well as the review of hundreds of documents such as contracts, real estate titles, and patents.

Paralegals collect, catalogue, and review the documents the other party is required to produce to close the transaction. They may also be responsible for preparing and producing documentation for the other party's review. Merger and acquisition work can require traveling and, at times, working long hours under pressure, but most paralegals who work in this area find it interesting and rewarding. Mergers and acquisitions offer just one example of a specialty for corporate paralegals.

Some other corporate specialty areas include the following:

- Securities
- International law
- Contracts
- Intellectual property
- Labor
- Business litigation

In-house paralegals may specialize in one or more of the following areas:

- Corporate governance
- Litigation
- Contracts
- Subsidiary maintenance
- Shareholder relations

The opportunities for corporate paralegals are vast and varied. If you are interested in beginning a career as a corporate paralegal, chances are there is a position with the right specialty, working conditions, and challenges to suit you.

Agency relationships can also arise between employers and independent contractors (such as real estate agents) who are hired to perform special tasks or services (such as the sale of property). An **independent contractor** is a person who is hired to perform a specific undertaking but who is free to choose how and when to perform the work.

EXAMPLE 18.11 Building contractors and subcontractors are independent contractors because the property owner does not control the details of the acts of these professionals. Similarly, truck drivers who own their equipment and hire themselves out to haul freight for various clients are independent contractors. However, truck drivers who drive company trucks on a regular basis are usually classified as employees.

independent contractor
A person who is hired to perform a specific undertaking but who is free to choose how to perform the work. An independent contractor may or may not be an agent.

Generally, courts look at the degree of control and supervision the employer exercises over the work performed to determine if the individual is an employee or an independent contractor. An independent contractor may or may not be an agent.

Agency Formation

Normally, agency relationships come about voluntarily by agreement of the parties. Although the parties often sign a contract (such as an agreement to list a house for sale with a real estate agent), the agreement need not be in writing.

> *EXAMPLE 18.12* If Deborah asks Lincoln, a gardener, to contract with others to landscape her yard and Lincoln agrees, an agency relationship is created. If Lincoln then contracts with a landscape architect to design Deborah's yard, Deborah, as the principal, is legally bound by that contract.

An agency agreement can also be implied by conduct.

> *EXAMPLE 18.13* Suppose that a hotel allows Dwight to park cars to earn tips, even though Dwight does not have an employment contract there. The hotel's manager tells Dwight when to work and where to park the cars. The hotel's conduct implies that Dwight has authority to act as a parking valet, and Dwight will be considered the hotel's agent for that purpose in case he should carelessly wreck the car of a hotel client.

An agency relationship can also arise if the *principal* causes a third person to reasonably believe that another person is his or her agent, thus creating the *appearance* of an agency that does not in fact exist.

> *EXAMPLE 18.14* Carmen, a sales representative, brings her friend with her to solicit orders from a customer and repeatedly refers to her friend as her assistant. The customer reasonably believes that the friend works with Carmen and later places an order with the friend. Carmen will not be allowed to deny that the friend is her agent.

Similarly, if a principal approves or affirms a contract after the fact—by filling orders placed with a person who was not truly an agent, for example—an agency relationship is created.

Fiduciary Duties

An important concept in agency law is that an agency agreement is a **fiduciary relationship**—one involving a high degree of trust and confidence. Because of this, certain fiduciary duties arise whenever an agency relationship comes into existence. Basically, this means that each party owes the other the duty to act honestly and to pursue faithfully the objective of the agency.

Duties of Agent and Principal

The principal is obligated to cooperate with the agent, provide safe working conditions for the agent, and reimburse the agent for work performed and for any expenses incurred while working on the principal's behalf. The agent, in turn, must perform agency tasks competently and must obey and be loyal to the principal. The duty of loyalty means that the agent's actions must be strictly for the benefit of the principal and must not result in any secret profit for the agent.

> *EXAMPLE 18.15* A real estate agent representing the seller of a house may not tell a prospective buyer that the seller is willing to accept 20 percent less than the asking price and is desperate to sell. The duty of the agent is to obtain the best price possible and follow the instructions of the seller (the principal).

In addition, the agent cannot represent two principals in the same transaction unless both know of the dual capacity and consent to it.

EXAMPLE 18.16 A real estate agent who represents both the seller and a buyer in a transaction must secure a written consent from each to effect the dual agency.

The agent also has a duty to notify the principal of all matters that come to his attention concerning the subject matter of the agency and to render an accounting to the principal of all property and funds received and paid out on behalf of the principal.

Rights of Agent and Principal

Duties also imply rights. In general, the agent has a right corresponding to every duty owed by the principal, and vice versa. When an attorney serves as an agent for a client (the principal), the attorney has a duty of loyalty to the client. The client, therefore, has a right to the attorney's loyalty. If you read through your state's ethical rules governing attorneys, you will find that many of the rules governing attorney-client relationships are rooted in these agency concepts.

Agency Relationships and Third Parties

Agency law also comes into play when disputes arise over who should be liable—the principal, the agent, or both—when an agent either forms a contract with a third party or causes injury to a third party. Generally, the principal is liable only for the authorized actions of the agent. Because the principal frequently has "deeper pockets" than the agent, the injured party usually seeks to hold the principal liable for the loss or damage caused by the agent. An employer, for example, can be expected to have greater resources with which to pay damages than an employee.

Contract Liability

If an agent is not authorized to enter into a contract on behalf of the principal, then normally the principal will not be bound by the contract unless she voluntarily accepts (ratifies) it. An agent may be clearly authorized, either orally or in writing, to form certain contracts. The agent's authority may also be implied by custom—that is, an agent normally has the authority to do whatever is customary or necessary to fulfill the purpose of the agency. A paralegal office manager, for example, has the implied authority to enter into a contract to purchase ordinary office supplies on behalf of the firm because the authority to purchase supplies is necessary to the duties of office manager.

Tort Liability

Obviously, any person, including an agent, is liable for his own torts. Whether a principal can also be held liable for an agent's torts depends largely on whether the agent was an employee and whether the agent was acting within the scope of employment at the time of committing the tort.

Under the doctrine of *respondeat superior*, the principal-employer is liable for harm caused to a third party by an agent-employee *acting within the scope of employment*. The doctrine imposes **vicarious liability** on the employer—that is, liability without regard to the personal fault of the employer—for torts committed by an employee in the course or scope of employment. The theory of *respondeat superior* is similar in this respect to the theory of strict liability covered in Chapter 14.

Courts consider a number of factors in determining whether a particular act occurred within the course and scope of employment. If the employer authorized the act or had reason to know that the employee would do the act in question, if the injury occurred during work hours, or if the employer furnished the means or

respondeat superior
A doctrine in agency law under which a principal-employer may be held liable for the wrongful acts committed by agents or employees acting within the scope of their agency or employment.

vicarious liability
Legal responsibility placed on one person for the acts of another.

tools (for example, a truck or a machine) that caused the injury, that fact would point toward employer liability. In contrast, if the injury occurred after work hours or while the employee was on a "frolic" of her own, having substantially abandoned the employer's business, the employer might not be held responsible. These factors are illustrated in the *Developing Paralegal Skills* feature below.

Liability for Independent Contractors' Torts

Generally, the principal is not liable for physical harm caused to a third person by the negligent act of an independent contractor in the performance of the contract. This is because the employer does not have the right to control the details of an independent contractor's performance. Exceptions to this rule are made in certain situations, however, as when exceptionally hazardous activities are involved or when the employer does in fact exercise a significant degree of control over the contractor's performance.

Employment Law

Whenever a business organization hires an employee, an employment relationship is established. In the United States, employment relationships traditionally were governed primarily by the common law, including, to a great degree, the law of agency,

DEVELOPING PARALEGAL SKILLS

A CASE OF *RESPONDEAT SUPERIOR*

Rosie Ball and her son Steven were driving home from the grocery store one evening. They were slowly making their way down an icy street. As they entered an intersection with a stop sign for oncoming traffic, their car was hit broadside by a driver who went through the stop sign at high speed. Steven sustained a severe head injury that resulted in irreparable brain damage. The driver of the other car, who worked for a large company, had gone out for several drinks after work with other employees before heading home.

Rosie contacted attorney Jared Mills, who is the supervising attorney for paralegal Thom Mintin. After meeting with Rosie, the attorney asked Thom to research the issue of whether the driver's employer could be held liable for the car accident under a theory of *respondeat superior*.

Thom learned that an employer is liable under *respondeat superior* for the negligent acts of an employee if the acts are committed in the scope of employment. The employer may also be liable for an employee's acts if the acts occur while the employee is on a brief "detour" from the employer's work. The employer is not liable, however, if the employee is on a "frolic" and is not engaged in an activity related to the work that he was hired to perform.

Checklist for Determining Liability under the Doctrine of *Respondeat Superior*

- Did the employee's act constitute a tort?
- Did the employee commit the act within the course and scope of employment?
- Was the act committed during work hours or after work hours?
- Did the employer authorize the act or have reason to know that the employee would do the act?
- Did the employer furnish the means by which the injury was inflicted (the car, for example)?
- Was the act committed during a brief detour from the employee's course of employment, or was the employee on a "frolic" of his own when the act occurred?

This hypothetical situation is relatively straightforward, as few employers send their employees out to bars during working hours. Change the facts: What if the employee had just taken pain medication prescribed by a company physician for the side effects of an earlier workplace injury? If the employee had simply stopped to pick up dry cleaning and was not intoxicated? These cases can be quite different in terms of determining liability.

which you read about in the preceding section. Today, though, federal and state statutes regulate the workplace and provide employees with many rights. Common law doctrines continue to apply to areas *not* covered by statutory law.

Because attorneys and paralegals are frequently involved in legal work relating to employment relationships, paralegals should have a basic understanding of employment law. In this section, we look at the common law doctrine governing employment relationships and at some of the ways in which the government regulates today's workplace.

Employment at Will

Traditionally, employment relationships have been governed by the common law doctrine of employment at will, as well as by the common law rules governing contracts, torts, and agency. Under the doctrine of **employment at will**, either party may terminate an employment relationship at any time and for any reason, unless a contract or statute specifically provides otherwise. This continues to be the basic rule in every state except Montana. So most employees still have the legal status of "employees at will."

Nonetheless, there are situations in which the doctrine is not applied. Sometimes, an employment contract limits the circumstances under which an employee can be fired. For example, many college teachers have a contract providing them with "tenure" that restricts the circumstances under which the college can fire them. Even in the absence of an express employment contract, some courts have held that an *implied* contract can exist—for example, when an employee manual states that, as a matter of policy, workers will be dismissed only for "good cause." For this reason, it is often important for a paralegal to read the employee manual when researching an employee's termination.

Also, as mentioned, federal and state statutes governing employment relationships override the at-will doctrine from being applied in a number of circumstances. Today's employer is not permitted to fire an employee if to do so would violate a federal or state employment statute, such as one prohibiting employment termination for discriminatory reasons (to be discussed shortly).

employment at will
A common law doctrine under which employment is considered to be "at will"—either party may terminate the employment relationship at any time and for any reason, unless a contract or statute specifies otherwise.

Restrictive Covenants

Many employers seek to restrict employees' ability to compete with them after the employees leave their job by asking employees to sign a **restrictive covenant** (also known as a *covenant not to compete*). In these agreements, employees agree not to enter into competing businesses or to solicit the employer's customers for a specified period after the end of their employment. Laws vary from state to state, with some states, such as California, refusing to enforce such agreements. States that allow such covenants require that the time limits on the ex-employee be reasonable, usually no more than two years, and be restricted to a geographic scope relevant to the particular profession. Paralegals may be asked to research the law to ensure that an employer's proposed restrictive covenant would be valid in all the states where the employer has employees.

restrictive covenant
An agreement between an employer and employee that the employee will not attempt to compete with the employer for a specified period after employment ends.

Wrongful Discharge

Whenever an employer discharges an employee in violation of an employment contract or a statutory law protecting employees, the employee may bring an action for **wrongful discharge**. For example, most states have a statute prohibiting employers from discharging an employee because the employee has filed a workers' compensation claim (discussed shortly), reported for jury duty, performed some other public duty, or refused to commit an illegal act.

wrongful discharge
An employer's termination of an employee in violation of an employment contract or statutory law.

EXAMPLE 18.17 An employee of a construction company is hit by a falling brick at a construction site. He suffers a serious injury. The employee files a claim for workers' compensation. The employer then fires the employee. The employee can sue for wrongful discharge.

Common Law Principles Apply

Wrongful discharge can also arise from the violation of a common law principle.

EXAMPLE 18.18 Cool Company hired Yvonne to be its representative in Detroit. She was to be paid a 20 percent commission for all business generated during the year. In November, Cool fired Yvonne and did not pay her a commission on business she had generated up to that time. Yvonne can sue for breach of contract and also for wrongful discharge.

Constructive Discharge

Sometimes, employees claim that they were "constructively discharged" from their jobs. **Constructive discharge** occurs when the employer causes the employee's working conditions to be so intolerable that a reasonable person in the employee's position would feel compelled to quit. This issue arises, for example, in some sexual-harassment cases, as we will soon review.

EXAMPLE 18.19 Mindy works for Megathon, Inc. Dustin is her supervisor. He constantly calls Mindy at home and bothers her at the office, insisting she date him. Even though Mindy complains to the human resources department, nothing is done. If Mindy finally quits to protect herself, she may sue Megathon on the grounds of constructive discharge.

constructive discharge
A termination of employment that occurs when the employer causes the employee's working conditions to be so intolerable that a reasonable person in the employee's position would feel compelled to quit.

Retaliatory Discharge

Employers sometimes fire employees in retaliation for making a complaint that the employer has engaged in allegedly discriminatory employment practices, has refused to provide required leave, or has violated health and safety laws. If an employer fires an employee because the employee made such a complaint to a supervisor or to a government regulator, the employer has engaged in *retaliatory discharge*. Similarly, cutting the employee's pay or hours can constitute *retaliation*. Many regulatory statutes prohibit retaliation and retaliatory discharge in any form.

EXAMPLE 18.20 Janice complains to the corporate human resources (HR) department that her manager, Pierre, is discriminating against her because he gives male employees the opportunity for overtime but does not give her the same opportunity. HR investigates but decides that there is no merit to Janice's complaint. Pierre is incensed that she complained about him and cuts her hours by half. Janice likely has a claim for retaliation.

Wage Laws

The Fair Labor Standards Act (FLSA) of 1938 established guidelines regulating overtime pay and minimum hourly wages. The act provided that if in any week a nonmanagerial employee works more than forty hours, the hours in excess of the first forty must be compensated at one and a half times the employee's regular hourly rate. As for the minimum hourly wage, it represents the minimum amount an employer can pay an employee per hour. The federal minimum wage rate, which is set by Congress, is changed periodically.

Many states also have minimum wage laws, which sometimes set higher minimums than exist under federal law (states may not set lower minimum wages than the federal government). Some cities also have their own minimum wage rate. All states also have wage payment statutes that require employers to pay employees promptly and limit what employers can deduct from employees' pay. Violating these statutes can expose employers to statutory penalties as well as damages; in some states, violations also carry criminal penalties.

Family and Medical Leave

The Family and Medical Leave Act (FMLA) allows employees to take time off work for family or medical reasons. Many states have similar laws, which may provide more generous benefits than the federal statute. The FMLA requires employers who have fifty or more employees to provide employees with up to twelve weeks of unpaid family or medical leave during any twelve-month period. During the employee's leave, the employer must continue the worker's health-care coverage and guarantee employment in the same or a comparable position when the employee returns to work. The act does not apply to employees who have worked less than one year or fewer than twenty-five hours a week during the previous twelve months. (This chapter's *Ethics Watch* feature reminds us that we must be careful when discussing FMLA or other laws with clients.)

Leave Rights

Generally, an employee may take family leave to care for a newborn baby, a newly adopted child, or a foster child just placed in the employee's care. An employee may also take medical leave when the employee or the employee's spouse, child, or parent has a "serious health condition" requiring care. For most absences, the employee must demonstrate that the health condition requires continued treatment by a health-care provider and includes a period of incapacity of more than three days. Employees suffering from certain chronic health conditions, such as asthma and diabetes, as well as employees who are pregnant, may take FMLA leave for their own incapacities that require absences of less than three days.

ETHICS WATCH

DISPENSING LEGAL ADVICE

Laura, a paralegal, was interviewing a client who was considering petitioning for bankruptcy. The client's right arm was in a sling. Laura asked him about the injury, and he described how it had happened. He said that he had been unable to work at his job for two weeks and that he was worried because his employer was threatening to fire him if he couldn't return to work within another week or two. Laura said, "I'm wondering how you could be fired, because employers are required by law to give their employees medical leave for up to twelve weeks during any one-year period."

Laura said that she would check with her supervising attorney about that matter, and then she continued the interview about bankruptcy. Thinking about what Laura said, the client later confronted his employer and demanded a twelve-week leave. The employer fired him. The employer had only a few employees and

was not subject to the leave requirements of the Family and Medical Leave Act.

Laura could be considered to have engaged in the unauthorized practice of law by giving legal advice to a client. That would be a violation of the NFPA *Model Code of Ethics and Professional Responsibility,* Section EC-1.8: "A paralegal shall comply with the applicable legal authority governing the unauthorized practice of law in the jurisdiction in which the paralegal practices." It would also violate NALA's *Code of Ethics,* Canon 4: "A paralegal must use discretion and professional judgment commensurate with knowledge and experience but must not render independent legal judgment in place of an attorney."

Remedies for Violation of FMLA

Remedies for violations of the FMLA include:

1. Damages for unpaid wages (or salary), lost benefits, denied compensation, and actual monetary losses (such as the cost of providing for care) up to an amount equivalent to the employee's wages for twelve weeks.

2. Job reinstatement.

3. Promotion.

The successful plaintiff is entitled to court costs, attorneys' fees, and—in cases involving bad faith on the part of the employer—double damages. Supervisors may also be subject to personal liability for violations of the act.

State Workers' Compensation Laws

workers' compensation laws
State statutes that establish an administrative procedure for compensating workers for injuries that arise out of or in the course of their employment, regardless of fault.

State **workers' compensation laws** establish an administrative procedure for compensating workers injured on the job. Instead of suing for costs resulting from the injury, an injured worker files a claim with the administrative agency or board that administers workers' compensation claims. State workers' compensation statutes normally allow employers to buy insurance from a private insurer or a state fund to pay workers' compensation benefits in the event of a claim. Most states also allow employers to be *self-insured*—that is, employers who show an ability to pay claims do not need to buy insurance, but they must provide benefits at the same level as the state-mandated program.

Requirements

The right to recover benefits is based on the existence of an employment relationship and the fact that an injury was *accidental* and *occurred on the job or in the course of employment*, regardless of fault. Intentionally inflicted self-injury, in contrast, would not be accidental and hence would not be covered. If an injury occurred while an employee was commuting to or from work, it usually would not be considered to have occurred on the job and hence would not be covered. Difficult cases involve employees who run personal errands while on the employer's business. If an employee on such an errand is injured while driving the employer's truck, the requirement for coverage by the employer varies by state.

The employee must notify the employer promptly of an injury (usually within thirty days of the injury's occurrence). Generally, the employee also must file a workers' compensation claim with the appropriate state agency or board within a certain period (sixty days to two years) from the time the injury is first noticed, rather than from the time of the accident. Employers may not retaliate against workers who file claims.

No Right to Sue

The existence of workers' compensation benefits bars the employee from suing for injuries caused by the employer's negligence.

EXAMPLE 18.21 Jim is hit by a falling brick while working at a construction site. He contacts an attorney who advises him that in his state, workers' compensation benefits will likely total about $200,000, given the nature of the injury. Jim wants to reject those benefits and sue his employer, the construction site operator, for more. That is not an option. Workers' compensation benefits are his exclusive remedy.

By barring lawsuits for negligence, workers' compensation laws also prevent employers from raising common law defenses to negligence. An employer cannot raise defenses such as contributory negligence or assumption of risk (see Chapter 14) to avoid liability for negligence. A worker may sue an employer who *intentionally* injures the worker, but such cases are not common. The *Developing Paralegal Skills* feature below reviews some procedures for workers' compensation claims.

Employment Discrimination

Federal and state laws prohibiting employment discrimination are key features of today's employment landscape. Some state and local laws protect employees to a greater extent than do federal laws. Some cities also ban appearance-based discrimination. The major federal laws prohibiting employment discrimination are the following:

- Title VII of the Civil Rights Act of 1964 (prohibits discrimination based on race, color, national origin, religion, and sex—including pregnancy, sexual orientation, and gender identity).

- The Age Discrimination in Employment Act of 1967 (prohibits discrimination based on age).

- The Americans with Disabilities Act of 1990 (prohibits discrimination based on disability).

DEVELOPING PARALEGAL SKILLS

ASSISTING WITH A WORKERS' COMPENSATION CLAIM

Calloway, an employee of GearHead Outlet, was on a ladder arranging tools when a box fell and knocked him to the floor. His wrist was broken in three places. Calloway submitted a workers' compensation claim to GearHead's human relations department two days after the incident. When the cast was removed, his physician prescribed physical therapy to alleviate the pain he experienced and to restore function to the wrist. GearHead's insurance provider, Delacroix Mutual, sent Calloway to another physician, who prescribed pain medication and declared the physical therapy unnecessary. Calloway's wrist continued to be in pain.

Two weeks later, Calloway contacted the law firm of Shapiro and Masters, which specializes in workers' compensation litigation. Attorney Melanie Shapiro conducted an initial interview with Calloway and accepted Calloway's case. After the interview, Shapiro asked paralegal Geena Tulane to gather evidence and prepare for a hearing before a workers' compensation judge.

Checklist for a Workers' Compensation Claim

- Review the employer's workers' compensation insurance policy with the attorney to clarify coverage terms.
- Collect all medical records and compensation claim forms from the client or employer.

- Assemble evidence regarding the medical condition the client has as a result of the work-related injury or illness. If possible, photograph the scene where the injury occurred, as well as any visible injuries that may assist in proving the claim. Gather statements from any witnesses.

- Check with state insurance regulators for a record of prior complaints against the insurer.

- Compile an estimate of all medical costs. Call the offices of the physicians to whom the client has been referred for treatment of the injury or illness to inquire about their fees for specific treatments.

- Keep a log of all communications with the insurer, including e-mails and recorded phone messages. Document when the claim was submitted to the insurer, how and when the insurer responded, what the insurer asked for, and what was provided.

- Draft a request for a workers' compensation hearing with the state commission or court responsible for settling workers' compensation claims.

- Before submitting claim information for the hearing, compile the information in a coherent, organized presentation. A well-documented claim is more likely to be successful.

Employment discrimination laws are enforced by the federal Equal Employment Opportunity Commission (EEOC), state employment opportunity agencies, and lawsuits brought by private parties. Typically, an employment discrimination complaint begins when an individual files an administrative complaint with the EEOC or equivalent state agency. After the agency has had a chance to investigate, it may seek to enforce the law or issue a "right to sue" letter to the individual filing the complaint, who can then file suit. The EEOC and state agencies frequently issue guidance documents explaining how they interpret the law. If you work in this area, you will want to keep up to date on the various agencies' views by reading these guidance documents.

Title VII of the Civil Rights Act of 1964

The most significant federal law prohibiting discrimination is the Civil Rights Act of 1964. One section of the act, Title VII, pertains to employment practices. Title VII prohibits employers with fifteen or more full-time employees from discriminating against employees or potential employees on the basis of race, color, national origin, religion, or sex.

In 1978, the Pregnancy Discrimination Act amended Title VII to expand the definition of sex-based discrimination to include discrimination based on pregnancy. In 2020, following the *Bostock v. Clayton County* Supreme Court decision discrimination in employment based on sexual orientation or gender identity is also a violation of Title VII. Cities and states may extend protections beyond those imposed by federal law.

Title VII has been interpreted by the courts to prohibit both intentional and unintentional discrimination. The latter occurs when certain employer practices or procedures have a discriminatory effect, even though they were not intended to be discriminatory. Courts call this "disparate impact" discrimination.

> **EXAMPLE 18.22** A city requires all firefighters to be at least six feet tall. In effect, that requirement discriminates against women, because few women are that tall. The effect of the rule is discriminatory, even though the intent in adopting the rule might have been to ensure an able-bodied firefighting crew. A proper test of physical ability for firefighters would be appropriate; height alone is not.

Job qualifications should focus on ability to perform job duties, not measures that can be discriminatory.

Sexual Harassment.   The courts have also extended Title VII protection to those who are subject to **sexual harassment** in the workplace. There are two types of sexual harassment. *Quid pro quo harassment* occurs when an employment superior gives awards (promotions, raises, benefits, or other advantages) to a subordinate in exchange for sexual favors. (*Quid pro quo*, a Latin term, means "this for that" or "something for something.")

In contrast, *hostile-environment harassment* occurs when an employee is subjected to offensive sexual comments, jokes, or physical contact in the workplace that make it difficult or impossible for the employee to perform a job satisfactorily. This generally requires that the harasser target employees of a particular sex rather than all employees. A supervisor who makes off-color jokes to male and female employees alike is poorly behaved and rude but is not likely to be engaged in sexual harassment. A supervisor who tells such "jokes" only to employees of one sex, however, is more likely to have engaged in sexual harassment.

Liability for Harassment.   Generally, under the doctrine of *respondeat superior* (discussed earlier), an employer may be held responsible (liable) for the conduct of certain employees, such as managers and supervisors. In a sexual-harassment case, if an

sexual harassment
In employment, (1) the hiring or granting of job promotions or other benefits in return for sexual favors (*quid pro quo* harassment) or (2) language or conduct that is so sexually offensive that it creates a hostile working environment (hostile-environment harassment).

employee in a supervisory position did the harassing, the employer will usually be held liable *automatically* for the behavior. Under the Supreme Court's decision in *Faragher v. City of Boca Raton*, however, employers can avoid liability for sexual harassment if they can show "(a) that the employer exercised reasonable care to prevent and correct promptly any sexually harassing behavior, and (b) that the plaintiff employee unreasonably failed to take advantage of any preventive or corrective opportunities provided by the employer or to avoid harm otherwise."

What Did the Employer Know?   If the person who did the harassing was not a supervisor but a co-worker, the employer will be held liable if the employer knew, or should have known, about the harassment and failed to take corrective action.

> **EXAMPLE 18.23** Elena was sexually harassed by a co-worker and complained to her supervisor several times, but nothing was done. If Elena later sued her employer for a Title VII violation, the employer could be held liable because the supervisor did not take steps to deal properly with the complaint.

An employer may even be held liable at times for the actions of nonemployees (customers or clients, for example) if the employer knew about the harassment and let it continue.

Note that Title VII prohibits not only sexual harassment but also the harassment of any employee on the basis of race, color, national origin, religion, or age. In other words, racial or ethnic slurs against an employee may give rise to a hostile work environment claim under Title VII, just as sexually offensive comments would.

Employers' Liability under Title VII.   An employer's liability under Title VII can be considerable. In general, the court can order injunctive relief against the employer (a judicial order to prevent future discrimination), retroactive promotions that were wrongfully withheld from the employee, and past wages to compensate the employee for any time he or she was wrongfully unemployed. Punitive damages are also available in cases involving *intentional* discrimination.

Discrimination Based on Age

The Age Discrimination in Employment Act (ADEA) prevents employers from discriminating against workers who are forty years of age or older on the basis of their age. For the ADEA to apply, an employer must have twenty or more employees. Procedurally, discrimination suits brought under the act are similar to suits brought under Title VII, and similar remedies are available.

Discrimination Based on Disability

The Americans with Disabilities Act (ADA) prohibits discrimination in the workplace against individuals with disabilities. Employers with fifteen or more employees are obligated to satisfy the requirements of the ADA. As defined by the ADA, disabilities include heart disease, cancer, blindness, paralysis, acquired immune deficiency syndrome (AIDS), serious emotional illnesses, and learning disabilities, among others. Conditions that interfere with one or more major life activities are considered disabilities under the law.

Reasonable Accommodation.   Under the ADA, an employer is not permitted to discriminate against a person with a disability if *reasonable accommodations* can be provided to assist the worker in satisfactorily performing the job. The employer must engage in an interactive process with the employee to determine if such an accommodation is possible.

> *EXAMPLE 18.24* Garrett must use a wheelchair as a result of spinal damage suffered in an auto accident. He cannot use a standard-issue computer desk because it is too high for him. Garrett's employer must provide him with a lower desk as a reasonable accommodation.

Hardship.   An employer is not required to accommodate a worker with a disability if the accommodation would constitute an undue hardship for the employer. If the cost of accommodating the employee is extremely high, the cost might constitute an undue hardship.

> *EXAMPLE 18.25* As the result of a neuromuscular disease, Aisha cannot lift more than five pounds. She applies for a job as a package handler at UPS. The company is not obligated to reorganize its method of package sorting so that only light packages would be directed to her. The cost of that accommodation would be very high.

Although enforcement of the ADA falls within the jurisdiction of the EEOC, the worker alleging discrimination in violation of the ADA may also file a civil lawsuit against the employer for violation of the act.

Religious Discrimination

Title VII bans discrimination based on religion. As the ADA does with disabilities, it requires employers to provide reasonable accommodations for employees when their religious beliefs conflict with their job duties, unless doing so would cause undue hardship for the employers. For example, providing flexible scheduling and voluntary shift substitutions to allow attendance at religious services would usually be a reasonable accommodation. Exempting an employee from working on weekends would not be.

> *EXAMPLE 18.26* Isaac wears a yarmulke (skullcap) as part of his expression of his Judaism. Isaac's employer has a "no hats in the workplace" policy. Refusing to allow Isaac to wear his yarmulke at work likely violates Title VII.

Employment Law and the Paralegal

As a legal professional, you may be involved in tasks relating to employment law. You may work in the corporate counsel's office of a large corporate enterprise, for example. As a paralegal in a law firm or a government agency, you might assist in work relating to claims of employment discrimination, which might require you to interact with the EEOC or a relevant state agency. Here are a few tasks that paralegals commonly undertake in the area of labor and employment law:

- Draft employment contracts for an employer.
- Assist in drafting an employee handbook.
- Prepare for and attend administrative hearings before a worker's compensation agency.
- Gather factual information to counter or support a claim for unemployment insurance.
- Prepare reports and furnish documentation in response to an EEOC investigation into an employee's claim of employment discrimination.
- Draft a policy manual for a business client concerning what actions constitute discriminatory employment practices.
- Research the EEOC's guidelines on sexual harassment and relevant case law to determine what types of policies and procedures will help a client avoid liability for sexual harassment.

- Prepare notices regarding a firm's employment policies.
- Assist in litigation involving multiple plaintiffs who are suing the same employer.

As a paralegal, you are also an employee and so are protected by many of the laws discussed in this chapter. If your supervisors engage in sexual harassment or make disparaging remarks based on race or another protected characteristic, you may have a claim that needs to be considered.

CHAPTER SUMMARY

BUSINESS ORGANIZATIONS AND EMPLOYMENT LAW

Forms of Business Organization

1. *Sole proprietorships*—This is the simplest form of business organization. Anyone who does business without creating a separate business entity is a sole proprietor. The owner is the business, even though he or she may hire employees to run the business.

   a. The owner is personally liable for all business debts and obligations.

   b. The owner pays personal income taxes on all profits.

   c. The proprietorship terminates on the death of the sole proprietor or the sale or transfer of the business.

2. *Partnerships*—Created by the written or oral agreement of the parties to do business jointly as partners. All partners share equally in management unless otherwise provided for in the partnership agreement. The partners may hire employees to assist them in running the business.

   a. Partners are personally liable for partnership debts and obligations.

   b. The partnership as an entity does not pay income taxes but files an informational tax return with the Internal Revenue Service each year. Each partner pays personal income tax on his or her share of the profits of the partnership.

   c. Partners have a fiduciary duty that sets a high legal standard for actions related to partnership business. A partnership may be terminated by the agreement of the partners or by the occurrence of certain events, such as the death or bankruptcy of a partner.

   d. A limited partnership is a special form of partnership involving two different types of partners—general partners and limited partners. Only the general partners may participate in management in a limited partnership. The general partners have unlimited personal liability. The liability of limited partners is limited to the amount of their investments.

3. *Corporations*—A corporation is created by a state-issued charter.

   a. The shareholders elect directors, who set policy and appoint officers to manage day-to-day corporate affairs. A corporation may be publicly held with many shareholders or be a close corporation with stock not freely traded.

   b. Shareholders have limited liability and are not personally liable for the debts of the corporation (beyond the amount of their investments).

   c. The corporation pays income tax on net profits; shareholders then pay income tax on profits distributed as dividends.

   d. A corporation may be terminated at the time specified in the articles of incorporation, by agreement of the shareholders and the board of directors, or by court decree.

4. *Limited liability organizations*—Other forms of business organization are the limited liability partnership (LLP), the limited liability company (LLC), and the professional corporation (PC). Generally, these organizations allow business owners to combine the tax advantages of a partnership with the limited liability of limited partners or corporate shareholders.

Agency Law

An agency relationship arises when one person (called the *agent*) agrees to act for or in the place of another person (called the *principal*).

1. *Employees versus independent contractors*— Employees who deal with third parties are normally considered to be agents of their employers.

An independent contractor differs from an employee in that the employer does not control the details of the independent contractor's job performance. The independent contractor may or may not be an agent.

2. *Agency formation*—An agency relationship may be formed by express agreement (oral or written) or implied by conduct. It can also arise if the principal causes a third party to believe the agency existed.

3. *Fiduciary duties*—The parties in an agency are held to certain obligations. The principal must cooperate with the agent, provide safe working conditions for the agent, and reimburse the agent for work performed and for any expenses incurred on the principal's behalf. The agent must perform his or her tasks competently, obey and be loyal to the principal, notify the principal of matters concerning the agency, and render an accounting to the principal of how and for what purpose the principal's funds were used.

4. *Agency relationships and third parties*—The principal normally is bound by any contract formed by the agent on behalf of the principal, as long as the action was authorized. If the action was not authorized, the principal will not be liable unless he or she voluntarily agrees to be bound by (ratifies) the contract. Agents are personally liable for the torts that they commit. If an agent commits a tort within the scope of his or her employment as an agent, the principal may also be held liable under the doctrine of *respondeat superior.* A principal is not generally liable for harm caused by an independent contractor's negligence.

Employment Law

1. *Employment at will*—Traditionally, the employment relationship has been governed by the doctrine of "employment at will"—that is, the relationship can be terminated at any time for any reason by either the employer or the employee—as well as by common law rules relating to contracts, torts, and agency. Most Americans have the legal status of "employees at will," but federal and state statutes prevent the doctrine from being applied in some circumstances.

2. *Restrictive covenants*—Employers may require employees to sign restrictive covenants, in which the employees agree not to enter into competing businesses or to solicit the employer's customers for a specified time after their employment ends. The law varies considerably across states in how such restrictions are viewed.

3. *Wrongful discharge*—Wrongful discharge occurs when an employer discharges an employee in violation of the law or of an employment contract.

4. *Wage laws*—The Fair Labor Standards Act established guidelines regulating overtime pay and minimum hourly wages. Many states also have minimum wage laws, which sometimes set higher minimums than exist under federal law.

5. *Family and medical leave*—The Family and Medical Leave Act of 1993 requires employers with fifty or more employees to provide their employees (except for key employees) with up to twelve weeks of unpaid family or medical leave during any twelve-month period. Generally, an employee may take family leave to care for a newborn baby, a newly adopted child, or a foster child just placed in the employee's care, as well as when the employee or the employee's spouse, child, or parent has a serious health condition requiring care.

6. *State workers' compensation laws*—Every state has an administrative procedure for compensating workers injured on the job.

7. *Employment discrimination*—Both federal and state laws prohibit discrimination against employees in the workplace. State laws sometimes afford greater protection. The major federal laws are:

   a. Title VII of the Civil Rights Act (1964), which prohibits employment discrimination against job applicants and employees on the basis of race, color, national origin, sex, sexual orientation, gender identity, or religion. The courts have interpreted Title VII to prohibit both intentional and unintentional discrimination. Discrimination based on pregnancy is also prohibited, as is sexual harassment.

   b. The Age Discrimination in Employment Act (ADEA) of 1967, which prohibits employment discrimination against employees who are forty years of age or older.

   c. The Americans with Disabilities Act (ADA) of 1990, which prohibits discrimination on the basis of disability against individuals qualified for a given job. Employers must reasonably accommodate the needs of persons with disabilities.

KEY TERMS AND CONCEPTS

agency relationship 553

agent 553

articles of incorporation 545

bylaws 545

certificate of incorporation 545

close corporation 547

constructive discharge 560

director 544

dissolution 543

dividend 549

employment at will 559

fiduciary relationship 556

general partner 544

independent contractor 555

joint and several liability 542

joint liability 542

limited liability company (LLC) 551

limited liability partnership (LLP) 552

limited partner 544

limited partnership 544

liquidation 551

officer 544

principal 553

professional corporation (PC) 552

publicly held corporation 546

respondeat superior 557

restrictive covenant 559

sexual harassment 564

share 544

shareholder 544

vicarious liability 557

winding up 543

workers' compensation laws 562

wrongful discharge 559

QUESTIONS FOR REVIEW

1. List and describe the three traditional forms of business entities. How is each entity created and terminated? Do the owners have personal liability? If so, describe.

2. What is a limited liability company? What advantages does this business organization offer to businesspersons? How does a limited liability company differ from a limited liability partnership?

3. How does an agency relationship arise? What is the difference between an employee and an independent contractor in an agency relationship? When is a principal liable for the contracts formed by an agent? For the torts of the agent?

4. What is a fiduciary obligation? In which relationships discussed in the chapter does a fiduciary obligation arise?

5. Which federal statutes prohibit employment discrimination? What kinds of discrimination are prohibited by these statutes? Which federal agency handles claims of employment discrimination?

ETHICS QUESTION

1. Peter works as a paralegal for a law firm. The firm's client is suing her former employer for wrongful termination of the employment relationship. The client has financial records that prove that her supervisor authorized nondisclosure of income to the Internal Revenue Service. Disclosing these records would seriously affect her supervisor's credibility and would strengthen the client's case. Peter contacts the client to obtain the records. She refuses, fearing the effect it might have on her ability to find another job. Peter's supervising attorney is adamant about the need to obtain these records. The attorney is concerned that the firm might be guilty of malpractice if it fails to introduce this evidence. To whom is Peter obligated, the client or the firm? Why? How should Peter resolve this conflict?

PRACTICE QUESTIONS AND ASSIGNMENTS

1. Identify whether each of the business firms described below is a sole proprietorship, a partnership, or a corporation, and explain why:

   a. Terrence and Lars have owned a business together for three months. Terrence contributed 60 percent of the capital needed to start the business, and Lars contributed the other 40 percent. Each owner is responsible for a proportionate share of the profits and losses of the business, and each owner participates in managing the business.

   b. Four wealthy individuals create a business for the purpose of funding the construction of a new commerce center to revitalize the downtown business district in their city. Each individual contributes 25 percent of the funds necessary for the project, and each individual is liable for only 25 percent of the firm's losses. They all sign an agreement.

   c. Ana Ing, David Goldberg, and Mike Werner are all certified public accountants. They decide to do business together. By the end of its first year, the firm has become very profitable. As a result, the firm has to pay a substantial amount in income taxes on its profits.

   d. Dr. Menendez practices medicine on his own; he has not incorporated his business.

   e. The Pear Co. is a for-profit business that has a charter issued by the state. The charter provides for the limited liability of the company's owners.

2. Michael Sánchez is an attorney who represents Aaron Tubman in his business ventures. Who is the principal, and who is the agent in this relationship? What duties does the principal owe to the agent? What duties does the agent owe to the principal?

3. Explain why the principal is (or is not) liable for the actions of the agent in each of the following situations:

   a. Attorney Arun Singh tells his paralegal, Aki Cho, to purchase litigation software.

   b. Attorney Jayne Sutterly leaves a written memo for her paralegal, David Hayes, instructing David to solicit bids for a computer network for the law firm from three computer consulting firms. David not only obtains three bids but also hires one of the firms to set up the network at a cost of $10,000.

   c. Paralegal Caitlin Bradley works for a sole practitioner and has office management duties in addition to her paralegal responsibilities. When the photocopier no longer functions, she enters into a lease for a new machine without discussing it with her supervising attorney. The cost of the new machine is the same as the cost of the old machine. Would it make any difference if the cost of the new machine were significantly greater than the cost of the old one?

4. Identify what type of employment discrimination, if any, is being practiced in each of the following hypothetical situations:

   a. Lana Ronsky, a female paralegal in an all-male law firm, is the object of frequent sexual jokes and comments and occasional uninvited touching—all of which are offensive to her and make it difficult for her to do her job.

   b. Monica Pierson, a partner in a large law firm, interviews seven potential paralegals, including an Asian American. Although the Asian American is the best qualified for the job, Monica does not hire him because he speaks English with an accent, which might offend some of the firm's clients.

   c. Diana Bekins, the manager of an insurance agency, makes it clear to Jacky McBride, a new sales representative, that she will promote him only if he provides sexual favors in return.

   d. A police department has a rule that only police officers who have been injured on the job may apply for light duty assignments. Six pregnant police officers, out of 150 on the force, were excluded from light duty assignments.

5. Samantha Elauf, a seventeen-year-old Muslim, wore a headscarf, or hijab, to a job interview with Abercrombie, a trendy clothing store for teenagers. During the interview, Ms. Elauf did not specifically request religious accommodation. Abercrombie did not hire Ms. Elauf on the grounds that wearing the scarf violated its "look policy" for members of the sales staff. Was it religious discrimination under Title VII to deny Ms. Elauf a job because she wore a headscarf?

GROUP PROJECT

Students will set up a limited liability company using the hypothetical information below, as well as forms from their state government's website, if one is available. If not, they should consult a state formbook from a law library.

Roberto Hernandez, a fifty-two-year-old mechanical engineer, lost his job. Unable to find similar work, he started a handyman business making repairs on rental properties. Roberto had a friend who owned thirty-eight rental properties and was willing to hire him to make repairs and do remodeling on the properties. Roberto started his business as a sole proprietorship called Roberto's R&R. He has done so well that he needs to hire a couple of carpenters and a painter to work for him. Roberto is concerned about possible liability, so he has consulted your supervising attorney, who has advised Roberto that he should form a single-member limited liability company.

Student one is responsible for finding out if the name Roberto's R&R is available for use. If so, he or she should print (or copy) and prepare the necessary forms to reserve it. If the name is not available, student one should recommend another name.

Student two is responsible for determining if an operating agreement is needed for a single-member limited liability company. If so, student two should do an Internet search to locate such an agreement.

Student three is responsible for learning about the state filing requirements, procedures, fees, and form(s) that Roberto must file to create his LLC, including obtaining the U.S. mail address, e-mail address, or fax number to which the forms should be sent.

Students three and four are responsible for preparing the form(s) located by student three and explaining to the class how a limited liability company is established in your state. In filling out the form(s), the students can use the following information:

- Purpose of the LLC—any legal purpose for which a business may be established in your state.
- Address (if required)—the school's address.
- Name of registered agent (if required)—Roberto's name.
- Duration of the business (if required)—"perpetual" duration, if that designation is allowed under your state's law.

CHAPTER
19

Bankruptcy and Environmental Law

CHAPTER OUTLINE

Introduction

The Bankruptcy Code

Liquidation Proceedings

Individual Repayment Plans

Reorganizations

Environmental Law

CHAPTER OBJECTIVES

After completing this chapter, you be able to:

- State the goals of bankruptcy law, and define the types of relief available for debtors under federal bankruptcy law.

- Summarize the basic procedures involved in an ordinary, or straight, bankruptcy proceeding.

- Summarize the basic procedures involved in an individual payment plan bankruptcy proceeding.

- Describe how bankruptcy law provides relief for corporate debtors and the basic procedures involved in corporate reorganizations.

- List and explain the major laws regulating environmental pollution.

- Discuss the basic purpose and provisions of Superfund.

Introduction

Historically, debtors had few rights. At one time, debtors who could not pay their debts faced harsh consequences, including imprisonment and involuntary servitude. Today, debtors have numerous rights. One of these rights is the right to petition for bankruptcy relief under federal law.

The 2005 Bankruptcy Reform Act is the most recent revision of federal bankruptcy law. The recession of 2008–2009 drove bankruptcy filings to about 1.5 million. Even so, the number of filings represents a great deal of legal work and means that there will continue to be a demand for paralegals in bankruptcy law.

In this chapter, you will read about the different types of relief offered under federal bankruptcy law and about the basic bankruptcy procedures required for specific types of relief. You will also learn about the major laws regulating environmental pollution. Although bankruptcy and environmental law are quite distinct areas of law, both are based largely on federal legislation and are areas in which paralegals may specialize.

The Bankruptcy Code

Bankruptcy relief is provided under federal law. Although state laws play some role in bankruptcy, particularly laws concerning property protection, the governing law is based on federal legislation, as required by the Constitution, and bankruptcy proceedings take place in federal courts.

Bankruptcy law comes from a statute called the Bankruptcy Code, or more simply, the Code. In 2005, Congress enacted the Bankruptcy Reform Act in a major revision of the Code. Paralegals may be involved in assisting individuals or firms with filing for bankruptcy to seek relief from their debts under the Code. Alternatively, they may help represent clients who are owed money by a debtor that has filed for bankruptcy. Some paralegals work for bankruptcy courts or for U.S. Trustee offices that help monitor and recover assets in bankruptcy cases.

Goals of Bankruptcy Law

Bankruptcy law has two main goals. The first is to provide relief and protection to debtors who have "gotten in over their heads." The second is to provide a fair means of distributing debtors' assets among the creditors. Thus, the law attempts to balance the rights of debtors and creditors.

Although the twin goals of bankruptcy remain the same, the balance between them has shifted over time. One of the major goals of the 2005 reform legislation was to require more consumers to pay more of their debts and have less debt fully extinguished in bankruptcy than before. Nonetheless, debtors remain able to discharge their debts while retaining their *exempt property*. That is, state law allows bankruptcy filers to keep certain property while they make a fresh start.

Bankruptcy Courts

Bankruptcy proceedings are held in federal bankruptcy courts, which are courts of limited jurisdiction under the authority of U.S. district courts. Rulings from bankruptcy courts can be appealed to the district courts, although in a minority of cases appeals go to a Bankruptcy Appellate Panel composed of three bankruptcy judges. A bankruptcy court fulfills the role of an administrative court for the federal district court concerning matters in bankruptcy. The bankruptcy court holds the proceedings required to administer the estate of the debtor in bankruptcy. Bankruptcy court judges are appointed for terms of fourteen years by the court of appeals in the circuit in which they will sit.

Depending on vacancies, there usually are 350 to 400 bankruptcy court judges. There is at least one such judge in each of the ninety-four federal districts.

A bankruptcy court can conduct a jury trial if the appropriate district court has authorized it and the parties to the bankruptcy consent, but that is not common. Bankruptcy courts follow the Federal Rules of Bankruptcy Procedure rather than the Federal Rules of Civil Procedure (see Chapter 10).

Types of Bankruptcy Relief

The Bankruptcy Code is contained in Title 11 of the *United States Code* (U.S.C.) and has eight chapters. Chapters 1, 3, and 5 of the Code include general definitional provisions and provisions governing case administration, creditors, the debtor, and the estate. These three chapters apply generally to all kinds of bankruptcies. Three chapters of the Code set forth the most important types of relief that debtors can seek:

- Chapter 7 provides for **liquidation** proceedings, in which all the debtor's nonexempt assets are sold and the proceeds distributed to creditors.

- Chapter 11 governs reorganizations and is mostly used by businesses.

- Chapter 13 provides for the adjustment of debts by persons with regular incomes.

In the following pages, we look at the specific type of bankruptcy relief provided under all three chapters. Note that the Code requires that a **consumer-debtor** (defined as a person whose debts are primarily consumer debts) be informed of the types of relief available. The clerk of the court must give all consumer-debtors written notice of the general purpose, benefits, and costs of each chapter under which they might proceed. In addition, the clerk must provide consumer-debtors with information on the types of services available from credit counseling agencies. In practice, an attorney, not a court clerk, handles these steps.

Liquidation Proceedings

Liquidation under Chapter 7 of the Bankruptcy Code is probably the most familiar type of bankruptcy proceeding and is often referred to as *ordinary*, or *straight*, bankruptcy. Put simply, a debtor in a liquidation bankruptcy states his or her debts and turns all assets over to be controlled by a **bankruptcy trustee**. The trustee sells the nonexempt assets and distributes the proceeds to creditors (the trustee's role will be discussed in more detail later in this chapter). With certain exceptions, the remaining debts are then **discharged** (extinguished), and the debtor is relieved of the obligation to pay the debts.

Any "person"—defined as including individuals and business entities—may be a debtor in a liquidation proceeding. A married couple may file jointly under a single petition. Insurance companies, banks, savings and loan associations, investment companies licensed by the Small Business Administration, and credit unions *cannot* be debtors in a liquidation bankruptcy. Rather, other chapters of the Bankruptcy Code or federal or state statutes apply to them.

A straight bankruptcy can be commenced by the filing of either a voluntary or an involuntary **petition in bankruptcy**—the document that is filed with a bankruptcy court to initiate bankruptcy proceedings. If a debtor files the petition, it is a *voluntary bankruptcy*. If one or more creditors file a petition to force the debtor into bankruptcy, it is an *involuntary bankruptcy*. We discuss both types of bankruptcy proceedings under Chapter 7 in the following subsections.

---

liquidation

A proceeding under Chapter 7 of the Bankruptcy Code (often referred to as *ordinary*, or *straight*, bankruptcy) in which a debtor lists his or her debts and turns all assets over to a trustee, who sells (liquidates) the nonexempt assets and distributes the proceeds to creditors. The remaining debts are then normally discharged, and the debtor is relieved of the obligation to pay the debts.

consumer-debtor

A debtor whose debts are primarily consumer debts—that is, debts for purchases that are primarily for household or personal use.

bankruptcy trustee

A person appointed by the bankruptcy court to administer the debtor's estate in the interests of both the debtor and the creditors. The basic duty of the bankruptcy trustee is to collect and reduce to cash the estate in property and to close up the estate as is compatible with the best legal interests of the parties.

discharged

Terminated, or extinguished. A discharge in bankruptcy terminates the debtor's obligation to pay the debts discharged by the court.

petition in bankruptcy

An application to a bankruptcy court for relief in bankruptcy; a filing for bankruptcy. The forms required for a petition in bankruptcy must be completed accurately, sworn to under oath, and signed by the debtor.

Voluntary Bankruptcy

To bring a voluntary petition in bankruptcy, a debtor files official forms designated for that purpose in the bankruptcy court. Before debtors can file a petition, they must receive *credit counseling* from an approved nonprofit agency within the 180-day period before the date of filing. Debtors filing a Chapter 7 petition must include a certificate proving that they have received individual or group credit counseling as required. One of your tasks as a paralegal may be to assist a debtor in locating and completing the required credit-counseling course (which may be online).

The Code requires consumer-debtors who have opted for liquidation bankruptcy proceedings to confirm the accuracy of the petition in bankruptcy that they have filed. They must state in the petition, at the time of filing, that they understand the relief available under other chapters of the Code and have chosen to proceed under Chapter 7. Attorneys representing consumer-debtors must file an affidavit stating that they have informed the debtors of the relief available under each chapter of the Bankruptcy Code. In addition, attorneys must reasonably attempt to verify the accuracy of consumer-debtors' petitions and schedules (described next).

Chapter 7 Schedules

The voluntary petition must contain the following schedules:

1. A list of secured and unsecured creditors, their addresses, and the amount of debt owed to each. A **secured creditor** is one who has a security interest in the collateral that secures the debt. For example, a lending institution that finances an automobile normally takes a security interest in the vehicle—the collateral for the loan. The borrower agrees, by contract, that the lender has the right to take the property financed by the loan in case payment is not made.

2. A statement of the financial affairs of the debtor.

3. A list of all property owned by the debtor, including property that the debtor claims is exempt.

4. A listing of current income and expenses.

5. A certificate from an approved credit-counseling agency.

6. Proof of payments received from employers within sixty days prior to the filing of the petition.

7. A statement of the amount of monthly income, itemized to show how the amount is calculated.

8. A copy of the debtor's federal income tax return (or a transcript of the return) for the year ending immediately before the filing of the petition.

The official forms must be completed accurately, sworn to under oath, and signed by the debtor. To conceal assets or knowingly supply false information on these schedules is a federal crime.

Most likely, the debtor will be required to file a tax return at the end of each tax year while the case is pending and provide a copy to the court. A request for a copy of the debtor's tax return may be made by the court, the **U.S. trustee**, or any party with a valid interest in the proceedings (such as a creditor). This requirement also applies to Chapter 11 and 13 bankruptcies (discussed later in this chapter). If you search online for "U.S. Trustee Program," you will see extensive discussions of the trustee's role on the U.S. Department of Justice website.

secured creditor
A lender, seller, or any other person who has a security interest.

U.S. trustee
A government official who performs administrative tasks that a bankruptcy judge would otherwise have to perform.

A paralegal meets with a couple filing for bankruptcy. What are some of the tasks that this paralegal must undertake to help this couple complete their filing?

Andrey_Popow/Shutterstock.com.

Means Test

A major focus of the bankruptcy proceeding is the *means test*. The purpose of the test is to keep upper-income people from abusing the bankruptcy process by filing for Chapter 7, as was thought to have happened in the past. The test forces more people to file for Chapter 13 bankruptcy (discussed later), rather than allow liquidation of debts.

Income Above or Below Median?   Debtors must complete the means test to determine whether they qualify for Chapter 7. The key element is the debtor's average monthly income for the past six months, adjusted for family size, compared with the median income in the geographical area in which the person lives. (The U.S. Trustee Program provides details on means testing on its website.) If the debtor's income is below the median income for the area in which the debtor lives, the debtor is usually allowed to file for Chapter 7 bankruptcy, as there is no presumption of bankruptcy abuse. (Median household income varies from state to state, from more than $80,000 in some states to about $45,000 in others.)

Allowances.   If the debtor's income is above the median income, then further calculations are made to project the debtor's income and expenses into the future. Recent monthly income is presumed to continue for the next sixty months. From that, the debtor subtracts the living expenses allowed by Internal Revenue Service (IRS) formulas. (The U.S. Trustee Program website also provides these numbers.) The IRS formula includes allowances for:

- Food.
- Clothing.
- Housekeeping supplies.
- Housing (including mortgage payment).
- Personal care products.
- Transportation (including car payment).
- Health care.
- Utilities.
- Other necessary expenses.

If the debtor's estimated future disposable income is more than an amount set annually by the U.S. Trustee Program, then debt abuse is presumed, and the debtor must file for Chapter 13, except in unusual circumstances.

Additional Grounds for Dismissal

A debtor's petition for Chapter 7 relief may be dismissed for abuse or for failing to provide the necessary documents (such as schedules and tax returns) within the specified time. In addition, a motion to dismiss a Chapter 7 filing may be granted in two other situations. First, if the debtor has been convicted of a violent crime, the victim can file a motion to dismiss the voluntary petition. Second, if after filing a petition the debtor fails to pay domestic-support obligations (which include child and spousal support), the court may dismiss the petition.

Order for Relief

If the voluntary petition for bankruptcy is found to be proper, the filing of the petition itself will constitute an **order for relief**. (An order for relief is a court's grant of assistance to a bankruptcy petitioner.) Once a consumer-debtor's voluntary petition has been filed, the clerk of the court or other appointee must give the trustee and creditors notice of the order for relief by mail not more than twenty days after entry of the order.

order for relief
A court's grant of assistance to a complainant.

Involuntary Bankruptcy

An involuntary bankruptcy occurs when the debtor's creditors force the debtor into bankruptcy proceedings. This generally means showing that the debtor has not been making payments owed to creditors. For an involuntary action to be filed, the following requirements must be met: If the debtor has twelve or more creditors, three or more of these creditors having unsecured claims totaling at least a specified amount (currently $16,750) must join in the petition. If a debtor has fewer than twelve creditors, one or more creditors having a claim of at least $16,750 may file.

If the debtor challenges the involuntary petition, a hearing will be held, and the bankruptcy court will enter an order for relief if it finds either of the following:

1. The debtor is not paying debts as they become due.

2. A general receiver, assignee, or custodian took possession of substantially all of the debtor's property within 120 days before the filing of the petition.

If the court grants an order for relief, the debtor will be required to supply the same information in the bankruptcy schedules as in a voluntary bankruptcy.

An involuntary petition should not be used as an everyday debt-collection device, and the Code provides penalties for the filing of frivolous petitions against debtors. Judgment may be granted against the petitioning creditors for the costs and attorneys' fees incurred by the debtor in defending against an involuntary petition that is dismissed by the court. If the petition is filed in bad faith, damages can be awarded for injury to the debtor's reputation.

Automatic Stay

The moment a petition in bankruptcy—either voluntary or involuntary—is filed, there exists an **automatic stay**, or suspension, of nearly all actions by creditors against the debtor or the debtor's property. In other words, once a petition has been filed, creditors cannot contact the debtor or start any legal proceedings to recover debts or to repossess property. In some circumstances, a creditor may petition the bankruptcy court for relief from the automatic stay, however.

automatic stay
A suspension of all judicial proceedings upon the occurrence of an independent event. Under the Bankruptcy Code, when a petition to initiate bankruptcy proceedings is filed, all litigation or other legal action by creditors against a debtor and the debtor's property is suspended.

All lawsuits against a debtor with a pending bankruptcy filing are stayed, and the plaintiffs must seek permission from the bankruptcy court to allow their claims to proceed. If a client of yours, for example, has sued her former employer for sex discrimination and the employer files for bankruptcy, your client's suit will be stayed (put on hold) until the bankruptcy court gives permission for the suit to continue.

Knowing Violation of the Automatic Stay

The Code provides that if a creditor *knowingly* violates the automatic stay (a willful violation), any party injured, including the debtor, is entitled to recover actual damages, costs, and attorneys' fees and may be entitled to recover punitive damages as well.

Exceptions to the Automatic Stay

There are several exceptions to the automatic stay. An exception is created for domestic-support obligations, which include any obligation owed to a spouse, a former spouse, a child of the debtor, the child's parent or guardian, or a governmental unit. In addition, proceedings against the debtor related to divorce, child custody or visitation, domestic violence, and support enforcement are not stayed.

Also excepted are investigations by a securities regulatory agency, proceedings to establish certain claims against real property (including property taxes), eviction actions on judgments obtained prior to the filing of the petition, and withholding from the debtor's wages for repayment of a retirement account loan.

Bankruptcy Estate

bankruptcy estate
In bankruptcy proceedings, all of the debtor's interests in property currently held and wherever located, as well as interests in certain property to which the debtor becomes entitled within 180 days after filing for bankruptcy.

At the beginning of a liquidation proceeding under Chapter 7, a **bankruptcy estate** (sometimes called an *estate in property*) is created. The estate consists of all the debtor's interests in property currently held, wherever located. Interests in certain property—such as gifts, inheritances, property settlements (divorce), and life insurance death proceeds—to which the debtor becomes entitled *within 180 days after filing* may also be part of the estate.

In contrast, contributions that the debtor has already made to an employee benefit plan, such as a retirement account, are excluded from the estate. Generally, though, the filing of a bankruptcy petition fixes a dividing line: property acquired prior to the filing of the petition becomes property of the estate, and property acquired after the filing remains the debtor's. An important role for paralegals in bankruptcy cases is locating property that should be included in the debtor's bankruptcy estate.

Creditors' Meeting

Within a reasonable time after the order for relief has been granted, the U.S. trustee must call a meeting of the creditors listed in the schedules filed by the debtor. The bankruptcy judge does not attend this meeting. The debtor is required to attend the meeting (unless excused by the court) and to submit to examination under oath by the creditors and the trustee. Failing to appear when required or making false statements under oath may result in the debtor's being denied a discharge in bankruptcy. The trustee ensures that the debtor is aware of the potential consequences of bankruptcy and of the ability to file for bankruptcy under a different chapter of the Bankruptcy Code.

Creditors' Claims

proof of claim
A document filed with a bankruptcy court by a creditor to inform the court of a claim against a debtor's property. The proof of claim lists the creditor's name and address, as well as the amount that the creditor asserts is owed to the creditor by the debtor.

To be entitled to receive a portion of the debtor's estate, each creditor normally files a **proof of claim** with the bankruptcy court clerk within ninety days of the creditors' meeting. The proof of claim lists the creditor's name and address, as well as the amount that the creditor asserts is owed to the creditor by the debtor. A creditor need not file a proof of claim if the debtor's schedules list the creditor's claim as liquidated (exactly determined) and the creditor does not dispute the amount of the claim. A proof of claim is necessary if there is any dispute concerning the claim. The *Developing Paralegal Skills* feature below reviews some steps that may be involved in filing a claim.

Exemptions

As mentioned, the bankruptcy trustee takes control over the debtor's property in a Chapter 7 bankruptcy, but an individual debtor is entitled to exempt (exclude) certain property from the bankruptcy. The Bankruptcy Code exempts (among other things) the following property:

1. Equity in the debtor's residence up to $25,150 (the *homestead exemption*, which will be discussed shortly).

2. Interest in a motor vehicle up to $4,000.

3. Up to $625 each for particular items, in household goods and furnishings, wearing apparel, appliances, books, animals, crops, and musical instruments (the aggregate total of all items is limited to $13,400).

DEVELOPING PARALEGAL SKILLS

PREPARING A PROOF OF CLAIM

Alonzo Smith works as a paralegal for a bankruptcy attorney. Alonzo has been assigned the task of preparing a proof-of-claim form to be filed with the bankruptcy court for a client. The client is Bill Peaslee, a farmer who supplies a number of local restaurants with organic produce. One of Peaslee's customers, Ashleigh Burke (the owner of Greenleaf Restaurant), owes Peaslee nearly $10,000 for orders placed in the previous six months.

Three weeks ago, when attempting to collect the past-due balance from Burke, Peaslee learned that Burke had filed for bankruptcy relief. Peaslee, as a creditor of an individual debtor filing for bankruptcy protection, must file a proof of claim with the bankruptcy court to establish the amount of his claim against Burke. After Alonzo's supervising attorney provides the necessary information, Alonzo turns to his computer.

Checklist for Preparing a Proof-of-Claim Form

- Retrieve the proof-of-claim form from the firm's forms database.
- Key in the client-creditor's name and address.
- Insert the amount that the debtor owes to the client.
- Enter the date, the debtor's name, and other required data.
- Print out the completed form, and proofread it carefully.

- Give the completed form to the supervising attorney to review.
- After the attorney has reviewed the form, make copies of it to send to the court for filing.

Other Considerations

Filling out a proof-of-claim form on the creditor's behalf is just the beginning of the paralegal's job. If you are in this situation, you should put yourself in the debtor's position and think about how you could hide assets from your creditors; then you need to look to see if any of those efforts have been made. Look for suspicious transactions close to the filing for bankruptcy, check for the beneficial owners of any entities to which significant assets were transferred, and, in general, use common sense to look for suspicious activities.

If you suspect there has been an effort to conceal assets, alert your attorney. It may be necessary to bring in a professional asset tracer to look for hidden assets. Such professionals can employ mathematical tools to search for clues. For example, Benford's Law can predict whether numbers are fraudulent (made up) based on the distribution of certain digits. When people invent fraudulent numbers, the numbers often contain patterns that violate Benford's Law. Fraud experts have a wide range of such tools that can be of significant help in an investigation.

4. Interest in jewelry up to $1,700.

5. Any tools of the debtor's trade up to $2,525.

6. Any unmatured life insurance contract owned by the debtor.

7. Employee contributions to a qualified pension plan.

8. Social Security and certain public assistance benefits, alimony and child support, unemployment compensation, disability compensation, certain retirement funds and pensions, and education savings accounts.

9. The right to receive personal-injury and other awards up to $25,150.

The amounts allowed are changed over time, and there are other categories, so you should always check to see the current allowances.

Individual states have the power to pass legislation precluding debtors from using the federal exemptions within the state. State exemptions are usually higher than the federal exemptions listed above and vary among states. (Do an online search for the latest information on exclusions in bankruptcy.) Furthermore, in some states, debtors may use only state, not federal, exemptions. In other states, debtors may choose either the exemptions provided under state law or the federal exemptions. In those states, paralegals often help attorneys determine which exemptions are most advantageous for debtors, given their circumstances.

The Homestead Exemption

homestead exemption
A law permitting the debtor to retain the family home, either in its entirety or up to a specified dollar amount, free from the claims of unsecured creditors or trustees in bankruptcy.

In some states, among them Florida and Texas, the state homestead exemption allows debtors petitioning for bankruptcy to shield unlimited amounts of equity in their homes from creditors. You must check exemption details on a state-by-state basis. The Bankruptcy Code requires the debtor to have lived in the state for two years prior to filing the petition to be able to use the state homestead exemption. In addition, if the homestead was acquired within forty months before the date of filing, the maximum equity that can be exempted is $170,350.

The Bankruptcy Trustee

Promptly after the order for relief in a liquidation proceeding has been entered, the U.S. trustee appoints an interim, or provisional, bankruptcy trustee. The bankruptcy trustee may be a bankruptcy attorney who is not involved in the case. The basic duty of the bankruptcy trustee is to collect and reduce to cash the nonexempt property in the bankruptcy estate. The trustee is held accountable for administering the debtor's estate in the interests of *both* the debtor and the creditors.

Duties for Means Testing

In Chapter 7 cases, the trustee is required to review promptly all materials filed by the debtor. After the first meeting of the creditors, the trustee must file a statement as to whether the case is presumed to be an abuse under the means test. The trustee must provide a copy of this statement to all creditors within five days. Not later than forty days after the first creditors' meeting, the trustee must either file a motion to dismiss the petition (or convert it to a Chapter 13 bankruptcy) or file a statement setting forth the reasons why the motion would not be appropriate.

Trustee's Powers

The trustee has the power to require persons holding the debtor's property at the time the petition is filed to deliver the property to the trustee. To enable the trustee to implement this power, the Code provides that the trustee occupies a position equivalent in rights to that of certain other parties, such as some types of creditors.

In addition, the trustee has specific *powers of avoidance*—that is, the trustee can set aside (avoid) an earlier sale or other transfer of the debtor's property, taking it back as a part of the debtor's estate. These powers include voidable rights available to the debtor, preferences, and fraudulent transfers by the debtor. Each is discussed in more detail below. Additionally, certain statutory liens (creditors' claims against the debtor's property) may be avoided by the trustee.

The debtor shares most of the trustee's avoidance powers. Thus, if the trustee does not take action to enforce one of the rights just mentioned, the debtor in a liquidation bankruptcy can enforce that right.

Voidable Rights.   A trustee steps into the shoes of the debtor. Thus, the trustee can use any reason that a debtor can use to obtain the return of property as well. These grounds include fraud, duress, incapacity, and mutual mistake (discussed in Chapter 15).

Preferences.   A debtor is not permitted to transfer property or to make a payment that favors—or gives a **preference** to—one creditor over others. The trustee is allowed to recover payments made by the debtor to one creditor in preference over another.

To make a recoverable preferential payment, a debtor generally must have transferred property for a preexisting debt within *ninety days* of the filing of the petition in bankruptcy. The transfer must give the creditor more than the creditor would have received as a result of the bankruptcy proceedings.

If a preferred creditor (one who has received a preference) has sold the transferred property to an innocent third party, the trustee cannot recover the property from the innocent party. The creditor, however, generally can be held accountable for the value of the property sold.

Fraudulent Transfers.   The trustee can avoid fraudulent transfers or obligations if they were made within two years of the filing of the petition or if they were made with actual intent to hinder, delay, or defraud a creditor. For example, suppose a debtor who is thinking about petitioning for bankruptcy sells his classic motorcycle, worth at least $20,000, to a friend for $500. The friend agrees that in the future he will "sell" the motorcycle back to the debtor for the same amount of money. This is a fraudulent transfer that the trustee can undo.

Distribution of Property

In the distribution of the debtor's estate in bankruptcy, secured creditors take priority over unsecured creditors. The Code provides that a consumer-debtor, within thirty days of filing a liquidation petition or before the date of the first meeting of the creditors (whichever is first), must file with the clerk a statement of intention with respect to the secured collateral. The statement must indicate whether the debtor will retain the collateral or surrender the collateral to the secured party. Also, if applicable, the debtor must specify whether the collateral will be claimed as exempt property and whether the debtor intends to redeem the property or reaffirm the debt secured by the collateral. The trustee is obligated to enforce the debtor's statement within forty-five days after it is filed.

Distribution to Secured Creditors

If the collateral is surrendered to the secured party, the secured creditor can enforce the security interest either by accepting the property in full satisfaction of the debt or by selling the collateral and using the proceeds to pay off the debt. Thus, the secured party has priority over unsecured parties as to the proceeds from the disposition of the

preference
In bankruptcy proceedings, a property transfer or payment made by the debtor that favors one creditor over other creditors. The bankruptcy trustee is allowed to recover payments made to one creditor in preference over another.

collateral. Should the collateral be insufficient to cover the secured debt owed, the secured creditor becomes an unsecured creditor for the difference.

Distribution to Unsecured Creditors

Bankruptcy law establishes an order of priority for classes of debts owed to unsecured creditors, and they are paid in the order of their priority. Each class of unsecured creditors must be fully paid before the next class is entitled to any of the remaining proceeds. If there are insufficient proceeds to pay fully all the creditors in a class, the proceeds are distributed proportionately to the creditors in the class, and classes lower in priority receive nothing. There are almost never sufficient funds to pay all creditors. The order of priority among classes of unsecured creditors is as follows (some of these classes involve claims against bankrupt businesses):

1. Claims for domestic-support obligations, such as child support and alimony.

2. Administrative expenses, including court costs, trustee fees, and attorneys' fees.

3. In an involuntary bankruptcy, expenses incurred by the debtor in the ordinary course of business.

4. Unpaid wages, salaries, and commissions earned within ninety days of the filing of the petition. The amount is capped for each claimant.

5. Unsecured claims for contributions to be made to employee benefit plans. The amount is capped for each claimant.

6. Consumer deposits given to the debtor before the petition was filed. The amount is capped for each claimant.

7. Certain taxes and penalties due to government units, such as income and property taxes.

8. Claims for death or personal injury resulting from the unlawful operation of a motor vehicle.

9. Claims of general unsecured creditors.

If any amount remains after the priority classes of creditors have been satisfied, it is turned over to the debtor. That is unlikely to happen. If the debtor had sufficient funds to satisfy the debtors, there would likely have been no bankruptcy filing.

Discharge

From the debtor's point of view, the primary purpose of liquidation is to obtain a fresh start through a discharge of debts. Certain debts, however, are not dischargeable in bankruptcy. Also, certain debtors may not qualify to have all debts discharged in bankruptcy. These situations are discussed next.

Exceptions to Discharge

Discharge of a debt may be denied because of the nature of the claim or the conduct of the debtor. Claims that are not dischargeable in a liquidation bankruptcy include the following:

1. Claims for back taxes accruing within two years prior to bankruptcy.

2. Claims for amounts borrowed by the debtor to pay federal taxes or any non-dischargeable taxes.

3. Claims against property or funds obtained by the debtor under false pretenses or by false representations.

4. Claims by creditors who were not notified of the bankruptcy. These claims did not appear on the schedules the debtor was required to file.

5. Claims based on fraud or misuse of funds by the debtor while acting in a fiduciary capacity or claims involving the debtor's embezzlement or larceny.

6. Domestic-support obligations and property settlements as provided for in a separation agreement or divorce decree.

7. Claims for amounts due on a retirement account loan.

8. Claims based on willful or malicious conduct by the debtor toward another or the property of another.

9. Certain government fines and penalties.

10. Certain student loans or obligations to repay funds received as an educational benefit, scholarship, or stipend—unless payment of the loans imposes an undue hardship on the debtor and the debtor's dependents.

11. Consumer debts of more than $500 for luxury goods or services owed to a single creditor incurred within ninety days of the order for relief.

12. Cash advances totaling more than $750 that are extensions of open-ended consumer credit obtained by the debtor within seventy days of the order for relief.

13. Judgments against a debtor as a result of the debtor's operation of a motor vehicle while intoxicated.

14. Fees or assessments arising from property in a homeowners' association, as long as the debtor retains an interest in the property.

15. Failure of the debtor to provide required or requested tax documents.

Objections to Discharge

In addition to the exceptions to discharge just listed, a bankruptcy court may also deny the discharge based on the debtor's conduct. In such a situation, the assets of the debtor are still distributed to the creditors, but the debtor remains liable for the unpaid portion of all claims. Some grounds for the denial of discharge based on the debtor's conduct follow:

1. The debtor's concealment or destruction of property with the intent to defraud a creditor.

2. The debtor's fraudulent concealment or destruction of financial records.

3. The granting of a discharge to the debtor within eight years prior to the petition filing.

4. Failure of the debtor to complete the required credit-counseling course.

5. Proceedings in which the debtor could be found guilty of a felony.

Effect of Discharge

The primary effect of a discharge is to void, or set aside, any judgment on a discharged debt and prohibit any action to collect a discharged debt. A discharge does not affect the liability of a co-debtor.

As this review of bankruptcy procedures makes clear, bankruptcy is a complicated process that requires attention to detail, as further explained in the *Developing Paralegal Skills* feature on the following page.

DEVELOPING PARALEGAL SKILLS

TOOLS NEEDED TO ASSIST BANKRUPTCY CLIENTS

Whether representing debtors or creditors, businesses or individuals, paralegals in bankruptcy practice need a mix of detective, accounting, and legal research skills. At the heart of a bankruptcy practice is the effort to negotiate a resolution of claims that exceed the assets available. In some cases, it takes detective skills to track down hidden assets or find flaws in creditors' accounts. Accounting ability is vital, since paralegals have to review the books and financial statements of debtors to sort out claims.

Negotiations, which are handled by attorneys, resolve most bankruptcy cases, as the creditors recognize that they will have to take less than full payment, and the main issue is how much of a "haircut" (reduced payment) each group will take on its claims.

Representing a debtor in bankruptcy matters often begins by interviewing the client and assembling his or her financial records to determine eligibility for particular forms of bankruptcy relief. The supervising attorney will review the information gathered and recommend the appropriate type of bankruptcy filing to the client.

The paralegal will then assist in drafting the bankruptcy petition, listing all debts and assets. The attorney will provide counseling for the client to ensure that she or he takes full advantage of the various exemptions provided by state and federal laws that protect certain assets (such as a home). Once the petition has been filed, the paralegal often assists in negotiations with creditors to resolve the claims.

Working as a paralegal for a creditor requires similar skills. An important part of the job is ensuring that the debtor applies the proper amount of assets to help pay debts owed to the creditor client.

Individual Repayment Plans

As noted earlier, some debtors who file for bankruptcy may prefer liquidation under Chapter 7, but due to the means test, may be required to file under Chapter 13. Chapter 13 of the Bankruptcy Code provides for "Adjustment of Debts of an Individual with Regular Income." Individuals (not partnerships or corporations) with regular income who owe fixed unsecured debts of less than $340,000 or fixed secured debts of less than $1 million may take advantage of bankruptcy repayment plans. Among those eligible are salaried employees and sole proprietors.

Many small-business debtors have a choice of filing a plan for reorganization (discussed later in this chapter) or for repayment. There are several advantages to repayment plans. One is that they are less expensive and less complicated than reorganization proceedings or liquidation proceedings.

Filing the Petition

A repayment-plan case can be initiated only by the filing of a *voluntary* petition by the debtor. In addition, certain liquidation and reorganization cases may be converted to repayment-plan cases with the consent of the debtor.

Upon the filing of a repayment-plan petition, a trustee, who will make payments under the plan, must be appointed. The automatic stay previously discussed also takes effect. Although the stay applies to all or part of a consumer debt, it does not apply to any business debt incurred by the debtor.

Filing the Plan

Only the debtor may file a repayment plan. This plan may provide either for payment of all obligations in full or, more likely, for payment of lesser amounts. The duration of the payment plan (three or five years) is determined by the debtor's median family income. If the debtor's income is greater than the state median income under the means test (previously discussed), the proposed time for repayment must be five years. The term may not exceed five years.

The Code requires the debtor to make "timely" payments from the debtor's disposable income, and the trustee is required to ensure that the debtor commences the payments. The debtor must begin making payments under the proposed plan within thirty days after the plan has been filed with the court. If the plan has not been confirmed, the trustee is instructed to hold the payments until the plan is confirmed and then distribute them accordingly. If the plan is denied, the trustee will return the payments to the debtor less any costs. Failure of the debtor to make timely payments or to begin payments within the thirty-day period will allow the court to convert the case to a liquidation bankruptcy or to dismiss the petition.

Confirmation of the Plan

After the plan is filed, the court holds a confirmation hearing, at which interested parties may object to the plan. The hearing must be held at least twenty days, but no more than forty-five days, after the meeting of the creditors. Confirmation of the plan is dependent on the debtor's certification that postpetition domestic-support obligations have been paid in full and all pre-petition tax returns have been filed. The court will confirm a plan with respect to each claim of a secured creditor under any of the following circumstances:

1. The secured creditors have accepted the plan.
2. The plan provides that secured creditors retain their claims against the debtor's property until payment is made in full or until the debtor receives a discharge.
3. The debtor surrenders the property securing the claim to the creditors.

Objections to the Plan

Unsecured creditors do not have a vote to confirm a repayment plan, but they can object to it. The court can approve a plan over the objection of the trustee or any unsecured creditor only in the following two situations:

1. When the value of the property to be distributed under the plan is at least equal to the amount of the claims.
2. When all of the debtor's projected disposable income to be received during the plan period will be applied to making payments. Disposable income is all income received *less* amounts needed to pay domestic-support obligations and/or amounts needed to meet ordinary expenses to continue the operation of a business.

Modification of the Plan

Prior to completion of payments, the plan may be modified at the request of the debtor, the trustee, or an unsecured creditor. If any interested party objects to the modification, the court must hold a hearing to determine approval or disapproval of the modified plan.

Discharge

After the completion of all payments, the court grants a discharge of the debts provided for by the repayment plan. Not all debts are dischargeable, however. Nondischargeable debts in a Chapter 13 bankruptcy include:

- Allowed claims not provided for by the plan.
- Certain long-term debts provided for by the plan.
- Claims for domestic-support obligations.
- Payments on retirement accounts.

- Debts for trust fund taxes or taxes for which returns were never filed or filed late (within two years of the bankruptcy filing).

- Student loans.

- Injury or property damage obligations arising from driving under the influence of alcohol or drugs.

- Debts arising from fraudulent tax obligations.

- Criminal fines and restitution.

- Debts arising from fraud by a person acting in a fiduciary capacity.

- Restitution payments due for willfully and maliciously causing personal injury or death.

If the debtor does not complete the plan, a hardship discharge may be granted if failure to complete the plan was due to circumstances beyond the debtor's control and if the value of the property distributed under the plan was greater than creditors would have received in a liquidation proceeding. A discharge can be revoked within one year if it was obtained by fraud.

Reorganizations

reorganization

A form of corporate bankruptcy under Chapter 11 of the Bankruptcy Code that allows the debtor and creditors to execute a plan enabling the debtor business to remain in operation in the hope of generating enough revenue over time to repay debts.

A type of bankruptcy proceedings often used by corporate debtors is the Chapter 11 **reorganization**. In a reorganization, the creditors and the debtor formulate a plan under which the debtor pays a portion of the debts and is discharged of the remainder. The debtor is allowed to continue in business. Although this type of bankruptcy is commonly a corporate reorganization, any debtor (except a stockbroker or a commodities broker) who is eligible for Chapter 7 relief is eligible for relief under Chapter 11. Railroads are also eligible. There is a "fast-track" Chapter 11 procedure for small-business debtors whose liabilities do not exceed $2 million and who do not own or manage real estate. This procedure does not require the appointment of committees and can save time and costs.

The same principles that govern the filing of a liquidation (Chapter 7) petition apply to reorganization proceedings. The case may be brought either voluntarily or involuntarily. The same principles govern the entry of the order for relief. The automatic-stay provision is also applicable in reorganizations. An exception from the automatic stay is triggered in the event that the debtor files for bankruptcy again within two years, and new grounds for dismissal (such as substantial abuse) or conversion of the case are established.

Workouts

workout

An out-of-court negotiation in which a debtor enters into an agreement with a creditor or creditors for a payment or plan to discharge the debtor's debt.

In some instances, to avoid bankruptcy proceedings, creditors may prefer a private, negotiated adjustment known as a **workout**. Often, out-of-court workouts are much more flexible and more conducive to a speedy settlement. Speed is critical, because delay is one of the most costly elements in a bankruptcy proceeding. Another advantage of workouts is that they avoid the administrative costs of bankruptcy proceedings.

Best Interests of the Creditors

After a petition for Chapter 11 bankruptcy has been filed, a bankruptcy court, after notice and a hearing, may dismiss or suspend all proceedings at any time if that would better serve the interests of the creditors. The Code also allows a court, after notice and a hearing, to dismiss a case under reorganization "for cause." Cause includes the absence of a reasonable likelihood of rehabilitation, the inability to effect a plan, and an unreasonable delay by the debtor that may harm the interests of creditors.

Debtor in Possession

On entry of the order for relief, the debtor generally continues to operate the business as a **debtor in possession (DIP)**. The court, however, may appoint a trustee (often referred to as a *receiver*) to operate the debtor's business if mismanagement of the business is shown or if appointing a trustee is in the best interests of the estate.

The DIP's role is similar to that of a trustee in liquidation proceedings. The DIP is entitled to avoid preferential payments made to creditors and fraudulent transfers of assets that occurred prior to the filing of the Chapter 11 petition. The DIP has the power to decide whether to cancel or assume obligations under executory contracts (contracts that have not yet been performed) that were made prior to the filing.

debtor in possession (DIP)
In Chapter 11 bankruptcy proceedings, a debtor who is allowed, for the benefit of all concerned, to maintain possession of the estate in bankruptcy (the business) and to continue business operations.

Creditors' Committees

As soon as practicable after the entry of the order for relief, a creditors' committee of unsecured creditors is appointed. This committee often is composed of the biggest suppliers to the business. The committee may consult with the trustee or the DIP concerning the administration of the case or the formulation of the reorganization plan. Additional creditors' committees may be appointed to represent creditors with special interests. Generally, no orders affecting the estate will be entered without either the consent of the committee or a hearing in which the judge hears the position of the committee.

The Reorganization Plan

A reorganization plan to rehabilitate the debtor is a plan to conserve and administer the debtor's assets in the hope of a return to successful operation and solvency. The plan must be fair and equitable and must do the following:

1. Designate classes of claims and interests.
2. Specify the treatment to be afforded the classes. The plan must provide the same treatment for each claim in a particular class.
3. Provide an adequate means for execution.
4. Provide for payment of tax claims over a five-year period.

Filing the Plan

Only the debtor may file a plan within the first 120 days after the date of the order for relief. This period may be extended, but not beyond eighteen months from the date of the order for relief. If the debtor does not meet the 120-day deadline or obtain an extension, and if the debtor fails to obtain the required creditor consent within 180 days, any party may propose a plan. The plan need not provide for full repayment to unsecured creditors. Instead, creditors receive a percentage of each dollar owed to them by the debtor. If a small-business debtor chooses to avoid creditors' committees, the time for the debtor's filing is 180 days.

Acceptance and Confirmation of the Plan

Once the plan has been developed, it is submitted to each class of creditors for acceptance. For the plan to be adopted, each class that is adversely affected by the plan must accept it. A class has accepted the plan when a majority of the creditors, representing two-thirds of the amount of the total claim, vote to approve it.

Even when all classes of creditors accept the plan, the court may refuse to confirm the plan if it is not "in the best interests of the creditors." This helps to protect the right of minority creditors, who may be pressured to agree by the majority. The plan can also be modified at the request of the debtor, the trustee, the U.S. trustee, or a holder of an unsecured claim. If an unsecured creditor objects to the plan, specific rules apply to the value of property to be distributed under the plan. Tax claims must be paid over a five-year period.

cram-down provision
A provision of the Bankruptcy Code that allows a court to confirm a debtor's Chapter 11 reorganization plan even though only one class of creditors has accepted it. To exercise this provision, the court must demonstrate that the plan does not discriminate unfairly against any creditors and is fair and equitable.

Even if only one class of creditors has accepted the plan, the court may still confirm the plan under the Code's so-called **cram-down provision**. In other words, the court may confirm the plan over the objections of a class of creditors. Before the court can exercise this right of cram-down confirmation, it must be demonstrated that the plan "does not discriminate unfairly" against any creditors and that the plan is "fair and equitable."

Discharge

The plan is binding on confirmation. Confirmation of a plan does not, however, discharge an individual debtor. For individual debtors, execution of the plan must be completed before discharge will be granted, unless the court orders otherwise. For all other debtors, the court may order discharge at any time after the plan is confirmed. The debtor at this time is given a reorganization discharge from all claims not protected under the plan. This discharge does not apply to any claims that would be denied discharge under liquidation.

Bankruptcy Law and the Paralegal

Today, roughly one in every five paralegals spends about half of his or her work time on bankruptcy law. Much of the work previously handled by attorneys can now be done by paralegals with expertise in this area. For example, a debtor-client who wants to petition for bankruptcy relief must provide the court with numerous forms stating in detail the debtor's assets and liabilities. These forms must be filled out accurately, and clients must follow procedures properly. The paralegal can assist in this process.

The specific types of work handled by bankruptcy paralegals vary, of course, depending on whether they work on behalf of the debtor, a creditor, or the bankruptcy trustee. Here are a few examples of paralegal tasks that you might be asked to perform if you were assisting a debtor-client (which could be an individual or a corporate representative) in petitioning for bankruptcy relief:

- Conduct an intake interview—and follow-up interviews as necessary—to obtain information concerning the debtor's income, debts, and assets.
- Verify the accuracy of the debtor's financial statements.
- Verify legal title status of property in which the debtor has an interest.
- Make arrangements for the debtor to receive credit counseling from an approved agency.
- Draft the bankruptcy petition based on the information obtained from the client.
- Verify the validity of creditors' claims that have been submitted to the bankruptcy court.
- Prepare the client for bankruptcy proceedings, such as creditors' meetings.
- Assist in work on the debtor's behalf in any legal actions relating to the bankruptcy proceedings.

- Research the Bankruptcy Code to verify that certain provisions are still effective, and keep up to date on bankruptcy law.

- Research state statutes governing property exemptions.

- Research case law to see how the courts have applied a certain provision of the Bankruptcy Code or a state law applicable to the bankruptcy proceedings.

Independent paralegals sometimes assist debtors by providing "do-it-yourself" bankruptcy kits. The bankruptcy process can be a daunting one, so it is imperative that independent paralegals understand their ethical role when it comes to providing services of this sort to the public, as this chapter's *Ethics Watch* feature explains.

Environmental Law

We now turn to a discussion of the various ways in which businesses are regulated by the government in its attempts to protect the environment. Remember from Chapter 2 that *environmental law* is defined as all law pertaining to environmental protection.

Environmental law is not new. Indeed, the federal government began to regulate some activities, such as those involving the pollution of navigable waterways, in the late 1800s. In more recent decades, however, the body of environmental law has expanded substantially as the government has attempted to control industrial waste and to protect natural resources. Because of the complexity of environmental law, firms often need legal assistance to make sure that they meet regulatory requirements. In this section, we look at some of the most significant environmental statutes and regulations.

ETHICS WATCH

THE PERILS OF INDEPENDENT PRACTICE

As you read in Chapter 2, independent paralegals provide services directly to the public (without attorney supervision). Some independent paralegals assist debtors by selling them "do-it-yourself" bankruptcy kits, preparing bankruptcy forms, and the like.

Although the Bankruptcy Code allows paralegals to act as bankruptcy petition preparers without attorney supervision, it contains strict requirements that must be followed. The law prohibits petition preparers from advising bankruptcy debtors about numerous issues and from offering legal advice. For example, petition preparers may not tell a debtor whether he or she will be able to retain certain property, such as a house or car, after filing for bankruptcy. They may not say whether a particular debt will or can be discharged. They may not tell debtors how to characterize an interest in property when filling out the forms, whether

to reaffirm a particular debt, or what tax consequences might be involved.

Violators may be subject to a fine; may be required to forfeit the fees they received from, or pay damages to, the debtor; and may even be ordered not to prepare bankruptcy petitions in the future. Because of the dangers involved, paralegals who prepare bankruptcy petitions without attorney supervision must be exceedingly careful to avoid pitfalls and potential lawsuits.

Such care is consistent with NALA's *Code of Ethics*, Canon 4: "A paralegal must use discretion and professional judgment commensurate with knowledge and experience but must not render independent legal judgment in place of an attorney."

Federal Regulation of the Environment

Congress has passed a number of statutes to control the impact of human activities on the environment. Some of these statutes were passed in an attempt to improve the quality of air and water. Some of them specifically regulate toxic chemicals and hazardous wastes. Exhibit 19.1 lists the major federal statutes that apply to various areas of the environment. Because regulations change frequently, a paralegal who works in the area will need to keep on top of the changes, as discussed in the accompanying *Developing Paralegal Skills* feature.

Environmental Regulatory Agencies

Much of the body of federal law governing business activities consists of the regulations issued and enforced by administrative agencies. The most well known of the agencies regulating environmental law is the Environmental Protection Agency (EPA), which was created by President Richard Nixon in 1970 to coordinate federal environmental responsibilities. Not only the EPA but also other agencies of the federal government, as well as the states, must take environmental factors into consideration when making significant decisions.

Many environmental laws provide that citizens can sue to enforce environmental regulations if government agencies fail to do so—or to limit enforcement if agencies go too far in their enforcement actions. Although we do not discuss state regulation here, each state has an environmental agency that parallels the EPA. Those agencies are often delegated major responsibilities by the EPA.

EXHIBIT 19.1

Federal Regulation of Environmental Pollution

Source: Meiners/Ringleb/Edwards, The Legal Environment of Business, 12E. © 2015 Cengage Learning.

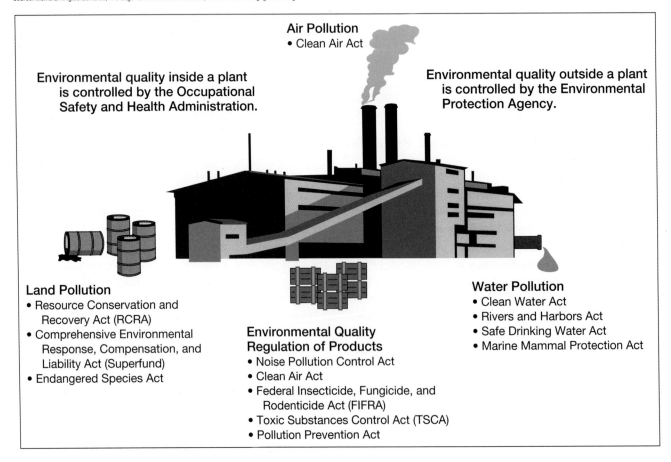

Air Pollution
• Clean Air Act

Environmental quality inside a plant is controlled by the Occupational Safety and Health Administration.

Environmental quality outside a plant is controlled by the Environmental Protection Agency.

Land Pollution
• Resource Conservation and Recovery Act (RCRA)
• Comprehensive Environmental Response, Compensation, and Liability Act (Superfund)
• Endangered Species Act

Environmental Quality Regulation of Products
• Noise Pollution Control Act
• Clean Air Act
• Federal Insecticide, Fungicide, and Rodenticide Act (FIFRA)
• Toxic Substances Control Act (TSCA)
• Pollution Prevention Act

Water Pollution
• Clean Water Act
• Rivers and Harbors Act
• Safe Drinking Water Act
• Marine Mammal Protection Act

DEVELOPING PARALEGAL SKILLS

MONITORING THE *FEDERAL REGISTER*

Robin Hayes is a paralegal for CARCO, Inc., a company that manufactures automobile parts. She works in the environmental law practice group within the corporation's legal department. One of her responsibilities is to monitor the *Federal Register* regularly for newly proposed environmental regulations and for changes to existing rules.

One day, Robin notices a change to the hazardous waste manifest, a form that CARCO is required to use when shipping hazardous waste to a disposal facility. The change requires the company to certify its efforts in reducing the amount of hazardous waste that it generates. Robin prepares a memo to the attorneys in the group, because they will need to inform company management of the change and be sure that the employees handling the waste complete the certifications.

Checklist for Monitoring the *Federal Register*

- Review the *Federal Register* regularly. This can be done online.
- Monitor the topics and subtopics to determine if notices, rules, or proposed rules have been issued on topics affecting your client.

- Skim through any notices, rules, and proposed rules that may apply to your client.
- Read in detail the relevant notices, rules, and proposed rules that may apply to your client.
- Print out relevant notices, rules, and proposed rules for circulation to the attorneys and others who should be advised of this information.
- Notify the attorneys and others of upcoming deadlines for comments on proposed rules and changes.

Don't Forget Social Media

In addition, read blogs, follow Twitter accounts, and listen to podcasts by commentators (or legal scholars) on the issues you are tracking. Use social media and the vast resources available online to help you learn about the latest changes and developments that may be relevant in your practice. Many law firms have employees who blog or use social media to monitor specific topics—find them and follow their news.

Environmental Impact Statements

The National Environmental Policy Act (NEPA) of 1969 requires that for every major federal action that significantly affects the quality of the environment, an **environmental impact statement (EIS)** must be prepared. Construction by a private developer of a ski resort on federal land, for example, may require an EIS. Building or operating a nuclear power plant, which requires a federal permit, or constructing a dam as part of a federal project would require an EIS. An EIS must analyze (1) the impact on the environment that the action will have, (2) any adverse effects on the environment and alternative actions that might be taken, and (3) irreversible effects the action might generate.

EISs have become instruments used by private citizens, consumer interest groups, businesses, and others to challenge federal agency actions on the basis that the actions improperly threaten the environment. A typical EIS is hundreds of pages long. Some environmental law paralegals assist in preparing and reviewing EISs.

environmental impact statement (EIS)

A statement required by the National Environmental Policy Act for any major federal action that will significantly affect the quality of the environment. The statement must analyze the action's impact on the environment and explore alternative actions that might be taken.

Air Pollution

Federal involvement with air pollution goes back to the 1950s, when Congress authorized funds for air-pollution research. In 1963, the federal government passed the Clean Air Act, which focuses on multistate air pollution and provides assistance to states.

Later amendments to the act, especially in 1970, 1977, and 1990, expanded the federal role in regulating air quality.

Mobile and Stationary Sources of Pollution

The Clean Air Act covers both mobile and stationary sources of pollution. Mobile sources include automobiles and other moving sources. Amendments to the act in 1970 require automobile manufacturers to cut new automobiles' exhaust emissions by a certain percentage by a given date. Every few years, the EPA reviews the standards and usually makes them tougher, so fewer emissions are allowed.

Stationary sources include manufacturing plants, electric utilities, and other nonmoving sources of pollution. The Clean Air Act authorizes the EPA to establish air-quality standards for these sources. The EPA sets the maximum levels of certain pollutants that may be emitted by stationary sources, and the states formulate plans to achieve those standards. Different standards apply to sources of pollution in clean areas and sources in polluted areas. Different standards also apply to existing sources of pollution and major new sources.

Performance standards for major sources require the use of "maximum achievable control technology" to reduce emissions from the combustion of fossil fuels (coal and oil). The EPA issues guidelines as to what equipment meets this requirement.

Penalties for Violating the Clean Air Act

The EPA can assess civil penalties of up to $25,000 per day for violations of emission limits under the Clean Air Act. Additional fines of up to $5,000 per day can be assessed for other violations, such as failing to maintain required records. To penalize those for whom it is more cost-effective to violate the act than to comply with it, the EPA is authorized to obtain a penalty equal to the violator's economic benefits from noncompliance. Persons who provide information about violators may be paid up to $10,000. Private citizens can also sue violators. Those who knowingly violate the act may be subject to criminal penalties, including fines of up to $1 million and imprisonment for up to two years (for false statements or failure to report violations).

Corporate officers are among those who may be subject to these penalties. The threat of penalties is not an empty one, as most years there are more than a hundred criminal indictments. Regulations in this and other areas change constantly and vary across states. Consequently, it is necessary to stay informed on relevant materials, as noted in this chapter's *Office Tech and Cybersecurity* feature.

Water Pollution

Federal regulations governing water pollution can be traced back to the Rivers and Harbors Act of 1899. Those regulations prohibited ships and manufacturers from discharging or depositing refuse in navigable waterways.

Navigable Waters

Navigable waters include coastal waters, freshwater wetlands, and lakes and streams used by interstate travelers and industry. In practice, most bodies of water and every stream are considered navigable and subject to federal regulation. In 1948, Congress passed the Federal Water Pollution Control Act (FWPCA), but its regulatory system and enforcement proved inadequate. In 1972, amendments to the FWPCA—known as the Clean Water Act—were enacted to (1) make waters safe for swimming, (2) protect fish and wildlife, and (3) eliminate the discharge of pollutants into the

OFFICE TECH AND CYBERSECURITY

ENVIRONMENTAL COMPLIANCE

Paralegals can quickly find an abundance of information not only on environmental laws but also on what businesses must do to comply with these laws. Here, we look at just a few online resources that paralegals can use to obtain such information.

Environmental Laws and Regulations

You can visit the EPA's website, at **epa.gov**, to find a wealth of detailed information on existing law as well as new regulations and proposed rules, proposed environmental legislation in Congress, and an explanation of how the EPA writes regulations.

More importantly, you can find the various types of informal documents through which EPA explains what it means at the Environmental Compliance website: **fedcenter.gov/programs/compliance**. Besides listing formal federal requirements in many areas, the site provides links to useful industry sites, such as one explaining how shipping ports comply with environmental rules at **portcompliance.org**.

When working with complex regulatory statutes, it is always a good idea to search agency websites for informal guidance documents and policy manuals to obtain insights into the agency's approach to enforcing a statute.

Another helpful website is **enviro.blr.com**. Here, you can find information on environmental laws and regulatory activity. Crucially, you can also find various tools (such as special forms and checklists) for monitoring and implementing a firm's compliance with regulatory requirements.

Compliance Assistance

The Environmental Compliance Assistance Platform, at **envcap.org**, is designed to help businesses comply with environmental regulations. The site includes links to compliance assistance for various industries and groups (for example, for automotive recycling) and to state regulations.

Technology Tip

When you are searching for government resources and are not sure where to go, remember that **usa.gov** is a gateway to all federal agencies and institutions. Offerings by private firms are expanding constantly, so searching to see what is available may reveal interesting results.

---

water. The amendments required that polluters apply for permits before discharging wastes into navigable waters.

Focus on Point-Source Emissions

The Clean Water Act focuses on pollutants that are emitted from *point sources*. These are sources that occupy small areas and have heavily concentrated outputs. The act, as amended over time, has five main elements:

1. National effluent (waste) standards set by the EPA for each industry.

2. Water quality standards set by the states under EPA supervision.

3. A *discharge permit* program that sets water quality standards to limit pollution.

4. Special provisions for toxic chemicals and for oil spills.

5. Construction grants and loans from the federal government for *publicly owned treatment works* (POTWs), primarily sewage treatment plants.

Discharge Permits. The Clean Water Act makes it illegal for any person, business, or government to dump pollutants into navigable waters without a discharge permit. These permits are issued under the National Pollution Discharge Elimination System. Any point source emitting pollutants into water must have a permit. Non-point-source pollution, such as runoff from farms, is not subject to much regulation.

Required Technology. As Exhibit 19.2 shows, there are two major categories of point-source discharges into the nation's waters. The first are POTWs, most of which are local sewage treatment plants. They must use the *best conventional technology* for treating waste in order to receive a permit to discharge. The EPA sets that technology standard. Subject to more strict controls are emissions from point sources such as factories. They must use the *best available technology* to treat their wastewater before returning the water to a waterway. When a firm shows that it is in compliance with the technology standard, it can then obtain a discharge permit.

Penalties for Violating the Clean Water Act

Because point-source water pollution control is based on a permit system, the permits are the key to enforcement. States have primary responsibility for enforcing the permit system, subject to EPA monitoring.

Discharging emissions into navigable waters without a permit, or in violation of pollution limits under a permit, violates the Clean Water Act. Firms that have discharge permits must monitor their own performance and file *discharge monitoring reports*. These reports are available for public inspection. Violators must report their violations and are subject to fines. Lying about a violation is more serious than admitting the truth about improper discharges.

Serious violations can result in criminal prosecutions, and every year people are sent to prison for dumping toxic pollutants. As with the Clean Air Act, citizens have the right to bring suits for pollutant violations that the EPA or a state environmental agency has not addressed properly.

Wetlands

Years ago, wetlands were seen as nuisances to be drained and filled with dirt. The Clean Water Act recognizes the ecological value of wetlands and protects them. *Wetlands* are any lands that support vegetation adapted to saturated soil conditions, such as swamps and bogs. They are protected no matter how large or small they are.

EXHIBIT 19.2

Primary Sources of Water Waste

Source: Meiners/Ringleb/Edwards, The Legal Environment of Business, 12E. © 2015 Cengage Learning.

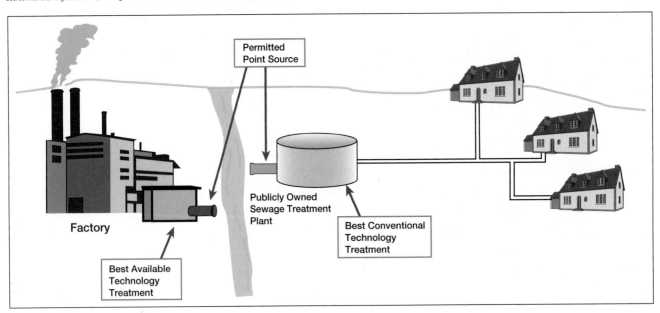

Under the Clean Water Act, anyone wanting to change a wetland, usually for construction purposes, must obtain a permit from the U.S. Army Corps of Engineers. Each year, the Corps issues more than 10,000 permits that involve significant wetland impact. The Corps reviews proposals for dredging or filling, and it often limits the work or requires work to be done elsewhere in exchange for the wetland lost to construction. The Corps issues another 75,000 permits annually for activities found to have "minimal adverse environmental effects" to wetlands. The EPA reviews the decisions of the Corps. Violators are subject to fines, which can be in the millions of dollars.

Toxic Chemicals

Originally, most environmental cleanup efforts were directed toward reducing smog and making water safe for fishing and swimming. Over time, however, control of toxic chemicals became an important part of environmental law.

Pesticides and Herbicides

The first toxic chemical problem to receive widespread public attention was that posed by pesticides and herbicides. Using these chemicals to kill insects and weeds has increased agricultural productivity, but their residue can remain in the environment. In rare instances, accumulations of this residue have killed animals, and scientists have identified potential long-term effects that are detrimental to humans.

Under the Federal Insecticide, Fungicide, and Rodenticide Act of 1947 (FIFRA), pesticides and herbicides must be registered before they can be sold. They may be used only for approved applications and in limited quantities when applied to food crops. If a substance is identified as harmful, the EPA can cancel its registration.

For a pesticide to remain on the market, there must be a "reasonable certainty of no harm" to people from exposure to the pesticide. This means that there must be no more than a one-in-a-million risk to people of developing cancer from exposure in any way, including eating food that contains residues from the pesticide.

Penalties for registrants and producers for violating the act include imprisonment for up to one year and a fine of no more than $50,000. Penalties for commercial dealers include imprisonment for up to one year and a fine of no more than $25,000. Farmers and other private users of pesticides or herbicides who violate the act are subject to a $1,000 fine and imprisonment for up to thirty days.

Hazardous Wastes

Some industrial, agricultural, and household wastes pose more serious threats than others. If not properly disposed of, toxic chemicals from a variety of sources may present a substantial danger to human health and the environment. If released into the environment, they may contaminate public drinking water resources and make land unsuitable for human use.

Resource Conservation and Recovery Act (RCRA). The Resource Conservation and Recovery Act (RCRA) requires the EPA to establish regulations to monitor and control hazardous waste disposal and to determine which forms of solid waste should be considered hazardous and thus subject to regulation. The EPA reports that waste amounting to approximately 3 billion tons a year at thousands of sites is subject to its control. The act authorizes the EPA to issue various technical requirements for some types of facilities for storage and treatment of hazardous waste. The act also requires all producers of hazardous waste materials to label and package properly any hazardous waste that is to be transported.

In practice, the RCRA imposes a "cradle-to-grave" system of controls on hazardous substances. As Exhibit 19.3 indicates, chemicals, besides being subject to regulatory

EXHIBIT 19.3

Regulation of Hazardous Substances

Source: Meiners/Ringleb/Edwards, The Legal Environment of Business, 12E. © 2015 Cengage Learning.

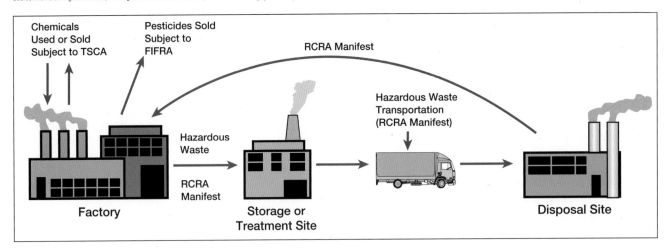

standards at the point of production and sale, are tracked as they are transported, used, and disposed of. The hazardous substance producer must attach a *manifest*, or data sheet, to all products that will become hazardous waste. The sellers of those substances must have an EPA permit. The manifests must accompany the substances down the chain of transportation, use, and disposal so parties in each category can be held responsible for the products. Firms that operate *treatment, storage, and disposal (TSD) sites* must meet all regulations regarding the proper handling, use, and destruction of hazardous materials.

Under the RCRA, a company may be assessed a civil penalty based on the seriousness of the violation, the probability of harm, and the extent to which the violation deviates from RCRA requirements. The assessment may be up to $25,000 for each violation. Criminal penalties include fines up to $50,000 for each day of violation, imprisonment for up to two years (in most instances), or both. Criminal fines and the time of imprisonment can be doubled for certain repeat offenders.

Superfund.   The Comprehensive Environmental Response, Compensation, and Liability Act (CERCLA), commonly known as Superfund, regulates the cleanup of disposal sites in which hazardous waste is leaking into the environment. A special federal fund was created for this purpose.

Superfund provides that when a release or a threatened release of hazardous chemicals from a site occurs, the following persons are responsible for cleaning up the site:

1. The person who generated the wastes disposed of at the site.

2. The person who transported the wastes to the site.

3. The person who owned or operated the site at the time of the disposal.

4. The current owner or operator.

A person falling within one of these categories is referred to as a **potentially responsible party (PRP)**. If the PRP does not clean up the site, Superfund authorizes the EPA to clean up the site and recover cleanup costs from the PRP.

Superfund imposes strict liability on PRPs. Also, liability under Superfund is usually joint and several—that is, a PRP who generated only a fraction of the hazardous waste disposed of at the site may nevertheless be liable for all of the cleanup costs. CERCLA authorizes a party who has incurred cleanup costs to bring a "contribution action" against any other person who is liable or potentially liable for a percentage of the costs.

Environmental Law and the Paralegal

A paralegal specializing in environmental law may work for a federal or state agency, for a law firm or corporate legal department, or with an organization interested in natural resource issues. As we have seen in this chapter, complex legal issues are involved. Some of the tasks that you might perform include:

- Draft and file permits with federal, state, or local agencies to use property in compliance with environmental and natural resource rules.

- Draft and file documents necessary to include another company as a potential defendant in an action brought by an agency.

- Monitor the *Federal Register* and state administrative regulations, as well as industry websites, to determine if new environmental requirements have been imposed.

- Research the scope and applicability of a regulation to determine if a client's planned action may violate that rule, whether a permit is required, and any other requirements.

- Prepare for and attend hearings before natural resource control agencies.

- Assist in negotiations between an environmental agency and a firm to settle a dispute over claimed violations of a regulation.

- Coordinate a client's environmental policies, and monitor corporate compliance with reporting requirements under various environmental statutes.

- Trace property histories to look for potential contributors to a Superfund site cleanup action.

Looking to the Future

In conclusion, we offer some words of wisdom from a seasoned paralegal in this chapter's *Featured Contributor* article that will give you a head start on succeeding in your paralegal career.

potentially responsible party (PRP)

A party that may be liable under the Comprehensive Environmental Response, Compensation, and Liability Act, or Superfund. Any party that generated hazardous waste, transported hazardous waste, owned or operated a waste site at the time of disposal, or currently owns or operates a site may be responsible for some or all of the cleanup costs involved in removing the hazardous substances.

FEATURED CONTRIBUTOR

LEARNING WELL AND FINDING YOUR PLACE

Kristine M. Condon

BIOGRAPHICAL NOTE

Kristine M. Condon is the program coordinator of the ABA-approved Paralegal Studies Program at Kankakee Community College, a program she established. She began her legal career as a deputy clerk to the Illinois Supreme Court as it established the first "paperless" office in the Illinois court system. She was the computer-training director for a top-ten, Chicago-based law firm and a senior trainer for the American Medical Association.

Dr. Condon is also a member of the Campaign for Legal Services Committee of Prairie State Legal Services, a provider of low-cost civil legal services to the poor and the elderly in Kankakee County. She has been published in the *Paralegal Educator*, the former magazine of the AAfPE.

Dr. Condon holds a bachelor of art's degree, *magna cum laude*, from Illinois Wesleyan University; a master of education degree from Loyola University Chicago; and a doctor of education degree from National Louis University.

I couldn't imagine what I had done wrong, yet I must have done something to be summoned to the justice's chambers. It was my first job out of paralegal school, in the plum job of my legal career as a deputy clerk with my state's highest court. Daily contact with three of the court's seven members, including the chief justice, was part of my routine. I thought I had been a model employee. Was my paralegal career over before it really started?

> ## Was my paralegal career over before it really started?

I made my way down the hall to the chambers of a justice who was the longest-serving member of the court. He had served as the dean of a Chicago-area law school. As the county's top prosecutor, he had secured the conviction of one of the nation's most notorious mass murderers. Yet his kind appearance and gentle demeanor belied his storied career. He greeted me warmly and asked me to sit.

President Lincoln's Legal Lesson for Paralegals

"Are you familiar with these?" the justice asked, as he gestured to a library bookcase filled with volumes of court opinions authored by his predecessors. I replied that I was. He made his way to a specific volume and thumbed to a well-worn page. He said, "This volume contains the opinion in Abraham Lincoln's first case before our Court."[a]

He continued, "Kris, Lincoln didn't have the tools we have today to argue before this Court, including paralegals. On some days, your job may be even more difficult as a paralegal than it would be as a lawyer, because we're asking you to anticipate everything we might possibly need. But Lincoln found his place in our profession by learning well as he studied the law. We want you to know that we're confident you learned well during your own schooling. You'll find your place here."

That was it. A conversation of a few minutes changed how and what I did for my career with the Court then and in the paralegal classroom now.

Tips to Finding Your Paralegal Place

How do *you* demonstrate to your employer that you learned well and have found your place as a paralegal? Here are some tips I learned along the way:

Tip 1: Come Prepared.

Try to anticipate what your supervisor might need from your research, and determine the time commitment involved.

Tip 2: Expect the Unexpected.

Anticipate the amount of time needed for a project, and add 10 percent to provide for the unexpected.

Tip 3: Be Ethical without Exception.

Your friends may think cases are fodder for lunch conversation. Don't ever give in to the temptation. Nonlawyers are subject to the same ethical guidelines as the attorneys for whom they work.

---

a. *Scammon v. Cline*, 3 Ill. 456, 2 Scam. 456, 1840 WL 2967 (1840).

Tip 4: Know How to Find Answers.

I never told a justice or an attorney, "I don't know." If they asked, I'd say, "I don't know at the moment, but I know how to find it." Then, I did.

Tip 5: Be Mindful of Cost.

A client paid for my mistakes and expenses: the taxpayer. In the case of online research, I often began my basic work in print and shifted to online when I had a solid lead to research.

Tip 6: Use a Variety of Sources.

The amount of digital content on the Internet is massive; it's your job as the paralegal to search for the relevant sources, legal and nonlegal.

Tip 7: Check and Double-Check.

Use notification tools, such as *KeyCite Alert* and *Shepard's Online*, to make sure your authority stays current from the time you draft until the time you submit.

Tip 8: Stay Current with Trends.

> " You will find your place . . . "

Some students think reviewing weekly legal publications is a waste of time, until an interviewer asks them whether they've read the latest bar journal article on a particular topic. Take full advantage of all the online sources to know the latest trends and events that affect your law firm's clients.

Tip 9: Pay Attention to the Details.

Legal writing requires a high degree of precision—beyond good grammar, spelling, and punctuation. Court rules are court rules. Know them inside and out, especially as they apply to formatting, citing, and preparing legal documents.

Tip 10: Value Different Perspectives.

Probably the most important lesson my justice imparted to me that day early in my career was that I needed to understand the past to anticipate the future. After all, even President Lincoln could not have anticipated the explosive growth of the legal profession and the increasingly important role paralegals play in shaping it. Take advantage of every opportunity to learn well in your paralegal education—and you, too, will find your place.

CHAPTER SUMMARY

BANKRUPTCY AND ENVIRONMENTAL LAW

Forms of Bankruptcy Relief Compared

	CHAPTER 7	CHAPTER 11	CHAPTER 13
Purpose.	Liquidation.	Reorganization.	Individual repayment plan.
WHO CAN PETITION	Debtor (voluntary) or creditors (involuntary).	Debtor (voluntary) or creditors (involuntary).	Debtor (voluntary) only.
WHO CAN BE A DEBTOR	Any "person" (including partnerships and corporations) except insurance companies, banks, savings and loan institutions, investment companies licensed by the Small Business Administration, and credit unions. Farmers and charitable institutions cannot be involuntarily petitioned. If the court finds the petition to be a substantial abuse of the use of Chapter 7, the debtor may be required to convert to a Chapter 13 repayment plan.	Any debtor (except a stockbroker or a commodities broker) eligible for Chapter 7 relief; railroads are also eligible.	Any individual (not partnerships or corporations) with regular income who owes specified amounts of fixed (liquidated) unsecured debt or fixed secured debt.
PROCEDURE LEADING TO DISCHARGE	Nonexempt property is sold with proceeds to be distributed (in order) to priority groups. Dischargeable debts are terminated.	Plan is submitted; if it is approved and followed, debts are discharged.	Plan is submitted (must be approved if debtor turns over disposable income for a three- or five-year period); if it is approved and followed, debts are discharged.
ADVANTAGES	On liquidation and distribution, most debts are discharged, and the debtor has the opportunity for a fresh start.	Debtor continues in business. Creditors can accept the plan, or it can be "crammed down" on them. Plan allows for reorganization and liquidation of debts over the plan period.	Debtor continues in business or retains possession of assets. If plan is approved, most debts are discharged after the plan period.

Environmental Law

1. *Federal regulation of the environment—*

   a. The federal Environmental Protection Agency (EPA) was created in 1970 to coordinate federal environmental programs. The EPA administers most federal environmental policies and statutes.

   b. The National Environmental Policy Act of 1969 imposes environmental responsibilities on all federal agencies and requires the preparation of an environmental impact statement (EIS) for every major federal action. An EIS must analyze the action's impact on the environment.

2. *Important areas regulated by federal law—*

   a. **AIR POLLUTION**—Regulated primarily by the Clean Air Act. The EPA sets allowable emission standards for various pollutants emitted from mobile sources (vehicles) and stationary sources (power plants, factories). Polluters must meet specific technological control standards.

b. WATER POLLUTION—Regulated primarily under the Clean Water Act. Polluters who dump waste into navigable waters must meet technical standards set by the EPA and enforced primarily by the states. The focus is on point sources such as sewage treatment plants and industrial sites, which must have discharge permits. The act also protects wetlands. Changing a wetland requires a permit from the Army Corps of Engineers.

c. TOXIC CHEMICALS AND HAZARDOUS WASTE—The Federal Insecticide, Fungicide, and Rodenticide Act controls pesticides and herbicides. The Comprehensive Environmental Response, Compensation, and Liability Act (CERCLA), commonly known as Superfund, requires sellers, transporters, users, and disposers to use manifests to track the history of the substances from production to disposal. The act also requires cleanup of polluted Superfund sites.

KEY TERMS AND CONCEPTS

automatic stay 577

bankruptcy estate 578

bankruptcy trustee 574

consumer-debtor 574

cram-down provision 588

debtor in possession (DIP) 587

discharged 574

environmental impact statement (EIS) 591

homestead exemption 580

liquidation 574

order for relief 577

petition in bankruptcy 574

potentially responsible party (PRP) 597

preference 581

proof of claim 578

reorganization 586

secured creditor 575

U.S. trustee 575

workout 586

QUESTIONS FOR REVIEW

1. What are the goals of bankruptcy law? What are the three most important types of relief available for debtors under federal bankruptcy law?

2. What is a liquidation proceeding under Chapter 7? How is it initiated? What is the difference between a voluntary bankruptcy and an involuntary bankruptcy? What is "means testing"?

3. What is an automatic stay? What effect does the filing of a bankruptcy petition have on creditors?

4. How does a Chapter 13 bankruptcy differ from Chapter 7 bankruptcy? What is a discharge? Are all debts dischargeable in bankruptcy? If not, give examples of the types of debt that are not dischargeable.

5. What happens when a company files for bankruptcy reorganization under Chapter 11? What is a debtor in possession? What procedure is followed after the bankruptcy is filed?

6. What is an environmental impact statement (EIS), and when is one required? What factors does an EIS evaluate?

7. What four environmental issues are regulated by federal environmental laws? List the major environmental laws that provide the regulatory framework in each area. What is Superfund? Which parties are responsible for the cleanup of hazardous waste sites?

ETHICS QUESTION

1. Marla, an independent paralegal, provides a variety of services for the public. Among other things, she provides debtors with bankruptcy forms and petitions. Mr. Ford has sought Marla's services in filing for bankruptcy. He takes home a set of Chapter 7 forms, reads through them, and begins to provide the information needed. He is not certain that he qualifies for Chapter 7 liquidation. He calls Marla and asks her if he has any other options. How should Marla answer Mr. Ford's questions?

PRACTICE QUESTIONS AND ASSIGNMENTS

1. Jamal earns a salary of $30,000 a year as a sales representative. He is married with two children in high school. In addition to his salary, he earns a 10 percent commission on what he sells. Over the past five years, Jamal earned annual commissions of $80,000 to $100,000. During this time, he purchased a $75,000 Cadillac and a $45,000 boat, and he incurred credit-card debt totaling $55,000. In the past six months, Jamal made only $10,000 in commissions, and he still owes $50,000 on the Cadillac and $30,000 on the boat. In all, he owes $135,000 to creditors. Jamal cannot pay his debts as they become due, and it does not appear that his financial situation will improve over the next two years in light of limited job prospects. As a result, he is thinking about filing for bankruptcy. If the median income in Jamal's state is $52,000 a year, would he be able to obtain a Chapter 7 liquidation? Why or why not?

2. Jon and Susan Bogren filed for voluntary bankruptcy under Chapter 7 and qualified by passing the means test. They own one car outright that has a value of $3,000, and they owe $10,000 to the bank for their second car. Their bankruptcy action will cause them to incur attorney's fees, trustee fees, and court costs. Jon owes alimony and child support to his former wife and children. Jon and Susan also owe income taxes and penalties from 2018, and Susan owes $35,000 in student loans. Is any property exempt? Are all of the debts dischargeable in bankruptcy? If not, indicate which ones are not dischargeable. List the priority in which the creditors will be paid.

3. The shoreline of Greers Ferry Lake is under the management of the U.S. Army Corps of Engineers. The Corps's 2019 Shoreline Management Plan (SMP) rezoned numerous areas along the lake and authorized the Corps to issue permits for the construction of new boat docks in the rezoned areas. No environmental impact statement (EIS) was required. The environmental group Save Greers Ferry Lake, Inc., filed a lawsuit in U.S. district court to order the Corps to prepare an EIS and stop it from issuing permits. When is an EIS required? What does an EIS analyze?

4. Identify the environmental law that applies to each of the following situations, and explain how it would address the problem:

    a. The foreman at a manufacturing plant disposes of a fifty-five-gallon drum of spent solvents, a toxic waste, every week by pouring it on the ground "out back."

    b. An investigation reveals that the local gas utility company has PCBs in its pipeline in excess of those allowed.

    c. An oil company releases oil into a local river, contaminating the river, which is a major source of drinking water for the area.

    d. A manufacturing plant that produces metallic paint for use on motor vehicles releases more pollutants into the air than the allowable emissions limits for its vicinity.

    e. Years ago, five large manufacturing companies disposed of hazardous waste by burying the waste on the property of a farmer forty miles away from the city and its inhabitants. The rural farm is now part of a suburb. The suburb's groundwater and drinking water are found to be contaminated by the waste buried on the site of the former farm. The citizens demand that the site be cleaned up.

GROUP PROJECT

This project involves researching the West Coast's frequent problems of drought and water shortages. Students should search for articles from authoritative news sources from the region's major newspapers, nonprofit organizations, environmental research studies, and the *Wall Street Journal*. Wikipedia should not be consulted.

Student one will do an Internet search for articles, photographs, and videos describing a specific area's drought and water crisis issues.

Student two will do an Internet search for articles explaining the causes of these water shortages and the effects of the region's increasing population on water consumption.

Student three will do an Internet search for articles about specific actions to address the drought and water crisis.

Student four will compile the information and present the group's findings to the class.

Appendix A

NALA's *Code of Ethics and Professional Responsibility*

A paralegal must adhere strictly to the accepted standards of legal ethics and to the general principles of proper conduct. The performance of the duties of the paralegal shall be governed by specific canons as defined herein so that justice will be served and goals of the profession attained. (See *Model Standards and Guidelines for the Utilization of Legal Assistants*, Section II.)

The canons of ethics set forth hereafter are adopted by the Paralegal Association, as a general guide intended to aid paralegals and attorneys. The enumeration of these rules does not mean there are not others of equal importance although not specifically mentioned. Court rules, agency rules, and statutes must be taken into consideration when interpreting the canons.

Canons of Ethics

Definition
Legal assistants, also known as paralegals, are a distinguishable group of persons who assist attorneys in the delivery of legal services. Through formal education, training and experience, legal assistants have knowledge and expertise regarding the legal system and substantive and procedural law which qualify them to do work of a legal nature under the supervision of an attorney.

Canon 1
A paralegal must not perform any of the duties that attorneys only may perform nor take any actions that attorneys may not take.

Canon 2
A paralegal may perform any task which is properly delegated and supervised by an attorney, as long as the attorney is ultimately responsible to the client, maintains a direct relationship with the client, and assumes professional responsibility for the work product.

Canon 3
A paralegal must not: (a) engage in, encourage, or contribute to any act which could constitute the unauthorized practice of law; and (b) establish attorney-client relationships, set fees, give legal opinions or advice, or represent a client before a court or agency unless so authorized by that court or agency; and (c) engage in conduct or take any action which would assist or involve the attorney in a violation of professional ethics or give the appearance of professional impropriety.

Canon 4

A paralegal must use discretion and professional judgment commensurate with knowledge and experience but must not render independent legal judgment in place of an attorney. The services of an attorney are essential in the public interest whenever such legal judgment is required.

Canon 5

A paralegal must disclose his or her status as a paralegal at the outset of any professional relationship with a client, attorney, a court or administrative agency or personnel thereof, or a member of the general public. A paralegal must act prudently in determining the extent to which a client may be assisted without the presence of an attorney.

Canon 6

A paralegal must strive to maintain integrity and a high degree of competency through education and training with respect to professional responsibility, local rules and practice, and through continuing education in substantive areas of law to better assist the legal profession in fulfilling its duty to provide legal service.

Canon 7

A paralegal must protect the confidences of a client and must not violate any rule or statute now in effect or hereafter enacted controlling the doctrine of privileged communications between a client and an attorney.

Canon 8

A paralegal must disclose to his or her employer or prospective employer any preexisting client or personal relationship that may conflict with the interests of the employer or prospective employer and/or their clients.

Canon 9

A paralegal must do all other things incidental, necessary, or expedient for the attainment of the ethics and responsibilities as defined by statute or rule of court.

Canon 10

A paralegal's conduct is guided by bar associations' codes of professional responsibility and rules of professional conduct.

NALA's *Model Standards and Guidelines for the Utilization of Paralegals*

Introduction

The purpose of this annotated version of NALA – The Paralegal Association's *Model Standards and Guidelines for the Utilization of Paralegals* (the Model) is to provide references to the existing case law and other authorities where the underlying issues have been considered. The authorities cited will serve as a basis upon which conduct of a paralegal may be analyzed as proper or improper.

The Model represents a statement of how the paralegal may function. The Model is not intended to be a comprehensive or exhaustive list of the proper duties of a paralegal. Rather, it is designed as guides to what may or may not be proper conduct for the paralegal. In formulating the Model, the reasoning and rules of law in many reported decisions of disciplinary cases and unauthorized practice of law cases have been analyzed and considered. In addition, the provisions of the American Bar Association's Model Rules of Professional Conduct, as well as the ethical promulgations of various state courts and bar associations, have been considered in the development of the Model.

This Model forms a sound basis for the paralegal and the supervising attorney to follow. It will serve as a comprehensive resource document and as a definitive, well-reasoned guide to those considering voluntary standards and guidelines for paralegals.

I. Preamble

Proper utilization of the services of paralegals contributes to the delivery of cost-effective, high quality legal services. Paralegals and the legal profession should be assured that measures exist for identifying paralegals and their role in assisting attorneys in the delivery of legal services. Therefore, the National Association of Legal Assistants, Inc., hereby adopts these Standards and Guidelines as an educational document for the benefit of paralegals and the legal profession.

The three most frequently raised questions concerning paralegals are: (1) How do you define a paralegal? (2) Who is qualified to be identified as a paralegal? and (3) What duties may a paralegal perform? The definition adopted by NALA answers the first question. The Model sets forth minimum education, training, and experience through standards which will assure that an individual utilizing the title "legal assistant" or "paralegal" has the qualifications to be held out to the legal community and the public in that capacity. The Model identifies those acts which the reported cases hold to be forbidden and gives examples of services which the paralegal may perform under the supervision of a licensed attorney.

This Model constitutes a statement relating to services performed by paralegals, as defined herein, as approved by court decisions and other sources of authority. The purpose of the Model is not to place limitations or restrictions on the paralegal profession. Rather, the Model is intended to outline for the legal profession an acceptable course of conduct. Voluntary recognition and utilization of the Standards and Guidelines will benefit the entire legal profession and the public it serves.

II. History

NALA adopted this Model in 1984. At the same time the following definition of a legal assistant was adopted:

> Legal assistants, also known as paralegals, are a distinguishable group of persons who assist attorneys in the delivery of legal services. Through formal education, training, and experience, legal assistants have knowledge and expertise regarding the legal system and substantive and procedural law which qualify them to do work of a legal nature under the supervision of an attorney.
>
> This definition continues to be used today.

III. Definition

A paralegal is a person qualified by education, training or work experience who is employed or retained by a lawyer, law office, corporation, governmental agency or other entity who performs specifically delegated substantive legal work for which a lawyer is responsible.

Comment

This definition emphasizes the knowledge and expertise of paralegals in substantive and procedural law obtained through education and work experience. It further defines a paralegal as the professional working under the supervision of an attorney as distinguished from a non-lawyer who delivers services directly to the public without any intervention or review of work product by an attorney. Such unsupervised services, unless authorized by court or agency rules, constitute the unauthorized practice of law.

Statutes, court rules, case law and bar association documents are additional sources for legal assistant or paralegal definitions. In applying the Standards and Guidelines, it is important to remember that they were developed to apply to the paralegal as defined herein. Lawyers should refrain from labeling those as paralegals or legal assistants who do not meet the criteria set forth in this definition and/or the definitions set forth by state rules, guidelines or bar associations. Labeling secretaries and other administrative staff as legal assistants/paralegals is inaccurate.

For billing purposes, the services of a legal secretary are considered part of overhead costs and are not recoverable in fee awards. However, the courts have held that fees for paralegal services are recoverable as long as they are not clerical functions, such as organizing files, copying documents, checking docket, updating files, checking court dates and delivering papers. As established in *Missouri v. Jenkins*, 491 U.S.274, 109 S.Ct. 2463, 2471, n.10 (1989), tasks performed by legal assistants must be substantive in nature which, absent the legal assistant, the attorney would perform.

There are also case law and Supreme Court Rules addressing the issue of a disbarred attorney serving in the capacity of a paralegal.

IV. Standards

A paralegal should meet certain minimum qualifications. The following standards may be used to determine an individual's qualifications as a paralegal:

- Successful completion of the Certified Paralegal (CP) certifying examination of NALA;
- Graduation from an ABA approved program of study for paralegals;
- Graduation from a course of study for paralegals which is institutionally accredited but not ABA approved, and which requires not less than the equivalent of 60 semester hours of class-room study;
- Graduation from a course of study for paralegals, other than those set forth in (2) and (3) above, plus not less than six months of in-house training as a paralegal;
- A baccalaureate degree in any field, plus not less than six months in-house training as a paralegal;
- A minimum of three years of law-related experience under the supervision of an attorney, including at least six months of in-house training as a paralegal; or
- Two years of in-house training as a paralegal.

For purposes of this Model, "in-house training as a paralegal" means attorney education of the employee concerning paralegal duties. In addition to review and analysis of assignments, the paralegal should receive a reasonable amount of instruction directly related to the duties and obligations of the paralegal.

Comment

This Model sets forth minimum qualifications for a paralegal. These minimum qualifications, as adopted, recognize legal-related work backgrounds and formal education backgrounds, both of which provide the paralegal with a broad base in exposure to and knowledge of the legal profession.

This background is necessary to assure the public and the legal profession that the employee identified as a paralegal is qualified.

The Certified Paralegal (CP) examination established by NALA in 1976 is a voluntary nationwide certification program for paralegals. The CP designation is a statement to the legal profession and the public that the paralegal has met the high levels of knowledge and professionalism required by NALA's certification program. Continuing education requirements, which all certified paralegals must meet, assure that high standards are maintained. The CP designation has been recognized as a means of establishing the qualifications of a paralegal in Supreme Court rules, state court and bar association standards and utilization guidelines.

On April 30, 2014, The National Commission for Certifying Agencies (NCCA) granted accreditation to the NALA Certified Paralegal program for demonstrating compliance with the NCCA Standards for the Accreditation of Certification Programs.

NCCA is the accrediting body of the Institute for Credentialing Excellence. The NCCA Standards were created to ensure certification programs adhere to modern standards of practice for the certification industry. The NALA Certified Paralegal program joins an elite group of more than 120 organizations representing over 270 certification programs that have received and maintained NCCA accreditation. The accreditation requires annual reports and renewal every five years to ensure standards.

Certification through NALA is available to all paralegals meeting the educational and experience requirements. Certified Paralegals may also pursue advanced certification in specialty practice areas through the APC, Advanced Paralegal Certification, credentialing program. Paralegals may also pursue certification based on state laws and procedures in California, Florida, Louisiana, North Carolina, and Texas.

V. Guidelines

These guidelines relating to standards of performance and professional responsibility are intended to aid paralegals and attorneys. The ultimate responsibility rests with an attorney who employs paralegals to educate them with respect to the duties they are assigned and to supervise the manner in which such duties are accomplished.

Comment

In general, a paralegal is allowed to perform any task which is properly delegated and supervised by an attorney, as long as the attorney is ultimately responsible to the client and assumes complete professional responsibility for the work product.

ABA Model Rules of Professional Conduct, Rule 5.3 provides: With respect to a non-lawyer employed or retained by or associated with a lawyer:

a) a partner in a law firm shall make reasonable efforts to ensure that the firm has in effect measures giving reasonable assurance that the person's conduct is compatible with the professional obligations of the lawyer;

b) a lawyer having direct supervisory authority over the non-lawyer shall make reasonable efforts to ensure that the person's conduct is compatible with the professional obligations of the lawyer; and

c) a lawyer shall be responsible for conduct of such a person that would be a violation of the rules of professional conduct if engaged in by a lawyer if:

    1) the lawyer orders or, with the knowledge of the specific conduct ratifies the conduct involved; or

    2) the lawyer is a partner in the law firm in which the person is employed, or has direct supervisory authority over the person, and knows of the conduct at a time when its consequences can be avoided or mitigated but fails to take remedial action.

There are many interesting and complex issues involving the use of paralegals. In any discussion of the proper role of a paralegal, attention must be directed to what constitutes the practice of law. Proper delegation to paralegals is further complicated and confused by the lack of an adequate definition of the practice of law.

Kentucky became the first state to adopt a Paralegal Code by Supreme Court Rule. This Code sets forth certain exclusions to the unauthorized practice of law:

For purposes of this rule, the unauthorized practice of law shall not include any service rendered involving legal knowledge or advice, whether representation, counsel or advocacy, in or out of court, rendered in respect to the acts, duties, obligations, liabilities or business relations of the one requiring services where:

- The client understands that the paralegal is not a lawyer;
- The lawyer supervises the paralegal in the performance of his or her duties; and
- The lawyer remains fully responsible for such representation including all actions taken or not taken in connection therewith by the paralegal to the same extent as if such representation had been furnished entirely by the lawyer and all such actions had been taken or not taken directly by the attorney. Paralegal Code, Ky.S.Ct.R3.700, Sub-Rule 2.

South Dakota Supreme Court Rule 97-25 Utilization Rule a(4) states: The attorney remains responsible for the services performed by the legal assistant to the same extent as though such services had been furnished entirely by the attorney and such actions were those of the attorney.

Guideline 1
Paralegals should:

- Disclose their status as paralegals at the outset of any professional relationship with a client, other attorneys, a court or administrative agency or personnel thereof, or members of the general public;
- Preserve the confidences and secrets of all clients; and
- Understand the attorney's Rules of Professional Responsibility and these Guidelines in order to avoid any action which would involve the attorney in a violation of the Rules or give the appearance of professional impropriety.

Comment

Routine early disclosure of the paralegal's status when dealing with persons outside the attorney's office is necessary to assure that there will be no misunderstanding as to the responsibilities and role of the paralegal. Disclosure may be made in any way that avoids confusion. If the person dealing with the paralegal already knows of his/her status, further disclosure is unnecessary. If at any time in written or oral communication the paralegal becomes aware that the other person may believe the paralegal is an attorney, immediate disclosure should be made as to the paralegal's status.

The attorney should exercise care that the paralegal preserves and refrains from using any confidence or secrets of a client and should instruct the paralegal not to disclose or use any such confidences or secrets. The paralegal must take any and all steps necessary to prevent conflicts of interest and fully disclose such conflicts to the supervising attorney. Failure to do so may jeopardize both the attorney's representation of the client and the case itself.

Guidelines for the Utilization of Legal Assistant Services adopted December 3, 1994 by the Washington State Bar Association Board of Governors states:

> "Guideline 7: A lawyer shall take reasonable measures to prevent conflicts of interest resulting from a legal assistant's other employment or interest insofar as such other employment or interests would present a conflict of interest if it were that of the lawyer."

In Re Complex Asbestos Litigation, 232 Cal. App. 3d 572 (Cal. 1991), addresses the issue wherein a law firm was disqualified due to possession of attorney-client confidences by a legal assistant employee resulting from previous employment by opposing counsel.

In Oklahoma, in an order issued July 12, 2001, in the matter of *Mark A. Hayes, M.D. v. Central States Orthopedic Specialists, Inc.*, a Tulsa County District Court Judge disqualified a law firm from representation of a client on the basis that an ethical screen was an impermissible device to protect from disclosure confidences gained by a non-lawyer employee while employed by another law firm.

In applying the same rules that govern attorneys, the court found that the Rules of Professional Conduct pertaining to confidentiality apply to non-lawyers who leave firms with actual knowledge of material, confidential information and a screening device is not an appropriate alternative to the imputed disqualification of an incoming legal assistant who has moved from one firm to another during ongoing litigation and has actual knowledge of material, confidential information. The decision was appealed, and the Oklahoma Supreme Court determined that, under certain circumstances, screening is an appropriate management tool for non-lawyer staff.

In 2004, the Nevada Supreme Court also addressed this issue at the urging of the state's paralegals. The Nevada Supreme Court granted a petition to rescind the Court's 1997 ruling in *Ciaffone v. District Court*. In this case, the court clarified the original ruling, stating "mere opportunity to access confidential information does not merit disqualification." The opinion stated instances in which screening may be appropriate and listed minimum screening requirements. The opinion also set forth guidelines that a district court may use to determine if screening has been or may be effective. These considerations are:

- substantiality of the relationship between the former and current matters
- the time elapsed between the matters
- size of the firm
- number of individuals presumed to have confidential information
- nature of their involvement in the former matter
- timing and features of any measures taken to reduce the danger of disclosure
- whether the old firm and the new firm represent adverse parties in the same proceeding rather than in different proceedings.

The ultimate responsibility for compliance with approved standards of professional conduct rests with the supervising attorney. The burden rests upon the attorney who employs a paralegal to educate the latter with respect to the duties which may be assigned and then to supervise the manner in which the paralegal carries out such duties. However, this does not relieve the paralegal from an independent obligation to refrain from illegal conduct. Additionally, and notwithstanding that the Rules are not binding upon non-lawyers, the very nature of a paralegal's employment imposes an obligation not to engage in conduct which would involve the supervising attorney in a violation of the Rules.

The attorney must make sufficient background investigation of the prior activities and character and integrity of his or her paralegals. Further, the attorney must take all measures necessary to avoid and fully disclose conflicts of interest due to other employment or interests. Failure to do so may jeopardize both the attorney's representation of the client and the case itself.

Paralegal associations strive to maintain the high level of integrity and competence expected of the legal profession and, further, strive to uphold the high standards of ethics. NALA's Code of Ethics and Professional Responsibility states "A paralegal's conduct is guided by bar associations' codes of professional responsibility and rules of professional conduct." On August 6, 2012, the American Bar Association approved revisions to the Model Rules of Professional Conduct, many of which specifically relate to technology. Changes include the Comment on Rule 1.1 Competence. The change to the Comment, now section 8 on Maintaining Competence, states:

> "To maintain the requisite knowledge and skill, a lawyer should keep abreast of changes in the law and its practice, including the benefits and risks associated with relevant technology, engage in continuing study and education and comply with all continuing legal education requirements to which the lawyer is subject."

With the increasing reliance on technology and the movement of the courts toward electronic filing and e-discovery, it is imperative that paralegals hold to the highest standards of professional and technological competence.

Guideline 2

Paralegals should not: establish attorney-client relationships; set legal fees; give legal opinions or advice; or represent a client before a court, unless authorized to do so by said court; nor engage in, encourage, or contribute to any act which could constitute the unauthorized practice of law.

Comment

Case law, court rules, codes of ethics and professional responsibilities, as well as bar ethics opinions now hold which acts can and cannot be performed by a paralegal. Generally, the determination of what acts constitute the unauthorized practice of law is made by state supreme courts. Numerous cases exist relating to the unauthorized practice of law. Courts have gone so far as to prohibit the paralegal from preparation of divorce kits and assisting in preparation of bankruptcy forms and, more specifically, from providing basic information about procedures and requirements, deciding where information should be placed on forms, and responding to questions from debtors regarding the interpretation or definition of terms. Cases have identified certain areas in which an attorney has a duty to act, but it is interesting to note that none of these cases state that it is improper for an attorney to have the initial work performed by the paralegal. This again points out the importance of adequate supervision by the employing attorney. An attorney can be found to have aided in the unauthorized practice of law when delegating acts which cannot be performed by a paralegal.

Guideline 3

Paralegals may perform services for an attorney in the representation of a client, provided:

- The services performed by the paralegal do not require the exercise of independent professional legal judgment;
- The attorney maintains a direct relationship with the client and maintains control of all client matters;
- The attorney supervises the paralegal;
- The attorney remains professionally responsible for all work on behalf of the client, including any actions taken or not taken by the paralegal in connection therewith; and
- The services performed supplement, merge with and become the attorney's work product.

Comment

Paralegals, whether employees or independent contractors, perform services for the attorney in the representation of a client. Attorneys should delegate work to paralegals commensurate with their knowledge and experience and provide appropriate instruction and supervision concerning the delegated work, as well as ethical acts of their employment. Ultimate responsibility for the work product of a paralegal rests with the attorney. However, a paralegal must use discretion and professional judgment and must not render independent legal judgment in place of an attorney.

The work product of a paralegal is subject to civil rules governing discovery of materials prepared in anticipation of litigation, whether the paralegal is viewed as an extension of the attorney or as another representative of the party itself. Fed.R.Civ.P. 26 (b) (3) and (5).

Guideline 4

In the supervision of a paralegal, consideration should be given to:

- Designating work assignments that correspond to the paralegal's abilities, knowledge, training and experience;
- Educating and training the paralegal with respect to professional responsibility, local rules and practices, and firm policies;
- Monitoring the work and professional conduct of the paralegal to ensure that the work is substantively correct and timely performed;
- Providing continuing education for the paralegal in substantive matters through courses, institutes, workshops, seminars and in-house training; and
- Encouraging and supporting membership and active participation in professional organizations.

Comment

Attorneys are responsible for the actions of their employees in both malpractice and disciplinary proceedings. In the vast majority of cases, the courts have not censured attorneys for a particular act delegated to the paralegal, but rather, have been critical of and imposed sanctions against attorneys for failure to adequately supervise the paralegal. The attorney's responsibility for supervision of his or her paralegal must be more than a willingness to accept responsibility and liability for the paralegal's work. Supervision of a paralegal must be offered in both the procedural and substantive legal areas. The attorney must delegate work based upon the education, knowledge and abilities of the paralegal and must monitor the work product and conduct of the paralegal to ensure that the work performed is substantively correct and competently performed in a professional manner.

Michigan State Board of Commissioners has adopted *Guidelines for the Utilization of Legal Assistants* (April 23, 1993). These guidelines, in part, encourage employers to support legal assistant participation in continuing education programs to ensure that the legal assistant remains competent in the fields of practice in which the legal assistant is assigned.

The working relationship between the lawyer and the paralegal should extend to cooperative efforts on public service activities wherever possible. Participation in pro bono activities is encouraged in ABA Guideline 10.

Guideline 5

In the supervision except as otherwise provided by statute, court rule or decision, administrative rule or regulation, or the attorney's rules of professional responsibility, and within the preceding parameters and proscriptions, a paralegal may perform any function delegated by an attorney, including, but not limited to, the following:

- Conduct client interviews and maintain general contact with the client after the establishment of the attorney-client relationship, so long as the client is aware of the status and function of the paralegal, and the client contact is under the supervision of the attorney.
- Locate and interview witnesses, so long as the witnesses are aware of the status and function of the paralegal.
- Conduct investigations and statistical and documentary research for review by the attorney.
- Conduct legal research for review by the attorney.
- Draft legal documents for review by the attorney.
- Draft correspondence and pleadings for review by and signature of the attorney.
- Summarize depositions, interrogatories and testimony for review by the attorney.
- Attend executions of wills, real estate closings, depositions, court or administrative hearings and trials with the attorney.
- Author and sign letters providing the paralegal's status is clearly indicated and the correspondence does not contain independent legal opinions or legal advice.

Comment

The United States Supreme Court has recognized the variety of tasks being performed by paralegals and has noted that use of paralegals encourages cost-effective delivery of legal services, *Missouri v. Jenkins*, 491 U.S.274, 109 S.Ct. 2463, 2471, n.10 (1989). In *Jenkins*, the court further held that paralegal time should be included in compensation for attorney fee awards at the market rate of the relevant community to bill paralegal time. Courts have held that paralegal fees are not a part of the overall overhead of a law firm. Paralegal services are billed separately by attorneys and decrease litigation expenses. Tasks performed by paralegals must contain substantive legal work under the direction or supervision of an attorney, such that if the paralegal were not present, the work would be performed by the attorney.

In *Taylor v. Chubb*, 874 P.2d 806 (Okla. 1994), the Court ruled that attorney fees awarded should include fees for services performed by paralegals and, further, defined tasks which may be performed by the paralegal under the supervision of an attorney including, among others: interview clients; draft pleadings and other documents; carry on legal research, both conventional and computer aided; research public records; prepare discovery requests and responses; schedule depositions and prepare notices and subpoenas; summarize depositions and other discovery responses; coordinate and manage document production; locate and interview witnesses; organize pleadings, trial exhibits and other documents; prepare witness and exhibit lists; prepare trial notebooks; prepare for the attendance of witnesses at trial; and assist lawyers at trials.

Except for the specific proscription contained in Guideline 1, the reported cases do not limit the duties which may be performed by a paralegal under the supervision of the attorney.

An attorney may not split legal fees with a legal assistant, nor pay a paralegal for the referral of legal business. An attorney may compensate a paralegal based on the quantity and quality of the paralegal's work and value of that work to a law practice.

Conclusion

These Standards and Guidelines were developed from generally accepted practices. Each supervising attorney must be aware of the specific rules, decisions and statutes applicable to paralegals within his or her jurisdiction.

NALS *Code of Ethics and Professional Responsibility*

Members of NALS are bound by the objectives of this association and the standards of conduct required of the legal profession.

Every member shall:

- Encourage respect for the law and the administration of justice;
- Observe rules governing privileged communications and confidential information;
- Promote and exemplify high standards of loyalty, cooperation, and courtesy;
- Perform all duties of the profession with integrity and competence; and
- Pursue a high order of professional attainment.

Integrity and high standards of conduct are fundamental to the success of our professional association. This Code is promulgated by the NALS and accepted by its members to accomplish these ends.

Canon 1

Members of this association shall maintain a high degree of competency and integrity through continuing education to better assist the legal profession in fulfilling its duty to provide quality legal services to the public.

Canon 2

Members of this association shall maintain a high standard of ethical conduct and shall contribute to the integrity of the association and the legal profession.

Canon 3

Members of this association shall avoid a conflict of interest pertaining to a client matter.

Canon 4

Members of this association shall preserve and protect the confidences and privileged communications of a client.

Canon 5

Members of this association shall exercise care in using independent professional judgment and in determining the extent to which a client may be assisted without the presence of a lawyer and shall not act in matters involving professional legal judgment.

Canon 6

Members of this association shall not solicit legal business on behalf of a lawyer.

Canon 7

Members of this association, unless permitted by law, shall not perform paralegal functions except under the direct supervision of a lawyer and shall not advertise or contract with members of the general public for the performance of paralegal functions.

Canon 8

Members of this association, unless permitted by law, shall not perform any of the duties restricted to lawyers or do things which lawyers themselves may not do and shall assist in preventing the unauthorized practice of law.

Canon 9

Members of this association not licensed to practice law shall not engage in the practice of law as defined by statutes or court decisions.

Canon 10

Members of this association shall do all other things incidental, necessary, or expedient to enhance professional responsibility and participation in the administration of justice and public service in cooperation with the legal profession.

NALA's Certification Program

The National Association of Legal Assistants (NALA)—also known as The Paralegal Association—offers a certification program for those who are interested. In the working environment, professional certification is a time-honored process respected by both employers and those within the career field. The following is a definition used by many to describe *professional certification*:

> Professional certification is a voluntary process by which a nongovernmental entity grants a time-limited recognition to an individual after verifying that the individual has met predetermined, standardized criteria. [Source: Rops, M., *Understanding the Language of Credentialing,* American Society of Association Executives, May 2002.]

The definition hits the high points. Certification is voluntary, not imposed by government. It is time limited, which means that those with the certification must fulfill ongoing educational requirements to keep the certification current, and the criteria for certification is recognized in the community.

The Purpose of NALA's Certified Paralegal Certification Program

Established in 1976, NALA's Certified Legal Assistant (CLA) program allowed the paralegal profession to develop a strong and responsive self-regulatory program offering a nationwide credential for paralegals. The current Certified Paralegal (CP) program establishes and serves as:

- A national professional standard for paralegals.
- A means of identifying those who have reached this standard.
- A credentialing program responsive to paralegal needs and responsive to the necessity of self-regulation to strengthen and expand paralegal career development.
- A positive, ongoing voluntary program to encourage the growth of the paralegal profession, attesting to and encouraging a high level of achievement.

The CP credential has been developed to recognize paralegals who have demonstrated entry-level knowledge and skill to provide competent assistance in the delivery of legal services for lawyers, law offices, corporations, or governmental agencies in the United States. The CP credential is a prestigious indicator to clients, potential clients, employers, and the public at large that the paralegal professional has proficiency in the legal services field.

When the CLA program was developed, the preferred term was *legal assistant* to designate a non-lawyer employee with specialized education who does work of a legal nature that, absent the legal assistant, the attorney would perform. Legal assistant time is billed to clients at market rates in the same manner as other legal professional staff. By 2004, the preferred term changed to *paralegal* even though bar association rules and guidelines and some statutes still used the term *legal assistant*. In 2004, NALA registered the certification mark CP® and in 2019 encouraged paralegals to use the CP®. Since 2011, the term *paralegal* is used almost exclusively, and the certification program is referred to as the Certified Paralegal program, which awards the Certified Paralegal credential.

Administration

The NALA Certifying Board is responsible for content, standards and administration of the Certified Paralegal Program. It is composed of paralegals who have received the Certified Paralegal certification designation, attorneys, and paralegal educators.

Accreditation of Certified Paralegal Program

The National Commission for Certifying Agencies (NCCA) has granted accreditation to the NALA Certified Paralegal program since 2014 for demonstrating compliance with the NCCA Standards for the Accreditation of Certification Programs. NCCA is the accrediting body of the Institute for Credentialing Excellence. The NCCA Standards were created to ensure certification programs adhere to modern standards of practice for the certification industry.

The NALA Certified Paralegal program joins an elite group of more than 120 organizations representing more than 270 certification programs that have received and maintained NCCA accreditation. More information on the NCCA is available online at www.credentialingexcellence.org/NCCA. To maintain accreditation, NCCA requires annual reports of all certification programs. Re-accreditation is required every five years.

The Certified Paralegal Credential

Use of the Certified Paralegal credential signifies that a paralegal is capable of providing superior services to firms and corporations. National surveys consistently show Certified Paralegals are better utilized in a field where attorneys are looking for a credible, dependable way to measure ability. The credential has been recognized by the American Bar Association as a designation, which marks a high level of professional achievement. The CP credential has also been recognized by more than forty-seven paralegal organizations and numerous bar associations.

Occasionally, paralegals call themselves "certified" by virtue of completing a paralegal training course, or another type of preparatory education. Although a school may award a certificate of completion, this is not the same as earning professional certification by an entity such as NALA. In this instance, the school's certificate is designation of completion of a training program.

The Certified Paralegal Examination

The Certifying Board provides oversight for the development and ongoing maintenance of the Certified Paralegal examination. The Certifying Board, NALA certification program staff, and trained subject matter experts, work in partnership with a qualified psychometric consultant to ensure the examination is developed and maintained in a manner consistent with generally accepted psychometric, educational testing practices, and national accreditation standards for certification programs.

Subject Matter Experts

The Certifying Board selects diverse groups of qualified subject matter experts (SMEs) to participate in exam development activities throughout the exam development and maintenance process. Activities that involve subject matter expert participation include creating job analysis surveys, creating test content outlines, writing and reviewing exam items, and establishing the passing point for exams. Ad-hoc committees and/or working groups of SMEs composed of Certifying Board members, paralegals, attorneys, educators, and other outside experts may be assembled for these tasks.

Qualified SMEs write and review items for the exam. Subject matter expert item writers and reviewers complete mandatory training on item writing/review for certification examinations. Items are subject to multiple levels of review and analysis before being used as graded items on the exam. The Certifying Board oversees a continual process of item writing, review and evaluation to ensure that exam content remains up-to-date, accurate, and consistent with the content outline.

Review of the Job Task Analysis Study

Job analysis studies are conducted periodically to identify and validate the knowledge and skills, which will be measured by the examination sections. The results of the job analysis studies serve as the basis for the exam specifications. These exam specifications, with weights for each content area, are approved by the Certifying Board.

In 2016, the NALA Certifying Board conducted its Job Task Analysis Study (Study). This Study examined the duties and responsibilities of paralegals in the workplace and the goals were to:

- Validate and update the Certified Paralegal examination content; and
- Ensure that NALA has current information about the roles and responsibilities of paralegals.

Based on analysis of the Study, improvements in technology, and recent refinements by the National Commission for Certifying Agencies (NCCA), and the advice of NALA's psychometricians, the Certifying Board approved a new structure for the Certified Paralegal examination effective January 2018. (NALA also modified some policies and procedures based upon best practices in credentialing programs, and they are posted on its website under the Certification link.)

The New Exam Format

The new Certified Paralegal examination format opened in March 2018 for one-month of post-administration analysis, scoring, and standard setting. With these modifications, the Certifying Board listened to member and nonmember paralegals working in the field, and applied findings of the Study to the examination. The Certifying Board works diligently to connect the Certified Paralegal examination directly to the day-to-day duties and responsibilities of paralegals in the workplace.

The modifications announced for the 2018 examination are part of the continued effort to ensure the Certified Paralegal examination remains an accurate and relevant reflection of today's paralegals. The Certified Paralegal examination now consists of two required sections taken in the following order:

1. The Knowledge Exam—The Knowledge Exam consists of multiple-choice questions covering the topic areas listed in the table below. The Knowledge Exam is administered on-demand, year-round at testing centers or with an approved exam proctor, with preliminary result reporting upon completion. Candidates must successfully complete the Knowledge Exam in order to be eligible to take the Skills Exam.

2. The Skills Exam—The Skills Exam will consist of a written assignment, and it is administered during four testing windows each year in February, April, July, and October. Successful completion of both the Knowledge and Skills Exams is required to obtain the Certified Paralegal credential.

Examination Points and Passing Scores

Once admitted to the Certified Paralegal credentialing program, examinees must successfully complete the two-part examination. The two exams' total points are as follows (see also Exhibit D.1):

Examination Name	Total Points
Knowledge Exam	100
Skills Exam	30

All NALA certification examinations are prepared and offered in English only. Special accommodations, such as requesting translation dictionaries, are not permitted. No language assistance will be authorized by the Certifying Board. See the NALA website at www.nala.org for more details on qualification for the Certified Paralegal program, as well as information about the Advanced Certified Paralegal Program.

EXHIBIT D.1

Certified Paralegal Exam
Specifications – Effective 2018

Knowledge Exam		100 Points Total
1	United States Legal System	15
1.A	Sources of Law	
1.B	Judicial System	
1.C	Remedies	
1.D	Administrative Law	
2	Civil Litigation	15
2.A	Jurisdiction	
2.B	Federal Rules of Civil Procedure	
3	Contracts	15
3.A	Formation, Rights, and Duties	
3.B	Enforcement and Defenses	
4	Corporate/Commercial Law	10
4.A	Business Organizations	
4.B	Rights and	
4.C	Responsibilities	
5	Criminal Law and Procedure	5
5.A	Criminal Law	
5.B	Criminal Procedure	
6	Estate Planning and Probate	5
6.A	Estate and Trusts	
6.B	Wills	
7	Real Estate and Property	10
7.A	Property Rights and Ownership	
7.B	Transactions	
8	Torts	10
8.A	Intentional	
8.B	Torts	
8.C	Negligence	
9	Professional and Ethical Responsibility	15
9.A	American Bar Association (ABA) Model Rules of Professional Conduct	
9.B	Unauthorized Practice of Law	

Continued

Skills Exam		30 Points Total
1	Writing	12
1.A	Grammar, Spelling, and Punctuation	6
1.B	Clarity of Expression	6
2	Critical Thinking	18
2.A	Reading Comprehension	6
2.B	Analysis of Information	6
2.C	Decision Making	6

EXHIBIT D.1

Certified Paralegal Exam Specifications – Effective 2018—Continued

NALS Certification

Obtaining a NALS certification demonstrates career commitment, builds credibility, showcases skills, and opens the doors of opportunity to enhance your career in the legal industry. NALS offers three unique certifications and four legal designations dedicated to the legal services profession.

The exams are of varying levels and are developed by professionals in the industry. Each certification is developed by NALS and takes advantage of the more than eighty-five-plus years of experience and dedication to the legal services industry only NALS has to offer. NALS has the certification for you, whether you are beginning a career in the legal industry or are a veteran paralegal ready to display your skills. Below is an overview of the three NALS certification programs.

1. **Accredited Legal Professional (ALP)**

   The ALP® is designed for students and entry-level professionals looking to get their foot in the door of the legal profession. It is often used as an exit exam for legal studies programs and serves as a great way to complement what has been learned in the classroom. Attaining this goal demonstrates commitment and aptitude for succeeding in the ever-changing legal environment and provides an opportunity to begin your career a rung above the competition.

2. **Professional Legal Secretary (PLS) and/or Certified Legal Professional (CLP)**

   The PLS® and/or CLP® is designed for individuals with a minimum of three years of legal work experience who are looking to establish their credentials nationwide as a Professional Legal Secretary or Certified Legal Professional. Attaining this goal demonstrates a mastery of office skills, the discipline to assume responsibility and exercise initiative and judgment, dedication to professionalism, and acceptance of the challenge to be exceptional.

3. **Professional Paralegal (PP)**

   The PP® is designed for students graduating from an ABA-approved legal studies or paralegal studies program OR individuals with a minimum of five years of paralegal/legal assistant experience who are looking to establish their credentials nationwide as a Professional Paralegal. Established in 2004 at our members' request, the PP® designation is an attainable goal for paralegals who wish to be identified as exceptional in all areas of the law. Attaining this goal demonstrates knowledge and understanding of legal terminology and procedures, as well as procedural and substantive law.

For information on the exams and materials, see the NALS website at www.nals.org.

The Constitution of the United States

Preamble

We the People of the United States, in Order to form a more perfect Union, establish Justice, insure domestic Tranquility, provide for the common defence, promote the general Welfare, and secure the Blessings of Liberty to ourselves and our Posterity, do ordain and establish this Constitution for the United States of America.

Article I

Section 1.   All legislative Powers herein granted shall be vested in a Congress of the United States, which shall consist of a Senate and House of Representatives.

Section 2.   The House of Representatives shall be composed of Members chosen every second Year by the People of the several States, and the Electors in each State shall have the Qualifications requisite for Electors of the most numerous Branch of the State Legislature.

No Person shall be a Representative who shall not have attained to the Age of twenty five Years, and been seven Years a Citizen of the United States, and who shall not, when elected, be an Inhabitant of that State in which he shall be chosen.

Representatives and direct Taxes shall be apportioned among the several States which may be included within this Union, according to their respective Numbers, which shall be determined by adding to the whole Number of free Persons, including those bound to Service for a Term of Years, and excluding Indians not taxed, three fifths of all other Persons. The actual Enumeration shall be made within three Years after the first Meeting of the Congress of the United States, and within every subsequent Term of ten Years, in such Manner as they shall by Law direct. The Number of Representatives shall not exceed one for every thirty Thousand, but each State shall have at Least one Representative; and until such enumeration shall be made, the State of New Hampshire shall be entitled to chuse three, Massachusetts eight, Rhode Island and Providence Plantations one, Connecticut five, New York six, New Jersey four, Pennsylvania eight, Delaware one, Maryland six, Virginia ten, North Carolina five, South Carolina five, and Georgia three.

When vacancies happen in the Representation from any State, the Executive Authority thereof shall issue Writs of Election to fill such Vacancies.

The House of Representatives shall chuse their Speaker and other Officers; and shall have the sole Power of Impeachment.

Section 3.   The Senate of the United States shall be composed of two Senators from each State, chosen by the Legislature thereof, for six Years; and each Senator shall have one Vote.

Immediately after they shall be assembled in Consequence of the first Election, they shall be divided as equally as may be into three Classes. The Seats of the Senators of the first Class shall be vacated at the Expiration of the second Year, of the second Class at the Expiration of the fourth Year, and of the third Class at the Expiration of the sixth Year, so that one third may be chosen every second Year; and if Vacancies happen by Resignation, or otherwise, during the Recess of the Legislature of any State, the Executive thereof may make temporary Appointments until the next Meeting of the Legislature, which shall then fill such Vacancies.

No Person shall be a Senator who shall not have attained to the Age of thirty Years, and been nine Years a Citizen of the United States, and who shall not, when elected, be an Inhabitant of that State for which he shall be chosen.

The Vice President of the United States shall be President of the Senate, but shall have no Vote, unless they be equally divided.

The Senate shall chuse their other Officers, and also a President pro tempore, in the Absence of the Vice President, or when he shall exercise the Office of President of the United States.

The Senate shall have the sole Power to try all Impeachments. When sitting for that Purpose, they shall be on Oath or Affirmation. When the President of the United States is tried, the Chief Justice shall preside: And no Person shall be convicted without the Concurrence of two thirds of the Members present.

Judgment in Cases of Impeachment shall not extend further than to removal from Office, and disqualification to hold and enjoy any Office of honor, Trust, or Profit under the United States: but the Party convicted shall nevertheless be liable and subject to Indictment, Trial, Judgment, and Punishment, according to Law.

Section 4.   The Times, Places and Manner of holding Elections for Senators and Representatives, shall be prescribed in each State by the Legislature thereof; but the Congress may at any time by Law make or alter such Regulations, except as to the Places of chusing Senators.

The Congress shall assemble at least once in every Year, and such Meeting shall be on the first Monday in December, unless they shall by Law appoint a different Day.

Section 5.   Each House shall be the Judge of the Elections, Returns, and Qualifications of its own Members, and a Majority of each shall constitute a Quorum to do Business; but a smaller Number may adjourn from day to day, and may be authorized to compel the Attendance of absent Members, in such Manner, and under such Penalties as each House may provide.

Each House may determine the Rules of its Proceedings, punish its Members for disorderly Behavior, and, with the Concurrence of two thirds, expel a Member.

Each House shall keep a Journal of its Proceedings, and from time to time publish the same, excepting such Parts as may in their Judgment require Secrecy; and the Yeas and Nays of the Members of either House on any question shall, at the Desire of one fifth of those Present, be entered on the Journal.

Neither House, during the Session of Congress, shall, without the Consent of the other, adjourn for more than three days, nor to any other Place than that in which the two Houses shall be sitting.

Section 6.   The Senators and Representatives shall receive a Compensation for their Services, to be ascertained by Law, and paid out of the Treasury of the United States. They shall in all Cases, except Treason, Felony and Breach of the Peace, be privileged from Arrest during their Attendance at the Session of their respective Houses, and in going to and returning from the same; and for any Speech or Debate in either House, they shall not be questioned in any other Place.

No Senator or Representative shall, during the Time for which he was elected, be appointed to any civil Office under the Authority of the United States, which shall have been created, or the Emoluments whereof shall have been increased during such time; and no Person holding any Office under the United States, shall be a Member of either House during his Continuance in Office.

Section 7. All Bills for raising Revenue shall originate in the House of Representatives; but the Senate may propose or concur with Amendments as on other Bills.

Every Bill which shall have passed the House of Representatives and the Senate, shall, before it become a Law, be presented to the President of the United States; If he approve he shall sign it, but if not he shall return it, with his Objections to the House in which it shall have originated, who shall enter the Objections at large on their Journal, and proceed to reconsider it. If after such Reconsideration two thirds of that House shall agree to pass the Bill, it shall be sent together with the Objections, to the other House, by which it shall likewise be reconsidered, and if approved by two thirds of that House, it shall become a Law. But in all such Cases the Votes of both Houses shall be determined by Yeas and Nays, and the Names of the Persons voting for and against the Bill shall be entered on the Journal of each House respectively. If any Bill shall not be returned by the President within ten Days (Sundays excepted) after it shall have been presented to him, the Same shall be a Law, in like Manner as if he had signed it, unless the Congress by their Adjournment prevent its Return in which Case it shall not be a Law.

Every Order, Resolution, or Vote, to which the Concurrence of the Senate and House of Representatives may be necessary (except on a question of Adjournment) shall be presented to the President of the United States; and before the Same shall take Effect, shall be approved by him, or being disapproved by him, shall be repassed by two thirds of the Senate and House of Representatives, according to the Rules and Limitations prescribed in the Case of a Bill.

Section 8. The Congress shall have Power To lay and collect Taxes, Duties, Imposts and Excises, to pay the Debts and provide for the common Defence and general Welfare of the United States; but all Duties, Imposts and Excises shall be uniform throughout the United States;

To borrow Money on the credit of the United States;

To regulate Commerce with foreign Nations, and among the several States, and with the Indian Tribes;

To establish an uniform Rule of Naturalization, and uniform Laws on the subject of Bankruptcies throughout the United States;

To coin Money, regulate the Value thereof, and of foreign Coin, and fix the Standard of Weights and Measures;

To provide for the Punishment of counterfeiting the Securities and current Coin of the United States;

To establish Post Offices and post Roads;

To promote the Progress of Science and useful Arts, by securing for limited Times to Authors and Inventors the exclusive Right to their respective Writings and Discoveries;

To constitute Tribunals inferior to the supreme Court;

To define and punish Piracies and Felonies committed on the high Seas, and Offenses against the Law of Nations;

To declare War, grant Letters of Marque and Reprisal, and make Rules concerning Captures on Land and Water;

To raise and support Armies, but no Appropriation of Money to that Use shall be for a longer Term than two Years;

To provide and maintain a Navy;

To make Rules for the Government and Regulation of the land and naval Forces;

To provide for calling forth the Militia to execute the Laws of the Union, suppress Insurrections and repel Invasions;

To provide for organizing, arming, and disciplining, the Militia, and for governing such Part of them as may be employed in the Service of the United States, reserving to the States respectively, the Appointment of the Officers, and the Authority of training the Militia according to the discipline prescribed by Congress;

To exercise exclusive Legislation in all Cases whatsoever, over such District (not exceeding ten Miles square) as may, by Cession of particular States, and the Acceptance of Congress, become the Seat of the Government of the United States, and to exercise like Authority over all Places purchased by the Consent of the Legislature of the State in which the Same shall be, for the Erection of Forts, Magazines, Arsenals, dock-Yards, and other needful Buildings;—And

To make all Laws which shall be necessary and proper for carrying into Execution the foregoing Powers, and all other Powers vested by this Constitution in the Government of the United States, or in any Department or Officer thereof.

Section 9. The Migration or Importation of such Persons as any of the States now existing shall think proper to admit, shall not be prohibited by the Congress prior to the Year one thousand eight hundred and eight, but a Tax or duty may be imposed on such Importation, not exceeding ten dollars for each Person.

The privilege of the Writ of Habeas Corpus shall not be suspended, unless when in Cases of Rebellion or Invasion the public Safety may require it.

No Bill of Attainder or ex post facto Law shall be passed.

No Capitation, or other direct, Tax shall be laid, unless in Proportion to the Census or Enumeration herein before directed to be taken.

No Tax or Duty shall be laid on Articles exported from any State.

No Preference shall be given by any Regulation of Commerce or Revenue to the Ports of one State over those of another: nor shall Vessels bound to, or from, one State be obliged to enter, clear, or pay Duties in another.

No Money shall be drawn from the Treasury, but in Consequence of Appropriations made by Law; and a regular Statement and Account of the Receipts and Expenditures of all public Money shall be published from time to time.

No Title of Nobility shall be granted by the United States: And no Person holding any Office of Profit or Trust under them, shall, without the Consent of the Congress, accept of any present, Emolument, Office, or Title, of any kind whatever, from any King, Prince, or foreign State.

Section 10. No State shall enter into any Treaty, Alliance, or Confederation; grant Letters of Marque and Reprisal; coin Money; emit Bills of Credit; make any Thing but gold and silver Coin a Tender in Payment of Debts; pass any Bill of Attainder, ex post facto Law, or Law impairing the Obligation of Contracts, or grant any Title of Nobility.

No State shall, without the Consent of the Congress, lay any Imposts or Duties on Imports or Exports, except what may be absolutely necessary for executing its inspection Laws: and the net Produce of all Duties and Imposts, laid by any State on Imports or Exports, shall be for the Use of the Treasury of the United States; and all such Laws shall be subject to the Revision and Controul of the Congress.

No State shall, without the Consent of Congress, lay any Duty of Tonnage, keep Troops, or Ships of War in time of Peace, enter into any Agreement or Compact with another State, or with a foreign Power, or engage in War, unless actually invaded, or in such imminent Danger as will not admit of delay.

Article II

Section 1. The executive Power shall be vested in a President of the United States of America. He shall hold his Office during the Term of four Years, and, together with the Vice President, chosen for the same Term, be elected, as follows:

Each State shall appoint, in such Manner as the Legislature thereof may direct, a Number of Electors, equal to the whole Number of Senators and Representatives to which the State may be entitled in the Congress; but no Senator or Representative, or Person holding an Office of Trust or Profit under the United States, shall be appointed an Elector.

The Electors shall meet in their respective States, and vote by Ballot for two Persons, of whom one at least shall not be an Inhabitant of the same State with themselves. And they shall make a List of all the Persons voted for, and of the Number of Votes for each; which List they shall sign and certify, and transmit sealed to the Seat of the Government of the United States, directed to the President of the Senate. The President of the Senate shall, in the Presence of the Senate and House of Representatives, open all the Certificates, and the Votes shall then be counted. The Person having the greatest Number of Votes shall be the President, if such Number be a Majority of the whole Number of Electors appointed; and if there be more than one who have such Majority, and have an equal Number of Votes, then the House of Representatives shall immediately chuse by Ballot one of them for President; and if no Person have a Majority, then from the five highest on the List the said House shall in like Manner chuse the President. But in chusing the President, the Votes shall be taken by States, the Representation from each State having one Vote; A quorum for this Purpose shall consist of a Member or Members from two thirds of the States, and a Majority of all the States shall be necessary to a Choice. In every Case, after the Choice of the President, the Person having the greater Number of Votes of the Electors shall be the Vice President. But if there should remain two or more who have equal Votes, the Senate shall chuse from them by Ballot the Vice President.

The Congress may determine the Time of chusing the Electors, and the Day on which they shall give their Votes; which Day shall be the same throughout the United States.

No person except a natural born Citizen, or a Citizen of the United States, at the time of the Adoption of this Constitution, shall be eligible to the Office of President; neither shall any Person be eligible to that Office who shall not have attained to the Age of thirty five Years, and been fourteen Years a Resident within the United States.

In Case of the Removal of the President from Office, or of his Death, Resignation or Inability to discharge the Powers and Duties of the said Office, the same shall devolve on the Vice President, and the Congress may by Law provide for the Case of Removal, Death, Resignation or Inability, both of the President and Vice President, declaring what Officer shall then act as President, and such Officer shall act accordingly, until the Disability be removed, or a President shall be elected.

The President shall, at stated Times, receive for his Services, a Compensation, which shall neither be increased nor diminished during the Period for which he shall have been elected, and he shall not receive within that Period any other Emolument from the United States, or any of them.

Before he enter on the Execution of his Office, he shall take the following Oath or Affirmation: "I do solemnly swear (or affirm) that I will faithfully execute the Office of President of the United States, and will to the best of my Ability, preserve, protect and defend the Constitution of the United States."

Section 2. The President shall be Commander in Chief of the Army and Navy of the United States, and of the Militia of the several States, when called into the actual Service of the United States; he may require the Opinion, in writing, of the principal Officer in each of the executive Departments, upon any Subject relating to the Duties of their respective Offices, and he shall have Power to grant Reprieves and Pardons for Offenses against the United States, except in Cases of Impeachment.

He shall have Power, by and with the Advice and Consent of the Senate to make Treaties, provided two thirds of the Senators present concur; and he shall nominate, and by and with the Advice and Consent of the Senate, shall appoint Ambassadors, other public Ministers and Consuls, Judges of the supreme Court, and all other Officers of the United States, whose Appointments are not herein otherwise provided for, and which shall be established by Law; but the Congress may by Law vest the Appointment of such inferior Officers, as they think proper, in the President alone, in the Courts of Law, or in the Heads of Departments.

The President shall have Power to fill up all Vacancies that may happen during the Recess of the Senate, by granting Commissions which shall expire at the End of their next Session.

Section 3.   He shall from time to time give to the Congress Information of the State of the Union, and recommend to their Consideration such Measures as he shall judge necessary and expedient; he may, on extraordinary Occasions, convene both Houses, or either of them, and in Case of Disagreement between them, with Respect to the Time of Adjournment, he may adjourn them to such Time as he shall think proper; he shall receive Ambassadors and other public Ministers; he shall take Care that the Laws be faithfully executed, and shall Commission all the Officers of the United States.

Section 4.   The President, Vice President and all civil Officers of the United States, shall be removed from Office on Impeachment for, and Conviction of, Treason, Bribery, or other high Crimes and Misdemeanors.

Article III

Section 1.   The judicial Power of the United States, shall be vested in one supreme Court, and in such inferior Courts as the Congress may from time to time ordain and establish. The Judges, both of the supreme and inferior Courts, shall hold their Offices during good Behaviour, and shall, at stated Times, receive for their Services a Compensation, which shall not be diminished during their Continuance in Office.

Section 2.   The judicial Power shall extend to all Cases, in Law and Equity, arising under this Constitution, the Laws of the United States, and Treaties made, or which shall be made, under their Authority;—to all Cases affecting Ambassadors, other public Ministers and Consuls;—to all Cases of admiralty and maritime Jurisdiction;—to Controversies to which the United States shall be a Party;—to Controversies between two or more States;—between a State and Citizens of another State;—between Citizens of different States;—between Citizens of the same State claiming Lands under Grants of different States, and between a State, or the Citizens thereof, and foreign States, Citizens or Subjects.

In all Cases affecting Ambassadors, other public Ministers and Consuls, and those in which a State shall be a Party, the supreme Court shall have original Jurisdiction. In all the other Cases before mentioned, the supreme Court shall have appellate Jurisdiction, both as to Law and Fact, with such Exceptions, and under such Regulations as the Congress shall make.

The Trial of all Crimes, except in Cases of Impeachment, shall be by Jury; and such Trial shall be held in the State where the said Crimes shall have been committed; but when not committed within any State, the Trial shall be at such Place or Places as the Congress may by Law have directed.

Section 3.   Treason against the United States, shall consist only in levying War against them, or, in adhering to their Enemies, giving them Aid and Comfort. No Person shall be convicted of Treason unless on the Testimony of two Witnesses to the same overt Act, or on Confession in open Court.

The Congress shall have Power to declare the Punishment of Treason, but no Attainder of Treason shall work Corruption of Blood, or Forfeiture except during the Life of the Person attainted.

Article IV

Section 1.   Full Faith and Credit shall be given in each State to the public Acts, Records, and judicial Proceedings of every other State. And the Congress may by general Laws prescribe the Manner in which such Acts, Records and Proceedings shall be proved, and the Effect thereof.

Section 2.   The Citizens of each State shall be entitled to all Privileges and Immunities of Citizens in the several States.

A Person charged in any State with Treason, Felony, or other Crime, who shall flee from Justice, and be found in another State, shall on Demand of the executive Authority of the State from which he fled, be delivered up, to be removed to the State having Jurisdiction of the Crime.

No Person held to Service or Labour in one State, under the Laws thereof, escaping into another, shall, in Consequence of any Law or Regulation therein, be discharged from such Service or Labour, but shall be delivered up on Claim of the Party to whom such Service or Labour may be due.

Section 3.   New States may be admitted by the Congress into this Union; but no new State shall be formed or erected within the Jurisdiction of any other State; nor any State be formed by the Junction of two or more States, or Parts of States, without the Consent of the Legislatures of the States concerned as well as of the Congress.

The Congress shall have Power to dispose of and make all needful Rules and Regulations respecting the Territory or other Property belonging to the United States; and nothing in this Constitution shall be so construed as to Prejudice any Claims of the United States, or of any particular State.

Section 4.   The United States shall guarantee to every State in this Union a Republican Form of Government, and shall protect each of them against Invasion; and on Application of the Legislature, or of the Executive (when the Legislature cannot be convened) against domestic Violence.

Article V

The Congress, whenever two thirds of both Houses shall deem it necessary, shall propose Amendments to this Constitution, or, on the Application of the Legislatures of two thirds of the several States, shall call a Convention for proposing Amendments, which, in either Case, shall be valid to all Intents and Purposes, as part of this Constitution, when ratified by the Legislatures of three fourths of the several States, or by Conventions in three fourths thereof, as the one or the other Mode of Ratification may be proposed by the Congress; Provided that no Amendment which may be made prior to the Year One thousand eight hundred and eight shall in any Manner affect the first and fourth Clauses in the Ninth Section of the first Article; and that no State, without its Consent, shall be deprived of its equal Suffrage in the Senate.

Article VI

All Debts contracted and Engagements entered into, before the Adoption of this Constitution shall be as valid against the United States under this Constitution, as under the Confederation.

This Constitution, and the Laws of the United States which shall be made in Pursuance thereof; and all Treaties made, or which shall be made, under the Authority of the United States, shall be the supreme Law of the Land; and the Judges in every State shall be bound thereby, any Thing in the Constitution or Laws of any State to the Contrary notwithstanding.

The Senators and Representatives before mentioned, and the Members of the several State Legislatures, and all executive and judicial Officers, both of the United States and of the several States, shall be bound by Oath or Affirmation, to support this Constitution; but no religious Test shall ever be required as a Qualification to any Office or public Trust under the United States.

Article VII

The Ratification of the Conventions of nine States shall be sufficient for the Establishment of this Constitution between the States so ratifying the Same.

Amendment I [1791]

Congress shall make no law respecting an establishment of religion, or prohibiting the free exercise thereof; or abridging the freedom of speech, or of the press; or the right of the people peaceably to assemble, and to petition the Government for a redress of grievances.

Amendment II [1791]

A well regulated Militia, being necessary to the security of a free State, the right of the people to keep and bear Arms, shall not be infringed.

Amendment III [1791]

No Soldier shall, in time of peace be quartered in any house, without the consent of the Owner, nor in time of war, but in a manner to be prescribed by law.

Amendment IV [1791]

The right of the people to be secure in their persons, houses, papers, and effects, against unreasonable searches and seizures, shall not be violated, and no Warrants shall issue, but upon probable cause, supported by Oath or affirmation, and particularly describing the place to be searched, and the persons or things to be seized.

Amendment V [1791]

No person shall be held to answer for a capital, or otherwise infamous crime, unless on a presentment or indictment of a Grand Jury, except in cases arising in the land or naval forces, or in the Militia, when in actual service in time of War or public danger; nor shall any person be subject for the same offence to be twice put in jeopardy of life or limb; nor shall be compelled in any criminal case to be a witness against himself, nor be deprived of life, liberty, or property, without due process of law; nor shall private property be taken for public use, without just compensation.

Amendment VI [1791]

In all criminal prosecutions, the accused shall enjoy the right to a speedy and public trial, by an impartial jury of the State and district wherein the crime shall have been committed, which district shall have been previously ascertained by law, and to be informed of the nature and cause of the accusation; to be confronted with the witnesses against him; to have compulsory process for obtaining witnesses in his favor, and to have the Assistance of Counsel for his defence.

Amendment VII [1791]

In Suits at common law, where the value in controversy shall exceed twenty dollars, the right of trial by jury shall be preserved, and no fact tried by jury, shall be otherwise reexamined in any Court of the United States, than according to the rules of the common law.

Amendment VIII [1791]

Excessive bail shall not be required, nor excessive fines imposed, nor cruel and unusual punishments inflicted.

Amendment IX [1791]

The enumeration in the Constitution, of certain rights, shall not be construed to deny or disparage others retained by the people.

Amendment X [1791]

The powers not delegated to the United States by the Constitution, nor prohibited by it to the States, are reserved to the States respectively, or to the people.

Amendment XI [1795]

The Judicial power of the United States shall not be construed to extend to any suit in law or equity, commenced or prosecuted against one of the United States by Citizens of another State, or by Citizens or Subjects of any Foreign State.

Amendment XII [1804]

The Electors shall meet in their respective states, and vote by ballot for President and Vice-President, one of whom, at least, shall not be an inhabitant of the same state with themselves; they shall name in their ballots the person voted for as President, and in distinct ballots the person voted for as Vice-President, and they shall make distinct lists of all persons voted for as President, and of all persons voted for as Vice-President, and of the number of votes for each, which lists they shall sign and certify, and transmit sealed to the seat of the government of the United States, directed to the President of the Senate;—The President of the Senate shall, in the presence of the Senate and House of Representatives, open all the certificates and the votes shall then be counted;—The person having the greatest number of votes for President, shall be the President, if such number be a majority of the whole number of Electors appointed; and if no person have such majority, then from the persons having the highest numbers not exceeding three on the list of those voted for as President, the House of Representatives shall choose immediately, by ballot, the President. But in choosing the President, the votes shall be taken by states, the representation from each state having one vote; a quorum for this purpose shall consist of a member or members from two-thirds of the states, and a majority of all states shall be necessary to a choice. And if the House of Representatives shall not choose a President whenever the right of choice shall devolve upon them, before the fourth day of March next following, then the Vice-President shall act as President, as in the case of the death or other constitutional disability of the President.—The person having the greatest number of votes as Vice-President, shall be the Vice-President, if such number be a majority of the whole number of Electors appointed, and if no person have a majority, then from the two highest numbers on the list, the Senate shall choose the Vice-President; a quorum for the purpose shall consist of two-thirds of the whole number of Senators, and a majority of the whole number shall be necessary to a choice. But no person constitutionally ineligible to the office of President shall be eligible to that of Vice-President of the United States.

Amendment XIII [1865]

Section 1. Neither slavery nor involuntary servitude, except as a punishment for crime whereof the party shall have been duly convicted, shall exist within the United States, or any place subject to their jurisdiction.

Section 2. Congress shall have power to enforce this article by appropriate legislation.

Amendment XIV [1868]

Section 1. All persons born or naturalized in the United States, and subject to the jurisdiction thereof, are citizens of the United States and of the State wherein they reside. No State shall make or enforce any law which shall abridge the privileges or immunities of citizens of the United States; nor shall any State deprive any person of life, liberty, or property, without due process of law; nor deny to any person within its jurisdiction the equal protection of the laws.

Section 2. Representatives shall be apportioned among the several States according to their respective numbers, counting the whole number of persons in each State, excluding Indians not taxed. But when the right to vote at any election for the choice of electors for President and Vice President of the United States, Representatives in Congress, the Executive and Judicial officers of a State, or the members of the Legislature thereof, is denied to any of the male inhabitants of such State, being twenty-one years of age, and citizens of the United States, or in any way abridged, except for participation in rebellion, or other crime, the basis of representation therein shall be reduced in the proportion which the number of such male citizens shall bear to the whole number of male citizens twenty-one years of age in such State.

Section 3. No person shall be a Senator or Representative in Congress, or elector of President and Vice President, or hold any office, civil or military, under the United States, or under any State, who having previously taken an oath, as a member of Congress, or as an officer of the United States, or as a member of any State legislature, or as an executive or judicial officer of any State, to support the Constitution of the United States, shall have engaged in insurrection or rebellion against the same, or given aid or comfort to the enemies thereof. But Congress may by a vote of two-thirds of each House, remove such disability.

Section 4. The validity of the public debt of the United States, authorized by law, including debts incurred for payment of pensions and bounties for services in suppressing insurrection or rebellion, shall not be questioned. But neither the United States nor any State shall assume or pay any debt or obligation incurred in aid of insurrection or rebellion against the United States, or any claim for the loss or emancipation of any slave; but all such debts, obligations and claims shall be held illegal and void.

Section 5. The Congress shall have power to enforce, by appropriate legislation, the provisions of this article.

Amendment XV [1870]

Section 1. The right of citizens of the United States to vote shall not be denied or abridged by the United States or by any State on account of race, color, or previous condition of servitude.

Section 2. The Congress shall have power to enforce this article by appropriate legislation.

Amendment XVI [1913]

The Congress shall have power to lay and collect taxes on incomes, from whatever source derived, without apportionment among the several States, and without regard to any census or enumeration.

Amendment XVII [1913]

Section 1. The Senate of the United States shall be composed of two Senators from each State, elected by the people thereof, for six years; and each Senator shall have one vote. The electors in each State shall have the qualifications requisite for electors of the most numerous branch of the State legislatures.

Section 2. When vacancies happen in the representation of any State in the Senate, the executive authority of such State shall issue writs of election to fill such vacancies: Provided, That the legislature of any State may empower the executive thereof to make temporary appointments until the people fill the vacancies by election as the legislature may direct.

Section 3. This amendment shall not be so construed as to affect the election or term of any Senator chosen before it becomes valid as part of the Constitution.

Amendment XVIII [1919]

Section 1. After one year from the ratification of this article the manufacture, sale, or transportation of intoxicating liquors within, the importation thereof into, or the exportation thereof from the United States and all territory subject to the jurisdiction thereof for beverage purposes is hereby prohibited.

Section 2. The Congress and the several States shall have concurrent power to enforce this article by appropriate legislation.

Section 3. This article shall be inoperative unless it shall have been ratified as an amendment to the Constitution by the legislatures of the several States, as provided in the Constitution, within seven years from the date of the submission hereof to the States by the Congress.

Amendment XIX [1920]

Section 1. The right of citizens of the United States to vote shall not be denied or abridged by the United States or by any State on account of sex.

Section 2. Congress shall have power to enforce this article by appropriate legislation.

Amendment XX [1933]

Section 1. The terms of the President and Vice President shall end at noon on the 20th day of January, and the terms of Senators and Representatives at noon on the 3d day of January, of the years in which such terms would have ended if this article had not been ratified; and the terms of their successors shall then begin.

Section 2. The Congress shall assemble at least once in every year, and such meeting shall begin at noon on the 3d day of January, unless they shall by law appoint a different day.

Section 3. If, at the time fixed for the beginning of the term of the President, the President elect shall have died, the Vice President elect shall become President. If the President shall not have been chosen before the time fixed for the beginning of his term, or if the President elect shall have failed to qualify, then the Vice President elect shall act as President until a President shall have qualified; and the Congress may by law provide for the case wherein neither a President elect nor a Vice President elect shall have qualified, declaring who shall then act as President, or the manner in which one who is to act shall be selected, and such person shall act accordingly until a President or Vice President shall have qualified.

Section 4. The Congress may by law provide for the case of the death of any of the persons from whom the House of Representatives may choose a President whenever the right of choice shall have devolved upon them, and for the case of the death of any of the persons from whom the Senate may choose a Vice President whenever the right of choice shall have devolved upon them.

Section 5. Sections 1 and 2 shall take effect on the 15th day of October following the ratification of this article.

Section 6. This article shall be inoperative unless it shall have been ratified as an amendment to the Constitution by the legislatures of three-fourths of the several States within seven years from the date of its submission.

Amendment XXI [1933]

Section 1. The eighteenth article of amendment to the Constitution of the United States is hereby repealed.

Section 2. The transportation or importation into any State, Territory, or possession of the United States for delivery or use therein of intoxicating liquors, in violation of the laws thereof, is hereby prohibited.

Section 3. This article shall be inoperative unless it shall have been ratified as an amendment to the Constitution by conventions in the several States, as provided in the Constitution, within seven years from the date of the submission hereof to the States by the Congress.

Amendment XXII [1951]

Section 1. No person shall be elected to the office of the President more than twice, and no person who has held the office of President, or acted as President, for more than two years of a term to which some other person was elected President shall be elected to the office of President more than once. But this Article shall not apply to any person holding the office of President when this Article was proposed by the Congress, and shall not prevent any person who may be holding the office of President, or acting as President, during the term within which this Article becomes operative from holding the office of President or acting as President during the remainder of such term.

Section 2. This article shall be inoperative unless it shall have been ratified as an amendment to the Constitution by the legislatures of three-fourths of the several States within seven years from the date of its submission to the States by the Congress.

Amendment XXIII [1961]

Section 1.   The District constituting the seat of Government of the United States shall appoint in such manner as the Congress may direct:

A number of electors of President and Vice President equal to the whole number of Senators and Representatives in Congress to which the District would be entitled if it were a State, but in no event more than the least populous state; they shall be in addition to those appointed by the states, but they shall be considered, for the purposes of the election of President and Vice President, to be electors appointed by a state; and they shall meet in the District and perform such duties as provided by the twelfth article of amendment.

Section 2.   The Congress shall have power to enforce this article by appropriate legislation.

Amendment XXIV [1964]

Section 1.   The right of citizens of the United States to vote in any primary or other election for President or Vice President, for electors for President or Vice President, or for Senator or Representative in Congress, shall not be denied or abridged by the United States, or any State by reason of failure to pay any poll tax or other tax.

Section 2.   The Congress shall have power to enforce this article by appropriate legislation.

Amendment XXV [1967]

Section 1.   In case of the removal of the President from office or of his death or resignation, the Vice President shall become President.

Section 2.   Whenever there is a vacancy in the office of the Vice President, the President shall nominate a Vice President who shall take office upon confirmation by a majority vote of both Houses of Congress.

Section 3.   Whenever the President transmits to the President pro tempore of the Senate and the Speaker of the House of Representatives his written declaration that he is unable to discharge the powers and duties of his office, and until he transmits to them a written declaration to the contrary, such powers and duties shall be discharged by the Vice President as Acting President.

Section 4.   Whenever the Vice President and a majority of either the principal officers of the executive departments or of such other body as Congress may by law provide, transmit to the President pro tempore of the Senate and the Speaker of the House of Representatives their written declaration that the President is unable to discharge the powers and duties of his office, the Vice President shall immediately assume the powers and duties of the office as Acting President.

Thereafter, when the President transmits to the President pro tempore of the Senate and the Speaker of the House of Representatives his written declaration that no inability exists, he shall resume the powers and duties of his office unless the Vice President and a majority of either the principal officers of the executive department or of such other body as Congress may by law provide, transmit within four days to the President pro tempore of the Senate and the Speaker of the House of Representatives their written declaration that the President is unable to discharge the powers and duties of his office. Thereupon Congress shall decide the issue, assembling within forty-eight hours for that purpose if not in session. If the Congress, within twenty-one days after receipt of the latter written declaration, or, if Congress is not in session, within twenty-one days after Congress is required to assemble, determines by two-thirds vote of both Houses that the President is unable to discharge the powers and duties of his office, the Vice President shall continue to discharge the same as Acting President; otherwise, the President shall resume the powers and duties of his office.

Amendment XXVI [1971]

Section 1. The right of citizens of the United States, who are eighteen years of age or older, to vote shall not be denied or abridged by the United States or by any State on account of age.

Section 2. The Congress shall have power to enforce this article by appropriate legislation.

Amendment XXVII [1992]

No law, varying the compensation for the services of the Senators and Representatives, shall take effect, until an election of Representatives shall have intervened.

Spanish Equivalents for Important Legal Terms in English

Abandoned property: bienes abandonados

Acceptance: aceptación; consentimiento; acuerdo

Acceptor: aceptante

Accession: toma de posesión; aumento; accesión

Accommodation indorser: avalista de favor

Accommodation party: firmante de favor

Accord: acuerdo; convenio; arregio

Accord and satisfaction: transacción ejecutada

Act of state doctrine: doctrina de acto de gobierno

Administrative law: derecho administrativo

Administrative process: procedimiento o metódo administrativo

Administrator: administrador (-a)

Adverse possession: posesión de hecho susceptible de proscripción adquisitiva

Affirmative action: acción afirmativa

Affirmative defense: defensa afirmativa

After-acquired property: bienes adquiridos con posterioridad a un hecho dado

Agency: mandato; agencia

Agent: mandatorio; agente; representante

Agreement: convenio; acuerdo; contrato

Alien corporation: empresa extranjera

Allonge: hojas adicionales de endosos

Answer: contestación de la demande; alegato

Anticipatory repudiation: anuncio previo de las partes de su imposibilidad de cumplir con el contrato

Appeal: apelación; recurso de apelación

Appellate jurisdiction: jurisdicción de apelaciones

Appraisal right: derecho de valuación

Arbitration: arbitraje

Arson: incendio intencional

Articles of partnership: contrato social

Artisan's lien: derecho de retención que ejerce al artesano

Assault: asalto; ataque; agresión

Assignment of rights: transmisión; transferencia; cesión

Assumption of risk: no resarcimiento por exposición voluntaria al peligro

Attachment: auto judicial que autoriza el embargo; embargo

Bailee: depositario

Bailment: depósito; constitución en depósito

Bailor: depositante

Bankruptcy trustee: síndico de la quiebra

Battery: agresión; física

Bearer: portador; tenedor

Bearer instrument: documento al portador

Bequest or legacy: legado (de bienes muebles)

Bilateral contract: contrato bilateral

Bill of lading: conocimiento de embarque; carta de porte

Bill of Rights: declaración de derechos

Binder: póliza de seguro provisoria; recibo de pago a cuenta del precio

Blank indorsement: endoso en blanco

Blue sky laws: leyes reguladoras del comercio bursátil

Bond: título de crédito; garantía; caución

Bond indenture: contrato de emisión de bonos; contrato del ampréstito

Breach of contract: incumplimiento de contrato

Brief: escrito; resumen; informe

Burglary: violación de domicilio

Business judgment rule: regla de juicio comercial

Business tort: agravio comercial

Case law: ley de casos; derecho casuístico

Cashier's check: cheque de caja

Causation in fact: causalidad en realidad

Cease-and-desist order: orden para cesar y desistir

Certificate of deposit: certificado de depósito

Certified check: cheque certificado

Charitable trust: fideicomiso para fines benéficos

Chattel: bien mueble

Check: cheque

Chose in action: derecho inmaterial; derecho de acción

Civil law: derecho civil

Close corporation: sociedad de un solo accionista o de un grupo restringido de accionistas

Closed shop: taller agremiado (emplea solamente a miembros de un gremio)

Closing argument: argumento al final

Codicil: codicilo

Collateral: garantía; bien objeto de la garantía real

Comity: cortesía; cortesía entre naciones

Commercial paper: instrumentos negociables; documentos a valores commerciales

Common law: derecho consuetudinario; derecho común; ley común

Common stock: acción ordinaria

Comparative negligence: negligencia comparada

Compensatory damages: daños y perjuicios reales o compensatorios

Concurrent conditions: condiciones concurrentes

Concurrent jurisdiction: competencia concurrente de varios tribunales para entender en una misma causa

Concurring opinion: opinión concurrente

Condition: condición

Condition precedent: condición suspensiva

Condition subsequent: condición resolutoria

Confiscation: confiscación

Confusion: confusión; fusión

Conglomerate merger: fusión de firmas que operan en distintos mercados

Consent decree: acuerdo entre las partes aprobado por un tribunal

Consequential damages: daños y perjuicios indirectos

Consideration: consideración; motivo; contraprestación

Consolidation: consolidación

Constructive delivery: entrega simbólica

Constructive trust: fideicomiso creado por aplicación de la ley

Consumer protection law: ley para proteger el consumidor

Contract: contrato

Contract under seal: contrato formal o sellado

Contributory negligence: negligencia de la parte actora

Conversion: usurpación; conversión de valores

Copyright: derecho de autor

Corporation: sociedad anónima; corporación; persona juridica

Co-sureties: cogarantes

Counterclaim: reconvención; contrademanda

Counteroffer: contraoferta

Course of dealing: curso de transacciones

Course of performance: curso de cumplimiento

Covenant: pacto; garantía; contrato

Covenant not to sue: pacto or contrato a no demandar

Covenant of quiet enjoyment: garantía del uso y goce pacífico del inmueble

Creditors' composition agreement: concordato preventivo

Crime: crimen; delito; contravención

Criminal law: derecho penal

Cross-examination: contrainterrogatorio

Cure: cura; cuidado; derecho de remediar un vicio contractual

Customs receipts: recibos de derechos aduaneros

Damages: daños; indemnización por daños y perjuicios

Debit card: tarjeta de dé bito

Debtor: deudor

Debt securities: seguridades de deuda

Deceptive advertising: publicidad engañosa

Deed: escritura; título; acta translativa de domino

Defamation: difamación

Delegation of duties: delegación de obligaciones

Demand deposit: depósito a la vista

Deposition: declaración de un testigo fuera del tribunal

Devise: legado; deposición testamentaria (bienes inmuebles)

Direct examination: interrogatorio directo; primer interrogatorio

Directed verdict: veredicto según orden del juez y sin participación activa del jurado

Disaffirmance: repudiación; renuncia; anulación

Discharge: descargo; liberación; cumplimiento

Disclosed principal: mandante revelado

Discovery: descubrimiento; producción de la prueba

Dissenting opinion: opinión disidente

Dissolution: disolución; terminación

Diversity of citizenship: competencia de los tribunales federales para entender en causas cuyas partes intervinientes son cuidadanos de distintos estados

Divestiture: extinción premature de derechos reales

Dividend: dividendo

Docket: orden del día; lista de causas pendientes

Domestic corporation: sociedad local

Draft: orden de pago; letrade cambio

Drawee: girado; beneficiario

Drawer: librador

Duress: coacción; violencia

Easement: servidumbre

Embezzlement: desfalco; malversación

Eminent domain: poder de expropiación

Employment discrimination: discriminación en el empleo

Entrepreneur: empresario

Environmental law: ley ambiental

Equal dignity rule: regla de dignidad egual

Equity security: tipo de participación en una sociedad

Estate: propiedad; patrimonio; derecho

Estop: impedir; prevenir

Ethical issue: cuestión ética

Exclusive jurisdiction: competencia exclusiva

Exculpatory clause: cláusula eximente

Executed contract: contrato ejecutado

Execution: ejecución; cumplimiento

Executor: albacea
Executory contract: contrato aún no completamente consumado
Executory interest: derecho futuro
Express contract: contrato expreso
Expropriation: expropriación

Federal question: caso federal
Fee simple: pleno dominio; dominio absoluto
Fee simple absolute: dominio absoluto
Fee simple defeasible: dominio sujeta a una condición resolutoria
Felony: crimen; delito grave
Fictitious payee: beneficiario ficticio
Fiduciary: fiduciaro
Firm offer: oferta en firme
Fixture: inmueble por destino, incorporación a anexación
Floating lien: gravamen continuado
Foreign corporation: sociedad extranjera; U.S. sociedad constituída en otro estado
Forgery: falso; falsificación
Formal contract: contrato formal
Franchise: privilegio; franquicia; concesión
Franchisee: persona que recibe una concesión
Franchisor: persona que vende una concesión
Fraud: fraude; dolo; engaño
Future interest: bien futuro

Garnishment: embargo de derechos
General partner: socio comanditario
General warranty deed: escritura translativa de domino con garantía de título
Gift: donación
Gift *causa mortis*: donación por causa de muerte
Gift *inter vivos*: donación entre vivos
Good faith: buena fe
Good faith purchaser: comprador de buena fe

Holder: tenedor por contraprestación
Holder in due course: tenedor legítimo
Holographic will: testamento ológrafico

Homestead exemption laws: leyes que exceptúan las casas de familia de ejecución por duedas generales
Horizontal merger: fusión horizontal

Identification: identificación
Implied-in-fact contract: contrato implícito en realidad
Implied warranty: guarantía implícita
Implied warranty of merchantability: garantía implícita de vendibilidad
Impossibility of performance: imposibilidad de cumplir un contrato
Imposter: imposter
Incidental beneficiary: beneficiario incidental; beneficiario secundario
Incidental damages: daños incidentales
Indictment: auto de acusación; acusación
Indorsee: endorsatario
Indorsement: endoso
Indorser: endosante
Informal contract: contrato no formal; contrato verbal
Information: acusación hecha por el ministerio público
Injunction: mandamiento; orden de no innovar
Innkeeper's lien: derecho de retención que ejerce el posadero
Installment contract: contrato de pago en cuotas
Insurable interest: interés asegurable
Intended beneficiary: beneficiario destinado
Intentional tort: agravio; cuasidelito intenciónal
International law: derecho internaciónal
Interrogatories: preguntas escritas sometidas por una parte a la otra o a un testigo
Inter vivos **trust:** fideicomiso entre vivos
Intestacy laws: leyes de la condición de morir intestado
Intestate: intestado
Investment company: compañia de inversiones
Issue: emisión

Joint tenancy: derechos conjuntos en un bien inmueble en favor del beneficiario sobreviviente
Judgment *n.o.v.*: juicio no obstante veredicto

Judgment rate of interest: interés de juicio
Judicial process: acto de procedimiento; proceso jurídico
Judicial review: revisión judicial
Jurisdiction: jurisdicción

Larceny: robo; hurto
Law: derecho; ley; jurisprudencia
Lease: contrato de locación; contrato de alquiler
Leasehold estate: bienes forales
Legal rate of interest: interés legal
Legatee: legatario
Letter of credit: carta de crédito
Levy: embargo; comiso
Libel: libelo; difamación escrita
Life estate: usufructo
Limited partner: comanditario
Limited partnership: sociedad en comandita
Liquidation: liquidación; realización
Lost property: objetos perdidos

Majority opinion: opinión de la mayoría
Maker: persona que realiza u ordena; librador
Mechanic's lien: gravamen de constructor
Mediation: mediación; intervención
Merger: fusión
Mirror image rule: fallo de reflejo
Misdemeanor: infracción; contravención
Mislaid property: bienes extraviados
Mitigation of damages: reducción de daños
Mortgage: hypoteca
Motion to dismiss: excepción parentoria
Mutual fund: fondo mutual

Negotiable instrument: instrumento negociable
Negotiation: negociación
Nominal damages: daños y perjuicios nominales
Novation: novación
Nuncupative will: testamento nuncupativo

Objective theory of contracts: teoria objetiva de contratos

Offer: oferta

Offeree: persona que recibe una oferta

Offeror: oferente

Order instrument: instrumento o documento a la orden

Original jurisdiction: jurisdicción de primera instancia

Output contract: contrato de producción

Parol evidence rule: regla relativa a la prueba oral

Partially disclosed principal: mandante revelado en parte

Partnership: sociedad colectiva; asociación; asociación de participación

Past consideration: causa o contraprestación anterior

Patent: patente; privilegio

Pattern or practice: muestra o práctica

Payee: beneficiario de un pago

Penalty: pena; penalidad

Per capita: por cabeza

Perfection: perfeción

Performance: cumplimiento; ejecución

Personal defenses: excepciones personales

Personal property: bienes muebles

Per stirpes: por estirpe

Plea bargaining: regateo por un alegato

Pleadings: alegatos

Pledge: prenda

Police powers: poders de policia y de prevención del crimen

Policy: póliza

Positive law: derecho positivo; ley positiva

Possibility of reverter: posibilidad de reversión

Precedent: precedente

Preemptive right: derecho de prelación

Preferred stock: acciones preferidas

Premium: recompensa; prima

Presentment warranty: garantía de presentación

Price discrimination: discriminación en los precios

Principal: mandante; principal

Privity: nexo jurídico

Privity of contract: relación contractual

Probable cause: causa probable

Probate: verificación; verificación del testamento

Probate court: tribunal de sucesiones y tutelas

Proceeds: resultados; ingresos

Profit: beneficio; utilidad; lucro

Promise: promesa

Promisee: beneficiario de una promesa

Promisor: promtente

Promissory estoppel: impedimento promisorio

Promissory note: pagaré; nota de pago

Promoter: promotor; fundador

Proximate cause: causa inmediata o próxima

Proxy: apoderado; poder

Punitive, or exemplary, damages: daños y perjuicios punitivos o ejemplares

Qualified indorsement: endoso con reservas

Quasi contract: contrato tácito o implícito

Quitclaim deed: acto de transferencia de una propiedad por finiquito, pero sin ninguna garantía sobre la validez del título transferido

Ratification: ratificación

Real property: bienes inmuebles

Reasonable doubt: duda razonable

Rebuttal: refutación

Recognizance: promesa; compromiso; reconocimiento

Recording statutes: leyes estatales sobre registros oficiales

Redress: reporacíon

Reformation: rectificación; reforma; corrección

Rejoinder: dúplica; contrarréplica

Release: liberación; renuncia a un derecho

Remainder: substitución; reversión

Remedy: recurso; remedio; reparación

Replevin: acción reivindicatoria; reivindicación

Reply: réplica

Requirements contract: contrato de suministro

Res judicata: cosa juzgada; res judicata

Rescission: rescisión

Respondeat superior: responsabilidad del mandante o del maestro

Restitution: restitución

Restrictive indorsement: endoso restrictivo

Resulting trust: fideicomiso implícito

Reversion: reversión; sustitución

Revocation: revocación; derogación

Right of contribution: derecho de contribución

Right of reimbursement: derecho de reembolso

Right of subrogation: derecho de subrogación

Right-to-work law: ley de libertad de trabajo

Robbery: robo

Rule 10b-5: Regla 10b-5

Sale: venta; contrato de compreventa

Sale on approval: venta a ensayo; venta sujeta a la aprobación del comprador

Sale or return: venta con derecho de devolución

Sales contract: contrato de compraventa; boleto de compraventa

Satisfaction: satisfacción; pago

Scienter: a sabiendas

S corporation: S corporación

Secured party: acreedor garantizado

Secured transaction: transacción garantizada

Securities: volares; titulos; seguridades

Security agreement: convenio de seguridad

Security interest: interés en un bien dado en garantía que permite a quien lo detenta venderlo en caso de incumplimiento

Service mark: marca de identificación de servicios

Shareholder's derivative suit: acción judicial entablada por un accionista en nombre de la sociedad

Signature: firma; rúbrica

Slander: difamación oral; calumnia

Sovereign immunity: immunidad soberana

Special indorsement: endoso especial; endoso a la orden de una person en particular

Specific performance: ejecución precisa, según los términos del contrato

Spendthrift trust: fideicomiso para pródigos

Stale check: cheque vencido

Stare decisis: acatar las decisiones, observar los precedentes

Statutory law: derecho estatutario; derecho legislado; derecho escrito

Stock: acciones

Stock warrant: certificado para la compra de acciones

Stop-payment order: orden de suspensión del pago de un cheque dada por el librador del mismo

Strict liability: responsabilidad uncondicional

Summary judgment: fallo sumario

Tangible property: bienes corpóreos

Tenancy at will: inguilino por tiempo indeterminado (según la voluntad del propietario)

Tenancy by sufferance: posesión por tolerancia

Tenancy by the entirety: locación conyugal conjunta

Tenancy for years: inguilino por un término fijo

Tenancy in common: specie de copropiedad indivisa

Tender: oferta de pago; oferta de ejecución

Testamentary trust: fideicomiso testamentario

Testator: testador (-a)

Third party beneficiary contract: contrato para el beneficio del tercero-beneficiario

Tort: agravio; cuasidelito

Totten trust: fideicomiso creado por un depósito bancario

Trade acceptance: letra de cambio aceptada

Trade name: nombre comercial; razón social

Trademark: marca registrada

Traveler's check: cheque del viajero

Trespass to land: ingreso no authorizado a las tierras de otro

Trespass to personal property: violación de los derechos posesorios de un tercero con respecto a bienes muebles

Trust: fideicomiso; trust

Ultra vires: fuera de la facultad (de una sociedad anónima)

Unanimous opinion: opinión unámine

Unconscionable contract or clause: contrato leonino; cláusula leonino

Underwriter: subscriptor; asegurador

Unenforceable contract: contrato que no se puede hacer cumplir

Unilateral contract: contrato unilateral

Union shop: taller agremiado; empresa en la que todos los empleados son miembros del gremio o sindicato

Universal defenses: defensas legitimas o legales

Usage of trade: uso comercial

Usury: usura

Valid contract: contrato válido

Venue: lugar; sede del proceso

Vertical merger: fusión vertical de empresas

Void contract: contrato nulo; contrato inválido, sin fuerza legal

Voidable contract: contrato anulable

Voir dire: examen preliminar de un testigo a jurado por el tribunal para determinar su competencia

Voting trust: fideicomiso para ejercer el derecho de voto

Waiver: renuncia; abandono

Warranty of habitability: garantía de habitabilidad

Watered stock: acciones diluídos; capital inflado

White-collar crime: crimen administrativo

Writ of attachment: mandamiento de ejecución; mandamiento de embargo

Writ of *certiorari*: auto de avocación; auto de certiorari

Writ of execution: auto ejecutivo; mandamiento de ejecución

Writ of *mandamus*: auto de mandamus; mandamiento; orden judicial

Chapter 1

[1] **www.nala.org**. This information is subject to updates and edits at any time. (p 3)

[2] Reprinted by permission of the National Federation of Paralegal Associations, Inc. (NFPA®), **www.paralegals.org**. (p 3)

[3] Reprinted by permission of the American Association for Paralegal Education. (p 4)

[4] California Business and Professions Code, Sections 6450–6456. Enacted in 2000. California Advanced Specialist (CAS) certification is also available as a specialty exam through NALA to paralegals who possess CLA or CP certification. For more information on this state-specific NALA certification, see Appendix F. (p 10)

Chapter 4

[1] Title 2 of the Texas Government Code, Section 81.101. (p 109)

[2] *Faretta v. California*, 422 U.S. 806 (1975). (p 111)

[3] *Oregon State Bar v. Smith*, 942 P.2d 793 (1997). (p 112)

[4] This law is codified in California Business and Professions Code, Sections 6400–6416. (p 112)

[5] *In re Nolo Press/Folk Law, Inc.*, 991 S.W.2d 768 (1999). (p 112)

[6] Texas Government Code Section 81.101(c) (Vernon Supp. 2000). (p 112)

Chapter 5

[1] 347 U.S. 483, 74 S.Ct. 686, 98 L.Ed. 873 (1954). (p 122)

[2] *In re Baby M*, 217 N.J.Super. 313, 525 A.2d 1128 (1987). (p 122)

[3] *Nature Conservancy v. Wilder Corporation of Delaware*, 656 F.3d 646 (2011). (p 124)

[4] 47 U.S.C. Section 223(d)(1)(B). Specifically, the CDA prohibited any obscene or indecent message that "depicts or describes, in terms patently offensive as measured by contemporary community standards, sexual or excretory activities or organs." (p 131)

[5] 521 U.S. 844, 117 S.Ct. 2329, 138 L.Ed.2d 874 (1997). (p 131)

[6] 47 U.S.C. Section 231. COPA made it a criminal act to post "material that is harmful to minors" on the Web. (p 131)

[7] *American Civil Liberties Union v. Mukasey*, 534 F.3d 181 (3d Cir. 2008). (p 131)

[8] *Cert.* denied, 129 S.Ct. 1032 (2009). (p 131)

Chapter 13

[1] The American Law Institute issued the Official Draft of the Model Penal Code in 1962. The Model Penal Code was designed to assist state legislatures in reexamining and recodifying state criminal laws. Uniformity among the states is not as important in criminal law as in other areas of the law. Crime varies with local circumstances, and it is appropriate that punishments vary accordingly. (p 383)

[2] *United States v. Park*, 421 U.S. 658, 95 S.Ct. 1903, 44 L.Ed.2d 489 (1975). (p 386)

[3] 384 U.S. 436, 86 S.Ct. 1602, 16 L.Ed.2d 694 (1966). (p 396)

Chapter 14

[1] 47 U.S.C. Section 230. (p 438)

[2] *Restatement (Second) of Torts*, Section 402a. (p 440)

[3] *Restatement (Third) of Torts: Products Liability*, Section 2, Comment h. (p 441)

Glossary

A

ABA-approved program A legal or paralegal educational program that satisfies the standards for paralegal training set forth by the American Bar Association.

acceptance In contract law, the offeree's indication to the offeror that the offeree agrees to be bound by the terms of the offeror's offer, or proposal to form a contract.

acquittal A certification or declaration following a trial that the individual accused of a crime is innocent, or free from guilt, in the eyes of the law and is thus absolved of the charges.

actionable Capable of serving as the basis of a lawsuit. An actionable claim can be pursued in a lawsuit or other court action.

active listening The act of listening attentively to the speaker's message and responding by giving appropriate feedback to show that you understand what the speaker is saying; restating the speaker's message in your own words to confirm that you accurately interpreted what was said.

actual malice Real and demonstrated evil intent. In a defamation suit, a statement made about a public figure normally must be made with actual malice (with either knowledge of its falsity or a reckless disregard of the truth) for liability to be incurred.

actus reus A guilty (prohibited) act. The commission of a prohibited act is one of the two essential elements required for criminal liability; the other element is the intent to commit a crime.

address block The part of a letter that indicates to whom the letter is addressed. The address block is placed in the upper left-hand portion of the letter, above the salutation (and reference line, if one is included).

adhesion contract A contract drafted by the dominant party and then presented to the other—the adhering party—on a "take-it-or-leave-it" basis.

adjudicate To resolve a dispute using a neutral decision maker.

administrative agency A federal or state government agency established to perform a specific function. Administrative agencies are authorized by legislative acts to make and enforce rules relating to the purpose for which they were established.

administrative law A body of law created by administrative agencies in the form of rules, regulations, orders, and decisions in order to carry out their duties and responsibilities.

administrative law judge (ALJ) One who presides over an administrative agency hearing and who has the power to administer oaths, take testimony, rule on questions of evidence, and make determinations of fact.

administrator A person appointed by a court to serve as a personal representative for a person who died intestate, who made a will but failed to name an executor, or whose executor cannot serve.

adoption A procedure in which persons become the legal parents of a child who is not their biological child.

Advanced Paralegal Certification (APC) A credential awarded by the National Association of Legal Assistants to a Certified Paralegal (CP) or Certified Legal Assistant (CLA) whose competency in a legal specialty has been certified based on an examination of the paralegal's knowledge and skills in the specialty area.

adversarial system of justice A legal system in which the parties to a lawsuit are opponents, or adversaries, and present their cases in the light most favorable to themselves. The impartial decision maker (the judge or jury) determines who wins based on an application of the law to the evidence presented.

affidavit A written statement of facts, confirmed by the oath or affirmation of the party making it and sworn before a person having the authority to administer the oath or affirmation.

affirm To uphold the judgment of a lower court.

affirmative defense A response to a plaintiff's claim that does not deny the plaintiff's facts but attacks the plaintiff's legal right to bring an action.

agency A relationship between two persons in which one person (the agent) represents or acts in the place of the other (the principal).

agent A person who is authorized to act for or in the place of another person (the principal).

agreement A meeting of the minds, and a requirement for a valid contract. Agreement involves two distinct events: an offer to form a contract and the acceptance of that offer by the offeree.

alimony Financial support paid to a former spouse after a marriage has been terminated. The alimony may be permanent or temporary (rehabilitative).

allegation A party's statement, claim, or assertion made in a pleading to the court. The allegation sets forth the issue that the party expects to prove.

alternative dispute resolution (ADR) The resolution of disputes in ways other than those involved in the traditional judicial process. Negotiation, mediation, and arbitration are forms of ADR.

American Arbitration Association (AAA) The major organization offering arbitration services in the United States.

American Association for Paralegal Education (AAfPE) A national organization of paralegal educators; the AAfPE was established in 1981 to promote high standards for paralegal education.

American Bar Association (ABA) A voluntary national association of attorneys. The ABA plays an active role in developing educational and ethical standards for attorneys and in pursuing improvements in the administration of justice.

annotation A brief comment, an explanation of a legal point, or a case summary found in a case digest or other legal source.

annulment A court decree that invalidates (nullifies) a marriage. Although the marriage itself is deemed nonexistent, children of a marriage that is annulled are deemed legitimate.

answer A defendant's response to a plaintiff's complaint.

appeal The process of seeking a higher court's review of a lower court's decision for the purpose of correcting or changing the lower court's judgment or decision.

appellant The party who takes an appeal from one court to another; sometimes referred to as the *petitioner*.

appellate court A court that reviews decisions made by lower courts, such as trial courts; a court of appeals.

appellate jurisdiction The power of a court to hear and decide an appeal; the authority of a court to review cases that have already been tried in a lower court and to make decisions about them without holding a trial.

appellee The party against whom an appeal is taken—that is, the party who opposes setting aside or reversing the judgment; sometimes referred to as the *respondent*.

appropriation In tort law, the use by one person of another person's name, likeness, or other identifying characteristic without permission and for the benefit of the user.

arbitration A method of settling disputes in which a dispute is submitted to a disinterested third party (other than a court) who issues a decision that may or may not be legally binding.

arbitration clause A clause in a contract providing that, in case of a dispute, the parties will determine their rights through arbitration rather than the judicial system.

arraignment A court proceeding in which the suspect is formally charged with the criminal offense stated in the indictment. The suspect then enters a plea (guilty, not guilty, or *nolo contendere*) in response.

arrest To take into custody a person suspected of criminal activity.

arrest warrant A written order, based on probable cause and typically issued by a judge, commanding that the person named on the warrant be arrested by the police.

arson The willful and malicious burning of a building (and, in some states, personal property) owned by another; arson statutes have been extended to cover the destruction of any building, regardless of ownership, by fire or explosion.

articles of incorporation The document filed with the appropriate state official, usually the secretary of state, when a business is incorporated. State statutes usually prescribe what kind of information must be contained in the articles of incorporation.

assault Any word or action intended to make another person apprehensive or fearful of immediate physical harm; a reasonably believable threat.

associate attorney An attorney working for a law firm who is not a partner and does not have an ownership interest in the firm. Associates are usually less experienced attorneys and may be invited to become partners after working for the firm for several years.

assumption of risk Voluntarily taking on a known risk; a defense against negligence that can be used when the plaintiff has knowledge of and appreciates a danger and voluntarily exposes himself or herself to the danger.

attorney-client privilege A rule of evidence requiring that confidential communications between a client and his or her attorney (relating to their professional relationship) be kept confidential, unless the client consents to disclosure.

authentication The process of establishing the genuineness of an item that is to be introduced as evidence in a trial.

automatic stay A suspension of all judicial proceedings upon the occurrence of an independent event. Under the Bankruptcy Code, the moment a petition to initiate bankruptcy proceedings is filed, all litigation or other legal action by creditors against a debtor and the debtor's property is suspended.

award In the context of alternative dispute resolution, the decision rendered by an arbitrator.

B

bail The amount of money or conditions set by the court to ensure that an individual accused of a crime will appear for further criminal proceedings. If the accused person provides bail, whether in cash or by means of a bail bond, then the person is released from jail.

bankruptcy court A federal court of limited jurisdiction that hears only bankruptcy proceedings.

bankruptcy estate In bankruptcy proceedings, all of the debtor's interests in property currently held and wherever located, as well as interests in certain property to which the debtor becomes entitled within 180 days after filing for bankruptcy.

bankruptcy law The body of federal law that governs bankruptcy proceedings. The twin goals of bankruptcy law are (1) to protect a debtor by giving him or her a fresh start and (2) to ensure that creditors competing for a debtor's assets are treated fairly.

bankruptcy trustee A person appointed by the bankruptcy court to administer the debtor's estate in the interests of both the debtor and the creditors. The basic duty of the bankruptcy trustee is to collect and reduce to cash the estate in property and to close up the estate as speedily as is compatible with the best interests of the parties.

battery The intentional and offensive touching of another without lawful justification.

beyond a reasonable doubt The standard used to determine the guilt or innocence of a person charged with a crime. To be guilty of a crime, a suspect must be proved guilty "beyond and to the exclusion of every reasonable doubt."

bigamy The act of entering into marriage with one person while still legally married to another.

billable hours Hours or fractions of hours that attorneys and paralegals spend in work that requires legal expertise and that can be billed directly to clients.

Bill of Rights The first ten amendments to the U.S. Constitution.

binder A written, temporary insurance policy.

binding authority Any source of law that a court must follow when deciding a case. Binding authorities include constitutions, statutes, and regulations that govern the issue being decided, as well as court decisions that are controlling precedents within the jurisdiction.

binding mediation A form of ADR in which a mediator attempts to facilitate agreement between the parties but then issues a legally binding decision if no agreement is reached.

bonus An end-of-the-year payment to a salaried employee in appreciation for that employee's overtime work, diligence, or dedication to the firm.

booking The process of entering a suspect's name, offense, and arrival time into the police log (blotter) following his or her arrest.

breach To violate a legal duty by an act or a failure to act.

breach of contract The failure, without legal excuse, of a contractual party to perform the obligations assumed in a contract.

briefing a case Summarizing a case. A case brief gives the full citation, the factual background and procedural history, the issue or issues raised, the court's decision, the court's holding, and the legal reasoning on which the court based its decision. It may also include conclusions or notes concerning the case made by the one briefing it.

burglary Breaking and entering onto the property of another with the intent to commit a felony.

business invitee A person, such as a customer or a client, who is invited onto business premises by the owner of those premises for business purposes.

business tort Wrongful interference with another's business rights.

bylaws A set of governing rules adopted by a corporation or other association.

C

case law Rules of law announced in court decisions.

case of first impression A case presenting a legal issue that has not yet been addressed by a court in a particular jurisdiction.

case on "all fours" A case in which all four elements (the parties, the circumstances, the legal issues involved, and the remedies sought) are very similar to those in the case being researched.

case on point A case involving factual circumstances and issues that are similar to those in the case being researched.

causation in fact Causation brought about by an act or omission without which an event would not have occurred.

cease-and-desist order An administrative or judicial order prohibiting a person or business firm from conducting activities that an agency or court has deemed illegal.

certificate of incorporation or corporate charter The document issued by a state official, usually the secretary of state, granting a corporation legal existence and the right to function.

certification Formal recognition by a private group or a state agency that a person has satisfied the group's standards of ability, knowledge, and competence; ordinarily accomplished through the taking of an examination.

Certified Paralegal (CP) A paralegal whose legal competency has been certified by the National Association of Legal Assistants following an examination that tests the paralegal's knowledge ad skills.

chain of custody A series describing the movement and location of evidence from the time it is obtained to the time it is presented in court. The court requires that evidence be preserved in the condition in which it was obtained if it is to be admitted into evidence at trial.

challenge An attorney's objection, during *voir dire*, to the inclusion of a particular person on the jury.

challenge for cause A *voir dire* challenge to exclude a potential juror from serving on the jury for a reason specified by an attorney in the case.

charge The judge's instruction to the jury setting forth the rules of law that the jury must apply in reaching its decision, or verdict.

checks and balances A system in which each of the three branches of the national government—executive, legislative, and judicial—exercises a check on the actions of the other two branches.

child support The financial support necessary to provide for a child's needs. Commonly, when a marriage is terminated, the noncustodial spouse agrees or is required by the court to make child-support payments to the custodial spouse.

chronologically In a time sequence; naming or listing events in the time order in which they occurred.

circumstantial evidence Indirect evidence offered to establish, by inference, the likelihood of a fact that is in question.

citation In case law, a reference to a case by the name of the case, the volume number and name of the reporter in which the case can be found, the page number on which the case begins, and the year. In statutory and administrative law, a reference to the title number, name, and section of the code in which a statute or regulation can be found.

citator A book or online service that provides the history and interpretation of a statute, regulation, or court decision and a list of the cases, statutes, and regulations that have interpreted, applied, or modified a statute or regulation.

citing case A case listed in a citator that cites the case being researched.

civil law Law dealing with the definition and enforcement of private rights, as opposed to criminal matters.

civil law system A system of law based on a code rather than case law, often originally from the Roman Empire; the predominant system of law in the nations of continental Europe and the nations that were once their colonies.

click-on agreement An agreement that arises when a buyer, engaging in a transaction on a computer, indicates his or her assent to be bound by the terms of an offer by clicking on a button that says, for example, "I agree"; sometimes referred to as a click-on license or a click-wrap agreement.

close corporation A corporation owned by a small group of shareholders, often family members; also called a closely held corporation. Shares in close corporations cannot be publicly traded on the stock market, and often other restrictions on stock transfer apply. Some close corporations qualify for special tax status as S corporations.

closed-ended question A question phrased in such a way that it elicits a simple "yes" or "no" answer.

closing In a letter, an ending word or phrase placed above the signature, such as "Sincerely" or "Very truly yours."

closing argument The argument made by each side's attorney after the cases for the plaintiff and defendant have been presented. Closing arguments are made prior to the jury charge.

code A systematic and topically organized presentation of laws, rules, or regulations.

common law A body of law developed from custom or judicial decisions in English and U.S. courts and not by a legislature.

common law marriage A marriage that is formed by mutual consent and without a marriage license or ceremony. The couple must be eligible to marry, have a present and continuing agreement to be a couple, live together as a couple, and hold themselves out to the public as a couple. Many states do not recognize common law marriages.

community property In certain states, all property acquired during a marriage, except for inheritances or gifts received during the marriage by either marital partner. Each spouse has a one-half ownership interest in community property.

comparative negligence A theory in tort law under which the liability for injuries resulting from negligent acts is shared by all persons who were guilty of negligence (including the injured party) on the basis of each person's proportionate carelessness.

compensatory damages A money award equivalent to the actual value of injuries or damages sustained by the aggrieved party.

complaint The pleading made by a plaintiff or a charge made by the state alleging wrongdoing on the part of the defendant.

concurrent jurisdiction Jurisdiction that exists when two different courts have the power to hear a case. For example, some cases can be heard in either a federal or a state court.

confirmation letter A letter that summarizes an oral conversation to provide a permanent record of the discussion.

conflict of interest A situation in which two or more duties or interests come into conflict, as when an attorney attempts to represent opposing parties in a legal dispute.

conflicts check A procedure for determining whether an agreement to represent a potential client will result in a conflict of interest.

consideration Something of value, such as money or the performance of an action not otherwise required, that motivates the formation of a contract. Each party must give consideration for the contract to be binding.

constitutional law Law based on the U.S. Constitution and the constitutions of the states.

constructive discharge A termination of employment that occurs when the employer causes the employee's working conditions to be so intolerable that a reasonable person in the employee's position would feel compelled to quit.

consumer A person who buys products and services for personal or household use.

consumer-debtor A debtor whose debts are primarily consumer debts—that is, debts for purchases that are primarily for household or personal use.

consumer law Statutes, agency rules, and judicial decisions protecting consumers of goods and services.

contingency fee A legal fee that consists of a specified percentage (such as 30 percent) of the amount the plaintiff recovers in a civil lawsuit. The fee is paid only if the plaintiff wins the lawsuit (recovers damages).

continuing legal education (CLE) program Courses through which attorneys and other legal professionals extend their education beyond school.

contract An agreement (based on a promise or an exchange of promises) that can be enforced in court.

contractual capacity The threshold mental capacity required by law for a party who enters into a contract to be bound by that contract.

contributory negligence A theory in tort law under which a complaining party's own negligence contributed to his or her injuries. Contributory negligence is an absolute bar to recovery in some jurisdictions.

conversion The act of wrongfully taking or retaining a person's personal property and placing it in the service of another.

copyright The exclusive right of an author (or other creator) to publish, print, or sell an intellectual production for a statutory period of time.

corporate law Law that governs the formation, financing, merger and acquisition, and termination of corporations, as well as the rights and duties of those who own and run the corporation.

counterclaim A claim made by a defendant in a civil lawsuit against the plaintiff; in effect, a counterclaiming defendant is suing the plaintiff.

court of equity A court that decides controversies and administers justice according to the rules, principles, and precedents of equity.

court of law A court in which the only remedies were things of value, such as money. Historically, in England, courts of law were different from courts of equity.

cram-down provision A provision of the Bankruptcy Code that allows a court to confirm a debtor's Chapter 11 reorganization plan even though only one class of creditors has accepted it. To exercise the court's right under this provision, the court must demonstrate that the plan does not discriminate unfairly against any creditors and is fair and equitable.

crime A broad term for violations of law that are punishable by the state and are codified by legislatures. The objective of criminal law is to protect the public.

criminal law Law that governs and defines those actions that are crimes and that subjects persons convicted of crimes to punishment imposed by the government (a fine or jail time).

cross-claim A claim asserted by a defendant in a civil lawsuit against another defendant or by a plaintiff against another plaintiff.

cross-examination The questioning of an opposing witness during the trial.

cyber crime A crime that occurs online, in the virtual community of the Internet, as opposed to the physical world.

cyberstalking The crime of stalking in cyberspace. The cyberstalker usually finds the victim through Internet chat rooms, newsgroups, bulletin boards, or e-mail and proceeds to harass that person or put the person in reasonable fear for his or her safety or the safety of his or her immediate family.

cyber tort A tort committed by use of the Internet.

D

damages Money awarded as a remedy for a civil wrong, such as a breach of contract or a tort (wrongful act).

debtor in possession (DIP) In Chapter 11 bankruptcy proceedings, a debtor who is allowed, for the benefit of all concerned, to maintain possession of the estate in bankruptcy (the business) and to continue business operations.

deception In consumer law, a material misrepresentation or omission in information that is likely to mislead a reasonable consumer to his or her detriment.

deceptive advertising Advertising that misleads consumers, either by unjustified claims concerning a product's performance or by failure to disclose relevant information concerning the product's composition or performance.

deed A document by which title to property is transferred from one party to another.

defamation Anything published or publicly spoken that causes injury to another's good name, reputation, or character.

default judgment A judgment entered by a clerk or court against a party who has failed to appear in court to answer or defend against a claim that has been brought against him or her by another party.

defendant A party against whom a lawsuit is brought.

defense The evidence and arguments presented in the defendant's support in a criminal action or lawsuit.

defense of others The use of reasonable force to protect others from harm.

defense of property The use of reasonable force to protect one's property from harm threatened by another. The use of deadly force in defending one's property is seldom justified.

demand letter A letter in which one party explains its legal position in a dispute and requests that the recipient take some action, such as paying money owed.

deponent A party or witness who testifies under oath during a deposition.

deposition A pretrial question-and-answer proceeding, usually conducted orally, in which a party or witness answers an attorney's questions. The answers are given under oath, and the session is recorded.

deposition transcript The official transcription of the recording taken during a deposition.

dicta A Latin term referring to nonbinding (nonprecedential) judicial statements that are not directly related to the facts or issues presented in the case and thus are not essential to the holding.

digest A compilation in which brief summaries of court cases are arranged by subject and subdivided by jurisdiction and court.

direct evidence Evidence directly establishing the existence of a fact.

direct examination The examination of a witness by the attorney who calls the witness to the stand to testify on behalf of the attorney's client.

director A person elected by the shareholders to direct corporate affairs.

disbarment A severe disciplinary sanction in which an attorney's license to practice law in the state is revoked because of unethical or illegal conduct.

discharge The termination of an obligation. A discharge in bankruptcy terminates the debtor's obligation to pay the debts discharged by the court.

discovery Formal investigation prior to trial. Opposing parties use various methods, such as interrogatories and depositions, to obtain information from each other and from witnesses to prepare for trial.

discovery plan A plan formed by the attorneys litigating a lawsuit, on behalf of their clients, that indicates the types of information that will be disclosed by each party to the other prior to trial, the testimony and evidence that each party will or may introduce at trial, and the general schedule for pretrial disclosures and events.

dissolution The formal disbanding of a partnership or a corporation.

diversion program In some jurisdictions, an alternative to prosecution that is offered to certain felony suspects to deter them from future unlawful acts.

diversity of citizenship Under the Constitution, a basis for federal district court jurisdiction over a lawsuit between (1) citizens of different states, (2) a foreign country and citizens of a state or states, or (3) citizens of a state and citizens of a foreign country. The amount in controversy must be more than $75,000 before a federal court can exercise jurisdiction in such cases.

dividend A distribution of profits to corporate shareholders, disbursed in proportion to the number of shares held.

divorce A formal court proceeding that legally dissolves a marriage.

docket The list of cases entered on the court's calendar and scheduled to be heard by the court.

double billing Billing more than one client for the same billable time period.

double jeopardy To place at risk (jeopardize) a person's life or liberty twice. The Fifth Amendment to the Constitution prohibits a second prosecution for the same criminal offense.

dram shop act A state statute that imposes liability on the owners of bars, as well as those who serve alcoholic drinks to the public, for injuries resulting from accidents caused by intoxicated persons when the sellers or servers of alcoholic drinks contributed to the intoxication.

due process of law Fair, reasonable, and standard procedures that must be used by the government in any legal action against a citizen. The Fifth Amendment to the U.S. Constitution prohibits the deprivation of "life, liberty, or property without due process of law."

duty of care The duty of all persons, as established by tort law, to exercise reasonable care in dealings with others. Failure to exercise due care, which is normally determined by the reasonable person standard, is the tort of negligence.

E

early neutral case evaluation A form of ADR in which a neutral third party evaluates the strengths and weaknesses of the disputing parties' positions; the evaluator's opinion forms the basis for negotiating a settlement.

easement The right of a person to make limited use of another person's real property without taking anything from the property.

elder law A relatively new legal specialty that involves serving the needs of older clients, such as estate planning and making arrangements for long-term care.

electronic filing (e-filing) system An online system that enables attorneys to file case documents with courts twenty-four hours a day, seven days a week.

elements The issues and facts that the plaintiff must prove to succeed in a tort claim.

emancipation The legal relinquishment by a child's parents or guardian of the legal right to exercise control over the child. Usually, a child who moves out of the parents' home and supports himself or herself is considered emancipated.

embezzlement The fraudulent appropriation of the property or money of another by a person entrusted with that property or money.

eminent domain The power of a government to take land for public use from private citizens for just compensation.

employment at will A common law doctrine under which employment is considered to be "at will"—that is, either party may terminate the employment relationship at any time and for any reason, unless a contract or statute specifies otherwise.

employment manual A firm's handbook or written statement that specifies the policies and procedures that govern the firm's employees and employer-employee relationships.

enabling legislation A statute enacted by a legislature that authorizes the creation of an administrative agency and specifies the name, purpose, composition, and powers of the agency being created.

environmental impact statement (EIS) A statement required by the National Environmental Policy Act for any major federal action that will significantly affect the quality of the environment. The statement must analyze the action's impact on the environment and explore alternative actions that might be taken.

environmental law All state and federal laws or regulations enacted or issued to protect the environment and preserve environmental resources.

equitable principles and maxims Propositions or general statements of rules of law that are frequently involved in equity jurisdiction.

e-signature An electronic sound, symbol, or process attached to or logically associated with a record and executed or adopted by a person with the intent to sign the record, according to the Uniform Electronic Transactions Act.

estate administration The process in which a decedent's personal representative settles the affairs of the decedent's estate (collects assets, pays debts and taxes, and distributes the remaining assets to heirs); the process is usually overseen by a probate court.

estate planning Making arrangements, during a person's lifetime, for the transfer of that person's property to others on the person's death. Estate planning often involves executing a will or establishing a trust fund to provide for others, such as a spouse or children, on a person's death.

ethical wall A term that refers to the procedures used to create a screen around an attorney, a paralegal, or another member of a law firm to shield him or her from information about a case in which there is a conflict of interest.

evidence Anything that is used to prove the existence or nonexistence of a fact.

exclusionary rule In criminal procedure, a rule under which any evidence obtained in violation of the accused's constitutional rights, as well as any evidence derived from illegally obtained evidence, will not be admissible in court.

exclusive jurisdiction Jurisdiction that exists when a case can be heard only in a particular court, such as a federal court.

executor A person appointed by a testator to serve as a personal representative on the testator's death.

expense slip A slip of paper on which any expense, or cost, that is incurred on behalf of a client (such as the payment of court fees or long-distance telephone charges) is recorded.

expert witness A witness with professional training or substantial experience qualifying him or her to testify as to his or her opinion on a particular subject.

eyewitness A witness who testifies about an event that he or she observed or experienced firsthand.

F

false imprisonment The intentional confinement or restraint of a person against his or her will.

family law Law relating to family matters, such as marriage, divorce, child support, and child custody.

federal question A question that pertains to the U.S. Constitution, acts of Congress, or treaties. It provides a basis for jurisdiction by the federal courts as authorized by Article III, Section 2, of the Constitution.

Federal Rules of Civil Procedure (FRCP) The rules controlling all procedural matters in civil trials brought before the federal district courts.

federal system The system of government established by the Constitution, in which the national government and the state governments share sovereign power.

fee simple absolute Ownership rights entitling the holder to use, possess, or dispose of the property however he or she chooses during his or her lifetime.

felony A crime—such as arson, murder, assault, or robbery—that carries the most severe sanctions. Sanctions range from one year in a state or federal prison to life imprisonment or (in some states) the death penalty.

fiduciary relationship A relationship involving a high degree of trust and confidence.

fixed fee A fee paid to the attorney by his or her client for having provided a specified legal service, such as the creation of a simple will.

forgery The fraudulent making or altering of any writing in a way that changes the legal rights and liabilities of another.

forms file A reference file containing copies of the firm's commonly used legal documents and informational forms. The documents in the forms file serve as models for drafting new documents.

foster care A temporary arrangement in which a family is paid by the state to care for a child for a limited period of time, often pending adoption.

fraudulent misrepresentation Any misrepresentation, either by misstatement or omission of a material fact, knowingly made with the intention of deceiving another and on which a reasonable person would and does rely to his or her detriment.

freelance paralegal A paralegal who operates his or her own business and provides services to attorneys on a contract basis. A freelance paralegal works under the supervision of an attorney, who assumes responsibility for the paralegal's work product.

friendly witness A witness who is biased against a client's adversary or sympathetic toward a client in a lawsuit or other legal proceeding.

G

garnishment A proceeding in which a creditor legally seizes a portion of a debtor's property (such as wages) that is in the possession of a third party (such as an employer).

general licensing Licensing in which all individuals within a specific profession or group (such as paralegals) must meet licensing requirements imposed by the state in order to legally practice their profession.

general partner A partner who participates in managing the business of a partnership and has all the rights and liabilities that arise under traditional partnership law.

genuineness of assent Knowing and voluntary assent to the contract terms. If a contract is formed as a result of mistake, misrepresentation, undue influence, or duress, genuineness of assent is lacking, and the contract will be voidable.

Good Samaritan statute A state statute stipulating that persons who provide emergency services to others in peril—unless they do so recklessly, thus causing further harm—cannot be sued for negligence.

grand jury A group of citizens called to decide whether probable cause exists to believe that a suspect committed the crime with which he or she has been charged and thus should stand trial.

guardian *ad litem* A person appointed by the court to represent the interests of a child or a mentally incompetent person before the court.

H

hacker A person who uses one computer to break into another.

headnote A note, usually a paragraph long, near the beginning of a reported case summarizing the court's ruling on an issue.

hearsay Testimony that is given in court by a witness who relates not what he or she knows personally but what another person said. Hearsay is generally not admissible as evidence.

holding The binding legal principle, or precedent, that is drawn from the court's decision in a case.

homestead exemption A law permitting the debtor to retain the family home, either in its entirety or up to a specified dollar amount, free from the claims of unsecured creditors or trustees in bankruptcy.

hornbook A single-volume scholarly discussion, or treatise, on a particular legal subject.

hostile witness A witness who is biased against your client or friendly toward your client's adversary in a lawsuit or other legal proceeding; an adverse witness.

hung jury A jury whose members are so irreconcilably divided in their opinions that they cannot reach a verdict. The judge in this situation may order a new trial.

hypothetical question A question based on hypothesis, conjecture, or fiction.

I

identity theft The theft of a form of identification, such as a name, date of birth, or Social Security number, which is then used to access the victim's financial resources.

impeach To call into question the credibility of a witness by challenging the truth or accuracy of his or her trial statement.

independent adoption A privately arranged adoption, as when a doctor, lawyer, or other person puts a couple seeking to adopt a child in contact with a pregnant woman who has decided to give up her child for adoption.

independent contractor A person who is hired to perform a specific undertaking but who is free to choose how and when to perform the work. An independent contractor may or may not be an agent.

indictment A charge or written accusation, issued by a grand jury, that probable cause exists to believe that a person has committed a crime for which he or she should stand trial.

information A formal criminal charge made by a prosecutor without a grand jury indictment.

informative letter A letter that conveys information to a client, a witness, an adversary's counsel, or some other person regarding a legal matter (such as the date, time, place, and purpose of a meeting) or a cover letter that accompanies other documents being sent to a person or court.

injunction A court decree ordering a person to do or to refrain from doing a certain act.

insider trading Trading in the stock of a publicly listed corporation based on inside information. One who possesses inside information and has a duty not to disclose it to outsiders may not profit from the purchase or sale of securities based on that information until the information is available to the public.

insurable interest An interest either in a person's life or well-being or in property that is sufficiently substantial to justify insuring against injury to or death of the person or damage to the property.

insurance A contract by which an insurance company (the insurer) promises to pay a sum of money or give something of value to another (either the insured or the beneficiary) to compensate for a specified loss.

intellectual property Property that results from intellectual, creative processes. Copyrights, patents, and trademarks are examples of intellectual property.

intentional infliction of emotional distress Intentional, extreme, and outrageous conduct resulting in severe emotional distress to another.

intentional tort A wrongful act knowingly committed.

international law The law that governs relations among nations. International customs and treaties are generally considered to be two of the most important sources of international law.

interrogatories A series of written questions for which written answers are prepared and then signed under oath by a party to a lawsuit (the plaintiff or the defendant).

interviewee The person who is being interviewed.

inter vivos **trust** A trust created by the grantor (settlor) and effective during the grantor's lifetime—that is, a trust not established by a will.

intestacy laws State statutes that specify how property will be distributed when a person dies intestate.

intestate The state of having died without a valid will.

investigation plan A plan that lists each step involved in obtaining and verifying facts and information relevant to the legal problem being investigated.

J

joint and several liability Shared and individual liability. In partnership law, joint and several liability means that a third party may sue all of the partners (jointly) or one or more of the partners separately (severally). This is true even if one of the partners sued did not participate in, ratify, or know about whatever gave rise to the cause of action.

joint custody Custody of a child that is shared by the parents following the termination of a marriage.

joint liability Shared liability. In partnership law, partners incur joint liability for partnership obligations and debts.

joint tenancy The joint ownership of property by two or more co-owners in which each co-owner owns an undivided portion of the property. On the death of one of the joint tenants, his or her interest automatically passes to the surviving joint tenant or tenants.

judgment The court's final decision regarding the rights and claims of the parties to a lawsuit.

judgment creditor A creditor who is legally entitled, by a court's judgment, to collect the amount of the judgment from a debtor.

jurisdiction The authority of a court to hear and decide a specific case.

justiciable controversy A controversy that is real and substantial, as opposed to hypothetical or academic.

K

KeyCite An online citator on Westlaw that can trace case history, retrieve secondary sources, categorize legal citations by legal issue, and perform other functions.

key number A number (accompanied by the symbol of a key) corresponding to a specific topic within West's key-number system to facilitate legal research of case law.

L

laches An equitable doctrine that bars a party's right to legal action if the party has neglected for an unreasonable length of time to act on his or her rights.

larceny The wrongful or fraudulent taking and carrying away of another person's personal property with the intent to deprive the person permanently of the property.

law A body of rules of conduct established and enforced by the controlling authority (the government) of a society.

law clerk A law student working as an apprentice with a law firm to gain practical experience.

lay witness A witness who can truthfully and accurately testify on a fact in question without having specialized training or knowledge; an ordinary witness.

leading question A question that suggests, or "leads to," a desired answer. Interviewers may use leading questions to elicit responses from witnesses who otherwise would not be forthcoming.

lease In real property law, a contract by which the owner of real property (the landlord) grants to a person (the tenant) an exclusive right to use and possess the property, usually for a specified period of time, in return for rent or some other form of payment.

legal administrator An administrative employee of a law firm who manages day-to-day operations. In smaller law firms, legal administrators are usually called office managers.

legal custody Custody of a child that confers on the parent the right to make major decisions about the child's life without consulting the other parent.

legalese Legal language that is hard for the general public to understand.

legal nurse consultant (LNC) A nurse who consults with legal professionals and others about medical aspects of legal claims or issues. Legal nurse consultants normally must have at least a bachelor's degree in nursing and significant nursing experience.

legal technician or independent paralegal A paralegal who offers services directly to the public without attorney supervision. Independent paralegals assist consumers by supplying them with forms and procedural knowledge relating to simple or routine legal procedures.

libel Defamation in writing or other published form (such as videotape).

licensing A government's official act of granting permission to an individual, such as an attorney, to do something that would be illegal in the absence of such permission.

limited liability company (LLC) A hybrid form of business organization authorized by a state in which the owners of the business have limited liability and taxes on profits are passed through the business entity to the owners.

limited liability partnership (LLP) A hybrid form of business organization authorized by a state that allows professionals to enjoy the tax benefits of a partnership while limiting in some way the normal joint and several liability of partners.

limited partner One who invests in a limited partnership but does not play an active role in managing the operation of the business. Unlike general partners, limited partners are only liable for partnership debts up to the amounts that they have invested.

limited partnership A partnership consisting of one or more general partners and one or more limited partners.

liquidation In regard to corporations, the process by which corporate assets are converted into cash and distributed among creditors and shareholders according to specific rules of preference. In regard to bankruptcy, a proceeding under Chapter 7 of the Bankruptcy Code (often referred to as *ordinary*, or *straight*, bankruptcy) in which a debtor states his or her debts and turns all assets over to a trustee, who sells the nonexempt assets and distributes the proceeds to creditors. With certain exceptions, the remaining debts are then discharged, and the debtor is relieved of the obligation to pay the debts.

litigation The process of working a lawsuit through the court system.

litigation paralegal A paralegal who specializes in assisting attorneys in the litigation process.

long arm statute A state statute that permits a state to obtain jurisdiction over nonresidents. The nonresidents must have certain "minimum contacts" with that state for the statute to apply.

M

mailbox rule A rule providing that an acceptance of an offer takes effect at the time it is communicated via the mode expressly or impliedly authorized by the offeror, rather than at the time it is actually received by the offeror. If acceptance is to be by mail, for example, it becomes effective the moment it is placed in the mailbox.

malpractice Professional misconduct or negligence—the failure to exercise due care—on the part of a professional, such as an attorney or a physician.

managing partner The partner in a law firm who makes decisions relating to the firm's policies and procedures and who generally oversees the business operations of the firm.

marital property All property acquired during the course of a marriage, apart from inheritances and gifts made to one or the other of the spouses.

material fact A fact that is important to the subject matter of the contract.

mediation A method of settling disputes outside of court by using the services of a neutral third party, who acts as a communicating agent between the parties; a method of dispute settlement that is less formal than arbitration.

memorandum of law A document (known as a *brief* in some states) that delineates the legal theories, statutes, and cases on which a motion is based.

mens rea A wrongful mental state, or intent. A wrongful mental state is a requirement for criminal liability. What constitutes a wrongful mental state varies according to the nature of the crime.

metadata Embedded electronic data recorded by a computer in association with a particular file, including location, path, creator, date created, date last accessed, hidden notes, earlier versions, passwords, and formatting. Metadata reveal information about how, when, and by whom a document was created, accessed, modified, and transmitted.

mini-trial A private proceeding that assists disputing parties in determining whether to take their case to court. Each party's attorney briefly argues the party's case before the other party and (usually) a neutral third party, who acts as an adviser. If the parties fail to reach an agreement, the adviser issues an opinion as to how a court would likely decide the issue.

***Miranda* rights** Certain constitutional rights of accused persons taken into custody by law enforcement officials, such as the right to remain silent and the right to counsel, as established by the United States Supreme Court's decision in *Miranda v. Arizona.*

mirror image rule A common law rule that requires that the terms of the offeree's acceptance adhere exactly to the terms of the offeror's offer for a valid contract to be formed.

misdemeanor A crime less serious than a felony, punishable by a fine or incarceration for up to one year in jail (not a state or federal penitentiary).

money laundering Falsely reporting income that has been obtained through criminal activity, such as illegal drug transactions, as income obtained through a legitimate business enterprise to make the "dirty" money "clean."

mortgage A written instrument giving a creditor an interest in the debtor's property as security for a debt.

motion A procedural request or application presented by an attorney to the court on behalf of a client.

motion for a change of venue A motion requesting that a trial be moved to a different location to ensure a fair and impartial proceeding, for the convenience of the parties, or for some other acceptable reason.

motion for a directed verdict A motion (also known as a *motion for judgment as a matter of law* in the federal courts) requesting that the court grant a judgment in favor of the party making the motion on the ground that the other party has not produced sufficient evidence to support his or her claim.

motion for a new trial A motion asserting that the trial was so fundamentally flawed (because of error, newly discovered evidence, prejudice, or other reason) that a new trial is needed to prevent a miscarriage of justice.

motion for judgment notwithstanding the verdict A motion (also referred to as a *motion for judgment as a matter of law* in federal courts) requesting that the court grant judgment in favor of the party making the motion on the ground that the jury verdict against him or her was unreasonable or erroneous.

motion for summary judgment A motion that may be filed by either party in which the party asks the court to enter judgment in his or her favor without a trial. A motion for summary judgment can be supported by evidence outside the pleadings, such as witnesses' affidavits, answers to interrogatories, and other evidence obtained prior to or during discovery.

motion *in limine* A motion requesting that certain evidence not be brought out at the trial, such as prejudicial, irrelevant, or legally inadmissible evidence.

motion to dismiss A motion filed by the defendant in which the defendant asks the court to dismiss the case for a specified reason, such as improper service, lack of personal jurisdiction, or the plaintiff's failure to state a claim for which relief can be granted.

motion to recuse A motion to remove a particular judge from a case.

motion to sever A motion to try multiple defendants separately.

motion to suppress evidence A motion requesting that certain evidence be excluded from consideration during the trial.

mutual mistake Mistake as to the same material fact on the part of both parties to a contract. In this situation, either party can cancel the contract.

N

National Association of Legal Assistants (NALA) One of the two largest national paralegal associations in the United States; formed in 1975. NALA is actively involved in paralegal professional development. Organization also called The Paralegal Association.

National Federation of Paralegal Associations (NFPA) One of the two largest national paralegal associations in the United States; formed in 1974. NFPA is actively involved in paralegal professional development.

national law Law that relates to a particular nation (as opposed to international law).

negligence The failure to exercise the standard of care that a reasonable person would exercise in similar circumstances.

negligence *per se* An action or failure to act in violation of a statutory requirement.

negotiation A process in which parties attempt to settle their dispute voluntarily, with or without attorneys to represent them.

networking Making personal connections and cultivating relationships with people in a certain field, profession, or area of interest.

no-fault divorce A divorce in which neither party is deemed to be at fault for the breakdown of the marriage.

nolo contendere Latin for "I will not contest it." A criminal defendant's plea in which he or she chooses not to challenge, or contest, the charges brought by the government. Although the defendant will still be convicted and sentenced, the plea neither admits nor denies guilt.

O

offer A promise or commitment to do or refrain from doing some specified thing in the future.

offeree The party to whom the offer is made.

offeror The party making the offer.

office manager An administrative employee who manages the day-to-day operations of a firm. In larger law firms, office managers are usually called legal administrators.

officer A person hired by corporate directors to assist in the management of the day-to-day operations of the corporation.

online dispute resolution (ODR) The resolution of disputes with the assistance of an organization that offers dispute resolution services via the Internet.

open-ended question A question phrased in such a way that it elicits a relatively unguided and lengthy narrative response.

opening statement An attorney's statement to the jury at the beginning of the trial. The attorney briefly outlines the evidence that will be offered during the trial and the legal theory that will be pursued.

opinion A statement by the court setting forth the applicable law and the reasons for its decision in a case.

opinion (advisory) letter A letter from an attorney to a client containing a legal opinion on an issue raised by the client's question or legal claim. The opinion is based on a detailed analysis of the law.

order for relief A court's grant of assistance to a complainant.

ordinance An order, rule, or law enacted by a municipal or county government to govern a local matter as allowed by state or federal legislation.

original jurisdiction The power of a court to take a case, try it, and decide it.

P

paralegal A person qualified by education, training, or work experience who is employed or retained by a lawyer, law office, corporation, governmental agency, or other entity and who performs specifically delegated substantive legal work, for which a lawyer is responsible.

paralegal manager An employee in a law firm who is responsible for overseeing the paralegal staff and paralegal professional development.

parallel citation A second (or third) citation for a given case. When a case is published in more than one reporter, each citation is a parallel citation to the other(s).

partner A person who operates a business jointly with one or more other persons. Each partner is a co-owner of the business firm.

partnership An association of two or more persons to carry on, as co-owners, a business for profit.

party With respect to lawsuits, the plaintiff or the defendant. Some cases involve multiple parties (more than one plaintiff or defendant).

passive listening The act of listening attentively to the speaker's message and responding to the speaker by providing verbal or nonverbal cues that encourage the speaker to continue; in effect, saying, "I'm listening, please go on."

patent A government grant that gives an inventor the exclusive right or privilege to make, use, or sell an invention for a limited time period.

paternity suit A lawsuit brought by an unmarried mother to establish that a certain person is the biological father of her child. DNA testing or a comparable procedure is often used to determine paternity.

peremptory challenge A *voir dire* challenge to exclude a potential juror from serving on the jury without any supporting reason or cause. Peremptory challenges based on racial or gender criteria are illegal.

performance In contract law, the fulfillment of duties arising under a contract; the normal way of discharging contractual obligations.

personal liability An individual's personal responsibility for debts or obligations. The owners of sole proprietorships and partnerships are personally liable for the debts and obligations incurred by their businesses. If their firms go bankrupt or cannot meet debts, the owners will be personally responsible for the debts.

personal property Any property that is not real property. Generally, any property that is movable or intangible is classified as personal property.

persuasive authority Any legal authority, or source of law, that a court may look to for guidance but on which it need not rely in making its decision. Persuasive authorities include cases from other jurisdictions, discussions in legal periodicals, and so forth.

persuasive precedent A precedent decided in another jurisdiction that a court may either follow or reject but that is entitled to careful consideration.

petition for divorce The document filed with the court to initiate divorce proceedings. The requirements governing the form and content of a divorce petition vary from state to state.

petition in bankruptcy An application to a bankruptcy court for relief in bankruptcy; a filing for bankruptcy. The official forms required for a petition in bankruptcy must be completed accurately, sworn to under oath, and signed by the debtor.

petty offense In criminal law, the least serious kind of wrong, such as a traffic or building-code violation.

plaintiff A party who initiates a lawsuit.

plea bargaining The process by which the accused and the prosecutor in a criminal case work out a mutually satisfactory disposition of the case, subject to court approval. Usually, plea bargaining involves the defendant's pleading guilty to a lesser offense in return for a lighter sentence.

pleadings Statements by the plaintiff and the defendant that detail the facts, charges, and defenses involved in the litigation.

pocket part A pamphlet containing recent cases or changes in the law that is used to update legal encyclopedias and other legal authorities. It is called a "pocket part" because it slips into a pocket, or sleeve, in the front or back binder of the volume.

policy In insurance law, a contract for insurance coverage. The policy spells out the precise terms and conditions as to what will and will not be covered under the contract.

potentially responsible party (PRP) A party who may be liable under the Comprehensive Environmental Response, Compensation, and Liability Act, or Superfund. Any person who generated hazardous waste, transported hazardous waste, owned or operated a waste site at the time of disposal, or currently owns or operates a site may be responsible for some or all of the cleanup costs involved in removing the hazardous substances.

prayer for relief A statement at the end of the complaint requesting that the court grant relief to the plaintiff.

precedent A court decision that furnishes authority for deciding later cases in which similar facts are presented.

predatory behavior Business behavior that is undertaken with the intention of unlawfully driving competitors out of the market.

preemption A doctrine under which a federal law preempts, or takes precedence over, conflicting state and local laws.

preference In bankruptcy proceedings, the debtor's favoring of one creditor over others by making payments or transferring property to that creditor at the expense of the rights of other creditors. The bankruptcy trustee is allowed to recover payments made to one creditor in preference over another.

preliminary hearing An initial hearing in which a judge or magistrate decides if there is probable cause to believe that the defendant committed the crime with which he or she is charged.

premium In insurance law, the price paid by the insured for insurance protection for a specified period of time.

prenuptial agreement A contract formed between two persons who are contemplating marriage to provide for the disposition of property in the event of a divorce or the death of one of the spouses after they have married.

pretrial conference A conference prior to trial in which the judge and the attorneys litigating the suit discuss settlement possibilities, clarify the issues in dispute, and schedule forthcoming trial-related events.

primary source of law In legal research, a document that establishes the law on a particular issue, such as a case decision, legislative act, administrative rule, or presidential order.

principal In agency law, a person who, by agreement or otherwise, authorizes another person (the agent) to act on the principal's behalf in such a way that the acts of the agent become binding on the principal.

privilege In tort law, the ability to act contrary to another person's right without that person's having legal redress for such acts. Privilege may be raised as a defense to defamation.

privileged information Confidential communications between certain individuals, such as an attorney and his or her client, that are protected from disclosure except under court order.

probable cause Reasonable grounds to believe the existence of facts warranting certain actions, such as the search or arrest of a person.

probate The process of "proving" the validity of a will and ensuring that the instructions in a valid will are carried out.

probate court A court having jurisdiction over proceedings concerning the settlement of a person's estate.

probation When a convicted defendant is released from confinement but is still under court supervision for a period of time.

procedural law Rules that define the manner in which the rights and duties of individuals are enforced.

product liability The legal liability of manufacturers, sellers, and lessors of goods to consumers, users, and bystanders for injuries or damages that are caused by the goods.

professional corporation (PC) A corporation formed by professionals, such as attorneys or accountants. Each member of the firm is liable for his or her own malpractice but is generally protected by limited liability as in the corporate form.

professional limited liability company (PLLC) An organizational form law firms may use in most states to help limit personal liability by separating individuals and the legal entity, the firm.

promise An assurance that one will or will not do something in the future.

promissory estoppel A doctrine under which a promise is binding if the promise is clear and definite, the promisee justifiably relies on the promise, the reliance is reasonable and substantial, and justice will be better served by enforcement of the promise.

proof of claim A document filed with a bankruptcy court by a creditor to inform the court of a claim against a debtor's property. The proof of claim lists the creditor's name and address, as well as the amount that the creditor asserts is owed to the creditor by the debtor.

property settlement The division of property between spouses on the termination of a marriage.

proximate cause Legal cause; exists when the connection between an act and an injury is strong enough to justify imposing liability.

public defender Court-appointed defense counsel. A lawyer appointed by the court to represent a criminal defendant who is unable to pay to hire private counsel.

public law number An identification number assigned to a statute.

publicly held corporation A corporation whose shares are eligible to be publicly traded in securities markets, such as the New York Stock Exchange.

public policy A governmental policy based on widely held societal values.

public prosecutor An individual, acting as a trial lawyer, who initiates and conducts criminal cases in the government's name and on behalf of the people.

punitive damages Money damages awarded to a plaintiff to punish the defendant and deter future similar conduct.

R

real estate Land and things permanently attached to the land, such as houses, buildings, and trees.

real property Immovable property consisting of land and the buildings and plant life thereon.

reasonable person standard The standard of behavior expected of a hypothetical "reasonable person"; the standard against which negligence is measured and that must be observed to avoid liability for negligence.

record on appeal The items submitted during the trial (pleadings, motions, briefs, and exhibits) and the transcript of the trial proceedings that are forwarded to the appellate court for review when a case is appealed.

recross-examination The questioning of an opposing witness following the adverse party's redirect examination.

redirect examination The questioning of a witness following the adverse party's cross-examination.

reference line The portion of the letter that indicates the matter to be discussed, such as "RE: Summary of Cases Applying the Family and Medical Leave Act of 1993." The reference line is placed just below the address block and above the salutation.

reformation An equitable remedy granted by a court to correct, or "reform," a written contract so that it reflects the true intentions of the parties.

Registered Paralegal (RP) A paralegal whose competency has been certified by the National Federation of Paralegal Associations after successful completion of the Paralegal Advanced Competency Exam (PACE).

relevant evidence Evidence tending to prove or disprove the fact in question. Only relevant evidence is admissible in court.

remand To send a case back to a lower court for further proceedings.

remedy The means by which a right is enforced or the violation of a right is prevented or compensated for.

remedy at law A remedy available in a court of law. Money damages and items of value are awarded as remedies at law.

remedy in equity A remedy allowed by courts in situations where remedies at law are not appropriate. Remedies in equity are based on rules of fairness, justice, and honesty.

reporter A book in which court cases are published, or reported.

reprimand A disciplinary sanction in which an attorney is rebuked for misbehavior. Although a reprimand is the mildest sanction for attorney misconduct, it is serious and may significantly damage the attorney's reputation in the legal community.

rescission A remedy in which the contract is canceled and the parties are returned to the positions they occupied before the contract was made.

respondeat superior A doctrine in agency law under which a principal-employer may be held liable for the wrongful acts committed by agents or employees acting within the scope of their agency or employment.

responsible corporate officer doctrine A common law doctrine under which the court may impose criminal liability on a corporate officer for actions of employees under her or his supervision regardless of whether she or he participated in, directed, or even knew about those actions.

restitution An equitable remedy under which a person is restored to his or her original position prior to loss or injury, or placed in the position that he or she would have been in had the breach not occurred.

restraining order A court order that requires one person (such as an abusing spouse) to stay away from another (such as an abused spouse).

restrictive covenants Agreements between an employer and employee that the employee will not attempt to compete with the employer for a specified period after employment ends.

retainer An advance payment made by a client to a law firm to cover part of the legal fees and/or costs that will be incurred on that client's behalf.

retainer agreement A signed document stating that the attorney or the law firm has been hired by the client to provide certain legal services and that the client agrees to pay for those services.

return-of-service form A document signed by a process server and submitted to the court to prove that a defendant received a summons.

reverse To overturn the judgment of a lower court.

reversible error A legal error at the trial court level that is significant enough to have affected the outcome of the case. It is grounds for reversal of the judgment on appeal.

risk A prediction concerning potential loss based on known and unknown factors.

risk management Planning that is undertaken to reduce the risk of loss from known and unknown events. In the context of insurance, risk management involves transferring certain risks from the insured to the insurance company.

robbery The taking of money, personal property, or any other article of value from a person by means of force or fear.

rulemaking The actions undertaken by administrative agencies when formally adopting new regulations or amending old ones.

rules of evidence Rules governing the admissibility of evidence in trial courts.

S

sales contract A contract for the sale of goods, as opposed to a contract for the sale of services, real property, or intangible property. Sales contracts are governed by Article 2 of the Uniform Commercial Code.

salutation In a letter, the formal greeting to the addressee. The salutation is placed just below the reference line.

search warrant A written order, based on probable cause and issued by a judge or public official (magistrate), commanding that police officers or criminal investigators search a specific person, place, or property to obtain evidence.

secondary source of law In legal research, any publication that indexes, summarizes, or interprets the law, such as a legal encyclopedia, a treatise, or an article in a law review.

secured creditor A lender, seller, or any other person in whose favor there is a security interest.

self-defense The legally recognized privilege to protect oneself or one's property against injury by another. The privilege of self-defense protects only acts that are reasonably necessary to protect oneself or one's property.

self-incrimination The act of giving testimony that implicates oneself in criminal wrongdoing. The Fifth Amendment to the Constitution states that no person "shall be compelled in any criminal case to be a witness against himself."

self-regulation The regulation of the conduct of a professional group by members of the group. Self-regulation involves establishing ethical or professional standards of behavior with which members of the group must comply.

sentence The punishment, or penalty, ordered by the court to be inflicted on a person convicted of a crime.

separate property Property that a spouse owned before the marriage, plus inheritances and gifts acquired by the spouse during the marriage.

service of process The delivery of the summons and the complaint to a defendant.

settlement agreement An out-of-court resolution to a legal dispute, which is agreed to by the parties in writing. A settlement agreement may be reached at any time prior to or during a trial.

sexual harassment In the employment context, (1) the hiring or granting of job promotions or other benefits in return for sexual favors (*quid pro quo* harassment) or (2) language or conduct that is so sexually offensive that it creates a hostile working environment (hostile-environment harassment).

share A unit of stock; a measure of ownership interest in a corporation.

shareholder One who has an ownership interest in a corporation through the purchase of corporate shares, or stock.

Shepard's An online citator on LexisNexis that provides a list of all the authorities citing a particular case, statute, or other legal authority.

shrink-wrap agreement An agreement whose terms are expressed in a document located inside the box in which the goods (usually software) are packaged.

slander Defamation in oral form.

slip opinion A judicial opinion published shortly after the decision is made and not yet included in a case reporter or advance sheets.

sole proprietorship The simplest form of business organization, in which the owner is the business. Anyone who does business without creating a formal business entity has a sole proprietorship.

specific performance An equitable remedy requiring exactly the performance that was specified in a contract; usually granted only when money damages would be an inadequate remedy and the subject matter of the contract is unique (for example, real property).

staff attorney An attorney hired by a law firm as an employee. A staff attorney has no ownership rights in the firm and will not be invited to become a partner in the firm.

standing to sue A sufficient stake in a controversy to justify bringing a lawsuit. To have standing to sue, the plaintiff must demonstrate an injury or a threat of injury.

stare decisis The doctrine of precedent, under which a court is obligated to follow earlier decisions of that court or higher courts within the same jurisdiction. This is a major characteristic of the common law system.

state bar association An association of attorneys within a state. In most states, an attorney must be a member of the state bar association to practice law in the state.

statute A written law enacted by a legislature under its constitutional lawmaking authority.

Statute of Frauds A state statute that requires certain types of contracts to be in writing to be enforceable.

statute of limitations A statute setting the maximum time period within which certain actions can be brought to court or rights enforced. After the period of time has run, no legal action can be brought.

statutory law The body of written laws enacted by the legislature.

strict liability Liability regardless of fault. In tort law, strict liability may be imposed on a merchant who introduces into commerce a good that is so defective as to be unreasonably dangerous.

submission agreement A written agreement to submit a legal dispute to an arbitrator or arbitrating panel for resolution.

subpoena A document commanding a person to appear at a certain time and place to give testimony concerning a certain matter.

substantive law Law that defines the rights and duties of individuals with respect to each other's conduct and property.

summary jury trial (SJT) A settlement method in which a trial is held but the jury's verdict is not binding. The verdict acts as a guide to both sides in reaching an agreement during mandatory negotiations that follow the trial. If a settlement is not reached, both sides have the right to a full trial later.

summons A document served on a defendant in a lawsuit informing the defendant that a legal action has been commenced against him or her and that the defendant must appear in court or respond to the plaintiff's complaint within a specified period of time.

supporting affidavit An affidavit accompanying a motion that is filed by an attorney on behalf of his or her client. The sworn statements in the affidavit provide a factual basis for the motion.

support personnel Employees who provide clerical, secretarial, or other support to the legal, paralegal, and administrative staff of a law firm.

supremacy clause The provision in Article VI of the U.S. Constitution that declares the Constitution, laws, and treaties of the United States "the supreme Law of the Land."

suspension A serious disciplinary sanction in which an attorney who has violated an ethical rule or a law is prohibited from practicing law in the state for a specified or an indefinite period of time.

syllabus A brief summary of the holding and legal principles involved in a reported case, which is followed by the court's official opinion.

T

tenancy in common A form of co-ownership of property in which each party owns an undivided interest that passes to his or her heirs at death.

testamentary trust A trust that is created by will and that does not take effect until the death of the testator.

testate The condition of having died with a valid will.

testator One who makes a valid will.

third party A person or entity not directly involved in an agreement (such as a contract), legal proceeding (such as a lawsuit), or relationship (such as an attorney-client relationship).

time slip A record documenting, for billing purposes, the hours (or fractions of hours) that an attorney or a paralegal worked for each client, the date on which the work was done, and the type of work done.

tort A civil wrong not arising from a breach of contract; a breach of a legal duty that causes harm or injury to another.

tortfeasor One who commits a tort.

trade journal A newsletter, magazine, or other periodical that provides a certain trade or profession with information (products, trends, or developments) relating to that trade or profession.

trademark A distinctive mark, motto, device, or emblem that a manufacturer stamps, prints, or otherwise affixes to the goods it produces so that they can be identified on the market and their origins made known. Once a trademark

is established (under the common law or through registration), the owner is entitled to its exclusive use.

trade name A term that is used to indicate part or all of a business's name and that is directly related to the business's reputation and goodwill. Trade names are protected under the common law (and under trademark law, if the business's name is the same as its trademark).

trade secret Information or processes that give a business an advantage over competitors who do not know the information or processes.

treatise In legal research, a work that provides a systematic, detailed, and scholarly review of a particular legal subject.

treaty An agreement, or compact, formed between two independent nations.

trespass to land The entry onto, above, or below the surface of land owned by another without the owner's permission.

trespass to personal property The unlawful taking or harming of another's personal property; interference with another's right to the exclusive possession of his or her personal property.

trial court A court in which cases begin and in which questions of fact are examined.

trial notebook Traditionally, a binder that contains copies of all the documents and information that an attorney will need to have at hand during the trial.

trust An arrangement in which property is transferred by one person (the grantor, or settlor) to another (the trustee) for the benefit of a third party (the beneficiary).

trust account A bank account in which one party (the trustee, such as an attorney) holds funds belonging to another person (such as a client); a bank account into which funds advanced to a law firm by a client are deposited. Also called an *escrow account*.

U

unauthorized practice of law (UPL) The performance of actions defined by a legal authority, such as a state legislature, as constituting the "practice of law" without authorization to do so.

unconscionable contract A contract that is so oppressive to one of the parties that the court will refuse to enforce the contract.

underwriter In insurance law, the insurer, or the one assuming a risk in return for the payment of a premium.

Uniform Commercial Code (UCC) Statutes adopted by all states, in part or in whole, that contain uniform laws governing business transactions as defined in the code.

unilateral mistake Mistake as to a material fact on the part of only one party to a contract. In this situation, the contract is normally enforceable against the mistaken party, with some exceptions.

unreasonably dangerous product A product that is defective to the point of threatening a consumer's health and safety. A product will be considered unreasonably dangerous if it is dangerous beyond the expectation of the ordinary consumer or if a less dangerous alternative was economically feasible for the manufacturer, but the manufacturer failed to produce it.

U.S. trustee A government official who performs administrative tasks that a bankruptcy judge would otherwise have to perform.

V

venue The geographic district in which an action is tried and from which the jury is selected.

verdict A formal decision made by a jury.

vicarious liability Legal responsibility placed on one person for the acts of another.

visitation rights The right of a noncustodial parent to have contact with his or her child. Grandparents and stepparents may also be given visitation rights.

voir dire A proceeding in which attorneys for the plaintiff and the defendant ask prospective jurors questions to determine whether any potential juror is biased or has any connection with a party to the action or with a prospective witness.

W

warranty An express or implied promise by a seller that specific goods to be sold meet certain criteria, or standards of performance, on which the buyer may rely.

white-collar crime A crime that typically occurs in a business context; popularly used to refer to an illegal act or series of acts committed by a person or business entity using nonviolent means.

wiki A Web page that can be added to and modified by anyone or by authorized users who share the site. The most famous example is Wikipedia.

will A document directing how and to whom the maker's property and obligations are to be transferred on his or her death.

winding up The process of winding up all business affairs (collecting and distributing the firm's assets) after a partnership or corporation has been dissolved.

witness A person who is asked to testify under oath at a trial.

witness statement The written record of the statements made by a witness during an interview, signed by the witness.

workers' compensation laws State statutes that establish an administrative procedure for compensating workers for injuries that arise out of or in the course of their employment, regardless of fault.

workers' compensation statutes State laws establishing an administrative procedure for compensating workers for injuries that arise in the course of their employment.

workout An out-of-court negotiation in which a debtor enters into an agreement with a creditor or creditors for a payment or plan to discharge the debtor's debt.

work product An attorney's mental impressions, conclusions, and legal theories regarding a case being prepared on behalf of a client. Work product normally is regarded as privileged information.

writ of certiorari A writ from a higher court asking a lower court to send it the record of a case for review. The United States Supreme Court uses certiorari to review most of the cases it decides to hear.

writ of execution A writ that puts in force a court's decree or judgment.

wrongful discharge An employer's termination of an employee's employment in violation of the law.

Index